"Yan Lianke is among the most controversial and sophisticated writers in contemporary China. He has a keen, journalistic sensibility with regard to social events and is capable of turning anything he touches into a dark carnival. This companion introduces Yan's extraordinary background, kaleidoscopic style, Kafkaesque sense of humor, and his deepest concern about the fate of China. This is a most comprehensive reader, demonstrating not only Yan's art and politics of fiction but also the construction and deconstruction of the 'China story' in our time."

—**David Der-wei Wang**, *Edward C. Henderson Professor of Chinese Literature at Harvard University, and Academician, Academia Sinica.*

"As the first English volume on this prominent, avant-garde, and controversial writer, the Routledge Companion to Yan Lianke is a magnificent pioneering work covering a rich array of literary criticism. With a kaleidoscopical treatment of Yan Lianke's novels, literary theory and essays, this book is a major achievement in addressing many pivotal themes such as mythorealism, absurdity, spirituality, history, gender, translation and reception."

—**Jianmei Liu**, *Professor of Chinese Literature, Hong Kong University of Science and Technology.*

"Encyclopedic in scope and comprehensive in coverage, the Routledge Companion to Yan Lianke presents a deep critical dive into the oeuvre of one of the most important Chinese writers of the past thirty years. For readers who want a more nuanced understanding of Yan Lianke's brilliant and twisted literary universe, this is the best place to start."

—**Michael Berry**, *Director, UCLA Center for Chinese Studies, Professor of Contemporary Chinese Cultural Studies Asian Languages & Cultures/Film, Television and Digital Media UCLA.*

"This volume brings together wide-ranging, comprehensive and compelling studies of the major contemporary Chinese fiction writer Yan Lianke, whose innovative writing frequently goes against the grain and persistently transgresses narratological frontiers. The editors are to be congratulated on putting together this tour-de-force. It will stand for many years to come as essential reading for anyone interested in Yan Lianke and the mythorealist mode he promotes."

—**Gregory B. Lee** *FHKAH, Founding Professor of Chinese Studies, Head of Department of Chinese Studies, Department of Chinese Studies, School of Modern Languages, University of St Andrews.*

THE ROUTLEDGE COMPANION TO YAN LIANKE

Yan Lianke is one of the most important, prolific, and controversial writers in contemporary China.

At the forefront of the "mythorealist" Chinese avant-garde and using absurdist humor and grotesque satire, Yan's works have caught much critical attention not only in the Chinese mainland, Hong Kong, and Taiwan but also around the world. His critiques of modern China under both Mao-era socialism and contemporary capitalism draw on a deep knowledge of history, folklore, and spirituality.

This companion presents a collection of critical essays by leading scholars of Yan Lianke from around the world, organized into some of the key themes of his work: Mythorealism; Absurdity and Spirituality; and History and Gender, as well as the challenges of translating his work into English and other languages. With an essay written by Yan Lianke himself, this is a vital and authoritative resource for students and scholars looking to understand Yan's works from both his own perspective and those of leading critics.

Riccardo Moratto is Full Professor of Translation and Interpreting Studies, Chinese Translation and Interpreting at the Graduate Institute of Interpretation and Translation (GIIT), Shanghai International Studies University (SISU), and Honorary Guest Professor at Nanjing Agricultural University. Prof. Moratto is a Chartered Linguist and Fellow Member of the Chartered Institute of Linguists (CIoL), Visiting Scholar at Shandong University, Honorary Research Fellow at the Center for Translation Studies of Guangdong University of Foreign Studies, and Expert Member of the Translators Association of China (TAC). Prof. Moratto is also an international conference interpreter and a renowned literary translator. He has published extensively in the fields of translation and interpreting studies and Chinese literature in translation.

Howard Yuen Fung Choy, Associate Professor at Hong Kong Baptist University, received his PhD in comparative literature from the University of Colorado. Chief editor of the Brill series *Hong Kong Culture and Literature* and *African and Asian Anthropocene: Studies in the Environmental Humanities*, co-editor of *Liu Zaifu: Selected Critical Essays* (2021), editor of *Discourses of Disease: Writing Illness, the Mind and Body in Modern China* (2016), the author of *Remapping the Past: Fictions of History in Deng's China, 1979–1997* (2008), and the assistant author of *The Illustrated Encyclopedia of Confucianism* (2005), he has also published articles and translations in major scholarly journals, including *positions*, *American Journal of Chinese Studies*, and *Asian Theatre Journal*.

Routledge Literature Companions

Also available in this series:

The Routledge Companion to Literature and Trauma
Edited by Hanna Meretoja and Colin Davis

The Routledge Companion to Literature and Disability
Edited by Alice Hall

The Routledge Companion to Death and Literature
Edited by Daniel K. Jernigan, Neil Murphy, and W. Michelle Wang

The Routledge Companion to Victorian Literature
Edited by Dennis Denisoff and Talia Schaffer

The Routledge Companion to Australian Literature
Edited by Jessica Gildersleeve

The Routledge Companion to Jane Austen
Edited by Cheryl A. Wilson and Maria H. Frawley

The Routledge Companion to Literature and Class
Edited by Gloria McMillan

The Routledge Companion to the British and North American Literary Magazine
Edited by Tim Lanzendörfer

The Routledge Companion to Literature and Emotion
Edited by Patrick Colm Hogan, Bradley J. Irish and Lalita Pandit Hogan

The Routledge Companion to Yan Lianke
Edited by Riccardo Moratto and Howard Yuen Fung Choy

The Routledge Companion to Korean Literature
Edited by Heekyoung Cho

The Routledge Companion to Humanism and Literature
Edited by Michael Bryson

For more information on this series, please visit: www.routledge.com/Routledge-Literature-Companions/book-series/RC4444

THE ROUTLEDGE COMPANION TO YAN LIANKE

Edited by
Riccardo Moratto
and Howard Yuen Fung Choy

LONDON AND NEW YORK

Cover image: Getty

First published 2022
by Routledge
2 Park Square, Milton Park, Abingdon, Oxon OX14 4RN

and by Routledge
605 Third Avenue, New York, NY 10158

Routledge is an imprint of the Taylor & Francis Group, an Informa business

© 2022 selection and editorial matter, Riccardo Moratto and Howard Yuen Fung Choy; individual chapters, the contributors

The right of Riccardo Moratto and Howard Yuen Fung Choy to be identified as the authors of the editorial material, and of the authors for their individual chapters, has been asserted in accordance with sections 77 and 78 of the Copyright, Designs and Patents Act 1988.

All rights reserved. No part of this book may be reprinted or reproduced or utilised in any form or by any electronic, mechanical, or other means, now known or hereafter invented, including photocopying and recording, or in any information storage or retrieval system, without permission in writing from the publishers.

Trademark notice: Product or corporate names may be trademarks or registered trademarks and are used only for identification and explanation without intent to infringe.

British Library Cataloguing-in-Publication Data
A catalogue record for this book is available from the British Library

Library of Congress Cataloguing-in-Publication Data
A catalog record has been requested for this book

ISBN: 978-0-367-70098-0 (hbk)
ISBN: 978-0-367-70097-3 (pbk)
ISBN: 978-1-003-14456-4 (ebk)

DOI: 10.4324/9781003144564

Typeset Bembo
by KnowledgeWorks Global Ltd.

CONTENTS

List of illustrations — xi
List of contributors — xii
Foreword: Reflections on darkness — xviii
Preface: Bounded experience and unbounded realness — xxvi
Editorial preface — xxxvi
Acknowledgment — xlviii
Editorial acknowledgment — l

PART I
Mythorealism and censorship — 1

1 Yan Lianke's mythorealist representation of the country and the city — 3
   Weijie Song

2 Building Chinese reality with language and metaphor: From socialist realism to mythorealism — 16
   Xiaolu Ma

3 Mythorealism, the absurd, and existential despair in Yan Lianke's memoir and fiction: Confronting the fate of Sisyphus in modern China's historical traumas — 28
   Ashley Liu

4 Magical realism, mythorealism, and the representation of history in the works of Yan Lianke — 37
   Raffael Weger

5 Mythorealism or pararealism? Yan Lianke's short fiction as a key to enter the author's representational world 49
Marco Fumian

6 Censure and censorship: Prohibition and presence of Yan Lianke's writings in China 70
Jessica Yeung

PART II
Absurdity and spirituality 91

7 The absurd as method: The Chinese absurdist hero, enchanted power, and the alienated poor in Yan Lianke's military literature 93
Haiyan Xie

8 Yan Lianke and Italo Calvino on the absurdity of urban life 104
Selusi Ambrogio

9 "Inverse Theology" in Yan Lianke's *The Four Books* and Franz Kafka's *The Trial* 122
Melinda Pirazzoli

10 Elements of modernism and the grotesque in Yan Lianke's early fiction 140
Nicoletta Pesaro

11 Representing the intellectuals in Yan Lianke's recent writing: An exile of the soul 154
Alessandra Pezza

12 The dream, the disease, and the disaster: on Yan Lianke's *Dream of Ding Village* 171
Shelley W. Chan

13 Yan Lianke's novel *Heart Sutra*: The kiss of the rock and the egg 184
Andrea Riemenschnitter

14 The redemption of the peach blossom spring: An examination of the human condition in Yan Lianke's *Zhongyuan* (*Zhongguo gushi*) 199
Di-kai Chao and Riccardo Moratto

PART III
History and gender   217

15 Creating a literary space to debate the Mao era: The fictionalization of the Great Leap Forward in Yan Lianke's *Four Books*   219
    Sebastian Veg

16 Disability, revolution, and historiography: Grandma Mao Zhi in *Lenin's Kisses*   238
    Zihan Wang

17 Corrective catachresis: Capitalist mystification derailed in *The Explosion Chronicles* and "The Story of Fertile Town"   250
    Kwan Yin Lee

18 Reconstructing the self through *herstory*: On Yan Lianke's *Tamen (Shes)*   266
    Sabrina Ardizzoni

19 Female labor, the third sex, and excrescence in Yan Lianke's nonfiction *tamen*   279
    Yijiao Guo

20 A geocritical study of Yan Lianke's *balou* mountain stories: The utopian cognitive mapping in post-1949 China   298
    Chen Wang

21 An ecocritical approach to Yan Lianke's Literary Works   311
    Minh Thương Nguyễn Thi and Riccardo Moratto

22 Paratextual encounters in Yan Lianke's fictional worlds: Reading between the lines   321
    Ronald Torrance

PART IV
Translation and reception   339

23 Ideological patterns in the critical reception of Yan Lianke: A comparative approach   341
    Chunli Shen

24 The challenge of translating Yan Lianke's literary creation   357
    Taciana Fisac

25	Yan Lianke in Basque: Notes on translating sensory images *Maialen Marin-Lacarta*	379
26	The translation and reception of Yan Lianke in France *Lu Gan*	391
27	The treacherous "news that stays news": *The Four Books* in Czech translation *Zuzana Li*	408
28	Translating the Chinese cultural other: Yan Lianke's *Shouhuo* in English translation *Baorong Wang*	417
29	The translation and reception of Yan Lianke in Japan *Dongli Lu and Riccardo Moratto*	437
30	The translation and reception of Yan Lianke's fiction in Vietnam *Van Hieu Do and Riccardo Moratto*	452
31	The reception and significance of Yan Lianke's works in Taiwan *Riccardo Moratto and Di-kai Chao*	467
32	The reception of Yan Lianke in Hong Kong *Carole Hang-fung Hoyan and Yijiao Guo*	489

Complete Chinese bibliography of Yan Lianke in chronological order — *506*
Index — *514*

LIST OF ILLUSTRATIONS

Figures

28.1	Toury's initial norm and the continuum of adequate and acceptable translation	418
32.1	Word cloud of scholarly works	495
32.2	Word cloud of book reviews on local English newspapers	498

Tables

28.1	Classification of translation strategies for CSIs in *Lenin's Kisses*	420
28.2	Statistical results of CSI translation strategies	420

CONTRIBUTORS

Selusi Ambrogio is Adjunct Professor of Chinese Literature, Chinese Philosophy, and Chinese Literary Translation at the University of Macerata and the University of Urbino in Italy. His research interests range from Chinese twentieth-century theater (Lao She), contemporary Chinese literary criticism (Yan Lianke), contemporary New Confucian philosophy with a focus on the historiography of philosophy, and the meeting of Chinese and Jesuits in Ming-dynasty China. He has published articles in several international peer-reviewed journals and has written two monographs. He currently serves as Vice-President of the European Association for Chinese Philosophy (EACP) and a member of the editorial board of *Asian Studies*.

Sabrina Ardizzoni has been teaching Chinese at the University of Bologna since 2003. She graduated in Oriental History in the same university and holds a PhD degree from Ljubljana University. She is a professional translator and community interpreter. Her research interests span from interlinguistic and intercultural issues to minorities education and gender studies. She has published various articles on Hakka culture, focusing on Hakka women and social transformation in Hakka communities in China and abroad.

Shelley W. Chan, Professor of Chinese Language and Cultural Studies at Wittenberg University, received her PhD from the University of Colorado-Boulder, her MA from the University of Wisconsin-Madison, and her BA from Hong Kong Baptist University. She is the author of *A Subversive Voice in China: The Fictional World of Mo Yan* (New York: Cambria Press, 2011) and the editor of *Mo Yan—Year 2000 Series: Close Readings on China* (Hong Kong: Ming Pao, 1999). She has published articles, translations, and book and film reviews on Chinese literature and culture in the United States, France, Germany, Australia, Sweden, China, Hong Kong, and Taiwan. Before joining Wittenberg University, she taught at Stanford University, Kalamazoo College, and Beloit College.

Di-kai Chao is a PhD candidate at the University of Canterbury in New Zealand. He obtained his BA in Chinese literature from National Chengchi University in Taiwan (NCCU), his first MA in Diplomacy studies from NCCU, and his second MA in teaching Chinese as a second language from National Taiwan Normal University. He is also a certificated Chinese language teacher. His research interests mainly focus on Sinophone literature and its relationship with world literature, ghost narrative in contemporary Sinophone fiction, and the lyrical tradition discourse.

Van Hieu Do is a Lecturer of Literary Theory at the Faculty of Philology, Hanoi National University of Education, Vietnam. He earned a PhD in literary theory at the School of Liberal Arts, Renmin University of China. His research focuses on literature reception, ecological criticism, and comparative literature, and he has authored over 40 papers in Chinese and Vietnamese journals.

Taciana Fisac is Professor of Chinese Language and Literature and Director of the Centre for East Asian Studies at the Autonomous University of Madrid. She has been a visiting scholar at various universities and institutes including Stanford University, Oxford University, Leiden University, the Chinese Academy of Social Sciences, Peking University, and Beijing Foreign Studies University, where she was appointed Honorary Professor in 2005. She has also held the title of Distinguished Professor at the Open University of Hong Kong. She has published extensively on gender, literature, and society in China, as well as translated modern and contemporary Chinese literature. In 2012, she was awarded the Special Book Award of China for her contribution to the promotion of Chinese literature.

Marco Fumian is Associate Professor of Chinese Studies at the Oriental University of Naples, Italy, where he teaches Mandarin language and modern Chinese literature. His main interests are in the areas of modern Chinese literature and popular culture, with a focus on their role in the production of mainstream ideological discourses in the PRC. He is the author of a number of articles on contemporary popular literature and a book-length study in Italian, which analyzes the emergence and development of writings by writers born after the 1980s. He is also an occasional translator of modern Chinese literature into Italian.

Lu Gan is a postdoctoral researcher at East China Normal University. Her research interests include translation studies, comparative literature, and world literature.

Yijiao Guo is an MPhil student from the Division of Humanities at Hong Kong University of Science and Technology. His primary research interests lie in contemporary Chinese literature, nonfiction literature, and independent documentary. His current thesis project concentrates on material culture, historiography in things, and lyrical documentation in the post-Cultural Revolution era. He received his BA in Translation from Hong Kong Baptist University.

Carole Hang-fung Hoyan received her PhD from the University of British Columbia. She is currently Associate Professor of the Department of Chinese Language and Literature and Director of the Yale-China Chinese Language Centre of the Chinese University of Hong Kong. Her research interests include modern Chinese fiction and drama, Eileen Chang studies, and Hong Kong literature. She is the author of *Re-Investigating Eileen Chang: Adaptation, Translation and Research* (2018), and *Revisiting Modern Chinese Literature: Close Reading, Data and Reception* (2020) and co-editor of *An Oral History of Hong Kong Drama* (2001). Her recent article is "'Include Me Out': Reading Eileen Chang as a World Literature Author" in *Ex-Position* (2019). She is an editorial committee member of the *Journal of Chinese Literature*.

Contributors

Kwan yin Lee is a PhD candidate in the Department of Comparative Literature at the University of Oregon, whose research dwells on written and filmic renditions of neoliberal realities across the Pacific.

Zuzana Li is a literary translator. She studied English and Chinese philology at Palacký University, Olomouc, and Modern Chinese Literature with Prof. Wen Rumin at Peking University. Her list of book translations consists thus far of eight novels, two collections of short stories, four nonfiction titles, two books for children, and a collection of poems. Her other translations, articles, book reviews, and interviews with writers and scholars have been published in various literary magazines. In 2016, she received the Special Book Award of China for Young Scholars.

Ashley Liu is a lecturer of modern Chinese literature at the University of Maryland. She graduated from the University of Pennsylvania with a PhD degree in East Asian Languages and Civilizations. She specializes in postmodern and postcolonial issues in Sinophone literature, especially literary connections among mainland China, Taiwan, and Hong Kong. Her latest book project, *Polyphonic Sinophone World and the Modern Dilemmas of Topolects, 1890s–1940s* (Amherst: Cambria Press, forthcoming), investigates the relationship between language activism and anti-colonialism in mainland China, Taiwan, and Hong Kong.

Dongli Lu is Associate Professor and Head of the Japanese Department in the School of Foreign Languages, Nanjing Agricultural University. Her research focuses on contemporary Chinese vernacular literature, science fiction literature, and the translation of contemporary poetry in Japan.

Xiaolu Ma is Assistant Professor at the Hong Kong University of Science and Technology. She was trained as a scholar of cultural studies at Harvard University, where she received her PhD degree in Comparative Literature. A native speaker of Chinese and fluent in Japanese and Russian, she engages in rigorous research and teaching in the areas of transculturation and world literature. She has published in English and Chinese on topics of translation theory and transcultural study concerning modern Chinese literature and its interactions with Japanese and Russian literature and culture.

Maialen Marin-Lacarta is a Researcher in the Department of Arts and Humanities at Universitat Oberta de Catalunya. Prior to joining UOC, she was Assistant Professor in the Department of Translation, Interpreting and Intercultural Studies at Hong Kong Baptist University. Among other authors, she has translated Yan Lianke and Mo Yan into Basque and Shen Congwen into Spanish. Her research areas include literary translation, modern and contemporary Chinese literature, literary reception, translation history, indirect translation, research methodologies, and digital publishing. Her publications have appeared in journals such as *Translation Studies*, *The Translator*, *Meta*, and *Perspectives*.

Riccardo Moratto is Full Professor of Translation and Interpreting Studies, Chinese Translation and Interpreting at the Graduate Institute of Interpretation and Translation (GIIT), Shanghai International Studies University (SISU), and Honorary Guest Professor at Nanjing Agricultural University. Prof. Moratto is a Chartered Linguist and Fellow Member of the Chartered Institute of Linguists (CIoL), Visiting Scholar at Shandong University, Honorary Research Fellow at the Center for Translation Studies of Guangdong University of Foreign Studies, and

Expert Member of the Translators Association of China (TAC). Prof. Moratto is also an international conference interpreter and a renowned literary translator. He has published extensively in the fields of translation and interpreting studies and Chinese literature in translation.

Minh Thương Nguyễn Thị earned her PhD in modern and contemporary Chinese literature at the School of Liberal Arts, Renmin University of China. Her research focuses on modern and contemporary Vietnamese literature, modern and contemporary Chinese literature, and comparative literature. She has authored or co-authored over twenty papers in specialized literary journals in Vietnam and China. Currently, she is a lecturer in the Department of Modern and Contemporary Studies at Hanoi National University of Education.

Nicoletta Pesaro is Associate Professor of Chinese Language, Literature and Translation at Ca' Foscari University of Venice, where she coordinates the MA program in Interpreting and Translation for Publishing and for Special Purposes. Her research interests focus on modern Chinese literature, narrative theory, and translation studies. She has published several articles and translations of modern Chinese literature. In 2013, she edited the book *The Ways of Translation: Constraints and Liberties in Translating Chinese* (Cafoscarina). She has recently co-authored with M. Pirazzoli a book on the history of Chinese fiction in the twentieth century: *La narrativa cinese del Novecento. Autori, opere, correnti* (Carocci, 2019). She is the Editor in Chief of the open-access book series *Translating Wor(l)ds*.

Alessandra Pezza obtained her PhD at INALCO in Paris and is currently a postdoctoral researcher at Università di Milano-Bicocca. Her research focuses mostly on the representation of forgotten and traumatic history and of cultural identity in contemporary Chinese literature. She is also interested in translation studies (participation in Officina workshop activities at Università Bicocca) and translating Chinese fiction (post-1980s fiction, flash fiction, *wuxia* literature). She is currently translating the second volume of Jin Yong's *She diao yingxiong zhuan* into Italian.

Melinda Pirazzoli is Adjunct Professor of Chinese Literature. She has published a study on classical Chinese poetry (Ananke, 2016) and a history of modern and contemporary Chinese fiction co-written with Nicoletta Pesaro (Carocci, 2019). She has published articles on modern and contemporary Chinese fiction. Her article on Yan Lianke's *Liven* and *Dream of Ding Village* has recently appeared on CLCWeb.

Andrea Riemenschnitter is Chair Professor of Modern Chinese Language and Literature at the University of Zurich. Her current research focuses on aesthetic, cultural, and literary negotiations of Sinophone modernities with a special interest in environmental humanities and art activism. Recent publications include *Anthropocene Matters: Envisioning Sustainability in the Sinosphere* (co-ed. special issue of ICCC, 2018) and *Hong Kong Connections Across the Sinosphere* (co-ed. special issue of *Interventions*, 2018). She is the organizer of the online course *Asian Environmental Humanities: Landscapes in Transition* (2018) and was invited as a research fellow and guest professor to universities in Europe, the United States, and East Asia.

Chunli Shen is a PhD candidate from Bangor University, UK. Her research interests include translation and ideology, translation and gender, and reception studies. Her article "Images of National Politics: The Reception and Translation of Yan Lianke's Fiction" is published in *Translation Quarterly*.

Contributors

Weijie Song is Associate Professor in the Department of Asian Languages and Cultures at Rutgers University. He is the author of *Mapping Modern Beijing: Space, Emotion, Literary Topography*, *From Entertainment Activity to Utopian Impulse: Rereading Jin Yong's Martial Arts Fiction*, and *China, Literature, and the United States: Images of China in American and Chinese-American Novel and Drama*. His new projects include "Ide©ology: Environmental Objects and Chinese Ecocriticism," "Chivalrous Psychogeography: Martial Arts, Avant-Garde, Sinophone Cinema," and "Reviving Northeast China: Contemporary Literature and Film Beyond the Great Wall." He is the (co)editor of *Selected Works of Xu Dishan* and *Environmental Humanities, Ecocriticism, Nature Writing*, as well as the (co)translator of *Repressed Modernities, Translingual Practice, Comparative Poetics*, *The Structural Transformation of Public Sphere*, *Understanding Popular Culture*, and *After the Great Divide: Modernism, Mass Culture, Postmodernism*.

Ronald Torrance studied at the University of Strathclyde, where he obtained his BA and MLitt. Ronald completed his PhD in contemporary Chinese literature at the University of Strathclyde. His thesis, entitled *The Re-presentation of History in the Works of Mo Yan, Ma Jian and Yan Lianke*, theorizes how significant historic events are symbolically represented in contemporary Chinese fiction. He is published in *Europe-Asia Studies*, the *Journal of the British Association for Chinese Studies*, and writes for *Cha: An Asian Literary Journal*.

Sebastian Veg is Professor of Intellectual History of Modern and Contemporary China, School of Advanced Studies in the Social Sciences at EHESS in Paris and an Honorary Professor at the University of Hong Kong, with interest in the history of intellectuals, social movements, and the public sphere, as well as in the recent history of Hong Kong. His latest book is *Minjian: The Rise of China's Grassroots Intellectuals* (Columbia UP, 2019).

Haiyan Xie is Associate Professor at Central China Normal University. She received her PhD degree from the program of Comparative Literature at the University of Alberta. She has published interviews with Yan Lianke and essays on his literature in some respectable journals, and two other essays are forthcoming in *MCLC* and *Texas Studies in Literature and Language*. She is now working on her book project tentatively titled *Mythorealism as Method: Form and Ideology in Yan Lianke's Fiction*. Her research interest covers Yan Lianke's research, the reception of contemporary Chinese literature in the Anglophone world, and translation and modernity around the May Fourth period.

Baorong Wang received his PhD in Translation Studies from the University of Hong Kong in 2012 and is currently a Distinguished Professor of Translation Studies at Hangzhou Normal University in Zhejiang, China. He is the author of two Chinese monographs: *The Experience of the Foreign: English Representations of Shaoxing Culture in Lu Xun's Fiction* (Zhejiang UP, 2015) and *Modes of Translation and Dissemination for Chinese Literature: With Special Reference to Modern Chinese Fiction in English* (Zhejiang UP, 2021). He has also published over 100 articles in both Chinese and international journals. His research interests include socio-translation studies, translation and dissemination of Chinese literature, and Chinese translation history.

Chen Wang received her PhD in Asian Literatures, Cultures, and Media with a graduate minor in Comparative Studies of Discourse and Society at the University of Minnesota-Twin Cities. She is currently a Visiting Assistant Professor of Chinese at Williams College. Her research interests include twentieth-century Chinese literature, translation theories, literary bilingualism, literary geocriticism, urban studies, and diaspora studies.

Zihan Wang completed his PhD in comparative literature at Purdue University. His research interests include medical humanities and modern Chinese literature and film. Inspired by his recent interest in digital humanities, he is pursuing an MS degree in computer science at Northeastern University, Seattle.

Raffael Weger studied Sinology and comparative literature at the University of Vienna and Peking University. He wrote a master's thesis on subversive representations of history in the works of Mo Yan and Yan Lianke with a special focus on their usage of magical realism and mythorealism. Since 2016 he has been working as an independent reviewer for Litprom's translation funding initiative, and in 2020 he was employed as a research assistant for a publication project on the Austrian writer Peter Waterhouse. His areas of research include contemporary Chinese fiction, metafiction, and magical realism.

Jessica Yeung is Associate Professor at the Department of Translation, Interpreting and Intercultural Cultural Studies, Hong Kong Baptist University. She is the author of *Ink Dances in Limbo: Gao Xingjian's Writings as Cultural Translation*, *The Third Way for Hong Kong: The Anarchist People's Theatre of Augustine Chiu-yu Mok* (in Chinese), and numerous articles on Chinese and Hong Kong literature and creative arts. She is also editor and translator of *Tharlo: Short Story and Film Script by Pema Tseden*. Her current research is on Uyghur cinema.

FOREWORD

Reflections on darkness

Carlos Rojas

Yan Lianke's first full-length novel, *The Prison-House of Emotion* (*Qinggan yu* 情感狱, 1991), is framed by two fractured betrothals. First, the work opens with the 20-year-old narrator learning that his fiancée has suddenly decided to break off their engagement because her father, the local village chief, wants her to marry the son of the deputy township mayor, who is about to be promoted to the position of township mayor. Second, the novel concludes a few months later, with the narrator rescuing the daughter of the local party secretary after she injures herself falling from a precipice. The narrator hopes the young woman will be willing to marry him, but she informs him that she has recently become engaged to a county official—explaining that after their people's commune is converted into a township and their production brigade is converted into a village, she hopes her fiancé will then be appointed township mayor, which in turn may enable her own father to be appointed village chief. The novel's coda then describes how the protagonist, disillusioned by these failed romances, decides instead to join the army but is initially passed over in favor of the nephews of the village's party secretary and of the director of the public security bureau, both of whom had failed the same military fitness exam that the narrator had already passed. Only after the narrator threatens to kill himself is he finally accepted into the army.

In addition to reflecting on the intricate imbrication of personal and political considerations at the beginning of the reform era (the conversion of brigades and communes into villages and townships, mentioned at the end of the work, occurred in 1983), *The Prison-House of Emotion* also offers an example of a self-referential gesture that will later become one of the distinctive features of many of Yan's later writings—in that the work's narrator shares the same name as the author, and the narrator's eventual decision to join the army at the age of twenty mirrors Yan's own decision to join the PLA when he was the same age.

Although, for the most part, *The Prison-House of Emotion* is structured as a conventional linear narrative, it does contain several non-narrative segments that anticipate the more experimental, self-referential style for which Yan Lianke will later become known.

For instance, after the narrator reveals, near the end of the first chapter, that the current fiancé of the village chief's daughter "is actually me, Yan Lianke," he immediately breaks to another, seemingly unrelated narrative:

> Let me tell you another story. In this story, our family has a house, behind which lie the Balou [耙耧] Mountains. In reality, however, they are not so much mountains as hills.

> Last spring, when the grass was fresh, the trees were green, and the fragrance was thick, I went out to weed the fields, whereupon I suddenly witnessed a miraculous sight: the hillside was suddenly covered in thousands upon thousands of wild rabbits that were all racing down the mountain. The rabbits blanketed the earth and sky, like flocks of large grey birds flying up and down around the mountain. The rabbits ran from west to east, as bright as mirrors. They sparkled in the sunlight, as though the sun itself were flickering on and off. As the rabbits tried to avoid the sunlight, they oriented their heads toward the ground, which was a vast expanse of darkness.[1]

In this passage, the narrator appears to be attempting to change the topic in order to avoid dwelling on the discomfort of his broken marital engagement. Curiously, though, imbedded within this narrative digression is another act of avoidance—in the specification that the rabbits racing down the mountain have their heads cocked down to avoid the sunlight. This evocative description of the rabbits staring down into "an expanse of darkness" (*yi pian hei'an* 一片黑暗), in turn, offers an uncannily prophetic description of Yan's subsequent literary trajectory. A recurrent theme throughout Yan's literary oeuvre, and particularly since the late 1990s, has involved a general avoidance of what might be regarded as the bright spots of China's development during the modern and contemporary periods, and a focus on a set of phenomena positioned in the shadows of this dominant narrative of political transformation and economic development.

Born in 1958 in rural Henan Province, Yan Lianke joined the People's Liberation Army (PLA) in 1978, the same year Deng Xiaoping launched the Reform and Opening Up Campaign, which catalyzed a period of rapid economic growth, more international contact, and a partial loosening of governmental controls over cultural production. The following year, Yan published his first story, "A Story of Gastrodia Orchids" (*Tianma de gushi* 天麻的故事, 1979), about a young man attempting to join the army. Over the next two and a half decades, Yan worked as a professional author for the PLA, and although many of his early works were relatively conventional social-realist narratives, beginning in the late 1990s, he began to shift to a more experimental style and attention to issues of oppression and exclusion, which is to say, the dark underbelly of modern China's vision of its own political and economic progress.

In particular, the first major work from the more experimental and socially engaged phase of Yan's career is arguably his fourth full-length novel, *Streams of Time* (*Riguang liunian* 日光流年, 1998). The novel, which is narrated in a reverse chronological fashion, beginning with the protagonist's death and then proceeding backward to his birth, focuses on a town whose residents suffer from a variety of physical ailments, and as a result, they invariably die before they reach the age of forty. Early on, the work reveals that a United Nations health team has determined that the town's health problems are caused by excessive amounts of fluoride in the community's water supply, and the work's plot focuses on the town's attempts to find an alternate water supply, one which, they hope, might help cure the disease that plagues them. In its implication that the elevated fluoride levels are caused by industrial contamination of some sort, the work presciently anticipates the debate over China's so-called cancer villages that the Chinese journalist Deng Fei 鄧飛 helped initiate a decade later.[2]

---

1 Yan Lianke 閻連科, *Qinggan yu* 情感獄 [The prison-house of emotion] (Beijing: Zhongguo renmin jiefangjun chubanshe, 1991), 1.
2 As early as 2009, Deng Fei compiled a Google map of Chinese villages with unusually high cancer rates. For a discussion, see Paulina Hartono, "A Map of China's Cancer Villages," China Digital Times, last modified 8 May 2009, https://chinadigitaltimes.net/2009/05/a-map-of-chinas-cancer-villages/.

Foreword

Published eight years after *Streams of Time*, Yan's 2006 novel *Dream of Ding Village* (*Dingzhuang meng* 丁莊夢) adopts a similarly unconventional narrative structure, insofar as roughly every other chapter is narrated in the voice of a young boy who is killed shortly before the novel begins, meaning that he is narrating the work from beyond the grave. The novel describes a remote Henan village that has been devasted by an outbreak of HIV/AIDS driven by contaminated blood-selling equipment, but unlike China's so-called cancer villages, which had not yet become a talking point at the time that Yan wrote *Streams of Time*, the nation's rural HIV/AIDS crisis had already received considerable attention by the time Yan began writing *Dream of Ding Village*. Yan actually made several trips to a Henan village that had been impacted by the epidemic, and he drew on his observations in this village when writing the resulting novel. As Yan later observes, however, in his novel, he deliberately downplayed some of the more horrific aspects of what he observed in this AIDS village, in an attempt to avoid problems with the censors.[3] As it turns out, however, even after this process of self-censorship, the novel was still recalled shortly after its initial publication.

After this frustrating experience in writing *Dream of Ding Village* (for which Yan feels he censored himself, only to have the work be banned anyway), Yan resolved—when writing about the politically sensitive topic of the Great Famine four years later—to approach the topic without consideration of how the novel might be received by the censors. The result was his 2010 novel *The Four Books* (*Sishu* 四書), which unfolds in a 1950s labor-reform camp for accused Rightists, with the latter portion of the work being set against the backdrop of the Great Famine (1959–62). The novel's title alludes to the way the work is composed of four interspliced texts, including two that were nominally composed by a fictional character known simply as "the Author." One of these texts, titled "Criminal Records," is a journalistic account of the illicit activities of some of the camp's other detainees, and we are told that the Author has agreed to compile these records for the authorities in order to secure greater leniency for himself. The other text, titled "Old Course," is an account of many of the same events recounted in "Criminal Records," but presented in a more literary style. We are told that the Author began compiling the latter text in secret, hoping to use it as the basis of a novel once he is released from the camp. With this juxtaposition of two fictional texts recounting the same events but for radically different purposes *The Four Books* foregrounds the challenge of how a contemporary author might reconcile his or her literary aspirations with the practical exigencies of working within a state-driven censorship system.

In addition to his focus on social crises in fictional works like *Streams of Time*, *Dream of Ding Village*, and *The Four Books*, Yan also reflects on issues of politics and aesthetics in many of his non-fictional works. For instance, in 2011, shortly after completing *The Four Books*, Yan published a volume of literary criticism titled *Discovering Fiction* (*Faxian xiaoshuo* 發現小說), in which he discusses developments in realist and neorealist fiction from the nineteenth century to the present, including a postrealist practice he calls "mythorealism," which he suggests is a distinguishing feature of some of his own recent works. Yan opens this study by alluding to the afterword he wrote for *The Four Books*, titled "A Traitor to Writing," in which he describes how, as he was writing the novel, he was sanguine about the fact that the novel had almost no chance of being published in China. He then explains that "many of the deviations from 'literary conventions' that appear in *The Four Books* are not true cases of betrayal, but rather they are merely preliminary

---

3 See, for instance, Yan's comments in a 2016 interview with Zhang Ying 張英, available in English translation at "Being Alive Is Not Just an Instinct," ESWN Culture Blog, 23 Mar. 2006, http://www.zonaeuropa.com/culture/c20060327_1.htm.

clues—hints of what I might write in the future. This, accordingly, is why I ultimately decided to call myself a traitor to writing."[4]

Yan Lianke reflects on related issues in his 2014 essay collection *Silence and Rest: Chinese Literature in My Experience* (*Chenmo yu chuanxi: Wo suo jingli de Zhongguo he wenxue* 沉默與喘息：我所經歷的中國和文學). Based on a series of twelve lectures Yan delivered at North American universities following the publication of the English translation of *Lenin's Kisses* in 2012, this volume addresses topics ranging from the relationship between what he calls "national amnesia" and "literary memory" to the condition of "living without dignity" yet "writing with honor." One of the most pointed essays in this collection, however, explicitly addresses the issue of literary censorship. Yan opens the essay by observing that, when he travels abroad, he is frequently introduced as China's "most censored author," but he specifies that this is definitely not something in which he takes any pride. He notes that we often celebrate banned works by famous authors like Solzhenitsyn, Pasternak, Nabokov, D. H. Lawrence, Borges, Vargas Llosa, Miller, Kundera, Rushdie, Pamuk, and Simail Kadare, but he contends that these works are not great because they were banned, but instead they are great works that happen to have been banned. Indeed, he argues that there is no inherent value in having one's works banned, as there are countless mediocre works that have been banned but which are largely forgotten. On the other hand, despite insisting that banned works are not necessarily good, Yan also notes that, given the specific political realities of contemporary China, if an author *never* runs into trouble with the state censorship apparatus, then that is rather suspicious in its own right.

Yan Lianke reflects even more explicitly on the political ramifications of his writing in his essay "The Person Selected by Heaven and Life to Experience Darkness" ("Shangtian he shenghuo xuanding nage ganshou hei'an de ren" 上天和生活選定那個感受黑暗的人) which he initially wrote as his acceptance speech upon winning the Franz Kafka Prize in 2014.[5] Yan opens the essay by recalling how, during the Great Famine, known euphemistically as the "three years of natural disaster," his mother observed to him that when people are starving, they will eat anything, even clay:

> After saying this, Mother went back inside to cook some food, leaving behind a shadow like dried-up leaves blowing in the wind. As for me, I stood on that edible clay gazing out at the sunset, the village, and the fields, as an enormous sheet of darkness gradually approached. From that point on, I proceeded to develop a very keen appreciation for darkness.[6]

After this opening prologue, Yan recalls an old blind man from his home village, and describes how "Every morning when the sun came up, [the blind man] would turn to the Eastern mountains and, facing the rising sun, would say to himself, 'It turns out that sunlight is actually black—but that is good!'" He recalls how, when the blind man went out at night, he would always take a flashlight—not to help him see, but rather to permit others to see him. Yan then suggests that when he later became an author, he took inspiration from this blind man:

> From this blind man, I came up with a new form of writing that is premised on a conviction that the darker it is, the brighter it becomes; and the colder it is, the warmer it

---

4 Yan Lianke, *Faxian xiaoshuo* (Taipei: Ink Publishing, 2011), 12.
5 An excerpt from this essay was published in English in a *The New York Times* op-ed titled "Finding Light in China's Darkness," 22 Oct. 2014, https://www.nytimes.com/2014/10/23/opinion/Yan-Lianke-finding-light-in-chinas-darkness.html, and a full translation will appear in the English version of *Silence and Rest*, forthcoming from Duke University Press.
6 Yan Lianke, "Shangtian he shenghuo xuanding nage ganshou hei'an de ren," 2014. This Chinese text can be found on several online sites, including https://www.aisixiang.com/data/79207.html.

becomes. The entire significance of this writing lies in permitting people to avoid its existence. My writing, in other words, is like the blind man with the flashlight who shines his light into the darkness to help others glimpse their goal and destination.[7]

Yan concludes that his receipt of the Kafka Prize is akin to the blind man receiving a lamp:

Because this lamp exists, that person who is fated to see only darkness can believe that in front of him there is light. Moreover, thanks to this light people can therefore perceive the existence of darkness, and consequently can more effectively ward off that same darkness and suffering. Meanwhile, that blind man can remain on the night road, and as people walk past him, he can illuminate the road in front of them—even if just for a short distance.[8]

Yan's twist on the original metaphor of the blind man can be found in his suggestion that the blind man's objective is not to use light to eliminate darkness, but rather to use light to help those around him to "[be able to] perceive the existence of darkness" (*neng kanjian hei'an de cunzai* 能看見黑暗的存在), so that they might then be able to attempt to ward off that same darkness and its implications.

Two recent works that use a self-referential conceit to help to explore themes of darkness and its potential illumination are the novels *The Explosion Chronicles* (*Zhalie zhi* 炸裂志, 2013) and *The Day the Sun Died* (*Rixi* 日熄, 2015). The narrator of *Explosion Chronicles* is a Beijing-based author named Yan Lianke, who has been recruited by his hometown mayor to compile and edit a local history of the municipality, which by that point is known as Explosion City. The fictional Yan Lianke accepts the assignment, and the implication is that the resulting chronicle corresponds roughly to the text of *Explosion Chronicles* itself. In particular, the text describes how, over the preceding decades, Explosion had enjoyed explosive growth as it grew from a small town into a vast megalopolis, obviously resonating with the explosive growth that China has enjoyed in the post-Mao era. In addition, through its focus on the fictional Yan Lianke's position as the designated author and editor of the local gazetteer, the novel underscores the role of chroniclers of all sorts, including historians, journalists, intellectuals, and novelists, in helping shape the narratives through which historical transformations may be viewed and understood.

The novel concludes with a twist, however, in that when the fictional Yan Lianke submits his manuscript to the mayor who commissioned the chronicle, the mayor is deeply displeased with the result—to the point that he not only refuses to accept the manuscript, he even burns it as the fictional Yan Lianke watches in horror:

The inch-thick bound copy of *The Explosion Chronicles* was placed neatly on the desk in front of [the mayor].

"Have you finished it?" I stammered. "It's a first draft and still needs to be revised."

"No need!" With this, the mayor took out a lighter and held it up to the manuscript, then set it on fire. As the fire was about to singe his hand, he threw the manuscript

---

[7] Yan, "The Person Selected by Heaven."
[8] Ibid.

down, then kicked it until the pages were reduced to ashes and all that remained was the spine and some burning embers. Then he looked up and said three things:

"As long as Explosion and I are here, you shouldn't even think about publishing this book in China.

"… If you try to publish this book anywhere outside China, you'll never be permitted to return to your hometown in the Balou Mountains as long as you live.

"… I want you to leave Explosion today. If you don't leave today, there's no telling what I'll do to you!"[9]

The mayor's reaction to the fictional Yan Lianke's manuscript resonates with the challenges that the real Yan Lianke was encountering during this same period—in that, although *Explosion Chronicles* was able to be published in mainland China, his preceding novel, *The Four Books*, was rejected by all of the Chinese publishers he contacted and, a few years earlier, *Dream of Ding Village* was recalled and banned shortly after its initial publication. In this respect, the novel reflects not only on some of the negative consequences of the nation's hyperbolic economic expansion and urbanization, it also comments on the way in which alternate perspectives and narratives are often relegated to the shadows of contemporary China's focus on progress.

Yan's following novel, *The Day the Sun Died*, meanwhile, similarly features a character who is loosely modeled on the author, and it concludes with a comparable act of textual immolation. In particular, in *The Day the Sun Died*, the fictional Yan Lianke is a neighbor of Li Niannian 李念念, the young boy who is the work's protagonist. Set in the town of Gaotian 皋田, the novel is narrated by Niannian, whose parents run a local funerary shop and whose uncle runs a crematorium. The work focuses on the events of a single night when most of the town's residents inexplicably begin to sleepwalk, leading to dramatic outbreaks of violence as many of the townspeople begin to act on impulses that were normally held in check when they were awake. The result is a bloodbath that leaves hundred dead or injured. The novel concludes with the fictional Yan Lianke visiting the narrator's home, where he pays his respects to the funeral portrait of the narrator's father, who had died during the night of the mass somnambulism:

[The visitor, Yan Lianke,] gazed at my father's funeral portrait without saying a word. He was silent for a long time—for what seemed like an entire day, an entire month, an entire year, and even an entire lifetime. Eventually, he began to remove several books from his suitcase, until he formed a pile—an enormous pile of books. The books had titles like *Kissing Lenin's Years* and like *Water, Ballad, Hymn, and Sun*; *Ding of Dream Village*; and *The Dead Books*. There was also *The Days, Months, Years* and *My Gaotian and Father's Generation*. The visitor placed the books in front of Father's funeral portrait, then lit them on fire. As he was doing so, he didn't kneel down, nor did he light any incense sticks. Rather, he merely stood there watching the fire, and looking at my father's black-and-white portrait. After the fire began to die down, the man gave Mother a final look, then caressed my face and patted my head.

---

9 Yan Lianke, *The Explosion Chronicles*, trans. Carlos Rojas (New York: Grove Atlantic, 2016), 448.

"If I don't succeed in writing the book your father asked me to write—a book that would function as a warm stove in winter and a cool electric fan in summer—then I won't ever return to this town."[10]

The titles listed here are all permutations of titles of works by the real Yan Lianke, just as the new book alluded to at the end of this passage is clearly a correlate of the novel *The Day the Sun Died* itself. In the end, however, it is unclear whether or not the fictional Yan Lianke ever finishes the book about the events described in *The Day the Sun Died*.

The fictional Yan Lianke's act of lighting on fire a pile of his earlier novels in this scene is paralleled by an earlier spectacular act of self-immolation. The novel had described how, as the somnambulistic night dragged on, time itself eventually froze just before sunrise. Concerned that the town's clocks would remain stuck at 6:00 a.m. and the sun would never come up, Niannian's father resolved to light himself on fire in the middle of a vast pool of "corpse oil" that his brother, Niannian's uncle, had collected over the years as a byproduct of the process of cremating human bodies:

> Father didn't cry or shout, and instead he stood there and let the burning oil envelop the kindling, branches, and clothing he was holding. The conflagration also continued to envelop his own body. He let the flames climb the pile of kindling, grass, and branches, and soon an enormous fireball emerged out of the fiery conflagration. The oil pit's burning surface was initially only as large as a tatami mat, but eventually it became larger than a house. In the blink of an eye, the fire enveloped the grass and kindling, and climbed up Father's fiery column. The fire reached upward and spread outward in all directions, quickly engulfing everything around it. There were red and blue flames, and when the fire reached the point where the oil touched the grass and kindling, it became a golden yellow fireball. I saw Father standing in the fire like a fireball on the spire of a fiery tower. That spire was swaying precariously back and forth, but didn't topple over.

"The sun has come out! Write me into your novel as a good person!"[11]

Not only does the father's self-immolation light up the night as though it were day, it also successfully summons the long-delayed sun to rise again, thereby bringing to an end what had threatened to become an interminable night. Ironically, however, even as this human fireball, fueled by the highly flammable "corpse oil" from countless earlier cremations, generates a radiant light that finally dispels the eerie darkness that had enveloped the town, it simultaneously serves as a reminder of the dark impulses the town's somnambulistic night had summoned forth.

With his final words being an entreaty to the fictional Yan Lianke to "write me into your novel as a good person," the father's death marks not only the end of the dark night that had engulfed his family and the entire town, but also the beginning of the process by which the fictional Yan Lianke endeavors to transform the preceding night's events into a coherent literary narrative. In this respect, the fictional Yan Lianke is perhaps not unlike the herd of rabbits that appears at the beginning of *The Prison-house of Emotion*—figuratively turning away from the sun-like conflagration of the father's self-immolation, and focusing instead on the underlying expanse of darkness that the father's death has helped illuminate.

---

10 Yan Lianke, *The Day the Sun Died*, trans. Carlos Rojas (New York: Grove Atlantic, 2018), 340.
11 Yan, *The Day the Sun Died*, 321–22.

Bibliography

Hartono, Paulina. "A Map of China's Cancer Villages." China Digital Times. Last modified 8 May 2009. https://chinadigitaltimes.net/2009/05/a-map-of-chinas-cancer-villages/.

Yan Lianke. *The Day the Sun Died*. Translated by Carlos Rojas. New York: Grove Atlantic, 2018.

———. *The Explosion Chronicles*. Translated by Carlos Rojas. New York: Grove Atlantic, 2016.

———. *Faxian xiaoshuo* 發現小說 [Discovering fiction]. Taipei: Ink Publishing, 2011.

———. "Finding Light in China's Darkness." *The New York Times*, 22 Oct. 2014. https://www.nytimes.com/2014/10/23/opinion/Yan-Lianke-finding-light-in-chinas-darkness.html.

———. *Qinggan yu* 情感獄 [The prison-house of emotion]. Beijing: Zhongguo renmin jiefangjun chubanshe, 1991.

———. *Silence and Rest*. Translated by Carlos Rojas. Durham: Duke University Press, forthcoming.

———. "Shangtian he shenghuo xuanding nage ganshou hei'an de ren" 上天和生活選定那個感受黑暗的人 [The person selected by heaven and life to experience darkness]. Last modified 23 Oct. 2014. https://www.aisixiang.com/data/79207.html.

PREFACE

Bounded experience and unbounded realness

Yan Lianke[1]

I would like to begin my preface with a quotation.

"I sat on the dock with the sun like a thin paper under my butt."[2] This is the opening sentence of the novel *Folk Ballad* (*Minyao* 民謠) written by the critic Wang Yao 王堯. It is hard to guess whether this novel will become a must-read or will be gradually forgotten; however, those who read it will most certainly remember this sentence. The two questions that arise from this statement are: (1) readers understand that it defies empirical logic because everyone knows that one cannot simply sit on the sun; it is the sun that sits in the sky. Yet why do readers not pursue this logic that defies common sense? (2) The sun is a symbol and metaphor for humanity, especially in China, where the sacredness of the "red sun" is a metaphor for supreme power, reminiscent of Dante's likening the sun to God in the *Divine Comedy*. Sitting the sun under one's buttocks defies the logic and experience of life; however, it seems to awaken a truer spiritual presence within people's hearts. From such a paradox of empirical logic, a series of questions about the experience and reality of literature are posed before us.

The seeds of experience

Literature originates with human beings' innate ability to remember and tell stories. Storytelling is essential to the development of cultures, ultimately leading to our multicultural world. Literature conveys all aspects of human life. Life forms have constantly been changing over the long course of history, creating the fluidity and changeability of literary reality. Thus, in literature, the truth flows and changes along with the flow of human life.

All views of reality and literature that cling to one literary truth will be but closed, authoritarian, and doubtable.

Human life is not immutable.

Likewise, literature does not have an immutable view of the truth and of what is real. Literature is, after all, a product of experience, and the experience spoken of here is none other than the variations of life forms. Every time we read literary publications, we find that almost all of them

---

1 This article was translated from Chinese by Riccardo Moratto and Haiyan Xie.
2 Wang Yao, *Minyao* (Nanjing: Yilin chubanshe, 2021), 1: 我坐在碼頭上，太陽像一張薄薄的紙墊在屁股下.

are depicting the same life experiences and the stories unfold in almost the same way. Writers seem to be purely experiential porters, the variations of whose work are only in the size and shape of the packing boxes. When we open these boxes, apart from stacks of life experiences, it is hard to glimpse even a bit of imaginable, but not practical, life experiences—like a mirror, our writing habitually reflects only the part of practical life experiences. In this regard, the life and truth of literature seem to be predetermined by this practicable life experience.

At least, this is true for contemporary China.

This is true of a significant portion, or the vast majority, of writing in today's China due to forces inherent in the literary development. We should think and ask why literature has to be so devoted to pleasing the practicable experiences. Within the literature, what power does the real, practical experiences of life have to decide that literary reality can only follow certain guidelines? What are the most universal and practicable experiences in human life and how do they influence and determine the literary truth?

Without a doubt, the most universal life experiences are food, clothing, and desire. Indeed, eating is the first event narrated at the beginning of Homer's *The Iliad* around 750 BC.

> Achilles' wrath, to Greece the direful spring
> Of woes unnumber'd, heavenly goddess, sing!
> That wrath which hurl'd to Pluto's gloomy reign
> The souls of mighty chiefs untimely slain;
> Whose limbs unburied on the naked shore,
> Devouring dogs and hungry vultures tore.[3]

Homer's epic, one of the earliest literary masterpieces, is almost exclusively devoted to gods and non-human heroes; however, the author does not forget to mention human life experiences, that is, the necessity of food and clothing even for gods and non-human heroes. In the Trojan War schemed by Zeus, the divinity sent Morpheus to inform the son of the god Atreus. When the non-human hero Agamemnon went to attack the city of Troy,

> Eager he rises, and in fancy hears
> The voice celestial murmuring in his ears.
> First on his limbs a slender vest he drew,
> Around him next the regal mantle threw,
> The embroider'd sandals on his feet were tied;
> The starry falchion glitter'd at his side;
> And last, his arm the massy sceptre loads,
> Unstain'd, immortal, and the gift of gods[4]

Food and clothing are assumed to be very insignificant and nearly negligible to the gods and non-human heroes, yet the poet never forgets to write about it and always provides a timely account. The main difference between gods and humans in the poet's writing is that gods feast on nectar, whereas humans live on plain food; non-human heroes wear "regal mantles," while common men wear simple straw coats.

In the Genesis, prior to the creation of man, God created plants and animals which would have been given to man as food: "And God said, Behold, I have given you every herb bearing

---

3 Alexander Pope, trans., The Project Gutenberg eBook of *The Iliad*, by Homer, 17 Nov. 2002, http://www.gutenberg.org/files/6130/6130-h/6130-h.htm#note_41 (last accessed 7 Aug. 2021).
4 Ibid.

Preface

seed, which is upon the face of all the earth, and every tree, in the which is the fruit of a tree yielding seed; to you it shall be for meat. And to every beast of the earth, and to every fowl of the air, and to everything that creepeth upon the earth, wherein there is life, I have given every green herb for meat: and it was so"; "And the Lord God took the man, and put him into the garden of Eden to dress it and to keep it. And the Lord God commanded the man, saying, of every tree of the garden thou mayest freely eat"; "And the eyes of them both were opened, and they knew that they were naked; and they sewed fig leaves together, and made themselves aprons."[5]

In *The Metamorphoses*, in Ovid's retelling of the first era of mankind, the "Golden Age," one can read:

> The teeming Earth, yet guiltless of the plough,
> And unprovok'd, did fruitful stores allow:
> Content with food, which Nature freely bred,
> On wildings and on strawberries they fed;
> Cornels and bramble-berries gave the rest,
> And falling acorns furnish'd out a feast.
> The flow'rs unsown, in fields and meadows reign'd:
> And Western winds immortal spring maintain'd.
> In following years, the bearded corn ensu'd
> From Earth unask'd, nor was that Earth renew'd.
> From veins of vallies, milk and nectar broke;
> And honey sweating through the pores of oak.[6]

When Dante woke up in the Dark Forest, he first encountered the leopard, representing lust, then the lion, representing pride, and soon thereafter the greedy she-wolf. Lust, pride, and greed are the three most primitive and universal human emotions and, in writing about them, the poet has struck at the heart of the human spirit. However, the supreme poet Dante Alighieri did not neglect some of the basic and most universal human desires. So, when it comes to the greedy she-wolf, Dante writes:

> Because this beast, at which thou criest out,
> Suffers not any one to pass her way,
> But so doth harass him, that she destroys him;
> And has a nature so malign and ruthless,
> That never doth she glut her greedy will,
> And after food is hungrier than before.
> Many the animals with whom she weds,
> And more they shall be still, until the Greyhound
> Comes, who shall make her perish in her pain.[7]

From Homer's *The Iliad* to the Bible, and from Ovid's *The Metamorphoses* to Dante's *Divine Comedy*, these works cover a wide range of time and space, from heaven to hell, the protagonists

---

[5] Genesis 1:29-30; 2:15-16; 3:7 (King James version).
[6] Sir Samuel Garth, et al., trans., The Internet Classics Archive, http://classics.mit.edu/Ovid/metam.html (last accessed 7 Aug. 2021).
[7] Henry Wadsworth Longfellow, trans., The Project Gutenberg eBook of *The Divine Comedy*, Hell, by Dante Alighieri, https://www.gutenberg.org/files/1001/1001-h/1001-h.htm (last accessed 7 Aug. 2021).

being gods, humans, non-human heroes, and symbolic animals. However, the authors never forget to mention that these non-human "characters" eat, dress, and have the same desires as human beings. Even in the epic of Gilgamesh, which was created nearly 4000 BCE, Gilgamesh is two-thirds god, (one-third human), and all the non-human beasts in the narrative present inclinations to food, clothing, and desire in their behavior.

Why did the earliest and greatest poets feel compelled to describe these most primitive and basic human desires? The earliest wise men, poets, and writers were aware of the fact that literature has insurmountable limitations: even if the "characters" in a literary work are gods, the author and the readers are all human beings. The dominance of perceptible and implementable life experiences in today's literature is inextricably linked to these early roots and seeds.

Human experiences replace the truths reflected in gods, immortals, and monstrous creatures

Human life experiences can be roughly classified into two categories: implementable and unimplementable. The former comprises food, clothing, desires, and various emotions that can be transformed into experiences. The latter may be exemplified in Zeus' informing Agamemnon that he could attack the city of Troy through the god of dreams or Dante's encounter with the leopard, the lion, and the she-wolf in the Dark Forest, as well as all the subsequent sights and experiences alongside the Roman poet Virgil through Hell and Purgatory. The former comprise the life experiences that almost all people have, while the latter is an imaginary life experience not conceivable to everyone. Homer would have never walked and chanted in ancient Greece under the stars had he not wanted his chants to be received by a wider audience. If the Bible was not intended to make more people believe in God, generations of missionaries would have lost the meaning of existence. Reception is the most basic demand for writing. It is for this reason that those life or imaginary experiences that cannot be practically implemented can only reach a larger readership, directly or indirectly, through the bridge of practicable experiences. Thus, food, clothing, and the most universal human desires are the bridges through which one writes about gods and demons, and through which one may convey one's true existence to readers. Ultimately, the implementable human life experiences which were initially used to prove the existence of gods, immortals, demons, and other non-human beings replace the status of gods, immortals, and demigods in writing, and become the orthodoxy and mainstream of literary creation.

I shall not clarify or explain from which day or starting with which work this implementable human life experiences substituted and replaced the writing of gods, demons, and immortal non-humans. It is fair to say that Dante, Shakespeare, Boccaccio, Geoffrey Chaucer, and Rabelais in the European Renaissance all made an outstanding contribution to this kind of writing. Rabelais' *The Life of Gargantua and of Pantagruel* perhaps could be described today as comically evocative, or even in slightly disrespectful terms, as crude and vulgar. The first and second volumes of this great work alone are said to have sold more copies in France in two months when they appeared in 1532 and 1533 than the Bible did in nine years. The work's popularity with the readers can be described as a "cheerful bustle." But what does Rabelais' *The Life of Gargantua and of Pantagruel* owe its success to? Of course, its success can be attributed to the Renaissance ideas, such as the critique of theocracy and the spirit of humanism. But the exaggeration of plot, scenes, details, and language, and the secularization of human experiences, namely, the substitution of unrealizable experience with authentic implementable life experiences, are even more essential and reliable factors in the success of this masterpiece.

Preface

While discussing the process in which human life experiences gradually appropriate and replace divine or non-human writings, classical Chinese literature, including works such as *In Search of the Supernatural* (*Sou shen ji* 搜神記), *The Investiture of the Gods* (*Feng shen bang* 封神榜), *Journey to the West* (*Xi you ji* 西遊記) and *Strange Tales from a Chinese Studio* (*Liaozhai zhi yi* 聊齋誌異), has outlined even more clearly such transitions. Among the above works, *Strange Tales from a Chinese Studio*, in particular, foregrounds the everyday human experiences in the most explicit way. It is arguably the most accomplished classic in that the non-human characters invariably share the same goal of living a human life and all experience human emotions and desires. Along this trajectory of literary imagination, we see more gods and immortals who live in the imaginary space of heaven in stories such as "The Fairy Maiden Pianpian" 翩翩, "The Island of the Immortals" 仙人島, "Jia Fengzhi" 賈奉雉; immortals and demons living in the ocean in "Yaksha Country" 夜叉國 and "Pink Butterfly" 粉蝶; ghosts and eerie creatures in the underworld and hell in "Zhang Ah Duan" 章阿端, "The Bureau of Examination Frauds" 考弊司, "Yu Qu'E" 于去惡, "In The Infernal Regions" 席方平, "Old Man Zhu" 祝翁, "Jinse" 錦瑟, etc., and finally, stories of animals, plants, birds, insects, and snakes that are transformed into human beings in "A Parrot" 阿英, "Ge Jin" 葛巾, "The Man Who Was Changed Into a Crow" 竹青, "Bai Qiulian" 白秋練. As is manifested in these stories, all non-human forms of life, whether gods, immortals, aliens, and spirits, crave for human experiences disregarding the trials and tribulations they would go through in the foreign space, whether for three or five hundred years, or even thousands of years, all in order to enjoy the pleasure of a few years, months or even just a few days of human joy, warmth, and other most mundane life experiences.

The main difference between *Strange Tales from a Chinese Studio* and Western masterpieces such as Homer's epic work and Dante's *Divine Comedy* lies in that while the latter demonstrates an intersection of life from two different spaces, in the former, the gods, immortals, demons, and aliens all have a definite yearning for and active integration into the worldly human life. For example, "Bird" 鴉頭 must be the most brilliant and classical short story among those collected in *Strange Tales from a Chinese Studio*. In the story, a family of fox spirits, comprising a mother and two daughters, are transformed into human beings after thousands of years of spiritual cultivation. The mother ends up running a brothel and instigating her two daughters, who are two dazzling beauties, to take on customers so that they can both indulge in carnal pleasure and enjoy an inexhaustible amount of money for food, drink, clothing, and lodging. The "fox spirit" pattern reveals a basic narrative structure, framing stories within the same logic, namely, a large number of fox spirits appear in the form of beautiful women and handsome men, and their basic demands and ultimately cherished wishes are to live and enjoy an earthly human life. Therefore, among the 200-odd short stories of fox spirits, we can see that in "Bird," the most representative work, Pu Songling 蒲松齡 writes with the softest and richest emotions about the allegiance and desire of the fox woman Bird who works as a prostitute attempting to experience romantic love in the human world. Pu has depicted these emotions in the same manner as those displayed in the story of "The Oil Vendor and the Song Girl" ("Maiyoulang du zhan huakui" 賣油郎獨佔花魁) collected in the tales of the *San yan er pai* 三言二拍 of the Ming-Qing period, and that in the short story "The Courtesan's Jewel Box" ("Du Shiniang nu chen baibaoxiang" 杜十娘怒沉百寶箱). Meanwhile, he has also illustrated the fox mother and her eldest daughter Nizi's longing and pursuing for the most banal human desires for treasures and physical pleasure. While Pu was deeply critical of the social reality and earthly desires, he has also provided an outlet for those otherworldly creatures to vent their desire and long for a worldly life.

In the great work *Strange Tales from a Chinese Studio*, Pu ingeniously writes all that is related to mankind. All human experiences eventually become the resource of literary creation. And everything that is true about human existence ultimately becomes the yardstick that measures literary truth. These internal laws of literature are clearly reflected in more than a hundred "fox spirit" stories similar to the "Bird."

If one contextualizes the great Chinese classic *Strange Tales from a Chinese Studio* in a broader context, one may realize that the pervasiveness of human practicable experiences in the creation of world literature begets literary realism.

Here I am not suggesting that *Strange Tales from a Chinese Studio* is a masterpiece with the same humanistic spirit as the great works of the European Renaissance. Pu wrote his fiction hundreds of years later than the *Decameron*, *The Canterbury Tales*, and *The Life of Gargantua and of Pantagruel*. However, compared to the latter, Pu makes it more obvious to Chinese readers that since ancient times literature always starts from and ends with human life experiences, the only evidence most directly and effectively proving the authenticity of literature.

The ultimate dominance of implementable experiences

The process through which implementable life experiences have ended up dominating over fiction may be likened to the growth of a gourd. The latter's long period of maturation resembles that of mankind from thousands of years BCE down to the Middle Ages. In the gourd case, the gourd dangling from the trellis like a little dwarf, remaining "little" for a relatively long period, suddenly comes to an "explosion" and matures with the arrival of autumn. Likewise, literature has gone through a long period of development, from the epic of Gilgamesh in the third or fourth millennium BCE to the Middle Ages, to the maturity and peak of development in the centuries following the Renaissance, namely in the eighteenth, nineteenth, and twentieth centuries, with thousands of years elapsing in the former and only nearly three hundred years in the latter. After the Renaissance, all gods, immortals, demons, and other eerie creatures were quickly and ruthlessly removed from literary human experiences, especially from the great realist works of the nineteenth century; all non-human experiences seem to have become insignificant and marginalized.

In the age of Homer, no one should have denied the possession, distribution, and arrangement of the city of Troy at the hand of the divinity: two worlds converged under the same sky, with men and gods on the opposite sides of the wall, yet interacting with each other. This was the truth of literature that nobody questioned. Yet by the time one gets to *Robinson Crusoe*, *Pride and Prejudice*, *Jane Eyre*, *Elective Affinities*, *The Sorrows of Young Werther*, *War and Peace* and all the works of the nineteenth century that are considered great masterpieces, it is unthinkable and intolerable that experiences or imaginings that no one could ever experience in everyday life would appear in realist writings.

Almost all great writers in twentieth-century literature were hailed, respected, admired, and discussed in their home country or in the language they used. For example, when *The Sorrows of Young Werther* was first published, it caused such a huge sensation throughout Europe that young people who felt lost in their life imitated the protagonist of the novel and committed suicide. Upon the publication of *Elective Affinities*, readers lined up in front of the bookstore in the middle of the night, like hungry people lining up in front of a bakery to buy bread. When Dickens' novels were serialized in the newspapers, the young people of the English countryside, squatting at the entrance of their village, would wait for the arrival of the mail coach, only to rush to read the next episode of the story. As for Turgenev's *Fathers and Sons*, the polemic over whether the characters in the novel were leftists or rightists led to parades and demonstrations that intermittently lasted three years and gave rise to episodes of vandalism, smashing, and burning throughout the city of St. Petersburg. Harriet Beecher Stowe's *Uncle Tom's Cabin* directly stimulated and led to the American civil war, a historical event that called for the abolition of slavery.

Examples of this kind are rare and almost non-existent in the twentieth century. This enables us to understand more objectively how deep and broad the concern of writers for people and the plight of their times was in nineteenth-century realist writings. If a great realist writer has no concern for the existence of human beings or for the most acute and widespread social conflicts in his/her time, s/he does not deserve the reputation of "engineers of the human soul."[8] In this light, human life and social experiences have become the only accepted literary benchmark.

In sum, today's literary truth resides in the fact that the implementable and perceptible human experiences have completely replaced those literary experiences that could only be perceived but not implemented.

Narrowed and restricted literary experience and reconceptualization of truth

A writer's brooding, inquisitive suspicion, and scrutiny of the literature of his or her times is what makes literature move forward. Thus, the great nineteenth-century literature, at the height of its heyday, embraced those genius authors' skepticism: why does writing have to be this way? Why should one's writing be overshadowed by one's predecessors? Why should literary reality be restricted to perceivable and practicable experiences even if human life is so rich, diverse, and all-encompassing? Does a person's individual experience have to be subject to the social experience? Why must one be contextualized in the grand narrative of the collective past instead of simply representing oneself as an individual? Is history greater than man or is man above and beyond history? Who decides that implementable experiences are the only criteria to verify the truth of literature? If so, does it mean that Zeus' sending the god of dreams to inform Agamemnon to attack the city of Troy was not part of our human life experiences? Should things such as the Hell, Purgatory, and Heaven depicted in Dante's story be removed from our writing because we cannot experience and verify them? Why has such imagination almost disappeared in today's classical writings?

The great literature of the nineteenth century succeeded in channeling human and social experiences to the "orthodox" path of writing, which emphasizes the supremacy of "realness," thus reaching the height and peak of literary creation. Nevertheless, it simultaneously caused the stagnation of literature and prevented it from moving forward or reaching a new height. Hence, the talented writers of the twentieth century began to write alternatively by exploring new expressions of literature.

Today, in China's literary criticism, the most common understanding of twentieth-century literature lies in a variety of formal innovations and literary -isms. There is an even more common and arbitrary comparison of the nineteenth- and twentieth-century literature, that is, the former is about "what to write," and the latter about "how to write." In this way, though, literature seems to lose its vitality and twentieth-century literary creations seem to have achieved nothing but an array of -isms.

I would like to move on by following the path of literary truth back to the literature of the nineteenth and twentieth centuries. If the great works of the eighteenth and nineteenth centuries finally brought the perceivable and implementable experiences of human life into its

---

8 Engineers of the human soul, in Russian Инженеры человеческих душ, in Chinese 人類靈魂的工程師, was a term applied to writers and other cultural workers by Joseph Stalin. Readers may refer to Frank Westerman, *Engineers of the soul. In the footsteps of Stalin's writers* (New York: Vintage, 2011).

narrative framework, twentieth-century literature nevertheless enabled the reader's re-identifying of human beings, or of one's own life experiences. Nineteenth-century literature was written for a wide audience, and it took upon itself the task of profoundly reaching a wider audience; twentieth-century literature took its way out of the mass audience and wrote for élite readers. However, it is certainly inaccurate to describe the latter as "élite writing and élite reading." Writers such as Joyce, Kafka, Proust, Woolf, and Faulkner wrote and succeeded in the first three decades of the twentieth century because of their unconventional response to the realist writings of the nineteenth century, a way of directing the readers who were used to realism to an alternative way of story-telling. It is very much like that in the field of poetry, where one poet's work is well received by a large number of readers and another poet is equally successful by writing poems that are more profound yet unintelligible to the former poet's readers. In the former case, the readers themselves can decode the poem; in the latter, however, the readers can only understand the poem through the intermediary of the critics.

It is fair to say that the greatness of nineteenth-century literature was perceived directly by the readers, a process in which the critics participated less often. In fact, the critics did not necessarily read more novels or understand novels better than the average readers. But in most cases, the average readers only had a general impression of a good piece of work whereas critics gave more precise comments. This is exemplified by the relationship between Dostoevsky, his readers, and Bakhtin, or later between Eileen Chang 張愛玲, her readers, and C. T. Hsia. However, the situation completely changed at the beginning of the twentieth century: the average reader was no longer the "first reader"; it was the literary critics who became the first readers. They took the lead in reading and analyzing the works and then reaching a consensus on how to interpret them and pass their messages on to the general readers. This was true not only with Kafka's *The Castle, The Trial, The Metamorphosis*, but also with works like *Ulysses, In Search of Lost Time* or authors like Woolf and Faulkner …. Only after reading literary critics' analyses of and commentaries on these works did the readers seem to have a sudden epiphany.

Thus, in their analysis and judgment, the concept of "élite writers" emerged, and various schools of thought and -isms emerged thereafter. In this way, twentieth-century literature became the carrier and interpreter of "-isms and forms." It is from this that we are today induced to recognize and understand the twentieth-century literary works by Joyce, Kafka, Proust, Woolf, Faulkner, Schultz, Musil, and later Beckett, Ionesco and Robbe-Grillet, Claude Simon, Nabokov, Calvino, and Borges. Readers of these writers and their works are classified into a first and a second readership, or an élite and a general readership. Unlike that of the nineteenth-century classics, the canonization of these writers and their works was accomplished by the collaboration of writers and critics.

However, there were also many works whose canonization indicates a process beyond the collaboration between writers and critics, such as that of Ernest Hemingway's masterpieces and many other writers' representative works produced in the gilded age of America. It was the same with an array of works, claimed by critics as magical realist and anti-utopian/dystopian, produced in the second half of the twentieth century, all becoming canonized due to a joint effort of the writer, the reader, and the critic.

It can be said that in the twentieth century, works were read and evaluated by the critics prior to being recommended to the readers; such a process has arguably altered and enriched the writer's individual experience in writing. Correspondingly, literary truth extended from a visible and tangible dimension to an invisible and intangible one, manifested in forms such as consciousness, subconsciousness, dreams, human visions, and hallucinations, which in many cases replaced the behaviorally implementable and testable truth. While we praise the uniqueness of twentieth-century literature, one must admit that the twentieth-century classics and creations completed with the co-participation of writers, critics, and writers (acting as critics) have expanded and deepened the unimplementable life experience, and have somehow led the literary realness to a more substantially spiritual existence.

One can sum up thousands of years of human life experiences by saying that literary writing is a process of narrowing experiences. In this narrowing process, the truth of literature is reversely deepened. Today, we believe in the absolute authenticity of human and perceptual experiences in literature, but at the same time, we do not doubt that the manifestations of gods, immortals, demons, and other eerie creatures in literature also, to some extent, are authentic from a literary point of view. While the realism of the nineteenth century pushed the reality of gods, immortals, demons, and other creatures from literature to the margins, the twentieth-century literature, however, has transformed this imaginary spiritual existence into man's spiritual consciousness, subconsciousness, dreams, visions, and hallucinations. The reality of literature is thus only centered on the human life experiences.

Regardless of how magical, mysterious, and great the literature of the distant past is, and how realistic or verisimilar the literature of today may be (or even how conscious, subconscious, dreamy, or illusory it may seem), what matters is that both classical and modern realist literature have both their own field of experience and interpretation of truth.

But what is the outstanding characteristic of twenty-first-century literature? Specifically, what characterizes the literary truth and experience of the twenty-first century? Human and historical experiences in literature have boundaries, and the truth of these experiences has perceptible and implementable guidelines, but literary truth has no boundaries and is infinitely expandable and explorable. In search of a new literary real in the field of unbounded literary truth, which direction should the literary realness of the twenty-first century take?

Literary truth in the twenty-first century

Let's return to the current writing in China and to the citation that I used at the beginning of this article. "I sat on the dock with the sun like a thin paper under my butt." Considering that this statement completely defies the logic of actual life experiences, what kind of real does it evoke within the reader's mind? What kind of life experience which cannot be perceived in life, yet exists in our mind, consciousness, and spirit, powerful and vivid, does it evoke within the reader's mind? The answer lies in the metaphorization of the sun as a spiritual symbol. Whether it is the hope of mankind, or a metaphor for the dominance of power, or as Dante describes in the *Divine Comedy* that only God is the Sun of mankind—when it becomes a thin sheet of paper under one's buttocks, it finally awakes people's collective unconscious. It arouses the reader's revulsion and reaction against blind obedience and authority, thus gaining a new sense of logic and realness. In the classical Chinese novel, *Romance of the Three Kingdoms* (*San guo yanyi* 三國演義), the writer's portrayal of Zhuge Liang 諸葛亮, the "divine man," was more successful, vivid, and animated than any other work since ancient times. In it, the author spared no effort to narrate and depict stories such as "Zhuge Liang summons an eastern wind" or "Zhuge Liang invented the wooden ox and the horse." The latter was meant to solve the problem of food transportation: Zhuge invented the wooden ox-horse, which was an impossible invention in real life. Critics who uphold realism would think such storylines are too unrealistic, considering the fact that the novel is a historical one and thus should be perceived, to some extent, as a quasi-historical documentary. Therefore, the plot and settings of Zhuge Liang, a realistic character, with his miraculous deeds have become the subject of criticism. But for readers, it is his miraculous deeds that make Zhuge Liang a powerful divine-like man and a most unique literary figure. Without such miraculous deeds and divine events, Zhuge Liang as a literary character would not poetically shine with radiance.

Such plots and details, in the logic of common sense would be paradoxical and impossible (just like "I sit on the dock with the sun like a thin paper under my butt"), but in the literary realness, they can be true.

The logic of life is a necessity of realistic empirical truth, while in writing beyond realism, there exists some kind of literary truth that necessarily transcends this logical experience. Such a literary truth is not merely a surreal reality but an even truer one. That "I sit on the dock with the sun like a thin paper under my butt" is something happening at the level of consciousness, whereas the stories about Zhuge Liang occur in the dimension of life experience. This gives rise to two different "story fields." The former is linked to twentieth-century literature, while the latter is similar to that of *The Iliad*, *The Odyssey*, *The Metamorphoses*, *The Divine Comedy*, and the "common domain of man and gods" in the stories of Journey to the West and Strange Stories from a Chinese Studio. The literary reality of the twentieth and nineteenth century have their respective story field, but what is the truth of literature in the twenty-first century? And where can we find its story field?

This is the dilemma of today's writing.

We do not know today what literary truth is and how it is different from that of the preceding three centuries, or where we should go for new literary truths and in what setting our stories should be situated. Reexamining contemporary Chinese literary creation in the light of this confusion and dilemma can shed light not only on what Chinese authors have written and accomplished in their stories, but how their writings are connected to and differentiated from the classical literature of the twentieth century, and also how they are different from their peer writers and what remains as unfinished in their writing.

Classical Chinese literature has accomplished and transcended the writing of gods, immortals and demons beyond the practical and perceivable human experiences. However, for many reasons, today's Chinese writers have not really completed the full coverage and replacement of literature with the experiences of human life and history in nineteenth-century writing. Nor have they really begun to experiment with and create twentieth-century literature that goes beyond implementable and perceivable human life and historical experiences to writing about individual richer life experiences such as consciousness, subconsciousness, dreams, and visions. In this respect, there are rarely any true classics in contemporary Chinese literature. Yet the richness, complexity, and absurdity of China's modern history and reality are in line with the similar symptom of the world, and arguably even more ahead of it. The great lag between reality and the overall life experience in literature constitutes a big gap between today's writing and reality, coupled with the harsh norms and constraints from the authority on today's writing imagination, which makes contemporary Chinese literature present huge blank spaces, gaps, and lags. But perhaps it is the time to seek and build a new literary reality on the basis of human life experiences now, one that can transcend perception and implementable experiences but differs from that of the nineteenth- and twentieth-century literature.

In a nutshell, human life experiences are tangible and sensible and have boundaries, whereas literary truth is unbounded and can be tangible and sensible, or sensible yet untouchable. Literature should not only exist for experience, but also for the truth that transcends the boundary of real-life experiences.

EDITORIAL PREFACE

Riccardo Moratto

Howard Y. F. Choy 蔡元豐

This international companion is an edited volume focusing on studies of Yan Lianke 閻連科, one of the most important and prolific writers as well as one of the most prominent avant-gardists in contemporary China. He is an author whose literary works have enjoyed an enormous readership and have caught much critical attention not only in the Chinese mainland, Hong Kong, and Taiwan but also in many other countries and regions around the world. The present volume is the first English book on Yan's studies, focusing on how Yan has been received in and beyond China, while presenting views of how Yan's main themes and literary topics have been understood, interpreted, and appreciated. By presenting the best original literary criticism on Yan by renowned as well as emerging scholars worldwide, the editors propose a new way to approach the topics of "mythorealism" (including its receptions in the West), absurdity and spirituality, and historical aspects in Yan's works.

Born in 1958, Yan is often defined and at times acclaimed as the most irreverent and censored writer at home. He has won prestigious literary awards in China and abroad, including the Lu Xun Literary Prize (*Luxun wenxue jiang* 魯迅文學獎), the Lao She Literary Award (*Lao She wenxue jiang* 老舍文學獎), the *Asiaweek* Best Ten Books Award (*Yazhou zhoukan zuijia shi ben shu jiang* 亞洲週刊最佳十本書獎), the Dream of the Red Chamber Award (*Hongloumeng jiang* 紅樓夢獎), the Franz Kafka Award, the Huazong Literary Award (*Huazong wenxue jiang* 花蹤文學獎) and the Newman Prize for Chinese Literature. It is with the novel *Lenin's Kisses* (*Shouhuo* 受活) that he was consecrated as an internationally renowned writer. *Le Monde* calls him one of the giants of literature and *The Guardian* a master of sarcasm. He has also been shortlisted for an array of prices including the International Man Booker Prize, the Independent Foreign Fiction Prize, and the Prix Femina étranger.

This volume will be a landmark resource for scholars in Chinese literature, Chinese studies, Asian studies, literary criticism, and cultural studies. To facilitate reading, the volume begins with a foreword by Carlos Rojas, Yan's main English translator, a preface written by Yan himself, this editorial preface, and is divided into four parts:

Part I: Mythorealism and Censorship
Part II: Absurdity and Spirituality
Part III: History and Gender
Part IV: Translation and Reception

Editorial preface

Yan regards himself as a rebel son of mainstream realism and coined the term "mythorealism" (*shenshi zhuyi* 神實主義) to elucidate the influence of Kafkaesque and Márquezan combinations of reality and absurdity on contemporary Chinese literature. In his anthology of critical essays, *Discovering Fiction* (*Faxian xiaoshuo* 發現小說), Yan writes:

> Mythorealism … abandons the seemingly logical relations of real life, and explores a "non-existent" truth, an invisible truth, and a truth concealed by truth. Mythorealism keeps a distance from any prevailing realism. The mythorealist connection with reality does not lie in straightforward cause-and-effect links, but rather relies on human souls, minds … and the authors' extraordinary fabrications based on reality. … Imaginations, metaphors, myths, legends, dreams, fantasy, demonization, and transplantation born from everyday life and social reality can all serve as mythorealist methods and channels.[1]

Yan's "mythorealism" challenges accepted conventions of a linear cause-and-effect relationship, often considered to be the driving force behind the development of literary narratives. In his *Discovering Fiction*, Yan makes distinctions between "complete cause-and-effect" (*quan yinguo* 全因果), "partial cause-and-effect" (*ban yinguo* 半因果), "internal cause-and-effect" (*nei yingu* 內因果), and "zero cause-and-effect" (*ling yinguo* 零因果), arguing that we should focus on an illogical logic and an irrational rationality that lie beyond conventional causality (171–73). The problem is that the concept of "mythorealism" has often been misunderstood by Western scholars and this is why we decided to address the issue of "mythorealism" in our first section by selecting and presenting the best scholarly critical essays on "mythorealism" and its receptions.

In Chapter 1, Weijie Song 宋偉杰 suggests that as an outstanding heir of Lu Xun, Yan regards himself as a rebel son of mainstream realism and coined the term "mythorealism" to elucidate the influence of Kafkaesque and Márquezan combinations of reality and absurdity on contemporary Chinese literature. His banned yet acclaimed works bravely enter the politically sensitive zones, fiercely confront the taboos of sex and politics, and vividly display the unhappy marriage of communism and capitalism. Yan's configurations of literary settings, from the metamorphosis of his rural hometown in Henan 河南 Province to the transfiguration of post-Maoist Beijing, illustrate his grotesque, comic, spectacular, miserable, absurd, and deformed imaginative world. This chapter considers Yan's literary method of "mythorealism," a creative and novel way of storytelling about silent China, especially evidenced in his *Lenin's Kisses* and *House No. 711* (*711 hao yuan: Beijing zuihou de zuihou jinian* 711號園：北京最後的最後紀念),[2] and examines Yan's post-Maoist representations of macro- and micro-mythoreality, political dystopia and ecocritical utopia, the articulated silence of the humiliated and insulted, and the large-scale ferocity and "slow violence" being committed in both the country and the city.

In Chapter 2, Xiaolu Ma 馬筱璐 puts forward the idea that in order to capture the elusiveness and absurdities of life in contemporary China, Yan has proposed the idea of "mythorealism," which elucidates the invisible truth underlying Chinese reality. According to Yan, the connection of "mythorealism" to life is constructed through three types of "spirits" (*shen* 神): "the spirit of god" (*lingshen* 靈神) invoked by folk culture and shamanism, "the human spirit" (*jingshen* 精神) reflected through the connections between human souls, and "the writer's spirit" (*chuangzuozhe de teshu yisi* 創作者的特殊意思) based on the writer's engagement with material reality.

---

1 Yan Lianke, *Faxian xiaoshuo* (Tianjin: Nankai daxue chubanshe, 2011), 181–82; Song Weijie, trans., "Yan Lianke's Mythorealist Representation of the Country and the City," *Modern Fiction Studies* 62, no. 4 (Winter 2016): 644.
2 The title of the simplified Chinese version is *Beijing, zuihou de jinian* 北京最後的紀念.

"Mythorealism" manifests Yan's ambition not only to probe the nature of reality and the depths of the human spirit, but also to transcend the commonly accepted tradition of realism in world literature. As a writer inspired by Western modernists including Franz Kafka, William Faulkner, and Gabriel García Márquez, Yan is generally considered a rebel against mainstream Chinese realism. In particular, he is seen as rejecting the dominant discourse of socialist realism, a literary trend that first flourished in Soviet Russia. However, as a child, Yan grew up reading revolutionary literature, which is rooted in canonical Russian realism. As a result, his writing cannot avoid profound engagement with that literary tradition. In fact, the relationship among the three key figures in Yan's mythorealism—the God, the humankind, and the author—is also central to the work of many classical Russian realists such as Gogol, Tolstoy, and Dostoevsky. Moreover, the relationship between everyday life and realism, which is crucial to Yan's definition of "mythorealism," was a subject heavily debated in Russia as well. By placing Yan's literary criticism and creative writing parallel to Russian discussions of realism in the nineteenth and early twentieth centuries, this chapter attempts to shed new light on Yan's "mythorealism," which represents a powerful Chinese contribution to the polymorphic and volatile world realist movement.

In Chapter 3, Ashley Liu 劉映雪 focuses on Yan's memoir *Three Brothers: Memories of My Family* (*Wo yu fubei* 我與父輩), in which Yan portrays the lives of his family as embodying the fate of Albert Camus' Sisyphus, enduring a lifetime of hardship to return to nothingness at the end. The Sisyphean fate of the Yan family blends reality and myth into a new type of "mythorealism" and reflects Yan's existential despair. In *Three Brothers* and *Dream of Ding Village* (*Dingzhuang meng* 丁莊夢), modern China's historical traumas enable the characters to understand the universal truths of existential meaning and meaninglessness and the absurd condition of living just to die. Yan's views on life and fate as expressed in *Three Brothers* allow a new interpretation of *Dream of Ding Village* that connects the fictional absurdity to the lived experience of Chinese modernity. His recognition of his family's dignified response to the cruelty of fate echoes the courageous stance to confront certain death taken by the characters in *Dream of Ding Village*. In both memoir and fiction, Yan combines reality and absurdity to portray lived historical traumas as a process of reflecting on existential despair and truths.

In Chapter 4, Raffael Weger presents the relationship between magical realism, mythorealism, and the re-presentation of history in the works of Yan. As Yan explains in his poetological volume *Discovering Fiction*, mythorealism is a way of writing that aims at making an irrational reality accessible again by unveiling its "inner truth" and "inner causality." Mythorealist works, like magical realist writing, convey an alternative conception of history, marked by frequent use of legends, myths, folklore, in short, what is usually called "the imaginary" as opposed to "the real." Embracing this dichotomy, magical realism, in the vein of what Eugene Arva calls "traumatic imagination," creates new meaning for historical events by raising the imaginary and the real to the same ontological level. Yan, in contrast, claims that mythorealism goes one step further, aspiring to fuse the two ontological states, striving to arrive at a new understanding of historical truths. By comparing the defining aspects of both magical realism and mythorealism, this chapter focuses not only on analyzing two of Yan's novels, *The Explosion Chronicles* (*Zhalie zhi* 炸裂志) and *The Four Books* (*Si shu* 四書) and their respective re-presentation of history, but also aims to answer the question whether mythorealism is merely a local adaptation of magical realism or instead should be seen as a new literary mode.

In Chapter 5, Marco Fumian presents a new approach to Yan's mythorealism. As emphasized by Fumian, besides being a prolific novelist, Yan is also well-known for his efforts to reflect upon and theorize his fictional approach. Deeply convinced of the inaptitude of Chinese realism to fully grasp the "invisible truths" of Chinese reality, he developed a writing style that he himself called *shenshi zhuyi*, a play on words that is now usually translated in English as "mythorealism."

Editorial preface

However, while we do find in several of Yan's novels a layer of mythical significations, the purpose of Yan's writing is definitely not that of transcending reality in a mythical way. Rather, as he has emphasized numerous times, his purpose is to find a form able to bring to the surface the most hidden aspects of the Chinese historical and social reality, especially highlighting the profound elements of absurdity that for him constitute the most significant and pervasive realities of contemporary Chinese society. Whereas Yan's novels tend to portray sweeping allegorical parables of modern and contemporary Chinese history and society, his short stories and novellas are instead mostly vignettes of rural life sketching out the mishaps of wretched individuals faced with unsustainable situations in their backward village settings. This chapter will analyze a number of these short stories to observe the functioning of Yan's critical representation of the rural structures of power and cultural psychology, highlighting as an important rationale of his representational style, which Fumian prefers to define in the case of his short fiction as "pararealism," the effort to use distorting fictional techniques as a means to grasp what he views as the objective distortions of reality.

In Chapter 6, the last of the first part of the volume, Jessica Yeung 楊慧儀 focuses on the issues of censure and censorship. Much attention has been paid to the censorship Yan has faced in mainland China. Close observation of the censure against his works shows that it operates in three forms: book bans, netizen censure, and transformation of public censure into pressure exerted on the novelist in the private domain. Compared with other critical writers and artists who have either left mainland China or are inconsistent in their critique of the state of affairs in the country, Yan's consistent critique and continuous presence in mainland China have highlighted a "structure of presence" of the critical subject which relies on networks of support to continue his presence in the country. On the one hand, these networks have enabled Yan's presence as a voice and a person in mainland China; on the other hand, Yan's critical writings also transform these infrastructural entities into a field of empowerment. Censorship, therefore, instead of being a one-dimensional imposition of power, could be viewed as a structure in which both restrictions and resistance play out.

The second section of this volume focuses on the themes of absurdity and spirituality, which are a common denominator in almost all of Yan's novels and short stories. We have selected the best scholarly critical essays covering the topics of absurdity and spirituality.

In Chapter 7, Haiyan Xie 謝海燕 focuses on the absurd as method: the Chinese absurdist hero, enchanted power, and the alienated poor in Yan's military literature. As one of the most prolific and outspoken contemporary Chinese writers, Yan has won international recognition for his writing from the margins. However, while his novels have been extensively studied, Yan's military literature has received much less scholarly attention. This chapter explores Yan's adaptation of the absurd in Western literature to Chinese military literature, investigates how he constructs Chinese absurdist heroes, and reconstructs the concepts of "the poor" and "power" in his narratives. Focusing in particular on his 2009 collection of military novellas *Prohibited Area Number Four* (*Sihao jinqu* 四號禁區), this chapter argues that the absurd in Yan's military texts serves not only as a formal experiment for exploring the alternative imagination of the alienated and marginalized peasant soldiers in contemporary China, but also as an implicit means of articulating Yan's own socio-political commentary, one which cannot allow itself to be explicitly political.

In Chapter 8, Selusi Ambrogio compares the description of the absurdity of urban life as presented by Yan with the one provided by the Italian Italo Calvino. Both authors' writing careers debuted from neorealism, but gradually shifted to a surrealistic style, which is named by Yan "mythorealism" and presented as the only way to look lucidly at the deepness of the contradictions present in contemporary human life. In 1972, at the peak of the Italian economic boom, Calvino wrote *Invisible Cities* as a narrative reflection on the utopian and dystopian aspects of urbanism. He presented 55 unrealistic cities, each one described by Marco Polo to the Mongol emperor Kublai Khan. Each city is a reflection of humanity, culture, development, memory and, finally, unlivableness. In a similar but even more excessive economic and urban context of development, Yan wrote the fiction *The Explosion Chronicles*. His aim was an "epic description" of the immoral beginning and despicable development of a metropolis, where economic growth and power alone constitute the unique human search at all costs, a kind of sacral faith. Opposed to this "extreme reality" of the city, Yan introduces natural elements, such as flowers, plants, insects, and clouds that always emerge as unrealistic reactions to human events. Their descriptions shed some light on human relationships with both cities and nature. However, while Calvino maintains, thanks to Polo, a detached and "light" narrative mood, Yan himself is the narrator or historian writing this tragic chronicle, and his truth-bearing act is rejected by authorities; therefore, for him, truth is always a "heavy task."

In Chapter 9, Melinda Pirazzoli suggests that *The Four Books* reflects Yan's Kafkian approach to art, human nature, the human quandary, and messianism. More specifically, Yan's *The Four Books* and Kafka's *The Trial* share many concerns: life as a form of confinement, a sense of impending horror, the self's loss of agency in the world, the interconnectedness between art and slander, the artist's connivance with (juridical) power, the interchangeability between the juridical realm and religion, the relationship between guilt and crime, and finally the relationship between life and shame. This study does not aim to compare *The Four Books* with *The Trial*. What will be argued instead is that while Yan relies on so-called Kafkian "inverse theology," the representation of a world forsaken by God, he ultimately crafts a diegetic world which also clearly reflects the Chinese cultural heritage. The reference to both the four gospels and the four Confucian classics suggests that Yan is attempting to convey an idea of culture which conflates Chinese and Western values in order to create a literary work that can simultaneously reflect and transcend local boundaries.

In Chapter 10, Nicoletta Pesaro aims to detect early signs of modernism and the grotesque in Yan's fiction from the 1990s, which is usually placed in the category of post-Maoist realism and, as a genre, is recognized as part of the "fiction of the native soil" (*xiangtu xiaoshuo* 鄉土小說). Most of the studies devoted to Yan's works focus on his latest novels, where his theory of the "mythorealism" or "spiritual realism" finds full expression. Indeed, an analysis of his early works can be of great interest in order to reconstruct the genesis of his peculiar style and vision of fiction. In particular, this chapter focuses on the novella "Gold Cave" ("Huangjin dong" 黃金洞), which openly challenges the assumptions of traditional *xiangtu xiaoshuo* with which Yan's early fiction has been initially identified and presents clear hints of a new aesthetics based on modernist techniques and strategies of bewilderment aimed to transcend reality in order to better express it.

In Chapter 11, Alessandra Pezza argues that the increasing presence and way of representation of intellectual characters in Yan's writing is a consequence of the author's troubled relationship with censorship. The varying possibility to publish within mainland China has had, all over Yan's writing years, a deep influence not only on his choice of topics, but also on his writing style, to the point that he defined his struggle with the possibility to publish in mainland China as an "exile of the soul." After a quick overview on how censorship has shaped Yan's writing over the years, from the declarations of self-censorship to the theorization of a literary writing style known as "mythorealism," which shows how deeply our author is influenced by politics in his conception of literature, Pezza discusses the increasing presence and satirical representation of intellectuals in Yan's writing in the decade 2008–18. It is argued that this representation has taken the form of a metatextual and avant-garde turn in Yan's writing as a new, creative literary response to the censors.

In Chapter 12, Shelley W. Chan 陳穎 focuses on *Dream of Ding Village*, the Chinese version of *The Plague* and a macabre story filled with death caused by AIDS, by the award-winning yet controversial writer Yan. It discusses how the daring novel shows concern for the biopolitical situation of the Chinese people, and how it spearheads its criticism on the "blood economy" that encouraged people to sell their blood and ended up causing an AIDS epidemic in central China in the 1990s. Through studying the mythorealistic elements such as the unconventional narrative voice and the experimental structure of the novel, this article examines the thanatopolitics characteristic of the story; it also demonstrates how the novel makes parts of the real illusory and imaginary, and how this technique serves to create a wider and deeper blurred space between reality and unreality to highlight the irrational and crazy materialistic desire of human beings, which leads to an absurd and ill-practiced modernization on the one hand, and makes it convenient for the author to practice self-censorship on the other hand, and how this practice affects the narrative in the artistic and realistic dimensions.

In Chapter 13, Andrea Riemenschnitter focuses on Yan's novel *Heart Sutra* (*Xinjing* 心經), a coming-of-age story about a Buddhist nun and a Daoist adept. Spending one year of further education at the Religious Studies Center of a fictitious university in Beijing, they fall in love, experience inner conflicts, suffer pressure from external forces, and end up returning to lay society without actually becoming part of it. The group of students studying together with them at the Center comprises leading representatives of mainland China's five officially recognized religions: Buddhism, Protestantism, Catholicism, Islam, and Daoism. Structurally, the novel is a generic bricolage consisting of a body of realist narrative complemented by some parts in italics, which give voice to different focalizers. In addition, a miniplay and a graphic story rendered in paper cuts with verbal glosses are included. While the Mahāyāna Buddhist sutra, which is widely known by the same title as the novel, reminds of the universal, mystical sediment of religious belief, namely the enigma of life and death, the Christian story of Jesus' crucifixion serves as a counterbalance to the detachment from the world as taught by the Buddhist and Daoist doxa. Consequently, the novel's protestant protagonist actively engages in social welfare while resisting the pressures of worldly power to the point of sacrificing his life. On the symbolic level, the tensions between sacred and mundane orthodoxies are played out in multiple encoded tug of war games and raise questions about individual sovereignty under the CCP regime. Yan's exploration of the encounter between the inner and outer spheres of religious faith is appositely captured in the image of a kiss between a rock and an egg, dwelling on the precarious, utopian moment of touching before one is crushed by the other.

In Chapter 14, the last of the second part, Di-kai Chao 趙帝凱 and Riccardo Moratto focus on Yan's recent novel *Central Plains* (*Zhongyuan* 中原). Yan completed the first draft of this novel in 2020, when China was ravaged by COVID-19. The novel was then revised at the end of the same year, when Yan was awarded the Newman Prize for Chinese Literature. *Zhongyuan* was first published in March 2021 in the second issue of the Chinese literary journal "Flower City" (花城 *Huacheng*). The same was later published on October 30, 2021 in a book form by Rye Field Publishing Co. (Maitian chubanshe 麥田出版社) in Taiwan in a slightly revised version with the new title *Zhongguo gushi* (中國故事, in English *Chinese Story* or *Story of China*). The production timing of this novel is indicative and meaningful. This chapter first conducts a textual analysis of *Central Plains*, arguing that the text embodies the alienation of people in daily life under capitalism and highlights the dominance of privileged mechanisms on the fixity of mobile meanings under the current globalization and transnationalism mobility. This chapter also interprets the spatial metaphors of Gaotian Township and Balou 耙耬 Mountains by drawing on the imagery of Peach Blossom Spring (*Taohuayuan* 桃花源). The imagery of utopia is closely linked to the discussion of the novel's theme. Since Yan seems to have more or less inadvertently mentioned the title of his acceptance speech for the Newman Prize at the end of the novel, that is "A Village Larger than the World" ("Yi ge bi shijie geng da de cunzhuang" 一個比世界更大的村莊), his acceptance speech may be interpreted as a subtext of the novel. It is argued that this subtext provides the context for researchers to place *Central Plains* within Sinophone literature, further highlighting the dialectical relationship between the novel's title and the outside world. This novel can be used as a research subject to validate the "human condition" under the discourse of Sinophone/Xenophone (*Huayifeng* 華夷風) initiated by David Der-wei Wang 王德威. Moreover, through the intertextuality with "A Village Larger than the World," the meaning of this novel is not limited to the alienated human relationships within the family or under capitalism, but also echoes the current discourse of Chinese nationhood by drawing on the imagery of Peach Blossom Spring.

The third part focuses on another pivotal theme in Yan's literary creation, namely history and gender. In Chapter 15, Sebastian Veg emphasizes that since the scar literature of the early 1980s, fiction and fictionalized autobiography have played an important role in bringing to light the mass violence of the Cultural Revolution (1966–76). However, these texts remained within a well-defined framework, in which the political system itself was not questioned. Over the last decade, by contrast, the Chinese literary field has focused more specifically on the 1950s with works like Yang Xianhui's 楊顯惠 *Chronicles of Jiabiangou* (*Jiabiangou jishi* 夾邊溝記事, 2002) and Yang Jisheng's 楊繼繩 *Tombstone* (*Mubei* 墓碑, 2008). This chapter focuses on Yan's *The Four Books* (2010), a full-fledged fictionalization in a fantastic mode of the famine of the Great Leap Forward in a village on the Yellow River. Considering literature in the context of theories of the public sphere, it suggests that Yan's book aims to broaden decisively the discussion on certain previously out-of-bounds aspects of the Mao era, an aim which was only partially thwarted by its failure to be published within mainland China. *The Four Books*, like Yang Xianhui's and Yang Jisheng's works, thus represents an attempt to call into question the original legitimacy of the PRC polity and to create a debate within the Chinese-speaking public sphere on the foundations of the current scenario.

In Chapter 16, Zihan Wang 王紫涵 argues that as one of Yan's most representative works, *Lenin's Kisses* has been widely discussed for its commercialization and alienation of bodies in the context of contemporary China. This chapter intends to examine the relationship between the body and the revolutionary past through the image of Grandma Mao Zhi 茅枝. By comparing Mao Zhi's story with similar narratives produced during the socialist period (1949–78), this article argues that the way Mao Zhi is represented not only deconstructs the revolutionary paradigm of writing disability, but also challenges the validity of official historiography.

In Chapter 17, Kwan Yin Lee 李焜妍 follows Keston Sutherland's and Sianne Ngai's call to heed what the figurative language employed in *Das Kapital* makes thinkable and palpable. Marx's likening of abstract labor to *Gallerte*, the German word for an edible gelatinous mass made from different animals' body parts, is catachrestic for the graphic image has abstract labor "sound confusingly *like* simple physiological human labor." Yet, it is precisely through catachresis that Marx highlights the violence inherent in the capitalist abstraction's reduction of concrete labor individual workers perform to undifferentiated labor power quantified by standardized time. The image of human brains, sinews, and bones mashed together as *Gallerte* for consumption also serves to nauseate readers and counter the normalization of exploitation. Recognition of this paradigm-shifting potential of catachrestic figurative language motivates the juxtaposition of Hong Kong writer Xi Xi's 西西 "The Story of Fertile Town" ("Feituzhen de gushi" 肥土鎮的故事, 1982) and Yan's *The Explosion Chronicles*. Instead of taking for granted the economic miracle narratives that bolster the supposed viability of capitalism, both texts recast the respective "economic miracles" in Hong Kong and in the Chinese mainland with catachrestic renderings that parody the elliptical and abstracting moves constituting such narratives. The two texts call for a Marxist close reading that unveils their unsuspected affinity and relevance to defanging global capitalism's ideological potency.

In Chapter 18, Sabrina Ardizzoni examines Yan's *Tamen* 她們, a book about Chinese rural women in the socialist and post-Socialist period. In proposing the English translation of the title as *Shes,* Ardizzoni highlights the main topics and ideas expressed by Yan, keeping in mind not only the gender-study framework suggested by Yan himself, but also Gayatri Spivak's categories of "subaltern studies." In fact, her categories, starting from the question "Can the subaltern speak?" may explain the male voice that speaks out in place of the "silenced subject" in Chinese history. The relationship between these stories and her-stories brings to surface other versions of modern China; these narratives dwell on taboo topics such as menstruation, female orgasm, homosexuality, prostitution, and a lavish repertoire of images linked to the body, as appurtenant to the author's style. These are subjects rural women do not wish to talk about; there are very few, if any, references to them in Chinese contemporary literature

In Chapter 19, Yijiao Guo 郭一驕 argues that in his 2020 nonfiction *Tamen,* Yan conducted an introspection on rural women's predicaments and the effaced female labor in the Great Leap Forward campaign. Yan argued that rural women, as the third sex in the PRC, suffered from the dual exploitations both inside and outside the domestic space. His proposition of excrescence, in particular, unraveled the paradox that females and femininity were inclusively excluded and consequently suspended in the patriarchy-dominated writing about history. By depicting rural women's disregarded talks-and-chats, life experiences, and social contributions, Yan reengaged the socialist history with a gender perspective, disclosed the amnesia scheme in the national narrative, and underscored the female subjectivity in history. Consequently, Yan's enriching corrections to the whitewashed history can be seen as a historical-narrative rhizome in formation that opens the prescribed gender discourse and connects females and femininity to other historical and narrative agencies.

In Chapter 20, Chen Wang 王琛 examines Yan's fictional stories set in the Balou Mountains from the perspective of literary geocriticism. Informed by Fredric Jameson's conceptualization of "cognitive mapping" and Robert T. Tally Jr.'s theory that the concept of utopia in contemporary times no longer refers to a concrete place or society, but a utopian impulse to re-situate humans in space and history, Wang focuses on land, place, environment and their dialectical relations with man as the subject matter in Yan's Balou Mountains narratives. Instead of reading Yan's Balou Mountains series as separate stories set in the same place, Wang reads them in their totality as a continuously expanding utopian cognitive map of the post-1949 China in Yan's literature. Concentrating on Yan's 1997 novella *The Years, Months, Days* (*Nian yue ri* 年月日) and the 2013 novel *The Explosion Chronicles*, this chapter argues that Yan has created a convoluted web of spatialized utopian attempts, which contradict, overwrite, and nullify one another or from within themselves. Serving as test cases, these utopian cognitive maps demonstrate Yan's intellectual endeavor to find a possible way out for and through a literature at the intersections between the rural and the urban, socialism and capitalism, the individual and the commune, as well as between human and space, which are pivotal issues for contemporary China and for the world at large.

In Chapter 21, Minh Thương Nguyễn Thi 阮氏明商 and Riccardo Moratto present an ecocritical approach to Yan's works. Yan is one of the most prolific writers in contemporary Chinese literature. The complexity and diversity of his works have drawn much scholarly attention. However, research from the perspective of ecocriticism remains a gap that not many have come to fill. In addition to *House No. 711*, which may be considered an ecological essay, other important novels by Yan, such as *The Four Books, Dream of Ding Village, Streams of Time* (*Riguang liunian* 日光流年), and *The Years, Months, Days,* to a certain extent all pose issues worth reflecting on the relationship between mankind and nature. This chapter approaches the works of Yan from the perspective of ecocriticism and explores the ecological dimension in his literary creation through the issues of ecological ethics, ecological philosophy, and ecological aesthetics.

In Chapter 22, the last of the third section, Ronald Torrance considers the ways in which ideas of Yan's authorship are portrayed in the authorial paratext to a selection of his contemporary novels. It posits that Yan's authorial paratext exhibits a unique forum for exploring the interplay between Yan as author, his readers, and the text. Within the context of literary censorship in China, and the contested reception of Yan's novels outside the mainland, this chapter illustrates Yan's unique literary response to the mechanisms of censorship in China, suggesting that his writing has developed in such a way over a prolonged period of literary creation in which he has, in his previous works, been subject to and complicit in the act of self-censoring his own writing. Drawing from existing debates on the use and implications of the paratextual constructs of the contemporary Chinese novel, this chapter argues that the creative framework of Yan's fiction is fundamentally significant in ascribing within contemporary Chinese literature a means by which Chinese writers might be able to successfully negotiate through fiction the ideological guidelines and mechanisms of literary censorship existent within China.

The fourth and final part of this volume focuses on the translation and reception of Yan's works in different countries and regions. In Chapter 23, Chunli Shen 沈春利 investigates the critical reception of Yan's works in China and the West from a comparative perspective. The Chinese reception tends to stress the literary aesthetics and universal significance of Yan's works, although they also convey some form of sociopolitical critique. By contrast, the Western reception promotes a framing of Yan's works, which not only attempts to invoke an autocratic image of China where oppressive censorship is prevalent, but also gives priority to highlighting his works as sociopolitical documents. Such disparate critical reception patterns are found to be contingent on the Chinese and Western ideological and poetic contexts. In China, loosening political restrictions after the Cultural Revolution allow Chinese intellectuals to have an easier access to Western literary trends and to experiment with various literary forms, which have stimulated a more aesthetic assessment of literature. Moreover, focusing on the literary value of Yan's works is also a safe way for Chinese scholars to maintain political correctness, as censorship remains constant in China. On the contrary, in the West, there are established stereotypes of modern and contemporary Chinese literature as sociopolitical documents with little literary value, which direct critics' attention to the repressive censorship in China via Yan's works.

In Chapter 24, Taciana Fisac aims at providing a comparative analysis of *The Four Books* in its translation into five different European languages: English, French, German, Italian, and Spanish. All the books used for this study are direct translations from the Chinese original and they provide insights into how translators have been dealing with the different levels of a literary translation. A comparison of the strategies used by the respective translators will be made in order to examine the extent of adjustments adopted to produce an equivalent of the original text in its target language, and thus illustrate how Yan's novel translated into European languages relates to his original literary writing. Rather than conducting an assessment, this chapter will examine what type of text non-Chinese readers of these languages have at their disposal and to what extent the literary richness of the original Chinese text can be perceived when reading *The Four Books* in translation. To that end, it is also essential to make an analysis of the original Chinese book and to know in depth the different literary features and levels displayed throughout the novel.

In Chapter 25, Maialen Marin-Lacarta examines Yan's translation into Basque. The Basque language, with around 750,000 speakers, of whom the majority reside in Spain and a small proportion in France, is a minority language with a peripheral literature, meaning that Basque does not have a big share in the world market of translated literature. Chinese, a dominant language with millions of speakers, has a similarly small share in the global market of translated literature. The peripheral position of these two literatures means that most translations from Chinese into Basque have so far been indirect, mediated by more central languages such as Spanish, English, and French (the Spanish translations used as source texts are also often indirect translations). The translation of Yan's *Balou Ballad* (*Balou tiange* 耙耬天歌) is an exception to this trend. Published in 2018 and translated directly from the Chinese by Maialen Marin-Lacarta and Aiora Jaka Irizar, it is one of the few direct translations of Chinese literature into Basque. This chapter examines Yan's poetic language through the analysis of the Basque translation of *Balou Ballad*. Marin-Lacarta compares their translation to the English translation by Carlos Rojas, entitled *Marrow*, published by Penguin in 2015, as a means to highlight the specificities of Yan's sensory images, as well as to emphasize our own choices in Basque. The examples show the multiple sensory images that proliferate in Yan's writing and the Basque translators' choice to seek creative solutions while remaining as close as possible to the author's style.

In Chapter 26, Lu Gan 甘露 focuses on the translation and reception of Yan in France. France has played a major role in introducing contemporary Chinese literature into Western countries. Since 2006, eleven books of Yan have been translated into French. In France, Yan has enjoyed a larger readership compared to other Chinese writers of our times, and his works have drawn quite a lot of critical attention. This chapter will start from presenting the general situation of the translation of Yan into French, especially the leading roles played by three translators, the literary agent, and the publishing house in the process of introducing the writer to France. In the second part, Gan uses a physiological framework borrowed from Albert Thibaudet to analyze the status quo and the characteristics of its reception. This chapter thus aims to conduct a general reflection on the current situation of Yan's translation and reception in France.

In Chapter 27, Zuzana Li provides an account of *The Four Books* in Czech translation as experienced and witnessed by one of the protagonists, the translator. It is the story of Yan and his writing as much as it is the story of the still continuing efforts of a small publisher and a group of Sinologists to bring contemporary Chinese writing to the attention of Czech readers. It is a story deeply embedded in literary practice, a multi-faceted story on how Yan is read in Czech, from the publisher's consideration via the translator's perspective to critical reception, a story that tackles some of the specifics of the Czech interactions with Yan's writing.

In Chapter 28, Baorong Wang 汪寶榮 analyzes *Lenin's Kisses* in English Translation. Yan's critically acclaimed novel features, among others, inventive use of regional dialect and a series of language and cultural notes. Embodying the Chinese cultural other, these dialect and cultural terms and phrases might pose a challenge to the translator and the success of the English edition depends much on their translation. Drawing on Gideon Toury's initial norm theory and Javier Franco Aixelá's taxonomy of translation strategies for treating culture-specific items, this chapter aims to examine Carlos Rojas's translation of these difficult terms and phrases. A quantitative analysis was manually conducted based on the data consisting of 100 Chinese terms and 100 Chinese phrases with their English renderings. The results show that on the whole, Rojas tries to strike a balance between adequacy-oriented translation and acceptability-oriented translation, though he is predisposed to preserve the cultural significance of these terms. The qualitative analysis with reference to specific examples demonstrates that Rojas translates the Chinese culture-specific items flexibly and resourcefully, transcending the binary opposition between foreignization and domestication. Driven by his professional habitus as a scholar-translator, his pursuit of adequacy in cultural translation offers English readers an opportunity to interact with the Chinese cultural other.

In Chapter 29, Dongli Lu 盧冬麗 and Riccardo Moratto focus on the translation and reception of Yan in Japan. Ten of Yan's books have been translated into Japanese thus far. Japan was first introduced to Yan's literature through *Dream of Ding Village*. However, it was *Lenin's Kisses* that brought him into the limelight. *The Years, Months, Days*, *The Explosion Chronicles*, and *Three Brothers* were all published in 2016. As a result, the Japanese media claimed that "the era of Yan" had finally arrived. The reception of the Japanese translation of Yan's novella "Pig Bristles, White Pig Bristles" ("Hei zhu mao bai zhu mao" 黑豬毛白豬毛) in Japan marked the consolidation of Yan's literary status. In translating Yan's literature into Japanese, his three translators have always respected the original text while attempting to appropriately find creative solutions to convey the deep layers of meaning in the original Chinese. Yan's Japanese publishers have contributed to promoting his literary works in Japan, while renowned Sinologists and critics have published book reviews in mainstream media which, in turn, have led to enhancing Yan's literary influence in Japan. Under the combined effect of various forces, Yan's literature has gained the close attention of Japanese readers. However, the focus of Japanese society gradually shifted from the societal aspects of his writings to the literariness of his work. Yan's translations in Japan show the commonality in the dissemination of contemporary Chinese literature in overseas contexts and provide an interesting point of reference for the translation of Chinese contemporary literature.

In Chapter 30, Van Hieu Do 杜文曉 and Riccardo Moratto focus on the translation and reception of Yan's fiction in Vietnam. Over the past twelve years, six of Yan's novels have been translated into Vietnamese and have been widely acclaimed by readers and critics alike. It can be said that Yan's novels occupy an important place in Vietnamese translated literature. Why do Vietnamese readers like to read his novels? How are Yan's novels translated and interpreted in Vietnam and how do Vietnamese readers understand and analyze the literary figure of Yan? Through the study of such research questions, this chapter aims to clarify the special relationship between Yan's fiction, Vietnamese readers, and contemporary Vietnamese literature in general. More broadly, this chapter also aims to analyze the reception of contemporary Chinese literature in Vietnam.

In Chapter 31, Riccardo Moratto and Di-kai Chao focus on the reception and significance of Yan's works in Taiwan. The analysis begins with the publication of Yan's first book in Taiwan, *Lenin's Kisses*. This essay focuses on how Yan's works are read and evaluated in the academia, the publishing industry, and the literary world, and examines why Yan is read in Taiwan and what his texts mean within the broader realm of Taiwanese literature. The study shows that when Taiwan first introduced *Serve the People!* (*Wei renmin fuwu* 爲人民服務), it paid special attention to Yan as a "banned author" from the Chinese mainland. Soon thereafter, the academia became concerned with the tensions between disease, poverty, and the discourse of state power in Yan's works and the inspiration that such literary creations brought to Taiwanese literature; therefore, the attention shifted to Yan's narrative techniques and universal issues. It is also suggested that in receiving Yan's texts, Taiwan has been thinking about the relevance and significance of Yan's literary creation with respect to Taiwanese literature. This reflection implies a deeper layer of thought, that is, Taiwan is pondering over the meaning of "Taiwan." Unlike the translation, circulation, and introduction of Yan's works as literature in other countries and regions, which are the usual topics of research in world literature, the reception of his works in Taiwan involves the circulation of texts among the Sinophone communities. By juxtaposing the differences in the degree of attention paid to Yan in the regions of Taiwan and Hong Kong, this essay also elevates the issue of Yan's reception history in Taiwan to the level of Sinophone literature research, pointing out that the process of Yan's reception in Taiwan reflects the continuous production of dynamic meanings of Sinophone texts in the continuous debates and dialogues between the self and the other in various places of the Sinosphere.

Editorial preface

In Chapter 32, the final chapter of this volume, Carole Hang-fung Hoyan 何杏楓 and Yijiao Guo focus on the reception of Yan in Hong Kong. Yan is a prolific and yet controversial mainland Chinese author who attracts global attention. Three of his novels and short-story collections banned in the mainland were published in Hong Kong, including *Serve the People!*, *The Years, Months, Days*, and *The Four Books*. He served as Visiting Professor of Chinese Culture at the Hong Kong University of Science and Technology and was conferred Doctor of Letters honoris causa. His two lecture collections review the dissemination and impacts of nineteenth- and twentieth-century world literature on China. What is the significance of Yan's encounter with Hong Kong? How do Hong Kong scholars and critics view Yan's mythorealist portrayal of the economic development of China in the age of globalization? This chapter investigates the reception of Yan in Hong Kong from a cross-regional perspective by analyzing Yan's literary works published in Hong Kong, his award-winning novel *The Day the Sun Died* (*Rixi* 日熄), *The Explosions Chronicles*, and *The Four Books* in particular. It also probes into the dynamics of how Yan and his writings travel to Hong Kong and beyond. The chapter draws on materials including anthologies reviews, journal papers, articles on local Chinese and English newspapers, academic conferences, graduate theses, and interviews. The quantitative approach of word cloud is employed to supplement the analysis. This chapter holds that Yan is perceived in Hong Kong as a controversial mainland author, who revealed through his mythorealist the "reality" hidden behind China's door that is half-opened and half-closed. Moreover, the significance of Yan's encounter with Hong Kong lies in its cross-regional publications and activities, which enable a censored writer to connect with global readers.

The volume closes with a complete Chinese bibliography of Yan in chronological order. This volume is not a mere edited collection of essays. It is a testament to life, the life of one of the greatest writers *tout court*. We are truly indebted to all the contributors of this volume, who provided the erudition and wisdom of each chapter. Working with scholars around the world has been a pleasure and, notwithstanding the names on the spine of the book, this volume is really yours.

ACKNOWLEDGMENT

Yan Lianke

Translated by Riccardo Moratto

Solitude is the most appropriate and noble word to describe the status of any writer in the world. Indeed, the yearning and reverence that writers feel for the word solitude are like the dark night gazing at the break of day far into the distance or the cold winter earnestly waiting for the arrival of spring.

> I do not long to be alone.
> I have never felt alone.

Even if the whole world thinks that your writing is like a hummingbird imprisoned in a boundless net, censored and oftentimes unpublished. Even if some of the books that were published in the past can no longer be reprinted. Even if you want your new books to be read by people sharing your mother tongue, yet you need to deliberately filter the subject matter, plot, and details. And then, after handing it over to the editor, you pay heed to their comments and suggestions, and work with them to revise it carefully or, with a smile on your face, you are to accept their abridgments and corrections. Your book is then finally published after numerous exchanges and innumerable recommendations as if one were burning joss sticks and worshipping Buddha. The book is now available to readers. Yet… just when your readership is beginning to discuss your work, for some arcane reason, the book can no longer be reprinted.

No one will tell you why. No explanation is required. It's just the way it is. Just like no one has ever asked God why He said let there be light and there was light; let there be water and there was water. I have become quite accustomed to all this: this is life or an inseparable part of it. Besides, there are so many people, near, far, who love literature and who are waiting to provide some help and assistance; just like when you are tired, there are always family members and relatives ready to pick up your bag and smile at you when you return home.

> I have never been a loner.
> I have almost never felt alone.

Sometimes I even feel that I have been given more understanding and love than others. A warm embrace is always awaiting me, stirring me to pursue my writing. The embrace of those colleagues who do everything in their power to help me get published, those who keep

Acknowledgment

apologizing for deleting a sentence or a minor detail, who believe that in literature, only imagination, freedom, and art count. I am really a very lucky person. In China and abroad, I can always meet understanding and warmth, and encounter fellow travelers who are bent on pursuing literature and art.

The *Routledge Companion to Yan Lianke* is an ordinary book, yet it is an extraordinary volume. The Sinologist Professor Dr. Riccardo Moratto decided to compile this volume over a few years ago. He then invited Dr. Howard Yuen Fung Choy, who readily accepted to co-edit this volume. Over the last two years, Prof. Dr. Riccardo Moratto has indefatigably invited scholars, critics, and translators from around the world. So many people have embraced and proceeded hand in hand, working hard and doing their utmost for the sake of literature. This is not a sheer edited volume but a call of kindred spirits welcoming spring. This is a ray of light and a source of warmth scattered over a cold and lonely road. However, despite this, I am convinced that we came together only for the sake of literature and this book was published for the sake of art.

I am by no means a lonely person, with so many fellow travelers all around me. In addition to thanking each and every one of you from the bottom of my heart, I also want to bow and give thanks to life. For any writer, as long as the pen is still there and the books are still in his or her studio, life will always be good. When there is a sunset, there will be a sunrise, and when there is a sunrise, there will always be a sunset.

Whether it is at sunrise or at sunset, as long as we keep walking forward, we will always encounter fellow travelers all around us.

February 3, 2021

Professor at the School of Liberal Arts, Renmin University of China
IAS Sin Wai Kin Professor of Chinese Culture and Chair Professor of Humanities, HKUST

EDITORIAL ACKNOWLEDGMENT

It's December 2019, just before the pandemic outbreak. Who could have known? Everyone was going about their lives, unaware and unperturbed, taking for granted those small daily freedoms, which in a few weeks, we would have all yearned for like water in the driest of deserts.

December 2019. Sofia, Bulgaria.

I (Riccardo Moratto) was in the Bulgarian capital as I had been invited to chair a session at the international conference "China and the World: Language, Culture, Politics", co-organized by the University of Sofia St Kliment Ohridski and Xi'an Jiaotong-Liverpool University. In those days, I had the opportunity to meet Dr. Howard Yuen Fung Choy, associate professor at Hong Kong Baptist University and also a presenter at the conference. After fruitful conversations, we exchanged WeChat on the third day; after that, we went our separate ways: I went back to Taiwan and he returned to Hong Kong.

In those days, we had talked a lot about modern and contemporary Chinese literature, and so I had learned that he was in contact with Yan Lianke 閻連科 as he was a member of the jury of the sixth Dream of the Red Chamber Award that Yan had won in 2017 with his *The Day the Sun Died* (*Rixi* 日熄).

After the pandemic broke out in January 2020, I decided to interview Yan. And that's when Dr. Choy was a great help to me, putting us in touch without any qualms.

The admiration I had nurtured for Yan over the years (I had read all his books even before he was discovered by Western publishers) had turned into anxiety and fear. "Who knows what he would think of me and of my interview?" I thought. Cobwebs of anxiety gripped my heart in a hold of apprehension and, at the same time, of unstoppable euphoria.

However, surpassing all my expectations, from the very first conversation, the great Yan never disappointed me, immediately presenting himself as a brother, friend, confidant, colleague, guide, and much more. Our interview was the beginning of a wonderful friendship and professional relationship that continues to this day.

Who is Yan Lianke?

Yan Lianke is one of us: a person with dreams, often broken, hopes, disappointments (countless), tenacity, immense courage, a lot of perseverance, and a boundless passion for writing. As he says, "writing is a creative process, a journey without a destination or a specific goal. Writing makes me feel alive. I have always used literature as a creative process aimed at finding the meaning of life."

Editorial acknowledgment

This volume is not a mere edited collection of essays. It is a testament to life, the life of one of the greatest writers *tout court*. We are truly indebted to all the contributors of this volume, who provided the erudition and wisdom of each chapter. Thank you for answering with patience our editorial queries and responding to our suggestions. Working with you has been a pleasure and, notwithstanding the names on the spine of the book, this volume is really yours.

I would also like to extend my most heartfelt gratitude to Di-kai Chao for his invaluable assistance, and gratefully acknowledge the support of the whole Routledge team. In particular, I would like to thank Simon Bates for his unwavering support and encouragement, Shubhayan Chakrabarti, and all the copyeditors and typesetters at Routledge. Thank you for your support and thank you all on behalf of Yan Lianke.

PART I

Mythorealism and censorship

1
YAN LIANKE'S MYTHOREALIST REPRESENTATION OF THE COUNTRY AND THE CITY[1]

Weijie Song

> When I look at contemporary China, I see a nation that is thriving yet distorted, developing yet mutated. I see corruption, absurdity, disorder and chaos. Every day, something occurs that lies outside ordinary reason and logic.
> —Yan Lianke, "Finding Light in China's Darkness"

On 16 February 1927, Lu Xun 魯迅 delivered his famous lecture "Silent China" ("Wusheng de Zhongguo" 無聲的中國) in Hong Kong, arguing that within the context of East-West cultural confrontation, warlord tyranny, and political censorship, "We have men but no voices, and how lonely that is! Can men be silent? No, not unless they are dead, or—to put it more politely—when they are dumb."[2] In what was then a British colony, Lu Xun addressed "literary revolution," "language reform," and "intellectual transformation," proposing that "we must speak our own language, the language of today, using the living vernacular to give clear expression to our thoughts and feelings."[3]

Lu Xun's call to articulate silences still rings around the world of post-Maoist, post-Cold War, and post-1989 Chinese literature. Yan Lianke 閻連科 is widely regarded as an outstanding heir of Lu Xun and develops "mythorealism" (*shenshi zhuyi* 神實主義) as a new literary method to tell the stories of silent China. His "banned at home, lauded abroad"[4] novel *Dream of Ding Village* (*Dingzhuang meng* 丁莊夢) bravely enters a politically sensitive zone: the blood-selling trade and subsequent AIDS epidemic in his home province of Henan. Another banned novel, *Serve the People* (*Wei renmin fuwu* 為人民服務), confronts the taboos

---

1 An earlier version of this essay was published as "Yan Lianke's Mythorealist Representation of the Country and the City," *MFS: Modern Fiction Studies* 62, no. 4 (2016): 644–58. © 2016 Purdue Research Foundation. Reprinted with permission of Johns Hopkins University Press.
2 Lu Xun, *Silent China: Selected Writings of Lu Xun*, ed. and trans. Gladys Yang (London: Oxford University Press, 1973), 164.
3 Ibid., 167.
4 Joy Lo Dico, "Banned at Home, Lauded Abroad: Vladimir Sorokin and Yan Lianke Make Man Booker Shortlist," *Independent*, 24 Jan. 2013, https://www.independent.co.uk/arts-entertainment/books/news/banned-home-lauded-abroad-vladimir-sorokin-and-yan-lianke-make-man-booker-shortlist-8466006.html (last accessed 8 Aug. 2013).

of sex and politics, Maoist rhetoric, and Mao fetishism. *Lenin's Kisses* (*Shouhuo* 受活), an absurdist and tragicomic representation of the lives of disabled rural villagers, describes the unhappy marriage of communism and capitalism—as well as, according to its book jacket, "the trappings and consequences of greed and corruption at the heart of humanity."[5] As a censored and major prize-winning author and university professor, Yan regards himself as a rebel son of mainstream realism and coined the term "mythorealism" to elucidate the influence of Kafkaesque and Márquezan combinations of reality and absurdity on contemporary Chinese literature. In his anthology of critical articles, *Discovering Fiction* (*Faxian xiaoshuo* 發現小說), Yan includes an essay "A Preliminary Explanation of Mythorealism" ("*Shenshi zhuyi de jiandan shishuo*" 神實主義的簡單釋說) and writes:

> Mythorealism … abandons the seemingly logical relations of real life, and explores a "nonexistent" truth, an invisible truth, and a truth concealed by truth. Mythorealism keeps a distance from any prevailing realism. The mythorealist connection with reality does not lie in straightforward cause-and-effect links, but rather relies on human souls, minds … and the authors' extraordinary fabrications based on reality …. Imaginations, metaphors, myths, legends, dreams, fantasy, demonization, and transplantation born from everyday life and social reality can all serve as mythorealist methods and channels.[6]

In 2016, after Yan was for the second time shortlisted for the Man Booker International Prize, he stated during an interview: "I feel that only in writing in a 'mythorealist' style am I truly able to probe the interior of reality and the depths of human spirit, and otherwise would only be able to engage with reality and history in a superficial fashion."[7]

Sun Yu 孫郁 traces the development of mythorealism over the course of Yan's career and points out that his 2001 novel *Streams of Time* indicates a narrative turn in Yan's realist concept and aesthetic imagery. *Hard as Water* and *Lenin's Kisses* strengthen this literary transition. Finally, *Dream of Ding Village*, *Ballad, Hymn, Ode*, *The Four Books*, and *The Explosion Chronicles* highlight Yan's mythorealist consciousness, innovative imagination, and creative literary praxis.[8] Yan's imaginative configurations of literary settings, from the metamorphosis of his hometown in Henan Province (in particular, the Balou 耙耬 Mountains and the Northwestern villages) to the transfiguration of post-Maoist Beijing (especially the

---

[5] See Yan Lianke, *Lenin's Kisses*, trans. Carlos Rojas (New York: Grove, 2012). Yan continues his mythorealist representations of the country and the city in his other works including *Streams of Time* (*Riguang liunian* 日光流年), *Hard as Water* (*Jianying ru shui* 堅硬如水), *Ballad, Hymn, Ode* (*Feng ya song* 風雅頌), *The Four Books* (*Si shu* 四書), *Garden No. 711: The Ultimate Last Memo of Beijing* (*711 hao yuan: Beijing zuihou de zuihou jinian* 711號園：北京最後的最後紀念), *The Explosion Chronicles* (*Zhalie zhi* 炸裂志), and *The Day the Sun Died* (*Rixi* 日熄). He has published numerous collections of novellas, short stories, and essays, including *Year Month Day* (*Nian yue ri* 年月日), *Marrow* (*Balou tiange* 耙耬天歌), and *My Elder Generation and I* (*Wo yu fubei* 我與父輩). He is the recipient of numerous literary awards, including the first and second Lu Xun Literary Prizes, the Lao She Award, the Dream of the Red Chamber Award, and the Franz Kafka Prize. *Lenin's Kisses* and *The Four Books* were shortlisted for the Man Booker International Prize, respectively, in 2013 and 2016.

[6] Yan Lianke, *Faxian xiaoshuo* (Tianjin: Nankai daxue chubanshe, 2011), 181–82. All English translations are mine unless otherwise indicated.

[7] See http://booker218.rssing.com/chan-5643463/all_p3.html (last accessed 8 Aug. 2021).

[8] Sun Yu, "Yan Lianke de 'shenshi zhuyi'" 閻連科的「神實主義」 [Yan Lianke's "mythorealism"], *Dangdai zuojia pinglun* 當代作家評論 [Contemporary writers review], 2013, no. 5: 13–21.

construction and destruction of his former home in that city, called Garden No. 711), illustrate his grotesque, comic, spectacular, miserable, absurd, and deformed literary world.

Yan's mythorealism challenges accepted conventions of linear cause-and-effect relationship, often considered to be the driving force behind the development of literary narratives. In his *Discovering Fiction*, Yan makes distinctions among "complete cause-and-effect" (*quan yinguo* 全因果), "partial cause-and-effect" (*ban yinguo* 半因果), "internal cause-and-effect" (*nei yinguo* 內因果), and "zero cause-and-effect" (*ling yinguo* 零因果), arguing that we should focus on an illogical logic and an irrational rationality that lie beyond conventional cause-and-effect associations.[9] Since the 1990s, the unpredictable and dynamic social, political, and cultural reality in mainland China has overwhelmed writers and scholars, pushing them to address the question raised sharply by Eileen Chang 張愛玲 decades ago: "What if the transformative era changes so drastically that fictional writings cannot follow reality?"[10] Yan's mythorealist writings can be read as persistent and painstaking efforts to follow, diagnose, and criticize this unpredictable and complex reality. This article considers Yan's *Lenin's Kisses* and *Garden No. 711*, focusing on Yan's post-Maoist representations of macro- and micro-mythoreality, political dystopia and ecocritical utopia, the articulated silence of the humiliated and insulted, and the large-scale ferocity and "slow violence" (Nixon's term) being committed in both the country and the city.[11] *Lenin's Kisses* and *Garden No. 711* serve as exemplary responses to what Lu Xun, in "Silent China," referred to as speaking "the language of today," "using the living vernacular," and giving "clear expression to our thoughts and feelings."[12] In fact, Yan goes even further by adopting mythorealism to resist oppression and violence amid political catastrophe and the environmental crisis in Maoist and post-Maoist China.

In terms of "the living vernacular," *Lenin's Kisses* gives new life to a bittersweet indigenous term—*shouhuo* (to liven)—used mostly in western Henan and eastern Henan's Balou Mountains. *Shouhuo* means to "experience 'enjoyment, happiness, and passion', and also carries connotations of finding pleasure in discomfort, or making pleasure out of discomfort."[13] Yan uses this unique, down-to-earth Northwestern vernacular in his depiction of the countryside of Henan, develops an experimental and mythorealist literary mode, and unfolds the novel's absurd story along the bifurcations and convergences of two major narrative structures within the text—the *zhengwen* 正文 (chapters portraying the "Story Proper," or the main body of the text) and the *xuyan* 絮言 ("Further Reading," or supplementary fragmented notes that punctuate the "Story Proper" and showcase Yan's innovative imagination).[14] The "Story Proper" focuses on new county official Chief Liu Yingque's 柳鷹雀 bold socialist-capitalist dream of borrowing Lenin's embalmed corpse from the bankrupt Soviet Union, relocating it to a memorial hall in the local Balou Mountains, which is the same size as Chairman Mao's Memorial Hall at Beijing's Tiananmen Square, and making vast profits from exhibiting the

---

9 Yan, *Faxian xiaoshuo* 發現小說, 171–73.
10 Eileen Chang, "Tan kanshu" 談看書 [On reading], in *Zhang kan* 張看 [Chang's observations] (Taipei: Huangguan, 1991), 188.
11 For "Slow Violence," see Rob Nixon, "Slow Violence and Environmental Storytelling," *Nieman Storyboard*, 13 June 2011, https://niemanstoryboard.org/stories/slow-violence-and-environmental-storytelling/ (last accessed 1 Oct. 2013); and his *Slow Violence and the Environmentalism of the Poor* (Cambridge, MA: Harvard University Press, 2011).
12 Lu Xun, *Silent China*, 167.
13 Yan, *Lenin's Kisses*, 4.
14 Liu Jianmei 劉劍梅 renders *zhengwen* as "Story Proper" in her *Zhuangzi and Modern Chinese Literature* (New York: Oxford University Press, 2016), 200. Carlos Rojas translates *xuyan* as "Further Reading" and sees it as "pretext for a series of flashbacks" and points out its "crucial structural and conceptual elements." See Rojas, Translator's Note, in *Lenin's Kisses*, viii.

body. Chief Liu is an orphan, an adopted nonconformist son of a local schoolteacher, and a newly appointed local authority with political ambition and economic dreams. He becomes a game-changer and trendsetter through the double baptism of Maoist ideology and post-Maoist economic reform.

The "Further Reading" section concentrates on Grandma Mao Zhi 茅枝婆 in the village of Liven, a small, independent, and isolated community occupied only by disabled residents. Mao Zhi was "the youngest female soldier in the Red Army," a "revolutionary orphan" who "lost three toes to frostbite and broke her leg falling into a ravine, leaving her unable to walk without the aid of a crutch."[15] After the founding of the People's Republic of China in 1949, Mao Zhi became "a bona fide revolutionary leader" and later the contemporary "ancestral mother" of Liven: "Thanks to her, therefore, Balou came to have glory, Liven came to have direction, and the villagers, despite being physically disabled, were able to live happy and fulfilled lives in the new society."[16] Yet Mao Zhi and her neighbors are forced to join in Chief Liu's carnivalesque, grotesque, and developmentalist dream over Lenin's corpse and become crippled clowns in Liu's socialist-capitalist dream-making—and later dream-breaking—stage performance.

From the beginning, the "Story Proper" is set within a pessimistic, gloomy, and bizarre mythoreality, starting with a seven-day hot snow that brings winter in the middle of a scorching summer.[17] Time "fell ill" and "out of joint," finally going downright "mad": "Overnight, everything degenerated into disorder and lawlessness."[18] The "Story Proper" of book 1, chapter 1 establishes an ominous, despairing tone for the entire novel as it laments the absurd, chaotic reality that dominates the countryside of contemporary China.

By contrast, in a quiet and pseudo-objective voiceover, the "Further Reading" section of book 1, chapter 1 combines historical accounts and fictional narratives, scholarly research, and imaginative descriptions, in which a lengthy endnote provides a concise local history of Liven as a distinctive community of disabled residents. Yan intentionally blends legendary prehistory and modern revolutionary history. He traces the history of the village back to the Ming dynasty, the large-scale migration in the Shaanxi and Henan areas, and the ancestral mother's kindness and generosity. Thanks to an old, deaf-mute woman's offer of food—an occasional meal of porridge—when he was poor and frustrated, a man who ultimately becomes the Ming dynasty's minister of migration bestows money and land to the deaf-mute woman and other disabled people so they could live a contented life in Liven. From neighboring villages and the adjacent county, the blind, the lame, the deaf, the crippled, and other disabled people flock to join the isolated village. Yan briefly depicts this deaf-mute woman, along with a blind man and a crippled young man, as constituting a household and living a "heavenly," paradisiacal life.[19]

However, Yan's main purpose is to present the mythoreality of the village of Liven in the context of and in contrast to Republican, post-1949, and post-1989 eras. The endnote

---

15 Yan, *Lenin's Kisses*, 9.
16 Ibid.
17 Ibid., 3.
18 Ibid.
19 A detailed description of the village of Liven is as follows, and in doing so, Yan designs a unique utopia led and occupied by the handicapped: "When word got out that a deaf-mute woman, a blind man, and a cripple had set up a household here and were enjoying a heavenly existence, disabled people from throughout the region began pouring in. The deaf-mute woman supplied them with land and silver, thereby permitting them to live comfortably, raise families, and establish a village. Although many of these villagers' descendants inherited similar physical handicaps, the deaf-mute woman continued to provide them with everything they need. The village came to known as Liven, and the old woman was recognized as the ancestral mother." See Yan, *Lenin's Kisses*, 8.

recounts that a 1980 local gazetteer "claims that Liven was not merely a location where disabled residents established a community, but a sacred revolutionary site where a soldier by the name of Mao Zhi from the Red Army's Fourth Regiment settled down to live."[20] As the narrative unfolds, the "Story Proper" and "Further Reading" sections intertwine, establishing a more complete picture of how Grandma Mao Zhi and her villagers follow the call of Maoist propaganda, step out from their ahistorical seclusion, and choose to join the utopian people's commune as new socialist citizens. But they profoundly suffer from the Maoist political movements and post-Maoist economic development—"The Iron Disaster," "The Year of the Great Plunder," "Black Disasters," "Red Difficulties," "Black Crimes," "Red Crimes," and "Admiration Hall"—reminding readers of stories of the Great Leap Forward, the People's Communization Movement, the Great Famine, the Five Black Categories, land reform prior to the post-Maoist market-economy miracle, and Chinese developmentalist fantasy.

The novel consists of odd-numbered chapters only (a reference to the characters' odd physical abnormalities and their strange stories) and evokes the sequential growth of plants in its eight book titles: "Rootlets," "Roots," "Stem," "Branches," "Leaves," "Flowers," "Fruit," and "Seeds." The "Story Proper" and "Further Reading" sections constitute a parallel structure, juxtaposing Chief Liu and Grandma Mao Zhi as symbolic double orphans. The two main narratives meet, dispute one another, and converge in correspondence with the contradictions and cooperation between the two worlds. In Yan's mythorealist imagination, Chief Liu is obsessed with a bold scenario: he uses his administrative power to raise seed money, organizes the disabled villagers of Liven as an eye-catching "Special-Skills Performance Troupe" to generate huge revenues, and allocates the funds to purchase Lenin's corpse, which he intends to relocate to a mausoleum in his administrative region, so as to attract millions of visitors and thus fulfill his political and economic ambitions. In the process he profits immensely but his unorthodox plan winds up causing his countrymen, including the villagers of Liven, more suffering and danger.

Liven's new ancestral mother, Mao Zhi, was injured in the revolutionary past, having experienced exile, abuse, insult, and pain, including her daughter being raped by Chief Liu. However, physical pain and bodily harm have not left the women of Liven traumatized; indeed, they seem to have survived by means of a healthy and forgiving amnesia. By contrast, political violence and injury, especially in the unexpected and traumatic aftermath of Mao Zhi and the villagers' attempt at *rushe* 入社 ("joining the commune" or "entering the world" of socialist China), bring Mao Zhi everlasting pain and sorrow, becoming an open wound in her memory. *Lenin's Kisses* ends with an unexpected compromise: Mao Zhi finally gets approval to withdraw from the commune from Chief Liu, who is about to be forced to resign from his position and soon has a traffic accident, loses his legs, and becomes disabled. He eventually settles as a newcomer in Liven, which returns to its original apolitical, ahistorical, self-contained, and marginalized state.

Liven demonstrates the mixture of literary and political dystopia manifested in the absurd reality of Maoist and post-Maoist China. Writing on the utopian, dystopian, irrational, antilogical, and grotesque characteristics in Yan's literary mythoreality, Chen Sihe 陳思和 points out that *Lenin's Kisses* "is not a writer's whimsical, nihilist joke of the international communist movement, but an allegory of the irrational world in the name of the red banner but in the crazy pursuit of capitalist profit."[21] Nan Fan 南帆 views *Lenin's Kisses* as "grotesque

20 Ibid.
21 Chen Sihe, "Diqijie Huazong wenxuejiang dezhu Yan Lianke de shoujiangci 第七屆花蹤文學獎得主閻連科的受獎辭 [The 7th Huazong Literature Award ceremony speech by Yan Lianke]," *Dangdai zuojia pinglun*, 2013, no. 5: 11.

realism" that conflates irony and the grotesque to provide a surreal picture: "*Streams of Time* blends with the structure of a myth, *Hard as Water* indulges in exaggerating political discourses, and *Lenin's Kisses* betrays an astonishing paradox."[22] Wang Yao 王堯 argues that *Lenin's Kisses* is in fact the origin of mythorealism, in which Yan began to consciously follow the "real heart" (*zhenshi de neixin* 真實的內心) and to question the so-called real life (*zhenshi de shenghuo* 真實的生活).[23] According to Wu Xiaodong 吳曉東, *Lenin's Kisses* reveals that the concepts of native soil and rural utopia are effectively erased by modern socialist and capitalist utopias.[24] As Wang Hongsheng 王鴻生 points out, *Lenin's Kisses* instead presents an anti-utopian utopia in which the Oriental Naturalist utopia resists the Western Communist utopia.[25] I contend that in this novel the tension among different types of utopia in China and the West highlights distinct differences in content but reveals a similar spirit, a critical utopian impulse toward absurd reality and social injustice. Paul Ricoeur, calling attention to different forms of utopia, explains, "Utopias (in the plural) do not easily yield a central meaning for Utopia (in the singular)."[26] I once argued that the presence of multiple visions of utopias within fictional narratives reflects specific and sometimes contradictory imaginations. Among the types of utopia I outlined are the lazy man's paradise, the remote refuge for the insulted and the injured, the hermit's "Peach Blossom Spring" (a vision of a perfect past), and the progressive, idealized future of modern society.[27] The spirit of utopia is connected with the impulse shared by authors, artists, and scholars to resist and fight for freedom, emancipation, salvation, social justice, and ideal life. In Paul Tillich's words, "it is the spirit of utopia that conquers utopia."[28]

I would also argue that from the beginning, Liven is not flawless: it is a paradise for the disabled and deformed residents, yet its door remains shut to healthy people. Yan never meant to retell the story of the classical Chinese "Peach Blossom Spring" or to present the equivalent of a pastoral hymn in the contemporary post-Maoist political and economic context. For centuries, Liven had farms and land and remained self-sufficient; before 1949, its people had never even heard of the Second Sino-Japanese War, the Chinese Civil War, or the founding of the People's Republic of China. Yet the reclusive and disabled villagers could not live a secluded pastoral life after Mao Zhi married into the village. Mao Zhi brought revolutionary information from the outside world, enabling the villagers to be continuously implicated in

---

22 Nan Fan, "*Shouhuo*: Guaidan ji qi meixue xipu" 《受活》: 怪誕及其美學系譜 [*Lenin's Kisses*: Grotesque and its aesthetic genealogy], *Shanghai wenxue* 上海文學 [Shanghai literature], 2004, no. 6: 67.
23 Wang Yao, "Zuowei shijieguan he fangfalun de 'shenshi zhuyi': *Faxian xiaoshuo* yu Yan Lianke de xiaoshuo chuangzuo" 作為世界觀和方法論的「神實主義」——《發現小說》與閻連科的小說創作 ["Mythorealism" as worldview and method: *Discovering Fiction* and Yan Lianke's fiction writing], *Dangdai zuojia pinglun*, 2013, no. 6: 9.
24 Wu Xiaodong, "Zhongguo wenxue zhong de xiangtu wutuobang ji qi huanmie" 中國文學中的鄉土烏托邦及其幻滅 [Rural utopia and its disillusionment in Chinese literature], *Beijing daxue xuebao* 北京大學學報 [Peking University journal] 43, no. 1 (2006): 79.
25 Wang Hongsheng, "Fan wutuobang de wutuobang xushi: Du *Shouhuo*" 反烏托邦的烏托邦敘事——讀《受活》 [Anti-utopian utopian narrative: Reading *Lenin's Kisses*], *Dangdai zuojia pinglun*, 2004, no. 2: 91.
26 Paul Ricoeur, *Lectures on Ideology and Utopia* (New York: Columbia University Press, 1987), 270.
27 Here I refer to the Peach Blossom Spring, a fable written by classical Chinese poet Tao Yuanming 陶淵明 during a chaotic political time. It describes an ahistorical, apolitical utopia where the residents live a pastoral and harmonious life, unaware of dynastic crisis and changes outside of their world. See Song Weijie 宋偉傑, "Wutuobang jianlun" 烏托邦簡論 [On utopia], *Yishu guangjiao* 藝術廣角 [Art panorama], 1998, no. 3: 11–12.
28 Paul Tillich, *Political Expectation* (New York: Harper & Row, 1971), 180.

the Maoist and post-Maoist political and economic campaigns. Tao Dongfeng 陶東風 reads *Lenin's Kisses* as a political allegory and writes that the characterization of healthy people as victimizers and the disabled villagers of Liven as victims somehow weakens the intensity of its political criticism.[29] However, I would say that the mythorealist juxtapositions of healthy people and disabled villagers underline the truth that Liven is not a homogeneous, abstract, rigid community but rather a complex, heterogeneous, partly closed, and partly open space full of contingent contradictions and temporary reconciliations.

Jianmei Liu labels the isolated and disabled villagers "collective Zhuangzis" 莊子.[30] To me, this is an idealized interpretation because the disabled group of pseudo-Daoist practitioners does not maintain a Zhuangzian (that is, Daoist) moral superiority over their corporeal deficiency. Stepping into the muddy reality of contemporary China, they turn from useless men into new citizens in socialist China, and their already deformed bodies are further tortured, tormented, and distorted by physical disability and human inferiority (greed, jealousy, calculation, and moral degeneration). They have lost the joy of life and encountered disillusionment in their painstaking struggle between "joining the commune" and *tuishe* 退社 (withdrawing from the commune).[31] The narrative structure and the looming disillusionment of the disabled villagers in *Lenin's Kisses* expose the negative and hesitant dimensions of the utopian imagination. The utopian imagination, in other words, can break down the absurdities of reality and social injustice. Through this imagination people can overcome their anxiety, fear, terror, depression, and schizophrenia, so as to gain hope, salvation, human freedom, and the possibility of liberation.

Political utopia pursues an ideal social system, and literary utopia constructs a poetic paradise. Yan does not make a distinction between the two but calls attention to the persistence of utopian dreams in his dialogue with critic Zhang Xuexin 張學昕:

> If there were not a utopian dream of Communism, how could our nation be so docile and obedient as to go through the Cultural Revolution and the three years of Great Famine? Weren't the decades of social development led by the beacon and lamp of communism moving forward? Didn't we conceive the dreams of a moderately prosperous society, a really affluent society, and a super-affluent society, as well as another dream of a powerful and wealthy nation-state? Isn't it yet another new utopian dream? People say that China is a nation without belief or religion, yet haven't utopias, one after another, become a national faith? Actually, utopia serves as a constant lamp in our dreams during the long process of human development, and remains a spiritual home for the human race to live and survive. Some time ago I was at home reading Tao Yuanming's poetry and biography. Carefully thinking about it, I recalled that the great Tao Yuanming was not only a poet and writer but also a philosopher and architect. After a thousand years, Peach Blossom Spring has become such a wonderful backyard for our modern civilization. Doesn't the pure land of Peach Blossom Spring constitute utopia for our entire prosperous society?[32]

---

29 Tao Dongfeng, "*Shouhuo*: Dangdai Zhongguo zhengzhi yuyan xiaoshuo de jiezuo" 《受活》: 當代中國政治寓言小說的傑作 [*Lenin's Kisses*: A masterpiece of contemporary Chinese political allegorical fiction], *Dangdai zuojia pinglun*, 2013, no. 5: 35.
30 Liu, *Zhuangzi and Modern Chinese Literature*, 205.
31 Ibid., 187.
32 Yan Lianke and Zhang Xuexin 張學昕, *Wo de xianshi, wo de zhuyi* 我的現實, 我的主義 [My Reality, my -ism] (Beijing: Zhongguo renmin daxue chubanshe, 2011), 77–78.

In *Discovering Fiction* Yan points out the desolation and coldness of being, yet in *Garden No. 711* the writer presents the warmth of being and the poetic light of utopia. Chen Xiaoming 陳曉明 uses the image of a destructively powerful wildfire to describe *Lenin's Kisses*, citing its explosive force and unprecedented challenge to native soil literature (*xiangtu wenxue* 鄉土文學) and existing modes of realism.[33] Interpreting the great transformation of Western literary criticism brought about by romanticism in the eighteenth century, M. H. Abrams "identifies two common and antithetic metaphors of mind," the mirror and the lamp, "one comparing the mind to a reflector of external objects, the other to a radiant projector which makes a contribution to the objects it perceives."[34] I would like to borrow these symbols to illustrate Yan's mythorealism and literary world: the mirror corresponds with a realist reflection of the world and the lamp with the mythorealist illumination of the absurd and intangible world. If *Lenin's Kisses* is a destructive wildfire, then *Garden No. 711* becomes a magic lamp; and if Yan's *The Four Books* might be regarded as a children's Bible, then *Garden No. 711* can be read as Yan's ecological *Exodus*. In the mythoreality of *Lenin's Kisses*, the villagers of Liven not only bear physical disabilities and psychological scars but also conceal their pain and trauma, withdrawing from the commune and retreating to their isolated village, an escapist and reclusive dreamscape. Yet *Garden No. 711* reconstructs an ideal home, having once existed as a real place but now turned into a literary symbol and warm memory after its brutal demolition by urban developers.

Yan declares *Garden No. 711* to be a tribute to Henry David Thoreau's *Walden*, and as a country person living in a city, expresses his fondness and familiarity with nature. *Walden* is his dream book, and Yan planned to write a similar book proposing that nature is part of human life and human beings are part of nature or an ecological text in which only nature exists and no humans are present. In the preface to *Garden No. 711*, Yan depicts his shock, humility, and sense of epiphany when he discovered the actual Garden no. 711, a seemingly magical yet real oasis surrounded by Beijing's concrete jungle:

> When I first stepped into that Garden, I was stunned and shocked by the endless green. The landscape hit my eyes and made a green-white sound, just like when Caribbean people first saw the ice and touched it, they found that the ice is like fire, hot and burning ....
>
> In Beijing's bustle, there is a quiet place like this, just as there is a religion for the secular world. Garden no. 711 is actually a church for a city to worship great nature. And we are just like the mundane people entering the church and being shocked by the holy and sacred.[35]

However, Yan found it impossible to fulfill the promise of writing a purely environmental work in which nature is the main and only protagonist with no human trace in the ecological garden. In Garden no. 711, nature occupies a small territory; it is only a tiny green space tightly besieged by the gigantic metropolis. Nevertheless, nature is not silent but full of magical sounds, colors, and emotions, and human beings are not entirely absent. They exist in and through traces or shadows. The first-person "I," for instance, is everywhere and provides an affective mapping of the coexistence and boundaries between nature and human beings

---

33 Chen Xiaoming, "Ta yinlai guihuo, ta hengsao yiqie" 他引來鬼火, 他橫掃一切 [He brings wildfire, he sweeps everything], *Dangdai zuojia pinglun*, 2007, no. 5: 68–69.

34 M. H. Abrams, *The Mirror and the Lamp: Romantic Theory and the Critical Tradition* (New York: Oxford University Press, 1953), vii.

35 Yan Lianke, *711 hao yuan: Beijing zuihou de zuihou jinian* (Taipei: Linking, 2012), 6.

in the southwestern corner of Beijing. Liu Jianmei outlines the diversified images of "I" in *Garden No. 711*:

> Choosing the "naturalization of humans" over "the "humanization of nature," Yan Lianke presents a self-image that cares more about nature than society, aligning himself more with Zhuangzi and Daoism than with Confucianism. The first-person narrator in this long essay appears as a writer aloof from any social entanglement, an amateur biologist studying animals and plants, "an idler," "a fribble," "a mental patient," "an orphan amid the crowd," and "an abandoner of the prosperous urban city of Beijing," as well as a "traitor to daily life and an enemy of reality." Yet this narrator is in fact the freest and happiest person, who has gained temporary relief from his anxiety of "national salvation" and retreated into his own little courtyard surrounded by vegetables and plants. In his beautiful natural garden, he has the luxury to perform Zhuangzi's "free and easy wandering," showing his passionate respect and love for nature, enjoying the state of "relying on nothing" and harvesting the true sense of happiness in life.[36]

Here, Liu understands the first-person narrator as a Zhuangzian figure who retreats from the city and resides in a pastoral garden. I would shift the scope of investigation to the construction and collapse of this ecological utopia, the order of things, the nuanced details of mythoreality, and the literary resistance to slow and fast violence in contemporary Beijing under the shadow of global commercialism and development.

Located in the southwest suburbs of Beijing, Garden no. 711 was once a wild, green park ignored by the city's twenty million residents. Almost no one set foot in this area of the city. Yan, meanwhile, presents it as an imperceptible entrance to an urban Peach Blossom Spring. *Garden No. 711* consists of eight chapters and subtly blends essay, fiction, and memoir into a single text. The first six chapters explore a complex ecological landscape, framed through an idealized rural life and the everlasting Chinese longing for a Peach Blossom Spring. Yan begins by describing shovels, hoes, and other garden tools, difficult to find in Beijing, which are incorporated into the mythical order of everyday life in Garden no. 711. Here, he captures not merely the extraordinarily long list of anti-urban objects but also tears and laughter, destiny and life. He connects these objects to wildflowers, vegetables, plants, and foodstuffs—the production and consumption of celery, gourds, and cabbage, among many others—as well as their magical and mythical prehistory and present story. Furthermore, Yan describes the flowers and trees inside and outside of his courtyard and creates a mythoreality in the botanical world: plants in possession of virtues, emotions, love, animosity, and even private hobbies. Yan also portrays the happiness and sadness of insects, birds, and animals, and he welcomes wandering, homeless cats and dogs as new residents of this garden. In his warm and touching history of an ecological utopia, he uses first-person narration to depict the tracks, traces, actions, and feelings of all kinds of nonhuman beings. Man and nature exist in peace, balance, and harmony.

In examining the genealogy of such magic-realist depictions of the country in contemporary Chinese novels, David Der-wei Wang 王德威 uses the terms "vegetarian" and "mineral" to compare the different rural spaces in Yan Lianke's and Mo Yan's 莫言 literary worlds:

---

36 Liu, *Zhuangzi and Modern Chinese Literature*, 206.

... it seems to me that Yan Lianke's concept of rural space is exactly the opposite of Mo Yan's. Heroes hide alongside ghosts, gods, and monsters among the red sorghum of Mo Yan's Jiaodong Plain, frequently creating confusion in the mundane world. The contaminated water of Lingyin canal runs through the wasteland that is Yan Lianke's Balou mountains, a place where the process of survival generates various kinds of bizarre phenomena. If Mo Yan's land is vegetarian, a place where plants spring forth and thrive, then Yan Lianke's land is mineral—devoid of growth and marked by silence and death.[37]

I would argue that Yan's "mineral" space becomes its opposite in *Garden No. 711*: a vegetarian space where "plants spring forth and thrive" on the margin of the rapidly growing metropolis, which is challenged by ecological crisis, climate change, air and water pollution, human construction and destruction, and the use and abuse of natural resources in the Chinese social, cultural, political, economic, physical, and psychological environments.

Yet predictably, this ecotopia could not last long. The journey from the political-economic dystopia in *Lenin's Kisses* to the ecological utopia of *Garden No. 711* ended abruptly in the winter of 2011 when the administrative authorities of the municipal and national governments decided to demolish the garden for the sake of a road-building project. If *Lenin's Kisses* envisions a macrolevel counter-utopia, *Garden No. 711* exhibits an ephemeral and microlevel ecotopia where natural order might be temporarily reestablished but is nevertheless destined to be deformed and destroyed according to the blueprint of "China and Beijing's crazy to insane economic development."[38]

In *Slow Violence and the Environmentalism of the Poor*, Rob Nixon forcefully argues that environmental calamities, ecological crises, sources of pollution, and transnational operations are often difficult to identify and trace. Because of this, there are few legal means to achieve justice. How, then, can poor, insulted, and injured people articulate their pain, anxieties, and trauma amid the overwhelming environmental crisis and ecological deterioration? When slow violence accumulates and grows into destructive violence, an ecological utopia like Garden no. 711 can be vehemently and rapidly removed, erased from the map of Beijing's South Fourth Ring Road by legally permitted intrusion and destruction.

Yan tried to become what Nixon calls an "environmental writer-activist."[39] He publicly protested the violation of human rights, wrote a petition to Chairman Hu Jintao 胡錦濤 and Prime Minister Wen Jiabao 溫家寶, and openly defended his property and rights through the mainstream media and blogosphere. Yan transformed an actual geographical site into a fictional text, and while the real-life Garden no. 711 was ultimately demolished, the garden remains alive in the literary world; the poetic and pastoral life Yan portrayed there stands as a true "last memo," surviving in his mythorealist representation.

Slow violence is not the wartime violence evidenced by corpses, wreckage, blood, or wounds. Instead, it appears in everyday life: demolitions, censorship, taboos, pollution, and the spread of chronic diseases. Yan's mythoreality serves as an intriguing case to illustrate the strategies of literary resistance Nixon conceived: its "reconfigur[ation]" of a "big stor[y] on a human scale" gives "shape to formless threats whose fatal repercussions are dispersed across space and time."[40] *Garden No. 711*'s last two chapters reveal a narrative rupture, continue its

---

37 Quoted in Liu, *Zhuangzi and Modern Chinese Literature*, 198.
38 Yan, *711 hao yuan*, 258.
39 Nixon, *Slow Violence and the Environmentalism of the Poor*, 5.
40 See Nixon, "Slow Violence and Environmental Storytelling."

mythorealist imagination, and confront the threat of violent destruction brought by the urban planning and development division. At the end of *Lenin's Kisses*, Chief Liu and Grandma Mao Zhi wake up from the nightmare of socialist-capitalist developmentalism.

The failure and frustration of public protest against the violation of human rights also pushed Yan to step out from his ecotopia and write about his shock and anger in 2010. He drafted two kinds of mythorealist resistance. The first is "Courtyard Album" (chapter 7), a mythorealist hologram meant to resist the violence of economic development. "Courtyard Album" vividly depicts gourds, watermelons, cherry blossoms, eggplants, hibiscus, henna, bamboo, and crows, a collection of items that might at first seem randomly chosen but in fact are fully charged with critical energy and creative imagination. "Fragmentary Records of the Courtyard," the last section of chapter 7, uses "striking visual imagery" and finds "powerful analogies that resonate"[41]: cypress twigs hit the ground with furious sounds and energetic resistance; the uncertain fate of peach trees indicates the future of the garden; the first-person "I" bids a tearful farewell to four toon trees; the garden and its plants claim victory over steel saws; ivies climb walls, demonstrating their vitality and adaptability; and finally, the physical shape and size of the courtyard become the methods of disclosing the author's anxiety, indignation, philosophical reflection, and literary representation of the dilemma of developmentalist myth and social injustice. Under Yan's mythorealist pen, *Garden No. 711*, like a high-resolution hologram, encodes and conveys Yan's literary ecotopia and his critique of the commercial society and the violence of demolition. "Courtyard Album" and *Garden No. 711* are thus no longer fictional texts of fragments, debris, or miscellany. Rather, they provide a holographic storage place that displays a nostalgic longing for a fleeting Peach Blossom Spring and a bygone ecotopia ruined by unequal economic growth and unhealthy environmental transformation. I would argue that a literary hologram can be an effective resistance strategy because even at its most fragmented, each fragment of the hologram is still capable of representing and reproducing the message of Yan's literary mythoreality.

The second resistance strategy appears in the final chapter, "Winter," which parallels the metaphors of four seasons developed by Northrop Frye in his "archetypal criticism."[42] Yan uses winter to indicate the collapse of Garden no. 711 and entitles his last section, "After the Winter," suggesting the possibility of rebuilding paradise. Yan continues to narrate *Garden No. 711* even as the garden comes tumbling down; he remains alone in the huge ruins, numb, dull-eyed, and silent until a homeless cat's gentle meow wakes him from his heartbreak and disillusionment. Yet Yan dreams another dream after this wake-up call:

> That night, I had a wonderful dream, in which a young woman, who loves nature and cats more than I do, accompanies me, and both of us lead a myriad of wild cats and dogs, flee from Beijing's bustle, expansion, and crowd all the way to a world with only blue sky, white clouds, rivers, birds, flower fragrance, lush vegetation, and numerous insects. We rebuild a new garden and courtyard, start a new life of writing and reading, planting and rearing, and feed and keep countless, countless cats and dogs. Every day, dragonflies and butterflies fly down from trees and flowers with love and aroma, and land on the cats' backs, the dogs' ears, and the point of my pen.[43]

---

41 Ibid.
42 Northrop Frye, "Archetypal Criticism: Theory of Myths," in his *Anatomy of Criticism: Four Essays* (Princeton: Princeton University Press, 1957), 131.
43 Yan, *711 hao yuan*, 283–84.

This dream allows Yan to bid farewell to the collapsed garden, embark on a sentimental, escapist journey with a passionate female partner, and build a new ecotopia. The dreamy ending makes *Garden No. 711* both an ecological *Exodus* and *Genesis*, wherein the author hopes to rearrange the sequence of flowers, birds, fish, and insects; reconstruct the spatial order of the garden and courtyard; and reorient the connection between man and nature.

But I would suggest another possibility and wonder if Yan could rewrite the myth of the Peach Blossom Spring by adding a mythorealist epilogue. Why can't the damaged tools and artifacts be reborn, resurrected, and even dance with the author, together moving into the imaginary garden? Why can't those flowers and birds become human and embark on the same journey together with the writer to the newly built pastoral courtyard? *Garden No. 711* already indicates this possibility, as the last section of the last chapter is titled "After the Winter"—and in the words of Percy Shelley, "If Winter comes, can Spring be far behind?" The construction, deconstruction, and reconstruction of ecotopia in *Garden No. 711*, to some extent, challenges the endings of *Lenin's Kisses*. Yan's ecotopia does not represent an explosive collapse or an implosive explosion; rather, it predicts an alternative rebirth and resurrection—creating, losing, separating from, and eventually returning to order.

Bibliography

Abrams, M. H. *The Mirror and the Lamp: Romantic Theory and the Critical Tradition*. New York: Oxford University Press, 1953.

Chang Eileen 張愛玲. "Tan kanshu" 談看書 [On reading]. In Chang, *Zhang kan* 張看 [Chang's observations], 155–97. Taipei: Huangguan, 1991.

Chen Sihe 陳思和. "Diqijie Huazong wenxuejiang dezhu Yan Lianke de shoujiangci" 第七屆花蹤文學獎得主閻連科的受獎辭 [The 7th Huazong Literature Award ceremony speech by Yan Lianke]. *Dangdai zuojia pinglun* 當代作家評論 [Contemporary writers review], 2013, no. 5: 11–12.

Chen Xiaoming 陳曉明. "Ta yinlai guihuo, ta hengsao yiqie" 他引來鬼火, 他橫掃一切 [He brings wildfire, he sweeps everything]. *Dangdai zuojia pinglun*, 2007, no. 5: 62–69.

Dico, Joy Lo. "Banned at Home, Lauded Abroad: Vladimir Sorokin and Yan Lianke Make Man Booker Shortlist." *Independent*, 24 Jan. 2013. https://www.independent.co.uk/arts-entertainment/books/news/banned-home-lauded-abroad-vladimir-sorokin-and-yan-lianke-make-man-booker-shortlist-8466006.html (last accessed 8 Aug. 2013).

Frye, Northrop. "Archetypal Criticism: Theory of Myths." In his *Anatomy of Criticism: Four Essays*, 131–242. Princeton: Princeton University Press, 1957.

Liang Hong 梁鴻. *Yan Lianke wenxue nianpu* 閻連科文學年譜 [Yan Lianke's literary chronicle]. Shanghai: Fudan daxue chubanshe, 2015.

Lin Jianfa 林建法, ed. *Yan Lianke wenxue yanjiu* 閻連科文學研究 [Literary study of Yan Lianke]. Kunming: Yunnan renmin chubanshe, 2013.

Lin Yuan 林源, ed. *Shuo Yan Lianke* 說閻連科 [Reading Yan Lianke]. Shenyang: Liaoning renmin chubanshe, 2014.

Liu, Jianmei 劉劍梅. *Zhuangzi and Modern Chinese Literature*. New York: Oxford University Press, 2016.

Liu Zaifu 劉再復. "Zhongguo chu le bu qi xiaoshuo: Du Yan Lianke de changpian xiaoshuo *Shouhuo* 中國出了部奇小說——讀閻連科的長篇小說《受活》[A strange novel has appeared in China: Reading Yan Lianke's fiction *Lenin's Kisses*]." *Mingbao yuekan* 明報月刊 (Ming Pao Monthly), 2004, no. 9: 104–06.

Lu Xun 魯迅. *Silent China: Selected Writings of Lu Xun*. Edited and translated by Gladys Yang. London: Oxford University Press, 1973.

Nan Fan 南帆. "*Shouhuo: Guaidan ji qi meixue xipu*《受活》: 怪誕及其美學系譜 [*Lenin's Kisses*: Grotesque and its aesthetic genealogy]." *Shanghai wenxue* 上海文學 [Shanghai literature], 2004, no. 6: 66–73.

Nixon, Rob. "Slow Violence and Environmental Storytelling." *Nieman Storyboard*, 13 June 2011. https://niemanstoryboard.org/stories/slow-violence-and-environmental-storytelling/ (last accessed 1 Oct. 2013).

———. *Slow Violence and the Environmentalism of the Poor*. Cambridge: Harvard University Press, 2011.

Ricoeur, Paul. *Lectures on Ideology and Utopia*. New York: Columbia University Press, 1987.
Song Weijie 宋偉傑. "Wutuobang jianlun" 烏托邦簡論 [On utopia]. *Yishu guangjiao* 藝術廣角 [Art panorama], 1998, no. 3: 40–45.
Sun Yu 孫郁. "Yan Lianke de 'shenshi zhuyi'" 閻連科的「神實主義」 [Yan Lianke's "mythorealism"]. *Dangdai zuojia pinglun*, 2013, no. 5: 13–21.
Tao Dongfeng 陶東風. "*Shouhuo*: Dangdai Zhongguo zhengzhi yuyan xiaoshuo de jiezuo" 《受活》:當代中國政治寓言小說的傑作 [*Lenin's Kisses*: A masterpiece of contemporary Chinese political allegorical fiction]. *Dangdai zuojia pinglun*, 2013, no. 5: 31–45.
Tillich, Paul. *Political Expectation*. New York: Harper & Row, 1971.
Wang David Der-wei 王德威. "Geming shidai de ai yu si: Lun Yan Lianke de xiaoshuo 革命時代的愛與死——論閻連科的小說 [Love and death in revolutionary time: On Yan Lianke's novels]." *Dangdai zuojia pinglun*, 2007, no. 5: 25–37.
Wang Hongsheng 王鴻生. "Fan wutuobang de wutuobang xushi: Du *Shouhuo* 反烏托邦的烏托邦敘事——讀《受活》 [Anti-utopian utopian narrative: Reading *Lenin's Kisses*]. *Dangdai zuojia pinglun*, 2004, no. 2: 89–98.
Wang Yao 王堯. "Zuowei shijieguan he fangfalun de 'shenshi zhuyi': *Faxian xiaoshuo* yu Yan Lianke de xiaoshuo chuangzuo" 作為世界觀和方法論的「神實主義」——《發現小說》與閻連科的小說創作 ['Mythorealism' as worldview and method: *Discovering Fiction* and Yan Lianke's fiction writing]." *Dangdai zuojia pinglun*, 2013, no. 6: 8–16.
Wu Xiaodong 吳曉東. "Zhongguo wenxue zhong de xiangtu wutuobang ji qi huanmie 中國文學中的鄉土烏托邦及其幻滅 [Rural utopia and its disillusionment in Chinese literature]." *Beijing daxue xuebao* 北京大學學報 [Peking University journal] 43, no. 1 (2006): 74–82.
Yan Lianke 閻連科. *711 hao yuan: Beijing zuihou de zuihou jinian* 711號園: 北京最後的最後紀念 [Garden no. 711: The ultimate last memo of Beijing]. Taipei: Linking, 2012.
———. *Faxian xiaoshuo* 發現小說 [Discovering fiction]. Tianjin: Nankai daxue chubanshe, 2011.
———. *Lenin's Kisses*. Trans. Carlos Rojas. New York: Grove, 2012.
——— and Zhang Xuexin 張學昕. *Wo de xianshi, wo de zhuyi* 我的現實, 我的主義 [My Reality, my -ism]. Beijing: Zhongguo renmin daxue chubanshe, 2011.

2
BUILDING CHINESE REALITY WITH LANGUAGE AND METAPHOR

From socialist realism to mythorealism

Xiaolu Ma

Among contemporary Chinese writers, Yan Lianke probably is one of the most self-conscious, reflecting on and conceptualizing his creative process like a literary critic. Alongside his many literary creations, he also produced books describing his reading and writing experiences, including *My Reality, My -ism* (*Wo de xianshi wo de zhuyi* 我的現實 我的主義, 2011), *Discovering Fiction* (*Faxian xiaoshuo* 發現小說, 2011) and two volumes of literary lectures (2017).[1] In fact, he coined the very term that has been used to characterize his literary creations: *shenshi zhuyi* (神實主義, commonly translated in English as "mythorealism").[2] This concept is generally recognized as drawing on the works of modernist writers such as Franz Kafka (1883–1924) and Gabriel García Márquez (1927–2014),[3] writers whom Yan often discusses in the courses he

---

1 Yan Lianke also published several books that compile his invited talks, including *Chenmo yu chuanxi: Wo suo jingli de Zhongguo he wenxue* 沉默與喘息: 我所經歷的中國和文學 [Silence and rest: My experience of Chinese literature] (Xinbei: Yinke wenxue shenghuo zazhi, 2014); *Yipai huyan: Yan Lianke haiwai yanjiang ji* 一派胡言: 閻連科海外演講集 [A Load of BS: Yan Lianke's overseas talks] (Beijing: Zhongxin chubanshe, 2012); *Chaijie yu dieping: Yan Lianke wenxue yanjiang* 拆解與疊拼: 閻連科文學演講 [Deconstruction and juxtaposition: Talks on literature by Yan Lianke] (Guangzhou: Huacheng chubanshe, 2008).
2 Ever since Yan coined "mythorealism" in his *Discovering Fiction*, many Chinese scholars consider this term the key to deciphering his literary works, especially those published after *Lenin's Kisses* (*Shouhuo* 受活, 2004). See Sun Yun 孫郁, "Yan Lianke de 'shenshi zhuyi'" 閻連科的「神實主義」 [Yan Lianke's "mythorealism"], *Dangdai zuojia pinglun* 當代作家評論 [Contemporary writers review], 2013, no. 5: 13–21; Sun Yu, "Cong *Shouhuo* dao *Rixi*: Zai tan Yan Lianke de shenshi zhuyi" 從《受活》到《日熄》——再談閻連科的神實主義 [From *Lenin's Kisses* to *The Day the Sun Died*: A further discussion of Yan Lianke's mythorealism], *Dangdai zuojia pinglun pinglun*, 2017, no. 2: 5–11; Wang Yao 王堯, "Zuowei shijieguan he fangfalun de 'shenshi zhuyi': *Faxian xianshuo* yu Yan Lianke de xiaoshuo chuangnzuo" 作為世界觀和方法論的「神實主義」——《發現小說》與閻連科的小說創作 [Mythorealism as worldview and methodology: Discovering fiction and Yan Lianke's fictional creation], *Dangdai zuojia pinglun*, 2013, no. 6: 8–16; Ding Fan 丁帆, "Zai 'shenshi zhuyi' yu 'huangdan pipan xianshi zhuyi' zhijian" 在「神實主義」與「荒誕批判現實主義」之間 [Between "mythorealism" and "absurdist critical realism"], *Dangdai zuojia pinglun*, 2016, no. 1: 4–11. In recent years, Chinese graduate students have produced at least twenty master's theses endeavoring to theorize the concept of mythorealism further.
3 Weijie Song 宋偉傑, "Yan Lianke's Mythorealist Representation of the Country and the City," *Modern Fiction Studies* 62, no. 4 (2016): 645. [A revised version appears as the first chapter in this edited volume. Eds.]

DOI: 10.4324/9781003144564-3

teaches in world literature and creative writing.[4] Yan has also several times described himself as an "unfilial son" of realism, including in the opening to *Discovering Fiction*, the book that elaborates his concept of mythorealism.[5]

Born in the rural region of Henan Province, Yan did not have access to a wide variety of literature until he joined the army in 1978. As a voracious reader, though, he has pursued widely ranging interests that have shaped his literary imagination and ideas. Amid this extensive reading, magical realism, modernism, and surrealism have stood out to many scholars as the basis—or counterparts—to Yan's mythorealism as the best approach for tackling the absurdity of contemporary Chinese reality. However, a close look at Yan's own analysis also reveals an entanglement with the more traditional forms of realism that flourished in the second half of the nineteenth century and have continued to exert a profound impact on twentieth-century Chinese literature in particular. More specifically, as this chapter demonstrates, Yan's conceptualization of mythorealism draws on not only nineteenth-century Russian realism but also the twentieth-century Soviet advocacy of socialist realism that shaped the Chinese literary imagination from the 1930s to the 1970s. After all, it is the Russian/Soviet realist tradition in which he was steeped as a young man as many other Chinese writers of his generation.

Realism may be a hydra that "opens up further vistas with each new exegesis,"[6] yet it has also shown itself uniquely responsive to the cultural and historical needs of Chinese writers throughout the twentieth century. Indeed, it is precisely the versatility and ambiguity of realism—or in Marston Anderson's words, its "protean quality"—"that accords it durability and power" and enables "it to continually accrue new meanings in response to changing cultural and historical conditions."[7] Raymond Williams, meanwhile, describes realism as offering "a valuing creation of a whole way of life, a society, that is larger than any of the individuals composing it, and at the same time valuing creations of individual human beings, who while belonging to and affected by and helping to define this way of life, are also, in their own terms, absolute ends in themselves."[8] For these reasons, regardless of its contradictory and problematic nature, realism has remained an important genre on which Yan has built.

Before delving into the relationship between Yan's mythorealism and Russian/Soviet literature, it is important to first tease out the connotations of Yan's Chinese term *shenshi zhuyi*, for which the English coinage "mythorealism" is in many ways an inaccurate approximation. Although this chapter adopts the standard English translation due to its wide usage, it is worth pointing out the limitations that may result in an overly narrow or even misleading interpretation of Yan's idea. In conversation with literary critic Taciana Fisac, Yan agreed that the more accurate translation might be "spirit(s) realism" or "divine realism," depending on whether one takes *shen* 神 to emphasize *jingshen* 精神 "spirit" or *shenling* 神靈 "deities."[9] Thus,

---

4 See Yan Lianke, *Yan Lianke de wenxue jiangtang: Shijiu shiji juan* 閻連科的文學講堂：十九世紀卷 [Yan Lianke's lectures on literature: The nineteenth century] (Hong Kong: Zhonghua shuju, 2017); Yan, *Yan Lianke de wenxue jiangtang: Ershi shiji juan* 閻連科的文學講堂：二十世紀卷 [Yan Lianke's lectures on literature: The twentieth century] (Hong Kong: Zhonghua shuju, 2017).

5 Yan Lianke, *Faxian xiaoshuo: Wenxue suibi* 發現小說：文學隨筆 [Discovering fiction: Essays on literature] (Tianjing: Nankai daxue chubanshe, 2011), 3.

6 Lilian R. Furst, *Realism* (London: Longman, 1992), 1.

7 Marston Anderson, *The Limits of Realism: Chinese Fiction in the Revolutionary Period* (Berkeley: University of California Press, 1990), 6.

8 Raymond Williams, "Realism and the Contemporary Novel," *Universities and Left Review*, no. 4 (1958): 22.

9 Taciana Fisac, "Ouzhou dui Zhongguo dangdai wenxue chuangzuo de yingxiang: Yi Yan Lianke weili" 歐洲對中國當代文學創作的影響——以閻連科為例 [The impact of europe on contemporary Chinese literary creation: A case study of Yan Lianke], *Nanfang wentan* 南方文壇 [Southern literary arena], 2019, no. 6: 89.

although *shenhua* 神話 "myth" or, more literally, "stories about deities" remains a reasonable interpretation of *shen*, there are other possible associations, including individual psyche. Consequently, mythorealism should not be treated as a direct derivation from magic realism or surrealism. As Yan himself argues, *shen* in *shenshi zhuyi* does not refer to the exaggeration, metamorphosis, or absurd distortion of reality, nor does mythorealism aim at verisimilitude. Mythorealism *is* reality.[10]

To make the possible interpretations of mythorealism more concrete, Yan envisions the connection between literary creation and reality in terms of three types of spirits (*shen* 神): the spirit of deities (*shenling* 神靈) invoked by folk culture and shamanism; the human spirit (*jingshen* 精神) reflected through the connections between human souls; and the writer's spirit (*chuangzuozhe de teshu yisi* 創作者的特殊意思) as it arises from the writer's engagement with material reality. These three links allow creative writing to supersede the superficial logic of life and reach for the truth that is invisible, concealed.[11] Put another way, as a writer, Yan is not trying to present the reality ordinary people perceive or the truth achieved through mass consensus, but the truth of his heart (the writer's spirit).[12]

The "absence" of socialist realism

Any discussion of the connection between Yan's mythorealism and Russian/Soviet literature must begin with an absence: specifically, the absence of socialist realism, which almost never appears in Yan's literary criticism. Yan's silence cannot be attributed to ignorance, as he grew up in a period when socialist realism and revolutionary literature were mainstream across China. Can we then attribute his silence to aversion? Yet Yan treats realism itself as his signature approach to literary creation. Why should he avoid socialist realism yet embrace realism more generally? Critics often focus on Yan's rebellious spirit, but it is equally important to recognize his undeniable kinship to that father, namely, mainstream Chinese realism that was constructed around socialist realism. It will be fruitful, therefore, to start our exploration with the debt Yan may owe to the tradition of socialist realism.

The widely accepted definition of socialist realism derives from a keynote speech given by Stalin's mouthpiece Andrei Zhdanov (1896–1948) at the First All-Union Congress of Soviet Writers in 1934:

> Социалистический реализм, являясь основным методом советской художественной литературы и литературной критики, требует от художника правдивого, исторически-конкретного изображения действительности в ее революционном развитии. При этом правдивость и историческая конкретность художественного изображения действительности должны сочетаться с задачей идейной переделки и воспитания трудящихся в духе социализма.

---

10 Zhu Youke, "Gushi he xianshi guosheng de shiqi: Yan Lianke fangtan lu," 故事和現實過剩的時期——閻連科訪談錄 [A period with excessive stories and reality: An interview with Yan Lianke], *Qingnian zuojia* 青年作家 [Young writers], 2017, no. 1: 10.
11 Yan, *Faxian xiaoshuo*, 181.
12 Yan Lianke and Zhang Xuexi, *Wo de xianshi wo de zhuyi: Yan Lianke wenxue duihua lu* 我的現實 我的主義:閻連科文學對話錄 [My reality my -ism: Records of conversations with Yan Lianke] (Beijing: Zhongguo renmin daxue chubanshe, 2011), 53.

Socialist realism, as the foundational method of Soviet artistic literature and literary criticism, demands from the artist a truthful, historically specific depiction of reality in its revolutionary development. At the same time, the truthfulness and historical specificity of the artistic depiction of reality must be combined with the task of the ideological transformation and education of the working people in the spirit of socialism.[13]

This doctrine offered the guiding principles for literary creation during the Stalinist period: truthfulness and historicity in combination with the ideological reshaping of the people. While the notions of truthfulness and historicity are relatively abstract, there is a concrete basis for the "ideological transformation and education" of the people, which emerges from the officially defined spirit of socialism according to the will of the party. This Stalinist legacy is reflected in Mao Zedong's "Talks at the Yan'an Conference on Literature and Art" ("Zai Yan'an wenyi zuotanhui shang de jianghua" 在延安文藝座談會上的講話, 1942) in which he advocates for a form of Chinese literature and art made by revolutionary writers and artists (the proletarian revolutionary utilitarians in Mao's terms). Such revolutionaries should process raw materials from people's everyday lives and give them ideologically meaningful literary and artistic forms in the service of the people, specifically, workers, peasants, soldiers, and the urban petty bourgeoisie. Mao denies the possibility of art for art's sake and declares proletarian literature and art a vital element of the proletarian revolutionary cause, and therefore subordinate to the revolutionary tasks set by the party.[14]

Mao's talks laid the foundation for the Chinese practice of literature and art, especially after the establishment of the PRC in 1949. In 1953 at the Second Congress of Chinese Literature and Art Workers (*Zhongguo wenxue yishu gongzuozhe di er ci daibiao dahui* 中國文學藝術工作者第二次代表大會), socialist realism was pronounced the highest principle of literary and artistic creation and criticism. Nor did the Chinese passion for socialist realism retreat throughout the 1950s, despite the changes taking place in the Soviet Union after Stalin's death in 1953 and the Sino-Soviet split during the late 1950s. The politicization of literary creation and criticism along ideological lines led to a kind of servility toward political expectations in Chinese literature.[15] Rather than attempting an accurate depiction of reality—traditionally the defining aim of realism—writers showed only the bright side of a society that permitted no darkness or ambiguity. By the same stroke, model revolutionary heroes superseded ordinary people as subject matter. The resulting literature accorded with an officially authorized, idealistic vision of reality. It was only in the late 1970s and early 1980s that the full scope of reality as a form of literary truth became a viable topic for discussion in China.[16]

In 1980, Chinese intellectuals proposed the idea of "socialist critical realism" (*shehui zhuyi pipan xianshi zhuyi* 社會主義批判現實主義). By adding the modifier "critical" (*pipan* 批判), this term shifts the subject matter of realism away from an idealistic utopia prioritizing the bright side of socialism and toward the exposure and criticism of social problems. Such "critical realism" might disclose internal conflicts among ordinary people or denounce

---

13 *Pervyi vsesoiuznyi s"ezd sovetskikh pisatelei. Stenograficheskii otchet* [The First All-Union Congress of Soviet Writers. Verbatim Report] (Moscow: Gosudarstvennoe izdatel'stvo khudozhestvennoi literatury, 1934), 716. The English translation is mine.
14 Mao Zedong, "Zai Yan'an wenyi zuotanhui shang de jianghua," in his *Mao Zedong xuanji* (Beijing: Renmin chubanshe, 1991).
15 Li Yuntuan 李運摶, *Zhongguo dangdai xianshi zhuyi wenxue liushi nian* 中國當代現實主義文學六十年 [Sixty years of modern Chinese realism] (Nanchang: Baihuazhou wenyi chubanshe, 2008), 62–90.
16 Cui Zhiyuan 崔志遠, *Xianshi zhuyi de dangdai Zhongguo mingyun* 現實主義的當代中國命運 [The destiny of realism in contemporary China] (Beijing: Renmin wenxue chubanshe, 2005), 355–70.

the shortcomings and backward aspects of Chinese society.[17] It manifested more specifically in what was called the "new realist fiction" (*xin xieshi xiaoshuo* 新寫實小說) initiated in 1988, based on the linked concepts of postrealism (*hou xianshi zhuyi* 後現實主義) and modern realism (*xiandai xianshi zhuyi* 現代現實主義).[18] The new wave of realism was a direct response to the social transformation of the time after the Chinese economic reform launched in 1978. The revelation of poverty and conservatism in the villages remained a consistent theme of the new form of realism, but this writing also addressed the ideological conflict and cultural shock brought by the introduction of market economy. In this way, it became an important manifestation of the spirit of a new era.

The 1990s saw the emergence of several trends that explored new ways of realistic depiction. These included "new historical fiction" (*xin lishi xiaoshuo* 新歷史小說), which deconstructed traditional grand narratives to reveal the fragmentation of history, as well as "women's literature" (*nüxing wenxue* 女性文學), which used body-writing to challenge the patriarchal cultural tradition. The common aim was to reveal the everyday life of ordinary people in an objective manner while exploring social dilemmas neglected by earlier socialist realism. At the same time, although Chinese writers adopted avant-garde literary techniques from foreign, especially Western, literature, the strong sense of social responsibility and the aspiration to truthful and historically specific depiction of reality—as proposed by Zhdanov—persisted down to the present day, just as the Chinese passion for realism remains. The primary difference in today's literature is the diminishing importance of a writer's class status and the decreased dominance of national and party ideology.

Such were the circumstances under which Yan Lianke entered the field of contemporary Chinese literature. Born in 1958, he grew up during the heyday of socialist realism and was only given revolutionary literature to read before he joined the army in 1978. As a young writer, Yan began his literary apprenticeship by emulating works available to him. His first published novel, *Mountain Village and Blood Fire* (*Shanxiang xue huo* 山鄉血火, 1975), told a story of class struggle and landowners' exploitation of the poor.[19] Four years later, his first published short story, "A Story of Gastrodia Elata" ("Tianma de gushi" 天麻的故事, 1979), likewise follows a plot broadly aligned with socialist realism: a noble political instructor educates a soldier, who tries to bribe him with the medicinal herb gastrodia elata in the hopes of becoming a party member.[20] Modeling his writing on the stories with which he was familiar, Yan produced fiction not far from the representative works of socialist realism.

As an unfilial son to realism, Yan makes clear that he is fully aware of his situation:

> 我在詛咒現實主義的時候, 最令我痛苦不安的, 是我靈醒明白, 我無法徹底地告別它們, 逃離它們; 更無法真正地一刀殺死它們, 置它們於死地而後快! 一如一個逆子把刀擱在父母的脖頸上時, 想起的卻是父母含辛茹苦的養育之恩。

> When I curse realism, what agonizes me most is my knowledge that I cannot bid it a final farewell and run way from it—not to say to kill it once and for all with a knife, and be content with its death! I am like an unfilial son who puts a knife against the neck of his parents, yet what he can think of is the troubles they had to endure to raise him up.[21]

---

17 Cui, *Xianshi zhuyi de dangdai Zhongguo mingyun*, 367.
18 Ibid., 425–26.
19 Yan and Zhang, *Wo de xianshi wo de zhuyi*, 12.
20 Ibid., 15.
21 Yan, *Faxian xiaoshuo*, 5.

From socialist realism to mythorealism

In 2011, 32 years after the publication of his first story, Yan published a book that proposed the concept of mythorealism. Yan describes this literary mode as a gesture of resistance to Western literature—as well as identification with that literature, given that it is impossible to completely jettison the influences of the West.[22] Among those influences was socialist realism. Even after Yan had spent decades developing his own literary voice and mode, he still upheld a core aspect of socialist realism: affinity to the people (*renminxing* 人民性), something to which socialist realists aspired in both their subject-matter and readership. This kinship with socialist realism is in keeping with Yan's claim that it is important for a writer to understand, respect, and love all the people in the world, including his enemies.[23]

Yan's commitment to the common people derives from his incisive observation of everyday life in China. When comparing Chinese with Russian literature and discussing the divergent upbringings and social contexts that led the writers of each country to create distinctive literature, Yan considers it crucial to explore the relation between lifestyle and writing. In particular, he questions the possibility of writers to maintain their dignity while living a wretched life. Yan acknowledges that Chinese spiritual life has a concrete material basis. He quotes Ling Mengchu's 凌濛初 (1580–1644) words in *Slapping the Table in Amazement II* (*Er ke pai an jingqi* 二刻拍案驚奇)—"If one is warm and well fed, one will think about wanton lust" (*baonuan si yinyu* 飽暖思淫慾)—to illustrate the material urges of the Chinese people for money, food, and sex.[24] Yan sees these desires as interfering with the search for answers to philosophical questions, such as where human beings have come from, or where they are heading to. In his lecture, he argues that this lack of inquiry into life's meaning condemns the Chinese people to live without dignity. This problem has, in turn, become the major issue of contemporary Chinese literature: "In a word, no one can live with dignity in front of reality. This is contemporary China's actuality and fact, the only and absolute." (一句話, 沒有誰可以在現實面前有尊嚴地活著和生活。這就是今天中國的現實和事實, 唯一和必然。)[25] Given this premise, a Chinese writer has only one choice: to recognize, understand, and love the mundanity of everyday life and to understand and love ordinary people while trying not to be assimilated into a society of individuals inkling toward power and vulgarity. This balancing act allows a writer to pen serious and elevated work despite the triviality of the life he leads.[26]

This perspective explains why Yan puts such emphasis on a writer's independence. For Yan, canonical Chinese revolutionary works lack individuality, which he characterizes as the absence of "I think" (*wo yiwei* 我以為). Rather than centering around a thinking voice, these works are based on political and revolutionary ideology, with characters that are alike in size, height, skin color, apparel, and hairstyle, in order to be ratified as politically appropriate.[27]

As cultural expectations loosened toward the turn of the twenty-first century, writers gained relative freedom: For Yan, the present-day relationship between the central government and writers has been transformed into that of a shepherd and his sheep.[28] Writers today participate in a well-established system of evaluation and publication regulated by the Writers' Association, which also loosely connects publishers, readers, and critics. Consequently, writers are primed to

---

22 Yan, *Chenmo yu chuanxi*, 101.
23 Yan and Zhang, *Wo de xianshi wo de zhuyi*, 65.
24 Yan, *Chenmo yu chuanxi*, 28.
25 Ibid., 30.
26 Ibid., 35–41.
27 Ibid., 226.
28 Ibid., 179.

abide by mainstream principles—including officially approved ideas of the true, the good, and the beautiful—which they may not share. Yan warns against such easy compliance: he praises Chinese writers born in the 1950s and 1960s who resist institutional oppression in order to portray the realities of modern Chinese life and history; he meanwhile cautions younger writers born in the 1980s and 1990s not to neglect a constructive spirit of self-conscious resistance.[29] Yan values the role of intellectuals as the social consciousness of Chinese society:

> 知識分子之所以還是知識分子，也正是他對社會、現實那種永存的懷疑精神；而文學、作家，之所以還有可敬——不僅僅可讀、可賞之處，也在於他對人與現實的描繪和懷疑。他對現實中的人生困境和精神窘境有著獨到、深刻的體悟和描摹。

> Intellectuals are able to remain intellectuals by persistently maintaining their skepticism towards society and reality. Literature and writers remain respectable not only because they can be read and appreciated, but also because of their depictions and wariness of people and the way things are: because of their unique and profound comprehension and delineation of life's predicaments and the psychological dilemmas in real life.[30]

Yan's interpretation of Chinese intellectuals and their place in society may remind us of the Russian concept of the intelligentsia, whose members, according to Isaiah Berlin, "thought of themselves as united by something more than mere interests in ideas; they conceived themselves as being a dedicated order, almost a secular priesthood," with the artist as a sacred vessel, "a wholly dedicated being … his fate … peculiarly sublime and tragic."[31] Both Russian and Chinese writers have experienced severe censorship over the past century and have endeavored to become wide-reaching voices of social critique. Yan similarly understands a writer as someone for whom speaking the truth is as important as breathing; for him, only such commitment can raise resistance against nationwide collective amnesia.[32]

This is the inner drive behind Yan's vision of mythorealism. His rebellious stance is directed toward maintaining his independence in his approach to theorizing and writing about the modern human experience. In his conception of mythorealism, he proposes to divide literary representations of reality into four categories, which he arranges in order from the most superficial and external to the most meaningful and internal:

1. Constructed realism (*konggou xianshi zhuyi* 控構現實主義): based on the reality of social construction (*shehui konggou zhenshi* 社會控構真實) and most common in authoritarian states. Yan accounts for *konggou* 控構 as a combination of controlled customization and fabrication (*kongzhi de dinggou he xugou* 控制的定構和虛構) that manifests dictatorship and national ideology.
2. Social realism (*shixiang xianshi zhuyi* 世相現實主義): based on the material experiences of reality (*shixiang jingyan zhenshi* 世相經驗真實). Social realism differs from constructed realism in that it depends not on an officially sanctioned narrative, but on the collective unconsciousness.

---

29 Ibid., 188–89.
30 Ibid., 194.
31 Isaiah Berlin, *Russian Thinkers*, ed. Henry Hardy and Aileen Kelly (London: Hogarth Press, 1978), 117, 28–29.
32 Yan, *Chenmo yu chuanxi*, 3.

3. Bio-realism (*shengming xianshi zhuyi* 生命現實主義): based on the reality of life experiences (*shengming jingyan zhenshi* 生命經驗真實). This type of realism is populated by typical characters that transcend their time and society.
4. Spiritual realism (*linghun xianshi zhuyi* 靈魂現實主義): based on the the reality of spiritual depth (*linghun shendu zhenshi* 靈魂深度真實). It is established on the foundation of bio-realism but investigates and elevates the significance of the human spirit.[33]

Yan admits the inseparability of these four levels of realism but elaborates the importance of treating them distinctly to fully comprehend their implications. By categorizing the literary genre of socialist realism as constructed realism, Yan unveils the superficiality of socialist realism that does not seek the truth of human life or the soul. Especially now that divergent forms of literary realism are allowed in contemporary China, Yan considers it imperative for writers to move beyond external censorship and self-censorship, as well as the inertia that keeps them in the comfortable first and second levels of realism, in order to fathom the reality of life experiences and spiritual depth.

Such a motivation pushes Yan toward what he calls the "internal cause-and-effect" (*nei yinguo* 內因果). Internal cause-and-effect differs from what Yan calls "complete cause-and-effect" (*quan yinguo* 全因果), typical in traditional realism, as well as "zero cause-and-effect" (*ling yinguo* 零因果), often found in modernism. Instead, "internal cause-end-effect" reflects an "inner truth" (*nei zhenshi* 內真實) based on the reality of the human soul and consciousness. Inner cause-and-effect need not be constrained by natural or social logic. It is allegorical and mystic. At the same time, it does not aim to prophesy or moralize; rather, it intrudes into real life and unveils the truth in an unexpected way.[34] From inner truth to inner cause-and-effect, Yan finds his path toward mythorealism, a mode that pursues inner truth by establishing connections between the human spirit and everyday life.

There is no question that Yan's mythorealism deviates remarkably from socialist realism, which Yan places in the first level, constructed realism. Nonetheless, the fundamental qualities Yan identifies in mythorealism—the desire to reach a certain kind of truth, the commitment to the people, and the intellectual's tenacious sense of social responsibility—all bring us back to the time in Yan's youth when socialist realism was still brewing, with ingredients from nineteenth-century Russian realism. And while Yan's literary criticism tends to downplay his interest in socialist realism, he frequently dwells on canonical Russian works of the nineteenth century, which are the focus of the next section.

Drawing on nineteenth-century Russian literature

The Chinese conceptualization of modern literature is rooted in nineteenth-century Russian literature. Russian literature was valued as the most important and influential foreign literature by Chinese readers in the 1950s and 1960s, as Yan's generation was growing up. In his literary criticism, Yan consistently praises the greatness of Russian realists such as Nikolai Gogol (1809–52), Ivan Turgenev (1818–83), Lev Tolstoy (1828–1910), and Fedor Dostoevsky (1821–81). He also uses these writers to explain his concept of mythorealism. In particular, he uses works by Tolstoy and Dostoevsky to illustrate the last two levels of realism, which are of paramount importance for him: bio-realism and spiritual realism.

---

33 Yan, *Faxian xiaoshuo*, 6–46.
34 Ibid., 172–73.

For example, in his discussion of bio-realism, Yan points to major novels by Tolstoy, contending that without characters like Anna Karenina and Katiusha Maslova, Tolstoy would not have been able to depict the real. By contrast with Turgenev's emphasis on the historical specificity of his works and characters, Tolstoy's interest in universal human nature has granted him more popularity in China. In other words, where Turgenev cares the social significance of his characters, Tolstoy focuses on their elementary qualities: "From the representative character Anna, we see the essence of human life, but from Bazarov, we see [only] leftist or rightist social trends." (我們從典型人物安娜身上，讀到的是人的生命的本質，而從巴紮羅夫這個人物身上，看到的他是左派還是右派的社會思潮。)[35]

Similarly, Yan draws on works by Dostoevsky to demonstrate the reality of spiritual depth. Yan teases out the difference between Dostoevsky versus Tolstoy and Turgenev: whereas literature by aristocrats or gentry such as Tolstoy and Turgenev largely deals with social complications and transformation, Dostoevsky's work rarely engages with grand historical moments. Instead, he aims to uncover the richness and colorfulness of the human soul.[36] Interestingly, Yan warns Chinese readers against attempting to emulate Dostoevsky's approach. For Yan, Dostoevsky has attained the highest realm of realism, yet this achievement also marks an endpoint for the school of realism: "This pursuit and elevation of spiritual realism is how Dostoevsky completes his transcendence of nineteenth-century realism and achieves the ultimate and exhaustive portrayal of truth. The consequence becomes that when late-comers approach reality—the main substance of realism—they feel like blades of grass growing reluctantly under a big tree, expending all their effort just to breath and wave under that tree." (這種對靈魂真實的追究和提升，是陀氏完成了對十九世紀現實主義的超越和對真實最終窮盡的刻寫，使後來者面對現實主義的主旨——真實時，宛若一棵小草在大樹下的無奈生長，所有的努力，都必須在那樹下呼吸和擺動。)[37]

Yan takes the depiction of the human soul as his goal, in common with Dostoevsky. In this respect, Yan's mythorealism, to an extent, represents one of his moves as a writer in competition with Dostoevsky. The elements condensed within the Chinese character *shen* (from Yan's original term for mythorealism, *shenshi zhuyi*) include fantasy (*shenqi* 神奇), mystery (*shenmi* 神秘), and psyche (*shenjing* 神經), all of which summarize literary aspects Yan introduces to traditional realism. *Shen* is what transports readers from daily reality to a more mysterious reality that may lie beyond sensory perception. While elements of *shen* can be grotesque and gaudy, mythorealism's emphases on inner truth and internal cause-and-effect uphold firm connection with realism. *Shen* becomes a vehicle by which Yan tries to reach the "real" (*shi* 實), thereby attaining "the 'new reality' and 'new truth': the reality and truth that cannot be achieved and revealed by the realism people generally adhere to" ("新的現實"和"新的真實"，是今天奉行的現實主義無法抵達和揭示的真實與現實).[38] For Yan, the focus of mythorealism is not *shen* but a form of *shi* that encompasses various types of reality including human beings (*ren* 人).[39]

Yan's conceptualization of mythorealism represents his effort to propose an alternative approach to realism while retaining the central mission of exploring reality and the human soul. Realism offers the opportunity to tackle the fundamental epistemological problem of art's relation to reality; such a temptation proves especially irresistible for Yan, who puts his

35 Ibid., 29.
36 This is not necessarily the case. Dostoevsky's works also engage closely with Russian society and politics; however, for Chinese readers unfamiliar with Dostoevsky's time, such exploration can easily be overshadowed by his breathtakingly psychological depictions.
37 Yan, *Faxian xiaoshuo*, 46.
38 Ibid., 194.
39 Ibid., 204.

faith in the kind of novel that "judges the quality of a whole way of living in terms of the qualities of persons."[40]

The path from *Shen* to *Shi*

The discussion in this chapter has thus far centered on unpacking the real (*shi*) in mythorealism. To understand more clearly how this approach to reality differs from other forms of realism in world literature, the remaining discussion will turn to deciphering the unique element of *shen*.

As I noted above, Yan's *shen* combines at least three layers of meaning: the spirit of deities, the human spirit, and the writer's spirit. While extant criticism generally attributes Yan's development of *shen* to the inspiration of modernism, I would argue that Yan's understanding of *shen* is particularly indebted to the Russian realist tradition. We have already seen how Yan values one element of *shen*—namely, the human spirit—as the ultimate subject matter of both his and Dostoevsky's writing. With regards to the writer's spirit, Yan again throws his lot in with the nineteenth-century realists: unlike modernist and postmodernist writers who contemplate the death of the author ("la mort de l'auteur" as Roland Barthes (1915–80) puts it), Yan trusts the author's autonomy in the creative process, emphasizing his efforts to use his heart to see reality through common people's eyes and to sing his own song.[41] Finally, while the spirit of deities and mythological elements akin to folklore might seem the point at which mythorealism comes closest to modernism, we can find nineteenth-century dimensions there too. Russian realism, particularly that of Gogol, often harkens back to folk culture and gives scope to the tradition of the grotesque, on which Yan's work builds.

In a lecture on nineteenth-century literature, Yan closely examines Gogol's short story "The Nose" ("Nos"). Gogol has been hailed the father of Russian realism thanks to the eminent Russian literary critic Vissarion Belinskii's (1811–48) reading of his story "The Overcoat" ("Shinel").[42] However, while "The Overcoat" takes a realistic approach, his story "The Nose" is quite different: a satirical comic fantasy that opens with collegiate assessor Kovalev waking up one morning to find his nose missing. The story becomes increasingly absurd as the nose is transformed into an important figure in an official uniform boasting a higher rank than Kovalev's own.

Critics have suggested that "The Nose" can be understood as a social satire about people's obsession with both olfactory perception and governmental ranking. Yet Yan has found this explanation too simplistic. He instead identifies parallels between "The Nose" and two modernist works, Marcel Aymé's (1902–67) "The Passer-through-walls" ("Le Passe-muraille") and Kafka's *The Metamorphosis* (*Die Verwandlung*). Yan notes that all three stories begin with the protagonist waking up one morning to discover their bodies transformed. "[The writers] were born almost a century apart," Yan remarks, "but their writings share striking similarities: exaggeration, romance, legend, satire, and care and attention towards the real life of the average 'nobody.'" (他們相差幾乎一個完整的世紀，可他們的寫作，卻有著驚人的相似和不同。誇張、浪漫、傳奇、諷刺和對現實中小人物的愛與關注。)[43]

Like the authors of the two later stories, Gogol does not explain how Kovalev loses his nose, nor how it eventually returns to his face. In other words, he does not attempt to render the plot plausible and depicts only the ludicrous world after the nose is lost. For Yan, the story proceeds as though starting from a small breeze (the loss of the nose) that unexpectedly

---

40 Williams, "Realism and the Contemporary Novel," 22.
41 Yan and Zhang, *Wo de xianshi wo de zhuyi*, 53.
42 Renato Poggioli, "Realism in Russia," *Comparative Literature* 3, no. 3 (1951): 257.
43 Yan, *Yan Lianke de wenxue jiangtang: Shijiu shiji juan*, 145.

uproots trees.[44] The cause might exist in that small breeze, but the result or the effect the loss of the nose causes far exceeds the cause's reasonable potential.

This conclusion leads Yan to consider different types of cause-and-effect, including what he calls zero, hidden, incoordinate, and misplaced cause-and-effect, which diverge from what we might think of as traditional, complete cause-and-effect.[45] Instead, these types of cause-and-effect lead to the exaggerations and absurdity of the story. Yan sees such incomplete forms of cause-and-effect as becoming increasingly common in modernist literature. By pointing to similarities between "The Nose" and narratives from twentieth-century literature, and by tracing the tradition of absurdity through *One Thousand and One Nights*, *The Decameron*, and *The Life of Gargantua and of Pantagruel*, Yan highlights the continuity of forms of exaggeration and illogicality in world literature. These elements, in turn, open for him new possibilities for understanding realism. The accommodation of imagination, allegory, legend, dream, fantasy, and magic in mythorealism finds its roots in earlier works, including works by writers such as Gogol that are frequently recognized as realist.

This study of Yan's literary concept of mythorealism began with socialist realism and proceeded to retrace Yan's broader engagement with Russian/Soviet literature. A close examination of Yan's own statements, compared with Russian/Soviet discourse, reveals inextricable connections that mark Yan's debt to Russian realism. He adapts aspects of the Russian/Soviet literature and its cultural context to meet his own goals. Just as with other inspirations, including modernism, magical realism, and surrealism, Yan chooses elements from various literary schools to enrich his writing but does not fall squarely within any one of them.

By examining Yan's ideas in relation to those of his predecessors, we can come closer to the origin of mythorealism. As this chapter reveals, Yan's mythorealism embraces the essence of Russian realism, with its "high seriousness, devotion to ideas and concern for spiritual values, as well as an unequalled power of psychological characterization."[46] Yan and the Russian realists share a fundamental goal of exposing social reality and the truth of the human soul. Yan himself has remarked that he values the literary ends more than the means. His major contribution to the school of realism, epitomized by the addition of *shen* to realism, is for him vital to attaining the ultimate truth and the reality, or *shi*, which determines the life a novel living among and through its readers.[47] In this way, Yan implies that realism must finally derive from a writer's profound love for human beings. Such an attitude aligns with the principal characteristic of traditional Russian realism: namely, universal love or sympathy toward human beings. This love, which D. S. Mirsky summarizes as the "philanthropic" attitude, necessarily draws writers' attention to the contemporary life of ordinary people.[48] It is precisely from this point that Yan's mythorealism finds its direction and goal, moving through a door that opens onto a possibly preposterous and ludicrous yet captivating and glamorous new reality.

Bibliography

Anderson, Marston. *The Limits of Realism: Chinese Fiction in the Revolutionary Period*. Berkeley: University of California Press, 1990.
Berlin, Isaiah. *Russian Thinkers*. Ed. Henry Hardy and Aileen Kelly. London: Hogarth Press, 1978.

---

44 Ibid., 155.
45 Ibid., 157.
46 Richard Freeborn, "The Nineteenth Century: The Age of Realism, 1855–80," in *The Cambridge History of Russian Literature*, ed. Charles Moser (Cambridge: Cambridge University Press, 1992), 331.
47 Yan, *Faxian xiaoshuo*, 215.
48 D. S. Mirsky, *A History of Russian Literature: From Its Beginnings to 1900*, ed. Francis J. Whitfield (New York: Vintage Books, 1958), 179.

Cui Zhiyuan 崔志遠. *Xianshi zhuyi de dangdai Zhongguo mingyun* 現實主義的當代中國命運 [The destiny of realism in contemporary China]. Beijing: Renmin wenxue chubanshe, 2005.

Ding Fan 丁帆. "Zai 'shenshi zhuyi' yu 'huangdan pipan xianshi zhuyi' zhijian" 在「神實主義」與「荒誕批判現實主義」之間 [Between "mythorealism" and "absurdist critical realism"]. *Dangdai zuojia pinglun* 當代作家評論 [Commentary on contemporary writers], 2016, no. 1: 4–11.

Fisac, Taciana. "Ouzhou dui Zhongguo dangdai wenxue chuangzuo de yingxiang: Yi Yan Lianke weili" 歐洲對中國當代文學創作的影響——以閻連科為例 [The impact of Europe on contemporary Chinese literary creation: A case study of Yan Lianke]. *Nanfang wentan* 南方文壇 [Southern literary arena], 2019, no. 6: 85–92.

Freeborn, Richard. "The Nineteenth Century: The Age of Realism, 1855–80." In *The Cambridge History of Russian Literature*, edited by Charles Moser, 248–332. Cambridge: Cambridge University Press, 1992.

Furst, Lilian R. *Realism*. London: Longman, 1992.

Li Yuntuan 李運摶. *Zhongguo dangdai xianshi zhuyi wenxue liushi nian* 中國當代現實主義文學六十年 [Sixty years of modern Chinese realism]. Nanchang: Baihuazhou wenyi chubanshe, 2008.

Mao Zedong 毛澤東. "Zai Yan'an wenyi zuotanhui shang de jianghua" 在延安文藝座談會上的講話 [Talks at the Yan'an forum on literature and art]." In *Mao Zedong Xuanji* 毛澤東選集 [Selected works of Mao Zedong], 804–35. Beijing: Renmin chubanshe, 1953.

Mirsky, D. S. *A History of Russian Literature: From Its Beginnings to 1900*. Edited by Francis J. Whitfield. New York: Vintage Books, 1958.

Pervyi Vsesoiuznyi S"Ezd Sovetskikh Pisatelei. Stenograficheskii Otchet [The First All-Union Congress of Soviet Writers. Verbatim Report]. Moscow: Gosudarstvennoe izdatel'stvo khudozhestvennoi literatury, 1934.

Poggioli, Renato. "Realism in Russia." *Comparative Literature* 3, no. 3 (1951): 253–67.

Song, Weijie 宋偉傑. "Yan Lianke's Mythorealist Representation of the Country and the City." *Modern Fiction Studies* 62, no. 4 (2016): 644–58.

Sun Yu 孫郁. "Cong *Shouhuo* dao *Rixi*: Zai tan Yan Lianke de shenshi zhuyi" 從《受活》到《日熄》——再談閻連科的神實主義 [From *Lenin's Kisses* to *The Day the Sun Died*: A further discussion of Yan Lianke's mythorealism]. *Dangdai zuojia pinglun*, 2017, no. 2: 5–11.

———. "Yan Lianke de "shenshi zhuyi" 閻連科的「神實主義」 [Yan Lianke's "mythorealism"]. *Dangdai zuojia pinglun*, 2013, no. 5: 13–21.

Wang Yao 王堯. "Zuowei shijieguan he fangfalun de 'shenshi zhuyi': *Faxian xianshuo* yu Yan Lianke de xiaoshuo chuagnzuo" 作為世界觀和方法論的「神實主義」——《發現小說》與閻連科的小說創作 ["Mythorealism" as worldview and methodology: *Discovering Fiction* and Yan Lianke's fictional creation]. *Dangdai zuojia pinglun*, 2013, no. 6: 8–16.

Williams, Raymond. "Realism and the Contemporary Novel." *Universities and Left Review*, no. 4 (1958): 22.

Yan Lianke 閻連科. *Chaijie yu dieping: Yan Lianke wenxue yanjiang* 拆解與疊拼: 閻連科文學演講 [Deconstruction and juxtaposition: Talks on literature by Yan Lianke]. Guangzhou: Huacheng chubanshe, 2008.

———. *Chenmo yu chuanxi: Wo suo jingli de Zhongguo he wenxue* 沉默與喘息: 我所經歷的中國和文學 [Silence and rest: My experience of Chinese literature]. Xinbei: Yinke wenxue shenghuo zazhi, 2014.

———. *Faxian Xiaoshuo: Wenxue suibi* 發現小說: 文學隨筆 [Discovering fiction: Essays on literature]. Tianjing: Nankai daxue chubanshe, 2011.

———. *Yan Lianke de wenxue jiangtang: Ershi shiji juan* 閻連科的文學講堂: 二十世紀卷 [Yan Lianke's lectures on literature: The twentieth century]. Hong Kong: Zhonghua shuju, 2017.

———. *Yan Lianke de wenxue jiangtang: Shijiu shiji juan* 閻連科的文學講堂: 十九世紀卷 [Yan Lianke's lectures on literature: The nineteenth century]. Hong Kong: Zhonghua shuju, 2017.

———. *Yipai huyan: Yan Lianke haiwai yanjiang ji* 一派胡言: 閻連科海外演講集 [A load of BS: Yan Lianke's overseas talks]. Beijing: Zhongxin chubanshe, 2012.

——— and Zhang Xuexi 張學昕. *Wo de xianshi wo de zhuyi: Yan Lianke wenxue duihua lu* 我的現實我的主義:閻連科文學對話錄 [My reality my -ism: Records of conversations with Yan Lianke]. Beijing: Zhongguo renmin daxue chubanshe, 2011.

Zhu Youke 朱又可. "Gushi he xianshi guosheng de shiqi: Yan Lianke fangtan lu" 故事和現實過剩的時期——閻連科訪談錄 [A period with excessive stories and reality—An interview with Yan Lianke]. *Qingnian zuojia* 青年作家 [Young writers], 2017, no. 1: 4–15.

3
MYTHOREALISM, THE ABSURD, AND EXISTENTIAL DESPAIR IN YAN LIANKE'S MEMOIR AND FICTION

Confronting the fate of Sisyphus in modern China's historical traumas

Ashley Liu

Introduction

Three Brothers: Memories of My Family is a memoir by Yan Lianke 閻連科, a prolific writer of absurdist fiction. In the memoir, Yan compares his uncle to Albert Camus' Sisyphus, a mythical icon of existential despair and awareness of life's absurd meaninglessness. To one extent or another, Yan and his family members, as depicted in the memoir, embody the fate of Sisyphus—enduring a lifetime of hardship to return to nothingness at the end. The Sisyphean fate of the Yan family blends reality and myth into a new type of mythorealism. Yan's existential despair is contextualized in the socio-economic and historical hardships of China's tumultuous modernization process. In *Three Brothers* and *Dream of Ding Village*, China's unique historical difficulties enable characters to understand the universal truths of existential meaning and meaninglessness and the absurd condition of living just to die. Yan's views on life and fate, as expressed in *Three Brothers*, allow a new interpretation of *Dream of Ding Village*. His recognition of his family's dignified response to the cruelty of fate echoes the courageous stance to confront certain death taken by characters in *Dream of Ding Village*. In both memoir and fiction, Yan combines reality and absurdity to portray lived historical traumas as a process of reflecting on existential despair and truths.

The absurd and mythorealism in *Three Brothers*

Three Brothers is a very special and sentimental work to Yan because it is a memoir, not a fiction. In his Preliminary Words, he states that this memoir was inspired by the deaths of the elders of his family and motivated by his genuine feelings toward them. In addition, this memoir embodies his love for his native village. In "The Home from which I Walked Away," he confesses his attachment to his village and the emotional toll of being forced away from it.[1] These statements establish this memoir as sincerely dedicated by Yan to his family and homeland.

The sincere nature of his artistic intention is again stressed in "Heart and Land," where he describes *Three Brothers* as a work without the kind of artificial construction common to his fiction:

> The writing of *Three Brothers* is precisely about giving your heart to the land …. I have written many fictions with intensive artistic experimentations: *Streams of Time*, *Hard Like Water*, *Lenin's Kisses*, *Dream of Ding Village*, and *Books of Odes*. I need a "return" that is without any artistic experimentation. I need to return to firm and solid land from the mountain peak that I have gone so far off to. I need to honestly return the grandiosity, ecstasy, and intentionally repressed emotions to the pureness and simplicity of the land. I need to remove the artifices and techniques from my writing until it is completely clean and blank and has nothing but heart and land.[2]

To Yan, *Three Brothers* is about connecting his heart and the land of his native village in the most simple and pure way possible; this book is special because it does not contain the daring artistic experimentations that define his other works. The difference between this memoir and his fictions lies in the lack of intentional construction and careful revising usually required to build his other story worlds.

Yan's pursuit of sincerity and simplicity in *Three Brothers* is a notable deviation from the usual fantastic nature of his fictions. How does this pursuit interact with his theory of literary creation and mythorealism? To Yan, imaginative construction is a necessary component of good literature. He points out the limitations of the type of realism that depicts reality as accurately as possible: "Realism is stuck on the aspect of the world that can be perceived; it cannot probe and explore the unperceivable existential absurdity and strangeness."[3] He describes literary creation as a process of inventing based on reality:

> To literature, reality is ultimately its raw material. When life becomes literature, it is no longer life; it is literature. Writing life as life is like a factory whose product is no different from the raw material. It is like neatly piling the scattered firewood and hay from the field in a storage house; despite the neat organization, they are ultimately just some firewood and hay. Thus, the firewood and hay must be burned in the heart of the writer and go through an energy transformation to become another novelty. Life is the pile of firewood and hay in the field. In it, some people see the passing of the four seasons, the prospering and decaying of a lifetime, and the fading of life. Some see the quarrels of the family and neighbourhood and the petty frustrations

---

1 Yan, *Three Brothers: Memories of My Family*, trans. Carlos Rojas (New York: Grove Press, 2020), 6–16.
2 Yan Lianke, *Yan Lianke wenlun* 閻連科文論 [On Yan Lianke] (Kunming: Yunnan renmin chubanshe, 2013), loc. 1925–29:

《我與父輩》的寫作，正是把心交給土地……我寫過很多帶著強烈嘗試的小說了，《日光流年》《堅硬如水》《受活》《丁莊夢>和《風雅頌》，我需要一次不帶任何嘗試的寫作和回歸，從走得很遠的絕峰回到踏踏實實、紮紮實實的土地上，讓寫作中的張揚、狂歡和有意壓抑的情感，一是一、二是二地回到土地的純淨和質樸中，把敘述中的技巧、技術從寫作中剔除到一乾二淨，窮窮白白，除了心和土地其餘什麼也沒有。

All quotations with original Chinese texts in the footnotes are translated by me.
3 Yan, *Yan Lianke wenlun*, loc. 4390–91: 現實主義只停留在一部分可以感知的世界上，而那些無法感知的存在的荒謬與奇異，現實主義則無法深求與探知。

of life. Some see poetry, the universe, and the stars. But for some, they can only see chaos and boredom.[4]

In his view, good literature is necessarily a processed and re-imagined version of life; the nature of the processing and re-imagining reflects the individual perception of the writer. He emphasizes one's own version of reality, as opposed to an objective reality perceived by all: "Please note that I am talking about 'my reality,' not 'our reality.' 'My' emphasizes the writer's own lived past and living experience; it is his own lived past and living experience."[5] This individual and personal nature of reality championed by Yan is the basis of his conception of mythorealism.

Although simplicity and sincerity are the explicit goals of *Three Brothers*, it does not mean that life, as depicted in it, has gone through no artistic imagination (or else it would be "just some firewood and hay"). The mythorealism present in Yan's experimental fiction is also prominent in this memoir, which is rooted in Yan's personal reality, lived past, and living experience contextualized in China's modern history. The connection between Yan's genuine feelings and mythorealism is established in the first paragraph of chapter 1: "In an instant, I finally understood that the function of all the toil and hardship, misfortune and kindness my father's generation experienced had been to permit them to continue living, to help them secure daily necessities, and to prepare them for the inevitable processes of aging, disease, and death."[6]

This somber way to begin his family's story reflects the genuine generational pain suffered by a family that lived through the impoverished years of the Maoist reign. It is also directly related to the myth of Sisyphus that Yan invokes later in the memoir, which establishes a myth as a central component of Yan's reality. In this book, the lives of Yan's father's generation are defined by endless backbreaking manual labor that resulted in very little improvement in the quality of life; all the toiling is for mere survival and living just to die. Yan describes that his First Uncle's life is filled with "daily struggles for survival [that] left him going in circles like an idling motor, unable to advance."[7] First Uncle is portrayed to be stuck in a cycle of making hard-earned money just to lose it all in failed business ventures and gambling. Yan compares this way of life to Sisyphus, a mythical figure who is condemned, for eternity, to push a heavy rock up a hill only for it to roll down every time it neared the top: "His situation resembled that of Sisyphus, and it was no longer important whether or not Sisyphus would be able to push that stone up to the mountaintop; the important thing was his fate and experience."[8] The Sisyphean fate of First Uncle accurately reflects the haunting image painted in the first paragraph of chapter 1.

Yan defines mythorealism as the attempt to portray a reality that cannot be perceived in the conventional depiction of reality:

> Mythorealism probably should have a simple explanation. It is abandoning the apparent pre-existing logical relationship of real life and exploring an "non-existent"

---

4 Yan, *Yan Lianke wenlun*, loc. 4359–64:

於文學而言，現實最終是它的原材料，當生活成為文學之後，它就不再是生活，而是文學。把生活寫成生活，一如一個工廠把原材料加工成了沒有變化的原材料，仿佛把田野凌亂的柴草搬移到整齊的庫房堆碼起來。可那整齊的碼放，也最終是一堆柴草而已。因為這樣，才要柴草在作家的心裡燃燒，能量轉化，生成別的奇異之物。生活就是那一堆、一片田野上的柴草，有人從中看到了春夏秋冬，歲月枯榮和生命的流逝；有人從中看到家長裡短，煩惱人生；還有人從中看到了詩和宇宙星辰。可也有人，只是從中看到了凌亂和無聊。

5 Yan, *Yan Lianke wenlun*, loc. 4223–25: 請注意，我說的是「我的現實」，而不是「我們的現實」。「我的」—— 它強調的是作家本人 的生活經歷和生活經驗，是他本人的生命經歷和生命體驗。
6 Yan, *Three Brothers*, 17.
7 Ibid., 180.
8 Ibid., 181.

reality: a reality that cannot be seen and a reality hidden by reality. Mythorealism distances itself from conventional realism. Its connection to reality is not the direct causal relationship of life; it is more reliant on the human soul and spirit ... and the artist's special imagination based on reality .... Imagination, allegory, myth, legend, fantasy, magical transformation, transplant, etc. based on everyday reality are all methods and channels through which mythorealism access truth and reality.[9]

The imagination of First Uncle as Sisyphus blends myth and reality. In the memoir, Yan and his father also suffer from the Sisyphean fate. In chapter 2, Yan recalls the hardship he endured to pursue education and the backbreaking physical labor he went through to improve his and his family's lives. The chapter ends with him finding out the futility of his efforts: country pumpkins like him had no chance at being admitted to a university and the book manuscript he worked hard on was burned by his mother for cooking.[10] The meaninglessness of hardship is also reflected in Yan's father's life. His father is described to have lived a life of tormenting physical labor that destroyed his health; at the end of his relatively short and sickly life, his family was so poor that it could not afford him the proper medical treatment or even a movie that he wanted to see before dying.[11] He endured a life of extreme hardship to improve his family's financial situation just to die in and because of abject poverty. The merging of the fate of Sisyphus and that of the Yan family allows access to a deeper reality—a mythorealist reality—that cannot be captured with conventional realism.

Absurdism is a prominent attribute of Yan's literature. To him, the absurdity of Chinese reality can be fittingly captured by the absurdist mythorealism:

> Everyone knows that the richness, complexity, absurdity, and strangeness of real life today are far greater than the complexity and absurdity in contemporary literature. Everyone is complaining that we don't have great works and great authors that can do justice to this era. But we have neglected one problem: for a long time, our literature has focused on depicting reality, not exploring reality .... The works that depict reality shoulder a great flag and sing songs of victory all the way; however, the works that explore reality are continuously questioned, debated, beaten, and scolded .... Thus, we have very few works that dare to truly challenge and question people and society.[12]

---

9 Yan, *Yan Lianke wenlun*, loc. 4350–54:

神實主義, 大約應該有個簡單的說法。即: 在創作中摒棄固有真實生活的表面邏輯關係, 去探求一種「不存在」的真實, 看不見的真實, 被真實掩蓋的真實。神實主義疏遠於通行的現實主義。它與現實的聯繫不是生活的直接因果, 而更多的是仰仗於人的靈魂、精神……和創作者在現實基礎上的特殊臆思……在日常現實土壤上的想像、寓言、神話、傳說、夢境、幻想、魔變、移植等等, 都是神實主義通向真實和現實的手法與管道。

10 Yan, *Three Brothers*, 67–70.
11 Ibid., 115–28.
12 Yan, *Yan Lianke wenlun*, loc. 4370–74:

誰都知道, 今天現實生活的豐富與複雜, 怪誕與奇異, 遠遠大於當代文學作品中的複雜與荒誕。誰都在抱怨, 我們沒有無愧於時代的大作品和偉大的作家, 可我們忽略了一個問題, 就是長期以來, 我們的文學注重於描摹現實, 而不注重於探求現實……描摹現實的作品肩扛大旗, 一路凱歌; 而探求現實的作品, 則被不斷的疑問、爭論所棒打與喝斥……所以, 我們很少有那些對人和社會敢於真正叩問和懷疑的作品。

In this passage, Yan criticizes realism's lack of ability to reflect the full extent of modern China's absurdity; he suggests that, unlike realism, mythorealism has the potential to "truly challenge and question people and society." *Three Brothers*' mythorealist representation of the cruel fate of Yan's family sees through surface-level reality and probes a deeper, terrifying truth of Chinese modernity.

In Albert Camus' "The Myth of Sisyphus," Sisyphus is condemned by the gods to suffer his endless toil. Who do the gods represent in Camus' myth? David Carroll argues that Camus' Sisyphus is comparable to "the worker in modern society" whose fate is absurd.[13] In this view, the gods who condemn one to repetitive work with little reward are the broader economic and societal conditions that foster this exploitation. The economic and societal conditions that condemn the Yan family are criticized in *Three Brothers*. The difference in wealth, education, and lifestyle between rural farmers like the Yan family and city dwellers is a recurring topic in the memoir. Yan recalls that when he was a child, he sat next to a girl from the city in class who consistently got better grades than him. He reflects, "The difference between our scores reflected a long-standing gulf between rural and urban life."[14] The rural-urban gap resurfaced when Yan encountered the "educated youths" from the cities. He remarks, "My most distinct impression was that their arrival confirmed that the gap between urban and rural life was far greater than people had thought."[15] The envy of city dwellers is Yan's fixation throughout the memoir. To him, city-living is "life" while rural-living is mere survival:

> People in the city refer to the process of living as "life," while those in the countryside refer to life as the process of "living." While this might appear to involve simply two different terms for the same thing, there is actually more fundamental difference between the two concepts. "Living" suggests a process of enduring day after day, with each day being the same, and implies a kind of monotony, boredom, hopelessness, and idleness. "Life," on the other hand, conveys a sense of richness, of progress and the future.[16]

This distinction between rural "living" and urban "life" is at the heart of the tragedy suffered by the Yan family. Camus contends that Sisyphus' fate is unspeakable cruelty because "there is no more dreadful punishment than futile and hopeless labor."[17] Yan's mythorealist portrayal of the Sisyphean fate of Chinese peasants reveals the heart-wrenching truth that the arbitrary rural-urban division in modern China has condemned hundreds of millions of innocent people to the cruelest form of punishment possible: to live without life and just to survive. The extent of cruelty imposed on such a vast population and the meaninglessness and hopelessness of their suffering render reality absurd; the absurdity of Chinese reality is beyond the reach of conventional realism and calls for an absurdist mythorealist representation.

Existential despair and truths in *Three Brothers*

The absurd and the mythorealist do not conflict with Yan's pursuit of the genuine in *Three Brothers*; rather, they facilitate the expression of sincere feelings. The mythorealist representation of the Yan family suffering the Sisyphean fate is a powerful reflection of Yan's genuine

---

13 David Carroll, "Rethinking the Absurd: Le Mythe de Sisyphe," in *The Cambridge Companion to Camus*, ed. Edward J. Hughes (Cambridge: Cambridge University Press, 2007), 64.
14 Yan, *Three Brothers*, 24.
15 Ibid., 50.
16 Ibid., 203.
17 Albert Camus, *The Myth of Sisyphus and Other Essays*, trans. Justin O'Brien (New York: Vintage Books, 1991), 23.

existential despair. As established in the first paragraph of chapter 1 quoted above, the meanings of life, fate, and mortality are central concerns in the memoir. An important function of Yan's memoir is to document the noble ways in which the Yan family faced existential despair and found their own existential truths. Camus' existentialism emphasizes "the human condition [as] characterized by the probability of suffering and the certainty of death—a fate which human reason cannot accept as reasonable."[18] To him, this renders the reality of life absurd. In *Three Brothers* and *Dream of Ding Village*, existential despair is often contextualized in the struggle against the absurdity of death's certainty and suffering's meaninglessness.

Yan praises his First Uncle for his dignified response to the cruelty of fate: "First Uncle, despite the fact that he couldn't read and was disinclined to discuss matters in any real depth, truly understood the meaning and implications of one crucial concept: dignity."[19] Despite the hardship of poverty, First Uncle honored promises and duty beyond his own well-being. After building a house for his children with his "sweat and blood," he announces to his family they must immediately get back to work to honor the obligation to pay debts.[20] Yan describes the impact First Uncle's dignity has exerted on him: "For more than half his life, First Uncle was tortured by the promises he made, but it was also for the sake of these promises that he lived, and they revealed the nobility and vulgarity of his humble peasant's view of life. These promises showed how First Uncle would leave a deeper and brighter mark than others on the land and on the road of life."[21] To Yan, the dignity of First Uncle is more noble than that of a privileged person: "I thought, if it is true that a king, for the sake of his own dignity, can decapitate someone, while commoners, to assert their dignity, must struggle to keep their backs straight while being decapitated, in order to show that their lives are not trivial and debased—then the dignity of the latter is, in fact, more worthy of respect than that of the former."[22] First Uncle's commitment to paying back his debt and endurance of backbreaking labor is like the commoner who asserts his dignity by standing straight while being decapitated: when fate has no mercy, the only dignified response is to face the mercilessness with pride. This is Frist Uncle's answer to the meaning of an existence defined by absurdly meaningless suffering.

Another aspect of First Uncle's dignity that left a deep impression in Yan is his calm acceptance of death: "First Uncle was not afraid of the leaf's falling or of death, and he sat there quietly waiting for the leaf to land and for the end that it would herald. It was as if he understood that life's endless toil and fatigue, rushing about and cycling around, was in the end all for the sake of this final moment—for death and oblivion."[23] What is impressive is not only First Uncle's lack of fear while facing death; it is his full acceptance that the endless suffering of his life was all for nothing more than just to die. In Yan's view, this acceptance stems from a sublime level of wisdom beyond what one can learn through education. He comments on his amazement at the potential connection between First Uncle's wisdom and illiteracy:

> Perhaps it was precisely on account of the fact that First Uncle was an illiterate peasant and, like everyone else from the countryside, was to a greater or lesser extent superstitious and believed in the afterlife, that he was therefore able to face death with such calmness. I thought, even if First Uncle didn't believe in the afterlife,

---

18 Ibid., 1.
19 Yan, *Three Brothers*, 157.
20 Ibid., 155–56.
21 Ibid., 154.
22 Ibid., 158.
23 Ibid., 194.

he certainly must have believed that human life has an origin and a destination. Therefore, it was precisely in the face of death that First Uncle could display this calmness and imperturbability, this peacefulness and self-sufficiency—that he could have such a secular yet transcendent sense of renewal and purpose in the face of life's road and homeward journey.[24]

First Uncle found peace in the very existence that condemned him to a cruel life: the existence as an illiterate, poor peasant. Through sheer spiritual nobility and inner strength, he transformed his curse into his blessing. His triumph over his fate is another way in which he resembles Camus' Sisyphus. Despite the eternal punishment imposed on him, Camus' Sisyphus proves superior to his fate and takes pride in his strength.[25]

Yan confesses that First Uncle's acceptance of death helped him get over his own fear of death.[26] At the end of the memoir, Yan describes his own thoughts regarding death. He compares the deaths of his father and uncles to the breaking of a "protective wall" that surrounds the family.[27] He states:

> In the end, however, it remains true that an entire section of that wall is now missing, and if we gaze out through that opening, we clearly see death and the notice it is carrying, and we can clearly hear its footsteps approaching and its low voice on the road. So we have no choice but to consider the answer and remuneration we will offer, just as we have no choice but to consider the attitude with which we will subsequently face our own death and fate, together with how we will respond to, argue with, and struggle against death. Life must always come to an end, and that final day will inevitably come, so it is necessary to consider those who will live on.[28]

In this passage, the older generation's deaths weaken the barrier between Yan and death, as their passing is a sign that his end is getting closer. The breaking of this barrier also allows him to face death more directly because the older generation's ability to accept death with dignity helped him in finding his own way of coming to terms with death and making sense of a lifetime of meaningless suffering. By documenting the lives of the three brothers of the older generation, Yan paves a path to lead himself from existential despair to existential truth. This ending reflects a profound understanding that life is ultimately about living on despite the absurdity of fate and the certainty of death.

Historical trauma and existential despair in *Dream of Ding Village*

In both memoir and fiction, Yan portrays China's modernization process as a lived experience of reflecting on existential meaning. The Yan family's despair that stemmed from their experience of living through the Maoist years lead them to transcendent visions of life, fate, and mortality. This process of living through historical traumas and seeking truths about the meaning of existence can also be found in *Dream of Ding Village*. The historical context of this fiction is the rural HIV epidemic in the 1990s, which was a direct result of rural residents

---

24 Ibid., 195.
25 Camus, *The Myth of Sisyphus*, 23.
26 Yan, *Three Brothers*, 196.
27 Ibid., 255.
28 Ibid., 256.

being systematically manipulated by governmental and private agencies to sell blood; due to the lack of proper medical standards, a large population was infected with HIV. Characters in this fiction are rural peasants who are coaxed into selling blood for money and dying of AIDS. As they struggle to find meaningful ways to live out their remaining lifespan in the face of certain death and unbearable pain, they embark on a journey of seeking out answers to life's most profound existential questions.

Like the Yan family, these rural dwellers with very limited education have come to understand the simple but sublime truth that life is about living on. Their attitudes toward the fate imposed on them are a combination of acceptance and defiance. Ding Liang and Lingling's journey from existential despair to finding meaning in life and welcoming death exemplifies the unimaginable courage behind both gestures of acceptance and defiance. Ding's existential despair emerges when he finds that living just to survive is absurd: even if he commits to living on for as long as possible by making healthy choices, what is the meaning of mere survival when his beloved wife would not even touch him? He asks himself, "What was the point of defying the odds, of going on living, if your life had no meaning?"[29] When life becomes merely surviving, Ding realizes the difference between living and life articulated by Yan in *Three Brothers*. Ding has his own Sisyphean fate: his exhausting and anguishing effort to keep moving is absurdly futile. The condition of living just to die is the absurdity that connects Yan's memoir and fiction.

Ding's hopelessness takes a sharp turn when he meets and falls in love with Lingling in the living quarter for AIDS patients. After making love, they re-discover the meaning of life.[30] Now, life is no longer about mere survival, as they help each other find reasons to muster the courage to confront their absurd fate: "'But what's the point,' she asked, 'when there's no reason to go on living?' 'There is no point, but every day you're alive, you have to find some reason to go on living.'"[31] Ding's response to Lingling's question demonstrates his acceptance of being condemned to an existence of meaningless suffering; it also reflects his defiant stance against this fate in trying to find reasons to live on despite the ultimate meaninglessness of his effort. This attitude is similar to that exhibited by Yan at the end of his memoir cited above, where he expresses that although death is certain, one must keep living until the end and choose how to face death.

Like Yan's First Uncle, Ding confronts his Sisyphean fate by transforming his curse into his blessing. When he makes love to Lingling, he finds the skin rashes caused by AIDS to be her unique beauty and the stimulus for his passion: "The spots that covered her body only seemed to highlight the tenderness of her youth, the pale softness of her skin .... He was mad for her."[32] Despite the opposition from his community, he insists on marrying Lingling and living out the rest of their short lives as an officially recognized couple. When harassed by others regarding his decision, he finds a refreshing sense of freedom in his lack of need to care about what others think and responds with "what the hell did it matter, anyway?"[33] He attains an even higher level of liberation from the oppression of his fate and community when an elderly man says to him, "Let them laugh. A lifetime is a lifetime, whether it's a long one or a short one."[34] Although fate has condemned him and Lingling to early deaths, it cannot take away their will and ability to spend a lifetime together. This is reminiscent of Camus' Sisyphus,

29 Yan Lianke, *Dream of Ding Village*, trans. Cindy Carter (New York: Grove Press, 2009), 64.
30 Ibid., 79.
31 Ibid., 129.
32 Ibid., 130.
33 Ibid., 208.
34 Ibid., 211.

whose last shred of dignity and defiance is beyond the reach of even the gods. Through sheer inner strength, Ding and Lingling have found a lifetime of blessing in their cursed existence.

When Ding and Lingling sense that death is near, they ponder on how they will face it. Lingling suggests that they commit suicide together. He is shocked to find that "Lingling—so gentle in life, so wild in bed—would be so steadfast in the face of death."[35] Her calmness stems from her belief that their suicide would be their last rebellion against the scorn from their fate and community: "'If we die together,' she declared, 'it will prove that our love was not in vain.'"[36] Here, Lingling resembles the commoner who asserts dignity by standing up straight when being executed in Yan's allegory quoted above; the story worlds of Yan's memoir and fiction connect in their characters' dignified defiance against crushing reality. Ding talks Lingling out of committing suicide: "No, let's not. Each day we're alive is better than being dead."[37] When he feels that he will die before Lingling, he urges her to keep living even if he dies: "Go on living. Take every day you can get."[38] His belief in living until the very end reflects a defiance against the absurd condition of the inherent conflict between the human will to live and the certainty of death. However, when he finds Lingling's corpse, he lays next to her and commits suicide.[39] This is perhaps a sign that he has given up on rebelling and finally accepted the absurd condition of death's certainty, or perhaps his suicide is his last stand against the control of fate and an attempt to take fate into his own hands by leaving this world with the love of his life.

Conclusion

The commonality of meaningless suffering in the face of certain death and the cursed existence of living just to die in both *Three Brothers* and *Dream of Ding Village* blurs the boundary between reality and fiction and that between reality and absurdity. The blurry boundaries attest to mythorealism's efficacy as a method that can truly capture the conditions of modern China and all its traumas. The genuine existential despair of the Yan family as documented in *Three Brothers* allows a profound insight into the artistic and philosophical vision of Yan Lianke and his fictions. This memoir transforms the reading experience of *Dream of Ding Village* by connecting the fictional absurdity to the memories of the generations who lived through the soul-crushing reality of Chinese modernity. In the era of "the death of the author," Yan's distinct authorial voice asserts the power of an artist's lived experience in enriching the story worlds he builds.

Bibliography

Camus, Albert. *The Myth of Sisyphus and Other Essays*. Translated by Justin O'Brien. New York: Vintage Books, 1991.
Carroll, David. "Rethinking the Absurd: Le Mythe de Sisyphe." In *The Cambridge Companion to Camus, Cambridge*, edited by Edward J. Hughes, 53–66. Cambridge: Cambridge University Press, 2007.
Yan Lianke. *Dream of Ding Village*. Translated by Cindy Carter. New York: Grove Press, 2009.
———. *Three Brothers: Memories of My Family*. Translated by Carlos Rojas. New York: Grove Press, 2020.
———. *Yan Lianke wenlun* 閻連科文論 [On Yan Lianke]. Kunming: Yunnan renmin chubanshe, 2013.

35 Ibid., 238.
36 Ibid., 239.
37 Ibid., 240.
38 Ibid., 248.
39 Ibid., 259.

4
MAGICAL REALISM, MYTHOREALISM, AND THE REPRESENTATION OF HISTORY IN THE WORKS OF YAN LIANKE

Raffael Weger

In his 1982 Nobel Prize acceptance speech, Gabriel García Márquez gave an overview of some of the most violent and gruesome events in Latin American history, speaking of an "outsized reality" that could not be accurately measured by Western rationalists with "the yardstick that they use for themselves." To solve "the quest of [their] own identity," it was necessary for Latin American intellectuals and artists to find a new mode of representation that would allow them to "render [their] lives believable."[1] Similarly, during the last decade, Yan Lianke has repeatedly stated that, in his opinion, contemporary China's reality is defined by an "incomprehensible absurdity":[2] "Every day, something occurs that lies outside ordinary reason and logic."[3] Since, according to him, neither traditional realism nor its contemporary Chinese offshoot is able to truly probe this "new reality" (*xin de xianshi* 新的現實), it has likewise become necessary to find a more adequate mode for expressing people's experiences and discovering reality's underlying "new truth" (*xin de zhenshi* 新的真實).[4] He calls this novel mode *mythorealism* (*shenshi zhuyi* 神實主義), emphasizing that it is not his or any other individual writer's invention; in fact, it "is not even strictly speaking a literary perspective at all, and instead it marks the very nature, origin, and identity of Chinese reality itself."[5]

Yan's line of argumentation suggests that, leaving aside its ontological precondition, in its concern with the nature of past and present reality and its representation, mythorealism as a literary mode can be understood not only as an extension of realism but also as a potential

---

1 Gabriel García Márquez, "The Solitude of Latin America," Nobel Lecture, https://www.nobelprize.org/prizes/literature/1982/marquez/lecture/ (last accessed 8 May 2021).
2 Yan Lianke, *The Explosion Chronicles*, trans. Carlos Rojas (London: Vintage, 2018), 451.
3 Yan Lianke, "Finding Light in China's Darkness," *The New York Times*, 23 Oct. 2014, https://www.nytimes.com/2014/10/23/opinion/Yan-Lianke-finding-light-in-chinas-darkness.html (last accessed 8 May 2021).
4 Yan Lianke, *Faxian xiaoshuo* 發現小說 [Discovering fiction] (Tianjin: Nankai daxue chubanshe, 2011), 194; Carlos Rojas, trans, *Discovering Fiction* (Durham: Duke University Press, 2022). Due to the translator's generosity in providing me with his manuscript, the quoted passages are all his translations.
5 Yan Lianke, *The Explosion Chronicles*, trans. Carlos Rojas (London: Vintage, 2018), 457.

derivative of magical realism. Even while stressing the necessity to "develop a modern writing style that is unique to us,"[6] he has repeatedly pointed out the huge influence that magical realism has had on modern Chinese literature and specifically on mythorealism.[7] Many scholars have convincingly argued that magical realism is not tied to a single geographic location, but is instead a global phenomenon, existing in different languages all over the world.[8] Wendy Faris has emphasized that one of the main challenges when analyzing the mode is the complexity of how it is adapted to local cultural needs and agendas.[9] By taking this challenge seriously, I aim to demonstrate that mythorealism is not merely a local adaptation of a global magical realism to the Chinese context. Rather, I will show that Yan's account of mythorealism constitutes a genuine development of magical realism, offering a related but unique approach to history and reality. To do so, I first consider truth, causality, trauma, myth, and their respective roles in magical realist and mythorealist writing. Following that, I turn to two of Yan's novels, *The Four Books* (*Si shu* 四書, 2011/2015) and *The Explosion Chronicles* (*Zhalie zhi* 炸裂志, 2013/2016), outlining the alternative perspectives of history they offer. By highlighting their respective structures, I demonstrate that these novels present divergent perspectives not as equally possible versions of the past but rather as fragments of a multifaceted, unified inner causality. This in turn allows them to go beyond the magical realist representation of traumatic events and actively explain, question, and even criticize their present manifestations, consolidating mythorealism's claim to being a mode distinct from magical realism.

Truth and causality

In his poetological volume *Discovering Fiction* (*Faxian xiaoshuo* 發現小說, 2011), Yan does his best to sketch out the contours of what he thinks mythorealism might eventually look like once it has managed to properly establish itself in contemporary Chinese literature. In order to do so, he devotes about the first two-thirds of the book to explaining all the things mythorealism is *not*: It is not nineteenth-century realism, with its dependency on full causality and its focus on the "materialism of the objective world" (*keguan shijie de weiwulun* 客觀世界的唯物論), nor is it Kafkaesque modernism, with its zero causality, murky symbolism, and emphasis on the "idealism of the subjective world" (*zhuguan shijie de weixinlun* 主觀世界的唯心論).[10] It is also not magical realism, whose partial causality, while typically characterized by its high density of "non-realistic" (magical) elements,[11] is still "always anchored in empirical reality."[12] Whereas, according to Yan, all of these literary modes ultimately point toward the outer truth of an external world, including society and the environment, and are thus driven by an outer causality (*wai yinguo* 外因果), mythorealism is guided by an inner causality

---

6 Yan Lianke, "*Bookforum* Talks with Yan Lianke," interview by Robert Anthony Siegel, Bookforum, 20 Dec. 2013, https://www.bookforum.com/interviews/bookforum-talks-with-yan-lianke-12668 (last accessed 8 May 2021).
7 See Yan, *Faxian xiaoshuo*, 203–04.
8 See Ouyang Wen-chin, "Magical Realism and Beyond: Ideology and Fantasy," in *A Companion to Magical Realism*, ed. Stephen M. Hart and Ouyang Wen-chin (Woodbridge: Tamesis, 2010), 15.
9 Wendy Faris, *Ordinary Enchantments: Magical Realism and the Remystification of Narrative* (Nashville: Vanderbilt University Press, 2004), 40.
10 Yan, *Discovering Fiction*, 154.
11 Anne Hegerfeldt, *Lies That Tell the Truth: Magic Realism Seen through Contemporary Fiction from Britain* (Amsterdam: Editions Rodopi, 2005), 51.
12 Taner Can, *Magical Realism in Postcolonial British Fiction: History, Nation, and Narration* (Stuttgart: Ibidem Press, 2015), 38.

(*nei yinguo* 內因果), which in turn is based on an inner truth, meaning the "truth of people's soul and consciousness" (*ren de linghuan yu yishi de zhenshi* 人的靈魂與意識的真實).[13]

It is important to note that Yan's definition of inner truth seems to be built upon an understanding of reality that runs contrary to that of traditional realism, which since the nineteenth century has operated with the idea that there is a real world "out there" and "that our senses give us a true report of it."[14] Yan, in contrast, calls this external reality merely the "surface level of the world" (*shijie de biaoceng* 世界的表層), adding to it an "imperceptible inner world" (*wufa ganzhi de shijie de neibu* 無法感知的世界的內部), namely the inner life of human beings, since "people and the world [make up] a single, indivisible whole" (*ren yu shijie shiwei buke fenge, boli de yiti* 人與世界視為不可分割、剝離的一體).[15] This is an essential point, as it not only constitutes a negation of realism's claim that it is possible, in a positivist manner, to mimetically depict reality[16] but also emphasizes humanity's power to actively shape reality, thus explaining mythorealism's aspiration to both "create reality and surpass realism" (*chuangzao xianshi he chaoyue xianshi zhuyi* 創造現實和超越現實主義).[17] While realism (and through it also historiography)[18] focuses first on the external world and from it derives people's inner life, mythorealism directs its attention at those underlying, hidden parts that traditional realism is unable to reach, the "interior of reality and the depths of human spirit."[19] By doing so, it in turn aims at discovering inner truths that shape the external world and govern human interactions with their environment.

As an example of inner truth, Yan mentions Wu Ruozeng's 吳若增 story "The Jadeite Cigarette Holder" ("Feicui yanzui" 翡翠煙嘴) in which the eponymous object, owned by an old peasant, is revered by him and his fellow villagers as a precious artifact, the possession of which is a cause for pride for the whole community. One day an antique expert visits the hamlet and, upon being shown the treasure, immediately realizes that what he is being presented with is actually a worthless fake. However, not only does he refrain from letting the villagers in on his knowledge, he even tells them that the item is priceless, warning them not to show it to anyone else.[20] While according to an outer truth, the cigarette holder is merely a cheap object, on the level of inner truth, it has a great impact on the people, effectively creating their reality, the truth of which is solely based on inner convictions. In this sense, when Yan talks about creating reality through literature, I believe his claim must be understood as an attempt to discover inner historical truths and through them represent the "unpresentable," signifying in this case that which cannot be experienced directly.[21]

Representation thus understood becomes a way of rationalizing a seemingly absurd reality, a method which, as García Márquez's quote in the opening passage of this article suggests, is

---

13 Yan, *Faxian xiaoshuo*, 207, 152.
14 Ian Watt, "Ian Watt on Realism and the Novel Form," in *Realism*, ed. Lilian R. Furst (London: Longman, 1992), 89.
15 Yan, *Faxian xiaoshuo*, 194, 205.
16 See Robert Scholes, *Fabulation and Metafiction* (Urbana: University of Illinois Press, 1979), 8, 51.
17 Yan, *Faxian xiaoshuo*, 182.
18 As Anne Hegerfeldt writes: "[T]he realist mode has been considered one of the strategies that enables historiography to produce a plausible and convincing account of events." Hegerfeldt, *Lies That Tell the Truth*, 174.
19 Yan Lianke "*The Four Books* Interview," Man Booker International Prize, 22 Mar. 2016, https://booker218.rssing.com/chan-5643463/all_p3.html.
20 See Yan, *Faxian xiaoshuo*, 189–90.
21 Jean-François Lyotard, "Answering the Question: What Is Postmodernism," in *The Postmodern Condition: A Report on Knowledge*, ed. Jean-François Lyotard (Minneapolis: University of Minnesota Press, 1984), 81.

not unique to mythorealism but has been equally employed by magical realism. One of the premises of the latter mode is, contrary to what realism claims, that there is not one universal truth, but rather truth depends on the beholder. Therefore, magical realism sheds any claim to mimetic objectivity and instead focuses on foregrounding alternative experiences of (historical) reality that, as in postcolonial Latin America, could be adequately represented neither through traditional realism nor through historiographic writing based on Western rationalist models.[22]

This is reflected in the way non-realistic elements are presented in magical realist writing. When using them to describe events, authors favor a "matter-of-fact manner," putting them side by side with realist elements, either set being equally part of an experienceable material reality.[23] Only by presenting both as possible can writers create what Suzanne Baker calls a "dual spatiality," meaning a space where "different perceptions of the world can be conceived."[24] This space is characterized by a negation of the ontological hierarchy between the "real" and the "imaginary."[25] When writing about historical events, magical realists often interfuse historiographical facts with legends, folklore, myths, and the like in order to not only emphasize the influence they have on people's perception of real events but also on the way they lead their lives: "Texts labeled magical realist draw upon cultural systems that are no less 'real' than those upon which traditional literary realism draws."[26] Nevertheless, while, in the manner of a *histoire des mentalités*, magical realism acknowledges the existence of inner truth, it still focuses on presenting a subjective interpretation of the external world rather than explaining or questioning individual views of past events, in clear opposition to mythorealism. Magical realism thereby offers alternative, unofficial versions of history, highlighting their importance when trying to understand the collective identity of a culture or society through its past.[27]

Trauma and myth

Apart from presenting different lived realities, there is a second historiographical function of magical elements in magical realist writing, one that is closely related to the above-mentioned goal of mythorealism to create reality: they help make sense of historical events that, at the time of their taking place, have at least partly escaped perception due to their traumatic nature.[28] Eugene Arva therefore calls this function "traumatic imagination," stating that only through imagination is it possible to reconstruct the gaps in our memory and give new meaning to reality by recreating it.[29] In other words, traumatic imagination is a way of making reality accessible again by representing the unpresentable, in this case, the traumata

---

22 See Lois Parkinson Zamora, "Magical Romance/Magical Realism: Ghosts in U.S. and Latin American Fiction," in *Magical Realism: Theory, History, Community*, ed. Lois Parkinson Zamora and Wendy Faris (Durham: Duke University Press, 1995), 500.
23 Maggie Ann Bowers, *Magic(al) Realism* (London: Routledge, 2004), 31.
24 Suzanne Baker, "Binarisms and Duality: Magic Realism and Postcolonialism," *Span: Journal of the South Pacific Association for Commonwealth Literature and Language Studies* 36 (1993), http://wwwmcc.murdoch.edu.au/ReadingRoom/litserv/SPAN/36/Baker.html.
25 See Stephen Slemon, "Magic Realism as Postcolonial Discourse," in Zamora, *Magical Realism*, 409–10.
26 Lois Parkinson Zamora and Wendy Faris, "Introduction: Daiquiri Birds and Flaubertian Parrot(ie)s," in *Magical Realism: Theory, History, Community*, ed. Lois Parkinson Zamora and Wendy Faris (Durham: Duke University Press, 1995), 3.
27 See Hegerfeldt, *Lies That Tell the Truth*, 63.
28 Ibid., 61.
29 See Eugene Arva, "Writing the Vanishing Real: Hyperreality and Magical Realism," *JNT: Journal of Narrative Theory* 38, no. 1 (Winter 2008): 68.

that have eluded rationalization. Such represented traumata can be individual but, in magical realist writing at least, are more often collective, e.g., either of the World Wars, colonialism, or the Great Chinese Famine.[30] Through focusing on empirical reality and the representation of past events, magical realist works therefore help people to reappropriate their own history and identity, effectively giving meaning to alternative lived experiences.[31]

A similar approach can be found in mythorealism, as Yan, too, highlights the importance of imagination when dealing with China's "unfathomable reality." Further, reality is not only imagination's source, but it also challenges "the limits of human imagination," making imagination the only way of grasping an unrationalizable reality.[32] I would therefore argue that Arva's traumatic imagination exists in both magical realism and mythorealism, with one important difference: While magical realism is characterized by an ontological de-hierarchization, Yan claims that mythorealism goes one step further, effectively fusing the "real" and the "imaginary" into something new, the "mythoreal."[33] Whereas magical realism strives to represent divergent, equally real-life experiences, mythorealism aims to explore the deeper reality that these lives are based on. Probing the mythoreal allows an author to not just represent but also explain past traumata, as well as question and possibly criticize their present manifestations.[34] I believe that stressing these latter objectives of mythorealism—its focus on making the past and, through it, the present understandable and graspable—is important since, as Yan explains, what "mythorealist writing absolutely cannot do is [to] pursue the mythoreal simply for the sake of the mythoreal" (*shenshi zhuyi chuangzuo, zui jueran buke de, shi zai xiezuo zhong weile shenshi er shenshi* 神實主義創作, 最決然不可的, 是在寫作中為了神實而神實), as this would lead to an alienation between "the real world" (*xianshi shijie* 現實世界) and "real 'humanity'" (*xianshi zhong de "ren"* 現實中的「人」).[35]

Bridging this gap is what "myth" is for. Myth must be understood as a very broad term, encompassing such diverse manifestations of inner truth as "imaginings, allegories, myths, legends, dreamscapes, and magical transformations" (*xiangxiang, yuyan, shenhua, chuanshuo, mengjing, huanxiang, mobian* 想像、寓言、神話、傳說、夢境、幻想、魔變).[36] Ultimately, however, they all serve the same goal: reconciling humanity and the real world or, in other words, representing "deep reality" (*shenke xianshi* 深刻現實) and "deep truth" (*shenceng zhenshi* 深層真實).[37] This approach to literature is reminiscent of what Robert Scholes calls the "cosmic imagination":

> [T]he great task of the human imagination for the present time is to generate, in literature and in life, systems that bring human desires into closer harmony with the systems operating in the whole cosmos. For this we need a cosmic imagination. We need to be able to perceive the cosmos itself as an [...] imaginative entity in which we can be as much at home as a character in a work of fiction. We must see

---

30 This last example must be seen as doubly unpresentable. Not only has it proven extremely traumatic for many Chinese, but the CCP has also prohibited its discussion through public channels, as can be seen by the banning of Yan's novel *The Four Books*.
31 See Bowers, *Magic(al) Realism*, 71.
32 Yan, *Explosion Chronicles*, 452.
33 Ibid., 452.
34 See Yan, *Faxian xiaoshuo*, 184.
35 Ibid., 202.
36 Ibid., 181–82.
37 Ibid., 215.

man as himself imagined and being re-imagined, and now able to play a role in the re-imagination of himself.[38]

What this comparison suggests, is that due to an emphasis on (re-)imagination, the same shift of perspective which I have argued magical realism has undergone, is also found in mythorealism: away from the alleged objective toward the subjective or individual. And indeed, Yan has repeatedly underlined that mythorealism concentrates on the individual, arguing that it is precisely through this subjective focus that collective sentiments can be explored or, in other words, that it becomes possible "to excavate the 'real' from the 'mythos'" (*cong "shen" xiang "shi" de juejin* 從「神」向「實」的掘金).[39]

When myth, in Yan's broad usage, is understood as an articulation of inner truth, it might be assumed that the latter has existed in narrative works for a long time. However, Yan claims that it has only become a prominent feature of literature during the twentieth century. He even pronounces that in modernist writings of the last century, the search for truth has, in reality, always been a search for inner truth.[40] He explains this shift in perspective through the tumultuous events and developments that have marked the previous century, i.e., two world wars as well as modern technological and social revolutions.[41] It seems thus that for Yan, inner truth is not only the driving force of inner causality in the present but itself a product of the past, of traumatic history. This helps explain why, even though their locus of meaning always lies in the present, in many of his novels, the past functions as a reference point, or even a mirror, essential for understanding the present.[42] This can be seen in two of his more recent works, which I will focus on for the remainder of this article: *The Four Books* and *The Explosion Chronicles*. As mythorealism depends on a subjective perspective, it should also be noted that it is as much a mode of reading as it is a mode of writing, depending on the reader to produce its meaning. While from a postmodern literary point of view, the structures of the two novels are nothing new in themselves, they nevertheless have some important ramifications for a mythorealist reading.

Multifaceted causality in *The Four Books*

This becomes apparent when looking at the polyphonic composition of *The Four Books*, constituting, as the title suggests, a collage of four fictitious "books." Parts of three of them are alternately presented to create one extensive, coherent narrative, a portrayal of life and survival in a re-education camp for intellectuals between 1958 and 1962, the period of the Great Leap Forward and the succeeding famine. The fourth "book" functions as a kind of philosophical epilogue. Although a single event is hardly ever described for a second time in the following "book," the fact that they are written in different styles, from the points of view of different characters and narrators, with different intentions, suffices to foreground the divergent perspectives that are being offered, and the complex, multifaceted inner causality on which they depend. This constellation of features illustrates not only the reliance of surface reality on inner truth but also that inner causality, as the structuring principle of mythorealist

---

38 Scholes, *Fabulation and Metafiction*, 217.
39 Yan, *Faxian xiaoshuo*, 197.
40 Ibid., 152.
41 Ibid., 159.
42 Ibid., 198.

narratives, is not based on a single source of causal logic but rather on multiple sources that need to be equally considered when trying to represent and explain past and present reality.[43]

This is depicted perfectly by the fate of one of the re-education camp's inmates. As a mathematician, he spent all his life trying to prove that one plus one equals two. After ultimately succeeding, however, to demonstrate that one plus one "*really* is equal to two," the only reaction from the higher-ups comes in the form of a rhetorical question: "Why don't we send this person for Re-Ed?"[44] Despite its brevity, this is a very telling example. There is a jarring disconnect between the discovery of a universal truth (the realism expressed by "one plus one equals two") and the external actions of the higher-ups. This sort of causal imbalance in China's recent history is exactly what Jeffrey Kinkley implies when he writes: "One mission of the aging children of Mao, who once accepted Mao's utopianism as a living faith, is to make the fanatical beliefs of their youth believable, so that these beliefs' historical culmination in dystopian outcomes [...] can be taken seriously."[45] *The Four Books* with its polyphonic structure can be seen as an attempted answer to this problem. By focusing on divergent perspectives that, as explanatory models, are each insufficient on their own, the novel highlights their respective relevance as fragments of a multifaceted, unified inner causality. In this specific case, the main focus lies both on a glorified self-representation of the Communist Party ("Heaven's Child") and a subjective, supposedly true account by one of the inmates, the Author ("Old Course" and, to a certain degree, "Criminal Records").

The gap between these two perspectives becomes especially obvious during a scene in which, to prepare them for the agrarian campaigns of the Great Leap Forward, the detainees are being sent to another camp to witness a theatrical play. The performance stars a professor who resists re-education and is unwilling to acknowledge the Party's utopian harvest targets, arguing that they are irrational and unscientific. After a long struggle, the other actors, with the approval of the audience, proceed to shoot the man. Only after a large pool of blood has appeared around the professor's head, though, do the attending intellectuals realize that what they have just witnessed was not mere make-believe but real. Still, as they make their way back to their own barracks, the Child, their camp commander, comments: "They performed very well. When they shot that man, it looked extremely realistic."[46] Truth, here, does ultimately depend on the subjective sentiments of each person, especially when they are interpreted as the driving force of inner causality and thus function to explain people's actions.

In this regard, one of the most noteworthy events described in the novel is the Author's attempt to grow giant wheat plants by watering them with his own blood.[47] This not only refers to the record harvests demanded by Mao and the Party's leadership but also demonstrates the belief which the Author, and almost all of the other detained intellectuals, despite their traumatic experiences at the re-education camp, still hold for the Party's utopian promises. I would therefore argue that when Laifong Leung 梁麗芳 states that the two books penned by the Author embody the "split mentality and moral dilemma" of Chinese writers in general—focusing on their own benefits or expressing their true feelings and beliefs—to it has to be added the meaning of "Heaven's Child," namely people's faith in the communist leadership.[48]

---

43 Ibid., 214.
44 Yan Lianke, *The Four Books*, trans. Carlos Rojas (London: Vintage, 2016), 166.
45 Jeffrey Kinkley, *Visions of Dystopia in China's New Historical Novels* (New York: Columbia University Press, 2014), 5.
46 Yan, *Four Books*, 53.
47 Ibid., 181–215.
48 Leung Laifong, "Yan Lianke: A Writer's Moral Duty," *Chinese Literature Today* 1, no. 2 (Winter/Spring 2011): 79.

Lastly, one should further include the implications of the fourth "book," "A new myth of Sisyphus," written by the Scholar, in which he voices his view that intellectuals need to readjust their focus, not acting as devoted disciples to their quasi-religiously venerated leaders anymore, but instead prioritizing the needs of the people. Only when keeping all these aspects in mind, the novel's structure suggests, can the meaning and the inner causality of the concrete unfolding of the event truly be understood. While the attempt to grow extraordinarily large wheat in exchange for his freedom indeed seems to suggest the pursuit of personal benefits, the fact that he quickly starts using his own blood to irrigate the seedlings proves his belief in the miracles demanded by the Party.

Although the Author's unusual method works, his undertaking ultimately still fails when the Scholar cuts all the remaining giant stalks down, leaving behind only a short message explaining that if the government were to see them, next year they would make the whole country bleed. The latter thus represents the critical part of intellectuals' consciousness that remains anchored in empirical reality, not letting himself be tricked by the Party's ideological illusions. Apart from the unrealistic size of the blood-fed crops, there is another mythorealistic element present in this event. As other inmates later fail to reproduce the miracle, it turns out that a necessary precondition for success was the fact that the Author's field was located directly above an emperor's tomb. This suggests an additional inner causal line of reasoning. In accordance with the glorification of the Party leadership in "Heaven's Child" and especially the omnipresent, symbolic equation of the Party with the sun, the magical qualities attributed to an emperor's tomb must be understood as resulting from a tradition of thought in which the ruler has not only been seen as a political representative but also as a semi-religious figure. This helps elucidate the unshakable assent with which all the detained intellectuals ultimately react to the higher-ups' orders, and simultaneously highlights their own complicity in keeping the system alive, something that Yan said he wanted to make visible due to its still lasting influence on intellectuals' self-portrayal in contemporary China.[49] Inner causality is therefore not only used to describe and explain historical circumstances but also to question and criticize them.

This can equally be seen in another mythorealist scene toward the end of the novel. As the detainees leave the camp without permission to try and return home, they arrive at a small town in which the headquarters of the re-education district is located. Try as they may, they are unable to skirt the place, leaving their hiding spot in the evening just to find themselves there again the next morning. On the third day, they finally send some of their own to scout ahead, at which point they discover that every night they have been stumbling through a vast graveyard encircling the whole town, filled with the corpses of starvation victims from the surrounding camps, many not even buried.[50] Their inability to successfully leave the horrific place behind can be interpreted in several ways. As the Author finally decides to enter the town and ask for permission to pass, he is told that the higher-ups have decreed that nobody can leave their respective area and that it is absolutely forbidden to share any information on the local number of deaths. Therefore, the impossibility of leaving the place behind can be seen as a physical manifestation of the intellectuals' political obedience and indoctrination. Then there is an unnamed detainee who confronts the Author with their situation, asking

---

49 See Sebastian Veg, "Literary and Documentary Accounts of the Great Famine: Challenging the Political System and the Social Hierarchies of Memory," in *Popular Memories of the Mao Era: From Critical Debate to Reassessing History*, ed. Sebastian Veg (Hong Kong: Hong Kong University Press, 2019), 128.
50 Yan, *Four Books*, 311–21.

why he had led them out of the camp if it was impossible to successfully traverse this field of corpses. Since the Author had been an informant in the past, representing and acting on behalf of the Party, this confrontation can be read as a direct critique of the policies of the Great Leap Forward: a promise to traverse into the future with modernization, but delivering only death and suffering. Lastly, the scene can also be interpreted as a critique of the intellectuals' collaboration with a system that promotes "state-sponsored amnesia," insinuating that as long as they ignore their past and choose not to face it, they will not be able to advance from where they are.[51]

Collective truth in *The Explosion Chronicles*

The Four Books deals with a specific traumatic historical event, representing a period that is still largely omitted from official discourse, and thus offering new meaning and potential for identity formation. *The Explosion Chronicles*, meanwhile, examines broader historical developments (the effects of the reform and opening-up policy) and tries to grasp a post-Mao, modern, globalized present, perceived as alien, irrational and, ultimately, unknowable.[52] The main narrative is presented in the form of a local gazetteer, a traditional Chinese form of historiography, and portrays the rapid growth of the village of Explosion into a megalopolis with more than twenty million inhabitants within the span of merely three decades (roughly between 1980 and 2010). It is framed by a fore- and afterword composed by the fictitious author Yan Lianke, in which he informs his readers that upon his request, the mayor permitted him to entirely rewrite an already existing version of the chronicles from an individual's point of view.[53] As the real Yan has repeatedly stated, writers, in his opinion, hold a privileged position that allows them to see and discover inner truths that remain out of sight for others, who therefore often take them to be purely imaginary.[54] As mentioned above, however, it is exactly through the imaginary—the myth—that mythorealism assumes truth can be found. In this regard, through the highlighting of its subjective nature, the narrative situation of *The Explosion Chronicles* can be seen as a mythorealist setting par excellence.

It is also thanks to this structure that the novel features two divergent endings: one allegorical, one "real." The latter tells of the return of the fictional Yan to Explosion and the handing over of the manuscript, which the mayor, unsatisfied with the historical representation, incinerates, thereby symbolically destroying individual history. Conversely, the former describes the ruin of the city as most of the inhabitants are led away by the richest and most powerful man in town to become part of a globalized workforce. Shortly after they leave, most of the clocks suddenly stop working, signifying not only the loss of millions of people (it has been established earlier in the narrative that whenever a clock stops, a person has died) but also a cessation of collective history and especially its economy-driven, teleological articulation as embodied by the mayor. What follows is a symbolic return of the remaining citizens to their past, represented by the fulfillment of their long-neglected traditional duty to visit their ancestors' graves. This finale therefore clearly emphasizes the above-mentioned function of the past as a reference point or mirror for the future. By implying that without a past, there

---

51 Yan Lianke, "On China's State-Sponsored Amnesia," *The New York Times*, 1 Apr. 2013, https://www.nytimes.com/2013/04/02/opinion/on-chinas-state-sponsored-amnesia.html.
52 See Anne Wedell-Wedellsborg, "Haunted Fiction: Modern Chinese Literature and the Supernatural," *The International Fiction Review* 32, no. 1–2 (2005): 31.
53 See Yan, *Explosion Chronicles*, 5.
54 See, for example, Yan Lianke, *Yan Lianke wenlun* 閻連科文論 [Yan Lianke's essays on literature] (Kunming: Yunnan renmin chubanshe, 2013), 155.

can be no future, Yan highlights the alienation between humanity and the real world, an issue which he has repeatedly broached all throughout the novel.

The two divergent endings represent exactly that problem, which, for him, is symptomatic of China's current "mythoreality": the gap between reality as it can be rationally grasped and reality as it is actually experienced. The former is represented by the afterword, the "real" ending, while the latter includes all the non-realistic elements described in the chronicles. Structurally speaking, therefore, neither *The Four Books* nor *The Explosion Chronicles* features a purely linear narration, but instead they both accentuate diverging perspectives, offering alternative accounts of history. Similar to magical realist novels, they highlight the fact that official history is just an interpretation of the past, serving the interests of those who write or commission it—as can be seen by the fact that the mayor, unsatisfied with the outcome, burns the fictional Yan's subjective account of the past.[55]

Contrary to *The Four Books*, which only features a handful of non-realistic elements, *The Explosion Chronicles* is permeated by magical occurrences, like the ability of official documents to make it snow or a character collecting shards of moonlight. These increase especially after Explosion's development has reached an unprecedented tempo, with buildings and streets being erected in a matter of weeks or even days, granting an absurd quality to a hyperbolic reality. The impossible speed of construction work is mirrored by plants blooming out of season, often coming alive within a matter of seconds and bearing fruit that are not natural to them. Mangoes and pomegranates growing on apricot trees are signs that the natural, external world is not in sync anymore with man-made reality.[56] This is especially accentuated by two scenes in which characters enter a place that has only been deserted for a couple of days but are confronted with a state of seemingly prolonged abandonment: trees grow out of cutting boards, tiny fish and shrimp swim around in porcelain sinks, and everything is overgrown with weeds.[57] Such sights highlight not only the intimate connection between the human and the natural world but also cause different layers of time—their past as a human habitat and their future return to nature—to merge in the present, effectively bringing the progress of time to a standstill. In this way, these places foreshadow the ultimate ruin of the city and its removal from a communist "temporal utopianism," which, based on a linear understanding of history, always justifies the present through its not-yet-fulfilled future.[58]

Compared to the "real" ending provided by the metafictional paratext, such occurrences not only highlight the split between experienced and "real" reality but also function as a kind of warning. As Yan writes, mythorealism is "like a fortune-teller who treats what he saw yesterday as a secret text anticipating what will happen tomorrow, and then tells other people" (*shi bugua xiansheng ba zuotian de suojian dangzuo mingbai yujian de miwen er gaosu taren* 是卜卦先生把昨天的所見當作明白預見的秘文而告訴他人).[59] Even though the downfall of the city does not "really" take place, it does, in the manner of the traumatic imagination, reveal a collective inner truth by pointing toward the alienation resulting from the perceived absurdity of reality caused by the city government's reckless, capitalistic pursuit of financial and political growth. This feeling is further enhanced by the fact that after the village is officially designated a town, the inhabitants' names disappear almost completely from the narration, turning a group of individuals into a nameless collective. The alienation finally reaches a

55 See Hegerfeldt, *Lies That Tell the Truth*, 63.
56 See Yan, *Explosion Chronicles*, 222.
57 Ibid., 190, 229.
58 Howard Y. F. Choy, *Remapping the Past: Fictions of History in Deng's China, 1979–97* (Leiden: Brill, 2004), 10.
59 Yan, *Faxian xiaoshuo*, 217.

horrific high point when thousands of amputated body parts are used to drastically speed up the building of a new airport, symbolizing the degradation of a human workforce into an expandable economic resource.

Conclusion

In some ways, mythorealism seems to resemble magical realism. Not only can both be understood as extensions of traditional realism, they each also focus on individual perspectives in order to make an outsized reality accessible again. However, while their similar approach of rationalizing a traumatic past and present moves them closer to each other, their understanding of truth seems to drive them apart. Whereas magical realism through its dual spatiality follows a more egalitarian approach, aiming to complement rather than completely replace the official narrative, functioning more inclusively and making the voices of often (historiographically) marginalized groups heard, mythorealism instead appears to seek to substitute the official narrative with a new, supposedly more comprehensive, more truthful version. This latter mode of representing history can be useful as it not only makes the past more comprehensible and graspable but also actively questions and criticizes it, as demonstrated in the above analyses. Nevertheless, the question arises whether by asserting that mythorealism is both denominating a new form of writing truth about reality and instantiating that "new reality" itself, Yan does not ultimately claim a degree of objectivity for the mode that puts it much closer to traditional realism than to the more egalitarian magical realism. To this can be added that whereas thanks to the work of scholars like Amaryll Chanady some level of agreement seems to exist about how to distinguish between magical realism and other similarly fantastic modes, it remains to be discussed what exactly makes a magical occurrence mythorealist.

Bibliography

Arva, Eugene. "Writing the Vanishing Real: Hyperreality and Magical Realism." *JNT: Journal of Narrative Theory* 38, no. 1 (Winter 2008): 60–85.
Baker, Suzanne. "Binarisms and Duality: Magic Realism and Postcolonialism." *Span: Journal of the South Pacific Association for Commonwealth Literature and Language Studies* 36 (1993). http://wwwmcc.murdoch.edu.au/ReadingRoom/litserv/SPAN/36/Baker.html.
Bowers, Maggie Ann. *Magic(al) Realism*. London: Routledge, 2004.
Can, Taner. *Magical Realism in Postcolonial British Fiction: History, Nation, and Narration*. Stuttgart: Ibidem Press, 2015.
Choy, Howard Y. F. *Remapping the Past: Fictions of History in Deng's China, 1979–97*. Leiden: Brill, 2004.
Faris, Wendy. *Ordinary Enchantments: Magical Realism and the Remystification of Narrative*. Nashville: Vanderbilt University Press, 2004.
García Márquez, Gabriel. "The Solitude of Latin America." Nobel Lecture. https://www.nobelprize.org/prizes/literature/1982/marquez/lecture/ (last accessed 8 May 2021).
Hegerfeldt, Anne. *Lies That Tell the Truth: Magic Realism Seen through Contemporary Fiction from Britain*. Amsterdam: Editions Rodopi, 2005.
Kinkley, Jeffrey. *Visions of Dystopia in China's New Historical Novels*. New York: Columbia University Press, 2014.
Leung, Laifong. "Yan Lianke: A Writer's Moral Duty." *Chinese Literature Today* 1, no. 2 (Winter/Spring 2011): 73–79.
Lyotard, Jean-François. "Answering the Question: What Is Postmodernism." In *The Postmodern Condition: A Report on Knowledge*, edited by Jean-François Lyotard, 71–82. Minneapolis: University of Minnesota Press, 1984.
Ouyang, Wen-chin. "Magical Realism and Beyond: Ideology and Fantasy." In *A Companion to Magical Realism*, edited by Stephen M. Hart and Wen-chin Ouyang, 13–20. Woodbridge: Tamesis, 2010.

Scholes, Robert. *Fabulation and Metafiction*. Urbana: University of Illinois Press, 1979.

Slemon, Stephen. "Magic Realism as Postcolonial Discourse." In *Magical Realism: Theory, History, Community*, edited by Lois Parkinson Zamora and Wendy Faris, 407–26. Durham: Duke University Press, 1995.

Veg, Sebastian. "Literary and Documentary Accounts of the Great Famine: Challenging the Political System and the Social Hierarchies of Memory." In *Popular Memories of the Mao Era: From Critical Debate to Reassessing History*, edited by Sebastian Veg, 115–36. Hong Kong: Hong Kong University Press, 2019.

Watt, Ian. "Ian Watt on Realism and the Novel Form." In *Realism*, edited by Lilian R. Furst, 87–94. London: Longman, 1992.

Wedell-Wedellsborg, Anne. "Haunted Fiction: Modern Chinese Literature and the Supernatural." *The International Fiction Review* 32, no. 1–2 (2005): 21–31.

Yan Lianke 閻連科. "*Bookforum* Talks with Yan Lianke." Interview by Robert Anthony Siegel. Bookforum, 20 Dec. 2013. https://www.bookforum.com/interviews/bookforum-talks-with-yan-lianke-12668 (last accessed 8 May 2021).

———. *Discovering Fiction*. Translated by Carlos Rojas. Durham: Duke University Press, 2022.

———. *The Explosion Chronicles*. Translated by Carlos Rojas. London: Vintage, 2018.

———. *Faxian xiaoshuo* 發現小說 [Discovering fiction]. Tianjin: Nankai daxue chubanshe, 2011.

———. "Finding Light in China's Darkness," *The New York Times*, 23 Oct. 2014. https://www.nytimes.com/2014/10/23/opinion/Yan-Lianke-finding-light-in-chinas-darkness.html (last accessed 8 May 2021).

———. *The Four Books*. Translated by Carlos Rojas. London: Vintage, 2016.

———. "*The Four Books* Interview." Man Booker International Prize. 22 Mar. 2016. https://booker218.rssing.com/chan-5643463/all_p3.html (last accessed 9 Aug. 2021).

———. "On China's State-Sponsored Amnesia." *The New York Times*, 1 Apr. 2013. https://www.nytimes.com/2013/04/02/opinion/on-chinas-state-sponsored-amnesia.html (last accessed 8 May 2021).

———. *Yan Lianke wenlun* 閻連科文論 [Yan Lianke's essays on literature]. Kunming: Yunnan renmin chubanshe, 2013.

Zamora, Lois Parkinson, and Wendy Faris, eds. *Magical Realism: Theory, History, Community*. Durham: Duke University Press, 1995.

———. "Introduction: Daiquiri Birds and Flaubertian Parrot(ie)s." In *Magical Realism: Theory, History, Community*, edited by Lois Parkinson Zamora and Wendy Faris, 1–11. Durham: Duke University Press, 1995.

Zamora, Lois Parkinson. "Magical Romance/Magical Realism: Ghosts in U.S. and Latin American Fiction." In *Magical Realism: Theory, History, Community,* ed. Lois Parkinson Zamora and Wendy Faris, 497–550. Durham: Duke University Press, 1995.

5
MYTHOREALISM OR PARAREALISM?
Yan Lianke's short fiction as a key to enter the author's representational world

Marco Fumian

Introduction

A prolific novelist as well as a painstaking theorist of his own fictional creations, Yan Lianke 閻連科 has always stood out for his efforts to define his particular mode of literary representation,[1] which eventually brought him to originate, some twelve years ago, the felicitous formula of *shenshizhuyi* 神實主義: a play on words that alters the Chinese word for *xianshizhuyi* 現實主義 'realism' by replacing its reference to "actual" existence (*xian* 現) with the "eerie" connotations of the character *shen* 神 'divine/marvelous/supernatural/weird/mysterious'. *Shenshizhuyi*, he wrote in a well-known and oft-quoted summary, is characterized by its purpose to break the "superficial logical relations which exist in real life," so as to explore a "nonexistent" truth that is "covered" by another "truth" and is therefore "invisible," and, as a way to grasp this elusive truth, by its having recourse to devices such as "fantasy, myth, legend, dream, illusion, magic and displacement."[2] Thus the conventional term that has been adopted so far in English to render this untranslatable play on words, first coined by Yan's translator Carlos Rojas, is "mythorealism," a word that highlights one particular connotation of the character *shen* insofar as the latter is a morpheme also used as a component of the word *shenhua* 神話 'myth'. Indeed, the term is to a good extent well-suited to make sense of a significant dimension of Yan's novelistic world, as many of his novels do in fact tend to present a layer of mythical significations, and sometimes they are even embedded in a mythical framework, mostly of biblical inspiration. Typically, in Yan's most renowned novels, history is turned into a fable, generally one with ghastly apocalyptic tones, whose parables are usually crafted as sweeping allegories of human nature and fate: the hubris of the powerful, the inane resistance of the powerless, the descent into degradation caused by greed, the Sisyphean

---

1 A mature attempt in this sense is already visible in a 2003 conversation with Li Tuo 李陀. See Li Tuo and Yan Lianke, "*Shouhuo*: Chaoxianshi xiezuo de xin changshi"《受活》——超現實寫作的新嘗試 [*Lenin's Kisses*: a New experiment of surrealist writing], *Dushu* 讀書 [Reading], 2004, no. 3: 44–54.
2 Yan Lianke, *Faxian xiaoshuo* 發現小說 [Discovering fiction] (2011; Beijing: Renmin wenxue chubanshe, 2014), 154.

frustration of all the efforts to change one's lot, the vengeful curses of nature and history, the annihilation of the body as the only way to find redemption, and so on. However, in spite of Yan's frequent "mythorealist" allegorizations of Chinese history, it is not to transcend history, turning it into a meta-historical scenario in which to enact some universal tales of vice and virtue, the most compelling purpose of Yan's elaboration of *shenshizhuyi*. Quite the opposite, what Yan is really aiming to, with his eerie transfigurations of Chinese history, is to find better ways to penetrate the hidden kernel of (modern) Chinese history and (contemporary) society in order to find a way, as he made clear, into the innermost recesses of the Chinese social reality and to illuminate the human life enmeshed in it. What he is looking for, he writes, is a "wedge" (*xiezi* 楔子), that is, a lever to unhinge, or perhaps a trick to circumvent, the "barrier" (*pingzhang* 屏障) that according to him usually blocks the Chinese realist writers, preventing them from questioning and criticizing society as any realist of serious endeavor for him should do; that barrier, simply put, is the cloak of ideology.[3] *Shenshizhuyi*, then, is not a way to supersede realism and to "mythicize" reality but is, in fact, a continuation of realism with other means, a circuitous way to do the job that realism in China is not able to do, mired as it is for Yan in its typically superficial and smugly complaisant representation of reality: *shen*, as he writes, is not an end in itself, but a *bridge*, whose purpose is to reach "the other shore of *shi*," namely the substance of (the social and historical) reality that is normally "invisible" as it is displaced, forgotten, ignored or evaded.[4] What Chinese realism is not able to do, in particular, is to grasp the profound elements of absurdity that for Yan constitute the most significant and pervasive realities of contemporary Chinese society ("reality is absurdity," as he stated in one passage of an interview)[5]: "realism," to quote his own words, "only stops at that part of the world that can be perceived, but it falls short in seeking and

---

3 Ibid., 158:

In our writing environment, every writer today is faced with the temptation of money, the lure of privilege and the restraints of the new ideology. This is the characteristic obstacle that causes contemporary Chinese literature to be incapable, as well as unwilling, to approach the most profound truths of realism. Such ideological restraints are not the prohibitions of the pre-reform era policies, but are rather stemming from the instinctive, unconscious unwillingness of the writers induced by the combined effects of politics and money surging from today's dramatic economic development. This drives the writers to voluntarily abandon the exploration of certain truths, preventing the soul to reach the core of social reality and the most authentic heart of the human being. This habit in the long run has produced in each and every writer, whether one admits it or not, a barrier that separates the self from the deepest layers of reality, nurturing in their writing a pervasive self-control and instinctive self-censorship.

在我們的寫作環境中，每個作家在寫作中所面臨的是經濟開放後金錢誘惑的包圍和特權的誘降與新意識形態的約束。這是中國當代文學無法、也不願走向現實主義深層真實的特色阻攔。這種新意識形態約束，不是改革開放前政策的「不准」、「不能」和「不允許」，而是今天經濟急劇發展後政治和金錢共同作用，促使並作用於作家本能的、無意識的「不願」。它使作家自願放棄心靈對某種真實的探求，不去主動讓靈魂抵達社會現實的最內部，抵達人的最真實的內心。久而久之的寫作習性，每個作家的內心，無論你承認與否，其實都有了一道自我與深層現實隔離的屏障，在寫作中點點滴滴地養成了自我的寫作管理和本能的寫作審查。

4 Ibid., 166. In a conversation with Zhang Xuexin 張學昕 in *Wo de xianshi wo de zhuyi: Yan Lianke duihua lu* 我的現實，我的主義——閻連科對話錄 [My "real" and my "-ism": Conversations with Yan Lianke], where he also illustrates the notion of *shenshizhuyi*, Yan even defines his writing, with regard to his most famous "mythorealistic" novels such as *Shouhuo* (*Lenin's Kisses*, 2004) and *Dingzhuang meng* 丁莊夢 (*Dream of Ding village*, 2006), as *realism*, however of an "alternative" sort. See *Wo de xianshi wo de zhuyi* (Beijing: Zhongguo renmin daxue chubanshe, 2010), 55.
5 Yan and Zhang, *Wo de xianshi wo de zhuyi*, 58.

probing those absurd and weird aspects of existence that cannot be perceived."[6] So the deep motive of *shenshizhuyi*, rather than the will to create some literary myths, is to seize and extract the absurd logic that for Yan fills up the body of modern Chinese history and contemporary society, so as to bring to the surface all that has been touched and warped by this logic exposing the sufferings that have been produced as a result. The alterations of reality conjured under the mode of *shenshizhuyi*, which include outright fantastic elements as much as simply incongruous depictions aimed to bend the "superficial logical relations of reality," are meant to be, in other words, subjective distortions of form whose aim is to capture the objective distortions of reality, as if the only way to apprehend the ambiguous and often ideologically mystified logic of modern and contemporary Chinese history and society could be that of adopting a deforming supply of techniques. For this reason, another term to translate *shenshizhuyi*, one perhaps more capable to make sense of Yan's most distinctive literary endeavor, could be in my opinion that of "pararealism." Derived from ancient Greek, the prefix para- refers to something close, contiguous, related, or similar to something else, which is yet *not quite the same*. Para- often points to a deviation, a deficiency or an aberration, as in the case of something that is false or tendentious (paralogism), that mocks and deforms the real thing (parody), that twists what is clear and normal (paranoia), that simply appears impossible in nature (paranormal), or that tries to say the same thing by changing the words (paraphrasis). Pararealism, then, sounds like a fairly suitable designation to name a literary form that imagines itself as tangent to realism but at the same time it strays from it, that aims to reproduce reality as it is but at the same time creates a paradoxical "para-reality" that mocks it and distorts it, that deviates from the familiar principles of verisimilitude only to dig out a more truthful "unfamiliar," and so on.

Even though Yan is chiefly known as a novelist, he also penned a number of significant short stories that offer a very interesting vantage point if one is not to investigate the author's more celebrated "mythorealistic" re-enactments of history, but prefers to observe the minute functioning of his "pararealistic" probing of social reality. Yan's landmark novels are almost all conceived, to varying degrees, as parables allegorizing the traumatic collective movements of modern Chinese history, with their monumental ambitions and calamitous failures.[7] Assuming the viewpoint of rural China, epitomized by the author's treatment of his West Henan (Yuxi 豫西) native region as a quintessential symbol of the ever-frustrated Chinese rural struggle for "catching up" (or at least to survive), many of these novels seek to lay bare the cannibalizations to which the relentless quest for "wealth and power" pursued by the Chinese authorities has repeatedly exposed the disadvantaged inhabitants of the Chinese countryside; their plots, then, are typically framed as counter-narratives that aim to satirize and tear apart, with jarringly tragicomic overtones, the master narratives of Chinese modernization. As a result, the individual psychological characterization does not feature prominently in these novels, as their characters are also to some extent conceived as allegorical personifications of some broad collective attributes or attitudes. The short stories, on the contrary, do not seek to portray any large historical movements, and instead they are, vice versa, mostly vignettes of rural life sketching out the mishaps of wretched individuals faced with unsustainable situations in their backward village settings, which normally tend to offer some disquieting epiphanies about the dynamics of power of the local rural life with the disrupting and corrupting effects they produce in the individual lives. Power is undoubtedly a very central element of Yan's

---

6 Yan, *Faxian xiaoshuo*, 158–59.
7 The novels I have in mind are mainly *Years Flowing in the Sun* (*Riguang liunian* 日光流年, 1998), *Lenin's Kisses*, *Dream of Ding Village*, *The Four Books* (*Sishu* 四書, 2011) and *The Explosion Chronicles* (*Zhalie zhi* 炸裂志, 2013).

poetic world, and I agree with Hong Zhigang 洪治綱 when he writes that a key goal of Yan's fiction is to provide a "deconstructive reflection" about how the "system of power" works in rural China producing the "external conditions of existence" at the base of the sufferings of the Chinese rural dwellers.[8] However, while the novels tend to concentrate on what we could call the "macro-system" of power—the unfathomable initiatives of the Chinese power-holders unceasingly launching their self-serving campaigns which end up producing devastating consequences into the lives of those below, the short stories vice versa focus on the "micro-system" of power, that is, that internalized structure of relations immanent to the local social life and that ultimately produces the rural psyche implanting its dominant social behaviors. In short, Yan's short stories often provide masterful representations of the cultural psychology of power in rural China (and in fact to some extent not only rural),[9] a psychology that feeds as much from traditional culture, with its cult of officialdom and hierarchical clan mentality, as from modern "socialist" politics, with their authoritarian ruling methods and mobilizing procedures, and the all-pervading marketization of contemporary society, with its tendency to commodify each and every aspect of life including the human body. This power, seen through Yan's representational lens, appears ubiquitous and irresistible, capable to exercise a destructive symbolic violence that ends up distorting all human behavior and social relations. Thus, as the main agent of distortion in Yan's social world seems precisely to be such embodied logic of power, we can also assume that this logic is the main target of Yan's pararealistic distortions of reality. But this treatment of social reality also places Yan very clearly in the lineage of the Chinese (critical) realist tradition—although as an "unfilial son," as he declared—with its exposure of the perversions of the national character and denunciation of the specific forms of oppression that characterize the Chinese social life. Obviously for these reasons, Yan has been often associated to Lu Xun 魯迅, the "father" of modern Chinese literature who, as pointed out by David Der-wei Wang 王德威, set the "discursive paradigm" of Chinese realism at the dawn of the modern literary revolution.[10] However, while acknowledging on several occasions his affinity with Lu Xun's critical approach as a writer and an intellectual, Yan also declared that his way of representing reality cannot be the same as that of Lu Xun, as well as it cannot be the same as that of Shen Congwen 沈從文. His effort, he said, is to find a "third way" in the representation of the Chinese rural "native soil" (xiangtu 鄉土), one that while not refuting the influence of the two masters, at the same time also consciously distances itself from them.[11]

This chapter attempts to observe how and why Yan's pararealistic representations converse and at the same time steer away both from the May Fourth "critical" realism of Lu

---

8 Hong Zhigang, "Xiangcun kunan de jizhi zhi lü: Yan lianke xiaoshuo lun" 鄉村苦難的極致之旅——閻連科小說論 [The extreme journey of rural suffering: On Yan Lianke's fiction], *Dangdai zuojia pinglun* 當代作家評論 [Contemporary writers review], 2007, no. 5: 70.

9 An important point to keep in mind is that the "rural," in Yan as well as in many other modern and contemporary Chinese authors, is used as a lens from which to reflect the historical and social problematic aspects of the whole China. For Yan, in particular, the disadvantaged "rural" often seems to become a prism to explore and criticize the overall dynamics of power formation and subjection to power that invest the Chinese society at large. On the use of the "native village" as a symbolic locus meant to supply a paradigmatic view of the disruptive Chinese social transformations, see the speech delivered by Yan on 22 Oct. 2014 at the awarding ceremony of the Franz Kafka Prize in Prague, "Zhe ge cunzhuang shi zui xianshi de Zhongguo" 這個村莊是最現實的中國 [This village is the most real China], 30 Dec. 2014, http://www.aisixiang.com/data/82017.html (last accessed 8 July 2021).

10 David Der-wei Wang, *Fictional Realism in Twentieth Century China: Mao Dun, Lao She, Shen Congwen* (New York: Columbia University Press, 1992), 1.

11 Yan, *Wo de xianshi wo de zhuyi*, 51.

Xun and the "lyrical" realism, as David Wang called it, of Shen Congwen.[12] One major reason for discarding the conventional principles of realism has obviously to do with the literary innovations that occurred in the Chinese literary field since the 1980s, when skepticism toward realism grew as a rebellion to the Communist ideological dogmas and a deep awareness of the importance of formal experimentalism as a medium to navigate the ambiguities of the real became widespread among the most contentious Chinese writers. But it also has to do, more significantly in my opinion, with the dominant contemporary conditions of social life as well as structures of perception shaped by ideology with which the Chinese writers today must deal and respond to when they create.

In 2017, I translated into Italian an anthology of some of Yan's best short stories published in China in the early 2000s, which includes "Three Strikes with a Club" ("San bang chui" 三棒槌, 2002), "Black Bristle, White Bristle" ("Hei zhumao bai zhumao" 黑豬毛白豬毛, 2002), "The Country Girl Goes to Market" ("Qu ganji de nizi" 去趕集的妮子, 2002), "Ideological-political work" ("Sixiang zhengzhi gongzuo" 思想政治工作, 2002), "Township Head Liu" ("Liu Xiangzhang" 劉鄉長, 2004), and the novella "Spring Awakening in the Peach Garden" ("Taoyuan chunxing" 桃源春醒, 2009).[13] In the remainder of this chapter, I will scrutinize some of these works to shed some light on the inner workings and motivations of Yan's pararealistic treatment of the reality as a way to talk about the contemporary Chinese society.

Life as a hog's bristle

While in this section I will focus mainly on the analysis of "Black Bristle, White Bristle," the best entry point to start this discussion about Yan's complex relation with the mainstream tradition of Chinese critical realism is the short story "Three Strikes with a Club." The plot is very simple. A guy named Shi Genzi 石根子, a cowardly man derided by the whole village, is bullied by a local tyrant named Li Mang 李蟒 (Li the Snake) who sleeps with his wife with the acquiescence of the latter and the complicity of the villagers. Exasperated by the continuous humiliations, in order to restore his dignity and prove that he is a "man" he eventually resolves to kill his tormentor, hitting him three times on the head with a club, with the consequence that he is finally executed. Thus, this is a story that recalls in its most basic elements what we could regard as the most typical Luxunian formulas: the indictment of the backward and cruel customs of the Chinese rural society with its marginalization and cannibalization of the weak conducted by the despotic elites under the gaze of the benighted, insensitive village spectators, which ultimately leads to the inevitable sacrifice of the victim. The point, however, is that the story is not set between the end of an agonizing feudal era and the beginning of a longed-for revolutionary rebirth, but in the present of a booming China that is embracing the market economy and is about to bring triumphally its "socialist market" into the ranks of the global world: Li Mang, in fact, is an upstart who got "tremendously rich" by dealing in herbal medicines and then became a "member of some sort of committee" as a result, thus gaining political power by virtue of his economic clout in a context in which the legitimate rules of the state are completely absent.[14] So the questions for a writer like Yan are: how to make sense of an arbitrary domination that was supposed to be wiped away by a

---

12 Wang, *Fictional Realism*, 201–46.
13 All the manuscripts, which I received from the author, correspond to the Chinese published version, apart from "Spring Awakening in the Peach Garden," as I will make clear in the final chapter. See Yan Lianke, *Il podestà Liu e altri racconti*, trans. Marco Fumian (Rome: Atmosphere, 2017).
14 Moreover, as if to celebrate his combination of wealth and power in culturally symbolic terms, Li Mang has built a sumptuous house in the style of the ancient residences of the officials.

revolution carried out in the name of the peasants' liberation and well-being, and that instead comes back now with a vengeance, cementing old feudal habits with new but no less heinous practices of oppression? How to deal with the reproduction of such a subjugation, especially considering that the very political force that had vowed to destroy the old social injustice is the one that allowed its revival, and even encouraged in many ways the ruthless exploitation of the peasant bodies in order to bolster the Chinese economic miracle?[15] How is it possible for a writer with a critical bent to simply expose, condemn, dissect, dividing past from future, evil from good, darkness from light, despair from hope as Lu Xun was ever struggling to do, when the Chinese modernization in rural China seems to be a looping journey without any hope of redemption, enlightenment or faith in social change?

When history repeats itself (it is even too easy to say in this case), it takes place first as a tragedy and then as a farce. Yan seems to know this very well as his story does not just climax with the tragic victimization, or desperate rebellion, of his downtrodden character, but finds its main narrative tension in the absurd dialogues between Shi Genzi and the judge who conducts the interrogation (the woes of Shi in the village are recounted as flashbacks), where an unexpected, counterintuitive inversion occurs: the judge who is in charge of sentencing him to death desperately tries to save him, encouraging him to falsify his confessions so as to hide his murderous intentions, whereas a paranoid Shi doggedly refuses to tell anything but the truth about his premeditated murder as he desperately wants to die in order to prove his manhood in the eyes of his wife and fellow villagers. This inversion in the end defamiliarizes a familiar narrative casting an ironic if not even parodic light on the May Fourth literary conventions, complicating in the process our view of the reality unraveled under the author's magnifying lens: on the one hand, Shi ultimately takes control of his destiny, but at the same time his twisted motives also sanction the triumph of the distorted cultural psychology which dominate his rural milieu—at the end of the story Shi is turned into an unlikely sort of folk hero worshipped by his superstitious fellow villagers. On the other hand, the story is an oblique sneer to the legitimacy of the official political power, as in spite of the sense of justice and humanity of the judge, the latter is nevertheless unable to redress the systematic injustice of Shi's world. Moreover, by depicting the protagonist's gestures as absurd and pathetic, Yan manages to "muffle" the subversive message resounding in those three strikes blown with all might on the villain's head, as if the only possible relief, for the irreparably aggrieved Chinese countryside, could be that of a rash and blind act of violence. In this way, the author is also able to intensify, rather than playing down, the emotional reception of Shi's tragic condition (the source of the tragic in the story is not so much his passive victimization, but his incapacity to deal with the whole situation in sensible terms), thus refreshing the otherwise worn-out May Fourth formula of compassion (tongqing 同情) as a device to arise sympathy for the plight of the weak.

If "Three Strikes with a Club" in our discussion only serves the purpose of setting up a problematic (how to treat, in literary terms, the predicament of the Chinese countryside in the "socialist market" era?), providing with its conclusion a paradoxical poetic catharsis as a fictional solution to the unsolvable problem of rural injustice, it is in "Black Bristle, White Bristle" that Yan attempts a more in-depth, pararealistic investigation into the structures of power that embed the rural social life delimiting its conditions of existence and (mis)shaping accordingly its prevailing social beliefs. The background of the story is as follows: the town head, a character that never shows up but that looms large behind the scenes as an inscrutable all-moving principle, has killed a twenty-year-old in a car accident; however, since it is simply unimaginable that a person of his caliber might pay his dues with the law and go to jail, it is

---

15 Clearly, this is the main theme of Yan's novels such as *Lenin's kisses* and *Dream of Ding Village*.

necessary to find a substitute willing to self-incriminate so to serve some time in prison in his place (is this a "typical situation"? That is, is this realistic in the sense that is something that is bound to happen with a certain frequency in China at the time Yan writes the story? Probably not, but this is precisely the sum of Yan's pararealism, which consists in his conjuring of *extreme* situations that are unlikely or simply impossible to happen in the real world, but that in fact with their paradoxical exaggerations are able to shed light on some significant and yet obscure dynamics of the social reality).

The focus of the story is then directed on the plight of Liu Genbao 劉根寶, a village resident whose cause of distress is that in spite of being already almost thirty, he has not yet managed to get married, first because his family is poor, second because they do not have any clan network of support or political ties in the village, third because he is too gentle and meek but this is perceived by the villagers as an unaffordable weakness, so he cannot by any means find a wife in an environment in which women seek in a husband mainly a protection to shield them from abuse: "Why on earth did you make me walk all these miles to come here and meet you?" (那你讓我跑十幾里路來和你見面幹啥？) shouts at Liu a hysterical woman paying him a visit for a potential marriage deal, after she finds out that his family does not have any status in the village, "Didn't the matchmaker tell you that my late husband hanged himself after he was beaten by someone stronger than him, and all that because of a fight about watering the fields? Didn't he tell you that I'm not after any money or property, but I only demand a man with a little bit of power, I'm not saying to bully other people, but at least not to be bullied by them!" (媒人沒和你說我原來的男人是因為和人爭水澆地，爭人家不過，被人打了一頓，回家上吊死了？沒說我不圖錢不圖財，就圖嫁個有勢力的男人，不說欺負別人，至少也不受人欺負！).

Thus the possibility of getting married eventually appears when Liu learns about the opportunity of going to jail as a substitute of the town head: confident that the official will not fail to satisfy his requests of finding a wife as a reward for his sacrifice, he walks out in the middle of the night to head toward the house of the butcher—another upstart who became rich by doing business and that is now acting as an intermediary between the town head and the villagers—only to find out that he is not the only candidate willing to sacrifice on behalf of the town head as there are at least three more adult men from the same village, each with his personal woe and consequent favor to submit to the politician, who are brooding the same thoughts as Liu's about serving some time in prison as a way to solve their personal problems. The butcher then arranges to call a lottery to decide who will be the winner: four pig bristles tucked in a folded piece of paper, three white and one black; and the one who will draw the black one will be the "lucky" one able to enjoy the privilege of going to jail (again, is this realistic? Surely, this is the most unlikely, deliberately distorted, and patently absurd situation of the whole story, but it shows very well the intent of Yan's pararealistic extremizations of reality. What does it mean that in order to achieve one's goals one must be ready to *compete* to self-immolate for a local politician? What does it mean to depend on a hog's bristle as a symbol of one's chances to determine one's fate? The heuristic value of such a technique lies in its metaphorical potential. This is what Yan means when he talks about uncovering a more profound truth that is hidden by another truth).

However, Liu in the end does not win, and dejected walks back toward his dilapidated home in the dead of night, where instead of finding his parents, he notices a bag full of freshly washed clothes and a pile of his most favorite fried pancakes that his mum lovingly prepared for him in anticipation of his imminent sojourn as a prison convict. Gutted, Liu goes out in the courtyard to look at the village and ponder over his own misery in what appears as the most heartrending lyrical moment of the story, until all of a sudden, a chatty and sexually attractive young lady pops in the courtyard to inform him that a wedding between him and her younger sister has already been arranged as a result of his lucky turn. Unable to tell her the truth and overwhelmed by his pent-up sexual frustration, he rushes to the house of the winner, a middle-aged man named Zhuzi 柱子, where he kneels down to beg him to let him be the one to act as a savior of the town head. Touched by his despair and under the promise that Liu will intercede for him with the town head once he has gained his favor, Zhuzi accepts.

Liu's good fortune, however, only lasts for a couple of hours, as the next morning, the absurd bubble that has nurtured his illusions abruptly explodes. The ending once again takes the form of a farce, one that, in its elated carnivalesque exaggeration, is able to deal a much more vicious blow in revealing Liu's impotence in changing his fate. Accompanied by the residents of the whole village, crowding to celebrate him as a hero and cheer him up for his sensational stroke of luck, the protagonist walks proudly out of the village, heading once again toward the home of the butcher, supposed to see him off to town where he will finally turn himself in: "Brother Genbao, now that you're running to meet your future don't forget about your brothers" (說根寶兄弟, 奔著前程了, 千萬別忘了你哥啊……) "What future are you taking about? I'm only going to jail in place of someone else …" (奔啥兒前程哩, 是去替人家蹲監呢), answers Genbao trying to bring the situation down to reality, but nonetheless complying with the absurdity of these celebrations, to which the villagers reply: "And in place of whom?! The town head! You're the savior of the town head, don't you think we don't know how big is the future awaiting for you!" (替誰呀? 是替鎮長哩, 你是鎮長的救命恩人呢, 還以為你哥我不知道你有多大前程嘛!). But at last, when the butcher's house is finally in sight, the butchers' assistants shout at him from afar to inform him that the deal with the town head has been called off, as the family of the victim did not charge the offender and only asked the town head to adopt their other son as a compensation for their loss, so there is no more need to find a replacement to go to prison in his place. Liu, feeling as if his legs are caving in, continues to walk away as he is not able to face the humiliation of telling the truth in front of the villagers.

So here is another story focused on the vicissitudes of a marginalized character seeking desperately to win social acceptance, however there is much more than that in the picture and the focus on Liu's bitter failure might be just a way of misdirecting the reader so as to hide the real gist of the tragedy. In order to delineate the coordinates of Liu's tragicomic fiasco, Yan draws a careful picture of the structures of inequalities, and the "structures of feelings" thereby determined, that appear to dominate the reality in which Liu is entrapped. Therefore we see an entangled web of factors old and new, from the clan-centered "differential mode of association" typical of the village social relations to the money crave triggered by the scrambles of the market economy,[16] from the backward views about marriage and manhood to the lack of sympathy caused by the struggle for survival in a lagged-behind environment, everything obviously presented in the expressionistic, exaggerated ways typical of the author (for example, to portray the twisted psychology of the woman who visits Liu, the author imagines that she first claims 50 yuan from him as a compensation for the time she wasted by traveling to meet him, then she asks him to beat her up to prove that he is a strong man that could protect her, swearing that in that case, she would be willing to marry him). But above all this, the tip that dominates such a structure of inequality, providing it with a system of shared meanings to justify its hierarchical syntax of inclusion and exclusion, is the political power of the officials, and the related cult of officialdom that symbolically sustains it. And

---

16 For the village social relations, see Fei Xiaotong 費孝通, *From the Soil: The Foundations of Chinese Society* (Berkeley and Los Angeles: University of California Press, 1992), 60–70.

this is not just because the story gravitates around the will of an official whose authority is so taken for granted that he does not even need to manifest himself in the lives of the villagers, but because the most scathing message that seems to be delivered by Yan is that in such social system the only reliable meter to determine one's social worth is the degree of one's proximity to the political power. In an environment apparently devoid of any legal guarantee, where ethics seem to have been distorted by greed and distrust, it is one's connection with the field of power, whether formal or informal, the best guarantee to secure one's personal safety and prosperity. Political power hence exudes a sort of all-pervasive *mana*, that is vicariously extended to and exerted by all those who have been blessed by its magic touch. The butcher, for example, is a former peasant who has upgraded his social position by making some money with his business, but what really makes him influential among the villagers is his having rubbed shoulders with some local officials, which allowed him to become a factotum entitled to act as an intermediary between the authorities and the villagers. Hilarious is the passage in which Yan describes how the butcher's business soared after the county Party secretary accidentally slept in one of his guest rooms after a car break, an event that allowed him to turn that room into a sort of reliquary in which everybody wished to stay so that they could use the same objects that had been touched by the Party secretary. And hilarious, although much more melancholic, is the scene in which Liu, upon his arrival at the butcher's house, discovers that on the external wall of the butcher's guest rooms there is not only a plaque reading "here slept county Party secretary Zhao" (縣委趙書記曾在此住宿), but also another one proclaiming "here slept county Chief Ma" (縣裏馬縣長曾在此住宿), a statement whose authenticity causes in Liu a vague perplexity. These passages reveal how the story to a large extent is meant to be a surrealist satire of the cult of power in rural China or, more precisely, of that supremacy of officialdom that is called by Chinese sociologists *guan benwei* 官本位 (or *guanbenzhuyi* 官本主義 'official-centrism'),[17] a satire which ridicules the psychological perversions that the hegemony of this internalized culture seems to produce in the rural population. This is the inherent tragedy of the countryside, the origin of that vicious system of distortion in which power has the prerogative to elevate everything it touches, but at the same time, it demands in return the infinite disposability of human life as a price to pay for those who enter this system as mere bodies without a social capital.[18] And this is likewise the main object of Yan's absurdist demystification. But absurdity, in Yan's story, is not conveyed primarily by the objective weirdness of the recounted situations. Certainly, persisting in one's resolution to go to jail in place of someone else is absurd, participating in a lottery to do it is even more so, not to mention holding a public gathering to congratulate the "hero" who succeeds in such an attempt. But the main target of Yan's criticism is not the absurdity of the objective situations. The real absurdity, instead, is that nobody is able to recognize these situations, for what they mean in symbolic terms, as absurd. Everybody in Liu's village finds it

---

17 For a treatment of the concept of *guan benwei*, see Yu Keping 俞可平, "Shenme zaocheng shehui de guan benwei wenhua" 什麼造成社會的官本位文化 [What has created the Chinese official-centric culture], Aisixiang 愛思想, 19 Oct. 2012, https://www.aisixiang.com/data/68654.html (last accessed 8 July 2021). As to Yan's criticism of this "official-centric" culture, see Shao Yanjun 邵燕君, "Huangdan haishi huangtang, xiesheng haishi xiedu? You Yan Lianke *Feng ya song* piping mou zhong buliang de xiezuo qingxiang" 荒誕還是荒唐，瀆聖還是褻瀆？——由閻連科《風雅頌》批評某種不良的寫作傾向 [Absurd or unreasonable, blasphemous or disrespectful? A criticism of certain poor writing inclinations through Yan Lianke's *Feng ya song*], *Wenyi zhengming* 文藝爭鳴 [Literary and artistic contentions], 2008, no. 10: 6–15.

18 Thus the typical stress on physical disablement and bodily self-consumption in much of Yan's fiction as a symbol of the peasants' "handicapped" position in the Chinese social structure.

normal to debase oneself to win the favor of a politician, to rival with each other to be (ab)used by him, and that it is even honorable to shatter one's dignity in such a way. This is the core of Yan's criticism, the main target of his pararealistic re-writing of reality, that in "Black Bristle, White Bristle" stages, on the one hand, an extreme scene of *obscene* power abuse and on the other a mindless, masochistic collective submission to it, leaving it to the reader to interrogate him or herself to what extent this incongruous situation might be realistic or not. Even Liu, although slightly more sensitive than the other villagers and capable to some degree of self-reflection, is not able to step out of this "slave mentality," simply because the only way to be integrated with his society is to go along with the rules of its system. Everybody is so inured to this structured inequality, and so indifferent to the cruelty thereby generated, that nobody sees, perhaps because they do not care about, the real tragedy of the story, which is unobtrusively played out by Yan in the background.

In fact, in spite of the carnivalesque climax mounted to dramatize even more Liu's abrupt disillusion, the background of the story is charged in every moment with a sinister atmosphere: the action is mostly set in the middle of the night, in a disturbing silence occasionally broken by the bone-chilling squeals of the pigs slaughtered by the butcher, whose function is on the one hand to amplify Liu's state of anguish, and on the other to serve as an ominous objective correlative of the ongoing act of cannibalization: "after all they are killing pigs, not people" (到底, 是殺豬, 又不是殺人), ruminates Liu in the attempt to get rid of his fear as he walks out of his house and heads to the butcher's. The cannibalization, however, in the end, is not that of Liu, who after all can still go back to his lackluster life of marginalization and subordination accepting his condition as a bachelor and poor peasant. The real cannibalization, rather, is that of the youth who was killed in the car accident, a tragedy that remains disguised in plain sight until the very end because nobody seems to be concerned about the fate of the victim, perhaps because he was from another village. And the most chilling, absurd aspect of this tragedy is that nobody is going to pay for his death: his life was so cheap, and the power of the local official is so absolute that even the family of the victim gave up seeking justice and instead "bought" a deal with the town head "selling" the other son to him in the hope of "gaining" for him a better life, thus suggesting again that in a society dominated by the "transactions of power and money" (*quan qian jiaoyi* 權錢交易). The best solution to guarantee one's future in life is to be "adopted" by someone in power, never mind if he is the killer of your brother. (Finally, to end this commentary between brackets: how realistic is this situation? This might be, after all, *very* realistic: how common has it been, in the years of the booming "socialist market" economy, the practice of settling a deadly incident with a cheap compensation, especially when crimes were committed by people in power at the expenses of the subaltern rural workers? Yan himself, in his speech about his village as a mirror of China's contemporary transformations, recounts as an example of the moral bankruptcy of the Chinese countryside an episode about a "little brother" of his, who complained because he was forced to pay as much as 30,000 yuan in compensation for having caused the death of a five year old, while in the same years the same situation was normally settled for a couple of 1,000, maximum 10,000 yuan.[19])

Two other short stories included in the abovementioned collection offer a very interesting representation of the Chinese peculiar syntaxes of power investigated by Yan, one is "Township Head Liu," and the other one is "Ideological-political work." However, since the first is mainly a satirical allegory of the Chinese rural authorities' quest for "catching up," and does not delve into the psychological condition of a peasant individual character, while the

---

19 Yan, "Zhe ge cunzhuang shi zui xianshi de Zhongguo."

second is about the psychological abuse of a peasant victim, but the abusing power is not that of the rural power system but that of the military, I will have to omit their discussion, and I will focus instead on two other works, the short story "The Country Girl Goes to Market" and the novella "Spring Awakening in the Peach Garden."

Intermission: On the impossibility of a pastoral redemption

The moon, in Liu Genbao's disquieting nocturnal adventure, often peeks out as if to offer, with its soothing light, an emotional foothold for the protagonist and a poetic relief for the reader. But what it manages to illuminate, in the end, is only the objective bleakness of Liu's surroundings and the subjective misery of his state of mind. Moreover, the moon also becomes, at some point, the helpless casualty of a sort of cannibalization, as it happens in the scene set in the butcher's courtyard, where the delicate moonlight shining upon the countryside is mercilessly swallowed by the unnatural blaze of two 200-watt bulbs switched on to floodlight the massive pig-slaughtering taking place in that location. This scene can be taken as a telling example of the author's attitude toward the "lyrical," and especially toward that particular mode of "pastoral" lyricism that has been typically associated, in the modern Chinese literary tradition, with the so-called genre of "native soil" fiction. As much as there is, in Yan, the desire to create poetic effects with his depictions of the rural natural sceneries as well as the simple, elemental ways of the country people, what we really find in his typical rural representations is not that ethic and aesthetic "unity of heaven and man" (*tian ren heyi* 天人合一) which is at the base of the traditional Chinese pastoral imagination, but rather the jarring evocation either of a cruel and crippling nature with which man can only wage a desperate struggle for survival, or the irreparable damage and distortion of an "original" nature, both *natural* and *human*, that has been raped, disfigured or destroyed by the corrupting forces of modernization. Nature in Yan does not possess any healing and nurturing beauty; the "poetic," if anything, stems in his fiction rather from the unequal human confrontation with nature's cruelty or corruption, a confrontation that is obviously tragic as it is always a losing one.

This brings us to our comparison with Shen Congwen, the master of the "romantic school" of the Chinese native soil fiction with whom Yan often compared himself,[20] underlining his unwillingness as well as the impossibility to follow in the footsteps of Shen's utopian rural imagination.[21] No story, perhaps, provides a better glimpse of the contrast between Shen's and Yan's rural poetics than "The Country Girl Goes to Market," given that the latter appears in some respects as a revisiting of Shen's masterpiece *The Border Town* (*Biancheng* 邊城), especially for what concerns the fate of the protagonist, similar and yet different from that of her elder sister Cuicui 翠翠, the main character of Shen's most famous work.

---

20 Ding Fan 丁帆, in his *Zhongguo xiangtu xiaoshuo shi* 中國鄉土小說史 [A history of the Chinese native soil fiction] (Beijing: Beijing daxue chubanshe, 2007), distinguishes between a realist "May Fourth" native soil fiction (*xieshi wusi xiangtu xiaoshuo* 寫實五四鄉土小說), which obviously includes Lu Xun as a trendsetter, and a "romantic native soil fiction" (*xiangtu langmanpai xiaoshuo* 鄉土浪漫派小說), with Fei Ming 廢名 and Shen Congwen as major representatives.

21 "Since I was young I always had a very clear feeling that in the countryside of the Central Plains everybody lives under the shadow of power; in the Central Plains you do not find any "peach springs beyond this world" (*shi wai taoyuan* 世外桃源) as in Shen Congwen's *Xiangxi* 湘西." See Yan Lianke and Yao Xiaolei 姚曉雷, "Xiezuo shi yinwei dui shenghuo de yanwu he kongju" 寫作是因為對生活的厭惡和恐懼 [I write out of fear and disgust toward life], *Dangdai zuojia pinglun*, 2004, no. 2: 80–88.

Cuicui, as we know, is an orphaned girl who is grown by her doting grandfather in a bucolic *locus amoenus* at the fringes of a serene and secluded "border town," untouched by the upheavals of modern Chinese history and immune to the conflicts caused by the disrupting social transformations (what makes the "border town" a modern version of the traditional utopia pictured in the classic Peach Blossom Spring). As she reaches the age of puberty, one day she comes to experience, for the first time on her own, the wonderful spectacle of the Dragon Boat Festival, where she is met for the first time with the mysterious promise of her sexual awakening and, at the same time, with the obscure threat that such promise brings along (as in the scene in which Cuicui, while waiting for the arrival of her granddad in the dusk, hears with a racing heart the singing of the prostitutes accompanied by the bawdy bantering of the sailors). However, even though this awakening will spark a chain of mournful events—one of Cuicui's suitors will perish in an accident caused indirectly by her granddad, and her granddad himself will die before being able to entrust her to the protection of a caring husband—in the end for Cuicui there is nothing to fear: in an organic society in which people's mores are chiseled out in sincere and honest ways by the benign influence of nature, and where human life regenerates itself continuously following the endless rhythms of the natural cycles, there seems to be no real danger of an irreparable catastrophe for the protagonist, and Cuicui will find a new home, she will be lovingly looked after and, perhaps, she will even be able to marry the handsome youth with whom she is in love.

Nothing of the sort in Yan's short story, where we also find an orphaned country girl raised by her loving grandmother nearing the end of her life, and is also about to approach sexual maturity and the hidden dangers that come along with it, but the sense of her experience, at the end of the story, is completely opposite to that of her literary antecedent. Impatient to become a "big girl," which for her means to show herself without any false prudery to be admired by those who want to see her, the girl's biggest dream is to go all alone to the town market, since the market is her "biggest happiness, as much as for a lamb is to be left free on an immense grassy hill" (趕集是妮子最快活的事情，就像一個羊羔兒被散在漫無邊際的草坡). But her grandma does not light-heartedly let her go away as Cuicui's granddad does, and instead tries by all means to keep her safe within the house, "guarding her like a little seedling from the bite of a farmyard animal" (奶奶守著她，就像守著生怕羊啃、豬拱的一株小苗兒). One day, however, foreboding her imminent death, her grandma allows her to go to the market on her own as she rapidly needs a reel of yellow thread to finish the sewing of her funeral dress. The girl then runs off to the town, elatedly visits all of the market areas, and, in spite of being disappointed because that day the market is almost desert, she watches all the scenes she runs into with great curiosity and excitement. Her journey, however, does not have the same luminous lightness of Cuicui's adventure, as she is always surrounded, in all of her wanderings, by the creeping desolation of the scenes she observes (the overworked animals sold for nothing at the end of their lives, the cheap broth soup made with the bones of these animals, the slick shopkeepers not even raising their eyes at her since she is not a buyer, the squalid shop of the lady who cheats her by selling her way more reels than she needs …) as well as by a sense of impending danger. At last, the climax of this mounting tension is the encounter, on the empty dirt road on the way home, with a thirty-year-old male peasant, who lures her with a trick into the sorghum fields with the intention to abduct her.

But this is not, in the end, the real danger that truly threatens the girl. The peasant, after all, promises that he will not touch her and only begs her, paralyzed as he is in a feverish fluster, to watch her body as she takes off her clothes in front of him, as in spite of being already a grown man he "has never, in all his life, seen the body of a woman" (一輩子還沒見到過女人的身子哩). Then, after he suddenly had an orgasm, he stares at her astounded by her naivety (again, she is equated in this passage to a lamb), as the girl is not only unaware of the tragedy she just skirted but is even happy and proud of having just been admired and praised by a man for her beauty: "Am I white? Am I beautiful?" (我白嗎? 漂亮嗎?) she asks him before leaving, "White ... Beautiful ... go home now" (白, 漂亮, 你走吧) answers the man flabbergasted. So rather than an encounter between a lamb and a wolf, the scene turns out as a rendezvous between two different types of victims, as suggested by the sympathy fleetingly betrayed by Yan toward this character (could it be Liu Genbao himself?) by describing him, through the objective voice of the impersonal narrator, as a "man deserving pity" (*kelian de da nanren* 可憐的大男人). It is another tragedy, instead, the one that the tension set up by this scene ushers into. As the country girl finally enters the village, eager to tell everybody about her adventures, she first meets, in the quiet scene of the village bathed by the last rays of the sunset, a man who tells her unsympathetically that she has to rush home because her grandma is dead. Then, when she finally makes it home, instead of finding the compassionate embrace of her fellow villagers, she stumbles into a neighbor, a "woman whom she usually called auntie" (一個她向人家叫嬸的婦女), who asks her matter-of-factly if the girl can give her one of the reels she bought because "now that your grandma has died, she won't need them anymore" (你奶奶不在了, 死了哩, 你買的絲線她也沒用了). To which the country girl, after a moment of astonishment, suddenly dashes off to go home dropping on the ground all the reels, while the woman, unfussed, bends down to pick them up.

So what Yan wants to tell us is that, unlike Shen's rural world, there is no place for innocence in his contemporary rural settings, and if you are on your own, without some close and reliable elder to protect you, you'd better put aside your naivety and learn quickly to fend for yourself, because there is no motherlike nature to embrace you and no organic society to adopt you, but a frenzied materialist society where callousness and greed have irredeemably replaced the traditional bonds of solidarity, as this is clearly illustrated in the long scene in which the country girl is conned by the woman who sells her the reels, a savvy peasant-turned-town-resident who does not hesitate to manipulate her fears about losing her grandma to coax her into spending almost all her money in the shop.

Shen, as we know, wrote in a time of turmoil and uncertainty in which the old traditional world, execrated by the May Fourth critical realists, was undergoing a painful erosion and was quickly disintegrating, so he decided to immortalize the memory of his archaic homeland, recreating it by means of his sublimating artistic imagination. Hence his effort to turn his native West Hunan (*Xiangxi* 湘西) into a lyrical utopia dominated by the "divinity" of nature (the border town as a "little Greek temple"), even though this utopia was a "damaged" one,[22] as David Wang noticed, as it was one that was never spared by the "shadows of death and violence" and constantly haunted by the ghosts of Eros and Thanatos.[23] But what about Yan? What are the primal historical experiences that constitute the foundations of his rural poetic imaginations? First, we see the traumas of the Maoist utopian struggles to "conquer nature," in the midst of which the author came to life (while the novella *The Years, Months, Days* can be read at one level as a universal parable of human endurance akin to *The Old Man and the Sea*,[24] I prefer to view it as a surrealist attempt to allegorize the traumatized peasant unconscious of the Big Leap famine, that broke out only one year after Yan's birth). Then, there are the struggles

---

22 Wang, *Fictional Realism*, 202.
23 Ibid., 205.
24 David Der-wei Wang, "Geming shidai de ai yu si: Lun Yan Lianke de xiaoshuo" 革命時代的愛與死——論閻連科的小說 [Love and death in a revolutionary age: On Yan Lianke's novel], *Dangdai zuojia pinglun*, 2007, no. 5: 25–37. Another allegory of this failing rural struggle against nature is *Years Flowing in the Sun* (*Riguang liunian* 日光流年, 1998).

to "modernize" of the Reform and Opening-up Era, during which, while many Chinese urbanites were "getting rich" and China was finally fulfilling its dream of "catching up" with the world, the Chinese countryside and peasants were once again left on their own in their Sisyphean struggles to change their unchangeable state of inferiority, with the ironic implication that the only possible utopia for them, as Yan suggested in *Lenin's Kisses* (*Shouhuo* 受活), seemed that of returning contentedly to a primitive state of pre-modern subsistence.[25] Yan's literary world therefore is also "cloaked" in a utopian imagination, as he himself observes,[26] but as the most significant purpose of his fiction is to bring to the surface the disruptions, deceptions, exploitations, and corruptions that the modernizing teleology has brought to the Chinese countryside and its inhabitants, the concrete expression of such imagination is, in the end, programmatically *anti*-utopian.[27] The countryside, in this sense, becomes in Yan the (distorted) mirror through which to reflect, magnifying them, the perverting effects of the Chinese relentless quest for modernity and prosperity; rather than an "imperfect paradise," as Jeffrey Kinkley defined Shen's fictional world,[28] it is a "perfect hell" which enacts the erosion, disintegration, frenzied reification and godless absence of piety that such quest has brought not only to the Chinese countryside but to the whole of China. A typical symbol of this degeneration is thus nature, either in the image of a beautiful rural landscape or an innocent human behavior, that instead of offering a lyrical consolation with its beauty in Yan appears frequently jeopardized by the danger of being violated, as it happens to the moon in "Black Bristle, White Bristle," or to the girl in "The Country Girl Goes to Market." Or, as it also happens in "Spring Awakening in the Peach Garden," the last story to be considered in this essay, where the "peach" theme is in no way a metaphor of utopia, but one symbolizing the sadomasochistic ghosts of self-destruction haunting the life of the contemporary Chinese countryside.

25 Jianmei Liu 劉劍梅, "Joining the Commune or Withdrawing from the Commune? A Reading of Yan Lianke's *Shouhuo*," *Modern Chinese Literature and Culture* 19, no. 2 (Fall 2007): 1–33.
26 "However, amid this change, I had the vague feeling that China woke up from one utopia just to find itself stepping into another utopia. As soon as it retreated from the Communist utopia, it leaped into a new utopia, this time a 'capitalist' one." (然而，在這種變化中，我隱隱地感覺到，中國是從一個烏托邦中醒來，又走進了另外一個烏托邦。從共產主義烏托邦中退出來，又一步跳進了「資本主義的烏托邦」，跳進了一個新的烏托邦。) See Yan Lianke, "'Wutuobang' longzhao xia de geren xiezuo: Zai Hanguo waiguoyu daxue de yanjiang" 「烏托邦」籠罩下的個人寫作——在韓國外國語大學的演講 [Personal writing under the cloak of utopia: Talk at the Hankuk University of Foreign Studies], 6 Feb. 2008, https://www.guishuji.cc/sanwen/9270/508963.html (last accessed 8 July 2021).
27 Ibid.

> [… a lot of social disasters and diseases that hit China since the 1990s …] at a superficial look seem to be to some extent "accidental," but, if we put all these "accidents" together, were they not to some extent necessary? And is this necessity somehow related to the ultra-rapid growth of today's China, to the utopian dream of "little," "medium" and "big" prosperity of a billion and three-hundred million people? Is this the symptom of a new utopian dream that is starting to break out like a disease on the body of the nation? Then there is the human heart, the dreadful human heart. During the Communist utopia, the Chinese people had a "collectivist" ideology. Now, in the new utopian dream of wealth and power, what we are left with is only an "ideology of private desire."

> 從表面上看，有許多的「偶然」成分，但把這些「偶然」合起來看，有沒有必然成分呢？這種必然和今天中國的飛速發展，和13億人口的「小康」、「中康」、「大康」的烏托邦夢境，有沒有關係呢？是不是一種新烏托邦夢的病症，在一個民族身上發作的開始呢？還有人心，可怕的人心。共產主義烏托邦時期，中國人都有「集體主義」思想。現在，在新的富裕和強大的烏托邦的夢境裏，我們現在只剩下了私欲主義。

28 Shen Congwen, *Imperfect Paradise: Twenty-Four Stories*, trans. Jeffrey Kinkley (Honolulu: University of Hawaii Press, 1995).

Conclusion: On the (im)possibilities of enlightenment

On the degeneration of the rural ethics (and aesthetics) is also "Spring Awakening in the Peach Garden," the only novella included in the abovementioned collection, which Yan personally recommended for me to translate, considering it one of his best pieces of short fiction. The story is about four friends in their late twenties who have returned to the countryside from the cities where they work. Since it is already spring, and the spring is "calling" them to do something, they arrange to meet in the peach garden at the edge of their village where after everybody has gotten drunk, the eldest of the group, Zhang Hai 張海, not having a clue about what else to do, proposes that each of them give a beating to their wives: "Zhang Hai pondered for a while, clenched his fist, waved it, and said: alright, I'm the eldest and you all listen to me, so today we'll all go home and beat our wives. He who doesn't beat is not a man. If one doesn't beat the shit out of his wife he's not our brother, but our grandson, our great grandson"[29] (張海思忖一陣, 把拳頭捏了一下, 揮了一下, 說好吧, 我是老大, 既然都聽我的, 今天就都回去把老婆揍了。說, 誰不打不揍不是男人。誰不往死裏去打去揍, 就是兄弟們的孫子、重孫子).[30] The result of this absurd pact is an outlandish escalation of violence that will lead to their own annihilation. Niu Lin 牛林 and Baozi 豹子, respectively second and fourth in the cast-iron age hierarchy of the group, take Zhang's invitation very literally, and hit their wives so hard that they send them to the hospital, one with a broken arm, the other with her belly pierced by a pair of scissors, even though she is pregnant. Zhang, feeling humiliated because he caused to his wife only a few scratches, while being the leader of the group he should have been the one to hit the hardest, goes home and burns his wife's hand badly to make up for his own weakness. But the most offensive affront comes from Musen 木森, the third in the rank, who had the nerve of not beating his wife at all with the excuse that she is still breastfeeding their baby, and if beaten, could lose her milk. Thus, the three brothers decide to teach him a lesson, setting him up with a prostitute and calling his wife, so that she can see his unfaithful behavior. Finally, after a scene in which Baozi is also humiliated and forced into submission by the powerful family of his wife, the story ends with the four of them convening again in the peach garden, where they repeat once more their initial mantra: "The spring has come, we need to do something" (說春天來了——做點事吧). Everyone then comes up with a vicious plan: Zhang proposes to bribe a few officials to win a bid; Niu suggests that they should frame the village authorities and take power in their place; Baozi insists that they should beat the member of his wife's family, who humiliated him and steal his money. It is nevertheless Musen, who so far has paid the highest price from their twisted pact having being forced by his wife to accept a divorce although he did not have any intercourse with the prostitute, to advance the most insane proposal: since they all are sworn brothers, and he has already divorced, everybody should divorce like him. As they are not able to agree on what to do, Baozi eventually has an "unimaginable" idea: they will have a race to fell down the peach trees of the garden, so that the one who will fell the most will decide what to do and the others will follow. Finding it a good idea, everybody rushes off to fetch an electric saw and begins to massacre the trees, all "in the prime of their life" (正值著壯年時辰), "more or less like them" (正是他們四個人平均年齡的數), until no one is left standing and the peach garden is razed to the ground. As the winner is Musen, the final say is that everybody will divorce.

29 Grandson (*sunzi* 孫子) in colloquial Chinese has a derogatory meaning similar to that of "son of a bitch."
30 All quotes of this story come from the original manuscript file received from the author.

Indeed, "Spring Awakening in the Peach Garden" is a little tour de force in which Yan's absurd deformations of reality achieve one of their most brilliant results. But it is not just the hard-core, over-the-top representation of a nonsensical outburst of violence that makes up the core of the author's pararealistic distortions here. The "eerie" element added by the *shen* component of his *shenshizhuyi* mode, here, played down or absent in the other stories so far investigated, is instead amplified to the extreme by the spectral presence of the peach trees of the garden that haunt from the beginning to the end the unfolding of the action, serving with their mute but evocative contours at least two symbolic functions. First, they constitute another parodic subversion of the loftiest tradition of the Chinese literary canon, as the pact that the four paranoid "brothers" strike among the peach trees in full bloom deliberately echoes, turning it on its head, the ultra-celebrated scene of the "Oath of the Peach Garden" of the *Romance of the Three Kingdoms* (*San guo yanyi* 三國演義), in which the three heroes Liu Bei 劉備, Guan Yu 關羽, and Zhang Fei 張飛, bent on saving the country and rescuing its people, swear that they will forever remain loyal to each other saying that even though they were not born as brothers, as brothers they will die. The four friends in Yan's story, however, do not have any great deeds to achieve, and instead they are mired in their own ignorance, aggressiveness, and the oppressiveness of their lives, so they turn the noblest values of the Chinese chivalric tradition into a vicious and self-defeating spiral of blind commitments. The story, then, appears first of all as an ironic overturning, and ingenious deconstruction, of the popular ethical construct of *yiqi* 義氣 (translatable as "spirit of brotherhood") glorified by the epic "oath": that bond of unbreakable mutual care and support between male friends, which turns friendship into consanguinity, that once has been transferred by Yan from the heroic landscapes imagined by the literati to the deprived (and according to Yan depraved) cultural terrain of the contemporary Chinese countryside, becomes a stifling shackle at the base of the latter's masochistic psychological makeup. Through this lens, Yan sketches out a disturbing picture of the most degraded and degrading cultural codes of masculine behavior with the most nefarious consequences they seem to engender: above all, a suffocating hierarchical bonding which feigns equality but produces subjugation, imposing duties according to one's rank, leading to the fear of losing face, desire to humiliate others, covert manipulation of their will, resentful allegiances which brood betrayal, not to mention the contempt toward those who are external to the group, as evinced in the misogynistic attitudes reserved to women and the hostility toward those who belong to other clans.

Following the twisted courses of action of the four brothers, then, we can observe another piercing dissection of the local psychology of power, in which power, this time, appears to spring forth not from the sweeping manipulations of those above but from the microscopic interpersonal confrontations of those at the bottom, for whom power becomes an implicit game to impose one's will in a system that explicitly recommends to adapt to the will of others. It is even too easy to see in this operation a typical Luxunian critique of the "bad roots" of the Chinese "national character" forever trapped in the backward soil of the Chinese countryside akin to that performed in "The True Story of Ah Q" ("A Q zhengzhuan" 阿Q正傳): and the comparisons with this novella could indeed be numerous, from the subversion of the noble idealizations of the official literary tradition through the caricatured enactment of some ignoble characters to the obvious "slave mentality" of the group members, with their inclinations to inflict upon those weaker than them the humiliations they receive, not to mention the "muddledness" of their resolutions that ultimately backfire against themselves. But obviously, there is more than that, as Yan's purpose is never that of simply criticizing the countryside and its people as the special repositories of the Chinese backward cultural elements, but always to problematize the disadvantaged position of the Chinese rural space within the contradictions of the Chinese modernizing process, showing the aberrations of the Chinese countryside as the extreme symptoms of the ailments afflicting the whole body of the modernizing Chinese society. Consequently, the four brothers depicted in the story are not only victimizers but also victims. As the social background of the story clearly reminds us, all of them are migrant workers tolling in the major cities of China (they mention Beijing and Canton), who returned to the village to visit their families for the New Year's break. Now that the spring is back, they are supposed to return to the cities, but as none of them wishes to do it (in fact, they betray an unspeakable fear of going back), they meet in the blossoming peach garden to fantasize about an alternative, a self-aggrandizing gesture that could give them a sense of purpose, but as there is no real alternative in place, the only gesture they can think of through the filter of their drunkenness is a (self-)destructive one, a misconceived attempt of self-empowerment unwittingly aimed at releasing their pent-up rage, and perhaps to exorcise their fears. What the story really aims to do, then, is to depict by oblique means the alienation of the characters, an alienation that is twofold insofar as the young migrants represented in the story appear alienated both from the cities to which they do not yet belong, where they veritably suffer another kind of violence that they have probably internalized and brought back home, and the countryside to which they do not entirely belong anymore (and from whose renewed structures of power they have already been marginalized). Reading the story from this point of view, we can also gain a more multifaceted understanding of the characters' twisted interpretation of the fantasies of *yiqi*: rather than viewing such articulation simply as the expression of the perpetual benightedness of the traditional rural ways, we should read it instead as the modern re-appropriation of a value resurrected by the disempowered subalterns as an armor to provide security in a time of anguish, a mask to prevent one's identity from crumbling in an environment that has lost its social bonds and cultural moorings. Similarly, the blind recourse to violence appears mostly as the result of the impossibility to verbalize and rationalize the causes of a painful distress, another symptom of their alienation. Significantly, a central element of the story is that of the incommunicability of the four brothers, their constitutional incapacity to reveal, to the others as well as to themselves, the hidden state of their intimate feelings, articulating them by means of frank and rational words: Zhang is always described as seething with rage, but on the surface he always appears wooden and tongue-tied, Baozi is only able to release his anger for the humiliations he received by fantasizing about killing his wife, Musen when summoned to divorce by his wife can only fence himself behind a hostile silence, while all the four brothers, when meeting to take their grave decisions with concern to their friendship, before taking up their nonsensical resolutions are always shrouded for some time by a speechless sense of suffocation, expressed in Chinese by the recurrent character *men* 悶, as if they were "locked in a dark room" (誰都如被關在黑屋) or "weighed down by a stone" (沉悶像石樣壓將下來).

Thereby we find the second function of the peach trees, the most important if we consider the metaphorical textual economy of Yan's pararealism. If the characters cannot express themselves, then the author makes sure that the trees can perform such expression in their place. Hence all the alienated gestures of the male protagonists are contoured and underlined by the chorus-like movements of the trees in the garden, whose function is to witness and comment, as if they were mysteriously alive, on the bewildering progression of their actions. When at the beginning of the story the four brothers lose control by getting drunk, the trees have just started to blossom, and the flower buds that are about to open up on the greening branches are also described as drunk, and on the verge of stripping naked in a somewhat lascivious way. As they start to put their wicked plans into practice, the trees are portrayed as progressively beginning to bloom, with their buds first looking as "drooling out their red like tempting lips" (再也含不住了紅色, 泄露出來, 唇樣的誘潤) and then, only a few hours later, "spreading out so thunderously" (轟轟隆隆盛開了) that the trees are made to look like "red balls of fire" (每棵桃樹都是一燃團團的火). Finally, when they go back for their last reunion in the garden, this already appears as "an ocean of scarlet, with each and every tree blooming with lustful audacity" (桃園已經大紅, 海海洋洋, 這一樹, 那一株, 皆著淫旺狂放.) What is this uncanny, carnivalesque orgy of natural life, recounted by Yan with virtuoso experimentalism, supposed to mean? Needless to say, the flowering trees in the midst of their "spring awakening" symbolize first of all the rebirth of nature, the renewal of life, and therefore the return of hope, optimism, and commitment. More specifically, in their "being in the prime of their life," more or less "like them," they symbolize the vigor of youth, thus functioning as a mirror for the youthful, vital energy of the characters. As the trees of the garden, however, are turned into the echo chamber of their raging frustration, they end up being transmogrified into something that is dark and threatening, savage and obscene, which seems to foment, shaking them violently, their worst instincts. Eventually, by severing the trunks of the peach trees in full bloom, they will do nothing but excise their own soul, and perhaps the last mooring to their original human nature before becoming alienated *for good*: and the cemetery of felled trees upon which they stand triumphally at the end of the story is none other than the antiphrastic conclusion of their work of self-destruction.

But the brothers depicted in this novella, we could say by way of conclusion, might be not alone in their difficulty to deal with the most unpleasant aspects of reality articulating them by means of language. Whereas the story I investigated corresponds to the original manuscript that I received directly from the author, the novella that was published in China features exactly the same plot but with a different ending, a mere 1,000 characters out of a total of almost 30,000 that are nevertheless sufficient to alter the general meaning of the story completely. Rather than coming from Baozi, the "unimaginable" idea in the amended version arrives from Musen, who instead of proposing to fell down all the trees, suggests that each of them pick up a peach flower and then throw it in front of them, so that the one who will throw it furthest will decide what to do. Then a marvelous thing happens, as while Zhang's, Niu's, and Baozi's flowers once thrown immediately drop down on their feet, Musen's flower, as if possessed by magic, first waves gently in the air for a while, then glides down quietly a few steps away, with the result that the one to take the final resolution is Musen. And, the resolution he takes, is no more that the brothers should all die with him in a ridiculous act of destructive solidarity, but a constructive one of collective amendment and a promise of good will: all the brothers will have to go home and, since it is already spring, they will have to buy a dress for their wife. Thus, my conclusive question is: Why this ending? What are the motivations of such an ending, an ending that, regardless of whether one appreciates it or not, appears by all means abrupt and contrived, extensively at odds with the inner logical development of a plot that appears so inexorably geared up, so as to climax with its absurd auto-da-fé? Was Yan somehow persuaded to opt for a blander finale because of censorship pressure? Or perhaps he thought that such a finale would be too depressing and thus, learning another lesson from Lu Xun, he decided to add a few "distorted strokes" (*qubi* 曲筆) in the conclusion to make it feel less pessimistic while giving at the same time a positive message of encouragement?

Interestingly enough, while the novella received very scant attention from the Chinese critics, perhaps a telling sign of the "difficulty" of its contents, the very few essays that tried to tackle it all focused on the positive messages conveyed by the conclusion. For one of them, "literature is a lamp, it always has to give some hope of moving forward" (文學是燈, 總要給人一點前行的希望), while Yan, who "does not wish to see the awakening of evil, has a hope to see the awakening of the good elements of human nature" (閻連科就是這樣, 他不希望看

到的總是邪惡甦醒, 期待人性的良善基因醒來). Hence, being an intellectual steeped in the May Fourth tradition, he gives himself the task to "reveal the pain of the disease and bring attention to the cure" (揭出病苦, 引起療救的注意).[31] For another, Yan with this story offers an imaginative solution to the problem of the damaged rural ethics, showing a "possibility" about how to "restore and reconstruct" its "emotional foundations": something that in turn also possesses some "enlightenment significance." In the same article, the author even goes as far as to greet this attitude as a "breakthrough" in Yan's otherwise repetitive "aesthetics of violence."[32]

However, is it really plausible to believe that Yan sees as his task that of enlightening the Chinese peasants? Does he wish to restore, together with their emotional foundations, the worn-out literary didacticism of the old days? A very quick look at what Yan wrote after he finished this novella will be sufficient for us to affirm that no "breakthrough" in Yan's "aesthetics of violence" has ever occurred since then, as Yan simply continued to write novels with grim apocalyptic endings that perhaps could offer to some degree a mild escapist consolation (indeed, another type of *qubi*), but definitely not positive messages or even imaginative "solutions" for change. Why then did it do it this time, in this particular text? The only tentative explanation that I am able to give, somehow cued by the above critical responses to the novella, is that there might be, in this novella, something that is particularly intractable, uncomfortable, perhaps unsayable, not simply for the official censorship but for the sensibility of the readers, especially the professional ones steeped in the habitudes of the Chinese intellectuals; something that thus needs to be treated, tamed, mitigated or exorcised. What we find, behind the "absurdized" explosion of violence of the story, is a radical social evil, a structured malaise that does not seem to have any imaginable solution (until the system in which the actions of the Chinese subalterns are embedded is not radically changed from above). Even more, hiding it under the mask of the characters' implausible behaviors, Yan has probably managed to touch the nerves of a profound psychological despair, something that might be so deeply rooted, in and out of the Chinese countryside as the characters represented here are in fact those that in reality constitute the underbelly of the Chinese urban *lumpenproletariat*, that no single act of resistance and redemption could really show the way to ease it up. However, as this *reality* seems a little too inconvenient to be fully brought to the surface with no abridgments, here it comes a convenient May Fourth "enlightenment" frame that rewrites the story inserting it into a mold that allows a much more reassuring interpretation: by suggesting that the possible "cure" to the "pain" of the characters' "disease" is an act of individual redemption and good will, the amended version of the story also suggests that the problem is not so much social as one of personal consciousness, and that it is after all a matter of personal responsibility to be able to get out, or not, of this state of alienation. This mechanism of interpolation, prompted by the literary and cultural "horizon of expectation" more than by the author's real poetic intentions, points to another important rationale for Yan's resorting to his pararealism as a way to grasp the most unpleasant aspects of social

---

31 Liu Ying 劉迎, "'Qimeng' lixing xia de xiangtu xiezuo: Ping Yan Lianke zhongpian xiaoshuo 'Taoyuan chunxing'" 「啟蒙」理性下的鄉土寫作——評閻連科中篇小說《桃園春醒》 [Native soil writing under the "enlightenment" reason: A critique of Yan Lianke's novella "Spring Awakening in the Peach Garden"], *Mingzuo xinshang* 名作欣賞 [Masterpieces review], 2010, no. 29: 76–78.

32 Cui Shaofeng 崔紹峰, "Chongjian xiangtu shehui biange zhong de qinggan lunli: Tan Yan Lianke xiaoshuo 'Taoyuan chunxing'" 重建鄉土社會變革中的情感倫理——談閻連科小說《桃園春醒》 [Reconstructing the emotional ethics of the transforming rural society: Discussing Yan Lianke's novel "Spring Awakening in the Peach Garden"], *Wenyi pinglun* 文藝評論 [Literature and art criticism], 2012, no. 3: 76–79.

reality. Pararealism, as we have intended it in this essay, mainly refers to the author's distorted representations of reality so as to bring to the surface its painful absurdities. But absurdity, by making reality seem "weird," also has the effect of reinforcing its elusiveness, thus providing for a multiplicity of interpretations. If, on the one hand, this technique is helpful to dig out the "invisible" truths that are usually hidden behind the filter of ideology, on the other hand, it is also able to screen these invisible truths with another filter, that by preserving the elusiveness of their meanings is also able to make them more socially acceptable.

Bibliography

Cui Shaofeng 崔紹峰. "Chongjian xiangtu shehui biange zhong de qinggan lunli: Tan Yan Lianke xiaoshuo 'Taoyuan chunxing'" 重建鄉土社會變革中的情感倫理——談閻連科小說《桃園春醒》[Reconstructing the emotional ethics of the transforming rural society: Discussing Yan Lianke's novel "Spring Awakening in the Peach Garden"], *Wenyi pinglun* 文藝評論 [Literature and art criticism], 2012, no. 3: 76–79.

Ding Fan 丁帆. *Zhongguo xiangtu xiaoshuo shi* 中國鄉土小說史 [A history of the Chinese native soil fiction]. Beijing: Beijing daxue chubanshe, 2007.

Fei Xiaotong 費孝通. *From the Soil: The Foundations of Chinese Society*. Berkeley and Los Angeles: University of California Press, 1992.

Hong Zhigang 洪治綱. "Xiangcun kunan de jizhi zhi lü: Yan Lianke xiaoshuo lun" 鄉村苦難的極致之旅——閻連科小說論 [The extreme journey of rural suffering: On Yan Lianke's fiction], *Dangdai zuojia pinglun* 當代作家評論 [Contemporary writers review], 2007, no. 5: 70–81.

Li Tuo 李陀 and Yan Lianke 閻連科. "*Shouhuo*: Chaoxianshi xiezuo de xin changshi《受活》——超現實寫作的新嘗試 [*Lenin's Kisses*: A New experiment of surrealist writing], *Dushu* 讀書 [Reading], 2004, no. 3: 44–54.

Liu, Jianmei 劉劍梅. "Joining the Commune or Withdrawing from the Commune? A Reading of Yan Lianke's *Shouhuo*," *Modern Chinese Literature and Culture* 19, no. 2 (Fall 2007): 1–33.

Liu Ying 劉迎. "'Qimeng' lixing xia de xiangtu xiezuo: Ping Yan Lianke zhongpian xiaoshuo 'Taoyuan chunxing'" 「啟蒙」理性下的鄉土寫作——評閻連科中篇小說《桃園春醒》[Native soil writing under the "enlightenment" reason: A critique of Yan Lianke's novella "Spring Awakening in the Peach Garden"], *Mingzuo xinshang* 名作欣賞 [Masterpieces review], 2010, no. 29: 76–78.

Shao Yanjun 邵燕君. "Huangdan hai shi huangtang, xiesheng haishi xiedu? You Yan Lianke *Feng ya song* piping mou zhong buliang de xiezuo Qingxiang" 荒誕還是荒唐, 瀆聖還是褻瀆?——由閻連科《風雅頌》批評某種不良的寫作傾向 [Absurd or unreasonable, blasphemous or disrespectful? A criticism of certain poor writing inclinations through Yan Lianke's *Feng ya song*], *Wenyi Zhengming* 文藝爭鳴 [Literary and artistic contentions], 2008, no. 10: 6–15.

Shen Congwen 沈從文. *Imperfect Paradise: Twenty-Four Stories*. Translated by Jeffrey Kinkley. Honolulu: University of Hawaii Press, 1995.

Wang, David Der-wei 王德威. *Fictional Realism in Twentieth Century China: Mao Dun, Lao She, Shen Congwen*. New York: Columbia University Press, 1992.

———. "Geming shidai de ai yu si: Lun Yan Lianke de xiaoshuo" 革命時代的愛與死——論閻連科的小說 [Love and death in a revolutionary age: On Yan Lianke's novel], *Dangdai zuojia pinglun*, 2007, no. 5: 25–37.

Yan Lianke. *Dingzhuang meng* 丁莊夢. Taipei: Maitian, 2006.

———. *Dream of Ding Village*. Translated by Cindy Carter. New York: Grove Atlantic, 2011.

———. *Explosion Chronicles*. Translated by Carlos Rojas. New York: Grove Atlantic, 2016.

———. *Faxian xiaoshuo* 發現小說 [Discovering fiction]. 2011; Beijing: Renmin wenxue chubanshe, 2014.

———. *The Four Books*. Translated by Carlos Rojas. New York: Grove Atlantic, 2016.

———. "Hei zhumao bai zhumao" 黑豬毛 白豬毛 [Black bristle, white bristle], *Mingzuo xinshang* 2008, no. 19: 119–26.

———. *Il podestà Liu e altri racconti*. Translated by Marco Fumian. Rome: Atmosphere, 2017.

———. *Lenin's Kisses*. Translated by Carlos Rojas. New York: Grove Atlantic, 2013.

———. "Liu Xiangzhang" 柳鄉長 [Township head Liu]. *Shanghai wenxue* 上海文學, 2004, no. 8: 102–8.

———. *Nian yue ri* 年月日 [The years, months, days]. Zhengzhou: Henan wenyi chubanshe, 2014.

———. "Qu gan ji de nizi" 去趕集的妮子 [The country girl goes to market]. *Hongyan* 紅巖 [Red cliff], 2002, no. 5: 40–47.

———. *Riguang liunian* 日光流年 [Years flowing in the sun]. Shenyang: Chunfeng wenyi chubanshe, 1998.

———. "San bang chui" 三棒槌 [Three strikes with a club], *Renmin wenxue* 人民文學 [People's literature], 2002, no. 1: 42–49.

———. *Shouhuo* 受活 [Lenin's kisses]. Shenyang: Chunfeng wenyi chubanshe, 2004.

———. *Sishu* 四書 [The four books]. Taipei: Maitian, 2006.

———. "Sixiang zhengzhi gongzuo" 思想政治工作 [Ideological-political work]. *Zhongshan* 鍾山 [Mountain Zhong], 2002, no. 3: 71–76.

———. "Taoyuan chunxing" 桃園春醒 [Spring awakening in the peach garden]. *Renmin wenxue* 人民文學 [People's literature], 2009, no. 7: 4–23.

———. "'Wutuobang' longzhao xia de geren xiezuo: Zai Hanguo waiguoyu daxue de yanjiang" 「烏托邦」籠罩下的個人寫作——在韓國外國語大學的演講 [Personal writing under the cloak of utopia: Talk at the Hankuk University of Foreign Studies]. 6 Feb. 2008. https://www.guishuji.cc/sanwen/9270/508963.html (last accessed 8 July 2021).

———. *Wo de xianshi wo de zhuyi: Yan Lianke duihua lu* 我的現實，我的主義———閻連科對話錄 [My "real" and my "-ism": Conversations with Yan Lianke]. Beijing: Zhongguo renmin daxue chubanshe, 2010.

———. *The Years, Months, Days*. Translated by Carlos Rojas. New York: Grove Atlantic, 2017.

———. *Zhalie zhi* 炸裂志 [Explosion chronicles]. Shanghai: Shanghai wenyi chubanshe, 2013.

———. "Zhe ge cunzhuang shi zui xianshi de Zhongguo" 這個村莊是最現實的中國 [This village is the most real China]. 30 Dec. 2014. http://www.aisixiang.com/data/82017.html (last accessed 8 July 2021).

——— and Yao Xiaolei 姚曉雷. "Xiezuo shi yinwei dui shenghuo de yanwu he kongju" 寫作是因為對生活的厭惡和恐懼 [I write out of fear and disgust toward life], *Dangdai zuojia pinglun*, 2004, no. 2: 80–88.

Yu Keping 俞可平. "Shenme zaocheng shehui de guan benwei wenhua" 什麼造成社會的官本位文化 [What has created the Chinese official-centric culture]. *Aisixiang* 愛思想, 19 Oct. 2012. https://www.aisixiang.com/data/68654.html (last accessed 8 July 2021).

6
CENSURE AND CENSORSHIP
Prohibition and presence of Yan Lianke's writings in China

Jessica Yeung

Introduction

Write-ups about Yan Lianke's 閻連科 novels and interviews with the novelist himself often include reference at some point in the text to the official bans and unofficial censure of his works in China.[1] One way to understand such attention to this aspect of Yan's career is that such strict control over literary and other expressions is a highly significant phenomenon that throws into sharp contrast life in China and that lived in what some might call "the free world."[2] One would expect this to be a major line of inquiry in the studies of Yan Lianke's works, but after thorough research, I have only found one such piece.[3] Studies on Chinese

---

1 Clarissa Sebag-Montefiore, "Blood Price of Fear and Greed : Yan Lianke's Novel Exposes the Truth about China's Hidden Epidemic," *Independent*, Oct. 2011, https://www.independent.co.uk/arts-entertainment/books/reviews/four-books-yan-lianke-book-review-looking-back-anger-mao-s-great-leap-forward-a109256.html (last accessed 10 July 2021); Lou Chengzhen 樓乘震, "Yan Lianke zui manyi zuopin *Si shu*: Cheng xiezuo shi mingyun de anpai 閻連科最滿意作品《四書》稱寫作是命運的安排 [*The Four Books* is Yan Lianke's most satisfactory work: He considers writing his fate]," *Shenzhen shangbao* 深圳商報 (Shenzhen Economic Daily), 3 Apr. 2014, http://culture.people.com.cn/BIG5/n/2014/0403/c22219-24819642.html (last accessed 10 July 2021); Fan Jiayang, "Yan Lianke's Forbidden Satires of China," *The New Yorker*, 8 Oct. 2018, https://www.newyorker.com/magazine/2018/10/15/yan-liankes-forbidden-satires-of-china (last accessed 10 July 2021); Lesley McDowell, "Yan Lianke: 'It's Hard to Get My Books Published in China'," *The Guardian*, 22 Sep. 2018, https://www.theguardian.com/books/2018/sep/22/yan-lianke-writers-in-china-day-the-sun-died-interview (last accessed 10 July 2021); Yuan Yang, "Yan Lianke : 'Propaganda Is a Nuclear Bomb,'" *Financial Times*, 3 Apr. 2020, https://www.ft.com/content/83b25396-7358-11ea-95fe-fcd274e920ca (last accessed 10 July 2021).
2 One example of the use of the expression "the free world" is in Mike Pompeo's speech given in an online commemoration event of the June Fourth Incident organized by Hong Kong dissidents in the United States. The speech starts at 42:35 at https://www.youtube.com/watch?v=E1efytDjwns. The description "the free world" designating mostly the Anglo-European world is certainly controversial, considering the numerous New Left critiques on liberalism and the postmodernist world. However, overt political censorship is, unfortunately, much more aggressive in China than in what Pompeo calls "the free world," and this almost justifies the expression as a relative term.
3 Lee Tong King, "China as Dystopia: Cultural Imaginings through Translation," *Translation Studies* 8, no. 3 (2015): 251–68.

DOI: 10.4324/9781003144564-7

censorship are indeed numerous, but most of them focus on the country's censorship of the internet,[4] and in particular about censorship of social media.[5] Studies have also been done on Chinese censorship from the legal perspective, such as from the point of view of international law.[6] This attention to China's internet and social media censorship is easy to understand, since they are indeed the channels of expression and communication with the most users and that manage to reach the majority of the country's population. If they really are the most impactful channels of communication, control over them would also be the most effective form of control over expression. Internet censorship is a colossal operation; it functions by means of comprehensive and sophisticated digital detective apparatuses such as keyword blockages. Feng Guangchao Charles and Steve Zhongshi Guo have investigated some of these structural mechanisms.[7] Other researchers have also studied tactics employed by netizens to bypass such mechanical censorship. One example is the survey on the numerous euphemisms that replace the allusion to the June 4th Tiananmen Incident.[8]

By comparison, studies of Chinese censorship on arts, literature, and other forms of writing account only for a small minority of Chinese censorship studies. The few examples include a study of queer documentaries under state censorship,[9] academic censorship against *The China Quarterly*,[10] and censorship in translation and in specific literary translation.[11] Particularly relevant to this present article is the aforementioned article by Lee Tong King discussing the censorship Yan's works are subject to. An analysis of the blurbs, introductions, and other paratextual marketing materials of the translations of Yan's novels leads the author to conclude that Yan's works are well received in the Anglophone literary market, because they feed into the Western imagination of China as "an overdetermined sign pointing to a repressive, dystopic Other."[12] He also suggests that the personality of Yan as a banned writer emphasized by his publishers and translator is nothing more than a kind of "literary victimization," since Yan still has very much enjoyed the status of a mainstream writer, although "a small number

---

4 Rebecca MacKinnon, "Flatter World and Thicker Walls? Blogs, Censorship and Civic Discourse in China," *Public Choice* 134, nos. 1–2 (2018): 31–46; Peter Lorentzen "China's Strategic Censorship," *American Journal of Political Science* 58, no. 2 (2014): 402–14; An Xiao Mina, "Batman, Pandaman and the Blind Man: A Case Study in Social Change Memes and Internet Censorship in China," *Journal of Visual Culture* 13, no. 3 (2014): 359–75; Wang Dakuo and Gloria Mark, "Internet Censorship in China: Examining User Awareness and Attitudes," *ACM Transactions on Computer-Human Interaction* 22, no. 6 (2015): 1–22; Han Rongbin, *Contesting Cyberspace in China* (New York: Columbia University Press, 2018); Chen Sally Xiaojin, *Resistance in Digital China: The Southern Weekly Incident* (London: Bloomsbury Academic, 2020).
5 Gary King, Jennifer Pan, and Margaret E. Roberts, "How Censorship in China Allows Government Criticism but Silences Collective Expression," *American Political Science Review* 107, no. 2 (2013): 326–43.
6 Ge Chen, "Piercing the Veil of State Sovereignty: How China's Censorship Regime into Fragmented International Law Can Lead to a Butterfly Effect," *Global Constitutionalism* 3, no. 1 (2014): 31–70.
7 Feng Guangchao Charles and Steve Zhongshi Guo, "Tracing the Route of China's Internet Censorship: An Empirical Study," *Telematics and Informatics* 30, no. 4 (2013): 335–45.
8 Anne Henochowicz, "Five Years of Sensitive Words on June Fourth," 1 June 2016, https://chinadigitaltimes.net/2016/06/five-years-sensitive-words-june-fourth (last accessed 10 July 2021).
9 Gareth Shaw and Zhang Xiaoling, "Cyberspace and Gay Rights in a Digital China: Queer Documentary Filmmaking under State Censorship," *China Information* 32, no. 2 (2018): 270–92.
10 Mathew Y. H. Wong and Ying-ho Kwong, "Academic Censorship in China: The Case of *The China Quarterly*," *PS: Political Science and Politics* 52, no. 2 (2019): 287–92.
11 Zaixi Tan, "Censorship in Translation: The Case of the People's Republic of China," *Neohelicon* 42, no. 1 (2015): 313–39.
12 Lee, "China as Dystopia," 251.

of his novels have been prohibited."[13] Along with other contemporary writers who are known for their critical works about China, such as Ma Jian 馬建, as cited by Lee, Yan's participation in feeding into the "sensational value that derives from publishing prohibited works in translation" has bought him the ticket to "a place in the Anglo-American publishing industry."[14] While Lee's points are eloquently argued and his evidence of the paratextual materials of Yan's novels are factually accurate, there are fundamental questions left unanswered by his argument. First and foremost, his doubt about Yan's status of being a prohibited writer in China begs the question: has Yan really been effectively banned, or prohibited, in China, or is it simply an overstatement created for marketing purposes? Secondly, if he is indeed effectively prohibited, what are the mechanisms at work that have managed to disguise the true situation from Lee? Thirdly, is Yan, as suggested by Lee, simply a pawn or an accomplice who has benefited in the global literary market by feeding into the China-bashing cultural politics adopted in the West? Or does the visibility of Yan and his works symbolize something important to China watchers in the West? This article will attempt to respond to these three questions. To do so, I will provide an account and an analysis in what follows of the official censorship and unofficial censure Yan and his works have been subjected to. This will be done in chronological order for the purpose of offering a comprehensive and contextualized account of the events. Details of those events are taken from Yan's own narratives and media reports, and confirmed by Yan in my numerous formal and informal interviews with him. To conclude, I will explore the implications of the continuous circulation of Yan's works in spite of the prohibitions imposed on them.

Book bans and individual agency

Judging from Yan's present relationship with the Chinese political establishment, it is difficult to imagine him beginning his career as an army writer and staying in that position for almost two decades. Like all works produced for military units, his early works read almost like soft propaganda. What has brought about the change and the critical dimension in his works is unknown but such dimension was first noticed in 1994.

The first controversy concerned his novella "Summer Sunset" ("Xia Riluo" 夏日落, 1992). It came as a surprise, since before that, the novella had been well received in the Chinese literary establishment. A good example of this positive reception is the award it received from the *Journal of Selected Novellas* (*Zhongpian xiaoshuo xuankan* 中篇小說選刊). The Fujian-based journal was well esteemed; not only was it included on the list of national core journals, but it also received congratulations in 1996 on its fifteenth anniversary from high-level political leaders including Xi Jinping 習近平, then-Deputy Secretary of Fujian Provincial CCP Committee. Yan's novella "Summer Sunset" is about the repercussions of the suicide of a soldier named Xia Riluo, literally "summer sunset." Xia never appears in the story but is repeatedly mentioned by his superiors in the regiment whose careers risked being ruined by his suicide. The story contains no obvious anti-establishment contents, except references to small-scale "string-pulling" (*guanxi* 關係) manipulations within the army, all due to human weaknesses such as bending rules to get advantages in order to fulfill familial responsibilities. It is true that the novella depicts the human side of soldiers rather than glorifying them in the typical manner as "heroes of the people," but it hardly constitutes any

---

13 Ibid., 259.
14 Ibid., 260.

real criticism of the army. This is why subsequent trouble came as such a surprise for Yan. It all started from the rave review it received in the Hong Kong-based *Chengming Magazine*, praising it for "portraying the fallen souls of army personnels."[15] Yan considers the cause of this sudden downturn of fortune being the approval given by this high-profile magazine, known for its critical stance on Chinese affairs. This is typical of Maoist politics, "We support whatsoever is opposed by our enemies, and oppose whatsoever is supported by them."[16] In other words, the offense caused by the novella was not something intrinsic of itself, but by its possible recuperation into the critical discourse against the Chinese authorities. This resulted in the interruption of Yan's publication plans. He had to abolish the plan to publish the novella in book form and in his collection of fictions, as well as recalling two other novellas already accepted by journals. The whole business only quietened down after six months' repeated self-criticism in meetings and written submissions. Although he was anticipating a more drastic penalty against him, it never came. The storm passed as unexpectedly as it had come. Yan was told months later by "someone in the know" that further actions against him were avoided because of overseas media attention to his case.[17] If what this person told Yan was true, it is almost ironic that he was let off because once again the military was concerned about the possible discursive affiliation of the novella. Both its prohibition and pardon seemed to have been imposed for the same reason, one that was extrinsic, rather than intrinsic, to the novella.

This traumatic experience brought to Yan by the proscription of "Summer Sunset" was followed by a rather peaceful period. The second half of the 1990s saw a drastic shift in the concerns and methods of his fictions. Although he was still working in the military unit, he no longer wrote about soldiers, but about farmers struggling to survive in his native Henan Province. While "Summer Sunset" is essentially a realist story, "The Golden Cave" ("Huangjin dong" 黃金洞, 1996) and *The Years, Months, Days* (*Nian yue ri* 年月日, 1997), the most representative of his works in this period, are structured with surrealist conceits which would develop into his later Mythorealist style.[18] With these works, he made major advancement in his career, and was awarded the first (announced in 1998 for works published in 1995–96) and second (announced in 2001 for works published in 1997–2000) Lu Xun Literary Prize (*Lu Xun wenxue jiang* 魯迅文學獎), for "The Golden Cave" and *The Years, Months, Days*, respectively. The Lu Xun Literary Prize is one of the most prestigious literary awards in China organized by the official Writers' Association.

However, these successes and his established fame did not guarantee him a smooth passage in publishing further works. In 2000, he ran into trouble again for his novel *Hard Like Water* (*Jianying ru shui* 堅硬如水, 2009). It is a compelling satire of the power craze manifested by numerous factions during the Cultural Revolution. The protagonists' destructive and ultimately self-destructive desires for sex and power were portrayed as being underpinned by the Maoist formulae for political struggles, as expressed by their frequent quotation of political slogans attributed to Mao. Soon after the novel's publication, complaints about its sexual

---

15 Yan Lianke, *Xia Riluo* 夏日落 [Summer sunset] (Hong Kong: Hong Kong City University Press, 2020), 164.
16 Yan Lianke, "Xianggang: Wo de shenhua yu chuanshuo 香港——我的神話與傳說 [Hong Kong is my myth and my legend]," in his *Tuikai Zhongguo de lingwai yi shan chuang: Haiwai suibi ji* 推開中國的另外一扇窗: 海外隨筆集 [Opening the door of China: Yan Lianke's collected overseas writings] (Hong Kong: Hong Kong City University Press, 2020), 106–09.
17 Yan, *Xia Riluo* 夏日落, 163–65.
18 Yan Lianke, *Faxian xiaoshuo* 發現小說 [Discovering fiction] (Taipei: INK, 2011).

descriptions and political incorrectness were made all the way to the CCP's Propaganda Department and the State Administration of the Press and Publication. The novel narrowly escaped banning only after the Wuhan-based publisher went to lobby authorities in Beijing, but a prohibition on any book promotion was imposed in order to limit its impact.[19]

The same fate repeated itself in 2003 for Yan's next novel *Lenin's Kisses* (*Shouhuo* 受活). By this time, he had adopted satire as his main literary method. The novel satirizes the cynicism of China's post-1989 reform era, where socialism was only a name without substance. The country's rapid transition to a market economy has provoked unrelenting greed. In the novel, the ambitious social climbing cadre takes advantage of the dissolution of the Soviet Union and buys the corpse of Lenin, houses it in a purpose-built hall, not for the veneration of the former Soviet leader, but as a tourist attraction. Also used as a money spinner are the disabled villagers who are herded into touring as a circus. The message of the novel is clear: China, as represented by the microcosm of this village, is selling out its Socialist ideology and exploiting its people for money. The authorities would certainly find such a book objectionable. The Propaganda Department took it very seriously, and dedicated a special meeting to discussing it. However, ready acclaim for the novel's partial serialization prompted the Department to be cautious in its sanction. In order to avoid boosting the novel's profile with an official prohibition, it decided to allow its circulation but no promotion, reviews, or discussions would be allowed. Yet, the reputation of the novel had already traveled. Media attention did not stop. In October of that year, after an interview with Yan by the Hong Kong-based Phoenix TV Channel was aired, he was dismissed from the army. Fortuitously, Yan was offered a job at exactly the same time with the Beijing Writers' Association.[20] What is particularly noteworthy is that, in spite of such objections from the authorities, the novel continued to have an impact. It even went on to receive the Lao She Literary Award (*Lao She wenxue jiang* 老舍文學獎) in 2005. This award was organized by the Beijing Municipal Federation of Literary and Art Circles. This diametrically different reception of the novel by the political and the literary establishments speaks volumes about the complicated tension and tug-of-war discourses among the various social and political forces in China, and how literature sometimes finds cracks in the "Great Wall" of censorship, and manages to break out into the public domain. These details concerning the publication and reception of *Hard Like Water* and *Lenin's Kisses* show that censorship is not always clear-cut and absolute. There are complex dynamics at work involving numerous stakeholders exercising their agency to either enforce or resist censorship. A decade later when Yan was asked about his difficulties of publishing in China as a controversial writer, he attributed the overcoming of such difficulties to the efforts of conscientious intellectuals in the publishing industry.[21] It is with these details in mind that I would argue that literary censorship in China should not be understood simplistically as a one-dimensional tool of political control. Instead, it should be observed as a site where multiple and nuanced dynamics of repression and resistance are played out, and individual stakeholders find space to exercise their agency, however narrow those spaces are.

---

19 Xiao Yi 蕭逸, "Yan Lianke ershinian wenxue kanke lu" 閻連科二十年文學坎坷路 [Yan Lianke walks on the rough path for twenty years], Open.com.hk. 7 Aug. 2013, www.open.com.hk/content.php?id=1447#.YOAweBOA63I (last accessed 10 July 2021).

20 Yan, "Xianggang," 107.

21 Echo Hui, "*Nanzao* Zhongwen zhuanfang Yan Lianke: Zhongguo chuban zhidu mei name zao" 南早中文專訪閻連科: 中國出版制度沒那麼糟 [*South China Morning Post* Chinese edition interviews Yan Lianke: The system of publishing in China isn't that bad], Nanzao.com, 4 Nov. 2013, http://ias.ust.hk/events/cwp/includes/media/2013/20131104_liu_zaifu_scmp.pdf (last accessed 10 July 2021).

Yan's next work, *Serve the People!* (*Wei renmin fuwu* 為人民服務, 2005), was given an even harsher treatment by the political establishment. The novella continues with the theme in *Hard Like Water* and lays bare how people's daily life is penetrated by politics in China, so much so that the personal can only be expressed when it is mediated and justified by the political. The main plot of the novella is an affair between a soldier and the wife of his superior. Like *Hard Like Water*, the couple's relationship is mediated by Maoist slogans and the political hierarchy they are steeped in, and depicted with an even sharper satirical edge by giving the iconic Maoist slogan "serve the people" a secondary meaning with reference to sexual favors. The first half of the novella was published in the first issue of the Guangzhou-based literary magazine *Huacheng* 花城 in 1995. Immediately the magazine received an instruction not only to halt publication of the rest of the novella in the next issue but also to recall the copies of the first issue that were still in circulation. An official ban was jointly issued by the Propaganda Department and the State Administration of Press and Publication and widely circulated in writing. This is unusual because most book bans in the PRC until that time had been executed by oral instructions, without official written records. This treatment for *Serve the People!* showed the seriousness of the situation. Criticisms were launched against the work for defaming Mao Zedong, defaming the noble spirit of Mao in "serving the people," defaming the people's army, defaming revolution and politics, indulging in sexual descriptions, causing bad influence on people's mind, and promoting wrong ideas from the West. These strongly worded criticisms were attributed to Li Changchun 李長春 and Liu Yunshan 劉雲山, both top-level members of the CCP leadership on the Standing Committee of the Political Bureau of the CPC Central Committee, and the latter also Chief of the Propaganda Department.[22]

Working with censorship has become routine for Yan since then. When *Dream of Ding Village* (*Dingzhuang meng* 丁莊夢), a novel about a village infested with AIDS, was published in 2006, the Propaganda Department and the State Administration of the Press and Publication requested the book to be submitted for censorship before it hit the market, and criticized the novel's pessimistic tone in its portrayal of AIDS in China.[23] For a while, the novel was taken off the shelf in bookshops across the country. Caution also needed to be exercised in adapting it into a film in 2011. The film's title *Love for Life* (*Zui'ai* 最愛) carried no reference to the novel. No mention was made in the film's production record about it being an adaptation of Yan's novel. His involvement in the script was also disguised by the pseudonym Yan Laoshi 言老施, homophones of "Teacher Yan," as Yan was addressed by his colleagues in the film production.[24] Similarly, in 2008, Yan's new novel *The Book of Song* (*Feng ya song* 風雅頌) was severely criticized for portraying academics and the academic establishment in China in a negative light, even though Yan had already incorporated many changes suggested to him in order to pass censorship.[25] The most difficult situation was encountered in the attempted publication of *The Four Books* (*Si shu* 四書). In 2011 Yan approached almost twenty publishers

---

22 Jiang Xun 江迅, "2005 nian diyi ben jinshu 'wei renmin fuwu'" 2005 年第一部禁書「為人民服務」 [The first banned book in 2005 *Serve the People!*], Inmedia, 16 Mar. 2005, https://www.inmediahk.net/node/20330 (last accessed 10 July 2021).
23 Jiang Xun, "Yongbao aizicun de wenxue guanhuai" 擁抱艾滋村的文學關懷 [Compassionate literature that embraces an AIDS infested village], *Yazhou zhoukan* 亞洲週刊 (Asia Week), 2006, no. 16, https://www.yzzk.com/article/details/文化/2006-16/1367466106046/擁抱艾滋村的文學關懷 (last accessed 10 July 2021).
24 Lou, "Yan Lianke zui manyi zuopin *Si shu*."
25 Renqi 人氣, "Yan Lianke: Yi zuojia de mingyi shenpan zhe ge guojia" 閻連科：以作家的名義審判這個國家 [Yan Lianke: In the name of an author he puts this country on trial], *Epoch Times*, 17 Jan. 2017, https://www.epochtimes.com/b5/17/1/17/n8713240.htm (last accessed 10 July 2021).

with the manuscript to no avail. He was told by almost all of these apologetic publishers that if they published it, their publishing company was almost sure to be closed down.[26] The novel was eventually published in Hong Kong and Taiwan. This powerful fiction set in a Chinese labor camp of the late 1950s during the Great Famine made it to the shortlist of the Man Booker Prize for 2016, and was responsible to a large extent for his Kafka Prize award in 2014. *The Four Books* has been translated into multiple languages but is yet to be published in mainland China to date. *The Day the Sun Died* (*Rixi* 日熄, 2015) and *Heart Sutra* (*Xinjing* 心經, 2020) were also only published in Taiwan and Hong Kong, respectively. In the case of *Heart Sutra*, the decision not even to approach publishers in the Chinese mainland was due to the novelist's reluctance to submit the manuscript to censorship reading.[27] One may conjecture that a similar decision regarding *The Day the Sun Died* was made for exactly the same reason.

The difference in the sizes of readership inside and outside the Chinese mainland could be fully appreciated by contemplating the following figures: one hundred and fifteen thousand copies of the first edition of *Dream of Ding Village* was printed by Shanghai Literature and Arts Publishing House,[28] but the first print of *The Four Books* published in Hong Kong only ran to five thousand copies. In spite of the small number of copies in circulation, publishing in Hong Kong and Taiwan had been a possible means of dissemination until the Chinese authorities clamped down on importing books from these two territories on the Chinese periphery. An iconic case in this change of circumstances was the Causeway Bay Books incident. In 2015, five Hong Kong booksellers of Causeway Bay Books were taken by the Chinese authority, in mainland China and allegedly in Hong Kong and Thailand, for publishing and bringing into mainland China books that were banned in the country.[29] Before that, there were a number of bookshops in Hong Kong specializing in selling books about Chinese affairs banned on the mainland. They served a sizeable clientele made up mainly of mainland Chinese tourists. Some Chinese readers also ordered those books from Hong Kong bookshops on the internet, and the booksellers would carry the books across the border to mail them in Shenzhen, since checking at the Hong Kong borders was still relatively relaxed. Yan's books, together with other banned authors such as Wang Lixiong 王力雄 and Yu Jie 余杰 were circulated in China through such means.[30] Once again, this shows the resourcefulness of literary stakeholders in coping with censorship by exercising individual agency.

---

26 Yan Lianke, "Sangjiaquan de yinian" 喪家犬的一年 [The year of the stray dog], in his *Tuikai Zhongguo de lingwai yi shan chuang*, 2.
27 Yan Lianke, "Fenhen yu ziji de xiezuo yu rensheng" 憤恨於自己的寫作與人生 [Resentment, my writings, and life]," in his *Tuikai Zhongguo de lingwai yi shan chuang*, vii–ix.
28 Tong Li 童立 and Cai Zhen 蔡震, "Yan Lianke wei aizicun zhuanggao chubanshe: Cheng buneng qipian duzhe" 閻連科為愛滋病村狀告出版社 稱不能欺騙讀者 [Yan Lianke sues his publishing for an AIDS infested village: He says one must not lie to readers], Xinlang 新浪(Sina), 4 Sep. 2006, http://book.sina.com.cn/news/c/2006-09-04/1104204423.shtml (last accessed 10 July 2021).
29 Ilaria Maria Sala, "Four Hong Kong Publishers Known for Books Critical of Chinese Regime Missing," *The Guardian*, 9 Nov. 2015, https://www.theguardian.com/world/2015/nov/09/hong-kong-publishers-gui-haiming-lu-bo-zhang-zhiping-lin-rongji-missing-china (last accessed July 2021).
30 Wang Lixiong is an influential social critic who advocates reform in China's political system, and has written extensively on the issue of ethnic minorities in China. He is the author of *Yellow Peril* (1991), *Sky Burial: The Fate of Tibet* (1998), and *West Region to Me, East Turkestan to You* (2007). Yu Jie is a dissident Chinese writer exiled to the United States since 2007.

Public prohibition and private regulation

"The Year of the Stray Dog" is a particularly moving essay in which Yan recorded his unhappy year of 2011.[31] That year, after the difficulty his son encountered in his job hunt and his own failure in publishing *The Four Books* in mainland China, he and his neighbors were notified that their houses on the outskirts of Beijing were to be demolished for a road-widening project. No official letters from any government departments were served to them, and no proper negotiations for compensation were conducted, although every household was offered a sum that would not even have bought a toilet in a respectable district in Beijing. They protested for months. On the eve of the demolition date, he posted an open letter on his blog addressed to then General Secretary of the CCP, Hu Jintao 胡錦濤, and State Premier, Wen Jiabao 溫家寶, to appeal for their intervention.[32] There was no official response to this letter, but it was reposted widely and aroused much attention from the media. Yet, this public attention did not prevent the demolition. A few days after that one of his neighbors was forcibly vacated and his house bulldozed. Eventually, they had no alternative but to comply.[33] Emotionally exhausted, Yan returned to his hometown during the Chinese New Year of 2012 (around the end of January and early February) to spend the festival with his mother and siblings. On the last day of his visit, his mother, elder brother, and elder sister all tried to persuade him not to write anything more to antagonize the government. In Yan's account of this incident, as he drove away from them and joined the expressway, he could not control his tears.

What happened on that leave-taking occasion on the last day of Yan's homecoming visit was a moment when censorship and prohibition in the public domain became transformed into constraint and regulation of behavior in the private domain. Such a transfer is certainly possible in any society when familial concern deters individuals from taking political risks. However, when this happens in rural China, the communal moral codes of the Chinese village endow it with very specific force. Fei Xiaotong 費孝通 characterizes the structure of traditional Chinese social relationships as one of "a differential mode of association."[34] In other words, radiating away from the self is a hierarchy of intimacy and shared interest. In this structure, familial ties are particularly binding, since they represent the immediate circle outside the self. Collective consensus or social values are always trumped by close familial or clannish associations. It is private morality defined by familial obligations rather than social contracts that imposes the most powerful restraints and regulations on individual behaviors.[35]

---

31 Yan, "Sangjiaquan de yinian."
32 Yan Lianke, "Zuojia Yan Lianke Weibo zhi zhongli gongkaixin: Shoudu qiangchai shijian" 作家閻連科微博致總理公開信: 首都強拆事件 [The writer Yan Lianke's open letter to the Premier on Weibo: On the incident of forced demolition in the capital], Xinlang Weibo 新浪微博 (Sina Weibo), 30 Nov. 2011, https://cul.sohu.com/20120209/n334240537.shtml (last accessed 10 July 2021).
33 In 2012, Yan published a collection of essays entitled *Beijing, zuihou de jinian: Wo yu 711 hao yuan* 北京, 最後的紀念: 我與711號園 [Beijing, the last remembrance: No 711 and me]. On the surface, the essays record the tranquil life the author had lived in that house in the rural setting, but the well-known fact of its forced demolition cast a shadow over the tranquil tone of the essays. The book becomes both a remnant and a symbol of the author's defiance not only in literary matters as a writer but in life as an ordinary member of society.
34 Fei Xiaotong, *From the Soil: The Foundations of Chinese Society* (Berkeley: University of California Press, 1992).
35 Ibid., 71–72.

Scholars have debated whether this has changed in contemporary China,[36] and Cao Jinqing 曹錦清 and Zhang Letian 張樂天 maintain that this model has continued into the modernization of the Chinese agricultural society, especially in the organization of modern rural entrepreneurs.[37] Many village and county-based agricultural businesses are contracted to fixed local families for long periods of time. Their setups and operations are almost a direct replica of the old familial-economic structure of pre-modern rural China. Xiong Feng 熊峰 and Yu Pan 余盼 basically concur with this view, but paint a more complicated picture.[38] According to them, in the 1950s familial association was indeed replaced by class comradeship. That was achieved not only by ideological didacticism but to a very large extent by hard measures in political campaigns and state recuperation of all production resources. When the family or clan as a unit lost its authority and function in resource distribution, the differential mode of association, privileging familial ties, as described by Fei, disintegrated. However, this was reversed in the 1980s when the contract system of production was introduced. The function of the family as a unit of economic production returned to some degree. This is particularly important since the absolute state power in the "socialist system with Chinese characteristics" still rendered ownership of private property unstable. As a result, familial associations still performed the function to bind and protect shared interests. Xiong and Yu describe this as a bonding of "affection + advantage." Individuals still need the help of their families, and therefore they take care to maintain close relationships with their families in order to secure their interests. "The individual is not only a family-self, but a site of relationships: he is an individual bound up in myriads of personal relationships."[39]

When Yan bade farewell to his family at the end of his Chinese New Year homecoming visit, he was bombarded by their well-meaning advice not to antagonize government authorities. The most poignant aspect of this is the positioning of his family in the scenario of Yan vs Authorities. While they showered him with familial love, they expressed no support for his position. Worse still, they objected to the reasons for his actions. I interpret Yan's emotional reaction to this, according to his own description, as a response to tremendous pressure which functioned on two levels. On one level, it was affection. Yan was aware of his family's worries for his safety and well-being. On the second level, it was advantage. The fact that his family actually voiced out their opinions on his business was a subtle reminder that he was an integral part of his family's network of interests. In a system where the interests of the individual and the family are bound up together, as in the Chinese rural structure, his family was concerned about their family members' relationship with the powerful state. There is one more important detail in this episode: it was the senior members of the family—his mother, elder brother, and elder sister—speaking through his

---

36 Du Heqi 杜何琪, Wang Ying 王熒, and Liu Shuo 劉碩, "Xiandaihua hui xueruo nongcun chuantong renji guanxi ma 現代化會削弱農村傳統人際關係嗎 [Does modernization weaken traditional interpersonal relationships in rural areas]," *Shanxi nongye daxue xuebao (shehui kexue ban)* (Journal of Shangxi Agricultural University [Social Science Edition]) 19, no. 4 (2020): 80–88.

37 Cao Jinqing and Zhang Letian, "Chuantong xiangcun de shehui wenhua tezheng: Renqing yu guanxi wang—Yi ge Zhebei cunluo de weiguan kaocha yu toushi" 傳統鄉村的社會文化特徵：人情與關係網——一個浙北村落的微觀考察與透視 [Social-cultural characteristics in traditional villages: Human feelings and networks of relationships—A micro-view and fieldwork in a north Zhejiang village], *Tansuo yu zhengming* 探索與爭鳴 [Exploration and free views], 1992, no. 2: 51–59.

38 Xiong Feng and Yu Pan, "Nongcun renji guanxi de jiegouxing yaosu ji qi bianqian" 農村人際關係的結構性要素及其變遷 [The structural factors of interpersonal relationships in rural villages and their changes], *Wuhan fangzhi daxue xuebao* 武漢紡織大學學報 (Journal of Wuhan Textile University) 28, no. 4 (2015): 84–87.

39 Ibid., 85–86; my translation.

nephew, who gave Yan the advice. In other words, the demand to comply with state authorities was spoken to him through the authority of the family elders.[40] This repression of Yan's will as an individual was not only transferred from the public to the private domain of the familial context but was also executed at maximum strength by the elders of his family.

Netizen censure

In the second half of the 2010s, Yan has taken up part-time residence in Hong Kong. He still publishes on the Chinese mainland occasional essays and less overtly political works, such as *Shes* (*Tamen* 她們), a non-fictional work about four generations of women in his family; some of his lectures and speeches delivered overseas are accessible to mainland Chinese readers on the other side of the country's digital Great Firewall; some are also reposted on Chinese websites and social media, sometimes in full, and sometimes in part as quotations. While these choices made by Yan might indicate his wish to get out of the frying-pan of state censorship, little did he know that he would be jumping into the fire of popular criticism on the internet. Indeed, he has become a frequent object of criticism by nationalistic writers of online media, bloggers, and netizens on social media. Those criticisms of Yan converge with the aggressive verbal attacks on public figures and international brands who have done or said something that "hurt the feelings of the Chinese people," a meme that is widely circulated in both Chinese diplomacy and patriotic posts by netizens. One famous example of this was the Dolce & Gabbana incident: a Chinese model was shown in a D&G advertisement eating Italian food with chopsticks. Nationalistic netizens interpreted this as an insult to the Chinese people and launched a boycott campaign against the brand.[41] Another example was the boycott campaign against a number of fashion brands including Nike, Adidas, Hugo, and H&M after they made the decision to cease using cotton from Xinjiang suspected of being produced through forced labor of the Uyghur population.[42]

One of the more serious recent internet attacks on Yan took place in 2020 in the early stage of the Covid-19 pandemic. During the total lockdown of the city of Wuhan, where the pandemic allegedly originated, the local writer Fang Fang 方方 published on the Weibo Social Media sixty essays in the form of a diary to record the situation of the city.[43] Not only was her Weibo account temporarily suspended, a huge backlash of Cultural-Revolutionary-style abusive warfare was also waged against her and her supporters.[44] Yan was one of her supporters.

---

40 An interesting discussion of the authority and function of the elderly in the rural areas of Hunan, Yan's home province can be found in Liu Yongqiang 劉永強 and Yao Linru 姚林茹, "Nongcun chuantong da jiating zhong laoren hexin ningjuli wenti de gean yanjiu: Yi Henansheng Y xiang S xiang G cun Liu shi da jiating weili" 農村傳統大家庭中老人核心凝聚力問題的個案研究——以河南省Y縣S鄉G村劉氏大家庭為例 [The elderly as core cohesion in rural traditional families: A case study of the extensive Liu family in G Village, S Township, Y County, Henan Province], *Laoling kexue yanjiu zazhi* 老齡科學研究雜誌 [Scientific research on aging] 3, no. 10 (2015): 60–71.
41 BBC, "'Racist' D&G Ad: Chinese Model Says Campaign Almost Ruined Career," 23 Jan. 2019, https://www.bbc.com/news/world-asia-china-46968750 (last accessed 10 July 2021).
42 Nik Martin, "Xinjiang Cotton Boycott Leaves Western Brands Reeling," DWnews, 8 Apr. 2021, https://www.dw.com/en/xinjiang-cotton-boycott-leaves-western-brands-reeling/a-57130450 (last accessed 10 July 2021).
43 Fang Fang, "Wuhan riji" 武漢日記 [Wuhan diary], Caixin wang 財新網, 25 Jan.–25 Mar. 2020, https://web.archive.org/web/20200327102104/http://m.app.caixin.com/m_topic_detail/1489.html (last accessed July 2021).
44 Hemant Adlakha, "Fang Fang: The 'Conscience of Wuhan' amid Coronavirus Quarantine," *The Diplomat*, 23 Mar. 2020, https://thediplomat.com/2020/03/fang-fang-the-conscience-of-wuhan-amid-coronavirus-quarantine/ (last accessed 10 July 2021).

He spoke out for her on two occasions. One was in a speech delivered in the Hong Kong University of Science and Technology, which was reprinted in a Hong Kong online media site.[45] The speech was entitled "What Happens after Coronavirus? On Community Memory and Repeating Our Own Mistakes."[46] In this speech, he asked his listeners to imagine the loss of our community memory without Fang Fang's record of Wuhan under lockdown. The second occasion was a comment he posted on social media: "We have to thank Fangfang for picking up the face that writers and literature have lost and trampled on the ground,"[47] lauding her for being the only writer with the courage to write about the situation of Wuhan against the government's attempt to block transparency. This comment has been widely quoted by netizens, some in support of him and Fang Fang, but many more are against them.

A few months after that, on 10 Mar. 2021, Yan gave his online speech as recipient of the Newman Prize for Chinese Literature. The speech was entitled "A Village Bigger than the World." He explained how his own worldview as expressed in his works had been informed by life in the village of his birth, and by his native language of Chinese, in order to argue for the relevance of the people and their experience in even the humblest corner of the world in the contexts of globalization and world literature. The content of the speech was apolitical and was not expected to cause any offense. However, some nationalistic netizens picked up on an episode he recounted in the speech and accused him of appeasing foreigners, specifically, the Japanese. The episode in question involves an old lady in Yan's village. In 1945 as a little girl, she watched the defeated Japanese soldiers retreat. One of the soldiers in tatters, and with wounds still bleeding, handed a candy to her. That was the first candy she had ever tasted. Now she was an old lady; every time she saw scenes on TV or heard villagers talk about the bad blood between the Chinese and the Japanese peoples, she would remember that soldier and want to bring something to him in Japan. Yan concluded this episode with a note of sympathy for the old lady. He said that in 2014 the first Japanese translation of his works was published. It was his way of bringing something to Japan on behalf of that old lady. This speech was given at a time when the controversy over Fang Fang's *Wuhan Diary* (*Wuhan riji* 武漢日記) still lingered, and the antagonism toward Japan (as an aftermath of the WWII eighty years ago) continued to be mobilized to nurture nationalistic sentiments.[48] Yan's innocuous

45 Yan Lianke, "Jing ci yijie, rang women chengwei you jixing de ren" 經此疫劫，讓我們成為有記性的人 [What happens after coronavirus? On community memory and repeating our own mistakes], Duan chuanmei 端傳媒 (Intimum Media), 21 Feb. 2020, https://theinitium.com/article/20200221-mainland-coronavirus-yanlianke (last accessed 10 July 2021).
46 Ibid.
47 Quoted in China Business Focus, "Naxie mingren gongkai zhichi Fang Fang?" 哪些名人公開支持方方？ [Which celebrities have openly supported Fang Fang?]" 25 Apr. 2020, https://www.163.com/dy/article/FB28CPO4053770WR.html (last accessed 10 July 2021); Sun Lan 孫瀾, "Fang Fang bei 'bangjia' yu silie de Zhongguo yulunchang" 被「綁架」的方方與撕裂的中國輿論場 [Fang Fang being 'hijacked' and the split in China's public opinions], DWnews, 8 Apr. 2020, https://www.dwnews.com/中國/60174801/新冠肺炎輿情被綁架的方方與撕裂的中國輿論場 (last accessed 10 July 2021); Guo Songmin 郭松民, "Fang Fang de lian yu Yan Lianke de lian" 方方的臉與閻連科的臉 [Fang Fang's face and Yan Lianke's face], Guanchazhe 觀察者 [Observer], 15 Apr. 2020, https://user.guancha.cn/main/content?id=287790 (last accessed July 2021).
48 Parks M. Coble, "China's 'New Remembering' of the Anti-Japanese War of Resistance, 1937–1945," *China Quarterly* 190 (2007): 394–410; Jeremy L. Wallace and Jessica Chen Weiss, "The Political Geography of Nationalist Protest in China: Cities and the 2012 Anti-Japanese Protests," *China Quarterly* 222 (2015): 403–29; Kevin Foley, Jeremy L. Wallace, and Jessica Chen Weiss, "The Political and Economic Consequences of Nationalist Protest in China: The 2012 Anti-Japanese Demonstrations," *China Quarterly* 236 (2018): 1131–53.

argument for literature being a means to create peace and empathy, even between former enemies, caught the attention of nationalistic writers on internet media and netizens who overinterpreted it as a sign of the treasonous tendency that they claimed Yan had promoted.[49] This is most unfortunate for the novelist, because discourses like this displace his consistent (internal) critique on the People's Republic of China after 1949, and equate it anachronistically to a treasonous pro-Japanese position during Japan's invasion of China, which had both occurred and ended before the PRC government took power. Such displacing tactics function for his opponents to claim the moral high ground and discredit Yan's critique on the PRC.

Many similar tactics to neutralize critiques of the Chinese government have been adopted as a measure of governance in China. It is true that the scale and diversity of expression enabled on the internet have presented a new challenge for the Chinese government in their regulation of dissent, but as Gary King, Jennifer Pan, and Margaret E. Roberts have obtained and analyzed empirical evidence to prove, the government has also made effective use of the internet to curb expressions of dissent by funding huge numbers of "50-centers" (*wumao* 五毛) to populate the virtual space with pro-government views and attack anti-government opinion holders.[50] These are social media users (among them many hold day jobs in government units) who are recruited to do this, and allegedly paid RMB 50 cents per post or comment. This works not only in tandem with official censorship to restrain dissent but also to engineer a pro-government social atmosphere. However, it is important not to hasten to conclude that all attacks on Yan on the internet are fabricated by government cheerleaders, since not all 50-centers are paid. Supporting the government alongside these paid government agents are individual netizens often referred to as "the voluntary 50-cents army" who champion the cause to defend the government.[51] Their passionate nationalistic orientation can be explained by the ideological changes in the country after 1989. After the Tian'anmen Square incident followed the dissolution of the *qimeng* 啓蒙 movement, advocacy for enlightened and critical reflection of the Chinese culture and society.[52] The moral vacuum resulting from the process, which Ci Jiwei describes as the desublimation of the *qimeng* ideal, has left an ideological space for nationalistic indoctrination by the state.[53] According to Han Rongbin, the cyber nationalism characterizing

---

49 Qingfeng 青鋒, "Yan Lianke de yi ke tang: Yaowei qilian huan bulai ai yu heping" 閻連科的一顆糖——搖尾乞憐換不來愛與和平 [Yan Lianke's candy: Love and peace cannot be found by getting down on your knees], zhihu.com, 16 Mar. 2021, https://zhuanlan.zhihu.com/p/357523085 (last accessed 10 July 2021); Gu Minghao 古明浩, "Bo Yan Lianke de rijun tangguo" 駁閻連科的日軍糖果 [Against Yan Lianke's candy of the Japanese soldier], Minzu fuxing wang 民族復興網 [Website of nation rejuvenation], 19 Mar. 2021, www.mzfxw.com/e/action/ShowInfo.php?classid=8&id=149269 (last accessed 10 July 2021); Xuezhong Fengche 雪中風車, "Yan Lianke: Gaoming er yinsun de 'yi kuai tang'" 閻連科: 高明而陰損的「一塊糖」 [Yan Lianke: The clever but vicious "candy"], 163.com, 25 Mar. 2021, https://3g.163.com/dy/article_cambrian/G5U8C8FP0523C0OR.html (last accessed 10 July 2021).
50 Gary King, Jennifer Pan, and Margaret E. Roberts, "How Censorship in China Allows Government Criticism but Silences Collective Expression," *American Political Science Review* 107, no. 2 (2013): 326–43.
51 Rongbin Han, "Defending the Authoritarian Regime Online: China's 'Voluntary Fifty-Cent Army'," *China Quarterly* 224 (Oct. 2015): 1006–25.
52 Xu Jilin 許紀霖, "Qimeng de mingyun: Ershi nian lai de Zhongguo sixiangjie" 啟蒙的命運——二十年來的中國思想界 [The fate of enlightenment: Chinese intellectuals in the past twenty years], *Twenty-First Century Bimonthly*, 1998, no. 50: 4–13.
53 Ci Jiwei, "The Dialectic of the Chinese Revolution Revisited: Desublimation and Resublimation in Post-Mao China," in *Contemporary Chinese Political Thought*, ed. Fred and Zhao Tingyang Dallmayr (Lexington: University Press of Kentucky, 2012), 173–78; Zhao Suisheng, "A State-Led Nationalism: The Patriotic Education Campaign in Post-Tiananmen China," *Communist and Post-Communist Studies* 31, no. 3 (1998): 287–302.

China of the new millennium is a continuation and manifestation of the post-1989 "state-fed nationalism."[54] The aim of this is to "stabilize the regime, not so much by legitimizing it, but by undermining the moral and factual grounds of regime challengers."[55]

This is exactly how popular censure against Yan on the internet operates. By labeling him unpatriotic and aligning him with the historical treasonous pro-Japanese position (although anachronistically), the 50-centers aim at discrediting him and thereby neutralizing his critiques of the Chinese society shaped by CCP policies. Observing the changes in the form of repression of Yan's expression from the early 1990s to the present would show a significant shift in strategy: the "authority vs Yan" model relying on book bans and censorship is no longer the only or main tactic. An alternative is now available to the state after decades of nationalistic education in the school system and through what Lagerkvist describes as "ideotainment," popular entertainment that fulfills ideological purposes.[56] With the vast armies of paid and voluntary 50-centers, a "people vs Yan" scenario is created. The repression of Yan's expression is turned into an act of public theatre of legitimizing the state with the voice of "the people." Yan's expression, and by extension other critical or dissenting voices, are therefore to be handled and probably made good use of, rather than repressed altogether. To the authorities, popular censure is therefore a more productive tactic than official censorship in some cases, and the two form a two-tier safety mechanism for the state to manage public opinions.

Some comparisons

In order to understand why Yan Lianke's particular circumstances represent an iconic case in the phenomenon of Chinese censorship, it is perhaps useful to compare his situation with a few of his contemporaries, who are also acclaimed for their critical literary creations. A good comparison is Jia Pingwa 賈平凹. Jia was born in 1952, six years earlier than Yan, but he started his writing career and found success much earlier. One of the representative writers of the Root-searching Movement of the 1980s,[57] he established his fame with the series of short stories set in Shangzhou ("Shangzhou xilie" 商州系列), which were poignant reflections of the social structures and human relationships in rural China. His novel *Turbulence* (*Fuzao* 浮躁, 1987) is one of the most influential contemporary Chinese novels, and explores and critiques the changes in the psychology of the rural population during China's modernization. His novel *The Ruined City* (*Feidu* 廢都), which was published in 1993, only four years after the 1989 Tian'anmen Square incident, satirizes the moral vacuum experienced by intellectuals in the post-1989 years. Its descriptions of sex and nihilism, coupled with frequent insinuations of censorship and self-censorship, got the novel banned very soon after its initial publication, and the ban lasted for seventeen years until 2009. His subsequent works are much more subtle, although he does not shy away from derogatory details about the system. One example of this is the novel *The Lantern Bearer* (*Dai deng* 帶燈, 2013). Many details and criticisms of

---

54 Han Rongbin, "Patriotism without State Blessing: Chinese Cyber Nationalists in a Predicament," in *Handbook of Protest and Resistance in China*, ed. Teresa Wright (Cheltenham, UK: Edward Elgar Publishing, 2019), 347.
55 Han, "Defending the Authoritarian Regime Online," 1021.
56 Johan Lagerkvist, "Internet Ideotainment in the PRC: National Responses to Cultural Globalization," *Journal of Contemporary China* 17, no. 54 (2008): 121–40.
57 A cultural and literary movement that advocated critical reflection of Chinese culture and Chinese modernization as a response to the traumatic years of the Cultural Revolution. See Han Shaogong 韓少功, "Wenxue de 'Gen'" 文學的根 [The 'roots' of literature], *Zuojia* 作家 [Writers], 1985, no. 4: 2–5.

the ineffective system of China's rural governance are included in the novel, yet the publication of this and the rest of his works seems to have been trouble-free. His subtle critiques of the system have found safe passage thanks to the low profile maintained by the novelist himself. His participation in the official literary establishment, such as taking up the position of the current Chairman of the Shaanxi Province Writers' Association, has also made him a very acceptable figure. There are many different ways to express critiques, and Jia has simply adopted strategies very different from Yan. Actions such as defying house demolition and writing an open petition to the country's leaders, as Yan has done, are simply unimaginable with Jia.

Another interesting contrast with Yan is the 2012 Nobel laureate Mo Yan 莫言. Like Jia, he found literary success early. His novella series, *Red Sorghum* (*Hong gaoliang jiazu* 紅高粱家族, 1988), is acclaimed to have inaugurated magical realism in contemporary Chinese literature. He shares a similar background with Yan, having come from a background of rural poverty and joined the military as an army writer, and then got into trouble with the military establishment for the critical works he wrote. He was dismissed from the army in 1996 for portraying Communists in a negative light and breaking sexual taboos in his novel *Big Breasts, Wide Hips* (*Fengru feitun* 豐乳肥臀). For decades he has been esteemed as one of the most critical writers. However, in recent years he has been criticized for aligning himself with Xi Jinping's authority.[58] A similarly ambivalent figure is the visual artist Ai Weiwei 艾未未. Having championed civil rights in China for years and having been detained by the Chinese police for 81 days in 2011, Ai has been criticized in recent years for having been inconsistent in his position by tweeting pro-democratic views in English but posting pro-government views on Chinese social media, especially against human rights activists' campaign for Liu Xiaobo's 劉曉波 release just before the death of the Nobel Peace laureate.[59] He has also come under fire for the comments he made in 2015 in Germany immediately after he left China, comments that sounded almost like a justification for the arrests of human rights lawyers in China.[60] The inconsistency of Mo Yan's and Ai Weiwei's public opinions stand in stark

---

58 Jiang Xun, "Mo Yan Nobei'er wenxue jiang xiaoying wenxue vs zhengzhi" 莫言諾貝爾獎效應文學vs政治 [The effect of Mo Yan's Nobel Prize for Literature: Literature vs politics], *Yazhou zhoukan*, 2012, no. 43, https://www.yzzk.com/article/details/封面專題%2F2012-43%2F1363610920983%2F莫言諾貝爾獎效應文學vs政治 (last accessed 10 July 2021); Hou Mingqing 侯明清, "Chumai linghun zhe neng huo Nuobei'er wenxue jiang ma?" 出賣靈魂者能獲得諾貝爾文學獎嗎? [Should a person who has sold his soul get the Nobel Prize for Literature?], Aisixiang 愛思想, 4 Oct. 2012, https://m.aisixiang.com/data/58089.html (last accessed 10 July 2021); Chen Can 陳燦 and Lin Lu 林露, eds., "Wendaihui zuodaihui lai la: Mo Yan Jiang Kun Xu Fan Liang Xiaosheng Huang Bo dou shuo le sha" 文代會作代會來啦: 莫言姜昆徐帆梁曉聲黃渤都說了啥 [The coming of representatives' meetings of China Writers' Association and China Federation of Literary and Art Circles: What have Mo Yan, Jiang Kun, Xu Fan, Liao Xiaosheng and Huang Bo said], People.cn. 1 Dec. 2016, http://culture.people.com.cn/BIG5/n1/2016/1201/c87423-28917794-2.html (last accessed 10 July 2021).
59 After the row with Liao Yiwu 廖亦武, Ai was interviewed by independent film director Zhang Zanbo 張贊波 in which he commented on his stance about the Liu Xiaobo affairs. In that interview, he also revealed that he did not whole-heartedly support Charter 08 but only put his signature down because Liu was arrested. Charter 08 was a Charter advocating for democracy and human rights in China. It was drafted by Liu Xiaobo et al. in 2008 and signed by over one thousand pro-democratic activists in China; Liao Yiwu, "Kan Ai Weiwei zenmo dihui Liu Xiaobo" 看艾未未怎麼詆毀劉曉波 [Look at how Ai Weiwei slandered Liu Xiaobo], Upmedia, 15 Aug. 2017, https://www.upmedia.mg/news_info.php?SerialNo=22711%0A2 (last accessed 10 July 2021).
60 Sang Pu 桑普, "Ai Weiwei de duoluo" 艾未未的墮落 [Ai Weiwei's fall from grace], *Minbao* 民報 (Taiwan People News), 17 Aug. 2015, https://www.peoplenews.tw/news/b0fdb818-05a4-40cf-9b73-c8c21d6c3527 (last accessed 10 July 2021).

contrast to Yan's unwavering critiques of contemporary Chinese history. Flexible views can be easily brushed aside, because the speakers are self-contradicting. Ai's case is a good example of this. Even though he has in recent times re-adopted his critical stance against the Chinese government, for example, on the Hong Kong social movement for greater autonomy of the territory,[61] his advocacy is no longer as effective as it was in the early 2010s, probably because many might now be taking his dissent with a pinch of salt.

Two other useful comparisons with Yan are Gao Xingjian 高行健 and Ma Jian 馬建. Both have lived in exile in order to avoid persecution for their critical writings. Gao has ceased writing about Chinese realities since his play *Fugitives* (*Taowang* 逃亡, 1990) which is a philosophical debate about living and dying between three fugitives of the June Fourth Tiananmen incident. His other works published since then are either set in France, or reminiscences of life in China during the Cultural Revolution. None of Gao's works are accessible in China, and discussions of his old works are also rare. From his present residence in London, Ma Jian has continued to publish poignantly critical works about the Chinese society and government in his latest fictions such as *The Dark Road* (*Yin zhi dao* 陰之道, 2012) and *China Dream* (*Zhongguo meng* 中國夢, 2018). He has also written occasional opinions and received interviews in the British mainstream media to air his critical views on China. However, like Gao, Ma's voice is not heard in China, since without continuous presence in China, as Yan has maintained,[62] Ma's channel of communication with the literary stakeholders in the country has been extremely limited, and therefore his voice is not represented at all.

Censorship and "the structure of presence"

By comparison with the (involuntary) absence of Gao Xingjian and Ma Jian from China, let's review Yan Lianke's presence and the functions of such presence. Yan is living most of the time in mainland China, although Hong Kong has become his second home, where he teaches for a few months every year. Most of his writings are accessible in China and, if not published in book form, appear on a good number of pirate websites. Many readers continue to be curious about his works, if not for appreciation of them, ironically, because of the internet attacks against him. He is also interviewed in the media, and is definitely active in teaching, and in exchange and other activities organized among the close-knit literary community of mainland China, Hong Kong, and Taiwan. In other words, he has maintained his role and participation as an active and influential stakeholder in the Chinese literary and cultural scenes, in spite of the censure and censorship launched against him. One might be surprised at the authority's toleration of this critical writer's ability to continue to do what he does, but a more nuanced observation will show that Yan's continuous presence is productive not only for himself but also for the Chinese authority. Firstly, the presence of this internationally high-profile and defiant critic of the country can be shown to the world outside to represent the CCP government's tolerance for dissenters. It can very well afford this when the internal threat posed by Yan's critical expression is being neutralized to an extent by attacks on the novelist by the fabricated "people" comprising 50-centers, paid and voluntary. Secondly, the restrictions on Yan's expression and the many subsequent pressures the novelist

---

61 Ai Weiwei, dir., *Cockroach* (Berlin: AWW Germany, 2020).
62 Unlike Gao Xingjian who has been persona non grata to China, Ma Jian has been able to enter the country occasionally, but only with a tourist visa on his British passport, until the mid-2010s. That has enabled him to conduct research for his books, such as the extended investigation he conducted for *The Dark Road*.

endures can also serve as a reminder for other writers of the need to self-censor, since they could be subject to the same restrictions or pressures. For Yan, however restricted his expression in China may be, his presence allows him a space for contestation about Chinese life and the history of the PRC. Even in the case of Fang Fang's *Wuhan Diary*, where the stakes are so high for the government, there are supporters rallying around her (such as Yan himself). Critical expression in China is possible, in both the cases of Yan and Fang Fang, with the presence of the authors on site. With them physically present on the scene, their voices have not been erased in the country in the way that Gao's and Ma's have been.

Judith Butler's study of the body's appearance in public space is relevant to this present discussion.[63] She stresses that the presence of the individual body in political assemblies cannot be isolated from its contextual circumstances, in other words, the conditions that have made such an appearance possible. For example, first and foremost, the protester needs the architectural support of the street or building to stand on (implicating the civil engineering systems of the place concerned); there are also the bus or tram networks that allow her to travel to the rally (transportation system), and her spouse who probably does not join the rally but is working on that day to earn the wages to maintain them both, or her mother who has washed and iron the clothes that she wears to the rally. Butler argues: "We cannot talk about a body without knowing what supports that body, and what its relation to that support—or lack of support—might be. In this way, the body is less an entity than a living set of relations; the body cannot be fully dissociated from the infrastructural and environmental conditions of its living and acting. Its acting is always conditioned acting, which is one sense of the historical character of the body."[64] She describes the body in assembly, or any body appearing in public protests, such as the Standing Man in Geze Park, Istanbul,[65] as a "heightened bodily exposure": "… heightened bodily exposure happens when assemblies deliberately expose their bodies to police power on the street or in public domains. It is also what happens daily under conditions of occupation, when walking down the street or trying to pass through a checkpoint, making the body available to harassment, injury, detention, or death."[66] This heightened bodily exposure (to risk) accentuates the precarity embodied in the individual. Such exposure is a powerfully performative moment that transforms not only the body into an active agent of political resistance but also the infrastructural networks that support this body into a field of empowerment. In the case of Yan, his heightened discursive exposure renders his person no less precarious than any bodies in a rally. This presence is also supported by a network of infrastructural conditions. This network is made up by, but not limited to, the publishing companies and journals that publish his works, the internet apparatuses that allow reporting about his works, the interviews with him, the pirate posting of his censored works, and reposting of his overseas speeches, the academic institutions that (although only very rarely) host conferences and discussions about his works, the literary establishments that (are inconsistent enough to) allow occasional awards to be given to him, alongside all the other

---

63 Judith Butler, *Notes Toward a Performative Theory of Assembly* (Cambridge, MA: Harvard University Press, 2015).
64 Ibid., 64.
65 On 17 June 2013, a man stood motionless for eight hours in Gezi Park, Istanbul, as a non-violent protest against the state and police violence during the Gezi Park demonstration in May. Butler has discussed this in relation to the network of supports for the body's appearance in protests (ibid., 168–69). A video recording of the *duran adam* (the standing man): https://www.youtube.com/watch?v=hQ1vRjJHWZE&t=383s.
66 Ibid., 125.

physical and social infrastructure that supports his bodily presence in the country. A two-way formative action is at work: when the structure made up of these infrastructure and networks supports Yan's continuous presence in China as a critical writer, his heightened discursive exposure also transforms the relevant infrastructure and networks into dynamic agents, and forms a structure of empowerment, at least in this particular instance of supporting Yan's presence. Therefore, Yan's continuous presence and discursive presence in mainland China should not be understood as a matter of luck or accident, but a phenomenon that is predicated on the negotiation of pressure distribution, the diplomacy tactics of the state, and the workings of a whole structure of presence on the part of the novelist.

Conclusion

I would argue that this more nuanced understanding of the censorship imposed in Yan Lianke's case can definitely be applied to other cases of literary censorship in China and other places. This could contribute to our understanding of literature beyond the text. I am certainly not advocating a pre-New Criticism ethos of biographical literary criticism. Instead, I am trying to show that there is a personal dimension in the historicization of literary texts. I hope that the above analysis of negotiation between censorship and the structure of presence in Yan's case has highlighted how the writing subject can and must cope with prohibitions of expression in repressive circumstances, thereby attesting to the importance of individual agency and resilience, which are the most important qualities that persons living under repressive circumstances must rely on.

I have started this article by asking three questions: Has Yan really been effectively censored? What are the mechanisms of censorship Yan is subject to? Is his fame in the West only a pawn in the Western-Chinese cultural politics?[67] I believe I have already answered the first two questions with the analysis above. The conclusion is: yes, his writings have been effectively prohibited by a combination of official censorship and netizen censure, and both forms of public restrictions have also been transformed into pressures the novelist must endure in the private sphere. The answer to the last question, however, is less straightforward. First, this question excludes the factor of literary quality in the Western reception of Yan's works. It would be naive to believe that ideology does not play any part in literary reception, but it is equally, if not more, naive to assume that the literary establishments nurtured by the traditions of Shakespeare, Goethe, Proust, and Falkner, to name but a few, would laud a body of works simply because it is critical of China. Let us not forget that in Levefere's sociological framework of literary translation studies, poetics is cited as an important factor alongside ideology and patronage.[68] Second, no doubt much attention is given in Western media and in the Western book market about the censorship Yan is subject to, but isn't resistance to restrictions of expression one important function of literature? And helping readers understand reality, at least the author's vision of it, another? If world literature manages to provide a space to share human concerns, it is because translations of works like Yan Lianke's are transforming this space into a supporting structure for the presence of heterogeneous voices.

---

67 I am using the description "Western" as a short-hand description of the Anglo-European cultural regions and the cultural spaces that have aligned themselves with their heritage and values. I am aware that this designation is as problematic as "the free world" that I have used earlier. I am using this word for want of a more convenient short-hand term.
68 André Lefevere, *Translation, Rewriting, and the Manipulation of Literary Fame* (London: Routledge, 2017).

Bibliography

Adlakha, Hemant. "Fang Fang: The 'Conscience of Wuhan' amid Coronavirus Quarantine." *The Diplomat*. 23 Mar. 2020. https://thediplomat.com/2020/03/fang-fang-the-conscience-of-wuhan-amid-coronavirus-quarantine/ (last accessed 10 July 2021).

Ai, Weiwei, dir. *Cockroach*. Berlin: AWW Germany, 2020.

BBC. "'Racist' D&G Ad: Chinese Model Says Campaign Almost Ruined Career." 23 Jan. https://www.bbc.com/news/world-asia-china-46968750 (last accessed 10 July 2021).

Butler, Judith. *Notes Toward a Performative Theory of Assembly*. Cambridge, MA: Harvard University Press, 2015.

Cao Jinqing 曹錦清 and Zhang Letian 張樂天. "Chuantong xiangcun de shehui wenhua tezheng: Renqing yu guanxi wan—yi ge Zhebei cunluo de weiguan kaocha yu toushi" 傳統鄉村的社會文化特徵:人情與關係網——一個浙北村落的微觀考察與透視 [Social-cultural characteristics in traditional village: Human feelings and networks of relationship—A micro-view and field work in a north Zhejiang village]. *Tansuo yu zhengming* 探索與爭鳴 (Exploration and free views), 1992, no. 2: 51–59.

Chen Can 陳燦 and Lin Lu 林露, eds. "Wendaihui zuodaihui lai la: Mo Yan Jiang Kun Xu Fan Liang Xiaosheng Huang Bo dou shuo le sha" 文代會作代會來啦：莫言姜昆徐帆梁曉聲黃渤都說了啥 [The coming of representatives' meetings of China Writers' Association and China Federation of Literary and Art Circles: What have Mo Yan, Jiang Kun, Xu Fan, Liao Xiaosheng and Huang Bo said]. People.cn. 1 Dec. 2016. http://culture.people.com.cn/BIG5/n1/2016/1201/c87423-28917794-2.html (last accessed 10 July 2021).

Chen, Ge. "Piercing the Veil of State Sovereignty: How China's Censorship Regime into Fragmented International Law Can Lead to a Butterfly Effect." *Global Constitutionalism* 3, no. 1 (2014): 31–70.

Chen, Sally Xiaojin. *Resistance in Digital China: The Southern Weekly Incident*. London: Bloomsbury Academic, 2020.

China Business Focus. "Naxie mingren gongkai zhichi Fang Fang?" 哪些名人公開支持方方？ [Which celebrities have openly supported Fang Fang?]. 25 Apr. 2020. https://www.163.com/dy/article/FB28CPO4053770WR.html (last accessed 10 July 2021).

Ci, Jiwei. "The Dialectic of the Chinese Revolution Revisited: Desublimation and Resublimation in Post-Mao China." In *Contemporary Chinese Political Thought*, edited by Fred Dallmayr and Zhao Tingyang, 173–184. Lexington: University Press of Kentucky, 2012.

Coble, Parks M. "China's 'New Remembering' of the Anti-Japanese War of Resistance, 1937–1945." *China Quarterly* 190 (2007): 394–410.

Du Heqi 杜何琪, Wang Ying 王熒, and Liu Shuo 劉碩. "Xiandaihua hui xueruo nongcun chuantong renji guanxi ma" 現代化會削弱農村傳統人際關係嗎 [Does modernization weaken traditional interpersonal relationships in rural areas], *Journal of Shangxi Agricultural University (Social Science Edition)* 山西農業大學學報 (社會科學版) 19, no. 4 (2020): 80–88.

Fan, Jiayang. "Yan Lianke's Forbidden Satires of China." *The New Yorker*, 8 Oct. 2018. https://www.newyorker.com/magazine/2018/10/15/yan-liankes-forbidden-satires-of-china (last accessed 10 July 2021).

Fang Fang 方方. "Wuhan riji" 武漢日記 [Wuhan diary]. Caixin wang 財新網. 25 Jan.–25 Mar. 2020. https://web.archive.org/web/20200327102104/http://m.app.caixin.com/m_topic_detail/1489.html (last accessed 10 July 2021).

Fei, Xiaotong. *From the Soil: The Foundations of Chinese Society*. Berkeley: University of California Press, 1992.

Feng, Guangchao Charles, and Steve Zhongshi Guo. "Tracing the Route of China's Internet Censorship: An Empirical Study." *Telematics and Informatics* 30, no. 4 (2013): 335–45.

Foley, Kevin, Jeremy L. Wallace, and Jessica Chen Weiss. "The Political and Economic Consequences of Nationalist Protest in China: The 2012 Anti-Japanese Demonstrations." *China Quarterly* 236 (2018): 1131–53.

Gu Minghao 古明浩. "Bo Yan Lianke de Rijun tangguo" 駁閻連科的日軍糖果 [Against Yan Lianke's candy of the Japanese soldier]. Minzu fuxing wang 民族復興網 [Website of nation rejuvenation]. 19 Mar. 2021. www.mzfxw.com/e/action/ShowInfo.php?classid=8&id=149269 (last accessed 10 July 2021).

Guo Songmin 郭松民. "Fang Fang de lian yu Yan Lianke de lian" 方方的臉與閻連科的臉 [Fang Fang's face and Yan Lianke's face]. *Guanchazhe* 觀察者 [Observer]. 15 Apr. 2020. https://user.guancha.cn/main/content?id=287790 (last accessed 10 July 2021).

Han, Rongbin. *Contesting Cyberspace in China*. New York: Columbia University Press, 2018.

———. "Defending the Authoritarian Regime Online: China's 'Voluntary Fifty-Cent Army'." *China Quarterly* 224 (Oct. 2015): 1006–25.

———. "Patriotism without State Blessing: Chinese Cyber Nationalists in a Predicament." In *Handbook of Protest and Resistance in China*, edited by Teresa Wright, 346–60. Cheltenham, UK: Edward Elgar Publishing, 2019.

Han Shaogong 韓少功. "Wenxue de 'Gen'" 文學的根 [The 'roots' of literature]. *Zuojia* 作家 [Writers], 1985, no. 4: 2–5.

Henochowicz, Anne. "Five Years of Sensitive Words on June Fourth." 1 June 2016. https://chinadigitaltimes.net/2016/06/five-years-sensitive-words-june-fourth (last accessed 10 July 2021).

Hou Mingqing 侯明清. "Chumai linghun zhe neng huo Nuobei'er wenxue jiang ma?" 出賣靈魂者能獲得諾貝爾文學獎嗎? [Should a person who has sold his soul get the Nobel Prize for Literature?]. Aisixiang 愛思想. 4 Oct. 2012. https://m.aisixiang.com/data/58089.html (last accessed 10 July 2021).

Hui, Echo. "*Nanzao* Zhongwen zhuanfang Yan Lianke: Zhongguo chuban zhidu mei name zao" 南早中文專訪閻連科：中國出版制度沒那麼糟 [*South China Morning Post* Chinese edition interviews Yan Lianke: The system of publishing in China isn't that bad]. Nanzao.Com. 4 Nov. 2013. http://ias.ust.hk/events/cwp/includes/media/2013/20131104_liu_zaifu_scmp.pdf (last accessed 10 July 2021).

Ilaria, Maria Sala. "Four Hong Kong Publishers Known for Books Critical of Chinese Regime Missing." *The Guardian*. 9 Nov. 2015. https://www.theguardian.com/world/2015/nov/09/hong-kong-publishers-gui-haiming-lu-bo-zhang-zhiping-lin-rongji-missing-china (last accessed July 2021).

Jiang Xun 江迅. "2005 nian diyi ben jinshu 'wei renmin fuwu'" 2005 年第一部禁書「為人民服務」 [The first banned book in 2005 *Serve the People!*]. Inmedia. 16 Mar. 2005. https://www.inmediahk.net/node/20330 (last accessed 10 July 2021).

———. "Yongbao aizicun de wenxue guanhuai" 擁抱艾滋村的文學關懷 [Compassionate literature that embraces an AIDS infested village]. *Yazhou zhoukan* 亞洲週刊 (Asia Week). 2006, no. 16. https://www.yzzk.com/article/details/文化/2006-16/1367466106046/擁抱艾滋村的文學關懷 (last accessed 10 July 2021).

———. "Mo Yan Nobei'er wenxue jiang xiaoying wenxue vs zhengzhi" 莫言諾貝爾獎效應文學vs政治 [The effect of Mo Yan's Nobel Prize for Literature: Literature vs politics]. *Yazhou zhoukan*, 2012, no. 43. https://www.yzzk.com/article/details/封面專題%2F2012-43%2F1363610920983%2F莫言諾貝爾獎效應文學vs政治 (last accessed 10 July 2021).

King, Gary, Jennifer Pan, and Margaret E. Roberts. "How Censorship in China Allows Government Criticism but Silences Collective Expression." *American Political Science Review* 107, no. 2 (2013): 326–43.

———. "How the Chinese Government Fabricates Social Media Posts for Strategic Distraction, Not Engaged Argument." *American Political Science Review* 111, no. 3 (2017): 484–501.

Lagerkvist, Johan. "Internet Ideotainment in the PRC: National Responses to Cultural Globalization." *Journal of Contemporary China* 17, no. 54 (2008): 121–40.

Lee, Tong King. "China as Dystopia: Cultural Imaginings through Translation." *Translation Studies* 8, no. 3 (2015): 251–68.

Lefevere, André. *Translation, Rewriting, and the Manipulation of Literary Fame*. London: Routledge, 2017.

Liao Yiwu 廖亦武. "Kan Ai Weiwei zenmo dihui Liu Xiaobo" 看艾未未怎麼詆毀劉曉波 [Look at how Ai Weiwei slandered Liu Xiaobo]. Upmedia. 15 Aug. 2017. https://www.upmedia.mg/news_info.php?SerialNo=22711%0A2 (last accessed 10 July 2021).

Liu Yongqiang 劉永強 and Yao Linru 姚林茹. "Nongcun chuantong da jiating zhong laoren hexin ningjuli wenti de gean yanjiu: Yi Henansheng Y xiang S xiang G cun Liu shi da jiating weili" 農村傳統大家庭中老人核心凝聚力問題的個案研究——以河南省Y縣S鄉G村劉氏大家庭為例 [The elderly as core cohesion in rural traditional families: A case study of the extensive Liu family in G Village, S Township, Y County, Henan Province]. *Laoling kexue yanjiu zazhi* 老齡科學研究雜誌 [Scientific research on aging] 3, no. 10 (2015): 60–71.

Lorentzen, Peter. "China's Strategic Censorship." *American Journal of Political Science* 58, no. 2 (2014): 402–14.

Lou Chengzhen 樓乘震. "Yan Lianke zui manyi zuopin Sishu: Cheng xiezuo shi mingyun de anpai" 閻連科最滿意作品《四書》稱寫作是命運的安排 [The *Four Books* is Yan Lianke's most satisfactory work: He considers writing his fate]. *Shenzhen shangbao* 深圳商報 [Shenzhen economic daily]. 3 Apr. 2014. http://culture.people.com.cn/BIG5/n/2014/0403/c22219-24819642.html (last accessed 10 July 2021).

MacKinnon, Rebecca. "Flatter World and Thicker Walls? Blogs, Censorship and Civic Discourse in China." *Public Choice* 134, nos. 1–2 (2008): 31–46.

Martin, Nik. "Xinjiang Cotton Boycott Leaves Western Brands Reeling." DWnews, 8 Apr. 2021. https://www.dw.com/en/xinjiang-cotton-boycott-leaves-western-brands-reeling/a-57130450 (last accessed 10 July 2021).

McDowell, Lesley. "Yan Lianke: 'It's Hard to Get My Books Published in China.'" *The Guardian*, 22 Sept. 2018. https://www.theguardian.com/books/2018/sep/22/yan-lianke-writers-in-china-day-the-sun-died-interview (last accessed 10 July 2021).

Mina, An Xiao. "Batman, Pandaman and the Blind Man: A Case Study in Social Change Memes and Internet Censorship in China." *Journal of Visual Culture* 13, no. 3 (2014): 359–75.

Qingfeng 青鋒. "Yan Lianke de yi ke tang: Yaowei qilian huan bulai ai yu heping" 閻連科的一顆糖——搖尾乞憐換不來愛與和平 [Yan Lianke's candy: Love and peace cannot be found by getting down on your knees]. Zhihu 知乎. 16 Mar. 2021. https://zhuanlan.zhihu.com/p/357523085 (last accessed 10 July 2021).

QQ.com. "Yan Lianke huojiang ganyan li, 'yi ke tang' bushi zhongdian, ershi 'chousha'" 閻連科獲獎感言裡，"一顆糖"不是重點，而是"仇殺" [In Yan Lianke's award recipient speech, the candy isn't the point, vendetta is]. 2021. https://new.qq.com/omn/20210329/20210329A07JQR00.html (last accessed, 10 July 2021).

Renqi 人氣. "Yan Lianke: Yi zuojia de mingyi shenpan zhe ge guojia" 閻連科：以作家的名義審判這個國家 [Yan Lianke: In the name of an author he puts this country on trial]. *Epoch Times*. 17 Jan. 2017. https://www.epochtimes.com/b5/17/1/17/n8713240.htm (last accessed 10 July 2021).

Sang Pu 桑普. "Ai Weiwei de duoluo" 艾未未的墮落 [Ai Weiwei's fall from grace]. *Minbao* 民報 (Taiwan People News). 17 Aug. 2015. https://www.peoplenews.tw/news/b0fdb818-05a4-40cf-9b73-c8c21d6c3527 (last accessed 10 July 2021).

Sebag-Montefiore, Clarissa. "Blood Price of Fear and Greed: Yan Lianke's Novel Exposes the Truth about China's Hidden Epidemic." *Independent*. Oct. 2011. https://www.independent.co.uk/arts-entertainment/books/reviews/four-books-yan-lianke-book-review-looking-back-anger-mao-s-great-leap-forward-a109256.html (last accessed 10 July 2021).

Shaw, Gareth, and Xiaoling Zhang. "Cyberspace and Gay Rights in a Digital China: Queer Documentary Filmmaking under State Censorship." *China Information* 32, no.2 (2018): 270–92.

Sun Lan 孫瀾. "Bei 'bangjia' de Fang Fang yu silie de Zhongguo yulunchang" 被「綁架」的方方與撕裂的中國輿論場 [Fang Fang being "hijacked" and the split in China's public opinions]. DWnews. 8 Apr. 2020. https://www.dwnews.com/中國/60174801/新冠肺炎輿情被綁架的方方與撕裂的中國輿論場 (last accessed 10 July 2021).

Tan, Zaixi. "Censorship in Translation: The Case of the People's Republic of China." *Neohelicon* 42, no. 1 (2015): 313–39.

Tong Li 童立 and Cai Zhen 蔡震. "Yan Lianke wei aizicun zhuanggao chubanshe: Cheng buneng qipian duzhe" 閻連科為愛滋病村狀告出版社 稱不能欺騙讀者 [Yan Lianke sues his publishing for an AIDS infested village: He says one must not lie to readers]. Xinlang 新浪 (Sina). 4 Sep. 2006. http://book.sina.com.cn/news/c/2006-09-04/1104204423.shtml (last accessed 10 July 2021).

Wallace, Jeremy L., and Jessica Chen Weiss. "The Political Geography of Nationalist Protest in China: Cities and the 2012 Anti-Japanese Protests." *China Quarterly* 222 (2015): 403–29.

Wang, Dakuo, and Gloria Mark. "Internet Censorship in China: Examining User Awareness and Attitudes." *ACM Transactions on Computer-Human Interaction* 22, no. 6 (2015): 1–22.

Wong, Mathew Y. H., and Ying Ho Kwong. "Academic Censorship in China: The Case of *The China Quarterly*." *PS: Political Science and Politics* 52, no. 2 (2019): 287–92.

Xiao Yi 蕭逸. "Yan Lianke ershi nian wenxue kanke lu" 閻連科二十年文學坎坷路 [Yan Lianke walks on the rough path for twenty years]. Open.com.hk. 7 Aug. 2013. www.open.com.hk/content.php?id=1447#.YOAweBOA63I (last accessed 10 July 2021).

Xiong Feng 熊峰 and Yu Pan 余盼. "Nongcun renji guanxi de jiegouxing yaosu ji qi bianqian" 農村人際關係的結構性要素及其變遷 [The structural factors of interpersonal relationships in rural villages and their changes]. *Wuhan fangzhi daxue xuebao* 武漢紡織大學學報 (Journal of Wuhan Textile University) 28, no. 4 (2015): 84–87.

Xu Jilin. 許紀霖. "Qimeng de mingyun: Ershi nian lai de Zhongguo sixiangjie" 啟蒙的命運——二十年來的中國思想界 [The fate of enlightenment: Chinese intellectuals in the past twenty years]. *Twenty-First Century Bimonthly*, 1998, no. 50: 4–13.

Xuezhong Fengche 雪中風車. "Yan Lianke: Gaoming er yinsun de 'yi kuai tang'" 閻連科：高明而陰損的「一塊糖」 [Yan Lianke: The clever but vicious "candy"]. 163.com. 25 Mar. 2021. https://3g.163.com/dy/article_cambrian/G5U8C8FP0523C0OR.html (last accessed 10 July 2021).

Yan Lianke 閻連科. *Faxian xiaoshuo* 發現小說 [Discovering fiction]. Taipei: INK, 2011.

———. "Fenhen yu ziji de xiezuo yu rensheng" 憤恨於自己的寫作與人生 [Resentment, my writings, and life]. In *Tuikai Zhongguo de lingwai yi shan chuan: Haiwai suibi ji* 推開中國的另外一扇窗：海外隨筆集 [Opening the door of China: Yan Lianke's collected overseas writings]. Hong Kong: Hong Kong City University Press, 2020.

———. "Jing ci yi jie, rang women chengwei you jixing de ren" 經此疫劫，讓我們成為有記性的人 [What happens after coronavirus? On community memory and repeating our own mistakes]. Duan chuanmei 端傳媒 (Intimum Media). 21 Feb. 2020. https://theinitium.com/article/20200221-mainland-coronavirus-yanlianke (last accessed 10 July 2021).

———. "Sangjiaquan de yinian" 喪家犬的一年 [The year of the stray dog]. In *Tuikai Zhongguo de lingwai yi shan chuan*. Hong Kong: Hong Kong City University Press, 2020.

———. *Xia Riluo* 夏日落 [Summer sunset]. Hong Kong: Hong Kong City University Press, 2020.

———. "Xianggang: Wo de shenhua yu chuanshuo" 香港—我的神話與傳說 [Hong Kong is my myth and my legend]. In *Tuikai Zhongguo de lingwai yi shan chuan*. Hong Kong: Hong Kong City University Press, 2020.

———. "Yi ge bi shijie geng da de cunzhuang" 一個比世界更大的村莊 [A village bigger than the world]. Initium Media. 2021. https://theinitium.com/article/20210310-notes-newman-prize-for-chinese-literature-yanlianke/ (last accessed 10 July 2021).

———. "Zuojia Yan Lianke Weibo zhi zongli gongkaixin: Shoudu qiangchai shijian" 作家閻連科微博致總理公開信：首都強拆事件 [The writer Yan Lianke's open letter to the premier on Weibo: On the incident of forced demolition in the capital]. Xinlang Weibo 新浪微博 (Sina Weibo). 30 Nov. 2011. https://cul.sohu.com/20120209/n334240537.shtml (last accessed 10 July 2021).

Yang, Yuan. "Yan Lianke: 'Propaganda Is a Nuclear Bomb.'" *Financial Times*, 3 Apr. 2020. https://www.ft.com/content/83b25396-7358-11ea-95fe-fcd274e920ca (last accessed 10 July 2021).

Zhang Zanpo 張贊波. "Ai Weiwei tan Liu Xiaobo: Ta de jiazhi bushi na Nobei'er jiang" 艾未未談劉曉波：他的價值不是拿諾貝爾獎 [Ai Weiwei on Liu Xiaobo: His value doesn't lie on getting a Nobel Prize]. *The Reporter*, 18 Oct. 2017. https://www.twreporter.org/a/interview-ai-weiwei-3 (last accessed 10 July 2021).

Zhao, Suisheng. "A State-Led Nationalism: The Patriotic Education Campaign in Post-Tiananmen China." *Communist and Post-Communist Studies* 31, no. 3 (1998): 287–302.

PART II

Absurdity and spirituality

7
THE ABSURD AS METHOD

The Chinese absurdist hero, enchanted power, and the alienated poor in Yan Lianke's military literature[1]

Haiyan Xie

Introduction

As an internationally influential Chinese writer, Yan Lianke 閻連科 is best known for his novels written during the past two decades, whereas a large number of his military-themed novellas, written earlier in the late 1980s and 1990s, have received much less scholarly attention. The prestigious scholar of military literature, Zhu Xiangqian 朱向前, has suggested two reasons for this lack of interest in Yan's military novellas: "first, when one considers the massive upsurge in formal experimentation in Chinese literature in the 1980s, Yan's writing may appear relatively conservative with respect to style; second, when in the 1990s the mainstream literary trend began to move towards the new realism (*xin xieshi zhuyi* 新寫實主義), Yan's writing was again ignored because it was not realistic enough."[2] Yan's military novellas feature a combination of realist and absurdist styles. By interweaving a latent strain of sociopolitical commentary into a kind of absurdist narrative that is itself a creative re-adaptation of the idea of the absurd in the Western literature, Yan has created a unique style of military writing that diverges sharply from mainstream Chinese military literature. His military works are praised by Zhu as the "herald of a new direction for [Chinese] military literature,"[3] one that deconstructs the stereotypes of the genre by introducing new thematic and stylistic elements. Yan's military novellas feature a particular group of peasant soldiers who, in Zhu's view, "show a complex appearance that is both typical and ordinary, both clear and vague, and both vivid and ambiguous."[4] The complexity of these characters and the surreality of the absurdist narrative function to destabilize conventional binary oppositions in military stories such that "readers have to 'suspend judgment' along with the author."[5]

---

1 This article first appeared in *Literature Compass*, 10 Mar. 2020, https://doi.org/10.1111/lic3.12568.
2 Zhu Xiangqian 朱向前, "Nongmin zhi zi yu nongmin junren" 農民之子與農民軍人 [The son of peasants and the peasant-soldiers], in *Yan Lianke wenxue yanjiu* 閻連科文學研究 [Studies of Yan Lianke's literature], vol. 1, ed. Lin Jianfa 林建法 (Yunnan: Yunnan renmin chubanshe, 2012), 59–60.
3 Ibid., 55.
4 Ibid.
5 Ibid.

By interpreting the absurd first and foremost as the method, this paper understands the absurd as a kind of analytical methodology and explores the absurd as a kind of formal experiment that covertly expresses Yan's socio-political views on the reality of contemporary China, here epitomized by the peasant soldiers' existential struggles. Meanwhile, "the absurd as method" also serves as a mode of literary analysis, one which takes the absurd as a starting point for looking into how the so-called "objectivity" of "social reality" as prescribed in literary realism and mainstream Chinese military literature is subverted and reconstructed in Yan's writing. Focusing in particular on Yan's 2009 collection of military novellas *Prohibited Area Number Four* (*Sihao jinqu* 四號禁區), this chapter explores how Yan adapts the Western absurdist narrative into his military writing. It argues that the absurd in Yan's military texts serves not only as a formal experiment that explores the alternative imagination of the alienated and marginalized peasant soldiers in contemporary China but also as an implicit means of articulating Yan's own socio-political commentary, one which cannot allow itself to be explicitly political. Here, by being explicitly political, it means openly and directly criticizing bureaucratic corruption in the military system, and promoting ideas that are antithetical to mainstream ideology, such as heroism and collectivism.

The absurd in Chinese literature and *Prohibited Area Number Four*

The absurd as an imported literary element from the West has appeared in a variety of genres in contemporary Chinese literature since the mid-1980s, a time that witnessed a boom in Chinese modernist fiction. Among these new modernist works, several have been particularly influenced by the Western philosophical trends of existentialism, absurdist fiction, and Theatre of the Absurd. For example, Liu Suola's 劉索拉 novella *You Have No Other Choice* (*Ni biewu xuanze* 你別無選擇, 1985) and Xu Xing's 徐星 *A Variation without a Theme* (*Wu zhuti bianzouqu* 無主題變奏曲, 1985) display styles and techniques which bear a close affinity to Joseph Heller's *Catch-22*.[6] Integrating the absurd into the local stories for the first time in modern Chinese literature, these two pieces are regarded as "marking the nascent Chinese modernist fiction."[7]

The absurd is also an important modernist technique favored by the avant-garde writers of the latter half of the 1980s. Among them, Can Xue 殘雪 stands out for her "ability to calmly reveal 'evil' and 'violence' by way of non-realistic imagery,"[8] something which consistently manifests itself in her own absurdist narratives. Greatly influenced by the Western absurdist writer Franz Kafka,[9] Can Xue conveys "the nightmarish quality of the absurd reality in a

---

6 Hong Zicheng 洪子誠, *A History of Contemporary Chinese Literature*, trans. Michael M. Day (Leiden: Brill, 2007), 384.

7 Chen Xiaoming 陳曉明, *Zhongguo dangdai wenxue zhuchao* 中國當代文學主潮 [Major trends in contemporary Chinese literature] (Beijing: Peking University Press, 2009), 320. Other works during this period "apparently influenced by Western absurdist literature" include Zong Pu's 宗璞 "absurdist fiction" series, Zhan Rong's 諶容 *Jianqu shi sui* 減去十歲 (Subtracting ten years), and Wu Ruozeng's 吳若增 *Lianpi zhaoling qishi* 臉皮招領啟事 (Face found and lost). See Feng Shounong 馮壽農, "Zhongguo xinshiqi wenxue dui Xifang huangdanpai wenxue de xishou he xiaorong 中國新時期文學對西方荒誕派文學的吸收和消融 [The absorption and dissolution of Western absurdist literature in Chinese new age literature]," *Xiamen daxue xuebao (zhexue shehui kexue ban)* 廈門大學學報 (哲學社會科學版) [Journal of Xiamen University (Arts & Social Sciences)], 1993, no. 3: 75.

8 Hong, *A History of Contemporary Chinese Literature*, 385.

9 In 1999, Can Xue 殘雪 published *Linghun de baolei: Lijie Kafuka* 靈魂的堡壘: 理解卡夫卡 (Castle of the soul: Understanding Kafka), which provides an interpretation of several of Kafka's important works from her own unique perspective, one which is markedly different from that of many Western canonical scholars.

nontraditional mode" and explores the absurdity of life and the unresolvedness of human nature through the theme of nihilism.[10] Perhaps the most influential piece of the absurdist genre in Chinese literature is the 2000 Nobel laureate Gao Xingjian's 高行健 famous play *The Bus-stop* (*Chezhan* 車站), with its blend of Chinese traditional theatrical elements with the Western-inspired Theatre of the Absurd.[11] Greatly inspired by Samuel Beckett's *Waiting for Godot*, *The Bus-stop* has "no character in conflict" and "no genuine action."[12] Gao's appropriation of the Western absurd in his work exemplifies what has become a common practice of Chinese authors using the absurd to express particularities of the Chinese literary and cultural context.

As a result of the innovative fusion of the Chinese literary tradition with the Western modernist technique of the absurd, these absurdist works have diverged sharply from their Western counterparts to take on new and unique forms. On the one hand, they have mostly curbed the abstract metaphysical impulses of Western philosophical thought by using the absurd to discuss the concrete reality of historical trauma. On the other hand, as it shows in Gao's plays, the absurd emerges in an ahistorical, irrational, and ideologically ambiguous context that evokes existential anxiety.

However, although the absurd is not uncommon in Chinese literature, either as a narrative technique or simply as a literary embellishment, military literature seems to be a "forbidden" zone. As Zhu observes, despite the fact that the landscape of Chinese military literature since the 1990s has changed significantly, it has never broken free from the limitations of mainstream political ideology.[13] In other words, the near-universal sense of "political correctness" inscribed within the generic parameters of Chinese military literature appears fundamentally incompatible with the absurdist narrative, which tends to undermine the supposed seriousness of military literature.

Yan Lianke is arguably the first contemporary Chinese writer to engage the absurd in Chinese military literature on a large scale. His use of the absurd to flirt with military subjects, in a manner that risks "political incorrectness" while simultaneously undercutting the seeming seriousness of any political critique, is an innovative and compelling strategy for attempting to shake the foundations of a literary genre that is heavily ideologically loaded. In order to understand Yan's idiosyncratic adaptation of the absurd, we must consider the specific meanings that he incorporates into his work. In his seminal work, *The Absurd in Literature*, Neil Cornwell observes that "for most commentators, absurdity is to be equated with nihilism" and that "the absurd […] is born of nihilism."[14] Martin Esslin similarly defines the common theme of the Theatre of the Absurd as "metaphysical anguish at the absurdity of the human condition."[15] Cornwell's and Esslin's interpretations of the absurd, albeit somewhat contentious, have largely informed the common understanding of absurdity in Western literature. While this article is not meant to offer a reductive reading of the absurd, especially

---

10　Rong Cai 蔡蓉, "In the Madding Crowd: Self and Other in Can Xue's Fiction," in *The Subject in Crisis in Contemporary Chinese Literature*, ed. Rong Cai (Honolulu: University of Hawai'i Press, 2004), 92.

11　Gao Xingjian wrote this play in 1981 when he was still a Chinese citizen. The play premiered in the Loft Space of the Beijing People's Art Theatre in 1983.

12　William Tay, "Avant-Garde Theatre in Post-Mao China: *The Bus-Stop* by Gao Xingjian," in *Soul of Chaos: Critical Perspectives on Gao Xingjian*, ed. Kwok-Kan Tam, (Hong Kong: Chinese University Press, 2001), 68.

13　Zhu Xiangqian, *Zhongguo junlü wenxue wushi nian* 中國軍旅文學五十年 [Chinese military literature in fifty years] (Beijing: Jiefangjun wenyi chubanshe, 2007), 7.

14　Neil Cornwell, *The Absurd in Literature* (Manchester: Manchester University Press, 2006), 4–5.

15　Martin Esslin, *The Theatre of the Absurd*, 3rd edn. (New York: Vintage Books, 2004), 23–24.

in light of its elusiveness and complexity as a concept, it does argue that, whereas Western absurdism focuses mostly on existential nihilism, Yan Sinicizes the notion of the absurd by reworking the existential meaning of nihilism into an alternative viewpoint that is itself closely tied up in the survival of the Chinese peasant soldiers in his stories. On the one hand, Yan's appropriation of the absurd stands in parallel to the absurdist narratives of his literary peers during the 1980s and 1990s; on the other, it demonstrates his unique interpretation and individual reworking of the absurd in the context of Chinese military literature.

Published in 2009, *Prohibited Area Number Four* is a collection of six of Yan's military novellas, each of which explores the concealed or repressed needs and anxieties of individuals and their confusion over the meaning of their struggle for life.[16] By foregrounding the conflict between the desire to break away from and the simultaneous impossibility of escaping the absurdity of existence, Yan's fictional world is less concerned with recounting military-related activities and appears rather to focus on the individual's quest for meaning. In addition to sharing similar thematic features which work to bind each separate story together, as manifestations of Yan's appropriation of the absurd, the stories are also stylistically different from conventional Chinese military literature. The narratives, modeled on Western absurdist fiction, are very loosely structured, with realist elements such as plot, characterization, and development mostly absent. In order to depict the mundanity of a routine existence, a recurring motif in this collection, the stories are told in plain and unembellished language. Yan describes thoughts and events in short, concise declarative sentences and in succinct, inanimate, and unemotional conversations as if the speakers' thoughts are drifting away. This is illustrated in the following conversation between Yu Qilin and his wife in "The War of Peace" ("Heping zhan" 和平戰):

"It is you who said divorce this time!"
"Yes, I said it."
"How about our property?"
"You decide."
"I want our daughter."
"Done."
"I have to take care of our daughter, so I will take the bank savings with me."
"Done."
"I don't watch TV, but our daughter can't go without it."
"You take it."
"You take the fridge."
"My hometown is in the countryside. I don't need a fridge there."
"What do you want?"[17]

The clipped and antagonistic manner in which these characters discuss their divorce mirrors the ineffable and escalating tension between the characters and life. Yu's repressed feelings of helplessness are implicitly conveyed in his seemingly indifferent and emotionally detached manner of speaking. The frequent occurrence of conversations such as this one throughout the collection creates an overall daunting reading experience, as readers are overwhelmed by

---

16 These six novellas were originally published in different years: "Sihao jinqu" (1995), "Heping zhan" (1994), "Zhongshi huanxiang" 中士還鄉 [The sergeant returning home] (1991), "Heping yuyan" 和平寓言 [The allegory of peace] (1993), "Daxiao" 大校 [The senior colonel] (1998), and "Jimo zhi wu" 寂寞之舞 [The dance of solitude] (2001).
17 Yan Lianke, *Sihao jinqu* (Shenyang: Beifang lianhe chuanmei, 2009), 56.

a linguistic world of monotony, dullness, purposelessness, and, most notably, a complete lack of moral judgment.

In addition to the use of short, unadorned narration and dialogue, Yan's writing is also pervaded with a sense of mystery that is manifested in supernatural elements, mysterious letters, inexplicable coincidences, and an overall sense of fate or destiny. Many of these stories begin in a similar manner to Kafka's *The Metamorphosis*, seeming to begin *in media res*.[18] For example, the opening sentence of *The War of Peace* is: "Luckily, Yu Qilin was re-diagnosed with cancer."[19] It is unclear why it would be lucky to be diagnosed with cancer, given that nothing is told of what has happened to the protagonist prior to the beginning of the story, and as it unfolds, the story itself does not provide any explicit explanations. In the opening lines to "The Dance of Solitude" ("Jimo zhi wu"), Major Guo's fate is described in terms that are both vague and contradictory: "This is how everything begins and is also how everything ends. Major Guo Songgang's fate came to its end just then, but paradoxically, it opened the real curtain of his fate."[20] These examples show that while the absurd in *Prohibited Area Number Four* shares several thematic and stylistic characteristics with its Western counterpart, there are also fundamental differences. Set mostly in rural China in the 1990s, Yan's fictional world reflects the pervasive alienation of modern existence and the inevitable absurdity of the larger world, not because of modernization as such, but because of the oppressive bureaucracy of the military system and the uncertainty of physical survival due to extreme poverty. Unlike Western absurdist fiction, Yan's stories happen in recognizable social and historical settings, indicating that his social criticism is not focused solely on abstract, universal questions of human existence.

Based on the similarities and differences between Yan's absurdism and Western absurdism, we may ask the following questions: why does Yan move away from realist writing in favor of the absurd? How does Yan's use of the absurd enable him to navigate the ideological challenges embedded in the discourse of military fiction? Do the absurdist elements in Yan's work weaken the critical power of his military stories? To answer these questions, the remainder of this article will focus on Yan's transformation of the Sisyphean hero of Western absurdist fiction into a Chinese one, and his reconstruction of the concepts of "the poor" and "power" in his military-specific discourse of the absurd.

The revision of the Sisyphean hero

In Western absurdist fiction, absurdist heroes are invariably "thrown" into an unreasonable world and generally come to accept their misfortune with austere resignation. Camus interprets such "passivity" as a kind of rebellion against the irrationality and indifference of the world, holding that the absurdist hero is "foreign to the society in which he lives" because "he does not play the game" that other people play to conform to the rules of the majority.[21] Without a doubt, the universally recognized prototype of the absurdist hero is Sisyphus,

---

18 There is much evidence that Yan has been greatly influenced by Kafka. For example, Yan is fascinated with the logic of Kafka's transforming a human being into an insect in *The Metamorphosis* without offering any reason for it. In his theoretical work *Faxian xiaoshuo* 發現小說 [Discovering fiction] (Beijing: Renmin wenxue chubanshe, 2001), 61–88, Yan devotes one chapter to elaborating on the opening lines of *The Metamorphosis*, which he calls "the issue of Gregor," interpreting it as a logic of "zero cause-and-effect" (*ling yinguo* 零因果).
19 Yan, *Sihao jinqu*, 56.
20 Ibid., 203.
21 As cited in David Sherman, *Camus* (Chichester: Wiley-Blackwell, 2009), 61.

whom Camus rehabilitates from a victim of divine punishment to a triumphant existential hero, famously claiming that "one must imagine Sisyphus happy."[22] According to Camus, this happiness consists of Sisyphus accepting life's absurdities and then facing and scorning them.

The existentialist implications of the Western absurdist hero, exemplified by Camus' Sisyphus, are very much present in Yan's military fiction. However, the peasant soldiers' ultimate failure to resist the absurdity of life does not so much evoke an existential revelation, as signify an interrogation of the alienating bureaucracy of the military system. In the novella entitled "Prohibited Area Number Four," the novella whose title was given to the collection, the orphan soldier Yuan Boy is left by himself to guard an abandoned military base. He strictly abides by the military protocol, each day checking every corner of the abandoned base, while at the same time, fighting loneliness and pushing back against the meaninglessness of these tasks and of his existence in general. One of the rules he must obey is that, for security reasons, soldiers are not allowed to have a girlfriend. This rule was made during wartime and does not serve any real purpose in peacetime, when the military base is functionally useless and abandoned. However, much like the base itself, this obsolete regulation has persisted.

The absurdity in this story, epitomized by the futility of Yuan Boy's endless assignment, is in many ways reminiscent of Sisyphus pushing a stone up a mountain for eternity. However, Yuan Boy's "scorn" for the absurdity of the world is manifested not only in his Camusian "scorn" in guarding the military base but also in his deliberate transgressing of the rules in secretly loving a neighborhood girl and protecting her from being taken away from him. Yan portrays Yuan Boy as an absurdist hero, one notably lacking the noble desire to sacrifice his own happiness for the sake of the country's safety. He is, in fact, uncertain whether his existence as a forgotten soldier guarding an abandoned military base is at all meaningful. He obeys orders and follows obsolete regulations without questioning their validity. However, his instinctive desire for love and companionship, though hindered by absurd regulations, motivates him to reflect on the meaning of his life. Thus, Yuan Boy's inner conflict is not so much a contest between responsibility and human nature, but rather an unconscious and silent resistance against an unreasonable military structure that reduces human existence to a bureaucratic function.

This absurdity manifests itself most hauntingly when the fragile balance between Yuan Boy's impassive carrying out of his duty and his deep-seated desire for love is destabilized in an incomprehensible and meaningless mission. Yuan Boy is notified that an inspection group composed of high-ranking officers and experts is coming to inspect the military base, and that this inspection "is decisive for the future of the company."[23] In order to prevent his girlfriend from approaching the entrance of the military base after the investigators arrive, Yuan Boy grudgingly shoots her, only to learn later that these officers have already decided to demolish the military base and turn it into a national park.

Similar dilemmas occur in most of the stories in *Prohibited Area Number Four*, whose protagonists must repress their feelings and desire for love in order to struggle toward what is ultimately revealed to be a hopeless future or to gain a sense of achievement, only to be ironically and invariably defeated by "destiny." Yan seeks here to expose the invisible hand that controls the fate of his characters, but he seems hesitant to reveal fully the nature of the invisible hand. This reticence is reflected in the nihilistic tone of his stories and seems to undermine his social critique.

---

22 Albert Camus, *The Myth of Sisyphus and Other Essays*, trans. Justin O'Brien (New York: Vintage Books, 1991), 123.
23 Yan, *Sihao jinqu*, 40.

Nevertheless, Yan's political commentary is expressed, even if unintentionally, by a piquant mixture of loosely structured plots, politically sensitive subject matter, and distinct, tangible military settings. Whereas the core of Western absurdist fiction lies in its search for "a possibility that is not historically determined and that accompanies man more or less eternally,"[24] Yan's absurdism turns the search for universality into a kind of particularity. That is to say, in Western absurdist fiction, the concrete social background is often deliberately ahistoricized. In so doing, the narrative's transcendence of immediate social reality inevitably moderates its sociopolitical significance. Yan, however, overcomes this limitation by placing his protagonists in the politically sensitive setting and involving them in a variety of contingencies that are unavoidably associated with government bureaucracy and the military system. Thus, his critical purpose is not merely a philosophical investigation of being, but more importantly, the interrogation of the powerful ideology and bureaucracy of the military system that renders meaningless the lives of individuals.

In addition to a feeling of existential emptiness resulting from adherence to a set of absurd and emotionally deadening military rules, most of Yan's characters also suffer from extreme poverty and must struggle relentlessly to survive. Thus, instead of expressing a theme of existential nihilism, Yan's military stories reveal an alternative sense of nihilism grounded in social marginalization, suggesting the fact that being physically marginalized eventually leads to existential marginalization. In subverting the notions of "the poor" and "power" that often appear in realist works, and in creatively integrating these notions into his own idea of the absurd, Yan demonstrates how the experience of poverty and the desire for power in rural politics has led to the soldiers' experience of alienation. However, instead of stating his case directly, Yan again obscures it within the theme of nihilism.

Enchanted power and the alienated poor

Many works of nineteenth- and twentieth-century Western literature are dominated by themes involving the plight of the poor. Chinese realist literature likewise—and perhaps even more so—represents sympathetically the plight of the impoverished classes. However, this preoccupation with society's poor and disenfranchised rarely appears in absurdist fiction, wherein it is much more often cast that, although the prosperity of modern society has brought people material comforts and enjoyments, the essence of human existence has become threatened by a lack of meaningful social connection. Unlike the city dwellers depicted in Western absurdist literature, the characters in Yan's military stories have not entered into the modern world in a real sense. They are at the very bottom level of China's social strata and are drawn from the faceless crowd that has not yet been claimed by modern civilization. Most of them are poor peasants who can only dream of changing their fate, and who thus have very different perceptions of "existence" than their more sophisticated Western counterparts. For them, the conundrum of existence is less a philosophical problem to be solved than a challenge or threat primarily resulting from scarcity.

Thus, Yan's integration of the motif of "the poor" into his absurdist narrative, tinged with a strong sense of irony, has subverted its conventional function in realist literature and thereby rendered his story a dark satire within the serious-minded genre of military literature. Rather than regarding poverty as a motivation for resistance and revolt, Yan reconceptualizes poverty as a kind of metaphor for human existence, a material representation of absurdity that is itself invested with existential implications. Poverty has been naturalized as a mode of existence,

24 Milan Kundera, *The Art of the Novel*, trans. Linda Asher (New York: Grove Press, 1988), 105.

one that exists in the characters' minds first and foremost as the material circumstances in which they live and from which they seek to escape, in the similar sense that human beings are doomed to die, but at the same time resist their mortality. It is this mentality that begets the soldiers' fascination with power.

The concept of power in these stories is somewhat different from Foucault's concept of disciplinary power, the process by which the state apparatus creates an obedient subject. For Yan's characters, power primarily signifies the ability to escape from poverty. Here power is depoliticized and stripped of ideology to become a kind of highly sought-after commodity. Although detailed depictions of poverty *per se* and of abuse of power are mostly absent from Yan's military novellas, these stories are intertextual to his novellas of other genres published during the same period, many of which feature the poor peasants, and in which the deterioration of the peasants' living conditions is frequently depicted as a vicious cycle powered by the ubiquitous corruption of rural politics. Having witnessed the rural leaders' abuse of power as a means of benefiting themselves, the poor villagers, who later go on to become the soldiers in Yan's military novellas, have by necessity developed their own strategy of becoming rich and powerful: first, join the army; second, join the Party; and third, retire from the army, return home, and get elected as the leader of the village. The following dialogue from "The Sergeant Returning Home" ("Zhongshi huanxiang" 中士還鄉), taking place between a brother and sister who are poor orphans, is exemplary in this respect:

Brother: "Sister, do you want me to become a successful person?"
Sister: "Yes."
Brother: "I want to join the army."
[…]
Sister: "Would that make you prosperous and successful?"
Brother: "I can join the Party in the army; then, I will be qualified to become a leader in our village when I return from the army."
Sister: "Then just do it. I will take care of our home."
Brother: "If you don't get married, I will be worried about you and I won't leave you."
Sister: "Anyway, I don't want to get married."
[…]
Sister: "If you can join the Party and become the Village Secretary, I agree to get married, even if I have to marry a blind and crippled man."[25]

This conversation between the siblings demonstrates the psychological struggles they must endure and the moral compromises they must make in their desperate attempts to improve their lives. Though joining the army is supposed to be an honorable, almost sacred act of patriotism, Yan's characters take the utilitarian view that it is first and foremost a way of making a living, a mockery of nationalist piety that displays in stark terms the unbearable heaviness of being.

Poverty inevitably leads to the pursuit of power. In their desire to escape their fate, Yan's soldiers do not resist or revolt but seek power, willing to become accomplices of the system that victimizes them. Like the army, the Party has long lost its sacredness in the soldiers' minds and has been reduced to as a means to an end. After many absurd twists and turns, the sergeant in "Sergeant Returning Home" leaves the army and returns home without having achieved anything, only to conclude that "life is meaningless, just like a bowl of water, tasteless."[26] The

25 Yan, *Sihao jinqu*, 103–5.
26 Ibid., 98.

story is permeated with a strong sense of nihilism. It turns out that the more effort the soldiers expend in their pursuit of power, the stronger a sense of nihilism they develop, largely a result of their repeatedly having been confronted with their inability to obtain it. These seemingly contradictory drives struggle against one another until nihilism eventually gains the upper hand, and the defeated protagonist retreats into apathy. Having lost his earlier impulse to seek a better life, the sergeant resigns himself to what has befallen him and is consumed by the lack of meaning in his existence. At the end of the story, he "peed towards the direction of the sunset and went home along the road from which he came."[27] This closing sentence is clearly symbolic: besides its literal meaning, it illustrates the absurdity and futility of the sergeant's life in that, after everything, he must return to the starting point from which he had sought to escape.

A sense of nihilism pervades every story in this collection, in which each protagonist's quest for a better life or a sense of achievement turns out to have been in vain. Yan's reconceptualization of "the poor" and "power" in these novellas carries a strong flavor of the absurd, something which, to some extent, dilutes the sense of reality in his writing. Rather than directly criticizing social and political realities, he uses the absurd to depict the powerlessness of individuals trapped in poverty as indicative of the human condition more generally. His stories are deeply pessimistic, offering no solution to the existential conundrums of his characters. This "non-solution," however, may well have an additional significance: not only are his peasant soldiers, despite their best efforts, ultimately unable to escape poverty, but also, on a stylistic level, the limitations of Yan's own poetics, and especially given his working environment, ultimately prevent him from directly challenging mainstream ideology and speaking openly for those on the margins.

Conclusion: Reclaiming self through the absurd

As Milan Kundera says, "All novels, of every age, are concerned with the enigma of the self. As soon as you create an imaginary being, a character, you are automatically confronted by the question: What is the self? How can the self be grasped?"[28] As is the case with any writer, Yan's construction of the absurdist hero is grounded in his own experience and perception of the world. All of his protagonists are, to varying degrees, allegorical self-portraits. Like them, Yan came from the poor countryside and dreamed of changing his fate by joining the army. Having served in the army for more than twenty years, he sought personal success within the military system by making reluctant compromises with power. In this, he was attempting to avoid ideological conflict by learning to "cooperate" with his superiors.

Given the army's purported valuing of heroism, patriotism, and collectivism, Yan's absurdist military novellas have sometimes been regarded as stigmatizing Chinese soldiers, and thus have attracted controversy. For example, his novella "Xia Riluo" 夏日落, first published in 1992, though winning him several awards, was banned in 1994 during the "Anti-Spiritual Pollution Campaign" because, as is the case with his other novellas, it was viewed as subverting the idealized image of the heroic soldier by "downgrading" him into an ordinary man.[29] Facing

---

27 Ibid., 128.
28 Kundera, *The Art of the Novel*, 23.
29 The "Anti-Spiritual Pollution Campaign" was a political campaign initiated by the Communist Party of China, lasting from March of 1983, when Zhou Yang 周揚 wrote an article condemning spiritual pollution in Chinese literature, until December of 1983. The campaign sought to curb Western-inspired liberal ideas among the Chinese populace, a byproduct of the economic reforms that had begun in 1978.

a dilemma between his deeply held conviction that "military literature should essentially return to respect for man" and the very real risks he could face for writing against the dominant ideology,[30] Yan himself has become like the absurdist heroes of his stories, inevitably bound by the limitations of his reality, such as his novels being banned in mainland China and removal from his posting in the army.[31]

Thus, the absurd in Yan's text not only articulates themes that are unconventional in Chinese military fiction but also insinuates his own existential struggle and necessarily repressed desire to criticize his society. Yan's complex feelings about soldiers, as presented in *Prohibited Area Number Four*, echo his consistent concern for underrepresented groups in Chinese society, which, as he himself has said, have "gradually become the core of [his] writing and may even become the center of all [his] future writing."[32] However, his persistence in expressing respect for humanity has had to be conducted in a roundabout way. That is to say, by using the absurd in his military works, Yan is able to transcend the thematic limitations of traditional military literature, shift its focus from heroism and collectivism to his concern for humanity's existential predicament and, most importantly, use the genre as a means of implicitly expressing his socio-political commentaries.

By using an absurdist style to ridicule the soldiers' reasons for joining the army, to depoliticize the issue of poverty, and to mock the ideology of power, Yan deliberately links the peasant soldiers' suffering with the "psychological pain of living in the world."[33] The absurd thus serves as a way of sidestepping the political implications of his writing and camouflaging Yan's own views within the trappings of existentialism while allowing him to adhere to his literary ideals. Yan's innovative rewriting of the absurd, especially with regard to the Chinese absurdist hero contextualized in a concrete historical moment and social context, as well as his reconceptualization of "the poor" and "power," has the effect of demystifying the absurd and revealing the hidden truth of a reality that is largely concealed in conventional military literature. His combination of realist and absurdist elements also constructs a literary world that sheds light on his own precarious existence, and that uncovers the hidden essence of the reality of his own world.

Bibliography

Cai, Rong 蔡蓉. "In the Madding Crowd: Self and Other in Can Xue's Fiction." In *The Subject in Crisis in Contemporary Chinese Literature*, edited by Rong Cai, 92–126. Honolulu: University of Hawai'i Press, 2004.

Camus, Albert. *The Myth of Sisyphus and Other Essays*. Translated by Justin O'Brien. New York: Vintage Books, 1991.

---

30 Yan Lianke and Liang Hong 梁鴻, *Wupo de hong kuaizi: Zuojia yu wenxue boshi de duihualu* 巫婆的紅筷子：作家與文學博士的對話 [A witch's red chopsticks: Dialogues between a writer and a doctor of literature] (Shenyang: chunfeng wenyi chubanshe, 2002), 44.
31 Leung Laifong 梁麗芳, *Contemporary Chinese Fiction Writers* (Milton Park, Abingdon, Oxon: Routledge, 2016), 87, 258; Liang Hong, *Yan Lianke wenxue nianpu* 閻連科文學年譜 [Literary chronicle of Yan Lianke] (Shanghai: Fudan daxue chubanshe, 2015), 87.
32 Yan Lianke and Li Tuo 李陀, "*Shouhuo*: Chaoxianshi xiezuo de zhongyao chanshi" 受活：超現實寫作的重要闡釋 [*Lenin's Kisses*: The significant experiment of surrealist writing]," in Lin Jianfa, ed., *Yan Lianke wenxue yanjiu*, vol. 2 (Yunnan: Yunnan renmin chubanshe, 2012), 305.
33 Yan Lianke, Huang Ping 黃平, and Bai Liang 白亮, "'Tudi,' 'renmin' yu dangdai wenxue zhi yuan" 「土地」、「人民」與當代文學之源 ["Land," "people" and contemporary literature resources], in *Yan Lianke yanjiu* 閻連科研究 [Studies of Yan Lianke], ed. Fang Zhihong 方志紅 (Kaifeng: Henan daxue chubanshe, 2015), 63.

Chen Xiaoming 陳曉明. *Zhongguo dangdai wenxue zhuchao* 中國當代文學主潮 [Major trends in contemporary Chinese literature]. Beijing: Peking University Press, 2009.

Cornwell, Neil. *The Absurd in Literature*. Manchester: Manchester University Press, 2006.

Esslin, Martin. *The Theatre of the Absurd*. 3rd edn. New York: Vintage Books, 2004.

Feng Shounong 馮壽農. "Zhongguo xinshiqi wenxue dui Xifang huangdanpai wenxue de xishou he xiaorong" 中國新時期文學對西方荒誕派文學的吸收和消融 [The absorption and assimilation of Western absurd literature in Chinese new period literature]. *Xiamen daxue xuebao (zhexue shehui kexue ban)* 廈門大學學報(哲學社會科學版) [Journal of Xiamen University (Arts & Social Sciences)], 1993, no. 3: 74–79.

Hong, Zicheng 洪子誠. *A History of Contemporary Chinese Literature*. Translated by Michael M. Day. Leiden: Brill, 2007.

Kundera, Milan. *The Art of the Novel*. 1st edn. Translated by Linda Asher. New York: Grove Press, 1988.

Liang Hong 梁鴻. *Yan Lianke wenxue nianpu* 閻連科文學年譜 [Literary chronicle of Yan Lianke]. Shanghai: Fudan daxue chubanshe, 2015.

Leung, Laifong 梁麗芳. *Contemporary Chinese Fiction Writers: Biography, Bibliography, and Critical Assessment*. Milton Park, Abingdon, Oxon: Routledge, 2016.

Sherman, David. *Camus*. Chichester: Wiley-Blackwell, 2009.

Tay, William. "Avant-Garde Theatre in Post-Mao China: *The Bus-Stop* by Gao Xingjian." In *Soul of Chaos: Critical Perspectives on Gao Xingjian*, edited by Kwok-Kan Tam, 67–76. Hong Kong: Chinese University Press, 2001.

Yan Lianke 閻連科. *Faxian xiaoshuo* 發現小說 [Discovering fiction]. Beijing: Renmin wenxue chubanshe, 2001.

———. *Sihao jinqu* 四號禁區 [Prohibited area number four]. Shenyang: Beifang lianhe chuanmei, 2009.

———, Huang Ping 黃平, and Bai Liang 白亮. "'Tudi,' 'renmin' yu dangdai wenxue zhi yuan" 「土地」、「人民」與當代文學之源 ["Land," "people" and contemporary literature resources]. In *Yan Lianke yanjiu* 閻連科研究 [Studies of Yan Lianke], edited by Fang Zhihong 方志紅, 56–67. Kaifeng: Henan daxue chubanshe, 2015.

——— and Li Tuo 李陀. "*Shouhuo*: Chaoxianshi xiezuo de zhongyao chanshi" 受活: 超現實寫作的重要闡釋 [*Lenin's Kisses*: The significant experiment of surrealist writing]. In *Yan Lianke wenxue yanjiu* 閻連科文學研究 [Studies of Yan Lianke's literature], vol. 1, edited by Lin Jianfa 林建法, 299–317. Yunnan: Yunnan renmin chubanshe, 2012.

——— and Liang Hong. *Wupo de hong kuaizi: Zuojia yu wenxue boshi de duihualu* 巫婆的紅筷子: 作家與文學博士的對話 [A witch's red chopsticks: Dialogues between a writer and a doctor of literature]. Shenyang: Chunfeng wenyi chubanshe, 2002.

Zhu Xiangqian 朱向前. "Nongmin zhi zi yu nongmin junren" 農民之子與農民軍人 [The son of peasants and the peasant-soldiers]. In *Yan Lianke wenxue yanjiu*, vol. 2, edited by Lin Jianfa, 47–61. Yunnan: Yunnan renmin chubanshe, 2012.

———. *Zhongguo junlü wenxue wushi nian* 中國軍旅文學五十年 [Chinese military literature in fifty years]. Beijing: Jiefangjun wenyi chubanshe, 2007.

8
YAN LIANKE AND ITALO CALVINO ON THE ABSURDITY OF URBAN LIFE

Selusi Ambrogio

Introduction

Italo Calvino was born in 1923, Yan Lianke 閻連科 in 1958. When young, both faced one of the most dramatic and violent events of the twenty-first century of their respective countries: the Second World War for the first author, the Cultural Revolution for the second one. Both reached their artistic maturity during the decades of the economic boom of each country. Calvino received international recognition as a writer in the 1960s, when the so-called Italian economic miracle completely changed the social, cultural, and urban landscape of the country. He rapidly became one of the most refined and complex interpreters of these dramatic changes. Yan published his first short story in 1979,[1] when Deng Xiaoping launched the opening-up policy. Yan's most renowned fictional works express concern for the consequences of Chinese economic growth on common people, particularly on the *shoukuren* 受苦人 (i.e., suffering people) of the countryside. Therefore, despite living in two different continents and in two different epochs, the social themes they describe with a personal touch are extremely similar. Both authors resort to surrealistic narrative solutions and omnipresent irony to write about reality. We will investigate one of these social themes, namely the absurdity of urban life, which denudes the unrealistic and unbelievable face of contemporary modern and developed societies.[2]

The spirit of the city in Calvino and Yan Lianke

Daniel A. Bell and Avner de-Shalit devoted a fascinating book to "the spirit of the cities," namely the peculiar identity that makes each city absolutely unique. They analyzed nine metropolises, selected because each one of them represents a specific value. Jerusalem is the

---

1 Liang Hong 梁鴻, *Yan Lianke wenxue nianpu* 閻連科文學年譜 [Chronology of Yan Lianke's literary activity] (Shanghai: Fudan daxue chubanshe, 2015), 11.
2 In this article, we are not concerned with the reception of Calvino in China; a wide body of literature, mostly in Italian, is already available on this topic. Calvino, despite being warmly received by several avant-garde and postmodernist Chinese authors (e.g., Ma Yuan 馬原, Can Xue 殘雪, Ge Fei 格非, Wang Shuo 王朔, Su Tong 蘇童, Yu Hua 余華, Mo Yan 莫言, Wang Xiaobo 王小波, etc.), did not reach the wider Chinese audience, likely because of his "minor" language, his style, and his lack of a Nobel Prize.

city of religion, Montreal of languages, Singapore of national building, Beijing of political power, Oxford of learning, Berlin of a mix of tolerance and intolerance, Paris of romance, and, lastly, New York is the city of ambition. Though these labels might seem quite stereotyped, the concrete analysis of the spirit of each city led to a variegated and not universal definition of civism. They use the word "ethos" to name this shared spirit of a community, thus a concept that implies both etic and social identity in a given urban space. According to their sociopolitical and historical investigation, there are six factors that could promote the birth and the development of the "urban ethos."

> First, the city does not have a huge gap between rich and poor or between ethnic and racial groups. … Second, the city has a long-term rivalry with another city, often in the same country. … Third, the city's identity/ethos is threatened by outside forces, and hence residents have a strong motivation to struggle to keep their identity. … Fourth, the city has substantial authority to enact laws (in the case of Singapore), ordinances, bylaws, and regulations that protect and nourish its particular identity or ethos. … Fifth, the cities have or had great city planners with the moral, political, and legal authority to enact transformative plans that help to realize a common public ethos. … Sixth, an external agency, such as an advertising campaign or a movie, brands a city as having particular characteristics. None of these six factors, taken alone, is necessary or sufficient to create or nourish an ethos. However, each factor does increase the likelihood of success, and the more such factors are present, the greater the likelihood of success.[3]

The first point concerns the vital energy of the urban context, the hybridization, and the tendency to englobe what originally comes from outside the city. This shows the importance of exchange that imparts vitality to this evolving urban identity. As the economist Edward Glaeser posits, the success of the city is due to the ability of humans to learn from each other and share their interests with one another.[4] The second and the third are about the historical relevance of the feeling of being in danger and encircled by forces that want to destroy "our" identity. The fourth aspect demands the political independence of the city's government to take innovative actions and to shape the urban identity. The fifth factor deals with the capacity to plan the city in order to physically represent and incentivize this ethos. Lastly, the marketing ability of the city to be perceived as unique is also relevant in order to communicate this specific urban identity to both inhabitants and strangers.

According to the Italian anthropologist Carlo Tullio-Altan, any social identity, particularly that of countries but also of cities, needs five conditions to find stability and recognition: *epos* (the common memory of the past), *ethos* (shared social norms and stable institutions that create values and thus civism), *logos* (a common language), *genos/ethnos* (ethnic lineage, common origins), *topos/oikos* (the territory as a symbolic space).[5] These five elements are what Bell and de-Shalit name, in a less structuralist fashion, the "spirit of the city." We will, in the first part of our investigation, compare how these five elements interact in the "invisible cities" of Calvino and in the city of Explosion described by Yan.

---

3 Daniel A. Bell and Avner de-Shalit, *The Spirit of Cities: Why the Identity of a City Matters in a Global Age* (Princeton: Princeton University Press, 2011), 11–13.
4 Edward Glaeser, *Triumph of the City* (New York: Penguin, 2011).
5 Carlo Tullio-Altan, *Ethnos e civiltà. Identità etniche e valori democratici* [Ethos and civilization: Ethnic identities and democratic values] (Milan: Feltrinelli, 1995).

Epos

We need to start our investigation with the narrative construction of the memory and history of the cities as described by the two authors since, as Walter Benjamin says, "memory is the epic faculty *par excellence*."[6] Both authors provide a refined historical setting that creates a strong epic flavor. Calvino makes use of Marco Polo, a narrator reminiscent of the ancient storytellers who adapt their stories to the audience and trap them in a web of fascinating labyrinths. Marco Polo describes to the Mongol emperor Kublai Khan fifty-five cities at the remotest corners of the Chinese empire, which he visited during his official trips as ambassador. The book opens by saying that the emperor most likely does not believe what his ambassador says about these incredible cities—he sometimes even tries to contest the validity of these descriptions. The more he resists, however, the more he is trapped within this surrealistic narration. The founder of this immense empire, after decades of winning battles, is starting to question himself about the meaning of what he has achieved, about the stability of the immense empire he has unified, and he feels a saddening voidness. Therefore, he needs Polo's accounts to find a reason for his actions and a renovated meaning for his reign: "Only in Marco Polo's accounts was Kublai Khan able to discern, through the walls and towers destined to crumble, the tracery of a pattern so subtle it could escape the termites' gnawing."[7] The cities belong to eleven series—memory, desire, signs, thin, trading, eyes, names, dead, sky, hidden, and continuous—with five in each one. They are presented in a non-serial order, which is interrupted by several exchanges between Polo and the emperor.

Therefore, the narrative context is apparently martial and official, but, in reality, Polo's descriptions are extremely vague, inward, and elusive. This official history/report, despite its granitic appearance, falls down under the weight of the loss of meaning. Only Polo's mesmerizing stories could trace some philosophical trajectories in this desert of sense. He responds to Kublai's desperation for the decaying empire: "Yes, the empire is sick, and, what is worse, it is trying to become accustomed to its sores. This is the aim of my explorations: examining the traces of happiness still to be glimpsed, I gauge its short supply. If you want to know how much darkness there is around you, you must sharpen your eyes, peering at the faint lights in the distance."[8] Therefore, Calvino provides his story through the appearance of official reports from an ambassador but, in reality, this is an anti-epic narrative. Polo does not exalt the richness of the country, does not celebrate Mongols' epic actions. He does not eternalize the sense of this conquest, predicting a bright future guaranteed by the *genos* or *ethnos* of the Mongol conquerors, namely Genghis Khan's lineage. This would have been a true *epos* for the empire and the cities. On the contrary, these cities are but traces of pale hope, which need to be composed together with difficulty in the mind of the reader into the shape of one livable city that still does not exist as such, but has already faded away.

When we analyze literary production in ancient and imperial China, it is evident that the historical dimension has always been preferred to the epic one. As Mao Dun 茅盾 already suggested in 1929, one of the reasons for China's presumed "loss of Epic" is the "historicization of the myths."[9] Myths and epics were mostly related to historical events, and in the

---

6 Walter Benjamin, "The Storyteller: Reflections on Nikolai Leskóv," in *Illuminations*, trans. Harry Zohn (New York: Schocken Books, 2007), 97.
7 Italo Calvino, *Invisible Cities*, trans. William Weaver (New York: Harvest Book, 1974): 5–6.
8 Ibid., 59.
9 Quoted in Li Gang, "20th Century Exploration of the 'Issue of the Chinese Epic,'" *Frontiers of Literary Studies in China* 4, no. 1 (2010): 38. This article presents an effective overview of the question of "Chinese loss of Epic" into a century of Chinese critical production. Li concludes that the "loss" is due to an uncritical application of Western literary paradigms presumed as universal, i.e., epic as the origin of literature, to the Chinese case.

histories, many mythological or epic sections could be found. Jaroslav Prusek interestingly advocates that Chinese historiography presents two main characteristics very distinct from the Greek ones. The first is a strong tendency to arrange events and material not according to a narrative chain, but rather to categories that could be pedagogically and philosophically meaningful. The second aspect is the scarce interest of the ancient Chinese historians in the peripetia and fate of the individuals, because the real aim of their writing was the general principle, the moral, and the systematic law of events that could be revealed through the historical narration.[10]

In *The Explosion Chronicles*, Yan Lianke shows all his mastery in creating a true contemporary epic that composes elements of Chinese historiography with elements of Greek historiography. From the latter, he acquires the pervading and critical role of the narrator, the strong epic taste, and the coherent narration. From Chinese historiography, he inherits the specific terminology, the tendency to provide extremely detailed descriptions of contexts, and the interest in investigating the flux of events in order to understand the underlying general law more than the singular event or personality. The narrative frame is the writing of the chronicles (*zhi* 志) of the growth of a village named Explosion (*Zhalie* 炸裂) from the Song dynasty (960–1279) to the early 2010s. The chronicles, as any effective historical work, start from the beginning, thus providing the explanation of the rare name of the village, which is due to the eruption of a volcano that forced the inhabitants of another countryside in the Henan region to mass migrate to this place. During the Yuan dynasty (1279–1368), this little newly established village of immigrants became a small marketplace that grew during the Ming dynasty (1368–1644). Because of the revolts and droughts during the late Qing dynasty (1644–1911), the residents left the village, and only under the Republic did the location start to repopulate. During the land redistribution movement, a concubine of the local landlord Zhu was reassigned to the family of Kong Mingliang, the grandfather of the "socialist heroes" at the core of the novel. Therefore, this contemporary communist model family was generated from a poor countryman surnamed Kong and an impure woman of the Zhu feudalistic family.

These chronicles were commissioned to exalt the men who made this growth possible. In the Preface (chapter 1), the fictional author of the chronicles, who shares not only a name with Yan Lianke but also many of his personal features, confesses having accepted this enormous task only because he was a native of this former village in the Balou 耙耧 mountains and because the reward for writing these chronicles was enormous. Despite presenting a long list of members of the editorial board, among whom appear the protagonists themselves, the author reports having obtained a complete freedom of writing. This freedom allowed him to compose the text from his individual point of view. In the detailed description of the (fictional) compilation process, we read that the book, after being released, was blocked and the author was exiled from the city. In the Postface (chapter 39) by the fictional Yan, he describes the violent reaction of the Mayor after having read the draft, the threats he received, and his ironic answer: "Thank you, Mayor Kong. You are this book's first reader, and your response reassures me that I have written a pretty good work."[11] From the paratextual material, it is evident that (the real) Yan's aim was challenging and discrediting the Chinese contemporary triumphal rhetoric of reforms and infinite growth. As Mencius said about Confucius's authorship of the *Spring and Autumn Annals*, "rebellious ministers and violent sons were struck with

---

10 Jaroslav Prusek, "History and Epics in China and in the West: A Study of Differences in the Conception of the Human Story," *Diogenes* 11, no. 42 (June 1963): 20–43.

11 Yan Lianke, *The Explosion Chronicles*, trans. Carlos Rojas (London: Chatto & Windus, 2017), 448.

terror" (*luanchen zeizi ju* 亂臣賊子懼) because of this historical writing.[12] Actually, the act of writing a history is dangerous for both the writer, as Mencius suggests in the same section, and the many "historical criminals" who have their true stories finally disclosed. The editorial board was looking for a glorifying chronology of the city, a true epic of its success, but what the members get is the epic of the immorality and desolation of their acts.

Yan is an intrusive narrator in *The Explosion Chronicles* but he never directly comments on characters. He does not search for their profound psychology because his characters are doers; they act according to a superior and general power, which is the true focus of the novel. Yan's characters represent the contemporary quest for the "national character" of the Chinese after the opening-up policy. However, while Lu Xun's 魯迅 Ah Q is a loser who pretends to be a winner according to the narrative "method of spiritual victory" (*jingshen shengli fa* 精神勝利法), the heroes of the city of *The Explosion Chronicles* are, speaking from the point of view of richness and power, perfect winners. For instance, Mayor Kong, the true protagonist of the story, is somebody who works crazily in order to achieve the dream of the promotion of Explosion from village to a metropolis comparable with Beijing, Shanghai, and Hong Kong. His blind desire seems to be driven and fed by a Nietzschean "will of power." Besides his burning ambition, he is a man without exceptional quality or ability, and his humanity gradually fades under the weight of ambition and power. The concrete achievement of this impossible and unrealistic dream enacts the outdoing of reality to this irrepressible "will of power."

The effective epic dimension of this novel is not to be found in the courage or heroism of the characters, but rather in the ambition to be upgraded, which is an incredible force. Characters are almost like puppets in the hand of this "superior power." The contrast between the two most relevant families, namely the Kong and Zhu, is presented as destiny instead of a human choice. In the second chapter, Kong Dongde, the impure ancestor of the family we reported before, in a kind of messianic prophecy (i.e., a new Noah), orders his four sons to leave home and to each go in a different cardinal direction, since they will find something on their path able to decide their future. The "heroic" young Mayor Kong encounters Zhu Ying, daughter of the chief village Zhu, fierce enemy of his clan. On the same night, each resident of Explosion has the same dream, namely Kong Dongde ordering him/her to get out in the middle of the night looking for his/her own destiny. The common dream is one of Yan's favorite narrative expedients.[13] In this novel, the following words introduce this surreal event: "There was a dynastic shift and an attendant process of geographic transformation, as place-names were all changed. The entire world was turned upside down, with black becoming white and white becoming black."[14]

In the Chinese original, Yan uses very specific expressions, such as *diyu yange* 地輿沿革, a historical term meaning an epoch of dramatic socio-political change, and *tianfan difu* 天翻地覆, a widely used idiom literally meaning that heaven and earth are turned upside down. Therefore, this apparently improbable event is the beginning of our story. After a few years, the two young characters compete one against the other to be elected chief of the village, and the man wins only because the woman opts to be his wife and fulfills the prophecy. They do not love each other, but both sacrifice their feelings in order to achieve the success

---

12 *Mencius* 3B.9; *Mencius*, trans. I. Bloom (New York: Columbia University Press, 2009), 71.
13 Marco Polo, presenting Zobeide, reports an extremely similar shared dream. The city is built according to a dream where every man runs after a beautiful naked lady in an unknown city at night and tries to trap her. In the end, the city is extremely ugly and unlivable because it has the suffocating shape of a trap. See Calvino, *Invisible Cities*, 45–46.
14 Yan, *The Explosion Chronicles*, 15. For the Chinese version, Yan Lianke, *Zhalie zhi* 炸裂志 [The explosion chronicles] (Zhengzhou: Zhongguo banben tushuguan, 2016), 14.

of the village, the only true driver of the narrative. As Yan explains in *The Discovery of Fiction* (*Faxian xiaoshuo* 發現小說), "improbability" (*bu keneng* 不可能) is the key for understanding "internal reality," the profound and not evident reality under the predictable surface we are used to seeing:

> … the aim of the internal causality (*nei zhenshi* 內真實) writings is not to arouse the feeling or reflection of mystery, allegory or esotericism, but rather to pioneeringly penetrate the concreteness of reality and of life. The essence and potentiality of internal causality is to start the writing of a new realism and of reality. Otherwise, internal causality would lose its meaning and it would be mortally suffocated by the two invisible hands of the fabulous and the mysterious.[15]

Yan names his narrative project "mythorealism" (*shenshi zhuyi* 神實主義) and he advocates that this is the third way between pure traditional realism, which is either controlled by authorities (i.e., revolutionary and patriotic) or typical of the superficial/hedonistic description of everyday life, and Western schools of fiction.[16] This could be the new Chinese way in literature, freeing Chinese writers from the formal obligation of adapting the Chinese narrative and soul to the various Western literary trends. He advocates that Western literary teachings and techniques cannot conform to the Chinese world, since the narrative art cannot be separated from a specific culture, epoch, and land.[17] He describes this new "Chinese narrative way" as follows:

> In the writing process it is necessary to abandon every superficial logical relations, in search of a "unmanifest reality" ("*bu cunzai*" *de zhenshi* 「不存在」的真實), namely an "invisible" reality that has been concealed by reality/realism. Mythorealism distances itself from the common understanding of realism. Its connection with reality is not based on the cause-and-effect relationship of everyday life, since it relies on human soul, the spiritual vitality (i.e., the connection between humans on one side, and the interaction of the essence of vitality with the interior of things on the other), and the subjective thought of the writer based on reality. Speaking just about what is visible and clear, we cannot cross the bridge between truth and reality. The techniques and means that bring together the mythorealism with truth and reality are imagination, allegory, mythology, legend, dream, fantasy, demoniac, metamorphic, etc., which all take place on the realistic soil of everyday life and society. Mythorealism is in no way a rejection of realism, but it strenuously creates reality and surpasses realism itself.[18]

In the last three decades, the narrative portrait of contemporary Chinese urban extraordinary transformations has been realized in several ways. The most common is the plain realistic description either of the hedonistic and successful metropolitan life, or of the personal crisis and misery that people can experience in such an unwelcoming environment (either high-class people or subalterns and migrants). A second way is to exaggerate the negative characteristics of the metropolis (i.e., sexuality, corruption, money, etc.), providing a bitter,

15 Yan Lianke, *Faxian xiaoshuo* (Tianjin: Nankai daxue chubanshe, 2011), 48. My translation.
16 Ibid., 181.
17 Ibid., 188–89.
18 Ibid., 48; my translation. A selection of this paragraph has already been translated in Song Weijie 宋偉杰, "Yan Lianke's Mythorealism Representation of the Country and City," *Modern Fiction Studies* 62, no. 4 (Winter 2016): 645.

parodistic, and sarcastic description, as for instance in the extraordinary masterpiece of Jia Pingwa's 賈平凹 *Ruined City* (*Feidu* 廢都, 1993).[19] A third way, at the moment one of the most flourishing, is the Sci-Fi approach, where a fantastic and imaginary city can provide a perfect mirror for real urban life, with the advantage of being free from censorship.[20] What Yan chooses is a fourth way that somehow brings together elements of these other three possible approaches. He describes the hedonism of success in contrast to the struggle of the *shoukuren*. However, he depicts these successful people as extremely empty, to the point of being perceived as soulless humans, unable even to benefit from their achievements. Their actions are described with a bitter and sarcastic tone full of flamboyant exaggerations that prevents any possible mimesis of the reader. Finally, the mythorealistic elements—shared dreams, rivers of money, unnaturalistic natural reactions, etc.—are his unrealistic insertions useful to investigate the truth behind reality. His setting is a fictional city, which experiences something very close to what happened to a real place like Shenzhen. Therefore, we can ask: is this city as unrealistic as the ones described by Sci-Fi narratives or not? Explosion is not a real Chinese city, it is a place where incredible things happen, but nothing unrealistic enough, or scientifically described, to be a Sci-Fi product.

Calvino's historical characters are effective historical and epic humans (i.e., Kublai Khan and Marco Polo), but his narrative is introverted, fragmented, and deeply philosophical. The historical setting and the fascinating flavor of each city provide an epic inward quest for the sense of human life, relationships, and society in a desert where any meaning seems lost. Polo travels around those diverse cities, but, in the end, he admits to searching for the features of his own hometown—i.e., Venice, La Serenissima—in each of these places. However, he is not a kind of heroic Ulysses; there is not an adverse fate or a divine force preventing him from going back home. His own human quest is the only reason for his adventures. This antiepic is typical of Calvino who, in *Our Ancestors* (1952–59), already provided a fascinating disintegration of literary heroic figures modeled on the epic poem *Orlando Furioso* by Ludovico Ariosto. On the contrary, Yan seems to know that there is a superior reason behind the actions of his characters, which are extreme and paradoxical but not epic (*etos*), since what is epical is only this indefinite power, this omnipresent mover that is ambition. Therefore, both authors present a clear epical narrative mode—although antiepic—to describe their cities, but their scope is very different.

Ethos

As we sketched out in the introductory section, the ethos is the second element necessary in the shaping and description of a city. Ethos is a composition of many aspects, such as rituals, values, and human relationships. We can anticipate that in the works of both authors, human relationships are very weak and loose. Only the interactions between Polo and the emperor

---

19 On these two kinds of urban fiction, see Robin Visser and Jie Lu, "Contemporary Urban Fiction: Rewriting the City," in *The Columbia Companion to Modern Chinese Literature*, ed. Kirk A. Denton (New York: Columbia University Press, 2016), 345–54.

20 Chen Qiufan 陳楸帆 paradigmatically affirms that "Sci-Fi is likely the most relevant realism because the Sci-Fi author can deal with issues ignored by mainstream literature as these could be sensitive topics (as smog, pollution, ethnic fight and struggle, etc.) and express his own opinions and reflections on them." See Dong Meiqi, "Chen Qiufan: Kehuan shi zuida de xianshizhuyi" 陳楸帆: 科幻是最大的現實主義 [Sci-Fi is the best realism], *Shangye jiazhi* 商業價值 [Business values], 10 Sep. 2015, http://www.chinawriter.com.cn/kehuan/2015/2015-09-10/253039.html (last accessed 25 July 2021). My translation.

are based on respect and reciprocity, but the two men are hierarchically very distant. What brings them together is the philosophical quest for the meaning of life and the meaning of the art of ruling. Their relationship is not based on friendship, love, or any other human feeling. At a certain point, they even doubt their own real presence in the garden as emperor and ambassador.[21] They are every man who is searching for truth. They are symbols of the human condition. This is the ethos between them.

We will try now to compose the complex and fragmentary ethos that is presented in some of the cities described by Polo. First of all, all these cities are oases in a desert (we will discuss this topic in the section on *topos*), isolated identities connected only by commercial roots. Therefore, residents are mostly merchants, by sea or by earth, and artisans, thus they are mostly devoted to commercial exchanges. Cities are like monads only connected by economic interest.

We can present the ethos of those cities under three categories: unhappy or impossible relationships, trickiness, and the relations with the dead. The more than fifty cities described by Polo are mostly unhappy, and when there is some happiness, it is extremely feeble. In Ersilia, human relationships are tied in order to be abandoned: "In Ersilia, to establish the relationships that sustain the city's life, the inhabitants stretch strings from the corners of the houses, white or black or gray or black-and-white according to whether they mark a relationship of blood, of trade, authority, agency. When the strings become so numerous that you can no longer pass among them, the inhabitants leave: the houses are dismantled; only the strings and their supports remain."[22]

The city is an unlivable skeleton of relationships that, when mature, are simply abandoned without remorse. Even the familial relationships, i.e., the roots of their *geno*, are left behind like unnecessary burdens or a corpse. In the metropolis of Chloe, when people see each other for the first time, they imagine their possible relationships, their conversations, and even their sexual life together. "Something runs among them," but they do not really meet, they do not speak. "A voluptuous vibration constantly stirs Chloe, the most chaste of cities."[23] The city is suspended between desire and reality. Something similar happens in Raissa, named the unhappy city, where people are always angry at each other and things can but go wrong. However, Polo observes, in this unhappiness, there are traces of possible happiness that residents suffocate under the weight of their negative mood. Calvino writes: "the unhappy city contains a happy city unaware of its own existence."[24] People are unable to be happy since urban life tricks them all the time. This is extremely evident in Anastasia, where any desire is furiously awakened in each mind, but every dream is impossible to realize. Happiness is always unachievable. Citizens "can only inhabit this desire and be content," because they are merely slaves of "the treacherous city."[25] They work extremely hard the whole day, and their labor feeds their unfulfillable desires.

The city is not only of the living residents but also of the dead. In Adelma, every person you meet reminds you of your dead ones, and you feel yourself as one of them. Both Eusapia and Laudomia are places where the dead people continue to create the ethos of the city. Eusapia has a perfect copy of itself in the underground where the dead still live their lives and are usually happier than the living people, because they can choose their most desired destinies.

21 Calvino, *Invisible Cities*, 103–04.
22 Ibid., 76.
23 Ibid., 51–52.
24 Ibid., 149.
25 Ibid., 12.

This is why the living people of these cities choose to imitate the life of the dead ones, and they enter a confraternity in order to be allowed to enter the underground as they please.[26] Laudomia is even triple: one copy for the living residents, one for the dead, and, finally, one for the unborn: "And to feel sure of itself, the living Laudomia has to seek in the Laudomia of the dead the explanation of itself ...."[27] The hermeneutical keys of those cities are the forged memories, the impossible desire, the loss of identity, the unhappiness, and the lack of sense: "... the charring of burned lives that forms a scab on the city, the sponge swollen with vital matter that no longer flows, the jam of past, present, future that blocks existences calcified in the illusion of movement: this is what you would find at the end of your journey."[28] After years of traveling, these are Polo's thoughts on these miserable but fascinating cities that he describes to Kublai. The lives in the cities are burned by desire and frustration.

While Calvino's ethos is very fragmented, Yan provides a very coherent and systematic ethos for Explosion that changes according to the dimension of the urban area. Since the Ming epoch, most of the residents of the village were surnamed either Kong or Zhu, and they pretend, without any evidence, to be descendants of the most relevant holy masters of Confucianism, namely Confucius (*Kongzi* 孔子) and the philosophic systematizer Zhu Xi 朱熹 (of the Song). These two philosophers represent the apex of the Chinese moral philosophy. Confucius is the first master who tried to restore the ancient moral and political tradition that goes back to the founder kings (*xianwang* 先王) of Chinese culture. Zhu Xi is the philosopher who composed the different aspects of this tradition with the influences from Daoism and Buddhism, and, in so doing, provided a moral thought that shaped the imperial culture of both the Ming and the Qing. Therefore, we would expect a very moral social context devoted to rituals and ethics. On the contrary, these villagers strenuously hate each other; the three most numerous families (Kong, Zhu, and Cheng 程) are sworn enemies.[29] But it is only in the revolutionary period that the true immoral nature of the village escalates; the two "destined lovers," full of ambition and resentment, choose their path of life: the boy becomes a thief who steals goods from trains and the girl becomes a whore in the nearby metropolis. In that way, both of them earn extremely large sums of money when compared to the poor local farmers (Yan's beloved *shoukuren*). He becomes the chief of a gang of thieves that, in a short time, includes almost all of the men of the village, who thus abandon farming. She instead recruits the most beautiful girls and boys to become prostitutes. The authorities try to fight this social drift, but money is like a flood impossible to arrest. As we said, Kong Mingliang becomes the chief of the village and, from this moment, his only aim is to transform the village into a city and, finally, the city into a metropolis like Beijing, Shanghai, Tokyo, and New York.[30]

This socio-political promotion of the village is based on bribery, prostitution, corruption, violence, and fraud. Both county politicians and foreign investors are easy to buy with money and prostitutes. The city is even transformed into a borderless Vietnamese whorehouse, only because the American investors have good memories of the local women during the Vietnam War.[31] The fake "Vietnamese parades" put in place are closed by horrific slogans such as: "After having killed so many of us, you should come here to invest! ... As long as you invest here, those dead Vietnamese will overlook the fact that you invaded and murdered them. ...

26 Ibid., 109–10.
27 Ibid., 141.
28 Ibid., 100.
29 We remark that also the surname Cheng is connected to Confucianism, being the surname of two Song philosophers, i.e., the Cheng brothers.
30 Yan, *The Explosion Chronicles*, 282.
31 Ibid., 284–91.

For the sake of your conscience, you should invest money here."[32] The forgiveness and absolution for having murdered and humiliated Asians for decades—we cannot but also think of the Chinese "century of humiliation of the nation" (*bainian guochi* 百年國恥)—can be bought through huge investments. We see clearly that the whole ethos of the city has a price and, if necessary, the Chinese city can be changed into a Vietnamese-style village, and citizens can become Vietnamese whores. When Kong Mingyao, the retired soldier among the brothers, who, for the sake of truth, has bought his undeserved medals, accuses Kong Mingliang of betraying the values of China and socialism, the latter "pushed Mingyao away, then slapped his face. 'The economy is the nation's top priority, you know? He howled, 'I'm telling you, all I need to do is give the word, and your mining company will immediately collapse, your assets will be seized, and your accounts will be frozen!'" Yan here cannot refrain from a political escalation and makes the mayor sarcastically remark: "China is now extraordinarily poor, but if it becomes rich then it would be able to purchase the US presidency."[33] All the angry former soldiers Mingyao reunited in military parades against the American investors unflinchingly turn back to their high-salary employments.

If the *ethos* and the *genos* of the entire village are submitted to what we named the "power of ambition," the private relationships are no more robust. For instance, Zhu Ying, blindly following the mythic dream and her ambitions, marries Kong Mingliang, the man who paid the villagers to drown his father, the former chief, under a Noahic flood of spittle that lasted an entire evening.[34] But the true emblem of social failure is the Kong family itself. Men are all driven by teenage sensual passion, even in old age. For example, the father Dongde leaves his wife in an attempt to satisfy his insatiable lust for young flesh, and thus he destroys his family. He falls in love with a young girl (the lover of one of his sons!) who leaves the family; he becomes extremely depressed, and his daughter-in-law consoles him with her young prostitutes. Zhu Ying tells Dongde that her girls can show the greatest "filial piety" or "filial love" to him, in Chinese *xiaoshun* 孝順,[35] where *xiao* is the pillar of Confucian moral system for both Confucius and Zhu Xi. The purity of this value is used to express sexual favors toward an old man.

We think it could be particularly effective, in order to represent the ethos of *The Explosion Chronicles*, to analyze some of the fourteen occurrences of the term *xiao* in the novel (alone or in compounds).[36] The first occurrence is when Kong Mingliang, after marrying Zhu Ying, celebrates and honors his father-in-law, who has been ironically killed by the spittle of the villagers he himself paid. The former chief Zhu was mourned as a martyr who pursued prosperity, together with all the thieves that died while subtracting goods from the trains. In this context, all the people have to *pima daixiao* 披麻戴孝, which means dress in deep mourning for the funeral of an elder member of the family.[37] Several occurrences express the fake devotion of Zhu Ying toward his father-in-law Kong Dongde. She always shows all her "filial devotion" and respect to the man who was the enemy of her father. In three occurrences, *xiao* means money, i.e., the money of inheritance and the money that mourning people give to the family of the dead. In order to avenge the father who died of a heart attack during sex

---

32 Ibid., 290.
33 Ibid., 297–98.
34 Ibid., 24.
35 Yan, *Zhalie zhi*, 153.
36 We did not count the four repetitions of *xiaobai* 孝白, namely the white color used for mourning the dead, because it is used by the former soldier Kong Mingyao in his accusations against the arrogant Western countries. Therefore, these occurrences are unrelated to familial values.
37 Ibid., 28.

with prostitutes, the mayor destroys his wife's brothel in order to fulfill his filial duty (*dui ni jinxiao le* 對你盡孝了).[38] However, when the Kong mother is severely sick, the good and weak brother Minghui stays day and night at her side, while the other brothers do not show up.[39] Minghui hates his work as bureau director as he was obliged by the mayor to take the job, and decides to leave his place and look after their sick mother. He makes three appointments with his brother's office manager, and when they finally meet, this is what happens: "When Mingliang heard Minghui's decision, he was furious, saying, 'You piece of shit. You're the youngest bureau director in the entire city. Don't you realize that?' Mingliang added, 'How many more days does our mother have to live? She has money and a nurse, so if we designate her a Mother of the Nation, we will have fulfilled our filial obligations.'"[40] Their mother has money and to designate her "Mother of the Nation" (*guomu* 國母) was enough to fulfill the filial piety or filial duty at the highest level (*daxiao* 大孝).[41] The last occurrence is again about the mother. When she dies, Mayor Kong answers to the brothers asking for his presence: "Throughout history, there has never been a hero who has mastered the ideals of both loyalty and filial piety."[42] Here we find the classical clash among Confucian values, the loyalty toward the empire and the love for parents. Classically, this clash is due to the impossibility of fulfilling both because, to a certain context, they turn out to be morally and socially incompatible. This is not the case in this context, however, and Mingliang is simply focused only on his ambition, completely disregarding his family and his social duties.

The ethos of the city of Explosion is clearly expressed by this disaggregated family full of hate and revenge. The father becomes an old sex maniac, and the mother is abandoned by most of her sons. The roots of the family are rotten, the *genos* is completely sick. Therefore, the family of the mayor cannot be in any way a positive model for the morality of the entire metropolis. Explosion's civism is based only on money and growth at any cost. Both our authors depict a dramatic involution of morality and human relations in the cities. As Polo describes, relationships are seen as a burden, not as a root.

Topos

Calvino's cities are of any kind and shape, but they share one relevant aspect: the desert encircles them. "Each city receives its form from the desert it opposes; and so the camel driver and the sailor see Despina, a border city between two deserts."[43] Each city is like an oasis in the desert, but the desert it opposes is not only a physical space, it is the desert of meaning. It is the human attempt to fight loss, diaspora, and dissolution. These "invisible cities" seem to be built out of a "superior architect" as ideal cities. However, this imagined perfection is always unreachable: "In every age someone, looking at Fedora as it was, imagined a way of making it the ideal city, but while he constructed his miniature model, Fedora was already no longer the same as before, and what had been until yesterday a possible future became only a toy in a glass globe."[44] The ideal cities are just glassy toys, fragile and cold, perfectly unlivable. When people start to construct those cities, they will endlessly try to reach the ideal shape, and they will never stop the construction process out of fear that the city will collapse. When Kublai

---

38 Ibid., 175.
39 Ibid., 249.
40 Yan, *The Explosion Chronicles*, 325.
41 For the Chinese original, see Yan, *Zhalie zhi*, 251.
42 Yan, *The Explosion Chronicles*, 374; Yan, *Zhalie zhi*, 287.
43 Calvino, *Invisible Cities*, 18.
44 Ibid., 31.

suggests that he has in his mind a perfect model city, one that perfectly corresponds to the norm, to which any other city just differs somehow, the wise Polo answers this model could but be "made only of exceptions, exclusions, incongruities, contradictions."[45] Therefore, these ideal cities are extremely disappointing, and the perfection they seek is a progressive distortion of human nature. Bersabea (Beersheba in the English translation) is designed by the most authoritative architects, with expensive materials to achieve the highest level of luxury. The residents are so intent on avoiding their natural needs and their imperfections that, as Calvino sarcastically comments: "Beersheba, a city which, only when it shits, is not miserly, calculating, greedy."[46]

The cities, despite being encircled by deserts, are overpopulated and limitless. Procopia becomes more and more overcrowded year after year, any natural element having been substituted by an "expanse of faces."[47] Even the sky has completely disappeared and been suffocated by them. In the local rest houses, you pay for a room that is already full of people on the ground. Both Trude and Penthesilea are endless, and any city will resemble them: "You have given up trying to understand whether, hidden in some sac or wrinkle of these dilapidated surroundings there exists a Penthesilea the visitor can recognize and remember, or whether Penthesilea is only the outskirts of itself. The question that now begins to gnaw at your mind is more anguished: outside Penthesilea does an outside exist? Or, no matter how far you go from the city, will you only pass from one limbo to another, never managing to leave it?"[48] These metropolises are like centerless and all-embracing octopuses that, after attracting residents with their apparent beauty, will strangle them. However, rather than humans, the true innocent victims are instead nature and animals. These cities are covered with expanses and mountains of rubbish and rusting sheet metal that menace the security of the same city.[49] The desert that divides one city from the others is covered with rubbish. "The boundaries between the alien, hostile cities are infected ramparts where the detritus of both support each other, overlap, mingle."[50]

Yan Lianke, who is widely known for the extreme precision of his special and naturalistic descriptions of environments that are inspired by his homeland, does not provide any detailed descriptions of Explosion. We can presume that the author is certainly more at ease with the natural countryside, but this lack of urban details is indeed revealing, since, at the same time, he offers extremely rich descriptions of the natural elements in the text (we will investigate them in the following section). Urban anonymity and repetitiveness are opposed to natural details and beauty. The extraordinary urban evolution of Explosion (i.e., natural village, social village, town, city, metropolis) is described through, on one side, human actions driven by the "power of ambition" and, on the other, by the official bureaucratic acts that approve each of these institutional promotions. We randomly know that the city's brothels are very beautiful and refined, and that extremely luxurious skyscrapers gradually dominate the skyline. Furthermore, factories and mines encircle this suffocating urban space. Farms are mostly abandoned. As we said, all these elements contribute to the creation of a perfectly anonymous city, completely centerless and, as Calvino depicts it, that "is only the outskirts of itself." We should bear in mind the aforementioned episode when the mayor is looking for American investments and he changes the city into a Vietnamese brother to please them. This episode is the vivid expression of both the immorality of economic growth and the complete lack of identity and civism of the city. The city is on sale.

45 Ibid., 69.
46 Ibid., 112.
47 Ibid., 147.
48 Ibid., 157.
49 Ibid., 104–05, 113–15.
50 Ibid., 114.

In chapter 15, we read that the city has hugely developed and changed its shape. The traces of the ancient village—the original main road—are still visible; however, the residents are no longer interested in this ancient-style area. Everybody wants to live in the luxurious attics that dominate the city:

> On account of this tension between reality and history, Explosion's old streets and the new city became divided into two distinct worlds. ... The glass surface of the buildings made the temperature in the city center always several degrees warmer than in the suburbs. Meanwhile, in the old city area, where there was a street named Explosion Street, there was barely anyone at all apart from a handful of people who came for sightseeing. Even Mayor Kong Mingliang and the city's richest resident, his brother Mingyao, rarely returned home to this street. It was as if they had already forgotten that they were originally from Explosion Street, and apart from New Year's or their mother's birthday, they almost never visited their former residence. They were all very busy as business took off.[51]

The lack of interest in the old city area coincides with the lack of filial piety toward the elders, and together they represent the rootless identity of this urban space devoted only to business, money, and success.

To some extent, the graves and the cemetery are described with a certain detail. The former chief of the village and father of Zhu Ying is buried in the same location where he was drowned by a river of spit in the square at the center of the village. When Kong Mingliang starts organizing a gang of thieves to steal goods from the trains, each one of them who accidentally dies in the meantime is proclaimed "martyr" (*lieshi* 烈士, hero or exemplary person who sacrifices himself for the wellbeing of a community), and he is buried in the same square.[52] When, in the end, the former village becomes a metropolis, the graves of the martyrs are relocated to an empty field in the mountains behind Explosion. Each one of them was proclaimed a city "pioneer" (*xianquzhe* 先驅者).[53] Evidently, the history of the city and the bodies of the dead are at the service of the new narrative of eternal growth. However, the last lines of the novel present a brotherly dialogue between Kong Mingguang and Kong Minghui, the least corrupted brothers; the second one says: "We should go weep at their graves. As Explosion has been transformed from a village to a town, from a town to a county, from a county to a city, and from a city to a provincial-level metropolis, the people of Explosion have lost the habit of weeping at the graves of their relatives."[54] Seeking forgiveness, the few remaining members of the Kong family who saved their humanity make a procession on their knees, leaving behind trails of blood.

The city and nature

Nature is not particularly evident in Calvino's *Invisible Cities*. It is mostly represented by the desert around the urban settlements. However, there is one city where the author refers to animals. Theodora, the "great cemetery of the animal kingdom, was closed, aseptic, over the final buried corpses with their last fleas and their last germs. Man had finally reestablished

---

51 Yan, *The Explosion Chronicles*, 323.
52 Ibid., 30; Yan, *Zhalie zhi*, 27.
53 Yan, *The Explosion Chronicles*, 322; Yan, *Zhalie zhi*, 249.
54 Yan, *The Explosion Chronicles*, 444.

the order of the world which he had himself upset: no other living species existed to cast any doubts." Humans have completely eradicated nature as it was a pestilence or a cancer. Since nature was a force that opposed the complete power of the humans, it became an unacceptable limitation. It is worth mentioning that Calvino closes this chapter on Theodora, suggesting that instead of animals and plants, a scary nature full of mythological creatures is preparing to resume possession of the city: "Sphinxes, griffons, chimeras, dragons, hircocervi, harpies, hydras, unicorns, basilisks."[55] Therefore, only mythic animals produced by human fears could avenge the violated nature.

Nature is similarly violated and subjugated for Yan. In this novel, the Chinese author reserves the use of mythorealism mostly to three issues: growth and money, floods of people (i.e., the military parades of the elder brother Kong Mingyao), and natural events. We already mentioned the first two, now we will focus on the last one. Besides the original eruption of the volcano, nature is always a passive protagonist in *The Explosion Chronicles*. It is described in terms opposed to the irrepressible power of ambition, growth, and richness. In this book, nature can only celebrate man's key acts. We calculated at least twenty unnatural natural events that were consequences of human acts. Those natural descriptions belong to circumstances such as the promotion of the urban space, the never-ending economic growth, and any arousing feeling or passion. For instance, when the village is promoted to town, all the dead plants in the mayor's office turn green again if touched by the letter of announcement.[56] Under the snow, red flowers start to blossom when the "heroic" Mingyao returns to the village and leaves the military training camp.[57] The economic investments of the Americans following the Vietnamization of the city are celebrated by tropical plants that blossom in early spring when it is usually still too cold for them in that season in Henan.[58] When Mingyao definitely abandons any hope for love and decides to create his own patriotic army, an eclipse obscures the sky.[59] And, when he organizes nationalist and anti-foreigner parades that could irritate the American investors, this is what happens:

> From the garden on the former site of the crematorium to the American investors' villa complex, and from the villa complex to the conference room in the villa's guildhall, every time Kong Mingliang [the mayor] said something, a different flower would wilt. As he apologized to the Americans, the leaves of the bamboo plants on the side of the road dried up. There were a pair of potted pines in the entranceway to the guildhall, but under the sound of his cursing the pots cracked and the soil and plants spilled onto the ground. This continued until he and the Americans were all seated on couches in the guildhall, and attendants brought them coffee, beer, and red wine.[60]

These events could also happen as consequences of private feelings, such as joy and anger. The birth of Mayor Kong's child is celebrated by flowers that even come out of pens.[61] A spit of anger and disdain produces seeds that instantly become plants full of fruits.[62]

---

55 Calvino, *Invisible Cities*, 159–60.
56 Yan, *The Explosion Chronicles*, 124–25.
57 Ibid., 257.
58 Ibid., 302.
59 Ibid., 269–71.
60 Ibid., 309.
61 Ibid., 237.
62 Ibid., 222.

However, Yan's favorite circumstance for incredible natural events is sexual excitement. When a woman takes off her clothes, not only are men completely under her power but even plants are also subjugated by her beauty. The most vivid example is when Little Cui says to the old Kong Dongde that she cannot have sex with him since she has been violated by one of his sons. These dramatic words come with colorful flowers that turn instantly to black. In order to avoid incest, she allows the old man only to see her naked. She calmly and sexually undresses, and thus an earthquake happens. Every smile she launches at the man is greeted by blossoming flowers around them. "Not until she finally opened her mouth to speak did the season finally returns to its proper place."[63] Something very similar happens again when Kong Mingyao, thanks to an experienced girl, learns for the first time how to have sex.[64] It is relevant to notice that in the desert of human feelings of this novel, these sexual acts are not connected to love but to lust and forms of power.

In the last pages of the novel, the metropolis ends up completely covered with a thick smog that prevents the sun from showing for thirty years. Plants, flowers, birds, and insects all die miserably. Residents cough blood from their sick lungs. This apocalyptic description is very common in several of Yan's most recent novels. In *Streams of Time* (*Riguang liunian* 日光流年, 1998) is a flood of dead animals that sinks all the hopes of a village decimated by pollution. *Dream of Ding Village* (*Dingzhuang meng* 丁莊夢, 2006) features an AIDS epidemic among a rural community. The historical setting of "The Years, Months, Days" ("Nian yue ri" 年月日, 1997) and *The Four Books* (*Si shu* 四書, 2010) includes a description of the dramatic famine that followed the Great Leap Forward (1959–61). More recently, in *The Day the Sun Died* (*Rixi* 日熄, 2015), the sun does not show and hundreds of people die during collective somnambulism. However, in the last pages of the *Chronicles of Explosion*, Yan provides a final hint of pale hope. The story is closed by the receding of the persistent smog, and the spontaneous sprouting of flowers and plants where, thirty years earlier, the last members of the Kong family proceeded on their knees toward the cemetery, leaving trails of fertile blood behind.[65] The remorse that guides this sacrificial act toward the ancestors is the nourishment for new sprouts.

As everyone familiar with Yan's writing knows, the author is originally a countryman. He lives in Beijing for work; however, his heart and inspiration remain in his rural village in Henan Province. In the capital, he bought a beautiful but dilapidated house with a big garden on the outskirts. The house and, particularly, the garden were his rural refuge from the suffocating metropolis; the place where he could write and stay in touch with nature, as the Suiyuan 隨園 (Garden of Accommodation) for Yuan Mei 袁枚 (1716–98). In 2011, his house and the surrounding neighborhoods were confiscated and demolished for a road-widening project.[66] The author did everything in his power to stop the demolition, even writing letters to Hu Jintao 胡錦濤 and Wen Jiabao 溫家寶, but his efforts were ultimately in vain. In 2012, in order to cherish his memories of the garden and unleash his sorrow, he wrote *Me and Garden No. 711: The Ultimate Last Memo of Beijing* (*Wo he 711 haoyuan: Beijing, zuihou de jinian* 我和711號園: 北京, 最後的紀念). This is a very nostalgic text, something between a memoir and an essay on nature. As Song Weijie suggests, this garden is a sort of urban "Peach Blossom Spring" (*Taohua yuan* 桃花源), a true ecotopia.[67] Or, as Liu Jianmei

---

63 Ibid., 185.
64 Ibid., 244–45. We notice that Kong Mingyao will remember this experience when reading the *Rouputuan* 肉蒲團 [The carnal prayer mat], ibid., 273.
65 These last lines strikingly remind to the poem "Chuntian" 春天 [Spring] by Mang Ke 芒克 (1951–).
66 Yan Lianke, "The Year of the Stray Dog," *The New York Times*, 20 Apr. 2021, https://www.nytimes.com/2012/04/21/opinion/the-year-of-the-stray-dog.html (last accessed 25 July 2021).
67 Song, "Yan Lianke's Mythorealism Representation of the Country and City," 653–56.

劉劍梅 richly argues, a Daoist retreat, something close to the Bamboo Grove for the Seven Sages.[68] Yan devotes several extremely detailed chapters to the description of gardening tools (almost impossible to find in Beijing), the vegetables he cultivated, the spontaneous vegetation (particularly flowers), plants, insects, and birds. Each extremely detailed description is combined with folk stories, funny and sentimental episodes. He recalls an episode when he was surprised by a copious rain under those trees:

> Standing [there], besides the quietness of the sound of pouring rain, of trees, and the absence of human voices, the rain filters through leaves and branches, it sounded like the laughter of a child. The pure water after pouring from your head down to your face, shoulders, trunk, legs, and feet, penetrates the mother earth (*dadi* 大地). You thus feel yourself and nature (*ziran* 自然) as melt in one unique body (*rong wei yi ti* 融為一體). You stand together with mother earth. You are lucky to become a son of the mother earth and nature. Your breath is the breath of nature. The life and death of vegetations is your own destiny. In that instant, … you are like a long-term separated child that is embraced again by his mother.[69]

This philosophical and lyric piece follows a beautiful short poem rich in pantheistic spirituality: "This wind coming from elsewhere/descends on this nameless and borderless earth/and brings rain from the sky, /thus, the deities of the altars of fertility/donate flowers and life."[70] Nature is the mother of all beings, and deities donate beauty and fertility to them. The whole cosmos is one body breathing to the same rhythm. At least, this is Yan's ecotopia, the private dream he lived in the Garden no. 711. The last chapter, which follows the demolition, is programmatically titled "Winter" ("Dongtian" 冬天) and provides a sort of heartfelt call for the whole of humanity. He says that we should stop blindly following scientific reasons and technological improvement. Experts of animals, ecology, and the environment are not better entitled to understand the future and the needs of humans than we are. As he suggested while describing the rain, the city and the country are in real danger.[71] The common people should decide to protect nature and the environment, following only "their feelings, their sentiments, and their discontent" (*qinggan, qingxu yu fennu* 情感、情緒與憤怒).[72]

Conclusions

Calvino and Yan Lianke describe the urban space in a dramatic and disconsolate way. For both authors, cities completely lack a true ethos, reject human relationships, and destroy nature (as the dangerous mirror that could show their true faces). They narrate a contemporary anti-epic of the human condition. Heroes are anti-heroes. The only values are growth, economic interest, and ambition. Calvino provides a fragmented text, which we already described as a labyrinth,[73] in which it is extremely hard to find any kind of *telos*. Polo and Kublai investigate

---

68 Liu Jianmei, "Yan Lianke's Vacillation: The Triumph of the Modern Zhuangzi," in her *Zhuangzi and Modern Chinese Literature* (New York: Oxford University Press, 2016), 205–10.
69 Yan Lianke, *Wo he 711 haoyuan: Beijing, zuihoude jinian* 我和711號園: 北京, 最後的紀念 [Me and garden no. 711: The ultimate last memo of Beijing] (Nanjing: Jiangsu renmin chubanshe, 2012), 89–90. My translation.
70 Ibid., 82. My translation.
71 Ibid., 90.
72 Ibid., 263.
73 Nick Bentley, "Postmodern Cities," in *The City in Literature*, ed. Kevin R. McNamara (Cambridge: Cambridge University Press, 2014), 175, 181–82.

together the meaning of life, ruling, and dwelling; but apparently, they do not find an answer to their questions. Polo simply suggests looking for the tiny traces of hope in a desert of sense. The philosophic and poetic writing of these short descriptions leaves the reader hanging in a sort of *epoché*, i.e., suspension of judgment. On the contrary, Yan's descriptions are extremely detailed and coherently organized. He wants to vivisect urban life without any scruples. In the novel, he gives voice to all his disdain toward the grand narrative of never-ending positive growth. Calvino does not have a precise cultural or political target; his quest is atemporal and immemorial. Yan has vividly in mind his object of criticism. After comparing their two anti-epics of the city, we suggest that while Calvino provides an anti-epic (a dissolution of an epic tale completely emptied of any *telos*), Yan offers a dystopian tale, where the *telos* is that of ambition, the true "will of power."[74] Yan's dystopia finds a hypothetical solution in the end with those sprouts, but this part of the story still needs to be written. We need to bear in mind that his urban ecotopia was demolished ten years ago. While Lu Xun urges "save the children," Yan is crying to save nature, rural people, and their culture.

We close with a last consideration for future investigations. We find Yan's production of the last years, and particularly *Me and Garden No. 711*, closer to a Neoconfucian philosophical stand (full of moral responsibility, social engagement, and ecologism)[75] than to a Daoist (i.e., Zhuangzi 莊子) relativist detachment. Yan's passion for ancient rituals, folk culture, social life, together with his frequent depiction of the dissolution of family lines, suggests a narrative engagement in the shaping of a renovated and moral China, able to find new ways to inhabit the world while walking on the paths left behind by its past. Calvino, with his praise for lightness, is certainly closer to the philosophical ironic nonsense of Zhuangzi. As the Italian author suggests: "We might say that throughout the centuries two opposite tendencies have competed in literature: one tries to make language into a weightless element that hovers above things like a cloud or better, perhaps, the finest dust or, better still, a field of magnetic impulses. The other tries to give language the weight, density, and concreteness of things, bodies, and sensations."[76] Calvino certainly belongs to the first group, while Yan belongs to the second. While in Italy for a conference in 2011, the Chinese author celebrated Calvino as an extraordinary writer, and he noticed that the Italian author did not achieve the great fame he deserves in China, that is, a wide public, because of his extreme attention to style, while Chinese readers care more about content.[77] Calvino always maintains a detached and "light" narrative mood composed of stylistic experiments, and philosophical enthusiasms for the unsaid. On the contrary, Yan is the narrator or "historian" writing a tragic chronicle, and his truth-bearing act is rejected by authorities (both in reality and in the metanarrative of *The Explosion Chronicles*); therefore, for him, truth is always a "heavy task." He prefers the solidity of soil, plants, and calloused hands.

---

74 Rob Latham and Jeef Hicks, "Urban Dystopias," in *The City in Literature*, ed. Kevin R. McNamara (Cambridge: Cambridge University Press, 2014), 163.
75 The Neo-Confucian (*xin rujia* 新儒家) philosopher Wang Yangming 王阳明 (1472–1529) uses very similar words (i.e., yiti 一體, "one/same body") in *Questions on The Great Learning* (*Daxue wen* 大学问); see Philip J. Ivanhoe, *Readings from the Lu-Wang School of Neo-Confucianism* (Indianapolis-Cambridge: Hackett Publishing Company), 160ff or Chan Wing-Tsit, *A Source Book in Chinese Philosophy* (Princeton: Princeton University Press, 1963), 659ff.
76 Italo Calvino, *Six Memos for the Next Millennium* (Cambridge: Harvard University Press, 1988), 15.
77 Yan Lianke, "Cong Kaerweinuo zai Zhongguo de lengyong shuoqi" 從卡爾維諾在中國的冷遇說起 [Talking about the cold welcoming of Calvino in China], in *Yipai huyan: Yan Lianke haiwai yangjiang ji* 一派胡言: 閻連科海外演講集 [Sheer nonsense: Collection of Yan Lianke's conference speeches abroad] (Beijing: Zhongxin chubanshe, 2012), 150.

Bibliography

Bell, Daniel A., and Avner de-Shalit. *The Spirit of Cities: Why the Identity of a City Matters in a Global Age*. Princeton: Princeton University Press, 2011.

Benjamin, Walter. "The Storyteller: Reflections on Nikolai Leskóv." In *Illuminations*. Translated by Harry Zohn. New York: Schocken Books, 2007.

Bentley, Nick. "Postmodern Cities." In *The Cambridge Companion to the City in Literature*, edited by Kevin R. McNamara, 175–87. Cambridge: Cambridge University Press, 2014.

Calvino, Italo. *Invisible Cities*. Translated by William Weaver. New York: Harvest Book, 1974.

———. *Six Memos for the Next Millennium*. Cambridge: Harvard University Press, 1988.

Chan, Wing-Tsit. *A Source Book in Chinese Philosophy*. Princeton: Princeton University Press, 1963.

Dong Meiqi 董美圻. "Chen Qiufan: Kehuan shi zuida de xianshizhuyi" 陳楸帆: 科幻是最大的現實主義 [Sci-Fi is the best realism]. *Shangye jiazhi* 商業價值 [Business values], 10 Sep. 2015. http://www.chinawriter.com.cn/kehuan/2015/2015-09-10/253039.html (last accessed 25 July 2021).

Glaeser, Edward. *Triumph of the City*. New York: Penguin, 2011.

Ivanhoe, Philip J. *Readings from the Lu-Wang School of Neo-Confucianism*. Indianapolis: Hackett Publishing, 2009.

Latham, Rob, and Jeef Hicks. "Urban Dystopias." In *The Cambridge Companion to the City in Literature*, edited by Kevin R. McNamara, 163–74. Cambridge: Cambridge University Press, 2014.

Li, Gang. "20th Century Exploration of the 'Issue of the Chinese Epic.'" *Frontiers of Literary Studies in China* 4, no. 1 (2010): 32–54.

Liang Hong 梁鴻. *Yan Lianke wenxue nianpu* 閻連科文學年譜 [Chronology of Yan Lianke's literary activity]. Shanghai: Fudan daxue chubanshe, 2015.

Liu, Jianmei 劉劍梅. *Zhuangzi and Modern Chinese Literature*. New York: Oxford University Press, 2016.

McNamara, Kevin R., ed. *The City in Literature*. Cambridge: Cambridge University Press, 2014.

Mengzi. *Mencius*. Trans. I. Bloom. New York: Columbia University Press, 2009.

Prusek, Jaroslav. "History and Epics in China and in the West: A Study of Differences in the Conception of the Human Story." *Diogenes* 11, no. 42 (June 1963): 20–43.

Song, Weijie 宋偉杰. "Yan Lianke's Mythorealism Representation of the Country and City." *Modern Fiction Studies* 62, no. 4 (Winter 2016): 655–58.

Tullio-Altan, Carlo. *Ethnos e civiltà. Identità etniche e valori democratici* [Ethos and civilization: Ethnic identities and democratic values]. Milan: Feltrinelli, 1995.

Visser, Robin, and Jie Lu. "Contemporary Urban Fiction: Rewriting the City." In *The Columbia Companion to Modern Chinese Literature*, edited by Kirk. A Denton, 345–54. New York: Columbia University Press, 2016.

Yan Lianke 閻連科. "Cong Kaerweinuo zai Zhongguo de lengyong shuoqi" 從卡爾維諾在中國的冷遇說起 [Talking about the cold welcoming of Calvino in China] (12 Sep. 2011). In *Yipai huyan: Yan Lianke haiwai yangjiang ji* 一派胡言: 閻連科海外演講集 [Sheer nonsense: Collection of Yan Lianke's conference speeches abroad], 145–51. Beijing: Zhongxin chubanshe, 2012.

———. *The Explosion Chronicles*. Translated by Carlos Rojas. London: Chatto & Windus, 2017.

———. *Faxian xiaoshuo* 發現小說 [The Discovery of fiction]. Tianjin: Nankai daxue chubanshe, 2011.

———. *Wo he 711 haoyuan: Beijing, zuihou de jinian* 我和711號園: 北京, 最後的紀念 [Me and Garden no. 711: The ultimate last memo of Beijing]. Nanjing: Jiangsu renmin chubanshe, 2012.

———. "The Year of the Stray Dog." *The New York Times*, 20 Apr. 2021. https://www.nytimes.com/2012/04/21/opinion/the-year-of-the-stray-dog.html (last accessed 25 July 2021).

———. *Zhalie zhi* 炸裂志 [The explosion chronicles]. Zhengzhou: Zhongguo banben tushuguan, 2016.

9
"INVERSE THEOLOGY" IN YAN LIANKE'S *THE FOUR BOOKS* AND FRANZ KAFKA'S *THE TRIAL*

Melinda Pirazzoli

Yan Lianke's 閻連科 *The Four Books* (*Si shu* 四書) is a complex and composite novel.[1] As Carlos Rojas has suggested, this title "evokes both a set of Confucian texts known as the Four Books as well as the Four Gospels within the Christian tradition."[2] It also refers to the four books or sections in the novel: "Criminal Records" ("Zuiren lu" 罪人錄), "Old Course" ("Gudao" 故道), "Heaven's Child" ("Tian de haizi" 天的孩子), and "A New Myth of Sisyphus" ("Xin Xixufu shenhua" 新西緒弗神話). The first three sections recount from different perspectives the vicissitudes of a group of intellectuals who, during the Great Leap Forward, were labeled as rightists and sent to a re-education compound called Zone 99. These intellectuals are strictly controlled, punished, and rewarded by a character named the Child. As Tsai Chien-hsin remarks in an editorial published on the website of *Modern Chinese Literature and Culture*, not only is the Child the protagonist around whom the first three narratives pivot, he is also the focus of "Heaven's Child." From the very offset of the novel, he is cast in a "Messianic light"[3] and is described as an "old youth," "who walks the thin line between good and evil."[4]

Sebastian Veg has argued that through this character, Yan is able to draw a parallel "between the Mao-state and Religion."[5] Not only is the Child's establishment of the re-education camp "recounted as a second Genesis," but the rules and regulations imposed by him are called "ten commandments."[6] In the beginning, he "wholeheartedly believes in the system and is prepared to sacrifice himself."[7] However, as Veg observes, the Child radically changes throughout the course of the novel. His personal interactions with the character named the Theologian, who tirelessly tells him stories from the Bible, his personal exposure to the Bible, the personal inadequacy entailed by his failure to organize the production of steel and wheat

---

1 In this study, I refer first to Carlos Rojas' English translation of *The Four Books* (New York: Grove Press, 2015) and then to the Chinese edition of *Si shu* (Taipei: Maitian chubanshe, 2011).
2 Carlos Rojas, "Translator's Note," in Yan, *The Four Books*: iv.
3 Ibid., 8.
4 Chien-hsin Tsai, "The Museum of Innocence: The Great Leap Forward and Famine, Yan Lianke and *Four Books*," *Modern Chinese Literature and Culture* (May 2011), https://u.osu.edu/mclc/online-series/museum-of-innocence/ (last accessed 25 July 2021).
5 Sebastian Veg, "Creating a Literary Space to Debate the Mao Era: The Fictionalization of the Great Leap Forward in *The Four Books*," *China Perspectives* 2014, no. 4: 11.
6 Ibid.
7 Ibid.

demanded by the political headquarters, the many deaths among the intellectuals of Zone 99 caused by the famine, and the episodes of cannibalism among the starving intellectuals seem to have a strong impact on him. In fact, in the end, the Child first awards the intellectuals the "red iron stars" they need to attain their long-awaited freedom and then crucifies himself. As Veg suggests, through the sacrifice of the Child, Yan perhaps "raises the question for the reader of whether, and how the Party can repent and atone for its sins."[8]

"Criminal Records" and "Old Course" are instead narrated by a diegetic character named the Author. The former is a journal, which he writes for the Child, and in which the Author describes not only the "crimes" of the intellectuals who live in Zone 99 but also their whereabouts. Relying on this journal, the Child makes his decisions about punishments and rewards. "Old Course," instead, is a narrative that the Author produces for no other purpose than himself.[9]

The last section is perhaps the most obscure part of the novel. Tsai suggests that it addresses, among other things, the question of the "writer's calling as he compares the task of the storytellers in Four Books to the endless Sisyphean labor,"[10] while Rojas reads it as "an allegorical commentary on the punitive conditions that hold sway in the compound itself."[11] In this section, Yan refers to a "strange hill' located outside of the northern Chinese city of Shenyang, where objects roll up the hill on their own accord but have to be pushed back down. He interprets this "as a commentary on the workings of power, but also on the possibility of either turning that power against itself or of finding a space of freedom within the soul-crushing conditions imposed by the same power."[12] So far, what has attracted the attention of Sinologists, particularly Sebastian Veg, has been Yan's attempt to deal "with the massive loss of life during the Great Leap Forward, and to offer reflections on how individuals, some of them highly educated, contributed to creating the climate of political terror in which the famine took place."[13] Yet, the hybrid nature of *The Four Books* and its composite structure have also prompted him to invite readers to "draw their conclusions as to how to reconcile the biblical profession of faith, the historical material, the fictional epic, and finally the philosophical reflection."[14]

This study is an attempt to reconcile all these aspects. It suggests that *The Four Books* is both a fictionalization of the Great Leap Forward and a metanarrative that revolves around ethical and aesthetic concerns about historical writing. More specifically, the traditional concepts of moral judgments and punishments, guiding principles of Confucian historiography,[15] are evoked in order to be deconstructed and transformed into an epic biopolitical account of human suffering during the tragic era of the Great Leap Forward, an aspect of the novel that will be addressed in the first section of this study. In particular, I shall suggest that the confinement of the intellectuals in Zone 99, with its cruel techniques of monitoring and surveillance of their bodies, brings about their dehumanization and criminalization. This novel, however, does not only address biopolitical concerns from an ethical perspective. The second section addresses the interconnectedness between (moral) judgments and the practice of writing. It will be argued that "Criminal Records" and "Old Course," two complementary

---

8 Ibid., 12.
9 Yan, *The Four Books*, 172; *Si shu* 211–12.
10 Tsai, "The Museum of Innocence," 5.
11 Rojas, "Translator's Note," ix.
12 Ibid.
13 Veg, "Creating a Literary Space to Debate the Mao Era," 10.
14 Ibid., 15.
15 In this regard, see Ann Van Auken Newell, "Killings and Assassinations in the *Spring and Autumn* as Records of Judgments," *Asia Major*, 3rd series, 27, no. 1 (2014): 1–31.

narratives written by the same author, allow Yan to express his engagement with the ethical implications of the authorial commitment to historiography as well as the ethics of storytelling in historiographical writing.

Yan focuses not merely on authorship but also on readership. The Child, the illiterate leader of Zone 99, at the beginning of the novel can be interpreted as a despot and as a (politically) brainwashed child. Seemingly, at the end of the novel, he is transformed by his proximity to the intellectuals that he himself should have reformed. Their stories, their books, and their ideas will apparently have such a radical impact on him that he will ultimately sacrifice himself to grant them freedom. This may be regarded as an expedient that Yan employs in order to evoke the transformative power of reading and listening.

In *The Four Books,* Yan describes the epic journey of a group of intellectuals. It begins with their confinement and ends with their release. While the intellectuals' final release can certainly be interpreted as a messianic light, a glimmer of hope, in my conclusive remarks, I will argue that Yan's messianism is very similar to Franz Kafka's "inverse theology."[16] The latter, as Hammer notes, is based on the assumption that "whatever hope there is for man can only be discerned by becoming aware of this damaged life."[17]

Yan's indebtedness to Kafka has been repeatedly acknowledged by Yan himself in his critical essays.[18] *The Four Books* also reflects Yan's Kafkian approach to art, human nature, the human quandary, and indeed messianism. More specifically, Yan's *The Four Books* and Kafka's *The Trial* share many notions and concepts: life as a form of confinement and caging, a sense of impending horror, the self's loss of agency in the world, the interconnectedness between art and slander, the connivance of the artist with (juridical) power, the interchangeability between the juridical realm and religion, the relationship between guilt and crime, and finally the relationship between life and shame.

This study does not aim to compare *The Four Books* with *The Trial*. What will be argued instead is that Yan also relies on such ideas. It will also be suggested that Yan manages to create his own culturally specific diegetic space. While there are many tropes in *The Four Books* which echo so-called Kafkian messianism, the diegetic world created by Yan also addresses the Chinese cultural heritage. The reference to both the Four Gospels and the Four Confucian Classics seemingly suggests Yan's attempt to convey an idea of culture which conflates Chinese and Western values in order to create a literary work that can simultaneously reflect and transcend local boundaries.

Cages: The *Homo Sacer* in Kafka and Yan Lianke

The Trial "centers on the description of a situation of confinement."[19] Although its protagonist, Joseph K., is charged with an obscure and unspecified crime, he is free to move and work. However, everywhere he goes, everyone seems to have judged him guilty of something

---

16 Peter E. Gordon, "Kafka's Inverse Theology," in *Kafka's* The Trial: *Philosophical Perspectives*, ed. Espen Hammer (Oxford: Oxford University Press, 2018), 23–54.
17 Espen Hammer, "Kafka's Modernism: Intelligibility and Voice," in *Kafka's* The Trial, ed. Espen Hammer (Oxford: Oxford University Press, 2018), 247.
18 Yan's indebtedness to Kafka is discussed in Melinda Pirazzoli, "From Franz Kafka to Franz Kafka Award Winner, Yan Lianke: Biopolitics and the Human Dilemma of *Shenshizhuyi* in *Liven* and *Dream of Ding Village*," *CLCWeb: Comparative Literature and Culture* 22, no. 4 (2020): 1–12, https://doi.org/10.7771/1481-4374.3437.
19 Dimitris Vardoulakis, *Freedom from the Free Will: On Kafka's Laughter* (New York: SUNY Press, 2012), 1.

indistinct, unexpressed, unknown. In other words, while Joseph K. can seemingly exercise his free will, this free will is exercised within a cage, "a cage without walls in which any vestige of ideal freedom is impossible."[20]

Zone 99 in *The Four Books* is also a space of confinement inhabited by intellectuals who are accused of different ideological crimes. These intellectuals, just like Joseph K., are constantly monitored, their movements traced and assessed, and their cases considered. Furthermore, just like Joseph K., they are not given a full name.[21] Significantly, these nameless characters are solely identified by the social role they used to perform before being labeled as rightists.

Their namelessness, which raises questions about their self-ownership and agency, prompts readers to address questions about the mission of intellectuals during the period of the Great Leap Forward as well as their destitution during the Maoist era. Besides the loss of their names and status, they are also compelled to endure the loss of their books. When, upon the Child's request, "they brought their books as though they were old shoes,"[22] they were implicitly compelled to relinquish the very capital on which they had constructed their own symbolic value. Not only are they compelled to disparage their own literary output, but they are also deprived of the possibility of professing their religious beliefs. For instance, the Author is compelled to refer to his own literary works as "dog shit,"[23] while the Theologian is forced to call himself "a pervert" because he owns a portrait of "Mary, Mother of God."[24]

From the moment Zone 99 is established, these intellectuals are subject to the Child's ten commandments, a list of prohibitions applicable only in Zone 99. These end up not only excluding the intellectuals from the rest of the world but also transforming their life into mere survival impulses: *zoe* (bare life). Alternatively put, these intellectuals' predicament is comparable to the condition of what Agamben defines as the *homo sacer*: "a human life which is included in the juridical order solely in the form of its exclusion—that is, of its capacity to be killed."[25]

Interestingly enough, Agamben's notion of *homo sacer* derives from his understanding of the representation of both the law and the human predicament in Kafka's *The Trial*:[26]

> Being in force without significance (*Geltung ohne Bedeutung*): nothing better describes the ban that our age cannot master than Scholem's formula for the status of law in Kafla's novel. What, after all, is the structure of the sovereign ban if not that of a law that is in force but does not signify anything? Everywhere on earth men today are subject to the ban imposed by a law and a tradition that are maintained solely as the "zero point" of their own content, and that include men within them in the form of

---

20 Ibid., 83.
21 Giorgio Agamben focuses on Joseph K.'s lack of a family name in his essay "K.," where he argues that K. stands for both Kalumnia and Kalumniator (Slander and Slanderer). See Justin Clemens, Nicholas Heron, and Alex Murray, eds., *The Work of Giorgio Agamben: Law, Literature, Life* (Edinburgh: Edinburgh University Press, 2012), 13–27.
22 Yan, *The Four Books*, 17; *Si shu*, 45.
23 Yan, *The Four Books*, 7; *Si shu*, 35.
24 Yan, *The Four Books*, 8; *Si shu*, 36.
25 Giorgio Agamben, *Homo Sacer: Sovereign Power and Bare Life*, trans. Daniel Heller-Roazen (Stanford: Stanford University Press, 1998), 8.
26 Kafka's influences on Agamben are thoroughly described in Gerhard Richter, "A Disease of All Signification: Kafka's *The Trial* between Adorno and Agamben," in *Kafka's* The Trial, ed. Espen Hammer (Oxford: Oxford University Press, 2018),111–38; and Carlo Salzani, "In a Messianic Gesture: Agamben's Kafka," in *Philosophy and Kafka*, ed. Brendan Moran and Carlo Salzani (Lanham: Lexington Books, 2013), 261–82.

a pure relation of abandonment. All societies and all cultures today (whether democratic or totalitarian, conservative or progressive) have entered into a legitimation crisis in which law (meaning any written tradition in its regulative form, whether the Jewish Torah or Islamic Shariah, Christian dogma or the *profanenomos*) is in force as the pure "Nothing of Revelation." But this is precisely the structure of the sovereign relation, and the nihilism in which we are living is, from this perspective, nothing other than the coming to light of this relation as such.[27]

The intellectuals of Zone 99 live under what Agamben defines as the "sovereign ban" in a state of exception. Indeed, they are stripped of their rights, they cannot take part in social activities, they cannot have sexual intercourse, and they cannot "read or write unnecessarily, nor think unnecessarily."[28] The only thing they are allowed to do is to work so as to fulfill the production targets established by the authorities. In other words, their exclusion from the rest of the world prevents them from living a fully fledged life (*bios*).

As already mentioned, the disconnectedness between Zone 99 and the rest of the world should not be overlooked. The dialectic tension between inclusion and exclusion is relatively a common trope in Yan's literary production. For instance, it is also apparent in some of Yan's earlier novels such as *Lenin's Kisses* (*Shouhuo* 受活)[29] and *Dream of Ding Village* (*Ding zhuang meng* 丁莊夢).[30] Both novels describe the human quandary of small and secluded communities living in a state of exception. In particular, Lupascu reads *Dream of Ding Village* as a biopolitical novel that focuses on the *homo sacer*.[31] According to her reading, it describes the way in which the dead bodies of poor human beings are used as an occasion of profit. Since *Dream of Ding Village* focuses mostly on the fictional representation of the blood market economy, Yan's biopolitical discourses are mainly deployed to address concerns about the newly implemented neoliberal practices.

In *The Four Books*, Yan presents an exacerbation of his previous biopolitical analysis of society and historical events. Here, however, the stakes are the interconnectedness between the ethical and juridical realms. Interestingly, unlike in *Dream of Ding Village*, the life of the intellectuals populating Zone 99 bears some resemblance to the life of Joseph K., a life in which the most innocent gesture can have the most extreme consequences. In a similar vein, also all the movements and gestures of the intellectuals in Zone 99, who are strictly controlled by the Child and by their fellow inmates, can have the most extreme consequences. They are aware that the Child has the power to control, reward, or punish them. As mentioned before, the Child is represented in all his ambivalence. On the one hand, he is the leader of Zone 99; on the other hand, he is a spokesman for the provincial authorities. Alternatively put, while he is the "guardian" of this banned community of intellectuals, he must also respond to the authorities for anything that happens in the re-education compound.

Awards and punishments soon become these intellectuals' obsession. From the very beginning of the novel, the Child's distribution of red blossoms as awards to those intellectuals who comply with his requests and of certificates to those who disobey the commandments serves as an expedient for Yan to describe the intellectuals' aspiration to freedom or dejection

27 Agamben, *Homo Sacer*, 51.
28 Yan, *The Four Books,* 2; *Si Shu*, 31.
29 Pirazzoli, "From Franz Kafka to Franz Kafka Award Winner, Yan Lianke," 5–8.
30 Victoria Lupascu, "Plasma Economy, Biopolitics of Blood and the Literary Specter of Aids," *Chinese Literature: Essays, Articles, Reviews (CLEAR)* 42 (2020): 133–57; Pirazzoli, "From Franz Kafka to Franz Kafka Award Winner, Yan Lianke," 9–12.
31 Ibid., 139.

at their confinement. The intellectuals' desire to be awarded the red blossoms needed to receive permission to leave the compound and attain freedom soon turns them into "tools of surveillance." Indeed, all the intellectuals inform on one another, thereby becoming factual accomplices of the system. Therefore, their tragic quandary notwithstanding, these intellectuals are never portrayed as mere victims.

The diegetic space portrayed by Yan leaves no room for hope, mutual trust, and affection. This is evidenced in those episodes describing the illicit romantic tryst between the Scholar and the Musician. Seemingly, Yan's assessments of the untenable relationship between emotional life and bare life in a state of exception do not differ from Lupascu's discussion about the representation of the tragic love affair between Lingling and Li Sanren in *Dream of Ding Village*. What is described in both novels is literally a ban on the natural outpouring of feelings. As Lupascu points out, the representation of Lingling and her love affair in *Dream of Ding Village* offers an occasion for Yan to further elaborate on classical Chinese views on human nature.[32] This also applies to the Musician in *The Four Books*. Just like Lingling in *Dream of Ding Village*, the Musician stands out among the crowd. Not only is she endowed with a "deep bourgeois sensibility,"[33] which is inadmissible in Zone 99 camp, but she is also determined to preserve her agency and subjectivity. I agree with Lupascu that in representing the tragedies of such strong-willed female characters, Yan is consciously harking back to Xunzi's 荀子 argument that "human nature is selfish and following one's desire can only lead to moral corruption and tragedies."[34] The Musician's desire to be admired and her concern about her bodily appearance, just as in Lingling's case, are described as the main cause of the disaster that befalls her.

What occurs in both cases is the internalization of the blame on the part of the female character. Such an internalization is particularly evident at the end of *The Four Books*, where the Musician, the sole inhabitant of Zone 99 to have maintained a beautiful body during the famine, initiates a tryst with an official living in a neighboring village. She exchanges her own body for food in order to allow herself, the Scholar, and the Author to live through the famine. She is eventually found dead in an "ugly posture:" "her pants ... pulled to her ankles, exposing her bare buttocks" and "[h]er mouth full of soybeans that she had not yet had the chance to swallow."[35] Needless to say, she is not the sole cause of her own tragedy. This is also the outcome of the way people judge and condemn her. The long and painful sessions of self-criticism for her tryst with the Scholar are followed by an even harsher moral condemnation by her beloved who, on the one hand, despises her for having an affair with the officer but, on the other, is willing to marry her in exchange for a bowl of soybeans.[36] In light of this, the Musician, as a character, allows Yan to focus on technologies of the self in order to represent, in the same way as in *Dream of Ding Village*, "biopolitical strategies of internalizing blame under the aegis of structural violence."[37]

In *The Four Books*, the internalization of blame is only one aspect of this complex novel. As will be argued in the following section, Yan also connects blame to the Kafkian representation of judgment (e.g., moral assessments, disparaging accusations, allegations).[38] In fact, each section of *The Four Books* can be regarded as expressing allegations against other people ("Criminal Records"), moral self-judgments ("Old Course"), or binding laws ("Heaven's Child").

32 Lupascu, "Plasma Economy, Biopolitics of Blood and the Literary Specter of Aids," 149–50.
33 Yan, *The Four Books*, 57; *Si shu*, 90–91.
34 Lupascu, "Plasma Economy, Biopolitics of Blood and the Literary Specter of Aids," 149.
35 Yan, *The Four Books*, 283; *Si shu*, 323.
36 Yan, *The Four Books*, 281; *Si shu*, 321.
37 Lupascu, "Plasma Economy, Biopolitics of Blood and the Literary Specter of Aids," 149.
38 Agamben, "K.,"14.

Recording crimes or writing the Old Dao?: "Criminal Records," "Old Course," and the construction of *The Four Books* as a metanarrative

The centrality and the role of writing and writers in *The Four Books* can hardly be overlooked. The references to both the Four Gospels and the Confucian Classics seemingly suggest that this novel may be read, among other things, as a metanarrative that dwells not only on a specific tragic historical event but also on the role and moral status of both writing and writers (i.e., intellectuals) living in a state of exception.

"Criminal Records" and "Old Course," the two books produced by the Author, provide complementary views and opposite assessments. In "Criminal Records," Yan brings to the fore questions about the guilt of intellectuals and their complicity with the system.[39] Just like Titorelli, the court painter in *The Trial*, in "Criminal Records," the Author plays an important role within the control apparatus.[40] By accepting the task of writing "Criminal Records," he ends up creating a narrative that *de facto* legitimates the Child's commandments.

The many pages dedicated to the illicitness of the love affair between the Scholar and the Musician and the reports about presumed thefts of blossoms on the part of the Technician, and about the Physician's possession of a pair of scissors, are only some of the many "crimes" described in Zone 99.[41] Such examples, which highlight the paradoxical nature of crime and crime control in Zone 99, compel readers to address questions about the notions of crime as well as its interrelation with the notion of guilt.

As mentioned earlier, since "Criminal Records" is a document produced for the Child, it would not be incorrect to consider it a criminal file that compels the inhabitants of Zone 99 to undergo endless "trials." Far from being presented as a mere list of factual crimes, it also contains slanderous reflections and oblique insinuations about the inmates. Hence, the collapse of clear-cut boundaries between legal accusations and malicious slander in this narrative casts light on the ambiguous and paradoxical situation that the intellectuals are forced to confront. On the one hand, the sixth commandment forbids gossip and slander; on the other, the Child awards the red blossoms in exchange for information about crimes and criminals. Hence, from the very outset, the intellectuals in Zone 99 are doomed to be guilty. Their predicament is not so different from Joseph K.'s: like him, they are all *kalumniatores* (false accusers) compelled to undergo a slanderous trial.[42] The Author's second narrative, entitled "Gudao" (a reference to the old riverbed of the Yellow River), offers, however, an alternative view on life, art, and humanity. Out of the four sections of this novel, this is seemingly the one that best reflects authorial ethical concerns. Yan's choice of this title may not be casual. While *gudao* refers to the riverbed of the river, it is also a

---

39 Veg, "Creating a Literary Space to Debate the Mao Era,"10.
40 For a detailed analysis of the function of art and the role of the artist in *The Trial*, see John Gibson, "On the Ethical Character of Literature," in *Kafka's* The Trial, ed. Espen Hammer (Oxford: Oxford University Press, 2018), 85–109. As Gibson remarks, through Titorelli, Kafka conveys the idea that "the modern artist who works in the service of power can no longer be an artist, since an artist whose relation to culture is uncritical and affirmative—who looks upon it and attempts to produce art by reproducing what he sees—is bound to run afoul of the aesthetic and cultural standards that govern the production of art" (94). Furthermore, the idea thoroughly articulated in *The Trail* that the artist's paintings do not belong to the artist, because "everything belongs to the court" (95) also applies to "Criminal Records," which is nothing but installments that the Author must submit to the Child on a regular basis.
41 Yan, *The Four Books*, 56; *Si shu*, 88–89.
42 Ibid., 13.

homophone of *gu Dao* 古道 'ancient Dao.' Considering the reference to the Four Gospels and the Four Confucian Classics in the main title, this may not be a coincidence.

The radical difference between "Old Course" and "Criminal Records" is highlighted by the Author himself:

> After returning home, I hoped to write a book about re-education through labor. This would be a true book (*zhenzhen shizai de shu* 真真實在的書), not like the installments of Criminal Records that I secretly gave the Child every month. I wanted to write an utterly sincere book (*zhenzheng shanliang* 真正善良)—writing it not for the Child, not for the People or for my readers, but rather just for myself. I had already began jotting down some fragments for this truly honest book (*zhen shu* 真書). I was prepared to leave all else behind.[43]

The repetition of "truly honest book" indeed catches the readers' eye and raises important questions about the genuineness and reliability of the information provided in "Criminal Records." Not only do the explicit mentions of the Chinese characters *zhen* 真 'true' and *shanliang* 善良 'good' evoke the three foundational principles of Chinese literature, namely *zhen*, *shan* 善 'good,' and *mei* 美 'beautiful,' but there may also be a veiled allusion here to the Mencian aesthetic proposition *chongshi zhi wei mei* 充實之謂美 ("he whose goodness and honesty have been completely filled up is what I call a beautiful man").[44]

Interestingly, the Author writes this statement of purpose of "Old Course" only after having obtained permission to reside outside Zone 99. While his excuse is that he wishes to find more fertile soil where to grow wheat, in order to contribute to the fulfillment of the production quota, his real aim is to establish a radically new harmonious relationship with the environment, so as to quell his urge to write:

> In the morning I would stand on the hill and look out at the rising sun, and in the evening, I would stand on the hillside and gaze at the setting sun. Sometimes I would lie down on the front of the hill and sun myself until my head was covered in sweat, whereupon I would go around to the back of the hill and lie down, enjoying the cool breeze as I stared up intently at the changing shapes of the clouds in the sky and listened to the sound of the moon and stars approaching. I yearned to write. Lying next to those plots of land, I would get so anxious to write that my hands would become covered in sweat. In order to quell that urge, I had no choice but to grasp a handful of cool sand and dirt, so that my feverish and trembling hands could calm down, like a pair of trapped rabbits.[45]

This exceptionally lyrical passage resonates with some important concepts in classical Chinese literature: the interaction between "interior emotion" (*qing* 情) and "exterior landscape" (*jing* 景), which "cooperate in a single process,"[46] the notion of *xing* 興, a "poetic incitement which refers to the '"direct arousal' of emotion … by *stimuli* from the external

---

43 Yan, *The Four Books*, 172; *Si shu*, 212.
44 Yi Wang and Xiaowei Fu, "An Exegetic Study of the So-Called Proposition of Confucian Aesthetics," *The Journal of Aesthetic Education* 42, no. 1 (2008): 83.
45 Yan, *The Four Books*, 188; *Si shu* 229.
46 Ling Hon Lam, *The Spatiality of Emotion in Early Modern China: From Dreamscapes to Theatricality* (New York: Columbia University Press, 2018), 3.

world,"⁴⁷ and finally the description of the process of writing as the product of an irrepressible physiological urge.⁴⁸

The passage mentioned above describes the Author's harmonious coexistence with the surrounding environment. As he looks at "the changing shapes of the clouds in the sky" and listens to "the sound of the moon and stars approaching," he feels that he himself is part of the cosmos. As his feelings merge with the exterior landscape, *stimuli* to write emerge. Far from being described as mere intellectual *stimuli*, they affect both his body and his mind. What apparently lurks behind such a harmonious coexistence between *qing* and *jing* is also the Confucian notion of *tian ren heyi* 天人合一 'the unity between heaven and man.'

As Yao Xinzhong points out, even if traditional Confucianism held that *tian ren heyi* was a human-centered philosophical fusion of humanity and nature, this concept is ambivalent because it can be viewed both as anthropocentric (*ren*-centered) and as nature-centric (*tian*-centered).⁴⁹ He also convincingly demonstrates that "*tian*-centered understanding establishes a metaphysical and religious framework for Confucian eco-ethical norms, in which ecological prohibitions and policies are built into the political and religious infrastructure, while the *ren*-centered orientation adds practical values and meanings to the ontological care of the human relation to the environment."⁵⁰ Both aspects are highlighted in *The Four Books*.

Initially, the Author tends to his wheat plants so well that they grow extraordinarily fast. Yet, the Child's visit to the Author marks the beginning of a series of tragedies. Amazed by the size and quality of the wheat, the Child demands the production of a disproportionate amount of enormous wheat ears in order "to be invited to the capital to pay tribute,"⁵¹ and the leaves of the plants begin to wilt. Refusing to accept the course of nature, the Author uses his own blood to irrigate the field:

> Eventually, I lost so much blood that I began to feel faint, and would become so dizzy after donating blood that I would have to kneel down immediately so as not to collapse. In fact, I had already passed out so many times, and in order to supplement my nutrition I began going to a distant pond to catch fish and crabs.⁵²

This passage not only shows total disrespect for the harmonious coexistence of *tian* and *ren*, but also highlights the sacralization of *zoe* (e.g., the life of the plants) at the expense of *bios* (human life). Arguably, this could be read as Yan's expedient to frame the collapse of the traditional Confucian precepts within a biopolitical discourse.

Interestingly, the violations of the Confucian principle of *tianren heyi* are described in two opposite ways in *The Four Books*. In the first part of the novel, Yan comments on a real historical event: the systematic devastation of forests in order to collect the wood needed for steel

---

47 Ibid.
48 As Stephen Owen suggests in *Readings in Chinese Literary Thought*, the process of writing as the product of an irrepressible physiological urge is clearly expressed in the "Great Preface" ("Da xu" 大序) to the *Classic of Poetry* (*Shijing* 詩經) and referred to the notion of *shi yan zhi* 詩言志 'poetry expresses intent': "The affections are stirred within and take on form in words. If words alone are inadequate, we speak them out in sighs. If sighing is inadequate, we sing them. If singing them is inadequate, unconsciously our hands dance them and our feet tap them." Owen, *Readings in Chinese Literary Thought* (Boston: Harvard University Press, 1996), 41.
49 Xinzhong Yao, "An Eco-Ethical Interpretation of Confucian 'Tianren Heyi,'" *Frontiers of Philosophy in China* 9, no. 4 (December 2014): 570.
50 Ibid.
51 Yan, *The Four Books*, 201; *Si shu*, 242.
52 Yan, *The Four Books*, 202; *Si shu*, 243.

production. Seemingly relying on a *tian*-centered approach, Yan identifies the lack of ecological consciousness as one of the causes of the Great Famine. The barren landscape in which the intellectuals live and the almost apocalyptic floods that devastate the crops are consistently presented as the premise upon which Yan constructs his representation of cannibalistic practices within Zone 99.

In the second part of the novel, the violation of the principle of *tianren heyi* is instead approached from an anthropocentric perspective. The Child's injunction to all the intellectuals of Zone 99 to follow the Author's example and to donate their blood to the plants is represented as both detrimental to the intellectuals of Zone 99 and useless for the crop—not only do the intellectuals lack the food necessary to their survival, but they are also physically harmed. The predicament of the *homo sacer* is recounted in a highly mimetic fashion by the Author and tragically commented on by one of the intellectuals: "A person's death is like a light being extinguished, after which it is no longer necessary to worry about trying to re-educate and reform them."[53] These words both allude to biopolitical discourses and seemingly establish a lineage within Confucian classical historiography.

The Author's commitment to good and honest writing leads him not only to describe the episodes of cannibalism in Zone 99 but also to address questions about his personal moral responsibilities for the tragic course of events. The Author's realization that both the Musician and the Scholar have read the pages of "Criminal Records" incriminating them—and know that all along he has been reporting their "crime"—is described as the very foundation of the Author's personal moral transformation. His sense of shame prompts him to "cut chunks of his own flesh"[54] and use them as nourishment for the starving Scholar. As Sebastian Veg has rightly observed, this could be interpreted as the Author's self-redeeming gesture.[55] While I agree that it is a "means of repentance," arguably it could also be read as Yan's strategy to both come to terms with the meaning of shame in a state of exception and to draw a clear-cut distinction between guilt and shame. As Ruth Leys puts it, whereas "guilt concerns your actions, that is, what you do, or what you wish or fantasize you have done," "shame is held to concern not your actions but who you are, that is, your deficiencies and inadequacies as a person as these are revealed to the shaming gaze of the other."[56] Such a distinction is also the foundation upon which Kafka's *The Trial* is constructed:[57] while throughout the novel, the protagonist tries to defend himself against his accusers and slanderers, he ultimately consigns himself to his soon-to-be killers because he finds it impossible to live with his shame. In this regard, Agamben has argued that Joseph K.'s shame must be considered "an index of the utmost, frightful proximity of human beings with themselves."[58] Considering this definition

---

53 Yan, *The Four Books*, 246; *Si Shu*, 246; emphasis mine. This passage may contain a veiled reference to Sima Qian's 司馬遷 (145–86) "Letter to Ren An" ("Bao Ren Shaoqing shu" 報任少卿書): "Surely, a man has but one death. That death may be as heavy as Mount Tai or as light as a goose feather. It is how he uses that death that makes all the difference!" Stephen Durrant et al., *The Letter to Ren An and Sima Qian's Legacy* (Seattle: University of Washington Press, 2016), 27.
54 Veg, "Creating a Literary Space to Debate the Mao Era," 4.
55 Ibid.
56 Ruth Leys, *From Guilt to Shame: Auschwitz and After* (Princeton: Princeton University Press, 2007), 11.
57 As the end of *The Trial* highlights, Joseph K. consigns himself to his killers because he cannot survive his shame: "But the hands of one of the men were placed on K.'s throat, whilst the other plunged the knife into his heart and turned it round twice. As his sight faded, K. saw the two men leaning cheek to cheek close to his face as they observed the final verdict. 'Like a dog!' he said. It seemed as if his shame would live on after him." Kafka, *The Trial*, 165.
58 Giorgio Agamben, *Idea of the Prose* (New York: SUNY, 1995), 69.

and representation of shame, it seems possible to argue that the Author's sacrifice has less to do with the relationship that he has established with the Scholar, than with the relationship he has with his own self.

It should be noted that it is not only his sacrifice (i.e., his self-redeeming gesture) but also his mission as an author that allows him to survive his shame. Indeed, he decides to reveal the "honest truth" about his guilt in "Old Course." Hence, the Author becomes simultaneously a *kalumniator* and the target of his own slander. While his "true honest" book does not erase his guilt, it nevertheless allows his readers to gain access to the truth.

As Sebastian Veg has observed, the representation of the use of the Author's body as nourishment for the Scholar may be related to the Luxunian indictment of cannibalism.[59] There may also be another allusion in the Author's self-redeeming gesture. Interestingly enough, the interrelatedness between *kalumnia* (with its related notions of guilt and shame) and writing is also regarded as the foundation of one of the most important historical documents in ancient China, *Historical Records* (*Shi ji* 史記). Its writer, Sima Qian, accepted to be castrated in order to accomplish something which he deemed to be more important than his own life, namely, to ponder on illustrious examples of virtuous deeds and historical wrongs and to redress previous historical misreading.[60] In light of this, the Author's representation of his self-mutilation within "Old Course" may be read as Yan's attempt to create a link with Sima's *Historical Records* and thereby to assert the primacy of ethics in historiographical writing.

Arguably, this may shed some light on the reference to the Four Confucian Classics in the title of this novel. It suggests that while *The Four Books* can certainly be read as a historical document that narrates the tragic years of the Great Famine, it cannot be qualified as reportage fiction (*baogao wenxue* 報告文學). The reference may be regarded as an expedient used by Yan to alert his readers that history should not be read as an assemblage of historical events. Through the dialectical tension between "Criminal Records," in which historical reality is fashioned in a way that "pleases the Child," and "Old Course," which offers an ethical approach to reality, Yan is able to represent both the dangers intrinsic to historiographical writing and the primary role of ethics in historiography.

In this regard, it should not be overlooked that *The Four Books* refers not only to the Four Confucian Classics but also to the Four Gospels. Interestingly enough, while there are no explicit references to the Confucian classic texts, the Bible is explicitly mentioned within the book entitled "Heaven's Child." In the following section, I shall suggest that if we consider *The Four Books* also as a metanarrative that revolves around ethical (or nonethical) spaces produced by the practices of writing and reading historical, religious, and philosophical texts, then also the character of the Child becomes more intelligible. While I am certainly not claiming that this is the only way to interpret this obscure text, it is nevertheless a tentative way to make sense of how and why the Child is at first depicted as a despot and in the end as a "savior" of the intellectuals that he himself has confined for such a long time.

---

59 Veg, "Creating a Literary Space to Debate the Mao Era," 12.
60 As Stephen Durrant, Wai-Yee Li, Michael Nylan, and Hans Van Ess note in *The Letter to Ren An and Sima Qian's Legacy*, 4, "[t]he letter presents Sima Qian struggling with the issue of why he did not commit suicide. In the end, he says, he chose to live on as 'a remnant of knife and saw' so as to complete a vast project of historical writing that had already occupied a good portion of his life. If only that history could be completed successfully, he says, 'then even if I were to suffer ten thousand public insults, how could I feel regret?'"

From confinement to release: On learning how to read, listen, and act ethically in "Heaven's Child"

As mentioned before, Kafka's and Yan's novels share many common concerns. Confinement in a state of exception, aspirations to freedom, expectations about the law during a state of exception and preoccupation with the decaying state of art. As mentioned earlier, at the beginning of the novel, the intellectuals' predicament shares many things in common with Joseph K.'s. They are confined, compelled to work, and yearn for freedom.

These novels, however, end in opposite ways. While in *The Trial* Joseph K. dies like a dog, in *The Four Books* the intellectuals are eventually released. Another striking difference between these two novels is constituted by the presence of an agent of control. In *The Trial* Joseph K. knows neither who is accusing him nor the nature of his crime. Instead, in *The Four Books* Zone 99 is under the control of the Child. He is the only one who can grant them freedom, which he eventually does.

I agree with Tsai Chien-hsin when he argues that "the Child develops from being selfish to mature and self-sacrificing."[61] Interestingly, the sections dedicated to him are entitled "Heaven's Child." What is emphasized in this title is not his position as a leader, but, on the contrary, the image of him as the child of a system that he reveres as if it were God. As Veg rightly notices, he clearly represents "the transformation of an entire nation of adults into brainwashed children."[62] As mentioned earlier, his first concern is to deprive all the intellectuals living in the re-education compound of their books. While he does not hesitate to burn most of them, he brings some of them to his lodging. He is ambivalently described as both omniscient and illiterate. As he himself admits at the beginning of the novel, he does not read the books he has collected in his room.[63] The books that he keeps there include an illustrated volume of the episodes from the Bible. His attitude toward the sacred book radically changes over the course of the story. The Child despises the Bible in the beginning, yet in chapter 2, he is described as fascinated by the book's illustrations:

> The Child *looked* first at the book, then at the illustrations. He *looked* at the pictures of the Heavenly Father, the birth of Jesus, and the Virgin Mary. *The Child laughed.* When *he saw* a picture of Christ bleeding on the cross, the Child *stared in shock.* When he saw the image of the birth of Christ, the Child closed the book.
>
> "For this volume," the Child said, "I'll give you a blossom for each pair of illustrations."
>
> The Theologian's *eyes* sparkled with delight. So it came to pass. The Theologian was awarded fifteen blossoms. He posted all fifteen above his bed, where they resembled a row of inextinguishable lights.[64]

This passage, which describes the Child's first encounter with the Bible, is strongly iconic. The emphasis on verbs such as "looking," "seeing," and "staring" suggests that such an encounter is of an emotional nature. He shows delight when he sees the pictures of the birth of Jesus, while he is shocked at the sight of the "picture of Christ bleeding on the cross." A

---

61 Tsai, "The Museum of Innocence," 7.
62 Veg, "Creating a Literary Space to Debate the Mao Era," 9.
63 Yan, *The Four Books*, 48; *Si shu*, 79.
64 Yan, *The Four Books*, 49; *Si Shu*, 80; emphasis mine.

question comes to mind: should we consider his intense emotional reaction as a "prolepsis" (according to Genette, a flashing forward to a later moment in the chronological sequence of events),[65] which foreshadows the Child's death, that is, his self-crucifixion to the cross?

While there is no definitive answer to this question, what is certain is that the Child is not only disobeying his own commandments but also awarding blossoms in exchange for the banned book. In short, this Bible could be read as marking an important crack in the self-contained world of the re-education compound. Furthermore, the Child's emotional reaction to the Bible suggests curiosity about the representation of both alternative ways of understanding the world and alternative value systems. Interestingly, while there are no theological discussions of the Bible in *The Four Books*, the Child's increasing interest in the Scripture can hardly go unnoticed. It even becomes pivotal in chapter 9, where the Child is forced to come to terms with a "strange event," which in the Gospels would easily fit into the category of "miracles": a cart containing the steel star that had to be consigned to the provincial authorities moves up the hill by itself. This inexplicable event occurs in the middle of a conversation in which the Theologian is explaining to the Child how Jesus was born of Mary, even though she still remained a virgin. As soon as the Child becomes annoyed because he feels unable "to get to the bottom of this" and threatens to "forfeit him his red blossoms,"[66] the strange event occurs:

> The Child then took the cart, the bottle, and the straw hat to the side of the hill facing the sun, and once again they started rolling up the hill on their own accord.
>
> The Child laughed.
>
> The Theologian also went to try. He announced, "This is indeed a strange hill."
>
> "No, it's not," the Child said. "You no longer need to explain how Jesus's mother could have gotten pregnant without there being a father."[67]

Passages like this suggest the function of the Bible in this novel: they are indexes of different ethical world that contain different value systems. The Child's final acceptance of the mystery shrouding Mary's virginity, while far from being described as a repudiation of his own faith in the system, nevertheless marks his entrance into a new state of awareness and openness to cultural, ethical, and religious values, which are in strident contrast with those imposed by the system. After this event, there are no other inexplicable events and the Child continues to control, award, and punish the intellectuals during their confinement.

Coincidentally, the ninth chapter of both *The Trial* and *The Four Books* contain parables.[68] Agamben has read the Kafkian parables as "Scriptures whose key has been lost."[69] This

---

65 Gerard Genette, *Narrative Discourse: An Essay in Method*, trans. Jane E. Lewin (Ithaca: Cornell University Press, 1980), 67.
66 Yan, *The Four Books*, 140; *Sishu*, 180.
67 Yan, *The Four Books*, 141–42; *Sishu*, 182.
68 The parable narrated to Joseph K. by the court chaplain in the chapter entitled "In the Cathedral" refers to a countryman who wishes to gain entry to "the Law" through the open doorway which gives access to it. "But the doorkeeper says he cannot let the man into the Law 'just now'. The countryman waits until he is about to die. Right before breathing his last, he asks the doorkeeper why no one else has come in all the years he has been there. The doorkeeper answers: 'No one else could be granted entry here, because this entrance was intended for you alone. I shall now go and shut it.'" Kafka, *The Trial*, trans. Mike Mitchell, ed. Ritchie Robertson (Oxford: Oxford University Press, 2009), 155.
69 Agamben, *Homo Sacer*, 83.

reading is also a useful key to "enter" not only the ninth chapter of *The Four Books* but also the novel as a whole. In fact, a similar "strange event" is also described in "A New Myth of Sisyphus." Arguably, the Child's inability "to get to the bottom of this" coincides with the beginning of his search for "the lost key." It should not be overlooked that while the Child is all too willing to comply with the authorities' orders, his inability to fulfill the steel and grain quotas compels him to come to terms with his own limitations. On many occasions, he is shown as all too willing to listen to the intellectuals' advice. He first relies on the Technologician's expertise to transform sand into steel, then he follows the Scholar's suggestion to create a pentagonal steel star, and finally heeds the Author's idea to use human blood to nourish the wheat plants.

Arguably, the ritualization of production can be read as the Child's attempt to impose the Author's (mis)reading of the principle of *tian ren heyi* on the whole re-education compound. Needless to say, his experiments all turn into total disasters. The Child's and the intellectuals' failed attempts to make sense of the disaster of the Great Famine lead them not only to evoke God on many occasions but also to draw parallels between the calamity of the famine and those described in the Bible. The emphasis on the Child's and the intellectuals' desperate search for interpretative keys for the disaster suggests that the intellectuals play a twofold role: on the one hand, they are informants or slanderers but, on the other, they convey values and meanings which are different from those proposed by the system.

I do agree with Veg and Tsai that the last chapters of "Heaven's Child" are the most obscure part of the novel. The reader is informed that the Child goes to Beijing, bringing not only the ears of wheat "grown with the blood of the writer,"[70] but also the chapters of "Old Course" which, as already observed, provide an honest and truthful description of the events in Zone 99. While his long stay in Beijing is shrouded in a halo of mystery, his decision to nail himself to a cross like Jesus is documented in detail:

> In the light of the sun, which had just risen in the east, the Child, who had nailed himself to the cross, had the faint smile of contentment of someone who had just endured an excruciating agony. Just as the sun was coming up, the Child had spread the red blossoms over the red ground and then nailed himself to the cross. No one knew what the Child had seen or encountered during the month he had spent in the capital, but the first thing he did upon returning was nail himself to that cross.[71]

Interestingly, in the text there is a reference not only to the cross but also to the red blossoms. Furthermore, immediately before dying, the Child also has the time to utter his final words. While this novel begins with his commandments, it ends on an almost opposite note: an invitation to all the intellectuals of Zone 99 to take not only the forty-four stars which will grant them freedom, but also the books which are in his room.[72] As the intellectuals enter his bedroom, they discover immaculate bookcases in a place covered with dust and find that his "bed was covered with more than a dozen children's book that the Child *had come to love, many of which were illustrated stories from the Bible.*"[73]

As is evident, from the beginning until his last journey, the Child is a character whose vision of the world is shaped by the authorities, by illustrated books, and by the stories of the intellectuals

---

70 Veg, "Creating a Literary Space to Debate the Mao Era," 12.
71 Yan, *The Four Books*, 325; *Si shu*, 367.
72 Yan, *The Four Books*, 326; *Si shu*, 369.
73 Ibid.

living in Zone 99. What is also clear is that while during his stay in Zone 99, he has always acted as a despot, he has nevertheless learned to love books. Given the centrality assigned to books in this novel and, above all, the fact that books are the Child's only legacy besides the red stars, some questions come to mind: Did the Child learn to read adult books during his stay in Beijing? Did he understand the transformative effect of reading? What is certain is that in Beijing, he had to consign both the ears of wheat and the Author's installments of his true and honest book, "Old Course." Hence, his stay in Beijing is presumably a final occasion for him to settle accounts with his own self. In his capacity as the leader of Zone 99, he is accountable not only for the many tragic deaths that have occurred in Zone 99, as well as the cases of cannibalism (described in detail in "Old Course"), but also for the criticism addressed against him in "Old Course."

The way in which the Child fashions his own death could be read as an attempt at self-redemption. By contrast to the Author who, like the Grand Historian Sima Qian, decides not to end his life because he has a mission to accomplish, the Child chooses to die as a savior and as an enlightened leader of Zone 99. While his decision to nail himself to the cross may suggest that he has internalized the Theologian's lessons about the meaning of Jesus (*Savior*),[74] his spreading of the red blossoms may arguably be read as an iconic legacy of his own past and background.

Yan's decision to have the Child grant freedom to the intellectuals of Zone 99 in many ways reverses the (pessimistic) Kafkian view about the state of exception. While in the famous Kafkian parable in *The Trial* the countryman is never allowed to pass through the gate that would lead him to the Law because the guardian shuts it before he can enter, the Child eventually decides to let the intellectuals make their way through that gate. As if to underscore the fact that this novel should not be interpreted as an invitation to convert to Christianity, none of the intellectuals in Zone 99 is shown as embracing the Christian faith. The Scholar, the only intellectual who willingly decides to remain behind, decides instead to devote his life to the study of Buddhism.

As will be discussed in the conclusion, in Yan Lianke, just as in Kafka, religion is present only in terms of inverse theology. What applies to Kafka – the idea that "religion survives only as a memory-trace of once-living belief"[75] – is also evident in Yan's *The Four Books*. The misread, camouflaged, or even erased Confucian values in the Author's texts, the forsaking of books on the part of the intellectuals, and the erasure of *bios* convey the idea of a diegetic world abandoned by God. Even if Yan seems relatively more optimistic than Kafka when he recounts the Scholar's decision to dedicate the rest of his life to the study of Buddhist scriptures, there is no eschatology in *The Four Books*: there are no factual descriptions of the human longing for the transcendental, let alone theological discussions.

In the last "book," entitled "A New Myth of Sisyphus," the concept of inverse theology is articulated clearly enough. Once again, Yan describes a "strange hill effect" (a clear link to the ninth chapter of *The Four Books* discussed above) and narrates the tragedy of the Eastern Sisyphus who, unlike the Western Sisyphus, is compelled by a ferocious God to push down the slope an enormous boulder which, as happened in the other chapter, spontaneously rolls upwards. I shall suggest that Yan wrote "A New Myth of Sisyphus" as a key to enter and read his complex and composite novel.

---

74 In the ninth chapter, the Theologian explains to Child: "*Jesus* means 'savior' and a *savior* refers to someone who will always go into adversity to rescue others." Yan, *The Four Books*, 139; *Si shu*, 179.
75 Gordon, "Kafka's Inverse Theology," 47.

Conclusion: Inverse theology and the recovery of humanity and humanness in "A New Myth of Sisyphus"

"A New Myth of Sisyphus" coincides with the sixteenth chapter of *The Four Books*, entitled "Manuscript." Not only does this section describe the different fates of the other three books, but it also presents this philosophical manuscript as the result of the many years that the Scholar has spent studying Buddhism. It recounts Sisyphus' toils as a "punishment by God," which became an "ordinary condition, to the point that he no longer regarded it as God's punishment for his transgression."[76] As decreed by God, Sisyphus pushes a boulder up a mountain every day. His ability to endure "absurdity, hardship, and punishment," in the Scholar's view, not only allows humanity to hold "a key and a spirit by which to shatter existing reality and create a new one," but also prompts Sisyphus to familiarize himself with his own tragic quandary.[77] His meeting with a child and his increasing fondness for this boy gives him an opportunity to partially escape "the prison house" created by his perpetual moving of the boulder and gives new meaning to his meaningless quandary. At the same time, this encounter also awakens the wrath of a God who cannot "permit Sisyphus to find familiarity and meaning in his punishment."[78] Accused of both loving the child and, even worse, having "become dependent" on pushing up the boulder, Sisyphus is then condemned to an opposite punishment: he has to move down the mountain a boulder that naturally moves up. God also declares that Sisyphus will be released from such a punishment if he "explains the principle underlying the strange hill."[79] Not only is Sisyphus unable to explain it, but he is even afraid that solving the riddle will bring him further punishments. The sight of a hermitage "with cows, sheep, and children playing outside" after so many years of toil gives him a fresh opportunity "to find new meaning in his punishment"—he even transforms such a punishment into a "precondition of his own existence."[80] Knowing that his contentment will make God upset, he simply pretends to be enduring his punishment as he used to.

I have dwelt on "A New Myth of Sisyphus" at length because it addresses questions that are very relevant for understanding this complex novel. Indeed, its emphasis on the human predicament, more specifically on the notions of punishment, entrapment, and confinement, allows readers not only to make sense of *The Four Books* as a whole but also to grasp the scope of Yan Lianke's project. The title of the novel, as already highlighted, points not only to the philosophical nature of this book, but also to its ethical relevance. As described in the "Manuscript," Yan's representation of the human quandary clearly reflects Kafkian views about radical estrangement and the fearful nihilism of a world abandoned by God. In "A New Myth of Sisyphus," God is not only present but also angry. He does not want Sisyphus to be content with his life and tries all possible methods to make him suffer.

"Our world is only a bad mood of God, a bad day of his,"[81] Kafka once said. This also applies to Yan's Sisyphus as well as to the intellectuals living in Zone 99. The overwhelming feeling that judgment comes from an unapproachable "elsewhere" is shared by Sisyphus, by the intellectuals of Zone 99, and ultimately by Joseph K., too, and this is part of Yan's and Kafka's messianism, which is bound to amount to a theological inversion. It is not redemption that is disclosed in "A New Myth of Sisyphus," but its opposite. In this regard,

---

76 Yan, *The Four Books*, 332; *Si shu*, 375.
77 Yan, *The Four Books*, 332; *Si shu*, 375.
78 Yan, *The Four Books*, 332; *Si shu*, 375.
79 Yan, *The Four Books*, 336; *Si shu*, 378.
80 Yan, *The Four Books*, 338; *Si shu*, 379.
81 Gordon, "Kafka's Inverse Theology," 30.

Kafka's vision of redemption, a condition by which the terror and hopelessness of the unredeemed world are brought into view, also applies to Yan's myth of Sisyphus, which represents a humanity condemned to suffer and be punished for no specific reason. One noticeable difference between *The Trial* and *The Four Books* is that while in *The Trial* the name of God is never mentioned, in *The Four Books,* it is consistently evoked, albeit solely as a name or an icon. In the main part of the story, it is an image in an illustrated textbook, a story told for the sake of the Child's entertainment, a reference.

Indeed, when God demands Sisyphus to explain "the principle underlying the strange hill," He is apparently referring to the keys that give access to an inaccessible world—keys that, as *The Trial* and "A New Myth of Sisyphus" teach us, have been lost with the advent of the modern era. Kafka's idea of an inaccessible reality is also apparent in his reflections about the relationship between art and reality/truth: "Art flies around truth, but with the definite intention of not getting burnt. Its capacity lies in finding in the dark void a place where the beam of light can be intensely caught, without this having been perceptible before."[82] These words appear to find a powerful echo in "A New Myth of Sisyphus," especially in those passages of Sisyphus's discovery of the hermitage. It is indeed a beam of light that Yan makes accessible to Sisyphus, albeit at a distance. While his toils and punishment continue, this light endows him with the meaning of his own existence.

While Kafka and Yan both represent an inverse theology, a world deserted by God, Yan's Eastern Sisyphus is different from the Kafkian tragic heroes. In the end, he is denied neither hope nor delight. Clearly, neither Sisyphus nor the intellectuals of Zone 99 are searching for God. They instead set out in search of a human environment where they can (possibly) live a fully fledged life. By focusing on the inaccessible "principle underlying the strange hill" in "A New Myth of Sisyphus," Yan also alerts his readers that *The Four Books* revolves around Scriptures which have now lost their meaning. Arguably, all tragedies of the present era are ascribable to the loss of the keys which give access to such Scriptures. Even if "A New Myth of Sisyphus" (like the rest of *The Four Books*) suggests, in a similar vein to Kafka, that those keys cannot be found, Yan nevertheless reminds readers of their existence and of their importance for the construction of historiographical, literary, philosophical, and cultural discourses.

Bibliography

Agamben, Giorgio. *Homo Sacer: Sovereign Power and Bare Life*. Translated by Daniel-Heller Roazen. Stanford: Stanford University Press, 1998.

———. "K." In *The Work of Giorgio Agamben: Law, Literature, Life*, edited by Justin Clemens, Nicholas Heron, and Alex Murray, 13–27. Edinburgh: Edinburgh University Press, 2012.

Durrant, Stephen, et al. *The Letter to Ren An and Sima Qian's Legacy*. Seattle: University of Washington Press, 2016.

Genette, Gerard. *Narrative Discourse: An Essay in Method*. Translated by Jane E. Lewin. Ithaca: Cornell University Press, 1980.

Gibson, John. "On the Ethical Character of Literature." In *Kafka's The Trial: Philosophical Perspectives*, edited by Espen Hammer, 85–109. Oxford: Oxford University Press, 2018.

Gordon, Peter E. "Kafka's Inverse Theology." In *Kafka's The Trial*, edited by Espen Hammer, 23–54. Oxford: Oxford University Press, 2018.

———, ed. *Kafka's The Trial: Philosophical Perspectives*. Oxford: Oxford University Press, 2018.

Hammer, Espen. "Kafka's Modernism: Intelligibility and Voice." In *Kafka's The Trial*, ed. Espen Hammer, 227–52. Oxford: Oxford University Press, 2018.

Kafka, Franz. *The Trial*. Translated by Mike Mitchell, edited by Ritchie Robertson. Oxford: Oxford University Press, 2009.

---

82 Richter, "A Disease of All Signification," 112–13.

Lam, Ling Hon. *The Spatiality of Emotion in Early Modern China: From Dreamscapes to Theatricality.* New York: Columbia University Press, 2018.

Leys, Ruth. *From Guilt to Shame: Auschwitz and After.* Princeton: Princeton University Press, 2007.

Lupascu, Victoria. "Plasma Economy, Biopolitics of Blood and the Literary Specter of Aids." *Chinese Literature: Essays, Articles, Reviews (CLEAR)* 42 (2020): 133–57.

Newell, Ann Van Auken. "Killings and Assassinations in the *Spring and Autumn* as Records of Judgments," *Asia Major*, 3rd series, 27, no. 1 (2014): 1–31.

Owen, Stephen. *Readings in Chinese Literary Thought.* Boston: Harvard University Press, 1996.

Pirazzoli, Melinda. "From Franz Kafka to Franz Kafka Award Winner, Yan Lianke: Biopolitics and the Human Dilemma of *Shenshizhuyi* in *Liven* and *Dream of Ding Village*." *CLCWeb: Comparative Literature and Culture* 22, no. 4 (2020): 1–12. https://doi.org/10.7771/1481-4374.3437.

Richter, Gerhard. "A Disease of All Signification: Kafka's *The Trial* between Adorno and Agamben." In *Kafka's The Trial*, ed. Espen Hammer, 111–38. Oxford: Oxford University Press, 2018.

Salzani, Carlo. "In a Messianic Gesture: Agamben's Kafka." In *Philosophy and Kafka*, ed. Brendan Moran and Carlo Salzani, 261–82. Lanham: Lexington Books, 2013.

Tsai, Chien-hsin. "The Museum of Innocence: The Great Leap Forward and Famine, Yan Lianke and *Four Books*." *Modern Chinese Literature and Culture* (May 2011): 1–14. https://u.osu.edu/mclc/online-series/museum-of-innocence/.

Vardoulakis, Dimitris. *Freedom from the Free Will: On Kafka's Laughter.* New York: SUNY Press, 2012.

Veg, Sebastian. "Creating a Literary Space to Debate the Mao Era: The Fictionalization of the Great Leap Forward in *The Four Books*." *China Perspectives*, 2014, no. 4: 7–15.

Wang, Yi and Xiaowei Fu. "An Exegetic Study of the So-Called Proposition of Confucian Aesthetics." *The Journal of Aesthetic Education* 42, no. 1 (2008): 80–89.

Yan Lianke 閻連科. *The Four Books.* Translated by Carlos Rojas. New York: Grove Press, 2015.

———. *Si shu* 四書 [The four books]. Taipei: Maitian chubanshe, 2011.

Yao, Xinzhong. "An Eco-Ethical Interpretation of Confucian 'Tianren Heyi.'" *Frontiers of Philosophy in China* 9, no. 4 (Dec. 2014): 570–85.

10
ELEMENTS OF MODERNISM AND THE GROTESQUE IN YAN LIANKE'S EARLY FICTION

Nicoletta Pesaro

The *Xiangtu Qingjie* (native-soil complex)

Yan Lianke 閻連科 (b. 1958) is indisputably one of the most important and controversial authors in contemporary China. Despite being considered a late bloomer in Chinese fiction,[1] through the numerous novels and short stories he has published since the late 1980s, he has created a new style, which has attracted scholarly attention both in China and abroad. His works were initially seen to fit within the well-known genre of the *xiangtu xiaoshuo* 鄉土小說 (fiction of the native soil),[2] but the author's first attempts to experiment with what was to become his signature style, which he himself has defined as spiritual realism or mythorealism (*shenshizhuyi* 神實主義), can be traced back to his early writings. These deserve to be analyzed, also in relation to his later achievements and to contemporary Chinese fiction as a whole.

In order to track the genesis of Yan's unique approach to *xiangtu* writing, this chapter focuses on his early fiction, namely the novella "Gold Cave" ("Huangjin dong" 黃金洞, 1995), which was awarded the prestigious Lu Xun Literary Prize for the best novella in 1998. The text deals with the story of a family conflict in a degraded rural village, where a father and his sons, haunted by a double lust for sex and money, vie for the same woman and for a cave of gold. The narrative is conveyed by the younger son, whose mental weakness and impaired cognitive functions make him an unreliable and yet highly perceptive narrator. This tense slice of life in a rural China facing the aggressive stimuli of Deng Xiaoping's economic reforms provides Yan with a literary opportunity to develop his aesthetics and ethics of fiction.

The critical literature on Yan's works has rapidly increased over the last two decades, mostly focusing on his outstanding novels, from *Lenin's Kisses* (*Shouhuo* 受活, 2004) and *Serve the People* (*Wei renmin fuwu* 為人民服務, 2005) to *Dream of Ding Village* (*Dingzhuang meng* 丁莊夢, 2006), *The Four Books* (*Si shu* 四書, 2011) and *The Day the Sun Died* (*Rixi* 日熄, 2015), just to name a few, which have aroused special interest and sparked some debates within the literary arena. Indeed, each of these novels has caused quite a stir, due to the writer's peculiar

---

1 Chen Xiaoming 陳曉明, "Zhemian kunan: Chongxie xiangtu Zhongguo" 直面苦難: 重寫鄉土中國 [Facing suffering: Rewriting rural China], in Chen, *Xiaoshuo shiping* 小說時評 [Review of current fiction] (Kaifeng: Henan daxue chubanshe, 2002), 60–66.
2 The term *xiangtu xiaoshuo* was created in the 1920s by Lu Xun 魯迅 and Zhou Zuoren 周作人, covering much of the 20th-century Chinese rural fiction.

way of tackling very crucial and often tragic issues related to contemporary Chinese history and society, through an approach that blends satire, the grotesque, and surrealism. Studies of his earlier fictional endeavors are, on the contrary, relatively rare, especially among Western scholars, while in Chinese literary research, we find a certain number of articles and reviews devoted to his 1990s works. Most of this literature builds upon Yan's alleged "native-soil complex" (*xiangtu qingjie* 鄉土情結), referring to the tight connection which binds him to his rural background and the fact that the majority of his works are set in the countryside, more specifically in his home village in Henan.

Yan defines himself as a *xiangtu* author, inspired by his native land and his own life experience. Engaging himself in literary writing is apparently an ethical choice for him, a way for him to contribute to his home village: "I feel that the land of my hometown has raised me, making me grow into a writer: in return, it requires me to express it, to narrate it" (我覺得我家鄉那片土地養育了我, 它把我培育成一個作家, 它要求的回報就是我去表達它, 敘述它).[3] This choice takes the form of an unavoidable ethical mission, but at the same time, it provides the writer with an inexhaustible literary resource:

> There's no way, because you are a peasant, and because you were born in that piece of land, therefore you must do whatever it takes for the relatives and the neighbours of that piece of land. ... I come from a small town in the countryside, a very big village. That village is an endless source of life for my writing: a source of emotions and images. In one word, it is the source of my inspiration. That small town is a land full of incomparable marvels, any fact of reality can be absurd or rational.[4]

As early as 1996, commenting on one of Yan's earliest collection of stories, including "Gold Cave," Wang Kan 王侃, despite considering Yan a representative of the *xiangtu* genre, noted: "Yan Lianke has by now built up a world of his own, recently his creation is tending toward the cultural fable and the narration of myths" (閻連科已經初步的構築了一個他的文學世界, 近期他的創作正趨向文化寓言與神話講述).[5] Acknowledging his skill in conceiving imaginary stories based on a crude reality, Wang seemingly foresees the author's progressive attempt to distance himself from the traditional nativist approach.

Nonetheless, most of the previous analyses provided by Chinese critics with respect to Yan's early works tend to place them in the field of realistic fiction as texts that are representative of the *xiangtu* genre. These studies emphasize his dependence on the traditional themes of "struggle for survival" (*shengcun* 生存), of illiterate peasants' subjection to their "fate" (*ming* 命) and of their endless "suffering" (*kunan* 苦難). According to Zhang Xitian 張喜田, Henan's specific social and cultural context is marked by narrow-mindedness and the acceptance of an obsolete heritage: "Lacking the opportunity of migration, people from Henan build their interpersonal relations on blood relations and not on an equality pact. The new generations

---

3 Yan Lianke and Zhang Xuexin 張學昕, *Wo de xianshi wo de zhuyi* 我的現實我的主義 [My reality, my -ism] (Tianjin: Nankai daxue chubanshe, 2011), 20. All translations are mine unless otherwise noted.

4 Ibid., 18-19: "這個事情沒辦法, 因為你是農民, 因為你出生在那塊土地上, 你就必須為那塊土地的親人、鄰居做你辦所能及的事情。……我家住在一個鎮子上, 那是一個很大的村莊。那個村莊是我寫作取之不盡的生活源泉、情感源泉、想像的源泉。一句話, 是我寫作的一切的靈感之源。那個鎮子奇妙無比, 任何現實中的一件事情都可能是荒誕的、合理的。"

5 Wang Kan, "Da beimin de qinghuai: Ping *Yan Lianke wenj*" 大悲憫的情懷——評《閻連科文集》[A deep sense of the tragic: Reviewing *Collected Essays of Yan Lianke*], *Quanguo xin shumu* 全國新書目 [National new books information], 1997, no. 5: 34.

must absolutely submit to the older ones. The bureaucratic system is based on the patriarchal system; 'filial piety' towards one's elders led to 'loyalty' towards officials."[6] Zhang claims that beyond this heavy cultural legacy, it is the "excess of soil" which condemns Henan writers, including Yan, to unduly indulge in a narrower vision of reality: "The native-soil spirit not only created Henan writers, but also wore them out, imposing unnecessary limits on their writing. The 'soil' is real, but when the 'soil' is too much, excess is like deficiency. By excessively sticking to the real soil, they lack the boldness of a view from above, ambitious goals and a broad vision."[7] This bond with the soil seemingly affects the vision and literary style of these writers, as their affection for relatives and neighbors in their village—something Yan himself emphasizes as the main motivation for his writing—keeps on haunting them like ghosts.[8]

The mythorealism that Yan gradually developed is further discussed and deeply analyzed elsewhere in this book. Arguably, it is the author's reaction to this "excess of soil" which allows his fiction to include, behind and beyond that soil, an invisible, surreal world within his depiction of reality, providing him with a broader view of rural China from both within and above. Yan's powerful rewriting of *xiangtu xiaoshuo* only came to be widely acknowledged by critics at the turn of the century, especially after the publication of *Streams of Time* (*Riguang liunian* 日光流年, 2004) where mythorealistic strategies are fully deployed. For his part, Chen Xiaoming also includes Yan among the most outstanding *xiangtu* writers: "Yan Lianke is well known in the literary world for reflecting the lifestyle of rural China. For many years, no one described the lives of Chinese peasants as persistently as he did. Although sometimes Yan Lianke exudes warm affection for rural China's human relations and customs, in most cases the suffering of peasants constitutes his recurrent theme."[9] While acknowledging the sense of despair which pervades Yan's representation of rural China, Chen denies that his point of view is passively pessimistic: "Despair is also a kind of force, a futile yet unyielding form of resistance" (絕望也是一種力量，一種徒勞而又並沒有屈服的反抗).[10] According to Chen, as an example of *xiangtu* writing, Yan's depiction of his home village and of Henan countryside, more generally, extends the concept of native-soil fiction beyond its three main configurations, namely, that devoted to "people's relations and customs" (such as in Fei Ming's 廢名 and Sheng Congwen's 沈從文 works), which later took a modernist form in the "root-seeking" school; the realistic approach focused on peasants' class struggle; and the tendency to depict the effects of reforms in the countryside, which emerged after China's opening up to the world. Chen states that the writer has adopted his own approach: by "getting rid of ideological biases and drawing upon his personal radical interpretation of rural China, he has carried out a powerful rewriting of mainstream 'native soil' literature"

---

6 Zhang Xitian 張喜田, "'Liantu': Yi ge jiuchan zhe Henan zuojia de qingjie" 「戀土」：一個糾纏著河南作家的情結 ["Loving the soil": A Complex haunting Henan writers], *Henan shifan daxue xuebao* 河南師範大學學報 [Journal of Henan Normal University] 23, no. 2 (1996): 58: "由於河南人缺少遷移，以血緣而居，人們之間的關係並不建立在平等的契約論的原理之上，而是建立在以出生論為基礎的血緣關係上，後代必然絕對服從前輩。家長制是長官制產生的基礎對長輩的「孝」直接導致了對當官的「忠」。"
7 Ibid., 60: "鄉土精神不僅造就了河南作家，而且也磨損了河南作家，使他們的創作出現了不應有的局限。「土」是實在，但太「土」，那就過猶不及。過於粘滯於現實的土壤使他們缺乏高屋建瓴的氣魄，缺乏宏大的目標和開闊的視野。"
8 Ibid., 57.
9 Chen, "Zhimian ku'nan," 60: "閻連科以反映鄉土中國的生活風習而著稱於文壇，這麼多年來，沒有人像他那樣執著地描寫中國農民的生活。雖然有時閻連科也沉浸於鄉土中國溫情脈脈的人倫風習，但大多數情況下，書寫中國農民的苦難構成他的持續主題。"
10 Ibid., 65.

(擺脫開意識形態的偏見，以他個人對鄉土中國的極端理解，對此前的鄉土中國的主流文學進行了一次強行的改寫).[11]

In his book on *xiangtu* fiction, Ding Fan 丁帆 praises Yan for his "artistic courage" (*yishu yonggan* 藝術勇敢) and talent (*caihua* 才華),[12] but finds it difficult to define him as a real *xiangtu* writer:

> Yan Lianke is extremely familiar with all the malpractices and shortcomings of the countryside and peasants, but his feelings for the countryside and its peasants could hardly be more profound, and he could hardly be more loyal to traditional culture and to the native-soil complex …. [He] undoubtedly touches on traditional culture, politics, the national character and people's essential survival with amazing sensitivity and sharpness. However, he only relies on the duties of "personal conscience" and the "spirit of enlightenment." Should this be regarded as a defect for a novelist with such a compelling talent and deep emotions?[13]

Later, in the same chapter of his book, when commenting on Yan's fiction from the second half of the 1990s, Ding concludes: "from that time, maybe even earlier, down to *Hard Like Water*, there is a qualitative leap in his investigation of suffering and evil; Yan Lianke has already taken the path … of metaphorical writing and can hardly be defined as a simple *xiangtu* fiction writer."[14]

Judging from this brief survey of Chinese critics' opinions on Yan's early fiction, it is clear that after his first literary achievements, he generally came to be labeled as a realistic *xiangtu* writer, even though early traces of modernism and surrealism were already perceivable in his fiction in the 1990s. The author himself, recalling his 1990s novellas, has stated: "my later works gradually developed along the path of earlier works, rather than appearing abruptly."[15] In a 2021 article, Zhou Yinyin 周銀銀 significantly speaks of "avant-gardist" or "experimental fiction of the native soil" (*xianfengshi xiangtu xiaoshuo* 先鋒式鄉土小說), citing Yan and Mo Yan 莫言 among the fundamental innovators of the genre, after a century of nativist fiction dominated by the realistic approach: "over the last hundred years in the history of Chinese literature, we can easily notice that it was traditional realism which ruled the roost: there has always been a distance between the artistic avant-garde of absurdity and distortion and the great rural motherland. The 'will o' the wisp' of modernism and postmodernism hardly managed to shine in the fiction of the native soil."[16]

---

11 Ibid., 64.
12 Ding Fan 丁帆, *Zhongguo xiangtu xiaoshuo shi* 中國鄉土小說史 [A history of Chinese native soil fiction] (Beijing: Beijing daxue chubanshe, 2007), 342.
13 Ibid., 343: "閻連科對農村和農民的一切弊端與缺陷在再熟悉不過，但對農村和農民的感情又再深不過，對傳統文化和鄉土中國情結再忠誠不過……毫無疑問地以驚人的敏感和銳利觸及到傳統文化、政治和國民性，觸及到人根本性的生存，卻只憑了「個人的良知」和「啟蒙精神」的任務，對於這樣一個才氣逼人而情感深沉的小說家，是否可以算做一種缺陷？"
14 Ibid., 344: "從這時或更早開始，直到《堅硬如水》，對苦難和罪惡的審視出現了質的飛躍，閻連科已經走向了真正意義上的隱喻式寫作，很難再用單一的鄉土小說界定他。"
15 Cited in Wang Yu, "Ghost Marriage in Twentieth-Century Chinese Literature: Between the Past and the Future," *Frontiers of Literary Studies* 10, no. 1 (2016): 99.
16 "執牛耳的一般是傳統寫實手法，荒誕變形式的先鋒藝術與厚重的鄉土大地總存在些許隔膜，現代主義與後現代主義的「鬼火」好像難以照進鄉土小說內部。" Zhou Yinyin, "20 shiji 90 niandai yilai xianfengshi xiangtu xiaoshuo de jiazhi guheng" 20世紀90年代以來先鋒式鄉土小說的價值估衡 [An appraisal of the value of the avantgardist fiction of the native soil in the 1990s], *Jiangsu keji daxue xuebao (shehui kexue ban)* 江蘇科技大學學報 [Journal of Jiangsu University of Science and Technology (Social Science Edition)] 21, no. 1 (2021): 42.

According to Zhou, "Yan Lianke did not take the avant-gardist path overnight: at different stages he continued to fight against realism and tear apart it: after experiencing 'dependence, estrangement, complicity, betrayals and breaks', he finally brought forth the way of mythorealism."[17] I would argue that Yan's famous literary concept and practice of the "mythorealism" stems from the blending of modernism and nativism he experimented as early as the 1990s by strewing fictional works such as "Gold Cave" with both grotesque and lyrical elements. This experimental writing resulted in a subjective form of "sensory" realism which, to some extent, can be compared to Faulkner's "rural modernism." As Jolene Hubbs puts it, "[r]ural modernism has not simply a geographic logic but also a sociopolitical significance. [It] critiques the conflation of the urban and the modern, in part by revealing how the country is used as a foil against which urban modernity is defined."[18] Regarding Faulkner's influence on Chinese literature, in an article on the reception of this American writer among contemporary Chinese authors, I noted: "If this stress on the local represented as universal drew Chinese writers' attention to Faulkner, the charm Faulkner exerted and still exerts on Chinese literary landscape sprang also from another crucial set of reasons: his individualism, and his ability to critique modernity and give voice to the contemporary man's crisis through an extraordinarily modern range of narrative techniques—such as interior monologues, constant shifts of narrative time, the free use of pronouns, etc."[19] In this chapter, I will show how, through a process similar to what we find at work in Faulkner's writing, the array of modernist devices adopted in "Gold Cave" provide Yan with a strategy to overcome his own "native-soil complex" and to reformulate the narration of Chinese rural society by disclosing, while at the same time demystifying its profound cultural substratum.

The story and its interpretations

"Gold Cave" is a tightly structured and beautifully written tale of family degradation, based on the development and consequences of desire-driven behaviors in a land whose historical, cultural, and ethical role has been perverted: the local peasants no longer till the soil, but have delved into the business of gold digging, dragging themselves and their families into a selfish competition for material success. This violation of the ancient pact between men and nature, set against the background of a China dominated by a Darwinist reformism and thirst for money, can be included among the traditional themes of *xiangtu* fiction: as I reported above, *shengcun* 'the struggle for survival' has often been associated with Yan, and *shengcun* is undoubtedly one of the pivotal elements of *xiangtu* fiction. But the new context in which this struggle takes place is the clash between the traditional rural values of self-restraint and frugality and the materialism rampant in contemporary society. This is strikingly epitomized by the gold cave and the urban lure exercised by the pivotal female character, Tao, in her total-red attires. Indeed, to Yan's eyes both cultural systems, the old and the new, are completely meaningless and dehumanizing. Throughout the narrative, the writer conducts a thorough critique of rural society, revealing how its fundamental tenets, still steeped in Confucian ethics and deeply rooted in Chinese peasants' moral subconscious, have been gradually distorted and disrupted.

17 Ibid.: "閻連科的先鋒之路並非一蹴而就。在不同階段，他與現實主義不斷搏鬥和撕扯，經由「依賴、疏離、糾結、背叛、決裂」後終於破繭成蝶，提出了「神實主義」的途徑。"
18 Jolene Hubbs, "William Faulkner's Rural Modernism," *The Mississippi Quarterly* 61, no. 3 (Summer 2008), *Special Issue on Faulkner, Labor, and the Critique of Capitalism*: 461.
19 Pesaro Nicoletta, "Faulkner and Chinese Modern Fiction: Between Nativism and Modernism," in *William Faulkner's Legacy*, ed. Pia Masiero (Venezia: Cafoscarina, 2012), 52.

In this conventional *xiangtu* setting, a small peasant family in Henan province, in addition to the bond with the soil, another Confucian value has been radically reversed: the harmony and order of kinship ties. Gong Gui, the father-master, is the despotic ruler of his family and of the gold-digging trade; he is a violent and coarse widower over the age of sixty, who is driven by his greed and hunger for sex with the young women who come from the city, dazzled by his sudden wealth. His two sons make a mockery of the long-standing virtue of filial piety (*xiao* 孝) as they hatch sordid plots against their father, to gain his lover's favor and reap the profits from the gold caves discovered under their family land. The term *xiao* and its symbols are scattered throughout the novella to express both empty boasting about traditional virtue and, at the same time, its sardonic violation.

Women's role in the novella is equally negative. This is especially true in the case of Tao, who becomes involved with both Gong Gui and the two brothers in an attempt to optimize her "gold digging." She represents the main obstacle preventing them from performing their proper roles as father and sons, respectively. Women from the city, with their immoral and seducing beauty, a traditional Confucianist bias and also a typical *xiangtu* motive,[20] symbolize the destructive power of the modern logic of profit. Even the older brother's wife, while performing her role as a wife and daughter-in-law quite decently, in her self-fulfilling prophecy ultimately embodies the worst violation of filial piety: "there are three ways you can fail to honor your parents, and the worst is to have no heir" (不孝有三，無後為大).[21] Indeed, toward the end of the novella, as predicted by his wife's oath in the first chapter, Laoda's lack of male heirs becomes a reality when the woman is sterilized after the birth of two girls and two miscarriages. Erhan, too, who, despite everything, strives to accomplish his last duty as a son—to bury his father's body in the family's first, now abandoned gold cave—commits a final act of abuse by having sex with Tao before his father's coffin.

Within such a gloomy and unethical landscape, which undermines even the theory of amoral familism,[22] as the family itself is disrupted by the moral corruption that haunts its members, Yan develops a radical critique of Chinese society and its backward rural culture vis-à-vis an equally insane modernity. The clash between traditional rural virtues and urban culture (hardly a new concept in Chinese *xiangtu* fiction)[23] has been envisaged by many critics as the pivotal theme of this text. Indeed, the novella has been mainly interpreted as a typical example of Yan's "world of Balou" (Balou *shijie* 耙耬世界) series, after the name of a mountain near the writer's home village in Henan. This world is both a real place and an imaginary one.[24] Most commentaries on the novella regard it as the literary exploration of an ethical

---

20 The trope of the identification of women with the city's modern and therefore immoral ways can be found in Sheng Congwen's fiction.
21 Mengzi 孟子, "Li Lou" 離婁, A.26; David Hinton, trans., *The Four Classics of Chinese Literature*, Kindle edn. (Berkeley: Counterpoint, 2013).
22 As discussed in Edward C. Banfield, *The Moral Basis of a Backward Society* (1958), the concept of amoral familism represents the selfish, even criminal behavior of the members of families in a backward social context, who sacrifice public interest for the sake of the family itself.
23 Wang Yu explores these conflicting values in his analysis of another novella by Yan, *Searching the Land* (*Xunzhao tudi* 尋找土地 1996), see Wang, "Ghost Marriage in Twentieth-Century Chinese Literature," 86–102.
24 In an interview with Riccardo Moratto, Yan claims: "耙耬山脈就是一個文學地理名稱而已。但「耙耬」兩個字，是中國的農具名稱，它代表著農耕文明、鄉村文明。這兩個字不來源於靈感，而是來自於現實。我老家有座山就叫做耙耬山，離我家只有幾里路。" See Moratto, "Zai yiqing liuxing de dangxia xunzhao ziwo he wenxue: Zhuanfang Yan Lianke" 在疫情流行的當下尋找自我和文學——專訪閻連科 [Looking for oneself and for literature during an epidemic: An interview with Yan Lianke], *Waiguo yuyan yu wenhua* 外國語言與文化 [Foreign languages and culture] 1 (20 Mar. 2020), https://mp.weixin.qq.com/s/_1FeqVY2_tjMxshZNcxA8g (last accessed 14 June 2021); also Moratto, "Intervista a Yan Lianke" [Interview with Yan Lianke], *Il Manifesto*, 27 Feb. 2020, https://ilmanifesto.it/yan-lianke-ansia-e-rabbia-da-virus-stanno-sfumando/ (last accessed 31 May 2021).

theme, connected with the clash of lifestyles and values between the countryside and the city.[25] Of course, it is also possible to frame Yan's story, as some critics have done, within the context of the long-standing debate about human nature (*renxing* 人性). In the most common interpretation, the cave symbolizes the dark recesses of human nature, the space of human beings' modern alienation.[26] To reinforce this interpretation, we may recall Hubbs' analysis of Faulkner's rural novels: "Faulkner uses the experimental forms associated with modernism to depict the impact of the sociocultural era called modernity, and the processes of urbanization and industrialization known as modernization."[27]

However, here and in other works related to the issue of ethics in the countryside, Yan does not engage in a nostalgic revival of classical Confucian virtues and values; as stated by Wang Yu with regard to another novella of the same period, he rather "announces the utter corruption, and therefore the death, of ethic-based society, suggesting that the only alternative is to confront the future as a road to hope rather than indulge in an illusion of the past."[28]

Modernism and the grotesque

In order to reflect on and debunk this illusion, in the Gong family saga Yan Lianke adopts a modernist approach by variously drawing upon the repertoire of modernist literature from an unreliable narrator to synesthetic language, from inner monologues to repetitions and non-linear time. Besides, the novella is also interspersed with grotesque elements. As a "sustained disruption of conventional logic,"[29] the modern grotesque provides fictional writing with a range of devices that enforce the alteration of reality and make readers see the story from a distorted yet illuminating perspective. The narrating voice in the novella is itself a manifestation of the grotesque. Indeed, the conflation between the rural and the urban vis-à-vis modernity is not the only similarity with Faulkner: the narrator of "Gold Cave" reminds us of Benjamin's utterances in *The Sound and the Fury*. Referring to the narrating voice in this novel, André Bleikasten states: "To have an idiot speak, then, would be to convey its essential simplicity, to give dumbness a tongue, to accede to a language without reflection and division. … To Faulkner he is first of all a being of language, an *idio-lect*."[30]

Gong Erhan plays the same role, by means of the obsessive sensoriality displayed in his monologue, he shows readers the world exactly as he perceives it. In this section of the chapter, I will provide a few examples of this language, which to some extent anticipates the atmosphere of later "mythorealistic" novels. In Yan's own words, his native land offers him stories in which "any fact of reality can be absurd or rational."[31] The most important features through which Yan

---

25 Zhang Lin 張琳, "Wenxue lunlixue shiye xia 'Huangjin dong' de wenben jiedu" 文學倫理學視野下《黃金洞》的文本解讀 [A textual interpretation of "Gold Cave" from the perspective of literary ethics], *Yancheng gongxueyuan xuebao (shehui kexue ban)* 鹽城工學院學報 (社會科學版) [Journal of Yancheng Institute of Technology (Social Science Edition)] 34, no. 1 (2021): 67.
26 Lei Nini 雷妮妮, "Tanxun renxing zhi dong: Yan Lianke 'Huanjing dong' zhong de yixian jietu" 探尋人性之洞——閻連科《黃金洞》中的意象解讀 [Searching the cave of human nature: A textual interpretation of the images in Yan Lianke's "Gold Cave"], *Xin xibu* 新西部 [New west], 2018, 7: 98, 19.
27 Hubbs, "William Faulkner's Rural Modernism," 461.
28 Wang, "Ghost Marriage in Twentieth-Century Chinese Literature," 86.
29 Debeveq Henning Silvie, "'La Forme In-Formante': A Reconsideration of the Grotesque," *Mosaic: An Interdisciplinary Critical Journal* 14, no. 4 (Fall, 1981): 109.
30 André Bleikasten, *The Ink of Melancholy: Faulkner's Novels from* The Sound and the Fury *to* Light in August (Bloomington: Indiana University Press, 2017), 56.
31 See note 4 above.

trespasses the boundaries and violates the conventions of traditional *xiangtu* literature are this iconic language and the use of the grotesque.³² Whereas Lu Xun's mad narrator embodies the allegorical potential of *xiangtu* fiction, by suspecting his own family of "cannibalistic" practices, Yan's mentally retarded narrator somehow mirrors a reality where these practices are ultimately perfectly integrated into the context of the family: they are shared and performed by the members of the Gong family throughout the novella. Only Gong Erhan, though, in his altered mental state, which paradoxically brings him closer to the truth, has the right to recount them. In the end, he describes the tragic deaths of his elder brother crushed by a landslide in the gold cave, and of his father, who deliberately leaves this world after a long illness, trying to carry as much gold as he can with himself into the realm of the dead.

By means of these artistic devices, the author here makes the first attempt to develop what in his more mature novels will become an "ethical aesthetics of fiction"; he drags the story out of its objective setting, pushing realism beyond its limits in order to shed light on the characters' minds and bodies. He designates the youngest character, the dumb son Gong Erhan, as the voice of "truth," a scandalous, cynical, and scorching truth that reflects the process of dehumanization. It is a visionary voice which candidly describes the lure of easy profit and mere sensory gratification—beyond the sexual power Tao exercises over each of the Gong family's men, through her rich and tasty cooking, she also satisfies their gluttony, substantiating the ancient saying: "Hunger for food and sex—that is nature" (*shi se, xing ye* 食色, 性也) debated by the ancient thinker Mencius.³³ As proof of "this descent into human nature's hell," a baffling ending closes the story: the two main contenders die losing both the woman and the cave, while Erhan "sublimates" his ultimate filial duty by engaging in a grotesque act of lovemaking by his father's tomb. Yan builds his harsh reflection about contemporary rural society in the advanced stage of Deng's reforms, by excavating the rural Confucian subconscious just as the Gong family and Tao greedily excavate their gold caves. While the technique is purely modern, or rather, a blending of modernism and nativism, the cultural substrate in the novella is represented and epitomized by the Balou mountains, a sort of immutable cultural space, where modernity has not yet completely set foot and primordial instincts are hardly contained by a range of internalized precepts surviving only perfunctorily.

The unspeakable passions of the characters are finally expressed by Erhan. Despite his dumbness, his figurative yet unfiltered narrating language allows us to dig deeper not only into his own inner world but also into the others' dark souls. All the characters in the novella share a variety of emotions and impulses, such as hate, disgust, suspicion, greed, and lust, which motivate their actions; however, only Erhan, by means of his endless and uncensored monologue, dares to explicitly display them through his twisted logic. The other characters' inner drives are blatantly revealed by the dumb youth, when he reports their conversations with him, for they do not consider him a real interlocutor and dare to confess their darkest secrets to him.

---

32 Indeed one can find some elements of the grotesque already in the *xiangtu xiaoshuo* of the 1920s, such as in Peng Jiahuang's 彭家煌 short stories, such as "Master Chen's Ox" ("Chen sidie de niu" 陳四爹的牛, 1927) or "Wedding Date" ("Xiqi" 喜期, 1927). Lu Xun himself spoke of grotesque with reference to Ah Q's story, see Lu Xun, "A Q zhengzhuan de chengyin" 阿Q正傳的成因 [How "The True Story of Ah Q" came about], in *Lu Xun zawen quanji* 魯迅雜文全集 [A complete collection of essays by Lu Xun] (1926; Qinyang: Henan renmin chubanshe, 1994), 251. However, in all these cases, the main narrative style is still realistic, the grotesque stemming merely from the plot and the narrated situations that blend irony and tragedy. Yan's modernist grotesque, on the contrary, not only emerges from absurd and conflicting situations but is deeply embedded in the author's language, syntax, and narrative patterns.

33 Mengzi, "Gaozi" 告子, 11.4; Hinton, *The Four Classics of Chinese Literature*.

This feature is typical of the classical unreliable narrator: Erhan is neither a liar nor a deceptive narrator, he just widely differs or departs from the implicit author's (and reader's) norms, but his words are not lies, as they perfectly reflect and express his perception of reality.

When his brother asks him to beat up Tao in order to make her loosen her grip on their father and the cave, by uttering his disorderly yet genuine thoughts, Erhan replies: "How could I beat Tao? Tao's skirt so red, her thighs so white and delicate; besides, she comes from the city. She brushes her teeth at dawn and dusk, so that they look so white. ... How to blame her? Blame Dad, better push him onto the bed and beat him, rather than beat Tao up."[34] When Erhan, this time instigated by the woman, tampers the ceiling beams in the gold cave, he thinks: "I want the cave to collapse onto Brother. If it crushes Dad, I will no longer be a good [*xiao*] son."[35] Later, when the father is indeed caught in the collapsed cave, Erhan speaks to himself: "You tell me, I have crushed Dad, and let Brother go, only one has been crushed. And not heavily, anyway."[36] His reasoning, although crudely brutal, has its own logic: "I suddenly felt that everyone in the village was digging for gold. Almost every family had a landslide. Every household had someone dead or with missing arms and broken legs. Only the Gong family is unscathed. The Gong family and Brother got away with little. Brother, you've got gold, you've got money, you've got a wife, you've got a new house, you've got arms and legs. Indeed, Brother got away with little."[37]

Although in his later novels the strategy of the grotesque is much more evident and further developed, Yan here exploits its ambiguity and its disrupting power by expressing an anomalous voice, "a liminal form of the grotesque which is not monstrous," similar to the concept of the "uncanny": "the experience of something being both foreign and familiar."[38] The same narrative function carried out by Erhan is characterized by unintentional black humor emerging from the grotesque descriptions of his own emotions. His storytelling is full of repressed fantasies and wishful visions of murder, as in the following case:

> Now I want to kill Tao. I just need to take a step forward and push her hard, and Tao will fall into the ditch beside me. The ditch is as deep as from Nanjing to Beijing, and there are a few secretly built gold refining plants at the bottom of the ditch, and there are anvils on the side of each plant. Tao falls down like a red persimmon onto the anvil, her arms and legs fly away, her body spreads out on the anvil like an iron persimmon, her head get crushed like a soft unripe walnut, juice and shell are mixed together splashing onto the bottom of the ditch. So you, Tao, won't have to share the bedding with Dad anymore, or to caress the broken leg of that old pig.[39]

---

34 Yan Lianke, "Huangjin dong," in Yan, *Heibai Yan Lianke: Zhongpian si shu* 黑白閻連科: 中篇四書 [Yan Lianke in black and white: Four novellas] (Beijing: Renmin wenxue chubanshe, 2014), 12: "怎麼打桃, 桃的裙子那麼紅色, 大腿那麼白嫩, 又是城裡的女人, 早上晚上都把牙刷得白白甜甜, ... 我說怪桃呀? 怪爹, 打桃一頓還不如把爹安在床上揍了。"
35 Ibid., 27.
36 Ibid., 29–30.
37 Ibid., 21: "我忽然覺得, 一個村落人都在挖金, 差不多家家都有塌方, 戶戶都有死人或缺胳膊斷腿, 唯這貢家完整, 這實在便宜了貢家, 便宜了老大。你老大有金子, 有錢, 有媳婦, 有新房, 還有胳膊有腿。"
38 Justin D. Edwards and Rune Graulund, *Grotesque*, Kindle edn. (London: Routledge, 2013).
39 Yan, "Huangjin dong," 40–41: "我現在就想殺了桃, 只消上前一步, 把桃用力一推, 桃就掉到身邊的溝裡了。溝有南京到北京那麼深, 溝底好幾個偷偷壘的煉金爐, 爐邊上都有鐵砧子。桃掉下去像一個紅柿子, 落在鐵砧上, 腿和胳膊飛丟了, 身子像鐵柿子樣攤在鐵砧上, 頭像敲碎的不熟的嫩核桃, 汁兒殼兒攪合著, 濺了一溝底。這樣妳桃就永遠不用去挨我爹的床褥了, 不用摸那老豬的斷腿了。"

Borrowing Edwards's and Graulund's words, Erhan's "ridiculously absurd logic makes him all the more terrifying and strange, because he appears in his own eyes to have been in earnest."[40] In some passages, the narrator's incapacity to decode other people's behaviors reminds us of Lu Xun's madman, who is unable to interpret his family's and the other villagers' sinister smiling, and suspects them of conspiring against him: "Seeing there is still a smile on Dad's face, I don't know why he's still smiling now that Brother and Tao have left; while Dad's smiling, I think it looks like when Brother almost strangled Dad on the bed" (我看著爹臉上依舊掛著笑，不知道老大和桃走了為啥還笑，爹笑著我想過去像老大把爹掐在床上).[41]

Grotesque elements are scattered throughout the novella, mainly in the form of physical sensations and bodily dysfunctions. One example is the father's illness and his missing leg, amputated after the cave accident: "Dad went to Luoyang to be hospitalised for four months, and he came back as soon as the spring started. When Dad walked into the village, his right leg was hollow, and his trousers seemed to float" (爹去洛陽住院了四個月，一開春爹就回來了。爹走進村裡時，右腿空空洞洞的，褲管像要飄起來).[42] Uncomfortable corporeal sensations haunt Erhan's *idio-lect*, as in the following passages:

Dad's footsteps entering the cave feel like he's stepping on my belly; one step after another makes me pee my pants.

爹進洞的腳步就像踩在我的肚子上，一下一下踩得我往褲上擠尿水。

I'm a little embarrassed, I don't know what to do. Sweat flows from my heart, all over me.

我有些為難，為難得不知如何是好了。汗從我的心裡流出來，了我一身。[43]

Many critics, both in China and abroad, have discussed the meaning and role of illness in Yan's fiction at length. Throughout his novels, from *Streams of Time* to *Lenin's Kisses* and *Dream of the Ding Village*, he adopts a consistent strategy of narrating contemporary China through the lens of sickness and deformity.[44] While in these later works, sickness is mainly a metaphorical tool hinting at Chinese society's moral decadence and corruption,[45] in "Gold Cave," it is adopted almost literally, and exploited to emphasize the creepy atmosphere of the degradation of human kinship bonds. Mental and physical illness convey a sense of ambiguity and distortion of reality, which can be seen to fit within the paradigm of the modern grotesque. Similarly, excrements and scatological needs, the representation of human beings as animals (pigs or snakes) and hallucinations are an integral part of Erhan's speech. He opens the novella by pontificating: "The world is like shit. I tried hard to think

---

40 Edwards and Graulund, *Grotesque*.
41 Yan, "Huangjin dong," 90.
42 Ibid., 31.
43 Ibid., 27, 54.
44 Concerning the bond between disease and the grotesque in Yan's works, Shelley Chan 陳穎 states: "Yan sees humans' hopeless struggle with fate as well as with absurd phenomena, including lust, greed, and corruption, in the grotesque post-Mao China through writing about illnesses." Chan, "Narrating Cancer, Disabilities, and AIDS: Yan Lianke's Trilogy of Disease," in *Discourses of Disease, Writing Illness, the Mind and the Body in Modern China*, ed. Howard Y. F. Choy 蔡元豐 (Leiden: Brill, 2016), 186.
45 Ibid., 182: "[A] metaphor for the diseased community signifying the suffering of the villagers as well as the defects of the leaders."

about it and then I remembered that it was just like shit" (世界像糞。我用力想呀想呀才想起原來像是糞).[46] The father, the older brother, Erhan himself, and even Tao are insistently described as pigs:

> … dad has been living alone for many years, bringing up my older brother and me, like two little pigs with nothing to eat.
>
> 好多年月裡爹都獨自過著，領著老大和我，像領著兩個沒啥兒喂的小豬。
>
> I hate Tao. I hate Dad, that old pig, and Brother.
>
> 我恨桃。恨爹這老豬和老大。
>
> Tao …. Are you alive or not? … You sow, you just hold on to our family.
>
> 桃——你走不走——你這母豬就賴在我們家。[47]

In the end, after having sex with Tao, Erhan has a vision of his dead father surging up from his coffin, "moving in great leaps and bounds towards the bean field, and in a blink of an eye, he runs away like a black pig with a missing leg." (一跳一跳朝著豆地那邊走去了，轉眼如一頭少了腿的黑豬一樣跑丟了。)[48]

Moreover, another fundamental modernist strategy adopted by Yan is the way he lets his narrator blend intra- and inter-subjectivity. Erhan keeps on reporting his own and the other characters' speeches, weaving an interpersonal web of complicated relationships within the family, which often blurs the boundaries between his own mind and that of the others. When expressing his own feelings of hate, greed, and disrespect, a self-other overlap takes place. As in Faulkner's experimental novel, *The Sound and the Fury*, in Yan's novella, the fact of giving voice to an idiot weakens or even neutralizes authorial control, erasing any possible value assessment or, rather, offering readers "a textual configuration of the chaos that undergirded the incoherence of modern life, and that allowed for new ways of producing meaning."[49] In his deeply sensory narration, Erhan often thinks and speaks in terms of colors, mostly gold and red, in order to describe what he sees and feels, as if the whole outside world were made out of these two elements. On the one hand, the color red conveys a sense of sexual arousal and burning passion; on the other hand, it is a sign of danger and bloody violence:[50] Tao embodies all these aspects at the same time and is constantly referred to as a "red fire" (*honghuo* 紅火). Gold is scattered throughout the text, with both its fascinating and corrupting symbolic power. Everything around the narrator is likened to gold or appears as gold:

> I open my eyes wide and see Dad's main room, the window is as bright as though it was covered with gold.
>
> 我睜開眼睛，看見爹的上房，視窗亮得像上有金子。

---

46 Yan, "Huangjin dong," 4.
47 Ibid., 8, 57, 59.
48 Ibid., 114.
49 Maurice Ebileeni, "Benjy's Howl: From Symptom to Sinthome in William Faulkner's *The Sound and the Fury*," *E-Rea* 12, no. 1 (2014).
50 See also Lei, "Tanxun renxing zhi dong," 98.

On the houses and the ground in the village, the color yellow is like a layer of golden water poured there.

村頭的房上和地上，黃的顏色像一層倒在那兒的黃金的水。

I want to touch Tao's calf, the tiny pimples on her calf must be like grains of gold.

我想去摸摸桃的小腿肚，小腿肚上的米粒疙瘩一定和黃金米粒一樣兒。[51]

Another modernist legacy is the extensive use of synesthetic language, a feature that will constantly appear in Yan's following novels. Here below, I list just a few examples:

The scent of shredded pork is just a red water line flowing in the snow.

燒肉絲的香味就紅紅的一條水線在雪地流著。

The scent of Tao's perfume is like the smell of a tender boiled jade bracelet, it is as clear and pure as a stream of water flowing through the yellow earth.

桃的香水味兒像煮嫩玉鐲的味，又清又純就像從黃土流過了一股水。

The smile on [Tao's] face is like oil floating on water.

[桃]臉上掛的笑像水上漂的油。

Tao passes by me like a red and cold wind blowing through.

桃從我身邊過去像刮過了又紅又涼的風。

When Dad speaks, he still faces inward, his voice is both thin and black …. The room is as quiet as the collapsed cave of gold sand, the sound of spiderwebs creaks under the bed.

爹說話時仍是面向裡，聲音又細又黑。……屋子裡靜得像塌過的金沙洞，蜘蛛網的聲音在床下吱兒吱兒響。

There is no sound in the ditch except that of crows. It's so quiet that you can hear the sound of the setting sun.

一條溝除了鴉叫再也沒有聲音了。靜得能聽見吱兒吱兒的落日聲。[52]

And again: "The village is so quiet that you can hear the sound of moonlight falling onto the ground" (村裡靜得能聽見月光的落地聲].[53]

---

51 Yan, "Huangjin dong," 13, 63, 113.
52 Ibid., 20, 47, 48, 77, 80, 87.
53 Ibid., 107.

Conclusion

The experimental intuition that Yan Lianke displayed in his works from the 1990s later developed into an accomplished artistic technique accommodating surreal or grotesque images within a realistic frame. In his harsh criticism of contemporary Chinese literature, Jing Kaixuan states: "Chinese writers try to get across the border of the real, not to better capture the real world but to escape from it."[54] I would argue, on the contrary, that in Yan's case, reality is not evaded, but ultimately better represented also in its invisible existence as a parallel world of inner, unconfessable sensations and irrationality, and then (re)created. In Yan's own words: "mythorealism never rejects realism, but strives to create reality and to transcend realism" (神實主義決不排斥現實主義, 但它努力創造現實和超越現實主義).[55]

It is precisely by adopting the device of the *idio-lect*, a language which, insofar as it deviates from conventional speech, comes closer to the ultimate reality, and the critical approach provided by modernism that Yan succeeds in creating an innovative style, blending the lyrical and the grotesque. In doing so, he achieves two goals, ethical and aesthetic, at the same time: on the one hand, this modernist style vividly enforces the nativist critique of society; on the other, it pushes the author's literary representations toward or beyond the boundary between fiction and reality. The weird paradox of a world steeped in compelling values constantly trampled upon and stifled by its own desire for modernity cannot be described except by molding reality into a modernist picture dominated by dazzling visions, colors, smells, sounds, and animals.[56] "Gold Cave" is a good example of Yan's unique rewriting of *xiangtu* fiction: the text operates as a powerful synthesis of the twentieth-century nativist fiction that sets its future evolution in the new century within a postmodern view of reality and art.

Bibliography

Bleikasten, André. *The Ink of Melancholy: Faulkner's Novels from The Sound and the Fury to Light in August*. Bloomington: Indiana University Press, 2017.
Chan, Shelley 陳穎. "Narrating Cancer, Disabilities, and AIDS: Yan Lianke's Trilogy of Disease." In *Discourses of Disease, Writing Illness, the Mind and the Body in Modern China*, edited by Howard Y. F. Choy 蔡元豐, 177–86. Leiden: Brill, 2016.
Chen Xiaoming 陳曉明. "Zhimian ku'nan: Chongxie xiangtu Zhongguo" 直面苦難: 重寫鄉土中國 [Facing suffering: Rewriting rural China]." In *Xiaoshuo shiping* 小說時評 [Review of current fiction], edited by Chen Xiaoming, 60–66. Kaifeng: Henan daxue chubanshe, 2002.
Debeveq Henning, Silvie, "'La Forme In-Formante': A Reconsideration of the Grotesque." *Mosaic: An Interdisciplinary Critical Journal* 14, no. 4 (Fall 1981): 107–21.
Ding Fan 丁帆. *Zhongguo xiangtu xiaoshuo shi* 中國鄉土小說史 [A History of Chinese native soil fiction]. Beijing: Beijing daxue chubanshe, 2007.
Ebileeni, Maurice. "Benjy's Howl: From Symptom to Sinthome in William Faulkner's *The Sound and the Fury*," *E-rea* 12, no. 1, online article. http://journals.openedition.org/erea/3949 (last accessed 7 June 2021).
Edwards, Justin D., and Rune Graulund. *Grotesque*. London: Routledge, 2013.
Hinton, David, trans. *The Four Classics of Chinese Literature*. Kindle edn. Berkeley: Counterpoint, 2013.
Hubbs, Jolene. "William Faulkner's Rural Modernism." *The Mississippi Quarterly* 61, no. 3 (Summer 2008), *Special Issue on Faulkner, Labor, and the Critique of Capitalism*: 461–75.

---

54 Jing Kaixuan, "Contemporary Chinese Fiction: Politics and Romance," *Macalester International* 18 (Spring 2017): 88.
55 Yan, *Faxian xiaoshuo* 發現小說 [Discovering fiction] (Tianjin: Nankai daxue chubanshe, 2011).
56 Whereas in Yan's fiction, animals epitomize human beings' dehumanization, in Mo Yan's vision, they demonstrate the symbiotic existence of humanity and animal nature in a post-human reality.

Lei Nini 雷妮妮. "Tanxun renxing zhi dong: Yan Lianke 'Huanjing dong' zhong de yixian jietu" 探尋人性之洞——閻連科《黃金洞》中的意象解讀 [Searching the cave of human nature: A textual interpretation of the images in Yan Lianke's "Gold Cave"]. *Xin xibu* 新西部 [New west], 2018, no. 20: 98, 19.

Lu Xun 魯迅. "A Q zhengzhuan de chengyin" 阿Q正傳的成因 [How "The True Story of Ah Q" came about]. In *Lu Xun zawen quanji* 魯迅雜文全集 [A complete collection of essays by Lu Xun], 249–51. Qinyang: Henan renmin chubanshe, 1994.

Moratto, Riccardo. "Intervista a Yan Lianke" [Interview with Yan Lianke]. *Il Manifesto*, 27 Feb. 2020. https://ilmanifesto.it/yan-lianke-ansia-e-rabbia-da-virus-stanno-sfumando/ (last accessed 31 May 2021).

———. "Zai yiqing liuxing de dangxia xunzhao ziwo he wenxue: Zhuanfang Yan Lianke" 在疫情流行的當下尋找自我和文學——專訪閻連科 [Looking for oneself and for literature during an epidemic: An interview with Yan Lianke]. *Waiguo yuyan yu wenhua* 外國語言與文化 [Foreign languages and culture] 1 (20 Mar. 2020). https://mp.weixin.qq.com/s/_1FeqVY2_tjMxshZNcxA8g (last accessed 31 June 2021).

Pesaro, Nicoletta. "Faulkner and Chinese Modern Fiction: Between Nativism and Modernism." In *William Faulkner's Legacy*, edited by Pia Masiero, 47–57. Venezia: Cafoscarina, 2012.

Wang Kan 王侃. "Da beimin de qinghuai: Ping *Yan Lianke wenji*" 大悲憫的情懷——評《閻連科文集》 [A deep sense of tragic: Reviewing *Collected Essays of Yan Lianke*]. *Quanguo xin shumu* 全國新書目 [National new books information], 1997, no. 5: 34.

Wang, Yu. "Ghost Marriage in Twentieth-Century Chinese Literature: Between the Past and the Future." *Frontiers of Literary Studies* 10, no. 1 (2016): 86–102.

Yan Lianke 閻連科. *Faxian xiaoshuo* 發現小說 [Discovering fiction]. Tianjin: Nankai daxue chubanshe, 2011.

———. "Huangjin dong" 黃金洞 [Gold cave]. In *Heibai Yan Lianke: Zhongpian si shu* 黑白閻連科：中篇四書 [Yan Lianke in black and white: Four novellas], edited by Yan Lianke, 4–114. Beijing: Renmin wenxue chubanshe, 2014.

——— and Zhang Xuexin 張學昕. *Wo de xianshi wo de zhuyi* 我的現實我的主義 [My reality, my -ism]. Beijing: Renmin daxue chubanshe, 2011.

Zhang Lin 張琳. "Wenxue lunlixue shiye xia 'Huangjin dong' de wenben jiedu" 文學倫理學視野下《黃金洞》的文本解讀 [A textual interpretation of "Gold Cave" from the perspective of literary ethics]. *Yancheng gongxueyuan xuebao (shehui kexue ban)* 鹽城工學院學報(社會科學版) [Journal of Yancheng Institute of Technology (Social Science Edition)] 34, no. 1 (2021): 67–70.

Zhang Xitian 張喜田. "'Liantu': yi ge jiuchan zhe Henan zuojia de qingjie" 「戀土」：一個糾纏著河南作家的情結 ["Loving the soil": A Complex haunting Henan writers]. *Henan shifan daxue xuebao* 河南師範大學學報 [Journal of Henan Normal University] 23, no. 2(1996): 57-60.

Zhou Yinyin 周銀銀. "20 shiji 90 niandai yilai xianfengshi xiangtu xiaoshuo de jiazhigu" 20世紀90年代以來先鋒式鄉土小說的價值估 [An appraisal of the value of the avantgardist fiction of the native soil in the 1990s]. *Jiangsu keji daxue xuebao (shehui kexue ban)* 江蘇科技大學學報 [Journal of Jiangsu University of Science and Technology (Social Science Edition)] 21, no. 1 (2021): 41–47.

11
REPRESENTING THE INTELLECTUALS IN YAN LIANKE'S RECENT WRITING

An exile of the soul

Alessandra Pezza

Yan Lianke's relationship with censorship and consequences on his writing

Yan Lianke's 閻連科 struggle with censorship and the possibility to publish in his own country starts as early as 1994 when, after the publication of the anti-heroic army novel *Summer Sunset* (*Xia riluo* 夏日落), he was forced to write self-criticism for a month.[1]

Consequences on his writing were fast and evident: from this episode, Yan abandoned the army as his main literary topic and started to seek an "escape in literature,"[2] especially in the countryside setting of the Balou Mountains (*Balou shanmai* 耙耬山脈), which is inspired by a real mountain range near his hometown.[3] While the focus on power dynamics and politics remains a constant, for instance, in *Streams of Time* (*Riguang liunian* 日光流年), it is somehow less evident until 2004, when the publishing of *Lenin's Kisses* (*Shouhuo* 受活), and

---

1 Yan Lianke, *Chenmo yu chuanxi: Wo suo jingli de Zhongguo he wenxue* 沉默與喘息: 我所經歷的中國和文學 [Silent and panting : My experience with China and literature] (Taipei: INK chubanshe, 2014), 135–36.
2 Ibid., 136: "我開始在文學上逃跑了。"
3 In an interview with Riccardo Moratto, when asked about the meaning and inspiration for this environment and its name, Yan states: "Balou Mountains are only a literary toponym. The name Balou, however, is used in the countryside, so it represents the agricultural and rural civilization. I did not draw it from my creativity, but from reality. There is a mountain named Balou in my natal village, only a few kilometers from my house." (耙耬山脈就是一個文學地理名稱而已。但「耙耬」兩個字, 是中國的農具名稱, 它代表著農耕文明、鄉村文明。這兩個字不來源於靈感, 而是來自於現實。我老家有座山就叫做耙耬山, 離我家只有幾里路。) Moratto, "Zai yiqing liuxing de dangxia xunzhao ziwo he wenxue: Zhuanfang Yan Lianke" 在疫情流行的當下尋找自我和文學——專訪閻連科 [Looking for oneself and for literature during an epidemic: An interview with Yan Lianke], *Waiguo yuyan yu wenhua* 外國語言與文化 [Foreign languages and culture] 1 (20 Mar. 2020), https://mp.weixin.qq.com/s/_1FeqVY2_tjMxshZNcxA8g (last accessed 31 May 2021). See also Moratto, "Intervista a Yan Lianke" [Interview with Yan Lianke], *Il Manifesto,* Feb. 27, 2020, https://ilmanifesto.it/yan-lianke-ansia-e-rabbia-da-virus-stanno-sfumando/ (last accessed 31 May 2021).

the subsequent interview on a Hong Kong television channel (*Fenghuang weishi* 鳳凰衛視), leads to Yan's forced resignation from the army.[4]

While the novel itself is not banned (it obtained, on the contrary, the Lao She 老舍 prize in 2005), not only did Yan's professional life undergo a drastic change but also his writing: in 2005 and 2006, he wrote respectively *Serve the People!* (*Wei renmin fuwu* 為人民服務) and *Dream of Ding Village* (*Dingzhuang meng* 丁莊夢) which both provoked some turmoil on the literary scene and were immediately banned. With respect to *Dream of Ding Village*, Yan declares to have practiced a rigorous self-censorship, in a (failed) attempt to prevent it from being banned. He stated, for instance, that the book's original project included the representation of international blood selling from China to the United States through enormous pipes,[5] an explicit political critique addressed to the central administration that he erased from the final version of the novel to ease the circulation of the books among Chinese readers, leaving him partially unsatisfied with the result.[6]

In the following years, Yan's publishing history goes through alternate phases: after the impossibility to publish *The Four Books* (*Si shu* 四書) despite several attempts in 2009–10,[7] *The Explosion Chronicles* (*Zhalie zhi* 炸裂志, 2013) is published (to Yan's own "great surprise"[8]) in mainland China, but in 2015, he proposes his last novel *The Day the Sun Died* (*Rixi* 日熄, 2015) directly to the Taiwanese Rye Field Publishing Co. (*Maitian chubanshe* 麥田出版社), without even attempting to publish it in mainland China.[9] In 2017, the semi-fictional novella *Want to Sleep Together Quickly* (*Su qiu gong mian* 速求共眠) appears first in the literary journal *Harvest* (*Shouhuo* 收穫) and is then published in Taiwan in 2018 and in mainland China in 2019. His novel *Heart Sutra* (*Xinjing* 心經) is published in January 2020 in Hong Kong, and his latest novel *Zhongyuan* 中原 appears in the literary journal *Harvest* in 2021.

Yan's dialectic struggle with power is, therefore, a constant rollercoaster made of openings and closures, "warm" and "cold" moments.[10] This alternance seems, however, to have led to an increasingly pessimistic stance with the passing of time. Since his expulsion from the army, Yan has begun to speak up more openly about the episodes of censorship he has been subject to, the apex of this denunciation being, until now, the collection of essays *Silent and Panting: My Experience with China and Literature* (2013), a re-edition of a series of speeches held in different universities in the United States, Canada, Japan, and Hong Kong, where he openly expresses himself about the struggles of publishing in mainland China and the limitations Chinese intellectuals are subjected to.

Matters of self-censorship, strategies of publishing, and mutism of the author, however, are not only widely discussed in Yan's essays, they are also a recurrent topic in his novels, both on a stylistic level and with concern to the topics addressed. This is precisely what will interest us in this chapter. As Perry Link states, in fact:

> … we must be able to distinguish between a non-literary intrusion and a literary response. We can rightly say that a political leader's command is extraneous to

---

4   Yan, *Chenmo yu chuanxi*, 136.
5   Jonathan Watts, "Censor Sees through Writer's Guile in Tale of China's Blood-Selling Scandal," zonaeuropa, 10 Sep. 2006, http://zonaeuropa.com/culture/c20060327_1.htm (last accessed 8 Jan. 2019).
6   Yan, *Chenmo yu chuanxi*, 96.
7   See Sebastian Veg, "Creating a Literary Space to Debate the Mao Era: The Fictionalization of the Great Leap Forward in Yan Lianke's *Four Books*," *China Perspectives*, 2014, no. 4: 7–15.
8   Yan Lianke, private interview by author, Feb. 2016.
9   Ibid.
10 For the meteorological metaphor, see Perry Link, *The Uses of Literature: Life in the Socialist Chinese Literary System* (Princeton: Princeton University Press, 2000).

literature, but it does not follow that the writer's response is also extraneous. Writers comply, resist or, more often, do a mixture of the two, and such responses might be carefully thought out, unconsciously reflexive, or somewhere in between. But all are genuine human responses, at least worth noting and often worth studying. Some, moreover, produce good literature. If works written in opposition to coercion seem wanting as "pure literature," they can nevertheless be very good ....[11]

The cases of "literary response" to censorship are, of course, extremely numerous, and Yan's example is part of a wider range that can only be quickly addressed in this chapter.

The perceived inference of power can bring, for instance, to complete mutism of the author in his/her native language, as in Li Peifu 李佩甫 and Wang Yaowen's 王耀文 cases in mainland China,[12] or Ha Jin's 哈金 case as an overseas writer. Ha Jin abandoned China following the Tiananmen massacre in 1989 and, after that, chose to write only in English. Perry Link underlines that this choice could partly be an attempt "to be sure that even subconscious influences do not affect his expression,"[13] a hypothesis recalling Li Tuo's 李陀 considerations on the omnipresence of the Mao discourse (Mao wenti 毛文體) and its underlying way of thinking in che Chinese literary scene.[14]

In other cases, the refusal concerns not the writing as such but the simple perspective of the publication. We can find one example in Gao Xingjian's 高行健 Nobel Prize acceptance speech, "The Case for Literature" ("Wenxue de liyou" 文學的理由): "I began writing my novel *Soul Mountain* to dispel my inner loneliness at the very time when works I had written with rigorous self-censorship had been banned. *Soul Mountain* was written for myself and without the hope that it would be published."[15]

This statement strikingly resonates with Yan's position in the essay "A Traitor of Literary Writing" ("Xiezuo de pantu" 寫作的叛徒, 2010):

> I always dreamt of writing as I wished, and not for publishing. *The Four Books* is a (partial) attempt to free myself from any restraints through abandoning any perspective of publishing. When I speak of freeing myself from restraints and writing following my heart, not thinking about publications, I do not merely mean adding despicable elements to the plot, mixing fine grains to the coarse ones, placing delightful flowers and moonlight along dog and chicken excrements. I mean to tell a story exactly in the way I want; being able to say something foolish, to make

11 Ibid., 4.
12 Their cases are mentioned by Yan himself in his "An Examination of China's Censorship System," ed. Andrea Bachner and Carlos Rojas, *The Oxford Handbook of Modern Chinese Literatures* (New York: Oxford University Press, 2016), 263–74.
13 Perry Link, "Does This Writer Deserve the Prize?" *The New York Review of Books*, 12 June 2012, https://www.nybooks.com/articles/2012/12/06/mo-yan-nobel-prize/ (last accessed 26 May 2021). See also Ha Jin's article on the topic, "The Censor in the Mirror: It's Not Only What the Chinese Propaganda Department Does to Artists, But What It Makes Artists Do to Their Own Work," *The American Scholar* 77, no. 4 (2008): 26–32.
14 Li Tuo, "Resisting Writing," in *Politics, Ideology and Literary Discourse in Modern China: Theoretical Interventions and Cultural Critique*, ed. Liu Kang 劉康 and Tang Xiaobing 唐小兵 (Durham: Duke University Press, 1993), 273–77.
15 "我的長篇小說《靈山》正是在我的那些已嚴守自我審查的作品卻還遭到查禁之時著手的，純然為了排遣內心的寂寞，為自己而寫，並不指望有可能發表。" Both the Chinese lecture and the English translation are available on the Nobel Prize website: Gao Xingjian, "Gao Xingjian: Nobel Lecture," NobelPrize.org, 2000, https://www.nobelprize.org/prizes/literature/2000/gao/25522-gao-xingjian-nobel-lecture-2000/ (last accessed 26 May 2021).

irresponsible comments, to obtain a real, complete freedom and liberation of expression and narration, and thus to build a new narrative structure. This is the biggest dream of every experienced writer. Writing *The Four Books* has been a wonderful vacation in my life as a writer. During this holiday, everything was back in my power. In this time, I was … not a slave of my quill, but the emperor of my writing.[16]

我總是懷著一次「不為出版而胡寫」的夢想。《四書》就是這樣一次因為不為出版而無忌憚的嘗試（並不徹底）。這裡說的不為出版而隨心所欲地肆無忌憚，不是簡單地說在故事裡種植些什麼粗糧細糧，花好月圓，或者雞糞狗屎，讓人所不齒。而是說，那樣一個故事，我想怎樣去講，就可能怎樣去講。胡扯八道，信口雌黃，真正地、徹底地獲得詞語和敘述的自由與解放，從而建立一種新的敘述秩序。建立新的敘述秩序，是每個成熟作家的偉大夢想。我把《四書》的寫作，當作寫作之人生的一段美好假期。假期之間，一切都歸我所有。而我——這時候是寫作的皇帝，而非筆墨的奴隸。[17]

As previously observed, however, politics seems to be deeply embedded in Yan's writing, and it is argued that the first layer of this relationship can be found in the theorization of his literary style, mythorealism (*shenshi zhuyi* 神實主義).

Mythorealism and politics

Yan Lianke fully describes and theorizes his "mythorealism" in the six-chapter essay *Discovering Fiction* (*Faxian xiaoshuo* 發現小說), first published in 2011. In the essay, Yan considers the problem of realism in literature from a historical and political point of view and distinguishes four kinds of realism: "society-controlled realism" (*shehui konggou zhenshi* 社會控構真實), "world-experienced realism" (*shixiang jingyan zhenshi* 世相經驗真實), "life-experienced realism" (*shengming jingyan zhenshi* 生命經驗真實), and "deep-spiritual realism" (*linghun shenke zhenshi* 靈魂深刻真實). Through a physiological metaphor,[18] he associates realism to a living body, where each layer corresponds to a function and the deepest ones cannot exist without the more superficial ones. In his representation, "world-experienced realism" corresponds to the skin, "life-experienced realism" to the skeleton, and "deep-spiritual realism," of which mythorealism is a part, to the marrow. "Society-controlled realism," however, corresponds to a "useless, or even harmful, appendix" (*youhai wuyi de lanwei* 有害無益的闌尾).[19]

The most transparent example of how Yan's analysis has a precise political target emerges precisely from his description of this last example of realism. Yan defines it as the way of writing imposed by an authoritarian power. In some conditions, he states, it satisfies both the authorities and the writers, but it essentially constitutes a betrayal of the reader. It is a "fiction coming from nothing" (*cong kongwu zhong pinbai xugou* 從空無中憑白虛構), derived from a "purchase order" (*dinggou* 定購) placed by the oppressive power to the author but benefitting

---

16 All Chinese citations were translated by the author unless otherwise specified.
17 Yan Lianke, "Xiezuo de pantu" 寫作的叛徒 [Betrayer of literature], *Shuo Yan Lianke* 說閻連科 [On Yan Lianke], ed. Lin Yuan 林源 (Shenyang: Liaoning renmin chubanshe, 2014), 10.
18 Association among politics and body are an extremely common topic in Yan's literature, see, for instance, the analysis of *Lenin's Kisses* by Tsai Chien-hsin 蔡建鑫, "In Sickness or in Health: Yan Lianke and the Writing of Autoimmunity," *Modern Chinese Literature and Culture* 23, no. 1 (Spring 2011): 77–104.
19 Yan Lianke, *Faxian xiaoshuo: Wenxue suibi* 發現小說: 文學隨筆 [Discovering the fiction: Essays on literature] (Tianjin: Nankai daxue chubanshe, 2011), 47.

the author as well: "It is a win-win transaction where, once the Authority has placed the order, the writer signs, pawns and buys with a cheque consisting in the loss of its integrity and conscience" (定購是權力在開好訂單之後，作家以良心和人格的喪失為支票，在那訂單上簽字、畫押、採購的互利買賣).[20] Yan considers it as a falsification of reality aiming to deceive the readers, a mere extension of propaganda. He mentions Nazi and Soviet literature as examples but, more importantly, he considers the style imposed in China since 1942 as a perfect expression of "society-controlled realism" and, at the same time, as the reason for a profound crisis in literary production in China up to today:

> In this realm, the realist novel erected a dam forbidding to go further in depth. It would be necessary to reform realism and to knock this dam over. Thousands of writers have been able to do it in the past, but today we are stagnant in front of this enormous threshold.
>
> 現實主義小說在這個境層上，築起了停歇深進的堤壩。改變現實主義和翻越這一築堤壩，竟成了這一寫作千人早已越過而今卻在此停滯的巨大門檻。[21]

The literary response that Yan finds to the failure of this superposition among literature and politics is not, however, the total separation of the two. On the contrary, for Yan, Chinese literature is due to be political and represent its country.[22] Aesthetical research is, as Liu Jianmei 劉劍梅 suggests, always connected in his writing to a moral, ethical and, therefore, political stance:

> Yan's aesthetic experiment never becomes a fetish detached from the political context; on the contrary, it persistently clings on his sense of social responsibility, as is often the case in the writing of Lu Xun and other leftist writers.[23]

The reply to the existing conflict between art and reality, especially as it takes the form of a political tension between the individual and power, is the new and most profound kind of realism, the one that Yan calls "deep spiritual realism" and of which "mythorealism" is a declination. Mythorealism emerges from the encounter between Chinese literary tradition and Western influences of absurd elements, surrealism, existentialism, and post-modernism, as well as South American "magical realism." In Yan's words, it means to "abandon, in the creative process, all relation to real life's superficial logics and search for a 'non-existent' reality, a hidden reality, the reality covered by reality."[24] One of the keywords in this otherwise rather

---

20 Ibid., 10.
21 Ibid., 58–59.
22 Yan Lianke, interview by author, Jan. 2018. Yan's statements evoke Jameson's: "All third-world texts are necessarily, I want to argue, allegorical, and in a very specific way: they are to be read as what I will call *national allegories*, even when, or perhaps I should say, particularly when their forms develop out of predominantly Western machineries of representation, such as the novel." Fredric Jameson, "Third-World Literature in the Era of Multinational Capitalism," *Social Text*, no. 15 (Autumn 1986): 69. China, however, can hardly be considered a third-world country today, as Wang Ning has argued in "A Reflection on Postmodernist Fiction in China: Avant-Garde Narrative Experimentation," *Narrative* 21, no. 3 (2013): 298.
23 Jianmei Liu, "To Join the Commune or Withdraw from It? A Reading of Yan Lianke's *Shouhuo*," *Modern Chinese Literature and Culture* 19, no. 2 (Autumn 2007): 19.
24 Yan, *Faxian xiaoshuo*, 181: "在創作中摒棄固有真實生活的表面邏輯關係，去探求一種「不存在」的真實，看不見的真實，被真實掩蓋的真實。"

obscure definition is "covered" (*yangai* 掩蓋), which implicitly hints at the political control on society that creates "alternative truths" for its scopes.

Mythorealism aims to reveal the essence of reality by showing those aspects we usually cannot, or do not want to, see. As Yan himself underlines, the choice of the character *shen* 神 'spirit/god' in *shenshi zhuyi* only indicates a device used to allow truths about humanity, society, and the world emerges. In Yan's words, "'myth' is the instrument, 'reality' is the goal" ("*shen*" *shi shouduamn,* "*shi*" *shi mude* 「神」是手段, 「實」是目的).[25]

Yan's analysis of realism is, therefore, strictly connected to his strong criticism of Chinese control on literature and has, therefore, and most importantly, a political significance.[26] The consequent theorization of "mythorealism," I argue, is therefore more the affirmation of a political stance than an innovative analysis of a literary trend. Even though they appear more than a decade after the emergence, and conclusion, of a postmodern wave in Chinese literature,[27] in fact, those traits and others characterizing Yan's writing and his theorization of "mythorealism" could otherwise be easily classified as post-modernist or avant-garde techniques, which Wang Ning summarizes as such: "Chinese postmodernist fiction is characterised by, among other features: (1) the short-circuiting of narration, (2) border crossing between history and fiction, (3) the mixing of the languages of high and low culture, (4) violation of established linguistic and aesthetic conventions, (5) a dehumanizing or posthumanizing tendency in the naming of characters."[28] All of those traits belong, in some way, to Yan's writing, and are, in most cases, employed in an allegorical way, with a polemical intention: the employment of absurd or paradoxical narrative strategies that Wang addresses as the "short-circuiting of narration," such as the inversion of the time of narration in *Streams of Time*, whose plot progresses through anti-chronological episodes, making the reader gradually aware of the villagers' amnesia of the past (and therefore of the Sisyphean nature of their efforts to deviate the course of the river); the moral prevalence of the disabled in *Lenin's Kisses* or the recurrent biological and partially cannibalistic plots or subplots where characters irrigate the soil with their own blood to make plants grow (*The Years, Months, Days, The Four Books*). The second point is to be found in the meticulous choice to situate almost every novel in a precise historical setting or to address a precise historical problem, such as *Hard Like Water* (*Jianying ru shui* 堅硬如水, 2000) on the Cultural Revolution, *Lenin's Kisses* on land collectivization, *The Four Books* on the Great Leap Forward and Anti-Rightist Movement, *The Explosion Chronicles* on the impromptu economic growth and narration of history, and *The Day the Sun Died* on the consequences of undigested collective trauma. Points three and four, i.e., the challenge of linguistic conventions, are the ones which confer a truly "mythical" effect to Yan's writing: the huge variation of language from one novel to another (and in the same novel sometimes, as in *Dream of Ding Village* or *The Four Books*), his use of lyricism, parody, dialects, and figures of speech are all employed to produce some effects of resonance with the reader. Different

25 Ibid., 215. Thanks to Taciana Fisac for an enlightening conversation on this topic.
26 The analysis of realism in modern and contemporary Chinese literature has been an essential topic of Chinese literary criticism since the May Fourth Movement, while the Maoist inference with literature since 1942 has made this reflection deeply linked to the political realm. See, for instance, Marston Anderson, *The Limits of Realism: Chinese Fiction in the Revolutionary Period* (Berkeley: University of California Press, 1990), and a well-known article by Liu Zaifu 劉再復, whose second version also points out the influence of politics on his analysis, "Lun wenxue de zhutixing" 論文學的主體性 [Subjectivity in literature], *Wenxue lilun* 文學理論 [Literary theory], 1985, no. 6: 11–26; Liu Zaifu, "The Subjectivity of Literature Revisited," in Liu and Tang, *Politics, Ideology and Literary Discourse in Modern China*, 56–69. Durham: Duke University Press, 1993.
27 Wang, "A Reflection on Postmodernist Fiction in China," 301.
28 Ibid., 299.

languages usually belong to different characters and points of view on the plot, and they provoke an effect of fragmentation which could open new perspectives and challenge the reader's perception of reality, thus suggesting a multi-discursive, dialogical, democratic approach to reality. As for the last point, the "dehumanizing or posthumanizing tendency in the naming of characters," it is especially applied to the intellectual characters that populate his writing in the decade 2008–18, which will be the topic of the second part of my chapter: describing the intellectuals, I argue, adds a new dimension to the avant-garde features of Yan's writing.

The presence of intellectuals in Yan's recent writing

Yan Lianke is utterly aware of the complex game between power and creativity at stake in the relationship between literature and censorship. In a paper from the 2016 *Oxford Handbook of Modern Chinese Literatures*, he speaks about the transition from "hard" to "soft" censorship, and how this could influence the quality standards of Chinese literature, pointing in particular to the heavy risks of this apparently less harmful control: "[A] new literary standard emerges, which in turn helps cultivate a new aesthetic sensibility. In this way, the regime is able to convince readers, authors, and theorists that if literature departs from this new standard, it will not be considered great; and even if it is not necessarily considered a bad work, it will still be quickly forgotten."[29] In this sense, a crucial role is played by the recent consumeristic turn of Chinese society, which not only aims to control its citizens' material and spiritual satisfaction, by trading their rights for a materialistic well-being,[30] but it also manages to influence literary production, by presenting the new conformity criteria as a "market exigence" instead of limitations to freedom of speech. Readers, in their role as consumers, become the ultimate censors: "[W]hen authors write for the sake of a group of readers, they ultimately come to accept the values held by those same readers. For instance, given that many contemporary readers are fond of hyper-nationalistic films, television programs, and novels, authors—if they wish to accommodate these interests in their writings—must necessarily accept the soft censorship role played by the readers."[31]

If we turn to Yan's fiction, we can find his "literary response" to this preoccupation: since 2008, Yan has, in fact, been introducing meta-reflections on the function of literature and of intellectuals within his novels. This aspect has become an increasingly important part of his writing, including a constant presence of an intellectual character with strongly autobiographical features, who becomes the victim of a striking satire.[32] As we anticipated above, Yan's representation of intellectuals, and of himself as an intellectual, is yet another

---

29 Yan, "An Examination of China's Censorship System," 268.
30 On this subject, Yan Lianke implicitly evokes Liu Xiaobo's 劉曉波 "Philosophy of the Pig" (*zhu zhexue* 豬哲學) in his "The Year of the Stray Dog," trans. Jane Weizhen Pan and Martin Merz, *The New York Times*, 20 Apr. 2012, http://www.nytimes.com/2012/04/21/opinion/the-year-of-the-stray-dog.html (last accessed 26 May 2021). See Liu Xiaobo, *La philosophie du porc et autres essais*, ed. Vaclav Havel, trans. Jean-Philippe Béja (Paris: Gallimard, 2011).
31 Yan "The Year of the Stray Dog," 270.
32 Metaliterary traits are not, by far, an exclusive trait in Yan's writing. We find ironical or even grotesque evocations of the author through a character in many contemporary Chinese works. Just to mention a few examples, it is a quite common trait in the works of Mo Yan 莫言, for example, *The Garlic Ballads* (*Tiantang suantai zhi ge* 天堂蒜薹之歌) and *The Republic of Wine* (*Jiuguo* 酒國); we have an ironical and pretentious self-introduction at the beginning of Ma Yuan's 馬原 "Fiction" ("Xugou" 虛構), and we can find a polemical representation of the intellectual's role and his relationship to power, among others, in Jia Pingwa's 賈平凹 *Decadent Capital* (*Feidu* 廢都).

postmodern feature of his writing, and contributes to situating him among many works that could be labeled using Linda Hutcheon's definition of "historiographical metafiction":[33] texts characterized by intertextuality and an explicit reflection on the writing process, as well as by a questioning of the meaning and truthfulness of historiographical narration. Wang Ning says it "demystified the scientificity of history."[34]

Setting aside the important role of these, and Yan's, literary works in helping to reconstruct "sensitive" episodes of Chinese history,[35] a topic that exceeds the scope of the present chapter,[36] it is interesting to analyze how the representation of intellectuals in Yan's fiction becomes a prominent topic in the novels published in the decade 2008–18, and it adds a meta-realistic feature to his writing. The choice of this time span is not fortuitous: 2008 is a crucial year in defining Yan's identity as an intellectual, because it is when, after being forced to resign from the army in 2004, he officially becomes a literature professor at Renmin University. In the same year, Yan publishes two important texts. The first is the essay collection *Three Brothers: Memories of My Family* (*Wo yu fubei* 我與父輩), possibly his most well-known non-fictional work in which Yan describes his rural origins, his family, and his conflictual choice to enroll in the army and start writing as strategies to escape the poor environment he was born in. *Three Brothers* is significant in our analysis because it helps Yan define his origins as a "rural" writer, in a moment when he is settling in a more urban and literate working environment. In the same year, the satirical novel *Ballad, Hymn, Ode* (*Feng ya song* 風雅頌) describes, in a polemical and carnivalesque tone, the hypocrisy of academia and, as a consequence, alienates him parts of the favors of the academic world.[37] The novel's protagonist is a Qingyan University 清燕大學 professor named Yang Ke 楊科—the ironical resonance with the author's name and profession is not casual. At the beginning of the novel, Yang comes back to his native village upon completing his commentary to the *Book of Odes* (*Shijing* 詩經), only to discover his wife cheating on him with the assistant of the university provost. From this moment on, his life will be a line of misadventures leading him to lose his wife and his career, to be locked up in a psychiatric asylum, where he ends up eliciting the enthusiasm of other patients by reading them the *Book of Odes*, and to try (and fail) in recreating an isolated and idyllic "city of Ancient Poetry" (*gushi cheng* 古詩城) along with other disappointed professors and prostitutes.

From the beginning, therefore, Yan's relationship to his new status as a full-time intellectual is represented as a conflictual one—as a desired yet guilty goal (like in *Three Brothers*), but also as a betrayal of his own origins and a delirium of nonsense (*Ballad, Hymn, Ode*). Most of

---

33 Linda Hutcheon, "Historiographic Metafiction: Parody and the Intertextuality of History," in *Intertextuality and Contemporary American Fiction*, ed. Patrick O'Donnell and Robert Con Davis (Baltimore: Johns Hopkins University Press, 1989), 3–32.

34 Wang, "A Reflection on Postmodernist Fiction in China," 299. Examples of fiction that could relate to this category in contemporary Chinese literature, besides Yan's, include Wang Xiaobo 王小波 (1952–97) *Future World* (*Weilai shijie* 未來世界, 1994), which is also a good example of tragicomical meta-representation of the author-character in his struggle to power, Chan Koonchung 陳冠中 (b. 1952) *The Fat Years* (*Shengshi: Zhongguo 2013* 盛世：中國 2013) and Zhang Kangkang's 張抗抗 (b. 1950) short story "Collective Memory" (*Jiti jiyi* 集體記憶, 2000).

35 Hutcheon, "Historiographic Metafiction," 4: "Historiographic metafiction works to situate itself within historical discourse without surrendering its autonomy as fiction."

36 See my article, "Un Monumento all'amnesia: Yan Lianke e la Traduzione della Storia Nazionale in Letteratura" [A monument to amnesia: Yan Lianke and the translation of contemporary history in literature], in *L'intraducibile: La comunicazione interculturale e la traducibilità*, ed. Alessandra Pezza (Milano: Mimesis, 2021).

37 Thanks to Prof. Chen Xiaoming for this suggestion (interview, 9 Jan. 2018).

Yan's writing in the following decade seems to be a struggle in coming to terms with his own identity as a full-time writer and professor and what it means to be an intellectual in China today, especially in what is perceived as a hostile environment.

Even though we can consider those two publications as a foreword to Yan's growing interest in the topic of intellectuals in Chinese society, and a desire to reflect on his own identity as such, Yan openly considers *The Four Books* to be his first novel entirely dedicated to intellectuals.[38] If the neglect of *Ballad, Hymn, Ode* is probably also due to the minor artistic value of the novel, it is true indeed that since the publication of *The Four Books*, as well as of the three subsequent novels, *The Explosion Chronicles*, *The Day the Sun Died* and *Want to Sleep Together Quickly*, the presence of writers and lettered becomes increasingly central, and the question arisen on their functions in society more urgent.

Between victimization and accusation: *The Four Books*

The Four Books, which Yan Lianke considers to be his chef-d'oeuvre, has at its center an allegory of the relationship between culture and politics.[39] The novel is set in a re-education camp for intellectuals during the years of the Great Leap Forward. The absurdity of the imprisonment and totalitarian control of authorities over intellectuals is symbolized by the constant reference to religion (in the novel, the parts fictionally extracted from the manuscript "Child of Heaven," written in a Bible-inspired language). The central character is the Child (*haizi* 孩子), head of the re-education camp and direct emanation of the Authorities (*shangbian* 上邊) who resembles an aspiring Jesus Christ and has an ambiguous narrative function, between the tyrannical "young fascist" (*shaonian faxisi* 少年法西斯)[40] and the (failed) savior of humanity, a role he assumes through the self-imposed crucifixion of the end and the discovery that he saved one copy of all the books he confiscated.

The ambiguous relationship the Child establishes with the other characters of the books, who are all intellectuals specialized in different fields, corresponds to the equally ambiguous relationship, made of control and submission, fear and respect, between culture and power in totalitarian systems. If we consider how the scholars are represented in the novel, we can start by noticing that the Hong Kong edition of *The Four Books* is dedicated to them: "This book is dedicated to all of those who have been forgotten by history, and to those millions of scholars who have lost their lives" (謹以此書獻給那被忘卻的歷史和成千上億死去與活著的讀書人).

In partial contradiction with the epigraph, however, the novel maintains a fundamental ambiguity between victimizing and accusatory tones. Scholars and intellectuals in the novel are not only brutally oppressed, but they also accept to cooperate with the Child in the vain

---

38 Yan Lianke, interview by author, Sep. 2018.
39 It is interesting to note that, though having claimed to be a spokesperson for the countryside (see for instance the essay "Shouzhu cunzhuang" 守住村莊 [Keeping the village], in *Yipai huyan: Yan Lianke haiwai yanjiang ji* 一派胡言: 閻連科海外演講集 [Selected overseas speeches of Yan Lianke] [Beijing: Zhongxin chubanshe, 2012]), or the positions held in *Three Brothers*, and being the author of magnificent depictions of rural life in Henan, both in essays and novels (*The Years, Months, Days*; *Lenin's Kisses*), Yan decided to make the intellectuals the main characters of a novel set in a highly sensitive historical period, the Great Leap Forward, which mostly hit the countryside and the peasants. We argue that this choice reveals the changing attitude of Yan toward his own identity and self-perception as an intellectual. In this regard, see how, only a few years later, he describes the growing distance to his family in the article "The Year of the Stray Dog" (2012).
40 Tsai Chien-hsin, "Quru de jiushu" 屈辱的救贖 [Redemption in humiliation]," in Yan Lianke, *Si shu* 四書 [The Four Books] (Taipei: Maitian chubanshe, 2011), 14.

hope to save their own life. Their culture and their prestige do not, in any way, make them morally superior to other human beings. After a first attempt to resist the foolishness of the agricultural politics of the Great Leap Forward, all characters find their own way to adapt to the situation (much like the "new Sisyphus" described in the final manuscript of the novel) and obtain the biggest privilege for themselves. The main drivers leading them to cooperate with the Child are first the egoistic desire to gain back their individual freedom by earning the small red flowers, and then the need for food they systematically hide from other inmates. They betray each other and their own beliefs, and when they accept to lie about the possibility to overproduce crops thanks to ideological willpower, they also become a part of the fraud. In the darkest hours of the famine, toward the conclusion of the novel, they even concede to cannibalism, thus losing even the most basic trait of humanity.

Their "dehumanization," however, starts much earlier in the novel and can even be traced back to their names (see Wang Ning's consideration mentioned above). The characters, in fact, are only called by the name of their professions: the Scholar (*xuezhe* 學者), the Author (*zuojia* 作家), the Theologian (*zongjiao* 宗教), the Musician (*yinyue* 音樂), and so forth. The choice to underline only the "professional," social and public role of the characters also gives an allegorical tone to the whole narration and focuses the attention of the reader on their unattended responsibilities toward society. All the intellectual characters are deeply anti-heroic figures, and at some point of the story, they betray, more or less symbolically, their profession: the Technician (*shiyan* 實驗) uses his knowledge to suggest to use the black sand to keep on the useless and destructive practice of smelting steel; the Theologian first disfigures Mother Mary's portrait in order to obtain a handful of beans from the Child and then vehemently insults Her on his deathbed for "making him a criminal"; the Physician (*nü yisheng* 女醫生) admits, emotionless, to having cooked and eaten human flesh.

It is interesting, in this respect, to consider the two central characters of the novel, the Author and the Scholar, who embody two symbolic and complementary attitudes toward power and society: the former represents corruption and compliance (though a problematic one) to the totalitarian power in exchange for personal advantages, while the latter symbolizes the complex, though failed, attempt to maintain a sort of moral integrity and a (traditional, Confucian) role as a guide for the governors.

In some way, they both attempt to serve the power, but in completely different ways and with different goals. The Author puts his quill and even his blood at the service of the Child for his personal benefit; he accepts to write the "Criminal Records" ("Zuiren lu" 罪人錄) to obtain paper and ink and write his own diary, which he hopes to publish after his liberation. He irrigates the wheat ears with his own blood in order to make them grow bigger and stronger and allow the Child to gain a reputation among the Authorities, as a way of earning his own release from the camp. When he gives his own flesh to the Scholar to eat, in an attempt to purify himself by sacrificing to his companion, he willingly contaminates the Scholar instead by transforming him into an (unaware) cannibal.

The Scholar, on the other hand, is the strongest opposer of the Child, he is the only one to drastically contradict his lies, for the stakes of his status as an intellectual. He accepts being the target of public humiliation only to protect his beloved Musician. He tries to take care of the whole community even in the darkest hours of the famine, and, in the conclusion of the novel, sacrifices himself by remaining by the Child's side in his self-martyrdom. He attempts to support the authorities by compiling the "A New Myth of Sisyphus" ("Xin Xixufu Shenhua" 新西緒弗神話), a philosophical uncompleted essay with the goal to guide the governors, which is described, however, in a fictional metatextual commentary in the last chapter of the novel as containing "eccentric and abstruse views on the survival of human society" (混淆, 晦澀難懂, 不知所云).[41] Even the morally irreprehensible Scholar is, in the conclusion, incapable of fulfilling a guiding role for his country. There is no entirely positive character in the novel: not the intellectuals, the living, nor the dead ones, and not the authorities, whose foolish politics are the cause for the Great Famine and who are incapable of protecting not only the people but also the privileged, and supposedly "essential" class of the lettered as well.

Censored literature is good literature: The conclusion of *The Explosion Chronicles*

In the less dramatic and more sarcastic *The Explosion Chronicles*, Yan Lianke makes the first explicit appearance as the novelized version of himself—though, as we have seen, a reference could also be found in the main character of *Ballad, Hymn, Ode*. In *The Explosion Chronicles*, with a metatextual narrative strategy, a character named "Yan Lianke" is entrusted with writing the chronicle of the village of Explosion (*Zhalie* 炸裂). His voice implicitly narrates the story and is only manifest at the beginning and at the end of the novel. The autobiographical references are evident: fictional "Yan Lianke" not only has the same name as the author, he is also from the Songyi County and writes the novel during his residence in Hong Kong, a customary practice in Yan's life for some time now. He is, however, also a morally ambiguous figure in his relationship with power, although in a more mundane way compared to *The Four Books*. He admits, for instance, that he wrote the manuscript in exchange for a huge amount of money which he needed "just as a man with too much testosterone needs a woman" (就像有太多男性荷爾蒙的人需要女人樣).[42] This allusion transforms the novel into the fruit of the same merchandizing society criticized in the novel itself, and its author in a mercenary ready to sell his intellect to the better offeror.

The authority, on the other hand, is only munificent and libertarian at the beginning since, after entrusting "Yan Lianke" with the task, it refuses the outcome because it is too harsh in its description of the Kong family, and forbids "Yan Lianke" from publishing it. We can read in this dynamic a polemical representation of the Chinese editorial scene: intellectuals don't hesitate to sell their work, while authorities have no measure in spending money to use culture as a tool of soft power and propaganda, but they ultimately refuse and censor the work when it does not correspond to the expected result. There is also an explicit hint to the "paradox of censorship,"[43] when the manuscript gains the attention of the whole town precisely because of its ban:

> September 2012, the manuscript of *The Explosion Chronicles* was distributed to the Explosion municipal government and to all levels of society, to read and evaluate. The work incited an uproar and received a steady string of critiques and denunciations,

---

41 Yan, *The Four Books*, trans. Carlos Rojas (New York: Grove Press, 2015, eBook version), chap.16.1, sec. 1; Yan, *Si shu*, 374.

42 Yan Lianke, *The Explosion Chronicles*, trans. Carlos Rojas (New York: Grove Press, 2016, eBook version), chap.1.1, sec. 2; Yan Lianke, *Zhalie zhi* 炸裂志 [The Explosion Chronicles] (Shanghai: Shanghai wenyi chubanshe, 2013), 3.

43 Michael Holquist, "Corrupt Originals: The Paradox of Censorship," *PMLA* 109, no. 1 (Jan. 1994): 14–25.

such that it became a legendary metropolitan chronicle that was privately circulated throughout Explosion.

2012年9月，《炸裂志》交炸裂市政府和各階層人員閱讀審定，引起一片譁然，聲討和咒罵連連不斷，使之成為炸裂私傳私閱的一本市志奇書。[44]

In the conclusion of the novel, fictional "Yan Lianke" reaches a maximum of paroxysms when he thanks Mayor Kong by stating that it is precisely the refusal of his manuscript by authorities that makes him completely sure of its worth:

> I gazed at the mayor's livid face, then smiled and said, "Thank you, Mayor Kong. You are this book's first reader, and your response reassures me that I have written a pretty good work." Then, I retreated from the mayor's office.

> 在那明亮的日光中，望著市長紫青色的臉，我對他笑笑說：「謝謝你，孔市長，你是這本書熱第一個讀者，你的話讓我知道我寫了一本還不錯的書。」然後我就從市長的辦公室力退將出來了。[45]

This paradoxical conclusion that not only multiple authors but even Yan Lianke himself contradict in multiple passages of his *Silent and Panting* reveals the deep frustration and level of exasperation that Yan wants to convey in the text. The metatextual references, along with the reflection on the process of historiographical research and its inner contradiction, moreover, allow us to classify this otherwise quite traditional novel as an example of "historiographical metafiction." The novels *The Day the Sun Died* and *Want to Sleep Together Quickly*, however, go even further in this meta-realistic representation of the intellectual and his position in society.

The incapable intellectual in *The Day the Sun Died*

In a Berkeley conference in 2013, while answering a question, Yan Lianke states that the only way Chinese writers can maintain a "dignified writing" (*zhuangyan de xiezuo* 莊嚴的寫作) is to completely give up the perspective of publishing in mainland China, and exploit the political and economic contradictions of the Chinese system by addressing themselves to Sinophone markets:

> Of course, I think Taiwan and Hong Kong constitute an excellent complement to publishing in [mainland] China. Chinese citizens have always considered these two territories as a part of China, but not for what concerns publishing. ... If Chinese writers acted like Yu Hua, who published in Hong Kong and Taiwan when he could not publish in [mainland] China, ... I think Chinese literature would be greatly advantaged.

> 我想當然臺灣香港是中國[大陸]出版非常好的補充，　中國的情況是中國人永遠認為臺灣和香港就是中國的一部分，　但他們認為它的出版又不是它的一部

---

44 Yan, *The Explosion Chronicles*, chap.1.1, sec. 15; Yan, *Zhalie zhi*, 6.
45 Yan, *The Explosion Chronicles*, chap.19, sec. 14; Yan, *Zhalie zhi*, 376.

分。……如果中國作家都可以像余華這樣，我的寫作不能在大陸出版那我在港臺出版，……我想中國的文學會有很大的改變。[46]

The impossibility to publish some of his novels in mainland China (*Serve the People!*, *Dream of Ding Village*, *The Four Books*) is, however, described as an experience of mutilation by Yan. In *Silent and Panting*, he describes it as such:

> When the novels you most wish your readers to read cannot be published in your mother tongue or in their native land, you experience a taste of "exile of the soul," as if you exiled your own soul in a faraway place.
>
> 你最希望讀者讀到的小說，不能用母語在本土出版時，你體會到一個人自己把自己的靈魂放逐到遠方的「靈魂流放」的味道了。[47]

Precisely this "exile of the soul" (*linghuan liufang* 靈魂流放) penetrates Yan's narrative and reverberates in the (already present) character of the oppressed or ridiculed intellectual. This is especially evident in the conclusion of *The Day the Sun Died*. In the last pages of the novel, the failed writer "Yan Lianke" finally manages to burn all of his books (something he has attempted to do all along the novel) and leaves for a self-imposed exile toward an unknown destination, possibly a Buddhist monastery. He takes his leave with these words, addressed to the young narrator:

> "If I don't succeed in writing the book your father asked me to write—a book that would function as a warm stove in winter and a cool electric fan in summer—then I won't ever return to this town."
>
> ... Then he left.
>
> 我要寫不出你爹讓我寫的那本書，寫不出冬天裡邊有火爐，夏天裡邊有電風扇的書，以後我就不再回這鎮上了。
>
> ……他就從這個世界消失了。[48]

The failure of fictional "Yan Lianke" is directly connected to his profession as a writer: he "used up his talent" (*Jianglang caijin* 江郎才盡),[49] is unable to write and, therefore, to speak to his readers and to tell what happens in the country.[50] As Carlos Rojas puts it, someone writes

---

46   Yan Lianke, "Living without Dignity and Writing with Integrity: Chinese Author Yan Lianke," UC Berkeley Events April 19, 2013, video of seminar, 1:23:20, https://www.youtube.com/watch?v=t6o0Agdmtp4. (last accessed 26 May 2021).
47   Yan, *Chenmo yu chuanxi*, 149.
48   Yan, *The Day the Sun Died*, trans. Carlos Rojas (London: Chatto & Windus, 2018), 340; Yan Lianke, *Rixi* (Taipei: Maitian chubanshe, 2015), 321.
49   Yan, *Rixi*, 18.
50   Arguably, not all writers write to speak to the people, let alone to tell what happens in a country. This seems, however, to have been Yan's goal in different occasions, as he openly told us in an interview (Jan. 2018) and as we can see from his representation of different crucial episodes of contemporary Chinese history in his novels. See Pezza, "Un Monumento all'amnesia."

about him, but he is unable to write.⁵¹ The narrator, a young boy named Li Niannian, deeply admires but is also unable to understand "Yan Lianke's" books. He mentions, for instance, *Liunian riguang* 流年日光, *Huo shou* 活受, *Si shu* 死書, and *Huo shou zhi liu shui ru nian* 受活之流水如年, which all represent a deformation of the original novels *Streams of Time*, *Lenin's Kisses*, *The Four Books*, possibly even a hint to *Hard Like Water*.

While arguably being part of a humorous and anti-realist trend that characterizes Yan's writing throughout his novels, this alteration, which also includes deformed quotations or even completely invented passages from the mentioned novels, suggests the impossible reception of the author's message, and the inevitable misunderstanding thereof. The relationship between author and power is completely denied in the novel, both on a textual level—the silence of the writer, who cannot speak up for his community—and on an implicit one, that is, the refusal to publish the novel in mainland China, that he already described as a (partially self-imposed) "exile of the soul" in 2013. The recurrent, altered metatextual references only reinforce the message of uselessness and impossible reception of the writer, whose reduction to silence is the only expectable outcome.

The hyper-realistic failure of "Yan Lianke" in *Want to Sleep Together Quickly*

This message of impossible reception is even stronger in *Want to Sleep Together Quickly*, subtitled *A Non-Fictional Piece About Me and Life* (*Wo yu shenghuo de yi duan fei xugou* 我與生活的一段非虛構, 2017), which represents the climax of metafictional and grotesque self-writing, as well as of other literary features of Yan Lianke's recent novels, such as the avant-gardist presence of different styles and genres in the same work and the presence of an urban setting.

Yan is both the narrator and the protagonist of this novella. In the opening of the text, a "Yan Lianke" approaching his fiftieth birthday suddenly decides that, since the literary scene will not reward his talent with any fame or money, he had better turn to the cinematographic market and become the director, scenarist, and main actor of a film inspired by a short story he has written. The plot follows his different attempts to transform an old short story inspired by a real incident, happened in his native village, into a movie. The "non-fictional" nature of the text is emphasized by some of the characters we encounter: apart from "Yan Lianke" himself and the protagonists of the incident, the reader meets the director Gu Changwei 顧長衛 and the young writer Jiang Fangzhou 蔣方舟, who are invited to be part of the filming, and have a relationship with Yan in real life: Gu is, for instance, the director of *Love for Life* (*Zui ai* 最愛, 2011), the movie inspired, although with many changes, by Yan's *Dream of Ding Village*.

From a stylistic point of view, the text is a literary *pastiche*—the parts directly narrated by "Yan Lianke" are alternated with the text of the "original" short story, transcripts of interviews with the protagonists of the incident, and the draft scenario. The hyper-realist tone of the text is also underlined by an apparent "obsession" of the narrator for an "objective" registration of all the facts. This is particularly evident in the last chapter, where two paragraphs are constituted by the sentence "suppressed here XX characters" (*ci chu shenglüe XX zi* 此處省略XX字) completed by an approximated figure allegedly indicating the number of censored characters, as well as by similar sentences all through the chapter, where the author demands permission from the reader to erase some dialogues.⁵² This stylistic solution immediately

---

51 Carlos Rojas, "*Rixi*: Lu Xun yu Qiaoyisi" 《日熄》: 魯迅與喬伊絲 [*The Day the Sun Died*: Lu Xun and Joyce], in Yan, *Rixi*, 7.

52 Yan Lianke, "Su qiu gong mian: Wo yu shenghuo de yi duan fei xugou," *Shouhuo* 收穫 [Harvest], special summer issue (Mar. 2017): 99, 101.

evokes Jia Pingwa's *Decadent Capital*, a novel Yan often mentions in his essays, and his exposed—and fictional—practice of self-censorship,[53] but, in the context of this narrator, also contributes to adding some doubt about the "reliability" of his version of the story.

"Yan Lianke" in fact gradually loses all his authority in the eye of the reader as we approach the conclusion. Not only does his project ultimately fail,[54] his status also drastically declines because of three climaxing discoveries that make him realize his complete failure as a writer. First, when he tries to interview some of the villagers about the events that inspired his short story, he encounters their complete disdain: they consider him a greedy man who does nothing with his life except take advantage of other people's life to make money; literature, on the other hand, is only a "legalized lie" ("造謠在嘴上就是犯罪了, 造謠在書上就成學問啦！").[55] Second, we learn that Li Jing, the young graduate who inspires the scenario, a talented scientist who is also an avid reader and good connoisseur of Chinese literature, thinks only the worst of his writing:

> Unexpectedly, she has read almost every contemporary Chinese writer. Mo Yan, Yu Hua, Su Tong, Ge Fei, Wang Anyi, Liu Zhenyun, Han Shaogong, Li Rui, Mai Jia, Li Er, Jia Pingwa, Bi Feiyu, Ah Lai, Chi Zijian, Lin Bai, Zhang Wei and so forth, from the earliest works of Wang Meng to the latest "post-Seventies" and "post-Eighties" generations and web writers. She is clearly extremely familiar with them all, she knows them like the palm of her hand. Although having fully undertaken a scientific major, she deeply loves the humanities …. According to her, there are only three authors she loathes, she throws their books away as soon as she sees their names. She said one of them is you ….
>
> "Yan Lianke's novels are scam, you cannot make head or tail of them."
>
> 我們誰都沒想到, 當代中國作家的小說, 她幾乎全讀過。莫言、余華、蘇童、格非、王安憶、劉震雲、韓少功、李銳、麥家、李洱、賈平凹、畢飛宇、阿來、遲子建、林白、張煒等, 甚至連更早的王蒙老師和再晚的「七〇後」「八〇後」的作家和網路作家們, 說出來她都瞭若指掌, 如數家珍。是一個地地道道的學理科卻深愛文科的人。……她說在中國作家中, 有三個作家她最為不喜歡, 看見名字就想扔了他們的書。在這三個作家中, 其中一個, 她說到了你……
>
> 「閻連科的小說太裝神弄鬼、莫名其妙了。」[56]

Finally, strolling along the bookshelves of his favorite bookstores in Beijing, "Yan Lianke" learns from a young bookseller, who does not recognize him, that even his most well-known novels have been removed from the shelves and sent back to the publishing house because "nobody ever read them" (閻連科的小說從來沒人看).[57]

The wounds inflicted to the protagonist have, at this stage, no apparent relationship with a political power; it is his incapacity to be "marketable" and obtain the attention of the

---

53 In Jia's novel, see Thomas Chen, "Blanks to Be Filled: Public-Making and the Censorship of Jia Pingwa's *Decadent Capital*," *China Perspectives*, 2015, no. 1: 15–22.
54 A movie with the same title, directed by Lü Yue 呂樂 on Yan's script, exists and has been presented at the 2018 Shanghai International Film Festival.
55 Yan, "Su qiu gong mian," 47.
56 Yan, "Su qiu gong mian," 94.
57 Ibid., 100–01.

readers-consumers that relegates him to a dark corner of the literary scene. It might also appear, however, as the fictional realization of the new "literary standard" consequent to the new regime of the "soft" censorship that Yan theorized in 2016, as mentioned above. The main traits chosen by Yan in representing intellectuals, and himself as an intellectual, are thus greed, moral deviation, and hypocrisy, accompanied, especially in the last part of his writing, by the representation of a frustrated desire to be a protagonist of the establishment which he also utterly criticizes, and an impossible desire to express oneself and to be understood.

The novels we consider thus offer a representation of different shades of the mourning toward the oppression of power Yan experienced with time, from the ironic denial of *Ballad, Hymn, Ode*, which expresses the illusory possibility of an escape in an idyllic retreat similar to the one described in *Lenin's Kisses*,[58] to the anger and (failed) bargaining with the power we can find in *The Four Books* and *The Explosion Chronicles*, up to the shift of the conflict to an apparently personal level in *The Day the Sun Died*, where no solution is left to the writer but to leave in a chosen and self-imposed exile, and *Want to Sleep Together Quickly*, where the writer is left licking the wounds inflicted to his narcissistic ego. On a stylistic level, however, this Sisyphean struggle seems to have led to an evolution in Yan's "mythorealistic" post-modern representation of reality: the progressive abandonment of absurd, impossible, or surreal elements, toward an ironical hyper-realism that super-exposes reality in its heaviest and most grotesque aspects and obliges the readers to face the challenges and contradictions of reality, reflecting the contradictory struggle of the author as an intellectual in contemporary China.

Bibliography

Anderson, Marston. *The Limits of Realism: Chinese Fiction in the Revolutionary Period*. Berkeley: University of California Press, 1990.

Chen, Thomas. "Blanks to Be Filled: Public-Making and the Censorship of Jia Pingwa's *Decadent Capital*." *China Perspectives*, 2015, no. 1: 15–22.

Gao Xingjian. "Gao Xingjian: Nobel Lecture." NobelPrize.org, 2000. https://www.nobelprize.org/prizes/literature/2000/gao/25522-gao-xingjian-nobel-lecture-2000/ (last accessed 26 May 2021).

Holquist, Michael. "Corrupt Originals : The Paradox of Censorship." *PMLA* 109, no. 1 (Jan. 1994): 14–25.

Hutcheon, Linda. "Historiographic Metafiction: Parody and the Intertextuality of History." In *Intertextuality and Contemporary American Fiction*, edited by Patrick O'Donnell and Robert Con Davis, 3–32. Baltimore: Johns Hopkins University Press, 1989.

Jameson, Fredric. "Third-World Literature in the Era of Multinational Capitalism." *Social Text*, no. 15 (Autumn 1986): 65–88.

Li Tuo. "Resisting Writing." In *Politics, Ideology and Literary Discourse in Modern China: Theoretical Interventions and Cultural Critique*, edited by Liu Kang 劉康 and Tang Xiaobing 唐小兵, 273–77. Durham: Duke University Press, 1993.

Lin Yuan 林源, ed. *Shuo Yan Lianke* 說閻連科 [On Yan Lianke]. 2 vols. Shenyang: Liaoning renmin chubanshe, 2014.

Link, Perry. "Does This Writer Deserve the Prize ?" *The New York Review of Books*, 12 June 2012. https://www.nybooks.com/articles/2012/12/06/mo-yan-nobel-prize/ (last accessed 26 May 2021).

———. *The Uses of Literature : Life in the Socialist Chinese Literary System*. Princeton: Princeton University Press, 2000.

Liu, Jianmei 劉劍梅. "To Join the Commune or Withdraw from It? A Reading of Yan Lianke's *Shouhuo*." *Modern Chinese Literature and Culture* 19, no. 2 (Autumn 2007): 1–33.

———. *Zhuangzi and Modern Chinese Literature*. New York: Oxford University Press, 2016.

---

58 For this parallel, see Jianmei Liu, *Zhuangzi and Modern Chinese Literature* (New York: Oxford University Press, 2016), 205–06.

Liu Xiaobo. *La philosophie du porc et autres essais*. Edited by Vaclav Havel. Translated by Jean-Philippe Béja. Paris: Gallimard, 2011.

Liu Zaifu 劉再復. "Lun wenxue de zhutixing" 論文學的主體性 [Subjectivity in literature]." *Wenxue lilun* 文學理論 [Literary theory], 1985, no. 6: 11–26.

———. "The Subjectivity of Literature Revisited." In Liu and Tang, *Politics, Ideology and Literary Discourse in Modern China*, 56–69. Durham: Duke University Press, 1993.

Moratto, Riccardo. "Intervista a Yan Lianke [Interview with Yan Lianke]." *Il Manifesto*, 27 Feb. 27, 2020. https://ilmanifesto.it/yan-lianke-ansia-e-rabbia-da-virus-stanno-sfumando/ (last accessed 31 May 2021).

———. "Zai yiqing liuxing de dangxia xunzhao ziwo he wenxue: Zhuanfang Yan Lianke" 在疫情流行的當下尋找自我和文學——專訪閻連科 [Looking for oneself and for literature during an epidemic: An interview with Yan Lianke]. *Waiguo yuyan yu wenhua* 外國語言與文化 [Foreign languages and culture] 1 (20 Mar. 2020). https://mp.weixin.qq.com/s/_1FeqVY2_tjMxshZNcxA8g (last accessed 31 May 2021).

Pezza, Alessandra. "Un Monumento all'Amnesia: Yan Lianke e la Traduzione della Storia Nazionale in Letteratura" [A monument to amnesia: Yan Lianke and the translation of contemporary history in literature]. In *L'intraducibile: La comunicazione interculturale e la traducibilità*, edited by Alessandra Pezza. Milano: Mimesis, 2021.

Rojas, Carlos. "*Rixi*: Lu Xun yu Qiaoyisi" 《日熄》: 魯迅與喬伊絲 [*The Day the Sun Died*: Lu Xun and Joyce]. In Yan Lianke, *Rixi*. Taipei: Maitian chubanshe, 2015.

Tsai Chien-hsin 蔡建鑫. "Quru de jiushu" 屈辱的救贖 [Redemption in humiliation]." In Yan Lianke, *Si shu* 四書 [The Four Books]. Taipei: Maitian chubanshe, 2011.

———. "In Sickness or in Health: Yan Lianke and the Writing of Autoimmunity." *Modern Chinese Literature and Culture* 23, no. 1 (Spring 2011): 77–104.

Veg, Sebastian. "Creating a Literary Space to Debate the Mao Era: The Fictionalization of the Great Leap Forward in Yan Lianke's *Four Books*." *China Perspectives*, 2014, no. 4: 7–16.

Wang Ning. "A Reflection on Postmodernist Fiction in China: Avant-Garde Narrative Experimentation." *Narrative* 21, no. 3 (2013): 296–308.

Watts, Jonathan. "Censor Sees through Writer's Guile in Tale of China's Blood-Selling Scandal." zonaeuropa, 10 Sep. 2006. http://zonaeuropa.com/culture/c20060327_1.htm (last accessed 8 Jan. 2019).

Yan Lianke. *Chenmo yu chuanxi: Wo suo jingli de Zhongguo he wenxue* 沉默與喘息: 我所經歷的中國和文學 [Silent and panting : My experience with China and literature]. Taipei: INK chubanshe, 2014.

———. *The Day the Sun Died*. Translated by Carlos Rojas. London: Chatto & Windus, 2018.

———. "An Examination of China's Censorship System." In *The Oxford Handbook of Modern Chinese Literatures*, edited by Andrea Bachner and Carlos Rojas, 263–74. New York: Oxford University Press, 2016.

———. *The Explosion Chronicles*. Translated by Carlos Rojas. New York: Grove Press, 2016, eBook version.

———. *Faxian xiaoshuo: Wenxue suibi* 發現小說: 文學隨筆 [Discovering the fiction: Essays on literature]. Tianjin: Nankai daxue chubanshe, 2011.

———. *The Four Books*. Translated by Carlos Rojas. New York: Grove Press, 2015, eBook version.

———. "Living without Dignity and Writing with Integrity: Chinese Author Yan Lianke." UC Berkeley Events, April 19, 2013, video of seminar. https://www.youtube.com/watch?v=t6o0Agdmtp4 (accessed May 26, 2021).

———. *Rixi* 日熄 [The Day the Sun Died]. Taipei: Maitian chubanshe, 2015.

———. *Si shu* 四書 [The Four Books]. Taipei: Maitian chubanshe, 2011.

———. "Su qiu gong mian: Wo yu shenghuo de yi duan fei xugou" 速求共眠——我與生活的一段非虛構 [A quick attempt to sleep together: A short nonfiction on myself and life]. *Shouhuo* 收穫 [Harvest], special summer issue (Mar. 2017): 4–104.

———. "The Year of the Stray Dog." Translated by Jane Weizhen Pan and Martin Merz. *The New York Times*, 20 Apr. 2012. http://www.nytimes.com/2012/04/21/opinion/the-year-of-the-stray-dog.html (last accessed 26 May 2021).

———. *Yipai huyan: Yan Lianke haiwai yanjiang ji* 一派胡言: 閻連科海外演講集 [Selected overseas speeches of Yan Lianke]. Beijing: Zhongxin chubanshe, 2012.

———. *Zhalie zhi* 炸裂志 [The Explosion Chronicles]. Shanghai: Shanghai wenyi chubanshe, 2013.

12
THE DREAM, THE DISEASE, AND THE DISASTER
On Yan Lianke's *Dream of Ding Village*[1]
Shelley W. Chan

Born in 1958, Yan Lianke 閻連科, a nationally and internationally known Chinese writer, has published more than ten novels, several dozens of novellas, short stories, and essays to date. He has been the recipient of major awards in China and abroad, including two consecutive Lu Xun 魯迅 Literary Prizes (1997 and 2001), Franz Kafka Prize (2014), Dream of the Red Chamber Award (2016), and The Newman Prize for Chinese Literature (2021). Nevertheless, this award-winning writer has been very controversial and, in fact, banned for a period of time in China, primarily because of the sensitive topics of his fiction. As observed by a research fellow of *Yazhou zhoukan* 亞洲週刊 (*Asiaweek*) in Hong Kong: "There has never been a writer like Yan Lianke, who has been labeled 'the most controversial writer with most banned books' besides the titles of 'master of absurd realism' and 'China's most likely Nobel Prize winner'. Such a label, neither an honor nor a criticism, makes Yan feel helpless. Indeed, no publishers in mainland China have published any of his books in the past five years."[2]

Yan is known for using illness to signify reality. Since the establishment of the new government in 1949 on the mainland, especially with the open-door policy that brought rapid economic growth after the Great Proletarian Cultural Revolution (1966–76), China has developed tremendously over the past four decades. Its recent achievements, including the 2008 Beijing Olympic Games, the 2010 Shanghai Expo, its rapid developments in space technology, its overtaking Japan to become the second-largest economic power, and its ambitious development strategies, such as the Belt and Road Initiative seen as an attempt of the Chinese dominance in world affairs, all in all have caught much attention from the rest of the world. As a result, many Chinese people believe that their country has shaken off its humiliating image as the "Sick Man of East Asia," which was the collective anxiety of the Chinese intellectuals in the late nineteenth and early twentieth centuries. Nevertheless, this anxiety

---

1 This article first appeared in *Literary and Visual Representations of HIV/AIDS: Forty Years Later*, ed. Aimee Pozorski, Jennifer J. Lavoie, and Christine J. Cynn (Lanham: Lexington Books, 2020), 89–104. A few minor changes have been made in the current version.
2 Yuan Weijing 袁瑋婧, "Yan Lianke: Wo xiang hui dao duzhe de huaibao zhong" 閻連科——我想回到讀者的懷抱中 [Yan Lianke: I would like to return to my readers], *Yazhou zhoukan* 亞洲週刊 (*Asiaweek*), 20 May 2018, medium.com/@cyanyuan/閻連科-我想回到讀者的懷抱中-6a4e5e0bb922?from=singlemessage&isappinstalled=0 (last accessed 23 Oct. 2018). My translation.

is still troubling some Chinese who see present-day China as an unhealthy and even morbid world wherein people are spiritually sick. Among them is Yan Lianke. For instance, *The New York Times* published his article "On China's State-Sponsored Amnesia" on 1 Apr. 2013, which was about how people in their 20s and 30s had no memories of important events such as the June 4 Tiananmen Incident of 1989. Yan has also published novels of disease, such as *Streams of Time* (*Riguang liunian* 日光流年, 1998), *Pleasure* (*Shouhuo* 受活, 2003),[3] and *Dream of Ding Village* (*Dingzhuang meng* 丁莊夢, 2006). These novels are about cancer sufferers, physical disabilities, and HIV patients, respectively.

This article focuses on *Dream of Ding Village* and discusses how the daring novel shows concern for the biopolitical situation of the Chinese people, and how it spearheads its criticism on the "blood economy" (*xuejiang jingji* 血漿經濟) in central China in the 1990s. Through studying the mythorealistic components, such as the unconventional narrative voice and the experimental structure of the novel, this article examines the thanatopolitics characteristic of the story and the possibility of the author's self-censorship. It also demonstrates how the novel makes parts of the real illusory and imaginary, and how this technique serves to create a wider and deeper blurred space between reality and unreality to highlight the irrational and crazy materialistic desire of human beings, which leads to an absurd and ill-practiced modernization.

Set in Henan Province in China, *Dream of Ding Village* is about how the local people engage in the infamous "blood economy" and get infected with AIDS. Henan Province in central China, believed to be the birthplace of the Chinese civilization, is a relatively less developed province where the per capita GDP is significantly lower than that of the more developed coastal or central areas. In Yan's own words: "Some of the most memorable events in history happened here, but, during my lifetime, it's become one of the poorest places in the country .... There is no dignity left, and because of that the people of Henan have felt a deep sense of loss and bitterness."[4] In the early to mid-1990s, the provincial government promoted a policy to "shake off poverty and attain prosperity" (*tuopin zhifu* 脫貧致富) and urged poor people to make money by selling their blood. The authority called this the "blood economy" or "plasma economy" and believed that this policy would make "the people rich and the nation strong" (*min fu guo qiang* 民富國強). To achieve the goal of the sovereign's administration by manipulating people's bodies fits the term "biopower" coined by Michel Foucault (1926–84), who points out: "During the classical period, there was a rapid development of various disciplines—universities, secondary schools, barracks, workshops; there was also the emergence, in the field of political practices and economic observation, of the problems of birthrate, longevity, public health, housing, and migration. Hence there was an explosion of the numerous and diverse techniques for achieving the subjugation of bodies and the control of populations, marking the beginning of an era of 'biopower.'"[5]

Perhaps this biopower in the context of China, which still claims to be a socialist country but in fact is more capitalist than many other countries that practice capitalism, is what Foucault calls "... an indispensable element in the development of capitalism,"[6] as we have seen similar

---

3 The title of *Shouhuo* is translated by Carlos Rojas as *Lenin's Kisses* (New York: Grove Press, 2012). I personally believe that "pleasure" is closer to the original meaning of the Chinese expression. As a result, I decide not to adopt Rojas' translation of the title in my discussion.
4 Fan Jiayang, "Yan Lianke's Forbidden Satires of China," *The New Yorker*, 15 Oct. 2018, http://www.newyorker.com/magazine/2018/10/15/yan-liankes-forbidden-satires-of-china?from=singlemessage&isappinstalled=0 (last accessed 23 Oct. 2018).
5 Michel Foucault, *The History of Sexuality*, vol. 1, *An Introduction*, trans. Robert Hurley (New York: Vintage Books, 1990), 140.
6 Ibid., 140–41.

practices in Yan Lianke's other works (such as selling skin and bodies in the above-mentioned novels of disease) as well as productions of other authors/artists, such as Yu Hua's 1995 novel *Chronicle of a Blood Merchant* [*Xu Sanguan maixue ji*] and Zhou Xiaowen's 1994 film *Ermo*. As Carlos Rojas, who has translated several novels of Yan Lianke, points out when he discusses the novel *Dream of Ding Village*: "[R]esidents of remote central Chinese villages are encouraged to join contemporary capitalist systems not by integrating their labor into those systems but rather by literally commoditizing their own bodies. The result is a process wherein the individual's relationship to the economic order is fundamentally transformed, as the subject's own body becomes a commodity in its own right."[7] Ironically, the blood economy that aimed at increasing the provincial government's revenue and improving people's wellbeing proved to be the most absurd joke and the main reason of a terrible outbreak. According to Dr. Gao Yaojie, China's most outspoken AIDS activist, this "blood economy" was a "blood disaster" (*xuehuo* 血禍) and "national calamity" (*guonan* 國難).[8]

Dream of Ding Village has eight volumes with irregular length. For instance, Volume One has only one page and Volume Eight has a little more than four pages, while other volumes have over 30, 40, or 50 pages. The longer volumes are further divided into chapters and sections. Like many of Yan's novels, the structure of this book is highly experimental, which is a mixture of reality and dreams of the narrator's grandfather. "Dream" appears in the title and is also the full content of the one-page Volume One, which consists of three short dreams: "The Cupbearer's Dream," "The Baker's Dream," and "The Pharaoh's Dream."[9] In fact, the dreams are part of and yet more eye-catching than the reality parts when they are printed in boldface and in a different font. To be precise, the narrative is often boldfaced and set in a special font throughout the entire book, mostly for Grandpa's dreams. Interestingly, Grandpa is often more clear-minded in his dreams than when he is awake in the daytime; when he dreams of something, he can always confirm it in reality, as if he has an extra-sensory perception. When the reader discovers that what is in Grandpa's dream is actually real, including the fact he is the one who is forced by the Director of Education to convince the villagers to sell their blood, they will gradually ignore the boundary between dreams and reality and wonder why the author chooses to present reality in the form of dream.

A Chinese version of *The Plague*, *Dream of Ding Village* is a macabre story filled with depictions of death:

They died like falling leaves.
Their light extinguished, gone from this world.

... for the past two years, people in the village had been dying. Not a month went by without at least one death, and nearly every family had lost someone. After more than forty deaths in the space of two years, the graves in the village cemetery were as dense as sheaves of wheat in a farmer's field ... *Died like falling leaves, their light gone from the world* ....[10]

---

7 Carlos Rojas, *Homesickness: Culture, Contagion, and National Transformation in Modern China* (Cambridge: Harvard University Press, 2015), 189.
8 See Gao Yaojie 高耀潔, *Gaojie de linghun: Gao Yaojie huiyilu* 高潔的靈魂：高耀潔回憶錄 [A Noble and Unsullied Soul: Gao Yaojie's Memoirs], rev. and enlarged ed. (Hong Kong: Ming Pao, 2010), 177. My translation.
9 Yan Lianke, *Dream of Ding Village*, trans. Cindy Carter (New York: Grove Press, 2004), 3.
10 Ibid., 9. Original italics.

The story is narrated by a twelve-year-old dead boy. His father, Ding Hui, is a blood head who collects blood from his fellow villagers and sells it to blood stations. After the outbreak of AIDS and people in almost every household die for selling blood, the villagers get revenge on Ding Hui by poisoning his chicken, then his pig, and eventually his son:

> I was only twelve, in my fifth year at the school, when I died. I died from eating a poisoned tomato I found on the way home from school ….

> I died not from the fever, not from AIDS, but because my dad had run a blood-collection station in Ding Village ten years earlier. He bought blood from the villagers and resold it for a profit. I died because my dad was the biggest blood merchant not just in Ding Village but in Two-Li Village, Willow Hamlet, Yellow Creek and dozens of other villages for miles around. He wasn't just a blood merchant: he was a blood kingpin.[11]

The narrator is right: his father is a merchant, a person who deals with buying and selling commodities for profit. His business is one that trades death, and everything he does is related to death. He is powerful among the villagers since he has the capital regardless of which means he collected it, and the power obtained from his wealth allows him to become the top predator. He gains profit by collecting and reselling the blood of his villagers at the expense of the lives of his own son and younger brother, who is also a blood seller and is, unfortunately, later infected with AIDS and dies. When more and more villagers die, the county government provides coffins to the families of the dead for free. The bloodsucker Ding Hui grabs the opportunity to make a fortune by controlling the distribution of the coffins and selling them: "No longer did my father have to do all the work himself. He had a crew of young men to unload coffins from the trucks and help villagers fill out their paperwork, while he sat at a separate table, sipping water and calling up the villagers one by one to collect their completed forms and payments. After he had counted the cash and stuffed it in his black leather case, he would issue a receipt and direct the person to the trucks to collect his or her coffin."[12]

Even worse, this blood head who will do anything to make money starts a new business—arranging marriages, not between living people but between the dead. He even sells the remains of his own son—the twelve-year-old boy—to the dead daughter of a local leader. This way, he becomes a relative of the leader, directly connecting himself to the authority and power. When questioned by Grandpa why he has found a dead girl who was a lot older than the boy, and who was physically handicapped, Ding Hui argues, "How could I have possibly found a better match? … Don't you know her father is moving up in the world? They just promoted him to mayor of Kaifeng!"[13] The dead first-person narrator, the innocent young boy who is saddled with his own father's sin and the villagers' hatred, serves to turn the entire novel into a thanato-narrative. Although Yan is not the first Chinese writer to use a dead first-person narrator—Fang Fang's 1987 novella "Landscape" ("Fengjing" 風景) is narrated by a dead child—the novel is greatly enriched by such an absurd element. On the one hand, the dead narrator creates one kind of alienation effect, better catching the reader's attention by providing a nonconventional reading experience. On the other hand, having a dead person tell the stories of the living, the boundary between the Netherworld and the human world is

11 Ibid., 10.
12 Ibid., 176.
13 Ibid., 328.

erased. That the Netherworld invades and eventually exercises control over the human world well fits the death theme of the novel. Furthermore, the binary opposition between the real and the unreal is also blurred, making the impossible possible.

In the beginning, the villagers of Ding Village are hesitant about selling blood. Grandpa sees/recollects clearly how Ding Village starts selling blood in one of his dreams. The county Director of Education urges the highly regarded Grandpa to organize people to pay a visit to Cai county, the richest county of Henan Province. The reason Cai county is able to get rid of dire poverty and become rich is through its people selling blood. The trip to Cai county is a great shock to the people of Ding Village:

> Crossing the county line was like driving into some sort of paradise. The villagers were startled to see both sides of the main road lined by modern, two-storey homes of red brick and tile …. There were flowers in every doorway, trees in every courtyard and broad avenues of poured concrete ….
>
> Inside the houses, even the household appliances and furnishings seemed standardized: refrigerators were to the left of the entry hall, televisions in the living room opposite the sofa, and washing machines in the bathroom opposite the kitchen. Door and window frames were shiny new aluminum alloy; chests, wardrobes and cabinets were red lacquer adorned with gold leaf. The beds were heaped with silk and satin quilts and woolen blankets, and every room smelled nice.[14]

The following descriptions remind the reader of the rosy pictures of communism: "Outside of the street, they ran into a group of laughing, chattering village women loaded down with bundles of fresh vegetables and bags of fish and meat. When the villagers asked the women if they'd been out shopping, the women answered that there was no need to shop, because the village committee gave away food for free. All you had to do was go to the committee headquarters and collect what you needed for the day."[15] This is the "model blood-selling village for the whole county, for the whole province," where "everyone … sells blood …."[16] This wealthy model village "had been made possible by selling blood."[17] The rosy pictures are also reminiscent of an economic and social campaign that occurred in the late 1950s to early 1960s: the Great Leap Forward. Launched and led by Mao Zedong (1893–1976), the campaign had its goal to rapidly construct the socialist China so as to catch up and surpass Western developed countries, such as the United Kingdom and the United States. The People's Communes were a product of the campaign: the agricultural collectivization and institutionalization that prohibited private farming. Private kitchens were abandoned; all people ate for free at the communal canteens, where everyone ate as they wished—an illusion of communism—the distribution principle of socialism is to distribute according to work, and that of communism is to distribute according to need. It was enjoyable for a short period of time, but very soon, the canteens experienced a lack of supply, and eventually had to be dissolved. The Great Leap Forward has been regarded as a failure that resulted in a great famine and millions of deaths.[18]

14 Ibid., 34–35.
15 Ibid., 35–36.
16 Ibid., 36.
17 Ibid., 37.
18 For more information on the Great Leap Forward and People's Communes, please consult Yang Jisheng 楊繼繩 et al., *Tombstone: The Great Chinese Famine, 1958–1962* (New York: Farrar, Straus and Giroux, 2012).

The practice of the communal canteens during the Great Leap Forward and that in the model village in Cai county of *Dream of Ding Village*, both based on the communist principle of distribution, are both ironically turned into deadly disasters that took away thousands and even millions of lives. What Carlos Rojas pinpoints can be a good summary of these disasters: "As Michel Foucault and others have argued, the modern state derives its authority and legitimacy from its biopolitical relationship to its citizens—a relationship that is predicated on the state's ability to nurture life. Embedded within this biopolitical logic, however, is an inverse necropolitical one, in that the state's ability to provide the conditions for nurturing life is inextricably intertwined with its parallel ability to withhold those same conditions."[19]

Foucault also points out: "For millennia, man remained what he was for Aristotle: a living animal with the additional capacity for a political existence; modern man is an animal whose politics places his existence as a living being in question."[20] Interestingly, the relation between the novel and the societal reality is similar to that between the dreams and the fictional reality in the novel. Despite the title, the story of *Dream of Ding Village* is a realistic reflection of the tragedy that occurred in China. The "blood economy" best exemplifies the post-revolutionary China as a wonderful setting for the sovereignty and biopolitics to be related: "… the culmination of a politics of life generated a lethal power that contradicts the productive impulse."[21] With the death of Mao and the official close of the Cultural Revolution, he launched that was later labeled as "ten years of disaster," China's socialism experienced a drastic change, gradually moving toward capitalism that had been denounced in China during the revolutionary period of time. Mao's theory and practice of class struggle had led the Chinese people to believe that the poorer the better, as rich people would be categorized as class enemies and punished. After Mao's death, Deng Xiaoping's (1904–97) open-door policy and economic reform not only unlocked the door of China but also changed the mindset of the Chinese people, whose materialistic desire that had been suppressed for decades was woken up, and honor was given to those who were able to accumulate capital. On discussing politics over life, Roberto Esposito asks: "How is it possible that a power of life is exercised against life itself? … Why does a power that functions by insuring, protecting, and augmenting life express such a potential for death? … Why does biopolitics continually threaten to be reversed into thanatopolitics?"[22] He quotes Foucault when he uses wars and the Beveridge Plan as examples:

> Foucault accents the direct and proportional relation that runs between the development of biopower and the incremental growth in homicidal capacity. There have never been so many bloody and genocidal wars as have occurred in the last two centuries, which is to say in a completely biopolitical period. It is enough to recall that the maximum international effort for organizing health, the so-called Beveridge Plan, was elaborated in the middle of a war that produced 50 million dead: "One could symbolize such a coincidence by a slogan: go get slaughtered and we promise you a long and pleasant life. Life insurance is connected with a death command."[23]

In the 1990s' China, with the increase of blood sellers, more and more public and private blood stations mushroomed, and the hygienic standards in the process of blood drawing and plasma production were not strictly controlled, leading to the outbreak of an AIDS epidemic,

---

19 Rojas, *Homesickness*, 188.
20 Foucault, *The History of Sexuality*, 1:143.
21 Roberto Esposito, *Bios: Biopolitics and Philosophy*, trans. Timothy Campbell (Minneapolis: University of Minnesota Press, 2008), 39.
22 Ibid.
23 Ibid.

exactly the same situation as described in *Dream of Ding Village*.[24] First of all, the post-Mao China appeared to have a post-traumatic symptom of the extreme shortage of supplies in the past decades: when the previous suppression of human materialist desire by communist doctrines was relaxed, planned economy was loosened up and market economy was practiced, people seemed to be driven into a frenzy for materialism and consumerism by fair means or foul, as if the Pandora's box was opened. In the past, it was the sovereignty that imposed the suppression, and later it was still the sovereignty that lifted the suppression and encouraged people to pursue wealth by making use of their own biological bodies; the relation of sovereignty and biopolitics was thus created. Secondly, the extreme monetary worship has turned China into a place wherein money is God and everything equating money with power. In other words, those who have a bigger accumulation of wealth have a bigger voice and power in the hierarchized society. In the case of the AIDS epidemic breakout, in both the fictional and the realistic worlds, the HIV patients contribute their own blood and even lives to the blood heads' accumulation of money. Behind the blood heads are the even bigger social apparatus, which have stronger destructive power once they are malfunctioned. May the intension of the blood selling policy be "in the name of a politics of power" or "in the name of the survival itself of populations that are involved"; "it is precisely what reinforces the tragic aporia of a death that is necessary to preserve life, of a life nourished by the deaths of others …."[25]

People in the West used to believe that AIDS often comes from homosexual communities. As Susan Sontag indicates: "Indeed, to get AIDS is precisely to be revealed … as a member of certain "risk group," a community of pariahs. The illness flushes out an identity that might have remained hidden from neighbors, job-mates, family, friends. It also confirms an identity and, among the risk group in the United States most severely affected in the beginning, homosexual men, has been a creator of community as well as an experience that isolates the ill and exposes them to harassment and persecution."[26] However, the identity is different in Yan's writing of AIDS in the Chinese context, though gay people in China are also treated as a "risk group." Yan's novel discloses a fact that the authorities would rather not face, and that is why *Dream of Ding Village* was banned in mainland China. Scholars believe that "not only is AIDS writing a literary act involving conscious decisions about what to say or what not to say and how to couch what is said, but that writing about that writing is also a political act."[27] The novelist visited the AIDS village in his hometown in Henan seven times, and he also communicated with Dr. Gao. As a matter of fact, it was in Dr. Gao's home where Yan first met with two HIV patients and learned about the absurd ways of blood collecting of the local blood heads and blood stations. He was driven by an impulse to write something for the victims of the "blood economy," in spite of the fact that many Chinese are misled to think that AIDS is always related to homosexuality and sexual promiscuity; in other words, AIDS has been turned into a metaphor for (im)morality. As Gao points out, "people generally believe that AIDS is one kind of 'moral disease' (*daodebing* 道德病) as a result of the immoral lifestyle of the patients. They [believe that AIDS sufferers] have only themselves to blame; other people, including the

---

24 For a detailed description of the epidemic outbreak, see Wang Jinping 王晋平, "Chongwen xuejiang jingji he aizibing de hunluan shidai: Yi shi wei jian" 重溫血漿經濟和愛滋病的混亂時代—以史為鑑 [A review of the chaotic times of the blood economy and AIDS: Benefit from history], *Huanqiu shibao* 環球時報 (*Global Times*), 31 Oct. 2008, http://www.haodf.com/zhuanjiaguandian/wangjinping_22943.htm (last accessed 28 June 2014).
25 Esposito, *Bios*, 39.
26 Susan Sontag, *Illness as Metaphor and Aids and Its Metaphors* (New York: Anchor Books, 1990), 112–13.
27 Suzanne Poirier, *Introduction to Writing AIDS: Gay Literature, Language, and Analysis*, ed. Timothy F. Murphy and Suzanne Poirier (New York: Columbia University Press, 1993), 5.

government, have no responsibility for it."²⁸ Yan's literary writing, however, boldly discloses the fact that in China, many AIDS patients, at least in the 1990s' central China, are victims of the "blood economy," for which the authority must take responsibility.

Critics compare *Dream of Ding Village* with Camus' *The Plague*. Yet Yan's work is darker than that of Camus because Camus' characters are not as hopeless as those created by Yan. As mentioned above, the blood head Ding Hui is a ruthless villain. When it comes to the characters inside the quarantine, the patients are equally hopeless, displaying the dark side of human nature: they steal, they cheat, they lie, they fight for power, and they publicly humiliate adulterers. It is not so much the illness as their evil human nature that makes these people ugly and repulsive. Yan once said: "*Dream of Ding Village* is more about AIDS, cancer, hepatitis ... in people's heart."²⁹ The entire Ding Village is physically and spiritually ill. While the quarantined town in Camus' *The Plague* is finally opened again and people are able to reunite with their loved ones, Ding Village becomes a dead world, and the neighboring villages are also deserted; no humans or animals are seen, and no trees or wooden furniture are left—all are used for making caskets. Interestingly, the word AIDS (*aizibing* 愛滋病) is not as frequently mentioned as the term "fever disease" (*rebing* 熱病) throughout the novel. *Rebing* not only refers to the fever associated with AIDS but also signifies people's irrational and crazy materialistic desire. One of the basic goals of the Chinese Communist Party was to overthrow (bureaucratic) capitalism. Ironically, the post-revolutionary ruling party continues the unfinished cause of capitalism in China in the high fever of materialistic modernization through a market blood economy.

Starting his writing career in the military, Yan was known for writing realistic fiction about the lives of soldiers and peasants in his early stage of literary creation. However, the 2001 novel *Hard Like Water* (*Jianying ru shui* 堅硬如水) marked the turning point of his writing style from realism to one that has become more and more experimental and absurd, resulting in his novels being labeled as absurdism, magical realism, or surrealism by critics. Nevertheless, Yan seems to believe that none of the existing labels would best represent the essence of his writing. As a result, he coins a term for his Kafkaesque writing style: "mythorealism" (*shenshi zhuyi* 神實主義) which, according to him, "abandons the seemingly logical relations of real life, and explores a 'non-existent' truth, an invisible truth, and a truth concealed by truth. Mythorealism keeps a distance from any prevailing realism. The mythorealist connection with reality does not lie in straightforward cause-and-effect links, but rather relies on human souls, minds …. Imaginations, metaphors, myths, legends, dreams, fantasy, demonization, and transplantation born from everyday life and social reality can all serve as mythorealist methods and channels."³⁰

When he was awarded the Franz Kafka Prize, Yan delivered a speech at the award ceremony entitled "The Man Chosen by Heaven and Life to Feel the Darkness."³¹ Obviously, he is that man who sees "a nation that is thriving yet distorted, developing yet mutated," who

---

28 Gao, *Gaojie de linghun*, 342. My translation.
29 Sun Li 孫麗, "Renwu zhuanfang: Zhuming zuojia Yan Lianke changtan xinzuo *Dingzhuang meng*" 人物專訪：著名作家閻連科暢談新作《丁莊夢》 [Special interview: Famous writer Yan Lianke speaks of his new book *Dream of Ding Village*], Zhengyi wang 正義網, http: live.jcrb.com/html/2006/93.htm (last assessed 23 Oct. 2018). My translation.
30 Yan Lianke, *Faxian xiaoshuo* 發現小說 [*The discovery of fiction*] (Tianjin: Nankai daxue chubanshe, 2011), 181–82; Weijie Song 宋偉杰, trans., "Yan Lianke's Mythorealist Representation of the Country and the City," *Modern Fiction Studies* 62, no. 4 (Winter 2016): 644.
31 This is my literal translation of the original Chinese title, which is translated as "Finding Light in China's Darkness" by Carlos Rojas.

also sees "corruption, absurdity, disorder and chaos."[32] "An enormous sheet of darkness gradually approached" this man, who "developed a keen appreciation for the somber side of ... existence" and "came to understand that darkness is not the mere absence of light, but rather it is life itself. Darkness is the Chinese people's fate."[33] In other words, the absurdity and seemingly impossibility in his fiction are in fact the "internal truth" of reality when he defines his mythorealism.[34] Perhaps only an absurd way of writing would be able to fully describe the absurd reality and express the love-and-hate complex of the novelist. In his own words: "The reality of China is so outrageous that it defies belief and renders realism inert."[35]

Indeed, the reality is so outrageous that it renders realism inert and impossible, and makes a more unrealistic style necessary. When the magical realistic fiction of the postcolonial Latin America could be seen as implicit social and cultural criticism, Yan's mythorealism which, according to some critics, is a Chinese version of magical realism, has its complexity of being subversive and submissive simultaneously. To take the first-person narrator and the dreams as an example, a dead narrator is doubtlessly an unreliable narrator, whose omnipresent point of view is questionable, setting a thanatopolitical tone for the story. Together with Grandpa's dreams, this unreliable narrator also adds a layer of uncertainty to the mythorealistic fiction. By making parts of the real illusory and imaginary, the author inserts an artistic dimension to the story, creating a wider and deeper blurred space between reality and unreality, highlighting the absurdity of the blood economy and human greediness, and leaving the reader to question the viability of such an ill-practiced modernization. In the meantime, narrating the cruel reality in the form of dream by a dead narrator so as to make it seem less real might be a strategy of self-censorship. As a result, they are subversive as they tactfully disclose the cruelty of the society and challenge/condemn the irresponsible policies of the authority under the disguise of unreliability and uncertainty on the one hand, and on the other hand, making use of unreliability and uncertainty can be seen as a submissive self-censorship, or an "internalization of external censorious impulses and practices."[36]

Paralleled to the evil force represented by the blood head Ding Hui, the image of Grandpa is more interesting. As mentioned above, Grandpa, although unwillingly, is the one who actually paves the way for the villagers to sell blood. The Director of Education has tried very hard to mobilize the peasants to sell their blood by talking "at length about the past, the future, the development of a 'plasma economy' and the need for a 'strong and prosperous China,'"[37] but he has not achieved much in Ding Village. Then he thinks of the educated and respected Grandpa, who is the bell ringer of the village school but has actually taught there for many years whenever the school is in need of a teacher. He hopes that Grandpa will be able to help him because villagers will listen to what he says, but the latter is too shocked to speak anything but: "Sell blood, did you say?" "My God ... you want them to sell blood?" "But good heavens, you're asking people to sell their blood?"[38] To his questions, the Director answers: "... you're an

---

32 Yan Lianke, "Shangtian he shenghuo xuanding na ge ganshou hei'an de ren" 上天和生活選定那個感受黑暗的人 [Finding Light in China's Darkness], trans. Carlos Rojas, *The New York Times*, 23 Oct. 2014, http://www.nytimes.com/2014/10/23/opinion/Yan-Lianke-finding-light-in-chinas-darkness.html?smid=tw-share&_r=0 (last accessed 23 Oct. 2018).
33 Ibid.
34 Yan, *Faxian xiaoshuo*, 182. My translation.
35 Fan, "Yan Lianke's Forbidden Satires of China."
36 Chien-hsin Tsai 蔡建鑫, "In Sickness or in Health: Yan Lianke and the Writing of Autoimmunity," *Modern Chinese Literature and Culture* 23, no. 1 (Spring 2011): 77.
37 Yan, *Dream of Ding Village*, 26.
38 Ibid., 28.

educated man. Surely you must know that the body's blood is like a natural spring: the more you take, the more it flows."³⁹ Grandpa, when recollecting how he was nominated a model teacher and approved by the Director so he got a cash bonus and an award certificate every year, agrees to give it a try. He rings the bell and leads the villagers to the riverbed.

> When Grandpa reached the riverbed, he searched around for a moist patch of sand, rubbed it between his hands and began to dig a small hole. Before long, the hole was half-filled with water. Grandpa produced a chipped ceramic bowl and began ladling the water from the hole and pouring it on to the sand. Again and again he ladled, pouring one bowl of water after another on to the sand. Just as if it seemed that the hole had gone dry, Grandpa paused. In a matter of moments, the water began to seep in, and the hole was once again full of water …. "Did you see that?" [Grandpa] asked, glancing around at the villagers. "Water never runs dry. The more you take, the more it flows." He raised his voice. "It's the same with blood. Blood always replenishes itself. The more you take, the more it flows."⁴⁰

Then we have the above-mentioned scenes that Grandpa leads the villagers to visit Cai county. After the trip to Cai county, villagers of Ding Village are finally convinced. More importantly, Ding Hui, the son of Grandpa and father of the narrator, becomes the first blood head after he sees what happened in the riverbed and Cai county. In the novel, Grandpa, who always has a sense of guilt, eventually kills Ding Hui. The novelist means to make Grandpa to embody a sober force to counteract the shocking irrationality. From the beginning, Grandpa constantly urges his son to apologize to the villagers for selling their blood and causing the "fever disease." Interestingly, he does not consider himself the origin of blood selling, although he "sees"—remembers—it clearly in his dream. When Ding Hui keeps refusing to apologize, Grandpa mobilizes all AIDS victims to move into the village school as quarantine and volunteers to take care of them. Everything he does is an attempt to redeem his son (and himself?). In the end, Grandpa's act to end Ding Hui's life suggests the author's belief that evil will not prevail over the good. This can be read as a victory of morality that Ding Hui's father wishes to uphold over the father-son bond, an important Confucian family ethic.⁴¹ If AIDS is regarded as a moral disease implying the immoral behavior of the patients, the killing of Ding Hui by his own father is an attempt to eliminate the cause of immorality and give the reputation back to the victims of the blood economy. An ultimate hope is revealed at the end in the last dream of Grandpa, in which he sees:

> *a woman, digging in the mud with the branch of a willow tree. With each flick of the branch, each stroke of the willow she raised a small army of tiny mud people from the soil. Soon there were hundreds upon thousands of them, thousands upon millions, millions upon millions of tiny mud people leaping from the soil, dancing on the earth, blistering the plain like so many raindrops from the sky.*
>
> *Grandpa found himself gazing at a new and teeming plain.*
>
> *A new world danced before his eyes.*⁴²

---

39 Ibid.
40 Ibid., 30–31.
41 Deng Hanmei 鄧寒梅 believes that Ding Hui's father has transcended the affection between father and son when he kills his son with the "stick of justice" (*zhengyi de gunbang* 正義的棍棒). See Deng, *Zhongguo xiandangdai wenxue zhong de jibing xushi yanjiu* 中國現當代文學中的疾病敘事研究 [A study of illness narratives in modern and contemporary Chinese literature] (Nanchang: Jiangxi renmin chubanshe, 2012), 224.
42 Yan, *Dream of Ding Village*, 341. Original italics.

After the death of the old world, a freshly created new world emerges with new people dancing before the eyes of Grandpa, the representative of the positive force. Undoubtedly, such an ending brings some hope to the reader to compensate for the heaviness and darkness of the story. The woman can be related to Nüwa, the legendary Chinese goddess who created human beings. At this point, an interesting discrepancy between the original and the translation plays an important role in the understanding of the ending. While the dreams are printed in boldface and in a different font in the Chinese text, they are printed in italics in the translation. The very last one-sentence paragraph is not boldfaced in the original Chinese text but in the same font as the non-dream parts of the novel. This indicates the author's belief in the certainty that a brand-new world will be created by the legendary Nüwa. In the translation, however, this last paragraph is also italicized, treating it as part of the dream and conveying a totally different message: the new world is but a dream and the reality has no redemption. Readers of the English translation will feel an implication of the author's despair; yet the more mysterious message is hidden in the original text where the font is the same as the real parts. Does it disclose the optimistic attitude of the writer who now sees China as a curable sick man? Or is it yet another example of the author's self-censorship? Yan does admit that he intentionally self-censored when he wrote *Dream of Ding Village*:

> In a rare insight, the author told the Guardian how he attempted [to] forestall a ban by doing the censors' work for them. Out went the novel's most ambitious features: the blood pipeline, the global trade angle and direct criticism of national politics. Instead he narrowed the focus to a single village, where blood is bought and sold with horrific consequences. "This is not the book I originally wanted to write," says Yan, who has won China's top two literary awards. "I censored myself very rigorously. I didn't mention senior leaders. I reduced the scale. I thought my self-censorship was perfect."[43]

Although Yan calculated much to conduct self-censorship so he could get his book published, he was not happy about it. He also told *The Guardian* that "he still regrets self-censoring when he wrote *Dream of Ding Village*, which deals with the blood-selling scandal that led to mass HIV infections in Henan province. He wanted to ensure it was published, he said; but now his priority was reaching the highest literary standard."[44]

It is not surprising that Yan regrets the self-censorship, as no matter how perfectly he thought he had self-censored himself, including demonizing Ding Hui and putting the blame on the blood head instead of the leadership, the book survived for three days only before it was banned. His "strategic anticipation of censorship—his internalization of external censorious impulses and practices—was ineffective," in the words of Tsai Chien-hsin.[45] Ironically, the biopolitical environment is unsatisfactory not only for people in reality and fictional characters but also for the fiction per se.

---

[43] Jonathan Watts, "Censor Sees through Writer's Guile in Tale of China's Blood-Selling Scandal," *The Guardian*, 8 Oct. 2006, http://www.theguardian.com/world/2006/oct/09/books.china (last accessed 14 Aug. 2021).

[44] Tania Branigan, "Chinese Intellectuals Avoid Key Issues Amid Censorship Fears, Says Author: Award-Winning Satirist Yan Lianke Says Chinese Intellectuals and Writers Must Push Leaders to Embrace Social Reform," *The Guardian*, 6 Feb. 2013, http://www.theguardian.com/world/2013/feb/06/chinese-writers-failing-censorship-concerns (last accessed 14 Aug. 2021).

[45] Tsai, "In Sickness or in Health," 77.

Nevertheless, the reader does find his novels being more optimistic. Take the three novels of disease as an example, the ending of each story becomes increasingly positive. *Streams of Light and Time* can be read metaphorically as the efforts to prolong people's lives and can be regarded as prescriptions to heal the sick society, but the society is so incurably ill that it is beyond any redemption after all attempts failed. When it comes to *Pleasure*, the author gives the novel a little hope by healing the insanity of Chief Liu even though the character's "wholeness" is taken away by being disabled. Yet being disabled is not a bad thing in Pleasure Village, particularly when the novelist paints a rosy picture of the paradise in the last "further reading" of the novel. Finally, we see a completely fresh and new world created by the presumed goddess Nüwa dancing before Grandpa's eyes in *Dream of Ding Village*, suggesting a hopeful future.

Interestingly, in his recent novels, Yan tends to create a "good man," perhaps in the hope of maintaining a balance in the otherwise totally dark and absurd stories. Besides Grandpa in *Dream of Ding Village*, another example is the character Li Tianbao in the 2015 novel *The Day the Sun Died* (*Rixi* 日熄). In the novel, somnambulism hits a small town called Gaotian, and all people of the town are sleepwalking and doing all kinds of evil things. The sun does not rise at daybreak, and therefore people will not wake up. Eventually, Li burns himself to create an artificial sun to wake people up, and thus brings the nightmare to an end. Does the pessimistic novelist still wish to search for a good soul as a remedy for the irrational and morbid society? When comparing Grandpa with Li, the reader finds an interesting similarity: both characters are meant to be moral models for the society, but neither of them is flawless. While Grandpa is not as perfect as some critics suggest due to the fact that he actually confirms and encourages Ding Village's blood-selling business, Li used to be an informant who exposed the secrets of the families that practiced ground burial when cremation was required by the government. Their extreme behaviors, i.e., killing his own son in the case of Grandpa and sacrificing himself in the case of Li, are seen as acts of redemptions. Does this reveal the hidden hope in the author's mind even though he appears to be pessimistic by conveying such a message: people can still be decent as long as they correct the mistakes they have made in the past, and so can a society?

In the speech at the Franz Kafka Prize award ceremony, Yan claimed: "It is a writer's job to find life within this darkness."[46] In the same speech, Yan told a story of a 70-year-old blind man. Every day he would look in the direction where the sun rose and said that the sunlight was dark. This same blind man had several flashlights since he was young. When he walked at night, he always turned one on and held it in his hand. This way, other people could see him from afar and so they would not bump into him. At the same time, passersby also benefited from his bright flashlight. In order to express their gratitude, villagers brought various flashlights to his funeral when he passed away. The blind man's story inspired Yan: there is one kind of writing—the darker it is, the brighter it gets; the colder it is, the warmer it becomes. The entire meaning of its existence is to allow people to avoid darkness. Yan believes that he and his writing are like the blind man who turned on the light in the dark. The reader has every reason to believe that *Dream of Ding Village* exactly belongs to this kind of writing.

Bibliography

Branigan, Tania. "Chinese Intellectuals Avoid Key Issues Amid Censorship Fears, Says Author: Award-Winning Satirist Yan Lianke Says Chinese Intellectuals and Writers Must Push Leaders to Embrace Social Reform." *The Guardian*, 6 Feb. 2013. http://www.theguardian.com/world/2013/feb/06/chinese-writers-failing-censorship-concerns (last accessed 14 Aug. 2021).

---

46 Yan, "Shangtian he shenghuo xuanding na ge ganshou hei'an de ren."

Deng Hanmei 鄧寒梅. *Zhongguo xiandangdai wenxue zhong de jibing xushi yanjiu* 中國現當代文學中的疾病敘事研究 [A study of illness narratives in modern and contemporary Chinese literature]. Nanchang: Jiangxi renmin chubanshe, 2012.

Esposito, Roberto. *Bíos: Biopolitics and Philosophy*. Translated by Timothy Campbell. Minneapolis: University of Minnesota Press, 2008.

Fan, Jiayang. "Yan Lianke's Forbidden Satires of China." *The New Yorker*, 15 Oct. 2018. http://www.newyorker.com/magazine/2018/10/15/yan-liankes-forbidden-satires-of-china?from=singlemessage&isappinstalled=0 (last accessed 23 Oct. 2018).

Foucault, Michel. "The History of Sexuality." In *An Introduction*. Translated by Robert Hurley, Vol. 1. New York: Vintage Books, 1990.

Gao Yaojie 高耀潔. *Gaojie de linghun: Gao Yaojie huiyilu* 高潔的靈魂: 高耀潔回憶錄 [*A noble and unsullied soul: Gao Yaojie's Memoirs*]. 2008. Rev. and enlarged edn. Hong Kong: Ming Pao, 2010.

Murphy, Timothy F., and Suzanne Poirier, eds. *Writing AIDS: Gay Literature, Language, and Analysis*. New York: Columbia University Press, 1993.

Rojas, Calos. *Homesickness: Culture, Contagion, and National Transformation in Modern China*. Cambridge, MA: Harvard University Press, 2015.

Song, Weijie 宋偉杰. "Yan Lianke's Mythorealist Representation of the Country and the City." *Modern Fiction Studies* 62, no. 4 (Winter 2016): 644–58.

Sontag, Susan. *Illness as Metaphor and Aids and Its Metaphors*. New York: Anchor Books, 1990.

Sun Li 孫麗. "*Renwu zhuanfang: Zhuming zuojia Yan Lianke changtan xinzuo Dingzhuang meng*" 人物專訪: 著名作家閻連科暢談新作《丁莊夢》[Special interview: Famous writer Yan Lianke speaks of his new book *Dream of Ding Village*], Zhengyi wang 正義網. http:live.jcrb.com/html/2006/93.htm (last assessed 23 Oct. 2018).

Tsai, Chien-hsin 蔡建鑫. "In Sickness or in Health: Yan Lianke and the Writing of Autoimmunity." *Modern Chinese Literature and Culture* 23, no. 1 (Spring 2011): 77–104.

Wang Jinping 王晉平. "Chongwen xuejiang jingji he aizibing de hunluan shidai: Yi shi wei jian" 重溫血漿經濟和愛滋病的混亂時代—以史為鑑 [A review of the chaotic times of the blood economy and AIDS: Benefit from history]. *Huanqiu shibao* 環球時報 [Global Times], 31 Oct. 2008. http://www.haodf.com/zhuanjiaguandian/wangjinping_22943.htm (last accessed 28 June 2014).

Watts, Jonathan. "Censor Sees through Writer's Guile in Tale of China's Blood-Selling Scandal." *The Guardian*, 8 Oct. 2006. http://www.theguardian.com/world/2006/oct/09/books.china (last accessed 14 Aug. 2021).

Yan Lianke 閻連科. *The Day the Sun Died*. Translated by Carlos Rojas. London: Chatto & Windus, 2015.

———. *Dingzhuang meng* 丁莊夢 [*Dream of Ding Village*]. Shanghai: Shanghai wenyi chubanshe, 2006.

———. *Dream of Ding Village*. Translated by Cindy Carter. New York: Grove Press, 2009.

———. *Faxian xiaoshuo* 發現小說 Discovering Fiction. Tianjin: Nankai daxue chubanshe, 2011.

———. *Lenin's Kisses*. Translated by Carlos Rojas. New York: Grove Press, 2012.

———. "On China's State-Sponsored Amnesia." *The New York Times*. 1 Apr. 2013. http://www.nytimes.com/2013/04/02/opinion/on-chinas-state-sponsored-amnesia.html?pagewanted=all&_r=0 (last accessed 27 June 2014).

———. *Riguang liunian* 日光流年 [*Streams of Time*]. Shenyang: Chunfeng wenyi chubanshe, 2004.

———. *Rixi* 日熄 [*The Day the Sun Died*]. Taipei: Meitian chubanshe, 2015.

———. "Shangtian he shenghuo xuanding na ge ganshou hei'an de ren" 上天和生活選定那個感受黑暗的人 [Finding Light in China's Darkness]. Translated by Carlos Rojas. *The New York Times*, 23 Oct. 2014. http://www.nytimes.com/2014/10/23/opinion/Yan-Lianke-finding-light-in-chinas-darkness.html?smid=tw-share&_r=0 (last accessed 23 Oct. 2018).

———. *Shouhuo* 受活 [*Pleasure*]. Shenyang: Chunfeng wenyi chubanshe, 2004.

Yang Jisheng 楊繼繩, et al. *Tombstone: The Great Chinese Famine, 1958–1962*. New York: Farrar, Straus and Giroux, 2012.

Yuan Weijing 袁瑋婧. "Yan Lianke: Wo xiang hui dao duzhe de huaibao zhong" 閻連科: 我想回到讀者的懷抱中 [Yan Lianke: I would like to return to my readers]. *Yazhou zhoukan* 亞洲週刊 (*Asiaweek*), 20 May 2018. medium.com/@cyanyuan/閻連科-我想回到讀者的懷抱中-6a4e5e0bb922?from=singlemessage&isappinstalled=0 (last accessed 23 Oct. 2018).

13

YAN LIANKE'S NOVEL *HEART SUTRA*

The kiss of the rock and the egg

Andrea Riemenschnitter

Introduction

The original *Heart Sutra* is one of Mahāyāna Buddhism's core texts; it fulfills an important ritual role in the daily life of Buddhists, as it is recited collectively before lecture and meditation sessions to lead everyone to a deeper understanding about the impermanence and emptiness of the real world.[1] According to Yan Lianke 閻連科, his novel *Heart Sutra* (*Xinjing* 心經) is however not about the 260 characters of this popular Buddhist sutra, best known by its short, vulgarized title.[2] Rather, and quite extraordinarily, the novel sets out to explore the lives of religious believers in contemporary China.[3] It is a story reflecting on "the encounter between the inner and outer spheres of religious faith," where "the exiting saints meet with the incoming secular world," Yan explains.[4] To try to capture this special, fleeting moment when, and location where, the two spheres converge is like dilating the instant of the collision of an egg and a rock: when they "rub against each other, touch, and kiss" (4). The story succeeds in magnifying this moment by temporarily disentangling the kiss from both its fleetingness and its material precarity.

In Buddhist thought, the experience of suffering is treated as an illusion that deceptively binds the embodied mind to the senses and their perceived reality. Therefore, the mind must liberate itself from this sensual reality and its sufferings in order to experience transcendental freedom, peace, and joy. In terms of the Freudian psychoanalytical reinterpretation of Abrahamic cosmological beliefs, libidinal energy constitutes the breath of life. It steers human

---

1 Tenzin Gyatso, *Essence of the Heart Sutra: The Dalai Lama's Heart of Wisdom Teachings*, ed. and trans. Geshe Thupten Jinpa (Boston, Mass.: Wisdom Publications, 2005), 8.
2 Yan Lianke, in his Epilogue, refers to an edition with 260 characters. Yan, *Xinjing* (Hong Kong: City University of HK Press, 2020), 424. Zhang counts a total of 313, and excluding the incantation, his edition still amounts to 275 characters. See Juyan Zhang, "Avalokiteśvara in the *Heart Sutra* Is the Buddha-to-Be: Intertextual Analyses between Three Mahāyāna Texts and the Northern Āgamas," *Studies in Humanist Buddhism* 9 (2019): 267.
3 Carlos Rojas, in his preface to the novel, also observes that despite a large number of religious believers in contemporary China, fiction about faith and spiritual orientations is extremely rare. See Rojas, Preface to Yan, *Xinjing*. xvi.
4 Yan, *Xinjing*, 4. Page references are henceforth cited parenthetically in the text; all citations are my translation.

personality formation and "points the way toward a circular model of existence, wherein life and death merge into an immortal, Divine plan. Here Eros and Thanatos can be viewed as a single cosmic force, at times distinguished through terrestrial occurrences, such as physical birth and death."[5] No matter which theory one favors, the symbolism of Yan's colliding forms points toward a sphere where ecstatic elevation from mundane reality can happen—the fleetingness of the event in real time notwithstanding. Due to the privileged perspective of the female protagonist, Buddhism, with its mix of popular stories and an esoteric philosophy, occupies more narrative space than the other four officially recognized religions featured in the novel.

Structure and intertextuality

When elaborating on what he did not intend his novel to be rather than describing what he thinks it is in his postscript, Yan Lianke mimics the religious sutra's negative rhetoric. The dialectics unfolds in the argument that *Heart Sutra* would neither resemble *The Scarlet Letter* (Nathaniel Hawthorne, 1850) or *The Brothers Karamazov* (Fyodor Dostoevsky, 1879–80), nor be like *The Magician of Lublin* (Isaac Bashevis Singer, 1960) and *The Power and the Glory* (Graham Greene, 1940), and also does not copy the epic mode of *Silence* (Chinmoku, Shūsaku Endō, 1966), *Deep River* (Fukai Kawa, Shūsaku Endō, 1993), and *History of the Soul* (*Xinling shi* 心靈史, Zhang Chengzhi 張承志, 1991). Rejected as models are furthermore *The Temple of the Golden Pavilion* (Kinkaku-ji, Yukio Mishima, 1956) and *The Satanic Verses* (Salman Rushdie, 1988) on behalf of their emphasis on obsession and strangeness. Later into the postscript, the movie *Hacksaw Ridge* (D. Mel Gibson, 2016) is added to Yan's list of influential works tackling religion. Some of these works explore how, under extreme pressure or hardship, is revealed what makes human beings human and the gods divine; others observe how human beings elevate themselves to the position of the gods or a god falls from grace to become human; and some imagine how the souls of human beings and gods can meet, touch and intertwine at their tip ends. That said, Yan believes that enough has been written on such weighty topics.

What the previous writers have left for him to do is a shift of perspective to the theme's fringes, its odds and ends or, as he also puts it, its lightness, for instance, the lightness of a fleeting rubbing of shoulders between two people, or a human and a divine being as they pass by each other—the one entering and the other exiting—at the doorway of religious faith. At this moment, they may smile at each other knowingly, or remain silent, or even harbor bitter feelings while not recognizing each other (426 f.). Yan explains that for his fictional exploration of the lightness of spiritual encounters, it is not important whether the stone tumbles toward the egg on its own or somebody throws the egg in the rock's direction. Rather, his story is meant to simulate and thus help us to understand what happens in the instant of their encounter: their light touch and the ephemeral perception of other realities resulting from it—before crushing into each other.

Following its own, negative logic, none from the long list of works that the novel is not supposed to resemble is excluded from having provided inspiration. Nor does Yan deny the strong impact of the ancient religious text by the same title. On the contrary, the author draws a parallel between what he calls his "mini-novel about the bitter-sweet self-knowledge resulting from the inevitable kiss between the secular world and the gods when they meet" (428) on the one hand, and the widespread, popular understanding of, as well as confusion

---

5 Andy Solomon, "Eros-Thanatos: A Modification of Freudian Instinct Theory in the Light of Torah Teachings," *Tradition: A Journal of Orthodox Jewish Thought* 14, no. 2 (1973): 99.

about, the Buddhist *Heart Sutra* on the other hand. As mentioned before, this latter folds into the main plot as a parallel narrative universe, represented by a series of paper cuts, which produce a new legend about the birth, adolescence, and adventurous love story between the Buddha Guanyin 觀音 and Laozi 老子.

The configuration of multiple plot lines—a preliminary miniplay centering around the crucifixion of Jesus, the visual narrative of Buddha and Laozi, and two intersecting textual layers relating the protagonists' inner and outer lives—raises the question of authorship, which is also addressed explicitly by Yan. In order to do so, the author first tells the story of his original inspiration. It refers to an experience he had roughly 20 years earlier, when he, in the company of a friend, visited an ancient temple near his hometown Luoyang. The temple and its natural surroundings appeared in a golden glow emanated by the autumnal sunset. As the visitors approached the building, a soft musical tune played on traditional instruments hung in the air and a group of six monks sat in the courtyard in a peaceful, serene posture, sorting the coins and bills of the temple's donation money into little piles. The enchanted scene left a deep imprint on Yan's memory, waiting to grow into a fictional text when the time would be ripe. In his view, this friend together with another acquaintance of his, who several years later told him about a friendship game of tug of war—and not to forget the cutout artist Shang Ailan 尚愛蘭,[6] who spent one and a half years producing her visual story made of more than 200 paper cuts for the novel—are the actual authors of *Heart Sutra*.[7] Yan furthermore credits the staff of Hong Kong City University Press as co-authors, only to define his own role as that of a mediator rather than as an individual author in the modern sense. By insisting on his not being the author, he impishly hints at an otherwise conspicuously absent saint, given this idol's prominent resurgence in today's China: Confucius, who two and a half thousand years ago made a similar claim. Having been blamed for China's backwardness during most of the twentieth century, he is presently venerated as the most important traditional source of the state-sanctioned value system. Some followers even established a Confucian clergy.[8] But beyond the question of authorship, Yan's rhetoric shows no trace of Confucianism. Indeed, even this denial resonates more strongly with Mahāyāna Buddhism's philosophy of the empty self and the poststructuralist paradigm of the death of the author.[9]

Coming of age

At the novel's core is a coming-of-age narrative. It relates the first encounter with sexuality, desire, and love by a Buddhist nun and a Daoist adept. They meet as students at a fictitious university in Beijing, start dating and, after having braved many turbulences, get married. Seen from a genre-historical perspective, the plot thus seemingly fulfills all requirements of a classical European Bildungsroman.[10] Yet, upon a closer look, this structure is only an

---

6 On the artist, see Xu Mingwei et al., "Shang Ailan: Jiang Fangzhou mama, yuwen laoshi haishi zuojia?" 尚愛蘭: 蔣方舟媽媽, 語文老師還是作家? ["Shang Ailan: Mother of Jiang Fangzhou, language teacher, or writer?"], *Pengpai* 澎湃 [The Paper], 8 Nov. 2019, https://www.thepaper.cn/newsDetail_forward_4891657 (last accessed 31 July 2021).

7 Yan mentions this number (428); however, only a little more than one hundred of them went into the print edition.

8 Ruiping Fan, ed., *The Renaissance of Confucianism in Contemporary China* (Dordrecht: Springer Science & Business Media, 2011).

9 Roland Barthes, *La Mort de l'Auteur* (1967); see also Jane Gallop, *The Deaths of the Author: Reading and Writing in Time* (Durham: Duke University Press, 2011).

10 Franco Moretti, *The Way of the World: The Bildungsroman in European Culture* (London: Verso, 2000); Sarah Graham, *A History of the Bildungsroman* (Cambridge: Cambridge University Press, 2019).

empty shell: the young lovers are sexually attracted to one another but do not trespass the threshold of hand-holding and kissing, they marry for the sake of a Beijing citizenship certificate and, after many corrosive experiences, refuse to integrate with, or adapt to, either of the two intersecting social spheres surrounding them: their religious communities and Beijing's secular city life.

Shang Ailan's paper cutouts are scattered across the novel. More often than not forming separate chapters, they sometimes also appear as a supplement within the chapter. The visual narrative's mythical storyline accompanies the personality formation of adolescent female protagonist Yahui 雅慧, an 18-year-old Buddhist nun from Xining and a gifted cutout artist. Her images tell a cosmic love story between Laozi and the Buddha, which mirrors and comments on the coming-of-age experience of the nun and her beloved, the Daoist Gu Mingzheng 顧明正. Both of them are non-regular students at the religious studies center, who, for different reasons, were exceptionally admitted into its further education and research program for clerical leaders. Besides an intense learning process resulting from the stormy encounters between the two adolescents, there are other lessons taken from their interaction with the classmates, the center's Director Gong 貢, and a grey eminence demanding to be addressed as Mr. Noname 無名氏.

While the nun Xia/Liu Yahui 夏/柳雅慧[11] and the adept Gu Mingzheng experience their adolescence as epic struggles with mundane temptations and conflicting moral demands, their adventures are spiritually sublimated in Yahui's papercuts. By staging such a parallel universe, the novel contemplates the two protagonists' formation from the point of view of both, its religious determination and the clashes with social reality they suffer underway. It can be argued that the two-fold narrative not only addresses the crisis-ridden process of individual religious subject formation in contemporary Chinese society but also critically interrogates the status of religious faith in national politics. Laliberté appositely describes how religion is currently politicized by the CCP in two different ways: a negative approach that treats religious belief as a threat to social stability and therefore strives to constrain its practitioners, and a positive strategy that attempts to use certain branches of religious tradition as a source of legitimation.[12]

One of the problems with this policy is that no clear distinction between the officially approved and the non-approved forms of faith can be drawn.[13] The believers' existential condition of uncertainty regarding these blurred limes of tolerance is accentuated in the bifurcated ending of the novel. On the one hand, the government unexpectedly rounds up and detains Yahui's classmates, despite their high social status as leading representatives of the five religions. During the tumultuous scene, all the gods moreover run away together with the help of Yahui's papercuts. But on the other hand, Yahui herself and Mingzheng, who is her legal husband by then, miraculously escape this crackdown and are shown to embark on a peaceful life as urban hermits. As readers learn earlier from Yahui's first visit to an apartment

---

11 Throughout the text, she is simply addressed as Yahui and her family background is not revealed. However, in part I on p. 91, Gu addresses her as Xia Yahui, whereas in part II, on p. 228, when Yahui returns from her temple in Xining to Beijing, she is announced with the surname Liu.
12 Fong and others moreover point out that religious leaders from the nation's peripheries, including Hong Kong and Taiwan, were coopted in the CCP's efforts to propel these populations' identification with the political center. See Brian C. H. Fong, Jieh-Min Wu, and Andrew J. Nathan, eds., *China's Influence and the Centre-Periphery Tug of War in Hong Kong, Taiwan and Indo-Pacific* (London: Routledge, 2021).
13 André Laliberté, "The Politicization of Religion by the CCP: A Selective Retrieval," *Asiatische Studien-Études Asiatiques* 69, no. 1 (30 Apr. 2015): 185–211, https://doi.org/10.1515/asia-2015-0010.

that she later buys, its location in Beijing's Haidian 海淀 district used to be an execution ground for religious leaders in the Republican era (1911–49). It is not told how and why all the classmates get there, or whether all of this happens in Yahui's imagination only. The previous scene merely describes the graduation ceremony in a campus lecture hall, during which Yahui is going amiss upon being sent to her room to fetch the marriage certificate. In a magical realist manner, she encounters a divine messenger outside the hall, who summons her to the apartment, where the gods have assembled and from where she is going to witness the other students' detainment by the security forces.

Despite the two adolescents' decision formally to abandon their religious congregations and "return into secular society" (*huansu* 還俗), they are not willing to forsake their religious beliefs and personal autonomy. Inasmuch as their journey toward maturity finds a kind of success ending, the traditional plot structure of coming-of-age fiction is not literally violated. Yet, their marriage is not going to contribute to national prosperity in the way genre theory and the CCP's doctrine of patriotic socialist citizenship would demand from the couple.[14] Rather, they choose to cultivate their spiritual wellbeing independently, shielded from the institutional engulfment by politics, their religious congregations, and society at large.

The novel's final scene highlights the undecidability, precariousness, and utopian dimensions of the individual's self-cultivation outside the control of the CCP. At the same time, the protagonists' decision aligns with emergent opposition to the economic domination of working people's lives as articulated in the trend of "lying flat" (*tangping* 躺平) in China's youth culture.[15] Dissatisfied by the frantic 996 working scheme, meaning six working days per week extending from nine a.m. to nine p.m.,[16] the *tangping* youth are content with taking only occasional jobs to sustain their modest living conditions. In the social media, they explain to have realized that such employment schemes as the 996 are not, or no longer, correlated to the government's promise of upward social mobility and a happy life in exchange for hard work. Therefore, they prefer to spend their extended leisure time reading, watching movies, writing blogs, hanging out together, or staying home by themselves. Minimal exposure to consumption stimuli is part of this lifestyle. In a similar vein, Yahui and Mingzheng renounce on the career opportunities offered to them by the CCP and their religious peers, respectively. It can be deduced from the decision the two protagonists make later that they will continue to live thriftily, maybe sustaining themselves by fulfilling minor administrative tasks at the department of religious studies or publishing Yahui's papercuts while remaining independent in their spiritual quest.

Storytelling

The plot covers one year in the life of a group of religious leaders from across the country, who attend a further educational program at the Center for Religious Studies at Beijing's fictitious University of State Affairs. They represent China's ca. 350 million religious believers,

---

14 Song Mingwei 宋明煒, *Young China: National Rejuvenation and the Bildungsroman, 1900–1959*, vol. 385, Harvard East Asian Monographs (Cambridge, Mass.: Harvard University Asia Center, 2015).
15 Oiwan Lam, "'Lying down Flat' as Passive Resistance in China," Global Voices, 13 June 2021, https://globalvoices.org/2021/06/13/lying-down-flat-as-passive-resistance-in-china/ (last accessed 31 July 2021). I would like to thank William A. Callahan, who mentioned this phenomenon when we discussed the novel.
16 *SCMP* reporters, "What Is China's 996 Work Culture That Is Polarizing Its Silicon Valleys?" *South China Morning Post*, https://www.scmp.com/tech/tech-trends/article/3136510/what-996-gruelling-work-culture-polarising-chinas-silicon-valley (last accessed 8 July 2021).

among whom ca. 200 million are affiliated with the five officially acknowledged religions: Buddhism, Daoism, the two main Christian branches of Protestantism and Catholicism, and Islam. According to statistical data, these institutionally established denominations amount to 16.6%, 0.4%, 7.4%, and 1.8%, respectively, of followers, whereas unaffiliated or unofficial agnostic and folk religious practitioners make up the majority of the registered believers.[17] Judging from the popularity of spiritual content in popular culture and the social media, it can be speculated that there is a much larger segment of latent, unregistered religious believers.[18] During the students' first semester at the University of State Affairs, the narrative reveals competition and occasional tension between the different religious groups but with time an ecumenical spirit of friendship, mutual support, and solidarity develops.

Entanglements between the religious and political spheres are accentuated on various planes throughout the novel. On the institutional level, the center of religious studies acts as the CCP's mouthpiece. Ideological submission to the Party line clearly stands out as the school's most important educational trajectory. The enrolled monks and nuns, priests, and imams (their age ranging from the youngest, 18-year-old Buddhist nun to an octogenarian Daoist abbot) are offered a variety of courses on the doctrines of the different congregations, but the exams are invariably concerned with the dominant role of CCP ideology. Moreover, the slogans decorating the walls of the center's dining hall spell out a clear message: "All religions must serve the people!"; "The relationship between the different religions represents a new kind of socialist relationship!"; "Buddha nature is Party nature, the glory of the Buddha is the glory of the Party"; or "The Great Unity of the religions is the Great Harmony of society" (131).

Storytelling plays an important role throughout the novel. It sometimes functions as a benevolent guide to spiritual enlightenment, while on other occasions, it becomes a tool for manipulation and delusion. Walter Benjamin, in his essay on storytelling, commented on the former category deploring the decline of the important social function of storytelling after the First World War. He claimed that societies continue to be in need for the storytellers' wisdom and the sacredness of good stories under the condition of floods of short-lived information produced in the mass media. Bound to death, memory and eyewitness experience, a sacred story thwarts the numbing effect of the information age while enabling community-building gestures such as listening, sharing, and transmitting.[19] In a similar vein, *Heart Sutra*'s sacred stories propel moral guidance, are imbued with ancient wisdom and appear in a panoply of vernacular, literary, and artistic forms comprising drama, legends, and folklore art comprising paper cuts and one popular opera song. On the other end of the spectrum, deceitful storytelling tends to cater to ad hoc purposes and mobilizes harmful affective energies. Two examples shall demonstrate the range of storytelling affordances played out in the novel.

The cover of the book's print edition comprises a short epigraph declaring its trajectory: "A story about the relationship between people and gods, the relationship between people, and the relationship between gods." A short play precedes the main narrative, cutting across and

---

[17] Eleanor Albert and Lindsay Maizland, "The State of Religion in China," Council on Foreign Relations, 25 Sep. 2020, https://www.cfr.org/backgrounder/religion-china (last accessed 31 July 2021). See also Sarah Cook, *The Battle for China's Spirit: Religious Revival, Repression, and Resistance under Xi Jinping* (Washington: Freedom House, 2017).

[18] See, for instance, some songs by the band "Haigui xiansheng" 海龜先生 [Mr. Sea Turtle], https://www.youtube.com/watch?v=ZowiFJh9njo; https://www.youtube.com/watch?v=ZdpSU2PwQCo. For this reference, I am indebted to Axel Schneider, who alerted me to the musicians' spiritual orientation.

[19] Walter Benjamin, *The Storyteller: Essays* (New York: New York Review of Books, 2019), 61–84.

connecting the three different categories of relationships mentioned on the cover: crucified Jesus suffers in death agony, while the Buddha, a human-embodied Dao, Holy Mary, and Mohammed arrive on the scene and offer advice, each from the point of view of their particular religion's doctrine. Buddha encourages him to step down, Dao offers to assist him in climbing even higher, Mary entreats him to put an end to his suffering presumably by means of a miracle, and Mohammed muses whether humankind wouldn't have been better off if Jesus had not accepted the ordeal. In response, Jesus points out that the purpose of his crucifixion is for every human being to understand that as humans, they inevitably must endure suffering. The conversation among the five divine representatives is interrupted by a group of human passersby who invite them to drink until everyone gets tipsy. With its grotesque plot, the miniplay not only anticipates how the three relationship categories will intersect in the main narrative, but moreover prepares the stage for the dialectics unfolding between religion and politics in the plot's contemporary Beijing. It does so by harking back to history: more than halfway through the story, the echo of the Roman imperial regime's trial resulting in the (non-)commandment to execute the Jewish rebel named Jesus Christ will resound in the suicide of an imprisoned protestant protagonist. Furthermore, the cosmic messengers' spiritual unity in diversity anticipates the novel's theme of friendship and respect among the different religious groups. Finally, the seemingly indifferent attitude of the passersby hints at a people's limited range of cultural articulation under an oppressive regime. Their drinking and merrymaking is thus an exemplary case for saturated meanings shrouded in interpretive silence—it can be understood as either a gesture of resignation, or a Dionysian counter-ritual, or carnivalesque laughter. But no matter whether its ambiguity leans more toward resistance or accommodation at any given moment, it is highly unlikely that the subversive aspects of the performed act can ever be controlled completely by a ruling power.[20]

Whereas the play observes the different attitudes of the characters, ranging from the state of exception's quintessential *homo sacer* to a deceptively detached crowd of spectators, its deterritorialized core story remains opaque while acquiring new elements in addition to the old gospel. As Giorgio Agamben recently observed, "the trial of Jesus is … one of the key moments of human history, in which eternity has crossed into history at a decisive point. All the more urgent, then, is the task of understanding how and why this crossing between the temporal and the eternal and between the divine and the human assumed precisely the form of a *krisis*, that is, of a juridical trial."[21] Jesus, who was put on trial but not judged, and finally abandoned by state power to face his death sentence "spoken" by a mob, has a human avatar in the novel. The protestant pastor Wang Changping will, however, not be exposed publicly, has no enemies except the impenetrable state apparatus, and commits suicide in prison. Arguably, he emerges as a symbol of modern history's doomed aspiration to redeem the people's hope for salvation by means of justice. The chapter relating an ecumenical memorial service for the deceased pastor enumerates several details hinting at the biblical, non-sacrificial sacredness of his death, among them a returned letter addressed to Jesus and Holy Mary. The letter, which must have been written before his detention, underscores both his premonition and his fate's radical otherness in relation to the way of the world at large, and justice in particular (345–52).

Benjamin's dictum of the sacredness of stories is willfully perverted in our example for the other, deceptive kind, when the most mysterious figure among the protagonists cunningly

---

20 Robert P. Weller, *Resistance, Chaos and Control in China: Taiping Rebels, Taiwanese Ghosts and Tiananmen* (Seattle: University of Washington Press, 1994), 3–29.
21 Giorgio Agamben, *Pilate and Jesus (Meridian: Crossing Aesthetics)*, trans. Adam Kotsko (Stanford: Stanford University Press, 2015), 2.

rehearses the importance of storytelling in order to lure 23-year old Gu Mingzheng onto a treacherous trail.[22] These are his words of wisdom: "Just take it as an opportunity to listen to a story …. Don't your religions all depend on stories so that they can have gods? Simply put, religious faith is made of faith stories. The world is governed by stories. Man only lives in the world so as to create stories." (195) This siren song of an advice is offered by retired PLA general Mr. Noname to Mingzheng, who has been brought up by the temple community as an orphan, but later learns that his biological father is from Beijing and may still be alive. Hoping to find a powerful patron for himself and his temple, he starts actively searching for him. Mingzheng is about to give up his quest when learning that his father is alive but sick and penniless, but then is encouraged by Mr. Noname to continue and seek an answer to the question of why he was abandoned as an infant. The old man poses as his mentor but is absent from the moment onward when Mingzheng returns from the visit of his destitute father and, in consequence, experiences a deep crisis.[23]

In contrast with Mr. Noname's exploitation of, and the government's suspicious attitude toward religious believers and their institutions, the relationship between the different gods is depicted as one of mutual recognition. On the level of the grassroots, the interaction between the human followers of the different spiritual traditions shows them to have much in common but also to be torn apart occasionally due to individual weaknesses and vulnerability. Still in the process of their personality formation, Yahui and Mingzheng repeatedly experience moral defeat, for example, when confronted with their bodies' sexual awakening or with culinary appetites that are taboo for them as monastic adepts. Yahui, despite feeling ashamed, cannot resist one or maybe even several secret meals of meat buns, and moreover, innocently enjoys flaunting her youthful beauty. Exchanging her monastic robe for pretty street clothes, she behaves like any secular girl when accepting Mingzheng's invitations to eat out or go to the zoo. However, their relationship is kept chaste even as her boyfriend, in a moment of uncontrolled arousal, sexually besieges Yahui in front of her dying mentor, Abbess Yuhui 玉慧. At the very last minute, Yuhui intervenes with a sigh and sharp admonishment from her deathbed. Although she successfully puts an end to Mingzheng's improper behavior, she will no longer be alive to protect Yahui from being knocked unconscious with drugs and raped by the old PLA retiree a few months later. Yet, the various crises and moral transgressions notwithstanding, the initial scene's utopian rays of light, where the divine messengers convene underneath the crucifix to consult with each other in their mission of saving humankind, accompany the narrative to its dystopian end, when the gods realize that they have forgotten how to save the world and withdraw. Yan's art of storytelling culminates in this conundrum: while the gods cannot remember, their human disciples compose a new gospel built from fragments of the different old ones: Yahui re-imagines Buddha and Laozi as lovers, Wang Changping follows in the footsteps of Jesus, and a Muslim Qin opera singer performs the funeral music for the protestant homo sacer.[24]

---

22 On the unabated, "brutally effective" social impact of basic types of storytelling in the contexts of populism and other forms of authoritarian delusion, see Ying Zhu, "Letter from the Editor," *Global Storytelling: Journal of Digital and Moving Images* 1, no. 1 (16 July 2021), https://doi.org/10.3998/gs.791. In the present context, Mr. Noname attempts to harness the young man's desire for a glorious (family) origin to his own scheme of building a network of religious leaders controlled by himself.
23 Yan, *Xinjing*, Part II, Preface no. 3, 182–214.
24 This song from the Qinqiang 秦腔 opera "Zhan Dan Tong" 斬單童 [Beheading Dan Tong] is first performed by the singer right after Wang's detention (278), and then again on the occasion of the funerary ceremony (350). For the text of the opera song, see https://twgreatdaily.com/zh/Wsu0yGwBJleJMoPMCVkj.amp.

Tug of war

In addition to the classroom activities Director Gong, the head of the center, insists on everyone to take part regularly in the center's tug of war games as either competitor or spectator. He is about to publish a book on the benevolent effects of the games on fostering a harmonious relationship between the different religions through friendship and reconciliation. Besides the project's intrinsic noble humanism, he expects his book to help him raise funds for a large-scale investment project, which is supposed to raise the institutional status of the center and, in this way, shall propel his personal career promotion. In the course of events, the center's tug of war games will take different shapes, functioning successively as health-threatening sports exercise, slapstick comedy, interreligious competition, and fundraising spectacle. In addition to the official exercises, a private game of tug of war is acted out between a Muslim contender and Yahui.

A popular game across the globe since ancient times, tug of war is documented as early as in a Tang-dynasty text, The *Notes of Feng* (*Feng shi wenjian ji* 封氏聞見記). The compendium describes the game as a part of the military training in the Spring and Autumn period (eighth to fifth century BE) and mentions the Xuanzong 玄宗 Emperor's (685–762) fondness of rope-pulling spectacles as entertainment.[25] Since then, tug of war became also linked to religious and ritual contexts and is still practiced today during seasonal festivals by some ethnic minorities in China.[26] A less edifying symbolic encoding of the game relates it to China's great-power aspirations on the political stage. The "center-periphery tug of war" the CCP has launched since the country's admission to international institutions such as the WTO and WHO was a game-changer, argue Fong, Wu, and Nathan.[27] Analyzing the major instruments and techniques of global influence employed so far, their edited book singles out the CCP's target agencies, among them international political and economic stakeholders, the information media and entertainment industries, and leaders of religious communities. The authors argue that China's heightened pressure on dissenting groups to submit to its sovereignty claims and jurisdiction is prone concomitantly to raise the extent and intensity of resistance. In this tug of war configuration between the mainland Chinese center and its peripheries, religious affiliations play a major part that has hitherto been under-researched, as Ying-ho Kwong observes.[28] The book's contributors shrewdly evaluate the growing influence of the CCP on religious and political authorities beyond the country's geographical borders. However, in view of how religious leaders are coopted into the inner circles of political power and vice versa in the novel, their research, including the symbolic encoding of tug of war, also provides an interpretive framework for the politics of religion within China.

---

25 Feng Yan 封演, "Bahe" 拔河 ["Tug of war"], in his *Feng shi wenjian ji*, juan 6, https://ctext.org/wiki.pl?if=gb&chapter=40115&remap=gb#%E6%8B%94%E6%B2%B3; Feng Yan, *Feng shi wenjian ji jiaozheng* 封氏聞見記校證 [*Miscellaneous notes of Feng Yen*], ed. Zhao Zhenxin 趙貞信, Harvard-Yenching Institute Sinological Index Series, supplement no. 7 (Taipei: Chinese Materials and Research Aids Service Center, 1966).

26 Ping Jie 平杰 and Yang Deming 楊德明, *Bahe Shiyong Jiaocheng* 拔河實用教程 [A Practical Tutorial of Tug of War Games] (Shanghai: Shanghai Lexicon Press, 2019); Shen Jiarong 沈嘉榮 and Shen Shan 沈杉, eds, *Zhongguo Lao Youxi* 中國老遊戲 [Ancient Chinese Games] (Beijing: Beijing Book Co. Inc., 2020), 198 f. There is also an entry on paper cutouts, see p. 8 f. On minority tug of war games see Zhang Tao 張濤, *Zhongguo Shaoshu Minzu Tiyu* 中國少數民族體育 [The Sports Activities of China's Ethnic Minorities] (Beijing: China Intercontinental Press, 2007), 5-14 and 100-107. My thanks to Helena Wu for tracing Zhang's book.

27 Fong, Wu, and Nathan, 3.

28 Ying-ho Kwong, "China's Influence on Hong Kong's Religions: Interreligious Comparison," in Fong, Wu, and Nathan, 157.

That tug of war as a leitmotif is lucidly laid out in the opening of the novel's first chapter, where Yahui muses on the Buddhist belief in fate and the confusion resulting from Director Gong's arrangement of tug of war games between five teams, each constituted by members of one singular religious affiliation:

Buddhists very much believe in fate, just like the Boddhisattva has faith in her fingers.[29]

But Yahui suspects that the affairs of the world aren't always determined by fate. For example, tug of war: the world of dust assumes that there are winners and losers just like there is black and white. But if it is tug of war between two religions, there is no clear distinction between black and white, or winner and loser. If there is a life-and-death competition between the Buddhist, Daoist, Protestant and Catholic teams— and not to forget the Muslims of the north-western provinces Ningxia and Gansu: who is the winner, who the loser? How could the outcome possibly be treated as determined by fate! (7)

Yahui then shifts her contemplation to the cycle of the four seasons and the different gods who are responsible for their regular coming and going. There can be a lot of confusion in this, too, she thinks, in case the gods lock up spring and autumn in hell and send winter and summer into a life-and-death battle. What if there were only alternating periods of extreme heat and cold, or if either of them even won a total victory over the other? Her doubts about the games are not just empty speculation. A flashback tells how Yahui's teacher, Abbess Yuhui, collapsed during one of the games. From her sickbed, she submitted several requests to Director Gong to end the games. Because they all went unnoticed, she later instructs Yahui to continue urging him and her classmates to abolish the competitions on her behalf. As the students gradually lose interest, Director Gong introduces monetary awards for the winners. From then on, the five teams become more and more engrossed in the game, to the point that a fundraising sportsbook is established, which generates an income of roughly one million *yuan*.

Because she needs to borrow money to buy her desired apartment, Yahui reluctantly allows herself to be drawn into a private competition for a loan based on the sportsbook funds by a Muslim woman, Ruan Zhisu 阮枝素. Not enthusiastic from the start, Yahui turns even more unwilling when Ruan announces it to be a spiritual power competition between Allah and Buddha. It quickly becomes apparent that the competition cannot end peacefully. Therefore, Yahui repeatedly requests to be qualified as the loser, not in the name of the Buddha, but as Buddha's unworthy disciple. Supported by a growing number of spectators, Ruan however insists on the game's continuation until Mingzheng arrives at the scene and volunteers to replace injured Yahui at the rope. At this instant, Ruan's husband intervenes by slapping his wife in the face, announcing that it is not Allah, but her husband punishing her (279–301). In this way, the most tension-ridden game of the novel ends drawn, but with Yahui, Mingzheng, and Ruan's husband emerging as equivocal spiritual winners. Tug of war, it may be concluded, functions as a catalyst of the emotional tensions circulating within and among the protagonists. These comprise Abbess Yuhui's abhorrence of the ignited agitation as such, Ruan's temporary religious fanaticism, and the Daoist team's humorous merrymaking by suddenly letting go of the rope on one occasion—not to forget the monetary reward system's arousal of unbefitting greed for material gains.

29 Kelsey Ables, "The Complex Meanings behind Hand Gestures in Buddhist Art," Artsy, 28 Mar. 2019, https://www.artsy.net/article/artsy-editorial-complex-meanings-hand-gestures-buddhist-art (last accessed 31 July 2021).

Sovereignty

If the rope used in the tug of war games symbolically binds the competitors to their earthly existence, and the different religions' sacred stories help believers to overcome their illusions and attachments, then political power, by claiming sovereignty over the clerical authorities, in various situations restricts, contests, and even violently denies the protagonists' freedom to act in accordance with their religious principles. The CCP representative Mr. Noname's anachronistic, obscene enactment of state sovereignty, abusing the ruling elite's legal immunity when turning his rape of Yahui into a cruelly perverted sacrificial ritual, flags up the desirability of an antinomian position, occupied in the novel by religion as the domain of the grass roots' spiritual autonomy. Sacred sovereignty thus transcends worldly power, postulating that everyone should be equally free to believe in a higher principle of justice and truth beyond the secular state.[30] It could also be argued that what looms behind the religious mask is a concept of popular sovereignty as, for example, defined by the Universal Declaration of Human Rights and by John Stuart Mill's famous dictum: "[O]ver himself, over his own body and mind, the individual is sovereign."[31] For lack of legal protection, Yahui and Mingzheng are driven to reclaim their personal sovereignty in a frightful way. As in Yan's earlier novel *Lenin's Kisses* (*Shouhuo* 受活),[32] the escape route chosen by Yahui and Mingzheng is self-mutilation. Their decision to disable their sexual organs highlights the libidinal rather than revolutionary encodings of the capitalist reform era.

While power in their case assaults both their bodies and minds, resistance to ideological domination can be observed even in the least combative confrontation between states and religious communities, argues Weller. It is embedded in certain, usually saturated rituals or symbols, and happens to be played out in precipitated interpretations whenever accommodation ceases to be a workable option. Quiet cultural resistance can thus turn into rebellion, as was the case with the Taiping or, to a lesser degree, the Tiananmen protests.[33] The novel's final scene alludes to such moments in China's recent history, but the protagonists' own resistance takes less radical or unified forms. From the students' deliberations on how (not) to answer those exam questions that threaten to compromise their religious loyalties to Wang Changping's suicide, their quest for "free space for resistance under socialism"[34] remains confined to individual choices.

Mingzheng, who wishes to track down his ancestors because he imagines them as revolutionary heroes, skips a compulsory lecture to be held by Mr. Noname in order to gain access to Babaoshan 八寶山 Revolutionary Cemetery. Upon his arrival, he learns that this monument of the Chinese revolution's heroes is not open to ordinary visitors. To work around the regulation, he stays longer than planned and clandestinely follows a group of school children into the compound. His search ends without any result like his next adventure, in which he follows Mr. Noname's arrangement to meet several candidates who are willing to

---

30 Robert A. Yelle, *Sovereignty and the Sacred: Secularism and the Political Economy of Religion* (Chicago: University of Chicago Press, 2018).
31 See "Universal Declaration of Human Rights," https://www.un.org/en/about-us/universal-declaration-of-human-rights (last accessed 14 Aug. 2021); also W. Michael Reisman, "Sovereignty and Human Rights in Contemporary International Law," *American Journal of International Law* 84, no. 4 (Oct. 1990): 867, https://doi.org/10.2307/2202838; John Stuart Mill, *On Liberty* (Kitchener: Batoche Books, 2001), 13.
32 Yan Lianke, *Shouhuo* (Beijing: Beijing shiyue wenyi chubanshe, 2009); Carlos Rojas, trans., *Lenin's Kisses* (New York: Grove Press, 2013).
33 Robert P. Weller, *Resistance, Chaos and Control in China: Taiping Rebels, Taiwanese Ghosts and Tiananmen* (Seattle: University of Washington Press, 1994).
34 Ibid., 29.

acknowledge him as their son. This brings Mingzheng to the Friendship Hotel, a historical monument where Mao Zedong and other revolutionary heroes used to receive foreign guests. He is supposed to meet a cadre who, he is made to hope, could be his father, but the man does not show up for the appointment. After a few more of such failed meetings, Mingzheng visits his biological father. He is so disgusted by the sight of the man's miserable life that he decides symbolically to dissever their blood ties by castrating himself. His earlier moral transgression at the Lama Temple Hospital may play a role, too, but the narrative does not discuss his motivation. The gruesome act leads to long hospitalization and Mingzheng's renunciation on both, his envisioned political career as a Daoist functionary and a secular future.

Yahui follows a similar path leading her from an innocent, youthful approach to her social environment to the ruination of her bodily integrity. Upon the death of the Xining temple's abbess, she is instructed by Director Gong to conceal the circumstances, including the corpse's cremation that is carried out without observation of the Buddhist funerary rites. In exchange for her silence, she is offered the position as Yuhui's successor, a substantial career boost at her young age, she is told. But Yahui returns to the Center after the winter break, telling Director Gong that her temple collapsed in the wake of heavy snowstorms, that there is no money to reconstruct it, and that she has nowhere else to go. Because Mingzheng is still on sick leave, she temporarily replaces him at the Center's office as Director Gong's secretary. When she accepts to "have a chat" with Mr. Noname, who promises to help her with the real estate acquisition, she has a vague idea about what he wants from her. The way the "transaction" happens in the hotel room is however unexpected and traumatizing. Drugged, knocked unconscious, and raped, she wakes up in terrible pain, unable to cope with her desecrated body. When being summoned for the next date with her rapist, she runs to her room instead and uses acid to vitriolize her sexual organs.

Besides the bodily consequences of their self-mutilation, the two protagonists render themselves inaccessible to Mr. Noname's power gambit. Though not challenging the system as a whole, their act of resistance implies that only such a radical gesture as sexual self-mutilation can buy them the freedom to escape the encroachment of politics, by means of pawning their bodies, on their spiritual life. The monstrous details of this liberation insinuate the grave social problems the regime's intolerance vis-à-vis cultural difference and alternative interpretive communities can create.

Conclusion

Similar observations were made by Sarah Cook, the author of a 2017 report on the religious revival, repression, and resistance under the Xi Jinping leadership: "The party's rigid constraints render it impossible for state-sanctioned institutions to meet the growing demand for religion in Chinese society. The result is an enormous black market, forcing many believers, from Taoists and Protestants to Tibetan Buddhists, to operate outside the law and to view the regime as unreasonable, unjust, or illegitimate."[35] Her report lists excessively repressive measures that however appear to yield the reverse effect, namely, a rapidly growing unofficial and extralegal space of religious practice. Its adherents' interpretive resistance can take many different forms, among them the refusal to engage with official campaigns, performative overenthusiasm, or the ironic subversion of authoritarian language. Naturally, religion is only one of several domains where storytelling escapes the control of the orthodoxy and can be mobilized for resistance,

---

35 Cook, *The Battle for China's Spirit*. See also https://freedomhouse.org/article/new-report-battle-chinas-spirit-religious-revival-repression-and-resistance-under-xi (last accessed 14 Aug. 2021).

but arguably it can be even more effective than literature. Weller explains: "The potential to develop organized and explicit resistance clearly lies within the multiple possibilities of these ironies, ambiguities, and refusals to interpret. The key questions for resistance lie less in finding some deeper level of meaning, than in understanding the chances for forging that critical combination of institution and interpretation that might support an active movement. The Taiping succeeded in this project, Taiwanese ghosts will probably never manage it, and Tiananmen was crushed before the process went very far."[36] In hindsight, he may have underestimated the role of Taiwanese religious practice in the process of the island's democratic reforms, but this does not disprove or devalue his argument. Yet, there is both, power and weakness in the dissemination of indeterminate meanings. Whatever resistant enunciation actively evades a clear message risks to trail off ineffectively. That said, it also seems clear that as long as the CCP's claims about good governance are undermined by its repressive violence and imposed silence, the affectively and symbolically saturated doxa of religious groups cannot but be perceived as a menace to its orthodoxy and, in the long run, social stability.

Yan wrote *Heart Sutra* during his time as IAS Sin Wai Kin Professor of Chinese Culture at the Hong Kong University of Science and Technology in the years of 2017 and 2018. The book is banned in mainland China, like several others from his pen. These novels are calls never to forget the dark moments in modern China's history, so as not to repeat the mistakes made in the past. On 21 Feb. 2020, when Yan offered a digital lecture on the Covid-19 pandemic, he warned about "triumphal songs" threatening to drown the mourning voices even before the victims are properly buried and while investigations into the extent of the global catastrophe have only just begun. This is the way of forgetfulness, he said, which ensures the return of the same kind of tragedies and disasters to haunt humankind in the future. The striking similarity between the 2002–04 SARS outbreak and Covid-19 makes them look like works by the same theater director. To prevent history from becoming "a collection of legends, of lost and imagined stories, that are baseless and unfounded," the students of his creative writing class should dedicate their lives to write, unearth the truth buried in deceptive stories, and make sure that memories are neither revised nor erased. There may be restrictions as to how truth can be spoken, yet the task of the storyteller is not to give up searching for ways to pass his or her memories on to future generations: "If we can't speak out loudly, then let us be whisperers. If we can't be whisperers, then let us be silent people who have memories."[37] In his speech, Yan referred to his previous novels addressing the Great Leap forward, the Cultural Revolution, the AIDS outbreak in Henan villages in the wake of a large-scale blood-selling campaign, and other human-induced tragedies. Among the "silent people who have memories" are the main protagonists of *Heart Sutra*, who were brought up as orphans and will not have offspring but are committed to preserving their higher principles and memories, even after the gods have forgotten and left the world. *Heart Sutra* may not belong to the kind of good stories Xi Jinping is currently asking his subjects to tell the world about China.[38] However, together with the religions it features, the novel will find eager

---

36 Weller, 219.
37 Yan, "Yan Lianke: What Happens after Coronavirus? On Community Memory and Repeating Our Own Mistakes," Literary Hub, 11 Mar. 2020, https://lithub.com/yan-lianke-what-happens-after-coronavirus/ (last accessed 31 July 2021).
38 David Der-wei Wang 王德威, *Why Fiction Matters in Contemporary China* (Waltham: Brandeis University Press, 2020). 1–2; David Bandurski, "Seeking China's New Narratives—China Media Project," China Media Project, 16 July 2021, https://chinamediaproject.org/2021/07/16/seeking-chinas-new-narratives/ (last accessed 31 July 2021).

audiences—and with a high degree of probability live longer than the ideology that is presently attempting to control them.

Bibliography

Ables, Kelsey. "The Complex Meanings behind Hand Gestures in Buddhist Art." Artsy, 28 Mar. 28, 2019. https://www.artsy.net/article/artsy-editorial-complex-meanings-hand-gestures-buddhist-art (last accessed 31 July 2021).

Agamben, Giorgio. *Pilate and Jesus (Meridian: Crossing Aesthetics)*. Translated by Adam Kotsko. Stanford: Stanford University Press, 2015.

Albert, Eleanor, and Lindsay Maizland. "The State of Religion in China." Council on Foreign Relations, 25 Sep. 2020. https://www.cfr.org/backgrounder/religion-china (last accessed 31 July 2021).

Bandurski, David. "Seeking China's New Narratives—China Media Project." China Media Project, 16 July 2021. https://chinamediaproject.org/2021/07/16/seeking-chinas-new-narratives/ (last accessed 31 July 2021).

Benjamin, Walter. *The Storyteller: Essays*. New York: New York Review of Books, 2019.

Cook, Sarah. *The Battle for China's Spirit: Religious Revival, Repression, and Resistance under Xi Jinping*. Washington: Freedom House, 2017.

Fan, Ruiping, ed. *The Renaissance of Confucianism in Contemporary China*. Dordrecht: Springer Science & Business Media, 2011.

Feng Yan 封演. *Fengshi wenjian ji jiaozheng* 封氏聞見記校證 [*Miscellaneous notes of Feng Yen*]. Edited by Zhao Zhenxin 趙貞信. Harvard-Yenching Institute Sinological Index Series. Supplement no. 7. Taipei: Chinese Materials and Research Aids Service Center, 1966.

Fong, Brian C. H., Jieh-Min Wu, and Andrew J. Nathan, eds. *China's Influence and the Centre-Periphery Tug of War in Hong Kong, Taiwan and Indo-Pacific*. London: Routledge, 2021.

Graham, Sarah. *A History of the Bildungsroman*. Cambridge: Cambridge University Press, 2019.

Gyatso, Tenzin. *Essence of the Heart Sutra: The Dalai Lama's Heart of Wisdom Teachings*. Edited and translated by Geshe Thupten Jinpa. Boston: Wisdom Publications, 2005.

Laliberté, André. "The Politicization of Religion by the CCP: A Selective Retrieval." *Asiatische Studien—Études Asiatiques* 69, no. 1 (30 Apr. 2015): 185–211. https://doi.org/10.1515/asia-2015-0010.

Lam, Oiwan. "'Lying down Flat' as Passive Resistance in China." Global Voices, 13 June 2021. https://globalvoices.org/2021/06/13/lying-down-flat-as-passive-resistance-in-china/ (last accessed 31 July 2021).

Mill, John Stuart. *On Liberty*. Kitchener: Batoche Books, 2001.

Moretti, Franco. *The Way of the World: The Bildungsroman in European Culture*. London: Verso, 2000.

Ping Jie 平杰 and Yang Deming 楊德明. *Bahe Shiyong Jiaocheng* 拔河實用教程 [*A Practical Tutorial of Tug of War Games*]. Shanghai: Shanghai Lexicon Press, 2019.

Reisman, W. Michael. "Sovereignty and Human Rights in Contemporary International Law." *American Journal of International Law* 84, no. 4 (Oct. 1990): 866–76. https://doi.org/10.2307/2202838.

Shen Jiarong 沈嘉榮 and Shen Shan 杉, eds. *Zhongguo Lao Youxi* 中國老遊戲 [*Ancient Chinese Games*]. Beijing: Beijing Book Co. Inc., 2020.

"What Is China's 996 Work Culture That Is Polarizing Its Silicon Valleys?" *South China Morning Post*, 9 June 2021. https://www.scmp.com/tech/tech-trends/article/3136510/what-996-gruelling-work-culture-polarising-chinas-silicon-valley (last accessed 8 July 2021).

Solomon, Andy. "Eros-Thanatos: A Modification of Freudian Instinct Theory in the Light of Torah Teachings." *Tradition: A Journal of Orthodox Jewish Thought* 14, no. 2 (1973): 90–102.

Song, Mingwei 宋明煒. *Young China: National Rejuvenation and the Bildungsroman, 1900–1959*. Vol. 385. Harvard East Asian Monographs. Cambridge: Harvard University Asia Center, 2015.

South China Morning Post Reporters. "What Is China's 996 Work Culture That Is Polarizing Its Silicon Valleys?" *South China Morning Post*, 9 June 2021. https://www.scmp.com/tech/tech-trends/article/3136510/what-996-gruellingwork-culture-polarising-chinas-silicon-valley (last accessed 8 July 2021).

Wang, David Der-wei 王德威. *Why Fiction Matters in Contemporary China*. Waltham: Brandeis University Press, 2020.

Weller, Robert P. *Resistance, Chaos and Control in China: Taiping Rebels, Taiwanese Ghosts and Tiananmen*. Seattle: University of Washington Press, 1994.

Xu Mingwei 徐明徽, et al. "Shang Ailan: Jiang Fangzhou mama, yuwen laoshi haishi zuojia?" 尚愛蘭: 蔣方舟媽媽, 語文老師還是作家? ["Shang Ailan: Mother of Jiang Fangzhou, language teacher, or writer?"]. *Pengpai* 澎湃 (The Paper), 8 Nov. 2019. https://www.thepaper.cn/newsDetail_forward_4891657 (last accessed 31 July 2021).

Yan Lianke 閻連科. *Lenin's Kisses*. Translated by Carlos Rojas. New York: Grove Press, 2013.

———. *Shouhuo* 受活 [*Lenin's Kisses*]. Beijing: Beijing shiyue wenyi chubanshe, 2009.

———. *Xinjing* 心經 [*Heart Sutra*]. Hong Kong: City University of Hong Kong Press, 2020.

———. "Yan Lianke: What Happens after Coronavirus? On Community Memory and Repeating Our Own Mistakes." Literary Hub, 11 Mar. 2020. https://lithub.com/yan-lianke-what-happens-after-coronavirus/ (last accessed 31 July 2021).

Yelle, Robert A. *Sovereignty and the Sacred: Secularism and the Political Economy of Religion*. Chicago: University of Chicago Press, 2018.

Zhang, Juyan. "Avalokiteśvara in the *Heart Sutra* Is the Buddha-to-Be: Intertextual Analyses between Three Mahāyāna Texts and the Northern Āgamas." *Studies in Humanist Buddhism* 9 (2019): 259–98.

Zhang Tao 張濤. *Zhongguo Shaoshu Minzu Tiyu* 中國少數民族體育 [The Sports Activities of China's Ethnic Minorities]. Beijing: China Intercontinental Press, 2007.

Zhu, Ying. "Letter from the Editor." *Global Storytelling: Journal of Digital and Moving Images* 1, no. 1 (16 July 2021). https://doi.org/10.3998/gs.791

14

THE REDEMPTION OF THE PEACH BLOSSOM SPRING

An examination of the human condition in Yan Lianke's *Zhongyuan* (*Zhongguo gushi*)[1]

Di-kai Chao and Riccardo Moratto

Introduction

Yan Lianke's 閻連科 works are often known for their magic realism and absurdity. His characters are always tough, serious, and death-defying vis-à-vis nature and the countryside, history and trauma, politics and violence. In recent years, however, it seems that Yan's work has become more adept at dealing with more abstract and "inward" issues such as spirituality and the human heart. In *Lenin's Kisses* (*Shouhuo* 受活), *The Explosion Chronicles* (*Zhalie zhi* 炸裂志), *Streams of Time* (*Riguang liunian* 日光流年), and *The Four Books* (*Si shu* 四書), the themes of capitalism and social conflicts, historical violence, and trauma all involve a grand narrative. With his novel *Heart Sutra* (*Xinjing* 心經), Yan begins to show a new attitude of "overcoming the strong by applying soft methods and conquering the unyielding with the yielding" (*yi rou ke gang, yi qing wei zhong de zitai* 以柔克剛、以輕為重的姿態).[2] In fact, from *The Day the Sun Died* (*Rixi* 日熄) onwards, Yan discusses the phenomenon according to which

---

1 *Zhongyuan* (中原, in English *Central Plains*) is Yan Lianke's most recent literary creation. This chapter was finalized and delivered to the publisher for printing on 25 December 2021]. *Zhongyuan* was first published in March 2021 in the second issue of the Chinese literary journal *Flower City* (花城 *Huacheng*). The same was later published on October 30, 2021 in a book form by Rye Field Publishing Co. (*Maitian chubanshe* 麥田出版社) in Taiwan in a slightly revised version with the new title *Zhongguo gushi* (中國故事, in English *Chinese Story* or *Story of China*). This essay was completed prior to the publication in Taiwan. An earlier version of this chapter first appeared in Chinese in Di-kai Chao and Riccardo Moratto, "Taohuayuan de jiushu: shilun Yan Lianke Zhongyuan de renjian qingjing" 桃花源的救贖: 試論閻連科〈中原〉的人間情境 [The Redemption of the Peach Blossom Spring: An Exploration of the Human Condition in Yan Lianke's "Zhongyuan"], *Yangzi jiang wenxue pinglun* 揚子江文學評論 [Yangtze Jiang Literary Review], November 2021, no. 6: 40–47. A few minor changes have been made in the current version, which to our best knowledge is the first English essay on Yan's latest literary creation.

2 Carlos Rojas, "Shen yu ren de anzhan yu fuhuan" 神與人的暗戰與復還 ["The dark war between God and man and the restoration"], in Yan Lianke, *Xinjing* (Hong Kong: City of University of Hong Kong Press, 2020), xviii.

people in contemporary Chinese society are generally situated in a "Chinese Dream" myth,[3] seeking the redemption of the human heart in contemporary society in the midst of collective sleepwalking and self-loss. If the depiction in *The Day the Sun Died* is still brutal and absurd, the narration in *Heart Sutra* is much more restrained: in it, Yan discusses the dialectical relationship between Chinese reality and religious life amidst the quarrels among different faiths. This inward turn may also be perceived in *Tamen* 她們. After exploring the human heart and religion in *Heart Sutra*, Yan allows his writing to return to the women of his family in *Tamen*, revealing his remembrance and nostalgia for family and human feelings through his detailed descriptions of the women in his family. In his latest novel *Central Plains* (*Zhongyuan* 中原), published in Taiwan with the title *Chinese Story* (*Zhongguo gushi* 中國故事),[4] Yan continues along the same notes, with a softer and more inward style compared to his early works.

Yan completed the first draft of *Zhongyuan* in 2020, when China was ravaged by COVID-19. The novel was then revised at the end of the year, when Yan was awarded the Newman Prize for Chinese Literature, and published in the bimonthly literary magazine *Flower City* (*Huacheng* 花城) in March 2021.[5] In this novel, Yan records (fictionalizes?) the narratives of three people in a family: a husband, a wife, and a son, revealing the emotional conflicts among the family members from the perspectives of each of the three people: the son wants to kill his father, the husband wants to kill his wife, and the mother wants to kill her son. The unusual, almost absurd emotions among the members of this family present a reflection on the nature of contemporary families. Yan also places himself in the narrative of the novel, just like in *The Day the Sun Died*, making his own perspective part of the novel and thus deepening the sense of metafiction.[6] Moreover, by creating the "narrative" and the "fictive objectivity" of these stories, the Yan-narrator who listens to the stories narrated by the three protagonists seems to be uncertain about the authenticity of the story itself, and at the same time, readers also question the authenticity of the stories, thus blurring the boundary between truth and fiction. In addition, the space in the novel revolves around the Central Plains of China and once again appropriates the spatial imagery of the Balou 耙耬 Mountains and their utopian metaphor, thus taking the novel beyond a mere story about a family and turning it into a discourse on the current Chinese nation.

The "killing" of the father, mother, and son

As far as the whole theme of the novel is concerned, *Central Plains* is a story about "killing the father, the wife, and the son." The novel is divided into four chapters, the first of which is the son's narrative of his long-standing desire to "kill his father," especially when the conflict between father and son is exacerbated by the father's disapproval of the son's will to study abroad. The second chapter is the husband's narrative about his idea of agreeing to a rich woman's request for an extramarital affair on condition that he divorce his wife; the husband even thinks about killing his wife in order to fulfill his wish of building a new house. The third chapter revolves around the mother's narrative, in which she is dissatisfied with her son's

---

3 Isabel Hilton, "*The Day the Sun Died* by Yan Lianke Review—The stuff of nightmares," *The Guardian*, 29 July 2018, https://www.theguardian.com/books/2018/jul/29/the-day-the-sun-died-yan-lianke-review-china (last accessed 15 July 2021).
4 Please refer to note number 1.
5 Yan Lianke, "Zhongyuan," *Huacheng*, 2021, no. 2: 5–79.
6 To clarify the difference between the intratextual narrator Yan Lianke and the extratextual author Yan Lianke, when necessary, we use the term Yan-narrator to refer to the former and Yan-author to refer to the latter.

fraudulent use of money in the name of college and the disgrace he has caused his family by being arrested for breaking the law, so she often secretly curses her son to death. The fourth chapter depicts the family's sudden departure out of town into the Balou Mountains, where they become reconciled. They end up living in a solitary abode in a village, leading an uneventful life aloof from the world. At the end of the novel, the writer ponders over the story of this family, while having trouble sleeping and eating.

The theme of the son killing his father is very outspoken: the son is constantly planning to kill his own father under the belief that "I am saving my mother by killing my father" (*shale die wo shi zai jiu niang a* 殺了爹我是在救娘啊).[7] Psychoanalytic scholars can make full use of the Oedipus complex to interpret the son's ambivalent feelings toward his father. This is especially true when the son recounts how he made up his mind to kill his father one morning when he was five years old, after seeing him naked on top of his mother, both of them drenched in sweat. This is a further confirmation of the Oedipus complex.

The Oedipus complex, however, is not the main point of the novel. As the son's narrative unfolds, we discover that the conflict between father and son is in fact far from the emasculating anxiety of the father's involvement in the mother-son relationship, as presupposed by psychoanalysis, but is due to very secular reasons, namely the generation gap and the ensuing different economic reality and societal values. The father believes that building a house is the right way to ensure the family's wealth and grandchildren's prosperity, while the son wants to emigrate to a "developed country" and leave the dilapidated and backward countryside behind him. As Yan reveals in *Three Brothers: Memories of My Family* (*Wo yu fubei* 我與父輩), his father and uncle had a lifelong belief in building houses.[8] This theme is repeated in many of his novels, including *Dream of Ding Village* (*Dingzhuang meng* 丁莊夢): rural people always take building houses as their lifelong endeavor and try to persuade their sons to stay in their hometowns. However, for the younger generation, striving to "go out" and taking advantage of the modern material conditions of globalization seems to be a more worthwhile goal to pursue in life. The son keeps thinking about how he can kill his father: his murder weapons range from hammers, bricks, and all the way to dichlorvos (rat poison); he broods over this matter for a long time. For the son, who is a university student, killing his father means escaping from the Central Plains area.

As for the father, his impulse to kill his wife stems from his desperate desire to build a new house. The narrative of the father begins as he is digging a hole for his new construction. He sees that the houses in the town are in better condition than his own, and naturally his depression and anger pile up inside. Until one day, the wife of the owner of a factory producing home appliances located on the west side of the town decides to take revenge on her husband, who previously had an extramarital affair but did not want to divorce to prevent the property from being split in half; therefore, she visits the father-protagonist to discuss with him the possibility of pretending to have an affair with her to repay her husband in kind and embarrass him. She promises to pay him for this favor but eventually starts to develop real feelings for him. She promises to give him a fair share of her wealth if he files for divorce. However, the father-protagonist's wife is not willing to divorce. He is therefore determined to kill her because he thinks she is the only obstacle preventing him from building a better and bigger house by starting a new life with the rich woman.

The father's desire to kill his wife is also aggravated by their inferior economic status and the conflict caused by the gap between rich and poor. Throughout the novel, he always pays attention to whose house is more refined, and he always makes sure to curse that family. If

---

7 Ibid., 15.
8 See Yan, "Gai fang" 蓋房 ["Building our home"], in *Wo yu fubei* (Taipei: Ink Literary, 2009), 61–67.

someone drives an expensive car, he hopes that person may end up in an argument and be beaten to death. Even when the owner of the fruit shop is willing to pay him a few extra bucks just to be called "general manager," he is not willing to lower his dignity and is reluctant to do so. The father ends up planning to strangle the mother with a hemp rope; however, the matter is dropped as the father's narrative comes to an end.

In contrast, the mother's desire for the son to die seems much milder: she does not actively plan her son's murder; at most, when her son goes to the well to get some water, she just secretly hopes he falls into the well and drowns. The mother's narrative begins when she goes to the police station to pick up her son, who is in trouble with the law for assisting in the illicit sale of examination questions. Through the mother's account, we learn that the college her son went to in the South is but a sham, and that the money he paid for tuition is thus wasted. The son keeps asking for money in order to move to the United States and pursue his studies there. Later, when he moves to Beijing, it is not to pursue his graduate studies but to run away with a girl he met in a hairdressing salon. They even have a child together. As we also learn from the mother's narrative, after he is released from the police station, he is keen on selling the land on which his father would have built a new house to earn some money to leave the town and lead a better life. Until finally, the son, seeing that he could not ask his parents to sell the new plot of land, directly asks his mother to bury him in the lime pit dug by his father. In short, the mother's disappointment with her son and embarrassment caused by him leads her to repeatedly curse him to death.

Alienated daily life

It is interesting to notice that none of these narratives has a final outcome: whether the son kills the father, whether the father strangles the mother, or whether the mother buries the son—all this is left suspended by the interruption of the narrative. Admittedly, knowing what happens next is not the main point of the novel. The real focus of *Central Plains* is that the author gives us a glimpse of real-life family conflicts by laying out the mutual complaints and curses of these family members, and the correspondence or rebuttals of the different narrators. However, rather than an exaggeration of modern family conflicts, this family of three wanting to kill each other is actually a metaphor for the alienated state of the modern world. This alienation corresponds to the theory of alienation that has long preoccupied Henri Lefebvre, that is, the modern world in which commodities, markets, and money have a tenacious logic and control over a daily life colonized by capitalism.[9] The South and the world metropolises represent the center of capitalist operations, making the son think that he must live in those developed places to survive and thrive, and he would not even hesitate one second to kill his father in order to achieve such a goal. By the same token, the construction of the new house and the town's reputation and sense of relative deprivation make the father willing to submit to the commodified interpersonal relationship agreed upon with the wife of the owner of a factory; he even plans to kill his own wife in order to fulfill that relationship. In addition, when the owner of the fruit shop is willing to pay in exchange to hear someone call her "general manager," it highlights the commercial transactional nature of such titles in the commercial logic.

In fact, this alienation of human beings under the operation of capitalist logic has been the subject of much effort in contemporary Chinese fiction. In *The Explosion Chronicles*, Lenin's

---

9 Henri Lefebvre, "Towards a Leftist Cultural Politics: Remarks Occasioned by the Centenary of Marx's Death," trans. David Reifman, in *Marxism and the Interpretation of Culture*, ed. Cary Nelson and Lawrence Grossberg (Urbana: University of Illinois Press, 1988), 79.

Kisses, Dream of Ding Village, The Four Books, The Day the Sun Died, Yan also deals with the odd depiction of people being reduced to commodities under economic development policies. In *Central Plains*, the alienation of human beings is also presented, but unlike the previous texts in which "events" are the main vehicle of presentation, *Central Plains* emphasizes the alienation of human beings in daily life and family relations. In short, in a daily life where the son is not a son, the husband is not a husband, and the mother is not a mother, people appear as being alienated.

Through the conflict between the different narratives of three people, Yan-author is in fact performing a Lefebvre-style "critique of everyday life": Yan-author emphasizes the pluralistic way of "de-ordinaryizing" everyday life, which is "the interrelationship of all aspects of life."[10] The fragments of the son's daily life present the situation of young people outside the world metropolises, under transnationalism and the globalized world system: the seemingly educational opportunities of pursuing knowledge, such as going to university and studying abroad, actually reveal the naked logic of capitalism (tuition and funding) concealed behind the façade. The father's daily life is presented as the situation of ordinary people in a mainland Chinese town under the game of economic and trade division: the father's dislike for the mother and his emotional contractual relationship with the wife of the owner of a factory present the complex relationship between marriage, economy, and law in Chinese society. Snippets from the mother's daily life are a reflection of women facing the double pressure of family expectations and neighbors. Each narrative presents a different spatial organization, from the perception of hometown and locality to the global inequality of world trade. Yan-author finds the shocking aesthetics of a glimpse in the trivial and seemingly boring details of daily life.

Interestingly, the story is narrated at a time that is symmetrical to the actual time in which the story occurs:[11] the son recounts the events happening at sunrise in the evening; the father recounts the events occurring around noon at midnight; and the mother recounts the events occurring after sunset shortly after the sun rises. In a similarly symmetrical fashion, Yan-narrator "sees" the family after they move up on the Balou Mountains on a winter night while he is on his way to the high-speed rail station at midday on a summer day. All the three protagonists lay out their respective stories in a linear time and in a monotonous rhythm of repetition and stagnation. We are reminded once again of what Lefebvre argues about everyday life in the modern world. For Lefebvre, the everyday is a concept that reflects the stereotypical, trivial, and repetitive quality of life under capitalism, and everydayness as a paradoxical state of the bureaucratic society of controlled consumption that appears to be organized but in fact lacks unity. This paradoxical state is full of linear changes, but at the same time, presents a constant recurrence and continuous repetition.[12] This everydayness of capitalist society is also a basis for the way Yan-author presents his characters, but in a more caricatured and exaggerated way,[13] for example, the planting of corn/wheat in *The Years, Months, Days* (*Nian yue ri* 年月日) or in *The Four Books*, the repetitive sleepwalking state in *The Day the Sun Died*, while in *Central Plains* the son and his father keep on emphasizing

---

10 Ben Highmore, *Everyday Life and Cultural Theory* (London: Routledge, 2001), 128.

11 Yan Lianke uses the phrase "two points in a line" (*yi tiao xian shang de liang ge dian* 一條線上的兩個點). See Yan, "Zhongyuan," 74.

12 Henri Lefebvre, "The Everyday and Everydayness," trans. Christine Levich, *Yale French Studies*, no. 73 (1987): 10.

13 Just as one can read in Yan's postscript interview with Li Tuo 李陀 in *Shouhuo* 受活 [*Lenin's Kisses*] (Taipei: Rye Field, 2007), the exaggerated depiction of the characters' interactive caricature reflects the commodification and objectification of human beings under capitalism.

their respective plans to study abroad and build a house, and in these repetitive actions, they continue to deepen the alienation of the self in the capitalist world.

These alienated states are fully revealed through each person's subjective and inner conversations, and are fully contrasted in the final section where the family suddenly moves away from Gaotian and goes to live a self-sufficient life on the Balou Mountains (a kind of anti-alienation decision, back to the basics and back to mother nature). Despite the family's grievances against each other, they finally reconcile, and this reconciliation is possible only when they are free from capitalist alienation. According to the narration of the Yan-narrator, the family switches house with a family that originally lived on the Balou Mountains, and they start living in a traditional compound made of grey bricks and tiles and built around a courtyard. The night after they move, the family sits under a religious painting that blends Christian and Buddhist elements and they eat food and drink together late into the night. They end up playing a game of drawing lots.

Here, Yan-author likens the lots game to the human nature in everyday life. This game has a total of nine sticks divided into three categories: Jesus, the cross, and the nails (crucifixion); the evil-doers, the hanged, and the hanging tree (sinners); the weeds, the dust, and the fawn (judgment). After the drawing of lots, the punishment is executed according to different categories (those who draw from the category of sinners are hanged, those who draw from the category of judgment execute the hanging, and those who draw from the category of crucifixion can decide whether to save someone or not). All three assume that they would draw the evil-doer lot and that they should all be punished, but it turns out that they all belong to the same category. We are all "passers-by, mortals and people, who have lived today and will live tomorrow" (*dou shi luren, fanren he baixing, dou shi guole jintian de rizi yao guo mingtian rizi de ren* 都是路人、凡人和百姓, 都是過了今天的日子要過明天日子的人); "the three of them all are equally evil-doers and should be hanged" (*tamen yi jia san ge dou yiyang shi xietu, yiyang gai shangdiao* 他們一家三個都一樣是邪徒, 一樣該上吊), and if no one can execute the punishment, then no one is executed.[14] Everyone in this family has mixed feelings: "The three of them look at each other without uttering a word, and finally all three of them shed a tear at the same time" (*san ge ren bici kan le kan, shei ye bu shuohua, zuihou san ge ren yan li tongshi you le lei* 三個人彼此看了看, 誰也不說話, 最後三個人眼裡同時有了淚),[15] for they finally acknowledge each other's inner dark consciousness.

This plot reflects the reality that people are both sinners and saints under the mechanisms of the modern world, both overseers and executioners. Everyone may judge or be judged, stand aside, or reach out to help. In any case, everyone is guilty, and therefore no one is qualified to condemn others. If alienation is a state of estrangement from nature, then the family's new life in a single-family village on the Balou Mountains is a metaphor, indicating the return to a natural pre-alienated state. This anti-alienation approach lies in a state of detachment from the logic of capitalist consumption. Yan-author here uses an imagery similar to that of the Peach Blossom Spring (*Taohuayuan* 桃花源) as the salvation of this family. This topic will be discussed more in detail in the following sections.

The allegory of spatial politics under the metaphor of globalization

The three characters have different reasons for wanting to kill each other; however, all motivations originate from pecuniary reasons. This financial conflict reflects the different degrees of economic development in contemporary China due to geographical differences. The title of this book is deliberately named after the Central Plains, which symbolize one of the origins of Chinese civilization, and is deliberately contrasted with the modernization of the Southern

---

14 Yan, "Zhongyuan," 78.
15 Ibid.

coastal cities, reflecting the backward position of the Central Plains and, by extension, China in the modernization process. Interestingly, this inconsistent development is depicted through the mother's temporal contrast (before vs. now) and the son's spatial contrast. Through the narratorial voice and the son's perspective, the writer uses spatial contrast to highlight the backwardness of the Central Plains in the process of globalization: "Some people say that China is like a big construction site. The South is a large construction site that has almost been completed and closed. Here we are rather a small site that has just been demolished in different pieces. There is another difference. The factories in the South have long since begun production. Here in the North, no one knows what we will end up producing."[16] What is presented here is the "North-South" problem, except that in China, the relationship between North and South is reversed: the South is an advanced, developed, and mature place, while the North seems to be a "junkyard"-like place with backward economic development, newly dismantled structures and in a general state of disarray. In addition, based on his own memories of studying in the South, the son uses the modern architecture and rich material life of the Southern coastal cities to contrast with the rustic architecture of the towns in the Central Plains. The South, in the son's eyes, is already a kind of reference to progress and civilization.

The son's narrative also places different cities in his North-South discourse in an attempt to conduct a geographic mapping in relation to the Central Plains, thus highlighting the spatial backwardness of the Central Plains, in spite of their "central" character, hence linked to the origin of Chinese civilization. The South is progressive in the same sense as New York City, Tokyo, Paris, and Rome; the Southern cities are near the sea, close to Macau, and the sea is always visible in almost all university campuses in the South, thus highlighting the openness and ability of the South to stay connected to the world: "The South is the leader and kaleidoscope of our age, like the urban skyscrapers and parks imagined by the peasants who live and die on the land."[17] The "sea" is used here as a metaphor for globalization and transnationalism that is "connected" and "mobile," while the imagery of New York, Tokyo, Paris, and Rome serve as symbols of metropolitan cosmopolitanism. By contrast, Gaotian Town is a place trapped inland. The backwardness of this town in the Central Plains always reflects the corny and old-fashioned characteristics of the hairdressing and beauty salon that plays a central part in the novel. This salon also uses the popular, yet old-fashioned, rotating stripe lamps which were popular in the past to indicate a hairdressing salon and to attract the attention of passersby, the only glimpse of modernity being the salon's "hair-washing method in a Southern-style" (*Nanfang xitou fa* 南方洗頭法).[18] The perfumes used in the salon are cheap fragrances, and sex services are also performed in this locale.

Here the South is a South that has been fetishized. Shu-mei Shih 史書美 argues that in globalization and transnationalism, the production of meaning is always captured in the flow of a specific space-time, depending on determinism and fixity.[19] While the South and other metropolises mastered and fixed globalized capital flows, the North, represented in this case by Gaotian Town, has become the "loser" in this unequal flow.

---

16 Ibid., 12:

   有人說中國就像一個大工地。南方那兒是差不多已經建成收工的大工地。我們這兒是剛剛大卸八塊正在拆遷的小工地。還有一個差別是，南方工地上的工廠早已開始生產了。而北方，中原咱們這鎮子，這個物雜千萬的破工地，還不知道將來生產什麼好。

17 Ibid., 21: "南方是這個時代的領頭羊和萬花筒，像死守土地的農民想像的城市高樓和公園樣。"
18 Ibid.
19 Shu-mei Shih, *Visuality and Identity: Sinophone Articulations across the Pacific* (Berkeley: University of California Press, 2007), 44.

The mother, meanwhile, reflects the decline and obsolescence of the Middle Kingdom towns through the technique of time correlation. The landscape on the way home when the mother picks her son up from the police station is one of depression after prosperity: the town has now fewer factories and companies than before: "Even Korean and Japanese investment in distilleries, beverage factories and pharmaceutical plants outside the town have lost money and moved away for no reason, leaving only those plants and company shells idling in and outside of the town."[20] Although the text does not directly reveal the cause of the depression in Gaotian Town, there are some clues indicating that it was caused by the trade war between the United States and China: on the road, someone stomps on a celebrity advertisement of "an old man with blond hair, high nose, and a full forehead with furrows."[21] As it turns out to be the former President of the United States, the person then yells: "So what if it's the President? I'll stomp on his face all the same! If it wasn't for him, my business wouldn't be so cold that I wouldn't be able to make ends meet."[22] The US President is supposed to be referring to former President Donald Trump, and the accusations in this paragraph reflect the role of the United States as a privileged institutional agent that dominates the world economy. Nonetheless, we are not arguing that Yan's work is intended to comment on the rights and wrongs of the US-China trade war. The spatial politics implied by the concepts of North and South, China and its periphery, and even China and the world, is what Yan has been reflecting over for a long time. In the desolate Gaotian Town, we seem to see the epitome of Wallerstein's world-system theory.[23]

This discernment of the North-South issue and the politics of space are also expressed in the mother's comments on the South. She believes that the source of all tragedies and misfortunes in their family derives from the desire and imagination for the South. "The South is a well, which has swallowed my child and my family. We hate the South and foreigners. We hate the United States, which is said to be a paradise. If there was no South, no United States and foreign countries, my child would not have ended at the town police station."[24] In a way, this family's view of the world seems to reflect the views of different groups of Chinese people facing the current world. While young people look forward to the "advanced" world of Europe and America and loathe the backwardness of the Central Plains, there is another group of people who hate the influence of foreign culture and believe that foreign influence is tearing China apart. If we look again at Shu-mei Shih's argument, we can find that the mother's comments on the South and foreign countries remind us of the current economic production and trade structures of capitalist globalization that also shape the current self-imagination of China. When China uses economic factors such as the world factory and the world market as political leverage, it is only putting itself at risk of falling into this North-South spatio-political dichotomization.

In chapter 4, Yan is preparing to return to Beijing and on his way to the high-speed railway station, he sees the former slogan of "Reform and opening up is a treasure, whoever embraces

---

20 Yan, "Zhongyuan," 62: "連韓國、日本在鎮外投資的酒廠、飲料廠和製藥廠，也都無緣由地賠錢了，無緣由地搬走了，只留下那些廠房、公司的房殼閑在鎮裡和鎮外。"
21 Ibid., 64: "老頭兒，金頭髮、高鼻樑，天庭飽滿的額上橫著溝渠紋。"
22 Ibid.: "總統又何呢？我踩的就是他，不是他我這生意也不會冷到出不敷入哩。"
23 Immanuel Wallerstein's world-system theory depicts the modern world as a capitalist system consisting of three zones: core, semi-periphery, and periphery. Each zone has its specific economic roles in the distribution of capitals. See Wallerstein, *Modern World-System: Capitalist Agriculture and the Origins of the European World-Economy in the Sixteenth Century* (New York: Academic Press, 1974).
24 Yan, "Zhongyuan," 56: "南方就是一口井，明明亮亮吞了兒娃吞了我一家。我們一家都些微多少恨南方，恨那外國人。都恨被人說成天堂的美國那地方。中國要是沒南方，沒有美國和外國，想我兒娃也不會去到鎮上派出所。"

it will be fine" (*gaige kaifang shi ge bao, shei qu yongbao shei jiu hao* 改革開放是個寶, 誰去擁抱誰就好) on the wall of the town changed into the red letters of "Revive our town, revitalize the Central Plains, revitalize China" (*fuxing wo zhen, fuxing Zhongyuan, fuxing Zhonghua* 復興我鎮、復興中原、復興中華).[25] This juxtaposition of the "connection" between mobility, openness, and "nodal points" with the hierarchical world picture of the Central Plains underlines China's self-imagined nationhood since the reform and opening up.[26]

Anti-flow metaphor: Peach Blossom Spring

The family of three, who initially seemed to be at odds with each other, suddenly and by chance move to the Balou Mountains at the end of the novel. In the surrounding area of their new home, there is absolutely no human population or even poultry; there is only a small courtyard in good condition left behind by their new home's previous owner. They do not even have water or electricity due to the government's initial policy of relocating the village. They have to start cultivating their own food for the days to come. They are the only family living in that particular area of the Balou Mountains: "A household is also a village. A village is a world."[27] The first night after they move into the new house, they open their hearts to each other and also feel the irony of everyone being a sinner while playing a game of drawing lots, thus forgetting all the tribulations they had previously experienced in Gaotian Town. This place can be said to be a modern version of Peach Blossom Spring.

Peach Blossom Spring is often used in Chinese literature as its counterpart "utopia" in Western literature. The term utopia was first coined by Thomas More (1478–1535) in his *Utopia* (1516), which combines the Greek word ὐ 'not' and τόπος 'place' to convey the meaning of "a place which does not exist." However, the Peach Blossom Spring in classical Chinese literature is different from Moore's concept of utopia. While the Western concept of utopia emphasizes the political ideal world of reason, man-made order, and the conquest of nature, Tao Yuanming's 陶淵明 prose "A Record of Peach Blossom Spring" ("Taohuayuan ji" 桃花源記) transcends historical time and religious mythology and returns to the true paradise of all things natural.[28] We argue that the utopian concept of modern contemporary Chinese fiction, influenced by Western literature, is already different from that of classical literature. The utopian imagination of Chinese fiction since the twentieth century combines an agenda of modernity, national construction, social renewal, political ideals, and cultural revival. The current imaginary of utopia in China persists despite the demise of the communist utopian myth.[29] As contemporary Chinese utopian discourse continues to develop, literary narratives

---

25 Ibid., 75.
26 The term "nodal point" is a concept formulated by Ernesto Laclau and Chantal Mouffe, which refers to a specific signifier or a discursive point to fix the fluid meaning of a "signifying chain." See Laclau and Mouffe, *Hegemony and Socialist Strategy* (London: Verso, 1985), 112.
27 Yan, "Zhongyuan," 79: "一戶人也是一個村。一個村就是一個世界呢。"
28 Lai Hsi-san 賴錫山, "'Taohuayuan ji bing shi' de shenhua, xinlixue quanshi: Tao Yuanming de Daojia shi 'leyuan' xintan" 〈桃花源記並詩〉的神話、心理學詮釋——陶淵明的道家式「樂園」新探 ["A mythological and psychological interpretation of 'A Record of Peach Blossom Spring, with Poem': A New Exploration of Tao Yuanming's Daoist 'Paradise'"], *Zhongguo wenzhe yanjiu jikan* 中國文哲研究集刊 [Bulletin of the Institute of Chinese Literature and Philosophy], 2008, no. 32: 27–29.
29 With China's growing political and economic influence since the twenty-first century, Chinese scholars have had different visions of China's future, which varies from political discourses of the rise of great power, the Chinese dream, a community with a shared future for mankind, and the great rejuvenation of the Chinese nation. These discourses are filled with confidence in China's political system, economic model and social mobilization, and optimism about the future world.

of dystopia and heterotopia have consistently questioned this political vision. Zhang Hao's 張灝 commentary on modern Chinese political thought points out that modern Chinese utopian discourse is "ultimately optimistic" in its mode of thinking.[30] David Der-wei Wang 王德威 further appropriates Zhang's term, "dark consciousness" as the fictional force of the novel, analyzing how it tends to bring despair, forbidden desires, and (ultimately optimistic) pent-up feelings stemming from an "obsession with China" (*gan shi you guo* 感時憂國) in the world of the novel.[31] In short, the utopian imagination of contemporary Chinese fiction is far from the world presented in Tao's fable.[32]

However, Yan's imagery of Peach Blossom Spring in *Central Plains* is not a practice of political discourse or a visionary imagination of the future world, nor is it a yearning for mechanical rationality or symbolic order (class or institutional organization), but a return to the natural state in Zhuangzi's 莊子 thought.[33] This utopian world may also be found in Liven Village in *Lenin's Kisses*, symbolizing a state of isolation without political intervention, and echoing Zhuangzi's natural theory of "the usefulness of the useless" (*wu yong zhi yong* 無用之用) to preserve the true nature and not be distorted by the world order.[34] It also appears in the epilogue of *The Four Books*, "The New Sisyphean Myth," which demonstrates a peaceful scene of a Zen garden with swirling cooking smoke (*chan yuan chuiyan tu* 禪院炊煙圖). Such images are used as the hope of the characters who are willing to endure suffering and live despite the oppression of the present world.[35] Yan's imagery of Peach Blossom Spring echoes Tao's, and in addition to emphasizing its "nature" (*ziran benxing* 自然本性), he places his imagery of Peach Blossom Spring in a cyclical view of time that abstracts from historical and linear time and reduces it to a mythological sense.

At the end of *Central Plains*, the boundary of the single-family village is demarcated by some farming tools that are no longer in use.[36] This means that the village is no longer subservient to the unifying mechanisms of the state apparatus or to the capitalist mode of production. Moreover, the useless farming tools also imply the imagery of Peach Blossom Spring through "the usefulness of the useless" of the farming tools. In other words, this boundary marker signifies their isolation from the other world. This world has no history. Just as Liven Village in *Lenin's Kisses* is not recorded on government documents or maps, the village where the family in *Central Plains* ends up is also a world outside of government town planning: "Here, time is nothing but morning and evening, each day and season. The years, the past and the future, have all disappeared. They have only the small time of this moment and that moment, but not the big time of the past and the future."[37] Just like in "A Record of Peach

---

30 David Der-wei Wang, "The Panglossian Dream and Dark Consciousness: Modern Chinese Literature and Utopia," in *Utopia and Utopianism in the Contemporary Chinese Context: Texts, Ideas, Spaces*, ed. David Wang, Angela Ki Che Leung, and Zhang Yinde (Hong Kong: Hong Kong University Press, 2020), 53.
31 Ibid.
32 For an English translation, see https://eastasiastudent.net/china/classical/tao-yuanming-taohua-yuan/ (last accessed 17 Aug. 2021).
33 Jianmei Liu 劉劍梅, "The Spirit of Zhuangzi and the Chinese Utopian Imagination," in *Utopia and Utopianism in the Contemporary Chinese Context*, 129.
34 Ibid., 143.
35 Yan, *Si shu* 四書 (Taipei: Maitian, 2011), 379–80.
36 Yan, "Zhongyuan," 79.
37 Ibid.: "在這兒，時間除了一天間的早晚和四季，年月、過去和未來，都已經消失不在了。他們只有這一會兒和那一會兒的小時間，而沒有過去和未來的大時間。"

Blossom Spring," they know nothing about the change of dynasties.[38] The time in this one-household village is divorced from the chronology of symbolic history, and does not have a branched view of time in the sense of past and future. Time here has only infinite cycles of "small time," but not "big time" in a linear sense.

If we juxtapose this village of Peach Blossom Spring with similar imagery in Yan's other books, we may see the emergence of Laozi's 老子 notions of "a small state with a small population"[39] and of governing by doing nothing that goes against nature (*wu wei er zhi* 無爲而治) in Yan's texts. However, we argue that it would also be underestimating *Central Plains* to simply see Yan's Peach Blossom Spring as a rewrite of Tao's Peach Blossom Spring without focusing on the significance of this phenomenon for Yan's times. In other words, why does Yan decide not to adopt the dystopia or heterotopia in *Central Plains* that he also previously used in *The Four Books* and that contemporary Chinese writers excel at, but he prefers to resort to the classic metaphor of Peach Blossom Spring, that is a return to the natural state of human nature and to the inherent quality of one's true natural self? It is argued that Yan's deliberate use of this "small state" imagery has its contemporary relevance, and can be said to be a reversal of the current "big power" discourse that is so popular in mainland China. At the same time, from the perspective of literary history, Yan's Peach Blossom Spring has formed another aspect of contemporary Chinese utopian imagination.

As mentioned above, the utopian imagination of Chinese novels since the late Qing period has carried the mission of enlightenment discourse, national imagination, social reform, and historical and cultural revival. It is through the imagination of a better world in the future and the argument that China will be strong and the heyday will return, that the writer completes the blueprint of China in the past and in the future. But the characteristic feature of this utopian imagination is that it completely ignores the "present" situation: the past and the future are commented in the "future perfect mood" with its "narrative fragment."[40] That is, the "present" is a blank space, not mentioned at all. Yan's Peach Blossom Spring is a counterpoint to this utopian imagination that lacks the "present" alone. When the family still lived in Gaotian Town, they were always projected into the future: a future in which the son would have migrated to a "developed country," a future where the father would have built a new house; but when the family moves to the Balou Mountains, the "past and the future are gone,"[41] all that is left is the present. In other words, what Yan's Peach Blossom Spring imagery highlights is precisely the recovery and emergence of "now."

As a village in a world without an economic production system and without alienated labor, the human body no longer has to be given pecuniary and exchange value. After moving to the Balou Mountains, the son no longer thinks about getting a new life in the South of China or moving to the United States. He even graciously announces that he would set his residence up on the Balou Mountains with his wife and daughter, in a world inhabited only by

---

38 "It turned out they hadn't even heard of the Han dynasty, let alone the Wei or the Jin dynasty." (乃不知有漢, 無論魏晉。) See https://eastasiastudent.net/china/classical/tao-yuanming-taohua-yuan/ (last accessed 17 Aug. 2021).

39 From the *Dao de jing*: "In a little state with a small population, I would so order it, that, though there were individuals with the abilities of ten or a hundred men, there should be no employment of them; I would make the people while looking on death as a grievous thing, yet not remove elsewhere (to avoid it)." ["小國寡民, 使有什伯之器而不用, 使民重死而不遠徙。"] https://ctext.org/dao-de-jing?filter=494852 (last accessed 19 July 2021).

40 David Der-wei Wang, *Fin-de-Siècle Splendor: Repressed Modernities of Late Qing Fiction, 1848–1911* (Stanford: Stanford University Press, 1997), 304–5.

41 Yan, "Zhongyuan," 79: "過去和未來, 都已經消失不在了。"

his own family. As for the parents, they no longer inquire about their son's past secret marriage and child, they only happily discuss the upcoming present. Perhaps this also symbolizes the subversion of the metaphor of flow. Flow only allows privileged institutions to fix meaning through the power of domination constructed by capital and discourse. Even if there are differences under such a flow, they are suppressed by privileged agents.[42]

Peach Blossom Spring is a world withdrawn from history: it does not participate in the flow of globalized transnationalism. The world of rationalism and capitalism is a production-centered logic that classifies everything in the world according to its utility, but Yan has already shown us the dialectical relationship between usefulness and uselessness in *Lenin's Kisses*, and thus deconstructed the myth of capitalist utopia. The village in *Central Plains* is a world that has withdrawn from globalization and national policies: it is different from Gaotian Town, which appears as depressed, bleak, and desolate due to the trade war between China and the United States; here, there is no need to try hard to imitate the South and the world metropolises. If we use David Wang's terminology, the excessive participation in the globalized flows of power domination may trigger a developmentalist anxiety, namely a "crisis consciousness." The crisis consciousness sometimes may lead people to be lost in the "dark consciousness," even to the point of distorted chaos. From this perspective, perhaps stopping participation in the world may not be pragmatic for the current society, but through echoing the metaphor of Peach Blossom Spring, Yan constructs a reality that others do not see in the real world.

Moreover, the juxtaposition of the Peach Blossom Spring narrative and religious elements make Yan's narrative different from the current dystopian and heterotopian narratives. After the publication of *The Day the Sun Died*, Yan began to use Gaotian Town as the chronotope for a series of novels centered around the Central Plains of China.[43] The novels in this Gaotian series are a metaphor for the Central Plains/China and a representation, by contrast, of other places, like the South or the United States in the case of this novel. While we can certainly see the use of different utopian imagery as the writer's quest for a breakthrough in writing techniques, we argue that this is another attempt by Yan to intervene in the real world.

The "orgiastic" bodily deformation in *Lenin's Kisses*, the sale of blood in *Dream of Ding Village*, the cannibalism in *The Four Books*, and the corpse oil in *The Day the Sun Died* bespeak Yan's ability to intervene in the real world with a dark power that makes people unable to sit or stand still. As for the relatively "clean" *Central Plains*, it is argued that Yan's deliberate adoption of the classical metaphor of Peach Blossom Spring in the text representing the Central Plains is a kind of murmur against the political utopian discourse since the post-Mao era, especially under the current grand narrative that constantly emphasizes the connectivity of "One Belt, One Road."

At the beginning of this chapter, we mentioned that Yan's writing style has become much milder since the publication of *Heart Sutra*, and that religious "salvation" has played an increasingly important role in his texts since *The Four Books*. This may reflect Yan's expectation of the current Chinese society. This kind of expectation is not necessarily an expectation of a specific religion, such as the Christian religion, but a belief in a religious spirit of salvation in a distorted and oppressive environment, such as the "love" and "compassion" presented in the passion of the Christ with Buddhist elements at the end of *Central Plains*. In other words, the world presented in dystopian or heterotopian narratives is one of deep despair, while Yan's narrative of Peach Blossom Spring is one in which there is still faith in hope after despair.

42 Shih, *Visuality and Identity*, 45.
43 Yan, personal communication, 4 July 2021.

Human condition in the Sinophone context

The first three chapters of the novel adopt the narrative perspective of internal focalization, carried out by the first-person subjective narrative mode. If Genette's classification of narrative genres is adopted, the first three chapters all present stories within stories and belong to the "intradiegetic-homodiegetic paradigm."[44] It is not until chapter 4 that the narrator goes from the characters back to the author himself (the textual Yan), and the narrative perspective changes back to the omniscient perspective. Thus, Yan-narrator in chapter 4 belongs to the "extradiegetic-heterodiegetic paradigm."[45] Yan-narrator, the extradiegetic narrator, recounts how, on his way back to Beijing, he sees from afar the family's return from a twisted psychology of wanting to kill each other to a simple life of idyllic pastoralism. This presence of an author surrogate is a common technique in Yan's texts, and it often serves as an important clue for us to observe Yan's texts wandering between fiction and truth. At the end of the fourth chapter, after the textual Yan has returned to Beijing, he keeps on thinking about the family's story and is not even able to write an article titled "A Village Larger than the World." We argue that this final chapter, short and with a clear referential meaning, is a crucial paratext of the whole novel.

"A Village Larger than the World" is also the title of Yan's acceptance speech for the 2021 Newman Prize for Chinese Literature.[46] At the beginning of his acceptance speech, Yan grasps the meaning of dispersion and return implied by the term *Huayu* 華語 and uses it to develop his interpretation of language and land. Accordingly, Yan also uses *The Odyssey* as a metaphor for the significance of the award to Sinophone literature.[47] Yan begins with the diasporic meaning of *Huayu* that signifies "the assessment and perception of a language and the literature it creates" by a group of people who have left the motherland of that language.[48] Of course, this metaphor presupposes a position of understanding Sinophone literature in terms of the imagery of "roots." Yan declares that his hometown is a big village that contains everything China imagines and desires for the world. This big village contains the ignorance, darkness, good and evil, love, hate, and cogitation of the *Huayu* world and of all humanity.

This speech drew criticism from some netizens who accused Yan of vilifying China: "village China" (*cunzhuang Zhongguo* 村莊中國), "servilism" (*chenqie zhuyi* 臣妾主義),[49] too Sinocentric, too arrogant, and too politically incorrect (in the acceptance speech, Yan

---

44 Gérard Genette, *Narrative Discourse: An Essay in Method* (New York: Cornell University Press, 1980), 248.
45 Ibid.
46 Yan Lianke, "Yi ge bi shijie geng da de cunzhuang" 一個比世界更大的村莊 ["A village larger than the world"], *Duan chuanmei* 端傳媒 [*Initum Media*], 10 Mar. 2021, https://theinitium.com/article/20210310-notes-newman-prize-for-chinese-literature-yanlianke/ (last accessed 10 Aug. 2021).
47 The term "Sinophone literature" is used here to highlight the tension between literature written in Chinese but produced in mainland China and literature not native to mainland China. Unlike the postcolonial and decentered connotations of scholars such as Shu-mei Shih, we use the term "Sinophone" here to echo the relationship between the paratext of *Central Plains* and the Newman Prize for Chinese Literature, emphasizing the discrepancy in the position of writing due to the geographic space difference.
48 Yan, "Yi ge bi shijie geng da de cunzhuang": "對這種語言和它所創造的文學的評估和認知。"
49 For example, Guo Songmin 郭松民, "Ping Yan Lianke jiang de liang ge gushi" 評閻連科講的兩個故事 ["On the two stories that Yan Lianke has recounted"], Kunlun ce 崑崙策, 14 Mar. 2021, http://www.kunlunce.com/e/wap/show2021.php?classid=176&id=151015&bclassid=1 (last accessed 10 Aug. 2021).

mentions a girl's compassion for Japanese soldiers).[50] These comments are too eager to make a big deal about the superficial meaning of language and words, ignoring the ambiguity and multiple referents of words as symbols themselves. In fact, if we place this acceptance speech within the context of the novel *Central Plains*, then we can clarify the meaning of village and even understand the meaning of Central, as in *Zhongyuan* (Central Plains) or *Zhongguo* 中國 (China. *Zhongguo* literally means Middle or Central Kingdom). Although *Central Plains* is basically a text in which family members complain to each other, it is thanks to the acceptance speech "A Village Larger than the World," which is also a paratext of the novel, that we might as well deepen our understanding of the concept of family and expand this "family" into a "Sinophone community."[51] This metaphor helps us to observe the differences and heterogeneity in the development of the various regions of the Sinophone world, and gives *Central Plains* a deeper layer of meaning within the Sinophone literary coordinates.

When we take a closer look at Yan's acceptance speech, we find that this village is representative of the Central Plains and, by extension, China because Yan is addressing a non-Chinese audience, while contemplating the meaning of Chinese literature in the world. Moreover, on the basis of Yan's acceptance speech, we find that this village can encompass the world, not because of geopolitics or the traditional Sino-barbarian dichotomy (*Hua yi zhi bian* 華夷之辨) discourse, but because of the various phenomena occurring in this village, which are universal to modern society. This village in the central part of the Central Plains of China presents the most divergent ideological differences and the most convergent desires; the conflict between the three family members reflects the difference between rich and poor in China under globalization and transnationalism, and the emotions derived from it, such as wanting to kill each other, also reflect the various responses, such as yearning, rejection or ambiguity, of the world's Sinophone community, including China, to all the different interpretations of "root" political metaphors such as *Zhongguo* and *Zhonghua* (中華).

In fact, this Chinese story written by Yan, a mainland Chinese writer from the very center of China, is very much a dialectical space between the Central Plains (*Hua* 華) and the outside world (*yi* 夷). For example, the inner monologue of the mother in the text can actually be understood as a kind of Sinophone vocalization. The mother's narrative is conducted in her own dialect because she believes that "as soon as I speak my native dialect, it all suddenly becomes clear in my head [...] if I have to speak official Mandarin, it can get messy sometimes and I can't sort out my thoughts."[52]

The tension between the official language and the dialect is pointed out here. The mother's dialect is regarded as the orthodox and ancient *Zhongyuan* dialect (*Zhongyuan hua* 中原話) and is also a derision of the current view of Mandarin as the orthodox status: the most original *Zhongyuan* dialect, the original language of the Central Plains, is not considered as the official dialect. What is even more interesting is that with the historical upheavals and population movements, the current dialects that have preserved the most authentic accent of "Central China" since the Song dynasty are instead found in the South: Hokkien (*Min* 閩),

---

50 Dahai li de zhen 大海裡的針, "Yan Lianke na pian 'Yi ge bi shijie geng da de cunzhuang,' ai ma yidian ye bu yuan" 閻連科那篇《一個比世界更大的村莊》，挨罵一點也不冤 ["Yan Lianke's article 'A Village Bigger than the World' is not unfairly scolded at all"], Zhi hu 知乎 [*Q&A website*], 19 Mar. 2021, https://zhuanlan.zhihu.com/p/358431006 (last accessed 10 Aug. 2021).

51 For Sinophone studies, it is still inappropriate to use home or family as a metaphor for the relationship among Sinophone communities. However, our reading here is a metaphor based on Yan's text and his acceptance speech.

52 Yan, "Zhongyuan," 54: "只要一說娘家話，許多事的攏來去處在我腦裡便明白條理了，紋絡抒順了 [...] 說你們都說的官話普通話，事情有時反倒麻亂一團著，理不出根藤毛鬢來。"

Hakka (*Kejia* 客家), Cantonese (*Yue* 粵), and *Wu* 吳. In particular, when the son in *Central Plains* asks the hairdresser to say "I love you" (*nong ai ni* 儂愛你) in the Shanghai dialect,[53] the fetish of the signifier South is obvious, and these plots highlight the fascination, or the fetish, of the Central Plains for the South. Here, the Central Plains, symbolizing China (*Hua*), become the slave of its master, the "South," the "America," and the "metropolises." The change or the reversal between *hua* and *yi* in the modern time is really sophisticated. When the theoretical starting point of Sinophone research lies in the diversity of accent and sound (or -phone if we use the Greek root), there seems to be more room for discussion on the identity of "Sino/Xeno"-phone, considering the historical context.

David Der-wei Wang has resorted to the concept of "human condition" proposed by Hannah Arendt to discuss the detectable field of Sinophone/Xenophone (*Huayifeng* 華夷風): rather than overly discussing right and wrong on the premise of sovereign politics, we should focus on all aspects including "community, geography, gender, age, class, psychology, social and ecological environment, etc. [...] and even on the 'post-human' imagination."[54] This human condition is the meaning of this village, which is "larger than the world." Yan emphasizes that this village, with a population of only a few thousand people, encompasses all kinds of human conditions and is therefore "a real representation of China and the world, and in many cases a concentration and an existence larger than China and the world."[55]

Yan's acceptance speech refers to *Central Plains* as a text presenting the current human condition, and the religious painting "The Cross of Jesus" described in the last chapter of the novel also becomes a picture of this human condition: the Chinese characters on the right-hand side of the picture read "Jesus–nail–cross" and represent the crucifixion, great love, and compassion, whereas on the left-hand side of the picture the characters read "evil–doer–tree–hanging-rope" and represent evil thoughts, sin and repentance; finally, the characters written on the upper part of the picture read "earth–grass–path" and represent the earth.

When we look again at the town of Gaotian in *Central Plains*, this place is indeed in this dual location of Central Plains/South and China/world, showing people's "seven affections and six desires" (*qi qing liu yu* 七情六欲): the son is crazy about foreign things and obsequious to foreigners, the employee at the hairdresser provides sexual services and even receives money for calling her customers whatever they want to be called (as in the case of the son wanting her to say "I love you" with a Southern accent), the father's extramarital affair and his obsession for building a new house, the mother's disappointment with her son, the love, hatred, and property entanglement between husband and wife who own the home appliances factory. In *Central Plains*, there is no famine as in *The Four Books*, no disease as in *Dream of Ding Village*, no sleepwalking as in *The Day the Sun Died*, but only common people and things that would appear around us in our everyday life. However, Yan uses once again the image of the "Crucifixion of Jesus" to resolve the various conflicts in the world. Such imagery has always played an important redemptive meaning in Yan's novels. The child in *The Four Books* follows the example of Jesus by crucifying himself and releasing the intellectuals of the re-education camp (*yuxin qu* 育新區). In *The Day the Sun Died*, Li Tianbao 李天保 finally douses himself with corpse oil and sets himself on fire in exchange for the light of day to return to Gaotian

---

53 Ibid., 23.
54 David Der-wei Wang, "Huayi zhi bian: Huayu yuxi yanjou de xin shijie" 華夷之變: 華語語系研究的新視界 (Sinophone/Xenophone Studies: Toward a Poetics of Wind, Sound, and Changeability), *Zhongguo xiandai wenxue* 中國現代文學 [Modern Chinese Literature Studies], 2018, no. 34: 21.
55 Yan, "Yi ge bi shijie geng da de cunzhuang": "又確確實實是完完整整的中國和世界, 且許多時候還是大於中國和世界的濃縮和存在。"

Town, as if to reenact the meaning of sacrifice and atonement. In *Central Plains*, this imagery of Jesus' crucifixion once again becomes the salvation of the protagonists of the novel, the contorted family comprising father, mother, and son.

Conclusion

Central Plains, or *Zhongyuan* in Chinese, is Yan's novel written after *Heart Sutra*. If *Heart Sutra* marks a change in Yan's literary style, *Zhongyuan* is the first novel that focuses on his hometown and on the Balou Mountains right after this style shift. *Zhongyuan* was first published in March 2021 in the second issue of the Chinese literary journal *Flower City* (花城 *Huacheng*). The same was later published on October 30, 2021 in a book form by Rye Field Publishing Co. (*Maitian chubanshe* 麥田出版社) in Taiwan in a slightly revised version with the new title *Zhongguo gushi* (中國故事, in English *Chinese Story* or *Story of China*). This essay was completed on July 10, 2021 prior to the publication in Taiwan. In terms of the relationship between the novel and the paratext, we are convinced that in "A Village Larger than the World," Yan also seems to ask for the "technologies of recognition" of current world literature with the title, *Zhongguo gushi*.[56]

We apply the terminology of Pierre Bourdieu's theory of field and argue that in the field of Sinophone novels, Yan has made full use of the symbolic capital of the Central Plains,[57] which has not only achieved a high degree of "distinction" for himself but also a "position" for his works that cannot be ignored, and has made his novels a presence that must be faced squarely under the "technologies of recognition" of world literature. Yan has long absorbed Western literature as his creative capital and fully presented stereotypically modern Chinese stories, thus attracting the attention of Chinese studies in Western academic circles and allowing his works to graft Chinese literature onto the broader realm of world literature.

Finally, the change of title from *Central Plains* to *Chinese Story* or *Story of China* marks Yan's attempt to speak to readers in different regions. For local Chinese readers, *Central Plains* refers to the dialectic of center and periphery; for non-local Chinese readers, *Chinese Story* or *Story of China* refers to a "story" from "China" within the context of Sinophone and world literature. *Central Plains* echoes the so-called "telling the good China story" (*jiang hao Zhongguo gushi* 講好中國故事). This Chinese story unfolds in "a village larger than the world," which shows the alienation of individuals and families in the repetitive daily life under the operation of capitalist logic. Unlike other writers' utopian/dystopian/heterotopian literary imaginations, which use the world of science fiction and fantasy to present the so-called "Chinese story," Yan adopts the most classical imagery of Peach Blossom Spring to respond to the current "Chinese story" discourse. Although this "Chinese story" is only a "fictional story" in the eyes of the wife and child of the textual Yan Lianke (i.e., Yan's self-censorship),[58] this story has nonetheless made the textual Yan think about it night and day. Perhaps the real "good"

---

56 The expression "technologies of recognition" represents Shu-Mei Shih's discussion of the potential discursive bias of Western scholarship in defining the so-called "the West" and "the rest." The West takes the so-called "West" as the criterion for all recognition of literary production in other regions, while the "rest" is merely waiting to be recognized. See Shu-Mei Shih. "Global Literature and the Technologies of Recognition," *PMLA* 119, no. 1 (2004): 16–30.
57 We argue that the closed geographical position of Yan's hometown contributes to his typicality to make a "distinction" in the literary field. The typicality and the distinction can be viewed as a sort of capital in world literature.
58 The reader may refer to Part I in this volume.

Chinese story lies in abandoning the compulsive obsession with the notions of development, mobility, and connection, in stepping away from the imagination in the "future perfect mood,"[59] and instead taking a good look at the present as well as looking deep within oneself.

Bibliography

Dahai li de zhen 大海裡的針. "Yan Lianke na pian 'Yi ge bi shijie geng da de cunzhuang,' ai ma yidian ye bu yuan" 閻連科那篇《一個比世界更大的村莊》，挨罵一點也不冤 [Yan Lianke's article "A Village Bigger than the World" is not unfairly scolded at all]. Zhi hu 知乎 [Q&A website], 19 Mar. 2021. https://zhuanlan.zhihu.com/p/358431006 (last accessed 10 Aug. 2021).

Chao Di-kai 趙帝凱, and Riccardo Moratto, "Taohuayuan de jiushu: shilun Yan Lianke Zhongyuan de renjian qingjing 桃花源的救贖：試論閻連科〈中原〉的人間情境 [The Redemption of the Peach Blossom Spring: An Exploration of the Human Condition in Yan Lianke's "Zhongyuan"]," *Yangzi jiang wenxue pinglun* 揚子江文學評論 [Yangtze Jiang Literary Review], November 2021, no. 6: 40–47.

Genette, Gérard. *Narrative Discourse: An Essay in Method.* New York: Cornell University Press, 1980.

Guo Songmin 郭松民. "Ping Yan Lianke jiang de liang ge gushi" 評閻連科講的兩個故事 ["On the two stories that Yan Lianke recounted"]. Kunlun ce 崑崙策, 14 Mar. 2021. http://www.kunlunce.com/e/wap/show2021.php?classid=176&id=151015&bclassid=1 (last accessed 10 Aug. 2021).

Highmore, Ben. *Everyday Life and Cultural Theory.* London: Routledge, 2001.

Hilton, Isabel. "*The Day the Sun Died* by Yan Lianke Review—The Stuff of Nightmares." *The Guardian*, 29 July 2018. https://www.theguardian.com/books/2018/jul/29/the-day-the-sun-died-yan-lianke-review-china (last accessed 10 Aug. 2021).

Laclau, Ernesto, and Chantal Mouffe. *Hegemony and Socialist Strategy.* London: Verso, 1985.

Lai Hsi-san 賴錫山. "'Taohuayuan ji bing shi' de shenhua, xinlixue quanshi: Tao Yuanming de Daojia shi 'Leyuan' xintan" 〈桃花源記並詩〉的神話、心理學詮釋——陶淵明的道家式「新園」新探 [A mythological and psychological interpretation of "A Record of Peach Blossom Spring, with poem": A new exploration of Tao Yuanming's Daoist "paradise"]. *Zhongguo wenzhe yanjiu jikan* 中國文哲研究集刊 [Bulletin of the Institute of Chinese Literature and Philosophy], 2008, no. 32: 1–40.

Lefebvre, Henri. "The Everyday and Everydayness," trans. Christine Levich. *Yale French Studies*, no. 73 (1987): 7–11.

———. "Towards a Leftist Cultural Politics: Remarks Occasioned by the Centenary of Marx's Death." Translated by David Reifman. In *Marxism and the Interpretation of Culture*, edited by Cary Nelson and Lawrence Grossberg, 75–88. Urbana: University of Illinois Press, 1988.

Liu, Jianmei 劉劍梅. "The Spirit of Zhuangzi and the Chinese Utopian Imagination." In *Utopia and Utopianism in the Contemporary Chinese Context: Texts, Ideas, Spaces*, edited by David Der-wei Wang, Angela Ki Che Leung, and Zhang Yinde, 129–46. Hong Kong: Hong Kong University Press, 2020.

Rojas, Carlos. "Shen yu ren de anzhan yu fuhuan" 神與人的暗戰與復還 ["The dark war between God and man and the restoration"]. In Yan Lianke, *Xinjing* 心經 [Heart Sutra], xiii–xix. Hong Kong: City of University of Hong Kong Press, 2020.

Shih, Shu-Mei. "Global Literature and the Technologies of Recognition." *PMLA* 119, no. 1 (2004): 16–30.

———. *Visuality and Identity: Sinophone Articulations across the Pacific.* Berkeley: University of California Press, 2007.

Wallerstein, Immanuel. *Modern World-System: Capitalist Agriculture and the Origins of the European World-Economy in the Sixteenth Century.* New York: Academic Press, 1974.

Wang, David Der-wei 王德威. *Fin-de-Siècle Splendor: Repressed Modernities of Late Qing Fiction, 1848–1911.* Stanford: Stanford University Press, 1997.

———. "Huayi zhi bian: Huayu yuxi yanjou de xin shijie" 華夷之變：華語語系研究的新視界 [Sinophone/Xenophone studies: Toward a poetics of wind, sound, and changeability]. *Zhongguo xiandai wenxue* 中國現代文學 [Modern Chinese Literature Studies], 2018, no. 34: 1–28.

---

59 David Der-wei Wang, *Fin-de-Siècle Splendor: Repressed Modernities of Late Qing Fiction, 1848–1911* (Stanford: Stanford University Press, 1997), 304.

———. "The Panglossian Dream and Dark Consciousness: Modern Chinese Literature and Utopia." In *Utopia and Utopianism in the Contemporary Chinese Context*, edited by David Wang, Angela Ki Che Leung, and Zhang Yinde, 53–70. Hong Kong: Hong Kong University Press, 2020.

Yan Lianke 閻連科. *Shuohuo* 受活 [Lenin's Kisses]. Taipei: Maitian, 2007.

———. *Si shu* 四書 [The Four Books]. Taipei: Maitian, 2011.

———. *Wo yu fubei* 我與父輩 [Three Brothers: Memories of My Family]. Taipei: Ink Literary, 2009.

———. "Yi ge bi shijie geng da de cunzhuang" 一個比世界更大的村莊 [A village larger than the world"]. Duan chuanmei 端傳媒 [Initum Media], 10 Mar. 2021. https://theinitium.com/article/20210310-notes-newman-prize-for-chinese-literature-yanlianke/ (last accessed 10 Aug. 2021).

———. "Zhongyuan" 中原 [Central plains]. *Huacheng* 花城 [Flower City], 2021, no. 2: 5–79.

PART III

History and gender

15
CREATING A LITERARY SPACE TO DEBATE THE MAO ERA

The fictionalization of the Great Leap Forward in Yan Lianke's *Four Books*[1]

Sebastian Veg

The post-Mao era is usually considered to have begun with the elimination of the Gang of Four and Deng Xiaoping's consolidation of power at the Third Plenum of the Eleventh Central Committee in Dec. 1978, two years after Mao's death. However, the Chinese regime has never entirely called into question Mao's role and importance as the founding father of the nation. Most recently, the current secretary general of the CCP, Xi Jinping, has put forward a complex theory of "two irrefutables" (*liang ge buneng fouding* 兩個不能否定), pointing out that the accomplishments of the Mao era could not be "refuted" by using the advances of the reform era.[2] In a recent essay, Joseph Fewsmith formulates the view that Mao's "legacy seems even more difficult to deal with today than it was 10 or 20 years ago."[3] The persistence of Mao's legacy has, of course, also been the subject of many scholarly studies; important ones include Geremie Barmé's *In the Red*, which points to the continued appeal of the figure of

---

1 This essay previously appeared in *China Perspectives* and *Perspectives Chinoises*, 2014, no. 4. The author would like to express his thanks for the permission to reprint it.
2 Xi began floating similar theories as early as 2011 in a talk for the 90th anniversary of the CCP. The classic formulation appeared in a Jan. 2013 speech to the 18th Central Committee. See "Haobu dongyao jianchi he fazhan Zhongguo tese shehui zhuyi: Zai shijian zhong buduan yousuo faxian yousuo chuangzao yousuo qianjin" 毫不動搖堅持和發展中國特色社會主義 在實踐中不斷有所發現有所創造有所前進 ["Unwaveringly uphold and develop socialism with Chinese characteristics: A practice of continuous discovery, creativity, and progress"], *Renmin ribao* 人民日報 [*People's Daily*], 6 Jan. 2013, http://politics.people.com.cn/n/2013/0106/c1024-20100407.html (last accessed 23 June 2014). This idea was reaffirmed in a long theoretical article authored by the Central Bureau of Party History and published in *People's Daily* on the eve of the Third Plenum: "Zhengque kandai gaige kaifang qianhou liang ge lishi shiqi" 正確看待改革開放前後兩個歷史時期 ["A correct view of the two historical periods before and after the reform and opening up"], *Renmin ribao*, 8 Nov. 2013, http://politics.people.com.cn/n/2013/1108/c1001-23471419.html (last accessed 23 June 2014).
3 Joseph Fewsmith, "Mao's Shadow," *China Leadership Monitor*, 2014, no. 43: 1, http://www.hoover.org/research/maos-shadow (last accessed 23 June 2014). Following an article published by Li Yongfeng in *Yazhou zhoukan* 亞洲週刊 [*Asiaweek*] in 2013, Fewsmith suggests that Xi's reappraisal of Mao may be inspired by an essay submitted by Zhu Jiamu of the Central Documents Research Office in 2007 prior to the 17th Congress and rejected by Jiang Zemin.

Mao in the cultural and intellectual field; Ching Kwan Lee's and Guobin Yang's *Re-envisioning the Chinese Revolution*, which turns to grassroots social representations of the "revolutionary era"; and Sebastian Heilmann's and Elizabeth Perry's *Mao's Invisible Hand*, in which the authors highlight the continuity in policy-making style between the Mao and post-Mao eras.[4]

The 1981 "Resolution on Certain Questions in the History of Our Party" laid out the general framework in which official historiography or other public writing could tackle the Mao era, in terms mainly of "errors" along the road of building socialism.[5] However, in parallel, the government enforced a politics of amnesia, by which public debate of the events of the pre-Reform era was actively discouraged in the public sphere. Fang Lizhi 方勵之, confined to the US embassy in Beijing shortly after the repression of the 1989 democratic movement, wrote the famous essay "The Techniques of Amnesia of the Communist Party" ("Gongchandang de yiwang shu" 共產黨的遺忘術), in which he sets out his idea of "generational break" (*duandai* 斷代), according to which the CCP's hold on power is linked to its ability to cut off the memory of generation after generation of democratic movements, so that each generation must start again from scratch, without knowledge of their predecessors' ideas and accomplishments.[6]

This is not to say that no debate has taken place in China about the years from 1949 to 1978; whether behind closed doors in the upper echelons of the Party or in popular, "unofficial" (*minjian* 民間) publications, there has been, over the years, a fair amount of soul-searching about the events of Mao's reign.[7] As early as 1978, even before the Third Plenum had consolidated Deng's power, the thaw in the literary and art world was signaled by the publication of two short stories, one of which (Lu Xinhua's 盧新華 "The Scar" ["Shanghen" 傷痕, first published in *Wenhuibao* in November 1978]) gave its name to a whole literary movement commemorating certain episodes of the Cultural Revolution. From the late 1970s, literature thus played the role of a substitute for the public discussion of the history of the Mao era. A systematic, public, and officially sanctioned discussion in China of the history and politics of the Mao era, allowing both historians and citizens (and children educated in schools) to better understand the mechanisms of the political persecution campaigns that began in the early 1950s, of the Great Famine of the late 1950s and early 1960s, and of the mass violence that took place throughout the country during the Cultural Revolution has obviously remained elusive, although such a public discussion has often been highlighted as an indispensable prerequisite for true political reform and democratization in China. However, writers

---

4 Sebastian Heilmann and Elizabeth Perry, eds., *Mao's Invisible Hand* (Cambridge, MA: Harvard University Asia Center, 2011); Geremie Barmé, *In the Red* (New York: Columbia University Press, 1999); Ching Kwan Lee and Guobin Yang, eds., *Re-Envisioning the Chinese Revolution: The Politics and Poetics of Collective Memory in Reform China* (Stanford: Stanford University Press, 2007).

5 For a general discussion of Mao's place in official historiography, see Arif Dirlik, "Mao Zedong in Contemporary Chinese Official Discourse and History," *China Perspectives*, 2012, no. 2: 17–28.

6 Fang Lizhi 方勵之, "The Chinese Amnesia," *New York Review of Books*, 27 Sep. 1990, http://www.nybooks.com/articles/archives/1990/sep/27/the-chinese-amnesia/ (last accessed 16 Oct. 2013).

7 Some recent examples of *minjian* voices would be the writings of Nanjing historian Gao Hua 高華 (1954–2012), whose study on Yan'an, *Hong taiyang shi zenyang shengqi de* 紅太陽是怎樣升起的 [*How the red sun rose*] (Hong Kong: Chinese University of Hong Kong Press, 2001), remains unpublished on the mainland; the review by economist Mao Yushi 茅于軾 calling to "bring Mao back to human stature" ["Ba Mao Zedong huanyuan cheng ren 把毛澤東還原成人"], *Caixin* 財新, 26 Apr. 2011; and lobbying by retired Party historian Xin Ziling 辛子陵 to have Mao's name removed from Party documents in late 2011 and early 2012. Retired Peking University Professor Qian Liqun 錢理群 also recently published a massive two-volume biography of Mao, *Mao Zedong shidai he hou Mao Zedong shidai (1949–2009): Ling yi zhong lishi shuxie* 毛澤東時代與後毛澤東時代：另一種歷史書寫 [*The Mao Zedong era and the post-Mao Zedong era (1949–2009): A different historical narrative*] (Taipei: Lianjing, 2012).

and publishers have continually sought to use the loopholes of the publishing system, the perceived greater tolerance for fiction, and the generally liberal sympathies of publishers and journal editors to spark a public discussion on various episodes of the Mao era. Literature thus represents one of the areas in which Chinese society has tried to circumvent the limitations imposed by official discourse.

This paper obviously does not aim to provide a comprehensive overview of intellectual debates on the Mao era, nor even to provide a full history of its literary treatment in China. It focuses more narrowly on one recent example of a fictional work that questions the previously well-defined borders of representing the Mao era in China. It is grounded in a theoretical framework that draws on Jürgen Habermas's definition of the public sphere and the role of literature in bringing about its historical institutionalization, complemented by John Searle's definition of fiction as a pragmatic act. In Habermas's understanding, the modern public sphere appeared in Europe in the eighteenth century in conjunction with an educated, bourgeois society of readers. The bourgeois public sphere, enabled by the press and other publications, can be defined as "the forum ... in which the private people—assembled as the public—gathered in order to constrain the public power to legitimate itself in front of public opinion." Habermas describes its advent as "the process during which the public, constituted of private individuals using reason, appropriates the public sphere controlled by authority, and establishes it as a sphere in which critique is directed at the power of the state, transforming a literary public sphere already endowed with a public and platforms of discussion."[8] Many discussions have been devoted to the normative dimension of Habermas's theory and its possible applications in China, a substantial review of which would go far beyond the scope of this paper. Undoubtedly, very strong constraints arise from writing inside what Perry Link has called the "socialist Chinese literary system."[9] Link considers that the "system" as such came to an end in the 1990s, but his recent publications continue to refer to the "system," highlighting that some of its practices survive.[10] However, despite continued censorship and

---

8 See Jürgen Habermas, *Strukturwandel der Öffentlichkeit* (1962; Frankfurt: Suhrkamp, 1990), 81, 116; my translations. Charles Taylor famously critiqued Habermas' definition of the public sphere in the name of a "politics of recognition" (a critique Habermas does not accept) grounded in a politics of difference that takes issue with the universalist politics of "equal dignity" inherent in Habermas's notion of the public. However, while the author is aware of this critique, this article does not construe Yan's questioning of the Mao era as an attempt to obtain recognition for a claim to an "authentic identity." See Taylor's and Habermas' contributions in Amy Gutman, ed., *Multiculturalism: Examining the Politics of Recognition* (Princeton: Princeton University Press, 1994).

9 Perry Link, *The Uses of Literature: Life in the Socialist Chinese Literary System* (Princeton: Princeton University Press, 2000). Link's approach, though it does not explicitly quote Bourdieu, is grounded in an empirical understanding of literature as a "spectrum of viewpoints," a Bourdieusian formulation Link uses on p. 56. Link defines this system by the combination of a bureaucracy borrowed from the USSR and an assumption of the relevance of literature widely shared in Chinese society. Its distinctive traits are the primacy of the relation between leaders and readers, to the detriment of writers, and its strong reliance on self-censorship, achieved through the "organized dependency" (Andrew Walder) of writers on the advantages offered by their work units.

10 For example, Perry Link writes: "Writers like Mo Yan are clear about the regime's strategy, and may not like it, but they accept compromises in how to put things. It is the price of writing inside the system ... Chinese writers today, whether 'inside the system' or not, all must choose how they will relate to their country's authoritarian government. This inevitably involves calculations, trade-offs, and the playing of cards in various ways." Link, "Does this Writer Deserve the Prize?" *New York Review of Books*, 6 Dec. 2012. Yan discusses this issue in his essay, "Zai gaodu jiquan yu xiangdui kuansong de shuangchong tiankong xia" 在高度集權與相對寬鬆的雙重天空下 [Under the twofold heavens of a high degree of power concentration and relative tolerance], in Yan, *Chenmo yu chuanxi* 沉默與喘息 [Silence and gasping] (Taipei, INK, 2014), 151–71.

control, it is undeniable that the economic reforms of the 1990s have created new spaces for publication and discussion, as Habermas set out in relation to eighteenth-century Europe. This paper builds on the idea that literary works and their discussion by private people, through the print media and in the press, can lead to a critique of the power of the state or of its dominant narratives. In this sense, it understands China to be endowed with an embryonic public sphere, that is in part a product of economic reforms, but also an emanation of a wider Sinophone public sphere, building on the freedoms of press and publication that, although they are not realized in mainland China, are guaranteed in Taiwan, Hong Kong (until recently) and on websites based outside the PRC. *Four Books* was ultimately not published in mainland China but has been made widely available on the internet including inside China (as discussed below); it can therefore be discussed in the framework of this wider Sinophone public sphere.

Furthermore, this paper relies on Searle's understanding of fictional discourse as a pragmatic act, endowed with intentionality (on the part of the author), communicational content, and a pragmatic effect on its readers, just like other types of discourse. While fiction may be "playful," it is therefore also understood as an intervention directed at a (potentially unlimited) group of addressees.[11] This explains why, in addition to the close textual reading of Yan's *Four Books*, the paper relies on two in-depth interviews with the author, in which the intentionality of the intervention can be better understood (though this should obviously not constitute a limit to possible readings and to its pragmatic effect). In parallel, public interviews are also quoted in which Yan makes similar points.[12] Based on this approach, this essay makes the argument for a possible turning point in the way contemporary Chinese intellectuals are prepared to publicly discuss the Maoist period in the PRC history.

The first section provides a brief historical overview, followed by an analysis of Yan's book and of its reception in China.

The debate on the Mao Era and the literary sphere: A historical overview

Since the scar literature of the late 1970s, fiction and fictionalized autobiography have played an important role in bringing to light the personal traumas of the Cultural Revolution. Lu Xinhua's "The Scar"[13] is about a young woman who breaks ties with her politically suspect family and goes to the countryside, only to find herself tainted by her family background. When her mother is eventually rehabilitated, she returns to Shanghai to look for her, only to discover she has just passed away. Texts like this one, often inspired by personal experience, nonetheless remained within a well-defined framework, in which the political system itself was never questioned; on the contrary, people's belief in the Party's and its ability to correct its own mistakes was often emphasized. This approach was largely mirrored in the 1981 resolution that followed a few years later, in which the final verdict on Mao remained positive, despite the "mistakes" made by the collective leadership as early as the 1950s and the full-scale condemnation of the Cultural

---

11 John Searle, "The Logical Status of Fictional Discourse," *New Literary History* 6 (1975): 319–32.
12 Yan's new collection of essays touching on censorship, amnesia, and other political issues (see n9 above) was published as the present article went to press; it can therefore only be referenced rather than fully discussed here.
13 See Lu Xinhua et al., *The Wounded: New Stories of the Cultural Revolution*, trans. Geremie Barmé et al. (Hong Kong: Joint Publishing, 1979).

Revolution as "erroneous."[14] Following its earlier practice (a similar resolution had been adopted in 1945), the CCP was thus able to weave the "error" of the Cultural Revolution into a larger narrative of modernization and the historical legitimacy of CCP rule.

Intellectuals in the 1980s were, to an extent, prepared to play by these rules. Within the larger context of a political consensus on modernization bringing together elites inside and outside the Party, the pervasive understanding of the Mao era was formulated in culturalist terms acceptable to the CCP: under Mao, the benighted forces of Chinese peasant tradition, in the form of ignorance and autocracy, as expressed most egregiously in the personality cult of Mao, had reappeared. Mao had been weighed down by the ignorance and lack of education of the Chinese population, both at the grassroots and among cadres. It was thus possible to denounce these forces in the name of enlightenment, and to give the Party credit for endorsing a new push toward more enlightenment.[15] This narrative had the additional advantage that intellectuals could be portrayed as victims: under Mao, the Party-State had betrayed the intellectuals' trust by siding with the large masses of the benighted peasantry; the intellectuals, however, had remained loyal, and were now once again prepared to work together with the State and the Party to overcome these obscure forces. These were, by and large, the terms of the original debate on Mao in the 1980s, although dissenting voices existed.[16]

One of these voices belonged to Liu Xiaobo 劉曉波 who, as early as 1986, wrote a famous essay entitled "Crisis!" in which he attacked intellectuals for only scratching the surface of the problems raised by the recent totalitarian past: "The rightist intellectuals in Zhang Xianliang's [張賢亮] works not only do not lose their sense of respect for humanity and its value among the inhuman conditions of reeducation through labor camps, on the contrary, thanks to the hard physical labor, by communing with ordinary people, in the kisses and caresses of sincere, simple, hard-working village girls, they even find their way back to the Marxist-Leninist worldview and regain their affection for the proletariat, which purifies their soul and elevates their moral feelings."[17] In Liu's view, despite Zhang Xianliang's unsparing

---

14 See "Resolution on Certain Questions in the History of Our Party Since the Founding of the People's Republic of China," Marxists Internet Archive, http://www.marxists.org/subject/china/documents/cpc/history/01.htm. For the Chinese original, see "Guanyu jianguo yilai dang de ruogan lishi wenti de jueyi" 關於建國以來黨的若干歷史問題的決議, Zhongguo zhengfu wang 中國政府網 [Chinese government website], http://big5.www.gov.cn/gate/big5/www.gov.cn/test/2008-06/23/content_1024934.htm (both last accessed on 25 June 2014). The key assessment on Mao and the 1956–66 decade is in paragraph 18: "In the course of this decade, there were serious faults and errors in the guidelines of the Party's work, which developed through twists and turns … All the successes in these ten years were achieved under the collective leadership of the Central Committee of the Party headed by Comrade Mao Zedong. Likewise, responsibility for the errors committed in the work of this period rested with the same collective leadership. Although Comrade Mao Zedong must be held chiefly responsible, we cannot lay the blame for all those errors on him alone." Paragraph 20: "The history of the 'cultural revolution' has proved that Comrade Mao Zedong's principal theses for initiating this revolution conformed neither to Marxism, Leninism nor to Chinese reality. They represent an entirely erroneous appraisal of the prevailing class relations and political situation in the Party and state."

15 See, for example, Jing Wang 王瑾, *High Culture Fever: Politics, Aesthetics, and Ideology in Deng's China* (Berkeley: University of California Press, 1996), in particular chap. 2, "High Culture Fever: The Cultural Discussion in the Mid-1980s and the Politics of Methodologies," 37–116.

16 See also Michael Berry's discussion of the dialectics of nostalgia and trauma in educated youth literature, focused on two more atypical authors, Wang Xiaobo and Ah Cheng 阿城, in his *A History of Pain* (New York: Columbia University Press, 2008), chap. 4, esp. p. 260.

17 Liu Xiaobo, "Weiji! Xin shiqi wenxue mianlin de weiji" 危機!新時期文學面臨的危機 ["Crisis! The crisis facing new era literature"], *Shenzhen qingnianbao* 深圳青年報 [*Shenzhen Youth Newspaper*], 3 Oct. 1986. See also my French translation in Liu Xiaobo, *La Philosophie du porc et autres essais* (Paris: Gallimard, 2011), 57–87.

descriptions of conditions in labor camps and of the humiliations undergone by intellectuals, his writing evacuates the institutional dimensions of Maoist policy as well as the intellectuals' role in supporting it.

New forms of writing appeared in the 1990s, when Wang Xiaobo's 王小波 novella *The Golden Age* (*Huangjin shidai* 黃金時代, 1993) marked a turning point. By trivializing the experience of rusticated educated youths, which is portrayed as a series of sado-masochistic sexual humiliations perpetrated by the state, Wang was the first to question the victim status of intellectuals, whose masochism stood for their consenting enjoyment of their victim role. Through this ironic indictment of the victims, Wang no doubt sought a more active role for civil society in debating Maoism.[18]

Most recently, writers have opened up new perspectives, both in moving beyond the Cultural Revolution back to the 1950s, and in more explicitly questioning the role of the Party in episodes of mass violence or death. Three recent works stand out, only one of which was published in mainland China. Yang Xianhui's 楊顯惠 *Chronicles of Jiabiangou* 夾邊溝記事 (Tianjin, 2002) was perhaps the pioneering work in dealing with the Anti-rightist movement and a deathly labor camp in Gansu during the great famine. Formally, it is presented as a collection of fictional stories, which allowed it to be published within the PRC, but it is largely based on survivor interviews.[19] Yang Jisheng's 楊繼繩 *Tombstone* 墓碑 (Hong Kong, 2008) is a work of citizen history, but also an essay in its own right, in the same tradition of Chinese reportage literature, based on interviews and documents. Finally, Yan Lianke's 閻連科 *Four Books* 四書 (Hong Kong, 2010) is a fictionalization of the famine of the Great Leap Forward in a labor camp on the banks of the Yellow River. Despite their formal differences, these works and their focus on the 1950s represent an attempt to call into question the original legitimacy of the PRC and to create a debate within the Chinese-speaking public sphere on the foundations of the current regime.[20]

In a first attempt to highlight how these works differ from past treatments of the Mao era, the following characteristics can be proposed as a working framework, which this essay will return to in detail below:

1. Breaking with the "safer" period of the Cultural Revolution, which was singled out as "completely erroneous" in the 1981 resolution and carefully circumscribed as a parenthesis in the PRC history, these works go back to the politically more "complex" foundational period of the 1950s.
2. Rather than revealing an "accident" in its development, these works question the nature of the PRC regime.
3. Rather than portraying intellectuals as victims, they attempt to address their "guilt" or at least complicity in the establishment and development of the regime.
4. Rather than focusing on the sufferings of the elite, they attempt to document the experience of ordinary people as victims of the regime and to endow them with agency.
5. While many previous publications focused on individual testimonies, making no claim as to the overarching political structures, these works attempt to go beyond purely individual narratives and to open a public debate on history.

18 See Sebastian Veg, "Utopian Fiction and Critical Reflection," *China Perspectives*, 2007, no. 4: 75–87.
19 See Sebastian Veg, "Testimony, History and Ethics: From the Memory of Jiabiangou Prison Camp to a Reappraisal of the Anti-Rightist Movement in Present-Day China," *The China Quarterly*, no. 218 (June 2014): 514–39.
20 There were a few isolated attempts to discuss the famine in literary works in the 1980s. Perry Link mentions the anonymous play *Wildfire* and novellas by Zhang Yigong 張一弓, "The Story of Criminal Li Tongzhong," and Qian Yuxiang 錢玉祥, "History, Be My Judge!" See Link, *The Uses of Literature*, 254–55.

Yan's singular novel raises specific questions about the sort of public sphere for the critique of official narratives that literature can attempt to open up, within certain limits, as highlighted by its non-publication in mainland China. It has, however, been made available and widely discussed on the Chinese internet. Read together with Yan's outspoken essay on amnesia published in the international media, it deals with the writer's responsibility to commemorate the past and fight forgetting. More practically, it raises the problem of the relationship between intentionality, as implicit in Searle's pragmatics, and literary form, which opens up a multitude of meanings for the reader. How can the responsibility to remember and the intention to commemorate be translated into an open literary form, without risking to be reduced to silence by the institutions of literary censorship in China? Perry Link, among others, has highlighted the risks inherent in engaging in the strategies of avoidance that are necessary to enter the Chinese public sphere.[21] Furthermore, how can a fictional narrative reestablish forgotten historical events? Finally, if what is most lacking today is an open debate within the public sphere about the mass violence of the Mao era, how can a work of fiction spark a historical debate, and leave the necessary space for polysemy and discussion?

Yan Lianke's *Four Books*

Yan Lianke's *Four Books*, first published in 2010 in Hong Kong, marks a new turn in the way Chinese literature has framed the historical events of the Mao era, attempting to engage with the massive loss of life during the Great Leap Forward, and to offer reflections on how individuals, some of them highly educated, contributed to creating the climate of political terror in which the famine took place. When discussing the motivations for writing a book about the great famine of 1958–61, Yan underlines that most writers after 1978 had limited themselves to writing about the Cultural Revolution: while this may have been natural for writers of his generation (he was born in 1958) who had experienced it, he criticizes the generation of his parents, who had lived through the Great Leap Forward and the famine, but failed to write about it. Perhaps, he hypothesizes, because in 1978 they were fully occupied reflecting on the Cultural Revolution, and because state politics were more restrictive regarding the "myth of the 1950s": the famine was never explicitly approved as an object of criticism in the same way as the Cultural Revolution in the 1981 resolution.[22] Liu Xiaobo in "Crisis!" had already mentioned that many writers did not dare to pursue their critique beyond the Cultural Revolution, because this would mean questioning the very foundations of the People's Republic that were laid down in the 1950s. For Yan, writings on the Cultural Revolution in the 1980s were both too uniform (*dandiao* 單調) and too fragmented: everyone wrote about their own memories rather than reflecting on the underlying political system.[23] There was no literary reflection of the variety of experiences—while 90 percent of the population has no ability to speak out, those that could speak out only speak about themselves. The CCP had invented the practice of *suku* 訴苦 or "airing grievances," by which peasants could

---

21 Perry Link refers to a "reverse magnet syndrome" that involves approaching problems like the Great Famine and then deflecting attention from their contentious aspects by using techniques such as "daft hilarity" (in the case of Mo Yan). Although the "socialist system of literature" as such is defunct, its technique of control relying on "organized dependency" continues to ensure that most writers will continue to make the "correct" choices of subject matter "in order to preserve (their) career prospects under Party rule." See Link, "Politics and the Chinese Language," *China File*, 24 Dec. 2012, http://chinafile.com/politics-and-chinese-language (last accessed 12 Aug. 2014).
22 Author's interview with Yan Lianke, Hong Kong, 11 Oct. 2013.
23 Ibid.

complain in public about their cruel treatment at the hands of landlords; for him much of the Cultural Revolution literature followed the *suku* model, in which intellectuals are only innocent victims. He therefore set out to write a book that was both more polyphonic and could question the role played by intellectuals.[24]

Memory and amnesia

Against state-sponsored amnesia, Yan believes that the writer's foremost duty is to write a well-constructed literary work, as only literary value can ensure the rebuilding of memory, as shown by the great Chinese novels that have survived to document bygone eras.[25] In April 2013, he published an op-ed in *The New York Times* entitled "On China's State-sponsored Amnesia" in which he denounced a state policy: "Lies are surpassing the truth. Fabrications have become the logical link to fill historical gaps." To him, writers working within the system are somehow complicit: "The state is not the only player to be blamed for the nation's amnesia in today's China. We must also look at Chinese intellectuals, as we appear to be content with this forced amnesia." He contrasts Chinese writers with Russian writers like Bulgakov and Pasternak, whose works "did not [simply] rebel against state power; they are more about preserving and restoring a nation's memories." In China, on the contrary, writers are eager to espouse the narrative sponsored by the state: "Naturally, we thus replace the forgotten past with fiction and build splendid lies over reality. And we do this without feeling any sense of moral guilt—it's all in the name of artistic creativity."[26]

While Yang Jisheng helps us to understand the facts (*zhenshi de shiqing* 真實的事情), Yan believes that his own writing can bring back the reality of feelings and memories (*zhenshi de ganqing* 真實的感情). Accordingly, although the idea for the novel was inspired by the discovery of historical traces (around 1989–90 when an army colleague in Lanzhou told Yan about finding bones in the desert that had belonged to rightists who died in a labor camp), he felt no need to undertake any historical research.[27] In the op-ed as well as the interview, Yan therefore presents his novel as the outcome of a deliberate strategy to counter *duandai* as defined by Fang Lizhi. Although some critics may find his pronouncements disingenuous and designed to curry favor with overseas readers,[28] in the final analysis, the "impurity" of authors' motivations is a defining fact of literature; it may therefore be more productive to study how these pronouncements tally with the design of the novel and the social effects of its reception. Relying on an international public sphere, in the age of the internet, may also be a strategy to transform the domestic one.

24 Author's interview with Yan Lianke, Hong Kong, 24 May 2012. On the *suku* model, see Sun Feiyu, *Social Suffering and Political Confession: Suku in Modern China* (Singapore: World Scientific, 2013). See also Yan Lianke "Kongju yu beipan jiang yu wo zhongsheng tongxing" 恐懼與背叛將與我終生同行 ["Fear and betrayal will accompany me all my life"], *Chenmo yu chuanxi*, 127–50.
25 Author's interview with Yan Lianke, Hong Kong, 11 Oct. 2013.
26 Yan Lianke, "On China's State-Sponsored Amnesia," *The New York Times*, 1 Apr. 2013, http://www.nytimes.com/2013/04/02/opinion/on-chinas-state-sponsored-amnesia.html?_r=0 (last accessed 25 June 2014). The Chinese version was first published in Yan's collection under the title "Guojia shiji yu wenxue jiyi" 國家失記與文學記憶 ["State amnesia and the memory of literature"], *Chenmo yu chuanxi*, 9–23.
27 Author's interview with Yan Lianke, Hong Kong, 24 May 2012.
28 *Four Books* has to date been translated into French by Sylvie Gentil, *Les Quatre Livres* (Arles: Picquier, 2012), but its publication seems to have received less international media coverage than *Serve the People* or Mo Yan's recent works. It has also been translated into Czech as *Čtyři knihy* by Zuzana Li and may have played a role in the awarding of the Kafka Prize to Yan in 2014 (I would like to thank an anonymous reviewer for pointing out this connection). The English translation by Carlos Rojas was published in 2016.

The structure of the novel stands out by its complexity. In this respect, as well as its subject matter, it reveals some continuities with Yan's earlier work, *Pleasure* (*Shouhuo* 受活, 2004, published in English as *Lenin's Kisses*), which is made up of a main narration and footnotes presented as "padding" (*xuyan* 絮言) that, as highlighted by Liu Jianmei 劉劍梅, are designed to document the past, as "Forgetting is our common sin."[29] Another similarity that confirms Yan's longtime preoccupation with the Mao era is the image of the commercial exploitation of a Lenin Memorial Hall in *Pleasure*, a metaphor for the Mao mausoleum in Tiananmen Square.

Four Books is divided into four narratives (in fact, each of these "books" is broken up into short extracts and presented in collage form, not continuously), each of which is linked with another, canonical, text. Events take place in a labor farm on the Yellow River (Zone 99, which may refer to "eternity" in Chinese), where about a hundred intellectuals are made to work, first to temper steel, then to grow astronomical outputs of wheat, under the direction of the "Child," the camp leader. Individuals are named after a personal characteristic (Writer, Laboratory, Music, Religion, etc.). The novel alternates between three narratives; the fourth "book" appears in a single chunk as an epilogue ("The New Myth of Sisyphus," rewriting the Greek myth). Two of the narratives are ostensibly written by one of the characters of the narrative, known as the "Writer": one to denounce other inmates to the authorities ("Account of Criminals"), the other is a "novel" entitled "The Old Bed," referring to the old riverbed of the Yellow River. The third one, "The Child of Heaven," is a third-person heterodiegetic narration centered on the character of the Child with strong biblical allusions and vocabulary.[30] The complexity of the structure therefore calls for some decoding and contextualization of each of the narratives, before any further interpretations are made.

Maoism as religion ("The Child of Heaven")

The use of religious vocabulary and biblical narration in "The Child of Heaven" is one of the most striking features of the novel. On the first page of the book, the establishment of the camp is recounted as a second genesis with the rhythmical repetition of the phrase "and it was so": "And it was so. God separated light from darkness. Light was called Day and Darkness was called Night. There was evening and morning" (30).[31] The Child returns to the great plain, proclaiming: "I have returned. From above, from the county-town. I will lay down ten commandments" (31). By comparing the Child to Moses, and the local bureaucrats to heavenly intercessors ("from above"), the author makes the comparison between the Mao-state and religion immediately explicit. It is of course an ironic one, as becomes even more apparent when the Child informs the men that they must produce 500 pounds of grain by *mu* 畝 of land to catch up with the United Kingdom and pass the United States, repeatedly threatening to kill himself if the men don't carry out his orders.[32]

29 This sentence appears on the cover of *Pleasure*. See Liu Jianmei, "To Join the Commune or Withdraw from It: A Reading of Yan Lianke's *Shouhuo*," *Modern Chinese Literature and Culture* 19, no. 2 (Fall 2007), 1–33, esp. 25.
30 Heterodiegetic narration, as defined by Gérard Genette, refers to a configuration in which the narrative voice cannot be identified as belonging to one of the characters in the narrative. This characteristic sets "The Child of Heaven" apart from the two other "Books" mentioned above, in which the narrator is the character named Writer.
31 Page numbers refer to Yan Lianke, *Si shu* 四書 [*Four books*] (Taipei: Maitian, 2011). See also chap. 7.4, entitled "Exodus," this chapter tells the "miracle" of making steel from the sands of the Yellow River.
32 Yan has previously used biblical allusions in the first chapter of *The Dreams of Ding Village*, where three of Joseph's dreams from the book of Genesis appear in the form of a prophecy; however, this is the first time he draws an explicit parallel with Maoism.

Throughout the novel, Yan develops a parallel between this biblical narrative and Maoist politics, a cult based on red flowers and stars, which the inmates can earn for their good deeds. The Child displays the naïve but unquestioning belief in revolution of the Red Guards, hinting at the transformation of an entire nation of adults into brainwashed children. The comparison is reinforced by the thematic use of a character called simply Religion. A Christian, he is persuaded by the Child to trample on and destroy his Bible and prints of the Virgin Mary. On one occasion, Religion is informed on by the Writer and discovered to have hidden a miniature bible inside Marx's *Capital*, a work the Scholar had helped translate (138). But the Child also shows some interest in the Bible: on one occasion, he asks Religion to tell him a story "from the Book you like most" (178); on another the inmates find him reading an album of *Stories from the Bible* and, when Religion begins to deface his last print of the Virgin Mary to obtain food from him, the Child stops him (289). More generally, the world of the labor camp rests upon acts of faith: the possibility of working miracles, by producing hitherto unheard-of quantities of grain per *mu*, or of making steel out of the silt of the Yellow River. Interestingly, Yan's interest in the ritual aspects of Maoist politics is in fact, quite similar to what sociologists have described as the "ritualization of processes of production," whereby the aim is no longer to produce but to "remold" peasants' representations.[33] Yan is no doubt also drawing on Mao's status as a worker of miracles in the countryside.[34]

The Child is a particularly puzzling character. Just as there is no explanation of the establishment of the camp, there is no given source for the narrative of "The Child of Heaven"—like the biblical narrative, it is omniscient and without an identifiable narrator. Yan underlines that the Child, similarly, has no biographical background and no psychological plausibility. He is what Tsai Chien-hsin 蔡建鑫 and Yan have termed "a little young Fascist," who wholeheartedly believes in the system and is prepared to sacrifice himself to it.[35] However, at the end of the novel, after traveling to Beijing, the Child also changes. He goes to Beijing with 18 gigantic ears of wheat, grown with the blood of the Writer, because he hopes to earn a special mention for his Zone; by this time, half of the inmates have died, and the Scholar entrusts him with a manuscript that is to reveal the truth of the situation to the central authorities. Although at this time, the inmates have already received the visit of a central leader whose physical description suggests a resemblance with Liu Shaoqi, and who has understood the extent of the famine, they still believe that the center can help them. However, when the Child returns, there is no account of his stay in Beijing, rather he distributes red stars "made of steel," (365) which will allow all inmates to return home and, the next evening, crucifies himself on a makeshift cross. Has he lost his childish faith in the system? Has his interest in

---

33 Guo Yuhua, "Folk Society and Ritual State," in *European and Chinese Sociologies: A New Dialogue*, ed. Laurence Roulleau-Berger and Li Peilin (Leiden: Brill, 2011), 220.
34 In an interview, Yan explicitly discusses the transformation of Mao into a Saint in the countryside, commenting that people are controlled by gods (*shen dui ren de guanli* 神對人的管理); in his view, Mao could be seen as a god—people have doubts, but venerate him because he holds power. Author's interview with Yan Lianke, Hong Kong, 24 May 2012.
35 See Tsai Chien-hsin, "The Museum of Innocence: The Great Leap Forward and Famine, Yan Lianke, and *Four Books*," *Modern Chinese Literature and Culture Resource Center*, May 2011, https://u.osu.edu/mclc/online-series/museum-of-innocence/ (last accessed 14 Aug. 2021). Yan has also used this expression, although obviously not in the novel. In an interview, he refers to him as a "young Fascist" (*xiao Faxisi* 小法西斯) whom thousands of intellectuals happily obey in the labor camp. See Xia Yu 夏榆, "Yan Lianke: Shenghuo de xiabian haiyou kanbujian de shenghuo" 閻連科: 生活的下邊還有看不見的生活 ["Yan Lianke: Below life there is another invisible life"], *Nanfang zhoumo* 南方周末 [*Southern Weekly*], 27 May 2011, http://www.infzm.com/content/59605 (last accessed 14 Aug. 2021).

the Bible led him to a kind of conversion that inspires his self-crucifixion? Tsai, in his preface to the Taiwanese edition of the book translated on the *Modern Chinese Literature and Culture* website, discusses the ambiguity of the character of the Child, who ultimately turns himself into a martyr to atone for his previous wrongdoings. As Tsai writes, his self-crucifixion "may well be a plea for absolution as well as a martyrdom motivated by true, altruist socialist ideals."[36] Most interestingly, perhaps, with the biblical simplicity of his Mao-like pronouncements, he raises the question for the reader of whether, and how, the Party can repent and atone for its sins.

An interesting point of detail in this regard is the narration in "The Child of Heaven" of how the great famine begins. In chapter 13, the third section begins with the following sentences: "This rain lasted for forty days, and boundless water covered the world. Noah insisted on making an Ark, and was thus able to succor the remaining men and animals" (268). While this narration seems to accredit the official narrative of a famine provoked by a natural catastrophe that cannot be mastered, we should note that no similar narration appears in the other chronicle of events. Perhaps the author is precisely suggesting that within the logic of Maoist faith, the failure to fulfill the quotas of grain could only stem from a heavenly curse of biblical dimensions.

The intellectuals' guilt ("The Old Course")

In another dramatic break with most previous writing about the Mao era, the author has structured *Four Books* as an indictment of intellectuals, who make up the mass of the inmates of the labor camp. Their guilt is twofold: they are accused of being among the perpetrators during the Mao era; but also of failing to face up to their own past in transmitting the memory of the events. This idea is strongly conveyed in the two other narratives that make up the bulk of *Four books*, both of which are ostensibly written by a character known as the Writer. He is something of a celebrity whose works have been extolled by the system before the campaign targeting intellectuals, in which he is designated for rustication by popular vote inside his work unit. However, the authorities take pity on him and agree to give him preferential treatment if he agrees to watch over the other inmates and deliver weekly written reports to the Child. While all the intellectuals in Zone 99 spend a large part of their time informing on others, in particular on possible illicit relationships, in the hope that they can earn enough red flowers to go home, the Writer surpasses all others in his systematic betrayal of all other inmates. He informs on the Scholar and Music, revealing their "crime of adultery" (*tongjian fan* 通奸犯) to the authorities; at the same time, he also double-crosses Laboratory (who is trying to catch them red-handed) in order to single-handedly pocket the benefits of his snitching. He again denounces those who have lied about the number of red stars after the Child's tent burns in chapter 11, and spies on Music even during the deadly famine in chapter 14. He is also always ready to participate in mass campaigns, and uses the last drop of his own blood to grow oversized ears of wheat. While all intellectuals are also victims, the Writer, in particular, is singled out as a perpetrator and avid collaborator in both the authorities' irrational production plans and ubiquitous surveillance.

36 See Tsai, "The Museum of Innocence," 7. Also noting that *Four Books* is the first full-fledged fictional inquiry into the great famine, Tsai reads it primarily as a moral inquiry, in conjunction with David Grossman's Holocaust novel *See Under: Love* and Lu Xun's two prose-poems "Revenge" I and II in *Wild Grass* (*Yecao* 野草). Just like the Christ-figure in "Revenge," Tsai reads the character of the Child as a probing of moral ambiguity, whose self-crucifixion reveals a mix of "sadistic autoeroticism and a disgraceful renunciation." By connecting it with Lu Xun's understanding of fiction as *pharmakon*, Tsai seems to suggest that the crucifixion of the Child can lead to a symbolic expulsion of the "poisonous" Maoist past from the city.

However, the Writer ends up unsatisfied with "Record of criminals," the reports with which he informs on others, and, while he is growing wheat far from the camp, turns to writing a fictional narrative as a complement (234). It is only in this narrative that the records of famine and cannibalism appear. Because of the pervasive famine, inmates are eating the dead bodies of other dead inmates in Zone 99—this is in keeping with the use of cannibalism as a trope in Chinese literature throughout the twentieth century to signify the debasement of the most basic ethics of humanity.[37] However, Yan ends up reversing this trope. The Writer, having informed on Music and her "adultery" with the Scholar, as well as with a well-connected official from a neighboring zone, who gives her food and whom the writer tries to blackmail, is alerted by the official that Music has died of overeating during a tryst with him. He then finds his own reports to the Child informing on her among her belongings. At this point, to request forgiveness both from her corpse and from her lover, the Scholar, the Writer cuts off two chunks of his own flesh from his calves and boils them. One is to be buried with Music, the other is served up to the starving Scholar as pork meat. When the Writer places the second piece together with his reports on Music's dead body, the Scholar understands what he has eaten and exclaims: "Ah, educated people ... educated people ..." (*Dushu ren ya ... dushu ren ...* 讀書人呀……讀書人……, 341). The trope of cannibalism is thus inverted: it becomes a means of repentance (*chanhui* 懺悔) for the intellectual, who is finally able to confront his own complicity in the system and understand his own role as a "cannibal." Although the term *chanhui* does not appear in the novel, Yan has used it in several public statements. Its religious connotations (mainly Christian but not only) suggest that, for Yan also, the main task in confronting the legacy of the Mao era is of a moral nature.[38]

In an interview, Yan highlights that, while intellectuals in China have always been very good at criticizing others, in this book they repent and criticize themselves: "Since Yan'an, all intellectuals have been both victims and guilty. How was it that intellectuals became the greatest collaborators of the regime? Worse than that: what they have told us are lies. Much worse than fake milk powder is the fake history they have produced. At least with milk powder, you can buy the real thing in Hong Kong. But our history textbooks have made a whole nation amnesic."[39] The Writer's repentance in the novel, as expressed in the act of cannibalism, therefore also leads to a reassessment of how to write about the events of the famine and to publish the novel that he began scribbling "in the blanks between the 'Reports on criminals' that I wrote for the Child" (212): "I want to write a really good book, not for the Child, not for the country, nor for this nation and its readers, only for myself." (211) This purely individual account, though it is a novel and thus not factual, may turn out to be the most truthful account of the famine. Beyond his moral critique, Yan therefore uses the two

---

37 See the comprehensive overview in Gang Yue 樂剛, *The Mouth That Begs: Hunger, Cannibalism, and the Politics of Eating in Modern China* (Durham: Duke University Press, 1999) and the enlightening critique in Katherine Edgerton-Tarpley, "Eating Culture: Cannibalism and the Semiotics of Starvation, 1870–2001," in *Tears from Iron: Cultural Responses to Famine in Nineteenth-Century China* (Berkeley: University of California Press, 2008), 211–33.

38 For example, Xia, "Yan Lianke": "In *Four Books*, one intellectual deeply repents [*chanhui*], and that is the Writer, who is also an informant. His repentance is more or less unprecedented among contemporary Chinese intellectuals." This is not entirely unprecedented: the first intellectual to call for "repentance" was Liu Zaifu 劉再復 in his 1986 essay "Wenxue yu chanhui yishi" 文學與懺悔意識 ["Literature and confession"], the publication of which was blocked by Bo Yibo until 1988. See Link, *The Uses of Literature*, 45, n109.

39 Author's interview with Yan Lianke, Hong Kong, 11 Oct. 2013.

accounts by the Writer to convey a narrative of history different from the official one and to illustrate the gap between the two.

The reception of *Four Books*: Opening a debate on history

It might seem paradoxical to initiate a discussion on the public sphere starting from a book that was not published in mainland China. However, contrary to what Tsai writes, Yan did not preemptively self-ban the novel by not submitting it to mainland publishers; rather it was submitted to several commercial publishers in succession, who turned it down, so that in the end, it had to be published in Hong Kong.[40] According to Yan, this was due to a lack of precaution on his behalf: if the first refusal had been kept secret, other publishers might have considered it seriously (as happened with his new book, just published, *Chronicle of Zhalie/Blow-up* (*Zhalie zhi* 炸裂志); as it was, news leaked out that no one would touch it, a self-fulfilling prophecy. Yan therefore points out that fiction is not necessarily easier to publish than documentary research; depending on whether the author is deemed "trustworthy," different standards may also apply.[41] Whatever the case may be, Yan did try to make the novel available to the mainland readership, even making certain changes to maximize its publication chances, so that "readers with the same mother tongue, history and culture, living on the same piece of earth could access a not too poor version of the book,"[42] and as of today, it is indeed available electronically on a mainland website.

Yan develops several strategies that can be understood as targeted at sparking a debate among mainland readers. And indeed, such a debate has taken place, to an extent, with the publication of newspaper reports and scholarly articles on the book by famous critics and academics like Sun Yu 孫郁 (Dean of Literature at People's University), Chen Xiaoming 陳曉明 (Peking University), and Wang Binbin 王彬彬 (Nanjing University), as well as other academics.[43] These articles appeared in the Chinese media at the same time as and in the context of other reports on the great famine, such as the investigative special feature of *Nanfang renwu zhoukan* 南方人物週刊 titled "The Great Famine" ("Da jihuang" 大饑荒) in May 2012.[44] The present section is therefore devoted to connecting the author's narrative strategies with the reality of the readings that took place in China. In particular, the polyphonic technique, as exemplified in the last "book" (Sisyphus), opens the possibility of multiple readings and debates about history. The fact that such debates took place, albeit in literary journals or on more obscure websites, highlights how the existence of a relatively autonomous sphere for the discussion of literature, as it emerged from the Chinese market reforms of the 1990s—in a way not unlike

---

40 Tsai, "The Museum of Innocence," 4. This reassessment is based on Yan's own assertion (interview, 2013, and his postface to the privately printed edn.) but is backed up by names of the many publishers he claims to have submitted the novel to and details of the process.
41 Author's interview with Yan Lianke, Hong Kong, 11 Oct. 2013. Yan jokes that if he had written *Frogs* on birth control, it would have been turned down, while under Mo Yan's signature, it was awarded the Mao Dun 茅盾 prize.
42 Yan Lianke, "Xiezuo de pantu (*Si shu* houji)" 寫作的叛徒(《四書》後記) "[The Writer as rebel: Postface to *Four Books*"], manuscript provided by the author.
43 See also presentations by Wang Yao 王堯, Suzhou University, and Cheng Guangwei 程光煒, People's University, at the conference on Yan Lianke and Yu Hua 余華 held at the Hong Kong University of Science and Technology on 10 Oct. 2013.
44 See "Da jihuang" ["The great famine"], *Nanfang renwu zhoukan* [*Southern People Weekly*], no. 299 (21 May 2012): 34–51.

the "literary public sphere already endowed with a public" described by Habermas—can indeed open up a wider social space of political discussion.

Reception in China

Although *Four Books* was not published in China, it has a distinct reception history on the mainland. *Beijing Youth Daily* (*Beijing qingnian bao* 北京青年報) reported as early as 28 Feb. 2011 that People's University Faculty of Literature, where Yan holds a professor position, organized a conference on *Four Books* and on an essay collection by Yan titled *Discovering Fiction* (*Faxian xiashuo* 發現小說) published simultaneously by People's University, on 26 Feb. 2011. The article quotes the author as well as comments by Sun Yu and writer Zhang Yueran 張悅然, and mentions that the book has been printed and a small number of copies presented to friends.[45] Around the same time, the first full reviews began appearing in Hong Kong and Singapore media, and circulating on the internet. In June, *Southern Metropolis Daily* (*Nanfang dushi bao* 南方都市報) printed a full-page article by an occasional contributor named Zhao Yong 趙勇, ostensibly devoted to the essay collection, but which describes in passing how he read a self-printed edition of the novel, which many friends around him were pressing him to finish and pass on to them.[46] Post-1980s writer Jiang Fangzhou 蔣方舟 mentions Yan's "publicity lecture tour" about this novel in another article published in Shenzhen under the telling title "Remedying Political Naiveté by Reading Books."[47] Liberal professor Wang Binbin, who also received a private copy as a gift, provides a full-fledged description of the plum-colored cover inscribed with the words *si shu* in Lu Xun's 魯迅 calligraphy and the author's afterword "The Writer as Rebel" ("Xiezuo de pantu" 寫作的叛徒).[48] Finally, the nomination and shortlisting of *Four Books* for the fourth Dream of the Red Chamber Award of Sinophone novels in July 2012 (awarded to Wang Anyi's 王安憶 *Heavenly Scent* [*Tian xiang* 天香]), unleashed a new wave of reporting in the mainland press.[49]

Wang Binbin, writing in the April 2011 issue of *Fiction Review* (*Xiaoshuo pinglun* 小說評論), introduces *Four Books* at length, and, after outlining its literary qualities, dwells particularly on its depiction of dehumanization and moral breakdown, as well as the act of self-redemption (*jiushu* 救贖) by the Writer who cuts off his flesh. He concludes with the "repentance" (*chanhui*) of the child, expressed in his self-crucifixion, and regrets that Yan does not use a more "mundane" (*shisu* 世俗) mode of redemption: "If he had died under the gun barrels of dictatorship, leading the inmates out of the concentration camp and attacking the control checkpoint, I would have been even more moved."[50] He nonetheless endorses the book and its critique of history.

---

45 Yan Lianke: "Wo yao nuli zuo yi ge xiezuo de huangdi, er fei bimo de nuli" 閻連科: 我要努力做一個寫作的皇帝, 而非筆墨的奴隸 [Yan Lianke: "I want to work hard on being a king of writers, not a slave of the pen"], *Beijing qingnian bao*, 28 Feb. 2011.
46 Zhao Yong, "Yan Lianke de zixing yishi" 閻連科的自省意識 ["Yan Lianke's self-reflexive consciousness"], *Nanfang dushi bao*, 26 June 2011.
47 "Tongguo kan shu lai huanjie zhengzhi youzhibing" 通過看書來緩解政治幼稚病 ["Relieving political infantilism by reading books"], *Nanfang dushi bao*, 16 July 2011.
48 Wang Binbin, "Yan Lianke de *Si shu*" 閻連科的《四書》["Yan Lianke's *Four Books*"], *Xiaoshuo*, 2011, no. 2: 18–22.
49 Yan later received the sixth Dream of the Red Chamber Award from Hong Kong Baptist University for his *Rixi* 日熄 [*The Day the Sun Died*] in 2017 edn.
50 Wang Binbin, "Yan Lianke de *Si shu*," 22.

Chen Xiaoming's article is similar in tone, though more scholarly in composition. Writing in *Review of Contemporary Writers* (*Dangdai zuojia pinglun* 當代作家評論) in late 2013, he focuses on what he terms "scenes of shock" (*zhenjing changjing* 震驚場景) in three of Yan's novels; the one in *Four Books* being the death of Music. He also discusses the Writer as a hero who, by cutting off his own flesh, becomes a fighter against "modernity" (a euphemism often used by left-leaning critics for the political regime). More prone to using theoretical references than Wang, he ends by quoting Foucault's idea of a "body branded by history" and concludes that the "shock scenes" allow Yan to rewrite the historical narrative, although he views his style as a critical continuation of the revolutionary legacy by comparing Yan's reinvention of realism to Hu Feng's 胡風.[51]

Sun Yu's scholarly article, dated October 2011 and probably originally presented at one of the conferences held in People's University to raise awareness about the book, was published by a small Beijing publisher, Dolphin Books (*Haitun chubanshe* 海豚出版社), jointly with *Zhongguo guoji chuban jituan* 中國國際出版集團 (CIPG) in a book of essays in May 2013. Sun describes the book as a "metaphysical fable," underlining its strangeness, achieved by a "zero causality realism" and the use of four conflicting narratives of the same events.[52] While he identifies "guilt" (*zuigan* 罪感) as the main theme, and takes care to the point that this is not a "Confucian style" guilt, he does not spell out its origin.

The "silent rebellion" contained in both the character Religion and the author's afterword to the private edition, which provides Sun Yu with the title of his own essay collection, *Xiezuo de pantu*, is associated with a struggle against the "old" language,[53] which readers can easily associate with the ideological tint of modern Chinese, especially when it is connected to the "quasi-religious mystical experience" in "times of fanaticism" (*kuangre de shihou* 狂熱的時候). Sun describes Yan's linguistic "self-awareness" (*zijue* 自覺) of his own dependency on Mao style (*Mao ti* 毛體) as the greatest discovery of the book. In fact, we may surmise that Yan's elaborate structure, using four different narrative voices, is also a way of breaking up the unity of the Mao style, which he has previously both parodied (*Serve the People!*) and tried to undermine by using dialect (*Shouhuo*).[54]

While they all highlight different aspects of the novel and discuss the historical events more or less explicitly, the fact that these three well-known scholars all published detailed discussions of a book that was not published in China shows how it can nonetheless enter the limited domestic public sphere.

---

51 Chen Xiaoming, "'Zhenjing' yu lishi chuangshang de qiangdu: Yan Lianke xiaoshuo xushi fangfa tantao" 「震驚」與歷史創傷的強度——閻連科小說敘事方法探討 ["'Shock' and the strength of historical trauma: A discussion of narrative technique in Yan Lianke's fiction"], *Dangdai zuojia pinglun* 2013, no. 5 (Oct. 2013), 22–30 (special issue on Yan Lianke). The question of realism is, of course, contentious. Yan defines his own style as "mythical realism" (*shenshi zhuyi* 神實主義), a form of writing that unearths the unreal within reality, notably by reconfiguring causal relations. Yan Lianke, *Faxian xiaoshuo* 發現小說 [*Discovering fiction*] (Taipei, INK, 2011), especially the last section, 172–200.

52 Sun Yu 孫郁, "Xiezuo de pantu" 寫作的叛徒 ["The Writer as rebel"], in *Xiezuo de pantu* (Beijing: Haitun chubanshe, 2012), 127. "Zero causality" is a concept developed by Yan in his *Faxian xiaoshuo*.

53 Sun Yu, "Zuozhe buduan de zhengtuo jiu de yuyan xiguan gei ziji dailai de yapo" 作者不斷地掙脫舊的語言習慣給自己帶來的壓迫 ["The writer is continually struggling against the pressure he experiences from the old language"] in his *Xiezuo de pantu*, 134.

54 See Tsai Chien-hsin's discussion in his "In Sickness or in Health: Yan Lianke and the Writing of Auto-immunity," *Modern Chinese Literature and Culture* 23, no. 1 (Spring 2011): 77–104, esp. 93–94.

Polyphonic structure and fictional reception

Although the polyphonic structure of the novel has already been noted, it is worth highlighting, in connection with its reception, that each of the "books" is provided with a distinct (fictional) publication and reception history in the introduction to the final chapter (374). "Records of Criminals" is the first to have been purportedly published as an internal Party document in the 1980s. It is the least threatening to the government, echoing the autobiographical and self-righteous personal bias of the intellectuals involved in the "scar literature" (*shanghen wenxue* 傷痕文學) movement. "The Old Course" is said to have been published in 2002 to little echo: readers are no longer interested in such old stories. "The Child of Heaven" is an anonymous volume that the narrator has allegedly found in an old second-hand store from a publisher specialized in myths and legends. Yan has thus inscribed within his own novel the nascent public sphere in which history can be discussed, in which various types of "interventions" may take place, mirroring the opening up of a sphere of discussion that he hopes to provoke in reality.

The fourth "book," the "New Myth of Sisyphus" raises several questions in its own right. Alone among the four books, it is not a narrative; we are only given to read the preface of a longer but unfinished manuscript described as "obscure and incomprehensible" (*huise nandong* 晦澀難懂), which the narrator has purportedly consulted in a research archive. It is ostensibly authored by the Scholar, the only one of the inmates to refuse to undergo reform through labor, and it is also the manuscript that the Child is to take to Beijing, which explains how it may have ended up in an archive. The preface consists of a rewriting of the myth of Sisyphus in which, just like a cart carrying the red star made of steel in one of the episodes of "The Child of Heaven" (chapter 9), to punish Sisyphus, who has gotten used to rolling his stone up the hill and meeting a mysterious child on the way, the gods make his stone roll up the hill by itself and force him to roll it down. Like the famous writers of the 1980s, Yan remains indebted to a form of cultural critique of Chinese civilization (perhaps also implicit in the idea of the "Old Course" of the Yellow River)—while Western intellectuals roll their stone upwards and strive for an ideal, Chinese intellectuals roll their stone downwards in search of more concrete advantages in the present world: food, riches, health, a large and prosperous family.[55] While the Western Sisyphus, accepting his punishment, is guilty of developing feelings for the child, the Eastern Sisyphus, when he adapts to pushing the rock downwards, "feels affection for the smoke and the temple" that stand for the human world at the bottom of the mountain. "The smoke of reality has given Sisyphus a new meaning in the midst of his punishment, the force to adapt" (380). Sun Yu reads this final revelation as a farewell to the illusions of transcendence, whether religious or political, and the acceptance of reality as the ultimate choice of reason: "On the one hand, Chinese people have no metaphysical life, however, at times of fanaticism, they have gone through a mystical experience comparable to religion. Yan Lianke's interest is in resisting both of these modes of existence."[56]

Conflicting narratives of history

With its title alluding both to the canonical texts of Confucianism, Four Books and Five Classics, and Lu Xun's indictment of the "cannibalism" they contain, and to the four gospels (four different accounts of a similar series of events), it immediately raises the question of

---

[55] Author's interview with Yan Lianke, Hong Kong, 11 Oct. 2013. Yan sums up this opposition as *jinsheng* 今生 'present life' vs. *houshi* 後世 'the next world.'
[56] Sun, "Xiezuo de pantu," 137.

conflicting, orthodox or heterodox, narratives of Chinese history. In the *New York Times* article, Yan criticizes the logic of official writing as a dampening of the critical mind: "Gradually we become accustomed to amnesia and we question people who ask questions." In *Four Books*, by contrast, the tension between the four accounts throws up questions that cannot be easily dismissed. Of the four books, three are narratives, while one is a discursive essay; two refer to canonical intertexts, the Bible and the myth of Sisyphus, while two others are a factual and a fictional version of the same events, ostensibly authored by the Writer. The title of the Writer's novel is *The Old Course* (*Gudao* 故道), which refers to the old course of the Yellow River. Yan glosses this as an alternative course of history, and as such, as a trope for fiction, as opposed to the documentary writing in the "Records of Criminals" ("Zuiren lu" 罪人錄): in one case, Yan argues, everything is true, the inmates' crimes have been faithfully noted; in the other, the novel *The Old Course*, the account may be fictionalized, in particular the episode of self-cannibalism, but it may well be truer than the informer's reports, in that it represents the Writer's sincere self-reflection.[57] As Yan puts it, the reality of feeling attracts more readers than historical investigation, because it allows an "individual judgment" (*geren de panduan* 個人的判斷), it starts out from the point of view of the individual.[58] The same story can therefore be told as a "gospel," a tenet of faith that cannot be questioned, as a series of informant's reports, or as fiction. Each of these narratives raises ethical questions about the status and stance of the narrator or alleged writer, and about the connection between the account and the historical events that serve as its point of reference. More importantly than reestablishing the "truth," which fiction is in any case ill-equipped to do, Yan therefore succeeds in opening up a space for discussion, using both narrative (conflicting stories) and linguistic (parody of different styles including *Mao ti*) polyphony.

Hence, while circumscribing his essay to an ostensibly aesthetic discussion, Sun makes clear that his interest in the book is motivated by the reexamination of "twentieth-century history" that it undertakes: "*Four Books* seems to be parodying history, but in fact, this struggle is a way of dealing with a cognitive void."[59] This readily accessible article deals directly with the major issues of the novel and the historical period, and points interested readers straight to the original work itself, which they may then read in pirated versions on the internet or purchase in Hong Kong.

This brief outline of the novel's reception attests to the growing complexity of the Chinese public sphere. The issue is no longer so much whether a book is censored or published within China—after all, even books that were published can go out of print, and publishers can be strategically prevented from reprinting them—but rather whether and in what terms it is publicly discussed, in academic venues, on the internet, in privately owned bookstores or cafes. In the case of Yan's novel, the academic, journalistic, and critical reception achieved by *Four Books* is sufficient to bring about a form of public discussion.

Yan Lianke has taken pains to both substantially transform the mainstream literary narrative of the Mao era, while leaving his text as open as possible. One of his narratives represents an indictment of Maoism as blind faith; however, it is only one of four narratives. In order to achieve openness, Yan leaves the relationship between the four "books" that make up his novel ambiguous, and leaves it to the readers to draw their own conclusions as to how to reconcile the biblical profession of faith, the historical material, the fictional epic, and finally the philosophical reflection. As Sun writes, this is a way of leaving a "void" (*kongbai* 空白) at the center

---

57 Author's interview with Yan Lianke, Hong Kong, 11 Oct. 2013.
58 Author's interview with Yan Lianke, Hong Kong, 24 May 2012.
59 Sun, "Xiezuo de pantu," 136.

of the novel. While the novel was in the end not published in mainland China, it was published in both Hong Kong and Taiwan, and circulated in pirate editions and on the Chinese internet. It was also discussed in various publications and academic conferences or other venues. In this sense, it represents a further contribution to the growing pool of interventions that actively call into question the official narrative of the history of the Mao era within China.

Bibliography

Barmé, Geremie. *In the Red*. New York: Columbia University Press, 1999.

Berry, Michael. *A History of Pain*. New York: Columbia University Press, 2008.

Chen Xiaoming 陳曉明. "'Zhenjing' yu lishi chuangshang de qiangdu: Yan Lianke xiaoshuo xushi fangfa tantao." 「震驚」與歷史創傷的強度——閻連科小說敘事方法探討 ["'Shock' and the strength of historical trauma: A discussion of narrative technique in Yan Lianke's fiction"]. *Dangdai zuojia pinglun* 當代作家評論 [*Review of Contemporary Writers*], 2013, no. 5: 22–30.

"Da jihuang" 大饑荒 ["The great famine"]. *Nanfang renwu zhoukan* 南方人物周刊 [*Southern People Weekly*], no. 299 (21 May 2012): 34–51.

Dirlik, Arif. "Mao Zedong in Contemporary Chinese Official Discourse and History." *China Perspectives*, 2012, no. 2: 17–28.

Edgerton-Tarpley, Katherine. *Tears from Iron: Cultural Responses to Famine in Nineteenth-Century China*. Berkeley: University of California Press, 2008.

Fang Lizhi 方勵之. "The Chinese Amnesia." *New York Review of Books*, 27 Sep. 1990. http://www.nybooks.com/articles/archives/1990/sep/27/the-chinese-amnesia/ (last accessed 16 Oct. 2013).

Fewsmith, Joseph. "Mao's Shadow." *China Leadership Monitor*, no. 43 (14 Mar. 2014): 1. http://www.hoover.org/research/maos-shadow (last accessed 23 June 2014).

Gao Hua 高華. *Hong taiyang shi zenyang shengqi de* 紅太陽是怎樣升起的 [*How the red sun rose*]. Hong Kong: Chinese University of Hong Kong Press, 2001.

Guo, Yuhua. "Folk Society and Ritual State." In *European and Chinese Sociologies: A New Dialogue*, ed. Laurence Roulleau-Berger and Li Peilin, 215–22. Leiden: Brill, 2011.

Gutman, Amy, ed. *Multiculturalism: Examining the Politics of Recognition*. Princeton: Princeton University Press, 1994.

Habermas, Jürgen. *Strukturwandel der Öffentlichkeit*. 1962. Frankfurt: Suhrkamp, 1990.

Heilmann, Sebastian, and Elizabeth Perry, eds. *Mao's Invisible Hand*. Cambridge, MA: Harvard University Asia Center, 2011.

Jiang Fangzhou 蔣方舟. "Tongguo kan shu lai huanjie zhengzhi youzhibing" 通過看書來緩解政治幼稚病 ["Relieving political infantilism by reading books"]. *Nanfang dushi bao* 南方都市報 [*Southern Metropolis Daily*], 16 July 2011.

Lee, Ching Kwan, and Guobin Yang, eds. *Re-envisioning the Chinese Revolution: The Politics and Poetics of Collective Memory in Reform China*. Stanford: Stanford University Press, 2007.

Link, Perry. "Does this Writer Deserve The Prize?" *New York Review of Books*. 6 Dec. 2012.

———. "Politics and the Chinese Language." China File, 24 Dec. 2012, http://chinafile.com/politics-and-chinese-language (last accessed 12 Aug. 2014).

———. *The Uses of Literature: Life in the Socialist Chinese Literary System*. Princeton: Princeton University Press, 2000.

Liu, Jianmei 劉劍梅. "To Join the Commune or Withdraw from It: A Reading of Yan Lianke's *Shouhuo*." *Modern Chinese Literature and Culture* 19, no. 2 (Fall 2007): 1–33.

Liu Xiaobo 劉曉波. "Weiji! Xin shiqi wenxue mianlin de weiji" 危機!新時期文學面臨的危機 ["Crisis! The crisis facing new era literature"]. *Shenzhen qingnianbao* 深圳青年報 [*Shenzhen Youth Newspaper*]. 3 Oct. 1986.

———. *La Philosophie du porc et autres essais*. Paris: Gallimard, 2011.

Lu Xinhua 盧新華 et al. *The Wounded: New Stories of the Cultural Revolution*. Translated by Geremie Barmé et al. Hong Kong: Joint Publishing, 1979.

Mao Yushi 茅于軾. "Ba Mao Zedong huanyuan cheng ren" 把毛澤東還原成人 ["Bring Mao back to human stature"]. *Caixin* 財新, 26 Apr. 2011.

Qian Liqun 錢理群. *Mao Zedong shidai he hou Mao Zedong shidai (1949–2009): Ling yi zhong lishi shuxie* 毛澤東時代和後毛澤東時代: 另一種歷史書寫 [*The Mao Zedong era and the post-Mao Zedong era, 1949–2009: A different historical narrative*]. Taipei: Lianjing, 2012.

Searle, John. "The Logical Status of Fictional Discourse." *New Literary History* 6 (1975): 319–32.

Sun, Feiyu. *Social Suffering and Political Confession: Suku in Modern China*. Singapore: World Scientific, 2013.

Sun Yu 孫郁. "Xiezuo de pantu" 寫作的叛徒 ["The writer as rebel"]. In Sun, *Xiezuo de pantu*. Beijing: Haitun chubanshe, 2012.

Tsai Chien-hsin 蔡建鑫. "In Sickness or in Health: Yan Lianke and the Writing of Auto-Immunity." *Modern Chinese Literature and Culture* 23, no. 1 (Spring 2011): 77–104.

———. "The Museum of Innocence: The Great Leap Forward and Famine, Yan Lianke, and *Four Books*." *Modern Chinese Literature and Culture Resource Center*, May 2011, https://u.osu.edu/mclc/online-series/museum-of-innocence/ (last accessed 14 Aug. 2021).

Veg, Sebastian. "Testimony, History and Ethics: From the Memory of Jiabiangou Prison Camp to a Reappraisal of the Anti-Rightist Movement in Present-Day China." *The China Quarterly*, no. 218 (June 2014): 514–39.

———. "Utopian Fiction and Critical Reflection." *China Perspectives*, 2007, no. 4: 75–87.

Wang Binbin 王彬彬. "Yan Lianke de *Si shu* 閻連科的《四書》" ["Yan Lianke's *Four Books*"]. *Xiaoshuo pinglun* 小說評論 [*Fiction Review*], 2011, no. 2: 18–22.

Wang, Jing. *High Culture Fever: Politics, Aesthetics, and Ideology in Deng's China*. Berkeley: University of California Press, 1996.

Xia Yu 夏榆. "Yan Lianke: Shenghuo de xiabian haiyou kanbujian de shenghuo" 閻連科: 生活的下邊還有看不見的生活 ["Yan Lianke: Below life there is another invisible life"]. *Nanfang zhoumo* 南方周末 [*Southern Weekly*]. 27 May 2011. http://www.infzm.com/content/59605 (last accessed 14 Aug. 2021).

Yan Lianke 閻連科. *Chenmo yu chuanxi* 沉默與喘息 [*Silence and gasping*]. Taipei: INK, 2014.

———. *Faxian xiaoshuo* 發現小說 [*Discovering fiction*]. Taipei: INK, 2011.

———. "On China's State-sponsored Amnesia." *The New York Times*, 1 Apr. 2013. http://www.nytimes.com/2013/04/02/opinion/on-chinas-state-sponsored-amnesia.html?_r=0 (last accessed 25 June 2014).

———. *Si shu* 四書 [*Four books*]. Taipei: Maitian, 2011.

———. "Wo yao nuli zuo yige xiezuo de huangdi, er fei bimo de nuli 閻連科: 我要努力做一個寫作的皇帝, 而非筆墨的奴隸 ["Yan Lianke: I want to work hard on being a king of writers, not a slave of the pen"]. *Beijing qingnian bao* 北京青年報 [*Beijing Youth Daily*], 28 Feb. 2011.

Yue, Gang 樂剛. *The Mouth That Begs: Hunger, Cannibalism, and the Politics of Eating in Modern China*. Durham: Duke University Press, 1999.

Zhao Yong 趙勇. "Yan Lianke de zixing yishi" 閻連科的自省意識 ["Yan Lianke's self-reflexive consciousness"]. *Nanfang dushi bao* 南方都市報 [*Southern Metropolis Daily*]. 26 June 2011.

16
DISABILITY, REVOLUTION, AND HISTORIOGRAPHY
Grandma Mao Zhi in *Lenin's Kisses*
Zihan Wang

Lenin's Kisses (*Shouhuo* 受活, 2003) is one of Yan Lianke's 閻連科 most acclaimed and controversial novels. Because of this work, Yan became the recipient of the Lao She 老舍 Literary Award in 2005. However, the novel also resulted in his forced departure from the army, where he had been working as a writer for more than 20 years, because his army superiors had run out of patience when dealing with his increasingly controversial writing that rattled official censors. *Lenin's Kisses* is unique for its two-part literary structure. The main storyline constructs a satirical allegory about how Liu Yingque, a county chief, attempts to purchase Lenin's embalmed corpse and have it relocated in his county to develop a new tourism site for more revenue. In order to achieve his crazy plan, he organizes a village of disabled people with different special skills into performance troupes to raise funds around the country. Along with this main plot, the complementary section offers endnote-like narratives (*xuyan* 絮言) explaining this village's history, customs, legends, and the like.

Scholars have been fascinated by the commercialization and alienation of the body in the novel, both disabled people and Lenin's corpse, to criticize contemporary Chinese society driven by money-making fever.[1] For instance, Liu Jianmei 劉劍梅 views this novel as Yan's effort to evaluate "the Chinese modernity project" because the exploit of disabled villagers as commodities is "a sign of alienation from the whole process of modernization."[2] Similarly, by analyzing the paradoxical implications of both Lenin's corpse and disabled performers, Carlos Rojas illustrates how "the continuation of the Chinese nation is grounded on the simultaneous rejection of and desire for embodied figures positioned at the symbolic margins of the body politic."[3] Tsai Chien-hsin 蔡建鑫 also touches upon the irony in the novel through

---

1 Also, see, for example, Shelley W. Chan 陳穎, "Narrating Cancer, Disabilities, and Aids: Yan Lianke's Trilogy of Disease," in *Discourses of Disease: Writing Illness, the Mind and the Boy in Modern China*, ed. Howard Y. F. Choy 蔡元豐 (Leiden: Brill, 2016), 184–88; Weijie Song 宋偉杰, "Yan Lianke's Mythorealist Representation of the Country," *MFS: Modern Fiction Studies* 62, no. 4 (Winter 2016): 646–50.
2 Jianmei Liu, "To Join the Commune or Withdraw from It? A Reading of Yan Lianke's *Shouhuo*," *Modern Chinese Literature and Culture* 19, no. 2 (Fall 2007): 4, 7; and her "Bianxing de wenxue bianzouqu" 變形的文學變奏曲 [Rhythm of metamorphic literature], *Zhongguo bijiao wenxue* 中國比較文學 [Comparative Literature in China] 37, no.1 (2020): 128.
3 Carlos Rojas, "Time Out of Joint: Commemoration and Commodification of Socialism in Yan Lianke's *Lenin's Kisses*," in *Red Legacies in China: Cultural Afterlives of the Communist Revolution*, ed. Jie Li and Enhua Zhang (Cambridge: Harvard University Asia Center, 2016), 308.

depictions of disabled villagers that follow a logic of autoimmunity: in order to prove that they are as economically valuable as abled ones, they have to inflict pain on their disabled bodies in their performance.[4]

In parallel with the bodies' implications to contemporary China, *Lenin's Kisses* also explores their association with the revolutionary past through the disability of Grandma Mao Zhi 茅枝婆, a PLA veteran and the matriarch of Liven village. In this chapter, I intend to compare how Mao Zhi's disability is narrated with that of similar stories in socialist narratives. In so doing, I argue that Mao Zhi's bodily sufferings and her past not only reveal Yan's effort to deconstruct the revolutionary paradigm of representing disability, which dominated during the socialist period (1949–78) but also bring to light Yan's doubt against the authority and legitimacy of official historiography.

Revolutionary way of representing disability

At the turn of the twentieth century, China was seen as "The Sick Man of East Asia" (*Dongya bingfu* 東亞病夫) because of its backwardness, especially after a series of military failures and its fate of "being torn apart like a melon" (*guafen* 瓜分) by other imperialist powers. In order to get rid of this morbid image, Chinese reformers and revolutionaries have been dedicated to renovating the nation and making it stronger. Anxiety over "The Sick Man of East Asia" inspired a great number of literary and cinematic characters with bodily or mental deformities as symbols of the nation's sick condition. In this context, disability was also constructed as "signs of racial degeneration and the nation's backwardness."[5]

The 1949 victory made it possible for the Chinese Communist Party (CCP) to imagine itself as the nation's savior that played a decisive role in transforming the previously weak China into a healthy body politic. Accordingly, the Communist authorities put representations of sick bodies under strict surveillance. For instance, in socialist literature and film, bodily sufferings of numerous proletariat subjects, such as illnesses, injuries, scars, and deaths, are always ascribed to imperialist abuse or the torture of the ruling class in the oppressive old society. In so doing, individual victims have been converted into symbols to embody the nation suffering international humiliation and domestic disorder. Representations of disabled bodies could not escape similar regulations. Readers or viewers during the socialist period could find disabled people in limited cultural representations mainly through two revolutionary scenarios: "1) the disabled characters' continuing contribution to the socialist development regardless of their disability led by war-related service; and 2) the miraculous recovery from their disability thanks to Maoism."[6] Regarding Mao Zhi's case in particular, her identity as a PLA veteran,

---

4 Chien-hsin Tsai, "In Sickness or in Health: Yan Lianke and the Writing of Autoimmunity," *Modern Chinese Literature and Culture* 23, no. 1 (Spring 2011): 87–91.
5 Xun Zhou, "The Discourse of Disability in Modern China," *Patterns of Prejudice* 36, no. 1 (2002): 104–12. See also Zihan Wang, "Revolutionary Appropriation of Disability in Socialist Chinese Literature and Film," *China Perspectives* 27, no. 2(2021): 61.
6 Wang, "Revolutionary Appropriation of Disability in Socialist Chinese Literature and Film," 61. Also see, for example, Emma Victoria Stone, "Reforming Disability in China: A Study in Disability and Development" (PhD diss., University of Leeds, 1998), 142–43; Sarah Dauncey, "Screening Disability in the PRC: The Politics of Looking Good," *China Information* 21, no. 3 (Nov. 2007): 481–90; Steven L. Riep, "A War of Wounds: Disability, Disfigurement, and Antiheroic Portrayals of the War of Resistance against Japan," *Modern Chinese Literature and Culture* 20, no. 1 (Spring, 2008): 137–38; and Riep, "Disability in Modern Chinese Cinema," in *The Oxford Handbook of Disability History*, ed. Michael Rembis, Catherine Kudlick and Kim E. Nielsen (New York: Oxford University Press, 2018), 408–10.

the association of her disability with the military past, and her determination to lead the revolution in Liven Village render her comparable to the fictional predecessors in the first scenario. Therefore, before moving directly to analyze Mao Zhi and Yan's writing, it is necessary to examine the relationship between revolution and disability during the socialist period.

To a large extent, these socialist stories of disabled veterans are similar to what is known as supercrip narratives favored by Western media, which usually highlight someone who overcomes the disability in ways that are seen as inspiring. To be more specific in the socialist Chinese context, the 1950s had witnessed a growing number of stories related to disabled veterans whose disability resulted from a series of revolutionary military activities that contributed to the CCP's final victory in 1949 and the defense of the newly established Communist regime during the Korean War (1950–53).[7] Regardless of their bodily loss, they continued to work for the revolutionary cause by overcoming various difficulties, and they were widely promoted as national inspirational models, like Pavel Korchagin and Wu Yunduo 吳運鐸, through various propaganda tools such as newspapers, literature, and movies.[8]

Compared with Western supercrip narratives that underscored how those with disabilities overcome their psychological or mental breakdown with their individual traits, such as individual willpower or determination,[9] the communist ideology placed a higher value on the Party's intervention than individualism and turned similar narratives into sites for the CCP to demonstrate its power over individuals. For example, the drama *The Party Brought Light to My Life* (*Dang chong gei le wo guangming* 黨重給了我光明, 1958) features the true story of Luo Muming 羅木命, a hero who loses his eyesight after an explosion in the middle of arms-producing services during the Korean War. In this play, when Luo becomes upset because of his disability, it is the factory leader, working as the Party secretary and thereby the representative of the Party, who encourages Luo "not to be a coward in front of difficulties."[10] This factory leader's words play a crucial role in restoring Luo's confidence so that he can make more industrial innovations and maintain his marriage.[11]

---

7 See Wang, "Revolutionary Appropriation of Disability in Socialist Chinese Literature and Film," 62.

8 To know how Pavel Korchagin and Wu Yunduo were turned into symbols of revolutionary awareness that could defeat any physical limitations, see Tina Mai Chen, "The Human-Machine Continuum in Maoism: The Intersection of Soviet Socialist Realism, Japanese Theoretical Physics, and Chinese Revolutionary Theory," *Cultural Critique* 80 (Winter 2012): 168–69; Hangping Xu, "Broken Bodies as Agents: Disability Aesthetics and Politics in Modern Chinese Culture and Literature" (PhD diss., Stanford University, 2018), 71.

9 Amit Kama, "Supercrips versus the Pitiful Handicapped: Reception of Disabling Images by Disabled Audience Members," *Communications* 29, no. 4 (Dec. 2004): 448; Catherine Scott, "Time Out of Joint: The Narcotic Effect of Prolepsis in Christopher Reeve's *Still Me*," *Biography: An Interdisciplinary Quarterly* 29, no. 2 (Spring 2006): 322; Sami Schalk, "Reevaluating the Supercrip," *Journal of Literary & Cultural Disability Studies* 10, no. 1 (2016): 73.

10 Ma Fei 馬飛 et al., "Dang chong gei le wo guangming" 《黨重給了我光明》[The Party brought light to my life], *Juben* 劇本 [Playscript] 1, no. 12 (1958): 20. Unless otherwise specified, all Chinese quotations are translated by me.

11 As for how this drama demonstrates the interaction between love and disability, see Wang, "Revolutionary Appropriation of Disability in Socialist Chinese Literature and Film," 62–64. To learn the Party's role in similar narratives, also see Feng Deying 馮德英, *Yingchunhua* 迎春花 [*Jasmine*] (Beijing: Jiefangjun wenyi chubanshe, 2007), 33–36; Zhou Changzong 周長宗, "Yi ge shuang mu shiming de canfei junren dangle gongchang de dangzhibu shuji" 一個雙目失明的殘廢軍人當了工廠的黨支部書記 [A blind veteran becomes the Party Secretary of a factory], *Renmin ribao* 人民日報 [People's Daily], 9 Nov. 1956.

The Party's influence was not limited within the text. When explaining the writing process, the writers of *The Party Brought Light to My Life* also powerfully reiterated the significance of the CCP's intervention in Luo's personal life in reality:

> What force made an almost disabled person resume the courage to stand up against difficulties and devote his youth to the revolutionary life? It was the Party. It was our great Party and the close relationship between the Party and the working class. Luo Muming turned out to be the most convincing example. When he got hurt, it was the Party that looked for good doctors and medicine for him, took him to the hospital in Harbin that was far away from his city, and rescued him from the dangerous status. When he became pessimistic about his future, it was the Party that comforted and encouraged him. When he made no progress in his career, it was also the Party that supported him mentally and financially. This was the truth of how an ordinary worker could become a heroic model. When we interviewed him, our hero particularly pointed out, "Without the Party, Luo Muming could not have survived and become a hero!"[12]

With its frequent references to the Party's greatness, this passage turned Luo into an object with little agency: he had nothing to do with his own recovery and waited passively to be rescued. As a result, it was no wonder that the title was changed from *Luo Muming* to *The Party Brought Light to My Life*, rendering the Party as the subject.[13] The writers also underlined the most important principle guiding their creation: "We felt that our script was not created for extolling only one individual hero. What was more important, through our creation we should praise our superior social system and our Party!"[14] That is to say, the writing of this drama was not so much a celebration of a disabled individual with revolutionary awareness as a demonstration of the advantages of Communism and the Party. The circulation of Luo's story was not solely because he was a strong man who could inspire others, but due to the fact that his disability was a chance to demonstrate the Party's merits.

In the early 1950s, the newly established People's Republic of China (PRC) was experiencing a transition from its war-torn status to socialist development. Therefore, how to deal with large numbers of disabled veterans returning from previous wars, particularly the Korean War, was important, because mistreatment of this group might turn them into a threat to social stability and discourage the passion of those who sacrificed themselves for the revolution. Therefore, propaganda materials participated in the project of comforting disabled veterans, and the Party had tightly produced, circulated, and controlled the meaning of these revolutionary supercrip narratives: the heroes' physical sacrifice for the revolution rendered them accessible to the Party's redemption, which motivated the heroes to overcome negative feelings, such as disappointment, sadness, and distress, caused by their physical loss. This transformation often made the disabled character look healthier, enjoy a happier relationship or marriage, and devote more efforts to the socialist development. At the same time, their stories were widely promoted as an evidence to authenticate the Party's glory. However, as we will see, the way Yan writes Mao Zhi deconstructs these socialist narratives and their implications.

12 Lian Yubin 連裕斌 et al., "Dang chong gei le wo guangming de chuangzuo jingguo" 《黨重給了我光明》的創作經過 [The process of creating "The Party Brought Light to My Life"], *Juben* 1, no. 12 (1958): 28.
13 Ibid.
14 Ibid.

Alternative writing of the revolutionary past

During the socialist period, revolution had been defined as *a priori* concept, namely a sacred cause that deserves one's whole-hearted devotion and sacrifice. Therefore, disabled veterans' bodily losses for revolution could give credence to their glory and made them qualified to be transformed by the Party. However, *Lenin's Kisses* does not follow this definition of revolution; instead, it explores some shady aspects of the communist revolution. Correspondingly, Yan manages to make use of Mao Zhi's story to demonstrate more complex dimensions between the collective and the individual as well as the ideal and the real. Mao Zhi is no longer a condensed symbol, readily manipulated by the dominating ideology for its political agendas.

Mao Zhi's tragedy is closely associated with the Long March and a series of political struggles in the CCP's central leadership before and during the march. After the broken alliance between the CCP and the Kuomingtang (KMT) in 1927, the ruling KMT's effort to wipe out its opponent gradually forced the CCP to shift from urban-oriented revolutionary strategies to rurally centered ones.[15] Among several rural hideouts established in mainly south China from the late 1920s, the largest one was the Chinese Soviet Republic (also known as the Central Revolutionary Base or Jiangxi-Fujian Soviet). Chiang Kai-shek, the president of KMT, gave the CCP and its Red Army little time to resurrect themselves and flourish. From 1930, Chiang launched several huge military operations, or what was known as encirclement campaigns (*weijiao* 圍剿), to eradicate these communist forces. Regardless of the Red Army's successful defense in the first four rounds against Chiang's suppression, the CCP and the Red Army failed to renew their victory in the fifth one, which resulted in what was later known as the Long March—three major divisions of the Red Army retreated from their original bases in 1934 and reunited in Yan'an in 1936 after a long journey with various difficulties. The Long March was not only an important historical event that allowed the CCP and its army to survive but also a valuable asset for one's political career: after the Long March, those who were not Party members could join the Party in accordance with Mao's instruction; cadres who experienced the Long March were largely protected from prosecutions in a series of political upheavals during the socialist period.[16] More importantly, the Long March became a discursive activity, whose significance has been consistently narrated and defined by the communist authorities, so that the Long March has become one of the foundational myths of the CCP's revolutionary history.[17] Particularly after the founding of the PRC in 1949, the Party gradually formed a mainstream understanding of this "Chinese exodus," which foregrounded the Red Army's heroism to overcome natural and physical ordeals, the Party members' fearless sacrifice, and Mao's tactful leadership in successfully directing the Party and the Army to reach Yan'an.[18]

Meanwhile, those who shaped the Long March myth have been vigilant against heterogenous voices. For instance, while three Divisions (the First, Second, and Fourth ones) of the Red Army were involved in the Long March, only the feat of the first one (also the central

---

15 Stephen C. Averill, "The Transition from Urban to Rural in the Chinese Revolution," *The China Journal* 48 (Jul. 2002): 87–88.
16 Gao Hua 高華, *Geming niandai* 革命年代 [Revolutionary times] (Guangzhou: Guangdong renmin chubanshe, 2010), 147–48.
17 Ibid., 139.
18 Enhua Zhang 張恩華, *Space, Politics, and Cultural Representation in Modern China: Cartographies of Revolution* (New York: Routledge, 2017), 72, 91.

one) led by Mao had been overwhelmingly celebrated, especially during the socialist period. In particular, Long March narratives have also become sites validating the power struggle within the Party: Mao's authority has been strengthened for his effort to thwart those, such as Wang Ming 王明 and Zhang Guotao 張國燾, who attempted to undermine the Party's solidarity and led the revolutionary cause to failure. For a long time, the official CCP's historiography has ascribed the Red Army's failure during the fifth encirclement campaign to Wang Ming's "leftist line." As an early CCP senior leader, Wang was one of Mao's chief opponents during the 1930s, and Chinese communists claimed that he led the CCP to disaster between 1930 and 1934 by blindly following a radical "left-opportunist line."[19] Similarly, Zhang Guotao, an experienced party leader and head of the Fourth Division, was labeled as "left separatist" and "traitor" in the CCP's historiography, because he intended to challenge the central party leadership by establishing his own central committee at the critical time of the Long March in 1935 and turned to the KMT in 1938.[20] Implicated by Zhang's misdeeds, the Fourth Division "was not given the credit they deserved in the battles against the KMT."[21]

Unlike mainstream Long March narrative paradigms, which often avoid discussing how individual lives, particularly female ones, were influenced by these political struggles, Yan's depictions of Mao Zhi, a member of the Fourth Division led by Zhang, sheds light on "the margin of the marginal" in cultural representations regarding the Long March.[22] In so doing, Yan manages to provide an alternative, and even subversive, interpretation of the CCP's historiography, and restore those repressed voices. For instance, instead of celebrating the Party cadres' care toward ordinary soldiers, how well-disciplined Red Army soldiers are, and the CCP's strong morality, some common topics in official Long March stories, Mao Zhi's Long March experience is filled with violence, conspiracy, and betrayal. In the process of breaking out of the KMT's fifth encirclement, Mao Zhi's mother is shot by a senior officer whom Mao Zhi viewed as an uncle because her mother is said to be a traitor, but later it turns out that this is a false accusation and her mother is a victim of Wang Ming's wrong political guideline. Although her mother's reputation is restored and Mao Zhi is recognized as a martyr's daughter, the loss makes her trapped in nightmares filled with the bullet sound that executed her mother. In addition, Mao Zhi loses three toes and becomes disabled during the Long March. However, after their arrival at Yan'an, without being assigned to some other important positions like her fictional predecessors who sacrifice for the revolution in the socialist representations, Mao Zhi, together with other injured and disabled soldiers in the Fourth Division, is dismissed by Zhang, who fears that these soldiers will disclose his ambition to separate from the Central leadership. Even worse, Mao Zhi is raped on her way to escape, probably by a brother-like colleague during a coma with fever. During these life-changing moments, Mao Zhi's position remains passive: she has little agency to change the misfortune imposed upon her from either someone who is too superior for her to know or those intimate ones. Revolution cannot always bring happiness to every individual who fights for it. By associating Mao Zhi's fate with central leaders' personal interests and the fellow soldiers' violence and highlighting her passivity, Yan exposes that revolution is not a purely glorious cause, upon which the communist authorities justify and maintain their legitimacy.

19 Cao Zhongbin 曹仲彬 and Dai Maolin 戴茂林, *Wangming zhuan* 王明傳 [A biography of Wang Ming] (Changchun: Jilin wenshi chubanshe, 1991), 221–35.
20 Xiaomei Chen, *Staging Chinese Revolution: Theater, Film and the Afterlives of Propaganda* (New York: Columbia University Press, 2017), 162, 242.
21 Zhang, 74.
22 Ibid., 92.

Mao Zhi finally arrives at Liven Village. However, dismissed from the army and without disclosing her previous experience, the Party has no chance to redeem her, and her sacrifice can not be automatically turned into glory, unlike what her fictional predecessors enjoy during the socialist period. Mao Zhi's Long March life also results in her psychological and emotional struggle toward the revolution. On the one hand, regardless of her tragedies, she cannot reconcile herself to the idea of staying in this village full of disabled people for the rest of her life. On the other hand, the past trauma prevents her from leaving the village and represses her desire to work for the revolution again, which also partly explains why she is reluctant to share her past with others. However, the news that the CCP has succeeded in building a new regime and encouraged rural cooperation re-ignites her revolutionary passion: "She wanted a revolution. She wanted to lead the people of Liven into a mutual aid team and a cooperative society."[23] Her effort to successfully lead the village to join the commune (*rushe* 入社) marks Mao Zhi's reconnection with the Party and the revolution. To follow the logic of socialist narratives, this should have turned her body into a healthier one, made her marriage happier, and led her villagers to a more prosperous life. However, none of these occurs.

First, her renewed contribution to revolution brings more harm to her body. Although Mao Zhi becomes disabled during the Long March, there is no fundamental difference between her and healthy people when she first arrives at the village. As the narrator stresses, "Her leg was somewhat lame, but not excessively so, and if she walked slowly no one could tell she was disabled."[24] However, during the Great Famine, when Mao Zhi attempts to prevent outsiders from looting grains from her villagers, those rioters begin to vent their anger on her and attack her legs because they believe that Mao Zhi, as a representative of those who cause the famine in the name of revolution, should be responsible for their loss of well-being. While cursing and kicking Mao Zhi, one rioter complains: "Blast your grandmother. It is all your fault that society has gotten messed up. If it hadn't been for the Revolution, our family would still have our ox and two *mu* of land. Thanks to your Revolution, we were designated as a rich peasant family and consequently lost both our ox and our land. During the famine, three out of the five members of my family starved to death."[25] Upon hearing these words, Mao Zhi suddenly becomes disillusioned toward the revolution, and it is also after this incident that she begins to walk like a more disabled person.

Liven Village has long been isolated from the outside world and is untouched by any communist influence; villagers, including Mao Zhi's husband, have no revolutionary consciousness. Therefore, her marriage is different from those during the socialist period because it is not the result of Mao Zhi and her husband's mutual commitment to the revolution. When she is asked by her husband about their marriage, she confesses that she regrets staying in the village. Their marriage does not become happier through the revolution, either. Her husband does not understand her devotion, and it is her revolutionary passion that finally leads to her husband's death due to starvation.

Mao Zhi's authority, which is established after the exposure of her revolutionary identity, is quickly interrupted in a series of political upheavals. Unlike her socialist predecessors, whose devotion to the revolution contributes to the development of the new communist regime, Mao Zhi fails to lead her villagers to a "heavenly" life and a promising future as indicated in the local gazetteer. Villagers resent her decision to "join the commune," which results in several severe disasters, and they want to "withdraw from the commune" by expressing that "Liven should

---

23 Yan Lianke, *Lenin's Kisses*, trans. Carlos Rojas (New York: Grove Press, 2012), 144.
24 Ibid., 134.
25 Ibid., 282.

never have been part of this commune, or this province."[26] Mao Zhi herself also realizes the mistake and, for the rest of her life, she spares no effort to withdraw Liven from the commune, so that the village can return to the original isolated status free from the Party's control.

As a result, Mao Zhi's stories completely undermine the socialist revolutionary logic of writing veterans' disability; the sublime feeling arising from the socialist narratives is accordingly deconstructed. This way of dealing with disability is likely ascribed to Yan's disillusion toward revolutionary myths. In an interview, he mentioned: "Before joining the army, I had read many classics related to military experience. However, after I became a PLA soldier, I found that the revolutionary heroism and romanticism did not exist .... I realized that those classics were fake. So I wrote some true depictions of people and stories, turning heroes into ordinary people and moving their stories from the battlefield to the land."[27] Mao Zhi turns out to be one of the examples demonstrating Yan's skepticism toward absolute values. Breaking down the grand narrative into small pieces, the novel is less interested in consolidating the glory of a revolutionary myth than illustrating the cruelty behind this myth.

Yan has been a brave and responsible writer because when others tended to avoid probing into the earlier years of the CCP's past and providing alternative interpretations, he insisted on doing so. As Sebastian Veg concludes, since the end of the Cultural Revolution, the CCP and Chinese intellectuals have worked together to form a mainstream understanding of Maoist period of the PRC history: public discussions "remained in a well-defined framework in which the political system itself was never questioned; on the contrary, people's belief in the Party and its ability to correct its own mistakes was often emphasized."[28] For the CCP, it "was thus able to weave the 'error' of the Cultural Revolution into a larger narrative of modernization and historical legitimacy of CCP rule."[29] Meanwhile, for intellectuals, it has gradually become a safe practice to limit criticism against the communist past within the decade of the Cultural Revolution without extending similar critical insights to earlier revolutionary history, because those ten years were defined as erroneous in the official 1981 resolution. Recent years have witnessed some attempts to break out of this comfort zone, and Yan's writings are outstanding. For instance, in *Four Books*, he "call[s] into question the original legitimacy of the PRC" and "creates a debate within the Chinese-speaking public sphere on the foundations of the current regime" through his fictional exploration into the Great Leap Forward and the succeeding famine in the 1950s.[30] In *Lenin's Kisses*, in addition to maintaining his efforts to reflect disasters in earlier PRC's history, Yan moves his focus to pre-PRC years and challenges the legitimacy of narratives regarding the Long March through a disabled veteran's experience.

A challenge to the official history writing

The intersection of disability and revolution reflected through Grandma Mao Zhi's body not only deconstructs the revolutionary paradigm of writing disability but also demonstrates Yan Lianke's endeavor to challenge the legitimacy of official historiography, as illustrated by his inclusion of the official local gazetteer at the end of the first chapter in the first part. According

---

26 Ibid., 284.
27 Shi Jianfeng 石劍鋒, "'Jinshu' shi zenme chansheng de" 「禁書」是怎麼產生的 [How to produce "banned books"], Tengxun wenhua 騰訊文化 [Tecent Culture], 4 Apr. 2014, https://cul.qq.com/a/20140404/018079.htm (last accessed 1 Nov. 2020).
28 Sebastian Veg, "Creating a Literary Space to Debate the Mao Era: The Fictionalisation of the Great Leap Forward in Yan Lianke's *Four Books*," *China Perspectives* 20, no. 4 (2014): 9.
29 Ibid.
30 Ibid.

to the Shuanghuai County gazetteer, in which the history of Liven is introduced: "Liven was not merely a location where disabled residents established a community, but a sacred revolutionary site where a soldier by the name of Mao Zhi from the Red Army's Fourth Regiment settled down to live."[31] The gazetteer further tells that Mao Zhi "became a revolutionary orphan" after her parents sacrificed for the revolution. In the middle of the Long March, "Mao Zhi lost three toes to frostbite and broke her leg falling into a ravine, leaving her unable to walk without the aid of a crutch."[32] She manages to survive and arrives at the village: "When she arrived at the Balou [耙耧] mountains and saw the disabled people living in Liven, she decided to stay with them. The gazetteer reports that while there was no record of Mao Zhi's having officially joined the Red Army, everyone in Liven—and throughout the entire county—regarded her as a bona fide revolutionary leader. Thanks to her, therefore, Balou came to have glory, Liven came to have direction, and the villagers, despite being physically disabled, were able to live happy and fulfilled lives in the new society."[33] This piece of recording, albeit short, encapsulates some characteristics of the socialist way of representing disabled veterans. However, other endnote-like narratives, which also touch upon Mao Zhi's life with varying reliability and authenticity in other chapters, are framed as counter-narratives to this official discourse of a revolutionary utopia established upon Mao Zhi's devotion. A comparison between the local gazetteer and other endnote-like narratives illustrates tellingly how the official ideology eases the tension between history and historiography by choosing selectively what to record and deleting any inconsistencies, embarrassments, failures, or mistakes. By including this official recording and then providing an alternative explanation that attempts to restore the accuracy of details and the complexity of realities, Yan not only exposes the teleological purpose hidden in the official interpretation of history to consolidate the validity of the CCP's rule but also makes it clear that the official historical account is a process of fabrication, more fictional than factual.

Yan was not the only contemporary cultural practitioner who intended to stay away from the cultural and political hegemony of the CCP's preferred perception of revolutionary history through representations of disabled veterans. For instance, in Nobel Prize-winner Mo Yan's 莫言 *Big Breasts and Wide Hips* (*Fengru feitun* 豐乳肥臀, 1996), the mute Sun Buyan 孫不言 becomes a soldier in a CCP-led troop and loses his legs in the war. Upon his return to the village, he rapes "my" third sister, which deconstructs the socialist image of a disabled Red Army soldier with strong moral responsibility. Besides, he fails to be rewarded with a happy marriage that could redeem his physical deficiency. When Sun returns for the second time, he becomes a hero and forces "my" eldest sister, who refused Sun several times and slept with others, to marry him. But she cheats on him and finally kills him when Sun witnesses her adultery. In addition, in Feng Xiaogang's 馮小剛 film *Youth* (*Fanghua* 芳華, 2017), adapted from a novel by Yan Geling 嚴歌苓, after the protagonist Liu Feng 劉峰 loses his arm during the Sino-Vietnam War, his devotion to the nation becomes meaningless in the post-socialist market-driven environment in which Maoism has yielded to capitalism. Without receiving any further support from the Party or the government, he has to rely on himself by selling books. This is not easy because this disabled veteran is manhandled and humiliated by thugs from the Public Order Office (*lianfangdui* 聯防隊) after his books are confiscated and he refuses to pay the unreasonable fine.

Compared with other cultural practitioners, Yan contrasts Mao Zhi's disability as it is written in the official local gazetteer with how it is narrated in other relevant narrative forms

---

31 Yan, *Lenin's Kisses*, 8.
32 Ibid., 9.
33 Ibid.

in the novel. As an outstanding example, this literary design demonstrates his consistent attempt to use various formal experiments to probe the tension between historiography, especially the official one, and corresponding historical events, which results in the questioning of absolute narratives and urges plurality of perspectives in fiction. In addition to *Lenin's Kisses*, he makes similar efforts in novels such as *Four Books* (*Si shu* 四書, 2011) and *The Explosion Chronicles* (*Zhalie zhi* 炸裂志, 2013), rendering them as reflexive sites that bring to light the fictional, instead of factual, nature of writing history. For instance, as demonstrated by Veg, each of the four accounts in *Four Books* "raises ethical questions about the status and stance of the narrator or alleged writer, and about the connection between the account and the historical events that serve as its point of reference."[34] In *The Explosion Chronicles*, Yan created an editor also called Yan Lianke within the novel who is responsible for writing chronicles of the Explosion city. The occasional appearance of this editor as a narrator addressing readers directly in the novel reminds readers of the constructed nature of the chronicles. In the final chapter, the fact that the mayor of the city burns the completed chronicles also indicates the tension between the writer's writing and the official writing sanctioned by the ruling power.

Conclusion

This chapter reads Yan Lianke's writing of disability in *Lenin's Kisses* against relevant narratives produced during the socialist period. Writers and filmmakers during the revolutionary years often represented characters as model types that should function according to their classes or how much revolutionary awareness they possess. Neither could fictional disabled veterans escape this discipline. Their identity as Red Army soldiers made them stay as inspirational role models to encourage themselves and others to keep working for the socialist development regardless of bodily losses. Whenever they feel frustrated to fulfill this duty, the Party would always intervene timely to assist these disabled veterans. However, Yan is hardly interested in following this line to represent disabled characters. His depiction of Grandma Mao Zhi deconstructs the revolutionary sublime aurora. Mao Zhi fails to become healthier, have a happier life with her partner, and lead her villagers to a more promising future. At the same time, the recount of Mao Zhi's stories through various resources in the novel also makes the revolutionary recording in the local gazetteer suspicious. As it turns out, official history writing is no more reliable than other forms of remembering the past.

Acknowledgment

I am grateful for the support received from Drs. Dino Franco Felluga, Chen Lin, Margret Tillman, and Hongjian Wang in the process of writing and revising this article. I would also like to thank the editors Prof. Dr. Riccardo Moratto and Dr. Howard Y. F. Choy for their time and efforts to develop this book project.

Bibliography

Anonymous Journalist. "Yi ke hongxin wei renmin: Ji canfei fuyuan junren, Yangjiaogou dadui geweihui fuzhuren Liu Baoren" 一顆紅心為人民——記殘廢復員軍人、羊窖溝大隊革委會副主任劉保仁 [A red heart for the people: The Story of a veteran Liu Baoren]. *Renmin ribao* 人民日報 [People's Daily], 30 Jan. 1970.

---

34 Veg, "Creating a Literary Space to Debate the Mao Era," 15.

Averill, Stephen C. "The Transition from Urban to Rural in the Chinese Revolution." *The China Journal* 48 (Jul. 2002): 87–121.
Cao Zhongbin 曹仲彬, and Dai Maolin 戴茂林. *Wangming zhuan* 王明傳 [A biography of Wang Ming]. Changchun: Jilin wenshi chubanshe, 1991.
Chan, Shelley W. 陳穎. "Narrating Cancer, Disabilities, and AIDS: Yan Lianke's Trilogy of Disease." In *Discourses of Disease: Writing Illness, the Mind and the Boy in Modern China*, edited by Howard Y. F. Choy 蔡元豐, 177–99. Leiden: Brill, 2016.
Chen, Tina Mai. "The Human-Machine Continuum in Maoism: The Intersection of Soviet Socialist Realism, Japanese Theoretical Physics, and Chinese Revolutionary Theory." *Cultural Critique* 80 (Winter 2012): 151–81.
Chen, Xiaomei. *Staging Chinese Revolution: Theater, Film and the Afterlives of Propaganda*. New York: Columbia University Press, 2017.
Dauncey, Sarah. "Screening Disability in the PRC: The Politics of Looking Good." *China Information* 21, no. 3 (Nov. 2007): 481–506.
Feng Deying 馮德英. *Yingchunhua* 迎春花 [Jasmine]. Beijing: Jiefangjun wenyi chubanshe, 2007.
Gao Hua 高華. *Geming niandai* 革命年代 [Revolutionary times]. Guangzhou: Guangdong renmin chubanshe, 2010.
Kama, Amit. "Supercrips versus the Pitiful Handicapped: Reception of Disabling Images by Disabled Audience Members." *Communications* 29, no. 4 (Dec. 2004): 447–66.
Lian Yubin 連裕斌 et al. "*Dang chong gei le wo guangming* de chuangzuo jingguo" 《黨重給了我光明》的創作經過 [The process of creating "The Party Brought Light to My Life"]. *Juben* 劇本 [Playscript] 1, no. 12 (1958): 27-28.
Liu Jianmei 劉劍梅. "Bianxing de wenxue bianzouqu" 變形的文學變奏曲 [Rhythm of metamorphic literature]. *Zhongguo bijiao wenxue* 中國比較文學 [Comparative Literature in China] 37, no.1 (2020): 114-30.
———. "To Join the Commune or Withdraw from It? A Reading of Yan Lianke's *Shouhuo*." *Modern Chinese Literature and Culture* 19, no. 2 (Fall 2007): 1–33.
Ma Fei 馬飛 et al. "Dang chong gei le wo guangming" 《黨重給了我光明》 [The Party brought light to my life]. *Juben* 1, no. 12 (1958): 7-23, 72.
Riep, Steven L. "Disability in Modern Chinese Cinema." In *The Oxford Handbook of Disability History*, edited by Michael Rembis, Catherine Kudlick, and Kim E. Nielsen, 407–24. New York: Oxford University Press, 2018.
———. "A War of Wounds: Disability, Disfigurement, and Antiheroic Portrayals of the War of Resistane against Japan." *Modern Chinese Literature and Culture* 20, no. 1 (Spring 2008): 129–72.
Rojas, Carlos. "Time Out of Joint: Commemoration and Commodification of Socialism in Yan Lianke's *Lenin's Kisses*." In *Red Legacies in China: Cultural Afterlives of the Communist Revolution*, edited by Jie Li and Enhua Zhang, 297–315. Cambridge: Harvard University Asia Center, 2016.
Schalk, Sami. "Reevaluating the Supercrip." *Journal of Literary & Cultural Disability Studies* 10, no. 1 (2016): 71–86.
Scott, Catherine. "Time Out of Joint: The Narcotic Effect of Prolepsis in Christopher Reeve's *Still Me*." *Biography: An Interdisciplinary Quarterly* 29, no. 2 (Spring 2006): 307–28.
Shi Jianfeng 石劍鋒. "'Jinshu' shi zenme chansheng de" 「禁書」是怎麼產生的 [How to produce "banned books"]. Tengxun wenhua 騰訊文化 [Tecent Culture], 4 Apr. 2014. https://cul.qq.com/a/20140404/018079.htm (last accessed 1 Nov. 2020).
Song, Weijie 宋偉杰. "Yan Lianke's Mythorealist Representation of the Country." *MFS: Modern Fiction Studies* 62, no. 4 (Winter 2016): 644–58.
Stone, Emma Victoria. "Reforming Disability in China: A Study in Disability and Development." PhD diss. University of Leeds, 1998.
Tsai, Chien-hsin 蔡建鑫. "In Sickness or in Health: Yan Lianke and the Writing of Autoimmunity." *Modern Chinese Literature and Culture* 23, no. 1 (Spring 2011): 77–104.
Veg, Sebastian. "Creating a Literary Space to Debate the Mao Era: The Fictionalisation of the Great Leap Forward in Yan Lianke's *Four Books*." *China Perspectives* 20, no. 4 (2014): 7-15.
Wang, Zihan. "Revolutionary Appropriation of Disability in Socialist Chinese Literature and Film." *China Perspectives* 27, no. 2 (2021): 61-69.
Wu Yunduo 吳運鐸. *Ba yiqie xian gei dang* 把一切獻給黨 [Everything for the Party]. Beijing: Gongren chubanshe, 1953.

Xiang Ming 向明 et al. "Zhenzheng de aiqing: Yi wei bianfang zhanshi weihunqi de zishu" 真正的愛情——一位邊防戰士未婚妻的自述 [True love: An account by a soldier's fiancée]. *Renmin ribao* 人民日報 [People's Daily], 14 Apr. 1979.

Xu, Hangping. "Broken Bodies as Agents: Disability Aesthetics and Politics in Modern Chinese Culture and Literature." PhD diss. Stanford University, 2018.

Yan Lianke. *Lenin's Kisses*. Translated by Carlos Rojas. New York: Grove Press, 2012.

Zhang, Enhua 張恩華. *Space, Politics, and Cultural Representation in Modern China: Cartographies of Revolution*. New York: Routledge, 2017.

Zhou Changzong 周長宗. "Yi ge shuang mu shiming de canfei junren dang le gongchang de dangzhibu shuji" 一個雙目失明的殘廢軍人當了工廠的黨支部書記 [A blind veteran becomes the Party Secretary of a factory]. *Renmin ribao*, 9 Nov. 1956.

Zhou, Xun. "The Discourse of Disability in Modern China." *Patterns of Prejudice* 36, no. 1 (2002): 104–12.

17

CORRECTIVE CATACHRESIS

Capitalist mystification derailed in *The Explosion Chronicles* and "The Story of Fertile Town"

Kwan Yin Lee

What if "wronging" a wrong can prove instrumental to righting it? What if, apart from denoting the limited reach of language, catachresis has the potential to throw one into a state of generative incertitude as opposed to idle mastery?

In broad strokes, this study examines the critical intervention catachrestic figurative language can make in the dominant capitalist discourse that invariably casts economic progress in a rosy light. Rather than at best serving decorative purposes or at worst obstructing genuine understanding of a phenomenon, figurative language illuminates as a "device of enstrangement"[1] and detains with its affective force. Its intentional "not-quite" jolts readers out of their complacency as knowing subjects but at the same time traps them within its haunting resonance. It shoves as it pulls. A case in point is Marx's likening abstract labor to *Gallerte*, the German word for an edible gelatinous mass made from different animals' bone, flesh, and connective tissues, in *Das Kapital*. Given the predominant "solicitude for conceptual literalism,"[2] this idiosyncratic analogy drawn by Marx is lost in both Ben Fowkes's and Samuel Moore's and Edward Aveling's English translations. Fowkes translates *Gallerte* into "congealed quantities"[3] whereas Moore and Aveling offer "congelation."[4] Both disregard *"the thinking that [Marx's figurative language] makes possible."*[5] While congelation as a process is reversible like ice melting back into water with heat, *Gallerte* is "the tremulous edible product of industrial *reduction* and *processing*,"[6] whose production/destruction is irreversible. The animal

---

1 Viktor Shklovsky, "Art, as Device," *Poetics Today* 36, no. 3 (2015): 162, 167. The Russian formalist first coined the term "enstrangement *ostranenie*" in his seminal work published in 1917. He posits that art in general is meant to shake us from automatized responses to things in life out of habit by enstranging them to "increas[e] the duration and complexity of perception." See the explanation offered by the translator in "Art, as Device," 152–54, Alexandra Berlina, for why the term should be spelt with an "n" instead of following the more common spelling for "estrangement."
2 Keston Sutherland, "Marx in Jargon," *World Picture* 1, no. 1 (2015), http://www.worldpicturejournal.com/WP_1.1/KSutherland.html (last accessed 29 Feb. 2020).
3 Karl Marx, *Capital*, trans. Ben Fowkes (London: Penguin, 1990), 128.
4 Karl Marx, *Capital*, ed. Friedrich Engels, trans. Samuel Moore and Edward Aveling (New York: Modern Liberary, 1936), 45.
5 Sutherland, "Marx in Jargon"; italics in the original.
6 Ibid; italics in the original.

substances boiled down together are indistinguishable in the final product. Nor can they ever regain their bodily integrity.

By using *Gallerte* as a metaphor for abstract labor, Marx highlights the violence inherent in the capitalist abstraction's reduction of concrete labor performed by different individual workers to undifferentiated, expendable labor power quantified by standardized time and retroactively valorized by the sales price of a commodity. The sanitized concept of abstract labor being the "congelation of homogeneous human labor,"[7] in Moore's and Aveling's translation, glosses over the heterogeneous material origins of the abstraction at work and its material impact on workers. Also forgone is the disgusted reaction to the image of human brains, sinews, and bones being mashed together as *Gallerte* evokes in readers, who are also the ones consuming this human gelatin day in and day out. As Sianne Ngai points out, the figurative language employed by Marx is catachrestic for the graphic image risks having abstract labor "sound confusingly *like* simple physiological human labor."[8] Yet, it is precisely through the catachresis that the "*socially binding or plasticizing action of capitalist abstractions*" is brought to the fore. "Visceral abstraction" is a term Ngai coins to designate the kind of catachrestic figurative language that "by triggering crude and elemental feelings" holds up a mirror to "the 'material force' of all capitalist abstractions."[9] If the latter intends to erase and convolute the human cost of capitalist advancement, the former insists on remembering and interrogating not only what the normalized abstract under capitalism draws from, but also what it feeds back into the concrete. With its irreverence for the supposed boundary separating the material and conceptual, figurative language is uniquely equipped to take on insidious capitalist abstractions with its own brand of abstraction that enstranges and resensitizes.

Refiguring the miraculous

It is the recognition of the paradigm-shifting potential of catachrestic figurative language that motivates this essay's juxtaposition of Xi Xi's 西西 "The Story of Fertile Town" ("Feituzhen de gushi" 肥土鎮的故事, 1982) and Yan Lianke's 閻連科 *The Explosion Chronicles* (*Zhalie zhi炸裂志*, 2013).[10] In "The Story of Fertile Town" (hereon abbreviated as "Fertile"), a wasteland that used to be an unofficial dumping ground for liquids from unspecified experiments, broken furniture, and everyday items starts yielding all kinds of gigantic flowers and produce spontaneously. The inexplicable godsend, which initiates the town's meteoric economic take-off, morphs into a nightmare as the ultra-fertile soil keeps expanding to the point of burying and even crushing everything in its wake. Equally outlandish but at times much more gruesome are scenes from *The Explosion Chronicles* (hereon abbreviated as *Explosion*). In its quest to be designated a megalopolis, a city called Explosion sees the completion of the construction of a super airport within two days' time. The expeditious process involves the

---

7   Marx, *Capital*, trans. Moore and Aveling, 45.
8   Sianne Ngai, "Visceral Abstractions," *GLQ: A Journal of Lesbian and Gay Studies* 21, no. 1 (2015): 44; italics in the original.
9   Ngai, "Visceral Abstraction," 54.
10 The original Chinese version of the short story was published in 1982 by a Hong Kong literary journal, *Suye wenxue* 素葉文學 [*Su Yeh Literature*]. The English version with Eva Hung as the translator was published by the Chinese University of Hong Kong Press in 1997 as part of a short story collection titled *Marvels of a Floating City and Other Stories*. Yan's original novel in Chinese was published in 2013 by Shanghai wenyi chubanshe 上海文藝出版社 [Shanghai Literature & Art Publishing House]; Grove Press published the English version in 2016 with Carlos Rojas as the translator.

military firing into a mountain with severed fingers and legs previously procured and planted there. Once the redesignation of Explosion as a provincial-level metropolis is approved by the central government, partly attributable to the said architectural feat, all seasonal fruits grow and ripen simultaneously regardless of what time of year it is.

With Fertile Town and Explosion as stand-ins, Xi Xi and Yan's works chart the so-called economic miracles in Hong Kong and mainland China, respectively. Considered one of the Asia's four little dragon economies, Hong Kong saw rapid industrialization and transformed into a leading international financial center in just two decades, 1960s and 1970s. Post-Mao China's economy snapped out of a deep slumber and the country has since been catapulted to the status of an unmistakable economic superpower with decades of close-to-double-digit economic growth, powered by manufacturing and exports. Yan rightly observes that "[c]ontemporary China is currently hurtling past a series of economic and developmental milestones that took Europe over two centuries to achieve."[11] This commentary is to a large extent applicable to Hong Kong in the second half of the twentieth century as well. The descriptor "miraculous" has come to be attached to both economies' developmental trajectories.

Curiously enough, the definition within economic studies of the term "miracle" diverges from its conventional designation of the unknowable with economists readily expounding on the making of the miracles and their supposed replicability. In an article drawing from his own monograph, *Demystifying the Chinese Economy*, Justin Lin asserts that developing countries can reproduce China's success by offering "transitory protections to unviable firms to maintain stability, but liberalizing entry into sectors in which the country has comparative advantages."[12] According to Lin, misallocation of resources, distortion of incentives, and repression of the labor-intensive sectors where China enjoyed a competitive edge held the country back from ascending in the global economic stage till the late 70s, when Deng Xiaoping introduced the Open Door Policy.[13] For Vladimir Popov and Jomo Kwame Sundaram, however, it is "the foundations established during the Mao period," such as the marked increase in literacy rates and people's life expectancy, that enabled the country to reap the benefits of liberalization.[14] Concerning Hong Kong's economic miracle, both Jean-Francois Minardi and Lawrence Reed commend John James Cowperthwaite, the Financial Secretary of Hong Kong from 1961 to 1971, for staunchly espousing non-intervention on the government's part, as in providing minimal social security and maintaining low tax rates.[15] Minardi goes so far as to proclaim Hong Kong as "one of the most striking and conclusive examples in the world of a society that succeeded in escaping underdevelopment by relying on economic freedom."[16]

Common to all these expository accounts is the ready acceptance of the premise—capitalism and its quest for perpetual growth are viable, not to mention desirable, as long as the right policies uphold a liberalized market. Differently put, the "invisible hand" can work miracles when it is properly left alone. Herein lies the crux of what Mark Fisher calls

---

11 Yan Lianke, *The Explosion Chronicles*, trans. Carlos Rojas (New York: Grove Press, 2016), 451.
12 Justin Lin, "Demystifying the Chinese Economy," *The Australian Economic Review* 46, no. 3 (2013): 266.
13 Ibid., 262.
14 Vladimir Popov and Jomo Kwame Sundaram, "Liberation, Not Liberalization, Responsible for China's Economic Miracle," *Inter Press Service*, Nov. 2019, http://www.ipsnews.net/2019/11/liberation-not-liberalization-responsible-chinas-economic-miracle/ (last accessed 15 Apr. 2020).
15 Lawrence K. Reed, "The Man Behind the Hong Kong Miracle," *Foundation for Economic Education*, Feb. 2014, https://fee.org/articles/the-man-behind-the-hong-kong-miracle/ (accessed Apr. 15, 2020).
16 Jean-François Minardi, "Hong Kong: The Ongoing Economic Miracle," *Montreal Economic Institute*, Nov. 2013, https://www.iedm.org/files/note1113_en.pdf (last accessed 15 Apr. 2020).

"capitalist realism," which functions as "a kind of anti-mythical myth."[17] As economists marshal facts to "demystify" and rationalize the "miraculous" growth rates recorded in Hong Kong and the mainland, they bolster the myth of market deregulation as what brings the economic progress all societies purportedly need to thrive. It is as if Latin American countries like Argentina did not lose a decade, 1998 to 2002, to a debilitating debt crisis even though extensive deregulation and privatization were carried out in accordance with the Washington Consensus; as if the interdependent yet asymmetrical relations between countries and regions under global capitalism were nothing but a nonissue; as if Hong Kong and mainland China were not plagued by vast income inequalities and intractable pollution.

For Fisher, "[c]apitalist realism can only be threatened if it is shown to be in some way inconsistent or untenable."[18] An approach to achieving this end can be laying out empirical evidence that sheds light on capitalist realism's incongruity. Though there is undoubtedly value in doing so, the extent to which all the information regarding the convoluted workings of the capitalist regime is digestible to a layperson is questionable. Another question that arises concerns whether a litany of facts can ever rival a magic show in terms of appeal. As Rebecca Karl rightly observes, "[a]s creative mediator, magic is crucial to the necessary ambiguity of modern everyday life," contributing to "the quotidian suturing of incommensurate temporalities and thus participat[ing] in the disjunctive rituals that comprise the everyday."[19] She goes on to note that "often more persuasively or in more saturated fashion," "magic is crucial as ideological illusion." Encapsulated in the narrative of economic miracles, capitalist realist "magic" captivates by offering dazzling spectacles that consist of impressive figures and perhaps panoramic shots of glistening skyscrapers, all the while posing as objective facts.

The catachrestic figurative language boldly employed in "Fertile" and *Explosion* flouts "the magician's code" as it takes the capitalist realist magic's elliptical and abstracting moves to their logical extremes. Rather than keeping a safe distance, the two texts explode the discursive terrain where fantasies are couched in ostensibly rational terms from within. Akin to Marx's *Gallerte*, Yan and Xi Xi's catachrestic renderings of the spectacular facades of and what lay behind the respective economic miracles unsettle readers on both the cognitive and affective levels. How *Explosion* and "Fertile" recast the economic miracle narratives calls for a Marxist close reading. They belong to the ranks of artwork that Anita Chari intriguingly describes to be "serv[ing] as a kind of theoretical Trojan horse: a gift unsuspectingly accepted by subjects in capitalist society that contains within it a critical weapon."[20] This paper examines how the two texts as Trojan horses collide with the capitalist train hurtling forward in "realistic" pursuit of profit.

Origin stories devoid of grandeur

In contrast with the stock image of a speeding train, *Explosion* offers that of a train "as though it were a smoldering pile of wet firewood or an enormous stove laboriously climbing the mountain,"[21] which paradoxically instigates Explosion Village's rise to prosperity. It is a

---

17 Mark Fisher, *Capitalist Realism: Is There No Alternative?* (Winchester: Zero Books, 2009), 10.
18 Ibid., 16.
19 Rebecca E. Karl, *The Magic of Concepts: History and the Economics in Twentieth-Century China* (Durham: Duke University Press, 2017), 9.
20 Anita Chari, *A Political Economy of the Senses: Neoliberalism, Reification, Critique* (New York: Columbia University Press, 2015), 171.
21 Yan, *The Explosion Chronicles*, 20.

train that transports coal and coke to the south from Shanxi, a province in North China.[22] The engine it runs on is not powerful enough to maintain a high velocity when hauling heavy loads up an incline. The mountain where the train slows to walking speed is just "several *li* away" from Explosion.[23] Stealing coal from the train as it struggles up the mountain and selling it in the city is the protagonist villager Kong Mingliang's "innovative" way of answering the government's call, after decades of outlawing private property ownership, for people to enrich themselves. Those who manage to save up to 10,000 *yuan* first would be eligible for a no-interest loan issued by the government. With the incorporation of Deng Xiaoping's famous dictum in the 1980s of allowing some to "get rich first,"[24] the fictional text clearly alludes to the pivotal moment in history when the post-Mao Communist Party of China set the stage for the country's economic take-off by de-collectivizing agriculture and advocating for entrepreneurship. However, the image readers are presented with as the origin of Explosion's speedy ascent to wealth is a man lifting coal from a lumbering freight train with a bamboo rake and depositing it in some baskets and hemp sacks.[25]

Rather than portraying exponential growth seamlessly activated as if by the flip of a switch, *Explosion*'s laggard locomotive conveys a disjuncture between grandiose economic aspirations and the actual capacity of existing infrastructure. The gap is made especially pronounced by Kong using an agricultural tool meant to loosen or smooth earth to "unload" from the train. The image's incongruity is further accentuated by a simile. Kong's action is described as analogous to "picking feathers from passing geese."[26] The expression is a literal translation of the Chinese proverb *yan guo ba mao* 雁過拔毛, which originally referred to one's dexterity as a martial arts practitioner but has come to be associated in a derogatory light with relentless opportunism. In addition to emphasizing the ease with which Kong manages to steal from the train and his "savviness," the ostensibly catachrestic analogy between coal and feathers brings into focus the former's "lightness of being." The labor Kong devotes to obtain a cart full of coal that he sells for two to three hundred *yuan* is minimal. The strenuous labor involved for miners to extract the rocks in the first place and the open wounds activities of this kind leave in nature are utterly elided in the transaction. Where the coal comes from cannot matter less for Kong and the buyers he deals with. Kong being exalted as "a nationally acclaimed model"[27] for being the first one in Explosion to have 10,000 *yuan* in his bank account completes the erasure.

With "a bowl-sized red blossom" pinned to his chest as he stands next to "a door-size copy of his bankbook," Kong has only one word of advice for his fellow villagers: diligence.[28] The pithy tip is followed by the mayor's hyperbolic elaboration: "as long as individuals had a diligent pair of hands, then even if they were blind or crippled, they could still gallop along the road to wealth." Here the text satirizes the self-made narrative that is habitually marshaled to gloss over injustices within a capitalist system. The catachrestic attribution of speedy accumulation of wealth to "honest hard work," rather than unchecked extractivism and direct or indirect exploitation of nature as well as workers, is made glaringly apparent when readers

---

22 Fictional places like Explosion and its neighboring villages coexist with "real" ones like Shanxi and Beijing in the narrative.
23 *Li* 里 *is a traditional Chinese unit of distance, corresponding to 500 meters or 1,640 feet.*
24 Yan, *The Explosion Chronicles*, 19.
25 Ibid., 20.
26 Ibid., 21.
27 Ibid.
28 Ibid., 22.

are privy to how Kong manages to save 10,000 *yuan*. The image of him leisurely pulling down coal from a train at walking speed connotes anything but industriousness. If anything, one sees a crafty beneficiary of an extractivist and industrializing economy. The fact that a high-ranking official makes it a point to validate Kong and his secret recipe for enrichment, entailing just a trait that everyone can supposedly cultivate, absolves the government from the responsibility to ensure the welfare of its subjects. This blatant form of state-sanctioned capitalist catachresis captured, complete with the description of a smirk on Kong's face as he stands before his fellow villagers,[29] taunts readers who may otherwise have been unsuspecting of or more likely, desensitized to how the golden rule of keeping one's nose to the grindstone rings hollow.

In "Fertile," the mayor also awards First Bloom and Second Bloom, the brothers whose experiments make a wasteland ultra-fecund, medals of honor at the town festival. Nonetheless, the recipients never show up to receive the award, let alone share the secret to their success like Kong does. In fact, they have no idea what exactly brings about the land's transformation and how to control it or replicate the results. Unlike *Explosion*, "Fertile" does not place readers in a privileged, knowing position. Narrated by First Bloom and Second Bloom's seven-or-eight-year-old niece, Everlasting Bloom, the sense of mystery is accentuated. As the only one who is relatively close to her reclusive uncles, Everlasting Bloom is the sole witness of their work. In a house full of bottles and colored water, she sees without comprehending why "the red liquid turn[s] violet and the green liquid turn[s] yellow when they [are] poured into different bottles ... *like magic*."[30] When she plays by the dumping ground her uncles' place looks out on, where people dispose of their furniture and household items by a tacit agreement, she enjoys waiting for them to throw the water they experiment with out of the windows. The liquid is "many-hued—sometimes violet, sometimes blue, always shimmering in the sunlight, like twinkling stars."[31] Over time, the dusty wasteland becomes a mud-plat and then transforms into a plot with soil that grows oversized ornamental plants and vegetables. Upon seeing the "barren, pitch-black mud-plat ha[ving] turned into an embroidered carpet of green,"[32] First Bloom wonders if Second Bloom has sowed any seeds when the latter believes the birds have done so. Neither can tell what exactly the soil is going to yield and count on knowing "soon enough."[33] The inexplicability of the phenomenon, as in coxcomb flowers in the size of rice bowls and bell peppers literally as big as church bells materializing in the mud-plat,[34] is of little concern to people eager to lay their hands on the soil. The town reaches a level of prosperity "beyond the townfolk's wildest dreams" with exponential growth in the export trade of soil, which in turn launches the tertiary industry. Sharing Everlasting Bloom's amazement, some experts studying the soil call it "a miracle" and the mud-plat "a veritable treasure trove."[35]

The image "Fertile" offers as the origin of Fertile Town's economic take-off turns out to be no less incongruous than that in *Explosion*. It involves seemingly scientific experiments in a secluded house likened to a magic show in the eyes of the child narrator and colored water as waste from the experiments splashed, sparkling the way stars do in a night sky, onto a "refuse

---

29 Ibid., 21–22.
30 Xi Xi, "Story of Fertile Town," *Marvels of a Floating and Other Stories*, trans. Eva Hung (Hong Kong: Chinese University of Hong Kong, 1997), 36; italics added.
31 Ibid., 39.
32 Ibid., 44.
33 Ibid., 46.
34 Ibid., 47.
35 Ibid., 36.

reservoir." While *Explosion* mobilizes catachresis to critique the immaterialization of exploitation and mock the tired refrain of hard work buttressing the capitalist system, "Fertile" belabors the catachrestic designation of meteoric economic growth as "miraculous" in a system that prides itself on being guided by rational calculation in pursuit of profit. It captures the illusion of calculability and predictability a capitalist regime offers and its built-in recourse to fantasies when calculation falls short. The text reflects on how, instead of raising concern over the inherent volatility and inconsistencies of the capitalist model, "success stories" of dramatic economic growth within a short period of time tend to capture one's imagination. Bafflement and fascination with the spectacles work in tandem to sustain or even bolster the appeal of capitalism.

Everlasting Bloom is not the only one in "Fertile" who is captivated by her uncles' experiments. Tourists flock to First Bloom's and Second Bloom's mansion in droves are entertained by employees hired specifically to throw colored water out of the windows.[36] Far from shedding light on what causes the exceptional fertility of the soil, the show only further mystifies its audience. For the employees who are no more knowledgeable than the tourists as to how the colored liquid transforms the dumping ground in the first place, their job is nothing but a "mechanical and monotonous" one.[37] With its uninspired portrayal of the staging of a "miracle," "Fertile" effectively dampens the excitement or wonder the term "an economic miracle" tends to elicit. Given the repetition, the unknown that characters in the text overlook or dismiss in favor of the spectacle lingers with readers, throwing doubt on the common catachrestic designation of rapid economic development as miraculous and thus, a cause for celebration.

Imaging value's metamorphoses

Apart from highlighting the hollowness of a miracle narrative, "Fertile" offers a visualization of processes within the capitalist system that tend to be taken for granted in highly abstract terms. In a sense, the figurative language used in the text directs readers' attention to capitalist abstractions with its own brand of catachrestic abstraction. Returning to the image of First Bloom's and Second Bloom's experiment, the changes in color when liquids are poured into different bottles quite literally call to mind market liquidity, how seamlessly assets can be converted into cash or vice versa. The image echoes how the capitalist system in general confers "shape-shifting power" on the objects it enlists and touches in pursuit of ever-growing profit. This is especially so when, as David Harvey rightly observes, "the money form is now unchained from any physical limitations such as those imposed by the money commodities."[38]

More explicitly registering this phenomenon is the enumeration of household items dumped at the wasteland, ranging from "leaky wash basins" to "worm-eaten wardrobes," from a "birdcage with an unhitched door" to "broken mirrors,"[39] and the description of their "speedy" disintegration, forming a key component of the "miraculously" fertile soil in addition to the mysterious colored liquids. Abnormally large fruits and vegetables emerge from the refuse of these non-essential objects likely from modest households and in turn the wealth such produce bestows on the townspeople transforms the composition of refuse disposal sites.

---

36 Ibid., 50.
37 Ibid., 51.
38 David Harvey, *Seventeen Contradictions and the End of Capitalism* (Oxford: Oxford University Press, 2014), 233.
39 Xi Xi, "The Story of Fertile Town," 37–38.

These sites become homes to "cigar boxes, fridges that did not defrost automatically, old sofas, spring mattresses with one bust spring, wigs, and high-heel shoes with skew-whiff heels ...."[40]

The shift in the content of the garbage, a result of commodities' "planned and sometimes instantaneous obsolescence" for the sake of "shorten[ing] turnover time,"[41] indicates the town's economic strides but readers are presented with a warped trajectory. The agricultural imagery seems out of place in a narrative tracing the further development of a town, not a bucolic village. However, agriculture as one of the most labor-intensive industries becoming one that requires no tilling, sowing or watering, and yields an array of beyond perfect produce automatically in "Fertile" can be an apt representation of the ultimate fantasy of a capitalist amassing wealth while bypassing workers and their "always-too-costly" labor. The glaring absence of workers in the picture brings home how "[t]he *devaluation* of the world of men is in direct proportion to the *increasing value* of the world of things."[42]

The fact that profitable cash crops grow from the soil "fertilized" by disintegrated, unwanted household goods also serves as a jarring catachresis that designates the arbitrariness of valorization within a capitalist system, how yesterday's trash can be today's treasure. This is to say the market value conferred on goods, not necessarily corresponding to the objects' "intrinsic" worth or the labor devoted to production, is highly abstract and mercurial. As Harvey points out succinctly, "[c]apital is not only about the production and circulation of value. It is also about the destruction or devaluation of capital."[43] Capital reproduces itself through ongoing processes of creative destruction with unpredictable ramifications. The rootlessness and volatility of this thing called value within capitalism is provocatively captured in the absurd image of produce springing from an unsown wasteland.

Moral depravity as convenient "truth"

At first blush, there seems to be an almost identical episode of refuse or worthless objects "shape-shifting" in *Explosion*. As the Explosion villagers manage to enrich themselves by "unloading" coals and different goods from cargo trains under Kong's "guidance,"[44] they have at their disposal the capital to industrialize and build their own factories. At a riverside agricultural processing plant, "mountain products such as walnuts, mushrooms, and tree fungus all went in smelling of dirt, only to emerge as highly refined swallow nest soup," whereas "[s]omeone's colorful plastic cup might be made from the rubber soles of that same person's shoes or sandals" and "tooth-brushing cup ... from former toilet plungers" at a rubber factory.[45] Diverging from "Fertile," where the element of chance with First Bloom's and Second Bloom's random pouring of liquids plays a dominant part in the transformation of a dumping ground, the "upgrade" of goods with little value in *Explosion* is attributed to conscious recycling and counterfeiting for the maximization of profit. It is relentless profiteering that works "magic," in this case.

In fact, the villagers' insatiable avarice and a glaring lack of scruples make up a prominent thread running through the narrative. Explosion's success story begins with Kong casually

---

40 Ibid., 54.
41 Harvey, *Seventeen Contradictions and the End of Capitalism*, 236.
42 Karl Marx, *Economic and Philosophic Manuscripts of 1844*, trans. Martin Milligan (Moscow: Progress Publishers, 1959), 28; italics in the original.
43 Harvey, *Seventeen Contradictions and the End of Capitalism*, 233.
44 Yan, *The Explosion Chronicles*, 28.
45 Ibid., 136–37.

stealing from passing trains. The whole village becomes rich when other villagers follow his lead to "unload" until the trains pick up speed with stronger engines and make unloading too risky.[46] Notwithstanding this momentary setback, people's resolve to "gallop along the road to wealth"[47] remains ever so strong. Eager to climb up the political ladder, the mayor and Kong as the village chief send all the young people from Explosion to a faraway city where they have to stay for at least half a year and figure out ways to earn enough money to "replace [their] thatched-roof house[s] with … tile-roof [ones]."[48] It is far from an innocuous coincidence on the plot level that the men resort to thievery and the women prostitution. So many of them get arrested that a police officer exclaims to the mayor, "Fuck! Your village really does specialize in producing thieves!"[49] On yet another occasion, the officer accosts the mayor with the caustic rhetorical question of whether his town "fucking specialize[s] in producing prostitutes?"[50] The insults echo the Chinese proverb *nan dao nü chang* 男盜女娼 'men robbing and women prostituting,' which is used to describe people being out-and-out scoundrels devoid of morality, involving an age-old misogynistic stigma attached to female sex workers.

Alongside the authorial choice to liken modern Chinese subjects under capitalism as either thieves or prostitutes and represent supposed human vices as the motor force of Explosion's whirlwind economic growth, Yan's proclamation in the Author's Note that his work "captures a hidden internal logic contained within China's reality" with its use of an original "mythorealist"[51] mode constitute a layer of catachresis marred by simplistic essentialism. Yan believes that "power and money have colluded to steal people's souls," resulting in "a string of terrifying incidents" in contemporary China.[52] Mythorealism, according to his conception, endeavors to "reveal the nine-tenths of an iceberg that lies hidden beneath the ocean waves" and "articulates the most basic spirit of contemporary Chinese history."[53] The accepted English translation of Yan's original term *shenshi zhuyi* 神實主義 as "mythorealism" is misleading for the word *shen* 神 does not refer to "myth" (*shenhua* 神話). Instead, based on the author's diagnosis of today's China quoted above, *shen* in the term more accurately designates "spirit" or "psyche" (*jingshen* 精神). Hence, the translation of the term into "psychical realism" can put the author's positioning into perspective more accurately. In an article titled "Finding Light in China's Darkness," Yan describes himself as "somehow fated to perceive darkness." Since he "sees" the "ugliness" of Chinese people as what is most worrying about the country's so-called economic miracle, he is dedicated to speaking "the truth."[54]

Granted, by casting himself as a metafictional character who cannot resist Kong's offer to pay him handsomely for penning the chronicles to glorify Explosion City, Yan does not necessarily place himself on a pristine moral high ground. Nevertheless, the exaggerated and monolithic portrayal of individuals' moral depravity as driving or plaguing China's economic take-off is a form of misguided catachresis that vastly understates the influence material and historical forces exert over people in a country which has had a fraught relationship with

---

46 Ibid., 40.
47 Ibid., 22.
48 Ibid., 51.
49 Ibid., 49.
50 Ibid., 51.
51 Ibid., 456.
52 Ibid., 451.
53 Ibid., 456–57.
54 Yan Lianke, "Finding Light in China's Darkness: Yan Lianke on Writing in China," *The New York Times*, 22 Oct. 2014, https://www.nytimes.com/2014/10/23/opinion/Yan-Lianke-finding-light-in-chinas-darkness.html (last accessed 24 Mar. 2018).

global capitalism. Equally concerning is the way *Explosion* perpetuates the grand-narrative elision of regular workers in the mainland as agents, albeit blatantly exploited, shaping the country's economic development. Charting the volume of labor unrest in the first decade of the twenty-first century, sociologist Ching Kwan Lee offers an important insight: "[f]ar from a docile lot, [Chinese] workers have staged significant resistance" against corruption and the severe lack of protection for workers' welfare.[55]

No miracle is an island

Pulling readers in a direction distinct from that taken by a sweeping claim on the ways of Chinese people are particular episodes in *Explosion* where the catachrestic figurative language provocatively employed designates the counterintuitive continuity between Maoist China and post-1978 China. They offer a pathway to developing a historicized examination of a distinctive facet of China's economic "miracle." One such episode is the gory construction of an airport mentioned earlier. To win the high-ranking officials' approval to promote Explosion's status into a metropolis, Kong Mingliang, who has become the mayor by then, makes the promise of having a one-hundred-kilometer subway line and the largest airport in Asia built in less than a week. Given his previous successes in making nature follow his orders, Kong tries to initiate the construction project with uttering imperatives alone. He is encouraged by his ability to have all the animals and insects in his garden gather in front of him by simply stating: "I am Mayor Kong, and all of you should show yourselves."[56] Unfortunately, nothing happens when he orders a structure to spring up at a spot he chooses: "I am Mayor Kong of Explosion. I am going to build a structure here …. I want to start building now, and since I am the mayor, what I say goes."[57] He tries again by waving the official documents endorsing the construction of an airport and the source of funding at the prospective site. After the fashion of God in the book of Genesis, he calls out emphatically but to no avail: "Let there be a runway. I am Mayor Kong."[58] Even though Kong's absurd experiments stem partly from his own delusion of grandeur, his belief in mind trumping matter echoes slogans widely popular during the Great Leap Forward (1958–62), for instance, "The bolder you are, the more fecund the land" (*ren you duo dadan, di you duo dachan* 人有多大膽, 地有多大產).

Not getting his way with mere authoritative commands, Kong turns to one of his brothers, Kong Mingyao, who owns a private army to accomplish the impossible mission. Mingyao has no problem building all the infrastructures in a few days' time provided that Mingliang can procure for him "five thousand severed legs and ten thousand severed fingers."[59] The general reasons: "Without severing that many legs and without cutting off that many fingers, and without thousands of people dying, do you think these construction projects can be completed?" The matter-of-fact message is hammered home as readers find themselves sitting through the process after which soldiers get "covered from head to toe in blood."[60] They first toss "in several dozen bloody fingers and then [stomp] on them" by the mountainside

---

55 Ching Kwan Lee, "Made in China: Labor as a Political Force?," paper presented at the Mansfield Conference, Missoula, 18–20 Apr. 2004), 1, https://www.umt.edu/mansfield/imx/conferencepdf/2004LeePaper.pdf.
56 Yan, *The Explosion Chronicles*, 384.
57 Ibid., 388.
58 Ibid., 391.
59 Ibid., 401.
60 Ibid., 403.

to get rid of the grass and thorns,[61] fire at the hill under which "hundreds of bloody fingers, toes, and severed legs" have previously been buried to create a flat surface,[62] and finally "trampl[e] the bloody ribs and leg bones that [litter] the ground," so that a standard airport runway materializes under their feet. The sole building materials literally being severed flesh and bones insist on having readers reckon with the exorbitant human cost involved in fulfilling the imperatives of economic progress that is deemed impressive enough. For exploited workers, displaced residents and those who fall through the cracks of the ever-dwindling safety net offered by a government prioritizing GDP growth rate, the mushrooming of large-scale infrastructures is likely more nightmarish than miraculous. No matter how the airport is lauded as the world's largest and most impressive one, it is unlikely to be able to erase from readers' mind the image of "a mountain blanketed in blood-covered finger and toe bones."

Again, one is reminded of the Great Leap Forward with the setting of a target impossible to reach and how the fulfillment of the target is placed before human lives. Back in the mid-twentieth century, China was eager to be self-sufficient through the collectivization of agriculture and industrialization. The goal was for the country to modernize as soon as possible and become independent from the Western powers, including the Soviet Union, to assume leadership of the communist and decolonizing movement worldwide. At play was what Roy Chan calls "fast socialism," which "rejected a temporal model of gradual transition into socialism" but instead "affirmed the need for a compressed period of productive accumulation to bring about the conditions for true socialism to flourish."[63] While the restlessness that undergirds the Great Leap Forward can be attributed to revolutionary zeal, idealism, or even "a suppressed desire for wealth,"[64] it also bespeaks a deep sense of insecurity within a hierarchical world order determined by one's level of development measured against the West. The urgency to gain a secure footing on the world stage would logically intensify rather than abate when the disastrous failure of the Great Leap forward and the chaos unleashed by the Cultural Revolution (1966–76) set the country back significantly. Aside from capturing capitalism's own brand of time compression for the lowering of cost, *Explosion*'s portrayal of an airport being built from scratch in a few days' time can be read as rendering in sharp relief an urgent desire, stemming from a perceived sense of lamentable belatedness to spare no effort in connecting and catching up with the r/west of the world. On the one hand, as Yu Hua 余華 puts it, "in [China's] economic miracle, there are both Great-Leap-Forward style revolutionary movement and Cultural-Revolution style revolutionary violence" (我們的經濟奇蹟裡, 既有大躍進式的革命運動, 也有文革式的革命暴力).[65] On the other, the excess characterizing China's economic miracle can partly be understood as embodying or carrying forward Maoist China's unfulfilled aspirations and unresolved anxiety in a globalized world with asymmetrical relationality governed by differential economic might.

Explosion's allusion to a hierarchical relationship between the developing China and the United States specifically is of interest here. To get an American automobile manufacturer

---

61 Ibid., 402.
62 Ibid., 403.
63 Roy Bing Chan, *The Edge of Knowing: Dreams, History, and Realism in Modern Chinese Literature* (Seattle: University of Washington Press, 2017), 140.
64 Carlos Rojas, "Introduction: Specters of Marx, Shades of Mao, and the Ghosts of Global Capital," *Ghost Protocol: Development and Displacement in Global China*, ed. Carlos Rojas and Ralph A. Lizinger (Durham: Duke University Press, 2016), 6.
65 Yu Hua, *Shi ge cihui li de Zhongguo* 十個詞彙裡的中國 [*China in Ten Words*] (Taipei: Maitian, 2011), 190; my translation.

to build their largest factory at Explosion, Kong Mingliang not only offers "the most favorable policies" but also treats the company's team to "the prettiest girls" and the finest food.[66] Somehow, the Americans still prefer establishing their factory on the coast because the CEO, having been in Vietnam for six years, finds "the girls [he] saw in Vietnam" are incomparable, "no matter how good Chinese girls may be."[67] Rather than leaving the group to their orientalist fantasies, Kong mobilizes everyone in Explosion to bring Vietnam from forty years back to indulge the Americans' nostalgia. Apart from having girls dress up in Vietnamese traditional clothing, sauntering up and down "a Vietnam street," and creating a "jungle made from plastic foam, wire, and pigment,"[68] Kong has his people stage the US army's massacre of Vietnamese guerrillas and civilians. The idyllic old Vietnam street becomes one "lined with piles of dead and wounded Vietnamese, their blood flowing like a river toward the American's feet."[69] As the team representing the automobile company finds themselves in need of a breather from the overblown re-enactment of the Vietnam War, the "Vietnamese" rush out in droves, kneel and kowtow to the Americans. They shout repeatedly and in unison: "For the sake of your conscience, you should invest your money here."[70] Shortly after, "the American industrialists signed an investment agreement with Explosion for tens of billions of *yuan*."[71]

Perhaps this farcical episode, with its liberal use of hyperbole, is meant as a form of corrective catachresis that critiques the overly eager courting of foreign investment in the mainland. The kneeling and kowtowing cast the people of Explosion as exceedingly sycophantic. The opportunist appropriation of Vietnam's historical trauma only adds to the characterization of these people as morally depraved. What this pointed catachrestic falls short of registering, though, is the mutually dependent and constitutive relationship between China and the then economic superpower teetering on its throne owing to the expenses of the Vietnam War and stagflation, among an array of factors. The former needed foreign capital to fulfill its aspiration to join the "developed" countries' club as much as the latter relied on the former to minimize production costs and temporarily fulfill the "necessity of escaping the material constraints to compound growth."[72] Together, the two countries added fuel to the faltering capitalist engine in the second half of the twentieth century.

In a subtle manner, "Fertile" also touches on the situatedness of Fertile Town (Hong Kong) in the world instead of presenting it as a closed-off space where something exceptional takes place. Before the unexpected success of First Bloom's and Second Bloom's experiments, the Bloom family owns a soft drink factory previously owned by a foreigner with blue eyes. When he is conscripted into the army by his home country, the foreigner leaves the factory to the patriarch of the family, Everlasting Bloom's grandfather. Equally noteworthy is the old grandmother's account of how her sons, First Bloom and Second Bloom, used to go fishing every day before becoming sailors. It remains a mystery as to "where their ship had taken them, or what sort of people they had met."[73] The only thing old grandmother is sure about is

---

66 Yan, *The Explosion Chronicles*, 284.
67 Ibid., 285.
68 Ibid., 286.
69 Ibid., 289.
70 Ibid., 290.
71 Ibid., 291.
72 Harvey, *Seventeen Contradictions and the End of Capitalism*, 238.
73 Xi Xi, "Story of Fertile Town," 42.

that they only start staying home and "bur[ying] themselves in their 'experiment'" after they return from their voyage abroad.

The catachrestic representation of the colonial legacy inherited by Hong Kong as a soft drink factory is intriguing for soft drinks are saccharine, pleasantly so for many, but far from nourishing. The miracle is partly built on the family owning the factory as it is what allows First Bloom and Second Bloom to keep experimenting to their hearts' desire, sustained by food and other necessities the staff are charged to deliver to them.[74] Similar to the soft drinks, the produce that emerges from the dumping ground transformed by unwanted liquids from the experiments may look and taste amazing but contain no real nutritional value. The backstory of the two having been abroad and returning home as changed people, obsessed with experimentation, are significant in that it attributes the subsequent economic take-off in part to the importation and mutation or adaptation of capitalist ideals and operating principles. As fuzzy as the attribution is, it counters the popular essentialist claim that ascribes Hong Kong's economic miracle to the "Lion Rock Spirit" as a virtue every Hongkonger possesses, generation to generation, of never giving up in the face of hardships and always putting in the hard work to succeed.

With both texts referencing the West in their narrativization of the respective economic miracles, the absence of the mainland in "Fertile" and that of Hong Kong in *Explosion* are striking given how heavily the two have figured in each other's developmental trajectories. Similar to the States, Hong Kong averted a potentially devastating economic downturn in the 1970s by tapping into the cheap labor available "just across the border in China."[75] It became one of the foremost international financial centers through capitalizing on its ideal geographical location to act as an intermediary between China and the world. When foreign investors were hesitant, some still are, to venture into mainland China's market given the inadequate legal protection offered, capital from Hong Kong served as the initial impetus to mainland China's economic development. The elision of Hong Kong and the mainland, respectively, in the two texts evinces the impulse to look to the West, specifically America and Western Europe, when it comes to identifying players that exert influence on the economic development of different parts of the world. The pervasiveness of capitalism globally, however, points to the sheer number of players and the decentering of historically dominant Western powers. The complex interlocking relationships that have emerged necessitate re-examinations that unravel how economic miracles came about, at the expense of who and what beyond the East-West dichotomy. In this regard, David Harvey's caution is well-taken: "The World Bank is fond of reassuring us that a rising tide of economic development is bound to lift all boats. Maybe a truer metaphor would be that exponentially rising sea levels and intensifying storms are destined to sink all boats."[76]

Unnatural disasters

Despite its publication in 1982 being one and a half decade before the 1997 Asian financial crisis, "Fertile" anticipated the rhetoric normalizing and glossing over the crash after the take-off. When the whole world raves about the miraculously fertile soil, some of the experts who study it warn: "This is a cancer of the soil; the cells of the mud-plat are propagating

---

74 Ibid., 40.
75 David Harvey, *A Brief History of Neoliberalism* (Oxford: Oxford University Press, 2005), 136.
76 Harvey, *Seventeen Contradictions and the End of Capitalism*, 245.

irregularly."[77] The warning is drowned out by the marveling of other "optimistic" experts and the general public. Over time, the cancerous nature of the soil becomes undeniably apparent and runs out of control. One of the outer walls of the building where numerous packages of the soil are stored comes crashing down as plants keep growing spontaneously from the soil with "entangled stems and runners ... like a huge expanding ice cube."[78] The soil itself "increase[es] in volume, expanding. It burst through the confines of the tin-foiled bags, scattered everywhere, then gathered itself together into a gigantic wriggling amoeba moving in every direction all at once."[79] No longer simply a material that generates profit in a docile manner, the soil takes on a life of its own. People try to get rid of it altogether by cutting up their plants and throwing away the soil but disposing it somewhere does not stop it from growing to the point that it "[seem] ready to devour the whole of Fertile Town."[80] They later resort to the drastic measure of burning all the plants and the soil. It is an unprecedented downpour and cyclone that ends up giving the town a clean slate, as if the soil never existed. The story ends with Everlasting Bloom's grandmother musing: "A town will not remain forever prosperous or forever poor. It's just the same as human beings; there's no everlasting happiness, and no endless sorrow either."[81]

When an economic miracle reveals itself to be a disaster in the making, the Zen notion of how transience is the only thing that lasts in life as a coping mechanism precludes critical reflection on how the disaster could have been averted in the first place. In this light, the capitalist boom and bust cycle is taken as the natural order of things, elusive and preordained. Both the designation of rapid economic growth as "miraculous" and that of an economic crisis as "natural" are part of a catachrestic discursive repertoire that helps the capitalist system covers its tracks, diverting attention away from the unnecessary evils it has unleashed and cultivated.

The image of the fertile soil as an ever-expanding "giant amoeba"[82] with a will of its own serves as a compelling visualization of a major cause of financial crises, namely unbridled speculation that becomes increasingly abstracted from material conditions and snowballs as a ticking time bomb. On top of exhibiting an unparalleled level of fertility when composed of broken furniture and yielding any kind of flowers or vegetables simultaneously, the soil can freely expand and alter its shape like an amoeba. These qualities combined to render the fertile soil menacing and volatile, creating a stark contrast with the common perception of soil as this organic matter to be manipulated in whichever way human beings see fit. By having an innocuous and inanimate matter morph into an indiscriminately destructive force in the narrative, "Fertile" alerts readers to the insidious effects of capitalism. The acts of speculation in the housing and stock market are represented in numbers and tend to have no immediate observable effects on our everyday reality. However, these gambles can stealthily add up to a breaking point when their reverberations are felt across the board, except for corporations deemed "worthy" of receiving bailouts from the government with taxpayers' money. Soil as the controlling image throughout the short story demands a serious consideration of the material impacts, conspicuous or otherwise, a capitalist system exerts on our lives.

---

77 Xi Xi, "Story of Fertile Town," 51.
78 Ibid., 57.
79 Ibid., 58.
80 Ibid., 59.
81 Ibid., 64.
82 Ibid., 58.

Unnatural death

To return to the temporal, if "Fertile" takes on the logic of economic cycles as the law of nature entailing only our resignation and adaptation, *Explosion* imagines what the sudden death of linear time would look like. Shortly after Explosion's promotion to a provincial-level metropolis, Kong Mingliang is assassinated by his drunk-in-power brother, Kong Mingyao, who helps him build the international airport in short order. The latter wants to "borrow the city's residents for three days"[83] to join his army on a quest to "fix all of America's problems, and then ... fix Europe's" before "proceed[ing] to fix China's problems, and even all of the world's."[84] The assassination is meant to forestall any attempt on Mingliang's part to sabotage his plan to save the world. With Mingyao getting his way, Explosion becomes a ghost town all of a sudden populated only by the elderly, the disabled, and children, who are not conscripted. Accompanying the narrator's solemn statements that "the city's prosperity abruptly [comes] to an end" and a "brilliant historical period reached its conclusion" is the depiction of "the city's trash bins, its gardens, and the ground ... littered with all sorts of discarded clocks and cheap watches that had suddenly stopped working and couldn't be fixed," for many of these clocks and watches, "their hour, minute, and second hands had completely fallen off."[85]

This image of Explosion "buried under a mountain of broken clocks and watches"[86] no doubt lends itself to the reading of "the linear logic of development ... reach[ing] its limit, resulting in its abrupt suspension."[87] Nevertheless, the expiration of the progress-oriented linear temporality envisioned and its premise paradoxically restricts readers' imagination for the takeaway seems to be that the capitalist train hurtling forward would eventually lose its steam. All that one can do, then, is to wait it out. The belief that the relentless drive for progress will implode in due time, coupled with the essentializing diagnosis of mainland Chinese people's soul being irredeemable, assures readers that there is nothing they can do about the dominance of the capitalist-driven linear conception of time. There is a world of difference between the hour, minute, and second hands of a clock falling off on their own versus those who toil under these hands' arbitrary command reclaiming their autonomy and ripping them off or rearranging them creatively on the clock face. Rather than dictating what the text should portray and how, the consideration of an alternative plot development is meant to demonstrate what the original conception precludes in terms of potentialities to take the conversation initiated by the text beyond the parameters it establishes.

By the same token, this comparative study's close examination of different forms and shades of catachresis in "Fertile" and *Explosion* is motivated by a desire to open up and sustain dialogues probing into the capitalist "success stories." The greater freedom fictional texts enjoy, given readers' general expectations, regarding the employment of catachrestic figurative language and their narrative structures allow for a dynamic engagement with official or widely accepted accounts of historical episodes. From this perspective, there is no reason for cultural scholars committed to thinking through and challenging the status quo saturated with capitalist normative principles to side-line fictional texts, assuming that they have no meaningful bearing on reality.

---

83 Yan, *The Explosion Chronicles*, 440.
84 Ibid., 439.
85 Ibid., 443.
86 Ibid.
87 Cao Xuenan, "Mythorealism and Enchanted Time: Yan Lianke's *Explosion Chronicles*," *Frontiers of Literary Studies in China* 10, no. 1 (2016): 108.

Acknowledgment

I would like to thank Dr. Roy Bing Chan for his feedback on previous versions of the essay and for his unwavering support as my advisor.

Bibliography

Cao, Xuenan. "Mythorealism and Enchanted Time: Yan Lianke's *Explosion Chronicles*." *Frontiers of Literary Studies in China* 10, no. 1 (2016): 103–12.
Chan, Roy Bing. *The Edge of Knowing: Dreams, History, and Realism in Modern Chinese Literature*. Seattle: University of Washington Press, 2017.
Chari, Anita. *A Political Economy of the Senses: Neoliberalism, Reification, Critique*. New York: Columbia University Press, 2015.
Fisher, Mark. *Capitalist Realism: Is There No Alternative?* Winchester: Zero Books, 2009.
Harvey, David. *A Brief History of Neoliberalism*. Oxford: Oxford University Press, 2005.
———. *Seventeen Contradictions and the End of Capitalism*. Oxford: Oxford University Press, 2014.
Karl, Rebecca E. *The Magic of Concepts: History and the Economics in Twentieth-Century China*. Durham: Duke University Press, 2017.
Lee, Ching Kwan. "Made in China: Labor as a Political Force?" Paper presented at the Mansfield Conference, Missoula, 18–20 Apr. 2004. https://www.umt.edu/mansfield/imx/conferencepdf/2004LeePaper.pdf.
Lin, Justin Yifu. "Demystifying the Chinese Economy." *The Australian Economic Review* 46, no. 3 (2013): 259–68.
Marx, Karl. *Capital*. Edited by Friedrich Engels. Translated by Samuel Moore and Edward Aveling. New York: Modern Library, 1936.
———. *Capital*. Translated by Ben Fowkes. London: Penguin, 1990.
———. *Economic and Philosophic Manuscripts of 1844*. Translated by Martin Milligan. Moscow: Progress Publishers, 1959.
Minardi, Jean-François. "Hong Kong: The Ongoing Economic Miracle." *Montreal Economic Institute*, Nov. 2013. https://www.iedm.org/files/note1113_en.pdf. (last accessed 15 Apr. 2020).
Ngai, Sianne. "Visceral Abstractions." *GLQ: A Journal of Lesbian and Gay Studies* 21, no. 1 (2015): 33–63.
Popov, Vladimir, and Jomo Kwame Sundaram. "Liberation, Not Liberalization, Responsible for China's Economic Miracle." *Inter Press Service*, 19 Nov. 2019. http://www.ipsnews.net/2019/11/liberation-not-liberalization-responsible-chinas-economic-miracle/ (last accessed 15 Apr. 2020).
Reed, Lawrence K. "The Man behind the Hong Kong Miracle." *Foundation for Economic Education*, 10 Feb. 2014. https://fee.org/articles/the-man-behind-the-hong-kong-miracle/ (last accessed 15 Apr. 2020).
Rojas, Carlos. "Introduction: Specters of Marx, Shades of Mao, and the Ghosts of Global Capital." In *Ghost Protocol: Development and Displacement in Global China*, edited by Carlos Rojas and Ralph A. Lizinger, 1–14. Durham: Duke University Press, 2016.
Shklovsky, Viktor. "Art, as Device," translated by Alexandra Berlina. *Poetics Today* 36, no. 3 (2015): 151–74.
Sutherland, Keston. "Marx in Jargon." *World Picture* 1, no. 1 (2008). http://www.worldpicturejournal.com/WP_1.1/KSutherland.html (last accessed 29 Feb. 2020).
Xi Xi 西西. "Story of Fertile Town." In *Marvels of a Floating City and Other Stories*, translated by Eva Hung, 31–64. Hong Kong: Chinese University of Hong Kong, 1997.
Yan Lianke 閻連科. *The Explosion Chronicles*. Translated by Carlos Rojas. New York: Grove Press, 2016.
———. "Finding Light in China's Darkness: Yan Lianke on Writing in China." *New York Times*, 22 Oct. 2014. https://www.nytimes.com/2014/10/23/opinion/Yan-Lianke-finding-light-in-chinas-darkness.html (last accessed 24 Mar. 2018).
Yu Hua 余華. *Shi ge cihui li de Zhongguo* 十個詞彙裡的中國 [China in Ten Words]. Taipei: Maitian, 2011.

18

RECONSTRUCTING THE SELF THROUGH *HERSTORY*

On Yan Lianke's *Tamen (Shes)*

Sabrina Ardizzoni

Introduction

For the translation of the title of Yan Lianke's *Tamen* 她們 'They (feminine)', I will use here an invented term, *Shes*, just like the gender-marked Chinese character *ta* 她 'she' is an invention of modern times.[1] While reading this book, so far untranslated in English, three points of enquiry came to my mind: (1) What is the main aim of this work, so peculiar and different compared to other writings by the same author? (2) Can we consider this a gap-filler in the writing of a *her*-story, complementary to *hi*story? and (3) What, if any, is the political value of this book? To answer these questions, I will go through the book, searching for the main topics and ideas expressed by the author, and cross-examining the text. In doing so, I will keep in mind not only the gender-study framework suggested by the author himself but also Gayatri Spivak's categories of subaltern studies. In fact, her categories, starting from the question "Can the subaltern speak?" help me to explain the male voice that speaks out in place of the women so brilliantly depicted in this literary work.

Upheld by many linguistic theories, the gender analysis here must take into account the fact that due to typological structure and discoursive practice, the Chinese language tends to

---

1 The character *ta* 她 is recorded in the *Shuo wen jie zi* 說文解字 [*Explanation of graphs and analysis of characters*] and *Kangxi* [康熙] *Dictionary*, but with a different pronunciation and meaning. In the 20th century, the feminine orthographic variation 她 was promoted by Liu Bannong 劉半農 (1891–1943), who used it in a poem in 1920: "Slim clouds floating in the sky,/Gentle wind blowing on the ground./Ah!/Light breeze ruffling my hair,/Tell me, how can I not think of her?" (天上飄着些微雲，/ 地上吹着些微風。/ 啊! / 微風吹動了我的頭髮，/ 教我如何不想她?). Its usage was very welcome by the intellectuals in the May Fourth Movement, like Lu Xun 魯迅 (1881–1936) and Guo Moruo 郭沫若 (1892–1978), who used it extensively in their vernacular (*baihua* 白話) production. It was widespread among the writers in the Written Vernacular Movement (*baihuawen yundong* 白話文運動) and it became official after the foundation of People's Republic of China in 1949. See Chris Shei, *The Routledge Handbook of Chinese Discourse Analysis* (London: Routledge), 2019, 148; also Sabrina Ardizzoni, "Revising the Chinese Translation of Verdi's Opera *La Traviata*: Linguistic and Methodological Issues," in *Diverse Voices in Chinese Translation and Interpreting*, ed. Riccardo Moratto and Martin Woesler (Singapore: Springer, 2021), 331.

under-represent women.[2] Chinese words do not recognize gender unless it is intentionally expressed, and the radical character for "woman," *nü* 女, when used as a semantic marker in word formation, often denotes a derogatory meaning.[3] Moreover, proper names do not express gender, unless otherwise specified by intertextual discourse markers. These linguistic features have played a part in connoting China's history, history of thought, literature, culture as generally "male." As widely accepted by historians and gender studies researchers, in traditional society, women occupied a well-delimited space or, more precisely, gender distinction was based on a rigid division of space: "women operate on the inside (*nei* 內), men on the outside (*wai* 外)."[4] Scope for action and its relevant functions were rigidly defined: women did not concern themselves of the *wai*, the public, political sphere, while men did not concern themselves of the *nei*, the domestic realm, the preservation of hearth-and-home and all that it contains. This Confucian tradition-derived separation, of which one finds traces in texts dating back to the pre-Qin Era,[5] merges with the division between *yin* 陰 and *yang* 陽, and the division between the sexes in social ethics that derives from it. Thus, within the dominating system, women were kept away from positions of power (deemed *wai* or "external"), wherefore their increasingly inevitable position of subordination, especially after the fourteenth century (i.e., the Ming-Qing period).

Indeed, as Spivak in her "Can the Subaltern Speak?" states the concept of subalternity is closely linked to a lack of access to hegemonic power.[6] The intellectual and political events of the modern age, from the mid-nineteenth century to the "Great Divide" marked by the foundation of the People's Republic of China in 1949, brought about an evolution of language and script, and a re-writing of female history, and this is also reflected in Yan's text.[7]

The twentieth- and twenty-first-century women depicted in Yan's three generations of *Shes* occupy a well-defined space: the author's home province, Henan, in the rural Central Plain. They are not victims or heroines who exhibit a revolutionary spirit of resistance against injustice as embodied in a phallocratic society, like in Lu Xun and the 1919 May Fourth Movement literature; they do not seek to achieve a personal subjectivity within a system which is, or is not, providing them with a space to position themselves, as shown in the literature of women writers like Ding Ling 丁玲 (1904–86) or Xiao Hong 蕭紅 (1911–42) during

---

2 Dali Tan, "Sexism in the Chinese Language," in *NWSA Journal* 2, no. 4 (1990): 635–39, defines the Chinese language, not different from the English language, as sexist in "defining, deprecating and ignoring women." Moreover, she states: "Women are commonly left out in the Chinese language."
3 Lan Li, "Gender Representation in Chinese Language," in *Analysing Chinese Language and Discourse across Layers and Genres*, ed. Wang Wei (Amsterdam: John Benjamins, 2020), 102–18, explores with a lexicographer's approach, the usage of the character *nü* 女 in the morphology of words and its implications in reflecting women's representation in social ideology.
4 On the *nei/wai* space division in classical gender study literature, see Patricia Ebrey, *The Inner Quarters: Marriage and the Lives of Chinese Women in the Sung Period* (Berkeley: University of California Press, 1993); Li-Hsiang Lisa Rosenlee, "Neiwai, Civility, and Gender Distinctions," *Asian Philosophy* 14, no.1 (2004): 41–58; and Sabrina Ardizzoni, "Women on the Threshold in the First Chapter of Liu Xiang's *Lienü zhuan*," *Asian Studies* 8, no. 3 (2020): 281–302.
5 It is referred to in "Neize" 內則 ["Family conduct"], the 12th chapter of the *Liji* 禮記, trans. James Legge, *Li Chi: Book of Rites*, 1:449–79 (New York: University Books, 1967). The "Neize" establishes the norm for man/woman differentiation (*nan nü zhi bie* 男女之別), as it emerges in the separation of spaces and spheres of action, of *inside* and *outside* (*nei/wai*), of studies, of ceremonial performance, and even of clothing, as well as family relationships.
6 Gayatri Chakravorty Spivak, "Can the Subaltern Speak?" in *Marxism and the Interpretation of Culture*, ed. Cary Nelson and Lawrence Grossberg (Urbana: University of Illinois Press, 1988), 271–313.
7 The original title of the book uses the character marked by the feminine *nü* 女 radical, which came into common use in the written language in the 1950s.

the Republican era (1911–49); they do not display rosy-red cheeks, long braids, and enthusiastic smiles in a vivid attempt to encourage the revolution, as does the "Iron Girls" narrative of the Mao era (1949–76); they are not skillful or naïve young urban workers, displaced from their rural hometown to explore muzzled topics like love, sex, loneliness, and become prey to heartless men who exploit them for money or leisure; nor are they charismatic community leaders, like in Yan's novel *Lenin's Kisses* (*Shouhuo* 受活, 2004) or *The Four Books* (*Si shu* 四書, 2011), or other fictional characters. They are actually all these things together. They display the complexity of women's world in contemporary China, from the author's personal point of view.

With this essay collection, *Tamen*, Yan has gone beyond the "spiritual" (*shen* 神) and "realistic" (*shi* 實), "mythorealistic" literary production that previously constituted the founding principle of his literature.[8] Here, he has found a space where, for once, the author, as a man, depicts his own positioning in History, and finds out it is actually a Herstory, like in a prismatic mirror. Yan himself has said of his book: "It's a tale about all the women in my family. … it is certainly an interesting cross-section of Chinese life, as well as a window on women's customs and social changes in the Chinese countryside over the last hundred years."[9] By rethinking his family history in a feminine way, he attempts to fill the gaps in official historiography and at the same time creates a gendered "We and You, together."

Chronologically, *Shes* is complementary to his *Three Brothers: Memories of My Family* (*Wo yu fubei* 我與父輩, 2009); spatially, it moves between the author's two spheres: the countryside and the city. Unlike in his 2009 work, the narrative line he draws here is not unidirectional but rather multidirectional. Yan spent ten years in reconstructing his family women's history and felt the need to address many women of European feminism, such as Simone de Beauvoir (*The Second Sex*, 1953) and Antoinette Fouque (*Il y a deux sexes*, 1995), and American women anthropologists and gender scholars like Susan Bordo (*Unbearable Weight*, 1993; *The Male Body*, 1999) and Judith Butler (*Gender Trouble: Feminism and the Subversion of Identity*, 1990; *Undoing Gender*, 2004), whose works were translated in the years straddling the twentieth and twenty-first centuries; finally, prominent intellectuals in the history of Chinese thought like Mao Zedong and the feminist intellectual Dai Jinhua 戴錦華 (*Zuori zhi dao* 昨日之島, 2015).

His writing, experiential and historically "reconstructionist," is *liminal* in that it is contained within the spatial borders of the author's village in the rural area around Luoyang, Henan Province, and within the temporal borders of the author's own lifespan; it is a deed of reminiscence, in search of erased narratives in order to shed light on the dark parts of history, a salvage of memories endangered by oblivion, a recomposition of divided memories.

---

8 On Yan's mythorealism, please refer to Part I in this book. I also relate to Carlos Rojas, "Speaking of the Margins: Yan Lianke," in *The Columbia Companion to Modern Chinese Literature*, ed. Kirk Denton (New York: Columbia University Press, 2016), 431–35; and Melinda Pirazzoli, "From Franz Kafka to Franz Kafka Award Winner, Yan Lianke: Biopolitics and the Human Dilemma of *shenshizhuyi* in *Liven* and *Dream of Ding Village*," *CLCWeb: Comparative Literature and Culture* 22, no. 4 (2020), https://doi.org/10.7771/1481-4374.3437.

9 Riccardo Moratto and Sabrina Ardizzoni, *Voci letterarie dal Levante—Dialoghi con autori cinesi in tempo di pandemia* [Literary voices from the East: Conversations with Chinese authors in pandemic time] (Bologna: Bonomo Editore, 2021), 18; also Riccardo Moratto, "Zai yiqing liuxing de dangxia xunzhao ziwo he wenxue: Zhuanfang Yan Lianke" 在疫情流行的當下尋找自我和文學——專訪閻連科 ["Looking for oneself and for literature during an epidemic: An Interview with Yan Lianke"], *Waiguo yuyan yu wenhua* 外國語言與文化 [Foreign Languages and Culture] 1 (20 Mar. 2020), https://mp.weixin.qq.com/s/_1FeqVY2_tjMxshZNcxA8g (last accessed 31 May 2021); Riccardo Moratto, "Intervista a Yan Lianke" ["Interview with Yan Lianke"], *Il Manifesto*, 27 Feb. 2020, https://ilmanifesto.it/yan-lianke-ansia-e-rabbia-da-virus-stanno-sfumando/ (last accessed 31 May 2021).

Gender and narrative structure

Tamen is a work of literary prose (*sanwen* 散文), a "non-fiction" (*feixugou* 非虛構) genre chosen by the author because it gives a wide berth to subjective expression. Its mainspring lies in the collection of oral testimony, as in the reflection on readings personally suggested by Liu Jianmei 劉劍梅, the feminist literary critic of Hong Kong University of Science and Technology who recommended to Yan gender studies classics from Western literature. The outcome is the fruit of a long and pondered meditation that led Yan to rethink the condition of women in "his" contemporary China; and the fact that it took ten years of writing proves that the process of textual production was subsequent to a long and meticulous period of data collection, not only objective data (women's histories) but also an introspection into one's own past. The book has seven chapters:

1. Shes;
2. Older Sister, Second Sister, Sister-in-Law;
3. Aunts;
4. Second Aunts;
5. Mother;
6. Third Sex: Third Person Feminine;
7. Shes; and
8. Coda Voice.

The stories in *Shes* are neither fictional nor metaphorical. The histories and memories Yan collects and shares with the reader are those of the women of his family, his village, and neighboring villages. Rural women, as distinct from urban ones. In Spivak's terms, "true subaltern groups, whose identity is their difference."[10]

The narrative form of the first part may be compared to a family book (*jiapu* 家譜) in the feminine. Usually, in traditional family books, only the male figures were recorded; in the few cases in which women's histories were annotated, the stories told were inevitably exceptional and, above all, exemplary. In the past, before the practice of keeping family and genealogy books (*zupu* 族譜) was deplored in Communist China as an ideological tool in the hands of the old patriarchal society, one would find narratives of virtuous women whose conduct was seen as especially adherent to Confucian ethics. When the compilation of family and genealogy books began again in the 1990s, in some cases, women were included. More specifically, this came about with women who expressed their support for a shared family or national project, or who could display their success in business, science, sports, media, or politics. But the women in *Shes* are common people who, in their common, rural lives, follow and construct *her*story with their very ordinariness:

> My mother's experience is only one of the most common and widespread among thousands of women during the period of socialist construction from the founding of new China in 1949 to the new era of Reform and Opening Up—it cannot even be considered a case.[11]

> 母親的經歷，只是一九四九年新中國成立至新時期改革開放前的社會主義大建設時期成千上萬的女性中最為通、普遍的一個或一列，連稱為一個案例都不算。

---

10 Spivak, 285.
11 Yan, *Tamen* (Zhengzhou: Henan wenyi chubanshe, 2020), 213. All Chinese citations were translated by the author unless otherwise specified.

In chapter 7, *Shes* displays a shift in narrative choice. The author here has gathered up a series of "mini-tales" of acquaintances or relatives—people he is familiar with, either personally or by hearsay. These are local chronicles of events known to village people: some are public stories, as they have been covered by local or national media; some are private, that is to say, they are not known outside of limited local groups. The literary form is reminiscent of the *zhiguai xiaoshuo* 志怪小說 of classical Chinese literature, which were closely related to the writing of history. Considered "strange tales" or "anomaly accounts," they related supernatural phenomena and local oddities.

The last chapter, "Coda Voice," is dedicated to the author's young granddaughter, to the innocence and tenderness of a little girl in a Beijing park under a blue sky with white clouds, representing hope in a future full of sweet-scented air and rainbow-colored flowers. The time structure of the text therefore connects past, present, and future, but holds fast to its temporal and spatial liminality, at the center of which the author's experience persists, directed or projected onto the female voices surrounding him. Narration is expressed in the first person to indicate that the center of the prism is the author himself.

The story-telling is interrupted by personal digressions, which the author calls *liaoyan* 聊言 and defines as "unbridled conversations" or "gossips" (*xin ma you jiang de xianhua* 信馬由韁的閒話).[12] In these inserts, he makes personal comments and remarks on the topics that came to the fore in previous chapters. He allows himself these interludes to take on the reader directly, often in very informal language, in line with the *sanwen* genre, and establishes an intimate relationship with his readership.

Even if this *jiapu* is communicated via writing, the transmission of the narratives may be considered an oral history, and the instrument of transmission is not a woman but a man. In the telling of women's tales, quasi-female autobiographies penned by a male hand, as well as in the "unbridled" sections, Yan always resorts to plain and simple language, to direct and transparent, albeit highly meaningful, metaphors. This kind of language characterizes his earlier works as well, but here it seems to be more straightforward, personal, colloquial: a learned conversation while sipping tea with his reader: "Hey—please don't read this chapter as an essay." (喂——請你千萬不要把這一章當成論文看。)[13]

Silenced subjects in *her*story

Silence, oblivion, the disappearance of women in the stories is a recurring theme. Yan resorts to it often in the course of his narratives and musings. For Yan, memory, especially women's memory in history, is an ethical one (*lunli huiyi* 倫理回憶), namely, a memory linked to the ethical system of the dominating culture. Whoever does not conform to this system will not be able to enter the memory circuit.

A fitting example of this aspect is expressed in the episode of his cousin, the daughter of his third paternal aunt. In an unspecified moment of her youth between 1958 and 1978, she is repudiated by the husband's family (and not by her husband) because "she is a compulsive sleeper" (*shishui* 嗜睡) as she falls into deep sleep and cannot perform her production duties in her husband's family. She is powerless against her narcolepsy, which keeps her from being a good wife, a good daughter-in-law, and this is enough for her husband's relatives to ordain her divorce. This is the revolutionary age, but in the countryside, many aspects of the revolution

---

12 Ibid., 18.
13 Ibid., 204.

have been accepted only partially, and a woman divorced not by her or her husband's choice but by that of her husband's family—"She 'was driven away' by the mother-in-law's house" (是「被」婆婆家裡離去的)[14]—is forced to quietly return to her parents' home. Her mother says: "it was too humiliating, something too humiliating for people to know and understand." (說是太丟人的事, 丟人到無法讓人知道讓人解.)[15] A divorcee, like a widow, may certainly remarry, but she must keep herself to certain precautions: the wedding must take place discreetly, without following the ritual practices required by local customs, everything must be hidden, both her return to her mother's home after the divorce and the second wedding. The woman must accept unfavorable conditions as well, like marrying a man with physical disabilities,[16] or not well-off, or with a low standard of living, perhaps a widower or a single man, with children and parents she will have to take care of. In her new marriage, the divorcee, or the widow, must show her intent to completely wipe out her personal desires, she must prove that she has completely submitted her power to the ethical system, thereby regaining the virtue which she lost in the infamy of divorce or widowhood. In this practice, the removal of the woman from the collective memory of family and village is paramount. When the cousin goes off with her new husband, her family imposes these terms on her: she must never return or have any contact with her hometown relatives. All the members of her family wipe her from their memory, nobody speaks about her anymore, they don't even know if she is dead or alive: "Whether in the city or in the countryside, in the family's ethical memory as molded by the patriarchal society, women are quickly erased from memory" (無論是城裡還是鄉下人, 在男權社會所左右的家族倫理記憶裡, 女性總是被記憶很快的遺忘抹去).[17]

The removal of this woman from memory is defined by the author "reasonably and emotionally erased" (*heqingheli de moqu* 合情合理的抹去), inasmuch as it is part of a rational and emotional system that provides for this kind of treatment. And the author remarks:

> If I hadn't written *Shes*, would I have remembered my cousin? Would I remember that because of that kind of minor disease of—or penchant for—sleepiness, her destiny was to be pushed by men (masculine) into the darkest and deepest of the unknown? And we are forgetful of her, and indifferent; likewise, we never forget to go honor the graves of our parents and grandparents every year for Qingming, full of sadness and memories, but never go to the graves of our aunts.
>
> 尚若不是為了寫「她們」我還能記住我的表姐呢? 能想起因為嗜睡著小而又小之病症或嗜好, 就被男人 (男性) 將其命運推入未知的黑暗和淵深裡, 而我們對她的遺忘與冷漠, 又如我們每年清明從未忘記去自己的父母、爺奶的墳頭祭奠、傷感和回憶, 卻從未去過姑娘們的墳上樣。[18]

These common rural women are the subaltern group inasmuch as, he suggests, they lack the power to speak for themselves, even if the space for them to speak is achieved.

---

14 Ibid., 119.
15 Ibid.
16 On physical disability in Yan's work, see Shelly W. Chan 陳穎, "Narrating Cancer, Disabilities and AIDS: Yan Lianke's Trilogy of Disease," in *Discourse of Disease-Writing Illness, the Mind and the Body in Modern China*, ed. Howard Y. F. Choy 蔡元豐 (Leiden: Brill, 2016), 177–99.
17 Yan, *Tamen*, 122.
18 Ibid., 123.

Let us consider his mother's example. Yan tells us that during the collectivization years, his mother was more than once honored with the prestigious title of "model worker" because she had successfully accomplished her duties outside (*wai*) the home. But the author-son as well as all the members of the production squads are perfectly aware that there is an undeclared chore, that of the domestic function of *nei*, historically inherited by the mother by the fact of being a woman, and never completely absorbed by the expanded function of the People's Commune. The mother, having been grown and educated in a rural environment, persistently sticks to her subaltern position and makes the commune's certificates of merit bestowed upon her disappear; she will not talk about it (silenced subject) and refuses to accept the merit conferred upon her in the public sphere. Quite the contrary, she wants to keep it hidden, because: "How embarrassing—I've always felt that women should not compete with men in this way." (多丟人——總覺得女人不該和男人一樣爭這些。)[19] Therefore, from the narratives collected here, what emerges is a herstory, the voices thereof have long been silenced or "normalized" by official history.

The third sex: The otherness of women

According to the author, "Even before being a woman, a woman is a person." All of chapter 6 is dedicated to the theorization of the "third sex," a concept developed starting from Simone de Beauvoir's *The Second Sex*. Yan quotes: "Woman? Very simple! She is a womb, an ovary,"[20] and recalls her confrontation with Antoinette Fouque.

This is something that lies between and outside of the two natural sexes of man and woman. He calls it "the otherness of women" (*nüxing zhong de taxing* 女性中的他性). It is compared to an excrescence, something superfluous yet ineluctable:

> In women, the third sex is a sort of excrescence. Whether born or acquired, an excrescence is a useless, meaningless and superfluous gall, but when you remove it, not only will you have persistent bleeding, but it will be such an unexpected evil that it will make you feel it would have been better to let it exist than to remove it.
>
> 女性中的他性是他們的一種疣贅物。
>
> 疣贅物無論是與生具來，還是後天生成，對人都是無用、無意義的多餘之瘻瘤，但如你將它割除時，你將流血不止，會有意外之惡，使你感覺讓疣贅存在要比割除好。[21]

The center of male power that in the male-oriented (*zhong nan qing nü* 重男輕女) society kept women tied down in the deepest of darknesses became the object of criticism during the revolution years and was rethought to the point that, in the name of equality, the differences were wiped out. Gender equality was the main goal of the political project, and this apparently was the same as a "genderless" society. But this gender-blind society was only apparent inasmuch as, both in the private and in the public realm the separation between sexes, as well as the biological, reproductive, and ethical duties were never completely challenged. At the same time, this

---

19 Ibid., 217.
20 Simone de Beauvoir, *The Second Sex* (New York: Alfred Knopf, 1952), 3.
21 Yan, *Tamen*, 207.

very political project transformed women in no-man/no-woman *persona*, what the author here defines a "third sex": something in-between and out of the binary definition of man/woman.

When quoting the opening line of "Childhood," the second chapter of *The Second Sex* ("One is not born, but rather becomes, a woman"), he points out that women are subjected to the limitations due to their biological sex, for instance, the cyclic nature of menstruation, menstrual pain, and childbirth pain; and, in addition, to those that are introduced by historical obligation and the dominant power, according to which women "must" make clothing, cook, and produce babies. To this, says the author, the women of his village add the task of being "workers in society," as imposed by culture, history, and the rural environment—this for him is the main meaning of "third sex."[22] This line of reasoning cannot but call to mind the 1927 "Report on an Investigation of the Peasant Movement in Hunan" ("Hunan nongmin yundong kaocha baogao" 湖南農民運動考察報告) in which Mao Zedong, when dealing with gender relations and the limitations imposed by society, stated that while peasants were subject to the oppressions of state, family system, and the world of spirits and underworld demons, peasant women were sorely oppressed by the patriarchal system.[23]

Besides common rural women, the author also mentions figures made public by the revolutionary narrative in 1958 (Yan's year of birth) during the Great Leap Forward years. At the time, thousands of youths were involved in the construction of the Ming Tombs Reservoir. The official narrative presented them as heroes and heroines who became part of the collective imagination, and their memories are still alive in our days as key cultural elements of twentieth-century China.. He quotes the Seven Girls of Shahe zheng Dongyi village (Liu Shumin 劉淑敏, Li Lianfang 李連芳, Wang Sumin 王素敏, Yan Shuqing 閆淑清, Li Guozhen 李國珍, Zhang Shuqing 張淑清, and Zhang Shuhua 張淑華), and the Nine Lan Girls Squad (Jiu Lanzu 九蘭組), all of whom teenagers between 15 and 19 years of age became part of the great narrative of History, reified because of their dedication and adherence to the nation's project.

And yet, the author invites the reader not to consider his a theoretical essay on gender. His literary invention of the "third sex" is meant to remain such, a literary digression, and does not want to be a pitch invasion in the field of gender studies.

Work and labor

Labor is one of the focuses of the whole book, and lies at the center of all its narratives. For peasant families, work is *the* existential dimension:

> My mother was always sitting there doing needlework, while my father was either peeling corn or packing up farming tools and broken bamboo baskets and willow baskets. It was a sin for them to sit there purely for rest. The most legitimate and solemn life and meaning of a farmer is to work constantly.
>
> 母親總是坐在在那兒做著針線活，父親不是剝著玉米，就是收拾著農具和破了邊的竹籃柳筐子。坐在那兒純粹之歇息，　在他們就是一種罪。不停地勞作才是農民最正當、莊嚴的人生和意義。[24]

---

22 See also Guo Yijiao's chapter in this book.
23 Mao Zedong, *Mao Zedong xuanji* 毛澤東選集 [*Selected works of Mao Zedong*], 4 vols. (Beijing: People's Publishing House, 1952), 12–42.
24 Yan, *Tamen*, 65.

The same existential value of labor is transferred to socialist China, where "working people didn't view their jobs as merely a means of making a living. A job meant an honorable vocation, and workers were endowed with dignity."[25]

In the twentieth century, changes in labor organization did not utterly modify family organization (women did housework, men farmed), but had a significant impact on the quantity of work: the shift from the small-scale subsistence agriculture structure that regulated village economy before 1949 to the collective organization of rural communes was focused on mobilizing resources in order to achieve large-scale projects. This change in the scale of labor required that women take up a far greater active role in *wai*-work than was customary in the past, and also brought about a change in the pace of life, but it did not effect substantial changes in the dynamics of *nei*:

> Before 1949, Chinese rural society was based on the individual family as a self-sustaining unit …. After 1949, … while the internal structure of the family remained unchanged, the external sphere of the family was infinitely enlarged by the sphere of socialist construction.
>
> 一九四九年前，中國的鄉村社會是以個體家庭為自存自在的單元形式的。…… 而在一九四九年後，……在家庭的內部結構仍然不變時，而家庭的外場域，因社會主義建設的場域無限地擴大增多了。[26]

As asserted by the feminist scholar Wang Zheng in her *Finding Women in the State*, during the revolutionary years, the positive representation of working women in the media had empowering effects on women who had previously been absent from cultural representations of China's drive for modernity.[27] And yet, despite the wide circulation of the slogan attributed to Mao, "Women can hold up half the sky" (the attribution is unverified), one huge issue was left standing, and remains apparently unresolved to this day: that of equality of wages. The redistribution of work-points according to tasks accomplished—"to each according to one's work" (按勞分配 *an lao fenpei*)—in taking into account age, strength, work attitude, and gender, in fact, left women constantly behind: "At the time, the strong laborers got ten work-points every day; the weak and cunning ones, just nine, which would then reduce their dignity. Women could get eight work-points per day, the weak and lazy ones, seven points." (那時壯勞力每天是十分工，弱的奸猾的，那就減去你的尊嚴為九分。婦女每天八分工，弱的懶的是七分。)[28] This disparity has never really been reversed.

From the onset of Deng's political and economic reforms, work began to be directed from the countryside to the city, and farmers all became peasant-workers (*nongmingong* 農民工), pouring into factories, construction sites, roadwork, restaurants, and urban services. In this new situation, women's labor remained very much like farm work: tireless and ceaseless; and the separation between the male and the female world, both as far as cohabitation and as tasks were concerned, was still an extremely clear-cut one.

If, in the pre-revolutionary period, the dominating culture imposed a division of the sexes and put a sex-based pressure on work, even in the age of revolution labor has preserved a gendered connotation. When speaking about the collectivization years, the author points

---

25 Wang, "Dignity of Labor," in Denton, 73.
26 Yan, *Tamen*, 214.
27 Wang Zheng, *Finding Women in the State: A Socialist Feminist Revolution in the People's Republic of China, 1949–1964* (Oakland: University of California Press, 2017), 228.
28 Yan, *Tamen*, 81.

out the linguistic difference between "workers" (*laodongzhe* 勞動者), the term used for men, and "laborers" (*laozuozhe* 勞作者), referring to women unless they became a "model female worker" (*laodong mofan* 勞動模範).[29] Here we see a linguistic distinction that highlights a male-centered gender vision on work. Women have to achieve more in order to be equal to men.

In the current times, characterized by market liberalization, de-politicization, and economic neo-liberalism, women voluntarily "inject themselves" (to use Yan's metaphor) with the obligation to comply with a male model of hyper-production and hyper-labor;[30] work thus wipes out all gender differences: women as well as men leave to go to "do temporary work" (*dagong* 打工), and engage in exacting seasonal jobs, because for each one of them: "This slave-like work was done today of her own free will and that of her sisters and their children." (這種如奴人一樣幹的活，今天完全是她和她的姐妹與兒女們自願的。)[31] Thus, work, any kind of work, is celebrated both by the rural and the socialist traditions. Today, ex-farmhands are dislocated, in their frantic search for economic success, in an often hostile urban environment, tainted by a depravity that gobbles up even the countryside: in the author's eye, and in that of the official narrative, it was supposed to remain a pure place, uncontaminated by immoral, unethical traits such as prostitution, drug abuse, and other deviations.

This condition is poignantly illustrated in the story of 24-year-old Zhao Yamin 趙雅敏, who has a fancy for watches.[32] In order to complete her collection of them, she sells herself in one of the many hairdresser's shops that in the 1980s harbored naïve girls in order to satisfy the appetites of successful businessmen. Her heart's desire is to return to her village after a few short years of "honest work," with her booty of one hundred watches acquired as a monetary exchange for her sex services in order to marry her fiancé and lead a normal life. What drives her is money, commodities, and the quest for a satisfaction of material desires (*wuwang* 物望).

This is what levels men and women today, and makes them equal in the face of society: men and women voluntarily take upon themselves the onus and obligations of the new forms of labor.

But Yan's book is, first and foremost, a literary work, and the author's lyricism in it is paramount. Work, the countryside, and childhood memories are well expressed in the "Coal" ("La mei" 拉煤") episode, in which he, still a child, and his slightly older sister, pull a cart on foot in order to go pick up coal at the quarry, traveling more than 40 km in one day.[33] The boy's pride in having such an honorable as well as grueling job marks his entry into adulthood, his belonging to a society of peasant-*laodongzhe*. At the same time, it represents the birth of his project of getting himself out of that world, as the lad says: "I really do not want to pull the cart like an ox or a horse" (我實在不想如牛馬一樣拉車出力了).[34] And in a few years, he will join the Army, which will allow him to study and become the writer that he is today.

Marriage

In traditional society, marriage is virilocal. This is already a starting point of disadvantage for women: "Married-out woman: spilled water." (嫁出去的人，潑出去的水。)[35] In rural culture, this is a common saying. Marriage is a central moment in the life of the rural woman,

---

29 Ibid., 189.
30 Ibid., 218.
31 Ibid., 239.
32 Ibid., 230–34.
33 Ibid., 84–94.
34 Ibid., 92.
35 Ibid., 123.

inasmuch as it marks her passage from one family to another, of which she will become an integral part.³⁶ In a society that traditionally practices ancestor cult, a woman leaves her birth family's line of descent to enter into that of her husband, but only if she adapts to society's and to that family group's ethical rules. The penalty for deviating from shared values is oblivion.

The prerequisites for marriage are the matchmaker, usually a woman, of whom our author presents a historical and literary analysis, pointing out the nuances and changes of meaning throughout history and "blind date" (*xiangqin* 相親). The author's mother herself is a matchmaker: "In the countryside, the matchmaker is not a profession, but a moral role of society." (在鄉村, 媒人不是一種職業, 但卻是一種社會的道德角色。)³⁷ In the past, the task of matchmaker (*meiren* 媒人 or *meipo* 媒婆) was mostly performed by women, and it was held in great consideration, as it was a predictive one. A *meiren* had to be able to predict whether a union could be harmonious, whether the couple would be able to have children together and grow old together. Today, this is performed by "introducers" (*jieshaoren* 介紹人), men and women alike, who merely resort to well-tested patterns to which they attribute new meanings and new practices.

Yan defines the figure of the go-between, previously utterly vilified in communist political and social analysis, as actually necessary for the advancement of society: "If there is marriage, the chain of human reproduction, survival, sexual needs, or love, without the existence of a matchmaker, how can human beings extend, advance and function?" (如果婚姻這一人類繁衍、生存、性需乃或說愛的環鏈中, 沒有媒人之存在, 人類又怎樣可以延展、推進和運行？)³⁸ The practice of *xiangqin* is a ritual of many meanings that emerge in the narratives of the book's first chapters. Meetings organized by a family to favor the encounter between a son and his possible future wife are as much concentrated on the compatibility between daughter-in-law-to-be and mother-in-law-to-be, as on the entente between the two presumptive fiancés.

Yan invites his readers not to give a binary, black and white, reading of events and persons, but to consider their multifaceted aspects. At the end of the game, he concludes, today's *jieshaoren*, the introducer who makes the future possible married couple meet, is merely continuing a tradition of change of signifier that conveys a signified that evolves in the course of time.

Conclusion

Tamen is a book about the representation of Chinese rural women in the socialist and postsocialist period. What emerges from this encounter between the reader and Yan's women is that on the one hand, women are achievers according to male-oriented models, on the other hand, they become subalterns in a still male-oriented society that manipulates them according to ludicrous models. After the 1980s, the gender-equality and gender-blindness of the revolutionary age are displaced by a framework that while offering multiple possibilities for individual choice, still unifies men and women within a channel of a common quest for material success and commodities, thereby implying conformity and sacrifice within the great country model. Like in the past, however, this quest does not remove women from their subaltern state

---

36 The passage from the state of *nü* 'maiden' to that of *fu* 婦 'married woman' repositions a woman's dyadic relationship from a father-daughter relationship to that of husband and wife, and is sanctioned by Confucius's system of values and those of later tradition. We are always dealing with a relationship of submissivity, within which a woman finds little in terms of visible spaces of subjectivity.
37 Yan, *Tamen*, 171.
38 Ibid., 167.

if they do not become "model female workers"; otherwise, they are forced to return to their traditional functions of child-bearing and domestic (*nei*) care.

Going back to the questions we posed at the beginning, we must remember that the women Yan speaks for are not representative of all of China, but are set in a well-defined space and time. For this reason, we can consider his work a *liminal* production. This is a book of many purposes. First of all, that of giving a voice to those who have not found one of their own yet. The women of this cross-section, according to Spivak's viewpoint, are subaltern groups. Yan represents them here to fill a gap in the great narrative of his country. In Spivak's terms, it is a "representation as speaking-for" not "re-presentation" as in art and philosophy.[39] Next, the author is also speaking about himself, his presence in the text is clearly declared, there is no intention of writing an objective text; as he himself often says, he does not want to hide behind the stratagems of a realistic work. His own personal history gets written through the polyphony of the women that surround him. So, the second purpose of the book would seem to be that of finding a memory of self-retrieval, of one's own identity.

As to the relationship between these stories and Herstory, besides bringing to surface other versions, other points of view, these narratives dwell on taboo topics such as menstruation, female orgasm, homosexuality, prostitution, and a lavish repertoire of images linked to the body, as appurtenant to the author's style. These are all subjects rural women do not wish to speak about, and we find no trace of them in literature. Those who do broach them are female writers, city-dwelling and educated, as well as inserted in a male-oriented value system. Yan's women, even when they veer away from the dominant model, preserve a dimension of subjectivity within the narrative context, and the author's mediation serves merely to enhance its worth. We can therefore consider this book a valued example, both for its writing on contemporary female society, and for breaking the silence to which common rural women are often confined to.

Lastly, on the political significance of *Shes*, though one cannot state that Yan's work has any direct political purpose, and despite the fact that the author distances himself from the theorization of women's history, his representation of women provides a focus on society that, as Gail Hershatter recently stated, "is always political."[40] His statements on muted identities, his efforts to shed light on the darker parts of society, his encouragement to rethink the categories of twentieth-century history not in black-and-white but keeping in mind their multifaceted aspects, finally, his considerations on language and on the institutions that are involved in the narratives collected here cannot but challenge the reader on the political level as well.

As a reprise of the lyricism that pervades the whole text, the image of the last chapter, dedicated to his granddaughter, sounds almost like a last will and testament: a final message of intergenerational love and faith in a future of white clouds and colored rainbows.

Bibliography

Ardizzoni, Sabrina. "Revising the Chinese Translation of Verdi's Opera *La Traviata*: Linguistic and Methodological Issues." In *Diverse Voices in Chinese Translation and Interpreting*, edited by Riccardo Moratto and Martin Woesler, 319–39. Singapore: Springer, 2021.

———. "Women on the Threshold in the First Chapter of Liu Xiang's *Lienü zhuan*." *Asian Studies* 8, no. 3 (2020): 281–302. https://doi.org/10.4312/as.2020.8.3.281-302.

---

39 Spivak, 275.
40 See Gail Hershatter, *Women in China's Long Twentieth Century* (Berkeley: University of California Press, 2007); also Hershatter, *The Gender of Memory: Rural Women and China's Collective Past* (Berkeley: University of California Press, 2011).

Bordo, Susan. *The Male Body: A New Look at Men in Public and in Private*. New York: Farrar, Straus and Giroux, 1999.
———. *Unbearable Weight-Feminism, Western Culture, and the Body*. Berkeley: University of California Press, 1993.
Butler, Judith. *Gender Trouble*. New York: Routledge, 1990.
———. *Undoing Gender*. New York: Routledge, 2004.
Choy, Howard Y.F. 蔡元豐, ed. *Discourse of Disease: Writing Illness, the Mind and the Body in Modern China*. Leiden: Brill, 2016.
Dai Jinhua 戴錦華. *Zuori zhi dao* 昨日之島 [*The Island of the Day Before*]. Beijing: Beijing University Press, 2015.
De Beauvoir, Simone. *The Second Sex*. 1949. New York: Alfred Knopf, 1952.
Denton, Kirk. *The Columbia Companion to Modern Chinese Literature*. New York: Columbia University Press, 2016.
Ebrey, Patricia. *The Inner Quarters: Marriage and the Lives of Chinese Women in the Sung Period*. Berkley: University of California Press, 1993.
Fouque, Antoinette. *Il y a deux sexes, Essais de féminologie, 1989–1995* [*There are two sexes: Essays in feminology, 1989–1995*]. Paris: Gallimard, 1995.
Hershatter, Gail. *The Gender of Memory: Rural Women and China's Collective Past*. Berkeley: University of California Press, 2011.
———. *Women in China's Long Twentieth Century*. Berkley: University of California Press, 2007.
Li, Lan. "Gender Representation in Chinese Language." In *Analyzing Chinese Language and Discourse across Layers and Genres*, edited by Wang Wei, 102–18. Amsterdam: John Benjamins, 2020.
Mao Zedong 毛澤東. *Mao Zedong xuanji* 毛澤東選集 [*Selected works of Mao Zedong*]. 4 vols. Beijing: People's Publishing House, 1952.
Moratto, Riccardo. "Intervista a Yan Lianke" ["Interview with Yan Lianke"]. *Il Manifesto*, 27 Feb. 27, 2020. https://ilmanifesto.it/yan-lianke-ansia-e-rabbia-da-virus-stanno-sfumando/ (last accessed 31 May 2021).
———. "Zai yiqing liuxing de dangxia xunzhao ziwo he wenxue: Zhuanfang Yan Lianke" 在疫情流行的當下尋找自我和文學——專訪閻連科 ["Looking for Oneself and for Literature during an Epidemic: An Interview with Yan Lianke"]. *Waiguo yuyan yu wenhua* 外國語言與文化 [*Foreign Languages and Culture*] 1 (20 Mar. 2020). https://mp.weixin.qq.com/s/_1FeqVY2_tjMxshZNcxA8g (last accessed 31 May 2021).
——— and Sabrina Ardizzoni. *Voci letterarie dal Levante—Dialoghi con autori cinesi in tempo di pandemia* [*Literary voices from the East: Conversations with Chinese authors in pandemic time*]. Bologna: Bonomo Editore, 2021.
Pirazzoli, Melinda. "From Franz Kafka to Franz Kafka Award Winner, Yan Lianke: Biopolitics and the Human Dilemma of *shenshizhuyi* in *Liven* and *Dream of Ding Village*." *CLCWeb: Comparative Literature and Culture* 22, no. 4 (2020). https://doi.org/10.7771/1481-4374.3437.
Rojas, Carlos. "Speaking of the Margins: Yan Lianke." In Denton, 431–35. New York: Columbia University Press, 2016.
Rosenlee, Li-Hsiang Lisa. "*Neiwai*, Civility, and Gender Distinctions." *Asian Philosophy* 14, no. 1 (2004): 41–58. https://doi.org/10.1080/0955236042000190473.
Shei, Chris, ed. *The Routledge Handbook of Chinese Discourse Analysis*. London: Routledge, 2019.
Spivak, Gayatri Chakravorty. "Can the Subaltern Speak?" In *Marxism and the Interpretation of Culture*, edited by Cary Nelson and Lawrence Grossberg, 271–313. Urbana: University of Illinois Press, 1988.
Tan, Dali. "Sexism in the Chinese Language." *NWSA Journal* 2, no. 4 (1990): 635–39. http://www.jstor.org/stable/4316075.
Wang, Ban. "Dignity of Labor." In Denton, 73–76. New York: Columbia University Press, 2016.
Wang, Zheng. *Finding Women in the State: A Socialist Feminist Revolution in the People's Republic of China, 1949–1964*. Oakland: University of California Press, 2017.
Yan Lianke 閻連科. *The Four Books*. Translated by Carlos Rojas. New York: Grove, 2015.
———. *Lenin's Kisses*. Translated by Carlos Rojas. New York: Grove, 2012.
———. *Tamen* 她們 [*Shes*]. Zhengzhou: Henan wenyi chubanshe, 2020.
———. *Three Brothers: Memories of My Family*. Translated by Carlos Rojas. New York: Grove, 2021.

19
FEMALE LABOR, THE THIRD SEX, AND EXCRESCENCE IN YAN LIANKE'S NONFICTION *TAMEN*

Yijiao Guo

This chapter delves into the subtle correlations between the portraits of women and Yan Lianke's 閻連科 refining endeavor to automatically form a feminist mindset in his nonfiction *Their Stories* (*Tamen* 她們). The following analyses begin with the effaced women's lives and labors in the Great Leap Forward period and the invisible gender of female in history. Women's historical status of excrescence, a distinctive type of historical material, and female gender as the third sex will be given special attention along with investigations through close readings on Yan's depictions of the local reservoir construction project, the disappearance of female labor in history narrative, and the publicized scene of menstruation. This chapter ends its discussion with an anticipatory reconfiguration of female history as a rhizome. Women and their lives in this sense may be perceived as tragic and insignificant but also as a vital alternative to narrative, gender, and history.

Reification and malady as two major paradigms have taken a dominant position in previous scholarly discussions on Yan's gender discourse, individual-society relation, and human objectification. People in Yan's stories are detached from their biological agency and societal autonomy, thereby bartering body parts, either physically or metaphorically, for economic capital and political capital. Carlos Rojas utilized the term "necropolitical logic" to describe how, despite gender, human beings in Yan's novels are dehumanized, commodified, and traded in the capitalist installation and pursuing of socioeconomic developments.[1] In addition, the representations on bodily deformation and human diseases correlate to the objectification of Yan's characters.[2] The essence

---

1 Carlos Rojas, *Homesickness: Culture, Contagion, and National Transformation in Modern China* (Cambridge, Mass.: Harvard University Press, 2015), 188–89 and 205; see also Rojas, "TIME OUT OF JOINT: Commemoration and Commodification of Socialism in Yan Lianke's *Lenin's Kisses*," in *Red Legacies in China: Cultural Afterlives of the Communist Revolution*, ed. Li Jie and Zhang Enhua (Cambridge, Mass.: Harvard University Asia Center, 2016), 297–309.
2 Liu Jianmei 劉劍梅, *Zhuangzi and Modern Chinese Literature* (New York: Oxford University Press, 2016), 188–96; also Liu, "Bianxin de wenxue bianzouqu" 變形的文學變奏曲 ["The variations of metamorphic literature"], *Comparative Literature in China*, 2020, vol. 118, no. 1: 128–29; Chan Shelley W. 陳穎, "Narrating Cancer, Disabilities, and AIDS: Yan Lianke's Trilogy of Disease," in *Discourses of Disease: Writing Illness, the Mind and the Body in Modern China*, ed. Choy Howard Y. F. 蔡元豐 (Leiden: Brill, 2016), 177–97.

of such a human and/or human body transaction is the state's control over one's life and death to actualize political ambitions and economic progressions.[3]

Putting forward a proposition different from the previous discussions, this chapter deciphers the productive potentialities of women in history narrative. Femininity, objectified notwithstanding, inhabits constitutive qualities in a metaphysical dimension that is not confined to sex limitations or gender troubles, but an overlapped realm that attributes female gender to an autonomous agency. This crafted agency in literature is an invention that inherits certain literary conventions and reiterates the discourses subscribed to the patriarchal matrix as in Judith Butler's words.[4] Whereas, this agency also holds an inextricable and inalienable autonomy as a historical subject. The historical subjectivity of femininity is neither ontologically inherent nor dependent on a prerequisite of (male) human animating practices. The aggregate of female lives and experiences, with morphogenetic capabilities, connects itself to the flows from other active agencies in history narratives and simultaneously follows these flows.[5] In consequence, Yan's gender representation does not, and shall not be, read in singularity and doomed to biopolitical plays, for it is a multi-layered embodiment, wherein subtleties, diversities, and perspectives can be found.

The focus here is not to understand gender commodification and the historical gender discourse as two negative factors, though aftereffects were indeed brought into beings. Instead, this chapter concentrates on conceiving the female gender as a commodified historical material that has wrought a new narrative sphere different from the ideologically-embedded narrative of history and the physiological concomitants in the androcentric, hazardous commodifying operations. This nascent layer of the gender-material narrative sphere pertains to the reevaluation of gender discourse, for it is the commodifiedness that tells the essence of the overlooked history of the very gender of female and the historical plight of the very social identity of femininity.

Now it is all about her

In recent years, Yan Lianke has been scrutinizing the ambivalence of women in history and unexpectedly refreshed his literary creation with a prospect that is no longer about absurdities in China's society, and a literary genre that is no longer novel. In February 2020, Yan published a long piece of nonfiction "Their Stories" in the famous literary bimonthly *Harvest* (*Shouhuo* 收穫), which was founded by Ba Jin 巴金 (1904–2005) and Jin Yi 靳以 (1909–59) in July 1957.[6] *Their Stories* is the latest open publication and legal circulation of Yan in the People's Republic of China (PRC) after the metafiction-cum-screenplay *Urgent Plea for Rest Together* (*Su qiu gong mian* 速求共眠) in 2018. It is also the first book-length essay collection that Yan specifically dedicates to women and female family members after his previous documentations about his father and uncles in *Me and My Father's Generation* (*Wo yu fubei* 我與父輩, 2009) and *Thoughts by One Person on Three Rivers* (*Yi ge ren de san tiao he* 一個人的三

---

3 Rojas, *Homesickness*, 188.
4 See Judith Butler, *Gender Trouble: Feminism and the Subversion of Identity* (New York: Routledge, 1990), 3–22.
5 Cf. Gilles Deleuze and Félix Guattari, *A Thousand Plateaus: Capitalism and Schizophrenia* (Minneapolis: University of Minnesota Press, 1987), 329.
6 *Their Stories* was published as a monograph in May 2020 by Henan wenyi chubanshe, and no differences exist between the two versions. In the interest of textual coherence and communicational convenience, this chapter uses Yan Lianke's 2020 book of *Their Stories* as the citation resource.

條河, 2013). In this nonfictional piece, Yan has recorded the life of and given voice to more than twenty-five rural women, including his failed dates, wife, mother, siblings, relatives, and female figures in or near his childhood village.

Their Stories contains seven chapters and a coda section. The first chapter is about Yan's love stories. The second to fourth chapters portray his siblings and other female relatives in the family. The fifth chapter is dedicated to his mother, who arguably made the most contribution in shaping how Yan reviewed all these rural females vis-à-vis history and culture. In the last two chapters, Yan launched a theoretical investigation on feminism within the PRC's milieu. The seventh chapter, in particular, is a dossier of eight women's melodramatic lives and misfortunes. Committing homicide, suicide, or other crimes and so-called sins, Zhao Yamin 趙雅敏, Tong Gaizhi 仝改枝, Yang Cui 楊翠, Wang Pingping 王萍萍, Wu Zhimin 吳芝敏, Fang Yuhua 方榆花, Yang Caini 楊采妮, and Zhao Zhizi 趙梔子 tell stories that resonate with but differ from the social context of Western feminism, which is theorized by Simon de Beauvoir, Simone Weil, Antoinette Fouque, Susan Bordo, Judith Butler, Monique Wittig, Amartya Sen, and Melanie Klein.

In the coda, Yan staged the story of the youngest woman in the family, his five-year-old granddaughter. Little as this girl was, she sensed the passing of time and the aging of her grandpa, and joked about getting married to him in the future. Yan, with joys of a grandfather, responded to his little girl's baby talk and ended the book with emotion: "Whirling the wheels and floating the water under the bridge, forward or backward both suits the earth. The clouds and rainbows stay in the world as always, resembling sunrise that occurs with no exceptions."[7]

Their Stories is more than a personal memoir or ethnography of village women in a small town of Henan Province. As Yan's most feminist writing hitherto, *Their Stories* is a story against memories fading in *history*. In the third chapter about his aunties, Yan discussed the severance between a female and her family once remarried in terms of memory removal:

> "A married woman is a woman of no connections." This is the cruelest and most hard-hearted social order in Chinese culture. It is a blunt knife that softly kills Chinese females …. As a consequence, a person with an egotistic and myopic ethic will never give a concern about their lives and fates. These women were murdered in memories, and nobody will take the moral blame.
>
> ……
>
> All of these are because they are women and female, rural women and female. It is just like that if a rural society is an antiquated, traditional, and chaotic wasted land, men and women were both reclaimed this land. When all people could leave this great earth, the inscribed names on the tombstones by the field land were only those of men. You can find no names of women as if they were never there and their tears, sweats, bloods had never existed.[8]

Although the form is not typically an oral history, *Their Stories* possesses the characteristics of what Gail Hershatter defines as a "good-enough story," which could accommodate female

---

7 Yan Lianke, *Tamen* (Zhengzhou: Henan wenyi chubanshe, 2020), 284; all translations are mine.
8 Yan, *Tamen*, 123–24.

voices as another perspective and alternative to constructing a history different from the official and male-experienced narratives.[9] Such a good-enough story is not a dispensable substitute or a spare component for a phallologocentric metanarrative that has been far too well reiterated. Rather, to tell the life story of rural women is to unveil a significant facet of history that was once manipulatively made opaque and obliterated, which will facilitate a more heterogenous conceptualization and a more inclusive understanding of the past.

Yan brought this nonfiction to his readers in a refreshing, if not surprising, way that it is possible for a male writer to write a story about women and the history they experienced. Even though such a shift in theme was unexpected, Yan loaded his female figures with historical concerns and narrative purposes in his novels. To a certain extent, his female character functioned as allegorical tropes, which could be categorized into recurrent archetypes of sex-industry tycoon, heroine, and Gaia-like goddess. For instance, Lan Sishi in *Streams of Time* (*Riguang liunian* 日光流年, 1998) and Zhu Ying in *The Explosion Chronicles* (*Zhalie Zhi* 炸裂志, 2013) exchanged their bodies for money and gradually built up an influential business in the sex industry. Thanks to their monopoly on the sex business, Lan and Zhu directly reshaped the local politics and male-centered power ecologies. The prominent female chief Grandma Mao Zhi in *Lenin's Kisses* (*Shouhuo* 受活, 2004) stepped into the power core of the mountain village Shouhuo and led a whole village to quit the people's commune during the consecutive political and economic disasters. As a Delacroixian personification of liberty, Mao Zhi removed all the obstacles in gender emancipation and women's political participation. The configuration of Ya Hui in *Heart Sutra* (*Xinjing* 心經, 2020) exemplifies Yan's idea of the unworldly purity and the transcendence at its most a female figure could achieve, who became a bodhisattva after detaching herself from romantic affection and sacrificing herself for all confined Buddhists, Daoists, Christians, Catholics, and Mohammedans.

The progression of *Their Stories*, in contrast, lies in the aspect that Yan closely examined female individuals and their lives, about whom and which he employed a sympathizing, caring tone to represent women in a documentary manner. Yan's contribution, or his unique perspective on history, displays voices for those rural women who faded away in history and historical narratives. To somehow hand over voices back to women, one discrete literary form, i.e., chats-and-talks (*liaoyan* 聊言), that Yan adopted in *Their Stories* is worthy of attention.

Yan defined *liaoyan* as talks and gossips that range wide and far in unlimited topics,[10] which is also designated as an inferior and minimal type of speech to women. Perhaps a coincidence or deliberate paraphrasing, such a definition is tantamount to the concept of *xiaoshuo* 小說, meaning gossips or trivial talks, in traditional Chinese literature, which was later translated as a correspondent term for fiction. In "Treaties of Arts of Literature" ("Yiwen zhi" 藝文志) in the *Book of Han Dynasty* (*Han shu* 漢書), literati and historian Ban Gu 班固 (32–92 CE) understood the genre of *xiaoshuo* as talks on streets and rumors based on unreliable sources.[11] All these trivial, fragmentary, and negligible words from the lower class embodied another side of history that was not included in official history writings and mainstream narratives.

---

9 Gail Hershatter, *The Gender of Memory: Rural Women and China's Collective Past* (Berkeley: University of California Press, 2011), 3.
10 Yan, *Tamen*, 18.
11 See Ban Gu, *Han shu*, Chinese Text Project, https://ctext.org/han-shu/yi-wen-zhi/zh (last accessed 15 Feb. 2021).

In this sense, *liaoyan* bears witness against and also upon history by revising while retelling history.[12]

Yan reversed the conceptual logic and epistemological rationale that what women experienced and talked about actually accounts for ontological and historical essences. These reversions do not mean an appraisal of women's competence to replace male narrators, nor do they stand for a requisite alignment with the conventional history-telling. Such a writing of infinitesimal and inconsequential things is to open the gendered telling about history, decipher the history agency embodied in women, and reiterate the historical subject of women. The female experiences in and about history, accordingly, are not an attachment or redundancy in a dispensable, if not stultifying, position of history rank. Women record history. Women lived in and through history. Women take a significant part in history. Women are history. Women's talks and chats institute and simultaneously constitute history. Women are both capable and endowed with the autonomy to tell history and facets about it. To illustrate this, Yan returned to the history scene of the Great Leap Forward and situated his reflections upon the pseudo-emancipation of female, women as the third sex, and the female's status of excrescence.

Female labor at Luhun, the third sex, and excrescence

From the late 1950s onward, the peculiar propagandist discourse on men-women equality and gender oneness came with the zealous dreams of socialism in sync. Especially in the urgent needs of the labor force, women were pushed out of their homes for heavy labor works in civil and industrial projects. One of the construction projects was Luhun 陸渾 Reservoir, a local water conservancy project in Tianhu 田湖 Town of Song 嵩 County, Yan's hometown.

The construction of Luhun Reservoir started on 31 Dec. 1959 and was completed in August 1965. Luhun Reservoir was one of the Sino-Soviet Cooperation Projects in the aims of Yellow River harnessing and hydroelectricity development.[13] The project recruited 80,000 to 100,000 laborers in total from nine surrounding counties and towns.[14] As *The Chorography of Song County* tells, all workers were put into three shifts from day to night with no breaks at the beginning stage of the construction. The "labor-intensive tactic," or *renhai zhanshu* 人海戰術 (*renhai* literally means a sea of people) in Chinese, was employed to replace machines with the paucity of heavy machinery.[15] People were used as excavators and earth trucks, digging out all the construction materials from nearby towns and river shoals by hands and transporting them to the dam site on foot, which was two to nine kilometers away.[16] Women, for sure, were not excluded from this urgent calling.

12 A witness "against history" refers to review and re-understand history in contrasts, which deviates from the collective or predestined history discourses and finds a historical agent that is not prescribed to trauma, nationalism, revolution, and other meta- and androcentric-narratives. See Yomi Braester, *Witness Against History: Literature, Film, and Public Discourse in Twentieth-Century China* (Stanford: Stanford University Press, 2003), 8–11.
13 Henan Songxian zhi bianzhuan weiyuanhui 河南嵩縣志編撰委員會, eds., *Songxian zhi* 嵩縣志 [*The Chorography of Song County*] (Zhengzhou: Henan renmin chubanshe, 1990), 202.
14 Zhang Zhengqing 張正青, "Jianshe Luhun shuiku de jianku suiyue" 建設陸渾水庫的艱苦歲月 ["The difficult years of building the Luhun Reservoir"], *Henan shuili yu nanshui beidiao* 河南水利與南水北調 [*Henan water resources & south-to-north water diversion*], 2007, no. 1: 62–63.
15 Zhang, "Jianshe Luhun shuiku de jianku suiyue," 62.
16 Ibid., 63.

Indeed, some history scholars conceded that the socialist reforms did bring job opportunities, hence emancipation to women, but history has a disparate say.[17] During the time when Luhun Reservoir was under construction, Song County, as well as the entire nation, suffered from the strike of an unprecedented famine. Hunger was ubiquitous. Because of the lunatic strive for communism and irrational planning of the economy, agricultural production was no longer profitable for peasants, who consequently stopped tilling the land. The total sum of grain production in Song County in 1961 was 90.63 billion *jin* 斤, a 40% decrease compared to 1959.[18] The arable land area declined from 7.20 billion *mu* 畝 in 1959 to 6.69 billion *mu* in 1961.[19] What made it worse was that in 1961 the amount of grain levy soared to 23.59 billion *jin*. It was the largest state levy on grain since 1949 and tantamount to 19.6% of the total grain production.[20] Under the great famine, death was also ubiquitous. The life-threatening edema became a common bodily feature, of which the causes were low protein intake and prolonged time of working. The outbreak of edema in Henan Province was notably serious. The mortality rate in Song County escalated from 14.2‰ in 1958 to 15.6‰ in 1960, the highest peak of death rate since 1949 to the status quo.[21]

The famine and long-time labor inflicted great harm to women's health. Due to malnutrition and lack of labor protection, around 2% of women encountered uterine prolapse. Malnutrition and overwork also resulted in 30% of women developing amenorrhea, which caused a direct influence on female fertility and generated a secondary fluctuation in the birth rate.[22] In 1960 in Song County, the natural increase rate dropped to 3‰, reaching the lowest point since 1949.[23]

---

17 For instance, Zang Jian held that the top-to-bottom of the CCP's enforcements on men-women equality, thanks to its coordination with the socialist planned economy, effectively eliminated gender differences in the social system and ideology. Many Chinese women even missed those achievements in the unemployment wave after the open-and-reform policy. Li Xiaojiang 李小江 argued that women stepped out from the home to society and gained equal status in legal and socio-systematical terms as a result of the socialist revolution. Doubtlessly, the post-1949 movements did achieve gender equality to a certain extent. However, it never applies to the concept that all women in the PRC were liberated once and for the rest. Nuances in the outcomes of gender equality movements, as Yan's stories tell, did exist between individual cases and different spatial localities. Instead of hallucinating a gender emancipation based on provisional selections of materials and problematic nostalgia, the matter-of-fact discussions on such matter demand more inclusive and accurate perspectives. See Zang Jian. "The Soviet Impact on 'Gender Equality' in China in the 1950s," in *China Learns from the Soviet Union, 1949–Present*, eds. Thomas P. Bernstein and Hua-Yu Li (Lanham: Lexington Books, 2010), 265–66; Li Xiaojiang, *Nuxing? zhuyi: Wenhua chongtu yu shenfen renting* 女性？主義——文化衝突與身份認同 [*Feminism? Cultural Conflicts and Identity*] (Nanjing: Jiangsu renmin chubanshe, 2000), 242–55.
18 Henan Songxian zhi bianzhuan weiyuanhui, *Songxian zhi*, 256. *Jin* is a standard weight unit in China; one *jin* equals a half kilogram or 1.1023 lb.
19 Ibid., 254. *Mu* is a standard unit of area in China; one *mu* equals 666.67 m² or 0.165 acre.
20 Henan Songxian zhi bianzhuan weiyuanhui, *Songxian zhi*, 124.
21 Ibid., 826–27.
22 The CCP Committee of Department of Health 衛生部黨組. "Zhonggong zhongyang pizhuan weishengbu dangzu 'Guanyu yufang dangqian zhuyao jibing de baogao'" 中共中央批轉衛生部黨組《關於預防當前主要疾病的報告》 [The Central Committee of the CCP approved and forwarded the "Report on the Prevention of Current Major Diseases" issued by the CCP Committee of Department of Health], Chinese Cultural Revolution Database, http://ccrd.usc.cuhk.edu.hk/Fulltext.aspx (last accessed 28 Feb. 2021).
23 Henan Songxian zhi bianzhuan weiyuanhui, *Songxian zhi*, 40.

Nevertheless, this tragic part of history was rephrased on account of its politically sensitive nature,[24] and the indifferences to women's untold sufferings. As an introspective response, Yan employed the social taboo of menstruation, redefined female gender as the third sex, and exposed the paradox in female's historical status as an excrescence to reverse the whitewashed past and revise the installed amnesia of history. Firstly, Yan captured her mother's effusive words about the absurd physical exploitation and the terrible conditions in the construction site of Luhun Reservoir. An embarrassing scene of publicized menstruation recalled female laborers' dual burdens in that harsh time:

> They [female laborers] physically quarried rocks and transported construction materials such as sands, stones, and peddles. My mother will burst into effusive words whenever she recalls these scenes. "People at the time went mad. People did not take people as humans. We all worked more than ten hours a day for months or more than half of a year. We were so exhausted that we fell on the ground asleep with a picul on the shoulder." Whenever she recalls all those "emancipated" women on the dam, mother will always wear an odd, puzzling smirk and muttered "Women were not treated as women. Even when our period came, we couldn't take a half-day-off. Some women on period still transported sands and quarried rocks. The blood flowed down to the earth along their legs and pants."[25]

An inhumane confrontation as such was not merely the inconsiderateness about women's needs or the lack of awareness as a result of ignorance. This form of inhumanity upon women was systematically forged, enforced, duplicated, and reaffirmed. In one aspect, male leaders and engineers did turn a blind eye to menstruation, for they never bothered with a female physiological phenomenon. Whereas, authorities within the patriarchal society did implement a conscious unawareness of women's needs.

The rationale of such a reckless and callous discounting of female experience and female need was legitimized by dint of the metanarrative of men-women equality and the dictation of coercive labor for the socialist developments. Since men do not have periods, such a trivial issue needed no consideration at all. Since men are capable of heavy physical labor, women could do the same kinds of work without caring about the physical adequacy. Put in another way, femininity was unnecessary and redundant to the homosocial structure. Because it was labor force in the very gender that was the real need for the society to consider, rather than the life and working conditions provided to this labor source. After all, labor is not gendered, at least not gendered in the shortage of labor force during the constructions.[26]

---

24 See Frank Dikötter, *The Cultural Revolution: A People's History, 1962–1976* (New York: Bloomsbury Press, 2016), 6–14.
25 Yan, *Tamen*, 212–13.
26 Cf. Li Yinhe 李銀河, "Zhongguo 'feixinghua' yu funü diwei" 中國「非性化」與婦女地位 ["Asexulization and women's role in China"], in *First International Conference on Women's Studies at Peking University, Beijing, Nov. 1992*, ed. Zang Jian 臧健 (Beijing: Women's Studies Center of Peking University, 1993), 21–22. Although differentiation and segregations still appeared between male and female laborers in terms of wages and social recognition during the Great Leap Forward, gender differences per se did not befit any requirements of and preferences in laborer recruitment during the late 1950s. This pseudo-equality partially explained why the CCP discourse generally endorses the discourse/ideology of sex equality and women emancipation: gender (identity) had not much to do with the governing, so the equality in gender would not fundamentally affect the political agendas of the party.

Despite the fact that men likewise were estranged as objects in the frenzy of industry and agricultural developments, the male was the reckoned social agency and subject. Women then shall metaphorically and physically abide by their male comrades, father, husband, and son (a parental substitution and/or potentiality) as an inferior adherent/laborer, who strived for the entitlement of masculinity but could never achieve so. The dogmatic directive on the abidance issued not only a disciplinary order but also epistemological confinement that qualified both women and gender discourse. After the founding of the PRC in 1949, women were transformed into a token of the liberated, the enlightened, and the emancipated in narratives. Chinese women were no longer victims and slaves of the hellish old society but absolutely loyal warriors for the new China, the Party, and the revolutionary crusades.[27] A socialist woman, desexualized to a quasi-masculinity, now became a topos that combined good wife and iron lady.[28] Or as Yan termed, women were turned into "the third sex" (*di san xing* 第三性).

Inspired by Simone de Beauvoir's notion in *The Second Sex* of how women and femininity were created, Yan regarded the third sex as a unique gender identity that was specially designed and designated to women in the PRC.[29] The designation of the third sex metamorphosed women from female to male. Such a metamorphosis bypassed the natural biological differences between females and males. The detoured operation intended to virilize female not physiologically but metonymically. As Mao's famous verse "Militia Women" ("Wei nübing tizhao" 為女民兵提照) reads, "China's daughters have high-aspiring minds. They love their battle array, not silks and satins."[30] The masculine paradigm became the socio-gender norm and the ultimate normative parameter, with which women must coordinate. Through and after the very process of metonymical virilization, masculinity integrated femininity into a subordinate singularity. Consequently, femininity and female subjectivity were conceptually tampered with, symbolically nullified, and socially canceled. Women's distinctive features were denied in the symbolic sense that the discreteness of femininity should not have existed in the female-liberated new China, for no differences shall exist between women and men.

27 Dai Jinhua 戴錦華, *Zuori zhi dao: Dai Jinhua dianying wenzhang zixuanji* 昨日之島: 戴錦華電影文章自選集 [*An island of yesterday: Dai Jinhua's self-selected works on film*] (Beijing: Peking University Press, 2015), 76–77.
28 Ibid., 80; see also Lu Tonglin 呂彤鄰, *Misogyny, Cultural Nihilism & Oppositional Politics: Contemporary Chinese Experimental Fiction* (Stanford: Stanford University Press, 1995), 4–8, 131.
29 The correspondent notion of the third sex was firstly addressed by Meng Yue 孟悅 and Dai Jinhua in their *Fuchu lishi dibiao: Xiandai funü wenxue yanjiu* 浮出歷史地表: 現代婦女文學研究 [*Emerging from the surface of history: A study of modern women's literature*] (Zhengzhou: Henan renmin chubanshe, 1989), 213–15, 268. Meng and Dai assessed that the alleged equality in gender was a gender homogeneity through the eliminations of gender differences and female subjective conscienceless. In socialist China, women could only be heard via men's narration or in male voices, and the degeneration of female gender became a "gender without gender" (*wu xing zhi xing* 無性之性). The pre-PRC female plight did not change in the "new China," where women were still trapped into the hallucination of equality that was nothing other than a de facto denial of female subjectivity and femininity. Yan acknowledges the intellectual inspiration he took from the two scholars in his *Tamen*, 220. The third sex, thus, can be traced in a genealogical affinity with Meng's and Dai's investigations upon the gender history in the PRC. Nevertheless, the unique contribution of Yan belongs to his shifted focus on the rural women in the Great Leap Forward movement. Yan put the notion of the third sex into perspective by reengaging with this group of people and this historical period that were somehow neglected by previous scholarly works.
30 Mao, "Militia Women," trans. Maoist Documentation Project, Marxists.org, https://www.marxists.org/reference/archive/mao/selected-works/poems/poems28.htm (last accessed 15 Mar. 2021).

This designation of femininity induced an ambiguity in the female's social gender role and its social perception, which can be examined from three aspects. First of all, the ambiguity that women laboring as men marked the basic feature of the third sex that the social gender role of female was mixed with that of male. It is something, as Yan said, "in-between and also outside male and female."[31] The ambiguity existed in the aspect that women were turned into "wo-men (*nü nanren* 女男人)," who had to take care of duties both inside and outside of the house.[32] The socialist manifestations of gender equality and equal employment opportunity during the Great Leap Forward assigned women with not only domestic duties but also the responsibility of heavy, physical labor, labor that would have been supposedly assigned to men but was loaded on to women. As a result, women were held responsible for labor both outside and inside the domestic sphere, and for gender roles both socially associated with females and males at the same time.[33] The perceptual parameter that demarcated what was conventionally and socially meant to be male and female was blurred. Women became stuck in the middle of nowhere to configure their gender role in society, for such an anchorage of coherence in gender perception had been removed from the socialist gender discourse in the name of man-women equality.

Such quality of "in-between and also outside" denoted the thirdness as in the third sex, which stood for a de facto suspension. The suspended status positioned women as an unnecessary attachment to the patriarchal entities. "Female comrades can also do what male comrades are capable of."[34] Mao's metaphor on young ladies' swimming competence precisely implied such a hierarchy that women, as duplications, in the workplace were not truly equivalent to men, who were the models, the origins, and the immense.[35] What men can do is the measuring scale and the standard. What women can do, then, is a copy of the male competencies, which shall befit the male scale of capacities. Women were no more than a fairly no-less-capable substitution for men, whose voices had to be articulated through Mao, the man of China, so as to be heard.

The presupposed and presumptuous consistencies in the female body and mindset to their prescribed male subject tolerated no incoordination but indistinction. Women were conceived not different from men by dint of gender singularity (in the name of equality and liberation) while they were not men. The bizarre indistinguishable discreetness applied the rationale that women were understood in terms of men while women cannot be men. One explicit example of this non-incoordination but indistinction can be seen in Yan's documentation of the publicized menstruation.

---

31 Yan, *Tamen*, 208.
32 "Wo-men" does not necessarily correlate to Judith Butler's notion on the performativity of the gendered body as subversive to the patriarchal matrix. Yan's proposition echoes Butler in terms of that the conventional gender discourse and the dichotomy in gender should be reexamined and debunked. However, as Yan said, the sociocultural context in *Their Stories* differs from it in Butler's discussions. Yan focused more on the historical gender maneuver, in and via which women and femininity were included while excluded, liberated but also oppressed, established while eliminated. See Yan, *Tamen*, 223; Judith Butler, *Bodies That Matter: On the Discursive Limits of "Sex"* (New York: Routledge, 1993), 1–31, 93–95, 244–45.
33 Yan, *Tamen*, 213.
34 Anonymous Journalist. "Mao zhuxi Liu zhuxi changyou Shisanlin shuiku" 毛主席劉主席暢遊十三陵水庫 ["Chairman Mao and President Liu paid a joyful visit to Ming Tombs Reservoir"], *People's Daily*, 27 May 1965, http://rmrb.egreenapple.com/index2.html (last accessed 14 Feb. 2021).
35 Lu, *Misogyny, Cultural Nihilism & Oppositional Politics*, 6.

Menstruation is one of the identifying marks that demarcates women and men physically. However, on the Luhun Reservoir, this screamingly identifying mark was paradoxically perceived as opaque and elusive to the social subject of male objects that acknowledged neither the classifying parameters nor the sex demarcation. Inasmuch as men did not menstruate, women at the reservoir construction site were deemed to have no menstruations. As Yan's mother recalled, women could not have a rest taken from the heavy physical labor even when they were menstruating. Functioning as a labor unit, women did not receive any relief but indifferences in using them as a supplementary of the labor force. The indistinction and indifference stemmed from the coercive gender coordination, the halt in sex nuances, and the Maoist homogeneity that women could do what men were capable of. Women were, indeed, treated as men, not legally and culturally but only physically.

Secondly, the ambiguity in the third sex also amplified the female predicament of dual exploitations, especially when there was a paucity in the labor force. From the late 1950s to the early 1960s, rural women were relocated from their domestic spaces to public construction sites for dikes, roads, railways, and other facilities. In the name of men-women equality and equal contributions to the country's development, women were forced into onerous jobs and encountered physical and physiological exploitations, neglects, and unfairness.[36] Meanwhile, women also took over all the housekeeping and other duties that had been unloaded from men and reloaded to them. Yan saw this nascent form of unfairness in labor distribution as a dual exploitation for rural women: "The traditional shackle of 'men as breadwinners and women as homemakers' was indeed broken after 1949. But after that, women didn't unload all the tasks assigned to them. Women were reloaded with a considerable proportion of tasks that had been pointed only to men. Women were breadwinners and homemakers. Women became female and male at the same time. All of that put women into a predicament of dual and even multiple exploitations, oppressions, occupations, and scarifies."[37] The duality in labor outputs made Chinese rural women face no options but to shoulder the tasks both outside and inside the home. In addition to build the reservoir by hands and foot, women were also obliged to take care of cooking, housekeeping, babysitting, tailoring all the clothes, washing dishes, doing laundry, serving their husbands, children, parents-in-law, and other aspects of daily chores. The dual oppressions and exploitations upon women can thus be configured as: Rural women had to work as men and rural women worked more than men did on the construction projects, despite their willingness and the terrible working conditions.

However, by no means could the abuse of treating women as men equal men-women equality and female emancipation. Living in an androcentric historical narrative, Chinese women acquired a lingering, hybrid status. Yan commented that "women are humans, but not men. But they have to be and act as men."[38] The thirdness, an awkward suspension between non-male and man-surrogate, renders women "mixtures of history and politics."[39] Females were recognized as a labor unit but far from qualified as male and being treated as so accordingly. Yan exposes how people turned a blind eye to women's physical outputs, rarely treated

---

36 The correspondent Chinese term for men-women equality is 男女平等, *nan nü pingdeng*. Although this slogan intended to address equality between two sexes, it should not be misused with gender equality, which was not widely adopted as an ideological orientation as well as a discursive device until the 1980s in China. See Zang, "Soviet Impact," 260–61.
37 Yan, *Tamen*, 214.
38 Ibid., 213.
39 Ibid.

women as laborers, and never regarded women's labors as real labors, but works.[40] Thus, the same amount of workload by women was counted less than it by men. Women's domestic and social contributions were taken for granted and reckoned inconsequential. Women were deprived of the entitlement to develop the society in the eyes of men, the alleged "true" producer, storyteller, and history writer.

The enigma here lies in the aspect that women, along with features and entities recognized as the constitutive elements of femininity, were inclusively excluded. The homosocial society of the PRC needed the working forces provided by females while it simultaneously deterred femininity and women from entering either society's center or the core streams of the history narrative. That is to say, thirdly, the overwhelming discourse based on the ambiguity and patriarchal superiority installed an obliteration-perception of history apropos gender as a socially designated entity. The history of women's lives and female experiences dissolved into times when their contributions had been dimmed out in memory and hidden from view. "The memory about this history became vague. Women's role to the memory also became vague. It disappeared," Yan noted.[41] When women were forgotten in history as prescribed, women's history was forgotten as planned.

The ruthless amnesia of history had crossed out women in the state's memory. "No matter in cities or rural places, women are invariably forgotten and effaced hurriedly in a patriarchal memory governed by familial ethics …. Passing away as someone's wife, a woman will only be remembered after her death as a minor detail or side issue attached to a male subject," Yan elucidated.[42] The amnesia scheme functioned in a programmed mode to detach women from the social memory machine and its encoding of time, namely the history-writing. Femininity in both of its presentations and representations was dodged; femininity in both of its presentations and representations became evasive and deviant. Women suffered from the amnesia enacted in the unfolding of the male-oriented history, which was invariably about farming, battle, industrial innovation, and revolution. As for women, they were conceptualized as an insignificant footnote to this male-comrade-made history and granted neither place nor legitimacy in its institution.

To keep accordance with the state's memory institution, the history narrative also positioned both women's presentations and representations as superfluous. The painful story about menstruation and heavy labor lived only in the *liaoyan* of Yan's mother. No official documentation or dossier would pen such a tabooed, trivial, and threatening detail about women's lousy living conditions in a history stage that itself read awkwardly for the state history/memory to either remember or process. In this regard, what Yan staged in the publicizing of menstruation were two enriching corrections to the installed amnesia of history.

The first enriching correction is the female life-cum-memory that would debunk the bogus history narrative of women's liberation and the glorification of the Great Leap Forward. Yan purported that in reality Chinese rural women encountered a divergent fate from the propaganda discourse. Chinese rural women's fates seem bound to be tragic on account of the dual oppression and the embarrassing identity of the third sex. This memory is particularly anchored by the taboo of the female physiological phenomenon of menstruation, which replaced the alleged decorum and indisputability of the phallogocentric event of history-remembering. Women's ordeals in the applauding of socialist frenzies, vague notwithstanding, exist as a

40 Ibid., 189–90.
41 Ibid., 217.
42 Ibid., 122.

historical fact and reconstitutes the history with their voices, their lives, their feelings, and their first-hand witnessing of the ruthless past.

The publicizing of this highly tabooed topic transformed menstruation into a bodily-historical entity. In conventional Chinese understanding, menstruation exemplifies the deficiency of female bodies and its characteristic of potential contamination. As a stigmatized physiological phenomenon, it stood for filth, embarrassment, and danger.[43] The flow of blood is a floating threat to the social order and the normal functioning of masculinity.[44] Whereas, the discharging of blood functioned as a myotonic sign of the body's writings on the ground, disclosed the taxing labor during periods of the Great Leap Forward, unraveled the lack of sanitation products, and exposed the unfair treatment that disqualified women as humans, viewing them only tools without feelings and needs.

Furthermore, Yan proposed a new term for the historical status of women, the third sex in the PRC, so as to rectify the whitewashed history. The third sex entails a sociocultural characteristic in its property, which Yan construed as excrescence (*youzhui* 疣贅). Yan explained: "No matter inherent or not, an excrescence to human beings is a useless, extra wart. If you cut it off, you bleed. This is an additional aversion that makes you feel it may be better to leave the excrescence there than removing it. With time going by, you get increasingly enclosed to the excrescence, and the excrescence becomes a part of your body and life. You stop sensing the excrescence as excrescent. It becomes a member or a property of your family. It is now a responsibility and task you have to take over and shoulder. (Oh my!)"[45] The Chinese word *youzhui* is compounded by two characters *you* and *zhui*, which means wart and superfluous/burdensome, respectively. A wart is a pathological growth and thickening on the skin and *zhui*, in particular, also shares the connotations of an extra appendage or a male member married into his wife's family and changed to his wife's family surname. In sum, *youzhui* suggests a diseased, unhealthy, and redundant attachment to a normal body or entity. An excrescence in this sense stands for a female shaping of history, which is included in the set of history narrative but also excluded as an extra and undesired element in this history set full of male stories and narrations.

The term excrescence has a correspondent meaning in Western language and political philosophy. Originated from the Latin word *excrescentia*, excrescence also means outgrowth. In Alain Badiou's categorization of the relations between membership and inclusion in political terms, excrescence refers to the situation when individuals were represented but not presented in the state.[46] Excrescent individuals were those who were included in society but were not members of society.[47] Namely, excrescence existed in the state, but it was not directly verified and recognized by the state or the sovereign. The existence of the excrescent was only verified and recognized inasmuch as it was in the status of the exceeded and the unregistered.[48] Giorgio Agamben, however, did not regard Badiou's theorization of excrescence as the whole

---

43 Ingrid Johnston-Robledo and Joan C. Chrisler, "The Menstrual Mark: Menstruation as Social Stigma," *Sex Roles* vol. 68, no. 1 (Jan. 2013): 10–14, https://doi.org/10.1007/s11199-011-0052-z.
44 Emily Martin. *The Woman in the Body: A Cultural Analysis of Reproduction* (Boston: Beacon Press, 1992), 27–53.
45 Yan, *Tamen*, 207.
46 In addition to excrescent, normal (presented and represented) and singular (presented but not represented) are other two situations. See Alain Badiou, *Being and Event* (London: Continuum, 2005), 99–101.
47 Giorgio Agamben, *Homo Sacer: Sovereign Power and Bare Life* (Stanford: Stanford University Press, 1998), 24.
48 Badiou, *Being and Event*, 100.

picture and assessed that *homo sacer*, sacred life, fits more adequately in terms of inclusive exclusion.[49]

Homo sacer exemplified the status of being included while excluded, for a sacred life may be killed but it cannot be sacrificed. The sovereignty's despotic power in the state would not be established and legitimized until homo sacer, reckoned the opposite to the state, had been exposed to abandonment, punishment, violence, and mortality in the state.[50] Meanwhile, homo sacer was excluded from the state's legal protection against homicide on account of its potential hazards to the state. Homo sacer was also excluded in the religious sphere as an impure entity that was not permitted to be sacrificed.[51] The result was that the inclusively excluded homo sacer became suspended in both the state/worldly and religious spheres. In such a paradoxical situation, the sovereignty's exclusion of homo sacer was only possible through including it and vice versa.[52]

At this point, one issue shall be clearly addressed that rural women during the Great Leap Forward as presented and represented in Yan's narratives do not entirely fit into either theorizations or the terminological realms of homo sacer. The perplexing paradox of the unverified membership in the state that is akin to women's predicament in history narrative notwithstanding, the political situation of excrescence and homo sacer shall not be deemed directly applicable and identical to the historical status of women in the PRC. However, this is not the case that women in socialist China, under a zealous movement, were exposed to necropolitics and registered as subjugated through biopolitics. In actual fact, rural women as Yan represented hardly registered any de facto politics and were hardly political in whatsoever forms, extent, and manners. This is the first eminent difference to be noted. Furthermore, women in the late 1950s in the PRC entailed contextual and historical meanings (either symbolically or in actuality), which differed from, say, the Jewish people in Nazi concentration camps and could only be analogously read vis-à-vis homo sacer in terms of the sovereignty's inclusive exclusion.

In *Their Stories*, the dual inclusive exclusions of rural women in both the narrative sphere and worldly sphere during the Great Leap Forward issued a distinctive suspension. Excrescence as a status of being or the way of being in itself constituted the mode of female labor on the construction site and women's historical circumstances in the patriarchal, homosocial society of the PRC. Women were included in history narratives only after they were simultaneously excluded as excrescences. To put in another way, women were recruited as a labor and cultural force without their contributions credited and experiences cited. The homosocial society and the PRC government needed women while women were denied by the same society and government as well. In this regard, Yan's proposition of excrescence formulates a counterfeit sacredness that may be obliterated in narratives but not excised.

As Yan described, one stops feeling and sensing the *youzhui* after time passes: "The excrescence becomes a part of your body and life. You stop sensing the excrescence as excrescence."[53] The ceasing of excrescence's existence on the body signifies the excrescence's emergence into the body, which assembles an inextricable segment of the body.[54] It is also a superfluous part of the body in either a physiological sense as an organism system or a political sense as the

---

49 Agamben, *Homo Sacer*, 25–28.
50 Ibid., 81–83.
51 Ibid., 75–80.
52 Ibid., 22.
53 Yan, *Tamen*, 207.
54 Ibid.

structure of a nation-state, whereas the dismembering of such body part integrated into the body will wound and stultify the body unity that functions on the basis of harmlessness. Nonetheless, excrescence is never entitled to forsake its pathological nature of hyperplasia. The immanent perniciousness of excrescence does not only originate in the undesirable and unneeded outgrowth but also in the impossibility to remove it. Yan reminded his readers that the consequential bleeding of excrescence excision will generate "an additional aversion."[55] Metaphorically taken, this bleeding, identical to menstruation, is an undesired and unexpected supplemental cost to the normal metabolism and functioning of the body, the society, the state.

The aversion does not have much to do with the excision operation, which technically causes the bleeding. Because this operation could have been avoided if the excrescence did not exist. Instead, it is the excrescence responsible for the preventable occurrences of the incision, the bleed, the aversion. In this sense, excrescence in itself is the aversion that needs a potential removal to diminish the tensions between the outgrown excrescence and the body. But excrescence can never receive this excision, this local hemorrhage on the body, this analogously vicarious castration of the homosocial body. Otherwise, the completeness and the masculinity of the body will no longer maintain and persist. In other words, besides the expenditure of severance that is too considerable to be allowed, the paradoxical impossibility of removing the outgrowth of excrescence is precisely because it is the excrescence that constitutes the sovereignty of the body and demarcates the body of the sovereignty from its excessive proliferation in the structure.

The paradox of inclusive exclusion found its echo in the history narrative. Rural women were obligatorily implicated as an obscure token with no substantiality and ontological substance in the phallologocentric narrative of history. Women with their gender identity were underestimated, effaced, and forgotten in history. This history written by men, spoken by men, and remembered by men did not accommodate any spaces for women. Nevertheless, the suspension of the feeling about the excrescence did not at all nullify and/or discharge the female in revolutionary stories, in which women played roles of every kind and for every purpose. Rather, it made those women, those roles, and those purposes everything if not nothing and consequently nothingness as in everything if anything. She who had been removed from the history narrative presented herself in the very plot the inclusive exclusion was staged. The inclusive exclusion of women in history narratives left a preordered vacuum to be fulfilled: the evacuation of women enabled the perpetuation of the superior male subject and the male narrator.

The fabricated hallucination of women's ephemeral and inconsequential existence was perpetuated as a vital and indispensable referent for the necessity of socialist construction projects and the revolutionary credos. "It is genuinely true that women made no less contributions than men, and always more than men. But after the joy of harvest, it was man who received applauses in speeches and words for his labors. It was forever man as the master of earth land who would be mentioned whenever praises for labor arises," Yan stated.[56] Women were outside of this collectivist ritual that celebrated and sanctified the revolution, for it was not the female that liberated the Chinese women and made better lives for the Chinese, but the CCP comrades and the Red Army/PLA soldiers.

---

55 Ibid.
56 Ibid., 216.

In speeches and writings about the history of the socialist period, women had no part in this political legitimacy and sanctification. Women shall wait to be freed by the heroic, brave soldiers. Women were in the queue to be enlightened as socialist subjects that would decipher the socialist teaching of men-women equality with the guidance from men who were CCP members. Women were sacred as sacrifices without sacredness, after which they became analogously comparable to men. She, who had been inclusively excluded from the history narrative, would allow the opposite sex its subjectivity and its social significance. The metaphorical rendering formulated an attendant absence in narratives, in which women were always present as a device that merely served for the sake of narration. Women were suspended in words and as words of nothingness and, therefore, inclusively excluded from the history narrative sphere.

However, this gendered token was too significant to be deleted in terms of its inextricability to the ideological concerns of men-women equality and the national propaganda machine. Since Chinese women would not have been liberated by men and their heroic revolutions, all the revolutionary endeavors must be regarded as legitimate because women were indeed liberated and extricated from the old, devilish society, where women had been nothing but slaves and victims. The underlying rationale indicates that revolution was legitimized and necessitated only after women were sacred as a suspended token. Such a token is detached from the history, in and through which the liberation of women was the indisputable truth. Accordingly, the revolution that had actualized this truth, this reality, this happy life in the status quo was inherently legitimate and necessary. The token of the liberated female was tantamount to the ultimate sacredness, which shall absolutely not be violated, thereby also excluding women from any queries that would nullify and/or debunk the narrative about this history in the worldly sphere.

Her stories as herstory? Rethinking *Liaoyan* and excrescence

In his discussion on exchange, Peter M. Blau (1918–2002) employed the notion of emergent properties to address the essential structure of social relations, wherein a societal system functions as an entity beyond individuals or individual components.[57] Within this particular structure, people are scattered into an emergence, an assemblage, a sum, of which the system possesses properties that are different from the properties of the composing parts and/or elements that consist of the system. Variables will occur when social exchange and interpersonal interaction are exercised. Xiang Biao 項飆 was sharp enough to point out that Blau took emergence as a sudden event and, therefore, somehow confined the analytical scope to the totality of society. For Xiang, attention should be paid to details and components within the entire structure of society, and one must decipher how individual components with their substantial details interact with and correlate to each other in society's complex networking.[58]

When the female's history and stories entered the complex narration machine and, by all means, counted one part of it, the disorganization of female and female experience as atoms will no longer ontologically exist, for the male-centered machine is partially consisted of this component and possesses the unique, inextricable characteristics of such component. As an actual consequence, the female's history is a segment of the history en bloc and this history

---

57 Peter M. Blau, *Exchange and Power in Social Life* (New York: John Wiley & Sons, 1964), 3–4.
58 Xiang Biao, *Kuayue bianjie de shequ: Beijing Zhejiangcun de shenghuo shi* 跨越邊界的社區: 北京「浙江村」的生活史 [*Transcending boundaries: Zhejiangcun, the story of a migrant village in Beijing*] (Beijing: Sanlian shudian, 2000), 14–17.

whole will not be as it is if the properties of the component of female history are de facto denied or deleted. That is because this whole is determined by its elements and the properties of this history are composed by properties of all elements inside, thereby rendering this history whole nothing if it is not composed in this way.[59] In addition, since emergence by definition is a matter of all proportions in differences, the internal relationship between the female's history as a component and the history as an emergence composed shall be taken as nonhierarchical and nonbinary. Such a history emergence does not form itself in a vertical structure where differences have to be determined for functioning and normal operation.

However, how can women forge their narratives and anchor their subjective autonomy after and in all that dreadfulness and abhorrence? Yan Lianke does not give any answers, at least not directly. His nonfictional documentation can hardly be regarded as an answer or solution to any sociocultural and gender troubles that are still puzzling, gnawing, and haunting Chinese women and feminist predicaments in the PRC. Instead, Yan managed to reveal women's stories, lives, contributions, and existences in a temporal apparatus, the history narrative, that has invariably been hostile and exclusive to women and femininity. In this sense, Yan's proposition of excrescence as women's historical status needs further thinking on its prospective potentialities and anticipatory competences.

Antecedent analyses demonstrated that excrescence epitomizes a suspension through inclusive exclusions, thereby positioning women in and outside of the narrative and worldly spheres. In the status of excrescence, female and female life were instantly passed in the memorization process of the national history machine. Ephemeral and trivial as deemed, the temporality fragments of women would not be converted to memories that are recorded and encoded in the national memory about history. Women were soon forgotten in the amnesia scheme and amnesiac mindset that women were never inhered within the sociocultural remembrance as time-independent sequences and tracings of consolidated events. All these scatterings of memento impermanence arouse only excrescent stimuli and even disruptions to the memory machine that begets and reiterates substantial values in permanence. Therefore, memories about female and female life shall be kept as time debris in disarray, as opposed to men and their enduring magnificence and great causes in the history.

Having said that, excrescence can also be understood as emergence in the social system. This assemblage of scattered memories in women's chats-and-talks, conceived excrescent and insignificant, constitutes a de facto narrative rhizome. Decentralized and heterogeneous in its compositions of utterances, the narrative rhizome remaps the obliterated faculties of female life experiences in the PRC history. Deleuze and Guattari take history as a unitary state apparatus that fixes at a sedimentary viewpoint and aims to reproduce long-term memory traces in the arborescent and hierarchical structure. In contrast, short-term memory is a rhizome that connects to multiplicities and maps an "acentered, nonhierarchical, nonsignifying system."[60] For Deleuze and Guattari, rhizome defines non-centralized multiplicities in a qualitative sense. Thus, history in the form of a rhizome is an immanent process rather than a finalized tracing and/or pivot within a hierarchical mechanism/organization governed by the state or sovereignty. History is more than what was. History is also about differences, non-linearity, and connectability to everything and everything else.[61] Following the very rationale,

---

59 To say history whole is not to take history as a seamless, exclusive, and enclosed singularity, but to remap history in a polymorphous compound that contains while integrates heterogeneous components or parts.
60 Deleuze and Guattari, *Plateaus*, 21.
61 Ibid., 20–25.

the female status of excrescence is fundamental and indispensable for history narrative and re-narrating of history.

Insofar as rewriting the PRC vis-à-vis rural women's life within and around a familial institution, Yan exposed a piece of acentered history about the silenced women and the veiled facts. He wrote, to a considerable extent, from female perspectives and experiences and provided voices for his female characters. But it remains questionable whether his depictions can be regarded as a contrast to the androcentric, logocentrism, and patriarchy-dominated history narrative and historiographical presentations/representations. Namely, does writing about women equal female writing? If yes, in which way and to what extent does it qualify as so? The ultimate question could be integrated into the query about whether women can be genuinely represented in the narrative if women do not present themselves in direct narrations.

Let potential misunderstandings be avoided, it is of no problem and inadequacy for a male writer to re-engage history from a feminist perspective, as Yan proposed in the preface to this nonfictional piece.[62] The actual problem, or one genuinely unideal aspect, is that Yan proposed a perspective of history-cum-literature narrative and a prospect for historical-cum-literary mindset that he is yet to fully actualize. What Yan configured in *Their Stories* are stories and events that happened to women, rather than femininity that is in itself answerable to the introspection of history narrative and symbolical refashioning. Yan refabricated women's life incidents and female existences into his needs of narration and narrative modes, wherein he provided his female characters with mediated voices. Women's voices were accorded and reintroduced to themselves, which heavily relied upon Yan's speak-out monologue and the third-person point of view in story-telling. Yan talked a lot about all those women. Those women were referred to, reflected upon, and sympathized with many times.

The complex ambivalences in a man's writing of herstory require more space for detailed discussion than this chapter can accommodate. Nonetheless, the radicle of narrative rhizome germinated within herstory, which Yan pinpointed, sustained its discrete meanings to reiterate and reassess the existence as well as the innovative significances of women as excrescent multiplicities to history and narratives. As Yan displayed, women are women but not men. Such a proposition implies neither gender hierarchy nor gender dichotomy but simply heterogeneousness that shall not be disregarded, which was brutally demolished in the PRC's history. The remedy Yan prescribed is to discern that all their stories are our stories. To say that means more than gender equality and gender visibility in history and narratives. The indistinguishable faculties between "their stories" and "our stories" request an unimplemented deconstruction of the dichotomies between women and men, femininity and masculinity, self and other.

Interestingly, it is never possible to implement this deconstruction in a Lacanian symbolic order. The indistinguishableness between "their stories" and "our stories" can never be fulfilled, for the (desire) subject forever needs the object to constitute itself, which will never be sought out.[63] Arguably, the alternative is not to appeal for the oneness of gender and gender history. It is rather about how one can see and understand gender as a rhizome, ceaselessly connecting to other power organizations and semiotic chains, producing new statements about the unconscious and desires, mapping decentered multiplicities and multiple entryways to other rhizomes that one would call history, gender, men, women, and everything in between and beyond.

---

62 Yan, *Tamen*, I–III.
63 Cf. Jacques Lacan, *The Psychoses, 1955–1956* (New York: W. W. Norton, 1993), 84–85.

Acknowledgment

I would like to express my great gratitude to my supervisor and mother-like mentor, Liu Jianmei 劉劍梅. No words can adequately express how blessed I am to have her guidance, care, and unconditional support. My sincere thanks are also due to Ma Xiaolu 馬筱璐, Wu Shengqing 吳盛青, Howard Y. F. Choy 蔡元豐, and Pang Laikwan 彭麗君 for their illuminating advice and help since the beginning of this project. I genuinely appreciate Riccardo Moratto and Howard Choy for their editorial efforts and for having been invariably helpful and efficient. I also thank Qiao Min 喬敏 and Zhuang Muyang 莊沐楊 for their scholarly suggestions.

Bibliography

Agamben, Giorgio. *Homo Sacer: Sovereign Power and Bare Life*. Stanford: Stanford University Press, 1998.

Anonymous Journalist. "Mao zhuxi Liu zhuxi changyou Shisanlin shuiku" 毛主席劉主席暢遊十三陵水庫 ["Chairman Mao and President Liu paid a joyful visit to Ming Tombs Reservoir"]. *People's Daily*, 27 May 1965. http://rmrb.egreenapple.com/index2.html (last accessed 14 Feb. 2021).

Badiou, Alain. *Being and Event*. London: Continuum, 2005.

Ban Gu 班固, comp. *Han Shu* 漢書 [*Book of the Han dynasty*]. Chinese Text Project. https://ctext.org/han-shu/yi-wen-zhi/zh (last accessed 15 Feb. 2021).

Blau, Peter M. *Exchange and Power in Social Life*. New York: John Wiley & Sons, 1964.

Braester, Yomi. *Witness against History: Literature, Film, and Public Discourse in Twentieth-Century China*. Stanford: Stanford University Press, 2003.

Butler, Judith. *Bodies That Matter: On the Discursive Limits of "Sex."* New York: Routledge, 1993.

———. *Gender Trouble: Feminism and the Subversion of Identity*. New York: Routledge, 1990.

CCP Committee of Department of Health 衛生部黨組. "Zhonggong zhongyang pizhuan weishengbu dangzu 'Guanyu yufang dangqian zhuyao jibing de baogao'" 中共中央批轉衛生部黨組《關於預防當前主要疾病的報告》 ["The Central Committee of the CCP approved and forwarded the 'Report on the Prevention of Current Major Diseases' issued by the CCP Committee of Department of Health"]. Database of Chinese Great Leap Forward & Great Famine. http://ccrd.usc.cuhk.edu.hk/Fulltext.aspx (last accessed 28 Feb. 2021).

Chan Shelley W. 陳穎. "Narrating Cancer, Disabilities, and AIDS: Yan Lianke's Trilogy of Disease." In *Discourses of Disease: Writing Illness, the Mind and the Body in Modern China*, edited by Choy Howard Y. F. 蔡元豐, 177–97. Leiden: Brill, 2016.

Dai Jinhua 戴錦華. *Zuo ri zhi dao: Dai Jinhua dianying wenzhang zixuanji* 昨日之島：戴錦華電影文章自選集 [*An island of yesterday: Dai Jinhua's self-selected works on film*]. Beijing: Peking University Press, 2015.

Deleuze, Gilles, and Félix Guattari. *A Thousand Plateaus: Capitalism and Schizophrenia*. Minneapolis: University of Minnesota Press, 1987.

Dikötter, Frank. *The Cultural Revolution: A People's History, 1962–1976*. New York: Bloomsbury Press, 2016.

Henan Songxian zhi bianzhuan weiyuanhui 河南嵩縣志編撰委員會, eds. *Songxian zhi* 嵩縣志 [*Chorography of Song County*]. Zhengzhou: Henan renmin chubanshe, 1990.

Hershatter, Gail. *The Gender of Memory: Rural Women and China's Collective Past*. Berkeley: University of California Press, 2011.

Johnston-Robledo, Ingrid, and Joan C. Chrisler. "The Menstrual Mark: Menstruation as Social Stigma." *Sex Roles* vol. 68, no. 1 (Jan. 2013): 9–18. https://doi.org/10.1007/s11199-011-0052-z

Lacan, Jacques. *The Psychoses, 1955–1956*. New York: W.W. Norton, 1993.

Li Xiaojiang 李小江. *Nüxing? zhuyi: Wenhua chongtu yu shenfen rentong* 女性？主義——文化衝突與身份認同 [*Feminism? Cultural Conflicts and Identity*]. Nanjing: Jiangsu renmin chubanshe, 2000.

Li Yinhe 李銀河. "Zhongguo 'feixinghua' yu funü diwei" 中國「非性化」與婦女地位 ["Asexulization and women's role in China"]. In *First International Conference on Women's Studies at Peking University, Beijing, Nov. 1992*, edited by Zang Jian 臧健, 19–22. Beijing: Women's Studies Center of Peking University, 1993.

Liu, Jianmei 劉劍梅. "Bianxin de wenxue bianzouqu" 變形的文學變奏曲 ["The variations of metamorphic literature"]. *Comparative Literature in China*, 2020, vol. 118, no. 1: 114–30.

———. *Zhuangzi and Modern Chinese Literature*. New York: Oxford University Press, 2016.

Lü Tonglin 呂彤鄰. *Misogyny, Cultural Nihilism & Oppositional Politics: Contemporary Chinese Experimental Fiction*. Stanford: Stanford University Press, 1995.
Mao Zedong 毛澤東. "Militia Women," Trans. The Maoist Documentation Project. Marxists.org. https://www.marxists.org/reference/archive/mao/selected-works/poems/poems28.htm (last accessed 15 Mar. 2021).
Martin, Emily. *The Woman in the Body: A Cultural Analysis of Reproduction*. Boston: Beacon Press, 1992.
Meng Yue 孟悅 and Dai Jinhua. *Fuchu lishi dibiao: Xiandai funü wenxue yanjiu* 浮出歷史地表：現代婦女文學研究 [*Emerging from the surface of history: A study of modern women's literature*]. Zhengzhou: Henan renmin chubanshe, 1989.
Rojas, Carlos. *Homesickness: Culture, Contagion, and National Transformation in Modern China*. Cambridge, Mass.: Harvard University Press, 2015.
———. "TIME OUT OF JOINT: Commemoration and Commodification of Socialism in Yan Lianke's *Lenin's Kisses*." In *Red Legacies in China: Cultural Afterlives of the Communist Revolution*, ed. Li Jie and Zhang Enhua, 297–315. Cambridge, Mass.: Harvard University Asia Center, 2016.
Xiang Biao 項飆. *Kuayue bianjie de shequ: Beijing Zhejiangcun de shenghuo shi* 跨越邊界的社區：北京「浙江村」的生活史 [*Transcending boundaries: Zhejiangcun, the Story of a migrant village in Beijing*]. Beijing: Sanlian shudian, 2000.
Yan Lianke 閻連科. *Tamen* 她們 [*Their Stories*]. Zhengzhou: Henan wenyi chubanshe, 2020.
Zang, Jian. "The Soviet Impact on 'Gender Equality' in China in the 1950s." *China Learns from the Soviet Union, 1949–Present*, edited by Thomas P. Bernstein and Hua-Yu Li, 260–73. Lanham: Lexington Books, 2010.
Zhang Zhengqing 張正青. "Jianshe Luhun shuiku de jianku suiyue" 建設陸渾水庫的艱苦歲月 ["The difficult years of building the Lukhun Reservoir"]. *Henan shuili yu nanshui beidiao* 河南水利與南水北調 [*Henan water resources & south-to-north water diversion*], 2007, no. 1: 62–63.

20
A GEOCRITICAL STUDY OF YAN LIANKE'S *BALOU* MOUNTAIN STORIES

The utopian cognitive mapping in post-1949 China

Chen Wang

Introduction

In his prefatory discussion of modern Chinese fiction in the canonical *Compendium of Modern Chinese Literature*, Lu Xun 魯迅 notes the particular devotedness to native soil literature in Beijing's publishing of the early 1920s. "The Beijing-based authors such as Qian Xian'ai who writes about Guizhou and Pei Wenzhong about Yuguan—despite that one claims his writing to be objective depictions or subjective expressions of thoughts and feelings—are writers of the native soil literature. Viewed from the fact that they reside in Beijing, these writers are also migrant writers," Lu Xun continues, "By entitling his first collection of short stories *The Homeland*, Xu Qingwen has also unconsciously identified himself as an author of the native soil literature. Prior to writing about the native soil, however, Xu has already been deported from his homeland, thus an exile to the land of foreignness."[1] According to Lu Xun, all Xu Qingwen was capable of doing was to recollect a non-existent garden, which could be more self-comforting than an actual garden that was inaccessible.

Lu Xun's remark acutely and prophetically unfolds two prominent features of modern Chinese native soil literature, which are found not only in early schools of writers including himself, Shen Congwen 沈從文 as well as revolutionary writers of the left wing in the pre-1949 China but also in the works by contemporary generations of native soil writers. First, native soil literature is in essence written by the displaced or the exiled. In other words, the native land can only be viewed and narrated about from afar, whose connection to its authorial subject is infinitely marked by a sense of distance. Second, although there has been a tradition of treating the native soil as the subject of critical revelation, ruthless ridicule, or melancholic nostalgia in the history of modern Chinese literature, it is precisely such distance from the native soil that enables modern Chinese writers to discover a moment of self-comfort, to retain a hope for possibilities, and to promise an emancipation from or transformation of the

---

1 Lu Xun, "Preface to *Zhongguo xinwenxue daxi (xiaoshuo er ji)*" 中國新文學大系 (小說二集) [Compendium of modern Chinese literature: fiction II], in *Lu Xun quanji* 魯迅全集 [Complete works of Lu Xun], vol. 6 (Beijing: Renmin wenxue chubanshe, 2005), 255.

DOI: 10.4324/9781003144564-23

bleak reality in native China. In short, it allows for a utopian, as Fredric Jameson terms it, "cognitive mapping" of one's native land in literature.[2]

Like many other his contemporaries, such as Mo Yan 莫言 who creates a village world rooted in the Gaomi 高密 county of Shandong, Jia Pingwa 賈平凹 writing on Shangzhou 商州 in the rural south of Shaanxi, and Han Shaogong 韓少功 on the West margin of Hunan, Yan Lianke 閻連科, winner of a Lu Xun Literature Prize, also gives reincarnation to his native land the Song 嵩 County in Henan Province, one of the most impoverished areas in China, in his series stories set in a fictional region called the Balou 耙耬 Mountain. Yan is recognized widely for his employment of mythorealism, a narrative mode through which the "non-existent," invisible and concealed truth is explored in the absence of logical relations in real life.[3] His 1997 novella *The Years, Months, Days* (*Nian yue ri* 年月日), for instance, places man in conditions of extremity where no desire is left but the drive for physical survival in a famine caused by drought, which ends up with striking images of human flesh and blood turning into fertilizer for a doomsday crop. His *Dream of the Ding Village* (*Dingzhuang meng* 丁莊夢) presents readers with a village's struggle in poverty and its dream of economic prosperity through blood trade, which is brutally shattered and turns into a nightmare of AIDS epidemic. Such themes and motifs as human's physical suffering backgrounded by social and historical movements in Maoist China like the Great Leap Forward and the Cultural Revolution or by the post-Mao conflict between humanity and capitalism recur in Yan's stories. However, it seems too convenient a critical job to simply draw a referential connection between Yan's work and the post-1949 China's reality, which is facilitated by these thematic recurrences. To put it alternatively, it begs the question as to whether Yan's works are for the mere sake of—and even stop short of transcending—an artistically sophisticated mimesis of the hidden social and historical truth. It is also worth asking whether Yan's works are, at best, an aesthetical test on his readers' physicality and mentality through depictions of historical traumas in the Maoist and post-Maoist China, using such literary techniques and rhetoric as mythorealism to invoke images and figures of the fantastic, the grotesque, the absurd, the mythical, and the appalling—some of the key terms used by scholars to identify the pivotal characteristics of Yan's fiction.

The major question here, therefore, concerns what possibilities of reality and ways of experiencing it Yan's works could help us envision after tearing open numerous social and historical scars in such a violent way. This chapter turns to the spatial dimension of human experiences in Yan's works. Instead of reading Yan's Balou Mountain series as separate stories set in a place under the same name, I read them in their totality. That is, from as early as the 1990s to recent years, Yan has created a serialized story, in which a cognitive map continuously expands. As narratives about the Balou Mountain accumulate, the landscapes covered on its map continue to enlarge and populations continue to grow and become demographically richer. By examining, in particular, the utopian "cognitive mapping" in Yan's 1997 novella *The Years, Months, Days* and 2013 novel *The Explosion Chronicles* (*Zhalie zhi* 炸裂志), this chapter argues that Yan has created a convoluted web of multiple and multi-layered utopian attempts, which (self-)contradict, overwrite, and nullify one another at the intersections of the rural and the urban, the individual and the commune, the dominating and the subaltern. I propose that, in this still-growing web, these utopian attempts serve as test cases to show Yan's

---

2 See Fredric Jameson, *Postmodernism, or, the Cultural Logic of Late Capitalism* (Durham: Duke University Press, 1991).
3 Yan Lianke, *Yan Lianke wenlun* 閻連科文論 [Yan Lianke's essays on literature] (Kunming: Yunnan renmin chubanshe, 2013), 155.

endeavors to explore the possibility of a way out. In that sense, a subtle transformation can be detected within the author's decade-long plowing and weeding of the same native soil. While the narration of utopian visions seems to result in more of an exhaustion of hopes, followed by pessimism and nihilism in Yan's earlier Balou Mountain stories such as *The Years, Months, Days*, his later works like *The Explosion Chronicles* start to show more a desire for solutions to the social and historical conundrums both he and his fictional characters face.

The original Greek word for utopia is literally translated as "no (ou) place (topos)." Its meaning was developed most famously by Thomas More, who used the word to refer to a perfect place or a place of impossibility. In this article, rather than understanding utopia in More's sense as an ideal society or state, I follow Robert T. Tally, Jr.'s conceptualization of it as being non-existent in the postmodern world, but instead as "a means of mapping the world."[4]

> Utopia in the age of globalization, as I see it, does not exist in this world, whether in its spaces or its times. Utopia is neither an attempt to locate a spatially accessible other-place apart from the places in which we live nor a form of imagining a temporal other-time, whether in the past or the future. Rather, utopia in the present configuration can only be a method by which one can attempt to apprehend the system itself. To put it another way, utopia is a means of mapping the world. Utopia is an attempt to construct or project a totality, and in this I associate it closely with Jameson's concept of "cognitive mapping." As in that model, the utopian impulse reflects an effort to situate oneself in space and in history, imaginatively projecting a world that enables one to represent the apparently unrepresentable totality of the world system. This act of figuration comes across in utopian texts as a form of literary cartography.[5]

The dialectics of man and space: *The Years, Months, Days*

In Yan Lianke's fictional world, the utopian impulse to reconfigure the space and one's relation to it is a central driving force and sustaining faith for, on the narrative level, many of his characters as well as for, on the discursive, the author/narrator. Even in works like *The Years, Months, and Days*, which depict more apparently, quite opposite to a utopia, an apocalyptic world, one nevertheless finds persistent utopian attempts of man to re-situate himself in the space. It is a Robinson Crusoe-like human survival story set in a village of the Balou Mountain area. The village is struck by an unprecedented drought. When all people leave the village to avoid famine, only a 72-year-old man called the Elder decides to stay simply because he has found a corn seedling in his field and is assured he could rely on it to survive. His only accompanies are an old blind dog and the immature corn plant. From the very outset, the Elder's connection to his environment differs from the traditional ways in which one perceives his native soil. His reluctance to leave the village is justified neither by a tie to the ancestral land nor by the fear of the unknown outside world. Rather, it is the sign of life embodied in the corn plant that breathes in him a faith toward the space in which he lives.

---

4 Robert T. Tally, Jr., ed., *Utopia in the Age of Globalization: Space, Representation, and the World-System* (New York: Palgrave Macmillan, 2013), viii–ix.
5 Ibid., ix.

As the narrative unfolds, it revolves around how the Elder relentlessly seeks for food to feed himself and the dog and for water sources to raise the only living crop in the village. Situating the protagonist in, as Jamie Fisher suggests, "the minimal staging [that] recalls a Beckett play,"[6] Yan brings to the forefront human's awareness of space *as such* in that the village is almost as nameless and unlocalizable as the Beckettian space. For instance, early in the story, the initial awe by the fact that he is the only person left behind in the village infuses a strong feeling of spatial alienation in the Elder from the surrounding environment: "The Elder stood at the end of his field until they [the villagers] vanished from sight, at which point a feeling of solitude struck his heart with a thud. His entire body began to tremble, as he suddenly realized that he, a seventy-two-year-old man, was now the only living soul in the entire village—and perhaps even the entire mountain range. There was a vast emptiness in his heart, as a sense of stillness and desolation enveloped his body."[7]

Whereas the Elder is enveloped in the stillness and desolation that separate him from what is in sight, the same emptiness also intensifies his sensitivity toward the space per se, because the village now becomes the sole possible source for him to continue to live. For instance, as the Elder roams about the entire village in the hope of finding something to eat, this walking experience suddenly awakens him to the fact that every villager's door is locked. The realization of the inaccessibility to others' places not only leads to the heightened awareness of his vulnerable position in the environing milieu but also complicates his identification with people who once occupied these spaces. When he stands on the empty street, the Elder sees "the sun's rays shone down, flowing through the village like a river of gold."[8] Such an image of warmth and glitter falls immediately into stark contrast with the deathly silence he experiences in front of these doors, leaving a paradoxical impact on the Elder's psyche. On the one hand, the space for him is no more than an object outside his subjective experience, which he feels driven to deconstruct and conquer: "*Did all of you fucking lock your doors just to stymie me?*" He thinks to himself, "*I'll climb your walls and pry open your doors, and find who has left behind any grain.*"[9] On the other, the impetus to cause destruction to the space mystically disappears when he literally confronts each locked door: "The Elder stood in the doorway of one family's house. This house belonged to one of his nephews with whom he shared a surname."[10] The doorway of an old widow's compound further reminds him of his connectedness to these owners: "When the widow was younger, she would give the Elder a pair of thick-soled boots every winter. Now she was dead, and her son had inherited this compound. The thought of this house gave the Elder a warm feeling that lingered in his empty heart."[11] In the end, he makes it through the entire village leaving everything intact.

This whole episode adds profound meanings to the Elder's existence in spatial terms, resulting in a transcendence of the object-subject binary between space and human. In other words, the space, at least for this moment, no longer functions as a mere material source outside the subject for the sake of his survival. Not only does the space become internalized as a part of the Elder, because the blood relation and the nuanced romantic memory embodied in

---

6 Jamie Fisher, "In the Brutality of the Chinese Countryside, 'Mythorealism' Reigns," *The New York Times*, 26 Jan. 2018, https://www.nytimes.com/2018/01/26/books/review/years-months-days-yan-lianke.html.
7 Yan Lianke, *The Years, Months, Days*, trans. Carlos Rojas (New York: Black Cat, 2017), 7.
8 Ibid., 17.
9 Ibid.; translator's italics.
10 Ibid.
11 Ibid.

these village houses beat the hollowness in the Elder and make him a more complete person, but the Elder himself also becomes an integral part of the space in that his intimate joyful recollections reshape what seems at the beginning to be a desolate and alienating figure of the village into, if not hopeful, at least something humane. In short, this is a transcendental moment in which the human-space dialectic in the story is reversed. Rather than an inorganic object producing that which human consumes for the sake of living, space is integrated organically into man. As a result, the guarding of and fighting for the maintenance of the space itself become equally important for man as the survival of his own body.

Although the Elder eventually would have no choice but to pry open these doors for food later in the story, such transformation of the human-space dynamic recurs as the narrative continues and culminates symbolically in the figure of the corn plant. As days on the barren land pass by, the Elder has to hunt around the village and in the mountain range for food and water, thus covering more and more expansive spaces. In these adventures, man seems to have become increasingly capable in terms of fighting against and conquering the space as the Other, despite the extreme difficulty in finding even the most nauseating food. To survive, the Elder consumes whatever is available to him, from weed to mud and rats. But curiously, it never occurs to him to eat the slowly growing ear of corn. Although the Elder decides to stay in the village originally because he believes that the corn plant will become a sufficient food source, he does not for once refer to it as food in his conversations with the blind dog. Throughout the story, every food-hunting adventure of the Elder serves the end to water the corn plant. He shares his drinking water with it until the last drop, speaks to it just as he talks to the dog, and identifies with it as if the word "corn" does not merely mean a type of grain, but the name of a living thing like his, the Elder, and the dog's, Blindy. The corn plant is viewed as another companion, which would later be pushed to the stage center of the narrative and take over the role of the protagonist.

It may be conveniently interpreted that the corn plant serves as the last string of hope that sustains the Elder's will to survive. Consuming it may help the protagonist live longer for a day or two, but would undoubtedly knock him down both physically and mentally. However, such interpretation of the Elder's reluctance to consume the corn is human-centered. On the contrary, readers slowly witness a fundamental transformation of the Elder's life goal from being human-centered to space-centered. After he exhausts all possible things in the environing milieu and his space of activity shrinks to his own field, the corn's survival outweighs everything including the Elder's own life. In one of the most desperate moments when the Elder could find nothing but a bowl of water, he holds back from the urge to drink it and says to himself, "*I can't drink anymore. That last bowl is for the cornstalk.*"[12] In several conversations with the dog, the Elder repeatedly makes remarks that eventually either the dog will eat him and then live with the cornstalk, or otherwise he will eat the dog and then live with the cornstalk.[13] Instead of viewing the corn as the ultimate food supply for him to live, keeping himself alive now serves as a means for the sake of ensuring the corn to live. Close to the end of the story, the faith in the corn that it would enable himself to survive the drought turns into the faith that the corn will make the whole village live again. "*Within three days, you and I will be so famished that we won't even have the energy to utter a word,*" he says to the dog, "*At that point, if you want to survive, you'll need to consume me piece by piece. Then you must guard this cornstalk, so that when the other villagers return, you can lead them over and let them pick the ear*

---

12 Ibid., 70; translator's italics.
13 Ibid., 81.

of corn."[14] Here, the horror of human carnivorism by an animal gives way to the resolution of guarding a crop at every cost. Is this faith an ethically noble wish of an individual for the survival of the greater human species, which again is human-centered? Or is it the result of a more philosophical repositioning of human and space in that they now enter a symbiotic relation, becoming mutually more dependent and integral part of each other? An answer might be found in the Elder's eventual decision to subject himself completely as fertilizer for the corn plant. He digs his grave under the corn plant and lies down in it "against the side where the roots of the cornstalk were."[15] When the other villagers make it back home one year after the disaster, they find a strikingly deformed human body in the Elder's grave, depicted in extreme details in the following paragraph:

> Each of the stalk's roots resembles a long and thin vine, and had a pinkish tint. The roots were growing into the Elder's body through the holds in his chest, thighs, wrists, and abdomen. There were several red roots as thick as chopsticks growing right through the Elder's decayed body and into his skull, ribs, and arm and leg bones. There were several reddish-white tendrils growing into his eye sockets and poking out through the back of his skull, gripping the packed earth along the bottom of the grave. Every joint and every piece of flesh has been transformed into a web of roots, tightly linking his body to the cornstalk itself.[16]

Reflecting upon his reading experience with Yan's works, Chen Sihe 陳思和 remarks that Yan's grotesque and evocative but also graphically vivid depictions always elicit successfully a visceral discomfort as well as excitement in his readers: "Reading Yan Lianke's works whips violently a pain into my soul. I am more often than not caught in astonishment, coupled with bone-biting afflictions."[17] Chen continues, however, by noting somehow regretfully that such an exciting reading experience is usually followed by a feeling of unsatisfactory, because humans in Yan's stories seem forever subjugated to fate or an inevitable victimization with no way out.[18] Chen laments, for instance, that the Elder's endeavor in *The Years, Months, Days* is nothing more than a Sisyphean tragedy, because the seven young men who stay behind for the second year with the seven seeds found in the Elder's corn at the end of the story "will evidently undergo another round of the same suffering."[19] Chen's interpretation, however, is clearly human-centered and justified by the subject-object binary of man versus space and, above all, pessimistic. But looking more closely at the passage quoted above from *The Years, Months, Days*, readers would find a highly vigorous scene of the space in itself. In this scene, the decay of the human body is organically absorbed and integrated into a much broader dimension, in which a robust cornstalk, with its thick vine-like roots and gripping tendrils, continues to grow and will surely expand to larger spaces. In short, man, standing alive or buried dead, is given a greater possibility in terms of his spatialized existence.

---

14 Ibid., 82; translator's italics.
15 Ibid., 93.
16 Ibid., 96.
17 Chen Sihe, "Du Yan Lianke de xiaoshuo zhaji zhi yi" 讀閻連科的小說劄記之一 [A note on reading Yan Lianke's fiction], in *Dangdai zuojia pinglun* 當代作家評論 [Contemporary writers review], 2001, no. 3: 44; my translation.
18 Ibid., 44–46.
19 Ibid., 46; my translation.

Overall, in *The Years, Months, Days*, there are two layers of utopian attempts in mapping the world. First, it is the Elder's original endeavor to keep himself alive in a deserted space destroyed both by nature and humans. In this sense, man is produced and cultivated by space because the latter is experienced as a material source for the sake of the former's survival. As a result, space is that which the human subject desires to discipline, overcome, and conquer. Second, it is the Elder's faith in keeping a seed of hope, which is embodied in the corn plant. Man, instead of being influenced by and dependent upon the environment, becomes a member of it and serves to ensure its survival. As the first layer of utopian cognitive mapping is gradually overwritten by the second in the story, Yan appeals to a reflective understanding of the human-space dynamic in our times, such as that of the Great Leap Forward in Maoist China, which clearly is alluded to as the story's historical background. The story, of course, could also be a harbinger for the foreseeable future of the world, which brings to the fore questions including though not limited to the following: Are there alternative ways for man to view his connection to space? By integrating into space rather than surveilling, navigating, and consuming it as an alienated object, what could the prospect of man be like?

Utopian space in the loss of time: *The Explosion Chronicles*

Yan's novella *The Years, Months, Days* recalls a Beckettian-style monodrama and closes with an evidently surrealistic ending. However, compared to his other works in the Balou Mountain series, it is a more realistic story in the conventional sense, tinged here and there by his characteristic mythorealism. Yan's novels set in the Balou Mountain present readers with cognitive maps featured by much more convoluted and absurd utopian attempts. Moreover, these utopian desires and endeavors in Yan's work contradict, ridicule, overwrite, and nullify one another or even themselves. *The Explosion Chronicles* originally published in 2013, among many others, is one of Yan's latest novels in the Balou series.

Before moving on to a close reading of the utopian world Yan creates in *The Explosion Chronicles*, I should note again that utopia in this chapter is understood as, in Tally's terms, a utopian impulse to (re-)project the world and one's position in it.[20] Two things are worth noting in this conceptualization. First, utopia does not refer to a concrete place, society, or state. Second, a utopian impulse is not necessarily ideal for everyone, at least not a universally recognized or unanimously appreciated way of thinking. In other words, utopia is relative, thus it could be problematic and inherently paradoxical, depending on whose perspective about the world and man's situation in this world the utopian thinking is subject to. *The Explosion Chronicles* is indeed an exemplary work that problematizes various utopian attempts and calls for alternative imaginations in the context of post-socialist China.

The novel is written as a double-layered narrative. Its central storyline is an account of the breathtaking transformation of an impoverished community called Explosion into a megalopolis during the post-Mao reform era. The actual story about Explosion's history is framed within a metanarrative written by a fictional Yan Lianke in the form of chronicles, informed by a traditional Chinese historical genre *fangzhi* 方志 or "local gazetteer." Explosion's growth involves three clans—the Kong family, the Zhu family, and the Cheng family—whose histories are intricately tied with one another. The key character Kong Mingliang, a rapacious and corrupted government official, is obsessed with numerous ambitious, sometimes insane, plans to reconstruct this rural community into a town, a county, a city, and a provincial-level

---

20 Tally, *Utopia in the Age of Globalization*, ix.

megalopolis. Implementation of these blueprints serves as a means for Kong to rise to power in political and economic senses. In the early years of China's economic reform, for instance, he leads the Explosion residents to steal, "to unload," as they call it, from cargo trains passing the mountain regions and sell the haul of goods to make fortunes. As a result, Explosion becomes a town-level community and Mingliang, as it is promised by his superior, is promoted as its head. His three brothers are given increasingly pivotal positions in the governmental offices, state-owned corporations, or education institutions so as to facilitate his aggressive schemes. In general, Explosion's incessant development and expansion mirror what one witnesses in many of the emerging Chinese metropolises during the economic reform since the 1980s. Floods of migrant workers are sent off into all corners of urban China to make money, the majority of whom, in Explosion's case, are women laborers trained by Mingliang's wife Zhu Ying and his mistress Cheng Jing to work as prostitutes or household servants. Coupled with the outsourcing of local laborers is the acquisition of state and foreign investments into Explosion to build factories, shopping malls, business centers, and subways.

Although a realistic reference is apparently made to contemporary China's conversion to economic capitalism in the novel, artistically it is Yan's another mythorealistic experiment with absurd, fantastical, surrealistic means of expressions to represent the real world underlined by his characteristic social and political sarcasm. The speed at which the community develops, for instance, is not measured by years but by months, days, minutes, and even literally a blink of eye in the story. Using his idiosyncratic literary rhetoric, the author depicts the overwhelmingly fast changes as visually impossible to be captured. Instead, they leave an auditory impact like explosives. "Once this [signing a secret oath about their 'train unloading' practice] was done, the village made a 'boom' sound and became rich."[21] Time is compressed the most for the sake of development, when Mayor Kong promises in front of an observational delegation from Beijing that he can build a one-hundred-kilometer subway line and the largest airport in Asia in less than a week. Such fetishization of speed and of the compressed temporality in a highly quantifiable fashion is subject to Yan's social critique, which symbolizes essentially the capitalist greed for power and state authoritarianism. "Yan satirizes the tactical aspect of speed," Cao Xuenan remarks, "presenting the rate of development as nothing but a bargaining chip for political power."[22] Cao further notes: "Mirroring the grandeur of China's development plans, Yan pushes the rhetoric of scientific precision to its extreme by having all projections be realized, no matter how far-fetched."[23] Time is warped in Explosion, to such an extent that a rational perception of temporality by the fictional characters, maybe also true for the readers, is overall missing in the story because changes take place too fast and time is reduced to nonsensical numbers. People no longer understand what "a short/long time" means. The most symbolic message about time is in the final episode when all Explosion residents clear from their houses clocks that mysteriously cease to work. Here, time stops, disappears, or is erased completely. It is impossible, in temporal terms, that one can find a solid meaning for his existence.

Whereas the Explosion residents seem to be seized *uniformly* in a whirlpool of meaningless time thanks to a fanatical addiction to speed, their spatialized awareness and practices are more varied. The narrative presents for readers diverse spatialized utopian attempts from

---

21 Yan Lianke, *Zhalie zhi* 炸裂志 [The explosion chronicles] (Shanghai: Shanghai wenyi chubanshe, 2013), 16; my translation.
22 Cao Xuenan, "Mythorealism and Enchanted Time: Yan Lianke's *Explosion Chronicles*," *Frontiers of Literary Studies in China* 10, no. 1 (May 2016): 107.
23 Ibid., 108.

varying perspectives of the fictional characters. However, it also unveils brutally the true side of reality that ridicules, problematizes, and discredits these utopian endeavors. In other words, Yan offers readers from within the novel symptomatic interpretations of the multiple spatialized experiences and, therefore, appeals to alternative possibilities for human and space. Mayor Kong, the master planner for the community, indeed justifies his existential meaning in Explosion almost exclusively depending upon his utopian cognitive mapping of an incessantly growing and hence empowering urban landscape. He is obsessed with the idea of leading the Explosion community to prosperity and making it to an upper tier of municipality, from a village to a provincial-level megalopolis. Yan's mythorealism pushes this ambition of subjugating the space to such extremes that Mayor Kong is deified in the story as the Creator. His speech and actions have power over not only humans but also nature. In one fantastical moment that strongly reminds readers of the rain-summoning rituals, villagers use an old yellowish piece of paper with Kong's signature, an allusion to the yellow-colored Daoist charm paper, to pray for snow. The villagers kneel down, wave the paper in the air, and chant that it is the mayor who is calling for snow. Snowflakes soon fill the air and fall onto the uncultivated fields.[24] The following scenario takes place after Mayor Kong hears discouraging news about his scheme to develop Explosion city into a megalopolis: "He stared at that flowerpot and suddenly had an evil thought. He wanted to stamp on that rosebush, but it had a single blossom, and the rest was only green leaves. When he went over and lifted his foot to stomp on that single rose, the flowerpot suddenly didn't have any green leaves left and instead, in the blink of an eye, dozens of red roses had bloomed, resembling layers upon layers of flames."[25]

However, underlying these utopian cognitive mapping of one's position in the space are ironic facts, rendering the seemingly well-intentioned utopia ridiculous. First, Kong's dream to expand Explosion is not at all some noble wish for the well-being of the community but, as noted earlier, for the sake of his own political and economic upward mobility. Second, from its initial transformation to a town and later to a megalopolis, the ways in which Explosion flourishes and measurements for its prosperity are expected to resemble, in its master designer's vision, any other big cities in China. Throughout the narrative, the newly emergent urban site is and has always been buttressed by two elements, industrial expansion and legitimization of prostitution, associated with losses of the rural land. When Explosion is re-designated as a town, for instance, a remapping of the space is conducted simply by packaging the local businesses with copycat names from other places such as the provincial cities in the south, with an attempt to either camouflage the place's nature as a brothel or give it a more appealing register. "For instance, if a sign read ZHANG FAMILY LOCKSMITH, it would have to be changed to read EXPLOSION TOWN LOCK CITY, and if a sign read WANG FAMILY SEWING, it would be changed to read EXPLOSION TOWN SEWING WORLD."[26] In other words, Kong's imagination about each new municipality is in essence based on a *lack* of imagination. Here, history is spatialized as the past and the present are convened into one space, but this particular space is banally flattened. Instead of producing the cartography of a new world and re-situating man in it, this utopia simply unveils symptomatically an image of homogeneity that features the urbanization process in the context of a capitalized and globalized China. The third and most ironic dimension in Kong's schemes is their resulting

---

24 Yan Lianke, *The Explosion Chronicles*, trans. Carlos Rojas (New York: Grove Press, 2016), 350.
25 Ibid., 420.
26 Ibid., 132; translator's capitalization.

polarizing impact on space and man. Despite his grandeur projection of Explosion to eventually grow into a provincial-level megalopolis, its desolate past lingers on stubbornly. When Explosion city is established, its reality and history are completely split as the urban space does.

On account of this tension between reality and history, Explosion's old streets and the new city become divided into two distinct worlds: "The city's east side, west side, and development zone extended along the river, where new buildings stretched out like a multicolored forest. The glass surface of the buildings made the temperature in the city center always several degrees warmer than in the suburbs. Meanwhile, in the old city area, where there was a street named Explosion Street, there was barely anyone at all apart from a handful of people who came for sightseeing [thanks to the mayor's old house and some abandoned constructions marked as cultural relic]."[27] Further reading the story, readers would find more shocking contrast between the dilapidated houses on the ghostly old streets, now inhabited by old and poor Explosion residents including the mayor's mother, and Mayor Kong's own extravagantly built house in the center of the garden-like courtyard of the city government with multiple halls, rooms, annexes, and corridors fenced by a vast wall. These spatialized contrasts are exemplary resonance to what one witnesses on the path of contemporary China's modernization. Rather than a total economic and social mobility, "a lucky minority have the power to seize resources, and the rest may be physically, economically, and socially displaced in the process."[28]

Mayor Kong's cognitive mapping is one of the many test cases in *The Explosion Chronicles*, which problematizes the nature of utopian thinking that emerges in post-socialist China's modernity, inherently marked by capitalism. An alternative case that tests the liminality of other possible utopian attempts in contemporary China is embodied, among various others, in Mayor Kong's younger brother Kong Mingyao. He also shows a heightened sensitivity toward space in his self-identification. An unfulfilled soldier for most of his army life, however, Mingyao is quickly appointed by Mayor Kong as the president of a state-owned mining corporation upon his return to town. Despite the wealth and power he enjoys, Mingyao is long disturbed by a subtle regret for leaving the army early. For the sake of self-consolation, he hires veterans as his employees, trains them like active soldiers, and even founds a secret army of his own in the remote corner of Balou Mountain a hundred miles away from Explosion.

Mingyao's utopian cognitive mapping of space is a Quixotic one, which is predetermined to be hilariously absurd but also devastating in terms of its consequence. His office in the mining company, for instance, is furnished more luxuriously than a general's war room. It is ornamented by globe and sand tables containing maps of the world, on which socialist countries and capitalist countries are painted in contrasting colors of red and black. Mingyao's spatialized sense is most hyperbolically embodied in the secret military base he establishes. What La Mancha is to Don Quixote is Balou Mountain to Kong Mingyao. The desolate grassland deep in the mountain that he sees is not what it truly is, but a battlefield for his navy. And they literally conduct naval drills on the sea-like grass field, using real cannons and fleets purchased with money Commander Kong makes (probably embezzles) from the mining corporation. Their objective is to one day defeat the Japanese as well as the US fleets and land on the US west coast whenever they want. For Mingyao, space is registered as an interface of conflicts, in this case, that of international ones. This allows him to project what he believes

---

27 Ibid., 323.
28 Jason McGrath, "Apocalypse, or, the Logic of Late Anthropocene Ruins," *Cross-Currents: East Asian History and Culture Review*, no. 10 (Mar. 2014): 114.

to be a nationalistic and patriotic self-identification. Situated at the center of these conflicts, his occupation of the space is understood to be an indication of the victory of nationalism, possibly over cosmopolitanism and globalization. Whereas it is worth noting that Mayor Kong's urbanization utopia is precisely a manifestation, though undoubtedly kitsch, of the ideal of cosmopolitanism. In this sense, it might not be difficult to understand the seemingly unfathomable ending of the story, that is, Mingyao suggests that Explosion will become an independent state and murders his brother Mayor Kong after his army invades the city government.

However, Mingyao's effort of using the historical conflict between China and former imperialist states to map the real outside world and his position in it is doomed to be a failed attempt. In fact, rather than reviving the spirit of nationalism that is dominant in republican and socialist China, his proposal for Explosion to become an independent state with him as its potential commander-in-chief paradoxically betrays his imperialist ambition. Moreover, underlying Mingyao's spatialized utopia is his frustration as a mediocre soldier back in the army and his unfulfilled responsibilities due to early retirement from the military. Viewed from this perspective, the utopia which calls for selfless patriotism is reduced to nothing but a compensation for his loss as a result of an incomplete personal history. Lastly, like Don Quixote, Mingyao is confused between the real and the fictional. Just as Sancho disenchants the knight hero from fighting the windmill giant, Mingyao's bubble of individual heroism is also pricked broken by the fact that the tranquil mountain is the farthest from a world war battlefield to make this ideal happen. His projection of space is indeed a literal "cognitive map."

With regard to personal heroism, nothing in the story problematizes the conceptualization of it more than Explosion's cartographical transformation through the construction of landmarks like memorial monuments and tombstones. These monuments and stone steles are spatialized utopian attempts to situate personal heroism at the center of a society and its history. However, personal heroism acquires varied and, in some cases, conflicting meanings from these symbolic constructions. More ironic is the fact that these incongruent symbols are often confusingly placed in juxtaposition by the Explosion residents. The first tombstone in the story, for instance, is erected for Zhu Ying's father, posthumously Mayor Kong's father-in-law. His death sounds like an impossible one, because he is drowned in villagers' spit, who are payed to do so by the then village head Kong Mingliang in order to settle the feud between their two families. Kong then allows Zhu Ying to bury her father in the center of the village square, and orders to leave an inscription on the gravestone: "TOMB OF THE MOST LOYAL OLD COMMUNIST, ZHU QINGFANG."[29] The inscription exemplifies the post-Mao representation of heroic models that bear strong Confucian moralism, which emphasizes an individual's connection to the state such as being loyal to it.[30] But such sublime orientation is completely deconstructed by reality. Is loyalty truly celebrated here? Does "old communist" refer to Mr. Zhu's long age or his being out-of-date? This kind of inherent paradox marks almost every memorial structure in the story. For instance, sixteen marble tombstones are erected in the center of the Explosion square for those who are killed in accidents when they "steal/unload" goods from trains. They are entitled as martyrs for people to emulate. When Zhu Ying returns to Explosion with tremendous fortune and opportunities for village

---

29 Yan, *The Explosion Chronicles*, 27.
30 Kirk A. Denton, *Exhibiting the Past: Historical Memory and the Politics of Museums in Postsocialist China* (Honolulu: University of Hawai'i Press, 2014), 155.

girls to work with her as prostitutes in other cities, villagers build her a stone monument at the entrance of the village to commemorate her contributions. It reads "TO GET RICH, LEARN FROM EXPLOSION/TAKE ZHU YING AS A MODEL."[31] Without any doubt, Mayor Kong has his own distinctive memorial structure, a bronze statue of him on a tall pedestal. Inscribed on its base is the word *"Trailblazer."*[32]

While these various utopian cognitive maps overwrite one another or are revealed as self-paradoxical, Yan provides readers with a once-for-all deconstruction of them by enveloping the story of Explosion in a metanarrative, a book of chronicles written by a fictional Yan Lianke. The narrator constantly reminds readers of the absurdity in these attempts. By noting that the content of his book is confronted with denial and is burnt by the furious Mayor Kong, the narrator raises readers' curiosity and suspicion as well as calls to attention the necessity to read and re-read it in order to find about the truth. "Dear readers," the fictional Yan Lianke writes in the prefatory chapter, "I have recorded all of this, though ordinarily it should not have been made public, just as a gentleman should not air his dirty laundry." He continues: "Go ahead and read it, and curse me."[33] If all those in Explosion are enchanted in the utopian cognitive maps they fabricate for themselves, there is at least a clear-minded narrator who is capable of creating a space for self-reflection and criticism.

In other words, what author Yan envisions as a possible alternative to these problematized utopian attempts in *The Explosion Chronicles* lies precisely in this narrator who, like a real martyr, voluntarily puts himself onto the execution ground. "You may curse me to death and drown me in an ocean of spittle—but before you bury me," the narrator writes, "I have but one request, like a criminal sentenced to death who wishes to make a final statement: Read these chronicles! Even if you read only a few pages, it will be as if you deposited a flower on my grave!"[34]

At the end of "My Old Home" ("Guxiang" 故鄉) Lu Xun closes with his version of a utopian cognitive mapping of space: "As I dozed, a stretch of jade-green seashore spread itself before my eyes, and above a round golden moon hung from a deep blue sky. I thought hope cannot be said to exist, nor can it be said not to exist. It is just like roads across the earth. For actually the earth had no roads to begin with, but when many men pass one way, a road is made."[35] It seems, from Lu Xun to Yan Lianke, writing about the native land is always an endeavor to look for the possible out of the impossible, the hopeful out of the disenchanted, and the utopian out of the dystopian.

Bibliography

Cao, Xuenan. "Mythorealism and Enchanted Time: Yan Lianke's *Explosion Chronicles*." *Frontiers of Literary Studies in China* 10, no. 1 (May 2016): 103–12.

Chen Sihe 陳思和. "Du Yan Lianke de xiaoshuo zhaji zhi yi" 讀閻連科的小說劄記之一[A note on reading Yan Lianke's fiction]. *Dangdai zuojia pinglun* 當代作家評論 [Contemporary writers review], 2001, no. 3: 44–47.

Denton, Kirk A. *Exhibiting the Past: Historical Memory and the Politics of Museums in Postsocialist China*. Honolulu: University of Hawai'i Press, 2014.

---

31 Yan, *The Explosion Chronicles*, 55.
32 Ibid., 267.
33 Ibid., 2–3.
34 Ibid., 3.
35 Lu Xun, "My Old Home," in *Lu Xun: Selected Works*, trans. Yang Xianyi and Gladys Yang, vol. 1 (Beijing: Foreign Languages Press, 1980), 101.

Fisher, Jamie. "In the Brutality of the Chinese Countryside, 'Mythorealism' Reigns." *The New York Times*, 26 Jan. 2018. https://www.nytimes.com/2018/01/26/books/review/years-months-days-yan-lianke.html (last accessed 31 July 2021).

Jameson, Fredric. *Postmodernism, or, the Cultural Logic of Late Capitalism*. Durham: Duke University Press, 1991.

Lu Xun 魯迅. "My Old Home." In *Lu Xun: Selected Works*, translated by Yang Xianyi and Gladys Yang, 1: 90–101. Beijing: Foreign Languages Press, 1980.

———. "Preface to *Zhongguo xinwenxue daxi (xiaoshuo er ji)* 中國新文學大系（小說二集） [Compendium of modern Chinese literature: fiction II]." In *Lu Xun quanji* 魯迅全集 [Complete works of Lu Xun], 6: 246–74. Beijing: Renmin wenxue chubanshe, 2005.

McGrath, Jason. "Apocalypse, or, the Logic of Late Anthropocene Ruins." *Cross-Currents: East Asian History and Culture Review*, no. 10 (Mar. 2014): 113–19.

Tally, Robert T., Jr., ed. *Utopia in the Age of Globalization: Space, Representation, and the World-System*. New York: Palgrave Macmillan, 2013.

Yan, Lianke. *The Explosion Chronicles*. Translated by Carlos Rojas. New York: Grove Press, 2016.

———. *Yan Lianke wenlun* 閻連科文論 [Yan Lianke's essays on literature]. Kunming: Yunnan renmin chubanshe, 2013.

———. *The Years, Months, Days*. Translated by Carlos Rojas. New York: Black Cat, 2017.

———. *Zhalie zhi* 炸裂志 [The explosion chronicles]. Shanghai: Shanghai wenyi chubanshe, 2013.

21
AN ECOCRITICAL APPROACH TO YAN LIANKE'S LITERARY WORKS

Minh Thương Nguyễn Thi and Riccardo Moratto[*]

Introduction

Yan Lianke 閻連科 is one of the most prolific writers in contemporary Chinese literature. His work addresses many broad and profound issues affecting reality, society, and history, as well as mankind's harsh struggle for survival. Yan is also ranked among the few authors who have formulated a specific literary conception with the proposal of the theory of "mythorealism" (*shenshi zhuyi* 神實主義), which has had a profound influence both in China and in the Western world.[1] The complexity and diversity of his literary works have drawn much scholarly attention. To date, there have been numerous studies on his works from the perspective of realism, mythorealism, life, survival, death, disease, humanity, love, ethics, etc. However, research from the perspective of ecocriticism has not been thoroughly explored. Aside from *House No. 711* (*711 hao yuan: Beijing zuihou de zuihou jinian* 711 號園: 北京最後的最後紀念),[2] which may be considered an ecological essay, his important novels all pose issues worth reflecting on and focus on the relationship between mankind and nature. This chapter approaches Yan's literary works from the perspective of ecocriticism and attempts to explore the ecological dimension in his literary creation through the issues of ecological ethics, ecological philosophy, and ecological aesthetics.

The rise of ecological thought

Eastern culture emphasizes the philosophical view of "unity between Heaven and man" (*Tian ren he yi* 天人合一), while Western culture focuses more on the opposition between human and nature. However, due to the deterioration of the ecological environment, Eastern traditional cultures have increasingly paid attention to ecological issues over the last decades, and this trend has become the theoretical root for the development of modern ecological thought.

---

[*] An earlier version of this chapter first appeared in Vietnamese in Minh Thương Nguyễn Thi, "Tư tưởng sinh thái trong sáng tác của Diêm Liên Khoa" [The Ecological Thought in Yan Lianke's Creation], *Tạp chí nghiên cứu văn học* [Literary Research Journal], August 2021, no. 8: 91–101. Minh Thương Nguyễn Thi is authorized to reuse and modify the paper. Several changes have been made in the current version.
1 For studies on "mythorealism," see the first section of this volume.
2 The title of the simplified Chinese version is *Beijing, zuihou de jinian* 北京, 最后的纪念.

The ecological conception in the thought of "unity between Heaven and man" comes from a society where agriculture was at its center; thus, in time, the relationship between Heaven, earth, and mankind has become a central issue that Eastern philosophy is particularly interested in. The "unity between Heaven and man" reflects the harmony between human as the subject and the world as the object, as well as the method of handling the relationship between human and nature, which tends to pursue an ideal living environment and affirms that human society progresses through co-existing in harmony with nature. Therefore, such a notion carries the spirit of humanism and has played an important role in the development of modern ecological culture. Confucianism and Daoism both emphasize the "unity between Heaven and man." However, the difference lies in the fact that Confucianism encourages humans to be active, while Daoism stresses that human beings must follow the laws of nature.

In the early modern period, along with the development of science and technology, Western people asserted their place in the world and formed the notion of "anthropocentrism," a human-centered *Weltanschauung*. The core of anthropocentrism is that man gives himself the right to conquer nature, to force nature to serve him, and sees the conquest of nature as a way to prove his values. Anthropocentrism is one of the root causes of the severe destruction of our environment. Therefore, the concept of "ecocentrism," one that does not take humans as the center, has appeared as a counterweight to protest against satisfying the self-interest of mankind, to deny the thought that man is the most important entity in the universe and to advise that humans must respect nature as well as the right to survive and the values of other non-human beings. The central part of this thought is: all beings in this world have the right to survive and thrive; however, if such a development exceeds the limit, it will eventually lead to extinction. Generally speaking, ecocentrism is consistent with the objective nature and laws of the world.[3] This thought can also be found in the works of Rousseau, who criticized the conquest and overpowering of nature as well as the lust, science, technology, and industrial civilization and praised a simple, back-to-nature lifestyle.[4]

Ecology is interested in how humans treat the right to survive of other beings. Ecological thought abandons the view that man is the conqueror and supports the belief that man is just an ordinary member of the ecosystem. In this system, each individual is an indispensable part, humans and other beings are equal in terms of survival rights and together create the sustainable development of the ecosystem. "Ecological holism advocates that ecological aesthetics is a harmonious unity between human beings and nature, human beings and society, and human beings and themselves, rather than human beings possessing, conquering, and transforming nature. It does not advocate the idea that labor creates beauty."[5]

Over the last decades, there have been numerous movies, TV shows, novels, poems, essays, and paintings focusing on ecological issues. These artistic works mainly express the love for nature or tragic scenes due to natural disasters or epidemics. Ecological literature seems to

---

[3] See Klaus Bosselmann, *When Two Worlds Collide: Society and Ecology* (Auckland: RSVP Publishing, 1999); Robyn Eckersley, *Environmentalism and Political Theory: Toward an Ecocentric Approach* (New York: State University of New York Press, 1992); Ned Hettinger and Bill Throop, "Refocusing Ecocentrism: De-Emphasizing Stability and Defending Wilderness," *Environmental Ethics* 21(1999): 3–21.

[4] Wang Nuo 王諾, *Ou Mei shengtai piping* 歐美生態批評 [European and American ecocriticism] (Shanghai: Xuelin chubanshe, 2008).

[5] Ji Qingben 季慶本, "Cong shengtai meixue kan shijian meixue" 從生態美學看實踐美學 [Practical aesthetics from ecological aesthetics], in *Zhongwai shengtai wenxue wenlun xuan* 中外生態文學文論選 [Selected literary essays on Chinese and foreign ecology], ed. Jing Yaping 荊亞平 (Hangzhou: Zhejiang gongshang daxue chubanshe, 2010), 148. All citations are translated by the authors unless otherwise specified.

remind humans to love and fear nature, as well as to raise our ecological awareness, improve our ecological culture and the sense of protecting the ecosystem. Western romantic literature also has many works praising nature and a quiet and wholesome life. Notably, William Wordsworth, a British romantic poet, composed numerous poems to praise nature and spring. Henry David Thoreau with his book *Walden* predicted the scourge brought by the industrial revolution due to its destruction of nature, as well as discovered the essence of the human-nature relationship. Meanwhile, the books *The Machine in the Garden: Technology and the Pastoral Ideal in America* by Leo Marx and *The Country and the City* by Raymond Williams both describe the complex development of attitude towards nature and the urban landscape. Not falling behind Western ecological literature, Chinese ecological literature has also flourished. Notable writers in contemporary Chinese literature, who have written numerous works that are rich in ecological elements, include Jia Pingwa 賈平凹, with *Wolves of Yesterday* (*Huainian lang* 懷念狼) and *The Lantern Bearer* (*Dai deng* 帶燈), Jiang Rong 姜戎 with *Wolf Totem* (*Lang tuteng* 狼圖騰), Zhang Wei 張煒 with *The Ancient Ship* (*Gu chuan* 古船) and *September's Fable* (*Jiuyue yuyan* 九月寓言), just to mention a few.

Man destroys the ecosystem and himself

Yan has written numerous influential novels. His novels do not necessarily fall in the category of country life and ecological literature, but hidden in the complex storylines are many ecological issues and themes. It can be said that his novels "are not really ecological literature but contain a strong ecological consciousness."[6]

Dream of Ding Village (*Dingzhuang meng* 丁莊夢) is a tragic story about a village, where people sell their blood to escape poverty. At that time, this activity was equal to selling AIDS, a disease that caused people to die "like falling leaves." The sale of blood, in defiance of all the principles of minimal hygiene and sanitation, directly changed the natural ecosystem in Ding village. The once clear pond is used in the novel as the place to wash the blood bags and turns into a bloody pond. The frogs in this pond used to sing like frogs elsewhere, with rhythms like flute and zither. But now, their cry is as harsh as the sound of clashing metal, their white belly turns dark red and is one and a half times the size of a normal frog's. Even the mosquitoes by the pond grow bigger, and the flapping of their wings resembles that of butterflies. The environment is completely changed and becomes stagnant and deadly due to devastating human actions. The rampant blood selling has changed the environment, making it monstrous and haunting.[7]

Dream of Ding Village has two intertwined storylines of dream and reality. The events occurring in Ding Shuiyang's dreams are magically connected to reality. In other words, the dream world extends and expands the dimensions of the real world. One of his haunting dreams is the one about the villagers of Ding cutting down trees to make coffins. Starting with the words from Zhao Dequan that people in the village are chopping down the trees, and that there won't be any left by the morning, Ding Shuiyang enters his dream, which is filled with the scent of white sawdust and the horrifying buzz of saws slicing timbers and the thud of axes chopping trees. People are excitedly cutting down the trees like they once did to

---

6 Van Hieu Do, "Shengtai piping de kequxing" 生態批評的可取性 [The plausibility of ecocriticsm], *Wenyi piping* 文藝批評 [Literary criticism], Sep. 2016: 45.
7 This section is a paraphrase of certain parts of the book and not a direct translation. Since *Dream of Ding Village* was banned in mainland China, the first author of this chapter, Minh Thương Nguyễn Thi, had to rely on an electronic draft version provided by Yan Lianke himself to translate this book into Vietnamese. Therefore, the printed page numbers are not available.

smelt the steel for constructing irrigation works. All of Ding Shuiyang's efforts to stop them are in vain, and every word he utters seems meaningless, as they are countered by the immoral actions of his own son. Ding Hui cheated the villagers and sold all the coffins distributed to them, so now they have to cut down the trees to make their own coffins. Each tree becomes raw material to make coffins, the containers of corpses. The chopping of trees thus becomes a symbol of the act of bringing people to death. The fact that people cut down trees means that they are killing themselves and destroying their own lives. Therefore, it is not coincidental that Yan describes the fact that the people of Ding village cut down the trees not as an ordinary labor, but as the execution of the death sentence for an innocent life. Moreover, that death sentence is carried out in a straightforward manner, with the announcement stamped by the village committee and the excitement of the executioners. From an ecological perspective, it can be seen that both consciously and unconsciously, man has given himself the right to destroy the environment and to force the trees to submit to his own needs. The sounds of trees being cut down roll back and forth like a cruel highlight in the dream. After only one night, there are no more trees in Ding village. The spring sun shines warm as usual, but without foliage or the shade of trees, the village feels scorching and unpleasant. This is an omen signaling a catastrophic drought that will happen soon.

The environment is only healthy when all species live together according to the principle of symbiosis, in which human is just a species among other species instead of the lord of nature. All foolish and subjective reformation of nature is doomed to fail. Like *Dream of Ding Village*, the novel *Streams of Time* (*Riguang liunian* 日光流年) deeply expresses Yan's ecological view about the foolish impact of mankind on nature.

In *Streams of Time*, the people of Sanxing Village suffer from a mysterious hereditary disease called "throat block syndrome" (*houduzheng* 喉堵症). Sanxing literally means three surnames, as the village was established by the three clans of Sima, Du, and Lan. In the late Ming dynasty and early Qing period, due to war and natural disasters, the three clans of Lan, Du, and Sima fled from their hometowns in Shandong, Shanxi, and Shaanxi, respectively, to the wild Balou 耙耧 Mountains, where they reclaimed the land and established a village. At first, they were like other people who lived up to the age of 60 and sometimes even 80. However, over many generations, their life expectancy sharply decreased and everyone's life expectancy would not exceed 40 years. When a person with this strange and incurable disease has swollen throat and vomits blood, s/he has set one foot out of the living realm, and death will approach as lightly as falling asleep. The people of the village grow up in that cursed environment, and they attempt to break the curse under the guidance of the village chiefs. The first village chief, Du Guaizi, encourages people to have many children. He believes that as long as there are many newborn children, living past 40 would not be a problem. However, this has no effect other than increasing the population. The second village chief, Sima Xiaoxiao, is naive enough to believe the words uttered by the elderly he met, who said that they have been eating rapeseed for generations, which is the secret of their long life. He encourages the villagers to grow rapeseed on a large scale. Even when a locust plague happens, he still orders people to sacrifice the food crops to keep the rapeseed, leading to a terrible famine. The third village chief, Lan Baisui, sees that the efforts of his predecessors were all in vain, and thinks that the problem may lie in the soil. He then mobilizes the villagers to turn up the topsoil of the entire village. Lan Baisui hopes that the crops grown on the new soil can cure the illness, but no matter how hard he tries, that wish cannot be fulfilled. All hopes then rest on the fourth village chief, Sima Lan, who believes that fate cannot be changed just by relying on the inner strength of the village. Thus, he kicks off the big project of digging the Lingyin canal to lead water from 40 miles away down to the village. This is the third time that

Sanxing villagers attempt to change nature. According to Sima Lan, if people drink the water from this canal, they can fulfill their wish to increase their life expectancy. After numerous efforts, the Lingyin canal is completed, but what it brings is not the fresh and sacred water they expected. Instead, the water reeks of the stench from garbage and dead rats. So, three generations of Sanxing people grew rapeseed, plowed the land, and channeled the water from the canal, but all of their efforts were futile. This also implies the complete failure of humans in their confrontation with nature. In order to break the deadly curse, Sanxing villagers try everything they can, even deploying the most cruel and painful options. To till more than 400 acres of land in 50–60 years, it takes a type of improved vehicle equivalent to ten healthy workers. They can make the trunk, but the wheels have to be bought. And the money to buy the wheels is earned from the skin on the thighs of the men in each family. Men and women have to sell their bodies in order to dig the canal and save their lives. Sima Lan mobilizes the entire village to build the canal, which leads to the death of 18 people. Meanwhile, six die from selling their own skin, and the women have to engage in prostitution more than 30 times, but after all this, what they get is just polluted and unusable water, which causes Sima Lan to break down and eventually die.

Yan skillfully integrates the tragic fate of the people in the Balou Mountains into the harsh natural environment. In such a context, people fight against nature to overcome the limits of their fate, thereby building the images of heroes in the struggle against nature and highlighting their greatness and tragedy. Despite being so heroic, why did the people of Sanxing village fail? The resistance to the tragic fate that befell them forces the villagers to go head-to-head with nature and use various methods to improve the natural environment and achieve a semblance of normal life. The natural environment on the Balou Mountains is the fundamental factor that determines their fate, so in order to change it, they must start with transforming nature. With *Streams of Time*, Yan has made readers realize that man cannot conquer nature. The harmony between human and nature is the only way for mankind to reproduce and survive. When humans fight against fate, they seem to end up in tragedy. A Chinese critic has pointed out: "The struggle of people like Sima Lan is a non-ecological struggle waged by a non-ecological fighting method in a non-ecological environment."[8] The fight for the survival of Sanxing Village is led by the blindness and the absurd will of their chiefs, causing them to act contrary to the laws of natural development. In such a confrontation with nature, the villagers fight desperately. This is Yan's profound reflection on the potential consequences of anthropocentrism. "The core idea of ecological holism is to consider the overall benefit of the ecosystem as the highest value rather than the benefit of human beings as the highest value, and to consider whether it is conducive to maintaining and protecting the perfect, harmonious, stable, and sustainable existence of the ecosystem as the fundamental measure of everything, and as the ultimate criterion for judging human lifestyles, technological progress, economic growth, and social development."[9]

The destruction that mankind brings upon the environment causes serious consequences. In *The Four Books* (*Si shu* 四書), people hack down an entire forest for the wide-scale steel smelting to catch up with the United States and the United Kingdom, leading to an enormous flood, a savage snowfall, and a terrible starvation with bodies all piled up. They eat everything

---

8 Xing Changyuan 邢長遠, "Shengtai shijiao xia *Riguang liunian* de jizhihua xushi celüe" 生態視角下《日光流年》的極致化敘事策略 [The polarizing narrative strategy of *Streams of Time* from an ecological perspective], *Shaoyang xueyuan xuebao (shehui kexue ban)* 邵陽學院學報 (社會科學版) [Journal of Shaoyang College (Social sciences edition)], 2012, no. 3: 101–4.

9 Wang, *Ou Mei shengtai piping*, 24.

they can to survive, including their own kind. Even the noble female musician dies a humiliating death after selling her dignity for food. As previously mentioned, in *Streams of Time*, due to a common belief that eating rapeseed could help people live past the age of forty, Sima Xiaoxiao orders everyone in the village to grow rapeseed. When the village is hit by the locust plague, he decides to protect the rapeseed instead of the food crops, leaving the villagers who are already facing the threat of the disease to starve to death. The locusts rage and quickly wipe out the entire village, without leaving a single blade of grass. The people of Sanxing Village try their best to chase them away, pray to the gods, and beat the gongs and drums, to no avail. As the villagers are starving, the first solution they think of is to eat the locusts. However, the famine does not subside but instead prolongs. They have to use the bones and flesh of their dead family members as bait to attract the crows, and survive by eating the birds.

In *Dream of Ding Village*, the cutting of trees to make coffins leads to the drought, an inevitable catastrophe. With the drought, the village completely becomes a barren land. There are only empty houses, as their owners have to evacuate to other places. Ding Village is still the same place, but all the people are gone. The streets are as silent as death, empty of man or beast. By destroying nature, man has also dug his own grave. It can be said that Yan has successfully built the motif of "nature's revenge" as the indignant and authoritative response of nature to the reckless and unscrupulous actions of mankind.

Thus, in the novels *Dream of Ding Village*, *Streams of Time*, and *The Four Books*, Yan describes the devastation and destruction inflicted by humans upon nature. It is because these "seeds of sin" are sowed that mankind has to suffer the severe punishment of nature. Droughts, floods, locusts, and diseases are inevitable consequences of the imbalance and disruption of the harmony and symbiosis of the ecosystem.

Misfortunes and the struggle to survive are recurring themes in Yan's literary works. Famines and epidemics have become the reagents to clearly display humanity. Men are often pushed to extreme humanity alienation. The stinky lumps of money earned from human blood in *Dream of Ding Village* culminate to cannibalism in *The Four Books*. Nguyen Thi Tinh Thy raises the questions: "From human to those who are 'disqualified as humans'. Did they turn into animals? No, that would be very bad for animals. Did they turn into evil beasts? No, in that case, the evil beasts would complain. Did they turn into demons? No, that would be too unfair to the demons. They turn into bizarre creatures, so terrifying that they could not be compared with any other species in this world."[10] Man's devastation of nature not only causes the ultimate destruction of nature but also causes humans to destroy themselves. Yan's works raise a painful and meaningful voice as a wake-up call to mankind about the consequences of environmental damage and degradation.

The life connection between humankind and nature

Yan not only writes about the act of destroying nature but also expresses a profound ecological thought when some of the characters of his novels use their own life to protect other life forms. The novella *The Years, Months, Days* tells about human struggle in an unusual drought, which occurs once in a thousand years, where everything is burned by the heat of the scorching sun. Faced with such a plight, other people in the village choose to leave this wasteland to find a new abode to live. Only an old man and his blind dog remain in the village. He chooses to

---

10 Nguyen Thi Tinh Thy, "Đinh Trang mộng: Nghẹt thở với vực thẳm nhân tính" [*Dream of Ding Village*: Suffocated in the humanity abyss], *Báo Thanh Niên* [Youth newspaper], Mar. 2019.

stay because he wants to protect the only hope left in the village—a single ear of corn. To protect it, he guards it day and night. The old man tries to nurture the corn seed that has germinated on a mountain top. He is devoted to this seedling, but, he experiences many difficulties: lacking water and food, he has to compete with the rats for things to eat and fights the wolves; however, he overcomes it all and is resilient even in grave danger. Finally, in order for the cornstalk to survive, he uses his own flesh as fertilizer. The cornstalk takes root deep in his body, survives the drought, and ends up producing seven precious kernels. When the drought returns to the village, the seven kernels have already sprouted into seven young cornstalks. Such a powerful narrative has given the village in the Balou Mountains hope even in its darkest days. *The Years, Months, Days* starts with a long drought and ends with another drought. The novella does not state a specific point in time, as if implying and emphasizing a long and cyclical return. However, even in the most miserable circumstances, man still proves his resilience and bravery. *The Years, Months, Days* reminds readers of Hemingway's *The Old Man and the Sea*, another work that praises the power of man to overcome adversity and his will to face the harshness of nature. The old man uses his body as fertilizer to feed the plant: this symbolizes the transformation between the physical body and the soul. Every time a man loses a part of his body, his soul becomes more resilient. Each time his body is damaged, his soul grows stronger. Even when the body disappears, what is reborn from that is the vitality of the soul. One message that can be read in Yan's novels is that in adverse circumstances, the human spirit seems to be stronger. Another aspect is that human and ecological life are interconnected and interdependent. The life of the cornstalk depends on the life of the elderly man. The fact that a human uses his own body and life to nurture and protect nature is not only the proof of the interdependence between the body and the soul but also a metaphor for the interconnectedness between humans and nature. The old man in the drought is a great man because he protects another life form. The life of the cornstalk and that of the old man have miraculously connected to create an immortal, never-ending life. Yan always seeks for even just a ray of light in the darkest hour, which can be the light of conscience or humanity. Here, the light comes from the survival of a small sprout in a dead time and space.

Ecological harmony and the dream of a carefree life

Wang Yao 王尧 once said: "Yan Lianke's tension with reality is evident in his works."[11] In Yan's novels, readers often see a stifling tension in the relationship between the writer and reality, between the characters and their living environment. Looking at his literary journey, notably in the topic of ecology, *House No. 711* is crucially important. Before *House No. 711*, Yan published a series of works about the destruction of the environment. With *House No. 711*, Yan regains balance in his ecological aesthetics. *House No. 711* is an essay about life immersed in idyllic nature. Unlike his other novels with a murky atmosphere, this essay is a refreshing departure where the writer immerses himself in nature and in his beloved garden, which he considers a beautiful place "beyond this world" because it no longer exists.[12] Born in the

---

11 Wang Yao, *Văn Học Trung Quốc Đương Đại, Tác Giả Và Luận Bình* [Contemporary Chinese literature, authors, and comments] (Hanoi: Social Sciences Publishing House, 2017).
12 *House No. 711* was originally named *House No. 711: Beijing, The Last Memory*. This is an essay written by Yan Lianke in memory of his house on the outskirts of Beijing. The house had a garden with trees and flowers and was located near a forest and a lake. There, he lived like a real farmer. In a June, Yan spent several dozen minutes walking in the garden and made the biggest decision in his life: he decided to use all of his savings to buy this garden and live "the most poetic and lavish part" of his life. However, in 2011, the house was demolished due to Beijing's urban development plan.

countryside, Yan especially loves a life associated with soil and plants. In the essay, he is able to understand the voice of the herbs, the insects, the animals, etc., and through such idyllic existences, he conveys simple yet profound contemplations as well as subtle and interesting feelings.

House No. 711 consists of eight chapters, which are divided into different topics, namely, farming tools (*nongju* 農具), farming and vegetables (*gengzuo yu shucai* 耕作與蔬菜), flowers (*huacao* 花草), forest and trees (*linmu* 林木), insects (*kunchongmen* 昆蟲們), a bird on the back of a deer (*lu bei shang de niao* 鹿背上的鳥), a courtyard photo album (*tingyuan zhaoxiangce* 庭院照相冊), and a final chapter set in winter (*dongtian* 冬天). Looking at the outline of the chapters, readers can see the idyllic atmosphere, a vivid ecosystem of flowers, herbs, vegetables, trees, animals, birds, fish, and insects, as well as the intra- and inter-species relationships. With this garden, Yan achieved his dream of a carefree life. In it, he had a world with blue sky, white clouds, lake and river, birds, plants, and insects, with no human trace. In this garden, he built a house, he used to write and read, plant the trees, spend time with dogs, cats, dragonflies, and butterflies. Every day, the love and scent of flowers and herbs would fall on the soft back of the cats, the ears of the dogs, and the tip of his pen. In that world, he used to live a life completely in harmony with nature: planting flowers and vegetables, picking mushrooms and vegetable leaves that still carried the night dew, observing and chatting with animals, insects, and flowers, sailing a boat to the center of the lake, watching the fish jumping out of the water, seeing the ants marching and helping them remove obstacles on their way, even climbing on a tree to reach a beehive, secretly hoping that bee venom could treat his cervical degenerative disc disease caused by protracted sitting and writing. In this book, he narrates the experience of a real farmer and conveys to readers the joys of buying farming tools, fertilizing the plants, and harvesting. In *House No. 711* Yan creates an ecological world with equality, where all creations with their own life and language are equal to humankind. For example, in "The Fate of a Shovel" ("Yi ba tiexian de mingyun" 一把鐵鍁的命運), he imagines how the shovel was shaped, the labors it did, and how the writer as its owner misused and broke it. He even holds a solemn ceremony for its retirement. In "The Autumnal Joy and Sorrow of the Grass" ("Cao qiu bei xi" 草秋悲喜), he perceives himself as the grass' soulmate who can hear its singing voice, at times characterized by a sad melody and at times by a rhythm of joy.

In *House No. 711* readers feel the earnest love of the author for nature, as well as his respect and Rousseauian desire to go back and live in harmony with it. Yan conveys to readers the refreshing feelings and his yearning for the natural world. In this garden, he makes every hour of his life poetic and artistic. His writing transmits his love for the natural world, his understanding of life, and the enlightenment of his soul.

This ecological space leads Yan as an author to contemplate about writing. When he lays on a newspaper in the shadow of a maidenhair tree, thinking about the ants that seem to have waged war for a grain of rice, he feels pain and sadness. When he arrives at the edge of the forest to see the sunset while a long train sweeps past with a loud whistling sound, he tells himself: "You write for your heart and not for anyone else. Why don't you write the way you want to write? The world is vast and life is short, shouldn't a writer express, portray and write for the innermost truth of his own heart?"[13] It is also here that he feels like he has come back to his roots. In chapter 4, "Forest and Trees" ("Linmu" 林木), through the wet body of each tree

---

13 Yan Lianke, *711 hao yuan* 711 號園 [House No. 711] (Nanjing: Jiangsu wenyi chubanshe, 2012), 87: "你的寫作是為了你的內心，並不為了別的人，你為什麼不想怎樣寫作就怎樣寫作呢？世界浩大，生命苦短，一個作家難道不應該為自己內心的最真實表達、描繪和入木三分的刻寫嗎？"

washed by the rain, looking at the trees that are still behind the curtain of rain in the distance, he feels like "a long-lost child returning to his mother's embrace, eager to cry, yet wanting to laugh at the same time."[14] Therefore, nature in *House No. 711* is not only an ecological space but also a sacred land that can purify and redeem human souls. Yan himself writes in the foreword: "In the midst of bustling Beijing, there is a calm and refreshing place and it feels like the mortal world finally has its religion. House no. 711 in fact is the church in the heart of the city that worships nature. And we are the mortals who enter the church and are shaken by the gods."[15] Yan is always concerned about finding a place to return to. In the novel *Books of Odes* (*Feng ya song* 風雅頌), the character Yang Ke constantly looks for somewhere he belongs to, but he cannot find any place like that in reality. Thus, he has to turn to the fictional world, the ancient city of *Shijing* 詩經 of more than a thousand years, and leads a primitive and debauched life with prostitutes. The despair for a place to return to in *Books of Odes* is resolved in *House No. 711*. It is in this place that Yan is enlightened, as he realizes that he can take refuge in the great natural world, that humankind can return to nature like a child coming back into his mother's arms, sit on his mother's lap, his homeland, and his lost memories.

House No. 711 is reminiscent of *Walden* by Henry David Thoreau. After the publication of *House No. 711*, some critics referred to Yan's work as directly influenced by *Walden*.[16] Both novels describe amazing ecological spaces where humans and nature can be ideally connected. However, while Walden Pond, with its long history, is included in the conservation list and always retains its pristine and eternal beauty, House no. 711 only existed for a short time—the rapid urbanization of Beijing caused it to be wiped out, and it only remains in the memory of the author as a beautiful, lavish but short-lived dream.

In conclusion, through his novels and essays, Yan may be defined as a writer with a profound ecological dimension. Through his skillful artistic writing, his work poses the issue of humankind destroying the environment and walking the path of self-destruction, as well as forecasts and warns about the disasters suffered by humankind when going against ecological laws. At the same time, Yan also realizes the interdependence between humans and nature, from which all forms of life are created. Yan's literary works also present the idea of the unity between Heaven and man, ecological equality, respect, admiration, and to a certain extent, even the sanctification of nature.

Bibliography

Bosselmann, Klaus. *When Two Worlds Collide: Society and Ecology*. Auckland: RSVP Publishing, 1999.
Do Van Hieu. "Shengtai piping de kequxing" 生態批評的可取性 [The plausibility of ecocriticsm]. *Wenyi piping* 文藝批評 [Literary criticism], Sep. 2016: 45, 50–55.
Eckersley, Robyn. *Environmentalism and Political Theory: Toward an Ecocentric Approach*. New York: State University of New York Press, 1992.
Guo Zeying 郭澤英. "Liang zhong meili, yi zhong qishi: *Waerdeng hu he Beijing, zuihoude jinian* zhi bijiao" 兩種美麗，一種啟示——《瓦爾登湖》和《北京，最後的紀念》之比較 [Two beauties, one inspiration: A comparison of *Walden* and *House No. 711*]. *Mingzuo xinshang* 名作欣賞 [Masterpieces review], 2013, no. 14: 124–25.

---

14 Ibid., 90: "你像一個失散多年的孩子回到了母親的懷抱般。想哭。也想笑。"
15 Ibid., 1: "北京的繁鬧裡，有這一處清靜，正是俗世有了它的宗教。711號園子，事實上就是一個城市對大自然膜拜的教堂。而我們，正是從凡塵進入教堂被神聖震撼的人世塵子。"
16 Guo Zeying 郭澤英, "Liang zhong meili, yi zhong qishi: *Waerdeng hu he Beijing, zuihoude jinian* zhi bijiao" 兩種美麗，一種啟示——《瓦爾登湖》和《北京，最後的紀念》之比較 [Two beauties, one inspiration: A comparison of Walden and House No. 711], *Mingzuo xinshang* 名作欣賞 [Masterpieces review], 2013, no. 14: 124.

Hettinger, Ned, and Bill Throop. "Refocusing Ecocentrism: De-Emphasizing Stability and Defending Wilderness." *Environmental Ethics* 21 (1999): 3–21.

Nguyen Thi Tinh Thy. "Đinh Trang mộng: Nghẹt thở với vực thẳm nhân tính" [*Dream of Ding Village*: Suffocated in the humanity abyss]. *Báo Thanh Niên* [Youth newspaper], Mar. 2019.

Ji Qingben 季慶本. "Cong shengtai meixue kan shijian meixue" 從生態美學看實踐美學 [Practical aesthetics from ecological aesthetics]. In *Zhongwai shengtai wenxue wenlun xuan* 中外生態文學文論選 [Selected literary essays on Chinese and foreign ecology], edited by Jing Yaping 荊亞平, 339–50. Hangzhou: Zhejiang gongshang daxue chubanshe, 2010.

Wang Nuo 王諾. *Ou Mei shengtai piping* 歐美生態批評 [European and American ecocriticism]. Shanghai: Xuelin chubanshe, 2008.

Wang Yao 王堯. *Văn Học Trung Quốc Đương Đại, Tác Giả Và Luận Bình* [Chinese contemporary literature, authors and comments]. Hanoi: Social Sciences Publishing House, 2017.

Xing Changyuan 邢長遠. "Shengtai shijiao xia *Riguang liunian* de jizhihua xushi celue" 生態視角下《日光流年》的極致化敘事策略 [The polarizing narrative strategy of *Streams of Time* from an ecological perspective]. *Shaoyang xueyuan xuebao (shehui kexue ban)* 邵陽學院學報 (社會科學版) [Journal of Shaoyang College (Social sciences edition)], 2012, no. 3: 101–4.

Yan Lianke 閻連科. *711 hao yuan* 711號園 [House no. 711]. Nanjing: Jiangsu wenyi chubanshe, 2012.

———. *Đinh Trang mộng* [Dream of Ding Village]. Translated by Minh Thương. Hanoi: Nhà xuất bản Hội Nhà văn và Công ty Sách Tao Đàn, 2018.

———. *Feng ya song* 風雅頌 [Books of odes]. Kunming: Yunnan renmin chubanshe, 2011.

———. *The Four Books*. Translated by Carlos Rojas. New York: Grove press, 2016.

———. *Riguang liunian* 日光流年 [Streams of time]. Tianjin: Tianjin renmin chubanshe, 2011.

22
PARATEXTUAL ENCOUNTERS IN YAN LIANKE'S FICTIONAL WORLDS

Reading between the lines

Ronald Torrance

When Yan Lianke's 閻連科 *The Day the Sun Died* (*Rixi* 日熄, 2015) was published in English in 2018, it evoked a reception within English-speaking literary circles unlike any of his recent publications to date. Yan, a prolific writer in his native Chinese, has published several novels over the course of the last decade, which have been translated into English mainly by Carlos Rojas. Yet none of Yan's previous translations have been received with the seemingly overnight acclaim with which *The Day the Sun Died* was met. An early review of the novel *The Day the Sun Died* by the *Economist* was among the first to connect the novel's central motif of a mass somnambulism experienced by the people of Gaotian Village, a fictionalized setting in modern-day central China, based loosely on Yan's ancestral home of Henan Province, to Xi Jinping's 習近平 "Chinese Dream" (*Zhongguo meng* 中國夢). The review claims: "Mr. Yan wrote *The Day the Sun Died* soon after China's leader Xi Jinping had sloganized the idea of the 'Chinese Dream.'"[1] The tenuous political analogy implied between Yan's writing of the novel and Xi's idea of the "Chinese Dream" gathered increasing momentum in subsequent reviews of the novel, with *The Irish Times* misinterpreting Carlos Rojas' introduction to *The Day the Sun Died* as supportive of Yan's political "critique of Chinese President Xi Jinping's slogan of the Chinese dream."[2]

The immediate correlation made among reviewers between the "mass dreamwalking" experience by Gaotian Village within *The Day the Sun Died* and the wider political context of the "Chinese Dream" seems to reflect Joel Kohen's review of the novel and suggestion that a more nuanced reading of Yan's fiction and Chinese literature, more generally, is required by

---

1 "Yan Lianke's Dark Satire of Modern China: A Novel of Looting, Murder and Economic Growth," *The Economist*, 26 July 2018, https://www.economist.com/books-and-arts/2018/07/26/yan-liankes-dark-satire-of-modern-china (last accessed 17 Aug. 2021).
2 Sean Hewitt, "*The Day the Sun Died* by Yan Lianke: A Brave, Masterful Novel," *The Irish Times*, 28 July 2018, https://www.irishtimes.com/culture/books/the-day-the-sun-died-by-yan-lianke-a-brave-masterful-novel-1.3558083 (last accessed 10 Jan. 2019).

Western audiences.[3] While Rojas' introduction to the novel indeed alludes to "marginalized figures" in contemporary China, and his hope that *The Day the Sun Died* will "draw attention to actual communities and social phenomena that remain hidden in the shadows of contemporary China's rapid growth," nowhere does he connect the novel's metaphor of somnambulism to the idea of the "Chinese Dream," an interpretation of the text which Yan has similarly rejected.[4]

Giving an interview in *The Guardian* while promoting the English-language publication of the novel, Yan responded to readings of *The Day the Sun Died* as a social and political critique of Xi's "Chinese dream": "When I first read some of the comments by critics here [in the U.K.] I was really surprised, because that hadn't been particularly my original intention. I wanted merely, through writing about sleepwalking, to reflect a lot of basic and fundamental truths about the human heart. A direct connection to the Chinese dream was not what I intended at all."[5] While it is necessary to take precautions in adhering to an author's interpretation of their own work, Yan is illustrative of a writer who has had considerable experience of falling afoul of China's censors. However, as contemporary Chinese critics, artists, and Yan himself frequently comments, the most ubiquitous form of censorship in China today is self-censorship, and Yan openly admits to having self-censored his earlier novels in an effort to have them published in mainland China.[6] Indeed, as Yan's own career trajectory ironically serves to illustrate, the state's banning of books has the unintended effect of bestowing targeted authors with prestige and legitimacy in China's literary field while bolstering their visibility both domestically and abroad. The censure of Yan's novel *Summer Sunset* (*Xia riluo* 夏日落, 1994), he suggests, was relaxed due to the positive attention the censorship of the novel received without China.[7] And yet, despite his own admissions of self-censorship, Yan has developed a more nuanced approach in his relationship with China's censors while maintaining a critical view on the state's intervention in China's literary field: mainland authors who have never been banned, he proposes, are held in suspicion by their peers. Conversely, he also exhibits suspicion toward writers who pursue censorship as a mark of distinction.[8] Yan's reflections therefore yield a key insight on censorship in contemporary China, namely that overt demonstrations of state power frequently fail to suppress the intended target, sometimes having directly the opposite outcome.

---

3 Joel Kohen, "Novelist Yan Lianke Underlines Nobel Prize Ambitions in 'The Day the Sun Died,'" *The Chronicle*, 26 Dec. 2018, https://www.dukechronicle.com/article/2018/12/novelist-yan-lianke-underlines-nobel-prize-ambitions-in-the-day-the-sun-died (last accessed 30 May 2021).

4 Carlos Rojas, Translator's Note in *The Day the Sun Died* (London: Chatto & Windus, 2018), vii.

5 Yan Lianke, "Yan Lianke: 'It's Hard to Get My Books Published in China,'" interview by Lesley McDowell, *The Guardian*, 22 Sep. 2018, https://www.theguardian.com/books/2018/sep/22/yan-lianke-writers-in-china-day-the-sun-died-interview (10 accessed Nov. 2018).

6 Describing the publication of his novel, *Lenin's Kisses*, Yan reflects: "I should have done much better with *Lenin's Kisses*. But I spent too much time on self-censoring. I wanted my book to be published." See Catherine Wong, "We Must Confront Our Dark Past of the Cultural Revolution to Avoid Repeating It, Says Chinese Novelist Yan Lianke," *South China Morning Post*, 9 May 2016, https://www.scmp.com/news/china/policies-politics/article/1942609/we-must-confront-our-dark-past-cultural-revolution (last accessed 10 Nov. 2018).

7 Yan Lianke, *Xia riluo* (Taipei: Lianjing, 2010), 185.

8 Harlan D. Chambers, "Writing with Care: Yan Lianke and the Biopolitics of Modern Chinese Censorship" (MA thesis, University of Texas, 2015), 7.

Imaginary spaces and paratextual construction

The combination of political authority and artistic control developed by the party-state in China has established a contemporary system of literary control in which writers like Yan Lianke play a critical role in defining the aesthetic trajectory of Chinese literature under an authoritarian regime. In his study of Yan in the context of modern Chinese censorship, Harlan D. Chambers approaches this dilemma from the "biopolitical" perspective of Yan's work and rather neatly summarizes how the Communist Party has established institutions that "completely fold life into politics" and thus "top-down techniques like censorship have reemerged in the bottom-up phenomenon of internalized censoring."[9] Chambers argues that the content of Yan's novels, which he interprets as restaging historical events in order to narrate confrontations between writers and institutions of power, is reflective in what he defines as Yan's "literary care" in his writing. Chambers convincingly concludes that Yan never neglects the relationship between life and politics but maintains that one is not reducible to the other. In so doing, Yan's novels show us how writers in China can "engage with political pragmatics so that [they] can better manipulate them, crafting out a way to care for [themselves] and others that transcends the violence of their exclusionary logic. This is certainly a decisive victory that Yan Lianke has won against the censors, gaining an international readership for his novels that has only served to place increased pressure on the authorities censoring him domestically."[10] One thread which is less convincing in Chambers' study, however, is his analysis of the literary techniques that Yan employs in his novels which he suggests are solely preoccupied with Yan's "literary care" in the face of internalized censorship. As my analysis of Yan's recent fiction in this chapter will illustrate, instances in which characters are shown by Chambers to disregard society's underlying disciplinary logic do so, not solely as a result of Yan's preoccupation with self-censorship, but in an attempt to create "thresholds" within his recent fiction that Yan employs as spaces of resistance against the restraints of the Chinese regime.[11] In this sense, Yan's fiction exhibits a new direction in contemporary Chinese literature, by which Chinese writers can use the constructs of metafiction as a tool in order to circumvent the censorship mechanisms existent within mainland China.

Yan's novels do not present society in a perfected form. Rather, his fiction reflects an unreal, or imagined, ontological space in which night replaces day, dreams are replaced by nightmares, and even fiction is contrasted with reality itself. These imagined spaces are illustrative of what Michel Foucault defines as "heterotopias," or sites that exhibit "the curious property of being in relation with all the other sites, but in such a way as to … invert the set of relations that they happen to designate, mirror or reflect."[12] The conceptual ambiguity of "difference" is crucial to Foucault's concept of heterotopias, yet it is in this area that scholars indicate his concept is at its weakest.[13] In their 2008 book, *Heterotopia and the City*, Michiel

---

9 Ibid., v.
10 Ibid., 99, 101.
11 The "Chinese regime" is here equated with the Chinese Communist Party (CCP). The Chinese government is also equated with the Chinese Communist Party, hereafter "CCP." The "one-party state," "Chinese government," "Chinese regime," "CCP" can all be used interchangeably.
12 Michel Foucault, "Of Other Spaces," trans. Jay Miskowiec, *Diacritics* 16, no.1 (1986): 24.
13 Kevin Hetherington, for example, argues that Foucault neglects to distinguish precisely how the spatial difference of heterotopias, which can include theatres, gardens, and carpets, should be determined and thus is too broad. See Kevin Hetherington, *The Badlands of Modernity: Heterotopia and Social Ordering* (London: Routledge, 1997), 7.

Dehaene and Lieven de Cauter attempt to navigate the multitudinous examples provided by Foucault by offering three frameworks that synthesize heterotopic spaces, grouping them as: the anthropological, the temporal, and the imaginary (i.e., illusionary). The last is my focus here. By considering Yan's fiction within the imaginary space of heterotopias, an analogous space most predisposed to literary analysis, I seek to illustrate how the paratextual construction of Yan's recent fiction provides a literary space in which the negotiation of China's historical and socio-political contexts can be played out and reinterpreted, acting as a space of resistance under the literary restraints of the Chinese party-state. This concept is expanded by Teresa Davis, who points out that Foucauldian thought often correlates heterotopias with "spaces of 'resistance' … in the sense that [heterotopias] are meant to be liminal and therefore spaces [from which] to challenge and question" dominant political forces.[14]

Recent studies of Yan's work have focused less on heterotopias in favor of either utopian, dystopian, or biopolitical interpretations of his novels; it is perhaps partly owing to these polarized readings of his novels that Yan has expressed frustration about Western readers' response to *The Day the Sun Died*.[15] By analyzing the construction of Yan's fiction through the lens of heterotopias, I hope to not only move interpretations of his novels away from polarized readings of utopias and/or dystopias but also to emphasize how his work illustrates different spaces which challenge and disturb other places around them and,[16] in doing so, to show how heterotopic spaces of resistance in contemporary Chinese literature offer ways of navigating the CCP's ideological vision for China's future in the twenty-first century.

Narrative thresholds and historical awakenings: *The Day the Sun Died*

Set over the course of one night in the Balou 耙耬 Mountains of Gaotian Village, *The Day the Sun Died* is narrated from the perspective of a 14-year-old boy Li Niannian 李念念 who comes to the realization that Gaotian's residents have succumbed to a "mass somnambulism" (*mengyou* 夢遊) as they carry on with their daily lives after the sun has gone down.[17] As Carlos Rojas recalls in his translator's note to the novel, the oneiric metaphors Yan employs equating history with sleep and dreams are evoked by James Joyce and Lu Xun 魯迅, two of the twentieth century's leading modernist authors whose works sought to "*awaken from* the nightmare that is history" (emphasis added) or, in the case of Lu Xun, "*awake into* a state of historical awareness" (emphasis in the original).[18] The metaphor of Gaotian's seemingly "endless" night is used by Yan to draw together Joyce and Lu Xun's concerns, calling upon his readers to *awaken from* the nightmare of history *into* a state of historical awareness.[19]

---

14 Teresa Davis, "Third Spaces or Heterotopias? Recreating and Negotiating Migrant Identity Using Online Spaces," *Sociology* 44, no. 4 (2010): 663.
15 While it is beyond the scope of this chapter to fully interrogate the cultural construction of China through the reading of Yan's novels in English translation, it is worth remembering that the essentialist characterization of China in the West is ubiquitously constructed as a dystopia arising from the systematicity with which China is discursively constituted through myriad forms of media, of which literary translations are a part. See T. K. Lee, "China as Dystopia: Cultural Imaginings through Translation," *Translation Studies* 8, no. 3 (2015): 255.
16 Heidi Sohn, "Heterotopia: Anamnesis of a Medical Term," in *Heterotopia and the City: Public Space in a Postcivil Society*, ed. Michiel Dehaene and Lieven De Cauter (London: Routledge, 2008), 44.
17 Yan Lianke, *The Day the Sun Died*, trans. Carlos Rojas (London: Chatto & Windus, 2018), 259.
18 Rojas, translator's note, iii.
19 Yan, *The Day the Sun Died*, 261. Further page numbers appear in the text.

One of the metaphors which expresses how Yan's characters in the novel "awaken" from the nightmare of history is ostensibly simple: Gaotian's residents awaken from their "somnambulistic state" (181) following the intervention of Li Niannian, his father Li Tianbao 李天保, and the town's resident author (one "Yan Lianke") as the night is ultimately overcome and the "sky … and everything under heaven [is] illuminated" (324), allowing the villagers of Gaotian to "[return] to the new day" (327) at the novel's conclusion. Yet while this metaphor of the sun rising, awakening Gaotian's residents in the process of transforming night into day, constitutes the overarching plot of the novel, it is intrinsically related to an ancillary plot relating to Li Niannian's family's storage of corpse oil: a thread throughout the text which appears, in either oversight or deliberate intent, to have been largely overlooked despite its significant role at the novel's climax.

Niannian's proximity to death is established early in the novel, in both literal and more nuanced configurations. His parents, owners of the New World funerary shop, make a living designing "bamboo frames and … papercuts" (14) while his uncle is the director in charge of Gaotian's crematorium: a place "devoted to cremating human corpses, and in this respect … marked a threshold through which people passed into another world" (38). Niannian remarks upon similar thresholds throughout the novel, using markers of physical and temporal space to describe Gaotian's mass somnambulism: "When people started dreamwalking," he observes, "they entered a different world" (127). Niannian's observation that his uncle's crematorium is a threshold by which people pass into another world is mirrored in Foucault's second principle of heterotopias in which he asserts: "a society, as its history unfolds, can make an existing heterotopia function in a very different fashion; for each heterotopia has a precise and determined function within a society and the same heterotopia can, according to the synchrony of the culture in which it occurs, have one function or another."[20] For Foucault, the cemetery is illustrative of a heterotopia as "it is a space that is … connected with all the sites of the city, state or society or village … since each individual, each family has relatives in the cemetery."[21] Gaotian's crematorium functions as Foucault's second principle of heterotopia outlines and, as Niannian discovers: "Originally, it *was* a cemetery—a cemetery where thousands or even tens of thousands of corpses were buried. Thousands, tens of thousands, an entire world of corpses—were all brought here in hearses, only to be reduced to ashes and taken away in urns." (emphasis in the original)[22] The correlation made here between the "threshold" space of Gaotian's crematorium and Foucault's concept of heterotopia returns to Teresa Davis' idea of how heterotopic spaces challenge and disturb other places around them and speaks to the novel's transcendence of "the nightmare that is history" through the metaphor of Gaotian's collective "dreamwalking" and subsequent (re-)awakening.

As Niannian navigates the "mass somnambulation" of Gaotian village, chaos ensues. The village's "dreamwalking" residents revert to a feudal state, presided over by a puppet military governor, who decrees the killing of anyone who is not from Gaotian (280). As the village's death toll rises over the course of the night, Niannian observes how his family, whose primary trade is in funerary arrangements for the dead, struggles to meet the demand for funerary goods. Niannian's uncle, taking advantage of the rising death toll and an unforeseen upturn in business, enforces the banning of burials and mandates cremation, thus producing the vast quantities of corpse oil which he sells to Niannian's father, who stores them in a nearby cave

---

20 Foucault, "Of Other Spaces," 25.
21 Ibid.
22 Yan, *The Day the Sun Died*, 76.

(89).²³ The lake of corpse oil prophetically imagined by Niannian comes to dramatic fruition at the novel's climax whereby his father immolates himself with the help of "Yan Lianke" by setting the lake on fire to "reflect ... the sun at dawn" (323), restoring the day and thus finalizing the overarching plot of the novel. Li Tianbao's sacrifice not only responds to the awakening from the nightmare of Gaotian's somnambulation but is followed by a narrative postface which speaks once more to Foucault's concept of heterotopia and is strategically placed by Yan at the end of the novel to call upon the reader to awaken into a state of historical awareness.

In his postface to *The Day the Sun Died*, Yan contrasts the different local and national "traces of existence" following Gaotian's "mass dreamwalking" and the eventual rising of the sun. Referring to the numbers of the dead, for example, Niannian recounts thirty-six of the 539 "people [who] died that night" (329) which is juxtaposed by the "county, city, and provincial ... announcement, stating that in Henan Province there had been only a small number of locations where dreamwalkers had managed to create a disturbance" (333). Returning one final time to his second principle of the heterotopia of the cemetery, Foucault notes that "from the moment when people are no longer sure that they have a soul or that the body will regain life, it is perhaps necessary to give much more attention to the dead body, which is ultimately the only trace of our existence in the world and in language."²⁴ This juxtaposition highlights the contrast between individual remembrance and state censorship in China, whereby local devastation is negated by a narrative posited by the state and thus the dead (i.e., "the only trace of our existence in the world") can be controlled by political factors without individual control. Niannian and his mother's remembrance of Li Tianbao highlights the importance of historical awareness as Gaotian village gradually reverts to its usual status quo after the sun has risen.

Had Yan concluded the novel at this narrative juncture, it could be argued that *The Day the Sun Died* could in fact be categorized as a dystopian novel as the combination of the Li family's loss and the erasure of Gaotian's "mass somnambulism" exhibits elements of dystopian literature, which Bobby Newman categorizes as "the unhappiness of the characters portrayed; suspicion of sources of control of behavior outside the individual; [and] suspicion of behavioral methods of governance."²⁵ However, a final scene in which the fictional version of Yan arrives at Niannian's home provides the most compelling case for *The Day the Sun Died* to be read as a heterotopic response to the wider context of contemporary Chinese literary censorship.

---

23 James Kidd suggests that Niannian's uncle's "sudden love affair with capitalism" places the novel within the context of "Deng Xiaoping's aspiration to make China gloriously rich." However, in a noteworthy case of life imitating art in July 2018, the same month in which *The Day the Sun Died* was published in English, authorities in southeast Jiangxi Province authorized a "zero burial" policy, effectively banning people from burying their dead with the aim to make cremation to sole approved method of disposing of people's remains. See "Bleak Reality Confronts the Chinese Dream in Yan Lianke's Gruesome, Gripping Novel, *The Day the Sun Died*," *South China Morning Post*, 1 Aug. 2018, https://www.scmp.com/magazines/post-magazine/books/article/2157656/bleak-reality-confronts-chinese-dream-yan-liankes (last accessed 10 Jan. 2019); and Mimi Lau, "Coffins Smashed, Seized, Exhumed in China as Province Bans Burials to Save Land," *South China Morning Post*, 31 July 2018, https://www.scmp.com/news/china/society/article/2157531/coffins-smashed-seized-exhumed-china-province-bans-burials-save (last accessed 20 Jan. 2019).
24 Foucault, "Of Other Spaces," 25.
25 Bobby Newman, "Discriminating Utopian from Dystopian Literature: Why Is Walden Two Considered a Dystopia?" *The Behaviour Analyst* 16, no. 2 (1993): 169.

In this closing sequence, the fictional Yan Lianke places "an enormous pile" of his own books next to the portrait of Niannian's father and, mirroring Li Tianbao's self-immolation, sets them alight. Alluding to Niannian's appeal at the beginning of the novel to "permit [Yan] to keep writing and keep living [and] to finish writing his *Night of the People* … so that he may then include my family in his narrative" (8),[26] the fictional Yan Lianke has seemingly thus succeeded in writing his book, which is materially manifested for the reader as the "real" Yan Lianke's *The Day the Sun Died*.

It is this revelation that situates the novel specifically within the framework of a heterotopia in the sense that Yan's literary imagination (i.e., the fictionalized account contained within the novel) provides an imagined space that reflects the socio-political constructs of contemporary China but is revealed to the reader to be an imaginary construct from which they must awake. Comparable to the fictional awakening of Gaotian's residents, *The Day the Sun Died* thus calls the reader to awaken into a state of historical awareness that challenges us to rethink the unwritten "traces of existence" which are otherwise narrated by the authoritarian institutions of state power in China. Unlike his other novels, in which he restages historical events in order to narrate confrontations between writers and the state, Yan's call for a state of historical awakening in the conclusion to *The Day the Sun Died* seems to suggest a pragmatic directional change for contemporary Chinese writers in the face of China's seemingly insurmountable political reality.

A paratextual prototype: *The Explosion Chronicles*

If *The Day the Sun Died* is illustrative of Yan Lianke's call for a state of historical awakening, an earlier prototype for this novel can be seen in *The Explosion Chronicles* (*Zhalie zhi* 炸裂志, 2013), Yan's first widely recognized literary achievement, which also marks his definitive professional break with the state propaganda apparatus.[27]

In *The Explosion Chronicles*, Yan explores the traumas that underlie contemporary China's economic development, the process by which China's political leaders attempted to restore the legitimacy of the Party and political system following the trauma of the Great Leap that resulted in man-made famines, the death of tens of millions, and later the disturbances of the Cultural Revolution. Comprised as a series of historical chronicles, the novel surveys more than a thousand years of "Explosion's explosive expansion" but notably centers its attention in the post-1949 era, particularly in the post-Mao period.[28] Recounting the fictionalized chronology of Explosion's (*Zhalie* 炸裂) rapid expansion, Yan symbolically transforms the exhaustion, pain, and trauma that underlies contemporary China's economic development by showing its effect on the community of Explosion's swift expansion as it capitalizes on the opportunity of economic expansion during the post-Mao period, metastasizing from a small village located in the Balou Mountain region of Henan province—the same region in which *The Day the Sun Died* is set—to a county, a city, and finally a provincial-level megapolis.

---

26 References to the "real" Yan Lianke's novels within *The Day the Sun Died* are all rendered as fictionalized amalgamations of his previous works or otherwise deliberately misquoted. For example, "*Kissing Lenin's Years*" functions as an amalgamation of *Lenin's Kisses* and *The Years, Months, Days*, while "*The Dead Books*" plays off *The Four Books*' homophonous association between the number four (*si* 四) and the Chinese word for "death" (*si* 死).
27 Chambers, "Writing with Care," 8.
28 Yan Lianke, *The Explosion Chronicles*, trans. Carlos Rojas (London: Chatto & Windus, 2017), 162.

The chronicle that the (fictional) Yan weaves deviates from Explosion's factual history, inventing a parallel narrative in which Explosion's unchecked development leads to the swift and absurd promotion of Kong Mingliang from village chief to town mayor, to county mayor, and city mayor before Explosion's uneven development is finally and fatally extinguished by an ill-fated war against the United States.[29] This conflict leaves Kong Mingliang dead (the result of an assassination by his younger brother, Kong Mingyao) and Explosion itself reduced to "a virtual ghost town" by the embedded novel's conclusion.[30]

By setting the novel against the backdrop of the post-Mao period, Yan explicitly correlates the development and fate of Explosion to the People's Republic, more widely: "After the founding of China in 1949, the history of Explosion Village replicated in miniature the pain and prosperity undergone by the nation itself."[31] Thus, the development of Explosion functions as a literary microcosm of the PRC's development within what D. W. Foster defines as the function of microcosms as "the need to understand a complex social situation" which underlies "the way in which the 'fictional world' is a microcosm of reality in the sense of a documentary miniature ... and no matter to what degree the writer follows an imperative to strive for a sense of the vastness and social fabric within it, the narrative can never be more than a coded map of the actual reality of social experience and the historical dynamic."[32] Therefore, by making the fictional growth of Explosion parallel to China's own economic development and political reforms, the novel symbolically aligns the projected futures of both Explosion and the PRC. While this imbues the novel with the narrative ability to reflect upon and thus examine the underlying traumas of the post-Mao period, the eventual collapse of Explosion functions as a fictionalized account of what Cai Rong 蔡蓉 terms the "Frankenstein's monster" of China's twentieth century, whereby Cai suggests that the social conditions that had given rise to the belligerence of Mao's Communist ideology may have been removed after his death, but have nevertheless remained a central concern for contemporary Chinese writers and are thus symbolically transformed into Explosion and played out by the conclusion of Yan's chronicles.[33] In this sense, by reinforcing "the glory and trauma [Explosion] shared with the People's Republic,"[34] *The Explosion Chronicles*' narrative trajectory of Explosion's rise and fall is distinctive; not singularly because Explosion serves as an allegorical depiction of China's urbanization, but rather for Yan's achievement in opening up an imaginary space that exposes the horror within the process of the mass social, political and economic development of China's twentieth century.

Structurally, *The Explosion Chronicles* exhibits the same literary devices of author surrogate and embedding, which Yan employs in *The Day the Sun Died*.[35] Consequently, *The Explosion*

---

29 Cao Xuenan, "Mythorealism and Enchanted Time: Yan Lianke's *The Explosion Chronicles*," *Frontiers of Literary Studies in China* 10, no.1 (2016): 5, 7.
30 Yan, *The Explosion Chronicles*, 442–43.
31 Ibid., 8.
32 David William Foster, *Violence in Argentine Literature: Cultural Response to Tyranny* (Columbia: University of Missouri Press, 1995), 75.
33 Rong Cai, *Subject in Crisis in Contemporary Chinese Literature* (Honolulu: University of Hawaii Press, 2014), 125.
34 Yan, *The Explosion Chronicles*, 9.
35 According to William Nelles, "Embedding," in *Routledge Encyclopedia of Narrative Theory*, ed. David Herman, J. Manfred, and M.-L. Ryan (London: Routledge, 2010), 134, "the most widely accepted use of the term 'embedding' in the context of narrative theory is to designate the literary device of the 'story within a story', the structure by which a character in a narrative text becomes the narrator of a second narrative text framed by the first one."

Chronicles is again a novel within a novel that recounts the transformation of Explosion from a small town to an international city, as recorded by a novelist under government commission, one "Yan Lianke." The inclusion of this fictionalized Yan Lianke, a prototype for the version of the author who appears in *The Day the Sun Died*, reminds us of Jukka Mikkonen's definition of "author surrogate," whereby an author may include a character within their fiction, "who represents the beliefs, views, and morality of the author who is often the main character and/ or narrator of the work."[36] Mikkonen distinguishes that there also exists "a large group of literary works in which an individual character does not directly represent the author's views but should rather be examined as part of the author's overall assertive act" and it is precisely within this framework that Yan's use of an author surrogate and his paratext functions.[37]

I highlight the paratext of *The Explosion Chronicles* because it is a significant example of Yan's "overall assertive act" within his works explored in this chapter. The text's paratextual merging of fiction and reality is not only symbolic of the *Chronicles*' own interplay between reality and fiction but also offers an imaginary space within which Yan inverts the relationship between reality and fiction. In doing so, Yan creates a literary space of resistance from which his fiction challenges and questions the socio-political and economic development of China in the twentieth century. In order to draw out Yan's interplay between reality and fiction in *The Explosion Chronicles*, the analysis that follows seeks to distinguish the novel's paratextual inclusions from what I will forthwith consider being the secondary embedded narrative of the text.

Drawing on the framework set out by Gérard Genette in his 1977 book, *Paratexts: Thresholds of Interpretation*, the following analysis of *The Explosion Chronicles* will consider how the structural composition of the text is produced in such a way as to juxtapose Yan's paratextual inclusions with the novel's secondary embedded narrative. By doing so, in relation to *The Explosion Chronicles*' primary narrative text, my analysis will thus show how Yan's structural composition of an imaginary heterotopic space within the text not only challenges and questions the socio-political and economic development of China in the twentieth century but also provides an imaginary space, which acts as a space of resistance against the artistic restraints of the CCP.

Yan's use of embedding in *The Explosion Chronicles* creates a narrative structure in which the fictionalized character of "Yan Lianke" narrates the second narrative (i.e., embedded) text. This structure is akin to the postface of *The Day the Sun Died*, in which Li Niannian implies that the inclusion of his family's narrative in the text signifies that the fictional Yan has completed his novel. This version of "Yan Lianke" who, throughout the novel, stands on the periphery of Li Niannian's embedded narrative is thus revealed in the novel's postface to have been responsible for the writing of the *"Night of the People,"* the text that Li Niannian invokes the fictional Yan to write at the opening of the novel, and is subsequently materially manifested to the reader as *The Day the Sun Died*. However, unlike the beginning of *The Day the Sun Died*, where the narrator-protagonist Li Niannian evokes (the fictional) Yan to finish writing his novel, the "Yan Lianke" of *The Explosion Chronicles* initiates the text as its primary narrator, leaving the reader under no illusion that the novel they are reading is in fact an embedded construct of a fictionalized Yan: "Esteemed readers, permit me to use this Note to clarify a few points. ... I agreed to put aside the novel on which I was working to accept the role of author and editor of *The Explosion Chronicles*. ... I spent quite a bit of time and effort

---

36 Jukka Mikkonen, *The Cognitive Value of Philosophical Fiction* (London: Bloomsbury, 2013), 71.
37 Ibid., 72.

on this project, not only for the sake of my readers and for Explosion City, but also to earn the vast sum of money specified in the contract."[38] Hence, in each primary narrative, the narrative frame (i.e., the text which Yan either delivers or completes in the postface of each respective novel) is revealed as a fictionalized version of Yan's writing of the book.

Significantly, however, the narrative frame of *The Explosion Chronicles* (i.e., the embedded narrative) is structurally juxtaposed against what Genette terms the "paratext" of the novel, a construct which he defines as "the means by which a text makes a book of itself and proposes itself as such to its readers, and more generally to the public."[39] From the above quotation by "Yan," we can see that the physical production of the chronicles is a concern for the fictionalized Yan, both in terms of how the chronicles are presented to its readers and for its representation of Explosion, but also that it meets the criteria that "*The Explosion Chronicles* Editorial Board" stipulates for Yan to receive "the enormous financial compensation" offered by Explosion City: "a sum so large," Yan reflects, that "it left me speechless."[40] This anxiety is not only reflected by a metatextual preface and postface written by the (fictional) Yan, which shows his concern for how *The Explosion Chronicles* is presented to its readers, but is framed by another narrative frame in the form of an "Author's Note" at the end of the book, in which (the real-life) Yan positions the novel in relation to a literary practice that he calls "mythorealism," which he defines as the use of a non-realistic narrative style to explore contemporary China's underlying reality.[41]

These multiple layers of narrative, demarcated by the novel's paratext, allow (the real-life) Yan to create what Genette conceptualizes as "a *threshold*, or … a 'vestibule' that offers the world at large the possibility of either stepping inside or turning back,"[42] an option which Yan himself invites the reader to partake in the novel's opening pages: "'Read these chronicles! Even if only a few pages, it will be as if you deposited a flower on my grave!'"[43] Once again, it is within this "threshold" space, manufactured by the paratextual constructs of the novel, that the narrative frame is juxtaposed against the primary narrative text of Yan's postface and wherein they function as heterotopic spaces.

Yan's paratextual conclusion to *The Explosion Chronicles* suggests a deliberate attempt by the author to separate the novel's integrative layers of narrative in order to invert the relationship between the embedded narratives and their paratextual constructs. The effect of this thus challenges the reader to question the relationship between reality (i.e., the book's paratextual construction) and fiction (the novel's narrative proper). The paratextual inclusion of a postface at the novel's conclusion thus constitutes the production of *The Explosion Chronicles*, which we, as readers, ultimately consume, and it is in the novel's conclusion that Yan symbolically transforms the fictitious censorship of the chronicles into an assertive act against the CCP's ideological vision for literature in China.

The narrative proper of Explosion's rise and fall is proceeded by a brief, closing postface in which the fictional Yan Lianke meets Explosion's city mayor, Kong Mingliang to deliver

---

38 Yan, *The Explosion Chronicles*, 1–2.
39 Gérard Genette, *Paratexts: Thresholds of Interpretation* (Cambridge: Cambridge University Press, 1977), 261.
40 Yan, *The Explosion Chronicles*, 1.
41 Carlos Rojas, Translator's Note to *The Explosion Chronicles*, by Yan Lianke (London: Chatto & Windus, 2017), v–x.
42 See Sally Bushell, "Paratext or Imagetext? Interpreting the Fictional Map," *Word & Image* 32, no. 2 (2016): 182; emphasis in the original.
43 Yan, *The Explosion Chronicles*, 3.

his completed manuscript. The meeting of "Yan Lianke" and Kong Mingliang whom, as we recall, was assassinated in Yan's fictive treatment, begins amicably as both men share a banquet hosted by Mayor Kong and exchange formalities before Yan submits his manuscript for the mayor's approval. The next morning, Yan is summoned to the mayor's office whereupon Mayor Kong sets Yan's newly completed manuscript alight and warns him: "As long as Explosion and I are here, you shouldn't even think about publishing this book in China. If you try to publish this book anywhere outside China, you'll never be permitted to return to your hometown in the Balou Mountains as long as you live."[44] Just as Yan's works in China are the target of coercive censorial action in China's literary system, *The Explosion Chronicle*'s fictional mayor censures the author by not only destroying his work but also by threatening his ability to publish without China and, perhaps more sinisterly, his ability to return to his homeland. The parallels established by Yan's real and fictive illustrations of Explosion's development akin to China, which are symbolically reinforced by the author's descriptive parallels between him and the chronicle's main character, also reveal the effect of censorship in the chronicle's destruction as a microcosm of China's censorship apparatus; as a symbol of censorship, Mayor Kong's burning of Yan's manuscript thus simultaneously erases the history of Explosion.

The conclusion of *The Explosion Chronicles* thus fictionally reimagines the difficulties which Yan encounters while evaluating the cultural-historical process of China's modernization and, more widely, highlights the challenges that contemporary Chinese writers encounter when addressing historical subjects inherent within the work of the post-1980s "generation of intellectuals who were otherwise bold and daring in their attempts to challenge the *status quo*."[45] Yet, the wider political and historical contexts of China show that it "is not a status quo country."[46] Within this context, D. K. Herzberger suggests that fiction's role in China thus seeks to open China to diversity and to empower the invented.[47] Consequently, the traditions of reading and writing associated with Herzberg's conclusion are reflected by the way in which Yan makes use of history and fiction within *The Explosion Chronicles*. The novel's paratextual conclusion, in which the fictive Yan's chronicles are destroyed highlights how fiction can negotiate the "official" historiography postulated under the CCP's authoritarian censorship system, symbolically transforming the secondary embedded narrative into the story we are reading.

By now turning to *The Four Books*, I show how the relationship between the reader and writer recurs as a thematic concern within Yan's wider oeuvre. However, these concerns are explicitly manifested and developed within *The Explosion Chronicle*'s multiple layers of embedded and paratextual narratives. Furthermore, the relationship between the reader within the wider context of the Chinese literary tradition is raised by Martin Kern and Robert E. Hegel, who stress that Chinese literature "has befallen not only the more technical issues involved in the history of literature but even some of the most basic concerns. Rarely do we see the fundamental questions that need to be asked anew for each period and

---

44 Ibid., 448.
45 Qian Suoqiao, *Liberal Cosmopolitan: Lin Yutang and Middling Chinese Modernity* (Leiden: Brill, 2011), 17; emphasis added.
46 Peter Hays Gries, *China's New Nationalism: Pride, Politics, and Diplomacy* (Berkeley: University of California Press, 2014), 11.
47 David K. Herzberger, "Cela and the Challenge to History in Francoist Spain," in *Spanish Literature: 1700 to the Present*, ed. David William Foster, Daniel Altamiranda, and Carmen de Urioste (New York: Garland, 2011), 11.

genre, namely: what is a text, and what is a book? What is an author, and what kind of social performance is the composition of (however defined) 'literature' in different periods under different circumstances?"[48] In *The Explosion Chronicles*, we can begin to see an answer to some of these questions through Yan's inclusion of preludial and postludial paratexts, which suggest that the novel is a significant move by Yan within his "overall assertive act."

This "overall assertive act," which Yan symbolically transforms within *The Explosion Chronicles* through Mayor Kong's censure of the chronicles, is reflected by the mayor's presumed victory in silencing Yan's fictive history of Explosion. Mayor Kong's triumph, however, is in fact mitigated and overcome by the novel's paratextual construction in which Yan's interplay of fiction and reality is transformed into the (real-life) Yan's book. Critically, this transformation, which occurs within the text's narrative and paratextual constructs, challenges Yan's readers to look beyond the novel's narrative proper to consider how the CCP's ideological vision for China, symbolized by the authoritarian figure of Mayor Kong, is a nihilistic method by which to shape out the world. This is a world in which, as *The Explosion Chronicles* shows us, literature, following primarily the task of imagination and simulation,[49] is called upon to validate past events and grant them authenticity under the mechanisms of an authoritarian regime.

Authorship and complicity in *The Four Books*

Notably, the censure of (the fictional) Yan Lianke's chronicles in *The Explosion Chronicles'* conclusion mirrors Yan's experience while attempting to publish his previous novel, *The Four Books* (*Si Shu* 四書, 2011), which is illustrative of Yan's first major break from the censors and marks a new turn in how Chinese literature has framed the historical events of the Mao era.[50] Attempting to engage with the massive loss of life during the Great Leap Forward and the Great Famine, *The Four Books* centers on a group of intellectuals undergoing compulsory re-education in a sprawling labor reform camp. The novel is told through fragments of the four fictional "books," referenced in the novel's title, two of which are written by the Author: a character identified according to his former profession, alongside his fellow inmates, similarly referred to throughout the text as the Musician, the Scholar, the Theologian, and the Technician.

While this chapter has previously highlighted works in which literary spaces of resistance are facilitated by Yan's use of metafiction, in *The Four Books*, the act of writing itself is symbolically transformed into an act of resistance against authoritarian control through the character of "the Author." As the novel's narrative unfolds, the Author records his experience of the re-education camp at the bequest of "the Child," a preadolescent Party officer in charge of the re-education camp, who delights in draconian rules, monitoring the intellectual inmates' behavior and confiscating their smuggled books.

While scholars, such as Leung Laifong 梁麗芳, have tended to focus on *The Four Books'* historical context and consequently, the novel as a critique of the Great Leap Forward and the ensuing disasters of the famine and the Cultural Revolution that followed, the technique

---

48 Martin Kern and Robert E. Hegel, "A History of Chinese Literature?" *Chinese Literature: Essays, Articles, Reviews* 26 (2004): 167.
49 Ulrike Altmann et al., "Fact versus Fiction: How Paratextual Information Shapes Our Reading Process," *Social Cognitive and Affective Neuroscience* 1, no. 1 (2014): 28.
50 Sebastian Veg, "Creating a Literary Space to Debate the Mao Era: The Fictionalization of the Great Leap Forward in Yan Lianke's *Four Books*," *China Perspectives*, 2014, no. 4: 10.

by which Yan juxtaposes the characters of the Child and the Author has been seemingly overlooked.[51] This omission is particularly striking given that this dynamic directly "reflects on issues of literary production and political supervision,"[52] two issues which, as we have seen in the concluding scene of *The Explosion Chronicles*, are once again symbolically reiterated by Yan in his fictional counterpart's confrontation with Kong Mingliang.

Speaking in an interview with Suman Gupta in 2008 while writing the Chinese version of *The Four Books*, Yan addressed the transactional relationship between artistic direction and state control in mainland China, in which he reflected: "I worry that in my writing I will unconsciously modify my standing and my artistic direction—that I will compromise in some way without realizing it, so that my writing will change in a way in which it shouldn't. ... In my new novel writing I am trying to find a balance between these two imperatives, ... [a]nd yet, I worry that this balancing is itself effectively a compromise, is a regressive step in my writing. Whether this is true I can only determine after the work is finished."[53] While Yan's concern about compromising his standing and artistic direction is manifested in the transaction between the Child and the Author, the metaphor Yan uses of the "balance between these two imperatives" is not fully realized until his subsequent writing and publication of *The Explosion Chronicles* in which, this chapter suggests, Yan manifests within his writing Foucault's concept of heterotopia in the novel's paratextual construction to highlight the *Chronicles*' central conceit of bypassing state censorship. However, no such overt conceit exists within *The Four Books*. While it would be tenuous to propose a reading of the novel akin to this chapter's earlier analysis of Yan's successive works, *The Four Books* is illustrative of a broader change in Yan's writing, one which is not, as Yan fears, "a regressive step," but which shows the development of his literature in finding a balance between his standing and artistic direction without compromising his writing.

The broader change in Yan's writing, as illustrated by *The Four Books*, is symbolically manifested in the transaction between the Child and the Author. Approaching novel from two aspects—first, to briefly consider the role of the Child in the novel as an enforcer of "the higher-ups" authority and as a metaphor of political supervision; and second, to illustrate the Author's response to the Child's directive—my reading of *The Four Books* shows how Yan's composition of the relationship between the Author and the Child functions as a symbolic representation of the censorship mechanisms of the CCP as it relates to literary production and political supervision of contemporary literature in China.

In his 2014 essay, "Creating a Literary Space to Debate the Mao Era," Sebastian Veg notes that "[t]he Child is a puzzling character ... who wholeheartedly believes in the system and is prepared to sacrifice himself to it."[54] Drawing from Tsai Chien-hsin's 蔡建鑫 analysis of the novel, Veg argues that the Child's trajectory, supported by "the biblical simplicity of his Mao-like pronouncements,... raises the question ... of whether, and how the Party can atone for its sins." Aside from *The Four Books*' title, which alludes to both the canonical texts of Confucianism and to the four Gospels of the Bible, the trajectory of the Child from the naïve enforcer of the "higher-ups" draconian rules to his sacrificial crucifixion, whereby "the

---

51 See Laifong Leung, "Yan Lianke: A Writer's Moral Duty," *Chinese Literature Today* 1, no. 2 (2011), 73–79.
52 Carlos Rojas, Translator's Note to *The Four Books*, by Yan Lianke (London: Chatto & Windus, 2017), vii.
53 Suman Gupta, "Li Rui, Mo Yan, Yan Lianke and Lin Bai: Four Contemporary Chinese Writers Interviewed," trans. Xiao Cheng, *Wasafiri* 23, no. 3 (2008): 34.
54 Veg, "Literary Space," 11–12.

Child [nails] himself to a cross covered with red blossoms,"[55] thus allowing the re-education camp's inmates to leave the compound, has particular implications for a reading of the text that correlates the Child as a metaphor for the authoritarianism of the CCP.

The ideological underpinnings of the Child over the course of the novel are gradually broken down and are emphasized by his reports on the re-education compound's inmates to the higher-ups in Beijing. Addressing the narrative trajectory of the Child over the course of *The Four Books* in an interview with the *South China Morning Post*, Yan reflected upon the symbolism of the character, whom he regards as "a unique presence not only in the novel, but also in Chinese literature, and even world literature. He is Evil but also a God. He can be Hitler or Mao. He is a very complex character who [is] both naïve, and equally capable of evil and good."[56] This contrast is illustrated upon the Child's first return from the capital whereby he relays the command to the inmates not to read, write or think unnecessarily and, later in the novel, when the Child, questioning the Author on the production levels of wheat in the compound, confides with the inmates that the higher-ups are pressuring him to produce results from the re-education camp.[57] Ultimately, the Child's capability of being "equally … evil and good" is fatefully illustrated by his sacrifice in defying the "higher-ups" and providing a means of escape for the re-education compound's inmates. By now turning to consider the transaction between the Child and Author at the beginning of *The Four Books*, I will show how the Child's act of atonement is a manifestation of his role as a symbolic representation of literary production and political supervision, while also considering the consequences of this control from the perspective of the Author.

Following his pronouncement mentioned earlier, in which he prohibits the re-education camp's inmates from reading or writing, nor thinking unnecessarily, the Child, whose ability to find prohibited books smuggled into the compound by its intellectual inmates makes him "[appear] to be omniscient,"[58] charges the Author with the task of chronicling the activities of the other inmates within the re-education compound, so that he can present a thorough record to his superiors. In return, the Child promises the Author that he will be permitted to return home if he provides enough incriminating material about his peers. Mirroring the threats which Kong Mingliang levels at the fictional Yan Lianke in the conclusion to *The Explosion Chronicles*, the Child's charge to the Author is a metaphor for the mechanisms of literary censorship in mainland China. Reflecting the targets of the CCP's censorship apparatus, the offer made by the higher-ups to "give" the Author another fifty sheets of paper per completed chapter reflects contemporary Chinese publications within the mainland that adhere to the CCP's ideological guidelines for literature.

By compromising the potential content of his book, the title of which is already predetermined by the higher-ups ("*Criminal Records*"), the Author enters into an agreement whereby the return investment on his work is nominally guaranteed. Furthermore, the higher-up's request is followed by a caveat in which the Author is promised premature release from the re-education compound and guarantees him preferential treatment in the process of literary production, as well as social and cultural standing as the leader of the country's writers in Beijing, provided that the Author meets the criteria established by the political ideology of his supervisors.

---

55 Yan Lianke, *The Four Books*, trans. Carlos Rojas (London: Chatto & Windus, 2015), 325.
56 Catherine Wong, "We Must Confront Our Dark Past of the Cultural Revolution to Avoid Repeating It."
57 Yan, *The Four Books*, 195.
58 Ibid., 16.

Although the Author enters into the agreement to watch over the other inmates of the re-education compound and deliver weekly written reports to the Child, thus becoming complicit in "single-handedly pocket[ing] the benefits of his snitching,"[59] the anxiety of what he should include and/or omit within "*Criminal Records*" soon becomes apparent. A point of detail in this regard is the Author's first response to his anxiety, whereby he reflects upon the wider political environment of the Mao era in which he and his fellow inmates find themselves. He observes: "I was keenly aware that we were in a state of political turmoil. ... 'If you're afraid that your handwriting might be recognized, you can simply imitate someone else's, write with your left hand, or even write with your eyes closed.'"[60] The Author's initial response to "write with [his] eyes closed" in the context of this environment appears to function as a metaphor for the act of self-censorship, an act of writing which Yan exercised while writing his 2006 novel *Dream of Ding Village* (*Dingzhuang meng* 丁莊夢).[61]

In his 2016 essay, "An Examination of China's Censorship System," Yan illustrates how "self-censorship arises out of an environment of terror, anxiety and fear, and while it is predicated on unwillingness and resistance, it eventually [generates] a kind of intuitive response."[62] Once again, the mechanisms of China's censorship apparatus are symbolically played out within *The Four Books* following the transaction between the Child and the Author as the latter's anxiety is manifested in his impulse to write an alternate account of the re-education compound: "I would get so anxious to write that my hands would become covered in sweat. ... I didn't want to write anything else for the Child and the higher-ups—not half a page, or even a few lines. Instead, I wanted to use this ink and paper to write what I really wanted to write. ... I wanted to write a true book. I didn't know what that book would be, but I was determined to write it nevertheless."[63] At this point in the narrative, the compromise that the Author accepts in his agreement with the higher-up's commission of "Criminal Records" is overcome and, no longer willing to chronicle the prescribed narrative of the higher-ups, his response is to compose another, "true," text entitled "Old Course." The Author's act of self-censorship in the earlier course of the novel is thus inverted: his composition of "Old Course" becomes his means of resistance while also functioning as a symbolic manifestation of the means by which the Author is finally able to confront his own complicity in the higher-up's system and understand his place and role as a writer.

Conclusion

Yan Lianke's fiction exhibits a uniquely nuanced approach to its historical referents. One reason for this is Yan's own experience and admission of self-censorship in his previous works, a concern which is symbolically manifested in *The Four Books*, wherein the character of the

---

59 Veg, "Literary Space," 12.
60 Yan, *The Four Books*, 20.
61 Intended as a carefully documented account of the AIDS crisis in Henan, Yan adopted fiction as a less "dangerous" form than the intended documentary account of his research. Following the novel's publication in 2006, Yan has since given multiple interviews in which he reflects upon the effect self-censorship had on his sense of his role as a writer while writing *Dream of Ding Village* in relation to the Chinese censorship apparatus. See, for example, Jonathan Watts, "Censors Sees through Writer's Guile in Tale of China's Blood-Selling Scandal," *The Guardian*, 9 Oct. 2006, https://www.theguardian.com/world/2006/oct/09/books.china (last accessed 25 Feb. 2019).
62 Yan Lianke, "An Examination of China's Censorship System," in *The Oxford Handbook of Modern Chinese Literatures*, ed. and trans. Carlos Rojas and Andrea Bachner (Oxford: Oxford University Press, 2016), 270.
63 Yan, *The Four Books*, 188.

Author resists the ideological commission from the "higher-ups" and, instead, produces an alternative novel, illustrating both his own awareness of his complicity but also his role as a writer under the censorial restrictions of the Chinese regime.

In my analysis of Yan's recent fiction, similar to the Author's growing awareness of the construction of texts in *The Four Books*, I have attempted to illustrate how Yan emphasizes the construction of fictional texts, placing emphasis on Yan as the author alongside the narrative and paratextual construction of his novels. By highlighting Yan's use of paratextual post- and prefaces in *The Day the Sun Died* and *The Explosion Chronicles* as examples of how Yan contains within the narrative proper an "imagined space" in which the author can reflect the socio-political concerns of contemporary China, this chapter points to his work as evidence of a new development within contemporary Chinese fiction, which emphasizes the role of the author alongside the content of the narrative text. Here, I take, for example, the paratextual construct of *The Day the Sun Died* and *The Explosion Chronicles*. In each of these texts, this chapter illustrates how the narrative proper is contained as an "imagined space" within the overall creative construct of the novel; in this sense, the paratextual post- and prefaces to each novel are employed by Yan in an effort to act as a continued literary space, in which the author reflects the socio-political constructs of contemporary China against the imaginary interpretations of the "fictionalized" China presented within each of these works. In its analysis of how Yan develops the paratextual construction of the novel, this chapter argues that Yan exhibits a uniquely literary response to the censorship mechanisms of the CCP, and that his writing has developed in such a way over a prolonged period of literary creation in which he has, in his previous works, been subject to and complicit in the act of self-censoring his own writing.

One problem this chapter raises in its discussion of Yan's recent fiction is the critical reception of contemporary Chinese fiction within Western readerships of his work which tend, more generally, to favor ideological underpinnings within contemporary Chinese fiction. For Yan, reception of *The Day the Sun Died* as a critique of Xi Jinping's underlying political strategy was surprising. By comparing Western reviews of the novel, which collectively align readings of *The Day the Sun Died* as a critical exposition of the "Chinese Dream" policy, this chapter emphasizes how the reality of critical discourse in China determines that this dialogue is limited by wider factors beyond the control of any individual author.

Finally, while this chapter considers the use and implications of the paratextual constructs of the Chinese novel,[64] further research is needed to identify if this system of literary resistance is evident and practiced in the paratextual construction of other works of fiction among a wider range of contemporary Chinese writers. If so, the implications may suggest that the creative framework of Yan's fiction is fundamentally significant in ascribing within contemporary Chinese literature a means by which a renewed emphasis on the role of the author, and the significance of the construction of narrative fiction itself, might be able to successfully circumvent, through fiction, the CCP's ideological guidelines and mechanisms of literary censorship existent in China today.

Bibliography

"Yan Lianke's Dark Satire of Modern China: A Novel of Looting, Murder and Economic Growth." *The Economist*, 26 July 2018. https://www.economist.com/books-and-arts/2018/07/26/yan-liankes-dark-satire-of-modern-china (last accessed 17 Aug. 2021).

---

64 See, for example, Frances Weightman, "Authoring the Strange: The Evolving Notions of Authorship in Prefaces to *Classical Supernatural Fiction*," *East Asian Publishing and Society* 8 (2018): 34–55.

Altman, Ulrike, et al. "Fact versus Fiction: How Paratextual Information Shapes Our Reading Process." *Social Cognitive and Affective Neuroscience* 1, no. 1 (2014): 22–29.
Bushell, Sally. "Paratext or Imagetext? Interpreting the Fictional Map." *Word & Image* 32, no. 2 (2016): 181–94.
Cai, Rong 蔡蓉. *Subject in Crisis in Contemporary Chinese Literature*. Honolulu: University of Hawaii Press, 2014.
Cao, Xuenan. "Mythorealism and Enchanted Time: Yan Lianke's *The Explosion Chronicles*." *Frontiers of Literary Studies in China* 10, no.1 (2016): 103–12.
Chambers, Harlan D. "Writing with Care: Yan Lianke and the Biopolitics of Modern Chinese Censorship." MA thesis, University of Texas, 2015.
Davis, Teresa. "Third Spaces or Heterotopias? Recreating and Negotiating Migrant Identity Using Online Spaces." *Sociology* 44, no. 4 (2010): 661–77.
Foucault, Michel. "Of Other Spaces," translated by J. Miskowiec. *Diacritics* 16, no.1 (1986): 22–27.
Genette, Gérard. *Paratexts: Thresholds of Interpretation*. Cambridge: Cambridge University Press, 1977.
Gries, Peter Hays. *China's New Nationalism: Pride, Politics, and Diplomacy*. 2nd ed. Berkeley: University of California Press, 2014.
Gupta, Suman. "Li Rui, Mo Yan, Yan Lianke and Lin Bai: Four Contemporary Chinese Writers Interviewed," translated by Xiao Cheng. *Wasafiri* 23, no. 3 (2008): 28–36.
Herzberger, David. K. "Cela and the Challenge to History in Francoist Spain." In *Spanish Literature: 1700 to the Present*, edited by David William Foster, Daniel Altamiranda, and Carmen de Urioste, 345–54. New York: Garland, 2001.
Hetherington, Kevin. *The Badlands of Modernity: Heterotopia and Social Ordering*. London: Routledge, 1997.
Hewitt, Sean. "*The Day the Sun Died* by Yan Lianke: A Brave, Masterful Novel." *The Irish Times*, 28 July 2018. https://www.irishtimes.com/culture/books/the-day-the-sun-died-by-yan-lianke-a-brave-masterful-novel-1.3558083 (last accessed 10 Jan. 2019).
Kern, Martin, and Robert E. Hegel. "A History of Chinese Literature?" *Chinese Literature: Essays, Articles, Reviews* 26 (2004): 159–79.
Kohn, Joel. "Novelist Yan Lianke Underlines Nobel Prize Ambitions in 'The Day the Sun Died'." *The Chronicle*, 26 Dec. 2018. https://www.dukechronicle.com/article/2018/12/novelist-yan-lianke-underlines-nobel-prize-ambitions-in-the-day-the-sun-died (last accessed 30 May 2021).
Lau, Mimi. "Coffins Smashed, Seized, Exhumed in China as Province Bans Burials to Save Land." *South China Morning Post*, 31 July 2018. https://www.scmp.com/news/china/society/article/2157531/coffins-smashed-seized-exhumed-china-province-bans-burials-save (last accessed 20 Jan. 2019).
Lee, Tong King. "China as Dystopia: Cultural Imaginings through Translation." *Translation Studies* 8, no. 3 (2015): 251–68.
Leung, Laifong 梁麗芳. "Yan Lianke: A Writer's Moral Duty." *Chinese Literature Today* 1, no. 2 (2011): 73–79.
Nelles, William. "Embedding." In *Routledge Encyclopedia of Narrative Theory*, edited by David Herman, Jahn Manfred, and Marie-Laure Ryan, 134–35. London: Routledge, 2010.
Newman, Bobby. "Discriminating Utopian from Dystopian Literature: Why Is Walden Two Considered a Dystopia?" *The Behavior Analyst* 16, no. 2 (1993): 167–75.
Qian, Suoqiao. *Liberal Cosmopolitan: Lin Yutang and Middling Chinese Modernity*. Leiden: Brill, 2011.
Rojas, Carlos. Translator's Note to *The Day the Sun Died*, by Yan Lianke, iii–x. London: Chatto & Windus, 2018.
———. Translator's Note to *The Explosion Chronicles*, by Yan Lianke, v–x. London: Chatto & Windus, 2017.
———. Translator's Note to *The Four Books*, by Yan Lianke, vii–xii. London: Chatto & Windus, 2015.
Sohn, Heidi. "Heterotopia: Anamnesis of a Medical Term." In *Heterotopia and the City: Public Space in a Postcivil Society*, edited by Michiel Dehaene and Lieven De Cauter, 41–50. London: Routledge, 2008.
Veg, Sebastian. "Creating a Literary Space to Debate the Mao Era: The Fictionalization of the Great Leap Forward in Yan Lianke's *Four Books*." *China Perspectives*, 2014, no. 4: 10.
Watts, Jonathan. "Censors Sees through Writer's Guile in Tale of China's Blood-Selling Scandal." *The Guardian*, 9 Oct. 2006. https://www.theguardian.com/world/2006/oct/09/books.china (last accessed 25 Feb. 2019).
Weightman, Frances. "Authoring the Strange: The Evolving Notions of Authorship in Prefaces to Classical Supernatural Fiction." *East Asian Publishing and Society* 8 (2018): 34–55.

Wong, Catherine. "We Must Confront Our Dark Past of the Cultural Revolution to Avoid Repeating It, Says Chinese Novelist Yan Lianke." *South China Morning Post*, 9 May 2016. https://www.scmp.com/news/china/policies-politics/article/1942609/we-must-confront-our-dark-past-cultural-revolution (last accessed 30 May 2021).

Yan Lianke 閻連科. *The Day the Sun Died*. Translated by Carlos Rojas. London: Chatto & Windus, 2018.

———. "An Examination of China's Censorship System." In *The Oxford Handbook of Modern Chinese Literatures*, edited by Carlos Rojas and Andrea Bachner, 263–74. Oxford: Oxford University Press, 2016.

———. *The Explosion Chronicles*. Translated by Carlos Rojas. London: Chatto & Windus, 2017.

———. *The Four Books*. Translated by Carlos Rojas. London: Chatto & Windus, 2015.

———. *Xia riluo* 夏日落 [Summer sunset]. Taipei: Lianjing, 2010.

———. "Yan Lianke: 'It's Hard to Get My Books Published in China.'" Interview by Lesley McDowell. *The Guardian*, 22 Sep. 2018. https://www.theguardian.com/books/2018/sep/22/yan-lianke-writers-in-china-day-the-sun-died-interview (last accessed 30 May 2021).

PART IV

Translation and reception

23
IDEOLOGICAL PATTERNS IN THE CRITICAL RECEPTION OF YAN LIANKE

A comparative approach

Chunli Shen

Yan Lianke 閻連科, who started publishing his works in 1979, is both influential and controversial in China, commonly seen as a promising candidate for the Nobel Literature Prize since he was awarded and shortlisted for several international literary prizes. Chinese official newspaper *China Daily* acclaims Yan as "a literary star" who might be "the next global literary sensation."[1] In contrast to China's emphasis on his international recognition, the West routinely introduces Yan as a banned and politically sensitive writer in China. For instance, the editor Becky Hardie from Chatto & Windus describes Yan as a "highly political writer" and a "teller of often dangerous truths."[2] Such divergent reception paths of Yan in terms of the controversial authorial status offer an intriguing point of departure for this chapter to explore how perceptions of an author and his literary works are transferred and mediated through literary criticism in different social, cultural, and ideological contexts. This chapter will engage with the critical reception of Yan and his works in China and the West from a comparative perspective. Through analyzing the Chinese and Western scholars' literary criticism published in books and journals, it attempts to identify the disparate reception patterns of Yan's works in China and the West. However, literary criticism does not occur in a vacuum but is mainly constrained by "the dominant ideological and poetological current" of a given culture and time.[3] From this perspective, this chapter will further explore the different ideological and poetological inclinations of Chinese and Western literary critics by locating the disparate reception in the Chinese and Western sociopolitical contexts.

---

1 See "A Literary Star Emerges from Countryside," *China Daily*, Mar. 2010, http://www.chinadaily.com.cn/life/2010-03/12/content_9579260.htm (last accessed 8 Dec. 2016).
2 See Becky Hardie, "The Dangerous Truths of Yan Lianke," Mar. 2015, https://www.penguin.co.uk/articles/2015/the-dangerous-truth-of-yan-lianke.html#L5R6RAcMbKjlIs6A.99 (last accessed 8 Dec. 2016).
3 André Lefevere, *Translation, Rewriting, and the Manipulation of Literary Fame* (London: Routledge, 1992), 8.

As Yan has published many fictional works, it is impossible to provide an exhaustive investigation of their literary criticism in the limited space here. Consequently, this chapter will focus on the literary scholarship on Yan's representative works at different stages of reception, including his Yaogou Series (*Yaogou xilie* 瑤溝系列),[4] *Streams of Time* (*Riguang liunian* 日光流年, 1998) and *Hard Like Water* (*Jianying ru shui* 堅硬如水, 2001),[5] and the eight works that have been translated into English by 2020.[6] To collect data of the Chinese scholarship on Yan's works, this chapter has consulted the important journals indexed by Chinese Social Sciences Citation Index and A Guide to the Core Journal of China in the database of China National Knowledge Infrastructure (CNKI). In this way, the chapter has found 477 articles in total, 281 of which are literary criticisms, from 1992 to 2020 by searching the subject "閻連科." As far as the Western discourse is concerned, the present chapter will examine the articles written in English and issued by American or British institutions regardless of the nationalities of their authors, given the fact that very few articles have been written by native American or British literary critics on Yan. According to these criteria, this chapter has obtained 24 critical articles about Yan's works by consulting the database of *Modern Chinese Literature and Culture* and the catalog of the British Library. In the following sections, this chapter will examine these collected data to shed light on the reception of Yan's works both in China and the West.

The reception of Yan Lianke's works in China: Literary aesthetics and universal significance

Chinese critical reception of Yan's works mainly revolves around their literary aesthetics and universal significance. It is noteworthy that these two reception patterns are in fact not clear-cut but rather intersect with each other. However, for the sake of a clear and nuanced illumination of each reception pattern, this chapter will discuss them in a relatively independent way and provide a chronological analysis of Yan's works in turn according to their publication year in China. In terms of the literary aesthetics, Chinese literary critics often focus on questions related to the narrative structure, narrative strategy, and rhetoric of Yan's works.

With respect to *Streams of Time*, Chinese scholars give special attention to its narrative structure of flashback and narratological strategy of synesthesia. For instance, calling Yan's narrative structure of flashback as "tracing origin style" (*suoyuanti* 索源體), Wang Yichuan 王一川 holds the view that it is instrumental in exploring the complex and cyclical relationship of death and life.[7] With an acknowledgment of Yan's unusual narrative, Li Er 李洱 contends that it empowers

---

4 The data from China National Knowledge Infrastructure (CNKI) reveals that occasional reviews on Yan's fiction in China emerged in the early 1990s, which focused on Yan's "Yaogou Series," in which Yan portrayed the people's life in the fictional world Yaogou on Balou 耙耬 Mountains.
5 After Yan published *Streams of Time* and *Hard Like Water*, he was acknowledged by Chinese literary critics as one of the most important Chinese writers. See Wang Yao 王堯 and Lin Jianfa 林建法, "Xiaoshuojia jiangtan: Zhuchiren de hua" 小說家講壇：主持人的話 [Forum for novelists: Chairperson's speech], *Dangdai zuojia pinglun* 當代作家評論 [Contemporary writers review], 2004, no. 2: 71.
6 *Serve the People!* (*Wei renmin fuwu* 為人民服務, 2005), *Dream of Ding Village* (*Dingzhuang meng* 丁莊夢, 2006), *Lenin's Kisses* (*Shouhuo* 受活, 2003), *The Four Books* (*Si shu* 四書, 2011), *The Explosion Chronicles* (*Zhalie zhi* 炸裂志, 2013), *Years Month Days* (*Nian yue ri* 年月日, 1997), *The Day the Sun Died* (*Rixi* 日熄, 2015), and *Three Brothers: Memories of My Family* (*Wo yu fubei* 我與父輩 2009).
7 Wang Yichuan, "Shengsi youxi yishi de fuyuan: *Riguang liunian* de suoyuanti tezheng 生死遊戲儀式的復原——《日光流年》的索源體特徵 [The recovery of the rituals of life and death: The feature of "suoyuanti" in *Streams of Time*], *Dangdai zuojia pinglun*, 2001, no. 6: 11.

the works to better illustrate themes such as fighting against doom.[8] In addition to the creative narrative structure, some scholars give prominence to Yan's creative employment of synesthesia in *Streams of Time* which, in their view, endows the work with a tense and serious atmosphere.[9]

When elaborating on *Hard Like Water*, Chinese scholars primarily focus on Yan's writing formula called "revolution plus love." According to David Der-wei Wang 王德威, this formula was widely used by Chinese writers to "invoke the romance as a symbol of the revolution" and present their revolutionary idealism.[10] In the view of Wang Zheng 汪政, by interweaving the passionate sexual affairs with the revolutionary zeal of the protagonists during the revolution periods in the fictional town Chenggang, *Hard Like Water* rewrites "revolution plus love" via satirizing a series of ridiculous aspects of the revolution.[11] Similarly, some other scholars also comment that such satirical effects are achieved mainly through the grotesque and carnivalesque narration of abundant sexual scenes permeated with frenzied revolutionary languages.[12]

When it comes to *Lenin's Kisses*, Chinese literary critics bring Yan's use of "supplementary notes" (絮言) and "the stems-and-branches" (天干地支, a kind of traditional calendrical system) to the fore. For example, Wang Hongsheng 王鴻生 and He Zhantao 何占濤 credit Yan's innovative use of "supplementary notes" for offering readers enough contextual information of the story and making the major text simple and logical to facilitating their understanding.[13] With a critical view of Yan's employment of the "the stems-and-branches," Shao Yanjun 邵燕君 maintains that telling his stories in such a traditional way without reference to modernism is not able to provide fruitful reflections on the modern history.[14] On the contrary, Liang Hong 梁鴻 praises "the stems-and-branches" for its cyclical feature, which preserves Chinese traditional idea of time and, more importantly, resists the temptation to reflect Chinese history in the scheme of world history in terms of continuous and evolving time.[15]

---

8   Li Er, "Yan Lianke de shengmu" 閻連科的聲母 [Yan Lianke's initial consonant], *Nanfang wentan* 南方文壇 [Southern cultural forum], 2007, no. 5: 46.
9   Feng Min 馮敏, "Siwang yu shijian: Changpian xiaoshuo *Riguang liunian* zhuti jieshi ji qita" 死亡與時間——長篇小說《日光流年》主題揭示及其他 [Death and time: On the theme and other aspects of *Streams of Time*], *Xiaoshuo pinglun* 小說評論 [Fiction review], 1999, no. 5: 83; Nan Fan 南帆, "Fankang yu beiju: Du Yan Lianke de *Riguang liunian*" 反抗與悲劇——讀閻連科的《日光流年》 [Revolt and tragedy: Reading Yan Lianke's *Streams of Time*], *Dangdai zuojia pinglun* 當代作家評論 [Contemporary writers review], 1999, no. 4: 85.
10 David Der-wei Wang, *The Monster That is History: History, Violence, and Fictional Writing in Twentieth-Century China* (Berkeley: University of California Press, 2004), 81.
11 Wang Zheng, "Yinxiang dianji (201–221): *Jianying ru shui* (changpian xiaoshuo)" 印象點擊 (201–221)——《堅硬如水》(長篇小說) [Impression (201–221): *Hard Like Water* (a novel)], *Dangdai zuojia pinglun*, 2011, no. 2: 67.
12 Zhang Zhizhong 張志忠, "*Jianying ru shui* (changpian xiaoshuo)," *Dangdai zuojia pinglun*, 2001, no. 3: 63; Lin Zhou 林舟, "*Jianying ru shui* (changpian xiaoshuo)," *Dangdai zuojia pinglun*, 2001, no. 5: 67–68.
13 Wang Hongsheng, "Fan wutuobang de wutuobang xushi: Du *Shouhuo* 反烏托邦的烏托邦敘事——讀《受活》 [Utopia narration of anti-utopia: Reading *Pleasure*], *Dangdai zuojia pinglun*, 2004, no. 2: 97; He Zhantao, "*Shouhuo* xuyan de xushi moshi" 《受活》絮言的敘事模式 [On the narrative mode of *Pleasure*'s "suoyanti"], *Xiaoshuo pinglun*, 2009, no. 4: 146.
14 Shao Yanjun, "Yu dadi shang de kunan ca jian er guo: You Yan Lianke *Shouhuo* kan dangdai xiangtu wenxue xianshi zhuyi chuantong de shiluo" 與大地上的苦難擦肩而過——由閻連科《受活》看當代鄉土文學現實主義傳統的失落 [Missing the hardship of rural areas: Looking into the loss of traditional realism of contemporary native soil literature from Yan Lianke's *Pleasure*], *Wenyi lilun yu piping* 文藝理論與批評 [Theory and criticism of literature and art], 2004, no. 6: 7.
15 Liang Hong, "Zhaohun, lunhui yu lishi de kaiqi: Lun *Shouhuo* de shijian" 招魂、輪迴與歷史的開啟——論《受活》的時間 [Summoning the soul, reincarnation and the beginning of history: On the time of *Pleasure*], *Dangdai zuojia pinglun*, 2013, no. 2: 25–26.

With regard to *Dream of Ding Village*, its innovative narrative techniques attract much attention. As Fang Yi 方奕 observes, the combination of realism and magical realism finds their full expression in Yan's blending of the narration of reality and dream.[16] With an appreciation of the narrative mode of the work, Hong Zhigang 洪治綱 comments that narrating the events through the perspective of the dead ghost alleviates the writer's intervention.[17]

In terms of *The Explosion Chronicles*, *The Four Books* and *The Day the Sun Died*, many Chinese critics are interested in the relation between Yan's creative aesthetic "mythorealism" (*shenshi zhuyi* 神實主義) in his writings and the Chinese realism tradition or the critical realism, and how Yan represents the concealed truth or reality through mythorealism. For instance, Wang Hongtu 王宏圖 and Wang Haitao 王海濤 associate *The Explosion Chronicles* with Gabriel García Márquez's *One Hundred Years of Solitude* (1967) and give credit to Yan for freeing himself from the realistic style that had been dominated in the early twentieth century to reveal the reality by means of eerie imagination.[18] In discussing *The Four Books*, Wang Yao 王堯 and Xu Ruowen 許若文 point out that the seemingly illogical narration of the protagonists called the Child and the Author is the writer's attempt to go beyond realism and capture the truth in life.[19] When analyzing *The Day the Sun Died*, Sun Yu 孫郁 compares Yan with Lu Xun 魯迅 and Franz Kafka, arguing that Yan similarly tries to reach the soul of people (how people perceive reality) by using eerie sentences and grotesque imagination.[20] Despite being highly acclaimed among Chinese scholarship, Yan's theory of mythorealism is also questioned by a handful of scholars. For instance, Ding Fan 丁帆 prefers to identify *The Four Books* as "absurd critical realism" (*huangdan pipan xianshi zhuyi* 荒誕批判現實主義) rather than mythorealism, since he observes that mythorealism cannot fully express the theme and form of *The Four Books*.[21] Xu Yong 徐勇 argues that Yan tends to abandon reality or real life in *The Day the Sun Died* while pursuing mythorealism via using satire in an extreme way.[22]

---

16 Fang Yi, "Yuwang, siwang, mengjing: Cong san ge guanjianzi jiedu *Dingzhuang meng*" 欲望·死亡·夢境——從三個關鍵字解讀《丁莊夢》 [Desire, death, dream: Reading *Dream of Ding Village* from three key words], *Mingzuo xinshang* 名作欣賞 [Appreciation of masterpieces], 2008, no. 22: 80–81.

17 Hong Zhigang, "Xiangcun kunan de jizhi zhi lü: Yan Lianke xiaoshuo lun" 鄉村苦難的極致之旅——閻連科小說論 [The extreme hardship in rural areas: On Yan Lianke's novel], *Dangdai zuojia pinglun*, 2007, no. 5: 78.

18 Wang Hongtu, "Xianshi zhuyi zai Zhongguo de mingyun" 現實主義在中國的命運 [The fate of realism in China], *Xueshu zhengming* 學術爭鳴 [Scholarly criticism], 2015, no. 6: 48-50.; Wang Haitao, "Bianhe shidai de shenshi xiezuo" 變革時代的神實寫作 [Mythorealism in revolutionary times], *Xiaoshuo pinglun*, 2014, no. 6: 98.

19 Wang Yao, "Zuowei shijiguan he fangfalun de 'shenshi zhuyi': *Faxian xiaoshuo* yu Yan Lianke de xiaoshuo chuangzuo" 作為世界觀和方法論的「神實主義」——《發現小說》與閻連科的小說創作 ["Mythorealism" as world view and methodology: *Explosion of Ficiton* and Yan Lianke's literary creation], *Dangdai zuojia pinglun*, 2013, no. 6: 11-12; Xu Ruowen, "*Si shu* zhong de ling yinguo yu silie xianshi zhuyi de wenti" 《四書》中的零因果與撕裂現實主義的文體 [Zero cause in *The Four Books* and the departure from realism], *Nanfang wentan*, 2012, no. 1: 125–30.

20 Sun Yu, "Cong *Shouhuo* dao *Rixi*: Zai tan Yan Lianke de shenshi zhuyi" 從《受活》到《日熄》——再談閻連科的神實主義 [From *Lenin's Kisses* to *The Day the Sun Died*: Revisiting Yan Lianke's mythorealism], *Dangdai zuojia pinglun*, 2017, no. 2: 5–11.

21 Ding Fan, "Zai 'shenshi zhuyi' yu 'huangdan pipan xianshi zhuyi' zhijian" 在「神實主義」與「荒誕批判現實主義」之間 [Between "mythorealism" and "absurd critical realism"], *Dangdai zuojia pinglun*, 2016, no. 1: 4–11.

22 Xu Yong, "Fengci xiezuo yu xiaoshuo chuangzuo de bianjie wenti: Lun Yan Lianke de *Rixi* jianji xiangguan chuangzuo" 諷刺寫作與小說創作的邊界問題——論閻連科的《日熄》兼及相關創作 [The boundary between satirical writing and fiction creation: On Yan Lianke's *The Day the Sun Died* and its related creations], *Wenyi yanjiu* 文藝研究 [Literature & art studies], 2017, no. 6: 26–34.

Aside from the literary aesthetics of Yan's works, their universal significance, which is exemplified by his exploration of universal themes such as life, death, love, desire, humanity, and redemption, is the primary focus of Chinese scholarship. For instance, as regards the thematic orientations of the Yaogou Series, an array of Chinese critics argue that Yan's works primarily deal with peasants' struggling for survival, their desires and failures and explore the contradictory love-hate complex of its protagonists toward their rural hometown.[23]

When discussing *Streams of Time*, some scholars incline to provide an ahistorical reading of the depiction that highlights death and tragedy. In the view of Nan Fan, the short life of the villagers in the Three Surname Village could not be attributed to any human factors, as they had not engaged in any political competitions, military confrontations, or complex modern economic competitions.[24] In a similar vein, Tao Dongfeng 陶東風 attempts to draw a clear line between the tragedy of the villagers in the Three Surname Village and the socio-historical movements such as the Great Leap Forward (1958–62) and the Great Famine (1959–61) depicted in the work by highlighting the mysteriousness of the villagers' tragedy.[25] Some other Chinese scholars also consistently draw readers' attention to Yan's exploration of the fundamental issues relating to human existence, like the universal human destiny and the touching stories about human struggles.[26]

With respect to *Hard Like Water*, Chen Sihe 陳思和 discusses its exploration of the psychological issue of "daimonic" and further brings the universality of the issue of daimonic to the fore by associating it with the concern of Socrates, Sigmund Freud, and George Gordon Byron.[27] From a different perspective, Zhang Xuexin 張學昕 and Yang Liang 楊亮 argue that *Hard Like Water* departures drastically from scar literature and reflective literature, since it explores the Cultural Revolution from the perspective of human nature and original desire, not merely from the restriction of specific social and historical conditions.[28] In this regard,

---

23 Zhao Shunhong 趙順宏, "Xiangtu de mengxiang: Lun Yan Lianke jinnian lai de xiaoshuo chuangzuo" 鄉土的夢想——論閻連科近年來的小說創作 [The dream of rural areas: Reviews on Yan Lianke's fiction writing in recent years], *Xiaoshuo pinglun*, 1993, no. 6: 9–13; Xu Guojun 徐國俊, "Nongmin qingjie: Nanyuan de meng—Yan Lianke xiaoshuo manping" 農民情結: 難圓的夢——閻連科小說漫評 [The complex of peasantry: A dream that is hard to fulfill—Reviews of Yan Lianke's fiction], *Dangdai zuojia pinglun*, 1993, no. 4: 84–88; Zhu Xiangqian 朱向前, "Nongmin zhi zi yu nongmin junren: Yan Lianke junlü xiaoshuo chuangzuo de dingwei" 農民之子與農民軍人——閻連科軍旅小說創作的定位 [The son of peasants and soldier peasants: The positioning of Yan Lianke's military fiction], *Dangdai zuojia pinglun*, 1994, no. 6: 59–70.
24 Nan Fan, "Fankang yu beiju," 80.
25 Tao Dongfeng, "Cong mingyun beiju dao shehui lishi beiju: Yan Lianke *Nian yue ri*, *Riguang liunian*, *Shouhuo* zonglun" 從命運悲劇到社會歷史悲劇——閻連科《年月日》《日光流年》《受活》綜論 [From destined tragedy to social-historical tragedy: Reviews of Yan Lianke's *Years Months Days*, *Streams of Time* and *Pleasure*], *Zhongguo xiandai wenxue yanjiu congkan* 中國現代文學研究叢刊 [Modern Chinese literature studies], 2016, no. 2: 175.
26 Feng Min 馮敏, "Siwang yu shijian: Changpian xiaoshuo *Riguang liunian* zhuti jieshi yu qita" 死亡與時間——長篇小說《日光流年》主題揭示及其他 [Death and time: On the theme and other aspects of *Streams of Time*], *Xiaoshuo pinglun*, 1999, no. 5: 83; Chen Sihe, "Du Yanlianke de xiaoshuo zhaji zhi yi" 讀閻連科的小說劄記之一 [Reading note of Yan's fiction (1)], *Xinan minzu daxue xuebao* 西南民族大學學報 [Journal of Southwest University for Nationalities] (Humanities & Social Sciences), 2001, no, 3: 45.
27 Chen Sihe, "Shilun Yan Lianke de *Jianying ru shui* zhong de e'moxing yinsu" 試論閻連科的《堅硬如水》中的惡魔性因素 [On the daimonic in Yan Lianke's *Hard Like Water*], *Dangdai zuojia pinglun*, 2002, no. 4: 36–40.
28 Zhang Xuexin and Yang Liang, "Quanli he yuwang jiaozhu de huayu kuanghuan: Lun Yan Lianke *Jianying ru shui*" 權力和欲望角逐的話語狂歡——論閻連科《堅硬如水》[Carnival discourse in the struggle for power and desire: On Yan Lianke's *Hard Like Water*], *Xiaoshuo pinglun*, 2006, no. 4: 80–84.

it is apparent that they foreground Yan's narration of negative aspects of humanity, which is definitely an important theme around the world, but tone down his critique of the Cultural Revolution in China.

For the reception of Yan's other fiction, Chinese scholars concentrate on their universal themes as well. For instance, a number of scholars stress the peasants' desires for power, money, and sex in *Lenin's Kisses*,[29] *Dream of Ding Village*,[30] and *The Explosion Chronicles*,[31] as well as the forces of evil in *The Day the Sun Died*.[32] A handful of scholars direct their attention to how Yan foregrounds problems caused by modern industrial civilization, such as the alienation of humanity in *Lenin's Kisses*[33] and *The Explosion Chronicles*.[34] Some other scholars are concerned with the common theme of humanity, repentance, and redemption in *The Four Books*.[35]

The reception of Yan Lianke's works in the West: Repressive censorship and sociopolitical documents

Unlike the reception of Yan's works in China, Western critics have a tendency to foreground the repressive censorship imposed on Yan's works in China and project them as sociopolitical documentaries. With an aim to bring the repressive censorship in China to the spotlight, they focus on the discussion of the state censorship and the self-censorship of Yan and publishing houses surrounding Yan's works. They consider the state censorship as a hindrance to literary creativity, as it is viewed as a powerful force to push Yan to self-censoring his own writing and Chinese publishing houses to conduct self-censorship in editing his works.

By featuring around keywords such as "banned," "controversial" and "sensitive," many scholars highlight the fact that Yan has been subject to various censorship in China, as his works have probed into the forbidden dimensions related to politics, governmental authorities, and

---

29 Lei Da 雷達, "Changpian xiaoshuo biji zhi ershi" 長篇小說筆記之二十 [Reading notes of novels (20)], *Xiaoshuo pinglun*, 2004, no. 3: 8; Wang hongsheng 王鴻生, "Fan wutuobang de wutuobang xushi—Du 'Shouhuo'" 反烏托邦的烏托邦敘事——讀《受活》[Utopia narration of anti-utopia—Reading of *Pleasure*], *Dangdai zuojia pinglu*, 2004, no. 2: 94.
30 Fang, "Yuwang, siwang, mengjing," 79–81; Ye Jun 葉君, "Xiangcun huangye: Xiangxiang yu feixugou—Cong Dingzhuang dao Liangzhuang" 鄉村荒野:想像與非虛構——從丁莊到梁莊 [Wildness of village: Imaginary and non-fictional——From Ding Village to Liang Village], *Tianjin shifan daxue xuebao (shehui kexue ban)* 天津師範大學學報 (社會科學版) [Journal of Tianjin Normal University (Social Science)], 2015, no. 1: 38–39.
31 Chen Hengjin 陳蘅瑾, "Ai hen jiaozhi de xiangtu qinggan" 愛恨交織的鄉土情感 [Love and hatred complex towards the rural hometown], *Xiaoshuo pinglun*, 2014, no. 6: 106.
32 Xu, "Fengci xiezuo yu xiaoshuo chuangzuo de bianjie wenti," 26.
33 Liu Zaifu 劉再復, "'Xiandaihua' ciji xia de yuwang fengkuangbing: *Jiuguo, Shouhuo, Xiongdi* sanbu xiaoshuo de pipan zhixiang" 「現代化」刺激下的欲望瘋狂病——《酒國》、《受活》、《兄弟》三部小說的批判指向 [Crazy desires motivated by "modernization": A Critical orientation towards *The Republic of Wine, Lenin's Kisses* and *Brothers*], *Dangdai zuojia pinglun*, 2011, no. 6: 51.
34 Fang Wei 房偉, "'Zhalie' de qishu: Ping Yan Lianke de xiaoshuo chuangzuo" 「炸裂」的奇書——評閻連科的小說創作 [The grotesque book of "explosion": On Yan Lianke's fictional writing], *Wenxue pinglun*, 2014, no. 3: 100; Wang, "Biange shidai de shenshi xiezuo," 98.
35 Cheng Guangwei 程光煒 and Qiu Huadong 邱華棟, "Chongshen shangheng wenxue lishi xushu de kenengxing: Yan Lianke xinzuo *Si shu, Faxian xiaoshuo* yantaohui jiyao" 重審傷痕文學歷史敘述的可能性——閻連科新作《四書》、《發現小說》研討會紀要 [Rethinking the possibility of the historical narrative of "scar literature": A summary of the seminar on Yan Lianke's *The Four Books* and *Faxian xiaoshuo*], *Dangdai zuojia pinglun*, 2011, no. 4: 54–55; Wang Binbin 王彬彬, "Yan Lianke de *Si shu*" 閻連科的四書 [Yan Lianke's *The Four Books*], *Xiaoshuo pinglun*, 2011, no. 2: 22–23.

Ideological Patterns in Critical Reception

sexual desire. For instance, Thomas Chen observes that Yan's writings like *Serve the People!* and *Dream of Ding Village* "consistently test the boundaries of state censorship" and are vulnerable to state censorship, due to their sensitive political and sexual plotlines.[36] Echoing Chen, Yang Jincai reveals that *Serve the People!* was banned since it is "extensive controversy" in depicting "vivid and colorful … sex scenes" and "items related to Mao and political issues."[37] In the view of Wang Jinhui, *Serve the People!* "irritated the authority so much" for the reason that it ironically parodies Mao's famous slogan "serve the people" (*wei renmin fuwu* 為人民服務), "deconstruct[ing] completely its authenticity and forcefully tear[ing] off the hypocritical veil of certain authorities."[38]

Some scholars dwell on Yan's self-censorship to reflect on the oppressive state censorship in China. For example, Tsai Chien-hsin 蔡建鑫 opens his article with a detailed discussion of Yan's self-censorship through the preemptive revision of *Serve the People!* and *Dream of Ding Village*, demonstrating Yan's helpless situations when it comes to the very strict state censorship.[39] Similarly, to demonstrate the severe state censorship in China on writings, Sebastian Veg also pays attention to Yan's self-censorship, revealing that Yan has made conscious efforts to "adopt fiction as a less dangerous form than a documentary account of his research."[40] With respect to *Serve the People!*, Ha Jin 哈金 points out that Yan has made a futile attempt to "cut more than 40,000 of the original 90,000 words" to deal with the state censorship and laments that such self-censorship makes it not like a piece of work anymore.[41]

A handful of scholars also pay attention to the difficult situation faced by Chinese publishing houses that try to publish Yan's works under strict state censorship. For example, the publisher of *Serve the People!* was requested to recall all copies from bookstores, which had an impact on the publisher's "commercial viability."[42] Being involved in the publication of *Serve the People!*, the editors were required by Chinese authorities to "perform self-criticism, examining their negligence and explaining the whole process of the publication to General Administrations of Press and Publication."[43] With Yan's *The Four Books*, no Chinese publishing houses were willing to take risks, leading to its "non-publication in mainland China."[44] In this respect, it is evident that the Chinese publishing industry is strictly monitored and repressed by China's censorship system with coercive forces or regulations and has to resort to self-censorship to guard against severe punishments.

Apart from the repressive censorship in China, the existing scholarship shows a keen interest in historical, social, and political issues in China. Phrases such as "the Great Leap Forward," "the Great Famine," "the Cultural Revolution," "the Mao era" (1949–76), "the

---

36 Thomas Chen, "Ridiculing the Golden Age: Subversive Undertones in Yan Lianke's Happy," *Chinese Literature Today* 1, no. 2 (2011): 66.
37 Jincai Yang, "Political Interrogation in Contemporary Chinese Fiction," *Neohelicon: Acta Comparationis Litterarum Universarum* 41, no. 1 (2014): 151.
38 Jinghui Wang, "'Serve the People' from 1944 to 2005," *Neohelicon* 43, no. 1 (2016): 52.
39 Chien-hsin Tsai, "In Sickness or in Health: Yan Lianke and the Writing of Autoimmunity," *Modern Chinese Literature and Culture* 23, no. 1 (2011): 95.
40 Sebastian Veg, "Eliminating Disharmony: Recent Examples of Censorship in Chinese Writing and Cinema," *China Perspectives*, 2007, no. 3: 66.
41 Ha Jin, "The Censor in the Mirror: It's Not Only What the Chinese Propaganda Department Does to Artists, but What It Makes Artists Do to Their Own Work," *American Scholar* 77, no. 4 (2008): 30.
42 Sebastian Veg, "New Spaces, New Controls: China's Embryonic Public Sphere," *Current History* 114, no. 773 (2015): 204.
43 Ha Jin, "The Censor in the Mirror," 31.
44 Sebastian Veg, "Creating a Literary Space to Debate the Mao Era: The Fictionalization of the Great Leap Forward in Yan Lianke's *Four Books*," *China Perspectives*, 2014, no. 4: 10.

Post-Mao era" and "the Economic Reform" recur frequently to set the historical background of Yan's stories. By placing Yan's works against the backdrop of these historical events or revolutionary upheavals, Western scholars primarily view his works as sociopolitical documentaries through which to shed light on the social and political problems in China, despite with some references to his writing styles.

Leung Laifong 梁麗芳 is the only researcher who conducts a panoramic overview of Yan's fictional works at different periods. She frames Yan's early works of Yaogou Series as a faithful representation of poverty-stricken rural areas in China by offering a complete study of Yan's harsh childhood experience and demonstrating that they evoke "a sense of autobiographical truth."[45] When elaborating Yan's works from the mid-1990s to 2003, she praises Yan for expanding his artistic horizons in terms of "blending fantasy and folk myth with the grotesque."[46] However, such artistic aspect is only given limited attention. Leung turns to conduct a lengthy review on "the failure" of the Sisyphean project (looking for ways to cure deadly disease) in *Streams of Time* and links it to "the many mega projects orchestrated during and after Maoist rule."[47] In this way, her interpretation of the work as a political critique toward the Maoist regime is brought to the fore. Furthermore, Leung comments on five individual works from 2004 onward, showing that their narrative is "grotesque," "satirical," "intensive," and "fantastic," and their thematic orientation is to satirize the army and beyond. For instance, she observes that Yan "has created a narrative that interweaves illusion and reality to critique that horrible page of recent Chinese history: the Great Leap Forward and its disastrous aftermath, the Great Famine" in *The Four Books*.[48] It is also noteworthy that her article ends with an emphasis on the authenticity of Yan's fictional works. Consequently, readers are left with the impression that the depictions of the dark side of China in Yan's literary oeuvre are reliable as documentary materials.

Unlike Leung, Carlos Rojas does not mention Yan's early works but focuses on his "increasingly provocative works" since the mid-1990s.[49] Rojas sets out to touch on Yan's mythorealism but only devotes one sentence to it. He then immediately turns to identify Yan as a "controversial" writer and spends the following three pages elaborating on Yan's works that are "either banned or recalled" with "politically sensitive topics."[50] This stark contrast suggests that Rojas downplays the literary style while highlighting the political critique of Yan's works, which is also self-evident in his subsequent reviews. For instance, his review of *Streams of Time* foregrounds "the recent attention to so-called Chinese cancer villages, in which industrial pollution is believed to be responsible for high rates of cancer."[51]

In another article, Rojas's discussion on the political dynamics of China is striking. Firstly, he expresses his general impression of China: "the Maoist era was characterized by a systematic process of political scapegoating to buttress the state's authority, the post-Mao era has witnessed a wide-scale process of sociopolitical disenfranchisement in the name of economic development."[52] Then he dwells on the suffering of rural-to-urban migrants in the post-Mao

---

45 Laifong Leung, "Yan Lianke: A Writer's Moral Duty," *Chinese Literature Today* 1, no. 2 (2011): 74.
46 Ibid., 76.
47 Ibid., 77.
48 Ibid., 79.
49 Carlos Rojas, "Speaking from the Margins: Yan Lianke," in *Columbia Companion to Modern Chinese Literature*, ed. Kirk A. Denton (New York: Columbia University Press, 2016), 432.
50 Ibid., 432.
51 Ibid., 432.
52 Carlos Rojas, "Time Out of Joint: Commemoration and Commodification of Socialism in Yan Lianke's *Lenin's Kisses*," in *Red Legacies in China: Cultural Afterlives of the Communist Revolution*, ed. Jie Li and Enhua Zhang 張恩華 (Cambridge, Mass.: Harvard University Press, 2016), 300.

era, such as the deprivation of their many basic social benefits despite their contribution to the economic growth.[53] Such readings foreground the political persecution in the Maoist regime and the breach of human rights in the post-Mao era. The fact that the Chinese socio-political issues are given a lengthy critique prior to the discussion of Yan's works indicates that Rojas gives priority to socio-political concerns. This point becomes more conspicuous when Rojas associates the contents in Yan's works with real historical events in China in the ensuing part. For example, Rojas contextualizes *Lenin's Kisses* "in the summer of 1998, precisely two decades after Deng Xiaoping's 1978 'Reform and Opening-Up' (*gaige kaifang* 改革開放) campaign, which helped catalyze China's strategic shift from high communism to hypercapitalism."[54] He also further attributes the polarization between the rural and urban areas in China to the "Reform and Opening-Up" policy before exploring a set of deep-rooted tensions in China's transition to hypercapitalism based on investigations of the contradictory associations implied in Lenin's corpse and the villagers' disabled bodies respectively.[55] In this respect, Rojas reads the works as a historically authentic account of the problematic side of the "Reform and Opening-Up" policy in China. His predilection for the social and political issues in Yan's works is also echoed by his own confession that he is fascinated by Yan's "attention to modern social concerns" and appreciates Yan's interrogations of an array of crises in China, which have been eschewed by most contemporary Chinese writers.[56]

In a similar way, Tsai shows no interest in Yan's early works but explores intensively the metaphorical dimension of *Streams of Time*, *Lenin's Kisses*, *Serve the People!* and *Dream of Ding Village* with the concept of "autoimmunity."[57] With respect to *Streams of Time* and *Serve the People!*, Tsai argues that "autoimmunity appears as an epistemological force that repeatedly challenges the principles and guidelines that define the Chinese Communist Party."[58] In his view, Yan's creative revision and reinterpretation of well-known political slogans help cast critical doubt on Maoist discourses on revolutionary ideals.[59] In this sense, Tsai presents these two works as satires on Maoist socialism. Furthermore, Tsai argues that *Lenin's Kisses* and *Dream of Ding Village* manifest such logic in the "ongoing negotiations between the capitalist transactions and socialist instructions in various communities that struggle for survival."[60] To be specific, they represent the logic of capitalism in communist China, which demands sacrifices of the individual body for the benefit of a larger social body.[61] Such interpretation satirizes China's contradictorily socialist and capitalist politics, which in turn reaffirms his presentation of Yan's works as sociopolitical documents.

Despite such an overtly emphasis on the sociopolitical documentary value of Yan's fiction, there are also a few scholars who swing between the sociopolitical reading and the generalized reading. For instance, Wang Jinghui views the work *Serve the People!* as a political criticism on

---

53 Ibid., 300.
54 Ibid., 301.
55 Ibid., 301–03.
56 Eric M. B. Becker, "Man Booker International Prize Q&A—Carlos Rojas," *WWB Daily*, May 2017, https://www.wordswithoutborders.org/dispatches/article/2017-man-booker-international-prize-qa-carlos-rojas-eric-m-b-becker) (last accessed 8 Oct. 2017).
57 Chien-hsin Tsai, "In Sickness or in Health: Yan Lianke and the Writing of Autoimmunity," *Modern Chinese Literature and Culture* 23, no. 1 (2011): 77–104.
58 Ibid., 80.
59 Ibid.
60 Ibid., 81.
61 Ibid.

political injustice in China on the one hand, and highlights the universal significance of the work in addressing the borderless topic of fear on the other.[62]

In addition, there is also an increasing discussion on how Yan approaches mythorealism to reflect on reality in recent years. However, it is worth noting that while Chinese scholarship tends to mention the socio-political reality in vague or metaphorical words, Western literary critics slant toward specifying the exact historical reality in China underlying Yan's works. For example, when exploring *The Explosion Chronicles*, the Chinese critic Wang Haitao reveals the function of mythorealism in exposing social illness in revolutionary societies without any references to China,[63] whereas the Western critic Cao Xuenan directly points to its interrogation on the logic of development in contemporary China.[64] By weaving a connection between the contents of Yan's works and the sociopolitical reality in China, Western criticism further accentuates the sociopolitical documentary function of his works.

Discussions of the disparate Chinese and Western reception

The critical reception of Yan's works in China and the West takes two distinct paths, namely, literary path and sociopolitical path. Following a literary path, the Chinese reception puts an emphasis on the literary aesthetics and universal significance of his works. This is achieved by shifting their focus away from the political satire and critical reflections on the contemporary Chinese society in Yan's works toward his sophisticated application of various narrative techniques like mythorealism and engagement with universal themes such as humanity, love, and death. By contrast, instead of putting much energy in discussing the literary merits of Yan's works, the Western reception takes a sociopolitical path with an inclination to laying bare the repressive censorship on his works and amplifying their functions as sociopolitical documents.

Such divergent reception of Yan's works in China and the West could be seen as the corollaries of the dominant ideology and literary tradition in China and the established perception of Chinese literature in the West. In China, Mao's Yan'an talks on art and literature, which urged cultural works to serve social and political functions rather than art for art's sake, has become a foundation and standard for the activities of Chinese critics and writers.[65] During the Cultural Revolution, when "the political ideology dominated the Chinese cultural polysystem," the then Chairman Mao's doctrine that "the political considerations should override the artistic ones" permeated every aspect of literature creation.[66] Influenced by such a totalitarian literary ideology, many Chinese scholars and writers were persecuted for deviating from the major political poetics of "socialist realism and socialist romanticism."[67]

After the Cultural Revolution, critics and writers were freed from the extremely political oppressions and were endowed with a relatively friendly environment for their literary criticism and creation. Meanwhile, due to the dismal and bleak literary landscape in China,

---

62 Wang, "'Serve the People' from 1944 to 2005," 45–57.
63 Wang, "Biange shidai de shenshi xiezuo," 99–100.
64 Xuenan Cao, "Mythorealism and Enchanted Time: Yan Lianke's *Explosion Chronicles*," *Frontiers of Literary Studies in China* 10, no. 1(2016): 103–12.
65 David Der-wei Wang, *Why Fiction Matters in Contemporary China* (Waltham: Brandeis University Press, 2020), 3.
66 Mingjian Zha, "Modern China's Translated Literature," in *A Companion to Modern Chinese Literature*, ed. Yingjin Zhang 張英進 (Chichester: Wiley Blackwell, 2016), 220.
67 Yiyan Wang, "Fiction in Modern China: Modernity through Storytelling," in Zhang, *A Companion to Modern Chinese Literature*, 204.

extensive translations of canonized Western literary works were introduced to China to rejuvenate its literary creativity. As a result, there emerged "a second movement towards 'openness', or 'moving toward the world' in modern and contemporary Chinese literature, led to the so-called second 'overall Westernization.'"[68] Drawing on the translations of Western literary works for creative inspiration, Chinese writers adapted, assimilated, and experimented with a variety of literary forms such as stream-of-consciousness and magical realism to modernize and expand the vision of Chinese literature. Besides, they were very concerned with the universal form of humanity, which not only allowed them to resume the "spirits of enlightenment and humanism"[69] but also helped them to move closer to world literature.[70]

It is admitted that Chinese government's control and intervention on literary creation, publication, and criticism have been gradually reduced since the end of the Cultural Revolution. However, a series of sensitive events ranging "from the 1979 'campaign against bourgeois liberalization' to the 1983 'anti-spiritual pollution campaign' to the June Fourth incident of 1989" nevertheless hindered the vigorous literary criticism in China.[71] Even today, ideological issues still impact many literary activities, despite the flourishing translations of foreign literary works and literary creations in China induced by relatively favorable cultural conditions. It is always necessary to keep the political correctness in mind, as censorship "has up to this day remained a socio-political and cultural constant" in China.[72]

In this context, it is no surprise that Chinese scholars shift their attention away from the controversial political topics in Yan's works in the interest of self-preservation and protection. Instead, they turn to focus on the discussions of the humanist themes and formal experimentation with literary techniques in Yan's works with universal resonance. Moreover, by highlighting the universal significance of Yan's works, they also strive for the international recognition of his works at a literary aesthetic level. Their efforts in constructing the literary meaning of Yan's works are in fact in tune with building up the literary fame of Chinese literature at the international level advocated by the cultural diplomacy of Chinese government.[73]

For the reasons underlying the Western reception of Yan's fiction, they are inextricably intertwined with the Western stereotypes toward modern and contemporary Chinese literature that are forged by the political stance and aesthetic standard of the West. In the first half of the twentieth century, the West generally viewed modern Chinese literature like May Fourth literature as "inferior imitations and adaptations of nineteenth- and twentieth-century Western models."[74] Besides, the West is also interested in the "historical perspective"

---

68 Ning Wang, "Editor's Introduction: Modern Chinese Literature from Local to Global," *Journal of Modern Literature* 44, no. 2 (2021): 4.
69 Zhang Yingjin, "Toward a Typology of Literary Modernity in China: A Survey of English Scholarship on Modern Chinese Literature," in his *A Companion to Modern Chinese Literature*, 491; Tao Dongfeng, "Thirty Years of New Era Literature: From Elitization to De-Elitization," in Zhang, *A Companion to Modern Chinese Literature*, 100.
70 Hongtao Liu, "Chinese Literature's Route to World Literature," *CLCWeb: Comparative Literature and Culture* 17, no. 1 (2015): 1–8.
71 Chen Sihe, "A Brief Overview of Chinese-Language Scholarship on Modern Chinese Literature," trans. Alvin Ka Hin Wong, in Zhang, *A Companion to Modern Chinese Literature*, 471.
72 Zaixi Tan, "Censorship in Translation: The Case of the People's Republic of China," *Neohelicon* 42 (2015): 335.
73 Mengying Jiang, "Translation as Cultural Diplomacy: A Chinese Perspective," *International Journal of Cultural Policy*, 2021, https://doi-org.nthulib-oc.nthu.edu.tw/10.1080/10286632.2021.1872554.
74 W. J. F Jenner, "Insuperable Barriers? Some Thoughts on the Reception of Chinese Writing in English Translation," in *Worlds Apart, Recent Chinese Writing and Its Audiences*, ed. Howard Goldblatt (New York: Routledge, 1990), 181.

of modern Chinese literature, thus often read modern Chinese literature as "historical documents than literature."[75]

The period between the 1960s and 1980s witnessed a growth of English-language scholarship on modern and contemporary Chinese literature. However, influenced by the Cold War precept "know thine enemy" in the Communist bloc, modern and contemporary Chinese literature was mainly approached by the West as "historical source materials" that helped them "understand Chinese social life."[76] Moreover, due to the interruption of cultural exchanges between China and the West caused by the Cultural Revolution, the West had a tendency to label modern and contemporary Chinese literature as "the stigma of communism," thus presenting and promoting it as "at best a source of political (preferably dissident) information on China, as worst as dully propagandistic."[77] Even after the Cultural Revolution, much of the Chinese literature of the 1980s was still perceived as "plagiarism" that imitated Western literary models, thus lacking creativity and imagination.[78] Certainly, this period also witnessed scholarly efforts toward interpreting Chinese literature through a literary approach. One of the most prominent examples is C. T. Hsia's seminal work *A History of Modern Chinese Fiction* (1961), which pioneered the study of modern Chinese literature with resort to Western literary theory.[79] Nevertheless, it is worth noting that Hsia's analysis was heavily imprinted with his "rightist position" and "the political tension" of the Cold War.[80] In other words, Hsia still adopted a documentary approach to the reception of modern Chinese literature.

Since the 1990s, there has been a rapid expansion in the discussion of modern and contemporary Chinese literature in the West. However, modern and contemporary Chinese literature remains "marginal"[81] or even "relegated to a kind of 'cultural ghetto'" in the global literary field.[82] Its quality is often assessed through "its political rather than its literary content."[83] Such reception manifests a contradictory pattern, in which "Chinese literature is both censured for being too political and then praised only for being political."[84] This reception of Chinese literature mainly for its sociopolitical interest has been informed by a specific world literary economy, that is non-Western literatures have rarely been prized for "their universal artistic qualities" but are mainly valued as "sociopolitical documents, as national obsessions."[85] Therefore, this chapter argues that the Western critical reception of Yan's works is governed by Western stereotypes of Chinese literature as sociopolitical documents with little literary value.

---

75 John Balcom, "Bridging the Gap: Contemporary Chinese Literature from a Translator's Perspective," *Wasafiri* 23, no. 3 (2008): 19.
76 Perry Link, "Ideology and Theory in the Study of Modern Chinese Literature: An Introduction," *Modern China* 19, no. 1 (1993): 4–5.
77 Julia Lovell, "Chinese Literature in the Global Canon: The Quest for Recognition," in *Global Chinese Literature: Critical Essays*, ed. Jing Tsu and David Der-wer Wang (Leiden: Brill, 2010), 202.
78 Bonnie S. Mcdougall, *Fictional Authors, Imaginary Audiences: Modern Chinese Literature in the Twentieth Century* (Hong Kong: Chinese University Press, 2003), 228–32.
79 Li-fen Chen, "The Cultural Turn in the Study of Modern Chinese Literature: Rey Chow and Diasporic Self-Writing," *Modern Chinese Literature and Culture* 12, no. 1 (2000): 46–47.
80 Ibid., 47.
81 Julia Lovell, *The Politics of Cultural Capital: China's Quest for a Nobel Prize in Literature* (Honolulu: University of Hawai'i Press, 2006), 32.
82 Andrew F. Jones, "Chinese Literature in the 'World' Literary Economy," *Modern Chinese Literature* 8, no. 1/2 (1994): 171.
83 Lovell, *The Politics of Cultural Capital*, 32.
84 Ibid., 36.
85 Ibid., 167.

Conclusion

Based on the comparative analysis of the Chinese and Western literary criticisms of Yan's works, this chapter has revealed two different modes of reception. Specifically, it demonstrates that Chinese scholarship on Yan's works tends to identify Yan as a nationally and internationally renowned author, who reflects on the essence of human existence, including human destiny, fighting, dreams, desires, and the meaning of life and death, transcending any political and historical boundaries. Moreover, it indicates that Chinese scholarship has tended to receive Yan as a creative writer who experiments with diverse literary techniques, for instance, the application of the narrative structure of flashback, metaphors, biblical language as well as surrealistic narration. By contrast, the Western discourse on Yan's works inclines to perceive them as sociopolitical documents that offer the pungent political and social criticism and are easily fallen prey to the state censorship. Such Western discourse is exemplified by foregrounding the futility of Yan's self-censorship faced with the state censorship and giving credit to his satire against the Maoist and post-Mao eras.

With respect to the salient differences between the reception of Yan's works in China and the West, this chapter further accounts for how his works come to be interpreted in these patterns. In China, rejuvenating Chinese literature and joining the ranks of world literature has been among the prioritized tasks since the late 1970s. Accordingly, Chinese writers actively learn literary techniques from Western literary works that have flooded into China via translations, which stimulate Chinese critics to devote their attention to humanity and literary techniques with universal appeals. Moreover, it is also safer to focus on the universal significance of Yan's works, as censorship to ensure political correctness remains constant in China. On the contrary, there is a deep-seated perception of Chinese literature as sociopolitical documents with little literary value in the West, which contributes to the dominance of a sociopolitical interpretation of Yan's works among the Western scholarship. Therefore, this chapter argues that the dominant literary traditions, political and cultural factors formulate the different reception of Yan's works in China and the West.

Acknowledgments

I appreciate Professor Helena Miguélez-Carballeira and Dr. Shasha Wang for their valuable comments on the earlier versions of this article. I am also grateful to China Scholarship Council for funding this research.

Bibliography

Anonymous. "A Literary Star Emerges from Countryside." *China Daily*, 12 Mar. 2010. http://www.chinadaily.com.cn/life/2010-03/12/content_9579260.htm (last accessed 8 Dec. 2016).

Balcom, John. "Bridging the Gap: Contemporary Chinese Literature from a Translator's Perspective." *Wasafiri* 23, no. 3 (2008): 19–23.

Becker, Eric M. B. "Man Booker International Prize Q&A—Carlos Rojas." *WWB Daily*. 1 May 2017. https://www.wordswithoutborders.org/dispatches/article/2017-man-booker-international-prize-qa-carlos-rojas-eric-m-b-becker) (last accessed 8 Oct. 2017).

Cao, Xuenan. "Mythorealism and Enchanted Time: Yan Lianke's *Explosion Chronicles*." *Frontiers of Literary Studies in China* 10, no. 1 (2016): 103–12.

Chen Hengjin 陳蘅瑾. "Ai hen jiaozhi de xiangtu qinggan" 愛恨交織的鄉土情感 [Love and hatred complex towards the rural hometown]. *Xiaoshuo pinglun* 小說評論 [Fiction Review], 2014, no. 6: 106–09.

Cheng Guangwei 程光煒, and Qiu Huadong 邱華棟. "Chongshen shangheng wenxue lishi xushu de kenengxing: Yan Lianke xinzuo *Si shu*, Faxian xiaoshuo yantaohui jiyao" 重審傷痕文學歷史敘述

的可能性——閻連科新作《四書》、《發現小說》研討會紀要 [Rethinking the possibility of the historical narrative of "scar literature": A summary of the seminar on Yan Lianke's *The Four Books* and *Faxian xiaoshuo*]. *Dangdai zuojia pinglun* 當代作家評論 [Contemporary Writers Review], 2011, no. 4: 52–59.

Chen, Li-fen. "The Cultural Turn in the Study of Modern Chinese Literature: Rey Chow and Diasporic Self-Writing." *Modern Chinese Literature and Culture* 12, no. 1 (2000): 43–80.

Chen, Sihe 陳思和. "A Brief Overview of Chinese-Language Scholarship on Modern Chinese Literature," translated by Alvin Ka Hin Wong. In *A Companion to Modern Chinese Literature*, edited by Yingjin Zhang, 465–82. Chichester: Wiley Blackwell, 2016.

———. "Du Yanlianke de xiaoshuo zhaji zhiyi" 讀閻連科的小說劄記之一 [Reading note of Yan's fiction (1)], *Xinan minzu daxue xuebao* 西南民族大學學報 [Journal of Southwest University for Nationalities (Humanities & Social Sciences)], 2001, no, 3: 44–47.

———. "Shilun Yan Lianke de *Jianying ru shui* zhong de e'moxing yinsu" 試論閻連科的《堅硬如水》中的惡魔性因素 [On the daimonic in Yan Lianke's *Hard Like Water*]. *Dangdai zuojia pinglun*, 2002, no. 4: 31–44.

Chen, Thomas. "Ridiculing the Golden Age: Subversive Undertones in Yan Lianke's Happy." *Chinese Literature Today* 1, no. 2 (2011): 66–72.

Ding Fan 丁帆. "Zai 'shenshi zhuyi' yu 'huangdan pipan xianshi zhuyi' zhijian" 在「神實主義」與「荒誕批判現實主義」之間 [Between "mythorealism" and "absurd critical realism"]. *Dangdai zuojia pinglun*, 2016, no. 1: 4–11.

Fang Wei 房偉. "'Zhalie' de qishu: Ping Yan Lianke de xiaoshuo chuangzuo" 「炸裂」的奇書——評閻連科的小說創作 [The grotesque book of "explosion": On Yan Lianke's fictional writing]. *Wenxue pinglun* 文學評論 [Literature Review], 2014, no. 3: 98–105.

Fang Yi 方奕. "Yuwang, siwang, mengjing: Cong san ge guanjianzi jiedu *Dingzhuang meng*" 欲望·死亡·夢境——從三個關鍵字解讀《丁莊夢》 [Desire, death, dream: Reading *Dream of Ding Village* from three key words]. *Mingzuo xinshang* 名作欣賞 [Appreciation of Masterpieces], 2008, no. 22: 79–81.

Feng Min 馮敏. "Siwang yu shijian: Changpian xiaoshuo *Riguang liunian* zhuti jieshi yu qita" 死亡與時間——長篇小說《日光流年》主題揭示及其他 [Death and time: On the theme and other aspects of *Streams of Time*]. *Xiaoshuo pinglun*, 1999, no. 5: 82–85.

Ha, Jin. "The Censor in the Mirror: It's Not Only What the Chinese Propaganda Department Does to Artists, But What It Makes Artists Do to Their Own Work." *American Scholar* 77, no. 4 (2008): 26–32.

Hardie, Becky. "The Dangerous Truths of Yan Lianke." Penguin, 25 Mar. 2015. https://www.penguin.co.uk/articles/2015/the-dangerous-truth-of-yan-lianke.html#L5R6RAcMbKjlIs6A.99 (last accessed 8 Dec. 2016).

He Zhantao 何占濤. "*Shouhuo* xuyan de xushi moshi" 《受活》絮言的敘事模式 [On the narrative mode of *Pleasure*'s "suoyanti"]. *Xiaoshuo pinglun*, 2009, no. 4: 146–49.

Hong Zhigang 洪治綱. "Xiangcun kunan de jizhi zhi lü: Yan Lianke xiaoshuo lun" 鄉村苦難的極致之旅——閻連科小說論 [The extreme hardship in rural areas: On Yan Lianke's novel]. *Dangdai zuojia pinglun*, 2007, no. 5: 70–81.

Jenner, W. J. F. "Insuperable Barriers? Some Thoughts on the Reception of Chinese Writing in English Translation." In *Worlds Apart, Recent Chinese Writing and its Audiences*, edited by Howard Goldblatt, 177–97. New York: Routledge, 1990.

Jiang, Mengying. "Translation as Cultural Diplomacy: A Chinese Perspective." *International Journal of Cultural Policy* (2021). https://doi-org.nthulib-oc.nthu.edu.tw/10.1080/10286632.2021.1872554.

Lefevere, André. *Translation, Rewriting, and the Manipulation of Literary Fame*. London: Routledge, 1992.

Lei Da 雷達. "Changpian xiaoshuo biji zhi ershi" 長篇小說筆記之二十 [Reading notes of novels (20)]. *Xiaoshuo pinglun*, 2004, no. 3: 8.

Leung, Laifong 梁麗芳. "Yan Lianke: A Writer's Moral Duty." *Chinese Literature Today* 1, no. 2 (2011): 73–9.

Liang Hong 梁鴻. "Zhaohun, lunhui yu lishi de kaiqi: Lun *Shouhuo* de shijian" 招魂、輪回與歷史的開啟——論《受活》的時間 [Summoning the soul, reincarnation and the beginning of history: On the time of *Pleasure*]. *Dangdai zuojia pinglun*, 2013, no. 2: 19–27.

Li Er 李洱. "Yan Lianke de shengmu" 閻連科的聲母 [Yan Lianke's initial consonant]. *Nanfang wentan* 南方文壇 [Southern Cultural Forum], 2007, no. 5: 45–48.

Link, Perry. "Ideology and Theory in the Study of Modern Chinese Literature: An Introduction." *Modern China* 19, no. 1 (1993): 4–12.

Lin Zhou 林舟. "*Jianying ru shui* (changpian xiaoshuo)" 《堅硬如水》(長篇小說) [*Hard Like Water* (a novel)], *Dangdai zuojia pinglun*, 2001, no. 5: 67–68.

Liu, Hongtao. "Chinese Literature's Route to World Literature." *CLCWeb: Comparative Literature and Culture* 17, no. 1 (2015). https://docs.lib.purdue.edu/cgi/viewcontent.cgi?article=2625&context=clcweb (last accessed 31 July 2021).

Liu Zaifu 劉再復. "'Xiandaihua' ciji xia de yuwang fengkuangbing: *Jiuguo*, *Shouhuo*, *Xiongdi* sanbu xiaoshuo de pipan zhixiang" 「現代化」刺激下的欲望瘋狂病——《酒國》、《受活》、《兄弟》三部小說的批判指向 [Crazy desires motivated by "modernization": A Critical orientation towards *The Republic of Wine*, *Lenin's Kisses* and *Brothers*]. *Dangdai zuojia pinglun*, 2011, no. 6: 50–52.

Lovell, Julia. "Chinese Literature in the Global Canon: The Quest for Recognition." In *Global Chinese Literature: Critical Essays*, edited by Tsu Jing and David Der-wer Wang, 197–218. Leiden: Brill, 2010.

———. *The Politics of Cultural Capital: China's Quest for a Nobel Prize in Literature*. Honolulu: University of Hawai'i Press, 2006.

Mcdougall, Bonnie S. *Fictional Authors, Imaginary Audiences: Modern Chinese Literature in the Twentieth Century*. Hong Kong: Chinese University Press, 2003.

Nan Fan 南帆. "Fankang yu beiju: Du Yan Lianke de *Riguang liunian*" 反抗與悲劇——讀閻連科的《日光流年》 [Revolt and tragedy: Reading Yan Lianke's *Streams of Time*]. *Dangdai zuojia pinglun*, 1999, no. 4: 80–87.

Rojas, Carlos. "Speaking from the Margins: Yan Lianke." In *Columbia Companion to Modern Chinese Literature*, edited by Kirk A. Denton, 431–35. New York: Columbia University Press. 2016.

———. "Time Out of Joint: Commemoration and Commodification of Socialism in Yan Lianke's *Lenin's Kisses*." In *Red Legacies in China: Cultural Afterlives of the Communist Revolution*, edited by Jie Li and Enhua Zhang, 297–315. Cambridge, Mass.: Harvard University Press. 2016.

Shao Yanjun 邵燕君. "Yu dadi shang de kunan ca jian er guo: You Yan Lianke *Shouhuo* kan dangdai xiangtu wenxue xianshi zhuyi chuantong de shiluo" 與大地上的苦難擦肩而過——由閻連科《受活》看當代鄉土文學現實主義傳統的失落 [Missing the hardship of rural areas: Looking into the loss of traditional realism of contemporary native soil literature from Yan Lianke's *Pleasure*]. *Wenyi lilun yu piping* 文藝理論與批評 [Theory and Criticism of Literature and Art], 2004, no. 6: 4–17.

Sun Yu 孫郁. "Cong *Shouhuo* dao *Rixi*: Zai tan Yan Lianke de shenshi zhuyi" 從《受活》到《日熄》——再談閻連科的神實主義 [From *Lenin's Kisses* to *The Day the Sun Died*: Revisiting Yan Lianke's mythorealism]. *Dangdai zuojia pinglun*, 2017, no. 2: 5–11.

Tan, Zaixi. "Censorship in Translation: The Case of the People's Republic of China." *Neohelicon: Acta Comparationis Litterarum Universarum* 42 (2015): 313–39.

Tao Dongfeng 陶東風. "Cong mingyun beiju dao shehui lishi beiju: Yan Lianke *Nian yue ri*, *Riguang liunian*, *Shouhuo* zonglun" 從命運悲劇到社會歷史悲劇——閻連科《年月日》《日光流年》《受活》綜論 [From destined tragedy to social-historical tragedy: Reviews of Yan Lianke's *Years Months Days*, *Streams of Time* and *Pleasure*]. *Zhongguo xiandai wenxue yanjiu congkan* 中國現代文學研究叢刊 [Modern Chinese Literature Studies], 2016, no. 2: 173–88.

———. "Thirty Years of New Era Literature: From Elitization to De-Elitization." In *A Companion to Modern Chinese Literature*, edited by Zhang Yingjin, 98–115. West Sussex: Wiley Blackwell. 2016.

Tsai, Chien-hsin 蔡建鑫. "In Sickness or in Health: Yan Lianke and the Writing of Autoimmunity." *Modern Chinese Literature and Culture* 23, no. 1 (2011): 77–104.

Veg, Sebastian. "Creating a Literary Space to Debate the Mao Era: The Fictionalization of the Great Leap Forward in Yan Lianke's *Four Books*." *China Perspectives*, 2014, no. 4: 7–15.

———. "Eliminating Disharmony: Recent Examples of Censorship in Chinese Writing and Cinema." *China Perspectives*, 2007, no. 3: 66–72, 161.

———. "New Spaces, New Controls: China's Embryonic Public Sphere." *Current History* 114, no. 773 (2015): 203–09.

Wang Binbin 王彬彬. "Yan Lianke de *Si shu*" 閻連科的四書 [Yan Lianke's *The Four Books*]. *Xiaoshuo pinglun*, 2011, no. 2: 18–23.

Wang, David Der-wei 王德威. *The Monster That Is History: History, Violence, and Fictional Writing in Twentieth-Century China*. Berkeley: University of California Press, 2004.

———. *Why Fiction Matters in Contemporary China*. Waltham: Brandeis University Press, 2020.

Wang Hongsheng 王鴻生. "Fan wutuobang de wutuobang xushi: Du *Shouhuo*" 反烏托邦的烏托邦敘事——讀《受活》[Utopia narration of anti-utopia: Reading *Pleasure*]. *Dangdai zuojia pinglun*, 2004, no. 2: 89–98.

Wang Haitao 王海濤. "Biange shidai de shenshi xiezuo" 變革時代的神實寫作 [Mythorealism in revolutionary times]. *Xiaoshuo pinglun*, 2014, no. 6: 97–101.

Wang Hongtu 王宏圖. "Xianshi zhuyi zai Zhongguo de mingyun" 現實主義在中國的命運 [The fate of realism in China]. *Xueshu zhengming* 學術爭鳴 [Scholarly Criticism], 2015, no. 6: 47–51.

Wang, Jinghui. "'Serve the People' from 1944 to 2005." *Neohelicon* 43, no. 1 (2016): 45–57.

Wang, Ning. "Editor's Introduction: Modern Chinese Literature from Local to Global." *Journal of Modern Literature* 44, no. 2 (2021): 1–5.

Wang Yao 王堯. "Zuowei shijiguan he fangfalun de 'shenshi zhuyi': *Faxian xiaoshuo* yu Yan Lianke de xiaoshuo chuangzuo" 作為世界觀和方法論的「神實主義」——《發現小說》與閻連科的小說創作 ["Mythorealism" as world view and methodology: *Explosion of Ficiton* and Yan Lianke's literary creation]. *Dangdai zuojia pinglun*, 2013, no. 6: 8–16.

——— and Lin Jianfa 林建法. "Xiaoshuojia jiangtan: Zhuchiren de hua" 小說家講壇: 主持人的話 [Forum for novelists: Chairperson's speech], *Dangdai zuojia pinglun*, 2004, no. 2: 71.

Wang Yichuan 王一川. "Shengsi youxi yishi de fuyuan: *Riguang liunian* de suoyuanti tezheng 生死遊戲儀式的復原——《日光流年》的索源體特徵 [The recovery of the rituals of life and death: The feature of "suoyuanti" in *Streams of Time*]. *Dangdai zuojia pinglun*, 2001, no. 6: 10–16.

Wang, Yiyan. "Fiction in Modern China: Modernity through Storytelling." In *A Companion to Modern Chinese Literature*, edited by Zhang Yingjin, 195–213. West Sussex: Wiley Blackwell, 2016.

Wang Zheng 汪政. "Yinxiang dianji (201–221): *Jianying ru shui* (changpian xiaoshuo)" 印象點擊 (201–221)——《堅硬如水》(長篇小說) [Impression (201–221): *Hard Like Water* (a novel)], *Dangdai zuojia pinglun*, 2011, no. 2: 67.

Xu Guojun 徐國俊. "Nongmin qingjie: Nanyuan de meng—Yan Lianke xiaoshuo manping" 農民情結: 難圓的夢——閻連科小說漫評 [The complex of peasantry: A dream that is hard to fulfill—Reviews of Yan Lianke's fiction]. *Dangdai zuojia pinglun*, 1993, no. 4: 84–88.

Xu Ruowen 許若文. "*Si shu* zhong de ling yinguo yu silie xianshi zhuyi de wenti" 《四書》中的零因果與撕裂現實主義的文體 [Zero cause in *The Four Books* and the departure from realism]. *Nanfang wentan*, 2012, no. 1: 125–30.

Xu Yong 徐勇. "Fengci xiezuo yu xiaoshuo chuangzuo de bianjie wenti: Lun Yan Lianke de *Rixi* jianji xiangguan chuangzuo" 諷刺寫作與小說創作的邊界問題——論閻連科的《日熄》兼及相關創作 [The boundary between satirical writing and fiction creation: On Yan Lianke's *The Day the Sun Died* and its related creations]. *Wenyi yanjiu* 文藝研究 [Literature & Art Studies], 2017, no. 6: 26–34.

Yang, Jincai. "Political Interrogation in Contemporary Chinese Fiction." *Neohelicon* 41, no. 1 (2014): 145–56.

Ye Jun 葉君. "Xiangcun huangye: Xiangxiang yu feixugou—Cong Dingzhuang dao Liangzhuang" 鄉村荒野:想像與非虛構——從丁莊到梁莊 [Wildness of village: Imaginary and non-fictional—From Ding Village to Liang Village]. *Tianjin shifan daxue xuebao (shehui kexue ban)* 天津師範大學學報 (社會科學版) [Journal of Tianjin Normal University (Social Science)], 2015, no. 1: 37–43.

Zha, Mingjian. "Modern China's Translated Literature." In *A Companion to Modern Chinese Literature*, edited by Zhang Yingjin, 214–27. West Sussex: Wiley Blackwell. 2016.

Zhang Xuexin 張學昕 and Yang Liang 楊亮. "Quanli he yuwang jiaozhu de huayu kuanghuan: Lun Yan Lianke *Jianying ru shui*" 權力和欲望角逐的話語狂歡——論閻連科《堅硬如水》 [Carnival discourse in the struggle for power and desire: On Yan Lianke's *Hard Like Water*]. *Xiaoshuo pinglun*, 2006, no. 4: 80–84.

Zhang, Yingjin 張英進. "Toward a Typology of Literary Modernity in China: A Survey of English Scholarship on Modern Chinese Literature." In *A Companion to Modern Chinese Literature*, edited by Zhang Yingjin, 483–500. West Sussex: Wiley Blackwell. 2016.

Zhang Zhizhong 張志忠. "*Jianying ru shui* (changpian xiaoshuo)." *Dangdai zuojia pinglun*, 2001, no. 3: 63.

Zhao Shunhong 趙順宏. "Xiangtu de mengxiang: Lun Yan Lianke jinnian lai de xiaoshuo chuangzuo" 鄉土的夢想——論閻連科近年來的小說創作 [The dream of rural areas: Reviews on Yan Lianke's fiction writing in recent years]. *Xiaoshuo pinglun*, 1993, no. 6: 9–13.

Zhu Xiangqian 朱向前. "Nongmin zhi zi yu nongmin junren: Yan Lianke junlü xiaoshuo chuangzuo de dingwei" 農民之子與農民軍人——閻連科軍旅小說創作的定位 [The son of peasants and soldier peasants: The positioning of Yan Lianke's military fiction]. *Dangdai zuojia pinglun*, 1994, no. 6: 59–70.

24
THE CHALLENGE OF TRANSLATING YAN LIANKE'S LITERARY CREATION

Taciana Fisac

Introduction

In a recent newspaper article, Mario Vargas Llosa, the Nobel Prize literary author, maintained that worthy literature and notably good novels are always subversive. In his opinion, critics should not only focus on philological studies but also on the relationship between fiction and social reality, as well as fabulation and politics, defending that good novels, among the various literary forms, are the best engines for social change.[1] In 1991, Vargas Llosa published another article with a similar perspective. On that occasion, he was extremely critical of aesthetics and ethic relativism in academia and praised dangerous literature as a tool for real life and social engagement. Precisely, in that article published more than thirty years ago, he mentioned some Chinese literary works as prominent examples of daring literature at that time.[2]

*The Four Book*s (*Si shu* 四書) is certainly a work that belongs to the above-mentioned description of dangerous novels.[3] Undoubtedly, it is one of Yan Lianke's 閻連科 masterpieces, abounding in creativity from the beginning to the end and touching very deeply upon an unhealed wound of twentieth-century Chinese history. The author makes use of all kinds of symbolic and linguistic devices at his disposal, creating an extremely powerful story that directly links to what occurred in China from 1957 to 1961. The narrated story could be equated with other atrocious holocausts of humanity, since its background is a real fact that truly ended with the death of several millions of people during Mao's time in power. The drama recreated in *The Four Books* takes us back to the Anti-Rightist Campaign, the Great Leap Forward and its aftermath. It is a story of immersion in the complexity of interpersonal relationships and the abuse of power in a dehumanized context. An effort was made to somewhat evoke factual episodes with the power of words, thus avoiding the oblivion of these episodes forever.

---

1 Mario Vargas Llosa, "La función de la crítica" [The function of literary review], *El País*, 2 Aug. 2020, https://elpais.com/opinion/2020-08-01/la-funcion-de-la-critica.html. All citations are of the author, unless otherwise specified.
2 Mario Vargas Llosa, "Saúl Bellow y los cuentos chinos" [Saul Bellow and the Chinese stories], *El País*, 1 Dec. 1991, https://elpais.com/diario/1991/12/01/opinion/691542011_850215.html.
3 Yan Lianke, *Si shu* (Taipei: Maitian, 2011).

Symbolism and realism in *The Four Books*

In 1956 Mao Zedong, the "great helmsman" of China, called on intellectuals and professionals who contributed to the reconstruction of the country. The Chinese Communist Party encouraged the questioning of its leaders' performance, promoting the growth of "flowers" at the cost of the proliferation of "weeds." Apparently, any well-founded criticism was considered constructive and welcomed. Such encouragement for criticism was part of a movement that aimed to correct improper tendencies within the communist organization. Paradoxically, an editorial published in the *People's Daily* (*Renmin ribao* 人民日報) on 8 June 1957 radically modified these criteria: numerous writers, professionals, and scholars from the most diverse specialties became victims of the so-called Anti-Rightist Campaign and were sent to labor camps to be "re-educated." Several hundred thousand professionals and scholars were consequently labeled as "rightists." This is the point in history where Yan Lianke's novel begins.

Throughout 1958 several political campaigns were launched with enormous impact on the population: the establishment of communes, the socialization of private housing, and the Great Leap Forward, a campaign that proposed to accelerate China's industrialization through large-scale iron and steel production. For this campaign, peasants were mobilized and assigned tasks related to metallurgy, causing the abandonment of fields and consequently leading to the decrease in cereal production. But the official propaganda spread successful news of bountiful harvests instead, showing photos of children jumping over extraordinarily bountiful rice fields. Years later, it would become clear that such images were crude manipulations. The dismantling of some communes provided proof of the failure of such social organization. It has been estimated that between 1959 and 1962, more than thirty million people died in rural areas as a result of this campaign.[4] Official accounts, however, continue to attribute these deaths to natural catastrophes. While the beginning of the new decade did bring with it droughts and floods, the great number of deaths was nevertheless a politically provoked catastrophe that is scarcely known both in and outside of China, an event that affected a significant part of China's population, especially in rural areas. In today's China, the responsibility of those who held the power then and the severity of what happened remain taboo issues preferably not talked about and even less written about.

For this reason, the first problem one encounters when translating *The Four Books* might be how to tell any reader unfamiliar with events in contemporary China that this novel must not be understood as only an imaginative display by the author, but is actually based on real facts. Yan's narrative leaves no one feeling indifferent, either because of the quality of his prose or his ability to dissect social reality, as he consistently offers a new and profound way to look at that social reality. His texts portray times of incredible hardships and complexities of life. The social responsibility of the writer that runs in the blood of some of the most prominent Chinese authors of the early twentieth century is still present in his writing. In China precisely, Yan has been labeled as "master of absurd realism" (*huangdan xianshi zhuyi dashi* 荒誕現實主義大師). This could be considered either as an effort to erase the socio-political implications of his narrative or to detach his works from reality. But Yan himself denies this alleged extravagance of his novels.[5] Some earlier works by Yan can be

---

4 See Yang Jisheng 楊繼繩, *Mubei: Zhongguo liushi niandai da jihuang jishi* 墓碑——中國六十年代大饑荒紀實 [Tombstone: A Chronicle of the Great Famine in China in the 1960s], 2 vols. (Hong Kong: Tiandi tushu, 2008).

5 During his visit to Spain in Oct. 2016, and on many occasions later in China, I had the opportunity to discuss several times this "label" with Yan.

described as allegorical and burlesque. In *The Four Books*, he does not completely resign from his characteristic parody to address dramatic and concrete events. Additionally, like in other previous works, he makes use of all the linguistic and poetic resources at his disposal with overwhelming creativity.

The original Chinese version of *The Four Books* was initially published in Hong Kong and Taiwan. For this analysis, the Taiwanese version will be used. The Taiwan edition comes with an introduction by Tsai Chien-hsin 蔡建鑫, who provides a clear historical background to the plot. In both the English and Spanish translations, an introduction was also included to explain the historical settings. In the case of the French version, there is a brief comment on the back cover of the book, while in the German version, one finds on the book flap the mentioning that the story is based on a historical episode still silenced today in China. The Great Leap Forward is cited as the background of the novel on the book flap of the Italian version. Somehow, all the translators were aware of the plot's link with Chinese twentieth-century history and related their translation to that history in varying degrees. Despite that, the main problem remains: will readers be able to understand the specific choice of words that appear in the text hinting at the author's criticism of the political campaigns and disasters of that period? It is undoubtedly an open question and unimportant whether referring to Chinese or foreign readers, since in both cases the lack of deep knowledge of that time is a general phenomenon. Yet, the author's primary inspiration for many incidents and anecdotes recounted throughout the pages of *The Four Books* is history, chiseled down to the most outrageous follies and tiniest details of real facts.

Translating Yan's literary works presents a significant challenge for anyone. As an author, Yan is continuously searching for a new literary language and trying to explore various relationships between form and content, innovating throughout the diverse levels of his text. The importance of structure and style along with the overlapping of form and content can be clearly identified in his works when reading them in Chinese. As he himself declares, he spends a lot of time rethinking what the skeleton of his story will be, meticulously intertwining it with the theme yet without forgetting other elements identifiable with literary language. In this manner, each of his novels develops a particularly elaborated style deeply linked with the structure of the text. The poetic elements in Yan's writings are also unquestionably overwhelming.

In *The Four Books,* he uses four interlocking texts around which he assembles his plot. In the original Chinese novel, formal elements were utilized to reinforce prose variances and even a distinctive font style was used for each of the four texts. For the translations, different font styles were also used in the French, Italian and Spanish versions. The English and German versions did not employ any such distinction and used only one font type throughout all four texts.

As it is quite obvious to anyone familiar with Chinese culture, the title of this novel has a direct relationship with *The Four Books* of the Confucian canon: "Great Learning" ("Daxue" 大學) "Doctrine of the Mean" ("Zhongyong" 中庸), *Analects* (*Lunyu* 論語), and *Mencius* (*Mengzi* 孟子). The Confucian code of ethics was collected in various texts, interpreted over time by many later sages, and attained the status of a moral standard until the modern period. Just as for generations intellectual elites studied and even memorized *The Four Books* in which the moral canon of the imperial period was collected, Yan's new "Four Books" is called to replace or perhaps complement the previous canon, becoming an obligatory reference not to forgetting the collective and individual destruction in which the madness of totalitarianism ended. The many nuances and double meanings of the title allow for multiple interpretations. Here, all five translations have kept the original meaning in Chinese. Titles are maintained with the original sense in most of the translations of Yan's books, but completely different in some cases. That was the particular case for *Shouhuo* 受活, a dialectal expression used in his region with the meaning of "enduring and enjoying life." When first published in 2009 in France, the title was translated as *Bons baisers de Lénine*, an alternative title that exercised an enormous influence on all other language versions. In English, this novel appeared as *Lenin's Kisses* (2012), in German as *Lenins Küsse* (2015), and even in Spanish as *Los besos de Lenin* (2015). Nevertheless, an absolute change of the original title remains an exception rather than a norm in the translation of Yan's literary works.

As for *The Four Books*, the first text, "Heaven's Child" ("Tian de haizi" 天的孩子), opens with the narrative of the establishment of the re-education camps where the "rightists" were confined. The echoing of the biblical account of Genesis resonates strongly in an amalgamation with classical concepts from Chinese traditional thought and religions, such as the supreme duality that rules everything in the universe: Heaven and Earth. Yan insisted on adopting an obscure language that is at times extremely challenging to translate, similar to that of the Bible in Chinese translation. In all five translations, it is recognizable that the text has been inspired by biblical language; probably, it would be easier for foreigners with Christian cultural roots rather than general Chinese readers to grasp his primary intention. The vision offered of events in this first book reveals the almost divine power of the Party, personified in an innocent and naive child, capable of the best and the worst. And this child, who rewards inmates with red flowers, an act of giving still done today in Chinese kindergartens, somehow imitates martyrs of the communist revolution or even Jesus Christ.

In the second book, "Old Course" ("Gudao" 故道), sublime levels of poetry are reached. The protagonist is the same imaginary author of the text. His everyday behavior contrasts with the greatness bestowed on the act of writing itself. Dignity and pettiness accompany him along with the rest of the scholars and fellow prisoners on his way to transform them into "new men." In this part of the novel, the influence of the Chinese poetic tradition is evident. Human feelings and emotions merge with nature. Interactions of human beings with the world are described with sounds, smells, tastes, colors, and textures in the manner of famous poems of the Tang dynasty. In the old Chinese way, Heaven and Earth, above and below, inside and outside make up a whole that encompasses the universe, including the literary creation itself. The description of the cycle of agriculture becomes a space for a vibrant exhibition of life, dreams, and desires, as an attempt to escape from confinement in the re-education camp. In the background of the story, the great and impetuous Yellow River, one of the most prominent symbols of Chinese civilization, as well as its ancient course are depicted. Chinese peasants are present in a beautiful allegory about blood, sweat, and tears shed on their land and crops.

The third book, "Criminal Records" ("Zuiren lu" 罪人錄) recreates reports on the anti-revolutionary behavior of the "rightist criminals" living in the concentration camp. The authorities requested the "Old Course" author to write down notes for the reports. A simple language goes along with the reproduction of phrases and expressions used for propaganda during the Maoist era. The annotation of the sayings and deeds of the inmates recalls the routine practice of denunciation during the period in which the action takes place.

As a culmination, "The New Myth of Sisyphus" ("Xin Xixufu shenhua" 新西緒弗神話) is the fourth and last book. It refers to a very well-known essay with almost similar title, written by Albert Camus (1913–60), a French author and philosopher. In his famous piece, Sisyphus, a character in Greek mythology, causes the anger of the gods and is punished to push a huge rock forever, showing the tragic and absurdity of his fate. It is a brief philosophical essay that Yan uses to propose a reflection on Chinese vital attitude toward suffering.

This novel has never been officially published in mainland China. Nevertheless, for private distribution, the author himself informally printed a few copies and circulated them among friends and translators. It seems that this informal edition, together with the published one, was used by the French translator, and presumably were known by the German and Italian counterparts, since both omit the title of the sections as in the case of this unofficial version.[6] In all the five translations compared, the integrity of the text has been maintained.[7] The text is divided into sixteen sections or chapters (*zhang* 章) with main subtitles in each of them. Within each one are included excerpts indicating the number of pages, as if they were related to an imagined complete volume of the four books.

Throughout all the texts, the translators of *The Four Books* faced the unavoidable necessity of making choices and decisions. Very often, the author introduces some subtle nuance that turns the phrase into something extraordinary. This happens even in the dedication of the book: "謹以此書獻給那被忘卻的歷史和成千上萬死去與活著的讀書人。"[8] In this sentence, Yan does not use the common word "intellectuals" (*zhishi fenzi* 知識分子), as is generally done when speaking of those who suffered the Anti-Rightist movement. The term intellectual is constructed with the combination of "knowledge" (*zhishi* 知識) and "element" or "member" (*fenzi* 分子). Intellectuals are those elements working with the intellect, as opposed to manual workers, distinctive of the proletariat. Yan, however, has not used the common "intellectuals" but a more traditional term, that is, *dushuren* 讀書人, literally "person who study books" in Chinese, which encompasses the meanings of "sage" or "scholar." The French, German and Italian translators decided to use "intellectuals," but the English and Spanish versions opted for "scholars" and "*estudiosos*," respectively, somehow maintaining the author's special choice of lexicon.

As hitherto mentioned, the beginning of the novel refers us directly to the Bible, although despite being relatively simple, the first sentence in the Chinese original has given rise to very different interpretations:

Original Chinese: "大地和腳, 回來了。"

English translation: "The great earth and the mortal path returned together."

French translation: "Ses pieds ont foulé la terre, il est revenu." [His feet have stepped on the ground, he came back.]

German translation: "Die Erde kehrte heim und mit ihr alle Kreatur." [The earth returned home and with it all creation.]

Italian translation: "I suoi piedi calpestavano la terra: era tornato." [His feet stepped on the earth: he had returned.]

---

6 Complete references of all five translations can be found in the Bibliography section at the end. On p. 35 of the French translation, the original Chinese text seems to use p. 15 of the author's version for distribution among his friends, not the printed edition in Taiwan.

7 It is not always the case in all translations. For example, when translated into French and Italian, Yan's *Wo yu fubei* 我與父輩 [My father's generation and me] was reduced to less than half of the original text.

8 One possible literal translation of this sentence could be: "To all those forgotten millions of scholars, dead or alive, and to the history that has been forgotten."

Spanish translation: "La madre tierra y los pies habían regresado." [The Mother Earth and the feet had returned.][9]

In fact, this sentence provides a very typical example of a topic-comment standard construction in Chinese, with the topic (*Dadi he jiao* 大地和脚 'the great earth and the feet') in the initial position of the sentence and separated with a comma, as a pause and topic marker.[10] In Chinese, this kind of sentence provides flexibility for establishing symbolic links and enriching narrative meanings. Topic-comment sentences are abundantly used by Yan and certainly pose many difficulties when translating into subject-predicate prominent languages. Most likely, for European-language-speaking translators, part of the apparent complexity of a relatively simple announcement has to do with the lack of a grammatical equivalent in the written discourse of European languages. The Spanish translation is the most literal one, maintaining *dadi* 大地 and *jiao* 脚 as subjects, but erasing the comma as a way of grammatically "domesticating" the sentence.[11] The French and Italian versions have both personalized the phrase in the third person, referring to the Child, despite the lack of person in the original Chinese text, and providing in this way a subject instead of a topic. For their part, the English and German translations have maintained "the earth" as the subject but have omitted "feet" and replaced it in both cases with other elements that accentuate the cosmological and mythological character of the statement. Meanwhile, "mortal path" was added in the English version, and "with it all creation" (*mit ihr alle Kreatur*) in the German version. As already stated by linguists, grammatical categories might carry a high semantic import, especially in poetry.[12] In the same breath, not only a lack of semantic but also a lack of syntactic equivalents in languages makes literary translations much more entangled and poses a significant challenge to translators. In this respect, grammatical features of the Chinese language itself provide Yan with a range of poetic narrative devices loaded with significance that are difficult to translate into Indo-European languages and require an interlingual transposition.

Without entering into an assessment on how the translators have "domesticated" this initial sentence of the text, it is clear that the author's intention in the first paragraphs of the novel is to refer to a kind of cosmological myth, in which the first chapters of Genesis resonate. For certain, any person familiar with the Old Testament can clearly identify the author's source of inspiration. And in this sense, foreign readers are more likely to have fewer problems for recognizing its linkage with the Bible. Despite this, foreigners would probably encounter

---

9 An English translation is provided for each of the examples from the other language editions. While the English rendition has been kept as close as possible to the translated texts in the other languages without any modifications for stylistic purposes and in order to facilitate a better understanding of the differences between them, it has been challenging as some words have nuances that are difficult to translate into English.

10 As it has been pointed out by Li and Thompson, this is a predominant phenomenon in the Chinese Language. See Charles N. Li and Sandra A. Thompson, "Subject and Topic: A New Typology of Language," in *Subject and Topic*, ed. Li (New York: Academic Press, 1976), 457–89. See also Charles N. Li and Sandra A. Thompson, *Mandarin Chinese: A Functional Reference Grammar* (Berkeley: University of California Press, 1981). Some linguists even state that almost all sentences in Chinese could be considered topic-comment structures. See Randy Lapolla, "Topic and Comment," in Rint Sybesma et al., eds., *Encyclopedia of Chinese Language and Linguistics*, vol. 4 (Leiden: Brill, 2017), 370–76.

11 Even if used before, I borrow this term as applied in Lawrence Venuti, *The Translator's Invisibility: A History of Translation*, 2nd ed. (London: Routledge, 2008).

12 Roman Jakobson, "On Linguistic Aspect of Translation," in *The Translation Studies Reader*, ed. Lawrence Venuti, 3rd ed. (London: Routledge, 2012), 126–31.

difficulties understanding that the use of a cosmological myth is far from new in Chinese literature and that it acquires a particular meaning. Some of the most classic texts, especially some master novels like *Dream of the Red Chamber* (*Hongloumeng* 紅樓夢), also begin with a kind of mythological cosmogony, fundamental for framing the story. Further, this narrative device is a feature present in many other famous Chinese works. The use of this strategy in classical Chinese novels has found resonance among Western specialists who have highlighted the importance of the symbolic in the conception and reading of such texts.[13] On the contrary, other scholars have emphasized that it is precisely in more realistic novels where the myth gives substance and form to the story.[14] Furthermore, such a reputable critic as C. T. Hsia 夏志清 disagrees with an interpretation that primarily highlights the mythical elements of *Dream of the Red Chamber*. In contrast, the mimetic aspects in this novel are predominant according to Hsia, since "*Dream* is by and large a realistic narrative,"[15] and there is a "vast amount of contemporary criticism (and not merely communist criticism) that regards *Dream* as a work of vital social and ideological significance in relation to the Chinese tradition as a whole and to its own times in particular."[16] Therefore, it would be plausible to consider that, from a traditional point of view, the use of myth and allegory in Chinese literature actually points toward a reading of historical and social reality rather than absurd realism, presumably Yan's intention would be the former. Undoubtedly, readers unfamiliar with Chinese culture will have trouble establishing a link with this distinctive feature.

In *The Four Books*, the main characters of the novel have no proper names in the natural use of the term. Instead, except for the single case of the Child (*haizi* 孩子), we find common nouns referring to the professional expertise of the personages. All of them have strong connotations substituting proper names and requiring a literal translation. At the beginning of the story, they are introduced very briefly as an author (*yi ge zuojia* 一個作家), a scholar (*yi ge xuezhe* 一個學者), a professor of religion (*zongjiao jiaoshou* 宗教教授), and a professor of music and female pianist (*yinyue laoshi, gangqinjia* 音樂老師, 鋼琴家).[17] Then, later on, a quite important secondary character appears on the scene: "a certain technician in the laboratory of a university" (*mou ge daxue shiyanshi de shiyanyuan* 某個大學實驗室的實驗員).[18] Along the text, their denomination is abbreviated in Chinese as "author" (*zuojia*), "scholar" (*xuezhe*) and "music or musician" (*yinyue*). While all the translations have adopted these same terms, there are differences in the case of *zongjiao* and *shiyan*. In the French and the Italian versions, "the Religious" (*le Religieux*, *il Religioso*) are used, whereas in the Spanish translation, "the One of the Religion" (*el de religion*), referring to a professor of religion, is used. In contrast, both English and German translators decided to use "the Theologian." For the secondary role, "the Researcher" was the translation chosen for *shiyan* in the French version (*le Chercheur*) and the Italian version (*il Ricercatore*), while "the Technician" was chosen for the English and German versions and "the lab's technician" (*el técnico de laboratorio*) for the Spanish version. In all but

---

13 For example, Andrew H. Plaks, *Archetype and Allegory in the Dream of the Red Chamber* (Princeton: Princeton University Press, 1976). He tried to underline the archetypal and allegorical elements of the text, in the specific case of *Dream of the Red Chamber*, relating them to Chinese cultural elements present in *Book of Changes* (*Yijing* 易經), the *yinyang* 陰陽 cosmogony and the so-called five agents (*wuxing* 五行).
14 Jean Levi, "Mythe et roman en Chine et en Occident," in *La Chine romanesque: Fictions d'Orient et d'Occident* (Paris: Éditions du Seuil, 1995), 211–19.
15 C. T. Hsia, *On Chinese Literature* (New York: Columbia University Press, 2004), 171–87, esp. 172.
16 Ibid., 176.
17 Yan, *Si shu*, 39.
18 Ibid., 57.

one case, capital letters have been used for outlining them as proper names. This is in fact already a normal practice in the German language, where names (proper or common) always begin with a capital letter. Spanish is an exception and has maintained the terms in lower case letters for underlining the nameless nature of its use in the original Chinese.

If we examine in more detail, we find that for "the Child" Yan uses the particular choice of words *haizi ta* 孩子他 38 times. Here we find a juxtaposition of two words: *haizi* 孩子 (child) and *ta* 他 (normally meaning "he," "him" or "his," but used also as apposition for emphasizing a person's name). Throughout the novel, except in one case, it functions as a sort of double topic in topic-comment constructions, most of the time with a comma as a topic marker. Only the Spanish translation has tried to replicate this expression as "*el niño ese*" [the child that one]. All the other translations omitted this special way of emphasizing this main character and simply used "the Child" in all cases. In the last chapter, apart from Sisyphus (Xixufu), other characters make their appearance: God or gods (*shen* 神) depending on how this was interpreted by each translator. The translators of the English and German versions opted for "God" in singular, while the translators of the Italian and Spanish versions went for "gods" in plural. In contrast, the translator of the French version in this specific case opted for domesticating the translation by using "Zeus," the specific Greek name of the king of gods of Olympus.

Lexical devices in Yan Lianke's work

Lexical devices used by Yan Lianke are extremely rich and complex for translators. One of them is the creation of new words. He invents them by making use of Chinese common word structures with either different character combinations or using them in other contexts, distinctive from the usual ones. For example, he repeats more than one hundred times *yuxin* 育新, formed with *yu* 'raise' or 'educate' and *xin* 'new' or 'renew,' in a sort of verb-object compound[19] In China, the use of *laojiao* 勞教 're-educate by physical labor' or *laodong gaizao* 勞動改造 'reform through labor' (abbreviated also as *laogai* 勞改) is commonplace. Since this novel refers to 1957, when many intellectuals (in the broad use of the term) were labeled as "rightists" and were interned in reform-through-labor detention camps, Yan invents this neologism combining it with *qu* 區 'district/region/area' to form the name *yuxiqu* 育新區. Furthermore, he also added the suffix *-men*, as a plural marker restricted to personal nouns in *yuxinmen* 育新們, and the suffix *-zhe* 者, as nominalizer with the meaning of 'doer' or 'one who' in *yuxinzhe* 育新者, while compounding *yuxin gaizao* 育新改造 as a synonym of the commonly used *laodong gaizao*.

All these are neologisms that have been rendered in the English translation as "Re-Education district" or just "Re-Ed." For the French translation, "*zone de novéducation*" and also as a verb (*se novéduquer*), which are clearly newly created words, are used. In the German version, the common verb *umerzogen* ("re-educate," also in a political sense) is used, as well as other already existent expressions with the same root, such as "*Umerziehungslager*" with the meaning of "indoctrination camp," which identified with communist regimes. The Italian version uses an ordinary vocable with the meaning of rehabilitation, reformation or re-education (*rieducazione, rieducare*), quite the opposite to "*re-formación*" in Spanish, which includes a hyphen between "re" and "training" as a way for highlighting its peculiar feature as well as a footnote mentioning that it is a neologism invented by Yan.

---

19 For this structure in Chinese, see Li and Thompson, *Mandarin Chinese*, 73–81.

Other lexical strategies include modification of the traditional order of disyllabic words to provide alternative meanings. For example, instead of *zhihui* 智慧 'wisdom/intelligence' and 'perfect wisdom in Buddhism,' where *zhi* 智 means "wisdom/resourcefulness/wit" and *hui* 慧 "wisdom/intelligence," he uses *huizhi huizhi* 慧智慧智. Reduplication turns the word into a manner adverb, modifying the verb, as can be identified by the position it occupies at the end of the sentence, located before the verb:

"孩子看了跟來的一人眼神後, 朝田頭, 圍了玉米桿的一棵楊樹慧智慧智走過去。"

English: "Upon noticing this, the Child turned toward the grove and walked deliberately toward one of the poplars at the edge of the cornfield."

French: "L'Enfant suivit un regard, puis s'en alla, l'air entendu, vers un de ces peupliers cernés de chaumes sur la bordure du champ." [The Child followed a gaze, then went away, seemingly having understood, to one of those poplars surrounded by stubble at the edge of the field.]

German: "Und in seiner Klugheit ging es zu einer der Pappeln am Ackerrand und trat gegen den Haufen von Maishalmen." [And in his cleverness, he went to one of the poplars at the edge of the field and stepped against the heap of maize stalks.]

Italian: "Seguendo lo sguardo di un detenuto, il Bambino scrutò verso l'estremità del campo e si diresse, con l'aria di saperla lunga, verso una catasta di fusti ammassati attorno a un pioppo." [Following the gaze of a prisoner, the Child peered to the far end of the field and, with the look of knowing a thing or two, went towards a pile of (corn) stalks heaped around a poplar.]

Spanish: "Tras observar la mirada de un hombre que le seguía, el niño se encaminó hacia el lindero, se dirigió a las cañas de maíz que había en torno a un álamo, con perspicaz sabiduría e insidiosa lucidez." [After observing the gaze of a man following him, the boy headed toward the edge of the field, made his way to the corn stalks around a poplar, with insightful wisdom and insidious lucidity.]

This expression has been domesticated in the English translation, and there is no trace of *huizhi huizhi* and its singularity.[20] In addition, the whole sentence has been simplified. The French version used *l'air entendu* as a manner adverb and stayed closer to the original sentence. The German version has also simplified the sentence but using the words "in his cleverness" (*in seiner Klugheit*). The Italian version has also utilized "with the air of knowing a thing or two" (*con l'aria di saperla lunga*) and is overall closer to the original. In Spanish, a more elaborate expression, "with insightful wisdom and insidious lucidity" (*con perspicaz sabiduría e insidiosa lucidez*), was used as a way of underlining some distinctive features in the primary text. In all translations but English, this expression was employed as a verb's modifier (a manner adverb), and in the Spanish translation, a footnote was added to explain the original pun.

There are also creations of new four-character idioms combining previously established Chinese sayings (*chengyu* 成語). The meaning of Chinese idioms is generally not derived from

20 Yan, *Si shu*, 36; English trans., 8; French, 16; German, 14; Italian, 18; Spanish, 27.

the literal meaning of the four characters and is a common way for metaphorical expression.[21] Due to their variety and frequency of use in the Chinese language, they often create translation challenges, more so in the case of newly created ones. For example, in *jinjing shensuan* 金睛神算 we find a mix of two traditional idioms. The first one is *huoyan jinjing* 火眼金睛 'fire-eyes-metal-pupils', used in *Journey to the West* (*Xi you ji* 西遊記) with the meaning of "penetrating insight" or "great powers of discernment," while the other one is *shenjing miaosuan* 神機妙算 'divine-stratagem-marvellous-scheme' known to have been introduced in *The Three Kingdoms* (*San guo yanyi* 三國演義) with the metaphoric meaning of "amazing foresight" and "a superb strategy" in military operations, among other meanings. This newly invented idiom appears twice in the following paragraph:

"收走幾本書。再又去搜鐵，金睛神算，知道誰把他的搪瓷鐵碗藏哪去。誰把他牙缸、不鏽鋼的調羹藏哪去。上邊的，金睛神算，到了也就找到了。上邊的，找了許多鐵。把孩子，叫到一邊說下許多話。"

English: "After collecting several books, he once again went off in search of iron. He magically seemed to know where each person had hidden their iron rice bowls, teeth-brushing cups, and stainless steel spoons. He then called the Child over, and they proceeded to have a long discussion."

French: "Il y confisqua quelques livres. Il y récupéra du fer. Cet homme avait un œil d'or et le don de divination: si quelqu'un avait caché des ustensiles en métal émaillé, il le savait et savait où les trouver. Si quelqu'un avait caché son verre à dents et sa cuillère en inox, il les trouvait. Les autorités sont clairvoyantes, il leur suffit de venir pour trouver. Il trouva du fer en grande quantité. Ensuite il prit l'Enfant à l'écart et lui parla longuement." [He confiscated some books there. He recovered iron there. This man had a golden eye and the gift of divination: if anyone had hidden utensils of enamelled metal, he knew it and knew where to find them. If someone had hidden his toothbrush cup and stainless spoon, he'd find them. The authorities are perspicacious (or clear-sighted), they just have to come to find (the things). He found iron in great quantities. Then he took the Child aside and spoke to him at length.]

German: "Er nahm einige Bücher an sich, dann suchte er nach Eisen. Und nichts entging seinem Blick. Er wusste, wer seine Emailleschüsseln, seine Zahnputzbecher und Löffel aus rostfreiem Stahl wo versteckt hatte. Auf wundersame Weise fand er, was es zu finden gab. Dann rief er das Kind zu sich und redete lange auf es ein." [He took some books, then he looked for iron. And nothing escaped his gaze. He knew who had hidden his enamel bowls, toothbrush cup and stainless-steel spoon and where. In a wondrous way he found what there was to find. Then he called the child to him and talked to him for a long time.]

Italian: "Sequestrò diversi libri. Poi si mise alla ricerca del ferro, dando prova di una miracolosa preveggenza e di una vista acutissima, dato che sapeva dove Tizio o Caio avevano nascosto la propria ciotola di metallo smaltato. O dove avevano infilato il

---

21 See Lei Wang et al., "A Study on Metaphors in Idioms Based on Chinese Idiom Knowledge Base," in *Chinese Lexical Semantics: CLSW 2014, LNAI 8922*, ed. Xinchun Su and Tingting He (Cham: Springer, 2014), 434–40.

bicchiere per sciacquarsi la bocca o il cucchiaio in acciaio inossidabile. L'uomo aveva una miracolosa preveggenza e una vista acutissima, gli bastò venire per trovare quello che cercava. Scovò una gran quantità di ferro. Poi chiamò in disparte il Bambino e gli parlò a lungo." [He sequestered several books. Then he went in search of iron, showing miraculous foresight and a very keen sight, for he knew where Tom, Dick and Harry/any of the guys had hidden their enamelled metal bowl. Or where they put the glass to rinse the mouth with or the stainless-steel spoon. The man had a miraculous foresight and a very keen vision, he only had to come to find what he was looking for. He discovered a great deal of iron. Then he called the Child aside and spoke to him at length.]

Spanish: "Recogió algunos libros y se los llevó. Y con pupilas doradas y predicción sobrenatural recogió también hierro; conocía exactamente el lugar donde escondían los utensilios de metal esmaltado y los tazones de hierro. Si alguien ocultaba su cuchara de acero inoxidable y el vaso del cepillo de dientes, allí iba. El de arriba, de pupilas doradas y predicción sobrenatural, allí iba y los hallaba. El de arriba encontró mucho hierro. Llamó al niño a un aparte y le dijo muchas cosas." [He picked up some books and took them away. And with golden pupils and supernatural prediction he also gathered iron; he knew exactly where the enamelled metal utensils and the iron bowls were hidden. If someone hid their stainless-steel spoon and the toothbrush cup, there he went. The higher-up, with golden pupils and supernatural prediction, went there and found them. The higher-up found a lot of iron. He called the boy aside and told him many things.]

In this case, for this newly created Chinese idiom (*jinjing shensuan*) the English translation uses "magically" as its choice in the first sentence it appears, but the whole sentence where this idiom was used for the second time was not included in the translation. As a whole, rhythm and vocabulary used in the original paragraph were simplified. Instead, the French version uses an explanatory translation the first time it appears: "*Cet homme avait un œil d'or et le don de divination*" (This man had a golden eye and the gift of divination), and then, in the second sentence, it was translated as "*être clairvoyant*" ("to be perspicacious" or "clear-sighted"). All the clauses of the paragraph have been maintained, and the most noticeable feature is the introduction of "he" (*il*) as a subject in all sentences, even employing it as a sort of anaphora instead of the one used originally in the novel (*shangbian de* 上邊的 'higher-ups'). Anaphora, the usage of the same repetitive words at the beginning of adjacent sentences for emphasis, is also a typical rhetoric device in Yan's works, even sometimes with lengthy sequences of words. As for the German translation of this sentence, an amalgam was made with the subsequent clause using "*Und nichts entging seinem Blick*" (And nothing escaped his gaze), and for the second time using "*Auf wundersame Weise*" (in a wondrous way). Nevertheless, it is evident that the paragraph has been partially simplified. As for the Italian (*una miracolosa preveggenza e di una vista acutissima*) and Spanish (*pupilas doradas y predicción sobrenatural*) versions, both have maintained the translation of this idiom in both clauses with a very similar structure, focusing more on the metaphorical sense in the first case and with a more literal translation in the second. In both cases, readers would be more likely to identify some distinctive features found in the Chinese original. Incidentally, the above-mentioned anaphora, as in the original text, is barely maintained in the Spanish translation.[22]

---

22 Yan, *Si shu*, 100; English, 65; French, 84; German, 72; Italian, 92–93; Spanish, 90–91.

Another lexical devise in Yan's texts is the introduction of reduplicate characters or even the invention of new ABB compounds of adjectives or adverbs. This kind of compounds, mostly trisyllabic or quadrisyllabic, very often have phonaesthetic elements such as affixes and incorporate the semantic feature of intensifying emotions or atmospheres. In fact, they were classified by Yuen Ren Chao 趙元任 as vivid reduplicates, since many of them are formed with vivid affixes (*shengdong houzhui* 生動後綴).[23] Generally speaking, these words are significantly associated with perceptive categories: vision, hearing, touch, taste, and smell. In Yan's narrative, it seems that those related with colors have augmented over the years and its usage frequency has increased in later works.[24] *The Four Books* is actually full of reduplicated adjectives and adverbs, newly created or employed in uncommon situations. While in Chinese, they would undoubtedly provide even more vivid description, for translators, even those generally used could be a nuisance.

"去看孩子臉。孩子望著人,目光哀灰灰的傷。"

English: "Then they turned to the Child, who looked back at them with a sorrowful expression in his eyes."

French: "Ils regardèrent l'Enfant. L'Enfant les observait et son regard était triste, blessé." [They looked at the Child. The Child watched them and his eyes (look or expression of his eyes) were sad, hurt.]

German: "Da schauten sie zum Kind, und das Kind schaute zurück, und sein Blick war voll Trauer." [Then they looked at the child, and the child looked back, and his gaze was full of sorrow.]

Italian: "Spostarono lo sguardo sul Bambino. Lui li guardava, con un'espressione ferita e piena di tristezza." [They shifted their gaze to the Child. He looked at them, with a wounded expression full of sadness.]

Spanish: "Dirigieron la vista hacia el rostro del niño. El niño contemplaba a los hombres con una mirada gris, triste y dolida." [They turned their gaze toward the boy's face. The boy contemplated the men with a grey, sad and painful look.]

In both English and German translations, *aihuihui de shang* 哀灰灰的傷 is domesticated as "sorrowful" and "full of sorrow." In the French and Italian versions, in addition to "sorrowful" (*triste* and *pieno di tritezza*), "hurt" (*blessé*) or "wounded" (*ferita*) was added. In the Spanish version, three adjectives: grey, sad and painful (*gris, triste y dolida*) were used.[25] In this case, the ABB-pattern adjective is an invention of the author. Despite that, throughout the

---

23 See Yuan Ren Chao, *A Grammar of Spoken Chinese* (1968; repr., Berkeley: University of California Press, 1970), 198–210.
24 See Zhu Dongping 祝東平, "Yan Lianke xiaoshuo yuyan ABB xing xingrongci de xingou" 閻連科小說語言ABB型形容詞的新構 [The new construction of ABB type adjectives in Yan Lianke's novel language], *Changchun daxue xuebao* 長春大學學報 [Journal of Changchun University] Aug. 2000, vol. 10, no.4: 59–61.
25 Yan, *Si shu*, 260–61; English, 219; French, 266; German, 228; Italian, 92–93; Spanish, 248.

texts, there are also many other such compounds that could be considered more ordinary, it is not unproblematic to incorporate them in translation. This is the case for the next example:

"半個鐘點後,紅薯的香味黃燦燦在爐的周圍飄。"

English: [This sentence is untranslated.]

French: "Une demi-heure plus tard, leur parfum jaune s'était mis à flotter." [Half an hour later, their yellow aroma started to float.]

German: "Als eine halbe Stunde später ihr goldgelber Duft in der Luft trieb." [When their golden-yellow aroma floated in the air half an hour later.]

Italian: "Dopo mezz'ora un profumo giallo si diffuse tutt'intorno." [After half an hour a yellow aroma spread all around.]

Spanish: "Media hora más tarde, por el entorno flotaba un reluciente aroma amarillo a batata." [Half an hour later, a shimmering sweet potato yellow aroma was floating around the surroundings.]

In this sentence, the common compound (*huangcancan* 黃燦燦 found in dictionaries as "bright yellow" or "golden") is used within an unusual context.[26] The vivid bright yellow color is applied to the aroma of sweet potatoes floating around a furnace. In the English version, this sentence is not translated, while the French translation merely employed "yellow" (*jaune*), as did the Italian version (*giallo*). In the German version "*goldgelb*" or "golden-yellow" is used, and the Spanish version added "shimmering" (*reluciente*) to "yellow" (*amarillo*).

Along with colors, onomatopoeias are equally used in profusion.[27] For example, the onomatopoeia with two distinct pronunciations and meanings *zhi/zi* 吱 appears in –23 sentences as *zhi* for small and shrill sound and as *zi* for the sound of small animals (equivalent to the English words "squeak," "chirp" or "peep"). It is introduced in four cases as a reduplicate, *zhizhi* (incisive sound in small broken bits), two cases as *zhizha* 吱喳 (noisy chatter), one case as a trisyllable, *zhizhizha* 吱吱喳, two other cases as a reduplicated disyllabic *zhizha zhizha* 吱喳吱喳 (sound of footsteps and of something tearing away), and one as *zizi zhazha* 吱吱喳喳 (sound of insects and birds under paper). There is also a combination with other onomatopoeias like *zhila* 吱啦 (sizzle), *zhicha* 吱嚓 (sound of wheels on the snow), or *zhiya* 吱呀 (door sound), and even a reduplicated *zhiya zhiya* 吱呀吱呀. This character also appears in a compound with green, *lüzhizhi* 綠吱吱, to suggest the sound of vegetation, another with grey, *huiming zhizhi* 灰鳴吱吱, to emulate the cry of birds/animals/insects, and in other combinations as quadrisyllabic compounds like *qinghong zhizhi* 青紅吱吱, *zuixi zhizhi* 碎細吱吱,

---

26 Yan, *Si shu*, 95; English, 61; French, 79; German, 68; Italian, 87; Spanish, 87.
27 See Xiao Shuangrong 肖雙榮, "Yan Lianke zuopin zhong nishengci de chaochang yunyong" 閻連科作品中擬聲詞的超常運用 [The extraordinary use of onomatopoeia in Yan Lianke's works], in Li Jianfa 林建法, *Yan Lianke wenxue yanjiu* 閻連科文學研究 [Studies on Yan Lianke's literature], vol. 2 (Kunming: Yunnan renmin chubanshe, 2013), 438–42. For a description of phonaesthetic features of Chinese language, see Yip Po-Ching, *The Chinese Lexicon: A Comprehensive Survey* (London: Routledge, 2007), 177–218.

369

jizhi jini 嘰吱嘰呢, and *zhiya jiji* 吱呀嘰嘰.[28] The diversity of onomatopoeias displayed by Yan is overwhelming. Using sound imageries, he explores different phonaesthetic features with alliteration, reduplication, assonance, and rhythm, while seeking new symbolic images and relationships. Translators no doubt encounter many difficulties in showing readers his inventiveness of onomatopoeias.

The use of allusions, similes, and metaphors

By far, the most evident poetic devices one encounters when reading *The Four Books* in Chinese are metaphorical comparisons (mainly allusions, similes, and partial or complete metaphors) extensively used throughout the work,[29] for which a comparative analysis would require considerable space. Along the text, Yan uses many allusions and literary quotations and profusely applies insinuations with direct or indirect reference to poems, traditional myths or classical passages, specific places, political events, or even concrete persons. For example, a famous sentence by a Tang poet, Xu Hun 許渾 (ca. 788–ca. 854) is introduced as a complete sentence. This verse can be found in dictionaries with the meaning of "ominous portents," "omen" or "portent." The allusion is translated with diverse strategies.[30]

"山雨欲來風滿樓。"

English: "They seemed to sense that this event heralded something much larger."

French: "Quand la tempête va s'abattre sur la montagne, le vent envahit le pavillon." [When the storm hits the mountain, the wind invades the pavilion.]

German: "Kommende Ereignisse schienen ihre drohenden Schatten vorauszuwerfen." [Coming events seemed to cast their looming shadows ahead.]

Italian: "Si sente nell'aria una minaccia di tempesta." [A menacing storm is felt in the air.]

Spanish: "La lluvia se abate sobre las montañas y el viento invade el pabellón." [The rain hit the mountains and the wind invades the pavilion.]

The English, German, and Italian versions opted for a translation of the sentence without making explicit any allusion to the literal words of the poem, but directly to its metaphorical meaning. In contrast to that, the French and Spanish versions provide a literal translation, with the Spanish version including a footnote to fully explain the allusion. There are plenty of allusions and various examples with much more complex structures and combinations, such as the following sentence:

"上邊說了，種上小麥，要摘月射日，大煉鋼鐵，你們平均每人每月，得煉出一爐鋼鐵，有文化能耐，不能比農民少缺。"

---

28 Yan, *Si shu*, 63, 135, 167, 178, 190, 208, 224, 237, 238, 239, 250, 263, 281, 284, 302, 310, 313, 315, 327, 343, 347, 364, 366.
29 For lexical feature of metaphorical comparisons and other rhetorical figures in Chinese, see Yip Po-Ching, *The Chinese Lexicon*, 219–64.
30 Yan, *Si shu*, 86; English, 54; French, 71; German, 61; Italian, 78; Spanish, 79.

English: "The higher-ups said that you should plant wheat and smelt steel. Everyone must smelt an average of a furnace-worth of steel every month. Given that each of you has cultural ability, you therefore cannot produce less than the peasants."

French: "Les autorités ont dit qu'après avoir semé le blé, il faudra décrocher la lune et fabriquer de l'acier à grande échelle, vous produirez en moyenne un fourneau par personne et par mois, vous êtes des hommes cultivés, des hommes capables, vous ne pouvez pas faire moins que les paysans." [The authorities said that, after sowing the wheat, it is necessary to take down the moon and make steel on a large scale; you will produce an average of one stove per person per month; you are cultured men, capable men; you cannot do less than the peasants.]

German: "Die Oberen sagen: Ihr sollt Weizen anbauen und Stahl schmelzen, und wenn ihr dafür die Sonne vom Himmel schießen müsst. Ein jeder von euch soll jeden Monat eine Ofenfüllung Stahl schmelzen. Ihr seid tüchtig und gebildet, ihr dürft nicht zurückbleiben hinter den Bauern." [The higher-ups say: You are to grow wheat and melt steel, and if you have to shoot the sun from the sky for that. Each of you must melt a steel furnace filling every month. You are capable and educated, you must not lag behind the peasants.]

Italian: "Lassù dicono che dopo la semina ci lanceremo nella produzione dell'acciaio, sarà uno sforzo epico per spezzare tutti gli ostacoli sul nostro cammino. Dovrete produrre in media il contenuto di una fornace per persona al mese, siete capaci e istruiti, non potete fare peggio dei contadini." [Up there they say that after the planting we will launch into steel production, it will be an epic effort to break all the obstacles in our path. You will have to produce an average of the contents of one furnace per person per month, you are skilled and educated, you cannot do worse than the peasants.]

Spanish: "Arriba lo han dicho: sembrad trigo, alcanzad la luna y disparad al sol, fundid hierro y acero a gran escala, una media de un horno por persona y mes. Tenéis aptitudes y cultura, no podéis quedar por debajo de los campesinos." [They (have) said it up above: sow wheat, reach the moon and shoot the sun, cast iron and steel on a large scale, an average of one furnace per person per month. You have skills and culture, you cannot fall below the peasants.]

In this sentence, *yao zhai yue she ri* 要摘月射日 resonates mixed allusions from multiple sources.[31] Since words are attributed to the highest leaders of the country, *zhai yue* 摘月 'pick the moon' could be considered an allusion to Mao Zedong. In one of his famous poems, he used a quite similar expression, *lan yue* 攬月 'take into one's arms the moon'. It is normally considered that his inspirations come from Li Bo's 李白 poems. Later on, this allusion to the moon becomes a popular saying with the meaning of "attaining the highest goals." A second allusion, *she ri* 射日 'shoot the sun', refers to the legend of Houyi 后羿. This ancient mythological story refers to a time when lands and fields were scorched due to the existence of ten suns. Houyi shoots his arrows and manages to eliminate nine of them, leaving a single sun,

---

31 Yan, *Si shu*, 32; English, 4; French, 12; German, 10; Italian, 13; Spanish, 24.

and hence making the planet's climate much more benign. This allusion to Houyi appears four times in the novel.³² In this first case, there is no trace of the double allusion in the English translation. In the French text, only the first allusion is partially translated: "take down the moon" (*décrocher la lune*). The German translation mentions the second allusion: "and if you have to shoot the sun from the sky for that" (*und wenn ihr dafür die Sonne vom Himmel schießen müsst*). The Italian translation uses both allusions, making a more explanatory translation: "it will be an epic effort to break all the obstacles in our path" (*sarà uno sforzo epico per spezzare tutti gli ostacoli sul nostro cammino*). Finally, the Spanish translation opted for a more literal translation of both: "reach the moon and shoot the sun" (*alcanzad la luna y disparad al sol*), accompanied by a footnote with the explanation of the allusions and their meaning.

Therefore, except in English, where both allusions are missing, various approaches to the translation of the allusions were made available to foreign readers: partial translation, descriptive equivalent or explanatory translation, and literal translation with detailed annotation. In fact, for Chinese readers, both allusions can be easily decoded when they are well-versed in mythology, history, and literary tradition. Reading in translation can add some difficulties to the in-depth grasping of the allusions to Chinese mythology or information related to double-level meanings, along with specific hints to the historical background and political movements of the period in which the story takes place. To understand these allusions and insinuations, footnotes can be a useful tool for translators and, in the case of Yan's literary translations such annotations can certainly be justified. Throughout the original novel, there are no notes,³³ but the Spanish version has 54 footnotes, 5 in the Italian version, and 1 in the German version. No annotations were added to the English or French versions.

Regarding comparative metaphors, different rhetorical devices (mostly the use of analogies, metonymies and specially similes) can be found. For the analysis of the translations in question, several words abundantly used by the author can be identified as comparative words that function as a sort of metaphorical markers. Precisely, the most used word is *ru* 如, meaning "like," "be like" or "such as." It appears 416 times throughout the text and is the 34th most used word. The word *yang* 樣 'manner/appearance' appears 191 times, including 141 times as the disyllabic *yiyang* 一樣 'same/equally/alike.' Meanwhile, *xiang* 像 'resemble/be like/look as' can be found 172 times and it is the 91st most used word. The term *si* 似 'be similar/like' occurs –67 times and *fangfu* 仿佛 'be like' 31 times. Finally, the word *ban* 般 'sort/kind' is used 42 times, *ruo* 若 'resemble' 7 times, and *wanruo* 宛若 'just like/as if' only once.³⁴ Every so often, these words are combined in the same sentence. Due to the extensive number of similes and metaphors used throughout the text, for this study, only 62 instances were compared. As a general result of the analysis, in the English translation, 7 were untranslated, 5 were partially translated, 21 were modified, and 29 adhered to the original text. As for the French translation, 2 were untranslated, 1 partially translated, 6 modified, and 53 adhered to the original text. In the German version, 11 were not translated, 7 were partially translated, 13 were modified, and 31 adhered to the original text. For the Italian version, 1 was untranslated, another one partially translated, 5 were modified, and 54 adhered to the original text. Finally, for the Spanish version, none were untranslated and of which 2 were partially translated, 3 modified, and 57 adhered to the original text.

---

32 Yan, *Si shu*, 32, 34, 121, 122.
33 Yan uses annotations as a literary device in his novel *Shouhuo*.
34 For words counting Voyant tools' Web application (https://voyant-tools.org) was used.

A few examples with diverse syntactic structures show how these figures of speech were dealt with in all five translations. The first example makes an appearance in the concluding sentence of the first chapter, with two poetic parallel clauses.[35]

"寂靜托著人的腳步，如水面托著它的浮物。"

English: "This stillness supported people's feet, as though they were floating on water."

French: "Le silence emporta le pas des hommes comme l'eau emporte les choses qui flottent." [Silence carried away men's steps as water carries away things floating.]

German: "Und die Stille trug die Menschen, als trieben sie auf dem Wasser." [And the silence carried the people as if they were floating on the water.]

Italian: "Il silenzio portava via l'eco dei passi come l'acqua porta via tutto ciò che galleggia sulla sua superficie." [The silence carried away the echo of the footsteps as water carries away everything that floats on its surface.]

Spanish: "El silencio sostenía los pasos de los hombres, al igual que la superficie del agua sostiene todo aquello que flota sobre ella." [Silence was upholding men's footsteps, just as the surface of the water upholds everything that floats on it.]

In the Chinese sentence, the verb is repeated in both clauses, with a durative aspect marker (*tuozhe* 托著 with the sense of "being held in the palm" or "being supported from under"). This is a syntactic aesthetic device that provides a parallel rhythm and structure. Since it is problematic to find a single-word verb with the same meaning in any of the five target languages, different choices were made. The English and German translations did not maintain clause parallelism, with the verb being modified in each clause, and the analogy of the second clause shortened to adapt to the meaning of the original text. The French and Spanish translations, on the other hand, both retain parallelism and are very close to the original sense. The same is seen in the Italian version, where "the echo" was added to complement "footsteps."

In the case of the following sentence, it poses several difficulties for translators, since a very descriptive image is provided with two similes, both introduced by *ru* 如 and both in between three *ba* 把 constructions.[36]

"為了跑得快，他把腳上的鞋子脫下來，拿在手裡如拿了兩隻船模型，因為跌倒甩掉了一隻去，他把另外一隻也索性扔在田地裡，把自己如甩出去的鞋樣朝著前邊衝。"

English: "In order to run faster, he took off his shoes and carried them in his hands. When he stumbled and dropped one shoe, then threw the other one into the field as well and continued hurtling forward, like the shoe he had just thrown away."

---

35 Yan, *Si shu*, 33; English, 5; French, 14; German, 11, Italian, 14; Spanish 25.
36 See Randy Lapolla, "Topic and Comment," 373. I adhere to his proposal, considering *ba* constructions as double topics constructions.

French: "Pour plus de célérité il s'était mis pieds nus et garda ses chaussures à la main comme deux maquettes de bateau jusqu'au moment où, en ayant fait tomber une en trébuchant, il lâcha l'autre et se mil à galoper à la même vitesse qu'il avait jeté sa savate." [For higher speed he went barefoot and kept his shoes in his hands like two models of a ship, until the moment when, having stumbled and dropped one, he let go of the other, and began to gallop at the same speed as he had thrown his old shoe.]

German: "Um schneller laufen zu können, zog er sich die Schuhe aus und nahm sie in die Hände. Als er ins Straucheln geriet und einen Schuh verlor, schleuderte er auch den anderen von sich und flog nun genauso davon wie sein Schuhwerk." [In order to be able to run faster, he took off his shoes and took them in his hands. When he stumbled and lost one shoe, he hurled the other one away and then flew away just like his footwear.]

Italian: "Per correre più i fretta si tolse le scarpe e le tenne in mano come fossero due barchette giocattolo, poi inciampò e gliene cade una, allora senza pensarci su gettò per terra anche l'altra continuando a galoppare in avanti con la stessa fretta precipitosa cui aveva buttato via la scarpa." [In order to run quicker, he took off his shoes and held them in his hand as if they were two toy boats, then he tripped and dropped one, now without thinking about it he threw the other one on the ground and kept on galloping forward with the same rushing haste as he had thrown away his shoe.]

Spanish: "Para correr rápido, se quitó los zapatos y los agarró en las manos, como quien lleva dos maquetas de barcos, pero al tropezar y caérsele uno, directamente tiró el otro al campo y se lanzó hacia adelante a la manera del zapato caído." [In order to run faster, he took off his shoes and grabbed them in his hands, as if he had two model boats, but when he tripped and dropped one, he threw the other straight into the field and threw himself forward like the fallen shoe.]

The first simile is untranslated in the English and German translations, but the second one was maintained. In both cases, there are domesticating practices, and the clauses are broken up with a full stop. In contrast, the French, Italian, and Spanish translations have kept both similes and are closer to the original.[37] In the next example, the first sentence introduces a metaphorical simile with *ru* 如 and then, a second one with *fangfu* 彷佛.[38]

"夜已經深到如同枯井般。月光在頭頂涼白涼白, 彷彿結在天空的冰。"

English: "The night was already as dark as the bottom of a well, but the moon was shining brightly overhead, as though frozen in the sky."

French: "La nuit était aussi profonde qu'un puits tari. Blanche et fraîche au-dessus de nos têtes, la lune semblait un bloc de glace solidifié dans le ciel." [The night was

---

37 Yan, *Si shu*, 58; English, 28–29; French, 40–41; German, 36, Italian, 44; Spanish, 50.
38 Yan, *Si shu*, 63; English, 33; French, 46; German, 39, Italian, 50; Spanish, 54.

as deep as a drained well, white and fresh above our heads, the moon looked like a solidified block of ice in the sky.]

German: "Die Nacht war tief wie der Grund eines versiegten Brunnens. Kalt und weiß schien der Mond über unseren Köpfen, als wäre er am Himmel gefroren." [The night was as deep as the bottom of a dried-up well. Cold and white shone the moon above our heads, as if it had frozen in the sky.]

Italian: "La notte era ormai profonda come un pozzo prosciugato e la luna sulle nostre teste aveva un freddo biancore, come ghiaccio solidificatosi nel messo del cielo." [The night was already as deep as a dried-out well and the moon above our heads had a cold whiteness, like ice solidified in the middle of the sky.]

Spanish: "La noche había alcanzado la profundidad de un pozo seco. La luz de la luna fría y blanca se alzaba sobre sus cabezas como hielo solidificado en el cielo." [The night had reached the depth of a dried-out well. The cold and white moonlight hoisted over their heads like solidified ice in the sky.]

In this context, the English translation uses the same pattern as before, domesticating and abridging metaphorical comparisons in both sentences. In the first one, the adjective "dried-up" before "well" was omitted. In the second one, the object for comparison (*bing* 冰 'ice') is absent. In comparison, the German version provides a complete translation of both the first and the second sentences. The French, Italian and Spanish versions have adhered to more literal translations. The French translation even retains the syntactic division and sentence rhythm. In the next case, several different lexical devices are presented, such as word repetition (*zuizui shangbian, shangbian* 最最上邊、上邊), two quadrisyllabic idioms (*yiliaobailiao* 一了百了 'solve the main problem and everything will follow' and *yingren'erjie* 迎刃而解 'be readily solved'), and a long simile introduced with *ru* 如.[39]

"以為最最上邊、上邊的國家領導來看了育新區, 所有的事, 都會一了百了, 迎刃而解, 如一團亂麻被國家的領導抽出了最有序的繩頭兒。"

English: "They had all believed that if the country's highest higher-ups came to visit the Re-Ed region, everything would be easily resolved, like unravelling a ball of thread."

French: "Ils s'imaginaient que la tournée du plus haut dignitaire de l'Etat dans les zones de novéducation allait régler leurs problèmes, sans exception, d'un coup de baguette magique. Comme s'il lui avait suffi de tirer le fil d'une pelote emmêlée pour que tout rentre dans l'ordre." [They imagined that the tour of the highest official of the state to the new-education zones would solve their problems, without exception, with the stroke of a magic wand. As if it was enough to pull the wire out of a tangled ball to get everything back to order.]

---

39 Yan, *Si shu*, 283; English, 242; French, 293; German, 251; Italian, 336; Spanish, 270.

German: "Nach dem Besuch eines unserer allerobersten nationalen Führer glaubten wir, nun wären mit einem Schlag alle unsere Probleme gelöst." [After the visit of one of our very highest national leaders, we believed that now all our problems would be solved in one fell swoop.]

Italian: "Credettero che la visita di uno dei massimi dignitari dello Stato al campo di rieducazione avrebbe portato con sé come per incanto la fine di tutte le loro disgrazie e la soluzione di ogni problema. Sarebbero venuti facilmente a capo delle difficoltà come quando, trovato il bandolo, si dipana una matassa intricata." [They believed that the visit of one of the highest dignitaries of the State to the re-education camp would bring with them, as if by magic, the end of all their misfortunes and the solution to every problem. Difficulties would have been easily solved like when an intricate skein is unravelled once its end is found.]

Spanish: "Creyeron que si los de más arriba, los más altos dirigentes del país habían venido al campo de re-formación, los problemas se solucionarían de una vez por todas y las cosas irían sobre ruedas. Era como si los dirigentes de la nación hubieran sacado el extremo de la madeja de un ovillo enmarañado." [They believed that if the higher-ups, the highest leaders of the country had come to the re-education camp, the problems would be solved once and for all and things would proceed smoothly. It was as if the nation's leaders had pulled the end of the skein out of a tangled ball.]

Once more, there is a partial translation of the clauses in English. Only one comparable idiom has been introduced and the final simile is not completely reproduced. In the German translation, there is an oversimplification. For the French, Italian and Spanish translations, there is an attempt to capture some of the rhetoric elements, introducing the two idioms with target language images, but shortening the simile to avoid reiteration of words that might not be well-considered in the target language. Word repetition in all five Indo-European languages can be interpreted as due to a lack of vocabulary richness when not used clearly as a rhetorical strategy, and this inevitably creates a challenge for translators. Chinese is a language where words repetition is much more accepted. In this specific case, only the Spanish translation has tried to reproduce the rhetoric word repetition at the beginning of the sentence.

Concluding remarks

According to Hans Georg Gadamer's hermeneutics, "reading is already translation, and translation is translation for the second time …. The process of translating comprises in its essence the whole secret of human understanding of the world and of social communications."[40] Therefore, reading as a professional translator can be considered a first translation and the process of rendering the text into another language a second translation. By this argument, foreign readers of a translated text thus perform a third act of translation. The production of a written translation takes place between its first reading and the translation being read by its target public. In this sense, the comparison of the five translations provides clearly different

---

40 Quoted in Rainer Schulte, "Interpretation," in *An Encyclopaedia of Translation: Chinese-English, English-Chinese*, ed. Chan Sin-Wai 陳善偉 and David Pollard (Hong Kong: Chinese University Press, 2001), 449.

readings of Yan Lianke's literary work. As for the English version produced by Carlos Rojas, his translation of *The Four Books* is primarily centered on the content of the story rather than on the style or other literary features of the novel. To some extent, the same could be applied to the German version done by Marc Hermann. Fluency in both texts, in terms of style and easy readability, are nearer to either Anglo-Saxon general readers' cultural domain or publishing current trends. Both could be considered as adherent of "domesticating practices" in Lawrence Venuti's sense.

As for the French, Italian, and my own Spanish translations, they are guided by Peter Newmark's statement: "the more important the language of a text, the more closely the language has to be translated."[41] These versions also try to be fluent in their target language, but efforts for accuracy with the original text make them all the more challenging for readers. Their closeness to the source language in terms of meaning and style requires a greater effort on the part of the readers to interpret the novel. The French translator, Sylvie Gentil even utilizes strategies for maintaining the rhythm of the clauses and sentences. The Italian translator, Lucia Regola sometimes provides a more domesticated translation while seeking for fidelity. As for my own Spanish version, annotations have been added as a strategy to alert readers about the richness of the original text.

This comparative analysis was originally undertaken with the aim of finding out what kind of strategies have been used by translators in order to reflect Yan's literary richness. Through the textual analysis, however, it was discovered that two particularly different approaches actually existed: one that searches for fluency and eliminates all kinds of foreignization as a deliberate choice, and the other more concerned with the search for an equivalent of the novel in a foreign language. As a result, the unique literariness of *The Four Books* is unfortunately rather imperceptible for English- and German-speaking readers. In contrast, the French, Italian and Spanish translations make Yan's extraordinary use of literary devices more recognizable. In their effort to reflect linguistic, poetic, and cultural differences, these translations provide a glimpse of the challenges of translating Yan's literary creation.

Bibliography

Chan, Sin-Wai 陳善偉, and David Pollard, eds. *An Encyclopaedia of Translation: Chinese-English, English-Chinese*. Hong Kong: Chinese University Press, 2001.

Chao, Yuan Ren 趙元任. *A Grammar of Spoken Chinese*. Berkeley: University of California Press, 1970.

Eoyang, Eugene, and Yao-fu Lin, eds. *Translating Chinese Literature*. Bloomington: Indiana University Press, 1995.

Hsia, C. T. *On Chinese Literature*. New York: Columbia University Press, 2004.

Jakobson, Roman. "On Linguistic Aspect of Translation." In *The Translation Studies Reader*, edited by Lawrence Venuti, 126–31. 3rd ed. London: Routledge, 2012.

Lapolla, Randy. "Topic and Comment." In *Encyclopedia of Chinese Language and Linguistics*, vol. 4, edited by Rint Sybesma et al, 370–76. Leiden: Brill, 2017.

Levi, Jean. *La Chine romanesque. Fictions d'Orient et d'Occident*. Paris: Éditions du Seuil, 1995.

Li, Charles N., and Sandra A. Thompson. *Mandarin Chinese: A Functional Reference Grammar*. Berkeley: University of California Press, 1981.

———. "Subject and Topic: A New Typology of Language." In *Subject and Topic*, edited by Charles N. Li, 457–89. New York: Academic Press, 1976.

Newmark, Peter. "Translation Procedures." In Chan and Pollard, *An Encyclopaedia of Translation: Chinese-English, English-Chinese*, 871–83. Hong Kong: Chinese University Press, 2001.

---

41 Peter Newmark, "Translation Procedures," in Chan and Pollard, *An Encyclopaedia of Translation*, 871.

Plaks, Andrew H. *Archetype and Allegory in the Dream of the Red Chamber*. Princeton: Princeton University Press, 1976.
Vargas Llosa, Mario. "La función de la crítica" [The function of literary review]. *El País*, 2 Aug. 2020. https://elpais.com/opinion/2020-08-01/la-funcion-de-la-critica.html.
———. "Saúl Bellow y los cuentos chinos" [Saul Bellow and the Chinese Stories]. *El País*, 1 Dec. 1991. https://elpais.com/diario/1991/12/01/opinion/691542011_850215.html.
Venuti, Lawrence. *The Translator's Invisibility: A History of Translation*. 2nd ed. London: Routledge, 2008.
Wang, Lei et al. "A Study on Metaphors in Idioms Based on Chinese Idiom Knowledge Base." In *Chinese Lexical Semantics: CLSW 2014, LNAI 8922*, 434–40, edited by Xinchun Su and Tingting He. Cham: Springer, 2014.
Xiao Shuanrong 肖雙榮. "Yan Lianke zuopin zhong nishengci de chaochang yunyong" 閻連科作品中擬聲詞的超常運用 [The extraordinary use of onomatopoeia in Yan Lianke's works]. In *Yan Lianke wenxue yanjiu* 閻連科文學研究 [Studies on Yan Lianke's literature], vol. 2, edited by Li Jianfa 林建法, 438–42. Kunming: Yunnan renmin chubanshe, 2013.
Yan Lianke 閻連科. *Los Cuatro Libros*. Translated by Taciana Fisac. Barcelona: Galaxia Gutenberg, 2016.
———. *The Four Books*. Translated by Carlos Rojas. New York: Grove Press, 2015.
———. *Les quatre livres*. Translated by Sylvie Gentil. Arles: Éditions Philippe Picquier, 2012.
———. *I quattro libri*. Translated by Lucia Regola. Milano: Nottetempo, 2018.
———. *Si shu* 四書 [The four books]. Taipei: Maitian, 2011.
———. *Die vier Bücher*. Translated by Marc Hermann. Frankfurt: Eichborn, 2017.
Yang Jisheng 楊繼繩. *Mubei: Zhongguo liushi niandai da jihuang jishi* 墓碑: 中國六十年代大饑荒紀實 [Tombstone: A chronicle of the great famine in China in the 1960s]. Hong Kong: Tiandi tushu, 2008.
Yip, Po-Ching. *The Chinese Lexicon: A Comprehensive Survey*. London: Routledge, 2007.
Zhu Dongping 祝東平. "Yan Lianke xiaoshuo yuyan ABB xing xingrongci de xingou" 閻連科小說語言 ABB 型形容詞的新構 [The new construction of ABB type adjectives in Yan Lianke's novel language]. *Changchun daxue xuebao* 長春大學學報 [Journal of Changchun University], Aug. 2000, vol. 10, no. 4: 59-61.

25
YAN LIANKE IN BASQUE
Notes on translating sensory images
Maialen Marin-Lacarta

Yan Lianke combines myth and realism in a unique way in this novel, narrating the difficult and hard life of the mountains through the means of dreams, fantasy and magic, and revealing the invisible realities hidden behind everyday life events. He addresses sensitive topics with beautiful language and provides an exact rhythm and perfect structure to the story.[1]

This is how the back cover of the Basque translation of *Balou tiange* (耙耧天歌), translated as *Balou mendikateko balada* (*Ballad of the Balou Mountain Range*), introduces Yan Lianke's 閻連科 work for the first time to Basque readers. In this blurb, the Basque editor condenses the novella's main stylistic features based on his reading of the translation and the introduction written by the translator. The novella, which is almost 33,600 Chinese characters long (and approximately 19,900 words in Basque), was first published in China in 2001 by Beiyue 北嶽 Literature and Art Publishing House and tells the story of You Sipo 尤四婆 (Fourth Wife You), a woman living in a remote village in the Balou mountains, who would do anything for her four mentally impaired children, including fighting with the dead and the living, and challenging the laws of nature. The translation, published in May 2018, is not only the first and only Basque translation of Yan's work to date but also one of the few direct translations from Chinese into Basque. A project by Maialen Marin-Lacarta in collaboration with Aiora Jaka Irizar, it is the first Chinese novel translated into Basque, as previous translations of Chinese literature focused on other genres.

From periphery to periphery: Translations of Chinese literature into Basque

Chinese and Basque literatures have in common that they can be considered peripheral literatures as they do not have a big share in the world market of translated literature. In terms of number of speakers or volume of literary production, Chinese is a central or dominant

---

1 The Basque original reads: "Mitoa eta errealismoa modu berezian uztartzen ditu Yan Liankek nobela honetan, mendialdeko bizitza zail eta gogorra kontatzeko ametsak, fantasia eta magia ere erabiliz, eguneroko bizitzaren azpian dautzan errealitate ikusezinak agerian jarriz. Gai gordinak hizkuntza eder baten bidez landuz eta kontakizunari erritmo doi eta egitura perfektua emanez." My translation.

language, but translations from Chinese have a less than one percent share in the world market of translated literature.[2] Basque is a minority language with 751,500 speakers as of 2016[3] and is spoken in a region that spans Northern Spain and Southwestern France. The majority of Basque speakers reside in Spain (93%)[4] and are bilingual speakers of Spanish (or French in France) in addition to this minority language, and often read and write in both languages. Since the end of the Francoist repression in the 1970s, the Basque agglutinative language, the only surviving pre-Indo-European language in Western Europe, has flourished again and has enjoyed an active literature and readership.[5]

Translations of Chinese literature into Basque are scarce, but it is worth introducing them before highlighting the uniqueness of Yan's novel in Basque. In a research conducted in 2013, we found 28 translations published in book form and in literary magazines, the earliest appearing in 1968.[6] These translations included Tang poetry (mainly Li Bo 李白, Wang Wei 王維 and Du Fu 杜甫), classical myths, legends and stories (such as those by Pu Songling 蒲松齡, often comparing them to Basque traditional stories), classical philosophical texts (such as *The Analects*, *Dao de jing* 道德經 and *The Art of War*), poems and essays by Mao Zedong, various contemporary poets translated by Itxaro Borda, and a collection of short stories by Mo Yan 莫言, translated after he was awarded the Nobel Prize. Surprisingly, no drama or novels had been rendered into Basque.

Most translations were initiated by translators who made proposals to publishers. These translators are often also Basque writers with an interest in Chinese literature (and world literature in general) and no knowledge of the Chinese language. Exceptions to this include Mo Yan's work, *Dao de jing* and *The Analects*. Translations of the *Dao de jing* and *The Analects* were included in a book series on world philosophy and religion commissioned by the editors, and the translation of Mo Yan's short story collection was also commissioned by the publisher from translators selected as part of a translation competition after the author was awarded the Nobel Prize. The book was chosen by the editor from the catalog of a literary agent in an international book fair, which is also the usual way for contemporary Chinese literature to reach the Spanish market in Spanish.[7]

Basque translators who showed an interest in Chinese literature and chose to translate it used translation as a strategy to enrich their creativity and knowledge of world literature. Instead of prioritizing closeness to the source text, they focused on the target culture and text, as is reflected in their free translation strategies and the lack of indication of the versions used as source texts for their translations. Most translations of Chinese literature in the 1980s and 1990s were done indirectly from Spanish. Some of these mediating texts were also indirect translations themselves, for example, Joseba Sarrionandia translated from the renderings of

---

2 Johan Heilbron and Gisèle Sapiro, "Outlines for a Sociology of Translation: Current Issues and Future Prospects," in *Constructing a Sociology of Translation*, ed. Michaela Wolf (Amsterdam: John Benjamins, 2007), 95–96.
3 Eusko Jaurlaritza, Nafarroako gobernua, and Euskararen Erakunde Publikoa "VI. Inkesta Soziolinguistikoa," 2016, https://www.irekia.euskadi.eus/uploads/attachments/9954/VI_INK_SOZLG-EH_eus.pdf?1499236557
4 Ibid.
5 Read, for example, the postnational history of Basque literature by Joseba Gabilondo, *Before Babel: A History of Basque Literatures* (Lansing: Barbaroak, 2016).
6 Aiora Jaka Irizar and Maialen Marin-Lacarta, "Txinatar literatura euskaraz: Zeharbidezko itzulpenetatik zuzenekoetara itzultzaile-bikoteen eskutik," *Uztaro* 89 (2014): 39–64.
7 Maialen Marin-Lacarta, "Mediated and Marginalized: Translations of Modern and Contemporary Chinese Literature in Spain (1949–2010)," *Meta* 63, no. 2 (2018): 318.

Octavio Paz, who translated from French and English, while Xabier Kaltzakorta used Borges's versions, which were based on English translations.[8] Basque translators from the French side, Itxaro Borda and Marcel Etchehandy used French as the mediating language instead of Spanish.[9] Josu Zabaleta exceptionally translated from French, English and Spanish versions in his 1989 translation of classical stories.[10] From 2000, the trend changed as translators started using more than one mediating text, often in various languages, and they indicated the source texts used for the translation. This new trend indicates the publishers' preference for direct translation and closeness to the source text.

Although Chinese literature has mainly been translated indirectly into Basque, we have found three direct translations published so far in addition to Yan's novel. These include Li Bo's poetry translated by Albert Galvany and Pello Otxoteko;[11] Li Bo, Wang Wei and Du Fu's poems by Rafa Egiguren, who has also written a book including poems by Bo Juyi 白居易 and fragments from *Zhuangzi* 莊子;[12] and a collection of short stories by Mo Yan, translated by Maialen Marin-Lacarta and Aiora Jaka Irizar.[13] Although Albert Galvany and Maialen Marin-Lacarta are native Basque speakers, in both cases, these Sinologists collaborated with more experienced Basque translators and poets (the latter is the case of Otxoteko) to ensure the correctness of the Basque text. Having two translators work together, a specialist in Chinese literature and a specialist in Basque, has been a suitable solution in these two cases.

Yan Lianke in Basque

I first met Yan in Hong Kong in 2016 and was honored to hear that he was interested in having his works, more specifically his novella *Balou tiange*, translated into Basque. My previous Basque translation, Mo Yan's *Shifu yuelaiyu youmo* 師傅越來越幽默, had been issued thanks to a fruitful collaboration with Aiora Jaka Irizar, a Basque translator and revisor, and Xabier Mendiguren, editor of Elkar, the leading Basque publisher. Both of them were supportive and agreed to work on the book with me. No translation of Chinese literature in Basque had been issued since our last publication, which demonstrates our immense responsibility in introducing major contemporary authors to Basque readers.

Balou tiange in Basque is unique for various reasons. To begin with, it is the first Chinese novel to have been translated into Basque; we have seen that previous translations covered poetry, stories (mostly classical stories in addition to Mo Yan's short story collection), and philosophy. Second, it is one of the few contemporary Chinese works that exist in Basque. Other modern or contemporary authors whose work has been rendered into Basque include Mo Yan, and poets such as Bian Zhilin 卞之琳, Gu Cheng 顧城, Ai Qing 艾青, Bei Dao 北島, and Shu Ting 舒婷. Their poems were translated by Itxaro Borda from French and included in

---

8 Joseba Sarrionandia, *Izkiriaturik aurkitu ditudan ene poemak* (Iruñea: Pamiela, 1985); Pu Songling, *Pu Songlingen ipuinak*, trans. Xabier Kaltzakorta (Bilbo: Labayru eta Bizkaiko Aurrezki Kutxa, 1988); *Ekialdeko ipuin miresgarriak*, trans. Xabier Kaltzakorta (Bilbo: Labayru eta Bizkaiko Aurrezki Kutxa, 1988).
9 Itxaro Borda, "Txinako poesiaz," *Maiatz* 10 (1985): 13–23; Marcel Etchehandy, "Xinatar ipui," *Maiatz* 10 (1985): 24–26.
10 *Txina zaharreko kontu zaharrak*, trans. Josu Zabaleta (Donostia: Erein, 1989).
11 Li Bo, *Urrutira bidalia*, trans. Albert Galvany and Pello Otxoteko (Irun: Alberdania, 2005).
12 Wang Wei, Li Bo, and Du Fu, *Mandarin Dotore: VIII. Mendeko olerkiak*, trans. Rafa Egiguren (Soraluze: Gaztelupeko Hotsak, 2003); Rafa Egiguren, *Gauza guztiak* (Iruñea: Pamiela, 2011).
13 Mo Yan, *Hori da umorea, maisu!*, trans. Maialen Marin and Aiora Jaka (Donostia: Elkar, 2013).

an issue of the *Maiatz* magazine in 1985. Third, this is one of the few direct translations from Chinese. We have seen that most translations so far are indirect, with the exception of three books. Fourth, this is probably the only translation that was initiated by the author himself, who chose the work to be translated. I suggested translating *The Years, Months, Days* (*Nian yue ri* 年月日) first, but he insisted on his choice. Previous translations were mostly initiated by Basque writers with an interest in Chinese literature, with the exception of Mo Yan's work and *The Analects* and *Dao de jing*, as explained above. Fifth, this translation prioritizes closeness to the source text, trying to transmit the stylistic features of the original as much as possible, while in most of the previous translations, translators had no access to the original and this was not important to them, as their aim was to enrich the target culture, literature and language.

As Jaka Irizar and I had already worked together for the translation of Mo Yan's short story collection, we had intuitively developed a method for Yan's Basque translation. First, I would do a draft in which I would often include more than one possible translation for the same sentence. I would share this with Jaka Irizar through an online folder that she would check when she was available. She would then gradually correct the translation, tracking the changes and adding comments to clarify corrections, to offer more than one possibility or to discuss specific topics and ask questions. After I had polished this version, we would have a final discussion to clarify some corrections in a video conference, as I was living in Hong Kong and she was living in Canada. Some passages needed more drafts than others, but our discussions always led to a better version, a version that reflected the style of the original and was correct in Basque.

A glimpse into Yan Lianke's poetic language through the Basque translation of *Balou tiange*

An examination of the translation drafts reveals that, among other challenges, we struggled and spent time reflecting on images, comparisons, metaphors, and descriptions in which Yan Lianke uses his characteristic poetic language.

In what follows, I will examine ten examples to illustrate Yan's poetic language, the various repetitive elements that make it distinctive, and the way we tried to convey them in Basque. Each Basque example will be followed by a literal translation into English, in brackets, and the published English translation by Carlos Rojas, preceded by the translator's initials (CR). The comparison with Rojas' translation, entitled *Marrow*, published in 2015 by Penguin, will help me to emphasize both Yan's unique style and the various choices we made in the translation.

Onomatopoeias are frequently used in contemporary Chinese literature, but they are often omitted in translation.[14] In addition to representing sounds, onomatopoeias have flexible grammatical functions in Chinese. They were first classified as adverbs, then adjectives, and later as interjections, and it is only since the 1990s that onomatopoeias have been considered a separate lexical category.[15]

---

14 Cheng Guanyu, "A traduçao indireta de literatura chinesa contemporânea para português europeu: o caso de Mo Yan" (PhD diss. Universidade Católica Portuguesa, 2021), 140.
15 Zhao Aiwu 趙愛武, "Jin ershi nian Hanyu xiangshengci yanjiu zongshu" 近 20 年漢語象聲詞研究綜述 [A review of the research on Chinese onomatopoeias in the last 20 years], *Wuhan daxue xuebao (zhexue shehui kexue ban)* 武漢大學學報(哲學社會科學版) [Wuhan University Journal of Humanities & Social Science] 61, no. 2(2008): 180–85.

The sound effect in the dynamic description of movements plays an important role in Yan's writing. Sometimes Yan is describing a real movement, as we will see in the first example (Example 25.1); in other cases, he uses onomatopoeias to describe movements in metaphoric expressions, as illustrated in Examples 25.2 and 25.3. In all cases, and especially in metaphoric expressions, we tried to maintain both the onomatopoeia and the metaphoric expression in Basque.

Example 25.1: Sound and Movement

Most of the examples I have chosen to explain some of the features of Yan's writing have to do with descriptions. However, this first example refers to an action, a movement. In the translation, we maintained the pictorial image (the boy's Adam's apple going up and down) together with the sound effect of the onomatopoeia *gugugege* 咕咕咯咯. Rojas' translation also renders both the image and the sound effect.

> 尤四婆把油饃從鍋裡揭將出來時，四傻的喉嚨裡咕咕咯咯響，喉結上上下下極快捷地蹟。[16]
>
> You Sipok opilak zartagitik atera zituenean, Laugarren Ergelaren zintzursagarra gora eta behera hasi zen, abiada bizian gur-gurka.[17]
>
> (When You Sipo took the buns out of the pan, Fourth Idiot's Adam's apple started moving quickly up and down, *gur-gurka*.)[18]
>
> CR: As Fourth Wife You was removing them from the skillet, Fourth Idiot began gurgling with anticipation, his Adam's apple bobbing up and down.[19]

Example 25.2: Sound and Metaphoric Movement

In the second example, the onomatopeia *dangdang dingding* 當當叮叮 acts as an adverb to the verb *jiben* 急奔 'to run hurriedly'. In Basque, knocking on the door (*ate joka*) is used as an expression for urgent matters and we added the Basque onomatopoeia *danba-danba* to describe the sound of knocking. In this case, Rojas translates the implicit meaning of the expression but does not retain the onomatopoeia.

> 本來她計劃著秋忙過後去看看大妞和二妞，可秋忙未過，三妞的出嫁當當叮叮急奔著又逼到跟前了。
>
> Hasiera batean, bi alabak udazkena pasatutakoan bisitatzea pentsatuta zeukan, baina, udazkeneko uzta amaitu baino lehen, Hirugarren Alaba ezkontzearen kontua danba-danba ate-joka iritsi zitzaion.[20]

---

16 The citations are from the manuscript provided by the author in a Word file, which is why there are no page numbers.
17 Yan Lianke, *Balou mendikateko balada*, trans. Maialen Marin-Lacarta and Aiora Jaka Irizar (Donostia: Elkar, 2018), 102.
18 I provide in brackets a word-for-word translation from Basque to allow readers to appreciate our translation choices, which is why it is not meant to be a fluent English text. The onomatopoeias are kept in Basque, shown in italics.
19 Yan Lianke, *Marrow*, trans. Carlos Rojas (Hong Kong: Penguin Books China), 95.
20 Yan Lianke, *Balou mendikateko balada*, 36.

> (She had originally planned to visit the two daughters after autumn, but before the autumn harvest was over, the matter of Third Daughter's marriage came *danba-danba* knocking at her door.)
>
> CR: Originally, Fourth Wife You had planned to visit her two daughters after the autumn harvest, but then the problem of her Third Daughter's marriage presented itself.[21]

Example 25.3: Sound, Metaphoric Movement, Natural Elements, and Parallelism

The second part of the following sentence was particularly difficult to translate.

> 那一天日光明麗，風像絲綢樣從梁上滑過去，然他們的日子卻一樣磕磕絆絆，不見風調，也不見雨順。
>
> Egun hartan, eguzkia bizi eta argitsu ageri zen, eta haizea zetazko oihal bat balitz bezala irristatzen zen mendikatean behera. Halere, haien bizitza, haizea bezain leuna edo euria bezain isurkorra izan beharrean, kinkili-kankala igaro zen.[22]
>
> (That day the sun was strong and bright, and the wind slipped down the mountain like a silk cloth. Their life, however, passed *kinkili-kankala*, instead of being smooth like the wind or fluid like water.)
>
> CR: The sun was shining brightly on the day of the wedding, and the wind was blowing down from the mountain ridge like a sheet of silk. Their lives, however, stumbled along.[23]

The onomatopeia *kekebanban* 磕磕絆絆 used here to describe their difficult life, like a bumpy road, was important for us not just in terms of semantics, but also because of the sound effect it creates. But this passage also posed other challenges, with *bu jian fengdiao* 不見風調 and *ye bu jian yushun* 也不見雨順, Yan not only creates a parallelism at the sentence level but also at the word level, between *fengdiao* and *yushun*, using natural elements, the wind and the rain, as the first part of the word. This sentence required a detailed description of the sense of each character on my part and led to discussions between the two translators before we agreed on the final version. Yan here demonstrates a masterful use of creative lexical choices, such as *fengdiao* and *yushun*, which is possible thanks to the flexibility of the Chinese language.

The English translation omits the play on words with the wind and the rain as well as the sound effect of the onomatopoeia. The semantic meaning of the onomatopoeia is, however, kept in the verb "stumbling." The use of natural elements, such as wind and rain, appears in other parts of the novella (see, for instance, Example 25.4), and so does the use of animals in comparative descriptions, as we will see in Example 25.5.

---

21 Yan Lianke, *Marrow*, 27.
22 Yan Lianke, *Balou mendikateko balada*, 35.
23 Yan Lianke, *Marrow*, 26.

Example 25.4: Dynamic Description and Comparison with Nature

In this case the comparison *yuguo tianqing* 雨過天晴 is part of a *chengyu* 成語, or "old idiom," mostly formed by four characters and widely used in Chinese, and could have been replaced by a semantic equivalent that overlooked the exact meaning of the image, but I chose to keep it, as it is consistent with Yan's use of natural elements in comparisons. The reader pictures the movement of clouds disappearing from the sky, which makes it a dynamic description. Rojas' translation also maintains the literal meaning of the *chengyu*.

> 待這次再見吳樹，她大大方方，那粉紅的淺羞雨過天晴一樣沒了。
>
> Wu Shu berriro ikusi zuen egun hartan, ordea, oso lasai eta natural jokatu zuen, eta lotsaren kolore arrosa desagertua zen haren aurpegitik, lainoak ekaitz osteko zerutik bezala.[24]
>
> (That day when she saw Wu Shu, she acted calmly and naturally, and the pink color of shame had disappeared from her face, like clouds from the sky after a storm.)
>
> CR: This time when she saw Wu Shu, Third Daughter was very friendly, and her blush of embarrassment had disappeared like storm clouds on a clear day.[25]

Example 25.5: Movement and Comparison with Nature

The next example was not particularly difficult to translate, but it led to a brief discussion between the two collaborators because the English translation was significantly different from my version, which is why Jaka Irizar asked me to verify the meaning.

> 從那果園邊上過時，尤四婆看見他挑水上坡，像出水的蝦米在旱坡上爬著走動。
>
> You Sipok, sagastiaren ondotik pasatzean, aldapan gora ura garraiatzen ikusi zuen herrena; uretatik ateratako izkira bat zirudien, aldapa lehorrean gora.[26]
>
> (When You Sipo walked past the apple grove, she saw the cripple carrying water; he looked like a shrimp pulled out of the water going up the dry slope.)
>
> CR: When Stone You passed by that orchard, he saw Cripple carrying the water up the hill, and the shrimp that had jumped out of the bucket were crawling around on the dry hillside.[27]

As she does not know any Chinese, Jaka Irizar checked my first draft against the English translation and she pointed out discrepancies whenever she saw them, but she always trusted my interpretation. In this case, the image of the cripple walking up the slope is described by Yan comparing him with a shrimp out of water, a powerful image that uses natural elements. However, the English translation missed the comic comparison and interpreted the sentence differently. The subject of the sentence is also mistaken, as it is Fourth Wife You (You Sipo) and not Stone You who walks past the apple grove.

---

24 Yan Lianke, *Balou mendikateko balada*, 58.
25 Yan Lianke, *Marrow*, 50.
26 Yan Lianke, *Balou mendikateko balada*, 46.
27 Yan Lianke, *Marrow*, 38.

In Examples 25.6 and 25.7, which have to do with space and spatial distribution, I have selected passages where Yan uses comparisons to describe the landscape in a pictorial way. They illustrate another characteristic of Yan's creative descriptive methods, but when looking at the whole novella, these static descriptions are less common, as Yan tends to offer a dynamic perspective.

Example 25.6: Pictorial Description of Landscape

In this example, in addition to the static comparison of space with a mat, we see the predominant use of colors in Yan's descriptions, a feature discussed later in this chapter with more evident examples. The yellow rocks become simply rocks in Rojas' English translation.

> 那空地在麥田和梁道的正中間，有草席樣一片，生了許多黃色礓石和茅草。
>
> Espazio hura lastozko estera bat bezala hedatzen zen galsoroaren eta mendiaren artean, harri horiz eta belar luzez beteta.[28]
>
> (That space expanded like a reed mat between the wheat field and the mountain, filled with yellow stones and long weeds.)
>
> CR: In an open space right between the wheat fields and the mountain ridge, there was an area that resembled a reed mat, full of rocks and weeds.[29]

Example 25.7: Pictorial Description of Landscape

Toward the end of the first chapter of the novella, a man who is flirting with You Sipo, the main character and mother of four mentally impaired children, offers to hoe her land in exchange for watching her half-naked body while he hoes. The description of the actions of the man hoeing the land is alternated with the dialogue between the two. This passage was not easy to translate as I had to imagine and picture how he was hoeing in one direction and then walking to the other end, instead of hoeing back, to be able to watch the woman the whole time. Toward the end, when he is about to finish, there is only some land left to hoe, as described in the following passage.

> ……一直坐到地被那男人翻剩下窄窄的一條，像一根灰色的布帶樣撐在溝邊上。這當兒那個男人也累了。男人想到了別的事。
>
> Erretenaren ertzean gerriko grisaxka bat bezala luzatzen zen lur zati estu bat baino ez zitzaion geratzen iraultzeko, baina, ordurako leher eginda, beste zerbaitetan pentsatzen hasia zen.[30]
>
> (He only had left to hoe a narrow patch of land, like a greyish belt running along the edge of the ravine, but by then he was exhausted and had started thinking about something else.)
>
> CR: … until only a narrow patch of land was left to be hoed, like a grey ribbon running along the edge of the ravine. By this point the man was tired and had something else on his mind.[31]

---

28 Yan Lianke, *Balou mendikateko balada*, 20.
29 Yan Lianke, *Marrow*, 11.
30 Yan Lianke, *Balou mendikateko balada*, 25.
31 Yan Lianke, *Marrow*, 15.

The challenge of translating this passage was understanding the image of the patch of land running along next to a ravine. My lack of knowledge of agricultural terminology both in Chinese and Basque meant that it took some research to understand what this *gou* 溝 was and how to translate it in Basque. Jaka Irizar's research and our discussions were key to finding the right term in Basque. Then we understood that the patch of land was not enveloping or going around the *gou*, which was my first interpretation, but that, instead, it ran along with it. Yan's comparison leads to a clear pictorial image of what the land looks like after the man's actions. Rojas' translation was also helpful, as he uses the verb "running along," which confirmed our interpretation.

Yan uses colors in a powerful way to describe moods and landscapes, among other things. In Examples 25.8 and 25.9, I illustrate the cumulative use of colors in the description, again adding a pictorial effect to his writing.

Example 25.8: Colorful and Dynamic Landscapes

In the following example, we have the redness of the sun and the purple color that covers the whole village. The description is dynamic, as the colors change and spread through the landscape, transmitting a sensory experience to readers, as viewers.

> 然後日頭就鮮紅豔豔地落山了，留下的一抹把吳家鋪子的房舍、樹木和街道洗染得紫紫褐褐，如夏季天邊奇怪的雲。
>
> Eguzki gorri-gorria mendien atzean ezkutatu zen, eta Wu herriko etxeak, zuhaitzak eta kaleak laino more batek estali zituen, udako hodei bitxi bat balitz bezala.[32]
>
> (The bright red sun set behind the mountains, and the houses, trees and streets of Wu village were covered by a purple mist, like a strange summer cloud.)
>
> CR: Then the bright red sun set behind the mountains, bathing the village's houses, trees, and streets in a purple glow, like a strange summer cloud.[33]

In the example above, I struggled with the *yi mo* 一抹, a faint trace left by the sun, and chose to translate it as mist in my first draft but explained what it was to Jaka Irizar. She agreed that mist (*laino*) was more suitable than trace (*arrasto*) because of its fluidity and suggested other possibilities, such as light, color, dye, and brightness. I decided to keep mist because it fit well with the later comparison with a cloud. Rojas chose the term "glow," which also fits perfectly with the image described by Yan.

Example 25.9: Colors and Comparison with Nature

I have selected the following example to confirm the importance of colors, comparisons, and movement in this novella. As illustrated in other examples, Yan uses various colors to describe the scene, employs a comparison with an animal, again introducing natural elements, and adds some movement to the scene with the swinging *huangdongzhe* 晃動著. Rojas' English translation maintains all elements in the translation. We see, in this case, that he has chosen to translate both colors, green grass and yellow stones, while

---

32 Yan Lianke, *Balou mendikateko balada*, 55.
33 Yan Lianke, *Marrow*, 48.

omitting the yellow stones in Example 25.6. This suggests that he also considered the colors and the parallelism between them important in this sentence.

> 日光把他的影兒曬得和蟬翼一樣薄, 且是一種灰白色, 在青茅草和黃礓石上晃動著。
>
> Haren itzal grisa, eguzkiaren argipean txitxar baten hegala bezain fina, belar berdeen eta harri horien artean kulunkatzen zen.[34]
>
> (His grey shadow, thin like a cicada's wing under the sunlight, swung between the green grass and the yellow stones.)
>
> CR: His grey shadow, thin as a cicada's wing, swayed between the green grass and the yellow stones.[35]

Example 25.10: Accumulation of Sensory Descriptions: Smells, Sounds, Colors

In addition to colors and sounds, smells are important elements in Yan's writing. The novella begins with the smell of autumn:

> 一世界都是秋天的香色。
>
> Udazken-usainak betetzen zuen mundu osoa.[36]
>
> (The autumn-scent filled the whole world.)
>
> CR: The entire world smelled of autumn.[37]

Yan frequently describes smells using colors, combining two sensory experiences. In the following example, we see a mix of all three sensory elements: colors, smells, and sounds. Both our translation and Rojas' maintain all elements, although the onomatopoeia *zizha sheng* 吱喳聲 becomes "sound of her hoeing," but Rojas maintains the parallelism between the two sounds, repeating "the sound of" and "the sound of" to render *zizha sheng* and *bixi sheng* 鼻息聲, prioritizing another important stylistic feature.

> 新翻的土地裡有一股清新潮潤的泥土味。泥土味是一種深紅色。旺茂的麥茬白亮亮在月光裡, 散發著溫熱膩人的白色的香, 那兩種紅白味道, 如煙如霧樣在夜裡流淌著, 還有她翻地的吱喳聲, 孩娃們睡著後的鼻息聲, 都在水樣的月色裡漫浸浸地流。
>
> Harrotu berri zuen alorrak lurraren usain freskagarri eta hezea zuen, usain gorri iluna. Galondo ugariek, ilargipean dir-dir, lurrin zuri bat isurtzen zuten, epel bezain gozoa. Usain gorria eta usain zuria, kea edo lainoa balira bezala, palaren txio-txioekin eta lo zeuden umeen arnasa sakonekin nahasten ziren.[38]
>
> (The field that he had just hoed had an earthy, moist and fresh smell, a dark red smell. The numerous wheat stubbles gleamed in the moonlight, producing a white aroma, both warm and sweet. The red and white smells, like smoke or

---

34 Yan Lianke, *Balou mendikateko balada*, 20.
35 Yan Lianke, *Marrow*, 11.
36 Yan Lianke, *Balou mendikateko balada*, 11.
37 Yan Lianke, *Marrow*, 1.
38 Yan Lianke, *Balou mendikateko balada*, 22.

> fog, mixed together with the *txio-txio* of the hoe and the deep breaths of the sleeping children.)
>
> CR: The freshly-hoed soil had a moist and earthy smell that resembled dark crimson. The wheat sprouts gleamed in the moonlight, producing a warm and alluring white aroma. The red and white odours mixed together in the night air, like smoke and fog, and the sound of her hoeing and the sound of her snoring children trickled lazily through the watery moonlight.[39]

Conclusion

The experience of translating Yan Lianke's *Balou tiange* into Basque has allowed me to examine various examples of the author's creative descriptions. Images full of sounds, smells, natural elements, colors, and a combination of various sensory elements abound in his writings. Although descriptions have often been considered timeless elements in the narrative,[40] in Yan's work, there is often movement and we have seen that there is a predominance of dynamic images.

Since there is no tradition of translating modern and contemporary Chinese literature into Basque, Jaka Irizar and I felt completely free to use our creativity to reflect Yan's style in Basque as closely as possible, maintaining colors, sounds, natural elements, and dynamic descriptions. Rojas' English translation sometimes omits onomatopoeias (as in Examples 25.2, 25.3, and 25.10), while maintaining them in others (example 25.1). He also omits the natural elements in Example 25.3 and colors in Example 25.6. Overall, however, the English translation also pays attention to the sensory elements in Yan's novella, which suggests that this is an important feature of the author's style.

While translating Yan's novella, I felt like a traveler trying to follow the dynamic and mobile point of view. I had to engage in a kind of mental act of movement and perception to understand the author's representation of human experience. Michel de Certeau saw our environment as an "instantaneous configuration of positions,"[41] which can be presented and interpreted in various ways. In this sense, I have tried to show how Yan interprets and presents the environment, the characters and some of their actions. I would like to conclude that translation, as an extremely detailed exercise in close reading, has allowed me to pay closer attention to these features.

Bibliography

Borda, Itxaro. "Txinako poesiaz." *Maiatz* 10 (1985): 13–23.
Cheng, Guanyu. "A traduçao indireta de literatura chinesa contemporânea para português europeu: o caso de Mo Yan." PhD diss., Universidade Católica Portuguesa, 2021.
De Certeau, Michel. *The Practice of Everyday Life*. Translated by Steven Rendall. Los Angeles: University of California Press, 1984.
Egiguren, Rafa. *Gauza guztiak*. Iruñea: Pamiela, 2011.

---

39 Yan Lianke, *Marrow*, 12.
40 Joshua Parker, "Conceptions of Place, Space and Narrative: Past, Present and Future," *Amsterdam International Electronic Journal for Cultural Narratology* 90 (2016), https://cf.hum.uva.nl/narratology/issue/7/a12_Joshua_Parker.html.
41 Michel de Certeau, *The Practice of Everyday Life*, trans. Steven Rendall (Los Angeles: University of California Press, 1984), 117.

Ekialdeko ipuin miresgarriak. Translated by Xabier Kaltzakorta. Bilbo: Labayru eta Bizkaiko Aurrezki Kutxa, 1988.

Etchehandy, Marcel. "Xinatar ipui." *Maiatz* 10 (1985): 24–26.

Eusko Jaurlaritza, Nafarroako gobernua, and Euskararen Erakunde Publikoa. "VI. Inkesta Soziolinguistikoa." 2016. https://www.irekia.euskadi.eus/uploads/attachments/9954/VI_INK_SOZLG-EH_eus.pdf?1499236557

Gabilondo, Joseba. *Before Babel: A History of Basque Literatures*. Lansing: Barbaroak, 2016.

Heilbron, Johan, and Gisèle Sapiro. "Outlines for a Sociology of Translation: Current Issues and Future Prospects." In *Constructing a Sociology of Translation*, edited by Michaela Wolf, 93–107. Amsterdam: John Benjamins, 2007.

Jaka Irizar, Aiora, and Maialen Marin-Lacarta. "Txinatar literatura euskaraz: Zeharbidezko itzulpenetatik zuzenekoetara itzultzaile-bikoteen eskutik." *Uztaro* 89 (2014): 39–64. Doi: 10.26876/uztaro.89.2014.3

Li Bo 李白. *Urrutira bidalia*. Translated by Albert Galvany and Pello Otxoteko. Irun: Alberdania, 2005.

Marin-Lacarta, Maialen. "Mediated and Marginalised: Translations of Modern and Contemporary Chinese Literature in Spain (1949–2010)." *Meta* 63, no. 2 (2018): 318.

Mo Yan 莫言. *Hori da umorea, maisu!* Translated by Maialen Marin and Aiora Jaka. Donostia: Elkar, 2013.

Parker, Joshua. "Conceptions of Place, Space and Narrative: Past, Present and Future." *Amsterdam International Electronic Journal for Cultural Narratology* 90 (2016): 74–101. https://cf.hum.uva.nl/narratology/issue/7/a12_Joshua_Parker.html

Pu Songling 蒲松齡. *Pu Songlingen ipuinak*. Translated by Xabier Kaltzakorta. Bilbo: Labayru eta Bizkaiko Aurrezki Kutxa, 1988.

Sarrionandia, Joseba. *Izkiriaturik aurkitu ditudan ene poemak*. Iruñea: Pamiela, 1985.

Wang Wei 王維, Li Bo, and Du Fu 杜甫. *Mandarin Dotore: VIII. Mendeko olerkiak*. Translated by Rafa Egiguren. Soraluze: Gaztelupeko Hotsak, 2003.

Yan, Lianke. *Balou mendikateko balada*. Translated by Maialen Marin-Lacarta and Aiora Jaka Irizar. Donostia: Elkar, 2018.

Yan, Lianke. *Marrow*. Translated by Carlos Rojas. Hong Kong: Penguin Books China, 2016.

Zabaleta, Josu, trans. *Txina zaharreko kontu zaharrak*. Donostia: Erein, 1989.

Zhao Aiwu 趙愛武. "Jin ershi nian Hanyu xiangshengci yanjiu zongshu" 近 20 年漢語象聲詞研究綜述 [A review of the research on Chinese onomatopoeias in the last 20 years]. *Wuhan daxue xuebao (zhexue shehui kexue ban)* 武漢大學學報(哲學社會科學版) [Wuhan University Journal of Humanities & Social Science] 61, no. 2(2008): 180–85.

26
THE TRANSLATION AND RECEPTION OF YAN LIANKE IN FRANCE

Lu Gan

The author of many excellent novels and the recipient of many literary prizes, Yan Lianke 閻連科 is one of the most prolific writers of contemporary Chinese literature. His major works have been translated into more than 20 languages, which greatly helped to expand the influence of contemporary Chinese literature worldwide. In 2020, Yan published his eleventh book in France, where the writer has developed a reputation as one of the greatest Chinese writers of our times. Since 2006, a large number of books by Yan have been translated into French in the unabridged version, including *Servir le peuple* (*Wei renmin fuwu* 為人民服務), *Le Rêve du village des Ding* (*Dingzhuang meng* 丁莊夢), *Les Jours, les mois, les années* (*Nian yue ri* 年月日), *Bons baisers de Lénine* (*Shouhuo* 受活), *Songeant à mon père* (*Xiangnian fuqin* 想念父親), *Les Quatre livres* (*Si shu* 四書), *La Fuite du temps* (*Riguang liunian* 日光流年), *Les Chroniques de Zhalie* (*Zhalie zhi* 炸裂志), *À la découverte du roman* (*Faxian xiaoshuo* 發現小說), *Un chant céleste* (*Balou tiange* 耙耬天歌), and *La Mort du soleil* (*Rixi* 日熄).[1]

Translating Yan Lianke in France

As one of the most influential novelists in contemporary Chinese literature, Yan Lianke's books have been translated into many languages. In France, the translation of Yan's works began in 2006, a year after the publication of his novella *Serve the People* in mainland China. This book

---

1 *Servir le peuple* is the title under which Claude Payen rendered *Wei renmin fuwu* (Arles: Éditions Philippe Picquier, 2006) into French; *Le Rêve du village des Ding*, the title Payen rendered *Dingzhuang meng* (Arles: Éditions Philippe Picquier, 2007) into French ; *Les Jours, les mois, les années*, the title Brigitte Guilbaud rendered *Nian yue ri* (Arles: Éditions Philippe Picquier, 2009) into French; *Bons baisers de Lénine*, the title Sylvie Gentil rendered *Shouhuo* (Arles: Éditions Philippe Picquier, 2009) into French; *Songeant à mon père*, the title under Guilbaud rendered *Xiangnian fuqin* (Arles: Éditions Philippe Picquier, 2010) into French, *Les Quatre livres*, the title Gentil rendered *Si shu* (Arles: Éditions Philippe Picquier, 2012) into French, *La Fuite du temps*, the title Guilbaud rendered *Riguang liunian* (Arles: Éditions Philippe Picquier, 2014) into French, *Les Chroniques de Zhalie*, the title Gentil rendered *Zhalie zhi* (Arles: Éditions Philippe Picquier, 2015) into French; *A la découverte du roman*, the title Gentil rendered *Faxian xiaoshuo* (Arles: Éditions Philippe Picquier, 2017) into French; *Un chant céleste*, the title Gentil rendered *Balou tiange* (Arles: Éditions Philippe Picquier, 2017) into French; *La Mort du soleil*, the title Guilbaud rendered *Rixi* (Arles: Éditions Philippe Picquier, 2020).

was first published by the publishing house Huacheng 花城 in 2005. Yan borrowed one of the most important slogans proposed by Mao Zedong in a speech titled "Serve the People," which is to commemorate the heroic death of a communist soldier, Zhang Side 張思德, as the title of this novella. In his novella, he features another PLA soldier, Wu Dawang 吳大旺, a model orderly of the Division Commander. In Yan's story, "serve the people," the role for Wu Dawang is to serve the Division Commander and his wife. Because of the political connotation behind the story, this book was soon recalled and banned by the Publicity Department of the Central Committee of the Communist Party of China (*Zhonggong zhongyang xuanchuanbu* 中共中央宣傳部) and the General Administration of Press and Publication (*Xinwen chuban zongshu* 新聞出版總署).

However, *Serve the people* gained more visibility after it was banned, and it attracted considerable attention both in mainland China and France. Defined by Michael Holquist as "the paradox of censorship," it "predictably creates sophisticated audiences."[2] Despite the ban, readers were even directed to look for the story and to find the satirical critique of the army, the revolution, and the political system. Aware of the enthusiasm among literary critics both in China and abroad, the publishing house Éditions Philippe Picquier swiftly introduced its French edition translated by Claude Payen. The French edition entitled *Servir le peuple* attracted considerable attention from the book market in France. With its success, Éditions Philippe Picquier published the author's second novel the following year, *Dream of Ding Village* (*Dingzhuang meng*), also translated by Payen.

In 2009, Éditions Philippe Picquier chose two other translators for Yan. *The Years, Months, Days* (*Nian yue ri*) is translated by Brigitte Guilbaud, and *Pleasure* (*Shouhuo*) by Sylvie Gentil. From this year on, these two people became the main translators of Yan's works in France. In 2010, Guilbaud translated a collection of short stories written by Yan under the title *Remembering My Father* (*Xiangnian fuqin*). In 2012, *The Four Books* (*Si shu*) was translated by Gentil, with its pocket edition published in 2015. In 2014 and 2015, *Streams of Time* (*Riguan liunian*) and *The Explosion Chronicles* (*Zhalie zhi*) were translated by Guilbaud and Gentil, respectively. In 2017, the publishing house acknowledged the literary criticism of this writer, and *Discovering Fiction* (*Faxian xiaoshuo*) was translated by Gentil. She also translated and published *The Song of Heaven of Balou* (*Balou tiange*) in the same year. In 2020, Guilbaud translated his eleventh book in France, *The Day the Sun Died* (*Rixi*).

The introduction of Yan to French readers is mostly attributed to the publishing house Éditions Philipper Picquier, a French publishing house specializing in books from the Far East, his literary agent Chen Feng 陳豐, and three translators named Claude Payen, Brigitte Guilbaud and Sylvie Gentil, all of whom are very influential in France.

Chen Feng and Éditions Philippe Picquier

Until 2020, almost all the works of Yan Lianke translated in France are published by the publishing house Éditions Philippe Picquier.[3] In the publishing industry, the publication of translated books is carried out through the work of a series of intermediaries: publishers,

---

2 Michael Holquist, "Corrupt Originals: The Paradox of Censorship," *PMLA* 109, no. 1 (1994): 14–25.
3 Except for *Amour virtuel et poil de cochon* (Visional Love and Pig Hair), a collection of five contemporary Chinese short stories by Dai Lai, Xu Kun, King Wen, Ye Mi and Yan Lianke, translated by Henri Gaubier and published by the publishing house Éditions des Riaux in 2006.

translators, literary agents, revisers, printers, bookbinders, graphic designers, etc. In this process, each publishing house has its own operating mechanism. From its foundation in 1986, Éditions Philippe Picquier has endeavored to introduce books from the Far East in France. When other publishing houses like Actes Sud, Éditions du Seuil, and Éditions Gallimard began to publish books of Asian literature by introducing certain collections, such as *Knowledge of the Orient* (*Connaissance de l'Orient*) of Gallimard, Éditions Philippe Picquier chose to translate and publish the Asian literature with more coherence, with the credo "Asia is large enough to only concern ourselves with."[4] "The publishing house relies on a solid network in Asia but also in Europe, made up of agents, authors, journalists, translators or specialists, and advisers."[5] The introduction and publication of his works is mainly attributed to its director of the Chinese collection, Chen Feng.

The literary agent and translator Chen Feng arrived in France after graduating from Peking University. After gaining a DEA in French literature, she earned her doctoral degree with a thesis entitled "The Discovery of the West: Anthropological Perspective of the First Chinese Diplomats in Western Europe: 1866–1894" ("La Découverte de l'Occident: Regard anthropologique des premiers diplomates chinois sur l'Europe occidentale: 1866–1894") at the EHESS in 1993.[6] Thereafter, "she worked for a long time as literary agent, importing in China more than a thousand French titles in social and human sciences and literature before becoming the deputy editor-in-chief at Shanghai 99 and then the deputy editor-in-chief at Thinkingdom."[7] In cultural and literary exchanges between France and China, literary agents play an important role in overcoming linguistic and editorial barriers. A good agent is sometimes the crucial element for the success of a book translated into French. By way of her education background in China as well as in France, Chen has an open horizon on Chinese and French culture and a lot of experience in the publishing industry. During an interview in 2004, she talks about her role as an intermediary between the two cultures: "In this job, regular communication matters a lot. Internet, mail and telephone allow me to stay in touch with my Chinese partners, to search for books and settle business. I spend two or three months in China every year to get a better sense of the atmosphere, and to learn about developments in the book market, particularly in terms of legislation. As an essential working tool, I have created my own catalogue of books for

---

4 Philippe Picquier, "La Maison d'édition," Éditions Philippe Picquier, last modified June, 2021, https://www.editions-picquier.com/la-maison-d-edition/ (accessed July 31, 2021).
5 Léonor de Nussac, "Philippe Picquier: 'Éditer, c'est convaincre'" [Philipper Picquier: "Edit, is to convince"], *Revue de l'association des bibliothèques français* [Journal of the Library Association] 13 (2004): 64–65.
6 DEA, Diplôme d'étude approfondies, a former university degree existing in France between 1964 and 2005, and in countries following the French model of higher education, such as Lebanon or those of the Maghreb. Today it is equivalent to the second year of a master's degree. Since 2005, it has been replaced by the reform LMD (reform of the undergraduate-master-doctor system). EHESS, École des hautes études en sciences sociales, the School for Advanced Studies in Social Sciences, is one of the most prestigious institutions for social science in France.
7 Established in 2004, "Shanghai 99" is one of the fastest growing publishing companies in China. It operates in book copyright-related business for the Chinese market, running a book club and an online bookstore. Thinkingdom Media Group" is a company in the publishing industry, focused on book planning, publishing and distribution. "L'excellence de la culture française en Chine," Faguo wenhua 法國文化 [French culture], last modified 19 Mar., https://www.faguowenhua.com/fr/event/la-littérature-chinoise-passée-à-la-loupe-les-grands-écrivains-chinois-vus-de-la-france (last accessed 31 July 2021).

which I have provided a notice in Chinese. Of the successful contracts, over 90% are for books that I have recommended."[8]

To better promote Chinese literature in France, French publishers need to know China better and become more informed. Chen remarks: "They should consider China, not only as a large potential market, but also as a country of great cultural and intellectual wealth, resulting in an editorial production that they must, in trade, consider against their own criteria."[9] Since 2002, Chen has directed the collections of Chinese literature for Éditions Philippe Picquier, introduced renowned contemporary Chinese writers to French readers, such as Lu Wenfu 陸文夫, Su Tong 蘇童, Wang Anyi 王安憶, Cao Wenxuan 曹文軒, and Bi Feiyu 畢飛宇. Yan Lianke's systematic translation in France also begins with Chen's recommendation. When she first read the novel *Pleasure*, she was enthralled by the writer's fascinating imagination. In 2006, she swiftly published *Serve the People*, which had just been censored upon publication in mainland China. Each time a new book is published, Chen has it translated. *The Day the Sun Died* was first entrusted to Sylvie Gentil and then to Brigitte Guilbaud in 2018. In 2019, Chen finally had the opportunity to publish an old book by the writer, *Hard Like Water* (*Jianying rushui* 堅硬如水), a satirical novel on the revolution, published in China in 2009. She entrusted the translation of this novel to Noël Dutrait, a well-known Sinologist and translator of the Nobel Prize winners Gao Xingjian 高行健 and Mo Yan 莫言.

Between 2006 and 2020, there was an expansion in the translations of Yan's works. In the beginning, Éditions Philippe Picquier entrusted Claude Payen with the translation of *Serve the People* and *Dream of Ding Village*. These two novels tackle ideological and realistic subjects in the Chinese society and were of great interest to French readers fond of contemporary Chinese literature. Subsequently, the publishing house sought to emphasize the literalness in Yan's works. As such, they approached the translators Guilbaud and Gentil to examine more serious novels by the writer.

Yan Lianke's three main translators in France

Being the first filter of linguistic, cultural, social, and philosophical signs, the translator plays a crucial role in the act of translating. If we consider translation as the rebirth of text in another language, it depends deeply on the talent and the strategy of the translator. As Mathieu Dosse remarks, "Reading a translation is always reading a translator."[10] In our case, despite the three translators interpreting Yan's novels differently, all played an important role in the progressive translation and reception of his works in France.

Claude Payen is not a professional translator, and it is only in retirement that he truly began a career translating works about China. At first, he translated from English into French. In 1969, he translated a book written by an American journalist, Agnès Smedley, who was a "war correspondent in China in the 1930s, and who, from 1938 to 1940, visited areas

---

8 Chen Feng and Bai Bing, "Entretiens avec Feng Chen (agent littéraire) et Bai Bing (Éditions Jieli)," Bureau International de l'Édition Française, last modified Apr. 2004, https://www.bief.org/Publication-2542-Article/Entretiens-avec-Feng-Chen-(agent-litteraire)-et-Bai-Bing-(Éditions-Jieli).html (last accessed 31 July 2021).
9 Mathieu Dosse, *Poétique de la lecture des traductions: Joyce, Nabokov, Guimaraes Rosa* [Poetics of reading translations: Joyce, Nabokov, Guimaraes Ros] (Paris: Classiques Garnier, 2006), 13.
10 Ibid.

controlled by the Communist forces and those of the Guomindang."[11] The translation is entitled *The Long March: Memoirs of the Marshal Zhu De* (*La Longue Marche: Mémoires du maréchal Zhu De*), prefaced by Lucien Bianco and published in two volumes by the publishing house Imprimerie nationale. "Because of his love of the Chinese language, he began studying it in 1962. After his retirement, he used his free time and devoted himself to translating Chinese novels. Fortuitously, he established contact with the publishing house Éditions Youfeng, and then gradually entered the Chinese novel translation market."[12]

In 1994, Payen conducted his first translation from Chinese into French for Éditions Youfeng. After his retirement in 1995, he successively translated about twenty works dealing with various subjects from Chinese into French. Before accepting the translation of *Serve the People*, Payen had already translated many contemporary Chinese novels, such as *Les Tambours* (*The Drum Singers* [*Gushu yiren* 鼓書藝人], 2001) by Lao She 老舍, *L'Opéra de la lune* (*The Moon Opera* [*Qingyi* 青衣], 2003) by Bi Feiyu, and *Je suis l'empereur de Chine* (*My Life as Emperor* [*Wo de diwang shengya* 我的帝王生涯], 2005) by Su Tong. When Éditions Philippe Picquier decided to translate Yan Lianke's works, Payen was invited to initiate the project. *Servir le peuple* sold 11,000 copies and *Le Rêve du village des Ding* 8,500 copies, which promoted the writer among French readers.

Despite his long career as a translator, the background of Payen remains unknown to French readers, as well as to researchers. In the era of mass media, almost no information about this translator is available on the internet. His name only appears with the titles of the works he has translated.[13] However, his work is essential for scholars when they study the translation of contemporary Chinese literature in France. The online Chinese newspaper *people.cn* published an interview with Payen on 27 Mar. 2018, entitled "The Neutral and Silent Translator" ("Yizhe zhongli, mo wu shengxi" 譯者中立，默無聲息). The interview allows us to better understand his philosophy and how he persists in working to introduce China to French readers through the literary translation.

For Payen, one of the purposes of translation is for the French reader to forget he or she is reading Chinese literature. In other words, the best translation should never look like a translation. In his work, he is primarily concerned with the translation's readability in the target language. For example, "Chinese literary works prefer the rhetoric of repetition. However, the French language pays more attention to the richness of the vocabulary. The translator must avoid repetition to find suitable synonyms to meet the reading habits of French readers."[14] Therefore, he indulges in reading classical French works, especially those with a beautiful and rich vocabulary, to polish his language. Regarding the selection of the text to translate, he believes that the

---

11 Brigitte Duzan, "'Ecrits de la maison des rats': quelques pages douces-amères pour mieux connaître Lao She," La nouvelle dans la literature chinoise contemporaine [The novels in contemporary Chinese literature], last modified 21 May 2010, http://www.chinese-shortstories.com/Actualites_16.htm (last accessed 31 July 2021).

12 Gong Ming 龔鳴, "Yizhe zhongli, mo wu shengxi" 譯者中立，默無聲息 [Translator are neutral and silent], Sohu 搜狐, last modified 27 Mar. 2018, https://www.sohu.com/a/226506736_630337 (last accessed 31 July 2021).

13 In 2010, Payen was involved in a polemic of translation against Pierre Kaser, professor and Sinologist of Université Aix-Marseille in France, around the translation of *The Plain* (*Pingyuan* 平原) by Bi Feiyu. For further information, see Pierre Kaser, "L'inaperçu de l'Inaperçu" [The unseen of the Unseen], Littérature d'Extrême-Orient, textes et traduction [Far Eastern literature, texts and translation], last modified 22 July 2010, http://jelct.blogspot.com/2010/07/linapercu-de-linapercu.html (last accessed 31 July 2021).

14 Gong, "Yizhe zhongli, mo wu shengxi."

translator should be "neutral, like a doctor seeing patients or a technician repairing a machine. There is no taste or aversion. What we can do is convey to Western audiences the typical Chinese elements, as well as Chinese literature and society."[15]

To achieve his objective of readability, Payen sometimes changes the structure of the original text and changes the original expressions of the writer. He also modifies the original text by the addition and deletion of certain sentences or phrases, especially when he feels they are not needed. If we analyze the following example from *Servir le peuple*:

有一天, 不知道師長從哪兒提著這塊刷了白漆、印了紅字, 並在字的左右兩側和下面, 用紅、黃漆套印了五星、長槍、水壺和麥穗的木牌回到家裏, 擺在餐桌上時, 師長肅穆地盯著正往桌上擺著飯菜的公務員兼炊事員的班長吳大旺, 說知道這木牌上的意思吧? 吳大旺專注地盯著看了一會, 細心地作了研解述說, 師長也就慢慢地微笑起來, 一臉舒展燦然, 說不錯、不錯, 的確不錯, 我師長家裏的公務員、炊事員也比他們覺悟高。[16]

Il ne savait pas d'où le général avait rapporté un jour cette pancarte avec des caractères rouges écrits sur fond blanc qui encadraient une étoile à cinq branches, un fusil, une gourde et des gerbes de blés peints en couleur rouge et jaune. Quand il l'avait ramené chez lui et posé sur la table, il avait fixé d'un regard grave Wu Dawang, son ordonnance qui faisait également office de cuisinier qui était en train de dresser la table. Il lui demanda s'il connaissait la signification de cette pancarte. Apres l'avoir regarder avec attention, Wu Dawang, en fit une explication détaillée. Le général se détendit, un sourire apparut progressivement sur son visage: pas mal, pas mal du tout, on ordonnance faisant office de cuisinier les dépasse par son niveau de conscience. [My trans.][17]

Il ne savait pas d'où le colonel avait un jour rapporté cette pancarte sur laquelle les étoiles, le fusil, la gourde et les gerbes de blé étaient peints en rouge et jaune sur fond blanc, mais il se rappelait que ce jour-là, le colonel l'avait longuement fixé avant de lui demander d'un ton solennel:

— Comprends-tu le sens de cette pancarte?

En regardant la pancarte avec la plus grande concentration, Wu Dawang en avait donné une explication minutieuse. Le colonel avait affiché un sourire radieux:

---

15 Ibid.
16 Yan Lianke, *Wei renmin fuwu* (Hong Kong: Wenhua yishu chubanshe, 2014), 6.
17 Here I propose my translation relatively more literal in order to be more close to the original text: "He did not know where the Division Commander had one day brought this sign with red characters written on a white background, which was framed with stars, rifle, canteen, and wheat painted in red and yellow. When he had brought it home and placed it on the table, he had gazed solemnly at Wu Dawang, his orderly who also acted as the cook, who is setting the table. He asked him if he knew the meaning of that sign. After watching it carefully, Wu Dawang produced a detailed explanation. The Division Commander relaxed, a smile gradually appeared on his face: not bad, not bad, really not bad, my orderly acting as the cook exceeds them by his level of consciousness."

— Pas mal, pas mal du tout. Mon ordonnance faisant office de cuisinier les dépasse tous par son niveau de conscience politique. [Payen's trans.][18]

As demonstrated, Payen divides the paragraph into several parts according to his understanding of the text. He emphasizes the dialogue between Wu Dawang and the colonel so that the French reader can better understand the narration. "This sign with red characters written on a white background which was framed with stars, rifle, canteen, and wheat painted in red and yellow" (這塊刷了白漆、印了紅字，並在字的左右兩側和下面，用紅、黃漆套印了五星、長槍、水壺和麥穗的木牌) is replaced by "cette pancarte sur laquelle les étoiles, le fusil, la gourde et les gerbes de blé étaient peints en rouge et jaune sur fond blanc" ("this sign on which the stars, the rifle, the canteen, and the wheat were painted in red and yellow on a white background"). This change of expression in a way simplifies the French translation and promotes the readability of the translated text.

In 1955, in his *The Translator's Invisibility: A History of Translation*, Lawrence Venuti talks about the invisible translator.[19] According to him, if one adopts the criterion of legibility (invisibility of the translator), he most often returns to the "quest for the Self at the cost of the Other, and would simultaneously consider the relations of domination maintained by the Anglo-American powers with the cultures they translate."[20] The "invisibility of the translation" is for Venuti the assimilation or violence of the dominant culture over the peripheral culture. He emphasizes that the translator should reveal the difference to tackle ethnocentric violence. Although Payen emphasizes the importance of the invisibility of the translator, he is often a "visible translator" according to the theory of Venuti. For example, he translated 說不錯、不錯、的確不錯，我師長家裏的公務員、炊事員也比他們覺悟高。 ("not bad, not bad, really not bad, my orderly acting as the cook exceeds them by his level of consciousness") by "pas mal, pas mal du tout. Mon ordonnance faisant office de cuisinier les dépasse tous par son niveau de conscience politique" ("not bad, not bad at all. My orderly acting as the cook surpasses them all in his level of *political* consciousness"). Here he translates the word *juewu* 覺悟 'level of consciousness' by "niveau de conscience politique" ("level of political awareness") to emphasize the political meaning in the colonel's speech. As Payen has observed, "Western audiences love the uniqueness of China. So, the translated works also have the task of discovering China and changing stereotypes."[21] The translator has the ambition to reveal

---

18 Yan Lianke, *Servir le peuple*, trans. Claude Payen (Arles: Éditions Philippe Picquier, 2006), 6:

He did not know where the colonel had one day brought this sign on which the stars, the rifle, the canteen, and the wheat were painted in red and yellow on a white background, but he remembered that on that day, the colonel had stared at him for a long time before asking him solemnly:

- Do you understand the meaning of this sign?

Looking at the sign with the greatest concentration, Wu Dawang gave a careful explanation. The colonel had displayed a radiant smile:

- Not bad, not bad at all. My orderly acting as the cook exceeds them all in his level of political awareness.

19 Lawrence Venuti, *The Translator's Invisibility: A History of Translation* (London: Routledge, 1995).
20 Corinne Durin, "Lawrence Venuti. *The Translator's Invisibility. A History of Translation*. London and New York: Routledge, coll. 'Translation Studies,' 1955, 353 pages," *Traduction, Terminologie, Rédaction* 8, no. 2 (Feb. 2007): 283–86.
21 Gong, "Yizhe zhongli, mo wu shengxi."

the specificity of Chinese culture and to avoid all kinds of clichés. Sometimes, when the "visible translator" chooses to focus above all on the differences between the two cultures and ideologies, the translation accentuates the danger of the violent ethnocentrism.

Brigitte Guilbaud is Yan's second translator. She translated *The Years, Months, Days* in 2009, *Remembering My Father* in 2010, *Streams of Time* in 2014, and *The Day the Sun Died* in 2020. She is also a writer and teacher of Chinese in France. In 2001, she published her prose work *La Saison d'Aurélia (Aurélia's Season)* and in 2004 *Une fronce dans le temps (A Fold in the Time)*. Guilbaud was born in the United States. After graduating from Inalco,[22] where she took evening classes, she joined a Chinese teaching association for seven years. Subsequently, she was appointed professor of Chinese at the Lycée Turgot in Paris. After publishing *Servir le peuple* and *Le Rêve du village des Ding*, the publishing house Éditions Philippe Picquier sought to translate *The Years, Months, Days* within three months. After a short meeting, Guilbaud accepted the job. It was also an opportunity for her to discover this Chinese writer and to gradually forge her own understanding of literary translation.

In contrast to Payen, Guilbaud puts a greater emphasis on the language of the novelist. For her, "Yan Lianke is particularly difficult to translate, because he has a unique, very personal, perfectly mastered language, which mixes the dialect of Henan with passages, often the most poetic, of the harshest Mandarin."[23] In her translation, she needs to capture not only the beauty of the story but also the beauty of his writing. The advantage of Guilbaud's translations is her understanding of the text and the emotions of the characters. She always tries to reproduce the style of the writer and maintain the literary value of the novel as much as possible. We will take this paragraph as an example:

田地裡的種子，都已被老鼠們吃得淨盡。先爺緩緩抬起頭，聽見遙遠的西邊，有了一聲嘰哇的慘叫，把目光投到最遠處，通過兩道山峰的中間，看到太陽被另一道山峰吞沒了，留下的紅燦燦的血漬，從山頂一直流到山底，又漫到先爺的身邊來。頃刻，一個世界無聲無息了，又將到一天中最為死靜的黃昏和傍黑之間的那一刻。要在往年往月，這一刻正是雞上架、雀歸巢的光景，滿世界的啁啾會如雨淋一樣降下來。可眼下什麼都沒了，沒了牲畜，沒了麻雀，連烏鴉也逃旱飛走了。只有死靜。先爺看著血色落日愈來愈薄，聽著那些紅光離他越來越遠如一片紅綢被慢慢抽去的響動，收拾著石窩裡的玉米黍穰，想又一天過去了，明兒天逼在頭頂該怎麼過呢？[24]

Les grains des semences ont été complètement dévorés par les rats. Il leva très lentement la tête. Du lointain, à l'ouest, lui parvenaient de misérables cris. Il porta son regard le plus loin possible. Il vit, entre deux faîtes, le soleil disparaître, englouti derrière une troisième cime. Restait un flot rouge brillant, s'écoulant du haut vers le bas de la montagne, se déversant jusque auprès de lui. Le monde entier se tut instantanément. C'était l'heure du silence le plus intense, entre le déclin du jour

---

22 Inalco, Institut national des langues et civilisations orientales, is a French higher education and research institution responsible for teaching languages and civilizations, excluding those of Westen Europe.
23 Brigitte Duzan, "Brigitte Guilbaud Présentation" [Brigitte Guilbaud presentation], La nouvelle dans la literature chinoise contemporaine [The novels in contemporary Chinese literature], last modified 19 Oct. 2018, http://www.chinese-shortstories.com/Traducteurs_et_editeurs_BrigitteGuilbaud.htm (last accessed 31 July 2021).
24 Yan Lianke, *Nian yue ri* (Zhengzhou: Henan wenyi chubanshe, 2014), 139.

et la tombée du la nuit. À cet instant-là, autrefois, on voyait les coqs monter sur leurs supports et les moineaux rentrer au nid, le monde s'emplissait d'une pluie de gazouillis. Mais aujourd'hui on ne voyait plus rien, ni bétail ni moineau, même les corbeaux avaient fui la sécheresse. Il n'y a plus que le silence. L'horizon rouge du couchant se faisait de plus en plus mince et l'aïeul entendait le froissement des rayons qui se retiraient comme un pan de soie. Ramassant les grains émiettés au creux de la pierre, il songea qu'une journée encore venait de s'achever, et qu'il ignorait comment il pourrait passer la suivante. [Guilbaud's trans.][25]

Compared to the translations of Payen, those of Guilbaud press closer to the original text and structure. In her translation, she also respects the continuity between sentences, connected in the Chinese text by commas, to evoke the extension of the landscape as well as the infinity of nature. Guilbaud hides behind the text and tries to remain invisible in her work.

Besides Payen and Guilbaud, Sylvie Gentil has also translated the majority of Yan Lianke's works in France: *Bons baisers de Lénine* (Pleasure), *Les Quatre livres* (The Four Books), *Les Chroniques de Zhalie* (The Explosion Chronicles), *Un chant céleste* (The Song of the Heaven of Balou) and *À la découverte du roman* (Discovering Fiction). She was born in 1958 in Saint-Maixent-l'Ecole and passed away in 2017 in Paris. After studying at Inalco with François Cheng and Jacques Pimpaneau as professors, she spent two years at Peking University from 1980 to 1982. From 1985, she moved to Beijing, first working as a translator of subtitles for the Chinese cinema and then as a proofreader of translations from Chinese into French. During the 1990s, she began to translate literary works. From then on, for almost thirty years, she translated several contemporary Chinese writers, including Xu Xing 徐星, Liu Suola 劉索拉, Feng Tang 馮唐, Mian Mian 棉棉, Li Er 李洱 and Mo Yan, and received the translation prize of Arles (prix Amédée Pichot) for *Bons baisers de Lénine* in 2010 and Chevalier de l'Ordre national du Mérite in 2014. She is not only a translator, but also a pilgrim between the two cultures. In 2016, she became the jury president for the Fu Lei Prize for Translation and Editing (*Fu Lei fanyi chuban jiang* 傅雷翻譯出版獎).

As a professional translator, she employs her own strategies in the field of Chinese translation. First of all, when it comes to choosing the text to translate, Gentil's attitude is not as neutral as that of Payen. According to her, a translator has to choose the text that he or she likes; otherwise the translation will be a torture. "Whether you read or translate, a book is

---

25 Yan Lianke, *Les Jours, les mois, les années*, trans. Brigitte Guilbaud (Arles: Éditions Philippe Picquier), 2014, 59–60:

All of the seeds in the fields were completely devoured by the rats. He raised his head very slowly, and heard miserable screams from the distant west. He peered into the distance as far as he could, and he saw, between the two mountain peaks, he could see the sun being swallowed by another mountain peak. The remaining shining-red stream flowed from the peaks down to the foot of the mountains, then back up to the Elder. The entire world fell completely silent. It was the hour of silence the most intense, between dusk and nightfall. In the past, at that moment, this would be when chickens returned to roost and sparrows went back to their nests, and the entire world would be filled with rain-like chirping. But today there wasn't a sound. There were no livestock, no sparrows, and even the crows had fled the drought. There was only silence. The red horizon of the setting sun grew fainter and fainter, and the Elder heard the rustling of the rays, like a sheet of silk. He collected the crumbled seeds in the stone mortar. He thought that another day had ended, but he did not know how he could get through the next day.

above all about love, but this is especially true when you translate."[26] At the start of her career, she produced translations that publishers commissioned. Shortly after, she began to make discoveries and adventures. The writers she translates are the ones she loves and it is thanks to her that these Chinese writers could be read in French. For example, when the editor Chen Feng of the publishing house Philippe Picquier searched in vain for translators of *Pleasure* because of the immense difficulty of its translation, Gentil volunteered to take on this task, with the condition that she is not time-limited.

Then, in relation to the idea proposed by Guilbaud to soak up the text, Gentil recommends making subsequent changes instead of carrying out a translation in one go. "When it comes to Chinese," says Gentil, "this direct approach is hardly possible: there is always a character that escapes you, you have to work step by step, dictionary in hand, and gradually soak up the style. It is only once this is clearly perceived that words and expressions come easily and naturally to mind."[27] At the same time, she shares the same principle as Guilbaud of mastering the target language in order to translate well.

Finally, regarding the transmission of style in the original text, Gentil emphasizes the importance of not removing its "strangeness." This "strangeness" is not only the primary quality for a translated work, but also an important value in creating literalness in the translation. She even suggests reinventing the appropriate language to "end up with a text that produces the same effect as the original."[28] This reinvention is, however, distinct from the translation style (rewriting) of Payen. Also, Gentil tries to create musicality in her translation, without going beyond the initial text. For example, we could look at the following paragraph from *Pleasure*:

天熱了，下雪了，時光有病了

你看喲，炎炎熱熱的酷夏裡，人本就不受活，卻又落了一場雪。是場大熱雪。

一夜間，冬天又折身回來了。也許是轉眼裡夏天走去了，秋天未及來，冬天繁步兒趕到了。這年的酷夏裡，時序亂了綱常了，神經錯亂了，有了羊角風，在一天的夜裡飄飄落落亂了規矩了，沒有王法了，下了大雪了。[29]

Il fait chaud, il neige, le temps est malade

Voyez-vous ça: c'était la canicule, on était mal benaise et il a neigé! Une neige chaude est tombée.

En une nuit l'hiver est revenu. Ou plutôt: après qu'en un clin d'œil l'été s'en est allé, sans laisser à l'automne le temps de se poser, à pas pressés il s'est installé. L'été était torride, et faisant fi de tout principe le temps s'est détraqué, nous a fait une crise

---

26 Brigitte Duzan, "Sylvie Gentil, pèlerin émérite des lettres chinoises" [Sylvie Gentil, pilgrim emeritus of Chinese letters], La nouvelle dans la literature chinoise contemporaine [The novels in contemporary Chinese literature], last modified 30 Apr. 2017, http://www.chinese-shortstories.com/Traducteurs_et_editeurs_Sylvie_Gentil.htm (last accessed 31 July 2021).
27 Ibid.
28 Ibid.
29 Yan Lianke, *Shouhuo* (Shenyang: Chunfeng wenyi chubanshe, 2003), 3.

d'épilepsie. Au mépris des lois les plus universelles, bouleversant les règles établies, en une nuit la neige s'est lourdement abattue. [Gentil's trans.]³⁰

In her translation, Gentil delicately changes the units of meaning between the sentences to render a poetic and literary style in her translation. This subtle adjustment gives the French text a musicality that exists alongside (but in a different way) in Chinese. For example, we may translate the sentences 你看哟, 炎炎熱熱的酷夏裡, 人本就不受活, 卻又落了一場雪。是場大熱雪。 literally by "Voyez-vous, pendant la canicule, les gens n'étaient pas benaise. Et il a neigé. C'était une neige chaude." In the Chinese text the endings of each sentence like *shouhuo* 受活, *yi chang xue* 一場雪 and *da re xue* 大熱雪 make up a harmonious rhyme, thus creating a rhythm of ascending gradations. To reproduce this literary effect in French, Gentil slightly modifies the words to obtain the following translation: "Voyez-vous ça: c'était la canicule, on était mal benaise et il a neigé! Une neige chaude est tombée." As a result, the French reader can feel the rhythm and coherence between sentences, without the translator betraying the original text.

To conclude, our analysis of the three translators of Yan shows that each translator has their own conception of translation, which will accordingly influence the strategies they use to translate. For example, Payen's perception of contemporary Chinese literature is closely linked to politics and ideology; therefore, he pays particular attention in his translation to the transposition of these two aspects. As for Gentil, she takes into account the use of dialect in the works of the writer and strives to translate this language style into her work by inventing expressions inspired by German and dialects from the South of France. The translator often bears a prejudice toward the text, which is based on his experiences of translation, his literary taste, or his knowledge of the literature he translates. Such prejudices can help the translator swiftly grasp the characteristics of the author's style and may also cause him or her to ignore other aspects of the novel.

In studying translation as a complex activity, we need to pay more attention to the active role of the translator and his or her prerogative. As Inger Hesjevoll Schmidt-Melbye pointed out in his article, "as a translation specialist, one is easily intrigued by certain choices made by the translator and, consequently, one often falls into the trap of condemning a translation without questioning the translator's own assessments."³¹ When we analyze the work of the three translators, we need to pay more attention to their conception of translation to better understand their translation strategies.

---

30 Yan Lianke, *Bons baisers de Lénine*, trans. Sylvie Gentil (Arles: Éditions Philippe Picquier, 2012), 7:

It's hot, it's snowing, the time is sick

Do you see that: it was a heatwave, people couldn't enjoy pleasure and it snowed! Warm snow fell.

Winter returned overnight. Or rather: after summer gone in the blink of an eye, without giving autumn time to settle down, it has stationed in haste. The summer was scorching, and ignoring any principle the time degenerated into disorder, gave us a crisis of epilepsy. In defiance of the most universal laws, overturning the established rules, the snow fell heavily the whole night.

31 Inger Hesjevoll Schmidt-Melbye, "Ambiguïté et hybridité – de la subjectivité dans le domaine de la traduction" [Ambiguity and hybridity : On the subjectivity in the field of translation], in *Pays Scandinaves* [Scandinavian Countries], 2002, no. 7: 31–41.

A physiological study of the status quo of the reception of Yan Lianke in France

By the end of 2020, 11 books had been translated and published in France. As we know, the publication of a book is the first step of reception. Thanks to Pascaline Garreau, production manager at Éditions Philippe Picquier, sales figures for Yan Lianke's works in France are now available (released at the end of 2019).

Books	Publication Dates	Copies	ISBN Numbers
Servir le people	2006.01	3,000	9782877308274
Servir le peuple (Poche)	2018.01	8,000	9782809713244
Le Rêve du village des Ding	2007.01	500	9782877309165
Le Rêve du village des Ding (Poche)	2009.02	8,000	9782809700855
Les Jours, les mois, les années	2009.02	6,000	9782809700961
Les Jours, les mois, les années (Poche)	2014.01	11,000	9782809709643
Bons baisers de Lénine	2009.10	5,000	9782809701333
Bons baisers de Lénine (Poche)	2012.08	4,000	9782809703542
Songeant à mon père	2010.04	3,000	9782809701715
Songeant à mon père (Poche)	2017.03	3,000	9782809712537
Les Quatre livres	2012.08	3,000	9782809703528
Les Quatre livres (Poche)	2015.09	3,000	9782809711165
La Fuites du temps	2014.01	3,000	9782809709636
La Fuite du temps (Poche)	2018.01	3,000	9782809713237
Les Chroniques de Zhalie	2015.09	3,000	9782809711158
Un chant céleste	2017.03	2,000	9782809712506
Un chant céleste (Poche)	2019.01	2,000	9782809713947
À la découverte du roman	2017.03	1,000	9782809712513

According to this table, the work that sells the best is *Les Jours, les mois, les années*. Six thousand paperbacks and 11,000 pocket books were sold up until the end of 2019. In addition, several thousand copies of *Servir le peuple* and *Bons baisers de Lénine* were also printed.

The translation and publication of a foreign work is always accompanied by commercial promotion as well as literary reviews, which influence the reception of a work by the public. As Yan's novels were introduced in France, there are different critics. Some of these are newspaper articles for advertising purposes, while others are comments by ordinary readers or literary critiques by professional researchers. Albert Thibaudet, in his *Physiologie de la critique* (*Criticism Physiology*), divides criticism into three categories: spontaneous criticism, professional criticism, and criticism of masters.[32] Thibaudet defined it: "Spontaneous criticism or 'criticism of decent people' is made by the public itself, or rather by the enlightened part of the public, and by its immediate interpretations. Professional criticism is made by specialists, whose job is to read books, to draw from these books a certain common doctrine, and to establish between books of all times and all places a kind of social space. The criticism of masters is made by the writers themselves, when they reflect on their art."[33] Through our studies on the reception of Yan's works in France, borrowing the theory of Thibaudet's classification of criticism, we could also find three typical subjects of criticism. In the case of spontaneous criticism, we have criticism made by internet users; in professional criticism we

---

32 Albert Thibaudet, *Physiologie de la critique* [Critism Physiology] (Paris: Éditions de la Nouvelle Revue Critique, 1930).
33 Ibid., 24–25.

find criticism exercised by journalists; finally, there is also the third kind of criticism—the criticism of researchers.

First of all, readers who state their opinions on the internet comprise much of the criticism of his works. In sites like *Babelio*, *Critique Libre*, individual or collective blogs, and even customer comments from *Amazon.fr*, we could find all kinds of reviews from internet users.[34] These comments reflect the writer's reception by the general public in France. They give instant responses to the work that they are reading, and the interpretations are sometimes devoid of deep reflections as well as theoretical foundations. However, in our age of mass culture, reactions from the general public remain important in assessing the reception of a writer in society. For example, on the page of *Critiques Libres*, in total, we find readers' comments on the ten books by Yan translated into French.[35] *Dream of Ding Village*, a novel audaciously uncovering the blood-selling scandal and consequent contamination of HIV/AIDS in Henan Province in the 1990s, gets fourteen reviews, compared to only one or two comments for each of Yan's other novels. On the website of *Babelio*, most comments center on books like *The Years, Months, Days*, *Dream of Ding Village*, and *Serve the People*. Besides the reason that those three books were translated earlier, this preference reflects how the French publics pay more attention to works dealing with realistic issues of contemporary China and novels that are easy to read.

Next, the criticism of journalists is made by specialists, whose job is to read books, write reviews for newspapers or magazines, establish a bridge between books and the common readers and promote the works. Articles on Yan's works often appear in *Le Monde*, *Le Temps*, *Le Figaro littéraire*, *Livres Hebdo*, and *Rue89*, etc. Indeed, the importance of journalistic criticism lies in the fact that it influences, to some extent, the general public's view of works. In *The Act of Reading*, Wolfgang Iser considers that the structure of the text and the act of reading are complementary but that the text is not imprinted directly on the reader's consciousness.[36] The field of criticism constructed by the distribution of the publishing house, the advertisements of the newspapers as well as the criticisms of the journalists constitutes "the social repertoire" for the general public.

Finally, there is the last step for translated works to continue life in a foreign country and to have the opportunity to become a literary classic—the criticisms made by researchers. Here we are talking about university professors, intellectuals, and men of letters. The scholars' review is not intended to promote the book or to make a journalistic observation. However, it is done because its author finds something important about the literary text, and such critique allows the work to officially enter the literary field of the host country.

From our study of the various critiques about the translation of Yan's works in France, and according to the reviews or comments concerning his works published there, we propose the following graph, "Numbers of the different critiques of Yan Lianke in France," listed in chronological order:

---

[34] *Babelio* is both a website and a mobile application dedicated to literature; it is also a social network where registered readers can share comments on literary works. *Critique Libre* is a free website dependent on the contribution of volunteers who use the internet to share their knowledge and reading experience; it contains book reviews and discussions for all types of literature.

[35] Also the collection of his short stories, *Amour Virtuelle et Poil de Cochon* [Visional love and pig hair].

[36] Wolfgang Isers, *The Act of Reading: A Theory of Aesthetic Response* (Baltimore: Johns Hopkins University Press, 1980).

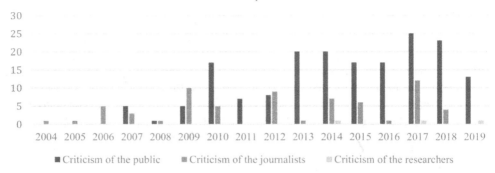

In the early years of Yan's translation in France, we could only find journalistic reviews. From 2007, a year after the first translation of his fiction, critiques from the general public began to emerge. Thanks to the progressive publication of Éditions Philippe Picquier, each year there have been a number of reviews from the journalistic world. However, until the end of 2019, only three reviews from researchers have been released, in 2014, 2017, and 2019, respectively. Through these statistics, we can see that the reception of Yan's works is quite limited, especially in the world of researchers.

In fact, Yan's reception in France still remains restricted, both quantitatively and qualitatively. There are few journalistic or general public reviews and even fewer reviews from researchers. When we examine the content of these critiques in more detail, we find that these criticisms are largely related to the "peripheral analyzes" of his works. Many of them focus on Chinese history and social reality rather than on the literary nature of his works. In other words, his works are above all a kind of literature from a distant land and a window through which the French readers can learn about the reality of today's China. Yan's works are viewed as what Pascale Casanova theorizes as "a reference to the history and to specificities in the national space."[37] In the case of our writer, all the labels on his works, for example, "censored novels," "by a controversial writer in mainland China," attest that readers pay particular attention to the peripheral aspects of his literature.

Gilles Deleuze and Félix Guattari have published a book called *Kafka: Pour une littérature mineure* (*Kafka: For a Minor Literature*), in which they talk about the difference between a dominant literature and a peripheral literature. According to the two theorists, the biggest symbol of the minor literature is that everything is political. "Each individual case is immediately plugged into politics."[38] In the critical field, we find that the majority of the critiques of Yan focus on politics and censorship in China today, but not on literary analysis of individual affairs of the novel. Those peripheral critiques reflect the modest reception of his works in France, for which we could assume several practical reasons.

First of all, Yan's works are part of a translated literature. When critics attempt to analyze one of his books, they immediately appeal to the literary field to which the book belongs.

---

37 Pascale Casanova, "La Guerre de l'ancienneté: Ou il n'y a pas d'identité nationale" [The war of antiquity: Or there is no national identity], in *Des literature combatives: L'internationale des nationalisemes littéraires* [Combative literature: The international of literary nationalisms], ed. Pascale Casanova (Paris: Éditions Raison d'Agir, 2011), 22.

38 Gilles Deleuze and Félix Guattari, *Kafka: Pour une littérature mineure* [Kafka: For a minor literature] (Paris: Minuit, 1975), 30.

The literary image constitutes what Hans Robert Jauss defines as a "horizon of expectation"[39] for readers and critics when they read foreign literature. In reality, mainly the media and the literary image of this culture generate the popular imagination of a foreign culture, which also constitutes a horizon of expectations for readers and influences their view of books from this foreign literature. For the works of Yan, the reference to Chinese literature has played an important role in its reception. When critics talk about his works, they often mention the regime, the politics, and the history of China. Starting from an economic criterion, Fredric Jameson, the American literary critic, Marxist political theorist, and student of Erich Auerbach, proposes a separation between the literature of the "Third World" and those of the "First World." The most obvious characteristic of provincial literature is its close connection with politics. "A popular or socially realistic Third World novel tends to present itself to us not immediately, but as already read. Between us and this foreign text, we feel the presence of another reading, the Other Reading, for which a story that appears conventional or naive to us has a freshness of information and a social interest that it is impossible for us to share."[40] According to Pascale Casanova, despising, minimizing, or discrediting the national belief in literature, as is often done in France, is one of the ways of reproducing the ethnocentric prejudices of French universalism. For Yan's works, which are considered provincial literature, preconceived ideas as well as an ignorance of Chinese literature weaken their reception in France. At the same time, when it comes to reading and receiving translated literature, the quality of the translation is undoubtedly an essential component. Foreign literature written in a foreign language is an obstacle not only for the translators but also for the readers.

Moreover, with regard to contemporary Chinese literature, due to ideological elements, French readers remain somewhat suspicious of the integrity of contemporary Chinese writers and their freedom to write. While at the same time, this constitutes a favorable element for the reception of Yan, who is considered a relatively free and courageous writer, often censored by his government. In critiques about the works of Yan in France, people talk a lot about censorship in China. This point of view, on the one hand, prevents French readers from accepting contemporary Chinese literature as literature worthy of the name and, on the other hand, encourages them to take a particular interest in the works of Yan, who is sometimes criticized and censored in mainland China. For example, in 2009, after the translation of *Pleasure* into French, an article in *Livres Hebdo* criticizes the censorship of literary works in China. "Since Yan Lianke saw himself, because of this book, kicked out of the army in 2002 and censored for the first time. He has never been imprisoned and may even travel abroad on his own. But his name was struck from the official delegation of Chinese writers invited to the recent Frankfurt Book Fair."[41]

In 2016, during his acceptance speech for the Dream of the Red Chamber Award,[42] Yan spoke about the censorship of publications in his country, which testifies to the inferiority of

---

39 Hans Robert Jauss, *Toward an Aesthetic of Reception*, trans. Timothy Bahti (Minneapolis: University of Minnesota Press, 1982).
40 Fredric Jameson, "La littérature du Tiers-monde à l'époque du capitalisme multinational" [Literature in the third-world in the era of multinational capitalism], in *Des literatures combatives: L'internationale des nationalisemes littéraires* [Combative literature: the international of literary nationalisms], ed. Pascale Casanova (Paris: Éditions Raison d'Agir, 2011), 39.
41 J.-C. P., "Le Grand cirque de Benaise" [The grand cirque of Benaise], *Livres Hebdo*, no. 794 (Oct. 23, 2009).
42 The Dream of the Red Chamber Award (*Hongloumeng jiang* 紅樓夢獎) is a literary prize created in 2006 by the Hong Kong Baptist University to recognize the best novels written in the Chinese language.

writers, literature, and art in the present day. He recalls a dream of his mother in which the writer committed a serious crime for writing books. This is why his mother insists on calling him before daybreak. The censorship system leaves a great abyss in Yan's heart. He criticizes the censorship and self-censorship of Chinese writers, arguing that these are undoubtedly harmful to contemporary Chinese literature and that any novelist while writing should be vigilant against this threat. However, he also delivers a rather tolerant and pragmatic reflection. As he states in his speech: "So here, all over the world, to talk about some literature, smiling, I would always say with frankness and honesty: The situation in China is much better than before, really much better. If it was over thirty years ago, and you had written something 'that should not be written' for literature and art, you risked being imprisoned, having your family broken up, your wife and children left. But today, am I not here in front of you? I can always accept this award, visit places, laugh and eat, and talk about literature and art with you."[43] For Yan Lianke, the existence of censorship testifies to the inferiority of literature to the reality of China today. The limitation of publication, the frustration of the writer, and the manipulation of political power create this feeling of inferiority. But this inferiority is also an essence of literature, and it is the task of a writer to represent the literary inferiority of his time. It is therefore up to Chinese writers to be aware of self-censorship, to make good use of this sense of inferiority, describe the reality, and recreate the reality in their works.

Bibliography

Casanova, Pascale. "La Guerre de l'ancienneté: ou il n'y a pas d'identité nationale" [The war of antiquity: Or there is no national identity]. In *Des literature combatives: L'internationale des nationalisemes littéraires* [Combative literature: The international of literary nationalisms], edited by Pascale Casanova, 22. Paris: Editions Raison d'Agir, 2011.

Chen, Feng 陳豐, and Bai Bing. "Entretiens avec Feng Chen (agent littéraire) et Bai Bing (Editions Jieli)," Bureau International de l' Édition Française, last modified Apr. 2004. https://www.bief.org/Publication-2542-Article/Entretiens-avec-Feng-Chen-(agent-litteraire)-et-Bai-Bing-(Éditions-Jieli).html (last accessed 31 July 2021).

Dai, Lai, et al. *Amour virtuel et poil de cochon* [Visional love and pig hair]. Paris: Éditions des Riaux, 2006.

De Nussac, Léonor. "Philippe Picquier: 'Editer, c'est convaincre'" [Philippe Picquier: Edit, is to convince]. In *Revue de l'association des bibliothèques français* [Journal of the library association] 13 (2004): 64–65.

Deleuze, Gilles, and Félix Guattari. *Kafka. Pour une littérature mineure* [Kafka: For a minor literature]. Paris: Minuit, 1975.

Dosse, Mathieu. *Poétique de la lecture des traductions: Joyce, Nabokov, Guimaraes Rosa* [Poetics of reading translations: Joyce, Nabokov, Guimaraes Ros]. Paris: Classiques Garnier, 2006.

Durin, Corinne. "Lawrence Venuti. *The Translator's Invisibility: A History of Translation*. London and New York: Routledge, coll. 'Translation Studies', 1955, 353 pages." *Traduction, Terminologie, Rédaction* 8, no° 2 (1995): 283–86.

Duzan, Brigitte. "Brigitte Guilbaud Présentation" [Brigitte Guilbaud presentation]. La nouvelle dans la literature chinoise contemporaine, last modified 19 Oct. 2018. http://www.chinese-shortstories.com/Traducteurs_et_editeurs_BrigitteGuilbaud.htm (last accessed 31 July 2021).

---

43 Lu Gan, "À la recherche de la force de l'infériorité. Une possibilité de la littérature dans la Chine d'aujourd'hui: discours de réception du prix Hongloumeng par Yan Lianke" [In Search of the Power of the Inferiority. A Possibility of the Literature in Today's China: The Acceptance Speech of the Hongloumeng Prize of Yan Lianke], in *Impressions d'Extrême-Orient* [Far East Impressions], June 30, 2021, doi: https://doi.org/10.4000/ideo.1639.

———. "'Ecrits de la maison des rats': quelques pages douces-amères pour mieux connaître Lao She." *La nouvelle dans la literature chinoise contemporaine* [The novels in contemporary Chinese literature], last modified 21 May 2010. http://www.chinese-shortstories.com/Actualites_16.htm (last accessed 31 July 2021).

———. "Sylvie Gentil, pèlerin émérite des lettres chinoises" [Sylvie Gentil, pilgrim emeritus of Chinese letters]. *La nouvelle dans la literature chinoise contemporaine*, last modified 30 Apr. 2017. http://www.chinese-shortstories.com/Traducteurs_et_editeurs_Sylvie_Gentil.htm (last accessed 31 July 2021).

Gan, Lu, "À la recherche de la force de l'infériorité. Une possibilité de la littérature dans la Chine d'aujourd'hui: discours de réception du prix Hongloumeng par Yan Lianke" [In search of the power of the inferiority: A possibility of the literature in today's China: The acceptance speech of the Dream of the Red Chamber Award of Yan Lianke]. *Impressions d'Extrême-Orient* [Far East impressions], no. 12, 30 June 2021. https://doi.org/10.4000/ideo.1639 (last accessed 31 July 2021).

Gong Ming 龔鳴. "Yizhe zhongli, mo wu shengxi" 譯者中立，默無聲息 [Translator are neutral and silent]. *Sohu* 搜狐, last modified 27 Mar. 2018. https://www.sohu.com/a/226506736_630337 (last accessed 31 July 2021).

Holquist, Michael. "Corrupt Originals: The Paradox of Censorship." *PMLA* 109, no. 1 (Jan. 1994): 14–25.

Isers, Wolfgang. *The Act of Reading: A Theory of Aesthetic Response*. Baltimore: Johns Hopkins University Press, 1980.

Jameson, Fredric. "La littérature du Tiers-monde à l'époque du capitalisme multinational" [The literature in the third-world in the era of multinational capitalism]. In *Des literatures combatives: L'internationale des nationalisemes littéraires* [Combative literature: The international of literary nationalisms], edited by Pascale Casanova, 39. Paris: Éditions Raison d'Agir, 2011.

Jauss, Hans Robert. *Toward an Aesthetic of Reception*. Translated by Timothy Bahti. Minneapolis: University of Minnesota Press, 1982.

J.-C. P. "Le Grand cirque de Benaise" [The grand cirque of Benaise]. *Livres Hebdo* no. 794, 23 Oct. 2009. https://www.editions-picquier.com/wp-content/uploads/2012/08/LH.jpg (last accessed 7 November 2021).

Kaser, Pierre. "L'inaperçu de l'Inaperçu" [The unseen of the Unseen]. *Littérature d'Extrême-Orient, textes et traduction* [Far Eastern literature, texts and translation]. last modified 22 July 2010. http://jelct.blogspot.com/2010/07/linapercu-de-linapercu.html (last accessed 31 July 2021).

Picquier, Philippe, et al. "L'excellence de la culture française en Chine," *Faguo wenhua* 法國文化 [French culture], last modified 19 Mar. 2018. https://www.faguowenhua.com/fr/event/la-littérature-chinoise-passée-à-la-loupe-les-grands-écrivains-chinois-vus-de-la-france (last accessed 31 July 2021).

Picquier, Philippe, "La Maison d'édition." *Édition Picquier*, last modified June 2021. https://www.editions-picquier.com/la-maison-d-edition/ (last accessed 31 July 2021).

Schmidt-Melbye, Inger Hesjevoll. "Ambiguïté et hybridité—de la subjectivité dans le domaine de la traduction" [Ambiguity and hybridity: On the subjectivity in the field of translation]. *Pays Scandinaves* [Scandinavian countries] no. 7 (2002): 31–41.

Thibaudet, Albert. *Physiologie de la critique* [Criticism physiology] Paris: Éditions de la Nouvelle Revue Critique, 1930.

Venuti, Lawrence. *The Translator's Invisibility: A History of Translation*. London: Routledge, 1995.

Yan Lianke 閻連科. *Bons baisers de Lénine* [Lenin's kisses]. Translated by Sylvie Gentil. Arles: Éditions Philippe Picquier, 2012.

———. *Les Jours, les mois, les années* [The years, months, days]. Translated by Brigitte Guilbaud. Arles: Éditions Philippe Picquier, 2014.

———. *Nian yue ri* 年月日 [The years, months, days]. Zhengzhou: Henan wenyi chubanshe, 2014.

———. *Servir le peuple* [Serve the people]. Translated by Claude Payen. Arles: Éditions Philippe Picquier, 2006.

———. *Shouhuo* 受活 [Pleasure]. Shenyang: Chunfeng wenyi chubanshe, 2003.

———. *Wei renmin fuwu* 為人民服務 [Serve the people]. Hongkong: Wenhua yishu chubanshe, 2014.

———. "Yan Lianke lingqu Hongloumeng jiang: Yinwei beiwei, suoyi xiezuo" 閻連科領取紅樓夢獎：因為卑微，所以寫作 [Yan Lianke receives Dream of the Red Chamber Award: Writing because of humility]. *Tengxun wenhua* 騰訊文化, last modified 22 Sep. 2016. https://cul.qq.com/a/20160922/034156.htm (last accessed 31 July 2021).

27

THE TREACHEROUS "NEWS THAT STAYS NEWS"

The Four Books in Czech translation

Zuzana Li

Yan Lianke's 閻連科 novel *The Four Books* (*Si shu* 四書) was published in Czech translation in October 2013.[1] Immediately after the book release, invited by his Prague publisher Verzone, Yan visited the Czech capital to present his new novel at Václav Havel Library and at Café Fra, two of Prague's top literary and intellectual venues. During his short stay, he gave interviews to Czech Radio and several prominent printed media. In March 2014, *The Four Books* was nominated for Magnesia Litera, the only national annual literary award. Together with two other novels published in Czech translation in 2013, Péter Esterházy's *Celestial Harmonies* and Sergio Álvarez's *35 Muertos*, it received a nomination in the category of Best Translated Book. On 22 May 2014, an international jury voted to select the fourteenth winner of the Franz Kafka Prize, the only Czech literary award of global scale, and the winner was Yan Lianke. In October 2014, Yan arrived in Prague again, this time to attend the award ceremony at Old Town Hall and collect a bronze statuette of Franz Kafka. Yan became the fourteenth recipient of the award, the first and up to now the sole Chinese and second Asian writer after Haruki Murakami, who received the award in 2006. Unlike many of the previous winners, Yan won the prize on his first nomination, the Franz Kafka Society disclosed.[2] For contemporary Chinese literature, grossly neglected in Czech translation at the time,[3] most of the above

---

1 Jen Lien-kche, *Čtyři knihy*, trans. Zuzana Li (Praha: Verzone, 2013), published with grant support from the Ministry of Culture of the Czech Republic and the Prague Center of the Chiang Ching-kuo Foundation for International Scholarly Exchange.
2 https://english.radio.cz/world-renowned-author-yan-lianke-awarded-franz-kafka-prize-8280061 (last accessed 18 Apr. 2021).
3 According to Olga Lomová's survey conducted in 2011, literary translation from Chinese was a marginal phenomenon already some time before but very much so after 1989. Forty-three titles by novelists or poets of Chinese ancestry, including British or American Chinese, were published in Czech translation in the 20 plus years between 1989 and 2011, more than half of which, 24 titles, were translations or retranslations from English. Only four titles published in the 20 plus years after 1989 were novels by writers who still lived and worked in mainland China, all of whom were published in the new millennium, and two of whom were retranslations from English: Wei Hui 衛慧, *Shanghai Baby* (*Shanghai baobei* 上海寶貝, 2003); Yu Hua 余華, *Chronicle of a Blood Merchant* (*Xu Sanguan mai xue ji* 許三觀賣血記, 2007), directly from Chinese; Yan Lianke, *Serve the People* (*Wei renmin fuwu* 為人民服務, 2008); and Jiang Rong 姜戎, *Wolf Totem* (*Lang tuteng* 狼圖騰, 2010),

DOI: 10.4324/9781003144564-31

mentioned was an unprecedented and highly surprising chain of events that came as a shock to everyone, including the author and myself, who served as translator.

The Four Books was published in Czech translation as the third volume of a new book series on modern and contemporary Chinese literature entitled Xin and established the previous year in a small and relatively new publishing house Verzone.[4] The first two titles in the Xin series were short story collections of masterpieces by Eileen Chang 張愛玲 and Shen Congwen 沈從文, a Czech debt to the "big names" of the first half of the twentieth century still untranslated. Initially, the third title planned in the Xin series was a novel by Mo Yan 莫言, which its translator Denis Molčanov had already been working on. When the Nobel laureate was announced in 2012, Verzone soon realized that a small publisher had little chance to win the now completely changed competition to obtain the publishing rights. Mo Yan, who was essentially unknown to Czech readers until October 2012, went on to be published by Mladá Fronta, one of the largest Czech publishing houses, and Verzone was left with an opening. The decision had to be quick. *The Four Books* ticked all the boxes required to attract attention in our intellectual environment.[5] Yan already had an international reputation as a rebel, as opposed to the recent Nobelist Mo Yan, generally pictured by Czech media as an apparatchik who was, mostly to their disillusionment, rewarded the Nobel Prize for Literature. *The Four Books* had not been published in mainland China, and a forbidden book is always a good choice in a post-socialist country. Yan had a previous book, *Serve the People* (*Wei renmin fuwu* 為人民服務),[6] published in Czech, a mediocre retranslation from English that went unnoticed by Czech critics. The existence, however, of the novel told us that we

---

directly from Chinese. See Olga Lomová, "Politika, exotika, erotika a ústup čínštiny" [The politic, exotic, erotic and receding of Chinese], *Plav*, 2011, no. 4: 45–51.

4   The name of the book series was inspired by the Chinese word *xin* 新 "new", an omnipresent concept in the modern Chinese context with arguably boundless multitudes of representations. The pronunciation is also rather close to the Latin stem of the word for China or Chinese, Sina, including Sinology. The Xin book series was launched by Czech Sinologists who felt the need to create a new space for publishing Chinese literary works that would have experienced difficulties to see the light based solely on market publishing strategies but who at the same time aimed higher and further than only becoming compulsory reading for students of modern Chinese literature. In the eight years since 2012, twenty books, including nine novels, eight short story collections, and three titles of non-fiction, have been published in the Xin series. Verzone also promotes its authors through launching literary events and inviting Chinese authors to Prague. Yan was invited to Prague several times, for the book launch of *The Four Books*, to receive the Franz Kafka Prize, and as a guest of the Prague Writers' Festival in 2016 when *The Explosion Chronicles* (*Zhalie zhi* 炸裂志) were published in Czech. Yu Hua stayed at the October Writers' Residence Prague in 2016 when another of his novels *The Seventh Day* (*Di qi tian* 第七天) was published in Czech, Sheng Keyi 盛可以 and Ning Ken 寧肯 were guests at the Book World Prague festival in 2019, also in connection with their books being published in Czech at the time.

5   After the Velvet revolution in 1989, censorship in literary and artistic creation has continued to be a prevalent issue and the unchallenged winner of public opinion when assessing contemporary Chinese literature, especially in intellectual circles where critics, journalists, and the majority of curious readers come from. It is a common belief that any free creation is essentially impossible in contemporary mainland China. Literary production from the PRC that reaches the West is perceived a priori with suspicion of the ill-intentions of Beijing propaganda, and the West is viewed as naïve for opening its doors to these dangers. The Cold War vocabulary continues to exist. In this perception, the only free literature worthy of the name is the works of Chinese dissidents and exiles (namely, Bei Dao 北島, Yang Lian 楊煉, Gao Xingjian 高行健, Duo Duo 多多, Bei Ling 貝嶺, and Liao Yiwu 廖亦武) and of Taiwanese writers.

6   Yan Lianke, *Služ lidu!*, trans. Petra Andělová (Praha: BB Art, 2008), retrans. from Julia Lovell's English rendition *Serve the People!*.

were not alone in our assessment of Yan's potential if another publisher, with no knowledge of Chinese literature, had chosen his title for publication earlier. The newly established book series needed something strong and powerful to draw attention to its production of modern and contemporary Chinese literature in the year of the Chinese Nobel laureate. Yan was a writer of the same generation, a juxtaposition to Mo Yan, a challenger and an antipode. He was someone who would both fit the popular narrative of censorship versus writer's freedom of creation and be able to challenge our understanding of censorship and self-censorship at the same time. Unlike his other internationally acknowledged novels, *The Four Books* was new; it had not been translated into English yet. In a world highly influenced and dominated by the English language,[7] we could present it as our "own discovery."[8] Several translation aspects also spoke in favor of the novel. But most of all, *The Four Books* is a spectacular literary masterpiece, truly dialogical and polyphonic, an exceptional narrative both in its content and form, an innovative approach to the tried and true story of how we as humankind keep playing games that prove to be lethal. It is a universal story deeply embedded in a specifically Chinese historical experience, on the symbolic level straddled between East and West, shattering both intellectually and emotionally, a tribute to and a daring defiance against literary creation, with messages of grave relevance. At the end of the day, it is a story of physical survival; on the metaphysical level it reveals how the stories we tell ourselves structure our minds and influence our lives, a story of psychological turmoil and redemption. Convinced of our choice, the publisher refuted all of Yan's London agent's arguments to start with one of his already famous titles, insisted on *The Four Books*, and later also asked Yan to write a preface for the Czech edition of the book he dedicated "to our forgotten past and to the millions of dead and living readers."

From the translator's point of view, *The Four Books* offered guidance to some of the most difficult challenges in translation from Chinese. Its composition, consisting of four stylistically distinctive narratives, not only established the voices for each of its narrations in the target language but also allowed me as the translator to make bolder moves on the microscopic but crucial scope of the linguistic detail. "Heaven's Child" ("Tian de haizi" 天的孩子) could draw inspiration from the *Old Testament*. Especially the *Book of Genesis* and *Ten Commandments* were a great help on the syntactic and lexical levels for the opening part of the book. "Criminal

---

7 According to the data published by the Association of Czech Booksellers and Publishers, translations represent almost 40% of the Czech book market, and translations from English represent more than half of all translated titles, 56% in 2019 with nearly 4,000 titles translated from English into Czech. Translations and retranslations from English also amount to more than half the number of annually translated books written by Chinese authors. Some of these Chinese authors do not live and work in the PRC and do not write primarily for Chinese readers but are generally perceived as Chinese for their ancestry or origin. There is a market of reasonable size for British or American Chinese novels in the tradition of Jung Chang's *Wild Swans* or Amy Tan's *Joy Luck Club*, but several titles of mainland novelists also reached the Czech lands through the global book market and were retranslated from English, as was the case with Yan's *Serve the People*, Mai Jia's 麥家 *Decoded* (*Jiemi* 解密) and *In the Dark* (*Ansuan* 暗算), several of Hong Ying's 虹影 novels, Wei Hui's 衛慧 *Shanghai Baby*, and Liu Cixin's 劉慈欣 *Three Body* (*Santi* 三體) trilogy. Retranslations from English are significantly more viable for a publisher as there is a multitude of skilled and experienced translators from English for all kinds of literary genres, who can work very quickly, while there were no professional literary translators from Chinese until recently. Translation from Chinese was even declared to be an academic endeavor and not a literary one by Jiří Levý in his still authoritative and valid classic *The Art of Translation* (1963).
8 *Stricto sensu*, the mere existence of *The Four Books* was initially brought to my attention through its French translation: Yan Lianke, *Les quatre livres*, trans. Sylvie Gentil (Arles: Philippe Picquier, 2012).

Records" ("Zuiren lu" 罪人錄) was in the style of ideological newspeak and could be modeled on the language from our own Czech history of the rule of the Communist Party, while the intended literary masterpiece "The Old Course" ("Gu dao" 故道) could make use of stylistic gestures perceived in the literary register in the Czech tradition. Finally, "The New Myth of Sisyphus" ("Xin Xixufu shenhua" 新西緒弗神話) was meant to be obscure, philosophical, and scholarly. All four styles would be familiar to the Czech reader, opening space for the translator to draw from our own linguistic tradition and creatively play with words, images and rhythm. The title of the book, in its dense expression often difficult to convey along the lines of its source's intent, charm, allusions, or multiple meaning, was not a major challenge in the case of *The Four Books*, which works perfectly well in its literal translation. Another considerable advantage of the story was the use of the names of the protagonists. Not being accustomed to Chinese names,[9] Czech readers often complain about the names being abstruse, incomprehensible, and hard to remember, but here we had characters whose names could be easily and unequivocally translated into common Czech words, thus amounting to one less obstacle in wider reception. The imagery and motifs, including their twisted linguistic representation, would in many cases also be familiar—the Above (*shangbian* 上邊) not having any names and faces but instantly giving orders and greatly influencing all aspects of lives of those below, the concept of re-education (*yuxin* 育新), unrealistic plans in agricultural and steel production, frantic ordering of quotas, slogans expressing the ultimate goal to prove better than the imperialistic West, forbidden books or songs or works of arts, people informing on their friends and neighbors—all of this is also known to readers in a country with its own experience with totalitarian rule and engineers of human souls, with the differences in the historical experience not being a serious obstacle in the case of a parable. I expected only one possible impediment to seamless, smooth reception of *The Four Books* by the Czech readership: the general acceptance of the game on the part of the ones below, "the criminals" or "sinners" (*zuiren* 罪人). The narratives we grow up in prefer to portray heroes who rebel against the power that is crushing them, or at least play a subversive fool. This type of narrative generally prevails also in the present Czech portrayal of the rule of the Communist Party of Czechoslovakia. But in *The Four Books,* the protagonists accept their given parts without protest, perhaps with the only exception of the Scholar who finally petitions the Above in Beijing. Unfortunately, none of the Czech reviewers dealt in depth with the central theme of guilt or with the notion of loyalty or "collaboration" in the novel.

The author's foreword to the Czech translation relies to a great extent on his postface initially written for the Chinese edition of the novel.[10] Yan called himself a traitor, literally *xiezuo de pantu* 寫作的叛徒, meaning "a traitor of (literary) writing" or "a writing traitor," the ambiguity of which gets lost in translation, and in his own words, "an honorary title he was not sure he was worthy of, similarly as Ah Q is not worthy of the surname Zhao," only with the exception that in the Czech preface he changed the simile into "similarly as those who

---

9 In official media and literature, Czech still uses its own transliteration of Chinese, so-called Standard Czech Transcription of Chinese, created by the Sinologists and linguists of the Academy of Sciences based on Czech rules of orthography. There is a tradition in translation of Chinese literature to render names semantically when suitable and possible to convey the meaning and often a certain tone behind the "speaking names" of Chinese characters, and to avoid clusters of letters unusual in the Czech text that make reading novels less accessible. This way of treating Chinese names has been receding recently, but there are still cases when names are rendered undogmatically and playfully.

10 The text was not published as originally planned but the first half about being a traitor can be found in Chinese as the opening to his prose on literature: Yan Lianke, *Faxian xiaoshuo* 發現小說 [Discovering fiction] (Tianjin: Nankai University Press, 2011), 3–4.

do not read fiction are not worthy of talking about Kafka." Yan discusses why he decided to call himself a traitor, talks about how he always dreamt of writing a book the way he pleased, without constraints and regardless of publishing (*bu wei chuban er hu xie* 不為出版而胡寫) and claims that *The Four Books* is such an experiment, a holiday in his writing career, an attempt to be the master and not the slave of the pen. He also describes, with his typical irony, his unsuccessful search for a publisher in China, and expresses his sympathy for all those editors who had no choice but to decline such a treacherous book, and his gratitude to the publishers and translators of Chinese books, thanking them that "literature can now better reveal its sanctity and solemnity."[11] As is the case of all books published in the Xin series, *The Four Books* has a postface. I borrowed Yan's own assessment of himself for the title of my afterword: "The Unworthy Son of Realism" provides insight into Yan's life and work, the relationship between reality and absurdity in his writing, introduces Yan's idea of "mythorealism" (*shenshi zhuyi* 神實主義)[12] and retells an allegory of the enlightenment of a clever and hard-working Buddhist monk to illustrate what literature means to Yan: "All solemnity is gone with the first smile, [I am] like a wanderer who stops at a teashop to have a chat but who will soon be back on his long journey all alone, with a bag on his back as if he was carrying time awaiting to become scribbled paper."[13]

Yan's open position as a rebel who does not follow the rules of literary writing but claims as much creative freedom for himself as possible certainly won him both sympathy and trust and awakened curiosity. It was, however, the literary quality of the novel, the philosophical issues raised, its exceptional imagery and bold treatment of motifs old and new, its overlaps with the roots of Judeo-Christian and Classical Chinese civilization, the structure of the narration, its powerful, impressive flow, and the excruciating experience portrayed in the timeless story that won him the nomination for Magnesia Litera in the category of Best Translated Book.[14] The symbolic and allegorical character of the work was mentioned repeatedly in interviews, reviews, and articles. The most frequently introduced aspects were the new Sisyphus, his reconciliation but not surrender, the possibility of finding meaning and beauty in hardship, the role

---

11 Jen Lien-kche, "Zrada literární tvorby" [Betrayal of literary writing], Preface to *Čtyři knihy*, 9–10. It is not common for novels at present to have a preface by the author written especially for the foreign readers. The only time it happened with a Czech translation of a Chinese book was in 1936 when Jaroslav Průšek asked Lu Xun, then already gravely ill, to write a few words for his first Czech rendering of *Call to Arms* (*Nahan* 吶喊), which was later published in 1937. The original copy of Průšek's letter to Lu Xun, preserved in Lu Xun's Museum in Beijing, is dated 21 July 1936. For further information, see Ge Baoquan 戈寶權, "Lu Xun he Pushike" 魯迅和普實克 [Lu Xun and Průšek], in *Lu Xun yanjiu ziliao* 魯迅研究資料 [Materials of Lu Xun studies], vol. 3 (Beijing: Wenwu chubanshe, 1979), 296–317.
12 To my knowledge, the term "mythorealism" was not coined as yet in English or any foreign language in 2013. Apart from explaining its meaning, I then rendered it into Czech as *sakrealismus* (sacrealism): *sacred* for the notion of the divine or deity (*shen* 神) from Latin *sacrare* 'to make holy/declare sacred/sanctify', in Czech with the Proto-Indo European root *sak*. Apart from the obvious compound of sacred + reality + ism, there is an old fashioned but still commonly used Czech swear word *sakra*, which is used in situations when things go wrong, similar to *damn* (compare French *sacré bleu*). It then seemed to correspond to what lay behind Yan's *shenshi zhuyi*.
13 Yan, *Faxian xiaoshuo*, 217; Zuzana Li, "Nehodný syn realismu," Afterword to *Čtyři knihy*, 306.
14 Every nomination is accompanied by a short text highlighting the qualities of the book nominated. See the Magnesia Litera online archive in Czech: https://www.magnesia-litera.cz/rocnik/2014/ (last accessed 21 Apr. 2021). Magnesia Litera is the only national literary award given annually in the spring for books published the previous year. It has many categories (prose, poetry, non-fiction, new discovery, etc.) but the main prize is reserved for Czech writers; all foreign literature is left only with the category of Best Translated Book. The criteria for nomination by a jury of renowned translators is both the quality of the original work and its translation.

of *The Bible* as not merely a stylistic inspiration for "The Heaven's Child" but also as an active imprint in the life of one of the protagonists, the story's setting on the banks of the Yellow River, once the cradle of Chinese civilization that now held a re-education camp, a prison without bars and an eventual tomb for unfaithful intellectuals, the costs of human lives in pursuit of utopian ideals, etc.[15] One of the book reviews concentrated on the voices of the four narratives: two voices belonging to the Author (the informer in "Criminal Records" and the writer of "The Old Course"), one to the Child, and one to the Scholar, comparing their respective stances in the same reality, their characters and behavior, pointing out the different types of pain of all of these individuals of flesh and blood hidden under the symbolic names.[16] Another book reviewer also noticed the contrast between the experienced reality portrayed in the book, the allegorical and mythological level of the story, and the symbolic deployment of the protagonists: the Child is in charge of the Musician, the Theologian, the Scholar, the Author and other characters representing various arts and sciences, and he plays a childish game with them that turns out to be grueling and humiliating with no chance to win and be rewarded freedom.[17]

The Franz Kafka Prize awarded to Yan in Prague by the Franz Kafka Society later that year not only for *The Four Books* but for Yan's literary oeuvre in its entirety attested to Yan's artistically exceptional literary creativity. The Franz Kafka Prize is awarded annually to contemporary authors whose work addresses readers regardless of their origin, nationality, and culture and contributes to cultural, national, language, and religious tolerance.[18] The Franz Kafka Prize Laudation was delivered by Oldřich Král, one of the members of the international jury.[19] "The Franz Kafka Prize is an international award, but its perspective is also a Czech and a Prague one. We look at what is happening in the world of literature throughout the languages and cultures at present and what resonates among Czech readers from that world in Czech translation in the perspective of Franz Kafka's legacy, as was the case with Yan's books recently." Despite Král's claim, however, his laudation revealed that his (and we can also assume the jury's) reading of Yan was not solely from a Prague point of view. It

---

15 Articles, interviews with the writer and book reviews appeared in print: daily newspaper *Právo*, the supplement of daily newspaper *Lidové noviny*, weekly periodicals *Respekt*, *Literární noviny*, biweekly *Tvar* and *A2*, the last one even with a drawing of Yan on the front cover of the periodical. Live interview on the Vltava Channel of Czech Radio and the nomination text for Magnesia Litera also mention some of these aspects.
16 Petra Martincová, "Zásadový, k jiným tolerantní" [Principled, tolerant to others], *Právo*, 12 Dec. 2013, S2.
17 "The hardship is so gruelling that the reader wishes for it to end but he too needs to endure it to get a taste of how impossible it is to reach the goal and be rewarded freedom … Yan's fascinating allegory reveals that in conditions when men die of hunger, his only aspiration is not freedom any longer but survival." Ondřej Nezbeda, "Pěticípá svoboda" [Five-pointed star liberty], *Respekt* 50 (2013): 67.
18 For criteria of awarding the Franz Kafka Prize, see the Franz Kafka Society official website in Czech and English: http://www.franzkafka-soc.cz/cena-franze-kafky/ (last accessed 20 Apr. 2021).
19 Oldřich Král (1930–2018) was a Czech Sinologist, translator, and professor of comparative literature at Charles University in Prague, whose extensive translation and academic oeuvre inspired poets, artists and scholars. It consists of Czech translations (always accompanied by his insightful commentaries) of literary and philosophical classical works that span centuries and genres: *Yijing* 易經, *Dao de jing* 道德經, *Zhuangzi* 莊子, "Daxue" 大學, "Zhongyong" 中庸, *Liuzu tanjing* 六祖壇經, *Wenxin diaolong* 文心雕龍, *Sunzi bingfa* 孫子兵法, *Wumenguan* 無門關, Tao Yuanming's 陶淵明 *Taohuayuan* 桃花源, *Kugua heshang huayu lu* 苦瓜和尚畫語錄, *Zhongguo hualun leibian* 中國畫論類編, *Rulin Waishi* 儒林外史, *Hongloumeng* 紅樓夢, Dong Yue's 董說 *Xi you bu* 西遊補, Li Yu's 李漁 *Rouputuan* 肉蒲團, *Jin Ping Mei* 金瓶梅 (unfinished). He is the author of *Čínská filosofie: Pohled z dějin* [Chinese philosophy: Perceived from history] (Lásenice: Maxima, 2005). He used to say that despite his many identities, he was always first and foremost a reader.

was also influenced by Král's knowledge of Chinese *literariness*, a term he liked to use rather than the term *literature*. In his speech, Král introduced the laureate's rebellious side as well as his acclaim and important literary prizes he was awarded in the PRC. Among Yan's literary works, he names *Summer Sunset* (*Xiariluo* 夏日落) in which the writer "denounced the contract he was living in" and *Lenin's Kisses* (*Shouhuo* 受活) as "a blend of a bitter comedy of human greed and an age-old Chinese utopia in search of the Peach Blossom Spring, under the nurturing corruption decomposing the vast Chinese burial ground of a great social utopia." He also mentions *Dream of Ding Village* (*Dingzhuang meng* 丁莊夢) and *Discovering Fiction*, in which "the author repeatedly and not in vain mentions *The Journey to the West* [*Xi you ji* 西遊記] or *Strange Tales from a Chinese Studio* [*Liaozhai zhi yi* 聊齋誌異] known in the Czech lands thanks to Jaroslav Průšek's translation."[20] Naturally, Král also comments on Yan's two books we then had in Czech translation: *Serve the People*, "with the Mao era almighty incantation on the cover of a black parody mocking all taboos including the sexual one, a story in which the tragic heroine disappears at the end in the style of a classical fox spirit," and *The Four Books*, with "again, a double ironic title, in the story of which we find nothing of the well-known Confucian bible or rather Neo-Confucian canon."[21] Král points out that "*The Four Books* is writing without boundaries,[22] or in the style of Yan's ironic diction, writing on a leave permit about something that is not allowed to be written and perhaps something that is even impossible to write about." According to the laudation,

> *The Four Books* is four genes of one big metaphor. At the beginning, a gate to a re-education zone of rebirth into the void opens for the Child, and at its end, the same Child, the same Creation of a New Man, encounters Sisyphus to teach him to push his boulder not uphill but downhill, reconciled because used to his punishment, secretly enjoying an occasional glimpse of a tree, a house, a village, smoke rising from a chimney and children playing at a gate, and so will that Eastern Sisyphus keep on pushing his rock downhill, somewhat carefree, somewhat content.

At the end of his speech, Král reflects on Yan calling himself a traitor, a deserter even. In Král's view, Yan betrays not only writing in the realistic gesture, but he also abandons all the past and present rules to create his own ones: "And so it goes with each and every one of his books, a different kind of game with a different set of rules, a different game of life, but always of that contemporary Chinese life with all its marvels, mysteries, ridiculous absurdities, and cruel pragmatism. And in that game, the good old Chinese lyricism is always present, that symbolism in its endless rhythm of changes and associations, all that in the boundless openness of Pound's 'news that stays news', in the end good news."[23]

---

20 Readers may also refer to the preface of this volume written by Yan Lianke and translated into English by Riccardo Moratto and Xie Haiyan.
21 Yan's other treacherous books—his account of the miraculous boom of the village of Zhalie was published in Czech after the Franz Kafka Prize: Jen Lien-kche, *Rozpukov—místopis čínského zázraku* [Boomville: Local history of the Chinese miracle], trans. Zuzana Li (Praha: Verzone, 2016).
22 Please refer to the preface of this volume.
23 Oldřich Král, "Laudatio Ceny Franze Kafky" [The Franz Kafka Prize Laudation]. The speech was delivered in Czech at the awarding ceremony at Old Town Hall in Prague on 22 Oct. 2014 and interpreted simultaneously. The manuscript of the speech is archived but not generally available. In this paragraph, my somewhat lengthy translation quotes the parts concerning Yan's novels as read by the late Sinologist in Czech, Chinese, English, and French to show the reasoning behind the Franz Kafka Prize awarded to Yan.

The story of *The Four Books* in Czech translation had a postscript as if written by the author himself. Czech President Miloš Zeman, who is often criticized by liberal intellectuals for his friendly attitude toward Russia and China, during his state visit to the PRC in October 2014 gave a lecture on political, cultural, and economic relations between the two countries at Renmin University, where he received a present from the university president Chen Yulu, the Czech translation of a literary work written by a professor of the School of Liberal Arts of Renmin University, Yan Lianke, who had just become the first Chinese writer in history to be awarded the Franz Kafka Prize in Prague four days earlier.[24] The official report does not name the title of the book, but we have it on good authority that under the general term "literary work" *The Four Books*, which was never published in the PRC, was hidden in their red book cover and red silky box.

Bibliography

[Anon.]. "The Chinese Writer Yan Lianke Will Be Awarded the Franz Kafka Prize." Franz Kafka Society, 22 Oct. 2014. http://www.franzkafka-soc.cz/clanek/the-chinese-writer-yan-lianke-will-be-awarded-the-franz-kafka-prize/ (last accessed 20 Apr. 2021).

[Anon.]. "Nominace Litera za překladovou knihu v roce 2014" [Nomination for Litera for translated book in 2014]. *Magnesia Litera*. https://www.magnesia-litera.cz/rocnik/2014/ (last accessed 21 Apr. 2021).

Cinger, František. "Vnímám touhy i strach z jejich naplnění" [I sense desires as well as fear of their fulfilment]. Interview with Yan Lianke. *Právo*, 24 Oct. 2014.

Fraňková, Ruth. "World-renowned Author Yan Lianke Awarded Franz Kafka Prize." *Radio Prague International*, 23 Oct. 2014. https://english.radio.cz/world-renowned-author-yan-lianke-awarded-franz-kafka-prize-8280061 (accessed 18 Apr. 2021).

Ge Baoquan 戈寶權 "Lu Xun he Pushike 魯迅和普實克" [Lu Xun and Průšek]. In *Lu Xun yanjiu ziliao 3* 魯迅研究資料 3 [Materials of Lu Xun studies 3], 296–317. Beijing: Wenwu chubanshe, 1979.

Jen Lien-kche 閻連科. *Čtyři knihy* [The Four Books]. Translated by Zuzana Li. 2011. Praha: Verzone, 2013.

———. "Zrada literární tvorby" [Betrayal of literary writing]. Preface to Jen Lien-kche, *Čtyři knihy*, 9–10. Praha: Verzone, 2013.

———. *Rozpukov – místopis čínského zázraku*. [The Explosion Chronicles]. Translated by Zuzana Li. 2013. Praha: Verzone, 2016.

Král, Oldřich. "Laudatio Ceny Franze Kafky" [The Franz Kafka Prize Laudation]. Unpublished manuscript archived by Franz Kafka Society.

Levý, Jiří. *Umění překladu* [The Art of Translation]. Praha: Československý spisovatel, 1963.

Li, Zuzana. "Nehodný syn realismu" [The Unworthy Son of Realism]. Afterword to Jen Lien-kche, *Čtyři knihy*, 299–306. Praha: Verzone, 2013.

———. "Pět dnů s autorem, který prošel sluncem" [Five Days with the Author Who Walked through the Sun]. *Literární noviny* 47 (21 Nov. 2013): 20.

Lomová, Olga. "Politika, exotika, erotika a ústup čínštiny" [The Politic, Exotic, Erotic and Receding of Chinese]. *Plav* 4 (2011): 45–51.

Martincová, Petra. "Zásadový, k jiným tolerantní" [Principled, Tolerant to Others]. Book review. *Salon* supplement to *Právo* daily, 12 Dec. 2013, S2.

Molčanov, Denis. "Dívat se. Psát. Neuhýbat" [Observe. Write. Do Not Dodge]. Interview with Yan Lianke. *Orientace* weekend supplement to *Lidové noviny* daily, 28 Dec. 2013, 26–27.

Nezbeda, Ondřej. "Pěticípá svoboda" [Five-pointed Star Liberty]. Book review. *Respekt* 50 (2013): 67.

———. "Čína je jako tekuté písky" [China Is Like Quicksand]. Interview with Yan Lianke. *Respekt* 50 (2013): 48–53.

Šimůnková, Tereza. "Hlavně to tu nějak přežít" [Crucial Is to Survive]. Interview with Yan Lianke. *Právo*, 12 Dec. 2013, S8.

---

24 See the report on Renmin wang 人民網 [people.com], http://edu.people.com.cn/n/2014/1026/c1006-25910128.html (last accessed 22 Apr. 2021).

Vimmrová, Pavlína. "Velký skok do tmy" [The great leap into darkness]. *A2* 25 (4 Dec. 2013): 5.
Yan Lianke 閻連科. *Dream of Ding Village*. Translated by Cindy Cater. New York: Grove Press, 2009.
———. *Faxian xiaoshuo* 發現小說 [Discovering fiction]. Tianjin: Nankai University Press, 2011.
———. *Lenin's Kisses*. Translated by Carlos Rojas. New York: Grove Press, 2012.
———. *Les quatre livres* [The four books]. Translated by Sylvie Gentil. Arles: Philippe Picquier, 2012.
———. *Xia riluo* 夏日落 [Summer sunset]. Shenyang: Chunfeng wenyi chubanshe, 2002.
———. *Služ lidu!* [Serve the people]. Translated by Petra Andělová. Praha: BB Art, 2008.
Zádrapová, Anna. "Dějiny dvacátého století ve Čtyřech knihách" [Twentieth-century history in *The Four Books*]. *Tvar*, no. 18 (2014): 21.
Zhao A'na 趙婀娜. "Jieke zongtong Zeman fangwen Zhongguo renmin daxue bing fabiao yanjiang" 捷克總統澤曼訪問中國人民大學並發表演講 [Czech President Zeman visits China Renmin University and gives a speech]. Renmin wang 人民網 [people.com], 26 Oct. 2014. http://edu.people.com.cn/n/2014/1026/c1006-25910128.html (last accessed 22 Apr. 2021).

28
TRANSLATING THE CHINESE CULTURAL OTHER

Yan Lianke's *Shouhuo* in English translation

Baorong Wang

Introduction

It is notoriously difficult to translate between Chinese and English, two completely distinct languages with no history or linguistic roots in common. Consequently, cultural translation between the two languages can be an insurmountable barrier. Howard Goldblatt, for example, admits that to tackle the historical, cultural, mythological, and political references in Chinese novels, he has tried many strategies but has yet to be fully satisfied with any. He even says, "In the main, however, I weigh the necessity of making every alien reference or concept clear to my reader; as often as not, I leave it unexplained, welcoming the reader to skip it, figure it out, or curse the translator."[1]

Meanwhile, there is a lot of dialect writing in contemporary Chinese fiction, notably by Lu Xun 鲁迅, Mo Yan 莫言, Yan Lianke 閻連科, Han Shaogong 韓少功, Jia Pingwa 賈平凹, Li Rui 李銳, etc. The use of literary dialect often manifests the author's artistic pursuits: to add local color to the story, to aid characterization of uneducated characters, to diversify or defamiliarize narrative language, or to constitute a key element of the narrative structure. In such cases, the translator is expected to represent at least part of this dialectal unfamiliarity in the translation, which is an equally challenging job.

These two cultural barriers loom large for translators of Yan Lianke's *Shouhuo* 受活 (*Lenin's Kisses* in English). Winner of China's prestigious Lao She 老舍 Literary Prize, *Shouhuo* is probably the most bizarre and hard-going contemporary Chinese novel ever published. Among other things, the author's inventive use of regional dialect and of a series of language and cultural notes labeled "Xuyan" 絮言 (literally "Additional Words," rendered as "Further Reading" by Carlos Rojas) make the novel both a stimulating and hard read not just for Western readers, but also for Yan's compatriots. The novel's storyline revolves around a local Chinese official's political ambition of bringing his county unimaginable wealth and his promotion. Liu Yingque's half-baked scheme is to purchase Vladimir Lenin's corpse from the Russians and install it in his home county to develop an extensive tourism industry around

---

1 Stephen Sparks, "Translating Mo Yan: An Interview with Howard Goldblatt," *Los Angeles Review of Books*, 26 May 2013, https://lareviewofbooks.org/article/translating-mo-yan-an-interview-with-howard-goldblatt/ (last accessed 27 July 2021).

this communist relic. But first he must find a way to raise the vast sum of money needed to buy the corpse. So he turns to an isolated village located at the outer margins of his county. He comes up with the clever idea of having the villagers perform their disabilities, reinventing themselves as spectacular commodities. As Rojas notes, owing to this isolation, the villagers speak a dialect of Chinese with many terms and phrases that would be unfamiliar to most outsiders. Some of these terms reflect actual usage in Yan's hometown in Henan Province, while others are merely his own invention. These obscure terms are given detailed interpretations in the "Xuyan" sections. According to Rojas, Yan uses the extensive notes as crucial structural and conceptual elements of the work itself. They "not only provide a convenient pretext for a series of flashbacks that help flesh out the histories of the protagonists and of the village itself but also exemplify the peculiar temporal disjointedness that is a central concern of the novel as a whole."[2]

Drawing on Gideon Toury's initial norm theory and Javier Franco Aixelá's taxonomy of translation strategies for treating culture-specific items, this chapter aims to examine Rojas's translation of these difficult terms and phrases. They are seen as signifiers of the Chinese cultural other, which is both bewildering and fascinating for the English reader. Whether they can have a meaningful dialogue with the Oriental other depends on how well the translator has done his job.

Theoretical framework

Toury observes three types of norms operating at different stages of the translation process. The basic initial norm refers to a general choice made by the translators. As shown in Figure 28.1 reproduced from Munday, if the translator "subjects him/herself to the original text, with the norms it has realized, ... the translation will tend to subscribe to the norms of the source text, and through them also to the norms of the source language and culture." This tendency is characterized as the pursuit of "adequate translation." In contrast, the translator's subscription to the norms originating in the target culture is seen as the pursuit of "acceptable translation." The poles of adequacy and acceptability are, however, on a continuum since no translation is ever totally adequate or totally acceptable. Shifts, be they obligatory or non-obligatory, are inevitable, norm-governed, and "a true universal of translation."[3] By analyzing the translation strategies adopted, we can find out whether the translator leans toward adequacy-oriented translation or acceptability-oriented translation or tries to reach a compromise between the two poles.

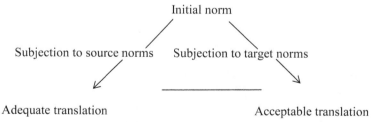

Figure 28.1 Toury's initial norm and the continuum of adequate and acceptable translation[4]

---

2 Carlos Rojas, "Translator's Note," in *Lenin's Kisses*, by Yan Lianke (New York: Grove Press, 2012), vi–vii.
3 Gideon Toury, *Descriptive Translation Studies and Beyond* (Amsterdam: John Benjamins, 1995), 56–57.
4 Jeremy Munday, *Introducing Translation Studies: Theories and Applications*, 2nd ed. (London and New York: Routledge, 2008), 113.

Since translation strategies that can achieve adequacy or acceptability are not explicitly theorized by Toury, here we need another analytical model, the taxonomy of translation strategies for treating culture-specific items (CSIs) developed by Aixelá. Culture-specific items refer to "those textually actualized items whose function and connotations in a source text involve a translation problem in their transference to a target text," often "due to the nonexistence or to the different value (whether determined by ideology, usage, frequency, etc.) of the given item in the target language culture."[5] Obviously, those cultural or dialectal terms and phrases in Yan's novel can be characterized as Chinese culture-specific items that would pose a big challenge to the translator.

Based on statistical analysis of data comprising English originals and their Spanish translations, Aixelá finds "all possible strategies applied to CSIs in translation." They are divided into two categories separated by the conservation or substitution of original references. Grouped in the category of conservation strategies are repetition (i.e., transference), orthographic adaptation (incl. transcription and transliteration), linguistic (non-cultural) translation, extratextual gloss, and intratextual gloss. Substitution translation strategies include synonymy, limited universalization, absolute universalization, naturalization, deletion, and autonomous creation. Moreover, Aixelá mentions other "potential strategies" like compensation, dislocation, and attenuation.[6] It follows that the conservation strategies help achieve adequate translation while the substitution ones lead to acceptability-oriented translation.

Given the peculiarity of language pairs, not all the translation strategies mentioned above apply to Chinese-English literary translation. For example, repetition involving the transference of a Chinese item to English is rarely used. Also rarely employed is autonomous creation, where the translator inserts into the translation a non-existent cultural reference in the source text.

Statistical analysis of CSI translation strategies

Data collection and analysis methods

In an attempt to pin down the translator's overall tendency in rendering Chinese culture-specific items in *Shouhuo*, a quantitative analysis was conducted based on the data consisting of 100 Chinese terms and 100 Chinese phrases with their corresponding English renderings. The original ones were randomly selected from the novel (on average, two terms were located every ten pages). These terms include dialect expressions, person names, place names, idioms, proverbs and aphorisms, time-specific jargon and slogans, etc. Then, each CSI translation is carefully checked against the translation strategies defined by Aixelá before determining which strategy has been employed in that case.

As far as our data is concerned, eight translation strategies were observed in the English version. As shown in Table 28.1, they are arranged into two categories: adequacy-oriented translation (or cultural conservation) and acceptability-oriented translation (or cultural substitution). Group A includes A1 (Linguistic translation), A2 (Linguistic translation plus gloss), A3 (Creative translation), A4 (Transliteration). Group B consists of B1 (Absolute universalization), B2 (Naturalization), B3 (Attenuation), B4 (Deletion).

---

5 Javier Franco Aixelá, "Culture-Specific Items in Translation," in *Translation, Power, Subversion*, ed. Roman Alvarez and M. Carmen-Africa Vidal (Clevedon: Multilingual Matters, 1996), 57–58.
6 Ibid., 61–64.

Table 28.1 Classification of translation strategies for CSIs in *Lenin's Kisses*

A	Adequacy-oriented translation	B	Acceptability-oriented translation
A1	Linguistic translation	B1	Absolute universalization
A2	Linguistic translation plus gloss	B2	Naturalization
A3	Creative translation	B3	Attenuation
A4	Transliteration	B4	Deletion

The culture-specific items in the original text are listed as per the page number. They are manually collected, sometimes assisted with Excel to re-verify the numbers. The results are summarized in the form of numbers and percentages. All these original data are shown in Appendices I and II. Table 28.2 shows only the statistical results of CSI translation strategies.

Statistical results and analysis

Table 28.2 shows that when handling these 100 words, the translator employs adequacy-oriented translation strategies (60%) more often than he does acceptability-oriented translation strategies (40%). It also indicates that linguistic translation plus gloss (38%) is the most commonly employed strategy. Absolute universalization (21%) is the second mostly commonly employed strategy, slightly outnumbering naturalization (16%), whereas deletion (1%) and attenuation (2%) are the least commonly used ones. And linguistic translation (12%) also plays an important role in the translator's pursuit of adequate translation. Creative translation (7%) must be emphasized here for its unique contribution to preserving the cultural meaning and strangeness of original CSIs. Surprisingly, transliteration accounts for only 3% as a basic way to retain the form of the original CSI.

Interestingly, Table 28.2 also indicates that when it comes to treating those phrasal CSIs, the translator strikes a perfect balance between acceptability-oriented and adequacy-oriented translation strategies. Of the several strategies used for treating the phrases, linguistic translation (40%) and absolute universalization (34%) appear to be the most commonly used, while transliteration (2%), creative translation (1%), and deletion (2%) are the least commonly employed.

Putting together the statistical data concerning CSI rendering at word and phrase level, we can see that adequacy-oriented translation strategies (55%) outnumber acceptability-oriented translation strategies (45%) by 10%. In his pursuit of adequacy, Rojas chiefly adopts linguistic translation (26%) and linguistic translation plus gloss (22.5%). Linguistic translation or literal

Table 28.2 Statistical results of CSI translation strategies

A	Adequacy-oriented translation	No. of words	No. of phrases	Total	Percentage
A1	Linguistic translation	12	40	52	26%
A2	Linguistic translation plus gloss	38	7	45	22.5%
A3	Creative translation	7	1	8	4%
A4	Transliteration	3	2	5	2.5%
Percentage		60%	50%	**55%**	
B	Acceptability-oriented translation	No. of words	No. of phrases	Total	Percentage
B1	Absolute universalization	21	34	55	27.5%
B2	Naturalization	16	13	29	14.5%
B3	Attenuation	2	1	3	1.5%
B4	Deletion	1	2	3	1.5%
Percentage		40%	50%	**45%**	

Translating the Chinese Cultural Other

translation appears to be his standard strategy for treating culture-specific items. For example, *liu le qingshan zai, na'er pa le mei chai shao* 留了青山在，哪兒怕了沒柴燒 is rendered into "as long as there is a verdant mountain, how can you be worried about not having enough wood for kindling?" Meanwhile, Rojas employs linguistic translation plus gloss mainly to deal with the dialectal or cultural terms explained in the "Xuyan" sections. That is, he follows the original format by translating their explanations directly, leading to much use of linguistic translation plus gloss. Though not frequently used, creative translation (4%) and transliteration (2.5%) are both impressive and stimulating.

Meanwhile, Rojas also pursues acceptability in his translation, though to a lesser extent. When a culture-specific item is judged to be incomprehensible or unacceptable to the English reader, it is treated mainly by absolute universalization (27.5%) and naturalization (14.5%). For example, *ya she ji zui* 鴨舌雞嘴 is translated as "to negotiate with" by absolute universalization, while *shibing* 柿餅 is naturalized into "pancake." Deletion is often employed when the translator decides that the words or phrases are repetitive and there is no need to translate them.

To sum up, the statistical results and analysis demonstrate that on the whole Rojas tries to strike a rough balance between adequacy-oriented translation and acceptability-oriented translation, though he is inclined to preserve the cultural significance of the original CSI. Our findings confirm his own claim that he has always tried to "maintain a balance between what you are calling preservationist and assimilative translation strategies."[7] As for a penchant for adopting preservationist or conservationist strategies, it might have been influenced by his professional habitus. A professor of modern Chinese literature and culture at Duke University, he naturally brings his scholar's habitus into the translation process and adopts a scholarly approach to translation.[8]

Textual analysis of CSI translation strategies

With reference to some typical examples, this section will probe into the decision-making process, including translator's appreciation of the denotative and connotative meanings of these culture-specific items, his assessment of target readers' cognitive level, and the employment of certain translation strategies.

Adequacy-oriented translation strategies

Linguistic translation

Non-cultural linguistic translation refers to the use of a denotatively very close reference to the original CSI[9] and hence is roughly equivalent to literal translation. For example:

ST-1: 可柳縣長不是那雞腸鴨肚的人。[10]

---

7 My email correspondence with Carlos Rojas, 29 Aug. 2015.
8 It is observed that scholar-translators tend to treat translation in the same way as they do scholarship. See Xu Minhui 徐敏慧, "Hanxuejia shiye yu xueshuxing fanyi: Jin Jiefu de Shen Congwen fanyi yanjiu" 漢學家視野與學術型翻譯：金介甫的沈從文翻譯研究 [Sinologists' horizons and scholarly translation: The case of Jeffrey Kinkley's translation of Shen Congwen's works], *Zhongguo fanyi* 中國翻譯 [Chinese translators' journal], 2019, no. 1: 60–67. English translations from the Chinese sources are all mine.
9 Aixelá, "Culture-Specific Items in Translation," 61–62.
10 Yan Lianke, *Shouhuo* [Happy] (Shenyang: Chunfeng wenyi chubanshe, 2004), 58. Further page numbers appear in the text.

TT-1: However, he was not a <u>wimpy chick-bellied, duck-gutted</u> loser.[11]

ST-2: ……她會忽然看見出演團的團長和縣裡的幾個圓全人,立在那雨水裡,人似了<u>落湯的雞</u>。(172)

TT-2: ... and that she would suddenly see the troupe director and several wholers from the country standing in the rain, looking like <u>chickens soaking in a pot.</u> (291)

ST-3: 「我一句話就能讓你家破人亡,就能讓你們名譽掃地,<u>成過街老鼠</u>。」 (269)

TT-3: "With one word, I can exterminate your entire family. I can drag your name through the mud, <u>reducing you to the status of a rat in the street.</u>" (453–54)

In the above examples, Rojas has used linguistic translation to deal with the animal-related phrases so that their cultural unfamiliarity is retained. The images of *ji* 雞, *ya* 鴨 and *laoshu* 老鼠 are all preserved. "Drowned rat, cat, or dog" might be an English equivalent for *luo tang de ji* 落湯的雞, but here it is translated faithfully as "chickens soaking in a pot." Likewise, *guojie laoshu* 過街老鼠 is rendered literally as "a rat in the street," for the translator assumes that with the help of the participial phrase inserted before it, English readers can work out its connotative meanings. *Ji chang ya du* 雞腸鴨肚, meaning "narrow-minded," is translated literally as "chick-bellied, duck-gutted." But it might prove bewildering to English readers. This reminds us of the deficiencies of literal translation. A gloss added to supplement the linguistic translation might help solve the problem.

Linguistic translation plus gloss

Sometimes an extratextual or intratextual gloss is added to supplement linguistic translation. The former takes the form of footnotes and endnotes or appears in the translator's notes, while the latter is inserted unobtrusively in the main body of the translation. Below is an example of intratextual gloss:

ST-4: 廟裡敬有菩薩、<u>關公</u>和受活莊的祖先受活婆。(23)

ST-4: a Buddhist temple adorned with statues of bodhisattvas; <u>Lord Guan, the god of war</u>; and Lady Livening, the town's sacred ancestor. (30)

Guan gong 關公 refers to Guan Yu 關羽 of the Three Kingdoms period (220–280 AD). Known for his gallantry and loyalty, he is widely revered and deified as the god of war by Chinese people around the world. Hence, the short explanation given of "Lord Guan" makes the historic figure more accessible to the English reader. Yet when the term appears again in "Further Reading," it is simply rendered as "Lord Guan" (365) with no explanation attached. In the same place, the legendary figure *Zhong Kui* 鍾馗 is explained as "the demon chaser" immediately after its name.

Where the culture-specific item is complicated and calls for detailed explanation, Rojas opts for giving an endnote which matches the original Chinese, while rendering the item literally. For example:

ST-5: 「……不同意了你就留在那兒受圓全人給你的<u>黑災紅難</u>吧。」 (213)

TT-5: "If you disagree, you are welcome to remain there and suffer the <u>black disasters and red difficulties</u> that the wholers will give you." (360)

---

11 Yan, *Lenin's Kisses*, 95.

Hei zai 黑災 alludes to the tumultuous Cultural Revolution (1966–76); in the story it refers specifically to "mass struggle sessions" (*pidouhui* 批鬥會) during which the "counter-revolutionary elements" would be publicly humiliated and tortured. *Hong nan* 紅難 alludes to the "Learn from *Dazhai* 大寨 Village" Movement launched by the central government in the mid-1960s when a revolutionary fervor was expressed through labor. As product of misguided politics, the two events resulted in socioeconomic chaos and brought untold sufferings to people. The two terms are coined by the author, though Yan claims to be from the local dialect. They are simply translated literally as "black disasters and red difficulties" in the main text since they are explained in a lengthy endnote included in "Further Reading." The endnote in English starts with these words: "These four terms are all equivalent. Only the people of Liven regularly use these words, and only villagers over the age of forty understand their historical meaning. The black and red crimes are not merely allusions, but rather they each have their own etymologies." (364) While Rojas is faithfully translating what the original says in "Further Reading," his renderings take the form of extratextual gloss. Nevertheless, for key terms like *hei zai hong nan*, it would render better service to English readers if they were explained briefly in a footnote.

Creative translation

Ingeniously employed by Rojas to retain the linguistic or cultural strangeness, creative translation is a special strategy of translating the original term by using such word-forming processes as coinage, blending, and derivation.

"Liven" for *shouhuo*, borrowed for both the name of the village and the novel's original title,[12] is a typical example of coinage. Rojas explains why he adopted such an approach:

> I adopted a different approach, in that I coined English words and phrases that contained a similar combination of familiarity and unfamiliarity as the ones Yan Lianke used in the novel. For instance, the novel's Chinese title, *Shouhuo*, is a dialect term used in regions of central China. The binome appears in the very first line of the novel, accompanied by an endnote explaining that it means "enjoyment, happiness, and passion, and also carries connotations of finding pleasure in discomfort." I rendered it into English as "liven"—a coinage that retains part of the semantic content of the Chinese binome (which could be rendered literally as "to receive life"),[13] while at the same time being a variant that does not exist in standard English, and consequently will be perceived as unfamiliar by English readers.[14]

---

12 The title itself, however, does not appear in English in the same way but is rendered as *Lenin's Kisses* borrowed from its French title, *Bon baisers de Lénine*. Initially, Rojas objected to using this title for the English version, but the publisher Grove Press insisted. Later he came to like this inspiring title. See Carlos Rojas and Zeng Jun 曾軍, "Cong *Shouhuo* dao *Liening zhi wen*: Duke Daxue Kaluosi Luojiesi fangtan lu" 從《受活》到《列寧之吻》: 杜克大學卡洛斯·羅傑斯訪談錄 [From *Happy* to *Lenin's Kisses*: An Interview with Carlos Rojas], *Dangdai zuojia pinglun* 當代作家評論 [Contemporary writers review], 2013, no. 5: 108.

13 This might be the translator's misinterpretation. According to Yan's own explanation of the dialect term, *shouhuo* should be rendered literally as "to enjoy life."

14 My email correspondence with Rojas, 22 July 2016.

One example of blending is "soc-ed" for *she jiao* 社教 in the following sentence:

ST-6: (耙耬)百姓覺悟低,需要教育和開導,國家需要開展社會主義教育運動,搞社教。(15)
TT-6: The people of Balou eventually came to realize that they needed knowledge and enlightenment, just as the nation needed to develop a socialist education movement, promote soc-ed. (19)

In the Chinese original, *she jiao* appears as the shortened form of *shehui zhuyi jiaoyu yundong* 社會主義教育運動, rendered literally as "socialist education movement." And "soc-ed" is created by combining the initial parts of "socialist" and "education." Given that its full form appears first, the blend itself should be accessible to the English reader. By the way, the main part of the translated sentence, "The people of Balou eventually came to realize that they needed knowledge and enlightenment," is wide of the mark, for the original sentence says: "The contented people of Balou were not enthusiastic about revolution,[15] so they needed education and enlightenment."

Some terms or expressions are translated creatively by derivation. For example, "這就讓柳縣長有些不消受了呢" (58) is rendered as "This made Chief Liu feel somewhat nonlivened." (95) As is explained in the original endnote, *bu xiaoshou* 不消受 is a Balou dialect expression meaning "unable to put up with"—this is an antonym of "liven." The word "nonlivened" is formed by attaching the negative prefix "non-" and the adjective suffix "-ed" to the coinage "liven." Here the use of derivation based on a coined word makes the novel term even more unfamiliar to the English reader. Yet presumably it should not be impenetrable while the linguistic strangeness is retained.

Another example of derivation is *yuan quan ren* 圓全人, explained in the original endnote as "a term of respect used in Liven to refer to healthy people. It is used to designate those of us who are normal and are neither blind, deaf, mute, nor missing any limbs." (14) In the English version it is ingeniously rendered as "wholers" by derivation.

Transliteration

Transliteration or transcription "is mainly used when the original reference is expressed in a different alphabet from the one which target readers use."[16] According to Catford, where languages such as Chinese are involved, the conversion of a source language form into a target language form is known as transcription.[17] By preserving "the visual relatedness between forms,"[18] transliteration might show the translator's respect for the original forms.[19] For example, *nongli bingzi nian qiu* 農曆丙子年秋 refers to the year of 1936 according to the Chinese calendar's 60-year "stem-and-branch" cycle. Rojas renders the phrase into English as "in the fall of the *bingzi* year, 1936" by both transliteration and intratextual gloss, trying to

---

15 The inhabitants of the remote Balou mountain region, including the village of Liven, in western Henan Province had enjoyed a "heavenly existence" for hundreds of years. Consequently, they never heard of and expected nothing of the communist revolution.
16 Aixelá, "Culture-Specific Items in Translation," 61.
17 John C. Catford, *A Linguistic Theory of Translation* (London: Oxford University Press, 1965), 68–70.
18 Ibid., 70.
19 Aixelá, "Culture-Specific Items in Translation," 61.

retain its unfamiliarity (*bingzi* in italics) while making it easy for the Western reader by adding Gregorian dates (1936). Below are two more examples:

ST-7: (他娘)如今不在了, 他想把他娘隆厚隆厚盛葬哩。(26)
TT-7: But now that she was deceased, he wanted to give her a magnificent *sheng* burial. (43)
ST-8: 且那奠字外邊的兩環圈繡中, 又都肩並肩地繡了銅錢般的小壽字, 使那奠字越發地透著了死人的氣息呢, 透出了逼人的陰氣呢。(204)
TT-8: In the two circles surrounding the character, there appeared an array of little *longevity* characters nestled against one other, giving the *libation* character even more of an aura of death, revealing a threatening *yin* quality. (346)

In the above examples, Rojas makes a special effort to transliterate two Chinese characters to highlight their foreignness for English readers. *Sheng zang* 盛葬, which can literally be translated as "magnificent burial," duplicates the meaning of *longhou longhou* 隆厚隆厚, rendered here as "magnificent." Likewise, *yin qi* 陰氣, which refers to the gloomy atmosphere of the world of the deceased, repeats the foregoing phrase "an aura of death." Despite this, the translator decides to preserve the unfamiliarity of *sheng* and *yin*. The two transliterated terms, *sheng* and *yin*, are specially italicized to remind the reader of their phonological strangeness.

Acceptability-oriented translation strategies

Translations that lean toward acceptability can be thought of as fulfilling the requirement of "reading as an original" written in the target language and consequently have a more natural "feel."[20] As shown above, Rojas's translation manifests a compromise between adequacy and acceptability. He employs absolute universalization, naturalization, attenuation, and deletion to minimize or erase the strangeness of Chinese culture-specific items for English readers.

Absolute universalization

Absolute universalization refers to the translation strategy where the translator prefers to delete any foreign connotations of the original CSI and chooses a neutral reference for the target reader.[21] By definition it is roughly equivalent to what is commonly known as "free translation." Below are just some examples:

ST-9: 鄉長就從魂魄山坐車, 用一大天時間到了縣裡邊, 向縣長鴨舌雞嘴了。(26)
TT-9: The township chief then spent the entire day driving down to the county seat to negotiate with the county chief. (43)
ST-10: 馬聾子那耳上放炮的節目是出演團的一齣大戲哩, 他不去, 那出演就少了一杆大臺柱子了。(77)
TT-10: Deafman Ma's Firecracker-on-the-Ear routine was one of the troupe's prize attractions, so if he didn't go, the troupe would lose one of its key assets. (129)

---

20 Mark Shuttleworth and Moira Cowie, *Dictionary of Translation Studies* (Manchester: St. Jerome, 1997), 2–3.
21 Aixelá, "Culture-Specific Items in Translation," 63.

Example 9 narrates that the town chief hurried to the county seat, complaining to County Chief Liu about the misconduct of the head contractor. *Ya she ji zui* can literally be translated as "duck tongues and chicken beaks," but that would make no sense to English readers. Here the free translation "to negotiate with" captures the metaphorical meaning of the dialectal expression, though its vividness is lost. *Tai zhuzi* 臺柱子, which literally means the wooden or bamboo pillars supporting the traditional Chinese stage, is used metaphorically to refer to the key performer in a troupe. Here it is rendered freely as "one of the troupe's key assets." Again, the meaning of the metaphor is adequately brought out while its form is not preserved.[22]

Generally speaking, Rojas employs absolute universalization or free translation with a sure hand that helps pave the way for English readers. Yet occasionally he goes a bit too far as to misinterpret the original meaning. Here is just one example:

ST-11: 柳縣長還看了一些受活人散落在各個景點的出演。他們半年來, 到外面世界風雨無阻地演絕術, 已經把那殘人的絕術出演得<u>爐火兒純青</u>了, (柳縣長) 想剪綵出演那一天, 必定是一場少見的完滿圓全的出演哩。(257)

TT-11: He also watched the residents of Liven perform their special-skills routines at different scenic spots throughout the region, but these routines were already <u>somewhat stale</u> after six months of continual performances, and he decided that for the ribbon-cutting ceremony they would need to develop a completely new routine. (433)

Luhuo chunqing 爐火純青, literally "the furnace fire has become perfectly blue," originally refers to the stage of Daoist alchemy where the pills of immortality are ready when the furnace fire turns perfectly blue. Today the idiom is often used metaphorically to refer to the state of perfection or a very high level of proficiency. The transparent idiom, however, is mistranslated as "somewhat stale." What is worse, the misinterpreted idiom leads to the mistranslated sentence starting with "and he decided that …." The original Chinese says to the effect that the troupe's performing skills are now near-perfect, so they must be able to stage a perfect performance at the ceremony.

Naturalization

Better known as "domesticating translation," naturalization refers to the replacement of an SL cultural term by a TL one. With this translation strategy, a transparent and fluent style is adopted to minimize the strangeness of the original text for target readers.[23] According to Venuti, it is an "ethnocentric reduction of the foreign text to target-language cultural values, bringing the author back home."[24] As the author is brought back to the translator's home, the ensuing translation no longer retains the exoticness of the foreign text but is made domestic and familiar to the target readers. Despite his apparent respect for the original forms, Rojas chooses to domesticate Chinese culture-specific items from time to time. Below are three examples:

ST-12: 柳鷹雀他死啦, 在下鄉社教的路上掉到溝裡<u>摔成柿餅</u>啦。(14)

---

22 I was wondering if *tai zhuzi* here can be translated more literally as "a pillar of the troupe."
23 Shuttleworth and Cowie, *Dictionary of Translation Studies*, 43–44.
24 Lawrence Venuti, *The Translator's Invisibility: A History of Translation* (London and New York: Routledge, 1995), 20.

TT-12: Liu Yingque had died, having been <u>crushed like a pancake</u> after falling into a ravine while promoting soc-ed in the countryside. (22)

ST-13: 「恭喜你打響了第一炮, 你要立馬<u>走紅</u>了。」 (110)

TT-13: "Congratulations on firing the first shot. You will quickly <u>become a sensation</u>." (184)

Shibing 柿餅, literally "persimmon cake," is a unique Chinese food made of dried persimmon fruit. The flattened preserved fruit looks like a cake and is very sweet, hence the name. Persimmon is also widely grown in Europe and America, where they are either eaten fresh as a dessert fruit, often with sugar or liqueur, or are stewed or cooked as jam.[25] Aware of the dietary differences, the translator replaces "persimmon cake" with "pancake" that is more familiar to English readers. Likewise, *zouhong* 走紅, literally "to become popular," is rendered as "to become a sensation." In *Merriam-Webster's Dictionary,* sensation is defined as "a cause or object of excited interest."[26] The word itself fits particularly well in the context where One-Legged Monkey performs his disabilities as a spectacular commodity just to satisfy the audience's excited interest.

Sometimes, dialectal terms are also naturalized by using English terms that the translator presumes correspond to the original ones. For example, *shangbian* 上邊 is explained in the original "Further Reading" as follows: "This refers to upper-level agencies and organizations. They are called this way by the people of Liven, of the Balou mountain region, and even of the entire province, and they elicit a feeling of awe among the common people." (67) Rojas finds an English equivalent for *shangbian* in this context: "higher-ups." (92) While its meaning is unmistakably clear to English readers, "higher-up" does not precisely convey the meaning of *shangbian* since it refers to a superior officer or official.[27]

Attenuation

Attenuation refers to the replacement, often on ideological grounds, of something "too strong" or unacceptable by something "softer" or what could in theory be expected by target readers.[28] That is, the original term is strategically "toned down" through translation to make it more comfortable or acceptable to target readers. By definition this strategy applies mainly to swearing, "a type of language use in which the expression (a) refers to something that is taboo and/or stigmatized in the culture; (b) should not be interpreted literally; (c) can be used to express strong emotions and attitudes."[29] Swearing is culture-specific and is often not used in a literal sense but in an emotive one,[30] hence the difficulty involved in translation. Swearing is often related to taboo subjects, including sex, religion, intimate bodily functions,

---

25 Encyclopaedia Britannica, s.v. "Persimmon," https://www.britannica.com/plant/persimmon (last accessed 19 Mar. 2020).
26 *Merriam-Webster,* s.v. "Sensation," https://www.merriam-webster.com/dictionary/sensation (last accessed 27 July 2021).
27 *Merriam-Webster,* s.v. "Higher-up," https://www.merriam-webster.com/dictionary/higher-up (last accessed 27 July 2021).
28 Aixelá, "Culture-Specific Items in Translation," 64.
29 Lars-Gunnar Andersson and Peter Trudgill, *Bad Language* (Oxford: Basil Blackwell, 1990), 53.
30 Ibid., 57.

and concealed parts of the human body.[31] Translators tend to dilute or downgrade sex-related terms, adopting either defensive or conservative translation strategies.[32] For example:

ST-14: 「賤! 賤! 你去看人家幹啥呀, 該死的你咋這樣賤!」 (74)
TT-14: "<u>How humiliating</u>! How could I have <u>debased myself</u> in this way?" (122)

In Chinese contexts, *jian* 賤, literally "cheap," "lowly," or "inferior," is often used to refer to a loose or disreputable woman, as in *jianhuo* 賤貨, literally "cheap goods," or used for swearing. Sometimes it is also used, like the above example, for cursing oneself. Hence, an English equivalent for *jian* is "bitch" though it sounds more vulgar and offensive. Here Jumei is blaming herself for paying a visit to Chief Liu, who had abandoned her while she was pregnant. The repeated *Jian! Jian!* is rendered as "How humiliating!" while the second *jian* is translated as "to debase oneself." But given that this time Chief Liu did not humiliate her, "How humiliating" is a toned-down and inaccurate rendering of the Chinese curse word. While "to debase oneself" is a faithful rendering of *jian*, it is not so vulgar as the latter. To preserve the vulgarity, the sentence could be translated as "Why do I have to behave like a bitch?"

For another example, during the row between the town chief and the head contractor, the town chief uttered twice the offensive swear expression *wo × ni ma* 我×你媽 and it is faithfully translated as "I will fuck your mother." Interestingly, the head contractor's twice retort, *ni bu yong × wo ma* 你不用×我媽, is significantly sanitized into "There is no need to insult my mother" and "You really don't need to talk about my mother." (42–43)

Deletion

As one of China's most critically acclaimed authors, Yan Lianke's literary achievement is compared to that of Mo Yan the Nobel laureate.[33] Nevertheless, Yan Lianke is sometimes criticized for writing with a rather crude, repetitive style. David Der-wei Wang 王德威 of Harvard University notes aptly: "because Yan is a prolific writer, the quality of his works is uneven. And as he writes with repetitive language and lengthy narrative structure, style-minded critics are generally not impressed by his writing."[34] When reviewing Yan's novel *The Day the Sun Died*, David Mills observes: "this is unsubtle and leaden stuff and the repetitive, rhetorical manner of the writing quickly grates."[35] *Shouhuo* is certainly not free of this problem. When Rojas decides that a culture-specific item is redundant in its context and need not be preserved, sometimes he deletes or condenses it to improve the fluency of his translation. For example:

ST-15: 人家說, 手裡有你這四個外甥女, 開了門咱們才可以<u>井水不犯河水</u>, 各做各的事, 各走各的路。(249)

---

31 Ana Maria F. Dobao, "Linguistic and Cultural Aspects of the Translation of Swearing: The Spanish Version of *Pulp Fiction*," *Babel* 52, no. 3 (2006): 223.
32 Jose Santaemilia, "The Translation of Sex, The Sex of Translation: *Fanny Hill* in Spanish," in *Gender, Sex and Translation: The Manipulation of Identities*, ed. Jose Santaemilia (Manchester: St. Jerome, 2005), 121.
33 Laifong Leung 梁麗芳, *Contemporary Chinese Fiction Writers: Biography, Bibliography, and Critical Assessment* (New York and London: Routledge, 2017), 265.
34 David Der-wei Wang, "Geming shidai de ai yu si: Lun Yan Lianke de xiaoshuo" 革命時代的愛與死——論閻連科的小說 [Love and death in the revolutionary era: On Yan Lianke's fiction], *Dangdai zuojia pinglun*, 2007, no. 5: 25.
35 David Mills, "Best Recent Novels from around the World: Review of *The Day the Sun Died*," *Sunday Times*, 9 July 2018, 39.

TT-15: He said, "Once we have your granddaughters in hand, we will open the door and <u>each go our separate ways</u>." (419)

ST-16: 是省裡和地區爭著想先把列寧遺體在他們城市裡擺放一些日子哦，才故意給雙槐出了難題兒，給柳縣長<u>做了小鞋穿</u>。(273)

TT-16: The reality was that both the district and the provincial seats had wanted to install the corpse in their respective cities for a few days, and had deliberately <u>created problems for</u> both Shuanghuai and Chief Liu. (461)

The Chinese adage *jingshui bu fan heshui* 井水不犯河水 literally means "the well water does not interfere with the river water." In the above example, the speaker simply intends to say "each of us minds his own business." Given that it repeats what is conveyed by *ge zuo ge de shi* 各做各的事 and *ge zou ge de lu* 各走各的路, the three phrases could be combined into one English expression: "each one minds his own business" or "each goes our separate ways." That is precisely what Rojas did, obviously to improve the repetitive manner of writing. Needless to say, the English version is stylistically more pleasing and acceptable, but the metaphorical form of *jingshui bu fan heshui* is lost. It is the same case with *zuo xiaoxie chuan* 做小鞋穿, which literally means "to make a pair of small shoes for someone's feet" and metaphorically refers to the malicious act of making things hard for someone. Since the translator assumes that it conveys the same meaning as *guyi chu le nanti* 故意出了難題, rendered here as "deliberately created problems," the former is deleted, again to make for more fluent reading.

Conclusion

Yan Lianke's critically acclaimed novel *Shouhuo* features ingenious use of dialect and cultural terms and phrases. As such terms embodying the Chinese cultural other are unfamiliar to the English reader and consequently pose a challenge to the translator, this chapter aims to investigate how American scholar-translator Carlos Rojas deals with these difficult terms and phrases. The quantitative analysis based on the data consisting of 100 Chinese terms and 100 Chinese phrases with their English renderings shows that on the whole Rojas tries to strike a balance between adequacy-oriented translation and acceptability-oriented translation, though he is predisposed to preserve the cultural significance of these terms. The qualitative analysis with reference to specific examples further demonstrates that Rojas translates the Chinese culture-specific items flexibly and resourcefully, transcending the binary opposition between foreignization and domestication. His pursuit of adequacy in cultural translation, largely driven by his professional habitus as a scholar-translator, offers English readers an opportunity to interact with the Chinese cultural other in the original novel or to give the target readers an alien reading experience. Meanwhile, his pursuit of acceptability in cultural translation derives from his full understanding of the linguistic and cultural divide between China and the West or of the asymmetrical literary and cultural relations between the two. Given that Anglo-American culture is for the most part "aggressively monolingual, unreceptive to the foreign, and accustomed to fluent translations,"[36] literary translators from the Chinese have to meet readers' expectations to ensure that their translations are read and sold.

Rojas's effort to preserve part of the dialectal and cultural unfamiliarity in the translation is laudable, as it might help rectify the Anglo-American readers' "narcissistic experience of

---

36 Venuti, *The Translator's Invisibility*, 15.

recognizing their own culture in a cultural other."[37] Even more positively, it might help contribute to cultural dialogue between China and the West. However, given the current East-West power imbalance and the paucity of world-class writing that can earn Chinese authors a firm place in the pantheon of world literature, there is still a long way for Chinese literature to meet with warm reception in the West. While Chinese authors safely enjoy the maximum freedom when it comes to depicting the Chinese cultural other in their works, the translator has to take a strategic decision on whether or not to preserve the cultural other in the translation. Either way, it has its pros and cons and will produce significant effects on the reception of Chinese literature in the West.

Bibliography

Aixelá, Javier Franco. "Culture-Specific Items in Translation." In *Translation, Power, Subversion*, edited by Roman Alvarez and M. Carmen-Africa Vidal, 52–78. Clevedon: Multilingual Matters, 1996.

Andersson, Lars-Gunnar, and Peter Trudgill. *Bad Language*. Oxford: Basil Blackwell, 1990.

Catford, John C. *A Linguistic Theory of Translation*. London: Oxford University Press, 1965.

Dobao, Ana Maria F. "Linguistic and Cultural Aspects of the Translation of Swearing: The Spanish Version of *Pulp Fiction*." *Babel* 52, no. 3 (2006): 222–42.

Leung, Laifong 梁麗芳. *Contemporary Chinese Fiction Writers: Biography, Bibliography, and Critical Assessment*. New York and London: Routledge, 2017.

Mills, David. "Best Recent Novels from around the World: Review of *The Day the Sun Died*." *Sunday Times*, 29 July 2018.

Munday, Jeremy. *Introducing Translation Studies: Theories and Applications*. 2nd ed. London and New York: Routledge, 2008.

Rojas, Carlos. "Translator's Note." In *Lenin's Kisses*, by Yan Lianke and translated by Carlos Rojas, v–ix. New York: Grove Press, 2012.

——— and Zeng Jun 曾軍. "Cong *Shouhuo* dao *Liening zhi wen*: Duke daxue Kaluosi Luojiesi fangtan lu" 從《受活》到《列寧之吻》: 杜克大學卡洛斯·羅傑斯訪談錄 [From *Happy* to *Lenin's Kisses*: An interview with Carlos Rojas]. *Dangdai zuojia pinglun* 當代作家評論 [Contemporary writers review], 2013, no. 5: 107–12.

Santaemilia, Jose. "The Translation of Sex, The Sex of Translation: *Fanny Hill* in Spanish." In *Gender, Sex and Translation: The Manipulation of Identities*, edited by Jose Santaemilia, 117–36. Manchester: St. Jerome, 2005.

Shuttleworth, Mark, and Moira Cowie. *Dictionary of Translation Studies*. Manchester: St. Jerome, 1997.

Sparks, Stephen. "Translating Mo Yan: An Interview with Howard Goldblatt." *Los Angeles Review of Books*, 26 May 2013. https://lareviewofbooks.org/article/translating-mo-yan-an-interview-with-howard-goldblatt/ (last accessed 27 July 2021).

Toury, Gideon. *Descriptive Translation Studies and Beyond*. Amsterdam: John Benjamins, 1995.

Venuti, Lawrence. *The Translator's Invisibility: A History of Translation*. London and New York: Routledge, 1995.

Wang Der-wei 王德威. "Geming shidai de ai yu si: Lun Yan Lianke de xiaoshuo" 革命時代的愛與死——論閻連科的小說 [Love and death in the revolutionary era: On Yan Lianke's fiction], *Dangdai zuojia pinglun*, 2007, no. 5: 25–37.

Xu Minhui 徐敏慧. "Hanxuejia shiye yu xueshuxing fanyi: Jin Jiefu de Shen Congwen fanyi yanjiu" 漢學家視野與學術型翻譯: 金介甫的沈從文翻譯研究 [Sinologists' horizons and scholarly translation: The case of Jeffrey Kinkley's translation of Shen Congwen's works], *Zhongguo fanyi* 中國翻譯 [Chinese translators' journal], 2019, no. 1: 60–67.

Yan Lianke 閻連科. *Lenin's Kisses*. Translated by Carlos Rojas. New York: Grove Press, 2012.

———. *Shouhuo* 受活 [Happy]. Shenyang: Chunfeng wenyi chubanshe, 2004.

---

37 Ibid.

Appendix I

List of 100 Chinese culture-specific terms in English translation

No.	Chinese original	Page number	English translation	Page number	Translation strategy
(1)	受活	2	to liven	3	A3
(2)	熱雪	2	hot snow	3	A2
(3)	圓全人	7	wholers	12	A3
(4)	死冷	11	cold dead	18	A2
(5)	社校娃	14	soc-school babe	22	A3
(6)	滿全臉	18	full face	29	A2
(7)	頂兒	20	peak	32	A2
(8)	田旁頭	23	field ends	38	A2
(9)	購列款	27	the Lenin Fund	45	A2
(10)	頭堂	27	head	46	A2
(11)	魂山	30	Spirit Mount	51	A2
(12)	受活慶	33	livening festival	56	A3
(13)	餛飩	34	flatbread	59	A2
(14)	洋相	40	make a spectacle of	67	B2
(15)	洋派	45	Westernized	75	B1
(16)	台踏子	46	stage-step	77	A2
(17)	中陰道	51	The Middle Shadows Path	84	A1
(18)	苦海	51	sea of bitterness	84	A1
(19)	不消受	58	nonlivened	95	A3
(20)	磕頭	60	kowtow	99	A4
(21)	對子	62	hanging couplets	103	A1
(22)	大鍋飯	66	a big pot of food	108	A2
(23)	強長	68	special skill	113	A2
(24)	實笨	70	mentally disabled	116	B3
(25)	賤	74	to debase oneself; humiliating	122	B3
(26)	壽衣	75	burial clothing	126	A1
(27)	進香	79	burn incense	132	A1
(28)	入社	79	enter society	132	A2
(29)	紅四	86	Red Fourth	143	A2
(30)	洋車子	88	foreign cart	148	A2
(31)	專區	90	the district	151	A1
(32)	鐵災	94	Iron Tragedy	157	A2
(33)	退社	96	withdraw from society	162	A2
(34)	駕樓	98	trucker's tower	166	A2
(35)	試演	106	dress rehearsal	178	B2
(36)	借涼	106	get out of the heat	178	B1
(37)	啞然	109	stunned silence	183	B1
(38)	走紅	110	become a sensation	184	B2
(39)	臉油	115	face cream	192	B2
(40)	狼邋子	118	ragged wolf	198	A2
(41)	敬仰堂	122	Hall of Devotion	206	A1
(42)	天書	123	empty words	209	B1
(43)	戶口本	125	residence permit booklet	211	B2
(44)	聖莊莊	129	divine	218	B1
(45)	門神	135	door gods	229	A1
(46)	念物	135	relics	229	A2

(Continued)

No.	Chinese original	Page number	English translation	Page number	Translation strategy
(47)	葛連	137	stay in touch	232	B1
(48)	包工頭兒	139	labor contractor	236	B2
(49)	蘿蔔頭兒	143	turnip-head	243	A1
(50)	甲子	146	sixty-year *jiazi* cycle	249	A2 A4
(51)	刷子辮	148	pigtail	253	B2
(52)	便當	152	convenient	259	B1
(53)	洋日子	154	the Western calendar	264	B2
(54)	大劫年	156	the Year of the Great Plunder	264	A2
(55)	正月	159	the first month	271	B1
(56)	王法	164	principles	278	B1
(57)	自留地	167	land	282	B4 (partial deletion)
(58)	難色	170	uncomfortable	287	B1
(59)	齊畢	172	complete	291	B1
(60)	冥錢	173	fake money	294	B1
(61)	天眉	180	skybrows	305	A3
(62)	頂門	180	sun panel	305	A3
(63)	廟會	185	a temple festival	314	A1
(64)	風水	188	scenery	319	A1
(65)	背集	191	the market was closed	325	A2
(66)	白搭搭	193	for nothing	328	A2
(67)	絕世	194	extraordinary	331	B1
(68)	天意	195	ideal	332	B1
(69)	琢磨	203	calculation	344	B1
(70)	陰氣	204	*yin* quality	346	A4
(71)	借	208	to borrow	354	A2
(72)	哨子	212	sentry	359	A2
(73)	黑罪紅罪	213	black crime and red crime	361	A2
(74)	人身影	214	shadows	362	A2
(75)	命道	221	path of fate	375	A2
(76)	梯田	223	lattice field	378	A2
(77)	糊弄	229	to fool	389	B2
(78)	犯事	230	in trouble	389	A2
(79)	井拔水	231	well water	391	A2
(80)	停當	232	thoroughly	392	B1
(81)	避諱	238	avoid one another	403	B1
(82)	歇晌	241	rest period	407	A2
(83)	決斷兒	246	decision	413	B2
(84)	天極	246	extremely	414	B1
(85)	闊綽	252	extraordinary	425	B1
(86)	糟蹋	254	to violate	427	B2
(87)	剪綵	259	ribbon-cutting ceremony	437	B2
(88)	天急	259	urgent	437	B1
(89)	足對足	265	pace by pace	446	A2
(90)	白枉枉	266	utterly wronged	448	A2
(91)	成全	269	to forgive	454	B2
(92)	意向兒書	271	intent-to-purchase statement	457	A2
(93)	衣冠塚	273	cenotaph	462	B2

(Continued)

No.	Chinese original	Page number	English translation	Page number	Translation strategy
(94)	偏興	275	fondness	465	A2
(95)	殉	280	departed	475	A2
(96)	野孩娃	281	a bastard child	477	B2
(97)	喜喪	285	a joyful funeral	483	A1
(98)	散地	288	loose earth	487	A2
(99)	功名	290	honor	492	B1
(100)	高壽	292	the advanced age	495	B2

Appendix II

List of 100 Chinese culture-specific phrases in English translation

No.	Chinese original	Page number	English translation	Page number	Translation strategy
(1)	時序亂了綱常了	2	time fell out of joint	3	B1
(2)	農曆丙子年秋	5	in the fall of the *bingzi* year, 1936	8	A2 A4
(3)	爭盼著做有頭有臉的事	9	tried to take the lead	14	B1
(4)	死冷狗皮上的虱	10	a flea on the corpse of a cold dead dog	17	A2
(5)	摔成柿餅	14	crushed like a pancake	22	B2
(6)	歇了七天腳	18	to cool his heels for a week	29	B2
(7)	地步著走	21	to proceed astep	34	A3
(8)	山流水轉	23	an upheaval	38	B1
(9)	你不用×我媽	25	There is no need to insult my mother.	42	B3
(10)	隆厚隆厚盛葬	26	a magnificent *sheng* burial	43	A4
(11)	掉到福窩	28	fall into a nest of riches	47	A1
(12)	你的嘴和茅廁一模樣	30	your mouth is like a toilet	49	A1
(13)	天東地西	34	throughout the land	59	B1
(14)	說的比唱的還要好聽	35	words are prettier than a song	60	A1
(15)	幾句話說動了心	36	steal a woman's heart with just a few words	61	B2
(16)	日有三竿的半晌	42	by the time the sun had risen three pole-lengths in the sky	70	A1
(17)	絕術表演	44	special-skills performances	74	A2
(18)	天堂的日子	40	heavenly days	82	A1
(19)	福如東海長流水	55	as fortunate as the eternally flowing eastern sea	90	A1
(20)	雞腸鴨肚	58	chick-bellied, duck-gutted	95	A1
(21)	磕頭謝恩	61	to bow down in gratitude	100	B1
(22)	天大的計畫	62	grandiose plan	101	B1
(23)	參天的搖錢大樹	66	an enormous tree of clarity	109	B1
(24)	盲四爺	68	Blind Fourth Grandpa	114	A1
(25)	冷不丁兒就有落處了	72	suddenly drop to the ground	120	B1
(26)	就了緒兒	75	get ready	125	B2
(27)	大臺柱子	77	key assets	129	B1
(28)	並頭齊肩	79	be on the same level	131	B1
(29)	合了鋪	82	slept together	137	B1
(30)	打倒地主（土豪）分田地	85	overturn landlords or local tyrants and divide up the land	142	A1
(31)	走走宿宿	89	walk all day and rest at night	148	A2
(32)	生產大隊	94	large production brigade	159	A1
(33)	多快好省	94	more, faster, and more efficiently	159	B1
(34)	心領神會	98	Spirit-Séance	165	B2
(35)	開水不響，響水不開	100	It wasn't safe to drink until it reached a full boil.	169	B1
(36)	白紙黑字	104	in the form of words on paper	174	B2
(37)	紅血公雞	105	blood red rooster	175	A2
(38)	打響了第一炮	110	fire the first shot	184	A1

(*Continued*)

No.	Chinese original	Page number	English translation	Page number	Translation strategy
(39)	壓台兒戲	111	the final event	185	B1
(40)	大出了人意	116	exceeded everyone's expectations	194	A1
(41)	水漲船高	116	a rising tide lifting all boats	195	A1
(42)	說一不二的人	124	a man of my word	210	B2
(43)	紅頭文件	124	official document	210	B1
(44)	兩情兩願	125	mutually agreeable to both parties	211	A1
(45)	水性楊花	129	skittish and unreliable	217	B1
(46)	白色恐怖	131	White Terror	222	A1
(47)	某日某月	136	on such-and-such month and such-and-such day	230	A1
(48)	做賣肉生意	137	sell their flesh	234	A2
(49)	一大段工夫兒	141	for a long time	240	B1
(50)	說到天東和地西	143	go on and on about this	243	B1
(51)	拉扯起來了	147	get under way	250	B1
(52)	一傳了十,十傳了百	150	Their stories grew and grew.	255	B1
(53)	高到了天上去	150	high enough to touch the sky	255	A1
(54)	剝臉皮	154	to have my dignity exploited	262	B1
(55)	大鬧天災了	157	an act of God	267	B2
(56)	解燃眉之急	160	to address this pressing matter	271	B1
(57)	沒良心	164	be lacking in compassion	278	B1
(58)	鋪天蓋地的糧荒	168	a full-fledged famine	284	B1
(59)	千年不遇的大劫難	169	once-in-a-millennium disaster	285	A1
(60)	落湯的雞	172	chickens soaking in a pot	291	A1
(61)	到了…的田地兒	173	having reached the point	299	B1
(62)	萬事俱備了,只欠了東風	180	Everything was ready, and all that was missing was the final touch.	304	B1
(63)	家長里短	181	details of families	306	A1
(64)	製造聲勢	183	to create some momentum	311	A1
(65)	如螞蟻搬家	186	like an anthill	317	A1
(66)	外國天大的人物	191	an enormous foreign figure	325	A1
(67)	機巧成千上萬	192	countless marvelous details	326	B1
(68)	沁潤人的心肺	195	moistening people's hearts	332	A1
(69)	耳聽是虛,眼見為實	197	Seeing is believing	336	B2
(70)	老死不相往來	203	never thought of coming over to visit	344	B1
(71)	吊胃口	204	to arouse their interest	346	B1
(72)	天塌地陷的事	208	something extraordinary	353	B1
(73)	留了青山在,哪兒怕了沒柴燒	210	As long as there is a verdant mountain, how can you be worried about not having enough wood for kindling?	356	A1
(74)	破新立舊	215	destroy the old and erect the new	365	A1
(75)	衣來伸手,飯來張口	218	They only had to reach out to get their clothes, and open their mouths to get food.	371	A1
(76)	罪加一等	219	commit another crime	372	A1
(77)	一場地覆天翻的事情	224	an earth-shattering event	381	A1
(78)	良心餵狗	230	fed our conscience to the dogs	390	A1

(Continued)

No.	Chinese original	Page number	English translation	Page number	Translation strategy
(79)	水米不打牙兒	235	hadn't had a taste of food and water	398	B1
(80)	隔著的一層窗紙終於捅破	236	had finally torn down the artificial façade	400	B1
(81)	體己的錢	238	cash stashed away on their persons	403	A2
(82)	在一片火上澆下了一桶水	240	had suddenly thrown water onto a burning fire	405	A1
(83)	我不是說話不作數的人	249	I'm good for my word.	419	B2
(84)	井水不犯河水	249	—	419	B4
(85)	一分一厘	251	a single cent	423	B2
(86)	任意發落著	252	whatever was to follow	424	B1
(87)	爐火兒純青	257	somewhat stale	433	B1 (mistranslated)
(88)	揮金如土	258	going through money like dirt	435	A1
(89)	十年寒窗	264	studying diligently for an exam for more than a decade	445	A1
(90)	悄無聲息	266	it could no longer be heard	448	B1
(91)	名譽掃地	269	drag your name through the mud	453	A1
(92)	成過街老鼠	269	reduce to the status of a rat in the street	454	A1
(93)	做了小鞋穿	273	—	461	B4
(94)	心裡悠忽一下子	274	one's heart skipped a beat	463	A1
(95)	人物兒樣	284	an important personage	480	A1
(96)	入土為安	286	be put to rest	483	B2
(97)	一旗又一旗	287	wave upon wave of	485	B2
(98)	安營紮寨	287	to pitch a camp and establish a village	487	A1
(99)	四季如春	290	like spring throughout the year	491	A1
(100)	尋短見	292	take my life	496	A1

29
THE TRANSLATION AND RECEPTION OF YAN LIANKE IN JAPAN

Dongli Lu and Riccardo Moratto[*]

Tsuyoshi Tanikawa 谷川毅, Yan Lianke's main Japanese translator, argues that: "In Japan, when one talks about Chinese literature, it is fair to say that many Japanese people look at it with a condescending attitude."[1] Compared to European and American literatures, which are popular among Japanese readers, the average circulation of translated books by Chinese authors in Japan is merely two to three thousand copies per title.[2] In an interview, Professor Fuji Shozo 藤井省三 once said:

> Japanese publishers are now very cautious for commercial reasons. Usually, the first printing is around 2,000 copies, and in many cases only 1,500, which is even less than the number of first printing copies thirty years ago, when the minimum was 2,500. The best time for Japanese publishing was around 1990, when the number of books and print runs was the largest. For example, in 1984, when I was an assistant in the Department of Literature at the University of Tokyo and published the book *The Shadow of Russia: Natsume Sōseki and Lu Xun* [ロシアの影: 夏目漱石と魯迅, the print run was 4,000 copies, an average number for academic books at that time. Today, thirty years have passed and I am Professor in the Department of Literature at the University of Tokyo; however, when I published my book *Lu Xun and Japanese Literature: From Natsume Sōseki and Mori Ōgai to Seichō Matsumoto and Murakami Haruki* [魯迅と日本文學: 漱石・鷗外から清張・春樹まで], the publisher printed only 2,000 copies.[3]

---

[*] An earlier version of this chapter first appeared in Chinese in Lu Dongli, "Riben de Yan Lianke shidai" 日本的閻連科時代 [The Era of Yan Lianke in Japan], *Nitchū hon'yaku bunka kyōiku kyōkai* 日中翻訳文化教育研究 [The Academic Journal of SETACS], 2019, no. 4: 32–40. Lu Dongli is authorized to reuse and modify the paper. A few changes have been made in the current version.

[1] Tanikawa Tsuyoshi, "Zhongguo dangdai wenxue zai Riben" 中國當代文學在日本 [Contemporary Chinese literature in Japan], *Zhongguo tushu pinglun* 中國圖書評論 [China book review], 2011, no. 5: 97: "在日本, 當我們提到中國 (文學), 確實有很多日本人持著居高臨下的態度觀望。" All citations are translated by the authors, unless otherwise specified.

[2] Liu Chengcai 劉成才 and Fujii Shōzō, "Mo Yan, dushi wenxue yu Zhong Ri wenxue jiaoliu: Dongjing daxue Tenjing Xingsan jiaoshou fangtan" 莫言、都市文學與中日文學交流——東京大學藤井省三教授訪談 [Mo Yan, urban literature and Sino-Japanese literary exchange: Interview with Professor Fuji Shozo of the University of Tokyo], *Shehui kexue luntan* 社會科學論壇 [Tribune of social sciences], 2020, no. 1: 8.

[3] Ibid., 180.

The market for translated Chinese literature is very small and the impact of the translations is minimal. Only a handful of contemporary Chinese writers have seen their works translated into Japanese, including Mo Yan 莫言, Can Xue 殘雪, Yan Lianke 閻連科, Jia Pingwa 賈平凹, Yu Hua 余華, Lu Yao 路遙, and Chi Zijian 遲子建. The reason is that the works of Chinese writers are far from the imagination of Japanese readers, especially those with rural themes, which are difficult for the average Japanese reader to understand.[4] With his novels, such as *Lenin's Kisses* (*Shouhuo* 受活), Yan succeeded in breaking the long silence of Chinese literature in Japan. Ten of Yan's books have been translated into Japanese thus far.[5] Yan was the first Asian writer to receive the Twitter Literary Award (Twitter 文學賞) in Japan for his book *Lenin's Kisses*.[6] With the publication of *The Years, Months, Days* (*Nian yue ri* 年月日), *The Explosion Chronicles* (*Zhalie zhi* 炸裂志) and *Three Brothers: Memories of My Family* (*Wo yu fubei* 我與父輩) in 2016, and *Hard Like Water* (*Jiangying ru shui* 堅硬如水) in 2017, the Japanese media declared that "the era of Yan Lianke in Japan" had arrived.[7] Yan's novels are rooted in the Chinese native soil and are highly local in character. Through Yan's books Japanese readers explore present-day Chinese society. Most importantly, Japanese mainstream media have paid unprecedented attention to Chinese literature thanks to the literary figure of Yan Lianke.

Medio-translatology perspective

Chinese traditional translation research mainly emphasizes "how to translate," the pragmatic functions of translation theory, and the "Chinese characteristics" of translation theory.[8] Nowadays, the "going out" or go-global strategy adopted by the Chinese government for the benefit of Chinese literature has expanded from mere translation research to communication and sociological studies. In recent years, medio-translatology (*yijiexue* 譯介學) research has focused on the unique value and significance of translation as a practical activity of cross-cultural communication,[9] and the focus of research has extended from the content

---

4 Izumi Kyoka 泉京鹿 and Chen Yan 陳言, "Nihonjin hon'yaku-ka kara mita Chūgoku no gendai bungaku" 日本人翻訳家から見た中国の現代文学 [Contemporary Chinese literature as seen by Japanese translators], *Renmin wang Riyu ban* 人民網日語版 [People.com in Japanese], http://j.people.com.cn/n/2015/1203/c94473-8985500.html (last accessed 9 June 2021).

5 *Serve the People* (人民に奉仕する), trans. Tanikawa Tsuyoshi (Tokyo: Bungeishunju, 2006); *Dream of Ding Village* (丁莊の夢), trans. Tanikawa Tsuyoshi (Tokyo: Kawade Shobō Shinsha, 2007; repr. 2020); *Lenin's Kisses* (愉楽), trans. Tanikawa Tsuyoshi, 2nd edn. (Tokyo: Kawade Shobō Shinsha, 201); *The Years, Months, Days* (年月日), trans. Izuka Yutori 飯塚容 (Tokyo: Hakusuisha Publishing, 2016); *Hard Like Water* (硬きこと水のごとし), trans. Tanikawa Tsuyoshi (Tokyo: Kawade Shobō Shinsha, 2017); *Black Pig Bristle, White Pig Bristle* (黒い豚の毛、白い豚の毛: 自選短篇集), trans. Tanikawa Tsuyoshi (Tokyo: Kawade Shobō Shinsha, 2019); *Three Brothers: Memories of My Family* (父を思う), trans. Izuka Yutori (Tokyo: Kawade Shobō Shinsha, 2016); *The Explosion Chronicles* (炸裂志), trans. Izumi Kyoka 泉京鹿 (Tokyo: Kawade Shobō Shinsha, 2016); and *Heart Sutra* (心経), trans. Izuka Yutori (Tokyo: Kawade Shobō Shinsha, 2021).

6 The Twitter Literary Award is a literary prize voted by Japanese readers via Twitter from the best Japanese novels of the year, and it is divided into two categories: domestic and overseas. Readers may refer to: https://twitter-bungaku-award.theblog.me/.

7 https://cul.qq.com/a/20170206/019744.htm (last accessed 15 June 2021).

8 Xie Tianzhen 謝天振, "Guonei fanyijie zai fanyi yanjiu he fanyi lilun renshi shang de wuqu" 國內翻譯界在翻譯研究和翻譯理論認識上的誤區 [Misunderstandings in translation research and translation theory in the domestic translation community], *Zhongguo fanyi* 中國翻譯 [Chinese Translators Journal] 22, no. 4 (July 2001): 4.

9 Xie Tianzhen 謝天振, "Zhongguo wenxue zou chuqu: Wenti yu shizhi" 中國文學走出去: 問題與實質 [Chinese literature going global: Problems and essence], *Zhongguo bijiao wenxue* 中國比較文學 [Comparative Chinese literature], 2014, no. 1: 3.

of translation to the five major elements of translation: subject, content, means, audience, and effect.[10] Drawing on the theoretical framework of medio-translatology, this chapter discusses the translation of Yan's literature in Japan from three aspects, namely the subject and content of translation, the way and mode of translation, and the effect of translation, and analyzes the characteristics of Yan's translation and reception in Japan.

Translations and reception of Yan's literary works in Japan

First works to be translated: Serve the People *and* Dream of Ding Village

Tsuyoshi Tanikawa has been a key figure in introducing Yan Lianke to Japanese readers. He has translated *Serve the People*, *Dream of Ding Village*, *Lenin's Kisses*, *The Years, Months, Days*, *Hard Like Water*, and *Black Pig Bristles, White Pig Bristles*. Tanikawa was introduced to Yan by Tian Yuan 田原, Professor at Josai International University. Before translating *Serve the People*, Tanikawa had already translated *Revolutionary Romanticism: Representative Short Stories of Yan Lianke* (*Geming langman zhuyi* 革命浪漫主義) and published it in the Chinese literary journal *Huoguozi* 火鍋子 in November 2004. After *Serve the People* was banned in mainland China in 2005, the publishing house Bungeishunju 文藝春秋 invited Tanikawa to translate the book and published it soon after in August 2006. The Japanese critic Fuji Shozo in an op-ed in the 27 Oct. 2014 issue of *Japan Economics Newspaper* (*Nihon Keizai Shimbun* 日本経済新聞) compared *Serve the People* to *Lady Chatterley's Lover*, depicting a grand modern Chinese story of love and politics.[11]

Dream of Ding Village was published in 2007 by the publishing house Kabushiki Kaisha Kawade Shobō Shinsha 株式会社河出書房新社. The book was promoted as grotesque literature with documentary overtones.[12] The Japanese title of *Dream of Ding Village* is 丁庄の夢——中国エイズ村奇談 (*Teishōnoyume—Chūgoku eizu-mura kidan*) which literally means "Dream of Ding Village: China AIDS Village Strange Story." The Japanese publisher opted for a subtitle emphasizing the "strangeness" of the story. The word "AIDS" sufficed to attract the attention of Japanese readers, and the subtitle "strange story" catered even more to the love of Japanese readers for strange and grotesque literature. The novel is narrated by a dead boy who recounts the story of an AIDS village, in which the realistic interpretation of human-ghost conversations and dreams perfectly reflects the characteristics of Japanese grotesque literature. *Dream of Ding Village* was even translated into Braille and published in Japan. Tanikawa describes this event as "shocking."[13]

---

10 Bao Xiaoying 鮑曉英, "Zhongguo wenhua 'zou chuqu' zhi yijie moshi tansuo: Zhongguo waiwenju fujuzhang jian zongbianji Huang Youyi fangtan lu" 中國文化「走出去」之譯介模式探索——中國外文局副局長兼總編輯黃友義訪談錄 [Exploring the translation and interpretation model of Chinese culture "going global": Interview with Huang Youyi, Deputy Director General and Editor-in-Chief of China Foreign Language Bureau], *Zhongguo fanyi*, 2013, no. 5: 63.
11 https://www.nikkei.com/article/DGXKZO78894720V21C14A0MZB001/ (last accessed 15 June 2021).
12 See Tanikawa, "Zhongguo dangdai wenxue zai riben," 98.
13 Zhang Yuan 張元, "Zhongguo dangdai xiaoshuo zai Riben de yijie yu chuanbo" 中國當代小說在日本的譯介與傳播 [The translation and dissemination of contemporary Chinese fiction in Japan], *Wenyi pinglun* 文藝評論 [Literary criticism], 2013, no. 5: 65.

The success of Lenin's Kisses

The Japanese translation of *Lenin's Kisses* was published at the end of 2014 by Bungeishunju. The first printing of 8,000 copies sold out and was reprinted three times within four months, with 3,000 copies each time, setting a new record for sales of Chinese authors in Japan.[14] Before that, only Jia Pingwa's *Ruined City* (*Feidu* 廢都) had been reprinted once in Japan, and the number of reprints was far less than that of *Lenin's Kisses*. On the back cover of the Japanese edition of *Lenin's Kisses* one can read: "A young man with broken feet who walks really fast, a hemiplegic embroidery master, and a blind woman who can distinguish the direction by listening to the sounds form a disabled stunt group with the ultimate goal to purchase Lenin's body and complete Lenin Memorial Hall. A masterpiece that strikes at the contradictions of modern China, making people laugh and weep at the same time." Some readers even admitted that the description of the disabled stunt group on the waistband evoked their desire to read the book.[15]

Tanikawa was shortlisted for the 2015 Japanese Literature Translation of the Year Award for the translation of this novel. It took ten years for *Lenin's Kisses* to be published in Japan. There are many reasons behind this delay. In an interview, Tanikawa explains that in addition to the difficulty of translating the work which brims with dialectal expressions from the province of Henan, other reasons include the anti-Japanese demonstrations in April 2005 in China, the cold relations between Japan and China, and the Japanese domestic publishing industry that is facing competition from the Internet and e-books and is therefore very cautious about publishing purely literary works.[16]

The era of Yan Lianke in Japan: The Years, Months, Days, The Explosion Chronicles, Three Brothers, *and* Hard Like Water

In 2016 Yan's *The Years, Months, Days* was published by Hakusuisha Publishing, while *The Explosion Chronicles* and *Three Brothers: Memories of My Family* were published by Kawade Shobō Shinsha. *Hard Like Water* was published the following year in 2017. The Japanese media and readers had a strong reaction and claimed that "the era of Yan Lianke" had finally arrived in Japan.[17] Tian Yuan claims: "It is rare for Japan to publish three books by the same contemporary Chinese writer with different publishers and translators within a year. Apart from Lu Xun, Yan Lianke is probably the only one who enjoys this honor."[18] *The Years, Months, Days* and *Hard Like Water* were also translated by Tanikawa. *The Years, Months, Days*, a novel recommended by the French Education Center as a book for secondary school students, depicts the story of life in the Balou 耙耬 Mountains in an allegorical way, shaping the course of human life within

---

14 Tian Yuan, "Yan Lianke *Shouhuo* Riwenban shangshi rexiao 4 ge yue nei zaiban 3 ci" 閻達科受活日文版上市熱銷4個月內再版3次 [The Japanese version of *Lenin's Kisses* has been selling well and has been reprinted three times within four months], *Beijing qingnian bao* 北京青年報 [Beijing Youth Daily], 26 Mar. 2015.

15 Readers may refer to the comments on the website 読書メーター: https://bookmeter.com/books/8236106 (last accessed 15 June 2021).

16 Lu Dongli 盧冬麗, "Fanyi shi xingfu er you manzu de guocheng: Yan Lianke Riyizhe Guchuan Yi fangtan lu" 翻譯是幸福而又滿足的過程——閻連科日譯者谷川毅訪談錄 [Translation is a happy and satisfying process: Interview with Tanikawa Tsuyoshi, Yan Lianke's Japanese translator], *Ri Zhong fanyi wenhua jiaoyu yanjiu* 日中翻譯文化教育研究 [Research on Japanese-Chinese translation, culture, and education], 2020, no. 5: 84–91.

17 See https://cul.qq.com/a/20170206/019744.htm (last accessed 15 June 2021).

18 Tian Yuan, personal communication, 2021.

the framework of a tragic text.[19] *Hard Like Water* describes the deformed, distorted, and even perverted lives, human nature, desires, pursuits, and greed of people in the particular context of the Cultural Revolution. *The Explosion Chronicles* was translated by Kyoka Izumi 泉京鹿. Written with the author's self-proclaimed mythorealist approach, it is an absurd, exaggerated and fantastical story of a village of a hundred people that instantly turns into a megalopolis of high-rise buildings. This novel was serialized since the 2014 autumn issue of *Waseda Literature* 早稲田文學 and then published in 2016 by Kawade Shobō Shinsha. Izumi is a professional translator; she has translated Yu Hua's *Brothers* (*Xiongdi* 兄弟), Tian Yuan's 田原 *Double Mono* (*Shui zhi bifang* 水之彼方), and Guo Jingming's 郭敬明 *Cry Me a Sad River* (*Beishang niliu cheng he* 悲傷逆流成河), just to mention a few. Her Japanese translations have been acclaimed by numerous writers and scholars. *Three Brothers* was translated by the renowned Japanese translator Yutori Iizuka 飯塚容, who has been translating contemporary Chinese literature for many years. Over the past 30 years, Iizuka has translated more than forty novels and plays by dozens of Chinese writers, including Lu Xun, Cao Yu 曹禺, Tie Ning 鐵凝, Wang Anyi 王安憶, and Yu Hua. Zhang Jing 張競, Professor at Meiji University 明治大學, highly rated Iizuka's translation of *Three Brothers*: "The translation is flawless and perfectly conveys the meaning of the original."[20]

Black Pig Bristles, White Pig Bristles, *and the consolidation of Yan's literary status*

Yan's *Black Pig Bristle, White Pig Bristle* was translated by Tanikawa and published by Kawade Shobō Shinsha on 25 July 2019. This novella contains four chapters focusing on rural themes, three on military themes, and two on religious themes, for a total of nine short stories. As soon as it was published in Japan, the response was so positive that it was beyond the publisher's expectations, and the book reviews came in so thick and fast that the publisher planned to print more copies at the end of the year.[21] The first printing of 3,000 copies and the additional printing within a few months was very unexpected in the Japanese publishing market. Tanikawa claims that the publication and positive reception of a collection of short stories in Japan is the most distinctive sign of a writer's consolidated status.[22] After the translation and publication of *Serve the People* and *Dream of Ding Village*, to the much-anticipated *Lenin's Kisses* published in Japan in 2014, the successive publication of four books translated by three different people from 2016 to 2018 along with *Black Pig Bristles, White Pig Bristles* in 2019 consolidated Yan's position in the Japanese literary scene and marked the positive reception of Yan's literature by his Japanese readership. The publication of five translations in two years is closely related to the diligence of the Japanese translators.

The Four Books was translated by Michio Kuwajima 桑島道夫, Professor at Shizuoka University, and will be published by Iwanami Shoten. *Discovering Fiction* (*Faxian xiaoshuo* 發現小說) and his other novel *The Day The Sun Died* (*Rixi* 日熄) are also being translated.[23] It can be said that the term "Yan Lianke era" is no exaggeration and will continue in the years to come.

---

19 Tian, "Yan Lianke *Shouhuo* Riwenban shangshi rexiao 4 ge yue nei zaiban 3 ci."
20 Zhang Jing 張競, "Seishin no sekihi ni nōmin seikatsu no jojishi kizamu" 精神の石碑に農民生活の敍事詩刻む [Engrave the epic of peasant life on the stone monument of the spirit], *Mainichi Shimbun* 每日新聞 [*Daily News*], 3 July 2016, Mai Saku 每索 database (last accessed 22 July 2021).
21 Tanikawa Tsuyoshi, personal communication, 2021.
22 Ibid.
23 This article was complete in June 2021.

Translation channels and modes

Publishers' preference for controversial novels

The role of publishers in the translation of Chinese literature is crucial and at times even decisive. Looking at Chinese literary works published in Japan, it is easy to see that publishers are selective in their translations of literary themes and have a preference for Chinese "problematic novels." It is undeniable that Yan's status as a "controversial writer" has stimulated the curiosity of Japanese readers, and the political narrative of the novel has induced their desire to pry into Chinese society. Most of his books are controversial and many are banned in mainland China; publishers use this as a major selling point to attract readers' attention. The lower part of the front cover of the Japanese translation of *Serve the People* reads "problematic novel" (問題小説). The blurb reads: "Set in the Cultural Revolution of the late 1960s, the novel depicts love hidden in the shadows and offers a fierce critique of the Chinese social system, making it a problematic novel." The entire cover of the Japanese translation shows Chinese women in traditional red high-necked *qipao* under a dimly lit shade, with their faces invisible and mysterious, giving an overwhelming and depressing impression. The head of Mao Zedong in the lower back corner highlights the novel's political background narrative, echoing the "problematic novel" written on the cover. The translator argues:

> Japanese readers generally prefer to read novels and other works that reveal the dark side of society or expose the dark reality. This is not only true for Chinese novels; many readers in different languages are curious about novels that take place in countries around the world and have a strong sense of dystopian reality, as in the case of *Serve the People*. As a business practice, this is certainly one of the important factors for publishers. *Serve the People* shows and describes the story surrounding the promiscuous relationship between the division commander's wife and the official squad leader. The combination of politics and sex not only gives Japanese readers a shot of adrenaline, but also provides them with great room for reflection and imagination. *Dream of Ding Village* is the story of an AIDS village. For Japanese readers, the noun phrase "AIDS village" seems to be enough to draw their attention. I believe that this word is very sensitive in many a country.[24]

Once the news that *Dream of Ding Village* was banned in mainland China started circulating, a Japanese translation was released early the following year, and the first edition was quickly sold out and later even translated into Braille; this was undeniably an important factor in the editor's urgency to publish the book. The book cover of the Japanese translations of *The Explosion Chronicles* and *Three Brothers* also highlighted Yan's status as a controversial writer in China. On the cover of the former, Yan himself shared the following words with his Japanese readers: "censorship has erected a wall, but there is no wall in the heart."[25]

Publishers' emphasis on pure literature

Publishers may use controversy as a booster to attract readers, but aside from that, what ultimately persuades readers is the literary quality of the novel. Even in the case of highly controversial

---

24 Lu, "Fanyi shi xingfu er you manzu de guocheng."
25 In Japanese: "検閲に壁はあるかもしれないが、わたしの心の中に壁はない."

novels, such as *Serve the People* and *Dream of Ding Village*, in addition to the political and disease narrative that shocked Japanese readers, what is more important is the author's gaze at the world and his profound revelation of the literary and human nature. In 2014, Kawade Shobō Shinsha positioned *Lenin's Kisses* as classic literature and priced it 3,600 *yen*; yet readers still flocked to it. The cover of the Japanese translation of *Lenin's Kisses* is very similar to the cover of the Japanese translation of *Blue Lard* by Vladimir Sorokin, the most controversial contemporary Russian writer, published in 1999.[26] On the cover of the Winter 2014 issue of *Waseda Literature*, *The Explosion Chronicles* is described as "a story told by a man born in darkness"; in the content recommendation, expressions such as winner of the Franz Kafka Prize and other descriptions are used to promote Yan's new work.

Yan's reception in Japan

The media's contribution to shaping Yan's image in Japan

The evaluation of Yan's works by Japanese mainstream media and critics has objectively created a "literary impression," which has largely influenced the reception of his literary works. Yan's works have received considerable attention from scholars as soon as they entered the Japanese market. The Nobel laureate Kenzaburō Ōe 大江健三郎 argues: "Yan Lianke's works are full of satire and criticism, and his character depiction is unparalleled, making him a literary master both at home and abroad."[27] Michio Kuwajima 桑島道夫 discusses the magical realism elements in *Dream of Ding Village*: "[This novel] brims with the characteristics of magic realism. The people of the remote countryside grew up in the birthplace of Chinese civilization, and their view of life and death (their obsession with the afterlife and coffins) is articulated with history and can only blossom and be expressed through the techniques of Latin American literature."[28]

When *Lenin's Kisses* was published in Japan, the most influential Japanese newspapers *Asahi Shimbun* 朝日新聞 and *Yomiuri Shimbun* 読売新聞 published several reviews of the book. Japanese novelist, writer, and actor Seiko Ito 伊藤正幸 praised Yan on *Asahi Shimbun*: "Yan Lianke inserts the political history into a mythical virtual existence of the village Liven. His creation has the power to dig into the earth, and its imagination can be extended infinitely like a cannonball. The language is sometimes literary and sometimes colloquial, and the narrative is [seemingly] unstructured and unpredictable, like a dragon soaring in the universe."[29] Fuji Shozo published a book review in *Nihon Keizai Shimbun* under the title "A Modern Chinese Allegory Full of

---

26 Lu Dongli and Li Hong 李紅, "Yan Lianke *Shouhuo* zai Riben de quanshi yu shourong: Jiyu Riyiben *Yuraku* fuwenben de fenxi" 閻連科《受活》在日本的詮釋與受容——基於日譯本《愉楽》副文本的分析 [The interpretation and reception of Yan Lianke's *Lenin's Kisses* in Japan: Analysis based on the paratext of the Japanese translation], *Wenyi zhengming* 文藝爭鳴 [Literary and artistic contentions], 2016, no. 3: 172.
27 Ōe Kenzaburō 大江健三郎, *Teigishu* 定義集 [A collection of definitions] (Tokyo: Asahi Shimbun Publications, 2012): 150.
28 Kuwajima Michio, "Yan Lianke no shōsetsu ni miru rinri (hon'yaku no 'rinri' o meguru sōgō-teki kenkyū" 閻連科の小説に見る倫理 (翻訳の〈倫理〉をめぐる総合的研究) [Ethics seen in Yan Lianke's novels (Comprehensive research on the ethics of translation)], *Hon'yaku no bunka/bunka no hon'yaku* 翻訳の文化／文化の翻訳 [Translating culture/cultural translation], 2015, no. 3: 83–89.
29 Ito Seiko 伊藤正幸, "Kenryoku o osorenu keta hazure no wanryoku" 権力を恐れぬケタ外れの腕力 [Out-of-order strength that is not afraid of power], *Asahi Shimbun*, 30 Nov. 2014, http://book.asahi.com/reviews/reviewer/2014120100009.html (last accessed 16 June 2021).

Deep Despair," comparing Yan with Lu Xun: "Lu Xun divided the history of China into two eras. The first is when one wants to be a slave but cannot be one, and the second is the era when one can be a slave without fear or hesitation. The creation of the third era, which has never existed before, is the destiny of modern youth. [...] After the 1990s Yan Lianke divides modern history into the era of imposed political slavery and the era of voluntary economic slavery. Yan's despair is deeper than Lu Xun's."[30]

Lenin's Kisses is very popular among readers in Japan. Tian Yuan believes that this has to do with the uniqueness and classicism of the work: "Yan's language is full of passion and poetry, utterly creative and rhetorical [...] His work is very unique, with a soaring imagination and a vast capacity for structural fiction. You rarely see the shadow of other Chinese writers in his work, and this is the essence of creativity. [...] Yan Lianke's profound revelation of human nature, the depth of his metaphors, his reflections on the current reality of China, and his unique imagination and ability to structure fiction, created a tremendous impact on Japanese readers."[31]

In 2016 three of Yan's books were published in the same year, namely *The Years, Months, Days*, *The Explosion Chronicles*, and *Three Brothers*. After the publication of these books, all major media outlets published book reviews claiming that the era of Yan Lianke in Japan had arrived. Tanikawa published an op-ed on *Chūnichi Shinbun* 中日新聞 titled "Who is Yan Lianke?,"[32] introducing Yan's life and his vigorous creative activities. The critic Ryouta Hukusima 福嶋亮大 also spoke highly of Yan's work in the *Nihon Keizai Shimbun*: "Yan Lianke's work is a breath of fresh air in the modern literary world, which is becoming increasingly anemic and dumb. The poignancy of his works is necessary to confront the imbalance of contemporary China, and is also similar to the works of Mo Yan, Yu Hua, and even Lu Xun's *Old Tales Retold*. The strong imagination of Chinese literature never fears violence and contamination."[33]

The Explosion Chronicles brims with strange and absurd episodes written with a magic realist touch. The villagers spit and drown the old village chief, the flowers on the graves wither and bloom instantly because of the utterance of a single word, the whole village gets rich by "unloading" a train, the navy is trained in the valley meadows …. Yan establishes a new narrative order in his book, in which the plot and characters have their own logical relationship, which is what the writer calls "mythorealism." Every detail seems to be impossible in life, but combined, one would not say it is impossible. The translator Yukiko Kousu 鴻巣友季子 claims: "To expose this internal cause-and-effect [*nei yinguo* 內因果] in Chinese society one must use mythorealism."[34] Zhang Jing further argues: "*The Explosion Chronicles* is not only

---

30 Fuji Shozo, "Fukai zetsubō komoru gendai Chūgoku no gūwa" 深い絶望こもる現代中國の寓話 [An allegory of modern China, filled with deep despair], *Nihon keizai shimbun*, 26 Oct. 2014, http://www.nikkei.com/article/DGXKZO78894720V21C14A0MZB001/ (last accessed 16 June 2021).
31 Tian, "Yan Lianke *Shouhuo* Riwenban shangshi rexiao 4 ge yue nei zaiban 3 ci."
32 In Japanese: "閻連科は誰？"
33 Hukusima Ryouta, "Taikin to hikikae ni 'ichi-shi' kaku"大金と引き換えに「市史」書く [Writing the "History of The City" in exchange for money], *Nihon Keizai Shimbun*, 11 Dec. 2016. http://style.nikkei.com/article/DGXKZO10523970Q6A211C1MY6001 (last accessed 16 June 2021).
34 Kousu Yukiko 鴻巣友季子, "Hakkin sakka ga 'kamumi shugi' de eguri dasu Chūgoku no kōtōmukeina rifujin-sa" 発禁作家が「神実主義」でえぐりだす　中國の荒唐無稽な理不盡さ [A banned writer uses "mythorealism" to reveal the absurd truth about China's absurdity], *Shukan shincho* 週刊新潮 [*Weekly News Magazine*], 22 Dec. 2016, https://www.bookbang.jp/review/article/523495 (last accessed 16 June 2021).

a reproduction of the corruption and degradation in the reform and opening up, but also a portrayal of the reality, which is exaggerated like a fairy tale."[35]

After the publication of the Japanese translation of *The Years, Months, Days*, the writer Kyoko Nakajima 中島京子, winner of the Naoki Prize and Izumi Kyōka Prize for Literature, wrote on *Daily News* (*Mainichi Shimbun* 毎日新聞): "The novel is an allegorical and soul-stirring story that discusses the meaning of life in all its forms, including humans, plants, animals, and the earth."[36] Renowned reviewer Yumi Toyosaki 豊崎由美 writes an even more emotional testimonial: "It moved me in a way I had never experienced before: my lips could not stop trembling."[37] Fuji argues: "The old man in *The Years, Months, Days* is as brave as the old fisherman Santiago in *The Old Man and the Sea*, but more compassionate than him, reminiscent of the *Little Prince*."[38]

Compared to the surrealist *The Years, Months, Days* and the mythorealist *The Explosion Chronicles*, *Three Brothers* stirred the hearts of Japanese readers with its nostalgia, hometown complex, warmth, and affection flowing through the brutal circumstances of poverty, hunger, and heavy physical labor. Zhang Jing argues that "*Three Brothers: Memories of My Family* is a narrative poem of peasant life carved on a spiritual stone. [...] The writer, with his unparalleled linguistic talent and stylistic refinement, is like wandering through a garden of words, trying to pick the brightest flowers, picking up the scattered notes that have lain dormant in the hearts of peasants for centuries, and weaving them into a magnificent symphony."[39]

Active promotion of Yan's works

The dissemination of Yan's works in Japan owes a lot to Japanese Sinologists, translators, and readers. Translators often have a dual or triple role. They are translators, readers, and critics at the same time. The major literary research associations and reading clubs have also played an important role in the dissemination of Yan's literature and in promoting the reception of his literature. On 15 Sep. 2016, the Society for the Study of Contemporary Chinese Literature in Japan held an open dialogue session at Komazawa University in Tokyo on the theme of "Dialogue with Author Yan Lianke: How to Read *Lenin's Kisses*," in which Yoshinobu Tokuma 德間佳信, Professor at Komazawa University, Tsuyoshi Tanigawa, Professor at of Nagoya University of Economics, and Yan Lianke himself held an open discussion on how Japanese readers understand *Lenin's Kisses*. The Society for the Study of Contemporary Chinese Literature in Japan is a private literary research organization. It was founded in

---

35 Zhang Jing, "Meruhen-tekina butai ni shakai chin genshō o kasha" メルヘン的な舞臺に社會珍現象を活寫 [Lively capture social rare phenomena on a fairy tale stage], *Mainichi Shinbun*, 11 Dec. 2016, http://mainichi.jp/articles/20161211/ddm/015/070/019000c (last accessed 16 June 2021).
36 See Nakajima Kyoko's endorsement on the cover of the Japanese edition of the novel, Hakusuisha, https://www.hakusuisha.co.jp/book/b251315.html (last accessed 17 June 2021).
37 See Toyozaki Yumi, "Mizou no kandō ni kuchibiru o furuwaseru" 未曾有の感動に唇を震わせる [Shake your lips with unprecedented excitement], Book Bang, https://www.bookbang.jp/review/article/529874 (last accessed 17 June 2021).
38 See Fuji Shozo, "Tōmorokoshi no nae o mamoru hanashi" 玉蜀黍の苗を守る話 [A story about protecting corn seedlings], ujikenorio's blog, 11 Dec. 2016, https://ujikenorio.hatenablog.com/entry/20161226/p4 (last accessed 24 Aug. 2021).
39 Zhang Jing, "Chichi o omou—aru Chūgoku sakka no jisei to kaiso" 父を想う—ある中國作家の自省と回想 [Thinking of my father: A Chinese writer's self-reflection and recollection], *Mainichi Shimbun*, 3 July 2016, http://mainichi.jp/articles/20160703/ddm/015/070/003000c (last accessed 16 June 2021).

1983 and has continued to exist for three decades without any official support. The members of the society come from all walks of life. Researchers of contemporary Chinese literature, employees of trading companies, translators, experts in Japanese literature have all supported the development of the society. The society regularly studies and discusses contemporary Chinese literature, and the one with Yan was its 302nd conference. It is worth mentioning that members of the World Literature Book Club also participated in this seminar. The members of this book club, who are now in their eighties, are pre-war Japanese girls' high school graduates who read a variety of books from around the world and meet regularly once a month to discuss the books they have read from various countries. The only Chinese works they have read are Lu Xun's *The True Story of Ah Q* and Yan's *Lenin's Kisses*. They have their own interpretation of *Lenin's Kisses*, and one old lady in particular was moved by the character of Grandma Mao Zhi 茅枝婆. During the exchange session with the writer, an old lady asked amusingly: "The character Yan 閻 used in your last name is the same as the one in Yama-raja, god of death and justice. What is the relationship between your last name and Yama-raja?" Yan humorously replied: "I did not know my last name had any relationship with anyone. But now I know, we must be relatives." Members of another Chinese literature reading club in Tokyo meet once a month out of their love for Chinese literature. So far, they have systematically discussed Yan's literary works four times.

Analysis of the characteristics of the translation and reception of Yan's works

The central role of translators and publishers

Translators are crucial in the dissemination of Chinese literature. In a letter to Japanese readers, Yan once wrote: "I can understand that translation is another creative process, although it is very different from the original work."[40] In translation, Yan emphasizes trust and respect and believes that the spiritual resonance between the original author and the translator, as well as the freedom of the translator, are particularly important. Yan argues: "I am willing to leave a margin of freedom to the translator; I would rather have the perfection of rhyme in translation than the completeness of words in a mechanical type of translation."[41] Yan's approach to translation focuses on the freedom of the translator and gives the translator a lot of room for creativity.

Tanikawa's translation of *Serve the People* was completed in a very short time; this was not unrelated to the publisher's request for an urgent publication. The publisher requested the translator to translate the book by respecting the original work as much as possible. Therefore, Tanikawa chose the foreignization strategy, trying to present the language and artistic atmosphere of the original work. The translation of *Dream of Ding Village*, *Lenin's Kisses*, and *The Years, Months, Days* were more centered on the readers' reception. In contrast to the "overly faithful" translation of *Serve the People*, *Dream of Ding Village* was named the best work in Japanese translation in 2007, and *Lenin's Kisses* was shortlisted for the 2015 Japanese Literature Translation of the Year Award. In an interview Tanikawa said: "The process of translating *Lenin's Kisses* was an unspeakably

---

40 Yan Lianke, "Nihon no dokusha no minasama e no tegami" 日本の読者の皆様への手紙 [A letter to Japanese students], in *Yuraku* 愉楽 (Lenin's Kisses), trans. Tanikawa Tsuyoshi, 2nd ed. (Tokyo: Kawade Shobō Shinsha, 2015), 447–48.
41 Gao Fang 高方 and Yan Lianke, "Jingshen gongming yu yizhe de 'ziyou': Yan Lianke tan wenxue yu fanyi" 精神共鳴與譯者的「自由」——閻連科談文學與翻譯 [Spiritual resonance and the translator's "freedom": Yan Lianke on Literature and Translation], *Waiguoyu* 外國語 [Journal of foreign languages] 37, no. 3 (May 2014): 22.

satisfying and blissful one, and the final recognition of the translation is largely due to the translation of the dialect [used by the author]."[42] In *Black Pig Bristles, White Pig Bristles* Yan deliberately uses the Henan dialect for his descriptions, and Tanigawa handled the language differently according to the atmosphere of the different short stories. In the interview Tanikawa says:

> Yan Lianke's trust and respect for my work makes me very happy; it is also a source of great encouragement. Any translator would feel lucky to meet such an author. It was on the basis of this attitude that my translation work was able to proceed "freely." However, this "freedom" does not entail "permissiveness." The translator should respect the original work and the wishes of the original author (in the case of a living writer), and should not arbitrarily delete, retranslate, edit or paraphrase. It is ideal for the translator to have some writing skills and creative experience. Although I have occasionally dabbled in writing, I can't say I have any extensive writing skills or creative experience. Writing and translating are two completely different activities, but I think both are creative processes.[…] After *Lenin's Kisses* was published in Japan, it immediately attracted the strong attention of the literary world and numerous critics, as well as Japanese writers and readers, perhaps because I was a little creative in the translation process. […] I try to reproduce the atmosphere of the original language as I perceive it when I translate the book.[43]

Izumi, the translator of *The Explosion Chronicles*, has translated numerous Chinese literary works. Izumi believes that the most difficult part of translation is not the language itself but the understanding of the meaning behind the words. Izumi often meets with the author to get a sense of his style by the way he moves, and she also visited the scenes of the novels to get a sense of the atmosphere from the environment.[44] Yan's works mostly focus on rural themes, which are difficult for Japanese readers to pick up. *The Explosion Chronicles* tells the story of how Explosion Village developed into a megalopolis. Izumi rode her bicycle several times to the places described by the author or to similar places, recorded the scenery, people, their movements, clothing, etc., and then expressed them in Japanese when she returned home.[45] Although this translation process is very slow and time-consuming, Izumi says, "I have a clear conscience if I can make the author feel at ease and the reader happy."[46] Therefore, Izumi's translation is less rigid and sluggish, more soft and fluent, full of true feelings.[47] To a certain extent, publishers play a decisive role in the translation and publication of overseas literature in Japan. The publisher determines the choice of subject matter and directly influences the translation style of the translator.

---

42 Lu, "Fanyi shi xingfu er you manzu de guocheng," 89.
43 Ibid.
44 Liu Chengcai 劉成才, "Jingyou wenxue fanyi lijie dangdai Zhongguo: Riben wenxue fanyijia Quan Jinglu fangtan" 經由文學翻譯理解當代中國——日本文學翻譯家泉京鹿訪談 [Understanding contemporary China through literary translation: Interview with Japanese literary translator Izumi Kyoka], *Zhongguo wenyi pinglun* 中國文藝評論 [China literature and art reviews], 2019, no. 8: 108.
45 Ibid.
46 Ibid.
47 Lu Dongli and Zhong Rizhou 鍾日洲, "Geng Yusong, Yan Lianke wenxue fangyan Riyi zelue de kaocha: Jiyu yizhe xingwei piping de shijiao" 耿玉淞.閻連科文學方言日譯策略的考察——基於譯者行為批評的視角 [An examination of the Japanese translation strategy of Geng Yusong's and Yan Lianke's literary dialect: Based on the perspective of translator's behavior criticism], *Ribenxue yanjiu* 日本學研究 [Japanese studies], 2020, no. 2: 73.

Serve the People was published by Bungeishunju, one of the largest publishing houses in Japan. Every year, they publish a wide range of books, from weekly magazines for the general public to monthly literary magazines for niche audiences and highly specialized magazines, with countless titles on literature, culture, history, science and technology, medical care, etc. As a powerful and large publishing house, publishing Yan's translations for the first time in Japan plays a certain role in promoting the writer's reception in Japan. Kawade Shobō Shinsha is a publisher of pure literature and has published five translations of Yan's works as of June 2021. Despite the relatively small size of the publishing house, it has published numerous works that have made a sensation in the Japanese literary world in recent years.

A shift of perspective

Initially, Japanese readers were exposed to Yan's novels *Serve the People* and *Dream of Ding Village*, focusing on the political narratives in the works to reveal the latent uneasiness of Chinese society and the social criticism of the heterogeneous Chinese social system and political context, satisfying the "voyeuristic and curious mindset of overseas readers towards Chinese society."[48] When it was sold in Japan, *Dream of Ding Village* was placed in the category of documentary reports of foreign countries rather than literary translations. It can be seen that initially Japanese readers were not exposed to Yan's works by focusing on the literary aspects of contemporary Chinese novels, but by looking at the social reality as presented in the novel. However, with the award-winning *Lenin's Kisses*, the focus of Japanese readers gradually shifted from the societal aspects to the literary value of Yan's works. Yan's French editor Chen Feng 陳豐 also acknowledges the literary value of Yan's works, arguing that the success of the French translation does not lie in the political cries of his works, but in the distinctive linguistic features and literary structure of the text: "Many people believe that political topics draw the attention of overseas readers for these reasons, but the writing itself is even more important."[49]

The poet Tian Yuan pointed out that the works by Yan that sold best in Japan and France were *Lenin's Kisses* and *Dream of Ding Village*, rather than *Serve the People*.[50] With *Serve the People* and *Dream of Ding Village*, Japanese readers heard Yan's political cries, tried to peek into the dark side of Chinese society, thus satisfying their inner curiosity; *Lenin's Kisses*, however, brings readers into Yan's literary world with his passionate and poetic language and magical storytelling ability. Yan's magical realism and mythorealism brought a whole new approach to writing and, thanks to his novels, for the first time since China's reform and opening up, Japan paid an unprecedented amount of attention to Chinese "pure literature."

Conclusion

Japanese readers are not as enthusiastic about Chinese literature as Chinese readers are about Japanese literature.[51] The reasons for the decline in the translation and dissemination of Chinese literature in Japan are both cultural and political. In the consciousness of many

---

48 Hu Anjiang 胡安江 and Zhu Yishu 祝一舒, "Yijie dongji yu chanshi weidu: Shilun Yan Lianke zuopin fayi ji qi chanshi" 譯介動機與闡釋維度——試論閻連科作品法譯及其闡釋 [The motivation of translation and the dimension of interpretation: On the French translation and interpretation of Yan Lianke's Works], *Xiaoshuo pinglun* 小說評論 [Fiction review], 2013, no. 5: 78.
49 Chen Feng 陳豐, "Yan Lianke zuopin zai Faguo de tuijie" 閻連科作品在法國的推介 [The promotion of Yan's works in France], *Dongwu xueshu* 東吳學術 (Soochow Academic), 2014, no. 5: 73.
50 Tian, "Yan Lianke *Shouhuo* Riwenban shangshi rexiao 4 ge yue nei zaiban 3 ci."
51 Tanikawa, "Zhongguo dangdai wenxue zai Riben," 97–98.

Japanese, they believe that their own works are superior; they look at Chinese literature in Japanese translation with a condescending attitude and, generally, they show a lukewarm attitude toward Chinese literature as a whole.[52] In addition, there is no greater struggle than the difficulty of understanding the political and historical context of China, especially after 1949. This adds to the challenge of understanding modern Chinese literature.[53] Tian Yuan argues that in terms of literature, Chinese writers are not broad-minded enough: "Chinese writers don't think much about worldwide thematic issues. It's normal for a writer to always write about what they are most excited about and familiar with, but they [Chinese writers] rarely think about how much these things mean in the world."[54] Tian also argues: "Many people think that language cannot be surpassed, but in fact, linguistic creativity can surpass one's native language. Yan's language is full of passion and poetry, utterly creative and rhetorical. His work is very unique, with a soaring imagination and a vast capacity for structural fiction. You rarely see the shadow of other Chinese writers in his work, it is very unique, and this is the essence of creativity."[55] In addition, the structure of the novel is also a problem. Many Chinese writers, as good as they are or might be in their native language, are overshadowed by translation and do not reach the heights expected by foreign readers. Regarding the success of his works in Japan, Yan believes: "The novels in Japanese literature are based on everyday life and human perspectives, which is very different from *Lenin's Kisses*, which has a spirited imagination. Perhaps the relevance of my novel to the Chinese reality and the psychological depiction of the characters have met the expectations of Japanese readers."[56]

Promotion by publishers and diverse reviews in mainstream media are crucial to the reception of translated works overseas. At present, Chinese literature is introduced abroad mainly through newspapers, literary magazines, reviews, and publications of research societies. With the growing development of the Internet and e-books, fewer people are buying paper books, and the situation is even more serious for pure literature. Japanese publishers have become very cautious in translating and publishing foreign pure literature books and lack confidence in marketing and online sales of works by excellent foreign pure literature writers. While this has had an impact on book translations, mass media can still open up new ways for the translation and dissemination of Chinese literature overseas. Diversified translation paths are thus warranted to help the international dissemination of contemporary Chinese literature.

Acknowledgments

Dongli Lu would like to acknowledge that this article was funded by the 2019 Jiangsu Provincial Research Project on Philosophy and Social Sciences in Higher Education, "Study on the Criticism and Reception of Yan Lianke's Vernacular Language in Japanese Translation" (Project No. 2019SJA0050), and by the Nanjing Agricultural University Humanities and Social Sciences Fund allocated through the Central Basic Research Funds for Universities (Project No. Y0201900131).

---

52 Ibid.
53 Ibid.
54 Tian, "Yan Lianke *Shouhuo* Riwenban shangshi rexiao 4 ge yue nei zaiban 3 ci."
55 Ibid.
56 Yan Lianke, "Dialogue with the Writer Yan Lianke: How to Read *Lenin's Kisses*," at the Society for the Study of Contemporary Chinese Literature in Japan, Komazawa University, Tokyo, 15 Sep. 2016.

Bibliography

Bao Xiaoying 鮑曉英. "Zhongguo wenhua 'zou chuqu' zhi yijie moshi tansuo: Zhongguo waiwenju fujuzhang jian zongbianji Huang Youyi fangtan lu" 中國文化「走出去」之譯介模式探索——中國外文局副局長兼總編輯黃友義訪談錄 [Exploring the translation and interpretation model of Chinese culture "going global": Interview with Huang Youyi, Deputy Director General and Editor-in-Chief of China Foreign Language Bureau]. *Zhongguo fanyi* 中國翻譯 [Chinese Translators Journal], 2013, no. 5: 62–65.

Chen Feng 陳豐. "Yan Lianke zuopin zai Faguo de tuijie" 閻連科作品在法國的推介 [The promotion of Yan's works in France]. *Dongwu xueshu* 東吳學術 [Soochow Academic], 2014, no. 5: 72–74.

Fuji Shozo 藤井省三. "Fukai zetsubō komoru gendai Chūgoku no gūwa" 深い絶望こもる現代中國の寓話 [An allegory of modern China, filled with deep despair]. *Nihon keizai shimbun* 日本經濟新聞 [Japan Economics Newspaper], 26 Oct. 2014. http://www.nikkei.com/article/DGXKZO78894720V21C14A0MZB001/ (last accessed 16 June 2021).

———. "Tōmorokoshi no nae o mamoru hanashi" 玉蜀黍の苗を守る話 [A story about protecting corn seedlings]. ujikenorio's blog, 11 Dec. 2016. https://ujikenorio.hatenablog.com/entry/20161226/p4 (last accessed 24 Aug. 2021).

Gao Fang 高方, and Yan Lianke 閻連科. "Jingshen gongming yu yizhe de 'ziyou': Yan Lianke tan wenxue yu fanyi" 精神共鳴與譯者的「自由」——閻連科談文學與翻譯 [Spiritual resonance and the translator's "freedom": Yan Lianke on literature and translation]. *Waiguoyu* 外國語 [Journal of foreign languages] 37, no. 3 (May 2014): 18–26.

Hu Anjiang 胡安江 and Zhu Yishu 祝一舒. "Yijie dongji yu chanshi weidu: Shilun Yan Lianke zuopin fayi ji qi chanshi" 譯介動機與闡釋維度——試論閻連科作品法譯及其闡釋 [The motivation of translation and the dimension of interpretation: On the French translation and interpretation of Yan Lianke's Works]. *Xiaoshuo pinglun* 小說評論 [Fiction review], 2013, no. 5: 75–82.

Hukusima Ryouta 福嶋亮大. "Taikin to hikikae ni 'ichi-shi' kaku" 大金と引き換えに「市史」書く [Writing the "History of The City" in exchange for money]. *Nihon Keizai Shimbun*, 11 Dec. 2016. http://style.nikkei.com/article/DGXKZO10523970Q6A211C1MY6001 (last accessed 16 June 2021).

Ito Seiko 伊藤正幸. "Kenryoku o osorenu keta hazure no wanryoku" 權力を恐れぬケタ外れの腕力 [Out-of-order strength that is not afraid of power]. *Asahi Shimbun* 朝日新聞 [*Asahi News*], 30 Nov. 2014. http://book.asahi.com/reviews/reviewer/2014120100009.html (last accessed 16 June 2021).

Izumi Kyoka 泉京鹿, and Chen Yan 陳言. "Nihonjin hon'yaku-ka kara mita Chūgoku no gendai bungaku" 日本人翻譯家から見た中国の現代文学 [Contemporary Chinese literature as seen by Japanese translators]. Renmin wang Riyu ban 人民網日語版 [People.com in Japanese]. http://j.people.com.cn/n/2015/1203/c94473-8985500.html (last accessed 9 June 2021).

Kousu Yukiko 鴻巣友季子. "Hakkin sakka ga 'kamumi shugi' de eguri dasu Chūgoku no kōtōmukeina rifujin-sa" 発禁作家が「神実主義」でえぐりだす 中国の荒唐無稽な理不尽さ [A banned writer uses "mythorealism" to reveal the absurd truth about China's absurdity]. *Shukan shincho* 週刊新潮 [*Weekly News Magazine*], 22 Dec. 2016. https://www.bookbang.jp/review/article/523495 (last accessed 16 June 2021).

Kuwajima Michio 桑島道夫. "Yan Lianke no shōsetsu ni miru rinri (hon'yaku no 'rinri' o meguru sōgō-teki kenkyū" 閻連科の小説に見る倫理 (翻訳の〈倫理〉をめぐる総合的研究) [Ethics seen in Yan Lianke's novels (comprehensive research on the ethics of translation)]. *Hon'yaku no bunka/bunka no hon'yaku* 翻訳の文化/文化の翻訳 [Translating culture/cultural translation], 2015, no. 3: 83–89.

Liu Chengcai 劉成才. "Jingyou wenxue fanyi lijie dangdai Zhongguo: Riben wenxue fanyijia Quan Jinglu fangtan" 經由文學翻譯理解當代中國——日本文學翻譯家泉京鹿訪談 [Understanding contemporary China through literary translation: Interview with Japanese literary translator Izumi Kyoka]. *Zhongguo wenyi pinglun* 中國文藝評論 [China literature and art reviews], 2019, no. 8: 105–13.

——— and Fujii Shōzō. "Mo Yan, dushi wenxue yu Zhong Ri wenxue jiaoliu: Dongjing daxue Tenjing Xingsan jiaoshou fangtan" 莫言、都市文學與中日文學交流——東京大學藤井省三教授訪談 [Mo Yan, urban literature and Sino-Japanese literary exchange: Interview with Professor Fuji Shozo of the University of Tokyo]. *Shehui kexue luntan* 社會科學論壇 [Tribune of social sciences], 2020, no. 1: 173–83.

Lu Dongli 盧冬麗. "Fanyi shi xingfu er you manzu de guocheng: Yan Lianke Riyizhe Guchuan Yi fangtan lu" 翻譯是幸福而又滿足的過程——閻連科日譯者谷川毅訪談錄 [Translation is a happy and satisfying process: Interview with Tanikawa Tsuyoshi, Yan Lianke's Japanese translator]. *Ri Zhong fanyi wenhua jiaoyu yanjiu* 日中翻譯文化教育研究 [Research on Japanese-Chinese translation, culture, and education], 2020, no. 5: 84–91.

——— and Li Hong 李紅. "Yan Lianke *Shouhuo* zai Riben de quanshi yu shourong: Jiyu Riyiben *Yuraku* fuwenben de fenxi" 閻連科《受活》在日本的詮釋與受容——基於日譯本《愉樂》副文本的分析 [The interpretation and reception of Yan Lianke's *Lenin's Kisses* in Japan: Analysis based on the paratext of the Japanese translation]. *Wenyi zhengming* 文藝爭鳴 [Literary and artistic contentions], 2016, no. 3: 170–75.

——— and Zhong Rizhou 鍾日洲. "Geng Yusong, Yan Lianke wenxue fangyan Riyi zelue de kaocha: Jiyu yizhe xingwei piping de shijiao" 耿玉淞.閻連科文學方言日譯策略的考察——基於譯者行為批評的視角 [An examination of the Japanese translation strategy of Geng Yusong's and Yan Lianke's literary dialect: Based on the perspective of translator's behavior criticism]. *Ribenxue yanjiu* 日本學研究 [Japanese studies], 2020, no. 2: 69–79.

Ōe Kenzaburō 大江健三郎. *Teigishu* 定義集 [A collection of definitions]. Tokyo: Asahi Shimbun Publications, 2012.

Tanikawa Tsuyoshi 谷川毅. "Zhongguo dangdai wenxue zai Riben" 中國當代文學在日本 [Contemporary Chinese literature in Japan]. *Zhongguo tushu pinglun* 中國圖書評論 [China book review], 2011, no. 5: 93–98.

Tian Yuan 田原. "Yan Lianke *Shouhuo* Riwenban shangshi rexiao 4 ge yue nei zaiban 3 ci" 閻連科受活日文版上市熱銷 4 個月內再版 3 次 [The Japanese version of *Lenin's Kisses* has been selling well and has been reprinted three times within four months]. *Beijing qingnian bao* 北京青年報 [Beijing Youth Daily], 26 Mar. 2015.

Xie Tianzhen 謝天振. "Guonei fanyijie zai fanyi yanjiu he fanyi lilun renshi shang de wuqu" 國內翻譯界在翻譯研究和翻譯理論認識上的誤區 [Misunderstandings in translation research and translation theory in the domestic translation community]. *Zhongguo fanyi* 中國翻譯 [Chinese Translators Journal] 22, no. 4 (July 2001): 2–5.

———. "Zhongguo wenxue zou chuqu: Wenti yu shizhi" 中國文學走出去: 問題與實質 [Chinese literature going global: Problems and essence]. *Zhongguo bijiao wenxue* 中國比較文學 [Comparative Chinese literature], 2014, no. 1: 1–10.

Yan Lianke 閻連科. *Chichi o omou* 父を思う [Three brothers: Memories of my family]. Tokyo: Kawade Shobō Shinsha, 2016.

———. *Jinmin ni hōshi suru* 人民に奉仕する [Serve the people]. Tokyo: Bungeishunju, 2006.

———. *Kataki koto mizu nogotoshi* 硬きこと水のごとし [Hard like water]. Tokyo: Kawade Shobō Shinsha, 2017.

———. *Kuroi buta no ke, shiroi buta no ke: Jisen tanpen-shū* 黒い豚の毛、白い豚の毛: 自選短篇集 [Black pig bristle, white pig bristle]. Tokyo: Kawade Shobō Shinsha, 2019.

———. *Nengappi* 年月日 [The years, months, days]. Tokyo: Hakusuisha Publishing, 2016.

———. *Sakuretsushi* 炸裂志 [The explosion chronicles]. Tokyo: Kawade Shobō Shinsha, 2016.

———. *Teishō no yume* 丁莊の夢 [Dream of Ding Village]. Tokyo: Kawade Shobō Shinsha, 2007.

———. *Yuraku* 愉楽 [Lenin's Kisses]. Tokyo: Kawade Shobō Shinsha, 2015.

Zhang Jing 張競. "Chichi o omou - aru Chūgoku sakka no jisei to kaiso" 父を想う—ある中國作家の自省と回想 [Thinking of my father: A Chinese writer's self-reflection and recollection]. *Mainichi Shunbun* 每日新聞 [*Daily News*], 3 July 2016. http://mainichi.jp/articles/20160703/ddm/015/070/003000c (last accessed 16 June 2021).

———. "Meruhen-tekina butai ni shakai chin genshō o kasha" メルヘン的な舞臺に社會珍現象を活寫 [Lively capture social rare phenomena on a fairy tale stage]. *Mainichi Shinbun*, 11 Dec. 2016. http://mainichi.jp/articles/20161211/ddm/015/070/019000c (last accessed 16 June 2021).

———. "Seishin no sekihi ni nōmin seikatsu no jojishi kizamu" 精神の石碑に農民生活の敘事詩刻む [Engrave the epic of peasant life on the stone monument of the spirit]. *Mainichi Shimbun*, 3 July 2016. Mai Saku 每索 database (last accessed 22 July 2021).

Zhang Yuan 張元. "Zhongguo dangdai xiaoshuo zai Riben de yijie yu chuanbo" 中國當代小說在日本的譯介與傳播 [The translation and dissemination of contemporary Chinese fiction in Japan]. *Wenyi pinglun* 文藝評論 [Literary criticism], 2013, no. 5: 62–66.

30

THE TRANSLATION AND RECEPTION OF YAN LIANKE'S FICTION IN VIETNAM

*Van Hieu Do and Riccardo Moratto**

Introduction

The reception of a writer in a foreign country relies on the readers who select his or her works. This selection is not just a personal or subjective choice. Many agents are involved in this process: translators, publishers, and the national culture as a whole. Such a selection is linked to the cultural tradition of a given nation and to the cultural reality of its present society. As a consequence of this process, a writer may gain a firm literary foothold in another country, making his or her literature a part of that country's literature, thus exerting a considerable influence on it, while being subject to a special understanding and interpretation by the target readers. Yan Lianke is a case in point: his works are the most representative writings of contemporary Chinese literature in Vietnam. Since 2008, when Yan's first novel was translated into Vietnamese, six novels have been translated, published, and studied. It can be said that Yan has become one of the most popular Chinese writers in Vietnam.

Why do Vietnamese readers like to read Yan's novels? How are his novels received in Vietnam? How do Vietnamese readers analyze and understand his fiction? What is the general understanding of Vietnamese readers of contemporary Chinese literature? Sorting out these questions will clarify not only the appeal of Yan's literature to Vietnamese readers but also the characteristics of Vietnamese readers' reception of contemporary Chinese literature as a whole.

The origin and popularity of Yan's reception

The publication of Yan's novels in Vietnam is not a coincidence but the result of objective and subjective factors; it is the expression of the special cultural relationship between China and Vietnam; it is the understanding and demand of Vietnamese readers for Chinese literature. In particular, it is the result of the convergence of various factors, including the magic of Yan's

---

* An earlier version of this chapter first appeared in Chinese in Van Hieu Do, "Xuanze yu zhushi: Yan Lianke xiaoshuo zai Yuenan de jieshou zhuizong" 選擇與注釋: 閻連科小說在越南的接受追蹤 [Selection and Annotation: The Reception of Yan Lianke's Fiction in Vietnam], *Zuojia zazhi* 作家雜志 [Writer Magazine], 2020, no. 11: 39–45. Van Hieu Do is authorized to reuse and modify the paper. Several changes have been made in the current version.

novels themselves. It can be said that the emergence and reception of Yan's novels in Vietnam has its own peculiar features compared to other countries.

The long-standing relationship between the cultures of China and Vietnam has fostered a special receptive mentality with regard to Chinese literature among Vietnamese readers. Considering the influence of ancient Chinese Confucianism and Daoism on Vietnam, ancient Chinese prose, novels, and poems have been translated into Vietnamese in large numbers. In the early twentieth century, although the crossover and collision between Vietnamese and Western cultures were more obvious and increased considerably, the reception of Chinese literature by Vietnamese readers was never interrupted. During the Vietnam War (1945–75), although Vietnamese literature was more influenced by Soviet literature, Vietnamese readers still paid attention to modern Chinese writers, such as the works by Lu Xun 魯迅. In 1986, after the reform and opening up, Vietnam began to form a diversified situation of cultural exchange with the rest of the world. Apart from ancient Chinese literature, which continued to receive the attention of the Vietnamese literary research community, the works of contemporary writers such as Mo Yan 莫言, Jia Pingwa 賈平凹, Yu Hua 余華, Li Rui 李銳, Wang Anyi 王安憶, Tie Ning 鐵凝, and other Chinese writers began to appear on the Vietnamese literary scene. Later, with the advent of the new century, the reception of contemporary Chinese literature in Vietnam became more diverse and complex. At this time, Chinese romance novels, detective novels, and online literature became the most important pastime for Vietnamese readers. Coupled with the influx of Western literature, this led to a decline in the reception of Chinese "pure" or proper literature.

It was in this context that Yan wrote *Serve the People!* (*Wei renmin fuwu* 為人民服務) in 2004, which was then widely acclaimed and translated around the world. The Sinologist Vũ Công Hoan noticed the special nature of this novel and contacted the writer himself. He then quickly translated the book and, after several efforts, finally published it in the spring of 2008 with Thanh Niên Publishing House. This rekindled the interest of Vietnamese readers in Chinese literature. In 2010 Yan's *Book of Odes* (*Feng ya song* 風雅頌)[1] was also translated by Vũ and published by Dân Trí Publishing House. Thereafter, from 2014 to 2019, *Hard Like Water* (*Jianying ru shui* 堅硬如水), *How are You, Pan Jinlian* (*Jinlian, ni hao!* 金蓮, 你好!), *Dream of Ding Village* (*Dingzhuang meng* 丁莊夢), and *The Four Books* (*Si hu* 四書) were all published by Hội Nhà văn Việt Nam, the Publishing House of Vietnam Writers' Association.

Why was it only in 2008 that Yan's novel was translated into Vietnamese? Why was *Serve the People!* his first book to be translated, instead of his other previous widely influential works, such as *The Years, Months, Days* (*Nian yue ri* 年月日), *Streams of Time* (*Riguang liunian* 日光流年) or *Lenin's Kisses* (*Shouhuo* 受活)?

Being translated is not the same as being received and accepted, nor is being published the same as being read. Yan's proper reception in Vietnam began in 2014, six years after the publication of *Serve the People!*. The translation and publication of *Hard Like Water* in 2014 can be indicated as the book that helped Vietnamese readers really get to know Yan. The publication of *Serve the People!* and *Book of Odes* merely helped Yan open the door to his connection with Vietnamese readers. His novel *Hard Like Water* was the true bridge to the hearts of Vietnamese people. As soon as the novel was released in Vietnam, it received wide attention from Vietnamese readers and critics, and in the same year, it won the Hanoi Writers' Association Award for Translated Fiction, which has great influence in Vietnam. At this stage, Yan was also shortlisted for and won various literary awards around the world, and these worldwide literary recognitions accelerated the wide and rapid reception of *Hard Like Water*

---

1 Literally *Ballad, Hymn, Ode*, also translated as *The Book of Songs* or *The Odes of Songs*.

in Vietnam, and in turn led to the reprinting of *Serve the People!* and *Book of Odes*. This series of events eventually led to Yan's "reading fever." Then came *How are You, Pan Jinlian* and the shockingly successive publications of *Dream of Ding Village* and *The Four Books*, thus creating an even more general "Yan fever" in Vietnam. Due to a certain confusion in Vietnamese publishing, we cannot exactly count how many editions or copies of Yan's novels have been printed thus far, but the following scenario can illustrate the love and appreciation of Vietnamese readers for Yan's books, that is, over the last ten years or so, due to the influence of the internet and reading on cell phones, many publishers have claimed that if the publication of a Chinese author does not lead to a financial loss, it can already be considered a victory; in spite of this trend, Yan's works are constantly reprinted and at times even pirated. Moreover, many excellent contemporary Chinese literary works are difficult to publish in Vietnam due to the marketization of Vietnamese books and the cultural background. This causes the small book market to experience even more difficulties when publishing these excellent works in Vietnam without financial support from the Chinese government. Against this background, Yan's works not only do not need government funding, but there are publishing houses in Vietnam willing to contact Yan's agent in Europe to negotiate for a one-time purchase of five of his works, namely *Explosion Chronicles* (*Zhalie zhi* 炸裂志), *The Day the Sun Died* (*Rixi* 日熄), *The Years, Months, Days, Discovering Fiction* (*Faxian xiaoshuo* 發現小說) and *House No. 711* (*711 hao yuan: Beijing zuihou de zuihou jinian* 711 號園: 北京最後的最後紀念)[2]. In Vietnam the reception of Yan's works has also led to the continuation and widening of the reception of literary works by other contemporary Chinese writers.

Analysis of Yan's reception in Vietnam

Today, Yan has become one of the most important contemporary Chinese writers in Vietnam. A neighboring country of China, today's Vietnam presents many approximations and similarities with China, both in historical and societal terms. At times, the Chinese reality may feel quite similar to the reality of Vietnam to Vietnamese readers. Therefore, when Vietnamese people read the works of Chinese writers, they use them to think about the reality of what is happening in Vietnam. For example, after the reform and opening up of Vietnam, the desire, helplessness, and loss of human dignity vis-à-vis reality, money, and power were the biggest source of confusion and desperation for Vietnamese people.

Against this background, in 2016 Yan's *How are You, Pan Jinlian* was published in Vietnam. The novel is about a country woman named Jinlian who is sent as a "gift" (with the pretext of working as a nanny) to a powerful and wealthy family in the city in exchange for possible favors. There, Jinlian has a love affair almost identical to the one between Pan Jinlian and Ximen Qing 西門慶 in the famous Chinese novel *Jin Ping Mei* 金瓶梅.[3] This novel may be read as a modern version of the ancient story of Pan Jinlian. The translator Nguyễn Thị Minh Thương states in the preface:

> From a new perspective, Yan Lianke formed a new character in a new space. Yan removes Pan Jinlian from her hometown of Qinghe in the province of Hebei (in the

---

2 The title of the simplified Chinese version is *Beijing, zuihou de jinian* 北京, 最后的纪念.
3 Translated into English as *The Plum in the Golden Vase* or *The Golden Lotus*.

original classic Chinese book) and places Jinlian in his personal literary space of the Balou [耙耬] mountains in the market economy storm of China's reform and opening up, and in the complex relationships of modern social life. By choosing to write the story in a new way, the writer intentionally taps into the reader's deep impressions of Pan Jinlian's image in past literature, allowing for a literary dialogue between the past and modern times, and with the market environment. This dialogue with Chinese modernity and market economy is in fact a dialogue with Vietnamese modernity and its market economy after the reform and opening-up. The heartache and anguish of the characters in the story over the destruction of humanity by power and lust is also the heartache and anguish of contemporary Vietnamese reality.[4]

It is thus evident that the translator and the publisher are mindful that Vietnamese readers will look to contemporary Chinese literature in the context of Vietnamese reality. It is easy to understand why Vietnamese readers would like Yan's novels in general and *How are You, Pan Jinlian* in particular, a novel that did not have much impact in China. Even Yan was surprised and puzzled by the publisher's choice to translate this novel.

From this analysis, it is possible to understand why novels such as *Hard Like Water* and *Book of Odes* are revered by readers in Vietnam. *Hard Like Water* is about revolution and love during the years of the Cultural Revolution (1966–76) in China. Vietnam did not experience such a drastic decade; however, Vietnam also underwent a period of land reform, just like China. The madness of people during the Vietnamese land reform is very similar to the madness depicted in *Hard Like Water*. Such a novel feels like a historical portrait of Vietnam. *Book of Odes* is Yan's second book published in Vietnam, and it was well received by readers and literary critics alike. In "*Book of Odes*: A Series of Tragedies of Cowardly Intellectuals,"[5] the critic Nguyễn Anh claims that the ideological value of this novel profoundly reflects the "social tragedy of intellectuals." However, this tragedy is not the tragedy of everyday life. It is not the tragedy that intellectuals often faced in the society of that time, but that of an intellectual facing the tragedy of power, of scholarship, of family and marriage, and of the relationship among intellectuals. In a nutshell, it is also the tragedy of Vietnamese intellectuals. At the beginning of the twentieth century, Vietnamese writers spoke of the tragedy of Vietnamese intellectuals, emphasizing the shattering of noble dreams in everyday life. After the reform and opening up, this theme continued to receive attention in Vietnamese literature. To a certain extent this contributed to making *Book of Odes* a continuation and development of Vietnamese literary thinking about intellectuals. Vũ Công Hoan, the translator of this novel, points out: "this novel is extremely critical and playful: the writer criticizes and plays with the cowardice, powerlessness, lack of temperament, lack of stand, and fear of commitment of contemporary Chinese intellectuals, who are used to flattering their superiors and dominating their subordinates. The problem of Chinese

---

4 Yan Lianke and Nguyễn Thị Minh Thương, "Nàng Kim Liên ở Trấn Tây Môn" [How are you, Pan Jinlian], in *Nàng Kim Liên ở Trấn Tây Môn* (Hanoi: Hội Nhà Văn Việt Nam, 2018), 5–8. All citations were translated by the authors unless otherwise specified.

5 Nguyễn Anh, "*Phong Nhã Tụng*—Chuỗi Bi Kịch Một Trí Thức Hèn" [*Book of Odes*: A series of tragedies of cowardly intellectuals], *Vietnamplus*, 14 Apr. 2011, https://www.vietnamplus.vn/phong-nha-tung-chuoi-bi-kich-mot-tri-thuc-hen/87718.vnp (last accessed 31 May 2021).

intellectuals is reflected amidst Vietnamese intellectuals."[6] In a comparative study and analysis of the image of intellectuals in *Book of Odes* and that in Ma Văn Kháng's *Marriage Without License*,[7] Trần Thị Thư provides a detailed analysis of the fate of intellectuals in the new era in Yan's novel and points out the falsehood and hypocrisy as well as the structural changes of intellectuals in reality.[8] In her thesis, Trần discusses this transformation in detail: "With the change of economic mechanisms and the entry of consumer spirit into all parts of life, the structure of intellectuals in society has also changed. Before Vietnamese and Chinese societies were influenced by the mechanisms of market economy and consumerism, intellectuals of the humanistic type enjoyed a high social status. However, after economy became the center of society, the status of these intellectuals was replaced by the economic and scientific intellectuals. Yang Ke, the associate professor in *Book of Odes* could very well be an intellectual called Yang Ke living and working in Vietnam."[9] It can be said that the realist aspects in Yan's novels mirror the reality of Vietnamese society. This also shows that the themes of Yan's novels go beyond China and have a global significance. With such a universal dimension, Vietnamese readers and researchers are inclined to read "Vietnameseness" in Yan's literary works.

Yan's fiction and Vietnamese literature: Connection and originality

For any writer to take root in another language, his or her work must be related, connected, and complementary to the literature of the target language. His or her work must become a part of the literature of that country, give inspiration to the writing and bring new creativity to the national literature. As far as Chinese literature is concerned, Lu Xun's works have long been acclaimed because of the significance of his writing within the field of Vietnamese literature. The works of writers such as Mo Yan and Jia Pingwa were later appreciated by Vietnamese readers, again because their works could bring readers the joy of reading and the novelty of originality. The same can be said for Yan's novels nowadays. The reflections in his works are also what Vietnamese writers are reflecting upon. The appearance of his novels made this pondering on the part of Vietnamese writers and literary critics all the more precise and clearer. For example, the weakness and plight of intellectuals during the period of reform and opening up in *Book of Odes*, the fate and suffering of intellectuals in *The Four Books*, the complexity of human nature, the cruelty, and the glimmer of light which in spite of the darkness can be found in the dimension of love in *Dream of Ding Village*—these are all aspects that Vietnamese literature needs to reflect upon. Therefore, the publication of Yan's novels created a resonance within Vietnamese literature: there was a connection of content and ideas. But, more importantly, the originality of his novels was perceived as something new and shocking to Vietnamese readers and writers. In *Hard Like Water*, for example, Vietnamese readers are familiar with revolutionary language, but in Vietnamese literature authors rarely write novels in this crazy, grotesque revolutionary language, nor do they tell the story

---

6 Vũ Công Hoan, "*Phong Nhã Tụng*: tiểu thuyết phê phán sự ươn hèn của giới trí thức" [*Book of Odes*: A novel that criticizes the weakness of intellectuals], Trieuxuan.info, 27 Sep. 2009, https://trieuxuan.info/phong-nha-tung-tieu-thuyet-phe-phan-su-uon-hen-cua-gioi-tri-thuc (last accessed 31 May 2021).
7 The original title in Vietnamese is *Đám cưới không có giấy giá thú*.
8 See Trần Thị Thư, "Hình tượng người trí thức trong 'Mùa lá rụng trong vườn' của Ma Văn Kháng (Việt Nam) và Phong Nhã Tụng của Diêm Liên Khoa (Trung Quốc)" [A comparative study of the image of intellectuals in Yan Lianke's *Book of Odes* and Ma Văn Kháng's *Marriage Without License*] (Master thesis, Hanoi National University of Education, 2014).
9 Ibid.

of revolutionary love in such a satirical and whimsical way. In terms of language, *Hard Like Water* is a great river of revolutionary language that sweeps readers away and takes them in at once. Combined with a crazy love story, these literary creations appear strange and surprising to the reader. Vietnam has had a similar history, but why has no writer gone on to write such novels? The language in *Dream of Ding Village* is yet completely different from *Hard Like Water*, with short rhythmic sentences, somber and poetic, resembling a tearful poem. In *The Four Books* the language has a strong biblical resonance. The Bible is one of the most popular and widely read religious classics in the world, and almost everyone has read or been exposed to it or parts of it, but it seems that no writer in the world has retold his or her literary story in the language of the Bible, at least not in Vietnamese literature or foreign literature translated into Vietnamese, before the publication of *The Four Books*. Therefore, when *The Four Books* was published in Vietnam, readers, writers, and scholars were all surprised and curious, considering it on a par with *Dream of Ding Village* as Yan's extravagant *chef d' œuvres*.

Vietnamese readers feel the originality of Yan's novels not only because of the different linguistic styles of his novels, but also because of the presence of four different linguistic voices in the structure of a novel like *The Four Books*: "Each book in the *Four Books* is written in a different language style, namely, biblical style, monologue style, political report style, and philosophical narrative style. This is really a showcase and testing ground for a writer's language."[10] Such a discourse not only illustrates the shock and creativity that Yan's fictional language brought to Vietnam but also bespeaks the writer's uniqueness and creativity in the structure of his novels, starting from language, just like a "kaleidoscope," with each novel having a different method of storytelling. Vietnamese readers also discovered many elements of intertextuality in Yan's novels.[11] In the *Book of Odes* Yan relies on the narrative of the *Classic of Poetry* (*Shijing* 詩經), which is also a familiar classic in Vietnamese culture. *How are You, Pan Jinlian* is also a new experimentation with metafiction. In *Dream of Ding Village* people discovered the "perspective of the dead" and the use of intermittent dreams, whereas in *The Four Books* readers were surprised by its labyrinthine structure. Thereby, readers and scholars alike began to marvel at this inventiveness of his, like spectators amazed by the narration of a magician-novelist.

The third aspect is the absurdity and allegorical nature of Yan's stories. They are at once realistic and absurd: Yan defines this style "mythorealism." This style has exerted a great impact on Vietnamese literature, which is traditionally more focused on realism. Almost every one of Yan's fictional stories will have countless surreal plots and details. These events are magical, yet they feel extremely real, as if they could absolutely happen in real life. When reading Yan's novels, readers do not feel any falsehood within that critical, satirical, and exaggerated allegorical style. In *Hard Like Water* the protagonists spend a year digging a tunnel that links their rooms just to satisfy their sexual hunger; in *Dream of Ding Village* we are confronted with

---

10 Nguyễn Thị Tịnh Thy, "'Tứ thư' của Diêm Liên Khoa: Nhìn lại một thời 'Đại nhảy vọt' kinh hoàng" [Yan Lianke's *The Four Books*: Revisiting the horrible Great Leap Forward], *Báo Thanh Niên* [Youth Daily], 17 Apr. 2019, https://thanhnien.vn/van-hoa/tu-thu-cua-diem-lien-khoa-nhin-lai-mot-thoi-dai-nhay-vot-kinh-hoang-1072148.html (last accessed 31 May 2021).

11 The structure of this novel is an issue of great importance to Yan in his creative process. He once told the authors of this paper: "I already have a lot of stories in my mind, and I'll write them when I find a suitable structure." However, it is difficult to discover the more hidden structures, such as the intertextuality. For instance, one cannot truly appreciate *How are You, Pan Jinlian* without a previous knowledge of the Ming-dynasty novel *Jin Ping Mei*. Likewise, without any previous knowledge of Chinese classic literature, one cannot appreciate that the structure of *Book of Odes* is deeply influenced by the *Classic of Poetry*.

people reselling coffins at a higher price; in *The Four Books* human blood is used to water the wheat. Similar details may seem unbelievable and are indeed unusually shocking but without a sense of falsity. Readers may feel chilled at times and will even feel like having to put the book down in order to breathe before continuing to read. Once the book is set down, most readers would keep on feeling a sense of loss and bewilderment as if they did not know what is going on in their life. Nguyễn Thị Tịnh Thy claims: "*Dream of Ding Village* is written as an allegory about the destruction of people. Yan Lianke puts the main characters at the doorstep of death in order to let them fully reveal their dark nature."[12] She deems Yan the "descendant of Lu Xun's dark fables": "Yan Lianke tells this thrilling and tragic story from the perspective of an omniscient dead narrator, and the tone of his storytelling is slow, quiet, and suffocatingly cold. The space is filled with death, blood, rotten smell, sick people, dead bodies, and coffins. This way of writing makes the reader feel that the social reality in the novel pours heavy rain directly on the reader, feeling dark and attractive, fearful and desperate, as if the reader is also a crawling insect in this dark fable."[13]

The Four Books, Yan's most recent novel published in Vietnam, is a masterpiece, just like *Dream of Ding Village*. When the novel was published in Vietnam, readers were surprised not only by the language and structure but also by the great uneasiness caused by the "mythorealist" details. Đặng Lưu's research article is very much in line with Yan's commentary on "mythorealism" in terms of understanding the surreal story. Đặng argues: "Mythorealism is the confrontation with the invisible reality, the reality that is concealed by reality and the unoccuring reality."[14] Đặng also claims: "After reading *The Four Books*, a novel that transcends reality at every turn, I felt a sense of panic throughout my body. Is it possible that this kind of fact really happened in this world? Could it be that our kind once experienced such a horrible calamity? Have the most absurd facts, the darkest, the most real yet surreal atrocities really occurred in human society?"[15] Đặng Lương analyzes several root causes of such a feeling of transcending reality. First of all, *The Four Books* is full of fearful details. In a novel of more than 300 pages, there is no deep philosophical talk; the author seems to disappear completely and there are only factual recorded statements. Secondly, Yan's greatness lies not in depicting the tragic death but in depicting how the human body slowly loses its vitality, making people feel that the cells in their body are dying one after another. Finally, Đặng claims that: "This novel is filled with a mission to return to reality, yet it brims with surreal details. One can imagine what a talented writer it takes to write a novel as great as *The Four Books*."[16] In short, Vietnamese readers consider *Dream of Ding Village* and *The Four Books* great novels full of all kinds of cruelty, poetry, experimentation, and transcendence dealing with the permanent human nature and human destiny.

In April 2019, Yan, together with three Chinese professors, namely Wang Yao 王尧, Ji Jin 季进, and Guo Bingru 郭冰如, went to Vietnam to exchange literary views with local literary

---

12 Nguyễn Thị Tịnh Thy, "Nghẹt thở với Đinh Trang mộng" [Choking with *Dream of Ding Village*], *Vanviet*, 28 Mar. 2019, http://vanviet.info/tren-facebook/nghet-tho-voi-dinh-trang-mong/ (last accessed 31 May 2021).

13 Ibid.

14 Đặng Lưu, "Một cái nhìn minh triết về con người (Đọc Tứ thư của Diêm Liên Khoa)" ["A clear and philosophical view of people: Reading Yan Lianke's *The Four Books*], *Tạp chí Văn hoá Nghệ An* [Nghe An Culture Magazine], no. 400 (Nov. 2019): n.p., http://www.vanhoanghean.com.vn/component/k2/nhung/13535-mot-cai-nhin-minh-triet-ve-con-nguoi-doc-tu-thu-cua-diem-lien-khoa-i (last accessed 31 May 2021).

15 Ibid.

16 Ibid.

figures. They also met with Vietnamese writers, critics, university professors, and readers and introduced the development of contemporary Chinese literature as a whole. This encounter enabled readers to understand the transcendence, complexity, and absurdity of Yan's novels.

Yan's novels have many original artistic features, but the versatility of language, richness, and structure complexity, as well as the novels' absurd, transcendental experimentation with mythorealism, constitute the most prominent Vietnamese understanding of his literary creations. These key features are another fundamental reason for the positive reception of his novels in Vietnam.

Translating Yan Lianke into Vietnamese

Any great writer who wishes to resonate, influence, and take root in the cultural soil of another country and in a new language needs to rely on translation. Although the market, publishers, and literary agents of the target language are important agents in this process, at the end of the day it is ultimately the translator who really brings the fundamentals of literature, including the language, ideas, meanings, characters, stories, and subtle rhythms, to the new linguistic and cultural environment. Oftentimes it is the translation of a novel that determines its success, or lack thereof, in the target language and culture.

If we also consider the translation of his essays and speeches, it can be said that there are six Vietnamese scholars who have translated his works; however, only three have translated his novels. One is the Sinologist Vũ Công Hoan, a Vietnamese translator of the older generation. Vũ Công Hoan has translated a large number of Chinese works, including *Wreaths at the Foot of the Mountain* (*Gaoshan xia de huahuan* 高山下的花環) by Li Cunbao 李存葆, as well as numerous other works by Zhang Kangkang 張抗抗, Jia Pingwa, and Yu Hua, just to mention a few. Yan's *Book of Odes* and *Serve the People!* were also translated by him into Vietnamese. The second translator is Nguyễn Thị Minh Thương. She translated *Hard Like Water*, *How are You, Pan Jinlian*, and *Dream of Ding Village*. Currently, she is translating *Explosion Chronicles* and preparing to translate *The Day the Sun Died*, *The Years, Months, Days*, and *Discovering Fiction*. The third translator is Châu Hải Đường. He has translated numerous Chinese literary works, such as Lu Xun's *Tang and Song Tales* (*Tang Song chuanqi* 唐宋傳奇), Feng Menglong's 馮夢龍 *Records of the States in the Eastern Zhou Dynasty* (*Dong Zhou lieguo lianhuanhua* 東周列國連環畫), and Shen Fu's 沈復 *Six Records of a Floating Life* (*Fusheng liu ji* 浮生六記), among others. On the recommendation of Nguyễn, Châu translated Yan's *The Four Books*.

The reason why we dedicate this section to Yan's Vietnamese translations is that his influence in Europe and America and the promotion of his works have been made possible thanks to his agent and mainly relied on the success of his French translation. To a considerable extent, translations all over the world have followed or somehow been influenced by the English and the French versions. Yan also agrees that his success in French and English has driven him to be translated and published almost all over the world. It is not clear how his work was introduced into the French language and became successful in France, but what is certain is that his success in Vietnam is not due to his previous success in Europe and America. Yan's influence in Vietnam is due entirely to the combined force of the translators and the quality of his work, while his influence in Europe and America only served to fuel and further consolidate his success in Vietnam. In Asia, especially in Vietnam, the significance of the translator is often greater than that of the publisher and agent. The translator may then be both the translator as well as the agent and promoter of the writer, and this is exactly the main factor that led to Yan's success in Vietnam.

Many Chinese writers and readers think that Yan's influence in Vietnam is due to his book *Serve the People!*, but this is actually not the case. That particular book was just a fortuitous chance and the beginning of his journey into Vietnam. Vũ discovered this book in 2005 and proceeded to translate it, trying to find a publisher. After the publication of *Serve the People!* and *Book of Odes*, the publishing environment in Vietnam changed significantly. Indeed, in 2011 after the publication of *Book of Odes* Vũ started to translate *The Four Books*. As soon as Yan finished writing the book in Chinese, he immediately sent the electronic version of the manuscript to Vũ. However, after translating the book, he could not find any publishing house willing to publish the novel. The reason is that the same caution and restrictions on publishing books that are highly controversial in China have also started in Vietnam. In some cases, this caution is even more prudent than China's. This is also why his acclaimed *Lenin's Kisses* has not yet been translated and published in Vietnam. It can be said that the publication of Yan's novels in Vietnam has been cautious and interrupted since *Book of Odes*. Vũ also had to stop translating and promoting his literary figure. However, at this time, Yan's second translator appeared on the scene: Nguyễn Thị Minh Thương, who was pursuing her doctoral studies at Renmin University of China. Her trust in and familiarity with Chinese culture and literature led her to completely abandon considerations of the Vietnamese book market and select authors and works that she personally enjoyed reading.[17] *Hard Like Water* is a very unique novel in terms of language style. It calls for a meticulous and careful translation in the selection of words. After one year, Nguyễn completed her translation. Yet she could find no publishing house willing to publish the novel. In the end, the publishing house of the Vietnam Writers' Association boldly accepted the book. The main reason is that the editor in charge of the publishing house is also a writer and also has a specific understanding and love for literature. *Hard Like Water* was thus published and was unexpectedly loved by readers, opening up new horizons for Yan's successive publications and driving the reprinting and new translations of his early works.

Yan's three main Vietnamese translators are all excellent and accomplished translators in their own right. However, Yan's ultimate success in Vietnam is due to Nguyễn, who is not only a translator and researcher of Chinese literature but also a writer of poetry; this allows her to convey the rhythm and nuances of the Chinese language in a profound way. The language of *Dream of Ding Village* was described in Vietnam as a "tearful prose poetry,"[18] and that of *Hard Like Water* as a "revolutionary stream."[19] A similar appreciation of the language of translation is due to the translator's creative experience and literary training. Therefore, it can be said that apart from the literary value of his works, Yan's successful reception in Vietnam is largely due to the translator's efforts. This, according to Yan himself, is largely true of his situation in South Korea and Mongolia as well.

An overview of the reviews of Yan's novels in Vietnam

Book of Odes

This is Yan's second book published in Vietnam and was well received by Vietnamese readers and literary critics upon its publication. In "*Book of Odes: A Series of Tragedies of Cowardly Intellectuals*,"[20] the critic Nguyễn Anh claims that the ideological value of this novel

---

17 Minh Thương Nguyễn Thị, personal communication, 2021.
18 Ibid.
19 Ibid.
20 Nguyễn, "*Phong nhã tụng.*"

profoundly reflects the "social tragedy of intellectuals." Nguyễn further argues: "It is not only a tragedy of intellectuals in Chinese society, but a common tragedy of intellectuals beyond the borders of China."[21] In a comparative study and analysis of the image of intellectuals in *Book of Odes* and that in Ma Văn Kháng's *Marriage Without License*,[22] Trần Thị Thư suggests that *Book of Odes* may be considered as part of the Vietnamese intellectual literature.[23] In her thesis, she pays attention to the narrative art of the two works. Her study of the three narrative spaces of *Book of Odes* has greatly inspired Vietnamese literature. The three spaces are: rural space, a past picture of peasants and countryside including decrepit houses and various survival techniques; urban space, including the sleeping room of Yang Ke and his wife at Qingyan University (these two are all in the present tense, with each scene deepening the tragedy of the characters); the third is the ancient time and sky referred to by the ancient city in the *Classic of Poetry* under the Balou Mountains. This ancient city carries more than two thousand years of forgotten memories and is actually an illusory space.

Hard Like Water

This is Yan's third novel translated into Vietnamese. It has received wide attention from Vietnamese readers and won the Literary Translation Award of the Hanoi Writers' Association in 2015. The translator Nguyễn Thị Minh Thương translated it and worked tirelessly to find a publisher, purely because of her love for Yan's novels. Vietnamese readers were amazed and shocked after reading this book. The critic Nguyễn Thị Thúy Hạnh comments: "This novel is a poignant reflection on the image and history of the soldier. Subverting the solemnity, nobility and sanctity of the peaceful warrior in history, it provides a new model for historical thinking in the Chinese literature of the new era."[24] *Hard Like Water* was also acclaimed by many liberal arts undergraduates and graduate students in Vietnam, who focused on various aspects of love, eroticism, characterization, and language in the novel. From the perspective of sexology and cultural semiotics, Lương Thị Bích explains the complex relationship and entanglement of desire and ontology, desire and love, desire and revolution, and language and body in this novel.[25]

How are You, Pan Jinlian

The publication of this novel can be said to be a way for the publisher to gauge the interest of Vietnamese readers. The translator Nguyễn Thị Minh Thương argues: "Yan Lianke intentionally opens up readers' deep impressions of Pan Jinlian in classical literature, forming a kind of cross-talk between old and new genres, old and new stories, and old and new characters, thus showing the pain of reality destroying humanity and awakening Vietnamese readers'

---

21 Ibid.
22 The original title in Vietnamese is *Đám cưới không có giấy giá thú*.
23 See Trần, "Hình tượng người trí thức trong 'Mùa lá rụng trong vườn' của Ma Văn Kháng (Việt Nam) và *Phong Nhã Tụng* của Diêm Liên Khoa (Trung Quốc)," n.p.
24 Nguyễn Thị Thúy Hạnh, "Diêm Liên Khoa—'Người đến muộn' tiên phong" [Yan Lianke: A pioneer writer who arrived late], *Văn Việt*, 12 Dec. 2017, http://vanviet.info/nghien-cuu-phe-binh/dim-lin-khoa-nguoi-den-muon-tin-phong/ (last accessed 31 May 2021).
25 See Lương Thị Bích, "Vấn đề tính dục trong tiểu thuyết 'Kiên ngạnh như thủy' của Diêm Liên Khoa" [The problem of sexuality in Yan Lianke's *Hard Like Water*] (Master's thesis, Ha Noi National University of Education, 2015).

memories of the classical Chinese novel *Jin Ping Mei*."[26] Trần Lê Hoa Tranh comments: "Yan Lianke's most complex and difficult allegory in this mundane yet extraordinary novel is how one can maintain one's truth in a reality full of pitfalls."[27] Thụy Anh points out: "The tragedy in *How are You, Pan Jinlian* does not lie in love, lust or instinctive desire. This work is about the deterioration of man, rotting like an old and unharvested wheat [...] It is an enchantingly beautiful novel, especially the vivid natural scenery in the four seasons of the Balou Mountains, which is simply poignantly beautiful."[28] Trần Khanh observes: "The form that dominates this novel is a form of rewriting. Shi Nai'an's [施耐庵] *Water Margin* [*Shuihu zhuan* 水滸傳], Lanling Xiaoxiao Sheng's [蘭陵笑笑生] *Jin Ping Mei*, and the fate of the characters Pan Jinlian, Wu Dalang [武大郎], Wu Erlang [武二郎] have all been rewritten and renarrated."[29]

Dream of Ding Village

As previously mentioned, the publication of *Hard Like Water* opened a new path for Yan's reception in Vietnam. The translation of *Dream of Ding Village* made him the heir of Lu Xun (in terms of care for the people) in the eyes of Vietnamese readers. There are numerous studies and discussions about the content of this novel in Vietnam. As far as the form of the novel is concerned, Nguyễn Đình Minh Khuê argues:

> Yan Lianke inherited and brought into play the writing tradition of dreams in Chinese literature [...]. In traditional Chinese literature, dreams have an allegorical tendency toward extinction, and Yan Lianke has inherited and developed this tendency [...]. The *Dream of the Red Chamber* [*Hong lou meng* 紅樓夢] builds a romantic atmosphere based on a vibrant dream, which is eventually destroyed by the author. In Yan Lianke it is the opposite: he starts off on the side of a waking dream disaster, full of death and destruction, but in the development of the story, one reads novelty, freshness and the intense vitality of people who are still alive. And in the end, he allows mankind to begin to regenerate. This may be perceived as an inversion of the parable of the dream in *Dream of the Red Chamber*.[30]

---

26 Nguyễn Thị Minh Thương, "Nàng Kim Liên ở Trấn Tây Môn," 3.
27 Trần Lê Hoa Tranh, "Soi chiếu xã hội qua Nàng Kim Liên ở trấn Tây Môn" [Reflecting on society through Jinlian in Ximen Town], *Báo Người Lao Động* [Nguoi Lao Dong News], 7 Aug. 2019, https://nld.com.vn/van-nghe/soi-chieu-xa-hoi-qua-nang-kim-lien-o-tran-tay-mon-20180806210043609.htm (last accessed 31 May 2021).
28 Thụy Anh, "Sắc dục và quyền lực trong câu chuyện nàng Kim Liên thời mới" [Jinlian, Lust and Power in the story of the new Jinlian], *Zingnews*, 2 July 2018, https://zingnews.vn/sac-duc-va-quyen-luc-trong-cau-chuyen-nang-kim-lien-thoi-moi-post856562.html (last accessed 31 May 2021).
29 Trần Khanh, "Từ nàng Kim Liên, nghĩ về một con đường của viết" [Thinking of a type of writing from Jinlian], *Báo Đại Đoàn Kết* [Dai Doan Ket News], 17 July 2019, http://daidoanket.vn/tu-nang-kim-lien-nghi-ve-mot-con-duong-cua-viet-442240.html (last accessed 31 May 2021).
30 Nguyễn Đình Minh Khuê, "Đọc Đinh Trang mộng của Diêm Liên Khoa, Minh Thương dịch, Tao Đàn & NXB. Hội nhà văn, 2019" [Dreaming and living: Reading Yan Lianke's *Dream of Ding Village* translated by Minh Thương, Tao Đàn & Translators' Association Publishing House, 2019], Department of Humanities and Social Sciences, Language and Literature Network, National University of Ho Chi Minh City, 25 Sep. 2019, http://www.khoavanhoc-ngonngu.edu.vn/nghien-cuu/luan-van-cua-ncs-hvch-sv/7489-m%E1%BB%99ng-m%E1%BB%8B-v%C3%A0-t%C3%ACnh-th%E1%BA%BF-c%E1%BB%A7a-s%E1%BB%B1-l%C3%A0m-ng%C6%B0%E1%BB%9Di.html (last accessed 31 May 2021).

The Four Books

This is Yan's latest publication in Vietnam. We will not engage in an in-depth discussion of the novel's story and its aspects related to Chinese history. According to the introduction on an online bookstore, "*The Four Books* is not only about the good nature of human beings, but also about their bad and evil intrinsic aspects. The writing refers to mythology and the Bible and brims with absurd and surreal details, creating a vast and dazzling space, in which reigns a chaos of good and evil."[31] Nguyễn Thị Tịnh Thy argues: "*The Four Books* is a fierce and painful reflection on history through the broad themes of history, life, and humanity. Yan also brilliantly inherits the motif of cannibalism created by Lu Xun."[32] Nguyễn Thị Tịnh Thy also pays special attention to the novel's language, structure, and cross-textuality while at the same time focusing on analyzing its mythical and allegorical nature. *The Four Books* is an allegorical book in which multiple stories intersect: the allegories of the Bible, the myth of Sisyphus, and all the characters representing different historical allegories.

Selected reviews

Among some comprehensive studies on Yan's novels, the following are worthy of attention: first of all, the research project (no. T.18-XH-02)) "Study on the Grotesque of Yan Lianke's Novels" by the literary critic Nguyễn Thị Tịnh Thy from Huế University. This research project takes Yan's published and partially unpublished works in Vietnam as the scope of research and studies various creations in Yan's novels focusing on his "mythorealism." In another article, Nguyễn Thị Tịnh Thy focuses on various intertextual genres of Yan's fiction.[33] The critic Trần Lê Hoa Tranh claims: "Yan Lianke is a truly realistic writer, a writer of the common people, introducing all aspects of the Chinese social reality of the underclass into his novels."[34] In 2021, Nguyễn Thị Tịnh Thy published a monograph titled *Dare to Look Back: Criticizing Contemporary Chinese Fiction*.[35] The book focuses on five contemporary Chinese writers, namely Li Rui, Mo Yan, Gao Xingjian 高行健, Yu Hua, and Yan Lianke, as the author considers them to be representative of the achievements of contemporary Chinese literature. It devotes approximately 40,000 words to analyzing Yan's novels published in Vietnam, arguing that he is a master of the grotesque, a writer with a mission. Nguyễn Thị Tịnh Thy argues that although Yan has repeatedly claimed that banned books are not necessarily good books and hopes that people will not introduce him as a writer with the greatest number of banned books, it seems that the research and media communities will not heed his wishes. Because for them, Yan's banned books are good books, tantamount to being strong and persistent, fierce, creatively independent, despite everything and "willing to give it all up, even the opportunity to

---

31 https://sachtaodan.vn/tu-thu (last accessed 31 May 2021).
32 Tịnh Thy Nguyễn Thị, "Tứ thư' của *Diêm Liên Khoa*."
33 Tịnh Thy Nguyễn Thị, "Liên Văn Bản Trong Tiểu Thuyết Của Diêm Liên Khoa" [Intertextuality in Yan Lianke's Novels], *Trường Đại Học Sư Phạm Tp Hồ Chí Minh Tạp Chí Khoa Học* [Ho Chi Minh City University of Education Journal of Science] 15, no. 8 (2018): 69–70.
34 Trần Lê Hoa Tranh, "Diêm Liên Khoa—Nhà văn hiện thực sâu sắc" [Yan Lianke: An outstanding writer of realism], *Tạp chí Tài hoa trẻ Báo Giáo dục và Thời đại* [Young Talent Magazine Education and Times Newspaper], no. 1023 (2019): 12–14.
35 Tịnh Thy Nguyễn Thị, *Dám Ngoái Đầu Nhìn Lại—Phê Bình Tiểu Thuyết Trung Quốc Đương Đại* [Dare to look back: Criticizing contemporary Chinese fiction] (Hanoi: Vietnam Writers' Association Publishing House, 2021).

publish his own works."³⁶ The success of his intellectual and artistic approach, rather than being taboo, has made Yan one of the few Chinese writers who have gained worldwide recognition without relying on the "go global" strategy promoted by the Chinese government.³⁷

The most systematic study of Yan's novels in Vietnam so far was conducted by Nguyễn Thị Thúy Hạnh. She suggests: "Yan Lianke's narrative is in line with Hayden White's view of history as narrative and Michel Foucault's view of sex as historical artifice."³⁸ In particular, she successfully defended her doctoral dissertation in December 2019, titled "The Narrative Art of Yan Lianke's Novels" (Vietnam Academy of Social Sciences, VASS). Her dissertation consists of four chapters. The first focuses on an overview of Yan's research in Chinese and Western literary studies. The second is "Yan Lianke's Mythorealism: From Conception to Creative Practice," which introduces Yan's views on mythorealism in detail and points out the development process of the writer from "reality" to "mythorealism." The third is "Yan's Narrative Techniques," which focuses on the following issues: (1) narrative allegorization; (2) narrative statement perspective; (3) narrative structure; (4) transcendentalism and narrative spacing. The fourth chapter is titled "Narrative Discourse and the Language of Fiction," which focuses on the dual discourse in the language of Yan's novels, the language of the post-revolutionary era, the anti-utopian discourse as a narrative feature, the language of parody, and the literary creation with dialects. Nguyễn Thị Thúy Hạnh's supervisor Nguyễn Thị Mai Chanh further comments: "Yan Lianke, Mo Yan and Gao Xingjian have the same high status in the history of Chinese literature. They all relentlessly pursue the innovation of fiction and among them Yan Lianke's mythorealism is the most unique reflection of China's deepest reality."³⁹

Today, Yan is not only one of the most important contemporary Chinese writers in Vietnam but also an important topic of research in Vietnamese academia. The publication of each of his novels, or even an article in the Vietnamese media, always arouses great interest among readers and the literary community.

Acknowledgements

Van Hieu Do would like to thank the Science Foundation Project "Contemporary Foreign Literary Theory and Innovation of Current Vietnamese Literary Theories" supported by the Vietnamese Ministry of Education (Project no. B2019—SPH-04) and a special thanks to Prof. Dr. Riccardo Moratto for his personal invitation to participate in such a landmark volume.

---

36 Yan Lianke, "*Si shu* shi zui manyi de zuopin, muqian zhiyou Taiwan ban" 《四書》是最滿意的作品 目前只有台灣版 [*The Four Books* is so far the work I am most satisfied with; currently only the Taiwanese edition is available], Tengxun wang 騰訊網, 3 Apr. 2014, https://cul.qq.com/a/20140403/017281.htm (last accessed 31 May 2021).

37 Nguyễn Thị Tịnh Thy, *Dám Ngoái Đầu Nhìn Lại - Phê Bình Tiểu Thuyết Trung Quốc Đương Đại*, 372.

38 Thúy Hạnh Nguyễn Thị, "Diêm Liên Khoa – "Người đến muộn" tiên phong." See also Nguyễn Thị Thúy Hạnh, "Diêm Liên Khoa: Từ quan niệm đến sự thực hành chủ nghĩa thần thực [Yan Lianke's mythorealism – From concept to creative practice], *Tạp chí Sông Hương* [Journal of Song Huong], no. 365 (August 21, 2019), http://tapchisonghuong.com.vn/tin-tuc/p0/c7/n28165/Diem-Lien-Khoa-Tu-quan-niem-den-su-thuc-hanh-chu-nghia-than-thuc.html (last accessed 31 May 2021).

39 Nguyễn Thị Mai Chanh, "Ba tác gia lớn của văn học đương đại Trung Quốc thời kì sau cải cách mở cửa" [Three major writers of contemporary Chinese literature after the Reform and Opening Up], *Tạp chí Khoa học trường Đại học Sư phạm Hà Nội* [Journal of Hanoi National University of Education] 64, no. 8 (2019): 3–11.

Bibliography

Đặng Lưu. "Một cái nhìn minh triết về con người (Đọc Tứ thư của Diêm Liên Khoa)" [A clear and philosophical view of people: Reading Yan Lianke's The Four Books]. Tạp chí Văn hoá Nghệ An [Nghe An Culture Magazine] 400 (Nov. 2019): n.p. http://www.vanhoanghean.com.vn/component/k2/nhung/13535-mot-cai-nhin-minh-triet-ve-con-nguoi-doc-tu-thu-cua-diem-lien-khoa-i (last accessed 31 May 2021).

Lương Thị Bích. "Vấn đề tính dục trong tiểu thuyết 'Kiên ngạnh như thủy' của Diêm Liên Khoa" [The problem of sexuality in Yan Lianke's Hard Like Water]. Master's thesis, Ha Noi National University of Education, 2015.

Nguyễn Anh. "*Phong Nhã Tụng*—Chuỗi Bi Kịch Một Trí Thức Hèn" [Book of Odes: A series of tragedies of cowardly intellectuals]. *Vietnamplus*, 14 Apr. 2011. https://www.vietnamplus.vn/phong-nha-tung-chuoi-bi-kich-mot-tri-thuc-hen/87718.vnp (last accessed 31 May 2021).

Nguyễn Đình Minh Khuê. "Đọc Đinh Trang mộng của Diêm Liên Khoa, Minh Thương dịch, Tao Đàn & NXB. Hội nhà văn, 2019" [Dreaming and living: Reading Yan Lianke's Dream of Ding Village translated by Minh Thương, Tao Đàn & Translators' Association Publishing House, 2019]. Department of Humanities and Social Sciences Language and Literature Network, National University of Ho Chi Minh City, 25 Sep. 2019. http://www.khoavanhoc-ngonngu.edu.vn/nghien-cuu/luan-van-cua-ncs-hvch-sv/7489-m%E1%BB%99ng-m%E1%BB%8B-v%C3%A0-t%C3%ACnh-th%E1%BA%BF-c%E1%BB%A7a-s%E1%BB%B1-l%C3%A0m-ng%C6%B0%E1%BB%9Di.html (last accessed 31 May 2021).

Nguyễn Thị Hương. "Giải mã Kiên ngạnh như thuỷ" [Decoding Yan Lianke's Hard Like Water]. Master's thesis, Hanoi National University of Education, 2015.

Nguyễn Thị Mai Chanh. "Ba tác gia lớn của văn học đương đại Trung Quốc thời kì sau cải cách mở cửa" [Three major writers of contemporary Chinese literature after the reform and opening up]. Tạp chí Khoa học trường Đại học Sư phạm Hà Nội [Journal of Hanoi National University of Education] 64, no. 8 (2019): 3–11.

Nguyễn Thị Minh Thương and Yan Lianke. Preface to Lời Giới Thiệu. In Nàng Kim Liên ở Trấn Tây Môn [How are you, Pan Jinlian], 5–8. Hanoi: Writers' Association Publishing House, 2018.

Nguyễn Thị Thúy Hạnh. "Diêm Liên Khoa—'Người đến muộn' tiên phong" [Yan Lianke: A pioneer writer who arrived late]. Văn Việt, 12 Dec. 2017. http://vanviet.info/nghien-cuu-phe-binh/dim-lin-khoa-nguoi-den-muon-tin-phong/ (last accessed 31 May 2021).

———. "Diêm Liên Khoa: Từ quan niệm đến sự thực hành chủ nghĩa thần thực" [Yan Lianke's mythorealism: From concept to creative practice]. Tạp chí Sông Hương [Journal of Song Huong] 365 (21 Aug. 2019). http://tapchisonghuong.com.vn/tin-tuc/p0/c7/n28165/Diem-Lien-Khoa-Tu-quan-niem-den-su-thuc-hanh-chu-nghia-than-thuc.html (last accessed 1 June 2021).

Nguyễn Thị Tịnh Thy. "Nghẹt thở với Đinh Trang mộng" [Choking with Dream of Ding Village]. Vanviet. http://vanviet.info/tren-facebook/nghet-tho-voi-dinh-trang-mong/ (last accessed 31 May 2021).

———. Dám Ngoái Đầu Nhìn Lại - Phê Bình Tiểu Thuyết Trung Quốc Đương Đại [Dare to look back: Criticizing contemporary Chinese fiction]. Hanoi: Vietnam Writers' Association Publishing House, 2021.

———. "Liên Văn Bản Trong Tiểu Thuyết Của Diêm Liên Khoa" [Intertextuality in Yan Lianke's novels], Trường Đại Học Sư Phạm Tp Hồ Chí Minh Tạp Chí Khoa Học [Ho Chi Minh City University of Education Journal of Science] 15, no. 8 (2018): 60–70.

———. "'Tứ thư' của Diêm Liên Khoa: Nhìn lại một thời 'Đại nhảy vọt' kinh hoàng" [Yan Lianke's The Four Books: Revisiting the horrible Great Leap Forward]. Báo Thanh Niên [Youth Daily], 17 Apr. 2019. https://thanhnien.vn/van-hoa/tu-thu-cua-diem-lien-khoa-nhin-lai-mot-thoi-dai-nhay-vot-kinh-hoang-1072148.html (last accessed 31 May 2021).

Thụy Anh. "Sắc dục và quyền lực trong câu chuyện nàng Kim Liên thời mới" [Jinlian, Lust and Power in the story of the new Jinlian]. Zingnews, 2 July 2018. https://zingnews.vn/sac-duc-va-quyen-luc-trong-cau-chuyen-nang-kim-lien-thoi-moi-post856562.html (last accessed 31 May 2021).

Trần Khanh. "Từ nàng Kim Liên, nghĩ về một con đường của viết" [Thinking of a type of writing from Jinlian]. Báo Đại Đoàn Kết [Dai Doan Ket News], 17 July 2019. http://daidoanket.vn/tu-nang-kim-lien-nghi-ve-mot-con-duong-cua-viet-442240.html (last accessed 31 May 2021).

Trần Lê Hoa Tranh. "Soi chiếu xã hội qua Nàng Kim Liên ở trấn Tây Môn" [Reflecting on society through Jinlian in Ximen Town]. *Báo Người Lao Động* [Nguoi Lao Dong News], 7 Aug. 2019. https://nld.com.vn/van-nghe/soi-chieu-xa-hoi-qua-nang-kim-lien-o-tran-tay-mon-20180806210043609.htm (last accessed 31 May 2021).

———. "Diêm Liên Khoa—Nhà văn hiện thực sâu sắc" [Yan Lianke: An outstanding writer of realism]. *Tạp chí Tài hoa trẻ Báo Giáo dục và Thời đại* [Young Talent Magazine Education and Times News], no. 1023 (2019): 12–14.

Trần Thị Thư. "Hình tượng người trí thức trong 'Mùa lá rụng trong vườn' của Ma Văn Kháng (Việt Nam) và Phong Nhã Tụng của Diêm Liên Khoa (Trung Quốc)" [A comparative study of the image of intellectuals in Yan Lianke's *Book of Odes* and Ma Văn Kháng's *Marriage Without License*]. Master's thesis, Hanoi National University of Education, 2014.

Vũ Công Hoan. "*Phong Nhã Tụng*: tiểu thuyết phê phán sự ươn hèn của giới trí thức" [*Book of Odes*: A novel that criticizes the weakness of intellectuals]. Trieuxuan.info, 27 Sep. 2009. https://trieuxuan.info/phong-nha-tung-tieu-thuyet-phe-phan-su-uon-hen-cua-gioi-tri-thuc (last accessed 31 May 2021).

Yan Lianke. "*Si shu* shi zui manyi de zuopin, muqian zhiyou Taiwan ban" 《四書》是最滿意的作品 目前只有台灣版 [*The Four Book* is so far the work I am most satisfied with; currently only the Taiwanese edition is available]. Tengxun wang, 3 Apr. 2014. https://cul.qq.com/a/20140403/017281.htm (last accessed 31 May 2021).

31
THE RECEPTION AND SIGNIFICANCE OF YAN LIANKE'S WORKS IN TAIWAN[1]

Riccardo Moratto and Di-kai Chao

Introduction

After 1949, the literature of Taiwan and that of the Chinese mainland have taken on different characteristics. The latter saw the development of "revolutionary" (*geming* 革命) literature, "scar" (*shanghen* 傷痕) literature, "root-seeking" (*xungen* 尋根) literature, and "nativist" (*xiangtu* 鄉土) literature, while Taiwan saw the rise of anti-communist (*fangong* 反共) and modernist (*xiandai zhuyi* 現代主義) literature, as well as the "debates on nativist literature" (*xiangtu wenxue lunzhan* 鄉土文學論戰) and post-modernist literature under the martial law of the KMT (Kuomintang 國民黨). Under the circumstances that the two sides of the Taiwan Strait have been isolated and cut off from each other for nearly 40 years, great differences in ideology, social systems, and even literary and aesthetic tastes are to be found between the two sides. Nevertheless, Taiwan gradually began to introduce mainland Chinese writers in the 1980s. At that time, Chen Yu-hang 陳雨航, who was then the publisher of Yuanliu Press (Yuanliu chubanshe 遠流出版社), started to introduce some mainland writers, such as Yu Hua 余華 and Mo Yan 莫言.[2] After Chen founded Rye Field Publishing (Maitian

---

1 An earlier version of this chapter first appeared in Chinese in Riccardo Moratto and Di-kai Chao, "Yan Lianke zuopin zai Taiwan de jieshou jiqi yiyi" 閻連科作品在臺灣的接受及其意義 [The Reception of Yan Lianke's Works in Taiwan and Its Significance], *Yanshan daxue xuebao (zhexue shehui kexue ban)* 燕山大學學報 (哲學社會科學版) [Journal of Yanshan University (Philosophy and Social Science Edition)] 22, no. 6 (November 2021): 36–45. A few minor changes have been made in the current version.

2 See the comments made by Hu Jin-lun 胡金倫, then editor-in-chief of Rye Field Publishing (Maitian chubanshe 麥田出版社), in 2007 on Maitian's introduction of mainland Chinese writers. When talking about Chen Yu-hang, Hu said: "He should be considered as the first person who introduced mainland writers to Taiwan" (*yinggai suan shi zui zao ba dalu zuojia yinjin Taiwan de ren* 應該算是最早把大陸作家引進台灣的人). See Sha Maomao 沙貓貓, ed., "Shuyou hui jilu: Wenxue zhubian tan Yan Lianke xinzuo *Shouhuo*" 書友會記錄: 文學主編談閻連科新作《受活》 [Reader's club minutes: Literary editors talk about Yan Lianke's new book *Lenin's Kisses*], Xiaoxiao shufang 小小書房 [Small life bookstore], 28 Jan. 2007, https://smallbooks.com.tw/2007/01/28/%E6%9B%B8%E5%8F%8B%E6%9C%83%E7%B4%80%E9%8C%84%EF%BC%9A%E6%96%87%E5%AD%B8%E4%B8%BB%E7%B7%A8%E8%AB%87%E9%96%BB%E9%80%A3%E7%A7%91%E6%96%B0E4%BD%9C%E3%80%8A%E5%8F%97%E6%B4%BB%E3%80%8B/ (last accessed 30 Aug. 2021).

chubanshe 麥田出版社, hereinafter referred to as Maitian), he continued to publish Chinese novels that were not limited to Taiwanese authors. One of the most important book series published by Maitian and edited by David Der-wei Wang 王德威 is the Contemporary Fiction Writers (*dangdai xiaoshuojia* 當代小說家) series. Under the academic guidance and influence of Wang, Maitian has also become one of the most important publishers for the introduction of Chinese literature not limited to Taiwanese authors. In addition to Maitian, in 1986, New Land Literature Press (Taipei xindi wenxue chubanshe 新地文學出版社) published the Contemporary Mainland Chinese Writers Series (*dangdai Zhongguo dalu zuojia congkan* 當代中國大陸作家叢刊), which actively introduced Chinese writers onto the Taiwanese literary scene. In 1989, Linbai 林白 Press published a series chief-edited by Bo Yang 柏楊, Literature by Mainland Chinese Writers (*Zhongguo dalu zuojia wenxue daxi* 中國大陸作家文學大系). This series also focused on works by writers of the "rightist" and "educated youth" (*zhiqing* 知青) generation.[3] However, due to the sensitivity of cross-strait politics, the reception of mainland Chinese writers in Taiwan's literary scene inevitably involves connotations of political and social changes.

Harold Bloom's observations on the production of classics can provide interesting insights for this study. Bloom argues: "Where they have become canonical, they have survived an immense struggle in social relations."[4] The social relations are reflected from aesthetic value emanating from "the struggle between texts: in the reader, in language, in the classroom, in arguments within a society."[5] In fact, the process of literature reception involves the connotation and evolution of the "horizon of expectation"[6] of the receiving place. This vision is strongly constrained by various local cultural, social, and historical factors as well as by readers' tastes. Therefore, when it comes to the reception of mainland Chinese writers, this issue also involves the construction and evolution of Taiwan's own cultural ideology.

Bloom's argument is directed at those Western texts that have been recognized as classics. However, the significance of Yan Lianke's 閻連科 textual creation and whether it has become a classic is yet to be ascertained. As Yan's creative path is ongoing, the meaning of the texts he has completed in the past continues to be interpreted in different ways as the needs of the times dictate. However, Bloom's perspective on the classics can also provide some insights into the circulation and reception of Yan's texts around the world. Yan's texts have been translated and received in Scandinavia, Eastern and Western Europe, the United States, Japan, and Vietnam, and have also been recognized by literary award mechanisms (including the Kafka Prize in Europe and the Newman Prize for Chinese Literature in the United States). Even this essay and this whole volume are involved in the process of classicizing Yan's textual creation. It cannot be denied that the cross-domain circulation of Yan's texts and the attention it has received from numerous places are phenomena worthy of detailed examination.

---

3 Huang Wen-Chien 黃文倩, "Mo Yan zai Taiwan de jieshou shi ji qi yiyi" 莫言在臺灣的接受史及其意義 [Acceptance history and meaning in Taiwan of the 2012 Nobel Prize laureate in literature Mo Yan], *Shida xuebao: Yuyan yu wenxue lei* 師大學報：語言與文學類 [Journal of National Taiwan Normal University: Language and literature] 60, no. 2 (2015): 5.
4 Harold Bloom, *The Western Canon: The Books and School of the Ages* (New York: Harcourt Brace, 1994), 38.
5 Ibid.
6 "Horizon of expectation," or in German *Erwartungshorizont*, is a term germane to German academic Hans Robert Jauss's reception theory.

However, unlike the translation, circulation, and introduction of Yan's works in other countries and regions, which are usual issues in the study of world literature, the reception of Yan's works in Taiwan deals with the issue of cross-strait literary exchange and even the circulation of texts among Sinophone communities and is thus different from the study of world literature under a comparative literary perspective. Sinophone literary texts certainly do not require literary translation because they share the same language and partly the same culture. However, the absence of a literary translation process seems to make it difficult, for some scholars, to meet the conditions of world literature.[7] It is hoped that the issue of the reception of Yan's works in Taiwan will not be limited to the meaning of cross-strait literary exchanges. In the following discussion, we will explore how Yan's works have been received in Taiwan's academia, publishing and literary circles, and attempt to examine why Yan is read in Taiwan and what the meaning of his textual creation is within the broader context of Taiwanese literature. In the conclusion of this essay, we shall attempt to go beyond the history of reception in Taiwan and propose future research topics by juxtaposing the differences in the degree of attention to Yan in Taiwan and Hong Kong. This chapter may thus serve as a reference for future research on the circulation of Sinophone texts, and in turn will facilitate our thinking about the true nature and deep significance of world literature.

Yan's reception in academia

Regarding the context in which Yan's texts are valued within Taiwanese academia, one should doubtlessly start with the figure of David Der-wei Wang as the first leading scholar to lead Yan's research in Taiwan. To our best knowledge, the earliest article ever published in Taiwan on Yan is "The Love and Death of the Revolution: On *Serve the People* by Yan Lianke, a Pioneer Writer in Mainland China."[8] Later on, Wang further elaborated on this article as the basis for an expanded discussion of Yan's other novels. His argumentation was then included as a readers' guide in the book *Serve the People* (*Wei renmin fuwu* 爲人民服務) published by Maitian.[9] Although Wang's articles on Yan are primarily linked to the publications of Yan's novels, Wang's essays have had a role in setting the tone for Yan's research in Taiwan's academia.

Wang has carefully traced the trajectory and important issues of Yan's work. Wang argues that what makes Yan's work special is that Yan offers a new reflection and imagination on the history of the PRC as he experienced it.[10] Wang also connects *Hard Like Water* (*Jianying ru shui* 堅硬如水) to Chiang Kuei 姜貴, who wrote anti-communist literature in Taiwan in the 1950s, and points out that Yan's farcical connection between revolution, violence, and sex highlights another kind of reflection and dialectic on the history of the Cultural Revolution.[11]

---

7   David Damrosch argues that only by "circulating out into a broader world beyond its linguistic and cultural point of origin," literary works may be included in world literature. See Damrosch, *What Is World Literature?* (Princeton: Princeton University Press, 2003), 6.
8   David Der-wei Wang, "Geming shidai de ai yu si: Lun dalu wentan fengtou zuojia Yan Lianke de *Wei renmin fuwu*" 革命時代的愛與死 論大陸文壇鋒頭作家閻連科的《為人民服務》 [Love and death in the age of revolution: On pioneer writer in mainland China's literary scene, Yan Lianke, and his *Serve the People*], *Lianhe bao* 聯合報 [United Daily News], 27 Dec. 2005.
9   David Der-wei Wang, "Geming shidai de ai yu si: Lun Yan Lianke de xiaoshuo" 革命時代的愛與死──論閻連科的小說 [Love and death in the age of revolution: On Yan Lianke's novel], foreword to *Wei renmin fuwu*, by Yan Lianke (2006; repr., Taipei: Maitian, 2018), 6.
10 Ibid.
11 Ibid., 12–13.

Wang also observes the significance of death in Yan's work and argues that Yan's scenes and metaphors of necrophilia reflect Yan's use of love and death as the *fil rouge* of his reflections on revolutionary history. In addition, Wang also points out that the difference between Yan's and Mo Yan's 莫言 work in terms of "soil complex" (*tudi qingjie* 土地情結) and "life consciousness" (*shengming yishi* 生命意識) lies in Yan's masochistic display of suffering and indulgence.[12] An even more important observation is that Wang has clearly seen the mixed feelings of the peasant-soldiers (*nongmin junren* 農民軍人) toward their "native soil" (*xiangtu* 鄉土), a feeling that was also revealed in Chen Baiqing's 陳栢青 interview in August 2010.[13]

In addition to Wang's pioneering research, graduate theses focusing on Yan have gradually emerged since 2007.[14] In her master's thesis, Chen Meng-Chun 陳孟君, one of the first students to conduct research on Yan in Taiwan, focuses on bodily metaphors from a psychoanalytic and genealogical standpoint. Chen conducts her study from three perspectives: the subject, the pathological body, and the national body, and analyzes the subject's "identity in the rural space, the sense of home/nationality flowing in the rural/city space, and the sense of life/death and historical trauma in the pathological space,"[15] and then discusses the meaning of existence and the cultural spirit of the era that Yan addresses in the text. Seven years later, in her doctoral dissertation Chen continues to explore Yan's literary work from a psychoanalytic perspective. This time she does not limit herself to a single author but compares Yan with other authors, namely, Mo Yan, Li Rui 李銳, and Chen Zhongshi 陳忠實. Chen Meng-Chun places Yan in the new historical narrative of the post-1980s social structure

---

12 Ibid., 24.

13 Ibid., 14. See also Chen Baiqing, "Wei ziji huxie yi hui, zhuanfang Yan Lianke" 為自己胡寫一回專訪閻連科 [Write for myself: Interview with Yan Lianke], *Wen hsun* 文訊 [Literary Newsletter Magazine], no. 298 (Aug. 2010): 31.

14 Chen Meng-chun, "Zhuti, bingi yu guoti: Yan Lianke xiangtu xiaoshuo de jingshen xipu" 主體、病體與國體：閻連科鄉土小說的精神系譜 [Subjects, sick bodies, and national bodies: The spiritual genealogy of Yan's nativist fiction] (MA thesis, National Chengchi University, 2007). Later there were doctoral and master's theses by Chu Yu-fang 朱玉芳, "Huang Chunming yu Yan Lianke kunan shuxie zhi bijiao" 黃春明與閻連科苦難書寫之比較 [Comparison of misery writing: Between Huang Chun-ming and Yan Lianke] (PhD diss., National Central University, 2009); Zhang Yongchen 張詠宸, "Yan Lianke xiangtu xiaoshuo zhong de guojia yu quanli" 閻連科鄉土小說中的國家與權力 [The state and power in Yan's nativist fiction] (MA thesis, National Tsing Hua University, 2010); Chang Li 張立, "Yan Lianke qianqi xiaoshuo zhong 'nongmin/juren' xingxiang yu shengming chujing" 閻連科前期小說中「農民／軍人」形象與生命處境 [The image of "peasants/military" and the life situation in Yan's early novels] (MA thesis, National Cheng Kung University, 2011); Chen Meng-Chun, "Shensheng yu xugou: Liang'an dangdai xiaoshuo zhong 'ghuojia shenhua' yu 'xin lishi xushi' zhi bianzheng" 神聖與虛構：兩岸當代小說中「國家神話」與「新歷史敘事」之辯證 [The sacred and the fictional: Dialectics of "national myths" and "new historical narratives" in contemporary cross-strait fiction] (PhD diss., National Taiwan University, 2014); Ng Jieyang 黃傑陽, "Lun Yan Lianke xiaoshuo ji qi shenshi zhuyi" 論閻連科小說及其神實主義 [Yan's fiction and its mythorealism] (MA thesis, Yuan Ze University, 2017); and Yang Sen 楊森, "Xiangtu de taoli yu huigui: Yan Lianke ji qi zuopin (1919–2013) yanjiu" 鄉土的逃離與回歸——閻連科及其作品(1979–2013) 研究 [Local escape and return: Researches on Yan Lianke and his literary works (1979–2013)] (PhD diss., National Chung Cheng University, 2017). Since doctoral dissertations are more in-depth and comprehensive, only doctoral dissertations will be mentioned in the following part of this essay. Although this article does not intend to introduce master's theses, Chen Meng-chun's master's thesis is the first thesis on Yan in Taiwan. Not only is the textual analysis and research vision complete and in-depth, but two of the chapters were also successfully submitted to anonymously reviewed journals. Her doctoral dissertation is also related to her master's thesis; therefore, this essay will still discuss Chen's master's thesis.

15 Chen, "Zhuti, bingi yu guoti," 1.

after the unbundling of the national myth. She regards these historical narratives as traumatic structures, "using the metaphors of patriarchal discipline and maternal reproduction to illustrate the relationship between the body and space,"[16] and then observes the similarities and differences between the new historical narratives of writers on both sides of the Strait.

Chu Yu-fang 朱玉芳 focuses on the narrative strategy and use of the theme of hardship (*kunan* 苦難), comparing the similarities and differences between Yan and Taiwanese writer Huang Chunming 黃春明 in writing about the hardships of the underclass. Chu discusses the similarities and differences between the two writers in terms of character narrative perspective, nativist imagery, and disease writing.[17] Yang Sen 楊森 focuses on how Yan's countryside embodies the writer's complex emotions of love and hate for his native soil, his desire to escape but also his longing to return. Yang also focuses on the revolutionary narrative, national allegory, capitalism, and mythological allegory inscribed in "body writing" (*shenti shuxie* 身體書寫). Yang likewise compares Yan with Huang Chunming's "nativist writing" (*xiangtu shuxie* 鄉土書寫), emphasizing the increasing importance of mythological elements in Yan's recent writing. Yang interprets this phenomenon as a manifestation of contemporary Chinese writers breaking out of the social realism writing mold, combining modernist and surreal elements to highlight the "reality" of the Chinese society.[18]

After master's and doctoral theses began to focus on Yan, Taiwanese scholars also started to conduct research on Yan's literary creation. Tang Yu-Li 唐毓麗 examined *Dream of Ding Village* (*Ding zhuang meng* 丁莊夢) by juxtaposing this text with Wu Jih Wen's 吳繼文 *Galaxies in Ecstasy* (*Tianhe liaoluan* 天河撩亂). Tang focuses on the co-constitution of disease and the body with the authoritarian politics of the state and discusses *Dream of Ding Village*'s use of disease and the body to interrogate historical memory in "Chinese Body Theory: The Metaphor of AIDS and Authoritarian Politics" (*Zhongguo shentilun: Aixi yinyu yu weiquan zhengzhi* 中國身體論：愛滋隱喻與威權政治). Tang's essay touches upon the complicity of the disease and the national narrative in Yan, which can be used as a reference for the study of social and cultural discursive construction in Taiwan under the authoritarian system of the KMT in the past.[19] Chiang Hsin-li 蔣興立 focuses on the comparison between the writing of poverty and illness in *Dream of Ding Village* and Chi Zijian's 遲子建 *Snow and Raven* (*Baixue wuya* 白雪烏鴉) and places Yan's writing about infectious diseases in his hometown in the context of criticism of policy power and the wave of modernity. Through the interconnection of body and disease, urban and rural areas, and poverty, the ethical value of "Chinese literature of the subaltern" is highlighted.[20] From the studies of Tang and Chiang, we can see that the subversive

---

16 Chen, "Shensheng yu xugou," 1.
17 Chu, "Huang Chunming yu Yan Lianke kunan shuxie zhi bijiao," 2.
18 Yang, "Xiandaihua licheng zhong de haixia liangan xiangtu wenxue: Yi Huang Chunming yu Yan Lianke wei guancha hexin" 現代化歷程中的海峽兩岸鄉土文學——以黃春明與閻連科為觀察核心 [Cross-straits local literature in the process of modernization: The comparison between Huang Chunming and Yan Lianke in local literature writing], *Gaoxiong shida xuebao* 高雄師大學報 [Kaohsiung Normal University Journal], no. 43 (Dec. 2017): 48.
19 Tang Yu-Li 唐毓麗, "Binghuan de yiyi: Tan *Tinge liaoluan* ji *Dingzhuang meng* de jiazu/guozu jishi yu shenti" 病患的意義——談《天河撩亂》及《丁莊夢》的家族／國族紀事與身體 [The Significance of Patients: On the Family/State Chronicle and Body of *Galaxies in Ecstasy* and *Dream of Ding Village*], *Xingda renwen xuebao* 興大人文學報 [Journal of Humanities College of Liberal Arts, National Chung Hsing University], no. 49 (2012): 145–81.
20 Chiang Hsin-li, "Lun *Dingzhuang meng* ji *Baixue wuya* zhong de pin bing shuxie" 論《丁莊夢》及《白雪烏鴉》中的貧病書寫 [Illness and bottom layer: A discussion of poverty and illness in *Dream of Ding Village* and *Snow and Raven*], *Gaoxiong shida guowen xuebao* 高雄師大國文學報 [Bulletin of Chinese Studies of National Kaohsiung Normal University], no. 24 (July 2016): 49–73.

power and possibility of the fictional narrative of the novel to deconstruct the historical discourse is a major focus of attention of the Taiwanese academia on Yan's works.

In addition to Tang and Chiang, Shih Hsiao-Feng 石曉楓 has also long been interested in Yan's works. In view of the fact that Chinese fiction studies in Taiwan have long focused on writers such as Yu Hua and Mo Yan, Shih hopes to broaden the understanding of contemporary Chinese fiction writers, and therefore she has been including Yan in her research field since 2011. In fact, Shih already wrote a book review of *Lenin's Kisses* (*Shouhuo* 受活) in 2007, and she is no stranger to Yan's background.[21] The research project Shih applied for in 2011 focused on Wang Xiaobo's 王小波 and Yan's narratives of the Cultural Revolution and the significance of body writing. Shih's project also examines the widespread use of Bakhtin's carnivalesque terminology in Taiwanese literary studies at the time of the dialogue, hoping to explore the applicability of Bakhtin's carnival theory to Chinese fiction through the observation of Wang's and Yan's physical carnival narratives.[22] In the essay completed for this research project, Shih uses David Der-wei Wang's discussion of Yan's *Hard Like Water* as the basis for an in-depth discussion of Yan's inheritance and redirection of the "revolution and love" (*geming jia lian'ai* 革命加戀愛) fiction formula in that book.[23] After completing her observations on the changing strategies of body writing in modern contemporary Chinese "revolution and love" novels, Shih turned to the ghost narratives of contemporary Chinese writers. Shih's next research project focused on the ghostly narratives of Mo Yan, Yan Lianke, Ye Zhaoyan 葉兆言, and Su Tong 蘇童 to observe the characteristics of ghostly narratives in mainland Chinese fiction.[24] The starting point of the study of ghost narratives in Chinese fiction can be said to echo the observations of David Der-wei Wang in his seminal article "Second Haunting" ("Hun xi guilai" 魂兮歸來). The article highlights the phenomenon of Chinese fiction since the 1980s that has gradually departed from the social realist tradition of the 1930s and has made extensive use of ghostly narratives in its writing.

In summary, David Der-wei Wang's initiation of a groundbreaking discourse on Yan has had the effect of setting the tone for the evaluation of Yan's work in Taiwan's academia. In the analysis of Yan's texts by some graduate students and scholars, we observe that Taiwanese researchers have paid attention to Yan in the two following general ways. First, they have conducted an analysis of Yan's nativist writing by comparing it with the different trends

---

21 Shih Hsiao-feng, "Zhengzhi kuangre xia de nongmin wange: Yan Lianke *Shouhuo* pingjie" 政治狂熱下的農民輓歌—閻連科《受活》評介 [The peasant's elegy under the political frenzy: Review of Yan Lianke's *Lenin's hsun*], *Wen hsun*, no. 258 (Apr. 2007): 102–3.

22 Shih Hsiao-feng, "Dalu wenge xiaoshuo zhong de shenti kuanghuan xushi ji qi yiyi: Yi Wang Xiaobo, Yan Lianke wei zhuyao taolun duixiang" 大陸文革小說中的身體狂歡敘事及其意義——以王小波、閻連科為主要討論對象 [Body carnival narratives and their meaning in mainland China's Cultural Revolution fiction: Wang Xiaobo and Yan Lianke as the main subjects of discussion], final report on National Science Council, Executive Yuan 行政院, Taipei, 21 Jan. 2013, 2, https://wsts.most.gov.tw/STSWeb/Award/AwardMultiQuery.aspx?year=110&code=QS01&organ=&name=%e7%9f%b3%e6%9b%89%e6%a5%93 (last accessed 31 Aug. 2021).

23 Shih Hsiao-feng, "Geming yu xing'ai de jile zhanchang: Yan Lianke *Jianying ru shui* zhong de shenti Shuxie" 革命與性愛的極樂戰場——閻連科《堅硬如水》中的身體書寫 [The happiest battle field of revolution and sex: Body writing in Yan Lianke's *Hard Like Water*], *Guowen xuebao* 國文學報 [Bulletin of Chinese], no. 51 (June 2012): 241.

24 Shih Hsiao-feng, "Zhongguo xin shiqi xiaoshuo zhong de guimei xushi ji qi yiyi (di 3 nian)" 中國新時期小說中的鬼魅敘事及其意義(第3年) [Ghost narratives and their meaning in Chinese new-age fiction (year 3)], final report on the project funded by the Ministry of Science and Technology, Taipei, 20 Oct. 2018, https://wsts.most.gov.tw/STSWeb/Award/AwardMultiQuery.aspx?year=110&code=QS01&organ=&name=%e7%9f%b3%e6%9b%89%e6%a5%93 (last accessed 11 Aug. 2021).

on both sides of the Strait; second, they have focused on the deconstruction of historical narratives and the national myth.

Publishing industry/literary arena

Of course, the academia's interest in Yan's literary figure in recent years is also due to the continued introduction of Yan's works in the publishing world. Yan's books have been published in Taiwan by Maitian, Linking (Lianjing 聯經), INK (Yinke wenxue 印刻文學), Fish&Fish (Er yu wenhua 二魚文化), and New Land Literature Press (Xindi wenxue chubanshe 新地文學出版社). We have compiled a list of publications of Yan's works in Taiwan as an appendix to this chapter. It can be seen that Maitian mainly publishes Yan's fiction, while INK mainly publishes his prose writings such as essays and literary theories. In addition, we can also see that *Serve the People* and *Dream of Ding Village* were the first novels to enter Taiwan in 2006.[25] At the same time, since *Lenin's Kisses* was awarded the Lao She 老舍 Literary Award in 2005, Maitian published the novel in 2007, one year after the publication of his first two novels in Taiwan. It was probably in 2005 that reports about Yan's work began to appear in the literary arts supplements of Taiwanese newspapers.[26]

Serve the People was censored in 2005. Perhaps it is because of the fame of the Literary Award that the "censored award-winning work" *Serve the People* has had an unexpectedly sensational effect, attracting the attention of Hong Kong and overseas media.[27] At the time, a Taiwanese critic whose *nom de plume* was Qingtian 青田 thought that the banning of a work may have a "sensational effect" (*hongdong xiaoying* 轟動效應) on a writer.[28] As a matter of fact, these two novels were published in Taiwan at the beginning of the following year. *Serve the People* was even serialized in *China Times* (*Zhongguo shibao* 中國時報) prior to its publication by Maitian, which shows the strong interest of the Taiwanese literary community in works banned by the mainland Chinese government.[29] In addition to Maitian, which actively introduces mainland Chinese writers including Yan, New Land Literature Press,[30] which has long been involved in cross-strait literary exchanges, has also published some of Yan's novels. In sum, considering

---

25 *Serve the People* was published in Jan. 2006, and *Dream of Ding Village* in May of the same year. According to our estimation based on the publication chronology, the publishing industry in Taiwan probably started to consult with Yan on publication-related matters in the first half of 2005, after his banned books became widely known.

26 We used the database Taiwan xinwen zhihui wang 台灣新聞智慧網 [Taiwan News Intelligence Network] to search for related news with "Yan Lianke" as the keyword. As a result, except for Yan's article "Tongnian wangshi: Fuqin de guanjiao" 童年往事 父親的管教 [Childhood stories: Father's discipline], which was first published on 14 Sep. 2001, the rest of the articles discussing Yan's works were all about the book banning incident that started in 2005, with the earliest news on 11 Mar. 2005.

27 For example, see Dumei bianji bu 獨媒編輯部, eds., "2005 nian di yi bu jinshu: 'Wei renmin fuwu'" 2005年第一部禁書：〈為人民服務〉 [The first banned book of 2005: *Serve the People*], *Duli meiti* 獨立媒體 [inmediahk], 16 Mar. 2005, https://bit.ly/3zH1epL (last accessed 30 Aug. 2021); Benjamin Kang Lim, "China's Censors 'Serve the People' with Ban on Novel," *The Seattle Times*, 16 Apr., 2005, https://www.seattletimes.com/nation-world/chinas-censors-serve-the-people-with-ban-on-novel/ (last accessed 30 Aug. 2021).

28 Qing Tian 青田, "Zhongguo dalu 2005 nian di yi jinshu de hongdong xiaoying: *Wei renmin fuwu* bei jin, Yan Lianke lülü huo jiang" 中國大陸2005年第一禁書的轟動效應《為人民服務》被禁，閻連科屢屢獲獎 [The stirring effect of mainland China's first banned book in 2005: *Serve the People* Banned, Yan Lianke awarded repeatedly], *Lianhe bao*, 31 May 2005.

29 *China Times* started to publish *Serve the People* from 16 to 22 Sep. 2005.

30 This publishing house closed in 2018.

the banning incidents and the timing of Yan's publication in Taiwan, it can be inferred that the initial reception of Yan's literary works in Taiwan was more or less due to his censorship. In other words, Yan became known to the Taiwanese literary world as a so-called "banned author."[31]

The year 2010 can be said to be the year when the Taiwanese literary world officially became fully acquainted with Yan's literary work. On 17 Apr. 2010, New Land Literature Press, a long-time promoter of literature from mainland China to Taiwan, held a "World Summit on Chinese Literature in the 21st Century" (*21 shiji shijie huawen wenxue gaofenghui* 21世紀世界華文文學高峰會議). The president of New Land Literature Press, Kuo Feng 郭楓, invited Chinese writers from around the world, including Yan, to Taiwan, and for the first time *China Times* devoted half a page to Yan, with an in-depth interview focusing on his past creative journey.[32] During the symposium, the writers were also arranged to deliver lectures at some universities in Taiwan. A few months later, Chen Baiqing, a graduate student then and a Taiwanese writer now, interviewed Yan, and the interview was published in the *Literary Newsletter Magazine* (*Wen hsun* 文訊).[33] This interview can be said to be a rather in-depth interview, introducing the themes of the countryside and peasant soldiers as the inspiration and *fil rouge* of Yan's literary creation, Yan's thoughts on censorship, his discussion of "reality" and other issues.

Yan's related information has been less active in Taiwan's paper press since 2011. This situation is probably due to the rise of new media in Taiwan in the 2010s and the gradual impact of online news on traditional paper-based media, with more readers reading news online.[34] It can be observed that the news about Yan in the past decade have all been on Hong Kong's Initium Media (Duan chuanmei 端傳媒), Taiwan's The Storm Media (Feng chuanmei 風傳媒), Up Media (Shangbao 上報), and People News (Minbao 民報).

The reception of Yan's works by the Taiwanese publishing community has to be assessed from a macro perspective, that is, the publishing market. Leaving aside academic works, historical fiction, popular literature, and online literature are the best sellers among mainland Chinese writers in the Taiwanese market, while fiction is the least popular within *élite* literature, even inferior to essays, miscellaneous articles, or casual writings by mainland Chinese writers.[35] Some observers argue that mainland fiction is unfamiliar to Taiwanese readers

---

31 Yang, "Xiandaihua licheng zhong de haixia liangan xiangtu wenxue," 35.
32 Lin Xinyi 林欣誼, "Huawen wenxue gaofenghui kamu: Dashi yunji" 華文文學高峰會開幕 大師雲集 [Chinese literature summit opens with a gathering of masters], *Zhongguo shibao*, 17 Apr. 2010.
33 Chen Baiqing, "Wei ziji hu xie yi hui: Zhuanfang Yan Lianke" 為自己胡寫一回 專訪閻連科 [Write for myself: Interview with Yan Lianke], *Wen hsun*, no. 298 (Aug. 2010): 29–35.
34 Zhang Yue-han 張約翰, "Xin meiti bu shi baoye yingxu zhi di, er shi bijing de xiantu" 新媒體不是報業應許之地　而是必經的險途 [New media is not a promised land for the newspaper industry, but a necessary and dangerous path], *Da shuju* 大數聚 [Big Data Group], 26 Feb. 2016, https://group.dailyview.tw/article/detail/252 (last accessed 16 July 2021). Since 2010, the internet has overtaken the newspaper as the main source of news, which means that people are reading the news on the internet while reducing their habit of reading newspapers. This has changed the ecology of literary production and reading in Taiwan since the 1980s, where newspaper supplements and newspaper literary awards were the main literary venues and literary acknowledgment mechanisms.
35 Zen, "Dalu changxiao shu zai Taiwan, huozhe shuo zai Taiwan changxiao de dalu chuban pin/Zuojia" 大陸暢銷書在台灣, 或者說在台灣暢銷的大陸出版品/作家 [Best-selling books from mainland China in Taiwan, or best-selling mainland Chinese publications/authors in Taiwan], *Zen da de Dunnan xin shenghuo* Zen 大的敦南新生活 [Mr. Zen's new life in Dunnan], 12 May 2011, https://zen1976.com/post-1322146939/ (last accessed 10 Aug. 2021).

because it involves too many local details.³⁶ Lin Hsiu-mei 林秀梅, then deputy editor-in-chief of Maitian, once said, "the 1990s were indeed the heyday of mainland literary works in Taiwan."³⁷ Lin believes that the significance of mainland China's literary works for the Taiwanese literary scene at that time was that their written themes helped Taiwan understand mainland China's development and changes and to learn from their writing techniques. However, with the differences in the development of life across the Strait and the changes in the ecology of text production, writer-reader relationship, and the rise of social media, literary works from mainland China have gradually lost their appeal in Taiwan's literary scene.³⁸ Such circumstance of losing their appeal for Taiwanese readers is also related to the characteristics of Taiwan's fiction reading market.

It is argued that when publishing mainland Chinese writers in Taiwan, perhaps the publishing industry temporarily suspends its alleged "reverence" for foreign novels. Reverence for foreign novels here mainly refers to the ecology and characteristics of Taiwan's fiction reading market. In fact, it is not because the Taiwanese market deliberately avoids works from mainland China, but because the vision of the Taiwanese reading market generally focuses on foreign works, making it difficult to pay attention to mainland Chinese writers.³⁹ The Taiwanese publishing industry has long favored European, American, and Japanese translated novels, leading to the myth that foreign novels are of better quality.⁴⁰ In addition, Taiwan's publishing industry has long relied on the foreign copyright market to earn profits as a kind of OEM (original equipment manufacturing), resulting in an over-reliance on knowledge and issues set by the West, which in turn "repressed" the development and originality of local issues.⁴¹ In other words, when publishing works from mainland China, the publishers would return to the core of literary production and cross-disciplinary circulation by thinking more sensitively about the following question: what kind of mainland Chinese writers or works are selling well in Taiwan?

This inevitably leads us to further consider another important factor. Yan's works are purely literary fiction and brim with local Chinese details, yet they have been published by four publishers in Taiwan in such a harsh publishing environment. Apart from his purported "banned author" status and the prestige derived from literary awards, as well as the high attention paid to Yan by the European and American academia, are there any other characteristics that can echo the horizon of expectation of the Taiwanese literary community?

---

36 Ibid.
37 Wu Wei-zhen 巫維珍, "'Zuojia zuopin ji' xie wenxue shi: Zhuanfang Maitian chuban fu zongbianji Lin Xiumei, bianji Lai Huiqi" 「作家作品集」寫文學史：專訪麥田出版副總編輯林秀梅、編輯賴惠琪 ["The Collection of Writers and Works" writing literary history: An interview with Lin Xiumei, deputy chief editor, and Lai Huiqi, editor of Rye Field Publishing], *Wen hsun*, no. 355 (May 2015): 83. According to the context of the interview, the 1990s (90 *niandai* 年代) here means the period of 1990–2010: "90 年代確實是大陸文學作品在台灣的盛世."
38 Ibid., 83–84.
39 Zen, "Dalu changxiao shu zai Taiwan, huozhe shuo zai Taiwan changxiao de dalu chubab pin/zuojia."
40 Yueliang Xiong 月亮熊, "Taiwan xiaoshuo mai bu chuqu: Quanyin shuizhun bi bu shang fanyi zuopin?" 台灣小說賣不出去 全因水準比不上翻譯作品？ [The reason why Taiwanese novels don't sell is because the standard is not as good as the translated works?], *Changyi* 倡議 [Advocacy], 23 Feb. 2019, https://ubrand.udn.com/ubrand/story/11815/3660715 (last accessed 10 Aug. 2021).
41 Fu Cha 富察, "Tantan Taiwan chuban jie de joushi yu ziwo xianzhi" 談談台灣出版界的優勢與自我限制 [Talking about the strengths and self-imposed limitations of Taiwan's publishing industry], *Liang'an gongping wang* 兩岸公評網, Apr. 2016, http://www.kpwan.com/news/viewNewsPost.do?id=1288 (last accessed 10 Aug. 2021).

The reception of Yan in Taiwanese literature: From mainland China as the other to concern for Yan's universality

When the martial law was lifted in Taiwan, active introduction of mainland Chinese writers on the part of publishing houses such as New Land Literature and Linbai Press was not simply a concern for the writing skills of these writers or for the purely literary nature of their work. Huang Wen-chien 黃文倩 has clearly pointed out that the concern of Taiwanese publishers for mainland Chinese writers right before and after the lifting of the martial law was in fact mostly to promote Taiwan's understanding of the reality of the mainland and, to a certain extent, even to strengthen the identity of the people on both sides of the Strait. At that time, Taiwan's attention to mainland China's literary works was mainly focused on texts with realistic overtones.[42] However, with the emergence of diverse trends in Taiwanese literature in the 1990s, including post-modernism, and the influence of David Der-wei Wang in the academia and Maitian in the publishing world, the trends of deconstructing the grand narrative and heteroglossia became increasingly popular, which in turn led to a shift in the perception and selection of mainland literary works: from an emphasis on a greater understanding of the realities of Chinese society to a focus on the ultimate negation of values in mainland works.[43] This can be seen in Mo Yan's work, which received earlier attention in Taiwan.

However, with the development of Western post-colonial discourse and the consciousness of "Taiwan subjectivity" after 2000,[44] Taiwanese literature has also become an emerging and independent field of study in academia, breaking away from its subordinate status to the Department of Chinese Literature.[45] The National Museum of Taiwan Literature, which is under the Ministry of Culture, was also established on 17 Oct. 2003.[46] Since 2000, the trend of Taiwan's subjective ideology, which integrates institutions, social perceptions, and national policies, has naturally made Taiwan less eager to understand the reality of mainland China and more obsessed with the identification of its self-image, the reinterpretation of its native soil,[47] and the discourse, interpretation, and contestation of the "privileged signifier" of Taiwan.[48] In the face of such a trend, Taiwan's literary community naturally and consciously tries to "relationalize" writers from the outside with Taiwan in order to "discover" Taiwan's

---

42 Huang, "Mo Yan zai Taiwan de jieshou shi ji qi yiyi," 5.
43 Ibid., 8–9.
44 For the debates and the development of post-colonialism in Taiwan since the 1990s, see Ping-hui Liao, "Postcolonial Studies in Taiwan: Issues in Critical Debates," *Postcolonial Studies* 2, no. 2 (1999): 199–211.
45 The current departments in Taiwan that study Taiwanese literature and culture were established between 1997 and 2005.
46 Guoli Taiwan wenxue guan 國立台灣文學館, eds., "Guoli Taiwan wenxue guan de dansheng" 國立台灣文學館的誕生 [The birth of National Taiwan Museum of Taiwanese Literature], Guoli Taiwan wenxue guan, https://www.nmtl.gov.tw/content_167.html (last accessed 30 Aug. 2021).
47 However, in the 1970s, the idea of nativist literature was concerned with the economic development, environmental protection, and urban-rural disparity of Taiwan's native soil on the premise that mainland China was not yet considered as the Other. The concept of native soil that emerged in the mid-1990s was clearly based on ideological premises to examine the authenticity of Taiwan.
48 Chuang Chun-mei has insightfully analyzed the postcolonial theoretical debate in Taiwan since the 1990s, which has overemphasized the signs and their referential activities. Such overemphasis has instead abandoned the exploration of the constructive premises, possibilities, and dynamic processes of considering Taiwan as an open signifier. See Chuang, *Houzhimin de yinxing qingjing: Yuwen, fanyi he yuwang* 後殖民的陰性情境: 語文、翻譯和慾望 [The postcolonial feminine situation: Language, translation and desire] (Taipei: Qunxue, 2012), chap. 5.

true identity, if any; vis-à-vis writers from "the Other," that is allegedly mainland China, it is difficult for Taiwanese literature to know and perceive them without trying to find inspiration for Taiwan in their works. In addition, this quest for Taiwan's subjectivity is accompanied by a critique of the past party-state system, including a questioning and deconstruction of the historical narrative of the KMT, as well as a repeated accusation of the white terror and state violence.

In such a context, some studies juxtapose Yan's native soil with the narrative of Taiwanese fiction's native soil. This perspective reflects the Taiwanese literary community's own concern for Taiwanese fiction. In fact, this is not the case only for Yan's works. According to Huang Wen-chien, since the early reception of Mo Yan's works in Taiwan, his nativist narrative has been used as an "other" to clarify and explore the multiple routes of Taiwan's own nativist narrative (modernism, nativism, post-modernism, neo-nativism, etc.).[49] In addition, Huang also compares the reception of Mo Yan and Lu Yao 路遙 in Taiwan,[50] highlighting the reading preference of Taiwan's literary community in terms of literary aesthetics, reflecting the favoring of post-modern aesthetics in Taiwan since the 1990s and the distance from the overly political realism.[51] Just like Mo Yan's nativist writing in the horizon of expectation of Taiwan's literary studies, the aforementioned comparison between Yan's nativist narratives and Huang Chunming's native writing by some graduate students and scholars actually reflects a major research issue in the comparison of nativist narratives between the two sides of the Strait. However, while we agree with Huang's view, we also argue that the reception of Yan's works by the Taiwanese literary community still involves a large part of Taiwan's interest in Taiwanese signifiers and the dimension of "mainland China as the Other." This orientation constitutes a major feature of the initial reception of Yan's works in Taiwan.[52]

Despite the fact that mainland China continues to be "the other" on which Taiwan's politics and society depend to establish the Taiwanese subjectivity, the reception of foreign works in Taiwan's literary community has transcended the framework of Taiwan as the ultimate benchmark. Numerous scholars have agreed that the writing of Taiwan's historical memory has been one of the deconstruction projects in Taiwanese literature since the 1990s.[53] The importance of this topic lies not only in Taiwan's urgent need to reconnect with the officially suppressed and distorted history of Taiwan after the martial law lifting but also in the need to construct a cultural memory. In fact, the discussion of memory construction and falsehood is an extremely serious issue in the Taiwanese literary scene. For example, the Sinophone-Malaysian (*Ma-Hua* 馬華) writer Li Zishu 黎紫書 won the 2000 United Press Literary Award for Short Stories (*Lianhebao wenxue jiang duanpian xiaoshuo dajiang* 聯合報文學獎短篇小說大獎) in Taiwan for her "Mountain Plague" ("Shan wen" 山瘟).[54] During the final evaluation, there was a heated discussion about whether the novel had too many local details (too much information about the Malaysian rainforest). The final decision on "Mountain Plague" by the jury lies in the fact that the text remains "universal" beyond the Malaysian locality:

---

49 Huang, "Mo Yan zai Taiwan de jieshou shi ji qi yiyi," 15.
50 According to Huang, Lu Yao's works have not yet entered Taiwan.
51 Ibid.
52 Of course, to this day, the distinctive Henan vernacular writing and the use of dialect in Yan's texts have been widely recognized by the Taiwanese literary community as having a strong "Chinese" character. The sense of otherness thus still exists. However, what we would like to say is that in recent years, the study of Yan in Taiwan has tended to focus more on his universal issues.
53 See Chen Fangming 陳芳明, *Taiwan xin wenxue shi* 台灣新文學史 [A history of modern Taiwanese literature] (Taipei: Linking Books, 2010), 39.
54 Li Zishu 黎紫書, "Shan wen" 山瘟 [Mountain plague], *Lianhe bao*, 25 Sep. 2000.

questioning the linguistic, historical, and narrative representation.⁵⁵ It is evident that this research focus is also another major issue in the current study of Taiwanese literature.

As mentioned above, some of the studies of Yan's works in Taiwanese literary circles have been juxtaposed to Taiwanese nativist narratives. However, other studies focus on the themes of disease, the national body, the national mythology, and the deconstruction of historical narratives. In contrast to Mo Yan's nativist narrative, which is full of energetic rural imagery, Yan's nativist writing starts with death and is filled with the hopelessness and despair of lifelessness and doomed death.⁵⁶ This negative and pessimistic tone comes from Yan's skepticism of the national grand narrative, as well as his examination of reality. Yan's exaggerated, distorted, absurd and magical style highlights the imperceptible reality of the physical world with his "mythorealism,"⁵⁷ deconstructing the official discourse, national narrative, and historical memory by "striking reality with fiction." This point echoes the questioning and deconstruction of history, memory, and discourse in Taiwan after the lifting of the martial law. In addition, the series Twenty Contemporary Novels edited by David Der-wei Wang presents his research interest and critical vision on the dialectical relationship between fictional and historical narratives.⁵⁸ In the book series Contemporary Fiction Writers II, Yan's *The Book of Odes* (*Feng ya song* 風雅頌) was the second novel to be included by Wang after Li Yongping's 李永平 *The End of the River* (*Da he jintou* 大河盡頭). It is evident that Wang is quite confident about Yan's achievement in questioning the authenticity of historical memory through the fictional nature of his narrative.

The concern for universality can also be observed in the phenomenon that Taiwanese writers no longer use the label of "mainland Chinese literature" for reading Yan's works. For Wu Ming-yi 吳明益, a Taiwanese writer and scholar, Yan's works differ greatly from those of Taiwanese writers. In a 2015 lecture on the writing trends of Taiwanese writers, Wu also mentioned his opinion of Yan's literary works and he particularly praised his storytelling skills. Wu believes that most Taiwanese writers work hard on rhetoric (*nuli yu xiuci* 努力於修辭) but less on the storytelling aspects; Yan's work has its own complete narrative and is concerned with how people face the "institution," and Wu further agrees with Yan's position in judging the state and the nation.⁵⁹

This comment by Wu in fact points out a long-standing weakness of Taiwan's fiction writing in general. Wu is not the only one to comment that Taiwanese writers "work hard on rhetoric." Chu Yu-hsun 朱宥勳, a writer and a scholar, has also pointed out the "collapse of the brand image" (*pinpai xingxiang de benghuai* 品牌形象的崩壞) of Taiwanese novels with

---

55 Zhan Min-xu 詹閔旭, "Duo di gong gou de Huayu yuxi wenxue: Yi Ma-Hua wenxue de Taiwan jingyu wei li" 多地共構的華語語系文學：以馬華文學的台灣境遇為例 [Sinophone literature as places-based production: On the predicament of Sinophone Malaysian literature in Taiwan], *Taiwan wenxue xuebao* 台灣文學學報 [Bulletin of Taiwanese Literature], no. 30 (June 2017): 101–2.
56 Wang, ""Geming shidai de ai yu si," 27–28.
57 Ibid. In addition, readers may refer to the first section of this volume.
58 Xu Deming 徐德明, "'Huawen yujing' zhong de dandai xiaoshuo piping shijie: Cong Wang Dewei de 'zhishi dili' tankan shuoqi" 「華文語境」中的當代小說批評視界——從王德威的「知識地理」探勘說起 [A critical perspective of contemporary fiction within the *Huawen* context: An exploration of David Der-wei Wang's "Geography of Knowledge"], *Shijie huawen wenxue luntan* 世界華文文學論壇 [Forum for Chinese literature of the world], 2002, no. 3: 18.
59 See Xu Qiu-ling 徐秋玲, "Huawen wenxue de chuzou yu guilai" 華文文學的出走與歸來 [The exodus and return of Sinophone literature], *Da ayi xiang tai duo* 大阿姨想太多 [Big auntie thinks too much], 25 Apr. 2015, https://blog.xuite.net/home14498/twblog/mosaic-view/312985708 (last accessed 10 Aug. 2021).

the sentence "the ability to 'plan a composition' is much stronger than the ability to write a book'" (*moupian de nengli bi moushu de nengli qiang de duo* 「謀篇」的能力比「謀書」的能力強得多).[60] Chu believes that the reason for this phenomenon is that Taiwanese writers have long been suppressed by their local culture and historical memory and have often tried to bear witness to history by writing *romans fleuve*, trilogies, and family histories in a very simple way, thus lacking narrative interest.[61] By synthesizing Wu's and Chu's discussions, we can observe that the originality of Yan's novels in terms of narrative technique and novel form was indeed the entry point for Yan's novels, such as *Lenin's Kisses*, to be praised by critics at the beginning.[62]

In addition to Yan's storytelling ability and formal innovation, perhaps the social concern intrinsic to his works was also an important inspiration for Taiwan's literary community. In 2011, Wu expressed his appreciation of *The Four Books* (*Si shu* 四書). He also praised Yan's *Discovering Fiction* (*Faxian xiaoshuo* 發現小說) for his macroscopic interpretation of the genealogy of Chinese writers and the significance of their writing from the perspective of fictional history.[63] Also in May 2012, he commented on Yan's *House No. 711* (*711 hao yuan: Beijing zuihou de zuihou jinian* 711號園：北京最後的最後紀念),[64] and observed that through the glory of a garden and the fate of its demolition, Yan uses his mythorealist method to profile the cold side of public power in the execution of urban planning.[65] In fact, Wu's review of *House No. 711* and the publication of the book in Taiwan coincided with the discussion of the Dapu Incident (*Dapu shijian* 大埔事件) that began the previous year in 2010.[66] At the same time, he also considers issues such as the tension between urban planning and people's property. The publication of this book review also reflects the emphasis in Taiwanese literary circles on the social and political critique in Yan's works.

For Chu, the drawback of Taiwanese fiction is not only the shortcomings of long narratives but also the total retreat of Taiwanese literary fiction from the public sphere. This has deprived fiction of its socially influential readership: intellectuals.[67] Chu attributes the lack of social engagement in Taiwan's fiction to the fact that Taiwanese literature has long been constrained by the tastes of the "lyrical tradition" (*shuqing chuantong* 抒情傳統) and the strict political atmosphere deriving from the martial law, allowing literature to focus only on "eternal

---

60 Chu Yu-hsun 朱宥勳, "Yijing huaihui de he zhengzai panzhang de: Taiwan xiaoshuo de cishi cike" 已經壞毀的和正在攀長的：台灣小說的此時此刻 [What's broken and what's growing: The here and now of Taiwanese fiction], Liang'an gongping wang, Apr. 2016, http://www.kpwan.com/news/viewNewsPost.do?id=1294 (last accessed 10 Aug. 2021).
61 Ibid.
62 Shih Hsiao-feng also praised Yan's narrative technique in *Lenin's Kisses*. See Shih, "Zhengzhi kuangre xia de nongmin wange."
63 Wu Ming-yi 吳明益, "Mongdong shi xiezuo xiaoshuo de zui hao zhuangtai" 懵懂是寫作小說的最好狀態 [Innocence is the best state for writing fiction], *Wen hsun*, no. 314 (Dec. 2011): 130–31.
64 The title of the simplified Chinese version is *Beijing, zuihou de jinian* 北京，最后的纪念.
65 Wu Ming-yi, "Na lengku beihou de fangxiang" 那冷酷背後的芳香 [The fragrance behind the ruthless], *Zhongguo shibao*, 19 May 2012.
66 The Dapu Incident was a controversy between the residents of Dapu village in Zhunan Township, Miaoli County, Taiwan, and the Miaoli County government. The residents disagreed about the expropriation and forced demolition of houses in the area led by the government's county chief, Liu Zheng-hong 劉政鴻. At that time, the Miaoli County government took land from the farmers without their consent, leading to a series of farmers' protests and intellectuals' criticism. For more information, see https://en.wikipedia.org/wiki/Dapu_incident (last accessed 28 Aug. 2021).
67 Chu, "Yijing huaihui de he zhengzai panzhang de."

human and literary values" (*yongheng de renxing yu wenxue jiazhi* 永恆的人性與文學價值).[68] To be fair, we do not agree with the explanation offered by Chu, because Chu confuses the lyrical tradition with the lyrical literary style that has been deliberately dominated by the KMT government in Taiwan since the 1950s.[69] However, Chu does indeed also touch on the long-standing phenomenon of lyrical exclusivity/superiority in Taiwanese literature. It seems that the critical nature of Yan's narrative and the judgment of the nation and nationality propagated by his works have awakened the dissatisfaction of the advocates of the nativist literature trend in Taiwan since the 1970s with the excessive emphasis on literary aesthetics in Taiwanese modernism. More importantly, Yan's fiction also demonstrates how literature can more actively engage with social, historical, and mainstream narrative goals.

Of course, not all of Yan's works are fully critical and absurd. Yan pursues stylistic diversity and presents a lyricism very much in line with the one Taiwanese literature is familiar with in *They* (*Tamen* 她們). In her review of Yan's *They*, Taiwanese writer Shih Fang-yu 石芳瑜 focuses on Yan's portrayal of strong and persevering women: "He also writes about women; however, unlike Bi Feiyu 畢飛宇, who is good at writing about women, he does not write about those who are lustful, but those who are simple and resolute, yet lovely in their own way."[70] Shih points out that the prose of *They* is different from the magical realism and the brushwork style of describing people and scenery but has a more lyrical style. This lyrical style is based on the interactions and events of daily life, which are written and piled up to reveal the personalities of the female characters and project the author's feelings for the women of his hometown. This style is not new to the Taiwanese literary scene, as lyrical prose has been the dominant aesthetic style in Taiwanese literature since the 1950s. In addition, Yan's expertise in the subject matter of Henan rural themes makes his depiction of rural women similar to the "lyrical native soil" (*shuqing xiangtu* 抒情鄉土) lineage of Taiwanese "nativist writing" (*xiangtu shuxie* 鄉土書寫).[71] In particular, this technique of projecting the writer's emotions through the description of external scenery is in line with the discourse on the lyrical tradition

---

68 Ibid.
69 For the influence of lyrical style on Taiwanese literature since the 1950s, please see Chang Sung-sheng Yvonne, *Modernism and the Nativist Resistance: Contemporary Chinese Fiction from Taiwan* (Durham: Duke University Press, 1993), chap. 1; Wang Yu-ting 王鈺婷, "Shuqing shi chengji, chuantong zhi yanyi—50 niandai nuxing sanwenjia meixue fengge ji qi celue yingyong 抒情之承繼, 傳統之演繹—五〇年代女性散文家美學風格及其策略運用 [Lyrical tradition and Taiwan women's prose writings in the 1950's]" (PhD diss. National Cheng Kung University, Tainan, 2009).
70 Shi Fang-yu, "Yan Lianke *Tamen* shuping: Miaoxie dadi wanwu shi wenzhi jiqi mohuan, tanlun aiqing shi que ruci jiandan" 閻連科《她們》書評: 描寫大地萬物時文字極其魔幻, 談論愛情時卻如此簡單 [Book review of Yan Lianke's *They*: The words are extremely magical when describing the earth and everything, but so simple when talking about love], Guanjian pinglun 關鍵評論 [The News Lens]. 28 Sep. 2020, https://www.thenewslens.com/article/140895 (last accessed 15 July 2021): "同樣寫女人, 和善寫女人的畢飛宇不同, 他不寫那些情慾纏綿, 而是那些樸拙堅毅, 卻也自有其可愛。"
71 The nativist literature that prevailed in Taiwan in the 1970s combined realism and made the realistic critique of sin and the communication of human goodness the mainstream of nativist literature. In contrast, although writers still have a sense of fondness and lyricism for the native soil, the lyrical *xiangtu* is still a tributary. See Liu Nai-Tzu 劉乃慈, "Richang de feichang: *Liushui zhang* de shuqing xiangtu yu xushi" 日常的非常——《流水帳》的抒情鄉土與敘事 [The extraordinary daily life: Lyrical native and narrative of *Running Account*], *Taiwan wenxue xuebao*, no. 20 (June 2012): 99–126.

in Taiwan since 1970,[72] which makes it possible to understand the high acceptance of the lyrical style in Taiwanese literature.

In addition to the preference for the lyrical taste, it is argued that the publication of *They* has further established the universal elements of Yan's literary creation. On the cover of *They*, Maitian in fact emphasizes the reflection on the subjectivity, dynamism, and subversiveness of women, even questioning the established gender mindset. According to Maitian's editor, Yan's *They* raises the hardly concealed disregard for women as "human beings" in mainstream discourse.[73]

To sum up, it is believed that the continued reception of Yan's works by the Taiwanese publishing community and even by the literary community *tout court* is not only because of his status as a "banned author" and the prestige of his literary awards. It is also because his works are a source of inspiration for Taiwan to think about the local situation, the universality of reconsidering the effectiveness of historical writing and memory discourse, and the fit between the literary style of Yan's works and Taiwan's reading tastes.

The significance of the circulation of Yan's works in Taiwan

In all fairness, Hong Kong is probably the place where the reception of Yan's works is most deeply appreciated in the Sinosphere outside of the Chinese mainland.[74] This is because Yan has been a visiting professor at the Hong Kong Baptist University and the Hong Kong University of Science and Technology since 2012. This not only allows Hong Kong experts and scholars to communicate directly with Yan and conduct more in-depth research but also provides Yan with the opportunity to publish more of his works through Hong Kong (university) presses. In contrast, the only way for Yan to be known in Taiwan is through the so-called "technologies of recognition" of the major literary awards and the academic influence of David Der-wei Wang.[75] Admittedly, Hong Kong offers a temporary escape from the "chaos" of Yan's life.[76] The deep friendship between Yan and Hong Kong has naturally made Hong Kong a major city for Yan's studies in the Sinosphere. Of course, Hong Kong and Taiwan have their own contexts of reception, and although they read the same texts, they can still have their

---

72 The lyrical tradition echoes the issue from comparative literature that Chinese literature specializes in lyrical genre but not in epics. No matter how deep this essentialist sense of discussion goes, David Der-wei Wang focuses on the "discourse" of the "lyrical tradition," and discusses the significance of the argument initiated by Chen Shih-Hsiang 陳世驤 and then by Kao Yu-kung 高有工 in the 1970s, and mainly developed by scholars from universities in Taiwan. See David Der-wei Wang, Introduction to his *The Lyrical in Epic Time: Modern Chinese Intellectuals and Artists Through The 1949 Crisis* (New York: Columbia University Press, 2015).
73 Chen Shuyi 陳淑怡, "Xian shi ren, cai shi nüren: 10 yue xian shu *Tamen*" 先是人，才是女人——10月選書《她們》 [First a man, then a woman: October's selected book *They*], *OKAPI Yuedu shenghuo zhi* OKAPT 閱讀生活誌 [OKAPI online reading & life magazine], 28 Sep. 2020, https://okapi.books.com.tw/article/13786 (last accessed 30 Aug. 2021.
74 For the reception of Yan's works in Hong Kong, readers may refer to the last chapter of this companion.
75 "Technologies of recognition" represent Shih Shu-Mei's 史書美 discussion of the potential discursive bias of Western scholarship in defining the so-called "the West" and "the rest." See Shu-Mei Shih, "Global Literature and the Technologies of Recognition," *PMLA* 119, no. 1 (2004): 16–30.
76 Yan Lianke, "Haibian de Yan Lianke: Lai Xianggang shi yi zhong taoli" 海邊的閻連科：來香港教書是一種逃離 [Yan Lianke by the sea: Coming to Hong Kong to teach is an escape], interview by Fu Ziyang 付子洋, Duan chuanmei 端傳媒 [Initium Media], 3 July 2018, https://theinitium.com/article/20180626-mainland-yanlianke/(last accessed 10 Aug. 2021).

own different standpoints. The different concerns between Taiwan and Hong Kong are also related to the differences in the reception of mainland Chinese writers' texts between Taiwan and Hong Kong. The question we would like to ask here is: does this reveal any tension within the Sinophone community? If Hong Kong sees Yan's texts as a window into the Chinese mainland, which in turn highlights Hong Kong's position of being in-between mainland China and the world, what does Taiwan's reception of Yan's texts mean or reveal for Sinophone literary studies?

In observing the classicization process of Hong Kong writer Huang Biyun 黃碧雲 (also known as Wong Bik-Wan in Cantonese), Lo Man Chi 盧敏芝 argues that Taiwanese female art scholars Chien Ying-ying 簡瑛瑛 and David Der-wei Wang's studies of Huang (Wong) focus on her transcendence, that is, the vision of transcending foreign literature and local literature, transcending the self and the other, as the Japanese Sinologist Yoshimi Takeuchi 竹內好 once said.[77] In particular, Wang's research has long been devoted to breaking through the framework of literary studies based on national boundaries, attempting to link literary works from all over the Sinosphere by means of Michel Foucault's genealogy, and transcending the framework of center-border literary studies from the standpoint of overseas Chinese literary studies (*haiwai Zhongguo wenxue yanjiu* 海外中國文學研究).[78] Both in Chien's feminist study of transnational/ethnic borders or in Wang's genealogical approach, we learn that only by transcending the national literary stereotypes can we free the literary works of the Sinosphere from being interpreted by researchers from the perspective of "mainland China as the Other" (*yi Zhongguo dalu zuowei tazhe* 以中國大陸作為他者), thus allowing Sinophone literature to break through the overly strong antagonistic posture of "excluding [mainland] China" (*paichu Zhongguo [dalu]* 排除中國[大陸]).

In this light, we come back to the reception of Yan's texts in Taiwan and what it may reveal. For Taiwan, Yan's work is still confined to the label of "banned author." Yan's *Serve the People* has even been a must-read for Taiwanese readers who are dissatisfied with the Chinese communist "regime" and are extremely critical of it and at times sarcastic. In the academia, Yan's nativist-writing texts were later used as a comparison to Taiwan's own nativist writing. It was only after 2010, with the successive publication of Yan's essay collections, that the academia and the literary community gradually paid attention to the universality behind Yan's text and the inspiration it might provide for Taiwanese literature.

Over the past thirty years, Taiwan has attempted to find an *a priori* Taiwanese subjectivity in post-colonial discourses and debates, but at the same time, has constructed a strongly exclusive literary position. However, as we observe from the perspective of the study of Yan's text within the academia, Wang's initial introduction has slowly led scholars to cut into Yan's textual creation from different angles. The papers and studies of scholars such as Chen Meng-chun, Shih Hsiao-feng, and Yang Sen, or even Wu Ming-yi's observation of Yan's narrative power, are a testament to the fact that the research scope of Taiwanese literature has moved from the original search for a subjectivity to transcending national boundaries, from reflecting on oneself to transcending oneself. This transcendence can be seen in the introduction to the recent publication of *They* in Taiwan. While emphasizing the controversial nature of Yan, Maitian published *They* in 2020, recommending the profound introspection of the

---

77 Lo Man Chi 盧敏芝, "Taiwan wenxue changyu yu Huang Biyun xiaoshuo de 'jingdian hua'" 台灣文學場域與黃碧雲小說的「經典化」 [The Literary Field of Taiwan and the "Canonisation" of Wong Bik-Wan's Fiction], *Taiwan wenxue yanjiu xuebao* 台灣文學研究學報 [Journal of Taiwan Literary Studies], no. 31 (Oct. 2020): 252.

78 Ibid., 257–59.

subjectivity and dynamism of women as "human beings" along other marginal transboundary concerns.

Perhaps the reception of Yan's texts in Taiwan highlights the relational and dynamic nature of meaning production within Sinophone literature. It is precisely because the relationship between Taiwan and Yan is not as direct and intimate as that with Hong Kong that the reception of Yan's works in Taiwan is a reflection of the attempt of Taiwanese literature to go beyond Taiwanese literature itself and to focus on the universality of Yan's texts. At the same time, it also highlights the infinite possibilities of the transnational characteristics and deterritorialization, in Deleuze's sense, of Sinophone literature itself. For Sinophone literature, the production of textual meaning does not lie in the assessment of a local dominant discourse or technologies of recognition but in the dynamic mirror of "relationality" that is constructed through continuous dialogue. This dialectical process of self and other, as well as the relational network of textual meaning production, is also the focus of discussion in world literature. The normative force and temporal nature of Yan's texts are also the world-making force of world literature advocated by Pheng Cheah.[79]

Conclusion and future research

It cannot be denied that the initial reception of Yan's novels in Taiwan was mainly focused on his satire of the revolutionary narrative of twentieth-century communist China, which in turn presented the ghosts of the anti-communist literature of those years. By presenting the ugliness and primitive desires of the characters in the history of the early PRC, Yan's novel develops a narrative of the Cultural Revolution that is different from the "scar" or "avant-guard literature" (*xianfeng wenxue* 先鋒文學). Moreover, the knowledge of Yan in Taiwan is largely due to the attention that Western academia has dedicated to Yan and the influence of David Der-wei Wang's scholarship in Taiwan, which has led to a gradual recognition of Yan's literary figure.

From what we have discussed thus far, we have learned that the reception of Yan's works in Taiwan, like that in Hong Kong or elsewhere, was initially focused on his label as a "banned author." At the same time, it also embraced the Western world's horizon of expectation of a dystopian communist China.[80] However, with the publication of Yan's novels and essays in Taiwan, the Taiwanese literary community has become increasingly concerned with how to see Taiwan rather than how to observe the Chinese mainland. In fact, while Hong Kong's literary and academic circles have gradually come to view Yan as a conduit for observing the political taboos and censorship mechanisms in mainland China, the reception of Yan's works in Taiwan is a reflection of its own position with the critical or aesthetic focus on Yan's works aiming to project a concern for the current political and social issues in Taiwan. In other words, the social reality of mainland China, the criticism of the state and nation, and even the reflection of the internal literary and political contestation in Yan's works[81] may not necessarily be what Taiwanese writers or readers are mostly interested in. Yan's suppression by political forces, his sharp critique, or the lyrical introspection that underlies his criticism have

---

79 Pheng Cheah, *What Is a World? On Postcolonial Literature as World Literature* (Durham: Duke University Press, 2016), 3–11.
80 Lee Tong King, "China as Dystopia: Cultural Imaginings through Translation," *Translation Studies* 8, no. 3 (2015): 251.
81 See Jessica Young's chapter in this companion.

been the long-term driving forces behind Taiwan's reception of Yan's literary creation because of their universality.

This universal concern also reflects the fact that Taiwan, in its reception of Yan's texts, is constantly thinking about the "relationality" and significance of Yan with regard to Taiwanese literature. Such a reflection thus means that Taiwan is reflecting on the significance of "Taiwan." In an essay written by Taiwanese author Li Ang 李昂 in her *Selected Novellas of the New Millenium* (*Jiushi nian xiaoshuo xuan* 九十年小說選), she argues that the "national" meaning of "Taiwan" in the literary field is diluted, and Taiwan is treated as an open and pluralistic signifier.[82] Chen Fang-ming argues that the liberal and democratic environment of Taiwanese literature has allowed the publication of banned books from mainland China, highlighting the tolerance of Taiwanese literature in the broader context of the Sinophone literary world. The fact that mainland Chinese writers, Hong Kong and Sinophone-Malaysian writers are published in Taiwan may help to build a fiction boom in Taiwan.[83] Regardless of the fact that the two remarks seem at first glance to be propaganda for the policy stance of the Taiwanese authorities, Li Ang's understanding of Taiwan as a signifier of openness is precisely the characteristic of Taiwanese literature as a part of Sinophone literature: beyond the framework of national literature, in the process of debating between the other and the self, literary works from outside Taiwan allegedly have meaning for Taiwan itself. In other words, it is suggested that in receiving Yan's texts, Taiwan has been thinking about the relevance and significance of Yan with respect to Taiwanese literature. This reflection implies a deeper layer of reflection; that is, Taiwan is pondering over the meaning of "Taiwan." Unlike the translation, circulation, and introduction of Yan's works as literature in other countries and regions, which are the usual topics of research in world literature, the reception of Yan's works in Taiwan involves the circulation of texts within the Sinophone community. By juxtaposing the differences in the degree of attention paid to Yan in Taiwan and Hong Kong, this chapter attempted to elevate the issue of Yan's reception history in Taiwan to the level of Sinophone literature research, pointing out that Yan's reception in Taiwan reflects the production of dynamic meanings of Sinophone texts in the continuous debates and dialogues between the self and the other in various places of the Sinosphere.

Yan Lianke's Publications in Taiwan

Title	Publisher	Year	Series	Language
丁莊夢	麥田	2006	麥田文學, no. 196	中文
為人民服務	麥田	2006	麥田文學, no. 179	中文
受活	麥田	2007	麥田文學, no. 208	中文
風雅頌	麥田	2008	麥田文學, no. 220 （當代小說家 II, 王德威主編）	中文
我與父輩	INK印刻文學	2009	印刻文學叢書, no. 229	中文
堅硬如水	麥田	2009	麥田文學, no. RL1226	中文
夏日落	聯經	2010	當代名家	中文
日光流年	聯經	2010	當代名家：閻連科作品集	中文
閻連科小說精選集	新地文化藝術	2010	世界華文作家精選集叢書	中文

(Continued)

82 Li Ang, "Xiangxiang Taiwan" 想像台灣 [Imagining Taiwan], in *Jiushi nian xiaoshuo xuan* 九十年小說選 [Selected novellas of the 1990s], ed. Li (Taipei: Jiuge, 2002), 14–15.

83 Feng Zichuan 馮子純, "Chen Fangming: Xiaoshuo de bai nian shengshi" 陳芳明: 小說的百年盛世 [Chen Fangming: A century of fiction in full bloom], *Wen hsun*, no. 309 (July 2011): 64–65.

Title	Publisher	Year	Series	Language
四書	麥田	2011	麥田文學, no. 240	中文
發現小說	INK印刻文學	2011	印刻文學叢書, no. 301	中文
711號園：北京最後的最後紀念	聯經	2012	當代名家：閻連科作品集.	中文
一個人的三條河	二魚文化	2013	文學花園, no. C098	中文
炸裂志	麥田	2013	麥田文學, no. 269	中文
黑白閻連科：中篇四書	二魚文化	2014	文學花園, no. C107	中文
沉默與喘息：我所經歷的中國和文學	INK印刻文學	2014	印刻文學叢書, no. 408	中文
黑白閻連科：中篇四書	二魚文化	2014	文學花園, no. C107-110	中文
兩代人的十二月	INK印刻文學	2015	印刻文學叢書, no. 452	中文
日熄	麥田、城邦文化	2015	麥田文學, no. 289	中文
速求共眠：我與生活的一段非虛構	INK印刻文學	2018	印刻文學叢書, no. 565	中文
她們	麥田	2020	麥田文學, no. 316	中文
中國故事	麥田	2021	麥田文學, no. 321	中文

Bibliography

Bloom, Harold. *The Western Canon: The Books and School of the Ages*. New York: Harcourt Brace, 1994.

Cheah, Pheng. *What Is a World? On Postcolonial Literature as World Literature*. Durham, NC: Duke University Press, 2016.

Chen Baiqing 陳栢青. "Wei ziji hu xie yi hui: Zhuanfang Yan Lianke" 為自己胡寫一回 專訪閻連科 [Write for myself: Interview with Yan Lianke]. *Wen hsun* 文訊 [Literary newsletter magazine], no. 298 (Aug. 2010): 29–35.

Chen Fangming 陳芳明. *Taiwan xin wenxue shi* 台灣新文學史 [A history of modern Taiwanese literature]. Taipei: Linking Books, 2010.

Chen Meng-Chun 陳孟君. "Shensheng yu xugou: Liang'an dangdai xiaoshuo zhong 'ghuojia shenhua' yu 'xin lishi xushi' zhi bianzheng" 神聖與虛構：兩岸當代小說中「國家神話」與「新歷史敘事」之辯證 [The sacred and the fictional: Dialectics of "national myths" and "new historical narratives" in contemporary cross-strait fiction]. PhD diss., National Taiwan University, 2014.

Chen Shuyi 陳淑怡. "Xian shi ren, cai shi nüren: 10 yue xian shu *Tamen*" 先是人，才是女人——10月選書《她們》 [First a man, then a woman: October's selected book *They*], *OKAPI Yuedu shenghuo zhi* OKAPT 閱讀生活誌 [*OKAPI Online Reading & Life Magazine*]. 28 Sep. 2020. https://okapi.books.com.tw/article/13786 (last accessed 30 Aug. 2021).

Chiang Hsin-li 蔣興立. "Lun *Dingzhuang meng* ji *Baixue wuya* zhong de pin bing shuxie" 論《丁莊夢》及《白雪烏鴉》中的貧病書寫 [Illness and bottom layer: A discussion of poverty and illness in *Dream of Ding Village* and *Snow and Raven*]. *Gaoxiong shida guowen xuebao* 高雄師大國文學報 [Bulletin of Chinese Studies of National Kaohsiung Normal University], no. 24 (July 2016): 49–73.

Chu Yu-fang 朱玉芳. "Huang Chunming yu Yan Lianke kunan shuxie zhi bijiao" 黃春明與閻連科苦難書寫之比較 [Comparison of misery writing: Between Huang Chun-ming and Yan Lianke]. PhD diss., National Central University, 2009.

Chu Yu-hsun 朱宥勳. "Yijing huaihui de he zhengzai panzhang de: Taiwan xiaoshuo de cishi cike" 已經壞毀的和正在攀長的：台灣小說的此時此刻 [What's broken and what's growing: The here and now of Taiwanese fiction]. *Liang'an gongping wang* 兩岸公評網 [Cross-strait public commentary website]. Apr. 2016. http://www.kpwan.com/news/viewNewsPost.do?id=1294 (last accessed 10 Aug. 2021).

Chuang Chun-mei 張君玫. *Houzhimin de yinxing qingjing: Yuwen, fanyi he yuwang* 後殖民的陰性情境: 語文、翻譯和慾望 [The postcolonial feminine situation: language, translation and desire]. Taipei: Qunxue, 2012.

Damrosch, David. *What Is World Literature?* Princeton: Princeton University Press, 2003.

Dumei bianji bu 獨媒編輯部, eds. "2005 nian di yi bu jinshu: 'Wei renmin fuwu'" 2005年第一部禁書:"為人民服務" [The first banned book of 2005: *Serve the People*], Duli meiti 獨立媒體 [inmediahk], 16 Mar. 2005. https://bit.ly/3zH1epL (last accessed 30 Aug. 2021).

Feng Zichuan 馮子純. "Chen Fangming: Xiaoshuo de bai nian shengshi" 陳芳明: 小說的百年盛世 [Chen Fangming: A century of fiction in full bloom]. *Wen hsun*, no. 309 (July 2011): 61–65.

Fu Cha 富察. "Tantan Taiwan chuban jie de joushi yu ziwo xianzhi" 談談台灣出版界的優勢與自我限制 [Talking about the strengths and self-imposed limitations of Taiwan's publishing industry]. Liang'an gongping wang. Apr. 2016. http://www.kpwan.com/news/viewNewsPost.do?id=1288 (last accessed 10 Aug. 2021).

Guoli Taiwan wenxue guan 國立台灣文學館, eds. "Guoli Taiwan wenxue guan de dansheng" 國立台灣文學館的誕生 [The birth of National Taiwan Museum of Taiwanese Literature]. Guoli Taiwan wenxue guan. https://www.nmtl.gov.tw/content_167.html (last accessed 30 Aug. 2021).

Huang Wen-chien 黃文倩. "Mo Yan zai Taiwan de jieshou shi ji qi yiyi" 莫言在臺灣的接受史及其意義 [Acceptance history and meaning in Taiwan of the 2012 Nobel Prize laureate in literature Mo Yan]. *Shida xuebao: Yuyan yu wenxue lei* 師大學報: 語言與文學類 [Journal of National Taiwan Normal University: Language and literature] 60, no. 2 (2015): 1–28.

Lee, Tong King. "China as Dystopia: Cultural Imaginings through Translation." *Translation Studies* 8, no. 3 (2015): 251–68.

Li Ang 李昂, ed. *Jiushi nian xiaoshuo xuan* 九十年小說選 [Selected novellas of the 1990s]. Taipei: Jiuge, 2002.

Li Zishu 黎紫書. "Shan wen" 山瘟 [Mountain plague]. *Lianhe bao* 聯合報 [United Daily News], 25 Sep. 2000.

Lim, Benjamin Kang. "China's Censors 'Serve the People' with Ban on Novel," *The Seattle Times*, 16 Apr. 2005. https://www.seattletimes.com/nation-world/chinas-censors-serve-the-people-with-ban-on-novel/ (last accessed 30 Aug. 2021).

Lin Xinyi 林欣誼. "Huawen wenxue gaofenghui kamu: Dashi yunji" 華文文學高峰會開幕 大師雲集 [Chinese literature summit opens with a gathering of masters]. *Zhongguo shibao* 中國時報 [China Times], 17 Apr. 2010.

Liu Nai-Tzu 劉乃慈. "Richang de feichang: *Liushui zhang* de shuqing xiangtu yu xushi" 日常的非常——《流水帳》的抒情鄉土與敘事 [The extraordinary daily life: Lyric native and narrative of *Running Account*]. *Taiwan wenxue xuebao* 台灣文學學報 [Bulletin of Taiwanese Literature], no. 20 (June 2012): 99–126.

Lo Man Chi 盧敏芝. "Taiwan wenxue changyu yu Huang Biyun xiaoshuo de 'jingdian hua'" 台灣文學場域與黃碧雲小說的「經典化」 [The literary field of Taiwan and the "canonisation" of Wong Bik-Wan's fiction]. *Taiwan wenxue yanjiu xuebao* 台灣文學研究學報 [Journal of Taiwan Literary Studies], no. 31 (Oct. 2020): 233–76.

Moratto, Riccardo, and Di-kai Chao, "Yan Lianke zuopin zai Taiwan de jieshou jiqi yiyi 閻連科作品在臺灣的接受及其意義 [The reception of Yan Lianke's works in Taiwan and its significance]," *Yanshan daxue xuebao (zhexue shehui kexue ban)* 燕山大學學報 (哲學社會科學版) [Journal of Yanshan University (Philosophy and Social Science Edition)] 22, no. 6 (November 2021): 36–45.

Qing Tian 青田. "Zhongguo dalu 2005 nian di yi jinshu de hongdong xiaoying: *Wei renmin fuwu* bei jin, Yan Lianke lülü huo jiang" 中國大陸2005年第一禁書的轟動效應《為人民服務》被禁, 閻連科屢屢獲獎 [The stirring effect of mainland China's first banned book in 2005: *Serve the People* Banned, Yan Lianke awarded repeatedly]. *Lianhe bao*, 31 May 2005.

Sha Maomao 沙貓貓, ed. "Shuyou hui jilu: Wenxue zhubian tan Yan Lianke xinzuo *Shouhuo*" 書友會記錄: 文學主編談閻連科新作《受活》 [Reader's club minutes: Literary editors talk about Yan Lianke's new book *Lenin's Kisses*]. Xiaoxiao shufang 小小書房 [Small life bookstore], 28 Jan. 2007. https://smallbooks.com.tw/2007/01/28/%E6%9B%B8%E5%8F%8B%E6%9C%83%E7%B4%80%E9%8C%84%EF%BC%9A%E6%96%87%E5%AD%B8%E4%B8%BB%E7%B7%A8%E8%AB%87%E9%96%BB%E9%80%A3%E7%A7%91%E6%96%B0%E4%BD%9C%E3%80%8A%E5%8F%97%E6%B4%BB%E3%80%8B/ (last accessed 30 Aug. 2021).

Shi Fang-yu 石芳瑜. "Yan Lianke *Tamen* shuping: Miaoxie dadi wanwu shi wenzhi jiqi mohuan, tanlun aiqing shi que ruci jiandan" 閻連科《她們》書評: 描寫大地萬物時文字極其魔幻, 談論愛情時卻

如此簡單 [Book review of Yan Lianke's *They*: The words are extremely magical when describing the earth and everything, but so simple when talking about love]. *Guanjian pinglun* 關鍵評論 [The News Lens]. 28 Sep. 2020. https://www.thenewslens.com/article/140895 (last accessed 15 July 2021).

Shih Hsiao-feng 石曉楓. "Dalu wenge xiaoshuo zhong de shenti kuanghuan xushi ji qi yiyi: Yi Wang Xiaobo, Yan Lianke wei zhuyao taolun duixiang" 大陸文革小說中的身體狂歡敘事及其意義——以王小波、閻連科為主要討論對象 [Body carnival narratives and their meaning in mainland China's Cultural Revolution fiction: Wang Xiaobo and Yan Lianke as the main subjects of discussion]. Final report on National Science Council, Executive Yuan 行政院, Taipei. 21 Jan. 2013. https://wsts.most.gov.tw/STSWeb/Award/AwardMultiQuery.aspx?year=110&code=QS01&organ=&name=%e7%9f%b3%e6%9b%89%e6%a5%93 (last accessed 11 Aug. 2021).

———. "Geming yu xing'ai de jile zhanchang: Yan Lianke *Jianying ru shui* zhong de shenti Shuxie" 革命與性愛的極樂戰場——閻連科《堅硬如水》中的身體書寫 [The happiest battle field of revolution and sex: Body writing in Yan Lianke's *Hard Like Water*]. *Guowen xuebao* 國文學報 [Bulletin of Chinese], no. 51 (June 2012): 241–66.

———. "Zhengzhi kuangre xia de nongmin wange: Yan Lianke *Shouhuo* pingjie" 政治狂熱下的農民輓歌—閻連科《受活》評介 [The peasant's elegy under the political frenzy: Review of Yan Lianke's *Lenin's Kisses*]. *Wen hsun*, no. 258 (Apr. 2007): 102–3.

———. "Zhongguo xin shiqi xiaoshuo zhong de guimei xushi ji qi yiyi (di 3 nian)" 中國新時期小說中的鬼魅敘事及其意義(第3年) [Ghost narratives and their meaning in Chinese new-age fiction (year 3)]. Final report on the project funded by the Ministry of Science and Technology, Taipei, 20 Oct. 2018. https://wsts.most.gov.tw/STSWeb/Award/AwardMultiQuery.aspx?year=110&code=QS01&organ=&name=%e7%9f%b3%e6%9b%89%e6%a5%93 (last accessed 11 Aug. 2021).

Shih, Shu-Mei. "Global Literature and the Technologies of Recognition." *PMLA* 119, no. 1 (2004): 16–30.

Tang Yu-Li 唐毓麗. "Binghuan de yiyi: Tan *Tinge liaoluan* ji *Dingzhuang meng* de jiazu/guozu jishi yu shenti" 病患的意義——談《天河撩亂》及《丁莊夢》的家族／國族紀事與身體 [The Significance of Patients: On the Family/State Chronicle and Body of *Milky Way is (Dazzling)* and *Dream of Ding Village*]. *Xingda renwen xuebao* 興大人文學報 [Journal of Humanities College of Liberal Arts, National Chung Hsing University], no. 49 (2012): 145–81.

Wang David Der-wei 王德威. "Geming shidai de ai yu si: Lun dalu wentan fengtou zuojia Yan Lianke de *Wei renmin fuwu*" 革命時代的愛與死 論大陸文壇鋒頭作家閻連科的《為人民服務》 [Love and death in the age of revolution: On pioneer writer in mainland China's literary scene, Yan Lianke, and his *Serve the People*]. *Lianhe bao*, 27 Dec. 2005.

———. "Geming shidai de ai yu si: Lun Yan Lianke de xiaoshuo" 革命時代的愛與死——論閻連科的小說 [Love and death in the age of revolution: On Yan Lianke's novel]. Foreword to *Wei renmin fuwu* 為人民服務 [Serve the people], by Yan Lianke, 5–38. 2006. Reprint, Taipei: Maitian, 2018.

Wu Ming-yi 吳明益. "Mongdong shi xiezuo xiaoshuo de zui hao zhuangtai" 懵懂是寫作小說的最好狀態 [Innocence is the best state for writing fiction]. *Wen hsun*, no. 314 (Dec. 2011): 130–31.

———. "Na lengku beihou de fangxiang" 那冷酷背後的芳香 [The fragrance behind the ruthless]. *Zhongguo shibao*, 19 May 2012.

Wu Wei-zhen 巫維珍. "'Zuojia zuopin ji' xie wenxue shi: Zhuanfang Maitian chuban fu zongbianji Lin Xiumei, bianji Lai Huiqi" 「作家作品集」寫文學史: 專訪麥田出版副總編輯林秀梅、編輯賴惠琪 ["The Collection of Writers and Works" writing literary history: An interview with Lin Xiumei, deputy chief editor, and Lai Huiqi, editor, of Rye Field Publishing]. *Wen hsun*, no. 355 (May 2015): 83–88.

Xu Deming 徐德明. "'Huawen yujing' zhong de dandai xiaoshuo piping shijie: Cong Wang Dewei de 'zhishi dili' tankan shuoqi" 「華文語境」中的當代小說批評視界——從王德威的「知識地理」探勘說起 [A critical perspective of contemporary fiction within the *Huawen* context: An exploration of David Wang's "Geography of Knowledge"]. *Shijie huawen wenxue luntan* 世界華文文學論壇 [Forum for Chinese literature of the world], 2002, no. 3: 17–22.

Xu Qiuling 徐秋玲. "Huawen wenxue de chuzou yu guilai" 華文文學的出走與歸來 [The exodus and return of Sinophone literature]. *Da ayi xiang tai duo* 大阿姨想太多 [Big auntie thinks too much], 25 Apr. 2015. https://blog.xuite.net/home14498/twblog/mosaic-view/312585708 (last accessed 10 Aug. 2021).

Yan Lianke. "Haibian de Yan Lianke: Lai Xianggang shi yi zhong taoli" 海邊的閻連科: 來香港教書是一種逃離 [Yan Lianke by the sea: Coming to Hong Kong to teach is an escape]. Interview by Fu

Ziyang 付子洋. Duan chuanmei 端傳媒 [Initium Media], 3 July 2018. https://theinitium.com/article/20180626-mainland-yanlianke/ (last accessed 10 Aug. 2021).

Yang Sen 楊森, "Xiandaihua licheng zhong de haixia liangan xiangtu wenxue: Yi Huang Chunming yu Yan Lianke wei guancha hexin" 現代化歷程中的海峽兩岸鄉土文學——以黃春明與閻連科為觀察核心 [Cross-straits local literature in the process of modernization: The comparison between Huang Chunming and Yan Lianke in local literature writing]. *Gaoxiong shida xuebao* 高雄師大學報 [Kaohsiung Normal University journal], no. 43 (Dec. 2017): 31–48.

———. "Xiangtu de taoli yu huigui: Yan Lianke ji qi zuopin (1919–2013) yanjiu" 鄉土的逃離與回歸——閻連科及其作品(1979–2013) 研究 [Local escape and return: Researches on Yan Lianke and his literary works (1979–2013)]. PhD diss., National Chung Cheng University, 2017.

Yueliang Xiong 月亮熊. "Taiwan xiaoshuo mai bu chuqu: Quanyin shuizhun bi bu shang fanyi zuopin?" 台灣小說賣不出去 全因水準比不上翻譯作品？ [The reason why Taiwanese novels don't sell is because the standard is not as good as the translated works?]. Changyi 倡議 [Advocacy], 23 Feb. 2019. https://ubrand.udn.com/ubrand/story/11815/3660715 (last accessed 10 Aug. 2021).

Zen. "Dalu changxiao shu zai Taiwan, huozhe shuo zai Taiwan changxiao de dalu chuban pin/Zuojia" 大陸暢銷書在台灣, 或者說在台灣暢銷的大陸出版品/作家 [Best-selling books from mainland China in Taiwan, or best-selling mainland Chinese publications/authors in Taiwan]. *Zen da de Dunnan xin shenghuo* Zen 大的敦南新生活 [Mr. Zen's new life in Dunnan], 12 May 2011. https://zen1976.com/post-1322146939/ (last accessed 10 Aug. 2021).

Zhan Min-xu 詹閔旭. "Duo di gong gou de Huayu yuxi wenxue: Yi Ma-Hua wenxue de Taiwan jingyu wei li" 多地共構的華語語系文學: 以馬華文學的台灣境遇為例 [Sinophone literature as places-based production: On the predicament of Sinophone Malaysian literature in Taiwan]. *Taiwan wenxue xuebao*, no. 30 (June 2017): 81–110.

Zhang Yue-han 張約翰. "Xin meiti bu shi baoye yingxu zhi di, er shi bijing de xiantu" 新媒體不是報業應許之地 而是必經的險途 [New media is not a promised land for the newspaper industry, but a necessary and dangerous path]. Da shuju 大數聚 [Big data group], 26 Feb. 2016. https://group.dailyview.tw/article/detail/252 (last accessed 16 July 2021).

32
THE RECEPTION OF YAN LIANKE IN HONG KONG

Carole Hang-fung Hoyan* and Yijiao Guo

Introduction

Yan Lianke 閻連科 is a prolific and controversial mainland Chinese author who attracts global attentions. Three of his novels and short stories collections banned in the mainland were published in Hong Kong, including *Serve the People!* (*Wei renmin fuwu* 為人民服務, 2005), *The Years, Months, Days* (*Nian yue ri* 年月日, 2009), and *The Four Books* (*Si shu* 四書, 2010). Yan was awarded The sixth Dream of the Red Chamber Award: The World's Distinguished Novel in Chinese organized by Hong Kong Baptist University (HKBU) for his novel *The Day the Sun Died* (*Rixi* 日熄) in 2017. He served as Visiting Professor of Chinese Culture at the Hong Kong University of Science and Technology (HKUST) and was conferred Doctor of Letters honoris causa. His two lecture collections review the dissemination and impacts of nineteenth-and-twentieth-century world literature on China. Despite Yan being connected to Hong Kong in many ways, not many previous studies thoroughly discussed his reception in this city, especially his reception in Hong Kong's academia.

What is the significance of Yan's encounter with Hong Kong? How do Hong Kong scholars and critics view Yan's mythorealist portrayal of the economic development of China in the age of globalization? This paper investigates the reception of Yan in Hong Kong from a cross-regional perspective, by analyzing Yan's literary works published in Hong Kong, his award-winning novel *The Day the Sun Died*, *The Explosions Chronicles* (*Zhalie zhi* 炸裂志), and *The Four Book* in particular. It also probes into the dynamics of how Yan and his writings travel to Hong Kong and beyond. It draws on materials including anthologies reviews, journal papers, articles on local Chinese and English newspapers, academic conferences, graduate theses, and interviews. The promotional strategies of the publishers and the quantitative approach

---

* An earlier version of this paper by Carole Hang-fung Hoyan, "The Reception of the Yan Lianke in Hong Kong," was presented at the conference panel "The Belt and Road of Banned Chinese Literature: The Global Receptions of Yan Lianke," organized and chaired by Howard Y. F. Choy, AAS-in-Asia 2020 Asia at the Crossroads: Solidarity through Scholarship, Association for Asian Studies, Kobe, 3 Sep. 2020. My thanks to Yip Ka Wing for helping with the collection of research materials, Xiang Yinkwan for helping with the generation of the word clouds, and Guo Yijiao for transcribing the presentation.

of word cloud will also be employed to supplement the analysis. This chapter resituates the reviews on Yan and his novels in the context of world literature and probes into the dynamics of how Yan's works have traveled to Hong Kong and other locations beyond mainland China. It holds that Yan is perceived in Hong Kong as a controversial mainland author, who revealed through his "mythorealism" the "reality" hidden behind China's door that is half-opened and half-closed. Moreover, the significance of Yan's encounter with Hong Kong lies in its cross-regional publications and activities, which enable a censored writer to reconnect with global readers.

A literary encounter: Yan Lianke's anthologies in Hong Kong

Before moving any further, a brief report on Yan's anthologies shall be made. The landscape of Yan's publishing is never limited to a single place; it ranges from mainland China, Hong Kong, and Taiwan to overseas. For instance, *Serve the People!* was published by both the local publisher Hong Kong Culture & Arts Publishing and Rye Field Publishing in Taipei in 2005. *The Years, Months, Days* was first published in the mainland by Xinjiang People's Publishing in 2002, of which two consecutive copies were made in 2009 by Ming Po 明報 Publications in Hong Kong and the Youth Book in Singapore. In the case of *The Four Books*, Rye Field republished this novel in 2011 after Ming Po Publications introduced it to the Hong Kong reader one year ago.

In 2020, The City University of Hong Kong Press (CityU Press) launched a book series titled Overseas Anthologies of Yan Lianke. This book series commenced with Yan's latest novel *Heart Sutra* (*Xinjing* 心經) on 1 January and was followed by the reprinting of his five previous works *Serve the People!*, *Summer Sunset* (*Xia riluo* 夏日落), *Dream of Ding Village* (*Dingzhuang meng* 丁莊夢), *The Day the Sun Dies*, and *The Four Books* on 20 March.[1] Three-volume omnibuses in the serial arrived on 1 July, which re-edited and reprinted his thoughts and reflections in recent years of overseas living, writing, and teaching into three anthologies: *With a Wild Voice: Yan Lianke's Collected Overseas Speeches* (*Ye sangzi: Haiwai yanjiang lu* 野桑子——海外演講錄), *Opening the Door of China: Yan Lianke's Collected Overseas Writings* (*Tuikai Zhongguo de ling yi shan chuang: Haiwai suibi ji* 推開中國的另一扇窗——海外隨筆集), and *Silence and Rest: My Experience with China and Chinese Literature* (*Chenmo yu chuanxi: Wo suo jingli de Zhongguo yu wenxue* 沉默與喘息——我所經歷的中國與文學).[2]

As the book introduction on the official website of CityU Press reads, the title *Opening the Door of China* vividly conveys a metaphor of "door" (or "window" in the Chinese title) that on the one hand summarized the sociohistorical context of the mainland after the reform policy that opened China's economy door to the world market.[3] On the other, it precisely captured the awkwardness in China's politics door that is described as "half opened and half closed," behind which China's history is intangible, the reality is mediated, and people's mind is obfuscated by the outrageous reality that is undistinguished from fiction.[4] The

---

1 For a full list of Yan's works published by CityU Press, please refer to https://www.cityu.edu.hk/upress/catalogsearch/result/?q=%E9%96%BB%E9%80%A3%E7%A7%91 (last accessed 12 Aug. 2021).
2 Ibid.
3 Ibid.
4 CityU Press, eds., "Opening the Door of China: Yan Lianke's Collected Overseas Writings," https://www.cityu.edu.hk/upress/opening-the-door-of-china (last accessed 25 Aug. 2021): "中國有兩扇窗，一扇「經濟」已經打開，另一扇「政治」卻在半開半閉間。"

predicament in today's China was taken as where Yan situated his writings made overseas into the retrospections upon China and the Chinese society and, accordingly, formulated his representative reception in the broad lands outside the PRC.

The significant publishing event of the Overseas Anthologies of Yan Lianke series has provoked multiple reviews. For instance, *Heart Sutra* was described as "a real story that subverts the distance between men and men, men and god, and gods and gods."[5] The awards-winning novel *Dream of Ding Village* was seen as a representative work that not only "earned Yan world acclaims" but also renowned him with controversy.[6] The contentious subject of Yan's literature creations was epitomized by *Serve the People!*, which became (in)famous for its reputation as a "censored book" and encountered six prohibitions (publishing, reprinting, reviewing, excerpting, reporting, and adapting) after publication in the PRC.[7] Nevertheless, the very novel has also been translated into twenty languages which, as the publisher stated, "aroused great concerns and heated discussions among medias and readers."[8]

In fact, the controversies around Yan started much earlier in his 1992 novel *Summer Sunset*. The story sets its background in the People's Liberation Army (PLA) during the Sino-Vietnamese War and "stroke the revolution in military literature and started Yan's life and writing of self-exile that last for half a year."[9]

Yan is perceived by the press as a storyteller who never fails to exert a poetically eerie feeling for his reader on account of his syntheses of absurdity and reality, which Yan names "mythorealism."[10] In the introduction to *The Day the Sun Died*, CityU Press elucidated that this novel manifested such a literary aesthetics in the manner that "the world is finally non-hypocritic on the day the sun died, but the reality is absurd and sad."[11] It also observed that Yan utilized a Bible-like language in *The Four Books* to remap the Anti-Rightist Campaign and the Great Famine history. The language style of this novel in particular received a comment that it "forms a collage of Eastern and Western religions and fables, mingling them with the

---

5 CityU Press, eds., "Heart Sutra," CityU Press, https://www.cityu.edu.hk/upress/heart–sutra (last accessed 25 Aug. 2021): "這是一部顛覆人與人、人與神、神與神距離的現實故事。"
6 CityU Press, eds., "Dream of Ding Village," https://www.cityu.edu.hk/upress/dream–of–ding–village-in–chinese (last accessed 25 Aug. 2021): "《丁莊夢》為閻連科贏得了世界聲譽"; "閻連科不是被爭議而廣為人知,而是廣為人知而備受爭議。"
7 CityU Press, eds., "Serve the People," https://www.cityu.edu.hk/upress/serve–the–people–in–chinese (last accessed 12 Aug. 2021): "一部禁書"; "不准發行、不准轉載、不准評論、不准摘輯、不准報導不准改編。"
8 Ibid.
9 CityU Press, eds., "Summer Sunset," https://www.cityu.edu.hk/upress/summer-sunset-in-chinese (last accessed 12 Aug. 2021): "引來了整個軍事文學的變革,開始了閻連科長達半年的檢討和自我放逐的人生與寫作。"
10 Cf. Howard Y. F. Choy 蔡元豐, "*You, you, you*: Yan Lianke de hei'an xiaoshuo *Rixi*" 遊、憂、幽——閻連科的黑暗小說《日熄》 [Itineraria, tristia, and darkness: Yan Lianke's dark novel *The Day the Sun Died*], Introduction to *The Sixth Dream of the Red Chamber Award: Collected Essays on Yan Lianke's The Day the Sun Died*, ed. Choy (Hong Kong: Infolink Publishing, 2018), ix–xi; Sun Yu 孫郁, "Yan Lianke de shengshi zhuyi" 閻連科的神實主義 [Yan Lianke's mythrealism], *Xindi wenxue* 新地文學 [New land literature], no. 26 (Dec. 2013): 147–56; Cao Xuenan, "Mythorealism and Enchanted Time: Yan Lianke's Explosion Chronicles," *Frontiers of Literary Studies in China* 10, no. 1 (May 2016): 103–12; Weijie Song 宋偉杰, "Yan Lianke's Mythorealist Representation of the Country and the City," *Modern Fiction Studies* 62, no. 4 (Winter 2016): 644–58.
11 CityU Press, eds., "The Day the Sun Died," https://www.cityu.edu.hk/upress/the–day–the–sun–died–in–chinese (last accessed 12 Aug. 2021): "日熄之日,世界終於不再虛偽,現實卻是荒誕又可悲。"

'realist'."[12] These two novels simultaneously brought Yan international fame and awards. *The Day the Sun Died* became the winners of the Dream of the Red Chamber Award, the Best Book of the Year by *Publishers Weekly*, and the Best Fiction in Translation Selection by *Kirkus Reviews*. Shortlisted for the Man Booker International Prize and the Prix Fémina, *The Four Books* also pinned its name on the winning list of the Franz Kafka Prize and honored Yan, the first Chinese author who won this international award.

The cross-regional travel experience from the mainland to Hong Kong also enhanced Yan's fame and earned him many recognitions in Hong Kong. The travel started with Yan's writer-in-residence at the HKUST in 2012 for two months. Yan served as IAS Sin Wai Kin Professor of Chinese Culture and Chair Professor of Humanities in 2013 and was conferred Doctor of Letters honoris causa in 2017 by the HKUST, where he has been teaching a creative writing course. His lecture series was later refashioned into a two-volume anthology *Yan Lianke's Writing Class: Twelve Lectures on the Literature in the Past Century* (*Bainian xiezuo shi'er jiang: Yan Lianke de wenxue jiangtang* 百年寫作十二講: 閻連科的文學講堂). Chung Hwa Book 中華書局 (Hong Kong) published this collection of lecture series in 2017, wherein Yan reviewed the dissemination and impacts of nineteenth- and twentieth-century world literature upon contemporary China and Chinese writers.

The reception of Yan in Hong Kong in this regard also involved world literature as one perspective of reading him, for the publication of his lecture series anchored the connection between him and the world literature in that Chinese literature and Chinese authors took rich resources from literature all over the regions and cultures. This publication made it tangible to juxtapose Yan's travel to Hong Kong with the literary interactions and intercultural communications between China and the world. As a result, the understanding of Yan as a mainland Chinese writer was intertwined with his efforts to transcend different cultural-geographical boundaries via both his literary creations and teaching in Hong Kong. The significance of the literary encounter between Yan and Hong Kong thus is more than the physical transportation and relocation that enabled more freedoms for a censored Chinese writer. Such an encounter also activated a mobility of narratives, which is seen in the trans-regional publications and reception of a censored writer with limited accessibility to world-wide readership. The following discussions will respond in detail to how Yan was viewed in Hong Kong through data generated from different local media.

Reviews in monographs, journal papers, articles, and theses

This section illustrates the general situation of how Yan's works were reviewed and understood in various media and publishing forms in Hong Kong, including but not limited to books, research publications, review articles, newspapers, and magazine journals. Three major categories of monograph, journal paper, and article will be considered primarily to demonstrate the receptions regarding Yan and his novel writing.

The presentation of Yan's image as a writer varies with the categories of publications. In general, newspaper and magazine articles tended to underline the censorial influences upon Yan and his identity as a censored Chinese writer, who also obtained many international literary awards. Meanwhile, scholarly works, graduate studies, and academic conferences concentrated on other topics such as the relationship between reality and absurdity, Yan's

---

12 CityU Press, eds., "The Four Books," https://www.cityu.edu.hk/upress/the-four-books-in-chinese (last accessed 12 Aug. 2021): "拼貼東西方宗教、神話與「最現實」的融合。"

proposition of mythorealism, and his role in Chinese literary history. Nonetheless, several recurrent descriptions regarding the identity of Yan as a writer and the meanings of his novels are found among all categories of media and these descriptions joined to read Yan in Hong Kong as a door to China's society and history.

In Hong Kong in 2018, the Faculty of Arts at HKBU published a monograph of essay-collection on Yan's *The Day the Sun Died* after this novel won the sixth Dream of the Red Chamber Award, which includes critique articles, book reviews, interview transcriptions, and nine appendixes contributed by scholars from all over the world. Chung Hwa Book in 2019 published another scholarly monograph authored by the mainland scholar Zhou Shubo 周述波. Zhou assessed Yan as "the master of absurd realism" and "the most excellent and controversial writer" in contemporary China.[13] He highlighted the necessity to situate Yan's novels as a dynamic unity into the reflections upon history and reality as well as thought and culture in the current period of social transformation.[14]

Articles published in both academic or non-academic journals edited and circulated in Hong Kong formed a receptive sphere and thus forged a rich touch of feedback regarding the role of Yan's works in literary history and the meaning of his narratives in the contemporary time. Most of these articles focused on *The Day the Sun Died*, the novel that won the aforementioned Hong Kong literature award, and *The Explosion Chronicles*, a work written in Hong Kong and inspired by the development model of the nearby mainland metropolis Shenzhen. In the aspect of academic journals, Chau Man Lut's 鄒文律 essay uttered a local voice in the discussions of Yan. Chau illustrated in detail the ideological relations between the utopia/paradise pictured in *Lenin's Kisses* and Maoist utopianism of "the ideal society" in Chinese Daoism through the case studies of the two protagonists Mao Zhi and Liu Yingque.[15] The author chose four keywords, "utopia," "paradise," "communism," and "post-Mao era," to analyze Yan's depictions of utopia and paradise in *Lenin's Kisses* and how Yan composed an anti-utopian writing by subverting Maoism and criticizing the pursuit of the "communist utopia" (i.e., "getting-rich-together") in the post-Mao era.[16] Nine articles in total can be found in local non-academic journals such as *Asiaweek* (*Yazhou zhoukan* 亞洲週刊), *Twenty-First Century* (*Ershiyi shiji shuangyuekan* 二十一世紀雙月刊), *Master Insight* (*Zhuojian mingjia* 灼見名家), *Initium Media* (*Duan chuanmei* 端傳媒), *Fleurs des Lettres* (*Zi hua* 字花), and *Ming Pao* 明報.[17] One special case is Lee Yee's 李怡 article "*The Explosion Chronicles*: The Latest Work

---

13 Zhou Shubo, "Xiangtu shang de cunzai zhi si yu nongcun chuanbo: Yan Lianke xiaoshuo chuangzuo lun" 鄉土上的存在之思與農村傳播：閻連科小說創作論 [Thinking of existence in the country and rural communication: On Yan Lianke's fictional creation], Chung Hwa Book Company, https://www.chunghwabook.com.hk/Index/book_detail/id/2833.html (last accessed 12 Aug. 2021): "荒誕現實主義大師"; "最優秀也最具爭議性的作家."

14 Ibid.: "將閻連科的小說視為一個有機發展的整體放在社會轉型期的歷史與現實、思想與文化中進行考察，力求呈現一個有關閻連科的全面完整的文學世界。"

15 Chau Man Lut, "Yi chu wutuobang zhi wai: Lun Yan Lianke *Shouhuo* de fan wutuobang Shuxie" 逸出烏托邦之外——論閻連科《受活》的反烏托邦書寫 [Escape from utopia: On the anti-utopian writing in Yan Lianke's *Lenin's Kisses*], *Zhongguo wenxue xuebao* 中國文學學報 [Journal of Chinese literature], vol. 8 (Dec. 2017): 151–86.

16 Ibid.

17 The nine articles are: Mao Ying 毛瑩, "Yan Lianke xie bei zhalie de ganqing" 閻連科寫被炸裂的感情 [Yan Lianke writes about exploded feelings], *Yazhou zhoukan*, 9–15 Dec. 2013, 49; Bu Lili 布莉莉 and Guo Quanzhao 郭全照, "Cang qiao yu tianran zhi zhong" 藏巧於天然之中 [Hiding ingenuity in the natural], *Ershiyi shiji shuangyuekan*, no. 135 (Feb. 2013): 145–50; Jiang Xun 江迅, "Yan Lianke huo Hongloumeng jiang qiyuan" 閻連科獲紅樓夢獎奇緣 [Yan Lianke wins the Dream of the Red Chamber Award], *Zhuojian mingjia*, 6 Oct. 2010, https://www.master-insight.

of the Most Censored Chinese Writer Yan Lianke," which was first aired in the radio program "One-Minute Reading" ("Yi fenzhong yuedu" 一分鐘閱讀) and later adapted into an article published on *ET Net* (*Jingji tong* 經濟通).[18]

As demonstrated above, terms such as controversy, censorship, and political association are commonly associated with how readers and publishers perceive Yan and his literary works. Yan was read as an author who invariably fell trapped by the censorship machine but kept writing fearlessly. Nevertheless, it remains opaque how Hong Kong scholars and critics in particular view Yan's mythorealist and reality-discoursive depictions of the changes in China during the particular socioeconomic era of globalization and market economy. The intermediality and multiplicity render a quantitative investigation especially informative for analyzing the diverse understandings of Yan and his novels. Consequently, a word cloud is utilized to analyze Yan's novels and directly visualize the ever-growing feedback of scholarly works. The word cloud (Figure 32.1) is generated from the commentaries on his novel *The Day the Sun Died* in the reviewing pieces previously mentioned. The size of a Chinese character or phrase corresponds to the frequency of its appearance in the reviewing pieces in the word cloud. The word cloud indicates that the diversified receptions of Yan in Hong Kong synchronize with the heterogeneity in his cross-regional publishing activities.

Large characters or terms such as "literature" (*wenxue* 文學), "writer" (*zuojia* 作家), "darkness" (*hei'an* 黑暗), "story" (*gushi* 故事), "reality" (*xianshi* 現實), "award" (*jiang* 獎), and "Hong Kong" (Xianggang 香港) reveal how scholars identified Yan as a Chinese writer and the novels *The Day the Sun Died* as a literary phenomenon. Small characters or terms such as "dream" (*meng* 夢), "absurdity" (*huangdan* 荒誕), "politics" (*zhengzhi* 政治), "controversy"

com/%E9%96%BB%E9%80%A3%E7%A7%91%E7%8D%B2%E7%B4%85%E6%A8%93%E5%A4%A2%E7%8D%8E%E5%A5%87%E7%B7%A3/ (last accessed 17 Aug. 2021); Cyan Yuan 袁瑋婧, "Wujin heian zhi zhong, ta de bi xia you guang" 無盡黑暗之中 他的筆下有光 [In the endless darkness, there is light under his pen], Cyan Yuan (blog), 21 June 2019, https://cyanyuan.medium.com/%E9%96%BB%E9%80%A3%E7%A7%91–%E7%84%A1%E7%9B%A1%E9%BB%91%E6%9A%97%E4%B9%8B%E4%B8%AD–%E4%BB%96%E7%9A%84%E7%AD%86%E4%B8%8B%E6%9C%89%E5%85%89–b1b36be250d0 (last accessed 17 Aug. 2021); Howard Y. F. Choy, "You, you, you: Yan Lianke de hei'an xiaoshuo Rixi," *Zhuojian mingjia*, 19 June 2018, https://www.master-insight.com/%E9%81%8A%E3%80%81%E6%86%82%E3%80%81%E5%B9%BD–%E9%96%BB%E9%80%A3%E7%A7%91%E7%9A%84%E9%BB%91%E6%9A%97%E5%B0%8F%E8%AA%AA%E3%80%8A%E6%97%A5%E7%86%84%E3%80%8B/ (last accessed 17 Aug. 2021); Howard Y. F. Choy, "Etuobang xiaoshuo *Rixi*" 惡托邦小說《日熄》 [Dystopia novel *The Day the Sun Died*], *Zhuojian mingjia*, 22 June 2018, https://www.master-insight.com/%E3%80%8A%E6%97%A5%E7%86%84%E3%80%8B%EF%BC%9A%E6%83%A1%E6%89%98%E9%82%A6%E5%B0%8F%E8%AA%AA/ (last accessed 17 Aug. 2021); Tang Ching-kin 鄧正健, "Xianshi zhuyi shuxie, ji qi zhenshi: Yan Lianke de *Faxian xiaoshuo*" 現實主義書寫, 及其真實——閻連科的《發現小說》 [Realistic writing, and its truth: Yan Lianke's *Discovering Fiction*], *Zi hua* 字花 [Fleurs des Lettres], Jan. & Feb. 2014, 47; Xie Xuan 謝璇, "'Zou chuqu' he 'zou huilai': Ji Yan Lianke Hongloumeng jiang jiangzuo 'Xianggang yu wo de wenxue yiyi'"「走出去」和「走回來」——記閻連科紅樓夢獎講座「香港於我的文學意義」 ["Going out" and "coming back": Dream of the Red Chamber Award lecture by Yan Lianke, "The literary significance of Hong Kong to me"], *Ming Pao*, 7 Nov. 2016, https://m.mingpao.com/pns/副刊/article/20161107/s00005/1478456523468/明藝–報道–「走出去」和「走回來」–記閻連科紅樓夢獎講座「香港於我的文學意義」 (last accessed 17 Aug. 2021).

18 "One-Minute Reading" is a program broadcasted on the local Cantonese-based radio channel RTHK Radio 1 (FM92.6–94.4) from Monday to Friday and posted on the RTHK website (rthk.hk). Lee Yee, "Zui chang zaojin de zuojia Yan Lianke xinzuo *Zhalie zhi*" 最常遭禁作家閻連科新作《炸裂志》 [The most frequently banned writer Yan Lianke's new work *The Explosion Chronicles*], Jingji tong 經濟通 [ET Net], 23 Nov. 2021, http://www.etnet.com.hk/www/tc/diva/art/oneminreading/21272 (last accessed 17 Aug. 2021).

Figure 32.1 Word cloud of scholarly works

(*zhenyi* 爭議), "society" (*shehui* 社會), "utopia" (*wutuobang* 烏托邦), and "Lu Xun" 魯迅 demonstrate the criteria for evaluating the writer Yan and the literary characteristics of this novel.

To put it into specific terms, the two most frequently occurred notional words, in addition to "Yan Lianke" as a general determiner, are "writer" and "China" (*Zhongguo* 中國), which were used 56 times and 50 times, respectively. "Darkness" as a general description occurred 25 times, and the term "Hong Kong" in particular occurred 23 times. The frequency slightly declined when the words were related to the styles or characteristics of the novel such as "story" (17 times), "reality" (16 times), "dream" (14 times), "world" (*shijie* 世界, 12 times), "life" (*shenghuo* 生活, 12 times), "dark" (*you* 幽, 12 times), "politics" (11 times), "absurdity" (10 times), "creation" (*chuangzuo* 創作, 10 times), "tradition" (*chuantong* 傳統, 10 times), "somnambulism" (*mengyou* 夢遊, 10 times), "doomed/fatalism" (*mingding* 命定, 9 times), "society" (9 times), "utopia" (9 times), "Lu Xun" (8 times), and "god/mythos" (*shen* 神, 7 times).

The term *you* in the cloud is worthy of further investigation. The "tradition of darkness" (*you chuantong* 幽傳統) as a counter-tradition has rooted in Chinese literary history, which was epitomized by myths, tales of the miraculous and the strange, and Lu Xun in the modern era.[19] Leo Ou-fan Lee 李歐梵 defined the tradition of *you* as the other side to light, which was about to enlighten the mass in the May Fourth Movement.[20] As in its original meaning of a small fire, *you* is the dimming light leading to the hope of illumination in the "doomed" darkness.[21]

In this regard, Yan's narrative in *The Day the Sun Died* was understood as an echo to his novelist predecessors, who delved into the unseen, intimidating depth to scrutinize the

---

19 Choy, "*You, you, you*," ix–xi.
20 Leo Lee, *Zhongguo wenhua de liu ge mianxiang* 中國文化的六個面向 [The Six Faces of Chinese Culture] (Hong Kong: Chinese University of Hong Kong Press, 2016), 253–57.
21 Choy, "*You, you, you*," xiv–xv.

illogical "world," the problematic Chinese "society" and the ambivalence of human nature in pursuance of reigniting humanity and reilluminating the world. Accordingly, the malady of "somnambulism" in the novel symbolizes not only an epidemic to people's bodies, but it also signifies a frenzy fueled by ruthless "politics" that strikes the entire nation and reloads people's minds with hollowness. As Howard Choy cited from the writer, this story reads like a "dream," in which one woke up from a "utopia" but only to find entering another.[22]

The word cloud indicates a receptive view that Yan intended to alienate "reality" from common sense and daily "life" through mythorealism in this fiction, which refashioned the "story" into a myth-like fictional "creation" where God became a young child. Such foreignizing and experimental narrative aesthetics compelled a divergent feeling among readers and literary critics. Thus, the term "controversy" (*zhengyi* 爭議, 8 times) in the word cloud displays a duality of dispute embodied in *The Day the Sun Died* that can be viewed from two dimensions. First at the textual-cum-narrative level, the controversy arose from the disturbing and horrific plots in the novel; and it was also originated from, at the sociocultural-cum-receptive level, the contestation over this book whereupon its denials by publishers in the mainland, its alternative publishing in Taiwan and Hong Kong, and its exceptional attainment of the Franz Kafka Prize. Therefore, terms such as "publication" (*chuban* 出版, 9 times), "mainland" (*dalu* 大陸, 10 times), and "hometown" (*guxiang* 故鄉, 10 times)" correlate to the suspensions of some intended publishing of Yan and the taboo status of his truth-confronting works in the PRC.

As an award-winning novel, there are also characters or terms that share connections to the achievement granted by the local university, such as "award," "literature," "award-winning" (*huo jiang* 獲獎, 8 times), "Dream of the Red Chamber" (*Hongloumeng* 紅樓夢, 10 times), and "Hong Kong Baptist University" (Xianggang jinhui daxue 香港浸會大學, 7 times). It shall also be noted that *Four Books* and *The Explosion Chronicles* won the Jury Award of the fourth and fifth of the Dream of Red Chambers Award in 2012 and 2014, respectively, which explains the appearances of words such as "explosion" (*zhalie* 炸裂, 21 times), "chronicle" (*zhi* 志, 12 times), and "*Four Books*" (*Si shu* 四書, 8 times) in the word cloud.

Interlingual receptions from newspapers, conferences, and interviews

As an inter-regional space, the language policy in the academia in Hong Kong sets its basic feature of multilingual practice, in which English has played an undeniable role in terms of academic language and performance. In consequence, Yan's receptions in the English world or English-orientated media instituted another discrete segment of how he is viewed and reviewed by Hong Kong scholars. The following parts in this section focus on four articles on Hong Kong-based newspapers, two academic symposiums held in local universities, three graduate student theses, and fourteen interviews Yan conducted with local (online) media so as to elaborate his receptions in English in Hong Kong. The four newspaper articles are selected from two leading English-language daily newspapers, *The Standard* and *South China Morning Post* (*SCMP*), in Hong Kong. Antoaneta Bezlova published a review article in the former newspaper on 28 May 2005 to reengage with the paradox that a banned book in China, saying the novella *Serve the People!* would cause troubles to the author while simultaneously guaranteeing fame and attention.[23] Bezlova also discussed that the explicit context

---

22 Ibid., xvi–xvii.
23 Antoaneta Bezlova, "Big Brother's Book Ban Blues," *The Standard*, 28 May 2005.

of "sex and political satire" triggered the censorial machine of the PRC government and the Party.[24] In her view, the utterly sensitive plot of adultery between a young soldier and the wife of an upper commander in the PLA crossed the bottom lines of many targeted subjects of party censor, which observers also understand as Yan's "sharp barb at corruption and vice in the army that earned it the axe."[25] Bezlova commented that the banning of this book "has stoked fervent anticipation for Yan's new work" that exposes the tragedies of the plasma economy and AIDS plight in his hometown Henan.[26] At the end of this article, Bezlova even forecasted that Yan would become "a literary star with foreign publishers" should his forthcoming book be censored and banned again, which later turned out to be true.[27]

Yan's two subsequent books, *The Four Books* and *The Day the Sun Died*, identically fell victims to the state's censorship and the suspension of publishing in the PRC. Cameron Deuck's article, posted on the *SCMP* on 17 Mar. 2015, tackled the desperate predicament of provisional publication for the specific overseas readership after Yan "abandoning any hope that it would be published in China even before he began writing it."[28] In Deuck's narrative, at this time, Yan found a distinguished approach for novel writing, for he filled *The Four Books* with "brilliantly chilling metaphors" and brought to life "the sadistic horror, robberies and denunciations caused by political misguidance."[29] Deuck continued to comment that adhering to the path of the literary tradition of *you*, this novel captures an aspect of Chinese life that is hard to imagine and understand for a foreigner, and Yan's depiction "reaffirms why he is China's most heralded and censored modern writer."[30]

Also posted on the *SCMP*, James Kidd's review dated 1 Aug. 2018 continued the discussion on the dark, absurd, and eerie writing style in *The Day the Sun Died*. Kidd noted that the political agenda in Yan's novel exposed the "abject horror" buried behind China's prosperity since the late twentieth century.[31] To do so, Yan as Kidd seen employed a regular habit in writing to compose a "national fable" wherein tiny things are compared to large things.[32] Kidd concluded that such a "highly fragmented and disjointed" story would fit both "the hallucinatory apocalypse enveloping Gaotian and Yan's broader political portrait of a planet out of joint."[33] Kidd's other review article on the *SCMP* on 8 Mar. 2020 also revealed a different aspect of Yan's literary creations that was family vis-à-vis history. Yan's 2020 book *Three Brothers: Memory of My Family* (*Wo yu fubei* 我與父輩) was read as a memoir that portrayed his father, uncles, and himself in youth. Kidd saw it in this work that Yan explored "poverty,

---

24 Ibid.
25 Ibid.
26 Ibid.
27 Ibid.
28 Cameron Deuck, "*The Four Books*—Biting Satire Offers Some Hope," *South China Morning Post*, 17 Mar. 2015, https://www.scmp.com/lifestyle/books/article/1742720/book-review-four-books-biting-satire-offers-some-hope (last accessed 17 Aug. 2021).
29 Ibid.
30 Ibid.
31 James Kidd, "Bleak reality confronts the Chinese dream in Yan Lianke's gruesome, gripping novel, *The Day the Sun Died*." *South China Morning Post*, August 1, 2018, https://www.scmp.com/magazines/post-magazine/books/article/2157656/bleak-reality-confronts-chinese-dream-yan-liankes (last accessed 17 Aug. 2021).
32 Ibid.
33 Kidd, "Bleak."

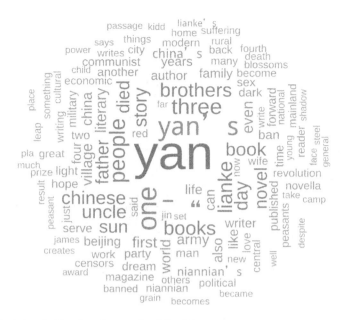

Figure 32.2 Word cloud of book reviews on local English newspapers

love, and the luxury of happiness" in this poignant nonfictional story, which was "as affecting as any of Yan's fictions."[34]

Another word cloud (Figure 32.2) generated from the four book reviews on local English newspapers is presented below. As the notable size of the word "Chinese" and "novel" indicates, many reviewers regarded these literary (the very term of "literary" per se occurred 11 times) works as Chinese literature despite the fact that they were published and mainly circulated and read in the overseas. Most of these abovementioned journalists also contributed words such as "author" and "writer" with "China" and "world" in their narratives about Yan, which reflected a trend of viewing him as a Chinese author. Nevertheless, Yan has spent a considerable time of his life in Hong Kong, penned more than nine novels and other works at the HKUST, and entered "world" (10 times) literature, or at least the literary landscape of the English-speaking world, long ago.

Suggesting the taboo in publication, the word "ban" and "banned" encapsulated the general impression of Yan's censored books, which directly points to the 6-time appearances of the word "censors." In correspondence, words such as "communist," "party," "sex," and "military" all occurred seven times, which underlines a cognitive rationale as well as result that the Chinese Communist Party (CCP) censored and banned Yan's novels because he depicted sex and negative contexts related to China's military faculties.

The receptions of the two reviewed books can be clearly classified in accordance with the different contexts that also share recurrent intertextual patterns. For *Serve the People!*, statistics tells that journalists utilized words such as "love," "political" and "revolution" (each

---

34 James Kidd, "Yan Lianke's Three Brothers honours his family and the struggle to survive in mid–20th century China," *South China Morning Post*, 8 Mar. 2020, https://www.scmp.com/magazines/post-magazine/books/article/3065106/yan-liankes-three-brothers-honours-his-family-and (last accessed 17 Aug. 2021).

with a frequency of occurrence of 6 times) to fathom the overall plot as a love story under political drives during an era of revolution, in which the signal of sex between Wu Dawang and Liu Lian was the revolutionary slogan of "serve the people" proposed by Mao Zedong. Words such as "peasants" and "economy" (each with a six-time frequency of occurrence) functioned as indicators of the underlying motivations of Wu and the overall background of the story.

As words "suffering," "home," "rural" and "death" (each with a frequency of occurrence of 5 times) indicate, *The Day the Sun Died* to Hong Kong readers was primarily a novel about ordeals, in which people sleepwalked in the hellish town in comma and human corpses were transacted as a commodity. Death was too common to astonish anyone any longer in this rural region that was so familiar to but can never qualify as home. Besides, similar to one reception by Hong Kong scholars, the event of winning the Kafka Prize occupied a central role in how Yan is viewed in Hong Kong, given that the word "prize" again appeared five times.

Both of the two novels were somehow seen as a response to the historical and political ecology in the disturbing times when the fetishisms of money, power, and a utopian hallucination surpassed all principles, ethics, laws, and even human dignity. Yan's writings were taken as one answer or one alternative of telling the outrageous problems in Chinese society and people that occurred after the opening of China's economy door. Villagers in *The Day the Sun Died* were reduced to a minimal status of animal, namely moving soulless beings, and craved for nothing other than the gratifications of desire, interest, and power even at the cost of autonomously relinquishing humanity and human subjectivity.

Alternatively, a view was also represented that the alleged counterrevolutionary acts or acts contradictory to the sublimity of the Cultural Revolution in *Serve the People!* formulated a de facto revolutionary effort abiding by the core of revolution spirits when the two protagonists were doomed into a minimal status, where all the worldly struggles and practices aimed at an apocalyptic liberation that would emancipate them from the sufferings and oppressions. The satiric paradox behind such is, as Kidd argued, the confrontation against the bleak reality while leaving a genuine hope in the darkness.[35]

In sum, the image of Yan in local English newspapers, resembling it in other media in Chinese, is heavily associated with the controversy of his novels and all the subtle tensions between a writer and the national political entities of the PLA and the CCP. Nevertheless, a differentiated angle that English journalists took was the highlighting of the market economy as an underlying rationale in his stories and the connection between Yan's novels and the history of the Cultural Revolution.

Receptions from conferences, theses, and interviews

Academic conference accounts for another important form of receiving Yan in Hong Kong. Two academic symposiums were held in Hong Kong that related to or specifically focused only on Yan and his novels. From 21 to 23 June 2017, the Chinese University of Hong Kong (CUHK) accommodated the Association of Chinese and Comparative Literature (ACCL) biennial conference: Text, Media, and Transcultural Negotiation. Panel 6, under the name of "Writing China: Reality and Absurdity," was held in Chinese and chaired by Yan himself and Liang Hong, a famous Chinese nonfiction writer and professor at Renmin University. Four

---

35 Kidd, "Bleak Reality."

panelists tussled with the subtle relationship between absurdity and reality in the narrative process in Chinese literature, among whom a consensus arrived that reality and absurdity were not mutually opposed concepts but rather mutually support and illuminate one another. Resembling a lamp and mirror or a pair of twins, absurdity to the panelists can be used to manifest reality as reality contains within itself an element of absurdity. The panel also discussed that absurdity and madness since Lu Xun have instituted an eminent tradition of representing reality in modern Chinese fictions, which has been continued by authors such as Yu Hua, Yan Lianke, and so forth in the 1980s. *The Seventh Day, Lenin's Kisses*, and *The Explosion Chronicles* all adopted a bizarrely imaginative approach to portray the reality of contemporary China. In a sense, such an absurd, mediated representation even rendered life and human existence more authentic to the underlying reality.[36] Thus, the notion of absurdity may assess the most essential aesthetic mode by which literature reflects reality in contemporary China, where a continual process of fragmentation unfolds itself in the ever-increasing gulf between rich and poor and increasingly jumbled concepts.

On 13 Dec. 2018, an international conference on "Disseminating Yan Lianke's *The Four Books*" was organized by Hong Kong Baptist University, in which Kevin Yau 丘庭傑 gave a presentation titled "Overseas Reviews of Yan Lianke's The Four Books," which is a case study of the reception of *The Four Book* in the non-Chinese language world of literature. By collecting over twenty reviews in English and several reviews in Korean, Deutsch, French, Spanish, and Czech, Yau investigated the overseas reception of *The Four Books* and demonstrated his preliminary findings to questions as follows: How have foreign readers evaluated and interpreted the narrative structure and language of this novel? In what way has the novel made a context for non-Chinese readership and accordingly was connected to readers' daily life and reading experience? What are the differences in study topics between Chinese academia and abroad? Yau also acknowledged a special issue regarding publishing that, banned in the PRC, *The Four Books* was translated into a number of languages and distributed widely in the world and the Czech edition helped him receive the Franz Kafka Prize in 2014. Such phenomenon urges that the relationship between censorship in the PRC and overseas publishing system should be thought.[37]

The attention of Hong Kong academia on Yan can also be noticed in the theses of graduate students from local universities. These graduate research projects intended to scrutinize Yan's novels and his literary world from different perspectives with various theoretical and analytical frameworks. They forged dialogues with multiple paradigms that resonate with how Yan was viewed in Hong Kong, as demonstrated above. For instance, Lin Yuan's 林源 ongoing PhD project at HKBU is a translation study on Yan's novels in English. Three graduate students at CUHK chose their research topics on Yan, which cover his utopian writing, the perspective of political theology, and somnambulism in *The Day the Sun Died*. Chau Man Lut in his PhD thesis looked into Yan's depiction of the tension between utopia and paradise, anti-utopia sentiments, and criticisms of the deeply-rooted and influential ideology of revolution in the Post-Mao era in *Lenin's Kiss*.[38] Cheung Kam Chuen's 張錦泉 article employed the theory of political theology to analyze how Yan's novels displayed the experience of religious

---

36 Yan Lianke, *Faxian xiaoshuo* (Taipei: INK Press, 2011): 176–86.
37 Sebastian Veg, "Creating a Literary Space to Debate the Mao Era: The Fictionalization of the Great Leap Forward in Yan Lianke's *Four Books*," *China Perspectives——Remembering the Mao Era: From Creative Practices to Parallel History* 4, no. 100 (Apr. 2014): 7–16.
38 Chau Man Lut, "A Study of Utopian Writing in Post-Mao Chinese Fictions" (PhD diss., Chinese University of Hong Kong, 2012), 106–43.

suffering in Chinese history after 1949. Cheung proposed that Yan's works used religious rhetoric and religious ideology to criticize the phenomena of political worship and capitalism in contemporary society.[39] Chan Wing Shan 陳穎珊 conducted a topic study on *The Day the Sun Died* and sleepwalking, in which she analyzed Yan's complex emotions toward the society that was hidden behind the metaphor of sleepwalking. Chan assessed that the intertextual representation of dream as a token in this novel and *Lenin's Kisses, Dream of Ding Village*, and *The Explosion Chronicles* delivered an author's message that, with the development of China's society, Chinese people gradually lost autonomy before desires and were even besieged by desires. These graduate studies contribute an image of Yan that is the storyteller of truths through pains. By telling the violence and monstrosity in China's history, Yan is portrayed as one who, besides knowing well about all those disregarded history fragments in the mainland, pieced the fragments of the painful history together. Yan's history-remapping operations were rationalized and theorized in these studies and, thus, these studies have extended his image from a writer to a story- and history-teller.

This chapter ends with the thirteen interviews Yan had as one last but not least parallel form of reception in Hong Kong.[40] The interviews played a vital role in presenting the image

---

39 Cheung Kam Chuen, "Taking God as a 'Way': A Study on Li Rui's, Yan Lianke's and Jia Pingwa's Religious Writing" (PhD diss., Chinese University of Hong Kong, 2020).

40 The thirteen interviews are: Yan Lianke, "Xianggang: Wo de shenhua yu chuanshuo" 香港: 我的神話與傳說 [Hong Kong: My mythology and legend], *Lichang xinwen* 立場新聞 [Stand News], 7 July 2019; Yan, "Haibian de Yan Lianke: Lai Xianggang shi yi zhong taoli" 海邊的閻連科: 來香港教書是一種逃離 [Yan Lianke by the sea: Coming to Hong Kong to teach is an escape], interview by Fu Ziyang 付子洋, *Duan chuanmei*, 3 July 2018, https://theinitium.com/article/20180626–mainland–yanlianke/ (last accessed 17 Aug. 2021); Yan, "Jing ci yi jie, rang women chengwei you jixing de ren" 經此疫劫, 讓我們成為有記性的人 [Through this epidemic, let us become people with memory], *Duan chuanmei*, 21 Feb. 2020, https://theinitium.com/article/20200221–mainland–coronavirus–yanlianke/ (last accessed 17 Aug. 2021); Yan; "Yi jie zhi xia, wuli, wuzhu he wunai de wenxue" 疫劫之下, 無力、無助和無奈的文學 [Powerless, helpless and helpless literature under the epidemic], *Duan chuanmei*, 12 Mar. 2020, https://theinitium.com/article/20200312-mainland-yanlianke-helpless-literature/ (last accessed 17 Aug. 2021); Yan, "Zai ruci jiaoza, daocuo de tiandi jian" 在如此交錯、倒錯的天地間 [In such an intertwined and inverted world], *Duan chuanmei*, 28 Apr. 2020, https://theinitium.com/article/20200428-mainland-yanlianke-upside-down/ (last accessed 17 Aug. 2021); Yan, "Dalu zhuming zuojia Yan Lianke: Wo jiu xiang sang jia zhi quan" 大陸著名作家閻連科: 我就像喪家之犬 [The famous mainland writer Yan Lianke: I am like a dog that lost its home], *Aboluo xinwen* 阿波羅新聞 [Apollo News], 28 Apr. 2016, https://hk.aboluowang.com/2016/0428/730558.html (last accessed 17 Aug. 2021); Yan, "Jin ci yi jie, rang women chengwei you jixin de ren," re-edited by Yuan Bin 袁斌, *Dajiyuan shibao* 大紀元時報 [The Epoch Time], 25 Feb. 2020, https://hk.epochtimes.com/news/2020–02–25/27731406 (last accessed 17 Aug. 2021); Yan, "Wo de jiazu yu Yingguo" 我的家族與英國 [My family and UK], *Zuojia* 作家 [Writer Magazine], vol. 21 (No. 2008): 56–58; Yan, "Yi ge weida de wenxue shidai yijing qiaoran jieshu" 一個偉大文學的時代已經悄然結束 [An era of great literature has come to a quiet end], interview by Shen Hexi 潘河西, Sina Hong Kong, 27 Dec. 2018, https://m.sina.com.hk/news/article/20181227/0/1/2/%E4%B8%80%E5%80%8B%E5%81%89%E5%A4%A7%E6%96%87%E5%AD%B8%E7%9A%84%E6%99%82%E4%BB%A3%E5%B7%B2%E7%B6%93%E6%82%84%E7%84%B6%E7%B5%90%E6%9D%9F%E5%B0%88%E8%A8%AA%E9%96%BB%E9%80%A3%E7%A7%91-9584816.html (last accessed 17 Aug. 2021); Yan, "Zuojia shenfen de jiaolü" 作家身份的焦慮 [The anxiety of writership], interview by Gun Lok 管樂, *Dagong wang* 大公網 [Da Kung newspaper website], 10 Oct. 2016, http://www.takungpao.com.hk/product/books/2016/1010/29800.html (last accessed 17 Aug. 2021); Yan, "Jinshu zuojia Yan Lianke: Ziwo shencha geng kepa" 禁書作家閻連科: 自我審查更可怕 [Censored writer Yan Lianke: Self-censorship is more horrible], *Hong Kong Economic Journal*, 8 Dec. 2016, https://www2.hkej.com/editorchoice/article/id/1444940/ (last accessed 17 Aug. 2021); Yan, "Fei changren: Yan Lianke: Women bei wenxue suo lei" 非常人: 閻連科　我

of the controversial writer as an ordinary human who genuinely cares about China, China's society, and the Chinese people. These interviewers were from local press, such as online media *Stand News* (*Lichang xinwen* 立場新聞), Initium Media, Aboluowang 阿波羅網, Sino Hong Kong (*Xinlang Xianggang* 新浪香港), and newspapers *The Epoch Times* (*Dajiyuan shibao* 大紀元時報), *Ta Kung Po* 大公報, *Hong Kong Economic Journal* (*Xinbao caijing xinwen* 信報財經新聞), *Apple Daily* (*Pingguo ribao* 蘋果日報, ceased publication since 24 June 2021), and *Wen Wei Po* 文匯報. These interviews covered a broad range of topics, including China's censorship, his helpless semi-exile, his teaching experience, his passion in NBA games, the outbreaks of COVID-19, and surely mythorealism, his novels, the identity of the author, and literature in general.

It is worth noting that these local press that reported Yan's interviews are of very different and even opposing backgrounds. In this sense, Yan was interviewed and thus represented by both camps and by viewers on different sides. While traditional print media, such as *Wen Wei Po* and *Ta Kung Po*, tend to focus on topics such as nation, human being, and the relationship between literature and society, online media, such as *Stand News* and *Initium Media*, built Yan's image more resembling an ordinary person who likes NBA as many of his readers do and has his own joys and sorrows in life as everyone else.

The latest interview Yan gave to a Hong Kong press was the conversation dated 3 Aug. 2020 with *Wen Wei Po* journalist Cheung Po Fung 張寶峰 on his new nonfiction work *Their Stories* (*Tamen* 她們). Cheung's article extolled this long prose writing about the four generations of women in Yan's hometown village. It regarded his records of the changes in Chinese women's life over the last century as a unique perspective of a male writer, which manufactured a "her world" for readers and set a new milestone for Chinese literature on women.[41] Cheung held the opinion that Yan's sincere care about, if not effusive obsession with, China's reality and the literary devices that may document reality as authentically as possible cannot be better seen in the following self-comments about this new work: "The novel *Heart Sutra* is a turning point in my writing, and the prose *Their Stories* is a more important and sharp turning point in my documentary writing."[42]

The reception from interviews with Yan somewhat displayed a different angle via the dialogues between Yan as the censored, controversial Chinese writer and the intended readers in Hong Kong. Yan was assessed and accessed in these interviews not merely as one who kept creating catching stories and troubles spelled by those stories, but also a person who lived a life as other ordinary people as readers themselves. The very model of reporting in interviews outlined Yan as a human being with real emotions, which simultaneously added-cum-underlined a humanitarian dimension to Yan, who is believed to strive for humanity utilizing his pen.

們被文學所累 [Non-ordinary person: Yan Lianke: We are burdened by literature], interview by Ju Baiyu 鞠白玉, *Zhonggup shuzi shidai* 中國數字時代 [China Digital Times], 2 Mar. 2013, https://chinadigitaltimes.net/chinese/281819.html?__cf_chl_jschl_tk__=pmd_28f3cac26f05f4eceb77145633f9ac016805bcf8-1628775661-0-gqNtZGzNAeKjcnBszQiO (last accessed 17 Aug. 2021); Yan, "Yan Lianke de 'ta shijie'" 閻連科的「她世界」 [Yan Lianke's "her world"], interview by Cheung Po Fung, *Wen Wei Po*, 3 Aug. 2020. http://paper.wenweipo.com/2020/08/03/BK2008030001.htm (last accessed 17 Aug. 2021).

41 Yan, "Yan Lianke de 'ta shijie.'"
42 Ibid. My translation.

Conclusion

The analyses above illustrate that the receptions of Yan in Hong Kong are represented by four words with the highest frequency of occurrence in the two word clouds: China, writer, prize, and controversy. This chapter concludes that Yan is perceived in Hong Kong as an unwelcome voice in the mainland, who invariably suffered from publication bans and other forms of censorial restrictions time after time. Yan is also perceived in Hong Kong as the winner of numerous international literature awards. The consistency of such a confrontation between overseas awards and domestic denials has interwoven a paradoxical while noteworthy dynamics in reception that Yan's literature is inextricably intertwined with politics and China's sociopolitical ecology.

Under such views, it is also the conclusion of this chapter that Yan is pictured as a holder and an observer by the gate of China's politics that is embarrassingly half-closed and half-opened. To put it in another way, Yan is read by Hong Kong scholars and critics in the way that his sense of responsibility as a writer has been increasingly heightened by such ambivalence he faced, which, in return, prescribed him with a repute of controversial mainland writer in Hong Kong. Shouldering up the onerous tasks of seeing the dark and offering perspectives, Yan's image is interpreted as a correlative symbol to the old flashlight-holder in his Kafka Prize acceptance speech, who guided the passersby in midnight without street lamps and shed lights against darkness.[43]

Last but not least, the significance of Yan's encounter with Hong Kong lies in the aspect that Yan re-anchoraged his accessibility to the readership in both China and overseas there. It also lies in the aspect that the connection between Yan as a mainland Chinese writer and world literature did not become possible until his travel to Hong Kong, wherein all the cross-regional publications and communications happened.

Bibliography

Bezlova, Antoaneta. "Big Brother's Book Ban Blues." *The Standard*, 28 May 2005.

Bu Lili 布莉莉, and Guo Quanzhao 郭全照. "Cang qiao yu tianran zhi zhong" 藏巧於天然之中 [Hiding ingenuity in the natural]. *Ershiyi shiji shuangyuekan* 二十一世紀雙月刊 [Twenty-First Century], no. 135 (Feb. 2013): 145–50.

Cao, Xuenan. "Mythorealism and Enchanted Time: Yan Lianke's *Explosion Chronicles*." *Frontiers of Literary Studies in China* 10, no. 1 (May 2016): 103–12.

Chau Man Lut 鄒文律. "A Study of Utopian Writing in Post-Mao Chinese Fictions." PhD diss., Chinese University of Hong Kong, 2012.

———. "Yi chu wutuobang zhi wai: Lun Yan Lianke *Shouhuo* de fan wutuobang Shuxie" 逸出烏托邦之外——論閻連科《受活》的反烏托邦書寫 [Escape from utopia: On the anti-utopian writing in Yan Lianke's *Lenin's Kisses*]. *Zhongguo wenxue xuebao* 中國文學學報 [Journal of Chinese literature], vol. 8 (Dec. 2017): 151–86.

Cheung Kam Chuen 張錦泉. "Taking God as a 'Way': A Study on Li Rui's, Yan Lianke's and Jia Pingwa's Religious Writing." PhD diss., Chinese University of Hong Kong, 2020.

Choy Howard Y. F. 蔡元豐. "Etuobang xiaoshuo *Rixi*" 惡托邦小說《日熄》 [Dystopia novel *The Day the Sun Died*]. *Zhuojian mingjia* 灼見名家 [Master Insight], 22 June 2018. https://www.master-insight.com/%E3%80%8A%E6%97%A5%E7%86%84%E3%80%8B%EF%BC%9A%E6%83%A1%E6%89%98%E9%82%A6%E5%B0%8F%E8%AA%AA/ (last accessed 17 Aug. 2021).

———. "You, you, you: Yan Lianke de hei'an xiaoshuo *Rixi*" 遊、憂、幽——閻連科的黑暗小說《日熄》 [Itineraria, tristia, and darkness: Yan Lianke's dark novel *The Day the Sun Died*]. In *Introduction to*

---

43 See Choy, "*You, you, you*," xv–xvi.

The Sixth Dream of the Red Chamber Award: Collected Essays on Yan Lianke's The Day the Sun Died, edited by Howard Y. F. Choy, ix–xvii. Hong Kong: Infolink Publishing, 2018.

———. "*You, you, you*: Yan Lianke de hei'an xiaoshuo *Rixi*." *Zhuojian mingjia*, 19 June 2018. https://www.master-insight.com/%E9%81%8A%E3%80%81%E6%86%82%E3%80%81%E5%B9%BD-%E9%96%BB%E9%80%A3%E7%A7%91%E7%9A%84%E9%BB%91%E6%9A%97%E5%B0%8F%E8%AA%AA%E3%80%8A%E6%97%A5%E7%86%84%E3%80%8B/ (last accessed 17 Aug. 2021).

Deuck, Cameron. "*The Four Books*—Biting Satire Offers Some Hope." *South China Morning Post*, 17 Mar. 2015. https://www.scmp.com/lifestyle/books/article/1742720/book-review-four-books-biting-satire-offers-some-hope (last accessed 17 Aug. 2021).

Jiang Xun 江迅. "Yan Lianke huo Hongloumeng jiang qiyuan" 閻連科獲紅樓夢獎奇緣 [Yan Lianke wins the Dream of the Red Chamber Award]. *Zhuojian mingjia*, 6 Oct. 2010. https://www.master-insight.com/%E9%96%BB%E9%80%A3%E7%A7%91%E7%8D%B2%E7%B4%85%E6%A8%93%E5%A4%A2%E7%8D%8E%E5%A5%87%E7%B7%A3/ (last accessed 17 Aug. 2021).

Kidd, James. "Bleak Reality Confronts the Chinese Dream in Yan Lianke's Gruesome, Gripping Novel, *The Day the Sun Died*." *South China Morning Post*, 1 Aug. 2018. https://www.scmp.com/magazines/post-magazine/books/article/2157656/bleak-reality-confronts-chinese-dream-yan-liankes (last accessed 17 Aug. 2021).

———. "Yan Lianke's Three Brothers Honors His Family and the Struggle to Survive in Mid-20th Century China." *South China Morning Post*, 8 Mar. 2020. https://www.scmp.com/magazines/post-magazine/books/article/3065106/yan-liankes-three-brothers-honours-his-family-and (last accessed 17 Aug. 2021).

Lee Leo Ou-fan 李歐梵. *Zhongguo wenhua de liu ge mianxiang* 中國文化的六個面向 [The Six Faces of Chinese Culture]. Hong Kong: Chinese University of Hong Kong Press, 2016.

Lee Yee 李怡. "Zui chang zaojin de zuojia Yan Lianke xinzuo *Zhalie zhi*" 最常遭禁作家閻連科新作《炸裂志》[The most frequently banned writer Yan Lianke's new work *The Explosion Chronicles*]. *Jingji tong* 經濟通 [ET Net], 23 Nov. 2021. http://www.etnet.com.hk/www/tc/diva/art/oneminreading/21272 (last accessed 17 Aug. 2021).

Mao Ying 毛塋. "Yan Lianke xie bei zhalie de ganqing" 閻連科寫被炸裂的感情 [Yan Lianke writes about exploded feelings]. *Yazhou zhoukan* 亞洲週刊 [Asiaweek], 9–15 Dec. 2013.

Song, Weijie 宋偉杰. "Yan Lianke's Mythorealist Representation of the Country and the City." *Modern Fiction Studies* 62, no. 4 (Winter 2016): 644–58.

Sun Yu 孫郁. "Yan Lianke de shengshi zhuyi" 閻連科的神實主義 [Yan Lianke's mythrealism]. *Xindi wenxue* 新地文學 [New land literature], no. 26 (Dec. 2013): 147–56.

Tang Ching-kin 鄧正健. "Xianshi zhuyi shuxie ji qi zhenshi: Yan Lianke de *Faxian xiaoshuo*" 現實主義書寫，及其真實——閻連科的《發現小說》 [Realistic writing, and its truth: Yan Lianke's *Discovering Fiction*]. *Zi hua* 字花 [Fleurs des Lettres], Jan. and Feb. 2014.

City University of Hong Kong Press, eds. "The Day the Sun Died." https://www.cityu.edu.hk/upress/the-day-the-sun-died-in-chinese (last accessed 12 Aug. 2021).

———, eds. "Dream of Ding Village." https://www.cityu.edu.hk/upress/dream-of-ding-village-in-chinese (last accessed 12 Aug. 2021).

———, eds. "Heart Sutra." https://www.cityu.edu.hk/upress/heart-sutra (last accessed 12 Aug. 2021).

———, eds. "Opening the Door of China: Yan Lianke's Collected Overseas Writings." https://www.cityu.edu.hk/upress/opening-the-door-of-china (last accessed 12 Aug. 2021).

———. "Serve the People." https://www.cityu.edu.hk/upress/serve-the-people-in-chinese (last accessed 12 Aug. 2021).

———, eds. "Yan Lianke." https://www.cityu.edu.hk/upress/catalogsearch/result/?q=%E9%96%BB%E9%80%A3%E7%A7%91 (last accessed 12 Aug. 2021).

Veg, Sebastian. "Creating a Literary Space to Debate the Mao Era: The Fictionalization of the Great Leap Forward in Yan Lianke's *Four Books*." *China Perspectives—Remembering the Mao Era: From Creative Practices to Parallel History* 4, no. 100 (Apr. 2014): 7–15.

Xie Xuan 謝璇. "'Zou chuqu' he 'zou huilai': Ji Yan Lianke Hongloumeng jiang jiangzuo 'Xianggang yu wo de wenxue yiyi'" 「走出去」和「走回來」——記閻連科紅樓夢獎講座「香港於我的文學意義」 ["Going out" and "coming back": Dream of the Red Chamber Award lecture by Yan Lianke, "The literary significance of Hong Kong to me"]. *Ming Pao* 明報, 7 Nov. 2016. https://m.mingpao.com/pns/副刊/article/20161107/s00005/1478456523468/明藝–報道–「走出去」和「走回來」–記閻連科紅樓夢獎講座「香港於我的文學意義」 (last accessed 17 Aug. 2021).

Yan Lianke 閻連科. "Dalu zhuming zuojia Yan Lianke: Wo jiu xiang sang jia zhi quan" 大陸著名作家閻連科：我就像喪家之犬 [The famous mainland writer Yan Lianke: I am like a dog that lost its home]. *Aboluo xinwen* 阿波羅新聞 [Apollo News], 28 Apr. 2016. https://hk.aboluowang.com/2016/0428/730558.html (last accessed 17 Aug. 2021).

———. *Faxian xiaoshuo* 發現小說 [Discovering fiction]. Taipei: INK Press, 2011.

———. "Fei changren: Yan Lianke: Women bei wenxue suo lei" 非常人：閻連科 我們被文學所累 [Non-ordinary person: Yan Lianke: We are burdened by literature]. Interview by Ju Baiyu 鞠白玉. *Zhonggup shuzi shidai* 中國數字時代 [China Digital Times], 2 Mar. 2013. https://chinadigitaltimes.net/chinese/281819.html?__cf_chl_jschl_tk__=pmd_28f3cac26f05f4eceb77145633f9ac016805bcf8-1628775661-0-gqNtZGzNAeKjcnBszQiO (last accessed 17 Aug. 2021).

———. "Hai bian de Yan Lianke: Lai Xianggang shi yi zhong taoli" 海邊的閻連科：來香港教書是一種逃離 [Yan Lianke by the sea: Coming to Hong Kong to teach is an escape]. Interview by Fu Ziyang 付子洋. *Duan chuanmei* 端傳媒 [Initium Media], 3 July 2018. https://theinitium.com/article/20180626-mainland-yanlianke/ (last accessed 17 Aug. 2021).

———. "Jing ci yi jie: Rang women chengwei you jixing de ren" 經此疫劫，讓我們成為有記性的人 [Through this epidemic, let us become people with memory]. *Duan chuanmei*, 21 Feb. 2020. https://theinitium.com/article/20200221-mainland-coronavirus-yanlianke/ (last accessed 17 Aug. 2021).

———. "Jing ci yi jie: Rang women chengwei you jixin de ren," re-edited by Yuan Bin 袁斌. *Dajiyuan shibao* 大紀元時報 [The Epoch Time], 25 Feb. 2020. https://hk.epochtimes.com/news/2020-02-25/27731406 (last accessed 17 Aug. 2021).

———. "Jinshu zuojia Yan Lianke: Ziwo shencha geng kepa" 禁書作家閻連科：自我審查更可怕 [Censored writer Yan Lianke: Self-censorship is more horrible]. *Hong Kong Economic Journal*, 8 Dec. 2016. https://www2.hkej.com/editorchoice/article/id/1444940/ (last accessed 17 Aug. 2021).

———. "Wo de jiazu yu Yingguo" 我的家族與英國 [My family and UK]. *Zuojia* 作家 [Writer Magazine], Nov. 2018, vol. 21: 56–58.

———. "Xianggang: Wo de shenhua yu chuanshuo" 香港：我的神話與傳說 [Hong Kong: My mythology and legend]. *Lichang xinwen* 立場新聞 [Stand News], 7 July 2019.

———. "Yan Lianke de 'ta shijie'" 閻連科的「她世界」 [Yan Lianke's "her world"]. Interview by Cheung Po Fung 張寶峰. *Wen Wei Po* 文匯報, 3 Aug. 2020. http://paper.wenweipo.com/2020/08/03/BK2008030001.htm (last accessed 17 Aug. 2021).

———. "Yi ge weida de wenxue shidai yijing qiaoran jieshu" 一個偉大文學的時代已經悄然結束 [An era of great literature has come to a quiet end]. Interview by Shen Hexi 潘河西. Sina Hong Kong, 27 Dec. 2018. https://m.sina.com.hk/news/article/20181227/0/1/2/%E4%B8%80%E5%80%8B%E5%81%89%E5%A4%A7%E6%96%87%E5%AD%B8%E7%9A%84%E6%99%82%E4%BB%A3%E5%B7%B2%E7%B6%93%E6%82%84%E7%84%B6%E7%B5%90%E6%9D%9F%E5%B0%88%E8%A8%AA%E9%96%BB%E9%80%A3%E7%A7%91-9584816.html (last accessed 17 Aug. 2021).

———. "Yi jie zhi xia, wuli, wuzhu he wunai de wenxue" 疫劫之下，無力、無助和無奈的文學 [Powerless, helpless and helpless literature under the epidemic]. *Duan chuanmei*, 12 Mar. 2020. https://theinitium.com/article/20200312-mainland-yanlianke-helpless-literature/ (last accessed 17 Aug. 2021).

———. "Zai ruci jiaoza daocuo de tiandi jian" 在如此交雜、倒錯的天地間 [In such an intertwined and inverted world]. *Duan chuanmei*, 28 Apr. 2020. https://theinitium.com/article/20200428-mainland-yanlianke-upside-down/ (last accessed 17 Aug. 2021).

———. "Zuojia shenfen de jiaolü" 作家身份的焦慮 [The anxiety of writership]. Interviewed by Gun Lok 管樂. *Dagong wang* 大公網 [Da Kung Newspaper website], 10 Oct. 2016. http://www.takungpao.com.hk/product/books/2016/1010/29800.html (last accessed 17 Aug. 2021).

Yuan, Cyan 袁瑋婧. "Wujin hei'an zhi zhong, ta de bi xia you guang" 無盡黑暗之中 他的筆下有光 [In the endless darkness, there is light under his pen]. Cyan Yuan, 21 June 2019. https://cyanyuan.medium.com/%E9%96%BB%E9%80%A3%E7%A7%91-%E7%84%A1%E7%9B%A1%E9%BB%91%E6%9A%97%E4%B9%8B%E4%B8%AD-%E4%BB%96%E7%9A%84%E7%AD%86%E4%B8%8B%E6%9C%89%E5%85%89-b1b36be250d0 (last accessed 17 Aug. 2021).

Zhou Shubo 周述波. "Xiangtu shang de cunzai zhi si yu nongcun chuanbo: Yan Lianke xiaoshuo chuangzuo lun" 鄉土上的存在之思與農村傳播：閻連科小說創作論 [Thinking of existence in the country and rural communication: On Yan Lianke's fictional creation]. Chung Hwa Book. https://www.chunghwabook.com.hk/Index/book_detail/id/2833.html (last accessed 12 Aug. 2021).

COMPLETE CHINESE BIBLIOGRAPHY OF YAN LIANKE IN CHRONOLOGICAL ORDER
閻連科著作書目

1. 小說（單行本、合集）

出版年份	作品	城市	出版社
1990	《情感獄》（長篇小說）	北京	解放軍文藝出版社 (1990)
		上海	上海文藝出版社 (2002)
		北京	人民日報出版社 (2007)（《閻連科文集》十二卷本）
		北京	現代出版社 (2009)
		天津	天津人民出版社 (2012)(精典博維·閻連科精品文集)
		鄭州	河南文藝出版社 (2014)
1992	《鄉里故事》（小說集）	天津	百花文藝出版社 (1992)
1993	《最後一名女知青》（長篇小說）	天津	百花文藝出版社 (1993)
		長春	時代文藝出版社 (2003)
		北京	人民日報出版社 (2007)（《閻連科文集》十二卷本）
		天津	天津人民出版社 (2012)
		昆明	雲南人民出版社 (2013)(精典博維·閻連科精品文集)
1994	《和平寓言》（小說集）	武漢	長江文藝出版社 (1994)
1995	《生死晶黃》（長篇小說）	濟南	明天出版社 (1995)
		北京	人民日報出版社 (2007)（《閻連科文集》十二卷本）
		昆明	雲南人民出版社 (2013)(精典博維·閻連科精品文集)
		鄭州	河南文藝出版社 (2016)

1995	《朝著天堂走》 （小說集）	北京	中國青年出版社 (1995)
		瀋陽	萬卷出版公司 (2009)
1996	《閻連科小說自選集》	鄭州	河南文藝出版社 (1996)
1996	《閻連科文集》五卷[1]	長春	吉林人民出版社 (1996)
1996	《黃金洞》 （中篇小說單行本）	長春	吉林人民出版社 (1996) (《閻連科文集》五卷)
		北京	中國文學出版社 (1998)
		重慶	重慶出版社 (2013) (更名為《世相書．黃金洞》)
		北京	中外文學出版社 (2013)
		合肥	黃山出版社 (2013)
1997	《金蓮，你好》 （中篇單行本和小說集）	北京	中國文學出版社 (1999) （更名為《陰晴圓缺：重說千古淫婦潘金蓮》）
		長春	時代文藝出版社 (2003) (更名為《潘金蓮逃離西門鎮》)
		北京	人民日報出版社 (2007) (《閻連科文集》十二卷本)
		天津	天地文化出版公司 (2012)
		南京	江蘇文藝出版社 (2013)
1998	《日光流年》 （長篇小說）	廣州	花城出版社 (1998)
		長春	時代文藝出版社 (2001)
		瀋陽	春風文藝出版社 (2004)
		北京	人民日報出版社 (2007) (《閻連科文集》十二卷本)
		北京	十月文藝出版社 (2009)
		臺北	聯經出版公司 (2009)
		天津	天津人民出版社 (2012) (精典博維·閻連科精品文集)
1998	《歡樂家園》（小說集）	北京	北京出版社 (1998)
2000	《朝著東南走》 （小說集）	北京	作家出版社 (2000)

---

[1] 《黃金洞》《青春谷》《和平窟》《情愛穴》《歷史窯》

閻連科著作書目

2001	《堅硬如水》（長篇小說）	武漢	長江文藝出版社 (2001)
		北京	人民日報出版社 (2007) (《閻連科文集》十二卷本)
		臺北	麥田出版 (2009)
		昆明	雲南人民出版社 (2009)
		昆明	雲南人民出版社 (2013) (精典博維·閻連科精品文集)
		南昌	百花洲出版社 (2013)
2001	《耙耬天歌》（小說集）	太原	北嶽文藝出版社 (2001)
2001	《穿越》（中篇小說）	北京	解放軍文藝出版社 (2001)
		天津	文化天地出版公司 (2012) （恢復原名《李師師和她的後裔》）
		南京	江蘇文藝出版社 (2013) (恢復原名《名妓李師師和她的後裔》)
2001	《鬥雞》（中篇小說單行本）	武漢	長江文藝出版社 (2001)
		天津	文化天地出版公司 (2012)
		南京	江蘇文藝出版社 (2013)
2002	《三棒槌》（短篇小說集）	北京	新世界出版社 (2002)
2002	《年月日：閻連科小說作品精選》（小說集）	烏魯木齊	新疆人民出版社 (2002)
2002	《鄉村歲月：大地蒼生的希望與失望》（小說集）	烏魯木齊	新疆人民出版社 (2002)
2002	《夏日落》（中篇小說）	瀋陽	春風文藝出版社 (2002)
		臺北	聯經出版公司 (2010)
		香港	香港城市大學出版社 (2020) (閻連科海外作品選集·小說卷)
2002	《中國作家經典文庫·閻連科卷》（小說集）	北京	光明日報出版社 (2002)
2004	《受活》（長篇小說）	瀋陽	春風文藝出版社 (2004)
		臺北	麥田出版社 (2007)
		北京	人民日報出版社 (2007) (《閻連科文集》十二卷本)
		北京	十月文藝出版社 (2009)
		天津	天津人民出版社 (2012) (精典博維·閻連科精品文集)
		北京	中國盲文出版社 (2014)

閻連科著作書目

2005	《為人民服務》 （長篇小說）	香港	香港文化藝術出版社 (2005)
		新加坡	玲子傳媒 (2005)
		臺北	麥田出版社 (2006)
		香港	香港城市大學出版社 (2020) (閻連科海外作品選集·小說卷)
2005	《革命浪漫主義：閻連科短篇小說代表作》（小說集）	瀋陽	春風文藝出版社 (2005)
2005	《天宮圖》 （中篇小說集）	南京	江蘇文藝出版社 (2005)
2006	《丁莊夢》 （長篇小說）	臺北	麥田出版社 (2006)
		香港	香港文化藝術出版社 (2006)
		上海	上海文藝出版社 (2006)
		新加坡	玲子傳媒 (2006)
		香港	香港城市大學出版社 (2020) (閻連科海外作品選集·小說卷)
2006	《母親是條河》 （長篇小說）	北京	大眾文藝出版社 (2006) (劇本被改編成小說，冠上書名)
2007	《瑤溝人的夢》 （中篇小說集）	瀋陽	春風文藝出版公司 (2007)
2007	《閻連科文集》十二卷[2]	北京	人民日報出版社 (2007)
2008	《風雅頌》 （長篇小說）	南京	江蘇人民出版社 (2008)
		臺北	麥田出版社 (2008)
		鄭州	河南文藝出版社 (2010)
		昆明	雲南人民出版社 (2012)
2009	《四號禁區》 （中篇小說集）	瀋陽	萬卷出版公司 (2009)
2009	《桃園春醒》 （中篇小說集）	合肥	黃山書社 (2009)
2009	《年月日》（中篇小說）	香港、新加坡	明報月刊出版社； 新加坡青年書局 (2009)
		鄭州	河南文藝出版社 (2010)
		南京	江蘇文藝出版社 (2021)

[2] 此《閻連科文集》十二卷本包括《金蓮，你好》《藝妓芙蓉》《生死晶黃》《黑豬毛白豬毛》《最後一名女知青》《寂寞之舞》《情感獄》《受活》《感謝祈禱》《堅硬如水》《日光流年》《鄉村死亡報告》，均使用同一國際書號。

閻連科著作書目

2010	《閻連科小說精選集》	臺北	新地文化藝術 (2010)
2010	《中國當代作家獲獎作品典藏·閻連科卷》（小說集）	鄭州	河南文藝出版社 (2010)
2010	《四書》（長篇小說)	自費印刷,分贈親友。	
		香港	明報月刊出版社 (2010)
		臺北	麥田出版社 (2011)
		香港	香港城市大學出版社 (2020) (閻連科海外作品選集·小說卷)
2011	《閻連科中篇小說編年》四輯[3]	杭州	浙江文藝出版社 (2011)
2013	《東京九流人物系列》（小說集）	昆明	雲南人民出版社 (2013) (精典博維·閻連科精品文集)
2013	《耙耬系列》上、下卷（小說集）	昆明	雲南人民出版社 (2013) (精典博維·閻連科精品文集)
2013	《和平軍旅系列》上、下卷（小說集）	昆明	雲南人民出版社 (2013) (精典博維·閻連科精品文集)
2013	《閻連科短篇小說精選》	昆明	雲南人民出版社 (2013) (精典博維·閻連科精品文集)
2013	《炸裂志》（長篇小說）	上海	上海文藝出版社 (2013)
		臺北	麥田出版社 (2013)
		鄭州	河南文藝出版社 (2016)
2013	《奴兒》（短篇小說集）	上海	上海文藝出版社 (2013)
		上海	華東師範大學出版社 (2017)
2014	《連科六短篇》	北京	海豚出版社 (2014)
2014	《親愛的,西班牙》（小說散文集）	南京	江蘇文藝出版社 (2014)
2014	《黑白閻連科．中篇四書》四卷[4]	北京	人民文學出版社 (2014)
2015	《中士還鄉》（中篇小說集）	上海	上海文藝出版社 (2015)

[3] 《藝妓芙蓉：閻連科中篇小說編年 1988-1990》(第1輯)、《中士還鄉：閻連科中篇小說編年 1991-1993》(第2輯)、《耙耬山脈：閻連科中篇小說編年 1993-1996》(第3輯)、《桃園春醒：閻連科中篇小說編年 1996-2009》(第4輯)
[4] 《黃金洞 尋找土地 中士還鄉》《年月日 朝著東南走 橫活》《耙耬天歌 大校 鄉村死亡報告》、《天宮圖 平平淡淡 瑤溝的日頭》

2015	《日熄》（長篇小說）	自費印刷,分贈朋友。	
		臺北	麥田出版社 (2016)
		香港	香港城市大學出版社 (2020) (閻連科海外作品選集·小說卷)
2018	《速求共眠》 （長篇小說）	新北	INK印刻文學生活 (2018)
		南昌	百花洲文藝出版社 (2019)
2019	《心經》 （長篇小說）	自費印刷,分贈朋友。	
		香港	香港城市大學出版社 (2020) (閻連科海外作品選集·小說卷)
2021	《中原》（長篇小說）	廣州	《花城》雜誌社 (2021)
		臺北	麥田出版社 書名改爲《中國故事》(2021)

2. 散文集

出版年份	作品	城市	出版社
1999	《褐色桎梏》	天津	百花文藝出版社 (1999)
2002	《返身回家》	北京	解放軍出版社 (2002)
2005	《沒有邊界的跨越：閻連科散文》	武漢	長江文藝出版社 (2005)
2008	《土黃與草青：閻連科親情散文》	廣州	花城出版社 (2008)
2008	《機巧與靈魂：閻連科讀書筆記》	廣州	花城出版社 (2008)
2009	《閻連科散文》	杭州	浙江文藝出版社 (2009)
2009	《我與父輩》 （長篇散文）	昆明	雲南人民出版社 (2009)
		新北	INK印刻文學生活 (2012)
		南京	江蘇人民出版社 (2014)
		北京	人民文學出版社 (2014、2016)
		鄭州	河南文藝出版社 (2019)
		南京	江蘇文藝出版社 (2021)
2011	《走著瞧》	上海	東方出版中心 (2011)
2011	《北京,最後的紀念：我和711號園》 （長篇散文）	南京	江蘇人民出版社 (2011)
		臺北	聯經出版公司 (2012) (更名爲《711號園：北京最後的最後紀念》)
		北京	人民文學出版社 (2014) (更名爲《711號園》)

2012	《一個人的三條河》	北京	中國人民大學出版社 (2012)
		臺北	二魚文化 (2013)
2013	《閻連科散文》[5]	昆明	雲南人民出版社 (2013) (精典博維·閻連科精品文集)
2014	《感念》	北京	人民文學出版社 (2014)
2014	《高壽的鄉村》	鄭州	河南文藝出版社 (2014)
2014	《走在別人的路上》	上海	上海人民出版社 (2014)
2014	《從田湖出發去找李白》 （長篇散文）	濟南	明天出版社 (2014)
		上海	上海文化出版社 (2018) (更名為《田湖的孩子》)
2015	《兩代人的十二月》 （蔣方舟合著）	新北	INK印刻文學生活 (2015)
2018	《獨自走過的日子都有餘溫》	長沙	湖南文藝出版社 (2018)
2020	《她們》 （長篇散文）	鄭州	河南文藝出版社 (2020)
		臺北	麥田出版社 (2020)
		南京	江蘇文藝出版社 (2021)
2021	《人生不過四季》	南京	江蘇文藝出版社 (2021)
2021	《生命於我, 就是笑著等待》	南京	江蘇文藝出版社 (2021)

3. 論述、演講、訪談

發表年份	作品	城市	出版社
2002	《巫婆的紅筷子: 作家與文學博士對話錄》 （與梁鴻對話）	瀋陽	春風文藝出版社 (2002)
		桂林	灕江出版社 (2014) (更名為《巫婆的筷子: 閻連科、梁鴻對談錄》)
2008	《拆解與疊拼: 閻連科文學演講》	廣州	花城出版社 (2008)
2011	《發現小說》	天津	南開大學出版社 (2011)
		新北	INK印刻文學生活 (2011)
		北京	中國人民文學出版社 (2014)
2011	《我的現實, 我的主義: 閻連科文學對話錄》 （與張學昕對話）	北京	中國人民文學出版社 (2011)

[5] 此本與 2009 年浙江文藝出版社的《閻連科散文》所收內容不同。

2012	《一派胡言：閻連科海外演講集》	北京	中信出版社 (2012)
2012	《寫作最難是糊塗》（文學隨筆）	北京	中國人民大學出版社 (2012)
2012	《丈量書與筆的距離》（讀書筆記）	北京	中國人民大學出版社 (2012)
2013	《閻連科文論》	昆明	雲南人民出版社 (2013) (精典博維·閻連科精品文集)
2013	《閻連科研究》上、下卷	昆明	雲南人民出版社 (2013) (精典博維·閻連科精品文集)
2014	《沉默與喘息：我所經歷的中國和文學》	新北	INK印刻文學生活
		香港	香港城市大學出版社 (2020) (略更名為《沉默與喘息：我所經歷的中國與文學》)
2017	《百年寫作十二講：閻連科的文學講堂》兩冊[6]	香港	中華書局 (2017)
2020	《推開中國的另一扇窗——海外隨筆集》	香港	香港城市大學出版社 (2020)
2020	《野嗓子——海外演講錄》	香港	香港城市大學出版社 (2020)

4. 其他 (混合文類)

發表年份	作品	城市	出版社
2004	《閻連科》	北京	人民文學出版社 (2004)
2012	《朝著東南走》[7]	瀋陽	遼寧人民出版社 (2012、2013)
2012–13	《閻連科作品集》十七卷	昆明 天津	雲南人民出版社 (2013) 天津人民出版社 (2013) (精典博維·閻連科精品文集)
2017	《閻連科自選集》	成都	天地出版社 (2017)

---

[6] 《百年寫作十二講：閻連科的文學講堂》(19 世紀寫作講稿)、《百年寫作十二講：閻連科的文學講堂》(20 世紀寫作講稿)。
[7] 不同於 2000 年作家出版社的小說集《朝著東南走》。

INDEX

711 hao yuan. See *Garden No. 711*

above, the, 30, 411
abstract labor, 250–51
abstraction, 251, 256
absurd, the, 5, 7–8, 10, 18, 25, 28, 32, 35–36, 39, 46, 51, 54–56, 58, 63–64, 66, 93–102, 141, 146–47, 149, 158–59, 171–74, 177, 179, 182, 200, 257, 259, 285, 304, 307, 315, 328, 344, 358, 363, 444, 458, 463, 478, 491, 493; absurdist fiction, 28, 94, 96–97, 99; absurdist hero, 93, 97–98, 101–2; absurdist narrative, 93–96, 99; absurdity, 3–4, 16, 26, 28–29, 31–37, 46, 50, 56–57, 68, 95–99, 101, 104, 137, 143, 162, 179, 199, 309, 360, 412, 444, 457, 459, 491–92, 494–95, 499, 500
acceptability-oriented translation. *See* translation
acceptance, 33–35, 37, 56, 134, 141, 156, 211–13, 234, 252, 405–6, 411, 481, 503
adequacy-oriented translation. *See* translation
aesthetics, 63, 67, 140, 147, 203, 311–12, 317, 342, 345, 350, 357, 477, 480, 491, 496; ecological aesthetics, 311–12, 317; literary aesthetics, 342, 345, 350, 477, 480, 491
Agamben, Giorgio, 125–27, 131, 134, 190, 290; *homo sacer*, 124–26, 131, 190–91, 291
agents, 86, 210, 259, 393, 452, 459
agglutinative language. *See* language
Ah Q, 64, 108, 411, 446
AIDS, 3, 35, 75, 118, 172–74, 176–78, 180, 196, 299, 313, 403, 439, 442, 471, 497
alienation, 41, 46, 65, 67, 97, 99, 146, 174, 202–4, 214, 238, 301, 316, 346
allegory, 9, 26, 31, 36, 58, 109, 162, 204, 238, 360, 363, 412–13, 443, 458, 462, 471; allegorical, 23, 45, 51, 101, 123, 147, 158–59, 163, 282, 328, 359, 363, 412–13, 440, 445, 457, 462–63
alliteration, 370

allusion, 129, 132, 164, 227, 260, 306, 370–72, 411, 423
amnesia, 7, 22, 45, 159, 172, 220, 225–26, 235, 285, 289, 294
Analects, 359, 380, 382
anthropocentrism, 312, 315
anti-epic, 106, 120
anti-hero, 119, 154, 163
Anti-Rightist Campaign, 357–58, 491
Anti-Spiritual Pollution Campaign, 101, 351
army writer, 72, 83
authorship, 107, 124, 186, 332
avant-garde, 20, 94, 104, 143, 160

Balou Ballad. See *Marrow*
Balou Mountains, 5, 12, 147, 154, 201, 203–4, 207, 209, 214, 315, 317, 331, 379, 461–62
Balou tiange. See *Marrow*
Ballad, Hymn, Ode (Feng ya song), 4, 75, 161–62, 164, 169, 319, 453, 478
Bamboo Grove, 119
Basque, 379–89
Belt and Road Initiative, 171
Bible, the, 10, 122, 132–35, 162, 228–29, 235, 333, 360–62, 413–14, 457, 463, 491
biopolitical, 123, 126–27, 130–31, 172, 176, 181, 280, 323–24
biopower, 172, 176
blind, 6, 54, 64–65, 100, 108, 182, 235, 254, 276, 285, 288, 300, 302, 316, 434, 440
blood, 20, 35, 43–44, 70, 80, 118, 126, 130–31, 135, 141, 155, 159, 163, 172–81, 195, 210, 228–29, 261, 285, 290, 299, 301, 313, 316, 358, 413, 434, 458; blood disaster, 173; blood economy, 172–73, 176–80; blood trade, 299
Book of Genesis, 227, 259, 410

514

Index

Borges, Jorge Luis, 381
bribery, 112
Buddhism, 112, 136–37, 184–86, 189, 365
Bulgakov, Mikhail, 226
burlesque, 359

C. T. Hsia, 352, 363
calculability, 256
Calvino, Italo, 104–6, 110–12, 114–17, 119–20
Camus, Albert, 28, 32–35, 97–98, 178, 360
Can Xue, 94–95, 104, 438
cancer village, 348
cannibalism, 123, 131–32, 136, 163, 210, 230, 234–35, 316, 463
capitalism, 4, 172, 176, 178, 199, 202–3, 210, 246, 251–53, 256–63, 299, 305, 307, 326, 349, 471, 501; capitalist, 5–8, 13, 46, 62, 172–73, 194, 202–4, 206, 208, 210, 214, 250–51, 253–57, 261–64, 279, 305, 307, 349; capitalist utopia, 8, 210; global capitalism, 253, 259
catachresis, 250–51, 254, 256–58, 261, 264
causality, 38, 42–44, 109, 233
cemetery, 66, 116, 118, 173, 194, 325–26
censorship, 3, 12, 22, 23, 50, 66–67, 70–86, 110, 154–56, 160, 164, 168–69, 172, 179, 181, 214, 221–22, 225, 322–23, 326, 330–35, 346–47, 350–51, 353, 392, 404–6, 409–10, 442, 474, 483, 494, 497, 500, 502; self-censorship, 23, 50, 82, 155–56, 168, 172, 179, 181, 214, 221, 322–23, 335, 346–47, 352, 406, 410; state censorship, 71, 79, 326, 333, 346–47, 353
Central Plains (Zhongyuan), 59, 199–214
Chi Zijian, 168, 438, 471
Chinese Communist Party (CCP), 41, 72, 74–75, 77, 82, 84, 178, 187–89, 194, 196, 219–20, 223, 225, 239–46, 284–85, 292–93, 323–24, 329–30, 331–34, 336, 349, 358, 498–99
Chinese cultural other, 417–18, 422–30
cognitive mapping, 298–300, 304, 306–7, 309
collectivism, 94, 101–2
Confucianism, 11, 112, 130, 186, 234, 312, 333, 453; Confucian canon, 359, 414; Confucian ethics, 144, 269; Confucian tradition, 267; Confucius 107, 112–13, 186, 276
corruption, 3–4, 59, 62, 94, 100, 109, 112, 127, 145–46, 149, 163, 179, 259, 414, 445, 497
creative translation. See translation
cruelty, 28, 32, 33, 58–59, 179, 245, 456, 458
Cultural Revolution, 9, 73, 82, 84, 104, 159, 171, 176, 196, 220, 222–26, 245, 260, 299, 322, 327, 332, 345–47, 350–52, 423, 441, 442, 455, 469, 472, 483, 499
Czech, 226, 408–15, 500

Daoism, 11, 112, 189, 312, 453, 493
darkness, 3, 19, 54, 106, 178–79, 181–82, 211, 227, 258, 272, 443, 456, 494–95, 499, 503

Day the Sun Died, The (Rixi), 4, 16, 76, 118, 140, 155, 159, 162, 165–67, 169, 182, 199–200, 203, 210, 213, 232, 321–22, 324, 326–29, 336, 344, 346, 392, 394, 398, 428, 441, 454, 459, 489, 491–97, 499–501
de Beauvoir, Simone, 268, 272, 281, 286
decadence, 149
dehumanization, 123, 147, 152, 163, 232
Deng Xiaoping, 104, 140, 176, 219, 252, 254, 326, 349
descriptive equivalent, 372
detective novel, 453
developmentalism, 13
dialect, 159, 212, 214, 233, 360, 398, 401, 417–19, 421–24, 426–27, 429, 440, 447, 464, 477
diaspora, 114; See also utopia
Dingzhuang meng. See *Dream of Ding Village*
direct translation. See translation
disability, 9, 238–41, 245–47
Discovering Fiction (Faxian xiaoshuo), 4, 5, 10, 16–17, 38, 157, 232, 392, 399, 414, 441, 454, 459, 479
disease, 12, 30, 67, 171–82, 213, 271, 279, 290, 311, 313–14, 316, 318, 348, 443, 471, 478; See also illness; sickness
dominant language. See language
Dostoevsky, Fyodor, 23–25, 185
Dream of Ding Village (Dingzhuang meng), 3–4, 28–29, 33–34, 36, 75–76, 118, 126–27, 140, 155, 159, 166–67, 171–82, 201, 203, 210, 213, 313–14, 316, 335, 344, 346–47, 349, 392–94, 403, 414, 439, 441–43, 446, 448, 453–54, 456–59, 462, 471, 473, 490–91, 501
Dream of the Red Chamber (Honglou meng), 363, 462, 496; Dream of the Red Chamber Award, 4, 171, 232, 405, 489, 492–93
dreamwalking, 321, 325–26

ecocriticism, 311–19; ecocritical, 5, 311–19
ecological aesthetics. See aesthetics
ecologism, 120; ecological ethics, 311; ecological philosophy, 311
economic development, 327–28; economic miracle, 54, 104, 252–53, 256, 258, 260, 262–63
ecotopia. See utopia
Eileen Chang, 5, 409
ethical mission 141
ethics, 57, 63, 67, 112, 124, 132, 140, 144, 146, 230, 267, 269, 289, 311, 359, 499; ecological ethics, 311
excrescence, 272, 279, 283, 285, 290–95
exile, 7, 84, 107, 154, 166–67, 169, 298, 409, 491, 502
existentialism, 33, 94, 102, 158
experimental, 5, 30, 143–44, 146, 150, 152, 172–73, 178, 496
explanatory translation. See translation

515

Index

Explosion Chronicles, The (Zhalie zhi), 4, 37–38, 41–42, 45–46, 107–8, 113, 117, 120, 155, 159, 162, 164, 169, 199, 202, 247, 250–51, 282, 299–300, 304, 307, 309, 327–34, 336, 344, 346, 350, 392, 399, 438, 440–45, 447, 454, 459, 493, 496, 500, 501

famine, 7, 9, 41–42, 61, 76, 118, 123, 127, 131–32, 135, 163, 164, 175, 213, 220, 224–25, 228–31, 244–45, 284, 299, 300, 314, 316, 327, 332, 345, 347, 348, 435, 491; Great Famine, 7, 9, 76, 131–32, 135, 164, 175, 220, 224–25, 229, 231, 244, 284, 332, 345, 347–48
fantasy, 4, 7, 24–26, 31, 49, 109, 178, 214, 257, 348, 379
fate, 13, 22, 28, 30–36, 43, 49, 55–56, 58–59, 70, 74, 97–101, 107, 110, 137, 141, 179, 190, 193, 243, 258, 281, 289, 303, 314–15, 318, 327, 360, 432, 456, 462, 479
Faxian xiaoshuo. See *Discovering Fiction*
fear, 9, 33–34, 58, 60–61, 64–65, 70, 114, 117, 137, 162, 243, 300, 313, 333, 335, 350, 444, 455, 458
femininity, 280, 285–87, 289, 294–95; female labor, 279, 283, 285, 291; female subjectivity, 286; *See also* gender; women
Feng ya song. See *Ballad, Hymn, Ode*
fetishism, 4, 499
figurative language. *See* language
filial piety, 113–14, 116, 142, 145
folk culture, 18, 25, 120; folklore, 189
Four Books, The (Si shu), 4, 10, 38, 42–43, 45–46, 75–77, 118, 122–38, 140, 155–57, 159, 162, 164, 166–67, 169, 199, 203, 208–10, 213, 219–36, 245, 247, 268, 315–16, 331–36, 344, 346, 347–48, 357–61, 368–69, 377, 392, 399, 408–15, 441, 453–54, 456–60, 463, 479, 489, 490–92, 496–97, 500
four gospels, 122, 124, 128–29, 132, 234, 333
France, 84, 360, 380, 391–406, 448, 459
Franz Kafka Prize, 4, 52, 171, 178, 182, 408–9, 413–15, 443, 492, 496, 500
free translation. *See* translation
freedom, 8–9, 21, 35, 44, 107, 123–27, 133, 135–36, 157, 160, 163, 184, 194–95, 222, 252, 264, 405, 410, 412–13, 430, 446–47, 492; freedom of speech, 160
Freud, Sigmund, 184, 345

Gang of Four, 219
Gao Xingjian, 84, 95, 156, 394, 409, 463, 464
Gao Yaojie, 173
Garden No. 711 (711 hao yuan), 4–5, 10–14, 77, 118–20, 311, 317–19, 454, 479, 485, 511
gender, 213, 266–69, 272–76, 279–80, 282–95, 481; gender emancipation, 282, 284; gender history, 286, 295; gender representation, 280; *See also* femininity
Genesis, 14, 122, 227, 259, 360, 362, 410

geocriticism, 298–309
global capitalism. *See* capitalism
Gogol, Nikolai, 23, 25–26
Great Famine. *See* famine
Great Leap Forward, 7, 42–43, 45, 118, 122–23, 125, 159, 162–63, 175–76, 196, 219, 224–25, 245, 259–60, 273, 279, 283, 285–87, 289–91, 299, 304, 332, 345, 347–48, 357–59
grotesque, 5–8, 24–25, 140–52, 167, 169, 190, 299, 303, 343–44, 348, 439, 456, 463
grotesque realism. *See* realism

Ha Jin, 156, 347
Hard Like Water (Jianying ru shui), 29, 73–75, 143, 159, 167, 178, 342–43, 345, 394, 438–39,
harmony, 11, 41, 145, 189, 312, 315–18, 440–41, 453, 455–57, 459–62, 469, 472
Heart Sutra (Xinjing), 76, 155, 184–97, 199–200, 210, 214, 282, 438, 490, 491, 502
hedonism, 110
Henan, 3–6, 17, 51, 73, 107, 117–18, 141–42, 144–45, 147, 162, 172, 175, 177, 181, 196, 267–68, 281, 284, 299, 321, 326–27, 335, 398, 403, 418, 424, 440, 447, 477, 480, 497
heroism, 94, 101–2, 108, 242, 245, 308
Herstory/Shes/They (Tamen), 266–77, 279–95, 480–82, 502
heterotopia. *See* utopia
historiography, 39, 45, 107, 123–24, 131–32, 220, 238–47, 268, 331
homo sacer. *See* Agamben, Giorgio
Hong Kong, 73, 74, 76, 79, 80, 84, 108, 155, 162, 164–65, 171, 186–87, 196, 222, 225, 230–32, 235–36, 252–53, 261, 262, 381–82, 469, 473–74, 481–84, 489–503
House No. 711 (711 hao yuan). *See Garden No. 711*
How are You, Pan Jinlian (Jinlian, ni hao!), 453–55, 457, 459, 461–62
human: human condition, 33, 95, 101, 111, 119, 199, 211, 213; human nature, 24, 49, 66, 95, 98, 115, 124, 127, 146–47, 178, 204, 209, 345, 441, 443, 444, 456, 458, 496; human quandary, 124, 126, 137; human spirit, 4, 18, 23, 25, 39, 317; *See also* inhumanity

idealism, 343
ideology, 6, 20–22, 50, 53, 62, 68, 74, 86, 94–95, 99–102, 189, 197, 240, 242, 246, 267, 284–85, 328, 334, 350, 401, 419, 467–68, 476, 500–1
idiolect, 146, 149
illness, 147, 149, 171, 177–78, 239, 301, 314, 350, 471; *See also* disease; sickness
imaginary, the, 14, 45; imaginative construction, 29
inhumanity, 285; *See also* human
intelligentsia, 22
inverse theology, 122–38
irony, 8, 99, 104, 147, 207, 238, 412

Index

Japan, 80–82, 171, 206, 212, 307, 437–49
Jesus, 133–35, 136, 162, 186, 190, 191, 204, 213–14, 360
Jia Pingwa, 82, 110, 168, 299, 313, 417, 438, 440, 453, 456, 459
Jianying ru shui. See *Hard Like Water*
Jinlian, ni hao! See *How are You, Pan Jinlian*

Kafka, Franz, 16, 25, 38, 40, 94, 97, 122, 124–25, 131, 133, 136–38, 178, 344, 404, 408, 412; *The Trial*, 122, 124–25, 128, 131, 133–34, 136, 138; *See also* Franz Kafka Prize
Korean War, 240–41
Kundera, Milan, 99, 101
Kuomingtang (KMT), 242–43, 467, 471, 477, 480

language: agglutinative language, 380; figurative language, 250–51, 253, 256, 259, 264; *See also* dialect; idiolect
Lao She Literary Award, 74
Laozi, 186–87, 191, 209
Lenin's Kisses (Shouhuo), 4–10, 12–14, 29, 62, 74, 126, 140, 149, 154, 159, 167, 169, 194, 199, 208, 210, 227, 238–39, 242, 245, 247, 268, 282, 322, 343, 346, 349, 360, 414, 417, 420, 423, 438–41, 443–49, 460, 472–73, 479, 493, 500–1
Li Peifu, 156
Li Tuo, 49, 156, 203
life-experienced realism. *See* realism
Ling Mengchu, 21
literal translation. *See* translation
literary aesthetics. *See* aesthetics
literary form, 51
literary production, 106, 126, 158, 160, 214, 268, 333–34, 379, 409, 474–75
literary space, 219–36
Liven (Shouhuo), 5–10, 124, 208, 239–40, 244–46, 423–24, 426–27, 431, 443
Long March, 242–46, 395
Lu Xun, 3, 5, 52, 54, 59, 66, 73, 108, 120, 140, 147, 149, 158, 171, 232, 234, 266–67, 298–99, 309, 324, 344, 412, 417, 437, 440–41, 444, 446, 453, 456, 458–59, 462–63, 495, 500
Lu Yao, 438, 477
lyricism, 59, 159, 275, 277, 414, 480

madman, 149
madness, 359, 455, 500
magical realism. *See* realism
Magnesia Litera Award, 408, 412–13
Mao Zedong, 19, 75, 175, 195, 223, 268, 273, 358, 371, 380, 392, 442, 499; Maoism, 224, 227, 235, 239, 246, 493
Marco Polo, 106, 108, 110
Marrow/Balou Ballad (Balou tiange), 4, 379, 381–82, 389, 391–92
masculinity, 286, 290, 292, 295

messianism, 124, 137
metanarrative, 120, 123, 128, 132, 282, 285, 304, 309
military literature, 93–102
Mladá Fronta, 409
Mo Yan, 11–12, 83, 143, 152, 168, 221, 225–26, 231, 246, 299, 380–82, 389, 394, 399, 409, 410, 417, 428, 438, 444, 453, 456, 463–64, 467, 470, 472, 476, 477–78
mystery, 24, 97, 109, 134–35, 255, 261
mythorealism, 1–86, 109, 117, 140, 142, 144, 152, 157–60, 179, 258, 299, 304, 306, 311, 330, 344, 348, 350, 412, 444, 448, 457–59, 463, 464, 478, 490–91, 493, 496, 502

national character, 52, 64, 108, 143, 483
native soil literature (xiangtu xiaoshuo), 10, 52, 140–47, 152, 467, 470–71, 480, 298
neorealism. *See* realism
nostalgia, 200, 261, 284, 298, 445
new historical fiction, 20
new realism. *See* realism
nihilism, 82, 95–96, 99, 101, 126, 137, 300
Nian yue ri. See *Years, Months, Days, The*

Old Testament, 362, 410
onomatopoeias, 369–70, 382–83, 389

paralogism, 51
paranoia, 51
paraphrasis, 51
pararealism. *See* realism
paratext, 211–12, 329
parody, 51, 159, 235, 359, 414, 464
partial translation. *See* translation
party-state, 223, 323–24, 477
Pasternak, Boris, 226
Patriotism, 100–1, 308
Peach Blossom Spring, 8–9, 11, 13, 14, 60, 118, 199–215, 414
People's Liberation Army (PLA), 191, 239, 245, 292, 392, 491, 497, 499
peripheral literature, 379, 404
plasma economy, 172, 179, 497; *See also* blood, blood economy
post-Mao era, 210, 219–20, 348–49, 353, 493, 500
postmodernism, 143
postrealism. *See* realism
Prohibited Area Number Four (Sihao jinqu), 94, 96–98, 102
prostitution, 112, 258, 275, 277, 306, 315
Průšek, Jaroslav, 107
psyche, 18, 24, 52
pure literature, 156, 442, 448–49

re-education, 42, 43, 44, 122, 126, 129, 133–35, 162, 213, 332, 334–35, 360, 364, 376, 411, 413–14

realism: bio-realism, 23–24; constructed realism, 22–23; critical realism, 19, 53; deep-spiritual realism, 157; life-experienced realism, 157; socialist realism, 16–21, 23, 26, 350; society-controlled realism, 157–58; magical realism, 17, 26, 37–38, 40–42, 47, 83, 158, 178–79, 344, 351, 443, 448, 480; new realism, 93, 109; pararealism, 49–68; postrealism, 20; world-experienced realism, 157
Red Army, 6–7
Red Guards, 228
redemption, 50, 54, 59, 67, 136–38, 181–82, 199–215, 232, 241, 345–46, 410
reflective literature, 345
reportage fiction, 132
rhizome, 279, 294–95
Riguang liunian. See *Streams of Time*
Rixi. See *Day the Sun Died, The*
romance novel, 453
romanticism, 10
root-seeking, 142
rural. *See* country
rural utopia. *See* utopia

"Sangjiaquan de yinian." See "Year of the Stray Dog, The"
satire, 25, 57, 73–74, 99, 141, 160, 344, 349, 350, 353, 443, 483, 497
scar literature, 222, 234, 345
sensory image, 379
Serve the People (Wei renmin fuwu), 3, 75, 140, 155, 166, 189, 226, 233, 347, 349, 391–92, 394–95, 403, 409, 410, 414, 439, 441–43, 446, 448, 453–54, 459–60, 469, 473, 482, 489, 490–91, 496, 498–99
Shen Congwen, 298, 409
shenshi zhuyi. See mythorealism
Shes. See *Herstory/Shes/They* (Tamen)
Shouhuo. See *Lenin's Kisses*
Si shu. See *Four Books, The*
Sick Man of East Asia, 171, 239
sickness, 149; *See also* disease; illness
Sihao jinqu. See *Prohibited Area Number Four*
simile, 254, 370, 372–73, 375–76, 411
sleepwalk. *See* dreamwalking
socialist realism. *See* realism
society-controlled realism. *See* realism
Somnambulism. *See* dreamwalking
Soviet literature, 17, 18, 26, 158, 453
spiritual realism. *See* mythorealism
Streams of Time (Riguang liunian), 4, 8, 29, 118, 142, 149, 154, 159, 167, 172, 199, 282, 314–16, 342–43, 345, 348, 349, 392, 398, 453
struggle for survival, 56, 59, 141, 144, 311, 349
Su qiu gong mian. See *Urgent Plea for Rest Together*
subjective world, 38
subversive, 54, 179, 190, 243, 287, 357, 411, 471, 481

Summer Sunset (Xia riluo), 72–73, 154, 322, 414, 490–91
surrealistic, 104, 106, 304–5, 353
symbolism, 38, 185, 334, 358, 414

Tamen. See *Herstory/Shes/They* (Tamen)
Tao Yuanming, 9, 207
Taoism. *See* Daoism
terror, 9, 108, 123, 138, 225, 334, 435, 477
thanato-narrative, 174; thanatopolitics, 172, 176
Theatre of the Absurd, 94, 95
They. See *Herstory/Shes/They* (Tamen)
third sex, the, 269, 272–73, 279–95
Thoughts by One Person on Three Rivers (Yi ge ren de san tiao he), 280
Three Brothers (Wo yu fubei), 4, 161, 201, 268, 280, 361, 438, 497
Three Years of Natural Disaster. *See* Great Famine
Tolstoy, Lev, 23–24
topos, 105, 111, 114, 286, 300
totalitarianism, 359
traitor, 11, 156, 243, 411, 412, 414
translated literature, 379–80, 404–5
translation: acceptability-oriented translation, 418–21, 425, 529; adequacy-oriented translation, 418–21, 429; creative translation, 418–21, 423; direct translation, 313, 379–82; explanatory translation, 367, 372; free translation, 380, 425–26; literal translation, 254, 363, 367, 370, 372, 375, 382, 411, 421, 422; partial translation, 372, 376; translation strategies, 380, 401, 418–21, 425, 428
transliteration, 411, 419–21, 424
traumatic imagination, 40–41, 46
trope, 124, 126, 230, 235, 282
Turgenev, Ivan, 23–24
Twitter Literary Award, 438

universalism, 405
urban life, 32, 104–20
urbanization, 146, 306, 308, 319, 328
Urgent Plea for Rest Together (Su qiu gong mian), 155, 280
utopia: ecocritical utopia, 5; ecotopia, 12–14, 118–20; heterotopia, 208–10, 214, 323–27, 333; rural utopia, 8; *See also* diaspora

Václav Havel Library, 408
veterans, 240–42, 245–47, 307
Vietnam, 452–66
violence, 5, 7, 11–13, 52, 54, 61, 63–65, 67, 85, 94, 112, 127, 150, 196, 199, 220, 224, 225, 243, 251, 260, 291, 323, 397, 397, 444, 469, 477, 501

Wang Yao, 8, 317, 344, 458
Wei renmin fuwu. See *Serve the People*
"What Happens After Coronavirus?", 89, 196

Wo yu fubei. See *Three Brothers*
women: rural women, 269, 271, 273, 276–77, 281–82, 286–89, 291–92, 295, 480; women's literature, 20; *See also* femininity; gender
world literature, 17, 25–26, 80, 86, 214, 334, 351, 353, 380, 430, 446, 469, 483, 484, 489–90, 492, 503
world-experienced realism. *See* realism

Xi Xi, 251–53
Xia riluo. See *Summer Sunset*
xiangtu xiaoshuo. *See* native soil literature
Xinjing. See *Heart Sutra*

Yang Jisheng, 224–26
"Year of the Stray Dog, The" (Sangjiaquan de yinian), 76–77
Years, Months, Days, The (Nian yue ri), 61, 73, 118, 159, 162, 203, 299–300, 303, 304, 316, 317, 382, 392, 398, 403, 438–40, 444–46, 453, 454, 459, 489–90
Yi ge ren de san tiao he. See *Thoughts by One Person on Three Rivers*
Yu Hua, 165, 168, 173, 260, 409, 438, 441, 444, 453, 459, 463, 467, 472, 500
Yuan Mei, 118

Zhalie zhi. See *Explosion Chronicles, The*
Zhang Hao, 208
Zhang Guotao, 243
Zhang Xuexin, 9, 345
Zhongyuan. See *Central Plains*
Zhu Xi, 112–13
Zhuangzi 9, 11, 120, 208, 381

CPSIA information can be obtained
at www.ICGtesting.com
Printed in the USA
BVHW060403080522
635598BV00003B/205